W9-DJN-901

WORLD
ENCYCLOPEDIA OF
PEACE

(SECOND EDITION)

WORLD ENCYCLOPEDIA OF PEACE

(SECOND EDITION)

VOLUME VI

Honorary Editor-in-Chief

Javier Perez De Cuellar

Editor-in-Chief

Young Seek Choue

OCEANA PUBLICATIONS, INC.®
NEW YORK

•

SEOUL PRESS

World Encyclopedia of Peace (Second Edition)

Published in the United States of America in 1999 and distributed exclusively throughout the world, except in Korea, by
Oceana Publications Inc.
75 Main Street
Dobbs Ferry, New York 10522
Phone: (914) 693-8100
Fax: (914) 693-0402

ISBN: 0-379-21404-0 (Volume VI)
ISBN: 0-379-21398-2 (Set)

Library of Congress Cataloging-in-Publication Data

World encyclopedia of peace / honorary editor-in-chief, Javier Perez de Cuellar, editor-in-chief, Young Seek Choue. -- 2nd ed.
   p. cm.
   Includes bibliographical references and indexes.
   ISBN 0-379-21398-2 (clothbound set : alk. paper)
   1. Peace Encyclopedias. I. Perez de Cuellar, Javier, 1920-
II. Young Seek Choue, 1921-
   JZ5533 .W67 1999
   327.1'03--dc21   99-34811
                                                              CIP

Published simultaneously in the Republic of Korea in 1999 by
Seoul Press
Jin Wang Kim, Publisher
Room 303, Jeodong Bldg., 7-2, Jeodong, Chung-ku
Seoul 100-032, Korea
Phone: (02) 2275-6566
Fax: (02) 2278-2551

ISBN: 89-7225-102-X   94330 (Volume VI)
ISBN: 89-7225-096-1 (Set)

Printed in the Republic of Korea by Seoul Press

TREATIES

The Treaties section comprises the texts of 95 treaties, agreements, conventions, and protocols of the twentieth century from 1919 to 1997. They have been selected for inclusion on the basis of their relevance to the issues of arms control, disarmament, and the prohibition of war and aggression. Treaties which concluded a war have been excluded except in cases where disarmament clauses constitute a significant element in the agreement, for example, the Treaty of Versailles. The Treaty texts have been reproduced in chronological order and the majority appear in full. In cases where treaties have been edited, summarized clauses are displayed in square brackets.

For a discussion of the nature of modern treaties, see the article in Volume V on *Treaties of the Modern Era*. Readers are also advised to refer to related articles in Volumes I, II, III, IV and V on international law. For more detailed treatments of specific aspects of arms control and disarmament, see the articles in Volumes I, II, III, IV and V: *Arms Control, Evolution of; Multilateralism*; and *Unilateralism*. Readers are advised to refer to companion articles in Volumes I, II, III, IV and V which discuss the significance of particular Treaties; these include: *Naval Limitation Treaties Between the World Wars; Non-Proliferation Treaty; Oceans: The Common Heritage* (for discussion of the Sea-Bed Treaty); and *Organization on Security and Cooperation in Europe (OSCE)*. Readers are also advised to refer to articles on Nobel Peace Prize Laureates in Volume VII for the significance of specific treaties of the interwar period.

CONTENTS

TREATIES

Treaty of Versailles (1919) 3

Treaty Concerning the Archipelago of Spitsbergen (1920) 23

Convention Relating to the Non-Fortification and Neutralisation
of the Aaland Islands (1921) 25

Treaty Between the United States of America, the British Empire, France,
Italy and Japan, for the Limitation of Naval Armament (1922) 27

Convention on the Limitations of Armaments of Central American States (1923) 39

Protocol for the Pacific Settlement of International Disputes (1924) 41

Protocol for the Prohibition of the Use in War of Asphyxiating, Poisonous
or Other Gases, and of Bacteriological Methods of Warfare (1925) 46

Treaty of Mutual Guarantee Between Germany, Belgium, France,
Great Britain and Italy (1925) 46

General Treaty for Renunciation of War as an Instrument
of National Policy (1928) 49

Anti-War Treaty (Non-Aggression and Conciliation) (1933) 50

Treaty for the Limitation of Naval Armament (1936) 53

Charter of the United Nations (1945) 61

Convention on the Prevention and Punishment of the Crime of Genocide (1948) 76

Geneva Convention Relative to the Protection of Civilian Persons in Time of War (1949) 78

The Antarctic Treaty (1959) 92

Declaration on the Neutrality of Laos (1962) 95

Memorandum of Understanding Between the United States of America
and the Union of Soviet Socialist Republics Regarding the Establishment
of a Direct Communications Link (1963) 97

Treaty Banning Nuclear Weapon Tests in the Atmosphere, in Outer Space
and Under Water (1963) 99

Treaty on the Principles Governing the Activities of States in the Exploration
and Use of Outer Space, Including the Moon and Other Celestial Bodies (1967) ... 100

Treaty for the Prohibition of Nuclear Weapons in Latin America (1967) 104

Treaty on the Non-Proliferation of Nuclear Weapons (1968) 113

Question Relating to Measures to Safeguard Non-Nuclear-Weapon States Parties
to the Treaty on the Non-Proliferation of Nuclear Weapons (1968) 117

Treaty on the Prohibition of the Emplacement of Nuclear Weapons and Other Weapons
of Mass Destruction on the Sea-bed and Ocean Floor and in the Subsoil Thereof (1971) ... 117

Agreements to Reduce the Risk of Nuclear War Between the United States
and the Union of Soviet Socialist Republics (1971) 120

Agreement Between the United States of America and the Union of Soviet Socialist Republics
on Measures to Improve the USA-USSR Direct Communications Link (1971) 121

Convention on the Prohibition of the Development, Production and Stockpiling
of Bacteriological (Biological) and Toxin Weapons and on their Destruction (1972) ... 122

Agreement Between the Government of the United States of America
and the Government of the Union of Soviet Socialist Republics on the Prevention
of Incidents on and over the High Seas (1972) 126

Treaty Between the United States of America and the Union of Soviet Socialist Republics
on the Limitation of Anti-Ballistic Missile Systems (1972) 128

Interim Agreement Between the United States of America and the Union
of Soviet Socialist Republics on Certain Measures with Respect
to the Limitation of Strategic Offensive Arms (1972) 131

Basic Principles of Negotiation on the Further Limitation
of Strategic Offensive Arms (1973) 132

Agreement Between the United States of America and the Union
of Soviet Socialist Republics on the Prevention of Nuclear War (1973) 133

Agreement Between the United States of America and the Union
of Soviet Socialist Republics on the Prevention of Nuclear War (1973) 134

Treaty Between the United States of America and the Union of Soviet Socialist Republics
on the Limitation of Underground Nuclear Weapon Tests (1974) 135

Protocol to the Treaty Between the United States of America and the Union
   of Soviet Socialist Republics on the Limitation of Anti-Ballistic Missile Systems (1974)   137

Document on Confidence-Building Measures and Certain Aspects
   of Security and Disarmament Included in the Final Act of the Conference
   on Security and Cooperation in Europe (1975)   138

Agreement Between the Government of the Republic of Korea and the International
   Atomic Energy Agency for the Application of Safeguards in Connection with
   the Treaty on the Non-Proliferation of Nuclear Weapons (1975)   140

Treaty Between the United States of America and the Union of Soviet Socialist Republics
   on Underground Nuclear Explosions for Peaceful Purposes (1976)   158

United Nations Convention on the Prohibition of Military or Any Other
   Hostile Use of Environmental Modification Techniques (1977)   169

Guidelines for Nuclear Transfers Agreed by the Nuclear Suppliers Group (1977)   173

Protocol I Additional to the Geneva Conventions of 1949 Relating to the Protection
   of Victims of International Armed Conflicts (1977)   179

Treaty Between the United States of America and the Union
   of Soviet Socialist Republics on the Limitation of Strategic Offensive Arms (1979)   193

United Nations Agreement Governing the Activities of States on the Moon
   and Other Celestial Bodies (1979)   210

Convention on the Physical Protection of Nuclear Material (1980)   215

Convention on Prohibitions or Restrictions on the Use
   of Certain Conventional Weapons Which may be Deemed
   to be Excessively Injurious or to Have Indiscriminate Effects (1980)   221

Charter of the Cooperation Council for the Arab States of the Gulf (1981)   225

Unified Economic Agreement Between the Countries of the Gulf Cooperation Council (1982)   230

Treaty for the Establishment of the Economic Community of Central African States (1983)   234

Memorandum of Understanding Between the United States of America and the Union
   of Soviet Socialist Republics on the USA-USSR Direct Communications Link (1984)   252

Agreement for Cooperation Between the Government of the United States of America and
   the Government of the People's Republic of China Concerning Peaceful Uses
   of Nuclear Energy (1985)   254

South Pacific Nuclear Free Zone Treaty (1985)   257

Contents

Agreement Between the UK and the USSR Concerning the Prevention of Incidents
  at Sea Beyond the Territorial Sea (1986)   260

Indo-Sri Lanka Agreement to Establish Peace and Normalcy in Sri Lanka (1987) 263

Text of Agreements by the Presidents of Central America (1987)   265

Agreement Between the United States of America and the Union of Soviet Socialist
  Republics on the Establishment of Nuclear Risk Reduction Centers (1987)   269

Treaty Between the United States of America and the Union of Soviet Socialist Republics on
  the Elimination of their Intermediate-Range and Shorter-Range Missiles (1987) 272

Agreement Among the United States of America and the Kingdom of Belgium,
  the Federal Republic of Germany, the Republic of Italy, the Kingdom of the Netherlands
  and the United Kingdom of Great Britain and Northern Ireland Regarding Inspections
  Relating to the Treaty Between the United States of America and the Union of Soviet
  Socialist Republics on the Elimination of their Intermediate-Range
  and Shorter-Range Missiles (1987)   297

Bilateral Agreement Between the Republic of Afghanistan and the Islamic Republic of
  Pakistan on the Principles of Mutual Relations in Particular on Non-Interference
  and Non-Intervention (1988)   301

Agreement Between the United States of America and the Union of Soviet Socialist
  Republics on Notifications of Launches of Intercontinental Ballistic Missiles
  and Submarine-Launched Ballistic Missiles (1988)   304

Agreement Between the Government of the United States of America and the Government
  of the Union of Soviet Socialist Republics on the Prevention of Dangerous Military
  Activities (1989)   305

Agreement Between the Government of the United States of America and the Government
  of the Union of Soviet Socialist Republics on Reciprocal Advance Notification of
  Major Strategic Exercises (1989)   308

Agreement Between the United States of America and the Union of Soviet Socialist
  Republics on Destruction and Non-Production of Chemical Weapons and on Measures
  to Facilitate the Multilateral Convention on Banning Chemical Weapons (1990) 309

Treaty Between the Federal Republic of Germany and the German Democratic Republic
  on the Establishment of German Unity—Unification Treaty (1990)   313

Treaty on Conventional Armed Forces in Europe (1990)   328

Agreement on a Comprehensive Political Settlement of the Cambodia Conflict (1991) 342

Resolution Adopted by the UN General Assembly on General
  and Complete Disarmament (1991)   347

Contents

Agreement Establishing the Commonwealth of Independent States (1991)   358

Agreement on Reconciliation, Nonaggression and Exchanges and Cooperation Between the South and the North (1991)   360

Agreement on Joint Measures with Respect to Nuclear Weapons (1991)   362

Joint Declaration of the Denuclearization of the Korean Peninsula (1992)   363

Agreement Between the Government of the Democratic People's Republic of Korea and the International Atomic Energy Agency for the Application of Safeguards in Connection with the Treaty on the Non-Proliferation of Nuclear Weapons (1992)   364

Treaty on European Union (1992)   382

Agreement to Establish a South-North Joint Nuclear Control Commission (1992)   413

Treaty on Open Skies (1992)   415

Agreement to Establish a South-North Joint Military Commission (1992)   433

Treaty of the Southern African Development Community (1992)   434

Protocol on the Compliance with the Implementation of Chapter II, Nonaggression, of the Agreement on Reconciliation, Nonaggression and Exchanges and Cooperation Between the South and the North (1992)   443

Central European Free Trade Agreement (1992)   445

Treaty Between the United States of America and the Russian Federation on the Further Reduction and Limitation of Strategic Offensive Arms (1993)   453

Convention on the Prohibition of the Development, Production, Stockpiling and Use of Chemical Weapons and on their Destruction (1993)   458

Preliminary Agreement Concerning the Establishment of a Confederation Between the Federation of Bosnia and Herzegovina and the Republic of Croatia (1994)   479

Agreement Establishing the World Trade Organization (WTO) (1994)   480

Agreements on the Gaza Strip and the Jericho Area (1994)   487

Convention on Nuclear Safety (1994)   493

Agreed Framework Between the United States of America and the Democratic People's Republic of Korea (1994)   500

Treaty of Peace Between the State of Israel and the Hashemite Kingdom of Jordan (1994)   502

Vienna Document 1994 (1994)   509

Agreement on the Establishment of the Korean Peninsula Energy Development
    Organization (1995)   532

Pelindaba Text of the African Nuclear-Weapon-Free Zone Treaty (1995)   537

General Framework Agreement for Peace in Bosnia and Herzegovina (1995)   541

Treaty on the Southeast Asia Nuclear-Weapon-Free Zone (1995)   542

Protocol on Prohibitions or Restrictions on the Use of Mines, Booby-Traps
    and Other Devices as Amended on May '96 (Protocol II as Amended on 3 May 1996)
    Annexed to the Convention on Prohibitions or Restrictions on the Use of Certain
    Conventional Weapons Which May be Deemed to be Excessively Injurious or
    to Have Indiscriminate Effects (1996)   549

Agreement on Normalization of Relations Between the Federal Republic of Yugoslavia
    and the Republic of Croatia (1996)   557

Comprehensive Nuclear Test Ban Treaty (1996)   559

The 1987 Montreal Protocol on Substances that Deplete the Ozone Layer Adjusted
    and Amended by the Ninth Meeting of the Parties (1997)   577

Convention on the Prohibition of the Use, Stockpiling, Production and Transfer of
    Anti-Personnel Mines and on their Destruction (1997)   591

Treaties

Treaty of Versailles

Date of signature: June 28, 1919
Place of signature: Versailles
Signatory states: the British Empire, France, Italy, Japan, the United States, Belgium, Bolivia, Brazil, China, Cuba, Czechoslovakia, Ecuador, Greece, Guatemala, Haiti, the Hedjaz, Honduras, Liberia, Nicaragua, Panama, Peru, Poland, Portugal, Roumania, the Serb-Croat-Slovene State, Siam, Uruguay, Germany

The United States of America, The British Empire, France, Italy and Japan,

These Powers being described in the present Treaty as the Principal Allied and Associated Powers,

Belgium, Bolivia, Brazil, China, Cuba, Ecuador, Greece, Guatemala, Haiti, the Hedjaz, Honduras, Liberia, Nicaragua, Panama, Peru, Poland, Portugal, Roumania, the Serb-Croat-Slovene State, Siam, Czechoslovakia and Uruguay,

These Powers constituting with the Principal Powers mentioned above the Allied and Associated Powers, of the one part;

and Germany

of the other part;

Bearing in mind that on the request of the Imperial German Government an armistice was granted on November 11, 1918, to Germany by the Principal Allied and Associated Powers in order that a Treaty of Peace might be concluded with her, and

The Allied and Associated Powers being equally desirous that the war in which they were successively involved directly or indirectly and which originated in the declaration of war by Austria-Hungary on July 28, 1914, against Serbia, the declaration of war by Germany against Russia on August 1, 1914, and against France on August 3, 1914, and in the invasion of Belgium, should be replaced by a firm, just and durable Peace.

For this purpose the High Contracting Parties . . .

Who having communicated their full powers found in good and due form have agreed as follows:

From the coming into force of the present Treaty the state of war will terminate. From that moment and subject to the provisions of this Treaty official relations with Germany, and with any of the German States, will be resumed by the Allied and Associated Powers.

PART I

THE COVENANT OF THE LEAGUE OF NATIONS

The High Contracting Parties;
In order to promote international co-operation and to achieve international peace and security

by the acceptance of obligations not to resort to war,

by the prescription of open, just and honourable relations between nations,

by the firm establishment of the understandings of international law as the actual rule of conduct among Governments, and

by the maintenance of justice and a scrupulous respect for all treaty obligations in the dealings of organized peoples with one another,

Agree to this Covenant of the League of Nations.

Article 1

The original Members of the League of Nations shall be those of the Signatories which are named in the Annex to this Covenant and also such of those other States named in the Annex as shall accede without reservation to this Covenant. Such accession shall be effected by a declaration deposited with the Secretariat within two months of the coming into force of the Covenant. Notice thereof shall be sent to all other Members of the League.

Any fully self-governing State, Dominion or Colony not named in the Annex may become a Member of the League if its admission is agreed to by two-thirds of the Assembly, provided that it shall give effective guarantees of its sincere intention to observe its international obligations, and shall accept such regulations as may be prescribed by the League in regard to its military, naval and air forces and armaments.

Any Member of the League may, after two years' notice of its intention so to do, withdraw from the League, provided that all its international obligations and all its obligations under this Covenant shall have been fulfilled at the time of its withdrawal.

Article 2

The action of the League under this Covenant shall be effected through the instrumentality of an Assembly and of a Council with a permanent Secretariat.

Article 3

The Assembly shall consist of Representatives of the Members of the League.

The Assembly shall meet at stated intervals and from time to time as occasion may require at the Seat of the League or at such other place as may be decided upon.

The Assembly may deal at its meetings with any matter within the sphere of action of the League or affecting the peace of the world.

At meetings of the Assembly each Member of the League shall have one vote, and may have not more than three Representatives.

Article 4

The Council shall consist of Representatives of the Principal Allied and Associated Powers, together with Representatives of four other Members of the League. These four Members of the League shall be selected by the Assembly from time to time in its discretion. Until the appointment of the Representatives of the four Members of the League first selected by the Assembly, Representatives of Belgium, Brazil, Spain and Greece shall be members of the Council.

With the approval of the majority of the Assembly, the Council may name additional Members of the League whose Representatives shall always be members of the Council; the Council with like approval may increase the number of Members of the League to be selected by the Assembly for representation on the Council.

The Council shall meet from time to time as occasion may require, and at least once a year, at the Seat of the League, or at such other place as may be decided upon.

The Council may deal at its meetings with any matter within the sphere of action of the League or affecting the peace of the world.

Any Member of the League not represented on the Council shall be invited to send a Representative to sit as a member at any meeting of the Council during the consideration of matters specially affecting the interests of that Member of the League.

At meetings of the Council, each Member of the League represented on the Council shall have one vote, and may have not more than one Representative.

Article 5

Except where otherwise expressly provided in this Covenant or by the terms of the present Treaty, decisions at any meeting of the Assembly or of the Council shall require the agreement of all the Members of the League represented at the meeting.

All matters of procedure at meetings of the Assembly or of the Council, including the appointment of Committees to investigate particular matters, shall be regulated by the Assembly or the Council, and may be decided by a majority of the Members of the League represented at the meeting.

The first meeting of the Assembly and the first meeting of the Council shall be summoned by the President of the United States of America.

Article 6

[The permanent Secretariat to be established at Geneva.]

Article 7

[Representatives and officials to enjoy diplomatic status.]

Article 8

The Members of the League recognize that the maintenance of peace requires the reduction of national armaments to the lowest point consistent with national safety and the enforcement by common action of international obligations.

The Council, taking account of the geographical situation and circumstances of each State, shall formulate plans for such reduction for the consideration and action of the several Governments.

Such plans shall be subject to reconsideration and revision at least every ten years.

After these plans shall have been adopted by the several Governments, the limits of armaments therein fixed shall not be exceeded without the concurrence of the Council.

The Members of the League agree that the manufacture by private enterprise of munitions and implements of war is open to grave objections. The Council shall advise how the evil effects attendant upon such manufacture can be prevented, due regard being had to the necessities of those Members of the League which are not able to manufacture the munitions and implements of war necessary for their safety.

The Members of the League undertake to interchange full and frank information as to the scale of their armaments, their military, naval and air programmes and the condition of such of their industries as are adaptable to war-like purposes.

Article 9

A permanent Commission shall be constituted to advise the Council on the execution of the provisions of Articles 1 and 8 and on military, naval and air questions generally.

Article 10

The Members of the League undertake to respect and preserve as against external aggression the territorial integrity and existing political independence of all Members of the League. In case of any such aggression or in case of any threat or danger of such aggression the Council shall advise upon the means by which this obligation shall be fulfilled.

Article 11

Any war or threat of war, whether immediately affecting any of the Members of the League or not, is hereby declared a matter of concern to the whole League, and the League shall take any action that may be deemed wise and effectual to safeguard the peace of nations. In case any such emergency should arise the Secretary General shall, on the request of any Member of the League, forthwith summon a meeting of the Council.

It is also declared to be the friendly right of each Member of the League to bring to the attention of the Assembly or of the Council any circumstance whatever affecting international relations which threatens to disturb international peace or the good understanding between nations upon which peace depends.

Article 12

The Members of the League agree that if there should arise between them any dispute likely to lead

to a rupture, they will submit the matter either to arbitration or to inquiry by the Council, and they agree in no case to resort to war until three months after the award by the arbitrators or the report by the Council.

In any case under this Article the award of the arbitrators shall be made within a reasonable time, and the report of the Council shall be made within six months after the submission of the dispute.

Article 13

[Disputes which cannot be settled by diplomacy to be submitted to arbitration.]

Article 14

The Council shall formulate and submit to the Members of the League for adoption plans for the establishment of a Permanent Court of International Justice. The Court shall be competent to hear and determine any dispute of an international character which the parties thereto submit to it. The Court may also give an advisory opinion any dispute or question referred to it by the Council or by the Assembly.

Article 15

[Disputes that are not submitted to arbitration to be submitted to the Council, who shall endeavour to effect a peaceful settlement.]

Article 16

Should any Member of the League resort to war in disregard of its covenants under Articles 12, 13 or 15, it shall *ipso facto* be deemed to have committed an act of war against all other Members of the League, which hereby undertake immediately to subject it to the severance of all trade or financial relations, the prohibition of all intercourse between their nationals and the nationals of the covenant-breaking State, and the prevention of all financial, commercial or personal intercourse between the nationals of the covenant-breaking State and the nationals of any other State, whether a Member of the League or not.

It shall be the duty of the Council in such case to recommend to the several Government concerned what effective military, naval or air force the Members of the League shall severally contribute to the armed forces to be used to protect the covenants of the League.

The Members of the League agree, further, that they will mutually support one another in the financial and economic measures which are taken under this Article, in order to minimise the loss and inconvenience resulting from the above measures, and that they will mutually support one another in resisting any special measures aimed at one of their number by the covenant-breaking State, and that they will take the necessary steps to afford passage through their territory to the forces of any of the Members of the League which are co-operating to protect the covenants of the League.

Any Member of the League which has violated any covenant of the League may be declared to be no longer a Member of the League by a vote of the Council, concurred in by the Representatives of all the other Members of the League represented thereon.

Article 17

In the event of a dispute between a Member of the League and a State which is not a Member of the League, or between States not Members of the League, the State or States not Members of the League shall be invited to accept the obligations of Membership of the League for the purposes of such dispute, upon such conditions as the Council may deem just. If such invitation is accepted, the provisions of Articles 12 to 16 inclusive shall be applied with such modifications as may be deemed necessary by the Council.

Upon such invitation being given the Council shall immediately institute an inquiry into the circumstances of the dispute and recommend such action as may seem best and most effectual in the circumstances.

If a State so invited shall refuse to accept the obligations of membership in the League for the purposes of such dispute, and shall resort to war against a Member of the League, the provisions of Article 16 shall be applicable as against the State taking such action.

If both parties to the dispute when so invited refuse to accept the obligations of membership in the League for the purposes of such dispute, the Council may take such measures and make such recommendations as will prevent hostilities and will result in the settlement of the dispute.

Article 18

Every treaty or international engagement entered into hereafter by any Member of the League shall be forthwith registered with the Secretariat, and shall as soon as possible be published by it. No such treaty or international engagement shall be binding until so registered.

Article 19

The Assembly may from time to time advise the reconsideration by Members of the League of treaties which have become inapplicable, and the consideration of international conditions whose continuance might endanger the peace of the world.

Article 20

The Members of the League severally agree that this Covenant is accepted as abrogating all obligations or understandings *inter se* which are inconsistent with the terms thereof, and solemnly undertake that they will not hereafter enter into any engagements inconsistent with the terms thereof.

In case any Member of the League shall, before becoming a Member of the League, have undertaken any obligations inconsistent with the terms of this Covenant, it shall be the duty of such Member to take immediate steps to procure its release from such obligations.

Article 21

Nothing in this Covenant shall be deemed to affect the validity of international engagements, such as treaties of arbitration or regional understandings like the Monroe doctrine, for securing the maintenance of peace.

Article 22

To those colonies and territories which, as a consequence of the late war, have ceased to be under the sovereignty of the States which formerly governed them, and which are inhabited by peoples not yet able to stand by themselves under the strenuous conditions of the modern world, there should be applied the principle that the well-being and development of such peoples form a sacred trust of civilization, and that securities for the performance of this trust should be embodied in this Covenant.

The best method of giving practical effect to this principle is that the tutelage of such peoples should be entrusted to advanced nations who, by reason of their resources, their experience, or their geographical position can best undertake this responsibility, and who are willing to accept it, and that this tutelage should be exercised by them as Mandatories on behalf of the League.

The character of the mandate must differ according to the stage of the development of the people, the geographical situation of the territory, its economic conditions, and other similar circumstances.

Certain communities formerly belonging to the Turkish Empire have reached a stage of development where their existence as independent nations can be provisionally recognised subject to the rendering of administrative advice and assistance by a Mandatory until such time as they are able to stand alone. The wishes of these communities must be a principal consideration in the selection of the Mandatory.

Other peoples, especially those of Central Africa, are at such a stage that the Mandatory must be responsible for the administration of the territory under conditions which will guarantee freedom of conscience and religion, subject only to the maintenance of public order and morals, the prohibition of abuses such as the slave trade, the arms traffic, and the liquor traffic, and the prevention of the establishment of fortifications or military and naval bases and of military training of the natives for other than police purposes and the defence of territory, and will also secure equal opportunities for the trade and commerce of other Members of the League.

There are territories, such as South-West Africa and certain of the South Pacific Islands, which, owing to the sparseness of their population, or their small size, or their remoteness from the centres of civilization, or their geographical contiguity to the territory of the Mandatory, and other circumstances, can be best administered under the laws of the Mandatory as integral portions of its territory, subject to the safeguards above mentioned in the interests of the indigenous population.

In every case of mandate, the Mandatory shall render to the Council an annual report in reference to the territory committed to its charge.

The degree of authority, control, or administration to be exercised by the Mandatory shall, if not previously agreed upon by the Members of the League, be explicitly defined in each case by the Council.

A permanent Commission shall be constituted to receive and examine the annual reports of the Mandatories and to advise the Council on all matters relating to the observance of the mandates.

Article 23

Subject to and in accordance with the provisions of international conventions existing or hereafter to be agreed upon, the Members of the League:

(a) Will endeavor to secure and maintain fair and humane conditions of labour for men, women and children, both in their own countries and in all countries to which their commercial and industrial relations extend, and for that purpose will establish and maintain the necessary international organisations.

(b) Undertake to secure just treatment of the native inhabitants of territories under their control.

(c) Will entrust the League with the general supervision over the execution of agreements with regard to the traffic in women and children, and the traffic in opium and other dangerous drugs;

(d) Will entrust the League with the general supervision of the trade in arms and ammunition with the countries in which the control of this traffic is necessary in the common interest;

(e) Will make provision to secure and maintain freedom of communications and of transit and equitable treatment for the commerce of all Members of the League. In this connection, the special necessities of the regions devastated during the war, of 1914-18 shall be borne in mind;

(f) Will endeavor to take steps in matters of international concern for the prevention and control of disease.

Article 24

There shall be placed under the direction of the League all international bureaux already established by general treaties if the parties to such treaties consent. All such international bureaux and all commissions for the regulation of matters of international interest hereafter constituted shall be placed under the direction of the League.

In all matters of international interest which are regulated by general conventions, but which are not placed under the control of international bureaux or commissions, the Secretariat of the League shall subject to the consent of the Council and if desired by the parties, collect and distribute all relevant information and shall render any other assistance which may be necessary or desirable.

The Council may include as part of the expenses of the Secretariat the expenses of any bureau or commission which is placed under the direction of the League.

Article 25

The Members of the League agree to encourage and promote the establishment and co-operation of duly authorised voluntary national Red Cross organisations having as purposes the improvement of health, the prevention of disease, and the mitigation of suffering throughout the world.

Article 26

Amendments to this Covenant will take effect when ratified by the Members of the League whose Representatives compose the Council and by a majority of the Members of the League whose Representatives compose the Assembly.

No such amendment shall bind any Member of the League which signifies its dissent therefrom, but in that case it shall cease to be a Member of the League.

Annex

Original Members of the League of Nations Signatories of the Treaty of Peace

United States of America	China
	Cuba
Belgium	Ecuador
Bolivia	France
Brazil	Greece
British Empire	Guatemala
Canada	Haiti
Australia	Hedjaz
South Africa	Honduras
New Zealand	Italy
India	Japan
Liberia	Roumania
Nicaragua	Serb-Croat-Slovene
Panama	State
Peru	Siam
Poland	Czecho-Slovakia
Portugal	Uruguay

States Invited to Accede to the Covenant

Argentine Republic	Persia
Chile	Salvador
Colombia	Spain
Denmark	Sweden
Netherlands	Switzerland
Norway	Venezuela
Paraguay	

PART II

BOUNDARIES OF GERMANY

Article 27

[The boundaries of Germany are determined in this article.]

Article 28

[The boundaries of East Prussia are determined in this article.]

Article 29

[This article specifies that the boundaries detailed in Articles 27-28 are drawn in red on a one-in-a-million map. The map was annexed to the original Treaty but is not included here.]

In the case of any discrepancies between the text of the Treaty and this map or any other map which may be annexed, the text will be final.

PART III

POLITICAL CLAUSES FOR EUROPE

Section I

Belgium

Article 31

Germany, recognizing that the Treaties of April 19, 1839, which established the status of Belgium before the war, no longer conform to the requirements of the situation, consents to the abrogation of the said treaties and undertakes immediately to recognize and to observe whatever conventions may be entered into by the Principal Allied and Associated Powers, or by any of them, in concert with the Governments, of Belgium and of the Netherlands, to replace the said Treaties of 1839. If her formal adhesion should be required to such conventions or to any of their stipulations, Germany undertakes immediately to give it.

Article 32

Germany recognizes the full sovereignty of Belgium over the whole of the contested territory of Moresnet (called *Moresnet neutre*).

Article 35

A Commission of seven persons, five of whom will be appointed by the Principal Allied and Associated Powers, one by Germany and one by Belgium, will be set up fifteen days after the coming into force of the present Treaty to settle on the spot the new frontier line between Belgium and Germany, taking into account the economic factors and the means of communication.

Decisions will be taken by a majority and will be binding on the parties concerned.

Section III
Left Bank of the Rhine

Article 42

Germany is forbidden to maintain or construct any fortifications either on the left bank of the Rhine or on the right bank to the west of a line drawn 50 kilometres to the East of the Rhine.

Article 43

In the area defined above the maintenance and the assembly of armed forces, either permanently or temporarily, and military maneuvres of any kind, as well as the upkeep of all permanent works for mobilisation, are in the same way forbidden.

Article 44

In case Germany violates in any manner whatever the provisions of Articles 42 and 43, she shall be regarded as committing a hostile act against the Powers signatory of the present Treaty and as calculated to disturb the peace of the world.

Section IV
Saar Basin

Article 45

As compensation for the destruction of the coal mines in the north of France and as part payment towards the total reparation due from Germany for the damage resulting from the war, Germany cedes to France in full and absolute possession, with exclusive rights of exploitation, unencumbered and free from all debts and charges of any kind, the coal mines situated in the Saar Basin as defined in Article 48.

Article 48

The boundaries of the territory of the Saar Basin, as dealt with in the present stipulations, [are fixed in this article].

Article 49

Germany renounces in favour of the League of Nations, in the capacity of trustee, the government of the territory defined above.

At the end of fifteen years from the coming into force of the present Treaty the inhabitants of the said territory shall be called upon to indicate the sovereignty under which they desire to be placed.

Section V
Alsace-Lorraine

The High Contracting Parties, recognising the moral obligation to redress the wrong done by Germany in 1871 both to the rights of France and to the wishes of the population of Alsace and Lorraine, which were separated from their country in spite of the solemn protest of their representatives at the Assembly of Bordeaux,

Agree upon the following Articles:

Article 51

The territories which were ceded to Germany in accordance with the Preliminaries of Peace signed at Versailles on February 26, 1871, and the Treaty of Frankfort of May 10, 1871, are restored to French sovereignty as from the date of the Armistice of November 11, 1918.

The provisions of the Treaties establishing the delimitation of the frontiers before 1871 shall be restored.

Article 52

The German Government shall hand over without delay to the French Government all archives, registers, plans, titles and documents of every kind concerning the civil, military, financial, judicial or other administrations of the territories restored to French sovereignty. If any of these documents, archives, registers, titles, or plans have been misplaced, they will be restored by the German Government on the demand of the French Government.

Article 60

The German Government shall without delay restore to Alsace-Lorrainers (individuals, juridical persons, and public institutions) all property, rights and interests belonging to them on November 11, 1918, in so far as these are situated in German territory.

Article 66

The railway and other bridges across the Rhine now existing within the limits of Alsace-Lorraine shall, as to all their parts and their whole length, be the property of the French State, which shall ensure their upkeep.

Section VI
Austria

Article 80

Germany acknowledges and will respect strictly the independence of Austria, within the frontiers which may be fixed in a Treaty between that State and the Principal Allied and Associated Powers; she agrees that this independence shall be inalienable, except with the consent of the Council of the League of Nations.

Section VII

Czecho-Slovak State

Article 81

Germany, in conformity with the action already taken by the Allied and Associated Powers, recognizes the complete independence of the Czecho-Slovak State, which will include the autonomous territory of the Ruthenians to the south of the Carpathians. Germany hereby recognizes the frontiers of this State as determined by the Principal Allied and Associated Powers and the other interested States.

Article 82

The old frontier as it existed on August 3, 1914, between Austria-Hungary and the German Empire will constitute the frontier between Germany and the Czecho-Slovak State.

Article 83

Germany renounces in favour of the Czecho-Slovak State all rights and title over the portion of Silesian territory defined [in this article].

Article 84

German nationals habitually resident in any of the territories recognized as forming part of the Czecho-Slovak State will obtain Czecho-Slovak nationality *ipso facto* and lose their German nationality.

Section VIII

Poland

Article 87

Germany, in conformity with the action already taken by the Allied and Associated Powers, recognizes the complete independence of Poland, and renounces in her favour all rights and title over the territory bounded by the Baltic Sea, the eastern frontier of Germany as laid down in Article 27 of Part 2 (Boundaries of Germany) of the present Treaty up to a point situated about 2 kilometres to the east of Lorzendorf, then a line to the acute angle which the northern boundary of Upper Silesia makes about 3 kilometres north-west of Simmenau, then the boundary of Upper Silesia to its meeting point with the old frontier between Germany and Russia, then this frontier to the point where it crosses the course of the Niemen and then the northern frontier of East Prussia as laid down in Article 28 of Part II aforesaid.

The provisions of this Article do not, however apply to the territories of East Prussia and the Free City of Danzig as defined in Article 28 of Part 2 (Boundaries of Germany) and in Article 100 of Section 11 (Danzig) of this Part.

The boundaries of Poland not laid down in the present Treaty will be subsequently determined by the Principal Allied and Associated Powers.

A Commission consisting of seven members, five of whom shall be nominated by the Principal Allied and Associated Powers, one by Germany and one by Poland, shall be constituted fifteen days after the coming into force of the present Treaty to delimit on the spot the frontier line between Poland and Germany.

The decisions of the Commission will be taken by a majority of votes and shall be binding upon the parties concerned.

Article 91

German nationals habitually resident in territories recognized as forming part of Poland will acquire Polish nationality *ipso facto* and will lose their German nationality.

German nationals' however, or their descendants who became resident in these territories after January 1, 1908, will not acquire Polish nationality without a special authorisation from the Polish State.

Within a period of two years after the coming into force of the present Treaty, German nationals over 18 years of age habitually resident in any of the territories recognized as forming part of Poland will be entitled to opt for German nationality.

Article 93

Poland accepts and agrees to embody in a Treaty with the Principal Allied and Associated Powers such provisions as may be deemed necessary by the said Powers to protect the interests of inhabitants of Poland who differ from the majority of the population in race, language, or religion.

Poland further accepts and agrees to embody in a Treaty with the said Powers such provisions as they may deem necessary to protect freedom of transit and equitable treatment of the commerce of other nations.

Section IX

East Prussia

Article 94

In the area between the southern frontier of East Prussia, as described in Article 28 of Part 2 (Boundaries of Germany) of the present Treaty, and the line described below, the inhabitants will be called upon to indicate by a vote the State to which they wish to belong: the western and northern boundary of *Regierung-sbezirk* Allenstein to its junction with the boundary between the *Kreise* of Oletsko and Angerburg; thence, the northern boundary of the *Kreis* of Oletsko to its junction with the old frontier of East Prussia.

Article 95

The German troops and authorities will be withdrawn from the area defined above within a period not exceeding fifteen days after the coming into force of the present Treaty. Until the evacuation is completed they will abstain from all requisitions in money or in kind and from all measures injurious to the economic interests of the country. [. . .]

Article 98

Germany and Poland undertake, within one year of the coming into force of this Treaty, to enter into Conventions of which the terms, in case of difference, shall be settled by the Council of the League of Nations, with the object of securing, on the one hand, to Germany full and adequate railroad, telegraphic and telephonic facilities for communication between the rest of Germany and East Prussia over the intervening Polish territory, and, on the other hand, to Poland full and adequate railroad, telegraphic and telephonic facilities for communication between Poland and the Free City of Danzig over any German territory that may, on the right bank of the Vistula, intervene between Poland and the Free City of Danzig.

Section XI

Free City of Danzig

Article 101

A Commission composed of three members appointed by the Principal Allied and Associated Powers, including a High Commissioner as President, one member appointed by Germany, and one member appointed by Poland, shall be constituted within fifteen days of the coming into force of the present Treaty for the purpose of delimiting on the spot the frontier of the territory as described above, taking into account as far as possible the existing communal boundaries.

Article 102

The Principal Allied and Associated Powers undertake to establish the town of Danzig . . . as a Free City. It will be placed under the protection of the League of Nations.

Article 103

A constitution for the Free City of Danzig shall be drawn up by the duly appointed representatives of the Free City in agreement with a High Commissioner to be appointed by the League of Nations. This constitution shall be placed under the guarantee of the League of Nations.

The High Commissioner will also be entrusted with the duty of dealing in the first instance with all differences arising between Poland and the Free City of Danzig in regard to this Treaty or any arrangements or agreements made thereunder.

The High Commissioner shall reside at Danzig.

Section XII

Schleswig

Article 109

The frontier between Germany and Denmark shall be fixed in conformity with the wishes of the population. [. . .]

Section XIII

Heligoland

Article 115

The fortifications, military establishments, and harbours of the Islands of Heligoland and Dune shall be destroyed under the supervision of the Principal Allied Governments by German labour and at the expense of Germany within a period to be determined by the said Governments.

The term "harbours" shall include the north-east mole, the west wall, the outer and inner breakwaters and reclaimed land within them, and all naval and military works, fortifications and buildings, constructed or under construction, between lines connecting the following positions taken from the British Admiralty chart No. 126 of April 19, 1918:

(a) lat. 54° 10′ 49″ N.; long. 7° 53′ 39″ E.;
(b) lat. 54° 10′ 35″ N.; long. 7° 54′ 18″ E.;
(c) lat. 54° 10′ 14″ N.; long. 7° 54′ 00″ E.;
(d) lat. 54° 10′ 17″ N.; long. 7° 53′ 37″ E.;
(e) lat. 54° 10′ 44″ N.; long. 7° 53′ 26″ E.;

These fortifications, military establishments and harbours shall not be reconstructed; nor shall any similar works be constructed in the future.

Section XIV

Russia and Russian States

Article 116

Germany acknowledges and agrees to respect as permanent and inalienable the independence of all the territories which were part of the former Russian Empire on August 1, 1914.

. . . Germany accepts definitely the abrogation of the Brest-Litovsk Treaties and of all other treaties, conventions and agreements entered into by her with the Maximalist Government in Russia.

The Allied and Associated Powers formally reserve the rights of Russia to obtain from Germany restitution and reparation based on the principles of the present Treaty.

PART IV

GERMAN RIGHTS AND INTERESTS OUTSIDE GERMANY

Article 118

In territory outside her European frontiers as fixed by the present Treaty, Germany renounces all rights, titles and privileges whatever in or over territory which belonged to her or to her allies, and all rights, titles and privileges whatever their origin which she held as against the Allied and Associated Powers.

Germany hereby undertakes to recognize and to conform to the measures which may be taken now or in the future by the Principal Allied and Associated Powers, in agreement where necessary with third Powers, in order to carry the above stipulation into effect.

In particular Germany declares her acceptance of the following Articles relating to certain special subjects.

Section I

German Colonies

Article 119

Germany renounces in favour of the Principal Allied and Associated Powers all her rights and titles over her overseas possessions.

Article 120

All movable and immovable property in such territories belonging to the German Empire or to any German State shall pass to the Government exercising authority over such territories . . . The decision of the local courts in any dispute as to the nature of such property shall be final.

Section II

China

Article 128

Germany renounces in favour of China all benefits and privileges resulting from the provisions of the final Protocol signed at Peking on September 7, 1901, and from all annexes, notes and documents supplementary thereto. She likewise renounces in favour of China any claim to indemnities accruing thereunder subsequent to March 14, 1917.

Section V

Morocco

Article 141

Germany renounces all rights titles and privileges conferred on her by the General Act of Algeciras of April 7, 1906, and by the Franco-German Agreements of February 9, 1909, and November 4, 1911. All treaties, agreements, arrangements and contracts concluded by her with the Sherifian Empire are regarded as abrogated as from August 3, 1914.

In no case can Germany take advantage of these instruments and she undertakes not to intervene in any way in negotiations relating to Morocco which may take place between France and the other Powers.

Article 142

Germany having recognized the French Protectorate in Morocco, hereby accepts all the consequences of its establishment, and she renounces the regime of the capitulations therein.

This renunciation shall take effect as from August 3, 1914.

Section VI

Egypt

Article 147

Germany declares that she recognizes the Protectorate proclaimed over Egypt by Great Britain on December 18, 1914, and that she renounces the régime of the Capitulations in Egypt.

This renunciation shall take effect as from August 4, 1914.

Section VIII

Shantung

Article 156

Germany renounces, in favour of Japan, all her rights, title and privileges—particularly those concerning the territory of Kiaochow, mines and submarine cables—which she acquired in virtue of the Treaty concluded by her with China on March 6, 1898, and of all other arrangements relative to the Province of Shantung.

All German rights in the Tsingtao-Tsinanfu Railway including its branch lines, together with its subsidiary property of all kinds, stations, shops, fixed and rolling stock mines plant and material for the exploitation of the mines, are and remain acquired by Japan, together with all rights and privileges attaching thereto.

The German State submarine cables from Tsingtao to Shanghai and from Tsingtao to Chefoo, with all the rights, privileges and properties attaching thereto, are similarly acquired by Japan, free and clear of all charges and encumbrances.

PART V

MILITARY, NAVAL AND AIR CLAUSES

In order to render possible the initiation of a general limitation of the armaments of all nations, Germany undertakes strictly to observe the military, naval and air clauses which follow.

Section I

Military Clauses

Chapter I

Effectives and Cadres of the German Army

Article 159

The German military forces shall be demobilised and reduced as prescribed hereinafter.

Article 160

1. By a date which must not be later than March 31, 1920, the German Army must not comprise more than seven divisions of infantry and three divisions of cavalry.

After that date the total number of effectives in the Army of the States constituting Germany must not exceed one hundred thousand men, including officers and establishments of depots. The Army shall be devoted exclusively to the maintenance of order within the territory and to the control of the frontiers.

The total effective strength of officers, including the personnel of staffs, whatever their composition, must not exceed four thousand.

2. Divisions and Army Corps headquarters staffs shall be organized in accordance with Table No. 1. ... [The table was annexed to this Section of the original Treaty but is not included here.]

The number and strengths of the units of infantry, artillery, engineers, technical services and troops laid down in the aforesaid Table constitute maxima which must not be exceeded.

The following units may each have their own depot:

An Infantry regiment;

A Cavalry regiment;

A regiment of Field Artillery;

A battalion of Pioneers.

3. The divisions must not be grouped under more than two army corps headquarters staffs.

The maintenance or formation of forces differently grouped or of other organizations for the command of troops or for preparation for war is forbidden.

The Great German General Staff and all similar organizations shall be dissolved and may not be reconstituted in any form.

The officers, or persons in the position of officers, in the Ministries of War in the different States in Germany and in the Administrations attached to them, must not exceed three hundred in number, and are included in the maximum strength of four thousand laid down in the third sub-paragraph of paragraph (1) of this Article.

Article 163

[How the reduction in strength of the German

military forces provided for in Article 160 is to be effected.]

Chapter II

Armament, Munitions and Material

Article 164

Up till the time at which Germany is admitted as a member of the League of Nations, the German Army must not possess an armament greater than the amounts fixed in Table No. 2 [the table was annexed to this Section of the original Treaty but is not included here] ... with the exception of an optional increase not exceeding one-twenty-fifth part for small arms and one-fiftieth part for guns, which shall be exclusively used to provide for such eventual replacements as may be necessary.

Germany agrees that after she has become a member of the League of Nations the armaments fixed in the said Table shall remain in force until they are modified by the Council of the League. Furthermore, she hereby agrees strictly to observe the decisions of the Council of the League on this subject.

[*Articles 165-167* specify the number of armaments and stock of munitions that Germany is allowed to maintain]

Article 168

The manufacture of arms, munitions, or any war material shall only be carried out in factories or works the location of which shall be communicated to and approved by the Governments of the Principal Allied and Associated Powers, and the number of which they retain the right to restrict.

Within three months from the coming into force of the present Treaty, all other establishments for the manufacture, preparation, storage or design of arms, munitions, or any war material whatever shall be closed down. The same applies to all arsenals except those used as depots for the authorized stocks of munitions. Within the same period the personnel of these arsenals will be dismissed.

Article 170

Importation into Germany of arms, munitions and war material of every kind shall be strictly prohibited.

The same applies to the manufacture for, and export to, foreign countries of arms, munitions and war material of every kind.

Chapter III

Recruiting and Military Training

Article 173

Universal compulsory military service shall be abolished in Germany.

The German Army may only be constituted and recruited by means of voluntary enlistment.

Article 177

Educational establishments, the universities, societies of discharged soldiers, shooting or touring clubs, and, generally speaking, associations of every description, whatever be the age of their members, must not occupy themselves with any military matters.

In particular they will be forbidden to instruct or exercise their members, or to allow them to be instructed or exercised, in the profession or use of arms.

These societies, associations, educational establishments and universities must have no connection with the Ministries of War or any other military authority.

Article 179

Germany agrees, from the coming into force of the present Treaty, not to accredit nor to send to any foreign country any military, naval or air mission, nor to allow any such mission to leave her territory, and Germany further agrees to take appropriate measures to prevent German nationals from leaving her territory to become enrolled in the Army, Navy or Air Service of any foreign Power, or to be attached to such Army, Navy or Air service for the purpose of assisting in the military, naval or air training thereof, or otherwise for the purpose of giving military, naval or air instruction in any foreign country.

The Allied and Associated Powers agree, so far as they are concerned, from the coming into force of the present Treaty not to enrol in nor to attach to their armies or naval or air forces any German national for the purpose of assisting in the military training of such armies, or naval or air forces, or otherwise to employ any such German national as military, naval or aeronautic instructor.

The present provision does not, however, affect the right of France to recruit for the Foreign Legion in accordance with French military laws and regulations.

Chapter IV

Fortifications

Article 180

All fortified works, fortresses and field works situated in German territory to the west of a line drawn fifty kilometres to the east of the Rhine shall be disarmed and dismantled.

Within a period of two months from the coming into force of the present Treaty such of the above fortified works fortresses and field works as are situated in territory not occupied by Allied and Associated troops shall be disarmed, and within a further period of four months they shall be dismantled. Those which are situated in territory occupied by Allied and Associated troops shall be disarmed and dismantled within such periods as may be fixed by the Allied High Command.

The construction of any new fortification, whatever its nature and importance, is forbidden in the zone referred to in the first paragraph above.

The system of fortified works of the southern and eastern frontiers of Germany shall be maintained in its existing state.

Section II

Naval Clauses

Article 181

After the expiration of a period of two months from the coming into force of the present Treaty the German naval forces in commission must not exceed:

6 battleships of the *Deutschland or Lothringen* type,

6 light cruisers,

12 destroyers,

12 torpedo boats,

or an equal number of ships constructed to replace them as provided in Article 190.

No submarines are to be included.

All other warships, except where there is provision to the contrary in the present Treaty, must be placed in reserve or devoted to commercial purposes.

Article 183

After the expiration of a period of two months from the coming into force of the present Treaty the total personnel of the German Navy, including the manning of the fleet, coast defences, signal stations, administration and other land services, must not exceed fifteen thousand, including officers and men of all grades and corps.

The total strength of officers and warrant officers must not exceed fifteen hundred.

Within two months from the coming into force of the present Treaty the personnel in excess of the above strength shall be demobilised.

No naval or military corps or reserve force in connection with the Navy may be organized in Germany without being included in the above strength.

Article 184

From the date of the coming into force of the present Treaty all the German surface warships which are not in German ports cease to belong to Germany, who renounces all rights over them.

Vessels which, in compliance with the Armistice of November 11, 1918, are now interned in the ports of the Allied and Associated Powers, are declared to be finally surrendered.

Vessels which are now interned in neutral ports will be there surrendered to the Governments of the Principal Allied and Associated Powers. The German Government must address a notification to that effect to the neutral Powers on the coming into force of the present Treaty.

Article 188

On the expiration of one month from the coming into force of the present Treaty all German submarines, submarine salvage vessels, and docks for submarines, including the tubular dock, must have been handed over to the Governments of the Principal Allied and Associated Powers.

Such of these submarines, vessels and docks as are considered by the said Governments to be fit to proceed under their own power or to be towed shall be taken by the German Government into such Allied ports as have been indicated.

The remainder, and also those in course of construction, shall be broken up entirely by the German Government under the supervision of the said Governments. The breaking-up must be completed within three months at the most after the coming into force of the present Treaty.

Article 190

Germany is forbidden to construct or acquire any warships other than those intended to replace the units in commission provided for in Article 181 of the present Treaty.

The warships intended for replacement purposes as above shall not exceed the following displacement:

Armoured ships................................10,000 tons,
Light cruisers ....6,000 tons,
Destroyers...800 tons,
Torpedo boats ....200 tons.

Article 191

The construction or acquisition of any submarine, even for commercial purposes, shall be forbidden in Germany.

Article 195

In order to ensure free passage into the Baltic to all nations, Germany shall not erect any fortifications in the area comprised between latitudes 55° 27′ N. and 54° 00′ N. and longitudes 9° 00′ E. and 16° 00′ E. of the meridian of Greenwich, nor install any guns commanding the maritime routes between the north Sea and the Baltic. The fortifications now existing in this area shall be demolished and the guns removed under the supervision of the Allied Governments and in periods to be fixed by them. [. . .]

Section III

Air Clauses

Article 198

The armed forces of Germany must not include any military or naval air forces.

Germany may, during a period not extending beyond October 1, 1919, maintain a maximum number of one hundred seaplanes or flying boats, which shall be exclusively employed in searching for submarine mines, shall be furnished with the necessary equipment for this purpose, and shall in no case carry arms, munitions or bombs of any nature whatever.

In addition to the engines installed in the seaplanes or flying boats above mentioned, one spare engine may be provided for each engine of each of these craft.

No dirigible shall be kept.

Article 199

Within two months from the coming into force of the present Treaty the personnel of the air forces on the rolls of the German land and sea forces shall be demolished. Up to October 1, 1919, however, Germany may keep and maintain a total number of one thousand men, including officers, for the whole of the cadres and personnel, flying and non-flying, of all formations and establishments.

Article 200

Until the complete evacuation of German territory by the Allied and Associated troops, the aircraft of the Allied and Associated Powers shall enjoy in Germany freedom of passage through the air, freedom of transit and of landing.

Article 201

During the six months following the coming into force of the present Treaty, the manufacture and importation of aircraft, parts of aircraft, engines for aircraft, and parts of engines for aircraft, shall be forbidden in all German territory.

Section IV

Inter-Allied Commissions of Control

Article 203

All the military, naval and air clauses contained in the present Treaty, for the execution of which a time limit is prescribed, shall be executed by Germany under the control of Inter-Allied Commissions specially appointed for this purpose by the Principal Allied and Associated Powers.

Article 204

The Inter-Allied Commissions of Control will be specially charged with the duty of seeing to the complete execution of the delivery, destruction, demolition and rendering things useless to be carried out at the expense of the German Government in accordance with the present Treaty.

They will communicate to the German authorities the decisions which the Principal Allied and Associated Powers have reserved the right to take, or which the execution of the military, naval and air clauses may necessitate.

Article 207

The upkeep and cost of the Commissions of Control and the expenses involved by their work shall be borne by Germany.

PART VI

PRISONERS OF WAR AND GRAVES

Section I

Prisoners of War

Article 214

The repatriation of prisoners of war and interned civilians shall take place as soon as possible after the coming into force of the present Treaty, and shall be carried out with the greatest rapidity.

Article 215

The repatriation of German prisoners of war and interned civilians shall, in accordance with Article 214, be carried out by a Commission composed of representatives of the Allied and Associated Powers on the one part and of the German Government on the other part.

For each of the Allied and Associated Powers a Sub-Commission, composed exclusively of Representatives of the interested Power and of Delegates of the German Government, shall regulate the details of carrying into effect the repatriation of the prisoners of war.

Article 217

The whole cost of repatriation from the moment of starting shall be borne by the German Government, who shall also provide the land or sea transport and staff considered necessary by the Commission referred to in Article 215.

Section II

Graves

Article 225

The Allied and Associated Governments and the German Government will cause to be respected and maintained, the graves of the soldiers and sailors buried in their respective territories. [. . .]

Article 226

The graves of prisoners of war and interned civilians who are nationals of the different belligerent States and have died in captivity shall be properly maintained in accordance with Article 225 of the present Treaty.

The Allied and Associated Governments on the one part and the German Government on the other part reciprocally undertake also to furnish to each other:

(1) A complete list of those who have died, together with all information useful for identification;
(2) All information as to the number and position of the graves of all those who have been buried without identification.

PART VII

PENALTIES

Article 227

The Allied and Associated Powers publicly arraign William 2 of Hohenzollern, formerly German Emperor, for a supreme offence against international morality and the sanctity of treaties.

A special tribunal will be constituted to try the accused, thereby assuring him the guarantees essential to the right of defence. It will be composed of five judges, one appointed by each of the following Powers: namely, the United States of America, Great Britain, France, Italy and Japan.

In its decision, the tribunal will be guided by the highest motives of international policy, with a view to vindicating the solemn obligations of international undertakings and the validity of international morality. It will be its duty to fix the punishment which it considers should be imposed.

The Allied and Associated Powers will address a request to the Government of the Netherlands for the surrender to them of the ex-Emperor in order that he may be put on trial.

Article 228

The German Government recognizes the right of the Allied and Associated Powers to bring before military tribunals persons accused of having committed acts in violation of the laws and customs of war. Such persons shall, if found guilty, be sentenced to punishments laid down by law. This provision will apply notwithstanding any proceedings or prosecution before a tribunal in Germany or in the territory of her allies.

The German Government shall hand over to the Allied and Associated Powers, or to such one of them as shall so request, all persons accused of having committed an act in violation of the laws and customs of war, who are specified either by name or by the rank, office or employment which they held under the German authorities.

Article 229

Persons guilty of criminal acts against the nationals of one of the Allied and Associated Powers will be brought before the military tribunals of that Power.

Persons guilty of criminal acts against the nationals of more than one of the Allied and Associated Powers will be brought before military tribunals composed of members of the military tribunals of the Powers concerned.

In every case the accused will be entitled to name his own counsel.

PART VIII

REPARATION

Section I

General Provisions

Article 231

The Allied and Associated Governments affirm and Germany accepts the responsibility of Germany and her allies for causing all the loss and damage to which the Allied and Associated Governments and their nationals have been subjected as a consequence of the war imposed upon them by the aggression of Germany and her allies.

Article 232

The Allied and Associated Governments recognize that the resources of Germany are not adequate, after taking into account permanent diminutions of such resources which will result from other provisions of the present Treaty, to make complete reparation for all such loss and damage.

The Allied and Associated Governments, however, require, and Germany undertakes, that she will make compensation for all damage done to the civilian population of the Allied and Associated Powers and to their property during the period of the belligerency of each as an Allied or associated Power against Germany by such aggression by land, by sea, and from the air, and in general all damages as defined in Annex I hereto [not included here]. . . .

Article 233

The amount of the above damage for which compensation is to be made by Germany shall be determined by an Inter-Allied Commission, to be called the *Reparation Commission* and constituted in the form and with the powers set forth hereunder and in Annexes II to VII inclusive hereto [not included here]. . . .

Article 235

In order to enable the Allied and Associated Powers to proceed at once to the restoration of their industrial and economic life, pending the full determination of their claims, Germany shall pay in such instalments and in such manner (whether in gold, commodities, ships, securities or otherwise) as the Reparation Commission may fix, during 1919, 1920, and the first four months of 1921, the equivalent of 20,000,000,000 gold marks. Out of this sum the expenses of the armies of occupation subsequent to the Armistice of November 11, 1918, shall first be met, and such supplies of food and raw materials as may be judged by the Governments of the Principal Allied and Associated Powers to be essential to enable Germany to meet her obligations for reparation may also, with the approval of the said Governments, be paid for out of the above sum. The balance shall be reckoned towards liquidation of the amounts due for reparation. Germany shall further deposit bonds as prescribed in paragraph 12 (*c*) of Annex II hereto.

Article 238

In addition to the payments mentioned above, Germany shall effect, in accordance with the procedure laid down by the Reparation Commission, restitution in cash of cash taken away, seized or sequestrated, and also restitution of animals, objects of every nature and securities taken away, seized or sequestrated, in the cases in which it proves possible to identify them in territory belonging to Germany or her allies. [. . .]

PART IX

FINANCIAL CLAUSES

Article 248

Subject to such exceptions as the Reparation Commission may approve, a first charge upon all the assets and revenues of the German Empire and its constituent States shall be the cost of reparation and all other costs arising under the present Treaty or any treaties or agreements supplementary thereto or under arrangements concluded between Germany and the Allied and Associated Powers during the Armistice or its extensions.

Up to May 1, 1921, the German Government shall not export or dispose of, and shall forbid the export or disposal of, gold without the previous approval of the Allied and Associated Powers acting through the Reparation Commission.

Article 249

There shall be paid by the German Government the

total cost of all armies of the Allied and Associated Governments in occupied German territory from the date of the signature of the Armistice of November 11, 1918, including the keep of men and beasts, lodging and billeting, pay and allowances, salaries and wages, bedding, heating, lighting, clothing, equipment, harness and saddlery, armament and rolling-stock, air services, treatment of sick and wounded, veterinary and remount services, transport service of all sorts (such as by rail, sea or river, motor lorries), communications and correspondence, and in general the cost of all administrative or technical services the working of which is necessary for the training of troops and for keeping their numbers up to strength and preserving their military efficiency. [. . .]

PART X

ECONOMIC CLAUSES

Section 1

Commercial Relations

Chapter 1

Customs, Regulations, Duties and Restrictions

Article 264

Germany undertakes that goods, the produce or manufacture of any one of the Allied or Associated States imported into German territory, from whatsoever place arriving, shall not be subject to other or higher duties or charges (including internal charges) than those to which the like goods the produce or manufacture of any other such State or of any other foreign country are subject.

Germany will not maintain or impose any prohibition or restriction on the importation into German territory of any goods the produce of manufacture of the territories of any one of the Allied or Associated States, from whatsoever place arriving which shall not equally extend to the importation of the like goods, the produce or manufacture of any other such State or of any other foreign country.

PART XI

AERIAL NAVIGATION

Article 313

The aircraft of the Allied and Associated Powers shall have full liberty of passage and landing over and in the territory and territorial waters of Germany,

and shall enjoy the same privileges as German aircraft, particularly in case of distress by land or sea.

Article 314

The aircraft of the Allied and Associated Powers shall, while in transit to any foreign country whatever, enjoy the right of flying over the territory and territorial waters of Germany without landing, subject always to any regulations which may be made by Germany and which shall be applicable equally to the aircraft of Germany and to those of the Allied and Associated countries.

Article 315

All aerodromes in Germany open to national public traffic shall be open for the aircraft of the Allied and Associated Powers, and in any such aerodrome such aircraft shall be treated on a footing of equality with German aircraft as regards charges of every description, including charges for landing and accommodation.

PART XII

PORTS, WATERWAYS AND RAILWAYS

Section I

General Provisions

Article 321

Germany undertakes to grant freedom of transit through her territories on the routes most convenient for international transit, either by rail, navigable waterway, or canal, to persons, goods, vessels, carriages, wagons and mails coming from or going to the territories of any of the Allied and Associated Powers (whether contiguous or not); for this purpose the crossing of territorial waters shall be allowed. Such persons, goods, vessels, carriages, wagons and mails shall not be subjected to any transit duty or to any undue delays or restrictions, and shall be entitled in Germany to national treatment as regards charges, facilities, and all other matters.

Goods in transit shall be exempt from all Customs or other similar duties.

Section II

Navigation

Chapter I

Freedom of Navigation

Article 327

The nationals of any of the Allied and Associated Powers as well as their vessels and property shall enjoy in all German ports and on the inland navigation routes of Germany the same treatment in all respects as German nationals, vessels and property. [...]

Chapter III

Clauses Relating to the Elbe, the Oder, the Niemen (Russstrom-Memel-Niemen) and the Danube

Article 331

The following rivers are declared international:
the Elbe (*Labe*) from its confluence with the Vltava (*Moldau*) and the Vltava (*Moldau*) from Prague;
the Oder (*Odra*) from its confluence with the Oppa;
the Niemen (*Russstrom-Memel-Niemen*) from Grodno;
the Danube from Ulm;

and all navigable parts of these river systems which naturally provide more than one State with access to the sea, with or without transhipment from one vessel to another, together with lateral canals and channels constructed either to duplicate or to improve naturally navigable sections of the specified river systems, or to connect two naturally navigable sections of the same river.

Section III

Railways

Chapter I

Clauses relating to International Transport

Article 365

Goods coming from the territories of the Allied and Associated Powers, and going to Germany, or in transit through Germany from or to the territories of the Allied and Associated Powers, shall enjoy on the German railways as regards charges to be collected (rebates and drawbacks being taken into account), facilities and all other matters, the most favourable treatment applied to goods of the same kind carried on any German lines, either in internal traffic, or for export, import or in transit, under similar conditions of transport, for example as regards length of route. The same rule shall be applied, on the request of one or more of the Allied and Associated Powers, to goods specially designated by such Power or Powers coming from Germany and going to their territories. [...]

Chapter IV

Provisions Relating to Certain Railway Lines

Article 372

When as a result of the fixing of new frontiers a railway connection between two parts of the same country crosses another country, or a branch line from one country has its terminus in another, the conditions of working, if not specifically provided for in the present Treaty, shall be laid down in a convention between the railway administrations concerned. If the administrations cannot come to an agreement as to the terms of such convention the points of difference shall be decided by commissions of experts composed as provided in the preceding article.

Section IV

Disputes and Revision of Permanent Clauses

Article 376

Disputes which may arise between interested Powers, with regard to the interpretation and application of the preceding Articles shall be settled as provided by the League of Nations.

Article 377

At any time the League of Nations may recommend the revision of such of these Articles as relate to a permanent administrative régime.

Section VI

Clauses Relating to the Kiel Canal

Article 380

The Kiel Canal and its approaches shall be maintained free and open to the vessels of commerce and of war of all nations at peace with Germany on terms of entire equality.

PART XIII

LABOUR

Section I

Organization of Labour

Whereas the League of Nations has for its object the establishment of universal peace, and such a peace can be established only if it is based upon social justice;

And whereas conditions of labour exist involving such injustice, hardship and privation to large numbers of people as to produce unrest so great that the peace and harmony of the world are imperilled; and an improvement of those conditions is urgently required: as, for example, by the regulation of the hours of work, including the establishment of a maximum working day and week, the regulation of the labour supply, the prevention of unemployment, the provision of an adequate living wage, the protection of the worker against sickness, disease and injury arising out of his employment, the protection of children, young persons and women, provision for old age and injury, protection of the interests of workers when employed in countries other than their own, recognition of the principle of freedom of association, the organization of vocational and technical education and other measures.

Whereas also the failure of any nation to adopt humane conditions of labour is an obstacle in the way of other nations which desire to improve the conditions in their own countries;

The High Contracting Parties, moved by sentiments of justice and humanity, as well as by the desire to secure the permanent peace of the world, agree to the following:

Chapter I

Organization

Article 387

A permanent organization is hereby established for the promotion of the objects set forth in the Preamble.

The original Members of the League of Nations shall be the original Members of this organization, and hereafter membership of the League of Nations shall carry with it membership of the said organization.

Article 388

The permanent organizations shall consist of:
(1) a General Conference of Representatives of the Members and,
(2) an International Labour Office controlled by the Governing Body described in Article 393.

Article 392

The International Labour Office shall be established at the seat of the League of Nations as part of the organization of the League.

[*Articles 393-397* specify the direction, organization,

and functions of the International Labour Office]

[*Articles 400-420* specify the procedures for the functioning of the International Labour Office]

Section II

General Principles

Article 427

The High Contracting Parties, recognizing that the well-being, physical, moral and intellectual, of industrial wage-earners is of supreme international importance, have framed, in order to further this great end, the permanent machinery provided for in Section I and associated with that of the League of Nations.

They recognize that differences of climate, habits and customs, of economic opportunity and industrial tradition, make strict uniformity in the conditions of labour difficult of immediate attainment. But, holding as they do, that labour should not be regarded merely as an article of commerce, they think that there are methods and principles for regulating labour conditions which all industrial communities should endeavour to apply so far as their special circumstances will permit.

Among these methods and principles, the following seem to the High Contracting Parties to be of special and urgent importance:

First—The guiding principle above enunciated that labour should not be regarded merely as a commodity or article of commerce.

Second—The right of association for all lawful purposes by the employed as well as by the employers.

Third—The payment to the employed of a wage adequate to maintain a reasonable standard of life as this is understood in their time and country.

Fourth—The adoption of an eight hour day or a forty-eight hour week as the standard to be aimed at where it has not already been attained.

Fifth—The adoption of weekly rest of at least twenty-four hours, which should include Sunday wherever practicable.

Sixth—The abolition of child labour and the imposition of such limitations on the labour of young persons as shall permit the continuation of their education and assure their proper physical development.

Seventh—The principle that men and women should receive equal remuneration for work of equal value.

Eighth—The standard set by law in each country with respect to the conditions of labour should have due regard to the equitable economic treatment of all workers lawfully resident therein.

Ninth—Each State should make provision for a system of inspection in which women should take part, in order to ensure the enforcement of the laws and regulations for the protection of the employed.

Without claiming that these methods and principles are either complete or final, the High Contracting Parties are of opinion that they are well fitted to guide the policy of the League of Nations; and that, if adopted by the industrial communities who are members of the League, and safeguarded in practice by an adequate system of such inspection, they will confer lasting benefits upon the wage-earners of the world.

PART XIV

GUARANTEES

Section I

Western Europe

Article 428

As a guarantee for the execution of the present Treaty by Germany, the German territory situated to the west of the Rhine together with the bridgeheads, will be occupied by Allied and Associated troops for a period of fifteen years from the coming into force of the present Treaty.

Section II

Eastern Europe

Article 433

As a guarantee for the execution of the provisions of the present Treaty, by which Germany accepts definitely the abrogation of the Brest-Litovsk Treaty, and of all treaties, conventions and agreements entered into by her with the Maximalist Government in Russia, and in order to ensure the restoration of peace and good government in the Baltic Provinces and Lithuania, all German troops at present in the said territories shall return to within the frontiers of Germany as soon as the Governments of the Principal Allied and Associated Powers shall think the moment suitable, having regard to the internal situation of these territories. These troops shall abstain from all requisitions and seizures and from any other coercive measures, with a view to obtaining supplies

intended for Germany, and shall in no way interfere with such measures for national defence as may be adopted by the Provisional Governments of Esthonia, Latvia and Lithuania.

No other German troops shall, pending the evacuation or after the evacuation is complete, be admitted to the said territories.

PART XV

MISCELLANEOUS PROVISIONS

Article 434

Germany undertakes to recognize the full force of the Treaties of Peace and Additional Conventions which may be concluded by the Allied and Associated Powers with the Powers who fought on the side of Germany and to recognize whatever dispositions may be made concerning the territories of the former Austro-Hungarian Monarchy, of the Kingdom of Bulgaria and of the Ottoman Empire, and to recognize the new States within the frontiers as there laid down.

The Present Treaty, of which the French and English texts are both authentic, shall be ratified.

The deposit of ratifications shall be made at Paris as soon as possible.

Powers of which the seat of the Government is outside Europe will be entitled merely to inform the Government of the French Republic through their diplomatic representative at Paris that their ratification has been given; in that case they must transmit the instrument of ratification as soon as possible.

A first procès-verbal of the deposit of ratifications will be drawn up as soon as the Treaty has been ratified by Germany on the one hand, and by three of the Principal Allied and Associated Powers on the other hand.

From the date of this first procès-verbal the Treaty will come into force between the High Contracting Parties who have ratified it. For the determination of all periods of time provided for in the present Treaty this date will be the date of the coming into force of the Treaty.

In all other respects the Treaty will enter into force for each Power at the date of the deposit of its ratification.

The French Government will transmit to all the signatory Powers a certified copy of the procès-verbaux of the deposit of ratifications.

Treaty Concerning the Archipelago of Spitsbergen

Date of signature: February 9, 1920
Place of signature: Paris
Signatory states: the United States, Great Britain, Ireland and the British Dominions, India, Denmark, the French Republic, Italy Japan, Norway, the Netherlands, Sweden

[The Signatories],
Desirous, while recognising the sovereignty of Norway over the Archipelago of Spitsbergen, including Bear Island, of seeing these territories provided with an equitable regime, in order to assure their development and peaceful utilisation, . . . have agreed as follows:

Article 1

The High Contracting Parties undertake to recognise, subject to the stipulations of the present Treaty, the full and absolute sovereignty of Norway over the Archipelago of Spitsbergen, comprising, with Bear Island or Beeren-Eiland, all the islands situated between 10° and 35° longitude East of Greenwich and between 74° and 81° latitude North, especially West Spitsbergen, North-East Land, Barents Island, Edge Island, Wiche Islands, Hope Island or Hopen-Eiland, and Prince Charles Foreland, together with all islands great or small and rocks appertaining thereto.

Article 2

Ships and nationals of all the High Contracting Parties shall enjoy equally the rights of fishing and hunting in the territories specified in Article I and in their territorial waters.

Norway shall be free to maintain, take or decree suitable measures to ensure the preservation and, if necessary, the re-constitution of the fauna and flora of the said regions, and their territorial waters; it being clearly understood that these measures shall always be applicable equally to the nationals of all the High Contracting Parties without any exemption, privilege or favour whatsoever, direct or indirect to the advantage of any one of them.

Occupiers of land whose rights have been recognised in accordance with the terms of Articles 6 and 7 will enjoy the exclusive right of hunting on their own land: (1) in the neighbourhood of their habitations, houses, stores, factories and installations, constructed for the purpose of developing their property, under conditions laid down by the local police regulations; (2) within a radius of 10 kilometres round the head-quarters of their place of business or works; and in both cases, subject always to the observance of regulations made by the Norwegian Government in accordance with the conditions laid down in the present Article.

Article 3

The nationals of all the High Contracting Parties shall have equal liberty of access and entry for any reason or object whatever to the waters, fjords and ports of the territories specified in Article 1; subject to the observance of local laws and regulations, they may carry on there without impediment all maritime, industrial, mining and commercial operations on a footing of absolute equality.

They shall be admitted under the same conditions of equality to the exercise and practice of all maritime, industrial, mining or commercial enterprises both on land in territorial waters, and no monopoly shall be established on any account or for any enterprise whatever.

Notwithstanding any rules relating to coasting trade which may be in force in Norway, ships of the High Contracting Parties going to or coming from the territories specified in Article 1 shall have the right to put into Norwegian ports on their outward or homeward voyage for the purpose of taking on board or disembarking passengers or cargo going to or coming from the said territories, or for any other purpose.

It is agreed that in every respect and especially with regard to exports, imports and transit traffic, the nationals of all the High Contracting Parties, their ships and goods shall not be subject to any charges or restrictions whatever which are not borne by the nationals, ships or goods which enjoy in Norway the treatment of the most favoured nation; Norwegian nationals, ships or goods being for this purpose assimilated to those of the other High Contracting Parties, and not treated more favourably in any respect.

No charge or restriction shall be imposed on the exportation of any goods to the territories of any of the Contracting Powers other or more onerous than on the exportation of similar goods to the territory of any other Contracting Power (including Norway) or to any other destination.

Article 4

All public wireless stations established or to be established by or with the authorisation of the Norwegian Government within the territories referred to in Article I shall always be open on a footing of absolute equality to communications from ships of all flags and from nationals of the High Contracting Parties, under the conditions laid down in the Wireless Telegraphy Convention of July 5th, 1912, or in the subsequent International Convention which may be concluded to replace it.

Subject to international obligations arising out of a state of war, owners of landed property shall always be at liberty to establish and use for their own purposes wireless telegraphy installations, which shall be free to communicate on private business with fixed or moving wireless stations, including those on board ships and aircraft.

Article 5

The High Contracting Parties recognise the utility of establishing an international meteorological station in the territories specified in Article 1, the organisation of which shall form the subject of a subsequent Convention.

Conventions shall also be concluded laying down the conditions under which scientific investigations may be conducted in the said territories.

Article 6

Subject to the provisions of the present Article, acquired rights of nationals of the High Contracting Parties shall be recognised.

Claims arising from taking possession or from occupation of land before the signature of the present Treaty shall be dealt with in accordance with the Annex hereto, which will have the same force and effect as the present Treaty.

Article 7

With regard to methods of acquisition, enjoyment and exercise of the right of ownership of property, including mineral rights, in the territories specified in Article 1, Norway undertakes to grant to all nationals of the High Contracting Parties treatment based on complete equality and in conformity with the stipulations of the present Treaty.

Expropriation may be resorted to only on grounds of public utility and on payment of proper compensation.

Article 8

Norway undertakes to provide for the territories specified in Article 1 mining regulations which, especially from the point of view of imports, taxes or charges of any kind, and of general or particular labour conditions, shall exclude all privileges, monopolies or favours for the benefit of the State or of the nationals of any one of the High Contracting Parties, including Norway, and shall guarantee to the paid staff of all categories the remuneration and protection necessary for their physical, moral and intellectual welfare.

Taxes, dues and duties levied shall be devoted exclusively to the said territories and shall not exceed what is required for the object in view.

So far, particularly, as the exportation of minerals is concerned, the Norwegian Government shall have the right to levy an export duty which shall not exceed 1% of the maximum value of the minerals exported up to 100,000 tons, and beyond that quantity the duty will be proportionately diminished. The value shall be fixed at the end of the navigation season by calculating the average free on board price obtained.

Three months before the date fixed for their coming into force, the draft mining regulations shall be communicated by the Norwegian Government to the other Contracting Powers. If during this period one or more of the said Powers propose to modify these regulations before they are applied, such proposals shall be communicated by the Norwegian Government to the other Contracting Powers in order that they may be submitted to examination and the decision of a Commission composed of one representative each of the said Powers. This Commission shall meet at the invitation of the Norwegian Government and shall come to a decision within a period of three months from the date of its first meeting. Its decisions shall be taken by a majority.

Article 9

Subject to the rights and duties resulting from the admission of Norway to the League of Nations, Norway undertakes not to create nor to allow the establishment of any naval base in the territories specified in Article 1 and not to construct any fortification in the said territories, which may never be used for war like purposes.

Article 10

Until the recognition of the High Contracting Parties of a Russian Government shall permit Russia to adhere to the present Treaty, Russian nationals and companies shall enjoy the same rights as nationals of the High Contracting Parties.

Claims in the territories specified in Article 1 which they may have to put forward shall be presented under the conditions laid down in the present Treaty (Article 6 and Annex) through the intermediary of the Danish Government, who declare their willingness to lend their good offices for this purpose.

The PRESENT TREATY, of which the French and English texts are both authentic, shall be ratified.

Ratifications shall be deposited at Paris as soon as possible.

Powers of which the seat of the Government is outside Europe may confine their action to informing the Government of the French Republic, through their diplomatic representative at Paris, that their ratification has been given, and in this case they shall transmit the instrument as soon as possible.

The present Treaty will come into force, in so far as the stipulations of Article 8 are concerned, from the date of its ratification by all the signatory Powers; and in all other respects on the same date as the mining regulations provided for in that Article.

Third Powers will be invited by the Government of the French Republic to adhere to the present Treaty duly ratified. This adhesion shall be effected by a communication addressed to the French Government, which will undertake to notify the other Contracting Parties.

Convention Relating to the Non-Fortification and Neutralisation of the Aaland Islands

Date of signature: October 20, 1921
Place of signature: Geneva
Signatory states: Germany, Denmark, Iceland, Estonian Republic, Republic of Finland, the French Republic, Great Britain, Ireland and the British Dominions, India, Italy, Republic of Latvia, Poland, Sweden
Ratifications: Germany, Denmark, Finland, France, the British Empire, Sweden, Italy, Poland, Latvia

[The signatories],
having agreed to carry out the recommendation formulated by the Council of the League of Nations in its Resolution of June 24, 1921, that a Convention should be concluded between the interested Powers with a view to the non-fortification and neutralisation of the Aaland Islands in order that these islands may never become a cause of danger from the military point of view;

Have resolved for this purpose to supplement without prejudice thereto, the obligations assumed by Russia in the Convention of March 30, 1856, regarding the Aaland Islands, annexed to the Treaty of Paris of the same date;

Who, having deposited their full powers, found in good and due form, have agreed upon the following provisions:

Article 1

Finland, confirming, for her part as far as necessary, the declaration made by Russia in the Convention of March 30, 1856, regarding the Aaland Islands, annexed to the Treaty of Paris of the same date, undertakes not to fortify that part of the Finnish Archipelago which is called "the Aaland Islands."

Article 2

I. This article gives the geographical position of the Aaland Islands.

II. The territorial waters of the Aaland Islands are considered to extend for a distance of three marine miles from the low-water mark on the islands, islets and reefs not permanently submerged, delimited above; nevertheless, these waters shall at no point extend beyond the lines fixed in section I of this Article.

III. The whole of the islands, islets and reefs delimited in paragraph I and of the territorial waters defined in paragraph II constitute the zone to which the following Articles apply.

Article 3

No military or naval establishment or base of operations, no military aircraft establishment or base of operations, and no other installation used for war purposes shall be maintained or set up in the zone described in Article 2.

Article 4

Except as provided in Article 7, no military, naval or air force of any Power shall enter or remain in the zone described in Article 2; the manufacture, import, transport and re-export of arms and implements of war in this zone are strictly forbidden.

The following provisions shall, however, be applied in time of peace:

(a) In addition to the regular police force necessary to maintain public order and security in the zone, in conformity with the general provisions in force in the Finnish Republic, Finland may, if exceptional circumstances demand, send into the zone and keep there temporarily such other armed forces as shall be strictly necessary for the maintenance of order.

(b) Finland also reserves the right for one or two of her light surface warships to visit the islands from time to time. These warships may then anchor temporarily in the waters of the islands. Apart from these ships, Finland may, if important special circumstances demand, send into the waters of the zone and keep there temporarily other surface ships, which must in no case exceed a total displacement of 6,000 tons.

The right to enter the archipelago and to anchor there temporarily cannot be granted by the Finnish Government to more than one warship of any Power at a time.

(c) Finland may fly her military or naval aircraft over the zone, but, except in cases of *force majeure*, landing there is prohibited.

Article 5

The prohibition to send warships into the zone described in Article 2 or to station them there shall not prejudice the freedom of innocent passage through the territorial waters. Such passage shall continue to be governed by the international rules and usages in force.

Article 6

In time of war, the zone described in Article 2 shall be considered as a neutral zone and shall not, directly or indirectly, be used for any purpose connected with military operations.

Nevertheless, in the event of a war affecting the Baltic Sea, Finland shall have the right, in order to assure respect for the neutrality of the Aaland Islands, temporarily to lay mines in the territorial waters of these islands and for this purpose to take such measures of a maritime nature as are strictly necessary.

In such a case Finland shall at once refer the matter to the Council of the League of Nations.

Article 7

I. In order to render effective the guarantee provided in the preamble of the present Convention, the High Contracting Parties shall apply, individually or jointly, to the Council of the League of Nations, asking that body to decide upon the measures to be taken either to assure the observance of the provisions of this Convention or to put a stop to any violation thereof.

The High Contracting Parties undertake to assist in the measures which the Council of the League of Nations may decide upon for this purpose.

When, for the purposes of this undertaking, the Council is called upon to make a decision under the above conditions, it will invite the Powers which are parties to the present Convention, whether Members of the League or not, to sit on the Council. The vote of the representative of the Power accused of having violated the provisions of this Convention shall not be necessary to constitute the unanimity required for the Council's decision.

If unanimity cannot be obtained, each of the High Contracting Parties shall be entitled to take any measures which the Council by a two-thirds majority recommends, the vote of the representative of the Power accused of having violated the provisions of this Convention not being counted.

II. If the neutrality of the zone should be imperilled by a sudden attack either against the Aaland Islands or across them against the Finnish mainland, Finland shall take the necessary measures in the zone to check and repulse the aggressor until such time as the High Contracting Parties shall in conformity with the provisions of this Convention, be in a position to intervene to enforce respect for the neutrality of the islands.

Finland shall refer the matter immediately to the Council.

Article 8

The provisions of this Convention shall remain in force in spite of any changes that may take place in the present *status quo* in the Baltic Sea.

Article 9

The Council of the League of Nations is requested

to inform the Members of the League of the text of this Convention, in order that the legal status of the Aaland Islands, an integral part of the Republic of Finland, as defined by the provisions of this Convention, may, in the interests of general peace, be respected by all as part of the actual rules of conduct among Governments.

With the unanimous consent of the High Contracting Parties, this Convention may be submitted to any non-signatory Power whose accession may in future appear desirable, with a view to the formal adherence of such Power.

Article 10

This Convention shall be ratified. The protocol of the first deposit of ratification shall be drawn up as soon as the majority of the signatory Powers, including Finland and Sweden, are in a position to deposit their ratifications.

The Convention shall come into force for each signatory or acceding Power immediately on the deposit of such Power's ratification or instrument of accession.

Deposit of ratification shall take place at Geneva with the Secretariat of the League of Nations, and any future instruments accession shall also be deposited there.

In faith whereof the plenipotentiaries have signed this Convention and have annexed their seals thereto.

Done at Geneva, on the twentieth day of October, one thousand nine hundred and twenty-one, in a single copy, which shall remain in the Archives of the Secretariat of the League of Nations. A certified copy shall be sent by the Secretariat to each of the signatory Powers.

Treaty Between the United States of America, the British Empire, France, Italy and Japan, for the Limitation of Naval Armament

Also known as: Washington Naval Treaty
Date of signature: February 6, 1922
Place of signature: Washington, DC
Signatory states: United States, the British Empire, France, Italy, and Japan

[The signatories],
Desiring to contribute to the maintenance of the general peace and to reduce the burdens of competition in armament;
Have resolved, with a view to accomplishing these purposes, to conclude a Treaty to limit their respective naval armament,
Who, having communicated to each other their respective full powers, found to be in good and due form, have agreed as follows:

CHAPTER I

GENERAL PROVISIONS, RELATING TO THE LIMITATION OF NAVAL ARMAMENT

Article I

The Contracting Powers agree to limit their respective naval armament as provided in the present Treaty.

Article II

The Contracting Powers may retain respectively the capital ships which are specified in Chapter II, Part I. On the coming into force of the present Treaty, but subject to the following provisions of this Article, all other capital ships, built or building, of the United States, the British Empire and Japan shall be disposed of as prescribed in Chapter II, Part 2.

In addition to the capital ships specified in Chapter II, Part I, the United States may complete and retain two ships of the *West Virginia* class now under construction. On the completion of these two ships, the *North Dakota* and *Delaware* shall be disposed of as prescribed in Chapter II, Part 2.

The British Empire may, in accordance with the replacement table in Chapter II, Part 3, construct two new capital ships not exceeding 35,000 tons (35, 560 metric tons) standard displacement each. On the completion of the said two ships, the *Thunderer, King George V, Ajax* and *Centurion* shall be disposed of as prescribed in Chapter II, Part 2.

Article III

Subject to the provisions of Article II, the Contracting Powers shall abandon their respective capital ship-building programmes, and no new capital ships shall be constructed or acquired by any of the Contracting Powers except replacement tonnage, which may be constructed or acquired as specified in Chapter II, Part 3.

Ships which are replaced in accordance with Chapter II, Part 3, shall be disposed of as prescribed in Part 2 of that Chapter.

Article IV

The total capital ship replacement tonnage of each of the Contracting Powers shall not exceed in standard displacement: for the United States, 525,000 tons (533,400 metric tons); for the British Empire, 525,000 tons (533,400 metric tons); for France, 175,000 tons (177,800 metric tons); for Italy, 175,000 tons (177,800 metric tons); for Japan, 315,000 tons (320,040 metric tons).

Article V

No capital ship exceeding 35,000 tons, (35,560 metric tons) standard displacement, shall be acquired by, or constructed by, for, or within the jurisdiction of, any of the Contracting Powers.

Article VI

No capital ship of any of the Contracting Powers shall carry a gun with a calibre in excess of 16 inches (406 millimeters).

Article VII

The total tonnage for aircraft-carriers of each of the Contracting Powers shall not exceed in standard displacement: for the United States, 135,000 tons (137, 160 metric tons); for the British Empire, 135,000 tons (137,160 metric tons); for France, 60,000 tons (60,960 metric tons); for Italy, 60,000 tons (60,960 metric tons); for Japan, 81,000 tons (82,296 metric tons).

Article VIII

The replacement of aircraft-carriers shall be effected only as prescribed in Chapter II, Part 3, provided, however, that all aircraft-carrier tonnage in existence or building on November 12, 1921, shall be considered experimental, and may be replaced, within the total tonnage limit prescribed in Article VII, without regard to its age.

Article IX

No aircraft-carrier exceeding 27,000 tons (27,432 metric tons) standard displacement shall be acquired by, or constructed by, for, or within the jurisdiction of, any of the Contracting Powers.

However, any of the Contracting Powers may, provided that its total tonnage allowance of aircraft-carriers is not thereby exceeded, build not more than two aircraft carriers, each of a tonnage of not more than 33,000 tons (33,528 metric tons) standard displacement, and in order to effect economy any of the Contracting Powers may use for this purpose any two of their ships, whether constructed or in course of construction, which would otherwise be scrapped under the provisions of Article II. The armament of any aircraft-carriers exceeding 27,000 tons (27,432 metric tons) standard displacement shall be in accordance with the requirements of Article X, except that the total number of guns to be carried, in case any of such guns be of a calibre exceeding 6 inches (152 millimeters), except anti-aircraft guns and guns not exceeding 5 inches (127 millimeters), shall not exceed eight.

Article X

No aircraft-carrier of any of the Contracting Powers shall carry a gun with a calibre in excess of 8 inches (203 millimeters). Without prejudice to the provisions of Article IX, if the armament carried includes guns exceeding 6 inches (152 millimeters) in calibre, the total number of guns carried, except anti-aircraft guns and guns not exceeding 5 inches (127 millimetres), shall not exceed ten. If, alternatively, the armament contains no guns exceeding 6 inches (152 millimetres) in calibre, the number of guns is not limited. In either case the number of anti-aircraft guns and of guns not exceeding 5 inches (127 millimetres) is not limited.

Article XI

No vessel of war exceeding 10,000 tons (10,160 metric tons) standard displacement, other than a capital ship or aircraft-carrier, shall be acquired by, or constructed by, for, or within the jurisdiction of, any of the Contracting Powers. Vessels not specifically built as fighting ships nor taken in time of peace under Government control for fighting purposes, which are employed on fleet duties or as troop transports or in some other way for the purpose of assisting in the prosecution of hostilities otherwise than as fighting ships, shall not be within the limitations of this Article.

Article XII

No vessel of war of any of the Contracting Powers hereafter laid down, other than a capital ship, shall carry a gun with a calibre in excess of 8 inches (203 millimetres).

Article XIII

Except as provided in Article IX, no ship designated in the present Treaty to be scrapped may be reconverted into a vessel of war.

Article XIV

No preparations shall be made in merchant ships in time of peace for the installation of warlike armaments for the purpose of converting such ships into vessels of war, other than the necessary stiffening of decks for the mounting of guns not exceeding 6 inches (152 millimetres) calibre.

Article XV

No vessel of war constructed within the jurisdiction of any of the Contracting Powers for a non-Contracting Power shall exceed the limitations as to displacement and armament prescribed by the present Treaty for vessels of a similar type which may be constructed by or for any of the Contracting Powers; provided, however, that the displacement for air craft-carriers constructed for a non-Contracting Power shall in no case exceed 27,000 tons (27, 432 metric tons) standard displacement.

Article XVI

If the construction of any vessel of war for a non-Contracting Power is undertaken within the jurisdiction of any of the Contracting Powers, such Power shall promptly inform the other Contracting Powers of the date of the signing of the contract and the date on which the keel or the ship is laid; and shall also communicate to them the particulars relating to the ship prescribed in Chapter II, Part 3, Section I (b), (4) and (5).

Article XVII

In the event of a Contracting Power being engaged in war, such Power shall not use as a vessel of war any vessel of war which may be under construction within its jurisdiction for any other Power, or which may have been constructed within its jurisdiction for another Power and not delivered.

Article XVIII

Each of the Contracting Powers undertakes not to dispose by gift, sale or any mode of transfer of any vessel of war in such a manner that such vessel may become a vessel of war in the Navy of any foreign Power.

Article XIX

The United States, the British Empire and Japan agree that the *status quo* at the time of the signing of the present Treaty, with regard to fortifications and naval bases, shall be maintained in their respective territories and possessions specified hereunder:

(1) The insular possessions which the United States now holds or may hereafter acquire in the Pacific Ocean, except (a) those adjacent to the coast of the United States, Alaska and the Panama Canal Zone, not including the Aleutian Islands, and (b) the Hawaiian Islands;

(2) Hong-kong and the insular possessions which the British Empire now holds or may hereafter acquire in the Pacific Ocean, east of the meridian of 110 east longitude, except (a) those adjacent to the coast of Canada, (b) the Commonwealth of Australia and its territories, and (c) New Zealand;

(3) The following insular territories and possessions of Japan in the Pacific Ocean, to wit: the Kurile Islands, the Bonin Islands, Amami-Oshima, the Loochoo Islands, Formosa and the Pescadores, and any insular territories or possessions in the Pacific Ocean which Japan may hereafter acquire.

The maintenance of the *status quo* under the foregoing provisions implies that no new fortifications or naval bases shall be established in the territories and possessions specified; that no measures shall be taken to increase the existing naval facilities for the repair and maintenance of naval forces, and that no increase shall be made in the coast defences of the territories and possessions above specified. This restriction, however, does not preclude such repair and replacement of worn-out weapons and equipment as is customary in naval and military establishments in time of peace.

Article XX

The rules for determining tonnage displacement prescribed in Chapter II, Part 4, shall apply to the ships of each of the Contracting Powers.

CHAPTER II

RULES RELATING TO THE EXECUTION OF THE TREATY—DEFINITION OF TERMS

Part I

Capital Ships which may be Retained by the Contracting Powers

In accordance with Article II, ships may be retained by each of the Contracting Powers as specified in this Part. [See Tables 1-5.]

Table 1

Ships which may be retained by the United States

Name:	Tonnage
Maryland	32,600
California	32,300
Tennessee	32,300
Idaho	32,000
New Mexico	32,000
Mississippi	32,000
Arizona	31,400
Pennsylvania	31,400
Oklahoma	27,500
Nevada	27,500
New York	27,000
Texas	27,000
Arkansas	26,000
Wyoming	26,000
Florida	21,825
Utah	21,825
North Dakota	20,000
Delaware	20,000
Total tonnage	500,650

On the completion of the two ships of the *West Virginia* class and the scrapping of the *North Dakota* and *Delaware*, as provided in Article II, the total tonnage to be retained by the United States will be 525,850 tons.

On the completion of the two new ships to be constructed and the scrapping of the *Thunderer, King George V, Ajax* and *Centurion*, as provided in Article II, the total tonnage to be retained by the British Empire will be 558,950 tons.

France may lay down new tonnage in the years 1927, 1929, and 1931, as provided in Part 3, Section II.

Italy may lay down new tonnage in the years 1927, 1929, and 1931, as provided in Part 3, Section II.

Part 2

Rules for Scrapping Vessels of War

The following rules shall be observed for the scrapping of vessels of war which are to be disposed of in accordance with Articles II and III.

Table 2

Ships which may be retained by the British Empire

Name:	Tonnage
Royal Sovereign	25,750
Royal Oak	25,750
Revenge	25,750
Resolution	25,750
Ramillies	25,750
Malaya	27,500
Valiant	27,500
Barham	27,500
Queen Elizabeth	27,500
Warspite	27,500
Benbow	25,000
Emperor of India	25,000
Iron Duke	25,000
Marlborough	25,000
Hood	41,200
Renown	26,500
Repulse	26,500
Tiger	28,500
Thunderer	22,500
King George V	23,000
Ajax	23,000
Centurion	23,000
Total tonnage	580,450

I. A vessel to be scrapped must be placed in such condition that it cannot be put to combatant use.

II. This result must be finally effected in any one of the following ways:

(a) Permanent sinking of the vessel;

(b) Breaking the vessel up. This shall always involve the destruction or removal of all machinery, boilers and armour, and all deck, side and bottom plating;

(c) Converting the vessel to target use exclusively. In such case all the provisions of paragraph III of this Part, except sub-paragraph (6), in so far as may be necessary, to enable the ship to be used as a mobile target, and except sub-paragraph (7), must be previously complied with. Not more than one capital ship may be retained for this purpose at one time by any of the Contracting Powers.

(d) Of the capital ships which would otherwise be scrapped under the present Treaty in or after the year 1931, France and Italy may each retain two sea-going vessels for training purposes exclusively, that is, a gunnery or torpedo schools. The two vessels retained by France shall be of the *Jean Bart* class, and of those retained by Italy one shall be the *Dante Alighieri*, the other of the *Giulio Cesare* class. On retaining these ships for the purpose above stated, France and Italy respectively undertake to remove and destroy their conning-towers, and not to use the said ships as vessels of war.

Table 3
Ships which may be retained by France

Name:	Tonnage (metric tons)
Bretagne	23,500
Lorraine	23,500
Provence	23,500
Paris	23,500
France	23,500
Jean Bart	23,500
Courbet	23,500
Condorcet	18,890
Diderot	18,890
Voltaire	18,890
Total tonnage	221,170

III.

(a) Subject to the special exceptions contained in Article IX, when a vessel is due for scrapping, the first stage of scrapping, which consists in rendering a ship incapable of further warlike service, shall be immediately undertaken.

(b) A vessel shall be considered incapable of further warlike service when there shall have been removed and landed, or else destroyed in the ship:

Table 4
Ships which may be retained by Italy

Name:	Tonnage (metric tons)
Andrea Doria	22,700
Caio Duilio	22,700
Conte Di Cavour	22,500
Giulio Cesare	22,500
Leonardo Da Vinci	22,500
Dante Alighieri	19,500
Roma	12,600
Napoli	12,600
Vittorio Emanuele	12,600
Regina Elena	12,600
Total tonnage	182,800

(1) All guns and essential portions of guns, fire-control tops and revolving parts of all barbettes and turrets;

(2) All machinery for working hydraulic or electric mountings;

(3) All fire-control instruments and range-finders;

(4) All ammunition, explosives and mines;

Table 5
Ships which may be retained by Japan

Name:	Tonnage
Mutsu	33,800
Nagato	33,800
Hiuga	31,260
Ise	31,260
Yamashiro	30,600
Fu-So	30,600
Kirishima	27,500
Haruna	27,500
Hiyei	27,500
Kongo	27,500
Total tonnage	301,320

(5) All torpedoes, war-heads and torpedo tubes;

(6) All wireless telegraphy installations;

(7) The conning-tower and all side armour, or alternatively all main propelling machinery; and

(8) All landing and flying-off platforms and all other aviation accessories.

IV. The periods in which scrapping of vessels is to be effected are as follow:

(a) In the case of vessels to be scrapped under the first paragraph of Article II, the work of rendering the vessels incapable of further warlike service, in accordance with paragraph III of this Part, shall be completed within six months from the coming into force of the present Treaty, and the scrapping shall be finally effected within eighteen months from such coming into force.

(b) In the case of vessels to be scrapped under the second and third paragraphs of Article II, or under Article III, the work of rendering the vessel incapable of further warlike service, in accordance with paragraph III of this Part, shall be commenced not later than the date of completion of its successor, and shall be finished within six months from the date of such completion. The vessel shall be finally scrapped, in accordance with paragraph II of this Part, within eighteen months from the date of completion of its successor. If, however, the completion of the new vessel be delayed, then the work of rendering the old vessel incapable of further warlike service, in accordance with paragraph III of this Part, shall be commenced within four years from the laying of the keel of the new vessel, and shall be finished within six months from the date on which such work was commenced, and the old vessel shall be finally scrapped in accordance with paragraph II of this Part, within eighteen months from the date when the work of rendering it incapable of further warlike service was commenced.

Part 3

Replacement

The replacement of capital ships and aircraft-carriers shall take place according to the rules in Section I and the tables in Section II of this Part.

Section I

Rules for Replacement

(a) Capital ships and aircraft-carriers twenty years after the date of their completion may, except as otherwise provided in Article VIII and in the tables in Section II of this Part, be replaced by new construction, but within the limits prescribed in Article IV and Article VII. The keels of such new construction may, except as otherwise provided in Article VIII and in the tables in Section II of this Part, be laid down not earlier than seventeen years from the date of completion of the tonnage to be replaced, provided, however, that no capital-ship tonnage, with the exception of the ships referred to in the third paragraph of Article II, and the replacement tonnage specifically mentioned in Section II of this Part, shall be laid down until ten years from November 12, 1921.

(b) Each of the Contracting Powers shall communicate promptly to each of the other Contracting Powers the following information:

(1) The names of the capital ships and aircraft-carriers to be replaced by new construction;

(2) The date of governmental authorisation of replacement tonnage;

(3) The date of laying the keels of replacement tonnage;

(4) The standard displacement in tons and metric tons of each new ship to be laid down, and the principal dimensions, namely, length at waterline, extreme beam at or below waterline, mean draft at standard displacement;

(5) The date of completion of each new ship and its standard displacement in tons and metric tons, and the principal dimensions, namely, length at waterline, extreme beam at or below waterline, mean draft at standard displacement, at time of completion.

(c) In case of loss or accidental destruction of capital ships or aircraft-carriers, they may immediately be replaced by new construction, subject to the tonnage limits prescribed in Articles IV and VII and in conformity with the other provisions of the present Treaty, the regular replacement program being deemed to be advanced to that extent.

(d) No retained capital ships or aircraft-carriers shall be reconstructed except for the purpose of providing means of defence against air and submarine attack, and subject to the following rules: The Contracting Powers may, for that purpose, equip existing tonnage with bulge or blister or anti-air attack deck protection, providing the increase of displacement thus effected does not exceed 3,000 tons (3,048 metric tons) displacement for each ship. No alterations in side armour, in calibre, number or general type of mounting of main armament shall be permitted except:

(1) in the case of France and Italy, which countries within the limits allowed for bulge may increase their armour protection and the calibre of the guns now carried on their existing capital ships so as not to exceed 16 inches (406 millimetres) and;

(2) the British Empire shall be permitted to complete, in the case of the *Renown*, the alterations to armour that have already been commenced but temporarily suspended.

Section II

Note Applicable to all the Tables in Section II

The order above prescribed in which ships are to be scrapped is in accordance with their age. It is understood that when replacement begins according to the . . . tables the order of scrapping in the case of the ships of each of the Contracting Powers may be varied at its option, provided, however, that such Power shall scrap in each year the number of ships above stated.

[See Tables 6-10]

Part 4

Definitions

For the purposes of the present Treaty, the following expressions are to be understood in the sense defined in this Part.

Capital Ship

A capital ship, in the case of ships hereafter built, is defined as a vessel of war, not an aircraft-carrier whose displacement exceeds 10,000 tons (10,160 metric tons) standard displacement, or which carries a gun with a calibre exceeding 8 inches (203 millimetres).

Aircraft-Carrier

An aircraft-carrier is defined as a vessel of war with a displacement in excess of 10,000 tons (10,160 metric tons) standard displacement designed for the specific and exclusive purpose of carrying aircraft. It must be so constructed that aircraft can be launched therefrom and landed thereon, and not designed and constructed for carrying a more powerful armament than that allowed to it under Article IX or Article X as the case may be.

Standard Displacement

The standard displacement of a ship is the displacement of the ship complete, fully manned, engined, and equipped ready for sea, including all armament and ammunition, equipment, outfit provisions and fresh water for crew, miscellaneous stores and implements of every description that are intended to be carried in war, but without fuel or reserve feed water on board.

The word "ton" in the present Treaty, except in the expression "metric tons", shall be understood to mean the ton of 2,240 pounds (1,016 kilos).

Vessels now completed shall retain their present ratings of displacement tonnage in accordance with their national system of measurement. However, a Power expressing displacement in metric tons shall be considered for the application of the present Treaty as owning only the equivalent displacement in tons of 2,240 pounds.

A vessel completed hereafter shall be rated at its displacement tonnage when in the standard condition defined herein.

Chapter III

Miscellaneous Provisions

Article XXI

If during the term of the present Treaty the requirements of the national security of any Contracting Power in respect of naval defence are, in the opinion of that Power, materially affected by any change of circumstances, the Contracting Powers will, at the request of such Power, meet in conference with a view to the reconsideration of the provisions of the Treaty and its amendment by mutual agreement.

In view of possible technical and scientific developments, the United States, after consultation with the other Contracting Powers, shall arrange for a conference of all the Contracting Powers which shall convene as soon as possible after the expiration of eight years from the coming into force of the present Treaty to consider what changes, if any, in the Treaty may be necessary to meet such developments.

Article XXII

Whenever any Contracting Power shall become engaged in a war which in its opinion affects the naval defence of its national security, such Power may after notice to the other Contracting Powers suspend for the period of hostilities its obligations under the present Treaty other than those under Articles XIII and XVII, provided that such Power shall notify the other Contracting Powers that the emergency is of such a character as to require such suspension.

The remaining Contracting Powers shall in such case consult together with a view to agreement as to what temporary modifications, if any, should be made in the Treaty as between themselves. Should such consultation not produce agreement, duly made in accordance with the constitutional methods of the respective Powers, any one of said Contracting Powers may, by giving notice to the other Contracting Powers, suspend for the period of hostilities its obligations under the present Treaty, other than those

Table 6

Replacement and Scrapping of Capital Ships-United States

Year	Ships laid down	Ships completed	Ships scrapped (age in parentheses)	Ships retained Summary	
				Pre-Jutland	Post-Jutland
			Maine(20), Missouri(20), Virginia(17) Nebraska(17), Georgia(17), New Jersey(17), Rhode Island(17), Connecticut(17), Louisiana(17), Vermont(16), Kansas(16), Minnesota(16), New Hampshire(15), South Carolina(13), Michigan(13), Washington(0), South Dakota(0), Indiana(0), Montana(0), North Carolina(0), Iowa(0), Massachusetts(0), Lexington(0), Constitution(0), Constellation(0), Saratoga(0), Ranger(0), United States(0)[1]	17	1
1922		A, B[2]	Delaware(12), North Dakota(12)	15	3
1923				15	3
1924				15	3
1925				15	3
1926				15	3
1927				15	3
1928				15	3
1929				15	3
1930				15	3
1931	C,D			15	3
1932	E,F			15	3
1933	G			15	3
1934	H, I	C, D	Florida (23), Utah (23), Wyoming (22)	12	5
1935	J	E, F	Arkansas (23), Texas (21), New York (21)	9	7
1936	K,L	G	Nevada (20), Oklahoma (20)	7	8
1937	M	H, I	Arizona (21), Pennsylvania (21)	5	10
1938	N,O	J	Mississippi (21)	4	11
1939	P,Q	K, L	New Mexico (21), Idaho (20)	2	13
1940		M	Tennessee (20)	1	14
1941		N, O	California (20), Maryland (20)	0	15
1942		P, Q	West Virginia class	0	15

1 The United States may retain the *Oregon* and *Illinois*, for non-combatant purposes, after complying with the provisions of Part 2 III (b). 2 Two West Virginia class. Note—A, B, C, D, etc., represent individual capital ships of 35,000 tons standard displacement, laid down and completed in the years specified.

Table 7
Replacement and Scrapping of Capital Ships—British Empire

Year	Ships laid down	Ships completed	Ships scrapped (age in parentheses)	Ships retained Summary	
				Pre-Jutland	Post-Jutland
			Commonwealth (16), Agamemnon (13), Dreadnought (15), Bellerophon (12), St. Vincent (11), Inflexible (13), Superb (12), Neptune (10), Hercules (10), Indomitable (13), Temeraire (12), New Zealand (9), Lion (9), Princess Royal (9), Conqueror (9), Monarch (9), Orion (9), Australia (8), Agincourt (7), Erin (7), 4 Building or projected[1]	21	1
1922	A,B[2]			21	1
1923				21	1
1924				21	1
1925	A, B		King George V (13), Ajax (12), Centurion (12), Thunderer(13)	17	3
1926				17	3
1927				17	3
1928				17	3
1929				17	3
1930				17	3
1931	C,D			17	3
1932	E, F			17	3
1933	G			17	3
1934	H, I	C, D	Iron Duke (20), Marlborough (20), Emperor of India (20), Benbow (20)	13	5
1935	J	E, F	Tiger (21), Queen Elizabeth (20), Warspite (20), Barnham (20)	9	7
1936	K, L	G	Malaya (20), Royal Sovereign (20)	7	8
1937	M	H, I	Revenge (21), Resolution (21)	5	10
1938	N, O	J	Royal Oak (22)	4	11
1939	P, Q	K, L	Valiant (23), Repulse (23)	2	13
1940		M	Renown (24)	1	14
1941		N, O	Ramillies (24), Hood (21)	0	15
1942		P, Q	A (17), B (17)	0	15

1 The British Empire may retain the *Colossus* and *Collingwood* for non-combatant purposes, after complying with the provisions of Part 2, III (b). 2 Two 35,000-ton ships, standard displacement. Note—A, B, C, D, etc., represent individual capital ships of 35,000 tons standard displacement laid down and completed in the years specified.

Table 8
Replacement and Scrapping of Capital Ships— France

Year	Ships laid down	Ships completed	Ships scrapped (age in parentheses)	Ships retained Summary Pre-Jutland	Post-Jutland
1922				7	0
1923				7	0
1924				7	0
1925				7	0
1926				7	0
1927	35,000 tons			7	0
1928				7	0
1929	35,000 tons			7	0
1930		35,000 tons	Jean Bart (17), Courbet (17)	5	(¹)
1931	35,000 tons			5	(¹)
1932	35,000 tons	35,000 tons	France (18)	4	(¹)
1933	35,000 tons			4	(¹)
1934		35,000 tons	Paris (20), Bretagne (20)	2	(¹)
1935		35,000 tons	Prpvemce (20)	1	(¹)
1936		35,000 tons	Lorraine (20)	0	(¹)
1937				0	(¹)
1938				0	(¹)
1939				0	(¹)
1940				0	(¹)
1941				0	(¹)
1942				0	(¹)

(¹) Within tonnage limitations; number not fixed. Note—France expressly reserves the right of employing the capital-ship tonnage allotment as she may consider advisable, subject solely to the limitations that the displacement of individual ships should not surpass 35,000 tons, and that the total capital-ship tonnage should keep within the limits imposed by the present Treaty.

Table 9

Replacement and Scrapping of Capital Ships—Italy

Year	Ships laid down	Ships completed	Ships scrapped (age in parentheses)	Ships retained Summary Pre-Jutland	Post-Jutland
1922				6	0
1923				6	0
1924				6	0
1925				6	0
1926				6	0
1927	35,000 tons			6	0
1928				6	0
1929	35,000 tons			6	0
1930				6	0
1931	35,000 tons	35,000 tons	Dante Alighieri (19)	5	([1])
1932	45,000 tons			5	([1])
1933	25,000 tons	35,000 tons	Leonardo da Vinci (19)	4	([1])
1934				4	([1])
1935		35,000 tons	Giulio Cesare (21)	3	([1])
1936		45,000 tons	Conte di Cavour (21), Duilio (21)	1	([1])
1937		25,000 tons	Andrea Doria (21)	0	([1])

([1]) Within tonnage limitations: number not fixed. Note—Italy expressly reserves the right of employing the capital-ship tonnage allotment as she may consider advisable, subject solely to the limitations that the displacement of individual ships should not surpass 35,000 tons, and the total capital-ship tonnage should keep within the limits imposed by the present Treaty.

Table 10

Replacement and Scrapping of Capital Ships—Japan

Year	Ships laid down	Ships completed	Ships scrapped (age in parentheses)	Ships retained Summary Pre-Jutland	Post-Jutland
			Hizen (20), Mikasa (20), Kashima (16),	8	2
			Katori (16), Satsuma (12), Aki (11),		
			Settsu (10), Ikoma (14), Ibuki (12),		
			Kurama (11), Amati (0), Akai (0), Kaga (0),		
			Tosa (0), Takao (0), Atago (0),		
			Projected programme 8 ships not laid down)[1]		
1922				8	2
1923				8	2
1924				8	2
1925				8	2
1926				8	2
1927				8	2
1928				8	2
1929				8	2
1930				8	2
1931	A			8	2
1932	B			8	2
1933	C			8	2
1934	D	A	Kongo(21)	7	3
1935	E	B	Hiyei (21), Haruna (20)	5	4
1936	F	C	Kirishima (21)	4	5
1937	G	D	Fuso (22)	3	6
1938	H	E	Yamashiro (21)	2	7
1939	I	F	Ise (22)	1	8
1940		G	Hiuga (22)	0	9
1941		H	Nagato (21)	0	9
1942		I	Mutsu (21)	0	9

1 Japan may retain the *Shikishima* and *Asahi* for non-combatant purposes, after complying with the provisions of Part 2, III (b). Note—A,B,C,D, etc., represent individual capital ships of 35,000 tons standard displacement, laid down and completed in the years specified.

under Articles XIII and XVII.

On the cessation of hostilities the Contracting Powers will meet in conference to consider what modifications, if any, should be made in the provisions of the present Treaty.

Article XXIII

The present Treaty shall remain in force until December 31st, 1936, and in case none of the Contracting Powers shall have given notice two years before that date of its intention to terminate the Treaty, it shall continue in force until the expiration of two years from the date on which notice of termination shall be given by one of the Contracting Powers, where upon the Treaty shall terminate as regards all the Contracting Powers. Such notice shall be communicated in writing to the Government of the United States, which shall immediately transmit a certified copy of the notification to the other Powers and inform them of the date on which it was received. The notice shall be deemed to have been given and shall take effect on that date. In the event of notice of termination being given by the Government of the United States, such notice shall be given to the diplomatic representatives at Washington of the other Contracting Powers, and the notice shall be deemed to have been given and shall take effect on the date of the communication made to the said diplomatic representatives.

Within one year of the date on which a notice of termination by any Power has taken effect, all the Contracting Powers shall meet in conference.

Article XXIV

The present Treaty shall be ratified by the Contracting Powers in accordance with their respective constitutional methods and shall take effect on the date of the deposit of all the ratifications, which shall take place at Washington as soon as possible. The Government of the United States will transmit to the other Contracting Powers a certified copy of the procès-verbal of the deposit of ratifications.

The present Treaty, of which the French and English texts are both authentic, shall remain deposited in the archives of the Government of the United States, and duly certified copies thereof shall be transmitted by that Government to the other Contracting Powers.

Convention on the Limitations of Armaments of Central American States

Date of signature: February 7, 1923
Place of signature: Washington, DC
Signatory states: Guatemala, El Salvador, Honduras, Nicaragua, Costa Rica
Ratifications: Nicaragua, El Salvador, Guatemala, Costa Rica, Honduras
Date of entry into force: November 24, 1924

[The signatories],
It being their desire and interest that in the future their military policy should be guided only by the exigencies of internal order, have agreed to conclude the present Convention.

After having communicated to one another their respective full powers, which were found to be in due form, the Delegates of the five Central American Powers assembled in the Conference on Central American Affairs at Washington, have agreed to carry out the said proposal in the following manner:

Article 1

The Contracting Parties having taken into consideration their relative population, area, extent of frontiers and various other factors of military importance, agree that for a period of five years from the date of the coming into force of the present Convention, they shall not maintain a standing Army and National Guard in excess of the number of men hereinafter provided, except in case of civil war, or impending invasion by another State.

Guatemala	5,200
El Salvador	4,200
Honduras	2,500
Nicaragua	2,500
Costa Rica	2,000

General officers and officers of a lower rank of the standing Army, who are necessary in accordance with the military regulations of each country, are not included in the provisions of this Article, nor are those of the National Guard. The Police Force is also not included.

Article 2

As the first duty of armed forces of the Central American governments is to preserve public order, each of the Contracting Parties obligates itself to establish a National Guard to cooperate with the existing Armies in the preservation of order in the various districts of the country and on the frontiers, and shall immediately consider the best means for establishing it. With this end in view the Governments of the Central American States shall give consideration to the employment of suitable instructors, in order to take advantage, in this manner, of experience acquired in other countries in organizing such corps.

In no case shall the total combined force of the Army and of the National Guard exceed the maximum limit fixed in the preceding Article, except in the cases therein provided.

Article 3

The Contracting Parties undertake not to export or permit the exportation of arms or munitions or any other kind of military stores from one Central American country to another.

Article 4

None of the Contracting Parties shall have the right to possess more than ten war aircraft. Neither may any of them acquire war vessels; but armed coast guard boats shall not be considered as war vessels.

The following cases shall be considered as exceptions to this Article: civil war or threatened attack by a foreign state; in such cases the right of defence shall have no other limitations than those established by existing Treaties.

Article 5

The Contracting Parties consider that the use in warfare of asphyxiating gases, poisons, or similar substances as well as analogous liquids, materials or devices, is contrary to humanitarian principles and to international law, and obligate themselves by the present Convention not to use said substances in time of war.

Article 6

Six months after the coming into force of the present Convention each of the Contracting Governments shall submit to the other Central American Governments a complete report on the measures adopted by said Government for the execution of this Convention. Similar reports shall be submitted semi-annually, during the aforesaid period of the five years. The reports shall include the units of the army, if any, and of the National Guard; and any other information which the Parties shall sanction.

Article 7

The present Convention shall take effect with respect to the Parties that have ratified it, from the date of its ratification by at least four of the signatory States.

Article 8

The present Convention shall remain in force until the first of January, one thousand nine hundred and twenty-nine, notwithstanding any prior denunciation, or any other cause. After the first of January, one thousand nine hundred twenty-nine, it shall continue in force until one year after the date on which one of the Parties bound thereby notifies the others of its intention to denounce it. The denunciation of this Convention by any of said Parties shall leave it in force for those Parties which have ratified it and have not denounced it, provided that these be not less than four in number. Any of the Republics of Central America which should fail to ratify this Convention, shall have the right to adhere to it while it is in force.

Article 9

The exchange of ratifications of the present Convention shall be made through communications addressed by the Governments to the Government of Costa Rica in order that the latter may inform the other Contracting States. If the Government of Costa Rica should ratify the Convention, notice of said ratification shall also be communicated to the others.

Article 10

The original copy of the present Convention, signed by all of the Delegates Plenipotentiary, shall be deposited in the archives of the Pan-American Union at Washington. A copy duly certified shall be sent by the Secretary-General of the Conference to each one of the Governments of the Contracting Parties.

Protocol for the Pacific Settlement of International Disputes

Date of signature: October 2, 1924
Place of signature: Geneva
Signatory states: Approved by the Assembly of the League of Nations on the above date

Animated by the firm desire to ensure the maintenance of general peace and the security of nations whose existence, independence or territories may be threatened;

Recognizing the solidarity of the members of the international community;

Asserting that a war of aggression constitutes a violation of this solidarity and an international crime;

Desirous of facilitating the complete application of the system provided in the Covenant of the League of Nations for the pacific settlement of disputes between states and of ensuring the repression of international crimes; and

For the purpose of realizing as contemplated by Article 8 of the Covenant, the reduction of national armaments to the lowest point consistent with national safety and the enforcement by common action of international obligations;

The undersigned, duly authorized to that effect, agree as follows:

Article 1

The signatory states undertake to make every effort in their power to secure the introduction into the Covenant of amendments on the lines of the provisions contained in the following articles.

They agree that, as between themselves, these provisions shall be binding as from the coming into force of the present protocol and that, so far as they are concerned, the Assembly and the Council of the League of Nations shall thenceforth have power to exercise all the rights and perform all the duties conferred upon them by the protocol.

Article 2

The signatory states agree in no case to resort to war either with one another or against a state which, if the occasion arises, accepts all the obligations hereinafter set out, except in case of resistance to acts of aggression or when acting in agreement with the Council or the Assembly of the League of Nations in accordance with the provisions of the Covenant and of the present protocol.

Article 3

The signatory states undertake to recognize as compulsory, *ipso facto* and without special agreement, the jurisdiction of the Permanent Court of International Justice in the cases covered by paragraph 2 of Article 36 of the Statute of the Court, but without prejudice to the right of any state, when acceding to the special protocol provided for in the said article and opened for signature on December 16, 1920, to make reservations compatible with the said clause.

Accession to this special protocol, opened for signature on December 16, 1920, must be given within the month following the coming into force of the present protocol.

States which accede to the present protocol, after its coming into force, must carry out the above obligation within the month following their accession.

Article 4

With a view to render more complete the provisions of paragraphs 4, 5, 6 and 7 of Article 15 of the Covenant, the signatory states agree to comply with the following procedure:

1. If the dispute submitted to the Council is not settled by it as provided in paragraph 3 of the said Article 15, the Council shall endeavor to persuade the parties to submit the dispute to judicial settlement or arbitration.

2.
(a) If the parties cannot agree to do so, there shall, at the request of at least one of the parties, be constituted a Committee of Arbitrators. The Committee shall so far as possible be constituted by agreement between the parties.

(b) If within the period fixed by the Council the parties have failed to agree, in whole or in part, upon the number, the names and the powers of the arbitrators and upon the procedure, the Council shall settle the points remaining in suspense. It shall with the utmost possible despatch select in consultation with the parties the arbitrators and their President from among persons who their nationality, their personal character and their experience, appear to it furnish the highest guarantees of competence and impartiality.

(c) After the claims of the parties have been formulated, the Committee of Arbitrators, on the request of any party, shall through the medium of the Council request an advisory opinion upon any points of law in dispute from the Permanent Court of International Justice, which in such case shall meet with the utmost possible despatch.

3. If none of the parties asks for arbitration, the Council shall again take the dispute under consideration. If the Council reaches a report which is unanimously agreed to by the members thereof other than the representatives of any of the parties to the dispute, the signatory states agree to comply with the recommendations therein.

4. If the Council fails to reach a report which is concurred in by all its members, other than the representatives of any of the parties to the dispute, it shall submit the dispute to arbitration. It shall itself determine the composition, the powers and the procedure of the Committee of Arbitrators and, in the choice of the arbitrators, shall bear in mind the guarantees of competence and impartiality referred to in paragraph 2 (b) above.

5. In no case may a solution, upon which there has already been a unanimous recommendation of the Council accepted by one of the parties concerned, be again called in question.

6. The signatory states undertake that they will carry out in full good faith any judicial sentence or arbitral award that may be rendered and that they will comply, as provided in paragraph 3, above, with the solutions recommended by the Council. In the event of a state failing to carry out the above undertakings, the Council shall exert all its influence to secure compliance therewith. If it fails therein, it shall propose what steps should be taken to give effect thereto, in accordance with the provision contained at the end of Article 13 of the Covenant. Should a state in disregard of the above undertakings resort to war, the sanctions provided for by Article 16 of the Covenant, interpreted in the manner indicated in the present protocol, shall immediately become applicable to it.

7. The provisions of the present article do not apply to the settlement of disputes which arise as the result of measures of war taken by one or more signatory states in agreement with the Council or the Assembly.

Article 5

The provisions of paragraph 8 of Article 15 of the Covenant shall continue to apply in proceedings before the Council.

If in the course of an arbitration, such as is contemplated by Article 4 above, one of the parties claims that the dispute, or part thereof, arises out of a matter which by international law is solely within the domestic jurisdiction of that party, the arbitrators shall on this point take the advice of the Permanent Court of International Justice through the medium of the Council. The opinion of the Court shall be binding upon the arbitrators, who if the opinion is affirmative, shall confine themselves to so declaring in their award.

If the question is held by the Court or by the Council to be a matter solely within the domestic jurisdiction of the state, this decision shall not prevent consideration of the situation by the Council or by the Assembly under Article 11 of the Covenant.

Article 6

If in accordance with paragraph 9 of Article 15 of the Covenant a dispute is referred to the Assembly, that body shall have for the settlement of the dispute all the powers conferred upon the Council as to endeavoring to reconcile the parties in the manner laid down in paragraphs 1, 2 and 3 of Article 15 of the Covenant and in paragraph 1 of Article 4 above.

Should the Assembly fail to achieve the amicable settlement:

If one of the parties asks for arbitration, the Council shall proceed to constitute the Committee of Arbitrators in the manner provided in sub-paragraphs (a), (b) and (c) of paragraph 2 of Article 4 above.

If no party asks for arbitration, the Assembly shall again take the dispute under consideration and shall have in this connection the same powers as the council. Recommendations embodied in a report of the Assembly, provided that it secures the measure of support stipulated at the end of paragraph 10 of Article 15 of the Covenant, shall have the same value and effect, as regards all matters dealt with in the present protocol, as recommendations embodied in a report of the Council adopted as provided in paragraph 3 of Article 4 above.

If the necessary majority cannot be obtained, the dispute shall be submitted to arbitration and the Council shall determine the composition, the powers and the procedure of the Committee of Arbitrators as laid down in paragraph 4 of Article 4.

Article 7

In the event of a dispute arising between two or more signatory states, these states agree that they will not, either before the dispute is submitted to proceedings for pacific settlement or during such proceedings, make any increase of their armaments or effectives which might modify the position established by the Conference for the Reduction of Armaments provided for by Article 17 of the present protocol, nor will they take any measure of military, naval, air, industrial or economic mobilization, nor, in general, any actions of a nature likely to extend the dispute or render it more acute.

It shall be the duty of the Council, in accordance with the provisions of Article 11 of the Covenant, to take under consideration any complaint as to infraction of the above undertakings which is made to it by one or more of the states parties to the dispute. Should the Council be of opinion that the complaint requires investigation, it shall, if it deems it expedient, arrange for inquiries and investigations in one or more of the countries concerned. Such inquiries and investigations shall be carried out with the utmost possible despatch and the signatory states undertake to afford every facility for carrying them out.

The sole object of measures taken by the Council as above provided is to facilitate the pacific settlement of disputes and they shall in no way prejudge the actual settlement.

If the result of such enquiries and investigations is to establish an infraction of the provisions of the first paragraph of the present article, it shall be the duty of the Council to summon the state or states guilty of the infraction to put an end thereto. Should the state or states in question fail to comply with such summons, the Council shall declare them to be guilty of a violation of the Covenant or of the present protocol, and shall decide upon the measures to be taken with a view to end as soon as possible a situation of a nature to threaten the peace of the world.

For the purposes of the present article decisions of the Council may be taken by two-thirds majority.

Article 8

The signatory states undertake to abstain from any act which might constitute a threat of aggression against another state.

If one of the signatory states is of opinion that another state is making preparations for war, it shall have the right to bring the matter to the notice of the Council.

The Council, if it ascertains that the facts are as alleged, shall proceed as provided in paragraphs 2, 4, and 5, of Article 7.

Article 9

The existence of demilitarized zones being calculated to prevent aggression and to facilitate a definite finding of the nature provided for in Article 10 below, the establishment of such zones between states mutually consenting thereto is recommended as a means of avoiding violations of the present protocol.

The demilitarized zones already existing under the terms of certain treaties or conventions, or which may be established in future between states mutually consenting thereto, may at the request and at the expense of one or more of the conterminous states, be placed under a temporary or permanent system of supervision to be organised by the Council.

Article 10

Every state which resorts to war in violation of the undertakings contained in the Covenant or in the present protocol is an aggressor. Violation of the rules laid down for a demilitarized zone shall be held equivalent to resort to war.

In the event of hostilities having broken out, any state shall be presumed to be an aggressor, unless a decision of the Council, which must be taken unanimously, shall otherwise declare:

1. If it has refused to submit the dispute to the procedure of pacific settlement provided by Articles 13 and 15 of the Covenant as amplified by the present protocol, or to comply with a judicial sentence or arbitral award or with a unanimous recommendation of the Council, or has disregarded a unanimous report of the Council, a judicial sentence or an arbitral award recognizing that the dispute between it and the other belligerent state arises out of a matter which by international law is solely within the domestic jurisdiction of the latter state; nevertheless, in the last case the state shall only be presumed to be an aggressor if it has not previously submitted the question to the Council or the Assembly, in accordance with Article 11 of the Covenant.

2. If it has violated provisional measures enjoined by the Council for the period while the proceedings are in progress as contemplated by Article 7 of the present protocol.

Apart from the cases dealt with in paragraphs 1

and 2 of the present article, if the Council does not at once succeed in determining the aggressor, it shall be bound to enjoin upon the belligerent an armistice, and shall fix the terms, acting, if need be, by a two-thirds majority and shall supervise its execution.

Any belligerent which has refused to accept the armistice or has violated its terms shall be deemed an aggressor.

The Council shall call upon the signatory states to apply forthwith against the aggressor the sanctions provided by Article 11 of the present protocol, and any signatory state thus called upon shall thereupon be entitled to exercise the rights of a belligerent.

Article 11

As soon as the Council has called upon the signatory states to apply sanctions, as provided in the last paragraph of Article 10 of the present protocol, the obligations of the said states, in regard to the sanctions of all kinds mentioned in paragraphs 1 and 2 of Article 16 of the Covenant, will immediately become operative in order that such sanctions may forthwith be employed against the aggressor.

Those obligations shall be interpreted as obliging each of the signatory states to cooperate loyally and effectively in support of the Covenant of the League of Nations, and in resistance to any act of aggression, in the degree which its geographical position and its particular situation as regards armaments allow.

In accordance with paragraph 3 of Article 16 of the Covenant the signatory states give a joint and several undertaking to come to the assistance of the state attacked or threatened, and give to each other mutual support by means of facilities and reciprocal exchanges as regards the provision of raw materials and supplies of every kind, openings of credits, transport and transit, and for this purpose to take all measures in their power to preserve the safety of communications by land and by sea of the attacked or threatened state.

If both parties to the dispute are aggressors within the meaning of Article 10, the economic and financial sanctions shall be applied to both of them.

Article 12

In view of the complexity of the conditions in which the Council may be called upon to exercise the functions mentioned in Article 11 of the present protocol concerning economic and financial sanctions, and in order to determine more exactly the guarantees afforded by the present protocol to the signatory states, the Council shall forthwith invite the econo-

mic and financial organizations of the League of Nations to consider and report as to the nature of the steps to be taken to give effect to the financial and economic sanctions and measures of cooperation contemplated in Article 16 of the Covenant and in Article 11 of this protocol.

When in possession of this information, the Council shall draw up through its competent organs:

1. Plans of action for the application of the economic and financial sanctions against an aggressor state;

2. Plans of economic and financial cooperation between a state attacked and the different states assisting it; and shall communicate these plans to the members of the League and to the other signatory states.

Article 13

In view of the contingent military, naval and air sanctions provided for by Article 16 of the Covenant and by Article 11 of the present protocol, the council shall be entitled to receive undertakings from states determining in advance the military, naval and air forces which they would be able to bring into action immediately to ensure the fulfilment of the obligations in regard to sanctions which result from the Covenant and the present protocol.

Furthermore, as soon as the Council has called upon the signatory states to apply sanctions, as provided in the last paragraph of Article 10 above, the said states may, in accordance with any agreements which they may previously have concluded, bring to the assistance of a particular state, which is the victim of aggression, their military, naval and air forces.

The agreements mentioned in the preceding paragraph shall be registered and published by the Secretariat of the League of Nations. They shall remain open to all states members of the League which may desire to accede thereto.

Article 14

The Council shall alone be competent to declare that the application of sanctions shall cease and normal conditions be reestablished.

Article 15

In conformity with the spirit of the present protocol, the signatory states agree that the whole cost of any military, naval or air operations undertaken for the repression of an aggression under the terms of the protocol, and reparation for all losses suffered by individuals, whether civilians or combatants, and for all material damage caused by the operations of both sides, shall be borne by the aggressor state up to the extreme limit of its capacity.

Nevertheless, in view of Article 10 of the Covenant, neither the territorial integrity nor the political independence of the aggressor state shall in any case be affected as the result of the application of the sanctions mentioned in the present protocol.

Article 16

The signatory states agree that in the event of a dispute between one or more of them and one or more states which have not signed the present protocol and are not members of the League of Nations, such non-member states shall be invited, on the conditions contemplated in Article 17 of the Covenant, to submit, for the purpose of a pacific settlement, to the obligations accepted by the states signatories of the present protocol.

If the state so invited, having refused to accept the said conditions and obligations, resorts to war against a signatory state, the provisions of Article 16 of the Covenant, as defined by the present protocol, shall be applicable against it.

Article 17

The signatory states undertake to participate in an International Conference for the Reduction of Armaments which shall be convened by the Council and shall meet at Geneva on Monday, June 15, 1925. All other states, whether members of the League or not, shall be invited to this Conference.

In preparation for the convening of the Conference, the Council shall draw up with due regard to the undertakings contained in Articles 11 and 13 of the present protocol a general programme for the reduction and limitation of armaments, which shall be laid before the Conference and which shall be communicated to the governments at the earliest possible date, and at the latest three months before the Conference meets.

If by May 1, 1925, ratifications have not been deposited by at least a majority of the permanent Members of the Council and ten other members of the League, the Secretary-General of the League shall immediately consult the Council as to whether he shall cancel the invitations or merely adjourn the Conference until a sufficient number of ratifications have been deposited.

Article 18

Wherever mention is made in Article 10, or in any other provision of the present protocol, of a decision of the Council, this shall be understood in the sense of Article 15 of the Covenant, namely that the votes of the representatives of the parties to the dispute shall not be counted when reckoning unanimity or the necessary majority.

Article 19

Except as expressly provided by its terms, the present protocol shall not affect in any way the rights and obligations of members of the League as determined by the Covenant.

Article 20

Any dispute as to the interpretation of the present protocol shall be submitted to the Permanent Court of International Justice.

Article 21

The present protocol, of which the French and English texts are both authentic, shall be ratified.

The deposit of ratifications shall be made at the Secretariat of the League of Nations as soon as possible.

States of which the seat of government is outside Europe will be entitled merely to inform the Secretariat of the League of Nations that their ratification has been given; in that case, they must transmit the instrument of ratifications as soon as possible.

So soon as the majority of the permanent members of the Council and ten other members of the League have deposited or have effected their ratifications, a *procès-verbal* to that effect shall be drawn up by the Secretariat.

After the said *procès-verbal* has been drawn up, the protocol shall come into force as soon as the plan for the reduction of armaments has been adopted by the Conference provided for in Article 17.

If within such period after the adoption of the plan for the reduction of armaments as shall be fixed by the said Conference, the plan has not been carried out, the Council shall make a declaration to that effect; this declaration shall render the present protocol null and void.

The grounds on which the Council may declare that the plan drawn up by the International Conference for the Reduction of Armaments has not been carried out, and that in consequence the present protocol has been rendered null and void, shall be laid down by the Conference itself.

A signatory state which, after the expiration of the period fixed by the Conference, fails to comply with the plan adopted by the Conference, shall not be admitted to benefit by the provisions of the present protocol.

Protocol for the Prohibition of the Use in War of Asphyxiating, Poisonous or Other Gases, and of Bacteriological Methods of Warfare

Also known as: Geneva Protocol
Date of signature: June 17, 1925
Place of signature: Geneva
Ratifications: France, Venezuela, Italy,
Austria, Belgium, Egypt, Poland, Serbs,
Croats and Slovenes, Germany, Finland,
Spain, Rumania, Turkey, Denmark,
Sweden, British Empire, India, Canada
Accessions: Liberia, Soviet Union, Persia, China,
Union of South Africa, Australia, New Zealand.

The Undersigned Plenipotentiaries, in the name of their respective Governments:
Whereas the use in war of asphyxiating, poisonous or other gases, and of all analogous liquids, materials or devices, has been justly condemned by the general opinion of the civilised world; and
Whereas the prohibition of such use has been declared in Treaties to which the majority of powers of the world are Parties; and
To the end that this prohibition shall be universally accepted as a part of International Law, binding alike the conscience and the practice of nations:

Declare:

That the High Contracting Parties, so far as they are not already Parties to Treaties prohibiting such use, accept this prohibition, agree to extend this prohibition to the use of bacteriological methods of warfare and agree to be bound as between themselves according to the terms of this declaration.

The High Contracting Parties will exert every effort to induce other States to accede to the present Protocol. Such accession will be notified to the Government of the French Republic, and by the latter to all signatory and acceding Powers, and will take effect on the date of the notification by the Government of the French Republic.

The present Protocol, of which the French and English texts are both authentic, shall be ratified as soon as possible. It shall bear today's date.

The ratifications of the present Protocol shall be addressed to the Government of the French Republic, which will at once notify the deposit of such ratification to each of the signatory and acceding Powers.

The instruments of ratification of and accession to the present Protocol will remain deposited in the archives of the Government of the French Republic.

The present Protocol will come into force for each signatory Power as from the date of deposit of its ratification, and, from that moment, each Power will be bound as regards other Powers which have already deposited their ratifications.

Treaty of Mutual Guarantee Between Germany, Belgium, France, Great Britain and Italy

Also known as: Treaty of Locarno
Date of signature: October 16, 1925
Place of signature: Locarno
Signatory states: Germany, Belgium, French
Republic, United Kingdom of Great Britain
and Ireland and the British Dominions, India,
Italy

[The signatories],
Anxious to satisfy the desire for security and protection which animates the peoples upon whom fell the scourge of the war in 1914-18;
Taking note of the abrogation of the treaties for the neutralisation of Belgium, and conscious of the necessity of ensuring peace in the area which has so frequently been the scene of European conflicts;

Animated also with the sincere desire of giving to all the signatory Powers concerned supplementary guarantees within the framework of the Covenant of the League of Nations and the treaties in force between them;

Have determined to conclude a treaty with these objects, and . . . have agreed as follows:

Article 1

The High Contracting Parties collectively and severally guarantee, in the manner provided in the following Articles, the maintenance of the territorial *status quo* resulting from the frontiers between Germany and Belgium and between Germany and France, and the inviolability of the said frontiers as fixed by or in pursuance of the Treaty of Peace signed at Versailles on June 28, 1919, and also the observance of the stipulations of Articles 42 and 43 of the said Treaty concerning the demilitarised zone.

Article 2

Germany and Belgium, and also Germany and France, mutually undertake that they will in no case attack or invade each other or resort to war against each other.

This stipulation shall not, however, apply in the case of:

(1) The exercise of the right of legitimate defence, that is to say, resistance to a violation of the undertaking contained in the previous paragraph or to a flagrant breach of Articles 42 or 43 of the said Treaty of Versailles, if such breach constitutes an unprovoked act of aggression and by reason of the assembly of armed forces in the demilitarised zone, immediate action is necessary;

(2) Action in pursuance of Article 16 of the Covenant of the League of Nations;

(3) Action as the result of a decision taken by the Assembly or by the Council of the League of Nations or in pursuance of Article 15, paragraph 7, of the Covenant of the League of Nations, provided that in this last event the action is directed against a State which was the first to attack.

Article 3

In view of the undertakings entered into in Article 2 of the present Treaty, Germany and Belgium, and Germany and France, undertake to settle by peaceful means and in the manner laid down herein all questions of every kind which may arise between them and which it may not be possible to settle by the normal methods of diplomacy:

Any question with regard to which the Parties are in conflict as to their respective rights shall be submitted to judicial decision, and the Parties undertake to comply with such decision.

All other questions shall be submitted to a conciliation commission. If the proposals of this commission are not accepted by the two Parties, the question shall be brought before the council of the League of Nations, which will deal with it in accordance with Article 15 of the Covenant of the League.

The detailed arrangements for effecting such peaceful settlement are the subject of special Agreements signed this day.

Article 4

(1) If one of the High Contracting Parties alleges that a violation of Article 2 of the present Treaty or a breach of Articles 42 or 43 of the Treaty of Versailles has been or is being committed, it shall bring the question at once before the Council of the League of Nations.

(2) As soon as the Council of the League of Nations is satisfied that such violation or breach has been committed, it will notify its finding without delay to the Powers signatory of the present Treaty, who severally agree that in such case they will each of them come immediately to the assistance of the Power against whom the act complained of is directed.

(3) In case of a flagrant violation of Article 2 of the present Treaty or of a flagrant breach of Articles 42 or 43 of the Treaty of Versailles by one of the High Contracting Parties, each of the other contracting Parties hereby undertakes immediately to come to the help of the Party against whom such a violation or breach has been directed as soon as the said Power has been able to satisfy itself that this violation constitutes an unprovoked act of aggression and that by reason either of the crossing of the frontier or armed forces in the demilitarised zone immediate action is necessary. Nevertheless, the Council of the League of Nations, which will be seized of the question in accordance with the first paragraph of this Article, will issue its findings, and the High Contracting Parties undertake to act in accordance with the recommendations of the Council, provided that they are concurred in by all the Members other than the representatives of the Parties which have engaged in hostilities.

Article 5

The provisions of Article 3 of the present Treaty

are placed under the guarantee of the High Contracting Parties as provided by the following stipulations:

If one of the Powers referred to in Article 3 refuses to submit a dispute to peaceful settlement or to comply with an arbitral or judicial decision and commits a violation of Article 2 of the present Treaty or a breach of Articles 42 or 43 of the Treaty of Versailles, the provisions of Article 4 of the present Treaty shall apply.

Where one of the Powers referred to in Article 3, without committing a violation of Article 2 of the present Treaty or a breach of Articles 42 or 43 of the Treaty of Versailles, refuses to submit a dispute to peaceful settlement or to comply with an arbitral or judicial decision, the other Party shall bring the matter before the Council of the League of Nations, and the Council shall propose what steps shall be taken; the High Contracting Parties shall comply with these proposals.

Article 6

The provisions of the present Treaty do not affect the rights and obligations of the High Contracting Parties under the Treaty of Versailles or under arrangements supplementary thereto, including the Agreements signed in London on August 30, 1924.

Article 7

The present Treaty, which is designed to ensure the maintenance of peace, and is in conformity with the Covenant of the League of Nations, shall not be interpreted as restricting the duty of the League to take whatever action may be deemed wise and effectual to safeguard the peace of the world.

Article 8

The present Treaty shall be registered at the League of Nations in accordance with the Covenant of the League. It shall remain in force until the Council, acting on a request of one or other of the High Contracting Parties notified to the other signatory Powers three months in advance, and voting at least by a two-thirds' majority decides that the League of Nations ensures sufficient protection to the High Contracting Parties; the Treaty shall cease to have effect on the expiration of a period of one year from such decision.

Article 9

The present Treaty shall impose no obligation upon any of the British dominions, or upon India, unless the Government of such dominion, or of India,

signifies its acceptance thereof.

Article 10

The present Treaty shall be ratified and the ratifications shall be deposited at Geneva in the archives of the League of Nations as soon as possible.

It shall enter into force as soon as all the ratifications have been deposited and Germany has become a Member of the League of Nations.

The present Treaty, done in a single copy, will be deposited in the archives of the League of Nations, and the Secretary-General will be requested to transmit certified copies to each of the High Contracting Parties.

FINAL PROTOCOL OF THE LOCARNO CONFERENCE

The representatives of the German, Belgian, British, French, Italian, Polish and Czechoslovak Governments, who have met at Locarno from October 5 to 16, 1925, in order to seek by common agreement means for preserving their respective nations from the scourge of war and for providing for the peaceful settlement of disputes of every nature which might eventually arise between them.

Have given their approval to the draft Treaties and Conventions which respectively affect them and which, framed in the course of the present Conference, are mutually interdependent:

> Treaty between Germany, Belgium, France, Great Britain and Italy (Annex A).
> Arbitration Convention between Germany and Belgium (Annex B).
> Arbitration Convention between Germany and France (Annex C).
> Arbitration Treaty between Germany and Poland (Annex D).
> Arbitration Treaty between Germany and Czechoslovakia (Annex E).

These instruments, hereby initialed *ne varietur*, will bear today's date, the representatives of the interested Parties agreeing to meet in London on December 1 next, to proceed during the course of a single meeting to the formality of the signature of the instruments which affect them.

The Minister for Foreign Affairs of France states that as a result of the draft arbitration treaties mentioned above, France, Poland and Czechoslovakia have also concluded at Locarno draft agreements in order reciprocally to assure to themselves the benefit of the said treaties. These agreements will be duly deposited at the League of Nations, but M. Briand holds copies forthwith at the disposal of the Powers represented here.

The Secretary of State for Foreign Affairs of Great Britain proposes that, in reply to certain requests for explanations concerning Article 16 of the Covenant of the League of Nations presented by the Chancellor and the Minister for Foreign Affairs of Germany, a letter, of which the draft is similarly attached (Annex F) should be addressed to them at the same time as the formality of signature of the above-mentioned instruments takes place. This proposal is agreed to.

The representatives of the Governments represent-ed here declare their firm conviction that the entry into force of these treaties and conventions will contribute greatly in bringing about a moral relaxation of the tension between nations, that it will help powerfully towards the solution of many political or economic problems in accordance with the interests and sentiments of peoples, and that, in strengthening peace and security in Europe, it will hasten on effectively the disarmament provided for in Article 8 of the Covenant of the League of Nations.

They undertake to give their sincere co-operation to the work relating to disarmament already undertaken by the League of Nations and to seek the realisation thereof in a general agreement.

General Treaty for Renunciation of War as an Instrument of National Policy

Also known as: Kellogg-Briand Pact, Pact of Paris
Date of signature: August 27, 1928
Place of signature: Paris
Signatory states: Germany, United States, Belgium, French Republic, Great Britain, Ireland and the British Dominions, India, Italy, Japan, Poland, Czechoslovakia
Accessions: Afghanistan, Abyssinia, Albania, Austria, Bulgaria, Chile, China, Costa Rica, Cuba, Denmark Free City of Danzig, Dominican Republic, Egypt, Estonia, Finland, Greece, Guatemala, Haiti, Honduras, Hungary, Iceland, Latvia, Lithuania, Luxembourg, Mexico, the Netherlands, Nicaragua, Norway, Panama, Paraguay, Peru, Persia, Portugal, Rumania, Kingdom of the Serbs, Croats and Slovenes, Siam, Spain, Sweden, Switzerland, Turkey, Soviet Union, Venezuela

[The signatories],
deeply sensible of their solemn duty to promote the welfare of mankind;

Persuaded that the time has come when a frank renunciation of war as an instrument of national policy should be made to the end that the peaceful and friendly relations now existing between their peoples may be perpetuated;

Convinced that all changes in their relations with one another should be sought only by pacific means and be the result of a peaceful and orderly process, and that any signatory Power which shall hereafter seek to promote its national interests by resort to war should be denied the benefits furnished by this Treaty;

Hopeful that, encouraged by their example, all the other nations of the world will join in this humane endeavour and by adhering to the present Treaty as soon as it comes into force bring their peoples within the scope of its beneficent provisions, thus uniting the civilized nations of the world in a common renunciation of war as an instrument of their national policy;

Have decided to conclude a Treaty and . . . have agreed upon the following articles:

Article I

The High Contracting Parties solemnly declare in the names of their respective peoples that they condemn recourse to war for the solution of international controversies, and renounce it as an instrument of national policy in their relations with one another.

Article II

The High Contracting Parties agree that the settlement or solution of all disputes or conflicts of whatever nature or of whatever origin they may be, which may arise among them, shall never be sought except by pacific means.

Article III

The present Treaty shall be ratified by the High

Contracting Parties named in the Preamble in accordance with their respective constitutional requirements, and shall take effect as between them as soon as all their several instruments of ratification shall have been deposited at Washington.

This Treaty shall, when it has come into effect as prescribed in the preceding paragraph, remain open as long as may be necessary for adherence by all the other Powers of the world. Every instrument evidencing the adherence of a Power shall be deposited at Washington and the Treaty shall immediately upon such deposit become effective as between the Power thus adhering and the other Powers parties hereto.

It shall be the duty of the Government of the United States to furnish each Government named in the Preamble and every Government subsequently adhering to this Treaty with a certified copy of the Treaty and of every instrument of ratification or adherence. It shall also be the duty of the Government of the United States telegraphically to notify such Governments immediately upon the deposit with it of each instrument of ratification or adherence.

In faith whereof the respective plenipotentiaries have signed this Treaty in the French and English languages both texts having equal force, and hereunto affix their seals.

Anti-War Treaty (Non-Aggression and Conciliation)

Also known as: Saavedra Lamas Treaty
Date of signature: October 10, 1933
Place of signature: Rio de Janeiro
Signatory states: Argentina, Brazil, Chile, Mexico, Paraguay, Uruguay

The States hereinafter named, in an endeavor to contribute to the consolidation of peace, and in order to express their adherence to the effort that all civilized nations have made to further the spirit of universal harmony;

To the end of condemning aggression and territorial acquisitions secured by means of armed conquest and of making them impossible, of sanctioning their invalidity through the positive provisions of this Treaty, and in order to replace them with pacific solutions based upon lofty concepts of justice and equity;

Being convinced that one of the most effective means of insuring the moral and material benefits the world derives from peace is through the organization of a permanent system of conciliation of international disputes, to be applied upon a violation of the hereinafter mentioned principles;

Have decided to record, in conventional form, these aims of non-aggression and concord, through the conclusion of the present Treaty, to which end they have appointed the undersigned plenipotentiaries, who, after having exhibited their respective full powers, which were found in good and due form, have agreed on the following provisions:

Article I

The High Contracting Parties solemnly declare that

they condemn wars of aggression in their mutual relations or against other States and that the settlement of disputes and controversies shall be effected only through the pacific means established by International Law.

Article II

They declare that between the High Contracting Parties, territorial questions must not be settled by resort to violence and that they shall recognize no territorial arrangement not obtained through pacific means, nor the validity of an occupation or acquisition of territory brought about by armed force.

Article III

In case any of the States engaged in the dispute fails to comply with the obligations set forth in the foregoing Articles, the Contracting States undertake to make every effort in their power for the maintenance of peace. To that end, and in their character of neutrals, they shall adopt a common and solidary attitude; they shall exercise the political, juridical or economic means authorized by International Law; they shall bring the influence of public opinion to bear; but in no case shall they resort to intervention either diplomatic or armed. The attitude they may have to take under other collective treaties of which said States are signatories is excluded from the foregoing provisions.

Article IV

The High Contracting Parties, with respect to all

controversies which have not been settled through diplomatic channels within a reasonable period, obligate themselves to submit to the conciliatory procedure created by this Treaty, the disputes specifically mentioned, and any others that may arise in their reciprocal relations, without any further limitations than those recited in the following Article.

Article V

The High Contracting Parties and the States which may hereafter accede to this Treaty may not formulate at the moment of signing, ratifying or adhering thereto limitations to the procedure of conciliation other than those indicated below:

(a) Controversies for the settlement of which pacifist treaties, conventions, covenants, or agreements, of any nature, have been concluded. These shall in no case be deemed superseded by this Treaty; to the contrary, they shall be considered as supplemented thereby insofar as they are directed to insure peace. Questions or issues settled by previous treaties are also included in the exception.

(b) Disputes that Parties prefer to settle by direct negotiation or through submission to an arbitral or judicial procedure by mutual consent.

(c) Issues that International Law leaves to the exclusive domestic jurisdiction of each State, under its constitutional system. On this ground the Parties may object to their being submitted to the procedure of conciliation before the national or local jurisdiction has rendered a final decision. Cases of manifest denial of justice or delay in the judicial proceedings are excepted, and should they arise, the procedure of conciliation shall be started not later than within the year.

(d) Questions affecting constitutional provisions of the Parties to the controversy. In case of doubt, each Party shall request its respective Tribunal or Supreme Court, whenever vested with authority therefor, to render a reasoned opinion on the matter.

At any time, and in the manner provided for in Article XV, any High Contracting Party may communicate the instrument stating that it has partially or totally dropped the limitations set thereby to the procedure of conciliation.

The Contracting Parties shall deem themselves bound to each other in connection with the limitations made by any of them, only to the extent of the exceptions recorded in this Treaty.

Article VI

Should there be no Permanent Commission of Conciliation, or any other international body charged with such a mission under previous treaties in force, the High Contracting Parties undertake to submit their controversies to examination and inquiry by a Commission of Conciliation to be reorganized in the manner hereinafter set forth, except in case of an agreement to the contrary entered into by the Parties in each instance: The Commission of Conciliation shall consist of five members. Each Party to the controversy shall appoint one member, who may be chosen from among its own nationals. The three remaining members shall be appointed by agreement of the Parties from among nationals of third nations. The latter must be of different nationalities, and shall not have their habitual residence in the territory of the Parties concerned, nor be in the service of either one of them. The Parties shall select the President of the Commission of Conciliation from among these their members. Should the Parties be unable to agree, they may request a third nation or any other existing international body to make those designations. Should the nominees so designated be objected to by the Parties, or by any of them, each Party shall submit a list containing as many names as vacancies are to be filled, and the names of those to sit on the Commission of Conciliation shall be determined by lot.

Article VII

Those Tribunals or Supreme Courts of Justice vested by the domestic law of each State with authority to interpret, as a Court of sole or final recourse and in matters within their respective jurisdiction, the Constitution, the treaties or the general principles of the Law of Nations, may be preferred for designation by the High Contracting Parties to discharge the duties entrusted to the Commission of Conciliation established in this Treaty. In this event, the Tribunal or Court may be constituted by the whole bench or may appoint some of its members to act independently or in Mixed Commissions organized with justices of other Courts or Tribunals, as may be agreed by the Parties to the controversy.

Article VIII

The Commission of Conciliation shall establish its own Rules of Procedure. Those shall provide, in all cases, for hearing both sides.

The Parties to the controversy may furnish, and the Commission may request from them, all the antecedents and data necessary. The Parties may be represented by agents, with the assistance of counsellors or experts, and may also submit every kind of evidence.

Article IX

The proceedings and discussions of the Commission of Conciliation shall not be made public unless there is a decision to that effect, assented to by the Parties.

In the absence of any provision to the contrary, the commission shall adopt its decisions by a majority vote; but it may not pass upon the substance of the issue unless all its members are in attendance.

Article X

It is the duty of the Commission to procure a conciliatory settlement of the disputes submitted to it.

After impartial consideration of the questions involved in the dispute, it shall set forth in a report the outcome of its work and shall submit to the Parties proposals for a settlement on the basis of a just and equitable solution.

The report of the Commission shall, in no case, be in the nature of a decision or arbitral award either in regard to the exposition or interpretation of facts or in connection with juridical consideration or findings.

Article XI

The Commission of Conciliation shall submit its report within a year to be reckoned from the day of its first sitting, unless the Parties decide, by common accord, to shorten or extend that term.

Once started, the procedure of conciliation may only be interrupted by a direct settlement between the Parties, or by their later decision to submit, by common accord, the dispute to arbitration or to an international court.

Article XII

On communicating its report to the Parties, the Commission of Conciliation shall fix a period of time, which shall not exceed six months, within which the Parties shall pass upon the bases of settlement it has proposed. Once this period of time has expired the Commission shall set forth in a final act the decision of the Parties.

Should the period of time elapse without the Parties having accepted the settlement, nor adopted by common accord another friendly solution, the Parties to the controversy shall regain their freedom of action to proceed as they may see fit within the limi-

tations set forth in Articles I and II of this Treaty.

Article XIII

From the outset of the procedure of conciliation until the expiration of the term set by the Commission for the Parties to make a decision, they shall abstain from any measure which may prejudice the carrying out of the settlement to be proposed by the Commission and, in general, from every act capable of aggravating or prolonging the controversy.

Article XIV

During the procedure of conciliation the members of the Commission shall receive honoraria in the amount to be agreed upon by the Parties to the controversy. Each Party shall bear its own expenses and a moiety of the joint expenses or honoraria.

Article XV

This Treaty shall be ratified by the High Contracting Parties, as soon as possible, in conformity with their respective constitutional procedures.

The original Treaty and the instruments of ratification shall be deposited in the Ministry of Foreign Affairs and Warship of the Argentine Republic, which shall give notice of the ratifications to the other signatory States. The Treaty shall enter into effect for the High Contracting Parties thirty days after deposit of the respective ratifications and in the order in which the same may be made.

Article XVI

This Treaty remains open to the adherence of all the States.

The adherence shall be made through the deposit of the respective instrument with the Ministry of Foreign Affairs and Warship of the Argentine Republic, which shall give notice thereof to the other States concerned.

Article XVII

This Treaty is concluded for an indefinite period, but it may be denounced by means of one year's previous notice, at the expiration of which it shall cease to be in force as regards the Party denouncing the same, but shall remain in force as regard the other States which may be Parties thereto under signature or adherence. Notice of the denunciation shall be addressed to the Ministry of Foreign Affairs and Warship of the Argentine Republic, which will transmit it to the other States concerned.

Treaty for the Limitation of Naval Armament

Also known as: London Naval Treaty
Date of signature: March 25, 1936
Place of signature: London
Signatory states: the United States, the French
Republic, Great Britain, Ireland and the
British Dominions, India
Ratifications: the United States, France,
United Kingdom, Canada, Australia, New
Zealand, India
Date of entry into force: July 29, 1937

[The signatories],
Desiring to reduce the burdens and prevent the dangers inherent in competition in naval armament;
Desiring, in view of the forthcoming expiration of the Treaty for the Limitation of Naval Armament signed at Washington on the 6th February, 1922, and of the Treaty for the Limitation and Reduction of Naval Armament signed in London on the 22nd April, 1930 (save for Part IV thereof), to make provision for the limitation of naval armament, and for the exchange of information concerning naval construction;
Have resolved to conclude a Treaty for these purposes . . . [and] have agreed as follows:

PART I

DEFINITIONS

Article 1

For the purposes of the present Treaty, the following expressions are to be understood in the sense hereinafter defined.

A.—Standard Displacement

(1) The standard displacement of a surface vessel is the displacement of the vessel, complete, fully manned, engined, and equipped ready for sea, including all armament and ammunition, equipment, outfit, provisions and fresh water for crew, miscellaneous stores and implements of every description that are intended to be carried in war, but without fuel or reserve feed water on board.

(2) The standard displacement of a submarine is the surface displacement of the vessel complete (exclusive of the water in non-watertight structure), fully manned, engined and equipped ready for sea, including all armament and ammunition, equipment, outfit, provisions for crew, miscellaneous stores and implements of every description that are intended to be carried in war, but without fuel, lubricating oil, fresh water or ballast water of any kind on board.

(3) The word "ton" except in the expression "metric tons" denotes the ton of 2,240 1b. (1,016 kilos).

B.—Categories

(1) *Capital Ships* are surface vessels of war belonging to one of the two following sub-categories:

(a) Surface vessels of war, other than aircraft-carriers, auxiliary vessels, or capital ship of sub-category (*b*), the standard displacement of which exceeds 10,000 tons (10,160 metric tons) or which carry a gun with a calibre exceeding 8 in. (203 mm.);

(b) Surface vessels of war, other than aircraft-carriers, the standard displacement of which does not exceed 8,000 tons (8,128 metric tons) and which carry a gun with a calibre exceeding 8 in. (203 mm.).

(2) *Aircraft-Carriers* are surface vessels of war, whatever their displacement, designed or adapted primarily for the purpose of carrying and operating aircraft at sea. The fitting of a landing-on or flying-off deck on any vessel of war, provided such vessel has not been designed or adapted primarily for the purpose of carrying and operating aircraft at sea, shall not cause any vessel so fitted to be classified in the category of aircraft-carriers.

The category of aircraft-carriers is divided into two sub-categories as follows:

(a) Vessels fitted with a flight deck, from which aircraft can take off or on which aircraft can land from the air;

(b) Vessels not fitted with a flight deck as described in (a) above.

(3) *Light Surface Vessels* are surface vessels of war other than aircraft-carriers, minor war vessels or auxiliary vessels, the standard displacement of which exceeds 100 tons (102 metric tons) and does not exceed 10,000 tons (10,160 metric tons), and which do not carry a gun with a calibre exceeding

8 in. (203 mm.).

The category of light surface vessels is divided into three sub-categories as follows:

(a) Vessels which carry a gun with a calibre exceeding 6.1 in. (155 mm.);

(b) Vessels which do not carry a gun with a calibre exceeding 6.1 in. (155 mm.) and the standard displacement of which exceeds 3,000 tons (3,048 metric tons);

(c) Vessels which do not carry a gun with a calibre exceeding 6.1 in. (155 mm.) and the standard displacement of which does not exceed 3,000 tons (3,048 metric tons).

(4) *Submarines* are all vessels designed to operate below the surface of the sea.

(5) *Minor War Vessels* are surface vessels of war, other than auxiliary vessels, the standard displacement of which exceeds 100 tons (102 metric tons) and does not exceed 2,000 tons (2,032 metric tons), provided they have none of the following characteristics:

(a) Mount a gun with a calibre exceeding 6.1 in. (155 mm.);

(b) Are designed or fitted to launch torpedoes;

(c) Are designed for a speed greater than twenty knots.

(6) *Auxiliary Vessels* are naval surface vessels the standard displacement of which exceeds 100 tons (102 metric tons) which are normally employed on fleet duties or as troop transports, or in some other way than as fighting ships, and which are not specifically built as fighting ships, provided they have none of the following characteristics:

(a) Mount a gun with a calibre exceeding 6.1 in. (155 mm.);

(b) Mount more than eight guns with a calibre exceeding 3 in. (76 mm.);

(c) Are designed or fitted to launch torpedoes;

(d) Are designed for protection by armour plate;

(e) Are designed for a speed greater than twenty-eight knots;

(f) Are designed or adapted primarily for operating aircraft at sea;

(g) Mount more than two aircraft-launching apparatus.

(7) *Small Craft* are naval surface vessels the standard displacement of which does not exceed 100 tons (102 metric tons).

C.—Over Age

Vessels of the following categories and sub-categories shall be deemed to be "over-age" when the undermentioned number of years have elapsed since completion:

(a) Capital ships.....26 years.

(b) Aircraft-carriers.....20 years.

(c) Light surface vessels, sub-categories (a) and (b):

(i) If laid down before lst January, 1920.....16 years.

(ii) If laid down after 31st December, 1919.....20 years.

(d) Light surface vessels, sub-category (c).....16 years.

(e) Submarines....13 years.

D.—Month

The word "month" in the present Treaty with reference to a period of time denotes the month of thirty days.

PART II

LIMITATION

Article 2

After the date of the coming into force of the present Treaty, no vessel exceeding the limitations as to displacement or armament prescribed by this Part of the present Treaty shall be acquired by any High Contracting Party or constructed by, for or within the jurisdiction of any High Contracting Party.

Article 3

No vessel which at the date of the coming into force of the present Treaty carries guns with a calibre exceeding the limits prescribed by this Part of the present Treaty shall, of reconstructed or modernised, be rearmed with guns of a greater calibre than those previously carried by her.

Article 4

(1) No capital ship shall exceed 35,000 tons

(35,560 metric tons) standard displacement.

(2) No capital ship shall carry a gun with a calibre exceeding 14 in. (356 mm.); provided however that if any of the parties to the Treaty for the Limitation of Naval Armament signed at Washington on the 6th February, 1922, should fail to enter into an agreement to conform to this provision prior to the date of the coming into force of the present Treaty, but in any case not later than the lst April, 1937, the maximum calibre of gun carried by capital ships shall be 16 in. (406 mm.).

(3) No capital ship of sub-category (a), the standard displacement of which is less than 17,500 tons (17,780 metric tons), shall be laid down or acquired prior to the lst January, 1943.

(4) No capital ship, the main armament of which consists of guns of less than 10 in. (254mm.) calibre, shall be laid down or acquired prior to the lst January, 1943.

Article 5

(1) No aircraft-carrier shall exceed 23,000 tons (23,368 metric tons) standard displacement or carry a gun with a calibre exceeding 6.1 in. (155 mm.).

(2) If the armament of any aircraft-carrier includes guns exceeding 5.25 in. (134 mm.) in calibre, the total number of guns carried which exceed that calibre shall not be more than ten.

Article 6

(1) No light surface vessel of sub-category (b) exceeding 8,000 tons (8,128 metric tons) standard displacement, and no light surface vessel of sub-category (a) shall be laid down or acquired prior to the lst January, 1943.

(2) Notwithstanding the provisions of paragraph (1) above, if the requirements of the national security of any High Contracting Party are, in His opinion, materially affected by the actual or authorised amount of construction by any Power of light surface vessels of sub-category (b), or of light surface vessels not conforming to the restrictions of paragraph (1) above, such High Contracting Party shall, upon notifying the other High Contracting Parties of His intentions and the reasons therefor, have the right to lay down or acquire light surface vessels of sub-categories (a) and (b) of any standard displacement up to 10,000 tons (10,160 metric tons) subject to the observance of the provisions of Part III of the Present Treaty. Each of the other High Contracting Parties shall thereupon be entitled to exercise the same right.

(3) It is understood that the provisions of paragraph (1) above constitute no undertaking expressed or implied to continue the restrictions therein prescribed after the year 1942.

Article 7

No submarine shall exceed 2,000 tons (2,032 metric tons) standard displacement or carry a gun exceeding 5.1 in. (130 mm.) in calibre.

Article 8

Every vessel shall be rated at its standard displacement, as defined in Article 1A of the present Treaty.

Article 9

No preparations shall be made in merchant ships in time of peace for the installation of warlike armaments for the purpose of converting such ships into vessels of war, other than the necessary stiffening of decks for the mounting of guns not exceeding 6.1 in. (155 mm.) in calibre.

Article 10

Vessels which were laid down before the date of the coming into force of the present Treaty, the standard displacement or armament of which exceeds the limitations or restrictions prescribed in this Part of the present Treaty for their category or sub-category, or vessels which before that date were converted to target use exclusively or retained exclusively for experimental or training purposes under the provisions of previous treaties, shall retain the category or designation which applied to them before the said date.

PART III

ADVANCE NOTIFICATION AND EXCHANGE OF INFORMATION

Article 11

(1) Each of the High Contracting Parties shall communicate every year to each of the other High Contracting Parties information, as hereinafter provided, regarding His annual Programme for the construction and acquisition of all vessels of the categories and sub-categories mentioned in Article 12 (a), whether or not the vessels concerned are constructed within His own jurisdiction, and periodical information giving details of such vessels and of any

alterations to vessels of the said categories or sub-categories already completed.

(2) For the purposes of this and the succeeding Parts of the present Treaty, information shall be deemed to have reached a High Contracting Party on the date upon which such information is communicated to His Diplomatic Representatives accredited to the High Contracting Party by whom the information is given.

(3) This information shall be treated as confidential until published by the High Contracting Party supplying it.

Article 12

The information to be furnished under the preceding Article in respect of vessels constructed by or for a High Contracting Party shall be given as follows; and so as to reach all the other High Contracting Parties within the periods or at the times mentioned:

(a) Within the first four months of each calendar year, the Annual Programme of construction of all vessels of the following categories and sub-categories, stating the number of vessels of each category or sub-category and, for each vessel, the calibre of the largest gun. The categories and sub-categories in question are:

Capital Ships:

  sub-category (a)

  sub-category (b)

Aircraft-Carriers:

  sub-category (a)

  sub-category (b)

Light Surface Vessels:

  sub-category (a)

  sub-category (b)

  sub-category (c)

Submarines.

(b) Not less than four months before the date of the laying of the keel, the following particulars in respect of each such vessel:

Name or designation;

Category and sub-category;

Standard displacement in tons and metric tons;

Length at waterline at standard displacement;

Extreme beam at or below waterline at standard displacement;

Mean draught at standard displacement;

Designed horse-power;

Designed speed;

Type of machinery;

Type of fuel;

Number and calibre of all guns of 3 in. (76 mm.) calibre and above;

Approximate number of guns of less than 3 in. (76 mm.) calibre;

Number of torpedo tubes;

Whether designed to lay mines;

Approximate number of aircraft for which provision is to be made.

(c) As soon as possible after the laying-down of the keel of each such vessel, the date on which it was laid.

(d) Within one month after the date of completion of each such vessel, the date of completion together with all the particulars specified in paragraph (b) above relating to the vessel on completion.

(e) Annually during the month of January, in respect of vessels belonging to the categories and sub-categories mentioned in paragraph (a) above:

(i) Information as to any important alterations which it may have proved necessary to make during the preceding year in vessels under construction, in so far as these alterations affect the particulars mentioned in paragraph (b) above.

(ii) Information as to any important alterations made during the preceding year in vessels previously completed, in so far as these alterations affect the particulars mentioned in paragraph (b) above.

(iii) Information concerning vessels which may have been scrapped or otherwise disposed of during the preceding year. If such vessels are not scrapped, sufficient information shall be given to enable their new status and condition to be determined.

(f) Not less than four months before undertaking such alterations as would cause a completed vessel to come within one of the categories or sub-categories mentioned in paragraph (a) above, or such alterations as would cause vessel to change from one to another of the said categories or sub-categories: information as to her intended characteristics as specified in paragraph (b) above.

Article 13

No vessel coming within the categories or sub-categories mentioned in Article 12 (a) shall be laid down by any High Contracting Party until after the expiration of a period of four months both from the date on which the Annual Programme in which the vessel is included, and from the date on which the particulars in respect of that vessel prescribed by Article 12 (b), have reached all the other High Contracting Parties.

Article 14

If a High Contracting Party intends to acquire a completed or partially completed vessel coming within the categories or sub-categories mentioned in Article 12 (a), that vessel shall be declared at the same time and in the same manner as the vessels included in the Annual Programme prescribed in the said Article. No such vessel shall be acquired until after the expiration of a period of four months from the date on which such declaration has reached all the other High Contracting Parties. The particulars mentioned in Article 12 (b), together with the date on which the keel was laid, shall be furnished in respect of such vessel so as to reach all the other High Contracting Parties within one month after the date on which the contract for the acquisition of the vessel was signed. The particulars mentioned in Article 12 (d), (e) and (f) shall be given as therein prescribed.

Article 15

At the time of communicating the Annual Programme prescribed by Article 12 (a), each High Contracting Party shall inform all the other High Contracting Parties of all vessels included in His previous Annual Programmes and declarations that have not yet been laid down or acquired, but which it is the intention to lay down or acquire during the period covered by the first mentioned Annual Programme.

Article 16

If, before the keel of any vessel coming within the categories or sub-categories mentioned in Article 12 (a) is laid, any important modification is made in the particulars regarding her which have been communicated under Article 12 (b), information concerning this modification shall be given, and the laying of the keel shall be deferred until at least four months after this information has reached all the other High Contracting Parties.

Article 17

No High Contracting party shall lay down or acquire any vessel of the categories or sub-categories mentioned in Article 12 (a), which has not previously been included in His Annual Programme of construction or declaration of acquisition for the current year or in any earlier Annual Programme or declaration.

Article 18

If the construction, modernisation or reconstruction of any vessel coming within the categories or sub-categories mentioned in Article 12 (a), which is for the order of a Power not a party to the present Treaty, is undertaken within the jurisdiction of any High Contracting Party, He shall promptly inform all the other High Contracting Parties of the date of the signing of the contract and shall also give as soon as possible in respect of the vessel all the information mentioned in Article 12 (b), (c) and (d).

Article 19

Each High Contracting Party shall give lists of all His minor war vessels and auxiliary vessels with their characteristics, as enumerated in Article 12 (b), and information as to the particular service for which they are intended, so as to reach all the other High Contracting Parties within one month after the date of the coming into force of the present Treaty; and, so as to reach all the other High Contracting Parties within the month of January in each subsequent year, any amendments in the lists and changes in the information.

Article 20

Each of the High Contracting Parties shall communicate to each of the other High Contracting Parties, so as to reach the latter within one month after the date of the coming into force of the present Treaty, particulars, as mentioned in Article 12 (b), of all vessels of the categories or sub-categories mentioned in Article 12 (a), which are then under construction for Him, whether or not such vessels are being constructed within His own jurisdiction, together with similar particulars relating to any such vessels then under construction within His own jurisdiction for a Power not a party to the present Treaty.

Article 21

(1) At the time of communicating His initial Annual Programme of construction and declaration of acquisition, each High Contracting Party shall inform each of the other High Contracting Parties of any vessels of the categories or sub-categories mentioned in Article 12 (a), which have been previously authorised and which it is the intention to lay down or acquire during the period covered by the said Programme.

(2) Nothing in this Part of the present Treaty shall prevent any High Contracting Party from laying down or acquiring, at any time during the four months following the date of the coming into force of the Treaty, any vessel included, or to be included, in His initial Annual Programme of construction or declaration of acquisition, or previously authorised, provided that the information prescribed by Article 12 (b) concerning each vessel shall be communicated so as to reach all the other High Contracting Parties within one month after the date of the coming into force of the present Treaty.

(3) If the present Treaty should not come into force before the lst of May, 1937, the initial Annual Programme of construction and declaration of acquisition, to be communicated under Articles 12 (a) and 14 shall reach all the other High Contracting Parties within one month after the date of the coming into force of the present Treaty.

PART IV

GENERAL AND SAFEGUARDING CLAUSES

Article 22

No High Contracting Party shall, by gift, sale or any mode of transfer, dispose of any of His surface vessels of war or submarines in such a manner that such vessel may become a surface vessel of war or a submarine in any foreign navy. This provision shall not apply to auxiliary vessels.

Article 23

(1) Nothing in the present Treaty shall prejudice the right of any High Contracting Party, in the event of loss or accidental destruction of a vessel, before the vessel in question has become over-age, to replace such vessel by a vessel of the same category or sub-category as soon as the particulars of the new vessel mentioned in Article 12 (b) shall have reached all the other High Contracting Parties.

(2) The provisions of the preceding paragraph shall also govern the immediate replacement, in such circumstances, of a light surface vessel of sub-category (b) exceeding 8,000 tons (8,128 metric tons) standard displacement, or of a light surface vessel of sub-category (a), before the vessel in question has become over-age, by a light surface vessel of the same sub-category of any standard displacement up to 10,000 tons (10,160 metric tons).

Article 24

(1) If any High Contracting Party should become engaged in war, such High Contracting Party may, if He considers the naval requirements of His defence are materially affected, suspend, in so far as He is concerned, any or all of the obligations of the present Treaty, provided that He shall promptly notify the other High Contracting Parties that the circumstances require such suspension, and shall specify the obligations it is considered necessary to suspend.

(2) The other High Contracting Parties shall in such case promptly consult together, and shall examine the situation thus presented with a view to agreeing as to the obligations of the present Treaty, if any, which each of the said High Contracting Parties may suspend. Should such consultation not produce agreement, any of the said High Contracting Parties may suspend, in so far as He is concerned, any or all of the obligations of the present Treaty, provided that He shall promptly give notice to the other High Contracting Parties of the obligations which it is considered necessary to suspend.

(3) On the cessation of hostilities, the High Contracting Parties shall consult together with a view to fixing a date upon which the obligations of the Treaty which have been suspended shall again become operative, and to agreeing upon any amendments in the present Treaty which may be considered necessary.

Article 25

(1) In the event of any vessel not in conformity with the limitations and restrictions as to standard displacement and armament prescribed by Articles 4, 5 and 7 of the present Treaty being authorised, constructed or acquired by a Power not a party to the present Treaty, each High Contracting Party reserves the right to depart if, and to the extent to which, He considers such departures necessary in order to meet the requirements of His national security;

(a) During the remaining period of the Treaty, from

the limitations and restrictions of Articles 3, 4, 5, 6, (1) and 7, and

(b) During the current year, from His Annual Programmes of construction and declarations of acquisition.

This right shall be exercised in accordance with the following provisions:

(2) Any High Contracting Party who considers it necessary that such right should be exercised, shall notify the other High Contracting Parties to that effect, stating precisely the nature and extent of the proposed departures and the reasons therefor.

(3) The High Contracting Parties shall thereupon consult together and endeavour to reach an agreement with a view to reducing to a minimum the extent of the departures which may be made.

(4) On the expiration of a period of three months from the date of the first of any notifications which may have been given under paragraph (2) above, each of the High Contracting Parties shall, subject to any agreement which may have been reached to the contrary, be entitled to depart during the remaining period of the present Treaty from the limitations and restrictions prescribed in Article 3, 4, 5, 6 (1) and 7 thereof.

(5) On the expiration of the period mentioned in the preceding paragraph, any High Contracting Party shall be at liberty, subject to any agreement which may have been reached during the consultations provided for in paragraph (3) above, and on informing all the other High Contracting Parties, to depart from His Annual Programmes of construction and declarations of acquisition and to alter the characteristics of any vessels building or which have already appeared in His Programmes or declarations.

(6) In such event, no delay in the acquisition, the laying of the keel, or the altering of any vessel shall be necessary by reason of any of the provisions of Part III of the present Treaty. The particulars mentioned in Article 12 (b) shall, however, be communicated to all the other High Contracting Parties before the keels of any vessels are laid. In the case of acquisition, information relating to the vessel shall be given under the provisions of Article 14.

Article 26

(1) If the requirements of the national security of any High Contracting Party should, in His opinion, be materially affected by any change of circumstances, other than those provided for in Articles 6 (2), 24 and 25 of the present Treaty, such High Con-

tracting Party shall have the right to depart for the current year from His Annual Programmes of construction and declarations of acquisition. The amount of construction by any Party to the Treaty, within the limitations and restrictions thereof, shall not, however, constitute a change of circumstances for the purposes of the present Article. The above mentioned right shall be exercised in accordance with the following provisions:

(2) Such High Contracting Party shall, if He desires to exercise the above mentioned right, notify all the other High Contracting Parties to that effect, stating in what respects He proposes to depart from His Annual Programmes of construction and declarations of acquisition, giving reasons for the proposed departure.

(3) The High Contracting Parties will thereupon consult together with a view to agreement as to whether any departures are necessary in order to meet the situation.

(4) On the expiration of a period of three months from the date of the first of any notifications which may have been given under paragraph (2) above, each of the High Contracting Parties shall, subject to any agreement which may have been reached to the contrary, be entitled to depart from His Annual Programmes of construction and declarations of acquisition, provided notice is promptly given to the other High Contracting Parties stating precisely in what respects He proposes so to depart.

(5) In such event, no delay in the acquisition, the laying of the keel, or the altering of any vessel shall be necessary by reason of any of the provisions of Part III of the present Treaty. The particulars mentioned in Article 12 (b) shall, however, be communicated to all the other High Contracting Parties before the keels of any vessels are laid. In the case of acquisition, information relating to the vessel shall be given under the provisions of Article 14.

PART V

FINAL CLAUSES

Article 27

The present Treaty shall remain in force until the 31st of December, 1942.

Article 28

(1) His Majesty's Government in the United Kingdom of Great Britain and Northern Ireland will, during the last quarter of 1940, initiate through the

diplomatic channel a consultation between the Governments of the Parties to the present Treaty with a view to holding a conference in order to frame a new treaty for the reduction and limitation of naval armament. This conference shall take place in 1941 unless the preliminary consultations should have shown that the holding of such a conference at that time would not be desirable or practicable.

(2) In the course of the consultation referred to in the preceding paragraph, views shall be exchanged in order to determine whether, in the light of the circumstances then prevailing and the experience gained in the interval in design and construction of capital ships, it may be possible to agree upon a reduction in the standard displacement or calibre of guns of capital ships to be constructed under future annual programmes and thus, if possible, to bring about a reduction in the cost of capital ships.

Article 29

None of the provisions of the present Treaty shall constitute a precedent for any future treaty.

Article 30

(1) The present Treaty shall be ratified by the signatory Powers in accordance with their respective constitutional methods, and the instruments of ratification shall be deposited as soon as possible with His Majesty's Government in the United Kingdom, which will transmit certified copies of all the *procès-verbaux* of the deposits of ratifications to the Governments of the said Powers and of any country on behalf of which accession has been made in accordance with the provisions of Article 31.

(2) The Treaty shall come into force on the 1st January, 1937, provided that by that date the instruments of ratification of all the said Powers shall have been deposited. If all the above-mentioned instruments of ratification have not been deposited by the 1st January, 1937, the Treaty shall come into force so soon thereafter as these are all received.

Article 31

(1) The present Treaty shall, at any time after this day's date, be open to accession on behalf of any country for which the Treaty for the Limitation and Reduction of Naval Armament was signed in London on the 22nd April 1930, but for which the present Treaty has not been signed. The instrument of accession shall be deposited with His Majesty's Government in the United Kingdom, which will transmit

certified copies of the *procès-verbaux* of the deposit to the Governments of the Signatory Powers and of any country on behalf of which accession has been made.

(2) Accessions, if made prior to the date of the coming into force of the Treaty, shall take effect on that date. If made afterwards, they shall take effect immediately.

(3) If accession should be made after the date of the coming into force of the Treaty, the following information shall be given by the acceding Power so as to reach all the other High Contracting Parties within one month after the date of accession:

(a) The initial Annual Programme of construction and declaration of acquisition, as prescribed by Articles 12 (a) and 14 relating to vessels already authorised, but not yet laid down or acquired, belonging to the categories or sub-categories mentioned in Article 12 (a).

(b) A list of the vessels of the above-mentioned categories or sub-categories completed or acquired after the date of the coming into force of the present Treaty, stating Particulars of such vessels as specified in Article 12 (b), together with similar particulars relating to any such vessels which have been constructed within the jurisdiction of the acceding Power after the date of the coming into force of the present Treaty, for a Power not a party thereto.

(c) Particulars, as specified in Article 12 (b), of all vessels of the categories or sub-categories above-mentioned which are then under construction for the acceding Power, whether or not such vessels are being constructed within His own jurisdiction, together with similar particulars relating to any such vessels then under construction within His jurisdiction for a Power not a party to the present Treaty.

(d) Lists of all minor war vessels and auxiliary vessels with their characteristics and information concerning them, as prescribed by Article 19.

(4) Each of the High Contracting Parties shall reciprocally furnish to the Government of any country on behalf of which accession is made after the date of the coming into force of the present Treaty, the information specified in paragraph (3) above, so as to reach that Government within the period therein mentioned.

(5) Nothing in Part III of the present Treaty shall

prevent an acceding Power from laying down or acquiring, at any time during the four months following the date of accession, any vessel included, or to be included, in His initial Annual Programme of construction or declaration of acquisition, or previously authorised, provided that the information prescribed by Article 12 (b) concerning each vessel shall be communicated so as to reach all the other High Contracting Parties within one month after the date of accession.

Article 32

The present Treaty, of which the French and English texts shall both be equally authentic, shall be deposited in the Archives of His Majesty's Government in the United Kingdom of Great Britain and Northern Ireland which will transmit certified copies thereof to the Governments of the countries for which the Treaty for the Limitation and Reduction of Naval Armament was signed in London on the 22nd April, 1930.

Charter of the United Nations

Date of signature: June 26, 1945
Place of signature: San Francisco
Signatory states: (All 51 Original Members)
Ratifications: Argentina, Australia, Belarus, Belgium, Bolivia, Brazil, Canada, Chile, China, Colombia, Costa Rica, Cuba, Czechoslovakia, Denmark, Dominican Republic, Ecuador, Egypt, El Salvador, Ethiopia, France, Greece, Guatemala, Haiti, Honduras, India, Iran (Islamic Republic of), Iraq, Lebanon, Liberia, Luxembourg, Mexico, Netherlands, New Zealand, Nicaragua, Norway, Panama, Paraguay, Peru, Philippines, Poland, Russian Federation, Saudi Arabia, South Africa, Syrian Arab Republic, Turkey, Ukraine, United Kingdom of Great Britain and Northern Ireland, United States of America, Uruguay, Venezuela, Yugoslavia
Date of entry into force: October 24, 1945

Preamble

WE THE PEOPLES OF THE UNITED NATIONS DETERMINED
to save succeeding generations from the scourge of war, which twice in our lifetime has brought untold sorrow to mankind, and
to reaffirm faith in fundamental human rights, in the dignity and worth of the human person, in the equal rights of men and women and of nations large and small, and
to establish conditions under which justice and respect for the obligations arising from treaties and other sources of international law can be maintained, and
to promote social progress and better standards of life in larger freedom,

AND FOR THESE ENDS
to practice tolerance and live together in peace with one another as good neighbors, and
to unite our strength to maintain international peace and security, and
to ensure by the acceptance of principles and the institution of methods, that armed force shall not be used, save in the common interest, and
to employ international machinery for the promotion of the economic and social advancement of all peoples,
HAVE RESOLVED TO COMBINE OUR EFFORTS TO ACCOMPLISH THESE AIMS
Accordingly, our respective Governments, through representatives assembled in the city of San Francisco, who have exhibited their full powers found to be in good and due form, have agreed to the present Charter of the United Nations and do hereby establish an international organization to be known as the United Nations.

Chapter I

Purposes and Principles

Article 1

The Purposes of the United Nations are:

1. To maintain international peace and security, and to that end: to take effective collective measures for the prevention and removal of threats to the peace, and for the suppression of acts of aggression or other breaches of the peace, and to bring about by peaceful means, and in conformity with the principles of justice and international law, adjustment or settlement of international disputes or situations which might lead to a breach of the peace;

2. To develop friendly relations among nations based on respect for the principle of equal rights and self-determination of peoples, and to take other appropriate measures to strengthen universal peace;

3. To achieve international cooperation in solving international problems of an economic, social, cultural, or humanitarian character, and in promoting and encouraging respect for human rights and for fundamental freedoms for all without distinction as to race, sex, language, or religion; and

4. To be a center for harmonizing the actions of nations in the attainment of these common ends.

Article 2

The Organization and its Members, in pursuit of the Purposes stated in Article 1, shall act in accordance with the following Principles.

1. The Organization is based on the principle of the sovereign equality of all its Members.

2. All Members, in order to ensure to all of them the rights and benefits resulting from membership, shall fulfill in good faith the obligations assumed by them in accordance with the present Charter.

3. All Members shall settle their international disputes by peaceful means in such a manner that international peace and security, and justice, are not endangered.

4. All Members shall refrain in their international relations from the threat or use of force against the territorial integrity or political independence of any state, or in any other manner inconsistent with the Purposes of the United Nations.

5. All Members shall give the United Nations every assistance in any action it takes in accordance with the present Charter, and shall refrain from giving assistance to any state against which the United Nations is taking preventive or enforcement action.

6. The Organization shall ensure that states which are not Members of the United Nations act in accordance with these Principles so far as may be necessary for the maintenance of international peace and security.

7. Nothing contained in the present Charter shall authorize the United Nations to intervene in matters which are essentially within the domestic jurisdiction of any state or shall require the Members to submit such matters to settlement under the present Charter; but this principle shall not prejudice the application

of enforcement measures under Chapter VII.

Chapter II

Membership

Article 3

The original Members of the United Nations shall be the states which, having participated in the United Nations Conference on International Organization at San Francisco, or having previously signed the Declaration by United Nations of January 1, 1942, sign the present Charter and ratify it in accordance with Article 110.

Article 4

1. Membership in the United Nations is open to all other peace-loving states which accept the obligations contained in the present Charter and, in the judgment of the Organization, are able and willing to carry out these obligations.

2. The admission of any such state to membership in the United Nations will be effected by a decision of the General Assembly upon the recommendation of the Security Council.

Article 5

A member of the United Nations against which preventive or enforcement action has been taken by the Security Council may be suspended from the exercise of the rights and privileges of membership by the General Assembly upon the recommendation of the Security Council. The exercise of these rights and privileges may be restored by the Security Council.

Article 6

A Member of the United Nations which has persistently violated the Principles contained in the present Charter may be expelled from the Organization by the General Assembly upon the recommendation of the Security Council.

Chapter III

Organs

Article 7

1. There are established as the principal organs of the United Nations: a General Assembly, a Security Council, an Economic and Social Council, a Trustee-

ship Council, an International Court of Justice, and a Secretariat.

2. Such subsidiary organs as may be found necessary may be established in accordance with the present Charter.

Article 8

The United Nations shall place no restrictions on the eligibility of men and women to participate in any capacity and under conditions of equality in its principal and subsidiary organs.

Chapter IV

The General Assembly

Article 9

Composition

1. The General Assembly shall consist of all the Members of the United Nations.

2. Each member shall have not more than five representatives in the General Assembly.

Functions and Powers

Article 10

The General Assembly may discuss any questions or any matters within the scope of the present Charter or relating to the powers and functions of any organs provided for in the present Charter, and, except as provided in Article 12, may make recommendations to the Members of the United Nations or to the Security Council or to both on any such questions or matters.

Article 11

1. The General Assembly may consider the general principles of cooperation in the maintenance of international peace and security, including the principles governing disarmament and the regulation of armaments, and may make recommendations with regard to such principles to the Members or to the Security Council or to both.

2. The General Assembly may discuss any questions relating to the maintenance of international peace and security brought before it by any Member of the United Nations, or by the Security Council, or by a state which is not a Member of the United Nations in accordance with Article 35, paragraph 2, and, except as provided in Article 12, may make recommendations with

regard to any such questions to the state or states concerned or to the Security Council or to both. Any such question on which action is necessary shall be referred to the Security Council by the General Assembly either before or after discussion.

3. The General Assembly may call the attention of the Security Council to situations which are likely to endanger international peace and security.

4. The powers of the General Assembly set forth in this Article shall not limit the general scope of Article 10.

Article 12

1. While the Security Council is exercising in respect of any dispute or situation the functions assigned to it in the present Charter, the General Assembly shall not make any recommendation with regard to that dispute or situation unless the Security Council so requests.

2. The Secretary-General, with the consent of the Security Council, shall notify the General Assembly at each session of any matters relative to the maintenance of international peace and security which are being dealt with by the Security Council and shall similarly notify the General Assembly, or the Members of the United Nations if the General Assembly is not in session, immediately the Security Council ceases to deal with such matters.

Article 13

1. The General Assembly shall initiate studies and make recommendations for the purpose of:

a. promoting international cooperation in the political field and encouraging the progressive development of international law and its codification;

b. promoting international cooperation in the economic, social, cultural, educational, and health fields, and assisting in the realization of human rights and fundamental freedoms for all without distinction as to race, sex, language, or religion.

2. The further responsibilities, functions and powers of the General Assembly with respect to matters mentioned in paragraph 1(b) above are set forth in Chapters IX and X.

Article 14

Subject to the provisions of Article 12, the General

Assembly may recommend measures for the peaceful adjustment of any situation, regardless of origin, which it deems likely to impair the general welfare or friendly relations among nations, including situations resulting from a violation of the provisions of the present Charter setting forth the Purposes and Principles of the United Nations.

Article 15

1. The General Assembly shall receive and consider annual and special reports from the Security Council; these reports shall include an account of the measures that the Security Council has decided upon or taken to maintain international peace and security.

2. The General Assembly shall receive and consider reports from the other organs of the United Nations.

Article 16

The General Assembly shall perform such functions with respect to the international trusteeship system as are assigned to it under Chapters XII and XIII, including the approval of the trusteeship agreements for areas not designated as strategic.

Article 17

1. The General Assembly shall consider and approve the budget of the Organization.

2. The expenses of the Organization shall be borne by the Members as apportioned by the General Assembly.

3. The General Assembly shall consider and approve any financial and budgetary arrangements with specialized agencies referred to in Article 57 and shall examine the administrative budgets of such specialized agencies with a view to making recommendations to the agencies concerned.

Voting

Article 18

1. Each member of the General Assembly shall have one vote.

2. Decisions of the General Assembly on important questions shall be made by a two-thirds majority of the members present and voting. These questions shall include: recommendations with respect to the maintenance of international peace and security, the election of the non-permanent members of the Secu-

rity Council, the election of the members of the Economic and Social Council, the election of members of the Trusteeship Council in accordance with paragraph 1(c) of Article 86, the admission of new Members to the United Nations, the suspension of the rights and privileges of membership, the expulsion of Members, questions relating to the operation of the trusteeship system, and budgetary questions.

3. Decisions on other questions, Composition including the determination of additional categories of questions to be decided by a two-thirds majority, shall be made by a majority of the members present and voting.

Article 19

A Member of the United Nations which is in arrears in the payment of its financial contributions to the Organization shall have no vote in the General Assembly if the amount of its arrears equals or exceeds the amount of the contributions due from it for the preceding two full years. The General Assembly may, nevertheless, permit such a Member to vote if it is satisfied that the failure to pay is due to conditions beyond the control of the Member.

Procedure

Article 20

The General Assembly shall meet in regular annual sessions and in such special sessions as occasion may require. Special sessions shall be convoked by the Secretary-General at the request of the Security Council or of a majority of the Members of the United Nations.

Article 21

The General Assembly shall adopt its own rules of procedure. It shall elect its President for each session.

Article 22

The General Assembly may establish such subsidiary organs as it deems necessary for the performance of its functions.

Chapter V

The Security Council

Article 23[2)]

1. The Security Council shall consist of fifteen Mem-

bers of the United Nations. The Republic of China, France, the Union of Soviet Socialist Republics, the United Kingdom of Great Britain and Northern Ireland, and the United States of America shall be permanent members of the Security Council. The General Assembly shall elect ten other Members of the United Nations to be non-permanent members of the Security Council, due regard being specially paid, in the first instance to the contribution of Members of the United Nations to the maintenance of international peace and security and to the other purposes of the Organization, and also to equitable geographical distribution.

2. The non-permanent members of the Security Council shall be elected for a term of two years. In the first election of the non-permanent members after the increase of the membership of the Security Council from eleven to fifteen, two of the four additional members shall be chosen for a term of one year. A retiring member shall not be eligible for immediate re-election.

3. Each member of the Security Council shall have one representative.

Functions and Powers

Article 24

1. In order to ensure prompt and effective action by the United Nations, its Members confer on the Security Council primary responsibility for the maintenance of international peace and security, and agree that in carrying out its duties under this responsibility the Security Council acts on their behalf.

2. In discharging these duties the Security Council shall act in accordance with the Purposes and Principles of the United Nations. The specific powers granted to the Security Council for the discharge of these duties are laid down in Chapters VI, VII, VIII, and XII.

3. The Security Council shall submit annual and, when necessary, special reports to the General Assembly for its consideration.

Article 25

The Members of the United Nations agree to accept and carry out the decisions of the Security Council in accordance with the present Charter.

Article 26

In order to promote the establishment and mainte-

nance of international peace and security with the least diversion for armaments of the world's human and economic resources, the Security Council shall be responsible for formulating, with the assistance of the Military Staff Committee referred to in Article 47, plans to be submitted to the Members of the United Nations for the establishment of a system for the regulation of armaments.

Voting

Article 27[3)]

1. Each member of the Security Council shall have one vote.

2. Decisions of the Security Council on procedural matters shall be made by an affirmative vote of nine members.

3. Decisions of the Security Council on all other matters shall be made by an affirmative vote of nine members including the concurring votes of the permanent members; provided that, in decisions under Chapter VI, and under paragraph 3 of Article 52, a party to a dispute shall abstain from voting.

Procedure

Article 28

1. The Security Council shall be so organized as to be able to function continuously. Each member of the Security Council shall for this purpose be represented at all times at the seat of the Organization.

2. The Security Council shall hold periodic meetings at which each of its members may, if it so desires, be represented by a member of the government or by some other specially designated representative.

3. The Security Council may hold meetings at such places other than the seat of the Organization as in its judgment will best facilitate its work.

Article 29

The Security Council may establish such subsidiary organs as it deems necessary for the performance of its functions.

Article 30

The Security Council shall adopt its own rules of procedure, including the method of selecting its President.

Article 31

Any Member of the United Nations which is not a member of the Security Council may participate, without vote, in the discussion of any question brought before the Security Council whenever the latter considers that the interests of that Member are specially affected.

Article 32

Any Member of the United Nations which is not a member of the Security Council or any state which is not a Member of the United Nations, if it is a party to a dispute under consideration by the Security Council, shall be invited to participate, without vote, in the discussion relating to the dispute. The Security Council shall lay down such conditions as it deems just for the participation of a state which is not a Member of the United Nations.

Chapter VI

Pacific Settlement of Disputes

Article 33

1. The parties to any dispute, the continuance of which is likely to endanger the maintenance of international peace and security, shall, first of all, seek a solution by negotiation, enquiry, mediation, conciliation, arbitration, judicial settlement, resort to regional agencies or arrangements, or other peaceful means of their own choice.

2. The Security Council shall, when it deems necessary, call upon the parties to settle their dispute by such means.

Article 34

The Security Council may investigate any dispute, or any situation which might lead to international friction or give rise to a dispute, in order to determine whether the continuance of the dispute or situation is likely to endanger the maintenance of international peace and security.

Article 35

1. Any Member of the United Nations may bring any dispute, or any situation of the nature referred to in Article 34, to the attention of the Security Council or of the General Assembly.

2. A state which is not a Member of the United Nations may bring to the attention of the Security Council or of the General Assembly any dispute to which it is a party if it accepts in advance, for the purposes of the dispute, the obligations of pacific settlement provided in the present Charter.

3. The proceedings of the General Assembly in respect of matters brought to its attention under this Article will be subject to the provisions of Articles 11 and 12.

Article 36

1. The Security Council may, at any stage of a dispute of the nature referred to in Article 33 or of a situation of like nature, recommend appropriate procedures or methods of adjustment.

2. The Security Council should take into consideration any procedures for the settlement of the dispute which have already been adopted by the parties.

3. In making recommendations under this Article the Security Council should also take into consideration that legal disputes should as a general rule be referred by the parties to the International Court of Justice in accordance with the provisions of the Statute of the Court.

Article 37

1. Should the parties to a dispute of the nature referred to in Article 33 fail to settle it by the means indicated in that Article, they shall refer it to the Security Council.

2. If the Security Council deems that the continuance of the dispute is in fact likely to endanger the maintenance of international peace and security, it shall decide whether to take action under Article 36 or to recommend such terms of settlement as it may consider appropriate.

Article 38

Without prejudice to the provisions of Articles 33 to 37, the Security Council may, if all the parties to any dispute so request, make recommendations to the parties with a view to a pacific settlement of the dispute.

Chapter VII

Action With Respect to Threats to the Peace, Breaches of the Peace, and Acts of Aggression

Article 39

The Security Council shall determine the existence of any threat to the peace, breach of the peace, or act of aggression and shall make recommendations, or decide what measures shall be taken in accordance with Articles 41 and 42, to maintain or restore international peace and security.

Article 40

In order to prevent an aggravation of the situation, the Security Council may, before making the recommendations or deciding upon the measures provided for in Article 39, call upon the parties concerned to comply with such provisional measures as it deems necessary or desirable. Such provisional measures shall be without prejudice to the rights, claims, or position of the parties concerned. The Security Council shall duly take account of failure to comply with such provisional measures.

Article 41

The Security Council may decide what measures not involving the use of armed force are to be employed to give effect to its decisions, and it may call upon the Members of the United Nations to apply such measures. These may include complete or partial interruption of economic relations and of rail, sea, air, postal, telegraphic, radio, and other means of communication, and the severance of diplomatic relations.

Article 42

Should the Security Council consider that measures provided for in Article 41 would be inadequate or have proved to be inadequate, it may take such action by air, sea, or land forces as may be necessary to maintain or restore international peace and security. Such action may include demonstrations, blockade, and other operations by air, sea, or land forces of Members of the United Nations.

Article 43

1. All Members of the United Nations, in order to contribute to the maintenance of international peace and security, undertake to make available to the Security Council, on its call and in accordance with a special agreement or agreements, armed forces, assistance, and facilities, including rights of passage, necessary for the purpose of maintaining international peace and security.

2. Such agreement or agreements shall govern the numbers and types of forces, their degree of readiness and general location, and the nature of the facilities and assistance to be provided.

3. The agreement or agreements shall be negotiated as soon as possible on the initiative of the Security Council. They shall be concluded between the Security Council and Members or between the Security Council and groups of Members and shall be subject to ratification by the signatory states in accordance with their respective constitutional processes.

Article 44

When the Security Council has decided to use force it shall, before calling upon a Member not represented on it to provide armed forces in fulfillment of the obligations assumed under Article 43, invite that Member, if the Member so desires, to participate in the decisions of the Security Council concerning the employment of contingents of that Member's armed forces.

Article 45

In order to enable the United Nations to take urgent military measures Members shall hold immediately available national air-force contingents for combined international enforcement action. The strength and degree of readiness of these contingents and plans for their combined action shall be determined, within the limits laid down in the special agreement or agreements referred to in Article 43, by the Security Council with the assistance of the Military Staff Committee.

Article 46

Plans for the application of armed force shall be made by the Security Council with the assistance of the Military Staff Committee.

Article 47

1. There shall be established a Military Staff Committee to advise and assist the Security Council on all questions relating to the Security Council's military requirements for the maintenance of international peace and security, the employment and command of forces placed at its disposal, the regulation of armaments, and possible disarmament.

2. The Military Staff Committee shall consist of the Chiefs of Staff of the permanent members of the Security Council or their representatives. Any Mem-

ber of the United Nations not permanently represented on the Committee shall be invited by the Committee to be associated with it when the efficient discharge of the Committee's responsibilities requires the participation of that Member in its work.

3. The Military Staff Committee shall be responsible under the Security Council for the strategic direction of any armed forces placed at the disposal of the Security Council. Questions relating to the command of such forces shall be worked out subsequently.

4. The Military Staff Committee, with the authorization of the Security Council and after consultation with appropriate regional agencies, may establish regional subcommittees.

Article 48

1. The action required to carry out the decisions of the Security Council for the maintenance of international peace and security shall be taken by all the Members of the United Nations or by some of them, as the Security Council may determine.

2. Such decisions shall be carried out by the Members of the United Nations directly and through their action in the appropriate international agencies of which they are members.

Article 49

The Members of the United Nations shall join in affording mutual assistance in carrying out the measures decided upon by the Security Council.

Article 50

If preventive or enforcement measures against any state are taken by the Security Council, any other state, whether a Member of the United Nations or not, which finds itself confronted with special economic problems arising from the carrying out of those measures shall have the right to consult the Security Council with regard to a solution of those problems.

Article 51

Nothing in the present Charter shall impair the inherent right of individual or collective self-defense if an armed attack occurs against a Member of the United Nations, until the Security Council has taken measures necessary to maintain international peace and security. Measures taken by Members in the exercise of this right of self-defense shall be immediately reported to the Security Council and shall not in any way affect the authority and responsibility of the Security Council under the present Charter to take at any time such action as it deems necessary in order to maintain or restore international peace and security.

Chapter VIII

Regional Arrangements

Article 52

1. Nothing in the present Charter precludes the existence of regional arrangements or agencies for dealing with such matters relating to the maintenance of international peace and security as are appropriate for regional action, provided that such arrangements or agencies and their activities are consistent with the Purposes and Principles of the United Nations.

2. The Members of the United Nations entering into such arrangements or constituting such agencies shall make every effort to achieve pacific settlement of local disputes through such regional arrangements or by such regional agencies before referring them to the Security Council.

3. The Security Council shall encourage the development of pacific settlement of local disputes through such regional arrangements or by such regional agencies either on the initiative of the states concerned or by reference from the Security Council.

4. This Article in no way impairs the application of Articles 34 and 35.

Article 53

1. The Security Council shall, where appropriate, utilize such regional arrangements or agencies for enforcement action under its authority. But no enforcement action shall be taken under regional arrangements or by regional agencies without the authorization of the Security Council, with the exception of measures against any enemy state, as defined in paragraph 2 of this Article, provided for pursuant to Article 107 or in regional arrangements directed against renewal of aggressive policy on the part of any such state, until such time as the Organization may, on request of the Governments concerned, be charged with the responsibility for preventing further aggression by such a state.

2. The term enemy state as used in paragraph 1 of this Article applies to any state which during the Second World War has been an enemy of any signatory of the present Charter.

Article 54

The Security Council shall at all times be kept fully informed of activities undertaken or in contemplation under regional arrangements or by regional agencies for the maintenance of international peace and security.

Chapter IX

International Economic and Social Co-operation

Article 55

With a view to the creation of conditions of stability and well-being which are necessary for peaceful and friendly relations among nations based on respect for the principle of equal rights and self-determination of peoples, the United Nations shall promote:

a. higher standards of living, full employment, and conditions of economic and social progress and development;

b. solutions of international economic, social, health, and related problems; and international cultural and educational co-operation; and

c. universal respect for, and observance of, human rights and fundamental freedoms for all without distinction as to race, sex, language, or religion.

Article 56

All Members pledge themselves to take joint and separate action in cooperation with the Organization for the achievement of the purposes set forth in Article 55.

Article 57

1. The various specialized agencies, established by intergovernmental agreement and having wide international responsibilities, as defined in their basic instruments, in economic, social, cultural, educational, health, and related fields, shall be brought into relationship with the United Nations in accordance with the provisions of Article 63.

2. Such agencies thus brought into relationship with the United Nations are hereinafter referred to as specialized agencies.

Article 58

The Organization shall make recommendations for the coordination of the policies and activities of the specialized agencies.

Article 59

The Organization shall, where appropriate, initiate negotiations among the states concerned for the creation of any new specialized agencies required for the accomplishment of the purposes set forth in Article 55.

Article 60

Responsibility for the discharge of the functions of the Organization set forth in this Chapter shall be vested in the General Assembly and, under the authority of the General Assembly, in the Economic and Social Council, which shall have for this purpose the powers set forth in Chapter X.

Chapter X

The Economic and Social Council

Composition

Article 61

1. The Economic and Social Council shall consist of fifty-four Members of the United Nations elected by the General Assembly.

2. Subject to the provisions of paragraph 3, eighteen members of the Economic and Social Council shall be elected each year for a term of three years. A retiring member shall be eligible for immediate re-election.

3. At the first election after the increase in the membership of the Economic and Social Council from twenty-seven to fifty-four members, in addition to the members elected in place of the nine members whose term of office expires at the end of that year, twenty-seven additional members shall be elected. Of these twenty-seven additional members, the term of office of nine members so elected shall expire at the end of one year, and of nine other members at the end of two years, in accordance with arrangements made by the General Assembly.

4. Each member of the Economic and Social Council shall have one representative.

Functions and Powers

Article 62

1. The Economic and Social Council may make or initiate studies and reports with respect to international economic, social, cultural, educational, health, and related matters and may make recommendations with respect to any such matters to the General Assembly, to the Members of the United Nations, and to the specialized agencies concerned.

2. It may make recommendations for the purpose of promoting respect for, and observance of, human rights and fundamental freedoms for all.

3. It may prepare draft conventions for submission to the General Assembly, with respect to matters falling within its competence.

4. It may call, in accordance with the rules prescribed by the United Nations, international conferences on matters falling within its competence.

Article 63

1. The Economic and Social Council may enter into agreements with any of the agencies referred to in Article 57, defining the terms on which the agency concerned shall be brought into relationship with the United Nations. Such agreements shall be subject to approval by the General Assembly.

2. It may coordinate the activities of the specialized agencies through consultation with and recommendations to such agencies and through recommendations to the General Assembly and to the Members of the United Nations.

Article 64

1. The Economic and Social Council may take appropriate steps to obtain regular reports from the specialized agencies. It may make arrangements with the Members of the United Nations and with the specialized agencies to obtain reports on the steps taken to give effect to its own recommendations and to recommendations on matters falling within its competence made by the General Assembly.

2. It may communicate its observations on these reports to the General Assembly .

Article 65

The Economic and Social Council may furnish information to the Security Council and shall assist the Security Council upon its request.

Article 66

1. The Economic and Social Council shall perform such functions as fall within its competence in connection with the carrying out of the recommendations of the General Assembly.

2. It may, with the approval of the General Assembly, perform services at the request of Members of the United Nations and at the request of specialized agencies.

3. It shall perform such other functions as are specified elsewhere in the present Charter or as may be assigned to it by the General Assembly.

Article 67

1. Each member of the Economic and Social Council shall have one vote.

2. Decisions of the Economic and Social Council shall be made by a majority of the members present and voting.

Procedure

Article 68

The Economic and Social Council shall set up commissions in economic and social fields and for the promotion of human rights, and such other commissions as may be required for the performance of its functions.

Article 69

The Economic and Social Council shall invite any Member of the United Nations to participate, without vote, in its deliberations on any matter of particular concern to that Member.

Article 70

The Economic and Social Council may make arrangements for representatives of the specialized agencies to participate, without vote, in its deliberations and in those of the commissions established by it, and for its representatives to participate in the deliberations of the specialized agencies.

Article 71

The Economic and Social Council may make suitable arrangements for consultation with non-governmental organizations which are concerned with matters within its competence. Such arrangements may be made with international organizations and, where appropriate, with national organizations after consultation with the Member of the United Nations concerned.

Article 72

1. The Economic and Social Council shall adopt its own rules of procedure, including the method of selecting its President.

2. The Economic and Social Council shall meet as required in accordance with its rules, which shall include provision for the convening of meetings on the request of a majority of its members.

Chapter XI

Declaration Regarding Non-Self-Governing Territories

Article 73

Members of the United Nations which have or assume responsibilities for the administration of territories whose peoples have not yet attained a full measure of self-government recognize the principle that the interests of the inhabitants of these territories are paramount, and accept as a sacred trust the obligation to promote to the utmost, within the system of international peace and security established by the present Charter, the well-being of the inhabitants of these territories, and, to this end:

a. to ensure, with due respect for the culture of the peoples concerned, their political, economic, social, and educational advancement, their just treatment, and their protection against abuses;

b. to develop self-government, to take due account of the political aspirations of the peoples, and to assist them in the progressive development of their free political institutions, according to the particular circumstances of each territory and its peoples and their varying stages of advancement;

c. to further international peace and security;

d. to promote constructive measures of development, to encourage research, and to cooperate with one another and, when and where appropriate, with specialized international bodies with a view to the practical achievement of the social, economic, and scientific purposes set forth in this Article; and

e. to transmit regularly to the Secretary-General for information purposes, subject to such limitation as

security and constitutional considerations may require, statistical and other information of a technical nature relating to economic, social, and educational conditions in the territories for which they are respectively responsible other than those territories to which Chapter XII and XIII apply.

Article 74

Members of the United Nations also agree that their policy in respect of the territories to which this Chapter applies, no less than in respect of their metropolitan areas, must be based on the general principle of good-neighborliness, due account being taken of the interests and well-being of the rest of the world, in social, economic, and commercial matters.

Chapter XII

International Trusteeship System

Article 75

The United Nations shall establish under its authority an international trusteeship system for the administration and supervision of such territories as may be placed thereunder by subsequent individual agreements. These territories are hereinafter referred to as trust territories.

Article 76

The basic objectives of the trusteeship system, in accordance with the Purposes of the United Nations laid down in Article 1 of the present Charter, shall be:

a. to further international peace and security;

b. to promote the political, economic, social, and educational advancement of the inhabitants of the trust territories, and their progressive development towards self-government or independence as may be appropriate to the particular circumstances of each territory and its peoples and the freely expressed wishes of the peoples concerned, and as may be provided by the terms of each trusteeship agreement;

c. to encourage respect for human rights and for fundamental freedoms for all without distinction as to race, sex, language, or religion, and to encourage recognition of the interdependence of the peoples of the world; and

d. to ensure equal treatment in social, economic, and

commercial matters for all Members of the United Nations and their nationals and also equal treatment for the latter in the administration of justice without prejudice to the attainment of the foregoing objectives and subject to the provisions of Article 80.

Article 77

1. The trusteeship system shall apply to such territories in the following categories as may be placed thereunder by means of trusteeship agreements:

a. territories now held under mandate;

b. territories which may be detached from enemy states as a result of the Second World War, and

c. territories voluntarily placed under the system by states responsible for their administration.

2. It will be a matter for subsequent agreement as to which territories in the foregoing categories will be brought under the trusteeship system and upon what terms.

Article 78

The trusteeship system shall not apply to territories which have become Members of the United Nations, relationship among which shall be based on respect for the principle of sovereign equality.

Article 79

The terms of trusteeship for each territory to be placed under the trusteeship system, including any alteration or amendment, shall be agreed upon by the states directly concerned, including the mandatory power in the case of territories held under mandate by a Member of the United Nations, and shall be approved as provided for in Articles 83 and 85.

Article 80

1. Except as may be agreed upon in individual trusteeship agreements, made under Articles 77, 79, and 81, placing each territory under the trusteeship system, and until such agreements have been concluded, nothing in this Chapter shall be construed in or of itself to alter in any manner the rights whatsoever of any states or any peoples or the terms of existing international instruments to which Members of the United Nations may respectively be parties.

2. Paragraph 1 of this Article shall not be interpreted as giving grounds for delay or postponement of the negotiation and conclusion of agreements for placing mandated and other territories under the trusteeship system as provided for in Article 77.

Article 81

The trusteeship agreement shall in each case include the terms under which the trust territory will be administered and designate the authority which will exercise the administration of the trust territory. Such authority, hereinafter called the administering authority, may be one or more states or the Organization itself.

Article 82

There may be designated, in any trusteeship agreement, a strategic area or areas which may include part or all of the trust territory to which the agreement applies, without prejudice to any special agreement or agreements made under Article 43.

Article 83

1. All functions of the United Nations relating to strategic areas, including the approval of the terms of the trusteeship agreements and of their alteration or amendment, shall be exercised by the Security Council.

2. The basic objectives set forth in Article 76 shall be applicable to the people of each strategic area.

3. The Security Council shall, subject to the provisions of the trusteeship agreements and without prejudice to security considerations, avail itself of the assistance of the Trusteeship Council to perform those functions of the United Nations under the trusteeship system relating to political, economic, social, and educational matters in the strategic areas.

Article 84

It shall be the duty of the administering authority to ensure that the trust territory shall play its part in the maintenance of international peace and security. To this end the administering authority may make use of volunteer forces, facilities, and assistance from the trust territory in carrying out the obligations towards the Security Council undertaken in this regard by the administering authority, as well as for local defense and the maintenance of law and order within the trust territory.

Article 85

1. The functions of the United Nations with regard

to trusteeship agreements for all areas not designated as strategic, including the approval of the terms of the trusteeship agreements and of their alteration or amendment, shall be exercised by the General Assembly.

2. The Trusteeship Council, operating under the authority of the General Assembly, shall assist the General Assembly in carrying out these functions.

Chapter XIII

The Trusteeship Council

Composition

Article 86

1. The Trusteeship Council shall consist of the following Members of the United Nations:

a. those Members administering trust territories;

b. such of those Members mentioned by name in Article 23 as are not administering trust territories; and

c. as many other Members elected for three-year terms by the General Assembly as may be necessary to ensure that the total number of members of the Trusteeship Council is equally divided between those Members of the United Nations which administer trust territories and those which do not.

2. Each member of the Trusteeship Council shall designate one specially qualified person to represent it therein.

Functions and Powers

Article 87

The General Assembly and, under its authority, the Trusteeship Council, in carrying out their functions, may:

a. consider reports submitted by the administering authority;

b. accept petitions and examine them in consultation with the administering authority;

c. provide for periodic visits to the respective trust territories at times agreed upon with the administering authority; and

d. take these and other actions in conformity with the terms of the trusteeship agreements.

Article 88

The Trusteeship Council shall formulate a questionnaire on the political, economic, social, and educational advancement of the inhabitants of each trust territory, and the administering authority for each trust territory within the competence of the General Assembly shall make an annual report to the General Assembly upon the basis of such questionnaire.

Voting

Article 89

1. Each member of the Trusteeship Council shall have one vote.

2. Decisions of the Trusteeship Council shall be made by a majority of the members present and voting.

Procedure

Article 90

1. The Trusteeship Council shall adopt its own rules of procedure, including the method of selecting its President.

2. The Trusteeship Council shall meet as required in accordance with its rules, which shall include provision for the convening of meetings on the request of a majority of its members.

Article 91

The Trusteeship Council shall, when appropriate, avail itself of the assistance of the Economic and Social Council and of the specialized agencies in regard to matters with which they are respectively concerned.

Chapter XIV

The International Court of Justice

Article 92

The International Court of Justice shall be the principal judicial organ of the United Nations. It shall function in accordance with the annexed Statute which is based upon the Statute of the Permanent Court of International Justice and forms an integral part of the present Charter.

Article 93

1. All Members of the United Nations are *ipso facto* parties to the Statute of the International Court of Justice.

2. A state which is not a Member of the United Nations may become a party to the Statute of the International Court of Justice on conditions to be determined in each case by the General Assembly upon the recommendation of the Security Council.

Article 94

1. Each Member of the United Nations undertakes to comply with the decision of the International Court of Justice in any case to which it is a party.

2. If any party to a case fails to perform the obligations incumbent upon it under a judgment rendered by the Court, the other party may have recourse to the Security Council, which may, if it deems necessary, make recommendations or decide upon measures to be taken to give effect to the judgment.

Article 95

Nothing in the present Charter shall prevent Members of the United Nations from entrusting the solution of their differences to other tribunals by virtue of agreements already in existence or which may be concluded in the future.

Article 96

1. The General Assembly or the Security Council may request the International Court of Justice to give an advisory opinion on any legal question.

2. Other organs of the United Nations and specialized agencies, which may at any time be so authorized by the General Assembly, may also request advisory opinions of the Court on legal questions arising within the scope of their activities.

Chapter XV

The Secretariat

Article 97

The Secretariat shall comprise a Secretary-General and such staff as the Organization may require. The Secretary-General shall be appointed by the General Assembly upon the recommendation of the Security Council. He shall be the chief administrative officer of the Organization.

Article 98

The Secretary-General shall act in that capacity in all meetings of the General Assembly, of the Security Council, of the Economic and Social Council, and of the Trusteeship Council, and shall perform such other functions as are entrusted to him by these organs. The Secretary-General shall make an annual report to the General Assembly on the work of the Organization.

Article 99

The Secretary-General may bring to the attention of the Security Council any matter which in his opinion may threaten the maintenance of international peace and security.

Article 100

1. In the performance of their duties the Secretary-General and the staff shall not seek or receive instructions from any government or from any other authority external to the Organization. They shall refrain from any action which might reflect on their position as international officials responsible only to the Organization.

2. Each Member of the United Nations undertakes to respect the exclusively international character of the responsibilities of the Secretary-General and the staff and not to seek to influence them in the discharge of their responsibilities.

Article 101

1. The staff shall be appointed by the Secretary-General under regulations established by the General Assembly.

2. Appropriate staffs shall be permanently assigned to the Economic and Social Council, the Trusteeship Council, and, as required, to other organs of the United Nations. These staffs shall form a part of the Secretariat.

3. The paramount consideration in the employment of the staff and in the determination of the conditions of service shall be the necessity of securing the highest standards of efficiency, competence, and integrity. Due regard shall be paid to the importance of recruiting the staff on as wide a geographical basis as possible.

Chapter XVI

Miscellaneous Provisions

Article 102

1. Every treaty and every international agreement entered into by any Member of the United Nations after the present Charter comes into force shall as soon as possible be registered with the Secretariat and published by it.

2. No party to any such treaty or international agreement which has not been registered in accordance with the provisions of paragraph I of this Article may invoke that treaty or agreement before any organ of the United Nations.

Article 103

In the event of a conflict between the obligations of the Members of the United Nations under the present Charter and their obligations under any other international agreement, their obligations under the present Charter shall prevail.

Article 104

The Organization shall enjoy in the territory of each of its Members such legal capacity as may be necessary for the exercise of its functions and the fulfillment of its purposes.

Article 105

1. The Organization shall enjoy in the territory of each of its Members such privileges and immunities as are necessary for the fulfillment of its purposes.

2. Representatives of the Members of the United Nations and officials of the Organization shall similarly enjoy such privileges and immunities as are necessary for the independent exercise of their functions in connection with the Organization.

3. The General Assembly may make recommendations with a view to determining the details of the application of paragraphs 1 and 2 of this Article or may propose conventions to the Members of the United Nations for this purpose.

Chapter XVII

Transitional Security Arrangements

Article 106

Pending the coming into force of such special agreements referred to in Article 43 as in the opinion of the Security Council enable it to begin the exercise of its responsibilities under Article 42, the parties to the Four-Nation Declaration, signed at Moscow October 30, 1943, and France, shall, in accordance with the provisions of paragraph 5 of that Declaration, consult with one another and as occasion requires with other Members of the United Nations with a view to such joint action on behalf of the Organization as may be necessary for the purpose of maintaining international peace and security.

Article 107

Nothing in the present Charter shall invalidate or preclude action, in relation to any state which during the Second World War has been an enemy of any signatory to the present Charter, taken or authorized as a result of that war by the Governments having responsibility for such action.

Chapter XVII

Amendments

Article 108

Amendments to the present Charter shall come into force for all Members of the United Nations when they have been adopted by a vote of two thirds of the members of the General Assembly and ratified in accordance with their respective constitutional processes by two thirds of the Members of the United Nations, including all the permanent members of the Security Council.

Article 109

1. A General Conference of the Members of the United Nations for the purpose of reviewing the present Charter may be held at a date and place to be fixed by a two-thirds vote of the members of the General Assembly and by a vote of any seven members of the Security Council. Each Member of the United Nations shall have one vote in the conference.

2. Any alteration of the present Charter recommended by a two-thirds vote of the conference shall take effect when ratified in accordance with their respective constitutional processes by two thirds of the Members of the United Nations including all the permanent members of the Security Council.

3. If such a conference has not been held before the tenth annual session of the General Assembly following the coming into force of the present Charter, the proposal to call such a conference shall be placed on the agenda of that session of the General Assembly,

and the conference shall be held if so decided by a majority vote of the members of the General Assembly and by a vote of any seven members of the Security Council.

Chapter XIX

Ratification and Signature

Article 110

1. The present Charter shall be ratified by the signatory states in accordance with their respective constitutional processes.

2. The ratifications shall be deposited with the Government of the United States of America, which shall notify all the signatory states of each deposit as well as the Secretary-General of the Organization when he has been appointed.

3. The present Charter shall come into force upon the deposit of ratifications by the Republic of China, France, the Union of Soviet Socialist Republics, the United Kingdom of Great Britain and Northern Ireland, and the United States of America, and by a majority of the other signatory states. A protocol of the ratifications deposited shall thereupon be drawn up by the Government of the United States of America which shall communicate copies thereof to all the signatory states.

4. The states signatory to the present Charter which ratify it after it has come into force will become original Members of the United Nations on the date of the deposit of their respective ratifications.

Article 111

The present Charter, of which the Chinese, French, Russian, English, and Spanish texts are equally authentic, shall remain deposited in the archives of the Government of the United States of America. Duly certified copies thereof shall be transmitted by that Government to the Governments of the other signatory states.

IN FAITH WHEREOF the representatives of the Governments of the United Nations have signed the present Charter.

DONE at the city of San Francisco the twenty-sixth day of June, one thousand nine hundred and forty-five.

Convention on the Prevention and Punishment of the Crime of Genocide

Also known as: Genocide Convention
Date of signature: December 9, 1948
Place of signature: Paris
Signatory states: Afghanistan, Albania, Algeria, Argentina, Australia, Austria, Bahamas, Barbados, Belgium, Brazil, Bulgaria, Burma, Byelorussia, Canada, Chile, Colombia, Costa Rica, Cuba, Czechoslovakia, Denmark, Ecuador, Egypt, El Salvador, Ethiopia, Fiji, Finland, France, Gambia, German Democratic Republic, Federal Republic of Germany, Ghana, Greece, Guatemala, Haiti, Honduras, Hungary, Iceland, India, Iran, Iraq, Ireland, Israel Italy, Jamaica, Jordan, Kampuchea, Republic of Korea, Laos, Lebanon, Lesotho, Liberia, Luxembourg, Mali, Mexico, Monaco, Mongolia, Morocco, Nepal, Netherlands, New Zealand, Nicaragua, Norway, Pakistan, Panama, Peru, Philippines, Poland, Romania, Rwanda, Saudi Arabia, Soviet Union, Spain, Sri Lanka, Sweden, Syria, Taiwan, Tonga, Tunisia, Turkey, United Kingdom, Upper Volta, Uruguay, Venezuela, Vietnam, Yugoslavia, Zaire
Date of entry into force: January 12, 1951

The Contracting Parties,
Having considered the declaration made by the General Assembly of the United Nations in its resolution 96 (I) dated 11 December 1946 that genocide is a crime under international law, contrary to the spirit and aims of the United Nations and condemned by the civilized world;
Recognizing that at all periods of history genocide has inflicted great losses on humanity; and
Being convinced that, in order to liberate mankind from such an odious scourge, international co-operation is required,
Hereby agree as hereinafter provided:

Article I

The Contracting Parties confirm that genocide, whether committed in time of peace or in time of war, is a crime under international law which they undertake to prevent and to punish.

Article II

In the present Convention, genocide means any of the following acts committed with intent to destroy, in whole or in part, a national, ethical, racial or religious group, as such:

(a) Killing members of the group;

(b) Causing serious bodily or mental harm to members of the group;

(c) Deliberately inflicting on the group conditions of life calculated to bring about its physical destruction in whole or in part;

(d) Imposing measures intended to prevent births within the group;

(e) Forcibly transferring children of the group to another group.

Article III

The following acts shall be punishable:

(a) Genocide;

(b) Conspiracy to commit genocide;

(c) Direct and public incitement to commit genocide;

(d) Attempt to commit genocide;

(e) Complicity in genocide.

Article IV

Persons committing genocide or any of the other acts enumerated in Article III shall be punished, whether they are constitutionally responsible rulers, public officials or private individuals.

Article V

The Contracting Parties undertake to enact, in accordance with their respective Constitutions, the necessary legislation to give effect to the provisions of the present Convention and, in particular, to provide effective penalties for persons guilty of genocide or of any of the acts enumerated in Article III.

Article VI

Persons charged with genocide or any of the other acts enumerated in Article III shall be tried by a competent tribunal of the State in the territory of which the act was committed, or by such international penal tribunal as may have jurisdiction with respect to those Contracting Parties which shall have accepted its jurisdiction.

Article VII

Genocide and the other acts enumerated in Article III shall not be considered as political crimes for the purpose of extradition.

The Contracting Parties pledge themselves in such cases to grant extradition in accordance with their laws and treaties in force.

Article VIII

Any Contracting Party may call upon the competent organs of the United Nations to take such action under the Charter of the United Nations as they consider appropriate for the prevention and suppression of acts of genocide or any of the other acts enumerated in Article III.

Article IX

Disputes between the Contracting Parties relating to the interpretation, application or fulfilment of the present Convention, including those relating to the responsibility of a State for genocide or for any of the other acts enumerated in Article III, shall be submitted to the International Court of Justice at the request of any of the parties to the dispute.

Article X

The present Convention, of which the Chinese, English, French, Russian and Spanish texts are equally authentic, shall bear the date of 9 December 1948.

Article XI

The present Convention shall be open until 31 December 1949 for signature on behalf of any Member of the United Nations and of any non-member State to which an invitation to sign has been addressed by the General Assembly.

The present Convention shall be ratified, and the instruments of ratification shall be deposited with the Secretary-General of the United Nations.

After 1 January 1950 the present Convention may be acceded to on behalf of any Member of the United

Nations and of any non-member State which has received an invitation as aforesaid.

Instruments of accession shall be deposited with the Secretary-General of the United Nations.

Article XII

Any Contracting Party may at any time, by notification addressed to the Secretary-General of the United Nations, extend the application of the present Convention to all or any of the territories for the conduct of whose foreign relations that Contracting Party is responsible.

Article XIII

On the day when the first twenty instruments of ratification or accession have been deposited, the Secretary-General shall draw up a *procès-verbal* and transmit a copy thereof to each Member of the United Nations and to each of the non-member States contemplated in Article XI.

The present Convention shall come into force on the ninetieth day following the date of deposit of the twentieth instrument of ratification or accession.

Any ratification or accession effected subsequent to the latter date shall become effective on the ninetieth day following the deposit of the instrument of ratification or accession.

Article XIV

The present Convention shall remain in effect for a period of ten years as from the date of its coming into force.

It shall thereafter remain in force for successive periods of five years for such Contracting Parties as have not denounced it at least six months before the expiration of the current period.

Denunciation shall be effected by a written notification addressed to the Secretary-General of the United Nations.

Article XV

If, as a result of denunciations, the number of Parties to the present Convention should become less than sixteen, the Convention shall cease to be in force as from the date on which the last of these denunciations shall become effective.

Article XVI

A request for the revision of the present Convention may be made at any time by any Contracting Party by means of a notification in writing addressed to the Secretary-General.

The General Assembly shall decide upon the steps, if any, to be taken in respect of such request.

Article XVII

The Secretary-General of the United Nations shall notify all Members of the United Nations and the non-member States contemplated in Article XI of the following:

(a) Signatures, ratifications and accessions received in accordance with Article XI;

(b) Notifications received in accordance with Article XII;

(c) The date upon which the present Convention comes into force in accordance with Article XIII;

(d) Denunciations received in accordance with Article XIV;

(e) The abrogation of the Convention in accordance with Article XV;

(f) Notifications received in accordance with Article XVI.

Article XVIII

The original of the present Convention shall be deposited in the archives of the United Nations.

A certified copy of the Convention shall be transmitted to each Member of the United Nations and to each of the non-member States contemplated in Article XI.

Article XIX

The present Convention shall be registered by the Secretary-General of the United Nations on the date of its coming into force.

Geneva Convention Relative to the Protection of Civilian Persons in Time of War

Date of signature: August 12, 1949   *Place of signature:* Geneva

Signatory states: *Afghanistan, Albania, Algeria, Argentina, Australia, Austria, Bahamas, Bahrain, Bangladesh, Barbados, Belgium, Benin, Bolivia, Botswana, Brazil, Bulgaria, Burundi, Byelorussia, Cameroon. Canada, Central African Republic, Chad, Chile, People's Republic of China, Colombia, Congo, Costa Rica, Cuba, Cyprus, Czechoslovakia, Denmark, Djibouti, Dominica, Dominican Republic, Ecuador, Egypt, El Salvador, Ethiopia, Fiji, Finland, France, Gabon, Gambia, German Democratic Republic, Federal Republic of Germany, Ghana, Greece, Grenada, Guatemala, Guinea-Bissau, Guyana, Haiti, Holy See, Honduras, Hungary, Iceland, India, Indonesia, Iran, Iraq, Ireland, Israel, Italy, Ivory Coast, Jamaica, Japan, Jordan, Kampuchea, Kenya, Democratic People's Republic of Korea, Republic of Korea, Kuwait, Laos, Lebanon, Lesotho, Liberia, Libya, Liechtenstein, Luxembourg, Madagascar, Malawi, Malaysia, Mali, Malta, Mauritania, Mauritius, Mexico, Monaco, Mongolia Morocco, Nepal, Netherlands, New Zealand, Nicaragua, Niger, Nigeria, Norway, Oman, Pakistan, Panama, Papua New Guinea, Paraguay, Peru, Philippines, Poland, Portugal, Qatar, Romania, Rwanda, Saint Lucia, Saint Vincent and the Grenadines, San Marino, Sao Tome and Principe, Saudi Arabia, Senegal, Sierra Leone, Singapore, Solomon Islands, Somalia, South Africa, Soviet Union, Spain, Sri Lanka, Sudan, Surinam, Swaziland, Sweden, Switzerland, Syria, Tanzania, Thailand, Togo, Tonga, Trinidad and Tobago, Tunisia, Turkey, Tuvalu, Uganda, Ukraine, United Arab Emirates, United Kingdom, United States, Upper Volta, Uruguay, Venezuela, Vietnam, Yemen Arab Republic, People's Democratic Republic of Yemen, Yugoslavia, Zaire, Zambia*
Date of entry into force: *October 21, 1950*

The undersigned Plenipotentiaries of the Governments represented at the Diplomatic Conference held at Geneva from April 21 to August 12, 1949, for the purpose of establishing a Convention for the Protection of Civilian Persons in Time of War, have agreed as follows:

PART I

GENERAL PROVISIONS

Article 1

The High Contracting Parties undertake to respect and to ensure respect for the present Convention in all circumstances.

Article 2

In addition to the provisions which shall be implemented in peacetime, the present Convention shall apply to all cases of declared war or of any other armed conflict which may arise between two or more of the High Contracting Parties, even if the state of war is not recognized by one of them.

The Convention shall also apply to all cases of partial or total occupation of the territory of a High Contracting Party, even if the said occupation meets with no armed resistance.

Although one of the Powers in conflict may not be a party to the present Convention, the Powers who are parties thereto shall remain bound by it in their mutual relations. They shall furthermore be bound by the Convention in relation to the said Power, if the latter accepts and applies the provisions thereof.

Article 3

In the case of armed conflict not of an international character occurring in the territory of one of the High Contracting Parties, each Party to the conflict shall be bound to apply, as a minimum, the following provisions:

(1) Persons taking no active part in the hostilities, including members of armed forces who have laid down their arms and those placed *hors de combat* by sickness, wounds, detention, or any other cause, shall in all circumstances be treated humanely, without any adverse distinction founded on race, colour, religion or faith, sex, birth or wealth, or any other similar criteria.

To this end, the following acts are and shall remain prohibited at any time and in any place whatsoever with respect to the above-mentioned persons:

(a) violence to life and person, in particular murder of all kinds, mutilation, cruel treatment and torture;

(b) taking of hostages;

(c) outrages upon personal dignity, in particular humiliating and degrading treatment;

(d) the passing of sentences and the carrying out of executions without previous judgment pronounced by a regularly constituted court, affording all the judicial guarantees which are recognized as indispensable by civilized peoples.

(2) The wounded and sick shall be collected and cared for.

Article 4

Persons protected by the Convention are those who, at a given moment and in any manner whatsoever, find themselves, in case of a conflict or occupation, in the hands of a Party to the conflict or Occupying Power of which they are not nationals.

Nationals of a State which is not bound by the Convention are not protected by it. Nationals of a neutral State who find themselves in the territory of a belligerent State, and nationals of a co-belligerent State, shall not be regarded as protected persons while the State of which they are nationals has normal diplomatic representation in the State in whose hands they are.

Article5

[Spies and saboteurs forfeit their rights under the Convention, but shall be treated humanely.]

Article 6

[The Convention applies throughout any conflict as defined in Article 2.]

Article 7

[Protected persons' rights shall not be adversely affected by special agreements.]

Article8

Protected persons may in no circumstances renounce in part or in entirety the rights secured to them by the present Convention, and by the special agreements referred to in the foregoing Article, if such there be.

Article 9

The present Convention shall be applied with the cooperation and under the scrutiny of the Protecting Powers whose duty it is to safeguard the interests of the Parties to the conflict. For this purpose, the Protecting Powers may appoint, apart from their diplomatic or consular staff, delegates from amongst their own nationals or the nationals of other neutral Powers. The said delegates shall be subject to the approval of the Power with which they are to carry out their duties.

Article 10

The provisions of the present Convention constitute no obstacle to the humanitarian activities which the International Committee of the Red Cross or any other impartial humanitarian organization may, subject to the consent of the Parties to the conflict concerned, undertake for the protection of civilian persons and for their relief.

Article 11

[Responsibility for protected persons may be entrusted to an organization such as the Red Cross.]

Article 12

[Disagreements over the application of the Convention shall be settled by arbitration.]

PART II

GENERAL PROTECTION OF POPULATIONS AGAINST CERTAIN CONSEQUENCES OF WAR

Article 13

The provisions of Part II cover the whole of the populations of the countries in conflict, without any adverse distinction based, in particular, on race, nationality, religion or political opinion, and are intended to alleviate the sufferings caused by war.

Article 14

[Hospitals and safety zones shall be established for the wounded, the sick, the aged, and children under fifteen.]

Article 15

Any Party to the conflict may, either direct or through a neutral State or some humanitarian organization, propose to the adverse Party to establish, in the regions where fighting is taking place, neutralized zones intended to shelter from the effects of war the following persons, without distinction:

(a) wounded and sick combatants or non-combatants;

(b) civilian persons who take no part in hostilities, and who, while they reside in the zones, perform no work of a military character.

When the Parties concerned have agreed upon the geographical position, administration, food supply and supervision of the proposed neutralized zone, a written agreement shall be concluded and signed by the representatives of the Parties to the conflict. The agreement shall fix the beginning and the duration of the neutralization of the zone.

Article 16

The wounded and sick, as well as the infirm, and expectant mothers, shall be the object of particular protection and respect.

As far as military considerations allow, each Party to the conflict shall facilitate the steps taken to search for the killed and wounded, to assist the shipwrecked and other persons exposed to grave danger, and to protect them against pillage and ill-treatment.

Article 17

The Parties to the conflict shall endeavour to conclude local agreements for the removal from besieged or encircled areas, of wounded, sick, infirm, and aged persons, children and maternity cases, and for the passage of ministers of all religions, medical personnel and medical equipment on their way to such areas.

Article 18

[Civilian hospitals shall be respected and protected at all times.]

Article 19

The protection to which civilian hospitals are entitled shall not cease unless they are used to commit, outside their humanitarian duties, acts harmful to the enemy. Protection may, however, cease only after due warning has been given, naming, in all appropriate cases, a reasonable time limit, and after such warning has remained unheeded.

The fact that sick or wounded members of the armed forces are nursed in these hospitals, or the presence of small arms and ammunition taken from such combatants and not yet handed to the proper service, shall not be considered to be acts harmful to the enemy.

Article 20

Persons regularly and solely engaged in the operation and administration of civilian hospitals, including the personnel engaged in the search for, removal and transporting of and caring for wounded and sick civilians, the infirm and maternity cases, shall be respected and protected.

Article 21

[Hospital trains and convoys shall enjoy absolute protection.]

Article 22

[Medical relief aircraft shall not be attacked.]

Article 23

Each High Contracting Party shall allow the free passage of all consignments of medical and hospital stores and objects necessary for religious worship intended only for civilians of another High Contracting Party, even if the latter is its adversary. It shall likewise permit the free passage of all consignments of essential foodstuffs, clothing and tonics intended for children under fifteen, expectant mothers and maternity cases.

Article 24

[The rights of orphans and children separated from their families are to be protected.]

Article 25

All persons in the territory of a Party to the conflict, or in a territory occupied by it, shall be enabled to give news of a strictly personal nature to members of their families, wherever they may be, and to receive news from them. This correspondence shall be forwarded speedily and without undue delay.

Article 26

Each Party to the conflict shall facilitate enquiries made by members of families dispersed owing to the war, with the object of renewing contact with one another and of meeting, if possible. It shall encourage, in particular, the work of organizations engaged on this task provided they are acceptable to it and conform to its security regulations.

PART III

STATUS AND TREATMENT OF PROTECTED PERSONS

Section I

Provisions Common to the Territories of the Parties to the Conflict and to Occupied Territories

Article 27

Protected persons are entitled, in all circumstances, to respect for their persons, their honour, their family rights, their religious convictions and practices, and their manners and customs. They shall at all times be humanely treated, and shall be protected especially against all acts of violence or threats thereof and against insults and public curiosity.

Women shall be especially protected against any attack on their honour, in particular against rape, enforced prostitution, or any form of indecent assault.

Without prejudice to the provisions relating to their state of health, age and sex, all protected persons shall be treated with the same consideration by the Party to the conflict in whose power they are, without any adverse distinction based, in particular, on race, religion or political opinion.

However, the Parties to the conflict may take such measures of control and security in regard to protected persons as may be necessary as a result of the war.

Article 28

The presence of a protected person may not be used to render certain points or areas immune from military operations.

Article 29

The Party to the conflict in whose hands protected persons may be, is responsible for the treatment accorded to them by its agents, irrespective of any individual responsibility which may be incurred.

Article 30

Protected persons shall have every facility for making application to the Protecting Powers, the International Committee of the Red Cross, the National Red Cross (Red Crescent, Red Lion and Sun) Society of the country where they may be, as well as to any organization that might assist them.

Article 31

No physical or moral coercion shall be exercised against protected persons, in particular to obtain information from them or from third parties.

Article 32

The High Contracting Parties specifically agree that each of them is prohibited from taking any measure of such a character as to cause the physical suffering or extermination of protected persons in their hands. This prohibition applies not only to murder, torture, corporal punishment, mutilation and medical or scientific experiments not necessitated by the medical treatment of a protected person, but also to any other measures of brutality whether applied by civilian or military agents.

Article 33

No protected person may be punished for an offence he or she has not personally committed. Collective penalties and likewise all measures of intimidation or of terrorism are prohibited.

Pillage is prohibited.

Reprisals against protected persons and their property are prohibited.

Article 34

The taking of hostages is prohibited.

Section II

Aliens in the Territory of a Party to the Conflict

Article 35

All protected persons who may desire to leave the territory at the outset of, or during a conflict, shall be entitled to do so, unless their departure is contrary to the national interests of the State. The applications of such persons to leave shall be decided in accordance with regularly established procedures and the decisions shall be taken as rapidly as possible. Those persons permitted to leave may provide themselves with the necessary funds for their journey and take with them a reasonable amount of their effects and articles of personal use.

Article 36

[The way in which such departures shall be carried out.]

Article 37

Protected persons who are confined pending proceedings or serving a sentence involving loss of liberty, shall during their confinement be humanely treated.

As soon as they are released, they may ask to leave the territory in conformity with the foregoing Articles.

Article 39

Protected persons who, as a result of the war, have

lost their gainful employment, shall be granted the opportunity to find paid employment. That opportunity shall, subject to security considerations and to the provisions of Article 40, be equal to that enjoyed by the nationals of the Power in whose territory they are.

Article 40

Protected persons may be compelled to work only to the same extent as nationals of the Party to the conflict in whose territory they are.

If protected persons are of enemy nationality, they may only be compelled to do work which is normally necessary to ensure the feeding, sheltering, clothing, transport and health of human beings and which is not directly related to the conduct of military operations.

Article 44

In applying the measures of control mentioned in the present Convention, the Detaining Power shall not treat as enemy aliens exclusively on the basis of their nationality *de jure* of an enemy State, refugees who do not, in fact, enjoy the protection of any government.

Article 45

Protected persons shall not be transferred to a Power which is not a party to the Convention.

This provision shall in no way constitute an obstacle to the repatriation of protected persons, or to their return to their country of residence after the cessation of hostilities.

In no circumstances shall a protected person be transferred to a country where he or she may have reason to fear persecution for his or her political opinions or religious beliefs.

Section III

Occupied Territories

Article 47

Protected persons who are in occupied territory shall not be deprived, in any case or in any manner whatsoever, of the benefits of the present Convention by any change introduced, as the result of the occupation of a territory, into the institutions or government of the said territory, nor by any agreement concluded between the authorities of the occupied territories and the Occupying Power, nor by any annexation by the latter of the whole or part of the occupied territory.

Article 49

Individual or mass forcible transfers, as well as deportations of protected persons from occupied territory to the territory of the Occupying Power or to that of any other country, occupied or not, are prohibited, regardless of their motive.

Nevertheless, the Occupying Power may undertake total or partial evacuation of a given area, if the security of the population or imperative military reasons so demand. Such evacuations may not involve the displacement of protected persons outside the bounds of the occupied territory except when for material reasons it is impossible to avoid such displacement. Persons thus evacuated shall be transferred back to their homes as soon as hostilities in the area in question have ceased.

Article 50

[Particular care is to be taken with children.]

Article 51

[Protected persons shall not be forced into military service. The nature of compulsory labour is determined.]

Article 52

No contract, agreement or regulation shall impair the right of any worker, whether voluntary or not and wherever he may be, to apply to the representatives of the Protecting Power in order to request the said Power's intervention.

Article 53

Any destruction by the Occupying Power of real or personal property belonging individually or collectively to private persons, or to the State, or to the State, or to other public authorities, or to social or cooperative organizations, is prohibited, except where such destruction is rendered absolutely necessary by military operations.

Article 54

The Occupying Power may not alter the status of public officials or judges in the occupied territories, or in any way apply sanctions to or take any measures of coercion or discrimination against them, should they abstain from fulfilling their functions for reasons of conscience.

Article 55

To the fullest extent of the means available to it, the Occupying Power has the duty of ensuring the food and medical supplies of the population; it should, in particular, bring in the necessary food-stuffs, medical stores and other articles if the resources of the occupied territory are inadequate.

The Occupying Power may not requisition food-stuffs, articles or medical supplies available in the occupied territory, except for use by the occupation forces and administration personnel, and then only if the requirements of the civilian population have been taken into account. Subject to the provisions of other international Conventions, the Occupying Power shall make arrangements to ensure that fair value is paid for any requisitioned goods.

Article 56

[The Occupying Power is responsible for maintaining hospital and medical services, and for public health and hygiene.]

Article 57

[Civilian hospitals shall be requisitioned only in emergencies, and then only temporarily.]

Article 58

The Occupying Power shall permit ministers of religion to give spiritual assistance to the members of their religious communities.

The Occupying Power shall also accept consignments of books and articles required for religious needs and shall facilitate their distribution in occupied territory.

Article 59

If the whole or part of the population of an occupied territory is inadequately supplied, the Occupying Power shall agree to relief schemes on behalf of the said population, and shall facilitate them by all the means at its disposal.

Such schemes, which may be undertaken either by States or by impartial humanitarian organizations such as the International Committee of the Red Cross, shall consist, in particular, of the provision of consignments of foodstuffs, medical supplies and clothing.

All Contracting Parties shall permit the free passage of these consignments and shall guarantee their protection.

Article 62

Subject to imperative reasons of security, protected persons in occupied territories shall be permitted to receive the individual relief consignments sent to them.

Article 63

[National Red Cross and comparable societies shall be enabled to carry out their humanitarian activities.]

Article 64

The penal laws of the occupied territory shall remain in force, with the exception that they may be repealed or suspended by the Occupying Power in cases where they constitute a threat to its security or an obstacle to the application of the present Convention. Subject to the latter consideration and to the necessity for ensuring the effective administration of justice, the tribunals of the occupied territory shall continue to function in respect of all offences covered by the said laws.

Article 65

The penal provisions enacted by the Occupying Power shall not come into force before they have been published and brought to the knowledge of the inhabitants in their own language. The effect of these penal provisions shall not be retroactive.

Article 71

No sentence shall be pronounced by the competent courts of the Occupying Power except after a regular trial.

Accused persons who are prosecuted by the Occupying Power shall be promptly informed, in writing, in a language which they understand, of the particulars of the charges preferred against them, and shall be brought to trial as rapidly as possible. The Protecting Power shall be informed of all proceedings instituted by the Occupying Power against protected persons in respect of charges involving the death penalty or imprisonment for two years or more; it shall be enabled, at any time, to obtain information regarding the state of such proceedings. Furthermore, the Protecting Power shall be entitled, on request, to be furnished with all particulars of these and of any other proceedings instituted by the Occupying Power against protected persons.

Article 74

Representatives of the Protecting Power shall have

the right to attend the trial of any protected person, unless the hearing has, as an exceptional measure, to be held *in camera* in the interests of the security of the Occupying Power, which shall then notify the Protecting Power. A notification in respect of the date and place of trial shall be sent to the Protecting power.

Article 76

Protected persons accused of offences shall be detained in the occupied country, and if convicted they shall serve their sentences therein. They shall, if possible, be separated from other detainees and shall enjoy conditions of food and hygiene which will be sufficient to keep them in good health, and which will be at least equal to those obtaining in prisons in the occupied country.

They shall receive the medical attention required by their state of health.

They shall also have the right to receive any spiritual assistance which they may require.

Women shall be confined in separate quarters and shall be under the direct supervision of women.

Proper regard shall be paid to the special treatment due to minors.

Protected persons who are detained shall have the right to be visited by delegates of the Protecting Power and of the International Committee of the Red Cross, in accordance with the provisions of Article 143.

Such persons shall have the right to receive at least one relief parcel monthly.

Section IV

Regulations for the Treatment of Internees

Chapter I

General Provisions

Article 79

The Parties to the conflict shall not intern protected persons, except in accordance with the provisions of Articles 41, 42, 43, 68 and 78.

Article 80

Internees shall retain their full capacity and shall exercise such attendant rights as may be compatible with their status.

Article 81

Parties to the conflict who intern protected persons

shall be bound to provide free of charge for their maintenance, and to grant them also the medical attention required by their state of health.

No deduction from the allowances, salaries or credits due to the internees shall be made for the repayment of these costs.

The Detaining Power shall provide for the support of those dependent on the internees, if such dependents are without adequate means of support or are unable to earn a living.

Article 82

The Detaining Power shall, as far as possible, accommodate the internees according to their nationality, language and customs. Internees who are nationals of the same country shall not be separated merely because they have different languages.

Throughout the duration of their internment, members of the same family, and in particular parents and children, shall be lodged together in the same place of internment, except when separation of a temporary nature is necessitated for reasons of employment or health or for the purposes of enforcement of the provisions of Chapter IX of the present Section. Internees may request that their children who are left at liberty without parental care shall be interned with them.

Wherever possible, interned members of the same family shall be housed in the same premises and given separate accommodation from other internees, together with facilities for leading a proper family life.

Chapter II

Place of Internment

Article 83

[Places of internment shall be communicated to the enemy, and shall be clearly identified from the air.]

Article 84

Internees shall be accommodated and administered separately from prisoners of war and from persons deprived of liberty for any other reason.

Article 85

The Detaining Power is bound to take all necessary and possible measures to ensure that protected persons shall, from the outset of their internment, be accommodated in buildings or quarters which afford every possible safeguard as regards hygiene and health, and provide efficient protection against the rigours of the climate and the effects of the war.

Article 86

The Detaining Power shall place at the disposal of interned persons, of whatever denomination, premises suitable for the holding of their religious services.

Article 87

Canteens shall be installed in every place of internment, except where other suitable facilities are available. Their purpose shall be to enable internees to make purchases, at prices not higher than local market prices, of foodstuffs and articles of everyday use, including soap and tobacco, such as would increase their personal well-being and comfort.

Article 88

[Air raid shelters shall be provided in all places of internment.]

Chapter III

Food and Clothing

Article 89

[Adequate food rations and supplies of drinking water shall be provided for all internees.]

Article 90

[All internees shall be provided with adequate clothing and footwear, including suitable working outfits.]

Chapter IV

Hygiene and Medical Attention

Article 91

Every place of internment shall have an adequate infirmary, under the direction of a qualified doctor, where internees may have the attention they require, as well as an appropriate diet. Isolation wards shall be set aside for cases of contagious or mental diseases.

Treatment, including the provision of any apparatus necessary for the maintenance of internees in good health, particularly dentures and other artificial appliances and spectacles, shall be free of charge to the internee.

Article 92

Medical inspections of internees shall be made at least once a month. Their purpose shall be, in particular, to supervise the general state of health, nutrition and cleanliness of internees, and to detect contagious diseases, especially tuberculosis, malaria, and venereal diseases. Such inspections shall include, in particular, the checking of weight of each internee and, at least once a year, radioscopic examination.

Chapter V

Religious, Intellectual and Physical Activities
Article 93

[Internees shall be free to practise their religious duties, and ministers of religion free to carry out their activities.]

Article 94

[Opportunities shall be provided for internees to follow intellectual, educational, and recreational pursuits.]

Article 95

[Internees shall not be employed against their wishes. Work shall not be degrading or humiliating.]

Chapter VI

Personal Property and Financial Resources
Article 97

Internees shall be permitted to retain articles of personal use. Monies, cheques, bonds, etc., and valuables in their possession may not be taken from them except in accordance with established procedure. Detailed receipts shall be given therefor.

The amounts shall be paid into the account of every internee as provided for in Article 98. Such amounts may not be converted into any other currency unless legislation in force in the territory in which the owner is interned so requires or the internee gives his consent.

Articles which have above all a personal or sentimental value may not be taken away.

A woman internee shall not be searched except by a woman.

Article 98

All internees shall receive regular allowances, sufficient to enable them to purchase goods and articles, such as tobacco, toilet requisites, etc. Such allowances may take the form of credits or purchase coupons.

Chapter VII
Administration and Discipline

Article 99

Every place of internment shall be put under the authority of a responsible officer, chosen from the regular military forces or the regular civil administration of the Detaining Power. The officer in charge of the place of internment must have in his possession a copy of the present Convention in the official language, or one of the official languages, of his country and shall be responsible for its application. The staff in control of internees shall be instructed in the provisions of the present Convention and of the administrative measures adopted to ensure its application.

The text of the present Convention and the texts of special agreements concluded under the said Convention shall be posted inside the place of internment, in a language which the internees understand, or shall be in the possession of the Internee Committee.

Regulations, orders, notices and publications of every kind shall be communicated to the internees and posted inside the places of internment, in a language which they understand.

Every order and command addressed to internees individually, must likewise, be given in a language which they understand.

Article 100

The disciplinary regime in places of internment shall be consistent with humanitarian principles, and shall in no circumstances include regulations imposing on internees any physical exertion dangerous to their health or involving physical or moral victimization. Identification by tattooing or imprinting signs or markings on the body, is prohibited.

In particular, prolonged standing and roll-calls, punishment drill, military drill and manoeuvres, or the reduction of food rations, are prohibited.

Article 101

Internees shall have the right to present to the authorities in whose power they are, any petition with regard to the conditions of internment to which they are subjected.

They shall also have the right to apply without restriction through the Internee Committee or, if they consider it necessary, direct to the representatives of

the Protecting Power, in order to indicate to them any points on which they may have complaints to make with regard to the conditions of internment.

Article 102

In every place of internment, the internees shall freely elect by secret ballot every six months, the members of a Committee empowered to represent them before the Detaining and the Protecting Powers, the International Committee of the Red Cross and any other organization which may assist them. The members of the Committee shall be eligible for re-election.

Internees so elected shall enter upon their duties after their election has been approved by the detaining authorities. The reasons for any refusals or dismissals shall be communicated to the Protecting Powers concerned.

Chapter VIII
Relations with the Exterior

Article 105

Immediately upon interning protected persons, the Detaining Powers shall inform them, the Power to which they owe allegiance and their Protecting Power of the measures taken for executing the Provisions of the present Chapter. The Detaining Powers shall likewise inform the Parties concerned of any subsequent modifications of such measures.

Article 106

[All internees permitted to inform their relatives of their detention, state of health, and their address.]

Article 107

[Internees permitted to send and receive letters and cards.]

Article 108

Internees shall be allowed to receive, by post or by any other means, individual parcels or collective shipments containing in particular foodstuffs, clothing, medical supplies, as well as books and objects of a devotional, educational or recreational character which may meet their needs. Such shipments shall in no way free the Detaining Power from the obligations imposed upon it by virtue of the present Convention.

Article 110

All relief shipments for internees shall be exempt

from import, customs and other dues.

Article 112

The censoring of correspondence addressed to internees or despatched by them shall be done as quickly as possible.

Article 116

Every internee shall be allowed to receive visitors, especially near relatives, at regular intervals and as frequently as possible.

As far as is possible, internees shall be permitted to visit their homes in urgent cases, particularly in cases of death or serious illness of relatives.

Chapter IX

Penal and Disciplinary Sanctions

Article 117

[The laws of the territory in which they are detained will continue to apply to internees. There shall be no double punishment.]

Article 118

The courts or authorities shall in passing sentence take as far as possible into account the fact that the defendant is not a national of the Detaining Power. They shall be free to reduce the penalty prescribed for the offence with which the internee is charged and shall not be obliged, to this end, to apply the minimum sentence prescribed.

Imprisonment in premises without daylight and, in general, all forms of cruelty without exception are forbidden.

Internees who have served disciplinary or judicial sentences shall not be treated differently from other internees.

The duration of preventive detention undergone by an internee shall be deducted from any disciplinary or judicial penalty involving confinement to which he may be sentenced.

Internee Committee shall be informed of all judicial proceedings instituted against internees whom they represent, and of their result.

Article 119

[Disciplinary punishment of internees shall not be inhuman, brutal, or dangerous for their health.]

Article 120

Internees who are recaptured after having escaped or when attempting to escape, shall be liable only to disciplinary punishment in respect of this act, even if it is a repeated offence.

Article 121

Escape, or attempt to escape, even if it is a repeated offence, shall not be deemed an aggravating circumstance in cases where an internee is prosecuted for offences committed during his escape.

Article 123

[Disciplinary punishment may be ordered only by the commandant of the place of internment.]

Article 124

Internees shall not in any case be transferred to penitentiary establishments (prisons, penitentiaries, convict prisons, etc.) to undergo disciplinary punishment therein.

The premises in which disciplinary punishments are undergone shall conform to sanitary requirements; they shall in particular be provided with adequate bedding. Internees undergoing punishment shall be enabled to keep themselves in a state of cleanliness.

Women internees undergoing disciplinary punishment shall be confined in separate quarters from male internees and shall be under the immediate supervision of women.

Article 125

[Basic rights of internees undergoing disciplinary punishment are safeguarded.]

Chapter X

Transfers of Internees

Article 127

The transfer of internees shall always be effected humanely.

Sick, wounded or infirm internees and maternity cases shall not be transferred if the journey would be seriously detrimental to them, unless their safety imperatively so demands.

If the combat zone draws close to a place of internment, the internees in the said place shall not be transferred unless their removal can be carried out in adequate conditions of safety, or unless they are exposed to greater risks by remaining on the spot than by being transferred.

Article 128

In the event of transfer, internees shall be officially advised of their departure and of their new postal address. Such notification shall be given in time for them to pack their luggage and inform their next of kin.

Chapter XI

Deaths

Article 129

[Regulations concerning the wills and death certificates of internees who die in custody.]

Article 130

The detaining authorities shall ensure that internees who die while interned are honorably buried, if possible according to the rites of the religion to which they belonged, and that their graves are respected, properly maintained, and marked in such a way that they can always be recognized.

Deceased internees shall be buried in individual graves unless unavoidable circumstances require the use of collective graves. Bodies may be cremated only for imperative reasons of hygiene, on account of the religion of the deceased or in accordance with his expressed wish to this effect. In case of cremation, the fact shall be stated and the reasons given in the death certificate of the deceased. The ashes shall be retained for safe-keeping by the detaining authorities and shall be transferred as soon as possible to the next of kin on their request.

Article 131

Every death or serious injury of an internee, caused or suspected to have been caused by a sentry, another internee or any other person, as well as any death the cause of which is unknown, shall be immediately followed by an official enquiry by the Detaining Power.

A communication on this subject shall be sent immediately to the Protecting Power. The evidence of any witnesses shall be taken, and a report including such evidence shall be prepared and forwarded to the said Protecting Power.

If the enquiry indicates the guilt of one or more persons, the Detaining Power shall take all necessary steps to ensure the prosecution of the person or persons responsible.

Chapter XII

Release, Repatriation and Accommodation in Neutral Countries

Article 132

[Internees shall be released as soon as circumstances permit.]

Article 133

Internment shall cease as soon as possible after the close of hostilities.

Internees in the territory of a Party to the conflict against whom penal proceedings are pending for offences not exclusively subject to disciplinary penalties, may be detained until the close of such proceedings and, if circumstances require, until the completion of the penalty. The same shall apply to internees who have been previously sentenced to a punishment depriving them of liberty.

Article 134

The High Contracting Parties shall endeavour, upon the close of hostilities or occupation, to ensure the return of all internees to their last place of residence, or to facilitate their repatriation.

Article 135

The Detaining Power shall bear the expense of returning released internees to the places where they were residing when interned, or, if it took them into custody while they were in transit or on the high seas, the cost of completing their journey or of their return to their point of departure.

Section V

Information Bureaux and Central Agency

Article 136

[Official Information Bureaux are to be established to receive and transmit information about internees.]

Article 137

[The Bureaux to forward information concerning protected persons, and to deal with all enquires.]

Article 138

The information received by the national Bureaux and transmitted by it shall be of such a character as to make it possible to identify the protected person exactly and to advise his next of kin quickly. The information in respect of each person shall include at least his surname, first names, place and date of birth, nationality, last residence and distinguishing characteristics, the first name of the father and the maiden name of the mother, the date, place and nature of the action taken with regard to the individual, the address at which correspondence may be sent to him and the name and address of the person to be informed.

Likewise, information regarding the state of health of internees who are seriously ill or seriously wounded shall be supplied regularly and possibly every week.

Article 139

[The Information Bureaux to be responsible for the personal valuables left by protected persons who have been released or who have escaped or died.]

Article 140

[A Central Information Agency to be created in a neutral country.]

Article 141

The national Information Bureaux and the Central Information Agency shall enjoy free postage for all mail, likewise the exemptions provided for in Article 110, and further, so far as possible, exemption from telegraphic charges or, at least, greatly reduced rates.

PART IV

EXECUTION OF THE CONVENTION

Section 1

General Provisions

Article 142

[The International Red Cross and similar agencies shall not be prevented from carrying out relief work.]

Article 143

Representatives or delegates of the Protecting Powers shall have permission to go to all places where protected persons are, particularly to places of internment, detention and work.

They shall have access to all premises occupied by protected persons and shall be able to interview the latter without witnesses, personally or through an interpreter.

Such visits may not be prohibited except for reasons of imperative military necessity, and then only as an exceptional and temporary measure. Their duration and frequency shall not be restricted.

The delegates of the International Committee of the Red Cross shall also enjoy the above prerogatives. The appointment of such delegates shall be submitted to the approval of the Power governing the territories where they will carry out their duties.

Article 144

[The Convention is to be fully disseminated in signatory countries, especially among civil, military, and police authorities.]

Article 146

The High Contracting Parties undertake to enact any legislation necessary to provide effective penal sanctions for persons committing, or ordering to be committed, any of the grave breaches of the present Convention defined in the following Article.

Article 147

Grave breaches to which the preceding Article relates shall be those involving any of the following acts, if committed against persons or property protected by the present Convention: wilful killing, torture or inhuman treatment, including biological experiments, wilfully causing great suffering or serious injury to body or health, unlawful deportation or transfer or unlawful confinement of a protected person, compelling a protected person to serve in the forces of a hostile Power, or wilfully depriving a protected person of the rights of fair and regular trial prescribed in the present Convention, taking of hostages and extensive destruction and appropriation of property, not justified by military necessity and carried out unlawfully and wantonly.

Article 148

No High Contracting Party shall be allowed to absolve itself or any other High Contracting Party of any liability incurred by itself of by another High Contracting Party in respect of breaches referred to in the preceding Article.

Article 149

At the request of a party to the conflict, an enquiry shall be instituted, in a manner to be decided between the interested Parties, concerning any alleged violation of the Convention.

If agreement has not been reached concerning the procedure for the enquiry, the Parties should agree on the choice of an umpire who will decide upon the procedure to be followed.

Once the violation has been established, the Parties to the conflict shall put an end to it and shall repress it with the least possible delay.

Section II

Final Provisions

Article 150

The present Convention is established in English and in French. Both texts are equally authentic.

The Swiss Federal Council shall arrange for official translations of the Convention to be made in the Russian and Spanish languages.

Article 151

The present Convention, which bears the date of this day, is open to signature until February 12, 1950, in the name of the Powers represented at the Conference which opened at Geneva on April 21, 1949.

Article 152

The present Convention shall be ratified as soon as possible and the ratifications shall be deposited at Berne.

A record shall be drawn up of the deposit of each instrument of ratification and certified copies of this record shall be transmitted by the Swiss Federal Council to all the Powers in whose name the Convention has been signed, or whose accession has been notified.

Article 153

The present Convention shall come into force six months after not less than two instruments of ratification have been deposited.

Thereafter, it shall come into force for each High Contracting Party six months after the deposit of the instrument of ratification.

Article 154

In the relations between the Powers who are bound by The Hague Convention respecting the Laws and Customs of War on Land, whether that of July 29, 1899, or that of October 18, 1907, and who are par-

ties to the present Convention, this last Convention shall be supplementary to Section II and III of the Regulations annexed to the above mentioned Conventions of The Hague.

Article 155

From the date of its coming into force, it shall be open to any Power in whose name the present Convention has not been signed, to accede to this Convention.

Article 156

Accessions shall be notified in writing to the Swiss Federal Council, and shall take effect six months after the date on which they are received.

The Swiss Federal Council shall communicate the accessions to all the Powers in whose name the Convention has been signed, or whose accession has been notified.

Article 157

The situations provided for in Articles 2 and 3 shall give immediate effect to ratifications deposited and accessions notified by the Parties to the conflict before or after the beginning of hostilities or occupation. The Swiss Federal Council shall communicate by the quickest method any ratifications or accessions received from Parties to the conflict.

Article 158

Each of the High Contracting Parties shall be at liberty to denounce the present Convention.

The denunciation shall be notified in writing to the Swiss Federal Council, which shall transmit it to the Governments of all the High Contracting Parties.

The denunciation shall take effect one year after the notification thereof has been made to the Swiss Federal Council. However, a denunciation of which notification has been made at a time when the denouncing Power is involved in a conflict shall not take effect until peace has been concluded, and until after operations connected with the release, repatriation and re-establishment of the persons protected by the present Convention have been terminated.

The denunciation shall have effect only in respect of the denouncing Power. It shall in no way impair the obligations which the Parties to the conflict shall remain bound to fulfil by virtue of the principles of the law of nations, as they result from the usages established among civilized peoples, from the laws of humanity and the dictates of the public conscience.

Article 159

The Swiss Federal Council shall register the present Convention with the Secretariat of the United Nations. The Swiss Federal Council shall also inform the Secretariat of the United Nations of all ratifications, accessions and denunciations received by it with respect to present Convention.

The Antarctic Treaty

Date of signature: December 1, 1959
Place of signature: Washington, DC
Signatory states: Argentina, Australia, Belgium, Chile, France, Japan, New Zealand, Norway, the Union of South Africa, the Soviet Union, the United Kingdom of Great Britain and Northern Ireland, the United States
Ratifications: Argentina, Australia, Belgium, Brazil, Chile, Czechoslovakia, Denmark, France, German Democratic Republic, Federal Republic of Germany, Italy, Japan, Netherlands, New Zealand, Norway, Papua New Guinea, Peru, Poland, Romania, Union of South Africa, the Soviet Union, United Kingdom of Great Britain and Northern Ireland, the United States, Uruguay
Accessions: Poland
Date of entry into force: June 23, 1961

[The signatories],
Recognizing that it is in the interest of all mankind that Antarctica shall continue forever to be used exclusively for peaceful purposes and shall not become the scene or object of international discord;
Acknowledging the substantial contributions to scientific knowledge resulting from international cooperation in scientific investigation in Antarctica;
Convinced that the establishment of a firm foundation for the continuation and development of such cooperation on the basis of freedom of scientific investigation in Antarctica as applied during the International Geophysical Year accords with the interests of science and the progress of all mankind;
Convinced also that a treaty ensuring the use of Antarctica for peaceful purposes only and the continuance of international harmony in Antarctica will further the purposes and principles embodied in the Charter of the United Nations;
Have agreed as follows:

Article 1

1. Antarctica shall be used for peaceful purposes only. There shall be prohibited, *inter alia*, any measures of a military nature, such as the establishment of military bases and fortifications, the carrying out of military maneuvers, as well as the testing of any type of weapons.

2. The present Treaty shall not prevent the use of military personnel or equipment for scientific research or for any other peaceful purpose.

Article II

Freedom of scientific investigation in Antarctica and cooperation toward that end, as applied during the International Geophysical Year, shall continue, subject to the provisions of the present Treaty.

Article III

1. In order to promote international cooperation in scientific investigation in Antarctica, as provided for in Article II of the present Treaty, the Contracting Parties agree that, to the greatest extent feasible and practicable:

(a) information regarding plans for scientific programs in Antarctica shall be exchanged to permit maximum economy and efficiency of operations;

(b) scientific personnel shall be exchanged in Antarctica between expeditions and stations;

(c) scientific observations and results from Antarctica shall be exchanged and made freely available.

2. In implementing this Article, every encouragement shall be given to the establishment of cooperative working relations with those Specialized Agencies of the United Nations and other international organizations having a scientific or technical interest in Antarctica.

Article IV

1. Nothing contained in the present Treaty shall be interpreted as:

(a) a renunciation by any Contracting Party of previously asserted rights of or claims to territorial sovereignty in Antarctica;

(b) a renunciation or diminution by any Contracting Party of any basis of claim to territorial sovereignty in Antarctica which it may have whether as a result of its activities or those of its nationals in Antarctica, or otherwise;

(c) prejudicing the position of any Contracting Party as regards its recognition or non-recognition of any other State's right of or claim or basis of claim to territorial sovereignty in Antarctica.

2. No acts or activities taking place while the present Treaty is in force shall constitute a basis for asserting, supporting or denying a claim to territorial sovereignty in Antarctica or create any rights of sovereignty in Antarctica. No new claim, or enlargement of an existing claim, to territorial sovereignty in Antarctica shall be asserted while the present Treaty is in force.

Article V

1. Any nuclear explosions in Antarctica and the disposal there of radioactive waste material shall be prohibited.

2. In the event of the conclusion of international agreements concerning the use of nuclear energy, including nuclear explosions and the disposal of radioactive waste material, to which all of the Contracting Parties whose representatives are entitled to participate in the meetings provided for under Article IX are parties, the rules established under such agreements shall apply in Antarctica.

Article VI

The provisions of the present Treaty shall apply to the area south of 60° South Latitude including all ice shelves, but nothing in the present Treaty shall prejudice or in any way affect the rights, or the exercise of the rights, of any State under international law with regard to the high seas within that area.

Article VII

1. In order to promote the objectives and ensure the observance of the provisions of the present Treaty, each Contracting Party whose representatives are entitled to participate in the meetings referred to in Article IX of the Treaty shall have the right to designate observers to carry out any inspection provided for by the present Article. Observers shall be nationals of the Contracting Parties which designate them.

The names of observers shall be communicated to every other Contracting Party having the right to designate observers, and like notice shall be given of the termination of their appointment.

2. Each observer designated in accordance with the provisions of paragraph 1 of this Article shall have complete freedom of access at any time to any or all areas of Antarctica.

3. All areas of Antarctica, including all stations, installations and equipment within those areas, and all ships and aircraft at points of discharging or embarking cargoes or personnel in Antarctica, shall be open at all times to inspection by any observers designated in accordance with paragraph 1 of this Article.

4. Aerial observation may be carried out at any time over any or all areas of Antarctica by any of the Contracting Parties having the right to designate observers.

5. Each Contracting Party shall, at the time when the present Treaty enters into force for it, inform the other Contracting Parties, and thereafter shall give them notice in advance, of:

(a) all expeditions to and within Antarctica, on the part of its ships or nationals, and all expeditions to Antarctica organized in or proceeding from its territory;

(b) all stations in Antarctica occupied by its nationals; and

(c) any military personnel or equipment intended to be introduced by it into Antarctica subject to the conditions prescribed in paragraph 2 of Article I of the present Treaty.

Article VIII

1. In order to facilitate the exercise of their functions under the present Treaty, and without prejudice to the respective positions of the Contracting Parties relating to jurisdiction over all other persons in Antarctica, observers designated under paragraph 1 of Article VII and scientific personnel exchanged under subparagraph 1 (b) of Article III of the Treaty, and members of the staffs accompanying any such persons, shall be subject only to the jurisdiction of the Contracting Party of which they are nationals in respect of all acts or omissions occurring while they are in Antarctica for the purpose of exercising their functions.

2. Without prejudice to the provisions of paragraph 1 of this Article, and pending the adoption of measures in pursuance of subparagraph 1 (e) of Article IX, the Contracting Parties concerned in any case of

dispute with regard to the exercise of jurisdiction in Antarctica shall immediately consult together with a view to reaching a mutually acceptable solution.

Article IX

1. Representatives of the Contracting Parties named in the preamble to the present Treaty shall meet at the City of Canberra within two months after the date of entry into force of the Treaty, and thereafter at suitable intervals and places, for the purpose of exchanging information, consulting together on matters of common interest pertaining to Antarctica, and formulating and considering, and recommending to their Governments, measures in furtherance of the principles and objectives of the Treaty, including measures regarding:

(a) use of Antarctica for peaceful purposes only;

(b) facilitation of scientific research in Antarctica:

(c) facilitation of international scientific cooperation in Antarctica;

(d) facilitation of the exercise of the rights of inspection provided for in Article VII of the Treaty;

(e) questions relating to the exercise of jurisdiction in Antarctica;

(f) preservation and conservation of living resources in Antarctica.

2. Each Contracting Party which has become a party to the present Treaty by accession under Article XIII shall be entitled to appoint representatives to participate in the meetings referred to in paragraph 1 of the present Article, during such time as that Contracting Party demonstrates its interest in Antarctica by conducting substantial scientific research activity there, such as the establishment of a scientific station or the despatch of a scientific expedition.

3. Reports from the observers referred to in Article VII of the present Treaty shall be transmitted to the representatives of the Contracting Parties participating in the meetings referred to in paragraph 1 of the present Article.

4. The measures referred to in paragraph 1 of this Article shall become effective when approved by all the Contracting Parties whose representatives were entitled to participate in the meetings held to consider those measures.

5. Any or all of the right established in the present Treaty may be exercised as from the date of entry into force of the Treaty whether or not any measures facilitating the exercise of such rights have been proposed, considered or approved as provided in this Article.

Article X

Each of the Contracting Parties undertakes to exert appropriate efforts, consistent with the Charter of the United Nations, to the end that no one engages in any activity in Antarctica contrary to the principles or purposes of the present Treaty.

Article XI

1. If any dispute arises between two or more of the Contracting Parties concerning the interpretation or application of the present Treaty, those Contracting Parties shall consult among themselves with a view to having the dispute resolve by negotiation, inquiry, mediation, conciliation, arbitration, judicial settlement or other peaceful means of their own choice.

2. Any dispute of this character not so resolved shall, with the consent, in each case, of all parties to the dispute, be referred to the International Court of Justice for settlement; but failure to reach agreement on reference to the International Court shall not absolve parties to the dispute from the responsibility of continuing to seek to resolve it by any of the various peaceful means referred to in paragraph 1 of this Article.

Article XII

1.

(a) The present Treaty may be modified or amended at any time by unanimous agreement of the Contracting Parties whose representatives are entitled to participate in the meetings provided for under Article IX. Any such modification or amendment shall enter into force when the depositary Government has received notice from all such Contracting Parties that they have ratified it.

(b) Such modification or amendment shall thereafter enter into force as to any other Contracting Party when notice of ratification by it has been received by the depositary Government. Any such Contracting Party from which no notice of ratification is received within a period of two years from the date of entry into force of the modification or amendment in accordance with the provisions of subparagraph 1 (a) of this Article shall be deemed to have withdrawn from the present Treaty on the date of the expiration of such period.

2.

(a) If after the expiration of thirty years from the date of entry into force of the present Treaty, any of the Contracting Parties whose representatives are entitled to participate in the meetings provided for under Article IX so requests by a communication addressed to the depositary Government, a Conference of all the Contracting Parties shall be held as soon as practicable to review the operation of the Treaty.

(b) Any modification or amendment to the present Treaty which is approved at such a Conference by a majority of the Contracting Parties there represented, including a majority of those whose representatives are entitled to participate in the meetings provided for under Article IX, shall be communicated by the depositary Government to all the Contracting Parties immediately after the termination of the Conference and shall enter into force in accordance with the provisions of paragraph 1 of the present Article.

(c) If any such modification or amendment has not entered into force in accordance with the provisions of subparagraph 1 (a) of this Article within a period of two years after the date of its communication to all the Contracting Parties, any Contracting Party may at any time after the expiration of that period give notice to the depositary Government of its withdrawal from the present Treaty; and such withdrawal shall take effect two years after the receipt of the notice by the depositary Government.

Article XIII

1. The present Treaty shall be subject to ratification by the signatory States. It shall be open for accession by any State which is a Member of the United Nations, or by any other State which may be invited to accede to the Treaty with the consent of all the Contracting Parties whose representatives are entitled to participate in the meetings provided for under Article IX of the Treaty.

2. Ratification of or accession to the present Treaty shall be effected by each State in accordance with its constitutional processes.

3. Instruments of ratification and instruments of accession shall be deposited with the Government of the United States of America, hereby designated as the depositary Government.

4. The depositary Government shall inform all signatory and acceding States of the date of each deposit of an instrument of ratification or accession, and the date of entry into force of the Treaty and of any modification or amendment thereto.

5. Upon the deposit of instruments of ratification by all the signatory States, the present Treaty shall enter into force for those States and for States which have deposited instruments of accession. Thereafter the Treaty shall enter into force for any accession.

6. The present Treaty shall be registered by the depositary Government pursuant to Article 102 of the Charter of the United Nations.

Article XIV

The present Treaty, done in the English, French, Russian and Spanish languages, each version being equally authentic, shall be deposited in the archives of the Government of the United States of America, which shall transmit duly certified copies thereof to the Governments of the signatory and acceding States.

Declaration on the Neutrality of Laos

Date of signature: July 23, 1962
Place of signature: Geneva
Signatory states: *Burma, Cambodia, Canada, People's Republic of China, Democratic Republic of Viet-Nam, France, India, Poland, Republic of Viet-Nam, Thailand, the Soviet Union, the United Kingdom of Great Britain and Northern Ireland, the United States*

[The signatories],

whose representatives took part in the International Conference on the Settlement of the Laotian Question, 1961-62;
Welcoming the presentation of the statement of neutrality by the Royal Government of Laos of July 9, 1962, and taking note of this statement, which is, with the concurrence of the Royal Government of Laos, incorporated in the present Declaration as an integral part thereof, and the text of which is as follows:

THE ROYAL GOVERNMENT OF LAOS

Being resolved to follow the path of peace and neutrality in conformity with the interests and aspirations of the Laotian people, as well as the principles of the Joint Communique of Zurich dated June 22, 1961, and of the Geneva Agreements of 1954, in order to build a peaceful, neutral, independent, democratic, unified and prosperous Laos,
Solemnly declares that:

(1) It will resolutely apply the five principles of peaceful co-existence in foreign relations, and will develop friendly relations and establish diplomatic relations with all countries, the neighbouring countries first and foremost, on the basis of equality and of respect for the independence and sovereignty of Laos;

(2) It is the will of the Laotian people to protect and ensure respect for the sovereignty, independence, neutrality, unity, and territorial integrity of Laos;

(3) It will not resort to the use or threat of force in any way which might impair the peace of other countries, and will not interfere in the internal affairs of other countries;

(4) It will not enter into any military alliance or into any agreement, whether military or otherwise, which is inconsistent with the neutrality of the Kingdom of Laos; it will not allow the establishment of any foreign military base on Laotian territory, nor allow any country to use Laotian territory for military purposes or for the purposes of interference in the internal affairs of other countries, nor recognise the protection of any alliance or military coalition, including SEATO;

(5) It will not allow any foreign interference in the internal affairs of the Kingdom of Laos in any form whatsoever;

(6) Subject to the provisions of Article 5 of the Protocol, it will require the withdrawal from Laos of all foreign troops and military personnel, and will not allow any foreign troops or military personnel to be introduced into Laos;

(7) It will accept direct and unconditional aid from all countries that wish to help the Kingdom of Laos build up an independent and autonomous national economy on the basis of respect for the sovereignty of Laos;

(8) It will respect the treaties and agreements signed in conformity with the interests of the Laot-

ian people and of the policy of peace and neutrality of the Kingdom, in particular the Geneva Agreements of 1962, and will abrogate all treaties and agreements which are contrary to those principles.

This statement of neutrality by the Royal Government of Laos shall be promulgated constitutionally and shall have the force of law.

The Kingdom of Laos appeals to all the States participating in the International Conference on the Settlement of the Laotian Question, and to all other States, to recognise the sovereignty, independence, neutrality, unity and territorial integrity of Laos, to conform to these principles in all respects, and to refrain from any action inconsistent therewith.

Confirming the principles of respect for the sovereignty, independence, unity and territorial integrity of the Kingdom of Laos and non-interference in its internal affairs which are embodied in the Geneva Agreements of 1954;

Emphasising the principle of respect for the neutrality of the Kingdom of Laos;

Agreeing that the above-mentioned principles constitute a basis for the peaceful settlement of the Laotian question;

Profoundly convinced that the independence and neutrality of the Kingdom of Laos will assist the peaceful democratic development of the Kingdom of Laos and the achievement of national accord and unity in that country, as well as the strengthening of peace and security in South-East Asia;

1. Solemnly declare, in accordance with the will of the Government and people of the Kingdom of Laos, as expressed in the statement of neutrality by the Royal Government of Laos of July 9, 1962, that they recognise and will respect and observe in every way the sovereignty, independence, neutrality, unity and territorial integrity of the Kingdom of Laos.

2. Undertake, in particular, that

(a) they will not commit or participate in any way in any act which might directly or indirectly impair the sovereignty, independence, neutrality, unity or territorial integrity of the Kingdom of Laos;

(b) they will not resort to the use or threat of force or any other measure which might impair the peace of the Kingdom of Laos;

(c) they will refrain from all direct or indirect interference in the internal affairs of the Kingdom of Laos;

(d) they will not attach conditions of a political

nature to any assistance which they may offer or which the Kingdom of Laos may seek;

(e) they will not bring the Kingdom of Laos in any way into any military alliance or any other agreement, whether military or otherwise, which is inconsistent with her neutrality, nor invite or encourage her to enter into any such alliance or to conclude any such agreement;

(f) they will respect the wish of the Kingdom of Laos not to recognise the protection of any alliance or military coalition, including SEATO;

(g) they will not introduce into the Kingdom of Laos foreign troops or military personnel in any form whatsoever, nor will they in any way facilitate or connive at the introduction of any foreign troops or military personnel;

(h) they will not establish nor will they in any way facilitate or connive at the establishment in the Kingdom of Laos of any foreign military base, foreign strong point or other foreign military installation of any kind;

(i) they will not use the territory of the Kingdom of Laos for interference in the internal affairs of other countries;

(j) they will not use the territory of any country, including their own for interference in the internal affairs of the Kingdom of Laos.

3. Appeal to all other States to recognise, respect and observe in every way the sovereignty, independence and neutrality, and also the unity and territorial integrity, of the Kingdom of Laos and to refrain from any action inconsistent with these principles or with other provisions of the present Declaration.

4. Undertake, in the event of a violation or threat of violation of the sovereignty, independence, neutrality, unity or territorial integrity of the Kingdom of Laos, to consult jointly with the Royal Government of Laos and among themselves in order to consider measures which might prove to be necessary to ensure the observance of these principles and the other provisions of the present Declaration.

5. The present Declaration shall enter into force on signature and together with the statement of neutrality by the Royal Government of Laos of July 9, 1962, shall be regarded as constituting an international agreement. The present Declaration shall be deposited in the archives of the Governments of the United Kingdom and the Union of Soviet Republics, which shall furnish certified copies thereof to the other signatory States and to all the other States of the world.

Memorandum of Understanding Between the United States of America and the Union of Soviet Socialist Republics Regarding the Establishment of a Direct Communications Link

Also known as: Hot-Line Agreement
Date of signature: June 20, 1963
Place of signature: Geneva
Signatory states: The United States, The Soviet Union

For use in time of emergency, the Government of the United States of America and the Government of the Union of Soviet Socialist Republics have agreed to establish as soon as technically feasible a direct communications link between the two governments.

Each government shall be responsible for the arrangements for the link on its own territory. Each government shall take the necessary steps to ensure continuous functioning of the link and prompt delivery of its head of government of any communications received by means of the link from the head of government of the other party.

Arrangements for establishing and operating the link are set forth in the Annex which is attached hereto and forms an integral part hereof.

ANNEX TO THE MEMORANDUM OF UNDERSTANDING BETWEEN THE UNITED STATES OF AMERICA AND THE UNION OF SOVIET SOCIALIST REPUBLICS REGARDING THE ESTABLISHMENT OF A DIRECT COMMUNICATIONS LINK

The direct communications link between Washington and Moscow established in accordance with the memorandum, and the operation of such link, shall be governed by the following provisions:

1. The direct communications link shall consist of:

A. Two terminal points with telegraph-teleprinter equipment between which communications shall be directly exchanged;

B. One full-time duplex wire telegraph circuit, routed Washington-London-Copenhagen-Stockholm-Helsinki-Moscow, which shall be used for the transmission of messages;

C. One full-time duplex radio telegraph circuit, routed Washington-Tangier-Moscow, which shall be used for service communications and for coordination of operations between the two terminal points.

If experience in operating the direct communications link should demonstrate that the establishment of an additional wire telegraph circuit is advisable, such circuit may be established by mutual agreement between authorized representatives of both governments.

2. In case of interruption of the wire circuit, transmission of messages shall be effected via the radio circuit, and for this purpose provision shall be made at the terminal points for the capability of prompt switching of all necessary equipment from one circuit to another.

3. The terminal points of the link shall be so equipped as to provide for the transmission and reception of messages from Moscow to Washington in the Russian language and from Washington to Moscow in the English language. In this connection, the USSR shall furnish the United States four sets of telegraph terminal equipment, including page printers, transmitters, and reperforators, with one year's supply of spare parts and all necessary special tools, test equipment, operating instructions and other technical literature, to provide for transmission and reception of messages in the Russian language. The United States shall furnish the Soviet Union four sets of telegraph terminal equipment including page printers, transmitters, and reperforators, with one year's supply of spare parts and all necessary special tools, test equipment, operating instructions and other technical literature, to provide for transmission and reception of messages in the English language. The equipment described in this paragraph shall be exchanged directly between the parties without any payment being required therefor.

4. The terminal points of the direct communications link shall be provided with encoding equipment. For the terminal points in the USSR, four sets of such equipment (each capable of simplex operation), with one year's supply of spare parts, with all necessary special tools, test equipment, operating instructions and other technical literature, and with all necessary blank tape, shall be furnished by the United

States to the USSR against payment of the cost thereof by the USSR.

The USSR shall provide for preparation and delivery of keying tapes to the terminal point of the link in the United States for reception of messages from the USSR. The United States shall provide for preparation and delivery of keying tapes to the terminal point of the link in the USSR for reception on messages from the United States. Delivery of prepared keying tapes to the terminal points of the link shall be effected through the Embassy of the USSR in Washington (for the terminal of the link in the USSR) and through the Embassy of the United States in Moscow (for the terminal of the link in the United States).

5. The United States and the USSR shall designate the agencies responsible for the arrangements regarding the direct communications link, for its technical maintenance, continuity and reliability, and for the timely transmission of messages.

Such agencies may, by mutual agreement, decide matters and develop instructions relating to the technical maintenance and operation of the direct communications link and effect arrangements to improve the operation of the link.

6. The technical parameters of the telegraph circuits of the link and of the terminal equipment, as well as the maintenance of such circuits and equipment, shall be in accordance with CCITT and CCIR recommendations.

Transmission and reception of messages over the direct communications link shall be effected in accordance with applicable recommendations of international telegraph and radio communication regulations, as well as with mutually agreed instructions.

7. The costs of the direct communications link shall be borne as follows:

A. The USSR shall pay the full cost of leasing the portion of the telegraph circuit from Moscow to Helsinki and 50 percent of the cost of leasing the portion of the telegraph circuit from Helsinki to London. The United States shall pay the full cost of leasing the portion of the telegraph circuit from Washington to London and 50 percent of the cost of leasing the portion of the telegraph circuit from London to Helsinki.

B. Payment of the cost of leasing the radio telegraph circuit between Moscow and Washington shall be effected without any transfer of payments between the parties. The USSR shall bear the expenses relating to the transmission of messages from Moscow to Washington. The United States shall bear the expenses relating to the transmission of messages from Washington to Moscow.

Treaty Banning Nuclear Weapon Tests in the Atmosphere, in Outer Space and Under Water

Also known as: Limited Test Ban Treaty, Partial Test Ban Treaty
Date of signature: August 5, 1963
Place of signature: Moscow
Signatory states: Afghanistan, Algeria, Australia, Austria, Belgium, Benin, Bolivia, Brazil, Bulgaria, Burundi, Byelorussia, Cameroon, Canada, Chad, Chile, Colombia, Costa Rica, Cyprus, Czechoslovakia, Denmark, Dominican Republic, Ecuador, Egypt, El Salvador, Ethiopia, Finland, Gabon, German Democratic Republic, Federal Republic of Germany, Ghana, Greece, Guatemala, Guinea-Bissau, Haiti, Honduras, Hungary, Iceland, India, Indonesia, Iran, Iraq, Ireland, Israel, Italy, Ivory Coast, Japan, Jordan, Republic of Korea, Kuwait, Laos, Lebanon, Liberia, Libya, Luxembourg, Madagascar, Malaysia, Mali, Mauritania, Mexico, Mongolia, Morocco, Nepal, Netherlands, New Zealand, Nicaragua, Niger, Nigeria, Norway, Pakistan, Panama, Paraguay, Peru, Philippines, Poland, Portugal, Romania, Rwanda, Samoa, San Marino, Senegal, Sierra Leone, Somalia, Soviet Union, Spain, Sri Lanka, Sudan, Sweden, Switzerland, Syria, Taiwan, Tanzania, Thailand, Togo, Trinidad and Tobago, Tunisia, Turkey, United Kingdom, United States, Upper Volta, Uruguay, Venezuela, Yemen Arab Republic, Yugoslavia, Zaire
Ratifications: Afghanistan, Australia, Austria, Bahamas, Belgium, Benin, Bhutan, Bolivia, Botswana, Brazil, Bulgaria, Burma, Byelorussia, Canada, Cape Verde, Central African Republic, Chad, Chile, Costa Rica, Cyprus, Czechoslovakia, Denmark, Dominican Republic, Ecuador, Egypt, El Salvador, Fiji, Finland, Gabon, Gambia, German Democratic Republic, Federal Republic of Germany, Ghana, Greece, Guatemala, Guinea-Bissau, Honduras, Hungary, Iceland, India, Indonesia, Iran, Iraq, Ireland, Israel, Italy, Ivory Coast, Japan, Jordan, Kenya, Republic of Korea, Kuwait, Laos, Lebanon, Libya, Luxembourg, Madagascar, Malawi, Malta, Mauritania, Mauritius, Mexico, Mongolia, Morocco, Nepal, Netherlands, New Zealand, Nicaragua, Niger, Nigeria, Norway, Papua New Guinea, Peru, Philippines, Poland, Romania, Rwanda, Samoa, San Marino, Senegal, Sierra Leone, Singapore, Somalia, South Africa, Soviet Union, Spain, Sri Lanka, Sudan, Swaziland, Syria, Taiwan, Tanzania, Thailand, Togo, Tonga, Trinidad and Tobago, Turkey, Uganda, United Kingdom, United States, Uruguay, Venezuela, People's Democratic Republic of Yemen, Yugoslavia, Zaire, Zambia
Date of entry into force: October 10, 1963

[The signatories],
Proclaiming as their principal aim the speediest possible achievement of an agreement on general and complete disarmament under strict international control in accordance with the objectives of the United Nations which would put an end to the armaments race and eliminate the incentive to the production and testing of all kinds of weapons, including nuclear weapons.
Seeking to achieve the discontinuance of all test explosions of nuclear weapons for all time, determined to continue negotiations to this end, and desiring to put an end to the contamination of man's environment by radioactive substances,
Have agreed as follows:

Article I

1. Each of the Parties of this Treaty undertakes to prohibit, to prevent, and not to carry out any nuclear weapon test explosion, or any other nuclear explosion, at any place under its jurisdiction or control:

(a) in the atmosphere; beyond its limits, including outer space; or underwater, including territorial waters or high seas; or

(b) in any other environment if such explosion causes radioactive debris to be present outside the territorial limits of the State under whose jurisdiction or control such explosion is conducted. It is understood in this connection that the provisions of this subparagraph are without prejudice to the conclusion of a treaty resulting in the permanent banning of all nuclear test explosions, including all such explosions underground, the conclusion of which, as the Parties have stated in the Preamble to this

Treaty, they seek to achieve.

2. Each of the Parties to this Treaty undertakes furthermore to refrain from causing, encouraging, or in any way participating in, the carrying out of any nuclear weapon test explosion, or any other nuclear explosion, anywhere which would take place in any of the environments described, or have the effect referred to, in paragraph 1 of this Article.

Article II

1. Any Party may propose amendments to this Treaty. The text of any proposed amendment shall be submitted to the Depositary Governments which shall circulate it to all Parties to this Treaty. Thereafter, if requested to do so by one-third or more of the Parties, the Depositary Governments shall convene a conference, to which they shall invite all the Parties, to consider such amendment.

2. Any amendment to this Treaty must be approved by a majority of the votes of all the Parties to this Treaty, including the votes of all of the Original Parties. The amendment shall enter into force for all Parties upon the deposit of instruments of ratification by a majority of all the Parties, including the instruments of ratification of all of the original Parties.

Article III

1. This Treaty shall be open to all States for signature. Any State which does not sign this Treaty before its entry into force in accordance with paragraph 3 of this Article may accede to it at any time.

2. This Treaty shall be subject to ratification by signatory States. Instruments of ratification and instruments of accession shall be deposited with the Governments of the Original Parties—the United States of America, the United Kingdom of Great Britain and Northern Ireland, and the Union of Soviet Socialist Republics—which are hereby designated the Depositary Governments.

3. This Treaty shall enter into force after its ratification by all the Original Parties and the deposit of their instruments of ratification.

4. For States whose instruments of ratification or accession are deposited subsequent to the entry into force of this Treaty, it shall enter into force on the date of the deposit of their instruments of ratification or accession.

5. The Depositary Governments shall promptly inform all signatory and acceding States of the date of each signature, the date of deposit of each instrument of ratification of and accession to this Treaty, the date of its entry into force, and the date of receipt of any requests for conferences or other notices.

6. This Treaty shall be registered by the Depositary Governments pursuant of Article 102 of the Charter of the United Nations.

Article IV

This Treaty shall be of unlimited duration.

Each Party shall in exercising its national sovereignty have the right to withdraw from the Treaty if it decides that extraordinary events, related to the subject matter of this Treaty, have jeopardized the supreme interests of its country. It shall give notice of such withdrawal to all other Parties to the Treaty three months in advance.

Article V

This Treaty, of which the English and Russian texts are equally authentic, shall be deposited in the archives of the Depositary Governments. Duly certified copies of this Treaty shall be transmitted by the Depositary Governments to the Governments of the signatory and acceding States.

Treaty on the Principles Governing the Activities of States in the Exploration and Use of Outer Space, Including the Moon and Other Celestial Bodies

Also known as: Outer Space Treaty
Date of signature: January 27, 1967
Place of signature: London, Moscow, and Washington, DC
Signatory states: Afghanistan, Argentina, Australia, Austria, Belgium, Bolivia, Botswana, Brazil, Bulgaria, Burma, Burundi, Byelorussian Soviet Socialist Republic, Cameroon, Canada, Central African Republic, Chile, China, Colombia, Congo (Kinshasa), Cyprus, Czechoslovakia, Denmark, Dominican Republic, Ecuador, Egypt, El Salvador, Ethiopia,, Finland, France, Federal Republic of Germany, Gambia, German Democratic

Republic, Ghana, Greece, Guyana, Haiti, Holy
See, Honduras, Hungary, Iceland, India,
Indonesia, Iran, Iraq, Iceland, Israel, Italy,
Jamaica, Japan, Jordan, Republic of Korea,
Laos, Lebanon, Lesotho, Luxembourg,
Malaysia, Mexico, Mongolia, Nepal,
Netherlands, New Zealand, Nicaragua, Niger,
Norway, Pakistan, Panama, Peru, Philippines,
Poland, Romania, Rwanda, San Marino,
Sierra Leone, Somalia, South Africa, Soviet
Union, Sri Lanka, Sweden, Switzerland,
Taiwan, Thailand, Togo, Trinidad and
Tobago, Tunisia, Turkey, Ukrainian Soviet
Socialist Republics, United Arab Republic,
United Kingdom, United States, Upper Volta,
Uruguay, Venezuela, Republic of Viet-Nam,
Yugoslavia, Zaire
Date of entry into force: *October 10, 1967*

The States Parties to this Treaty,

Inspired by the great prospects opening up before mankind as a result of man's entry into outer space,

Recognizing the common interest of all mankind in the progress of the exploration and use of outer space for peaceful purposes,

Believing that the exploration and use of outer space should be carried on for the benefit of all peoples irrespective of the degree of their economic or scientific development,

Desiring to contribute to broad international cooperation in the scientific as well as the legal aspects of the exploration and use of outer space for peaceful purposes,

Believing that such co-operation will contribute to the development of mutual understanding and to the strengthening of friendly relations between States and peoples,

Recalling resolution 1962 (XVIII), entitled "Declaration of Legal Principles Governing the Activities of States in the Exploration and Use of Outer Space," which was adopted unanimously by the United Nations General Assembly on 13 December 1963,

Recalling resolution 1884 (XVIII), calling upon States to refrain from placing in orbit around the Earth any objects carrying nuclear weapons or any other kinds of weapons of mass destruction or from installing such weapons on celestial bodies, which was adopted unanimously by the United Nations General Assembly on 17 October 1963,

Taking account of United Nations General Assembly resolution 110 (II) of 3 November 1947, which condemned propaganda designed or likely to provoke or

encourage any threat to the peace, breach of the peace or act of aggression, and considering that the aforementioned resolution is applicable to outer space,

Convinced that a Treaty on Principles Governing the Activities of States in the Exploration and Use of Outer Space, including the Moon and Other Celestial Bodies, will further the Purposes and Principles of the Charter of the United Nations,

Have agreed on the following:

Article I

The exploration and use of outer space, including the moon and other celestial bodies, shall be carried out for the benefit and in the interests of all countries, irrespective of their degree of economic or scientific development, and shall be the province of all mankind.

Outer space, including the moon and other celestial bodies, shall be free for exploration and use by all States without discrimination of any kind, on a basis of equality and in accordance with international law, and there shall be free access to all areas of celestial bodies.

There shall be freedom of scientific investigation in outer space, including the moon and other celestial bodies, and States shall facilitate and encourage international co-operation in such investigation.

Article II

Outer space, including the moon and other celestial bodies, is not subject to national appropriation by claim of sovereignty, by means of use or occupation, or by any other means.

Article III

States Parties to the Treaty shall carry on activities in the exploration and use of outer space, including the moon and other celestial bodies, in accordance with international law, including the Charter of the United Nations, in the interest of maintaining international peace and security and promoting international co-operation and understanding.

Article IV

States Parties to the Treaty undertake not to place in orbit around the Earth any objects carrying nuclear weapons or any other kinds of weapons of mass destruction, install such weapons on celestial bodies, or station such weapons in outer space in any other manner.

The moon and other celestial bodies shall be used by all States Parties to the Treaty exclusively for peaceful purposes. The establishment of military bases, installations and fortifications, the testing of any type of weapons and the conduct of military maneuvers on celestial bodies shall be forbidden. The use of military personnel for scientific research or for any other peaceful purposes shall not be prohibited. The use of any equipment of facility necessary for peaceful exploration of the moon and other celestial bodies shall also not be prohibited.

Article V

States Parties to the Treaty shall regard astronauts as envoys of mankind in outer space and shall render to them all possible assistance in the event of accident, distress, or emergency landing on the territory of another State Party or on the high seas. When astronauts make such a landing, they shall be safely and promptly returned to the State of registry of their space vehicle.

In carrying on activities in outer space and on celestial bodies, the astronauts of one State Party shall render all possible assistance to the astronauts of other States Parties.

States Parties to the Treaty shall immediately inform the other States Parties to the Treaty or the Secretary-General of the United Nations of any phenomena they discover in outer space, including the moon and other celestial bodies, which could constitute a danger to the life or health of astronauts.

Article VI

States Parties to the Treaty shall bear international responsibility for national activities in outer space, including the moon and other celestial bodies, whether such activities are carried on by governmental agencies or by non-governmental entities, and for assuring that national activities are carried out in conformity with the provisions set forth in the present Treaty. The activities of non-governmental entities in outer space, including the moon and other celestial bodies, shall require authorization and continuing supervision by the appropriate State Party to the Treaty. When activities are carried on in outer space, including the moon and other celestial bodies, by an international organization, responsibility for compliance with this Treaty shall be borne both by the international organization and by the States Parties to the Treaty participating in such organization.

Article VII

Each State Party to the Treaty that launches or procures the launching of an object into outer space, including the moon and other celestial bodies, and each State Party from whose territory or facility an object is launched, is internationally liable for damage to another State Party to the Treaty or to its natural or juridical persons by such object or its component parts on the Earth, in air space or in outer space, including the moon and other celestial bodies.

Article VIII

A State Party to the Treaty on whose registry an object launched into outer space is carried shall retain jurisdiction and control over such object, and over any personnel thereof, while in outer space or on a celestial body. Ownership of objects launched into outer space, including objects landed or constructed on a celestial body, and of their component parts, is not affected by their presence in outer space or on a celestial body or by their return to the Earth. Such objects or component parts found beyond the limits of the State Party to the Treaty on whose registry they are carried, shall be returned to that State Party, which shall, upon request, furnish identifying data prior to their return.

Article IX

In the exploration and use of outer space, including the moon and other celestial bodies, States Parties to the Treaty shall be guided by the principle of co-operation and mutual assistance and shall conduct all their activities in outer space, including the moon and other celestial bodies, with due regard to the corresponding interests of all other States Parties to the Treaty. States Parties to the Treaty shall pursue studies of outer space, including the moon and other celestial bodies, and conduct exploration of them so as to avoid their harmful contamination and also adverse changes in the environment of the Earth resulting from the introduction of extraterrestrial matter and, where necessary, shall adopt appropriate measures for this purpose. If a State Party to the Treaty has reason to believe that an activity or experiment planned by it or its nationals in outer space, including the moon and other celestial bodies, would cause potentially harmful interference with activities of other States Parties in the peaceful exploration and use of outer space, including the moon and other celestial bodies, it shall undertake appropriate international consultations before proceeding with any such activity or experiment. A State Party to the Treaty which has reason to believe that an activity or experiment planned by another State Party in outer space, including the moon and other celestial bodies, would cause potentially harmful interference with activities in the peaceful exploration and use of outer space, including the moon and other celestial bodies, may request consultation concerning the activity or experiment.

Article X

In order to promote international co-operation in the exploration and use of outer space, including the moon and other celestial bodies, in conformity with the purposes of this Treaty, the States Parties to the Treaty shall consider on a basis of the equality any requests by other States Parties to the Treaty to be afforded an opportunity to observe the flight of space objects launched by those States.

The nature of such an opportunity for observation and the conditions under which it could be afforded shall be determined by agreement between the States concerned.

Article XI

In order to promote international co-operation in the peaceful exploration and use of outer space, States Parties to the Treaty conducting activities in outer space, including the moon and other celestial bodies, agree to inform the Secretary-General of the United Nations as well as the public and the international scientific community, to the greatest extent feasible and practicable, of the nature, conduct, locations and results of such activities. On receiving the said information, the Secretary-General of the United Nations should be prepared to disseminate it immediately and effectively.

Article XII

All stations, installations, equipment and space vehicles on the moon and other celestial bodies shall be open to representatives of other States Parties to the Treaty on a basis of reciprocity. Such representatives shall give reasonable advance notice of a projected visit, in order that appropriate consultations may be held and that maximum precautions may be taken to assure safety and to avoid interference with normal operations in the facility to be visited.

Article XIII

The provisions of this Treaty shall apply to the activities of States Parties to the Treaty in the exploration and use of outer space, including the moon and other celestial bodies, whether such activities are carried on by a single State Party to the Treaty or jointly with other States, including cases where they are carried on within the framework of international intergovernmental organizations.

Any practical questions arising in connection with activities carried on by international inter-governmental organizations in the exploration and use of outer space, including the moon and other celestial bodies, shall be resolved by the States Parties to the Treaty either with the appropriate international organization or with one or more States members of that international organization, which are Parties to this Treaty.

Article XIV

1. This Treaty shall be open to all States for signature. Any State which does not sign this Treaty before its entry into force in accordance with paragraph 3 of this article may accede to it at any time.

2. This Treaty shall be subject to ratification by signatory States. Instruments of ratification and instruments of accession shall be deposited with the Governments of the United States of America, the United Kingdom of Great Britain and Northern Ireland and the Union of Soviet Socialist Republics, which are hereby designated the Depositary Governments.

3. This Treaty shall enter into force upon the deposit of instruments of ratification by five Governments including the Governments designated as Depositary Governments under this Treaty.

4. For States whose instruments of ratification or accession are deposited subsequent to the entry into force of this Treaty, it shall enter into force on the date of the deposit of their instruments of ratification or accession.

5. The Depositary Governments shall promptly inform all signatory and acceding States of the date of each signature, the date of deposit of each instrument of ratification of and accession to this Treaty, the date of its entry into force and other notices.

6. This Treaty shall be registered by the Depositary Governments pursuant to Article 102 of the Charter of the United Nations.

Article XV

Any State Party to the Treaty may propose amendments to this Treaty. Amendments shall enter into force for each State Party to the Treaty accepting the amendments upon their acceptance by a majority of the States Parties to the Treaty and thereafter for each remaining State Party to the Treaty on the date of acceptance by it.

Article XVI

Any State Party to the Treaty may give notice of its withdrawal from the Treaty one year after its entry into force by written notification to the Depositary Governments. Such withdrawal shall take effect one year from the date of receipt of this notification.

Article XVII

This Treaty, of which the English, Russian, French, Spanish and Chinese texts are equally authentic, shall be deposited in the archives of the Depositary Governments. Duly certified copies of this Treaty shall be transmitted by the Depositary Governments to the Governments of the signatory and acceding States.

Treaty for the Prohibition of Nuclear Weapons in Latin America

Also known as: Treaty of Tlatelolco
Date of signature: February 14, 1967
Place of signature: Mexico City
Signatory states: Antigua & Barbuda, Argentina, Bahamas, Barbados, Belize, Bolivia, Brazil, Chile, People's Republic of China, Colombia, Costa Rica, Cuba, Dominica, Dominican Republic, Ecuador, El Salvador, France, Grenada, Guatemala, Guyana, Haiti, Honduras, Jamaica, Mexico, Netherlands, Nicaragua, Panama, Paraguay, Peru, St. Kitts/Nevis, St. Lucia, St. Vincent Gredadines, Surinam, Trinidad and Tobago, Soviet Union, United Kingdom, United States, Uruguay, Venezuela
Date of entry into force: April 22, 1968

Preamble

In the name of their peoples and faithfully interpreting their desires and aspirations, the Governments of the States which have signed the Treaty for the Prohibition of Nuclear Weapons in Latin America,
Desiring to contribute, so far as lies in their power, towards ending the armaments race, especially in the field of nuclear weapons, and towards strengthening a world at peace, based on the sovereign equality of States, mutual respect and good neighbourliness,
Recalling that the United Nations General Assembly, in its resolution 808 (IX), adopted unanimously as one of the three points of a co-ordinated programme of disarmament "the total prohibition of the use and manufacture of nuclear weapons and weapons of mass destruction of every type",
Recalling that militarily denuclearized zones are not an end in themselves but rather a means for achieving general and complete disarmament at a later stage,

Recalling United Nations General Assembly resolution 1911 (XVIII), which established that the measures that should be agreed upon the denuclearization of Latin America should be taken "in the light of the principles of the Charter of the United Nations and of regional agreements",
Recalling United Nations General Assembly resolution 2028 (XX), which established the principle of an acceptable balance of mutual responsibilities and duties for the nuclear and non-nuclear powers, and
Recalling that the Charter of the Organization of American States proclaims that it is an essential purpose of the organization to strengthen the peace and security of the hemisphere,
Convinced:
That the incalculable destructive power of nuclear weapons has made it imperative that the legal prohibition of war should be strictly observed in practice if the survival of civilization and of mankind itself is to be assured,
That nuclear weapons, whose terrible effects are suffered, indiscriminately and inexorably, by military forces and civilian population alike, constitute, through the persistence of the radioactivity they release, an attack on the integrity of the human species and ultimately may even render the whole earth uninhabitable,
That general and complete disarmament under effective international control is a vital matter which all the peoples of the world equally demand,
That the proliferation of nuclear weapons, which seems inevitable unless States, in the exercise of their sovereign rights, impose restrictions on themselves in oder to prevent it, would make any agreement on disarmament enormously difficult and would increase the danger of the outbreak of a nuclear conflagration,
That the establishment of militarily denuclearized zones is closely linked with the maintenance of peace

and security in the respective regions,

That the military denuclearization of vast geographical zones, adopted by the sovereign decision of the States comprised therein, will exercise a beneficial influence on other regions where similar conditions exist,

That the privileged situation of the signatory States, whose territories are wholly free from nuclear weapons, imposes upon them the inescapable duty of preserving that situation both in their own interests and for the good of mankind,

That the existence of nuclear weapons in any country of Latin America would make it a target for possible nuclear attacks and would inevitably set off, throughout the region, a ruinous race in nuclear weapons which would involve the unjustifiable diversion, for warlike purposes, of the resources required for economic and social development,

That the foregoing reasons, together with the traditional peace-loving outlook of Latin America, give rise to an inescapable necessity that nuclear energy should be used in that region exclusively for peaceful purposes, and that the Latin American countries should use their right to the greatest and most equitable possible access to this new source of energy in order to expedite the economic and social development of their peoples,

Convinced finally:

That the military denuclearization of Latin America—being understood to mean the undertaking entered into internationally in this Treaty to keep their territories forever free from nuclear weapons—will constitute a measure which will spare their peoples from the squandering of their limited resources on nuclear armaments and will protect them against possible nuclear attacks on their territories, and will also constitute a significant contribution towards preventing the proliferation of nuclear weapons and a powerful factor for general and complete disarmament, and that Latin America, faithful to its tradition of universality, must not only endeavour to banish from its homelands the scourge of a nuclear war, but must also strive to promote the well-being and advancement of its peoples, at the same time co-operating in the fulfilment of the ideals of mankind, that is to say, in the consolidation of a permanent peace based on equal rights, economic fairness and social justice for all, in accordance with the principles and purposes set forth in the Charter of the United Nations and in the Charter of the Organization of American States,
Have agreed as follows:

Obligations

Article 1

The Contracting Parties hereby undertake to use exclusively for peaceful purposes the nuclear material and facilities which are under their jurisdiction, and to prohibit and prevent in their respective territories:

(a) The testing, use, manufacture, production or acquisition by any means whatsoever of any nuclear weapons, by the Parties themselves, directly or indirectly, on behalf of anyone else or in any other way; and

(b) The receipt, storage, installation, deployment and any form of possession of any nuclear weapon, directly or indirectly, by the Parties themselves, by anyone on their behalf or in any other way.

2. The Contracting Parties also undertake to refrain from engaging in, encouraging or authorizing, directly or indirectly, or in any way participating in the testing, use, manufacture, production, possession or control of any nuclear weapon.

Definition of the Contracting Parties

Article 2

For the purposes of This treaty, the Contracting Parties are those for whom the Treaty is in force.

Definition of territory

Article 3

For the purposes of this Treaty, the term "territory" shall include the territorial sea, air space and any other space over which the State exercises sovereignty in accordance with its own legislation.

Zone of application

Article 4

1. The zone of application of the Treaty is the whole of the territories for which the Treaty is in force.

2. Upon fulfilment of the requirements of Article 28, paragraph 1, the zone of application of the Treaty shall also be that which is situated in the western hemisphere within the following limits (except the continental part of the territory of the United States of America and its territorial waters): starting at a point located at 35° north latitude, 75° west longitude; from this point directly southward to a point at 30° north latitude, 75° west longitude; from there, directly eastward to a point at 30° north latitude, 50°

west longitude; from there along a loxodromic line to a point at 5° north latitude, 20° west longitude; from there directly southward to a point at 60° south latitude, 20° west longitude; from there directly westward to a point at 60° south latitude, 115° west longitude; from there directly northward to a point at 0° latitude, 115° west longitude; from there along a loxodromic line to a point at 35° north latitude, 150° west longitude; from there directly eastward to a point at 35° north latitude, 75° west longitude.

Definition of nuclear weapons

Article 5

For the purposes of this Treaty, a nuclear weapon is any device which is capable of releasing nuclear energy in an uncontrolled manner and which has a group of characteristics that are appropriate for use for warlike purposes. An instrument that may be used for the transport or propulsion of the device is not included in this definition if it is separable from the device and not an indivisible part thereof.

Meeting of signatories

Article 6

At the request of any of the signatories, or if the Agency established by Article 7 should so decide, a meeting of all the signatories may be convoked to consider in common question which may affect the very essence of this instrument, including possible amendments to it. In either case, the meeting will be convoked by the General Secretary.

Organization

Article 7

1. In order to ensure compliance with the obligations of this Treaty, the Contracting Parties hereby establish an international organization to be known as the "Agency for the Prohibition of Nuclear Weapons in Latin America", hereinafter referred to as "the Agency". Only the Contracting Parties shall be affected by its decisions.

2. The Agency shall be responsible for the holding of periodic or extraordinary consultations among member States on matters relating to the purposes, measures and procedures set forth in this Treaty and to supervision of compliance with the obligations arising therefrom.

3. The Contracting Parties agree to extend to the Agency full and prompt co-operation in accordance with the provisions of this Treaty, of any agreements they may conclude with the Agency and of any agreements the Agency may conclude with any other international organization or body.

4. The headquarters of the Agency shall be in Mexico City.

Organs

Article 8

1. There are hereby established as principal organs of the Agency a General Conference, a Council and a Secretariat.

2. Such subsidiary organs as are considered necessary by the General Conference may be established within the purview of this Treaty.

The General Conference

Article 9

1. The General Conference, the supreme organ of the Agency, shall be composed of all the Contracting Parties; it shall hold regular sessions every two years, and may also hold special sessions whenever this Treaty so provides, or, in the opinion of the Council, the circumstances so require.

2. The General Conference:

(a) May consider and decide on matters or questions covered by the Treaty, within the limits thereof, including those referring to powers and functions of any organ provided for in this Treaty.

(b) Shall establish procedures for the control system to ensure observance of this Treaty in accordance with its provisions.

(c) Shall elect the members of the Council and the General Secretary.

(d) May remove the General Secretary from office if the proper functioning of the Agency so requires.

(e) Shall receive and consider the biennial and special reports submitted by the Council and the General Secretary.

(f) Shall initiate and consider studies designed to facilitate the optimum fulfilment of the aims of this Treaty, without prejudice to the power of the General Secretary independently to carry out similar studies for submission to and consideration by the Conference.

(g) Shall be the organ competent to authorize the conclusion of agreements with Governments and other international organizations and bodies.

3. The General Conference shall adopt the Agency's budget and fix the scale of financial contributions to be paid by member States, taking into account the systems and criteria used for the same purpose by the United Nations.

4. The General Conference shall elect its officers for each session and may establish such subsidiary organs as it deems necessary for the performance of its functions.

5. Each member of the Agency shall have one vote. The decisions of the General Conference shall be taken by a two-thirds majority of the members present and voting in the case of matters relating to the control system and measures referred to in article 20, the admission of new members, the election or removal of the General Secretary, adoption of the budget and matters related thereto. Decisions on other matters, as well as procedural questions, and also determination of which questions must be decided by a two-thirds majority, shall be taken by a simple majority of the members present and voting.

6. The General Conference shall adopt its own rules of procedure.

The Council

Article 10

1. The Council shall be composed of five members of the Agency elected by the General Conference from among the Contracting Parties, due account being taken of equitable geographical distribution.

2. The members of the Council shall be elected for a term of four years. However, in the first election three will be elected for two years. Outgoing members may not be re-elected for the following period unless the limited number of States for which the Treaty is in force so requires.

3. Each member of the Council shall have one representative.

4. The Council shall be so organized as to be able to function continuously.

5. In addition to the functions conferred upon it by this Treaty and to those which may be assigned to it by the General Conference, the Council shall, through the General Secretary, ensure the proper operation of the control system in accordance with the provisions of this Treaty and with the decisions adopted by the General Conference.

6. The Council shall submit an annual report on its work to the General Conference as well as such special reports as it deems necessary or which the General Conference requests of it.

7. The Council shall elect its officers for each session.

8. The decisions of the Council shall be taken by a simple majority of its members present and voting.

9. The Council shall adopt its own rules of procedure.

The Secretariat

Article 11

1. The Secretariat shall consist of a General Secretary, who shall be the chief administrative officer of the Agency, and of such staff as the Agency may require. The term of office of the General Secretary shall be four years and he may be re-elected for a single additional term. The General Secretary may not be a national of the country in which the Agency has its headquarters. In case the office of General Secretary becomes vacant, a new election shall be held to fill the office for the remainder of the term.

2. The staff of the Secretariat shall be appointed by the General Secretary, in accordance with rules laid down by the General Conference.

3. In addition to the functions conferred upon him by this Treaty and to those which may be assigned to him by the General Conference, the General Secretary shall ensure, as provided by Article 10, paragraph 5, the proper operation of the control system established by this Treaty, in accordance with the provisions of the Treaty and the decisions taken by the General Conference.

4. The General Secretary shall act in that capacity in all meetings of the General Conference and of the Council and shall make an annual report to both bodies on the work of the Agency and any special reports requested by the General Conference or the Council or which the General Secretary may deem desirable.

5. The General Secretary shall establish the procedures for distributing to all Contracting Parties information received by the Agency form governmental sources, and such information from non-governmental sources as may be of interest to the Agency.

6. In the performance of their duties, the General Secretary and the staff shall not seek or receive instructions from any Government or from any other authority external to the Agency and shall refrain from any action which might reflect on their position as international officials responsible only to the Agency; subject to their responsiblilty to the Agency, they shall not disclose any industrial secrets or other confidential information coming to their knowledge by reason of their official duties in the Agency.

7. Each of the Contracting Parties undertakes to respect the exclusively international character of the responsibilities of the General Secretary and the staff

and not to seek to influence them in the discharge of their responsibilities.

Control system

Article 12

1. For the purpose of verifying compliance with the obligations entered into by the Contracting Parties in accordance with Article 1, a control system shall be established which shall be put into effect in accordance with the provisions of Articles 13-18 of this Treaty.

2. The control system shall be used in particular for the purpose of verifying:

(a) That devices, services and facilities intended for peaceful uses of nuclear energy are not used in the testing or manufacture of nuclear weapons;

(b) That none of the activities prohibited in Article 1 of this Treaty are carried out in the territory of the Contracting Parties with nuclear materials or weapons introduced from abroad, and

(c) That explosions for peaceful purposes are compatible with Article 18 of this Treaty.

IAEA Safeguards

Article 13

Each Contracting Party shall negotiate multilateral or bilateral agreements with the International Atomic Energy Agency for the application of its safeguards to its nuclear activities. Each Contracting Party shall initiate negotiations within a period of 180 days after the date of the deposit of its instrument of ratification of this Treaty. These agreements shall enter into force, for each Party, not later than eighteen months after the date of the initiation of such negotiations except in case of unforeseen circumstances of force majeure.

Reports of the parties

Article 14

1. The Contracting Parties shall submit to the Agency and to the International Atomic Energy Agency, for their information, semi-annual reports stating that no activity prohibited under this Treaty has occurred in their respective territories.

2. The Contracting Parties shall simultaneously transmit to the Agency a copy of any report they may submit to the International Atomic Energy Agency which relates to matters that are the subject of this Treaty and to the application of safeguards.

3. The contracting Parties shall also transmit to the Organization of American States, for its information, any reports that may be of interest to it, in accordance with the obligations established by the inter-American System.

Special reports requested by the General Secretary

Article 15

1. With the authorization of the Council, the General Secretary may request any of the Contracting Parties to provide the Agency with complementary or supplementary information regarding any event or circumstance connected with compliance with this Treaty, explaining his reasons. The Contracting Parties undertake to co-operate promptly and fully with the General Secretary.

2. The General Secretary shall inform the Council and the Contracting Parties forthwith of such requests and of the respective replies.

Special inspections

Article 16

1. The International Atomic Energy Agency and the Council established by this Treaty have the power of carrying out special inspections in the folowing cases:

(a) In the case of the International Atomic Energy Agency, in accordance with the agreements referred to in article 13 of the Treaty;

(b) In the case of the Council:

(i) When so requested, the reasons for the request being stated, by any Party which suspects that some activity prohibited by this Treaty has been carried out or is about to be carried out, either in the territory of any other Party or in any other place on such latter Party's behalf, the Council shall immediately arrange for such an inspection in accordance with article 10, paragraph 5.

(ii) When requested by any Party which has been suspected of or charged with having violated the Treaty, the Council shall immediately arrange for the special inspection requested, in accordance with Article 10, paragraph 5. The above requests will be made to the Council through the General Secretary.

2. The costs and expenses of any special inspection carried out under paragraph 1, sub-paragraph (b),

sections (i) and (ii) of this article shall be borne by the requesting Party or Parties, except where the Council concludes on the basis of the report on the special inspection that, in view of the circumstances existing in the case, such costs and expenses should be borne by the Agency.

3. The General Conference shall formulate the procedures for the organization and execution of the special inspections carried out in accordance with paragraph 1, sub-paragraph (b), sections (i) and (ii) of this article.

4. The Contracting Parties undertake to grant the inspectors carrying out such special inspections full and free access to all places and all information which may be necessary for the performance of their duties and which are directly and intimately connected with the suspicion of violation of this Treaty. If so requested by the Contracting Party in whose territory the inspection is carried out, the inspectors designated by the General Conference shall be accompanied by representatives of the authorities of that Contracting Party, provided that this does not in any way delay or hinder the work of the inspectors.

5. The Council shall immediately transmit to all the Parties, through the General Secretary, a copy of any report resulting from special inspections.

6. Similarly, the Council shall send through the General Secretary to the Secretary-General of the United Nations for transmission to the United Nations Security Council and General Assembly, and to the Council of the Organization of American States for its information, a copy of any report resulting from any special inspection carried out in accordance with paragraph 1, sub-paragraph (b), sections (i) and (ii) of this article.

7. The council may decide, or any Contracting Party may request, the convening of special session of the General Conference for the purpose of considering the reports resulting from any special inspection. In such a case, the General Secretary shall take immediate steps to convene the special session requested.

8. The General Conference, convened in special session under this article, may make recommendations to the Contracting Parties and submit reports to the Secretary-General of the United Nations to be transmitted to the Security Council and the General Assembly.

Use of nuclear energy for peaceful purposes

Article 17

Nothing in the provisions of this Treaty shall prejudice the rights of the Contracting Parties, in confor-

mity with this Treaty, to use nuclear energy for peaceful purposes, in particular for their economic development and social progress.

Explosions for peaceful purposes

Article 18

1. The Contracting Parties may carry out explosions of nuclear devices for peaceful purposes—including explosions which involve devices similar to those used in nuclear weapon—or collaborate with third parties for the same purpose, provide that they do so in accordance with the provisions of this article and the other articles of the Treaty, particularly Articles 1 and 5.

2. Contracting Parties intending to carry out, or co-operate in the carrying out of such, an explosion shall notify the Agency and the International Atomic Energy Agency, as far in advance as the circumstances require, of the date of the explosion and shall at the same time provide the following information:

(a) The nature of the nuclear device and the source from which it was obtained;

(b) The place and purpose of the planned explosion;

(c) The procedures which will be followed in order to comply with paragraph 3 of this article;

(d) The expected force of the device;

(e) The fullest possible information on any possible radioactive fall-out that may result from the explosion or explosions, and the measurfauna, and territories of any other Party or Parties.

3. The General Secretary and the technical personnel designated by the Council and the International Atomic Energy Agency may observe all the preparations, including the explosion of the device, and shall have unrestricted access to any area in the vicinity of the site of the explosion in order to ascertain whether the device and the procedures followed during the explosion are in conformity with the information supplied under paragraph 2 of the present article and other provisions of this Treaty.

4. The Contracting Parties may accept the collaboration of third parties for the purpose set forth in paragraph 1 of the present Article, in accordance with paragraphs 2 and 3 thereof.

Relations with other international organizations

Article 19

1. The Agency may conclude such agreements

with the International Atomic Energy Agency as are authorized by the General Conference and as it considers likely to facilitate the efficient operation of the control system established by this Treaty.

2. The Agency may also enter into relations with any international organization or body, especially any which may be established in the future to supervise disarmament or measures for the control of armaments in any part of the world.

3. The Contracting Parties may, if they see fit, request the advice of the Inter-American Nuclear Energy Commission on all technical matters connected with the application of the Treaty with which the Commission is competent to deal under its Statute.

Measures in the event of violation of the Treaty

Article 20

1. The General Conference shall take note of all cases in which, in its opinion, any Contracting Party is not complying fully with its obligations under this Treaty and shall draw the matter to the attention of the Party concerned, making such recommendations as it deems appropriate.

2. If, in its opinion, such non-compliance constitutes a violation of this Treaty which might endanger peace and security, the General Conference shall report thereon simultaneously to the Security Council and the General Assembly through the Secretary-General of the United Nations and to the Council of the Organization of American States. The General Conference shall likewise report to the International Atomic Energy Agency for such purposes as are relevant in accordance with its Statute.

United Nations and Organization of American States

Article 21

None of the provisions of this Treaty shall be construed as impairing the rights and obligations of the Parties under the Charter of the United Nations or, in the case of States members of the Organization of American States, under existing regional treaties.

Privileges and immunities

Article 22

1. The Agency shall enjoy in the territory of each of the Contracting Parties such legal capacity and such privileges and immunities as may be necessary for the exercise of its functions and the fulfillment of its purposes.

2. Representatives of the Contracting Parties accredited to the Agency and official of the Agency shall similarly enjoy such privileges and immunities as are necessary for the performance of their functions.

3. The Agency may conclude agreements with the Contracting Parties with a view to determining the details of the application of paragraphs 1 and 2 of this Article.

Notification of other agreements

Article 23

Once this Treaty has entered into force, the Secretariat shall be notified immediately of any international agreement concluded by any of the Contracting Parties on matters with which this Treaty is concerned; the Secretariat shall register it and notify the other Contracting Parties.

Settlement of disputes

Article 24

Unless the parties concerned agree on another mode of peaceful settlement, any question or dispute concerning the interpretation or application of this Treaty which is not settled shall be referred to the International Court of Justice with the prior consent of the parties to the controversy.

Signature

Article 25

1. This Treaty shall be open indefinitely for signature by:

(a) All the Latin American Republics;

(b) All other sovereign States situated in their entirety south of latitude 35° north in the western hemisphere; and, except as provided in paragraph 2 of this article, all such States which become sovereign, when they have been admitted by the General Conference.

2. The General Conference shall not take any decision regarding the admission of a political entity part or all of whose territory is the subject, prior to the date when this Treaty is opened for signature, of a dispute or claim between an extra-continental country and one or more Latin America States, so long as the dispute has not been settled by peaceful means.

Ratification and deposit

Article 26

1. This Treaty shall be subject to ratification by signatory States in accordance with their respective constitutional procedures.

2. This Treaty and the instruments of ratification shall be deposited with the Government of the United States of Mexico, which is hereby designated the Depositary Government.

3. The Depositary Government shall send certified copies of this Treaty to the Governments of signatory States and shall notify them of the deposit of each instrument of ratification.

Reservations

Article 27

This Treaty shall not be subject to reservations.

Entry into force

Article 28

1. Subject to the provisions of paragraphs 2 and 3 of this Article, this Treaty shall enter into force among the States that have ratified it as soon as the following requirements have been met:

(a) Deposit of the instruments of ratification of this Treaty with the Depositary Government by the Governments of the States mentioned in Article 25 which are in existence on the date when this Treaty is opened for signature and which are not affected by the provisions of Article 25, paragraph 2;

(b) Signature and ratification of Additional Protocol I annexed to this Treaty by all extra-continental and continental States having de jure or de facto international responsibility for territories situated in the zone of application of the Treaty;

(c) Signature and ratification of the Additional Protocol II annexed to this Treaty by all powers possessing nuclear weapons;

(d) Conclusion of bilateral agreements on the application of the Safeguards System of the International Atomic Energy Agency in accordance with Article 13 of this Treaty.

2. All signatory States shall have the imprescriptible right to waive, wholly or in part, the requirements laid down in the preceding paragraph. They may do so by means of a declaration which shall be annexed to their respective instruments of ratification and which may be formulated at the time

of deposit of the instrument or subsequently. For those States which exercise this right, this Treaty shall enter into force upon deposit of the declaration, or as soon as those requirements have been met which have not been expressly waived.

3. As soon as this Treaty has entered into force in accordance with the provisions of paragraph 2 for eleven States, the Depositary Government shall convene a preliminary meeting of those States in order that the Agency may be set up and commence its work.

4. After the entry into force of the Treaty for all the countries of the zone, the rise of a new power possessing nuclear weapons shall have the effect of suspending the execution of this Treaty for those countries which have ratified it without waiving the requirements of paragraph 1, sub-paragraph (c) of this article, and which request such suspension; the Treaty shall remain suspended until the new power, on its own initiative or upon request by the General Conference, ratifies the annexed Additional Protocol II.

Amendments

Article 29

1. Any Contracting Party may propose amendments to this Treaty and shall submit their proposals to the Council through the General Secretary, who shall transmit them to all the other Contracting Parties and, in addition, to signatories in accordance with article 6. The Council, through the General Secretary, shall, immediately following the meeting of signatories, convene a special session of the General Conference to examine the proposals made, for the adoption of which a two-thirds majority of the Contracting Parties present and voting shall be required.

2. Amendments adopted shall enter into force as soon as the requirements set forth in Article 28 of this Treaty have been complied with.

Duration and denunciation

Article 30

1. This Treaty shall be of a permanent nature and shall remain in force indefinitely, but any Party may denounce it by notifying the General Secretary of the Agency if, in the opinion of the denouncing State, there have arisen or may arise circumstances connectd with the content of the Treaty or of the annexed Additional Protocols I and II which affect its supreme interests and the peace and security of one or more Contracting Parties.

2. The denunciation shall take effect three months

after the delivery to the General Secretary of the Agency of the notification by the Government of the signatory State concerned. The General Secretary shall immediately communicate such notification to the other Contracting Parties and to the Secretary General of the United Nations for the information of the Security Council and the General Assembly of the United Nations. He shall also communicate it to the Secretary General of the Organization of American States.

Authentic texts and registration

Article 31

This Treaty, of which the Spanish, Chinese, English, French, Portuguese and Russian texts are equally authentic, shall be registered by the Depositary Government in accordance with Article 102 of the United Nations Charter. The Depositary Government shall notify the Secretary-General of the United Nations of the signatures, ratifications and amendments relating to this Treaty shall communicate them to the Secretary General of the Organization of American States for his information.

Transitional Article

Denunciation of the declaration referred to in Article 28, paragraph 2, shall be subject to the same procedures as the denunciation of the Treaty, except that it shall take effect on the date of delivery of the respective notification.

ADDITIONAL PROTOCOL I

The . . . Plenipotentiaries, furnished with full powers by their respective Governments,
Convinced that the Treaty for the Prohibition of Nuclear Weapons in Latin America, negotiated and signed in accordance with the recommendations of the General Assembly of the United Nations in resolution 1911 (XVIII) of 27 November 1963, represents an important step towards ensuring the non-proliferation of nuclear weapons,
Aware that the non-proliferation of nuclear weapons is not an end in itself but rather a means of achieving general and complete disarmament at a later stage,
Desiring to contribute, so far as lies in their power, towards ending the armaments race, especially in the field of nuclear weapons, and towards strengthening a world at peace, based on mutual respect and sovereign equality of States,
Have agreed as follows:

Article 1

To undertake to apply the status of denuclearization in respect of warlike purposes as defined in Articles 1,3,5 and 13 of the Treaty for the Prohibition of Nuclear Weapons in Latin America in territories for which, de jure or de facto, they are internationally responsible and which lie within the limits of the geographical zone established in that Treaty.

Article 2

The duration of this Protocol shall be the same as that of the Treaty for the Prohibition of Nuclear Weapons in Latin America of which this Protocol is an annex, and the provisions regarding ratification and denunciation contained in the Treaty shall be applicable to it.

Article 3

This Protocol shall enter into force, for the States which have ratified it, on the date of the deposit of their respective instruments of ratification.

ADDITIONAL PROTOCOL II

The . . . Plenipotentiaries, furnished with full powers by their respective Governments,
Convinced that the Treaty for the Prohibition of Nuclear Weapons in Latin America, negotiated and signed in accordance with the recommendations of the General Assembly of the United Nations in resolution 1911 (XVIII) of 27 November 1963, is an important step towards ensuring the non-proliferation of nuclear weapons,
Aware that the non-proliferation of nuclear weapons is not an end in itself but rather a means for achieving general and complete disarmament at a later stage,
Desiring to contribute, so far as lies in their power, towards ending the armaments race, especially in the field of nuclear weapons, and towards promoting and strengthening a world at peace based on mutual respect and sovereign equality of States,
Have agreed as follows:

Article 1

The status of denuclearization of Latin America in respect of warlike purposes, as defined, delimited and set forth in the Treaty for the Prohibition of Nuclear Weapons in Latin America of which this instrument is an annex, shall be fully respected by the Parties to this Protocol in all its express aims and provisions.

Article 2

The Governments represented by the . . . Plenipotentiaries undertake, therefore, not to contribute in any way to the performance of acts involving a violation of the obligations of Article 1 of the Treaty in the territories to which the Treaty applies in accordance with Article 4 thereof.

Article 3

The Governments represented by the . . . Plenipotentiaries also undertake not to use or threaten to use nuclear weapons against the Contracting Parties of the Treaty for the Prohibition of Nuclear Weapons in Latin America.

Article 4

The duration of this Protocol shall be the same as that of the Treaty for the Prohibition of Nuclear Weapons in Latin America of which this Protocol is an annex, and the definitions of territory and nuclear weapons set forth in articles 3 and 5 of the Treaty shall be applicable to the Protocol, as well as the provisions regarding ratification, reservations, denunciation, authentic texts and registration contained in articles 26, 27, 30 and 31 of the Treaty.

Article 5

This Protocol shall enter into force, for the States which have ratified it, on the date of the deposit of their respective instruments of ratification.

Treaty on the Non-Proliferation of Nuclear Weapons

Also known as: Non-Proliferation Treaty, NPT
Date of signature: July 1, 1968
Place of signature: London, Moscow, and Washington DC
Signatory states: Afghanistan, Australia, Austria, Barbados, Belgium, Benin, Bolivia, Botswana, Cameroon, Canada, Chad, Colombia, Costa Rica, Cyprus, Czechoslovakia, Denmark, Dominican Republic, Ecuador, Egypt, El Salvador, Ethiopia, Finland, Gambia, German Democratic Republic, Federal Republic of Germany, Ghana, Greece, Guatemala, Haiti, Honduras, Hungary, Iceland, Indonesia, Iran, Iraq, Ireland, Italy, Ivory Coast, Jamaica, Japan, Jordan, Kenya, Republic of Korea, Kuwait, Laos, Lebanon, Lesotho, Liberia, Libya, Luxembourg, Madagascar, Malaysia, Maldives, Mali, Malta, Mauritius, Mexico, Mongolia, Morocco, Nepal, Netherlands, New Zealand, Nicaragua, Nigeria, Norway, Panama, Paraguay, Peru, Philippines, Poland, Romania, San Marino, Senegal, Singapore, Somalia, Sri Lanka, Sudan, Swaziland, Sweden, Switzerland, Syria, Taiwan, Togo, Trinidad and Tobago, Tunisia, Turkey, Soviet Union, United Kingdom, United States, Upper Volta, Uruguay, Venezuela, Yemen Arab Republic, People's Democratic Republic of Yemen, Yugoslavia, Zaire
Ratifications: Afghanistan, Australia, Austria, Bahamas, Bangladesh, Barbados, Belgium, Benin, Bolivia, Botswana, Bulgaria, Burundi, Cameroon, Canada, Cape Verde, Central African Republic,

Chad, Congo, Costa Rica, Cyprus, Czechoslovakia, Denmark, Dominican Republilc, Ecuador, Egypt, El Salvador, Ethiopia, Fiji, Finland, Gabon, Gambia, German Democratic Republic, Federal Republic of Germany, Ghana, Greece, Grenada, Guatemala, Guinea-Bissau, Haiti, Holy See, Honduras, Hungary, Iceland, Indonesia, Iran, Iraq, Ireland, Italy, Ivory Coast, Jamaica, Japan, Jordan, Kampuchea, Kenya, Republic of Korea, Laos, Lebanon, Lesotho, Liberia, Libya, Liechtenstein, Luxembourg, Madagascar, Malaysia, Maldives, Mali, Malta, Mauritius, Mexico, Mongolia, Morocco, Nepal, Netherlands, New Zealand, Nicaragua, Nigeria, Norway, Panama, Paraguay, Peru, Philippines, Poland, Portugal, Romania, Rwanda, Saint Lucia, Samoa, San Marino, Senegal, Sierra Leone, Singapore, Solomon Island, Somalia, Sri Lanka, Sudan, Surinam, Swaziland, Sweden, Switzerland, Syria, Taiwan, Thailand, Togo, Tonga, Tunisia, Turkey, Tuvalu, Soviet Union, United Kingdom, United States, Upper Volta, Uruguay, Venezuela, People's Democratic Republic of Yemen, Yugoslavia, Zaire
Date of entry into force: March 5, 1970

The States concluding this Treaty, hereinafter referred to as the "Parties to the Treaty",
Considering the devastation that would be visited upon all mankind by a nuclear war and the consequent need to make every effort to avert the danger

of such a war and to take measures to safeguard the security of peoples,

Believing that the proliferation of nuclear weapons would seriously enhance the danger of nuclear war,

In conformity with resolutions of the United Nations General Assembly calling for the conclusion of an agreement on the prevention of wider dissemination of nuclear weapons,

Undertaking to co-operate in facilitating the application of International Atomic Energy Agency safeguards on peaceful nuclear activities.

Expressing their support for research, development and other efforts to further the application, within the framework of the International Atomic Energy Agency safeguards system, of the principle of safeguarding effectively the flow of source and special fissionable materials by use of instruments and other techniques at certain strategic points,

Affirming the principle that the benefits of peaceful applications of nuclear technology, including any technological by-products which may be derived by nuclear-weapon States from the development of nuclear explosive devices, should be available for peaceful purposes to all Parties to the Treaty, whether nuclear-weapon or non-nuclear-weapon States,

Convinced that, in furtherance of this principle, all Parties to the Treaty are entitled to participate in the fullest possible exchange of scientific information for, and to contribute alone or in co-operation with other States to, the further development of the applications of atomic energy for peaceful purposes,

Declaring their intention to achieve at the earliest possible date the cessation of the nuclear arms race and to undertake effective measures in the direction of nuclear disarmament,

Urging the co-operation of all States in the attainment of this objective,

Recalling the determination expressed by the Parties to the 1963 Treaty banning nuclear weapon tests in the atmosphere, in outer space and under water in its Preamble to seek to achieve the discontinuance of all test explosions of nuclear weapons for all time and to continue negotiations to this end,

Desiring to further the easing of international tension and the strengthening of trust between States in order to facilitate the cessation of the manufacture of nuclear weapons, the liquidation of all their existing stockpiles, and the elimination from national arsenals of nuclear weapons and the means of their delivery pursuant to a Treaty on general and complete disarmament under strict and effective international control,

Recalling that, in accordance with the Charter of the United Nations, States must refrain in their international relations from the threat or use of force against the territorial integrity or political independence of any State, or in any other manner inconsistent with the Purposes of the United Nations, and that the establishment and maintenance of international peace and security are to be promoted with the least diversion for armaments of the world's human and economic resources,

Have agreed as follows:

Article I

Each nuclear-weapon State Party to the Treaty undertakes not to transfer to any recipient whatsoever nuclear weapons or other nuclear explosive devices or control over such weapons or explosive devices directly, or indirectly; and not in any way to assist, encourage or induce any non-nuclear-weapon State to manufacture or otherwise acquire nuclear weapons or other nuclear explosive devices, or control over such weapons or explosive devices.

Article II

Each non-nuclear-weapon State Party to the Treaty undertakes not to receive the transfer from any transfer or whatsoever of nuclear weapons or other nuclear explosive devices or of control over such weapons or explosive devices directly, or indirectly; not to manufacture or otherwise acquire nuclear weapons or other nuclear explosive devices; and not to seek or receive any assistance in the manufacture of nuclear weapons or other nuclear explosive devices.

Article III

1. Each non-nuclear-weapon State Party to the Treaty undertakes to accept safeguards, as set forth in an agreement to be negotiated and concluded with the International Atomic Energy Agency in accordance with the Statute of the International Atomic Energy Agency and the Agency's safeguards system, for the exclusive purpose of verification of the fulfillment of its obligations assumed under this Treaty with a view to preventing diversion of nuclear energy from peaceful uses to nuclear weapons or other nuclear explosive devices. Procedures for the safeguards required by this Article shall be followed with respect to source or special fissionable material whether it is being produced, processed or used in any principal nuclear facility or is outside any such facility. The safeguards required by this Article shall

be applied on all source or special fissionable material in all peaceful nuclear activities within the territory of such State, under its jurisdiction, or carried out under its control anywhere.

2. Each State Party to the Treaty undertakes not to provide: (a) source of special fissionable material, or (b) equipment or material especially designed or prepared for the processing, use or production of special fissionable material, to any non-nuclear-weapon State for peaceful purposes, unless the source or special fissionable material shall be subject to the safeguards required by this Article.

3. The safeguards required by this Article shall be implemented in a manner designed to comply with Article IV of this Treaty, and to avoid hampering the economic or technological development of the Parties or international co-operation in the field of peaceful nuclear activities, including the international exchange of nuclear material and equipment for the processing, use or production of nuclear material for peaceful purposes in accordance with the provisions of this Article and the principle of safeguarding set forth in the Preamble of the Treaty.

4. Non-nuclear-weapon States Party to the Treaty shall conclude agreements with the International Atomic Energy Agency to meet the requirements of this Article either individually or together with other States in accordance with the Statute of the International Atomic Energy Agency. Negotiation of such agreements shall commence within 180 days from the original entry into force of this Treaty. For States depositing their instruments of ratification or accession after the 180-day period, negotiation of such agreements shall commence not later than the date of such deposit. Such agreements shall enter into force not later than eighteen months after the date of initiation of negotiations.

Article IV

1. Nothing in this Treaty shall be interpreted as affecting the inalienable right of all the Parties to the Treaty to develop research, production and use of nuclear energy for peaceful purposes without discrimination and in conformity with Articles I and II of this Treaty.

2. All the Parties to the Treaty undertake to facilitate, and have the right to participate in, the fullest possible exchange of equipment, materials and scientific and technological information for the peaceful uses of nuclear energy. Parties to the Treaty in a

position to do so shall also co-operate in contributing alone or together with other States or international organizations to the further development of the applications of nuclear energy for peaceful purposes, especially in the territories of non-nuclear weapon States Party to the Treaty, with due consideration for the needs of the developing areas of the world.

Article V

Each Party to the Treaty undertakes to take appropriate measures to ensure that, in accordance with this Treaty, under appropriate international observation and through appropriate international procedures, potential benefits from any peaceful applications of nuclear explosions will be made available to non-nuclear-weapon States Party to the Treaty on a non-discriminatory basis and that the charge to such Parties for the explosive devices used will be as low as possible and exclude any charge for research and development. Non-nuclear-weapon States Party to the Treaty shall be able to obtain such benefit, pursuant to a special international agreement or agreements, through an appropriate international body with adequate representation of non-nuclear-weapon States. Negotiations on this subject shall commence as soon as possible after the Treaty enters into force. Non-nuclear-weapon States Party to the Treaty so desiring may also obtain such benefits pursuant to bilateral agreements.

Article VI

Each of the Parties to the Treaty undertakes to pursue negotiations in good faith on effective measures relating to cessation of the nuclear arms race at an early date and to nuclear disarmament, and on a treaty on general and complete disarmament under strict and effective international control.

Article VII

Nothing in this Treaty affects the right of any group of States to conclude regional treaties in order to assure the total absence of nuclear weapons in their respective territories.

Article VIII

1. Any Party to the Treaty may propose amendments to this Treaty. The text of any proposed amendment shall be submitted to the Depositary Governments which shall circulate it to all Parties to the Treaty. Thereupon, if requested to do so by one-third or more of the Parties to the Treaty, the Deposi-

tary Governments shall convene a conference, to which they shall invite all the Parties to the Treaty, to consider such an amendment.

2. Any amendment to this Treaty must be approved by a majority of the votes of all the Parties to the Treaty, including the votes of all nuclear weapon States Party to the Treaty, and all other Parties which, on the date the amendment is circulated, are members of the Board of Governors of the International Atomic Energy Agency. The amendment shall enter into force for each Party that deposits its instrument of ratification of the amendment upon the deposit of such instruments of ratification by a majority of all the Parties, including the instruments of ratification of all nuclear-weapon States Party to the Treaty and all other Parties which, on the date the amendment is circulated, are members of the Board of Governors of the International Atomic Energy Agency. Thereafter, it shall enter into force for any other Party upon the deposit of its instrument of ratification of the amendment.

3. Five years after the entry into force of this Treaty, a conference of Parties to the Treaty shall be held in Geneva, Switzerland, in order to review the operation of this Treaty with a view to assuring that the purposes of the Preamble and the provisions of the Treaty are being realised. At intervals of five years thereafter, a majority of the Parties to the Treaty may obtain, by submitting a proposal to this effect to the Depositary Governments, the convening of further conferences with the same objective of reviewing the operation of the Treaty.

Article IX

1. This Treaty shall be open to all States for signature. Any State which does not sign the Treaty before its entry into force in accordance with paragraph 3 of this Article may accede to it at any time.

2. This Treaty shall be subject to ratification by signatory States. Instruments of ratification and instruments of accession shall be deposited with the Governments of the United Kingdom of Great Britain and Northern Ireland, the Union of Soviet Socialist Republics and the United States of America, which are hereby designated the Depositary Governments.

3. This Treaty shall enter into force after its ratification by the States, the Governments of which are designated Depositories of the Treaty, and forty other States signatory to this Treaty and the deposit of their instruments of ratification. For the purposes of this Treaty, a nuclear-weapon State is one which has manufactured and exploded a nuclear weapon or other nuclear explosive device prior to 1 January, 1967.

4. For States whose instruments of ratification or accession are deposited subsequent to the entry into force of this Treaty, it shall enter into force on the date of the deposit of their instruments of ratification or accession.

5. The Depositary Governments shall promptly inform all signatory and acceding States of the date of each signature, the date of deposit of each instrument of ratification or of accession, the date of the entry into force of this Treaty, and the date of receipt of any requests for convening a conference or other notices.

6. This Treaty shall be registered by the Depositary Governments pursuant to Article 102 of the Charter of the United Nations.

Article X

1. Each Party shall in exercising its national sovereignty have the right to withdraw from the Treaty if it decides that extraordinary events, related to the subject matter of this Treaty, have jeopardized the supreme interests of its country. It shall give notice of such withdrawal to all other Parties to the Treaty and to the United Nations Security Council three months in advance. Such notice shall include a statement of the extraordinary events it regards as having jeopardized its supreme interests.

2. Twenty-five years after the entry into force of the Treaty, a conference shall be convened to decide whether the Treaty shall continue in force indefinitely, or shall be extended for an additional fixed period or periods. This decision shall be taken by a majority of the Parties to the Treaty.

Article XI

This Treaty, the English, Russian, French, Spanish and Chinese texts of which are equally authentic, shall be deposited in the archives of the Depositary Governments. Duly certified copies of this Treaty shall be transmitted by the Depositary Governments to the Governments of the signatory and acceding States.

Question Relating to Measures to Safeguard Non-Nuclear-Weapon States Parties to the Treaty on the Non-Proliferation of Nuclear Weapons

Resolution 255 (1968) of 19 June 1968 Adopted at the 1433rd meeting by 10 votes to none, with 5 abstentions (Algeria, Brazil, France, India and Pakistan)

The Security Council,

Noting with appreciation the desire of a large number of States to subscribe to the Treaty on the Non-Proliferation of Nuclear Weapons, and thereby to undertake not to receive the transfer from any transfer or whatsoever of nuclear weapons or other nuclear explosive devices or of control over such weapons or explosive devices directly or indirectly not to manufacture or otherwise acquire nuclear weapons or other nuclear explosive devices, and not to seek or receive any assistance in the manufacture of nuclear weapons or other nuclear explosive devices.

Taking into consideration the concern of certain of these States that, in conjunction with their adherence to the Treaty on the Non-Proliferation of Nuclear Weapons, appropriate measures be undertaken to safeguard their security.

Bearing in mind that any aggression accompanied by the use of nuclear weapons would endanger the peace and security of all States.

1. Recognizes that aggression with nuclear weapons or the threat of such aggression against a non-nuclear-weapons State would create a situation in which the Security Council, and above all its nuclear-weapon State permanent members, would have to act immediately in accordance with their obligations under the United Nations Charter;

2. Welcomes the intention expressed by certain States that they will provide or support immediate assistance, in accordance with the Charter, to any non-nuclear-weapon State Party to the Treaty on the Non-Proliferation of Nuclear Weapons that is a victim of an act or an object of a threat of aggression in which nuclear weapons are used;

3. Reaffirms in particular the inherent right, recognized under Article 51 of the Charter, of individual and collective self-defense if an armed attack occurs against a Member of the United Nation, until the Security Council has taken measures necessary to maintain international peace and security.

Treaty on the Prohibition of the Emplacement of Nuclear Weapons and Other Weapons of Mass Destruction on the Sea-Bed and the Ocean Floor and in the Subsoil Thereof

Also known as: Sea Bed Treaty
Date of signature: February 11, 1971
Place of signature: London, Moscow, and Washington, DC
Signatory states: Afghanistan, Argentina, Australia, Austria, Belgium, Benin, Bolivia, Botswana, Brazil, Bulgaria, Burma, Burundi, Byelorussia, Cameroon, Canada, Central African Republic, Colombia, Costa Rica, Cyprus, Czechoslovakia, Denmark, Dominican Republic, Equitorial Guinea, Ethiopia, Finland, Gambia, German Democratic Republic, Federal Republic of Germany, Ghana, Greece, Guatemala, Guinea, Honduras, Hungary, Iceland, Iran, Iraq, Ireland, Italy, Jamaica, Japan, Jordan, Kampuchea, Republic of Korea, Laos, Lebanon, Lesotho, Liberia, Luxembourg, Madagascar, Malaysia, Mali,

Malta, Mauritius, Mongolia, Morocco, Nepal, Netherlands, New Zealand, Nicaragua, Niger, Norway, Panama, Paraguay, Poland, Romania, Rwanda, Saudi Arabia, Senegal, Sierra Leone, Singapore, South Africa, Soviet Union, Sudan, Swaziland, Sweden, Switzerland, Taiwan, Tanzania, Togo, Tunisia, Turkey, Ukraine, United Kingdom, United States, Uruguay, Yemen Arab Republic, People's Democratic Republic of Yemen, Yugoslavia
Ratifications: Afghanistan, Australia, Austria, Belgium, Botswana, Bulgaria, Byelorussia, Canada, Cape Verde, Central African Republic, Congo, Cuba, Cyprus, Czechoslovakia, Denmark, Dominican Republic, Ethiopia, Finland, German Democratic Republic, Federal Republic of

Germany, Ghana, Guinea-Bissau, Hungary, Iceland, India, Iran, Iraq, Ireland, Italy, Ivory Coast, Japan, Jordan, Laos, Lesotho, Malaysia, Malta, Mauritius, Mongolia, Morocco, Nepal, Netherlands, New Zealand, Nicaragua, Niger, Norway, Panama, Poland, Portugal, Qatar, Romania, Rwanda, Sao Tome, Saudi Arabia, Seychelles, Singapore, Solomon Islands, South Africa, Soviet Union, Swaziland, Sweden, Switzerland, Taiwan, Togo, Tunisia, Turkey, Ukraine, United Kingdom, United States, Vietnam, People's Democratic Republic of Yemen, Yugoslavia, Zambia,
Date of entry into force: *May 18, 1972*

The General Assembly,
Recalling its resolution 2602 F (XXIV) of 16 December 1969,
Convinced that the prevention of a nuclear arms race on the sea-bed and the ocean floor serves the interests of maintaining world peace, reducing international tensions and strengthening friendly relations among States,
Recognizing the common interest of mankind in the reservation of the sea-bed and the ocean floor exclusively for peaceful purposes,
Having considered the report of the Conference of the Committee on Disarmament, dated 11 September 1970, and appreciative of the work of the Conference on the draft Treaty on the Prohibition of the Emplacement of Nuclear Weapons and Other Weapons of Mass Destruction on the Sea-Bed and the Ocean Floor and in the Subsoil Thereof, attached to the report,
Convinced that this Treaty will further the purposes and principles of the Charter of the United Nations,

1. *Commends* the Treaty on the Prohibition of the Emplacement of Nuclear Weapons and Other Weapons of Mass Destruction on the Sea-Bed and the Ocean Floor and in the Subsoil Thereof, the text of which is annexed to the present resolution;

2. *Requests* the depositary Governments to open the Treaty for signature and ratification at the earliest possible date;

3. *Expresses the hope* for the widest possible adherence to the Treaty.

ANNEX

Treaty on the Prohibition of the Emplacement of Nuclear Weapons

and Other Weapons of Mass Destruction on the Sea-Bed and the Ocean Floor and in the Subsoil Thereof

The States Parties to this Treaty,
Recognizing the common interest of mankind in the progress of the exploration and use of the sea-bed and the ocean floor for peaceful purposes,
Considering that the prevention of a nuclear arms race on the sea-bed and the ocean floor serves the interests of maintaining world peace, reduces international tensions, and strengthens friendly relations among States,
Convinced that this Treaty constitutes a step towards the exclusion of the sea-bed, the ocean floor and the subsoil thereof from the arms race,
Convinced that this Treaty constitutes a step towards a treaty on general and complete disarmament under strict and effective international control, and determined to continue negotiations to this end,
Convinced that this Treaty will further the purposes and principles of the Charter of the United Nations, in a manner consistent with the principles of international law and without infringing the freedom of the high seas,
Have agreed as follows:

Article I

1. The States Parties to this Treaty undertake not to emplant or emplace on the sea-bed and the ocean floor and in the subsoil thereof beyond the outer limit of a sea-bed zone as defined in Article II any nuclear weapons or any other types of weapons of mass destruction as well as structures, launching installations or any other facilities specifically designed for storing, testing or using such weapons.

2. The undertakings of paragraph 1 of this Article shall also apply to the sea-bed zone referred to in the same paragraph, except that within such sea-bed zone, they shall not apply either to the coastal State or to the sea-bed beneath its territorial waters.

3. The States Parties to this Treaty undertake not to assist, encourage or induce any State to carry out activities referred to in paragraph 1 of this Article and not to participate in any other way in such actions.

Article II

For the purpose of this Treaty the outer limit of the sea-bed zone referred to in Article I shall be the coterminous with the twelve-mile outer limit of the zone referred to in Part II of the Convention on the Territorial Sea and the Contiguous Zone, signed in

Geneva on 29 April 1958, and shall be measured in accordance with the provisions of Part I, Section II, of this Convention and in accordance with international law.

Article III

1. In order to promote the objectives of and ensure compliance with the provisions of this Treaty, each State Party to the Treaty shall have the right to verify through observation the activities of the States Parties to the Treaty on the sea-bed and the ocean floor and in the subsoil thereof beyond the zone referred to in Article I, provided that observation does not interfere with such activities.

2. If after such observation reasonable doubts remain concerning the fulfilment of the obligations assumed under the Treaty, the State Party having such doubts and the State Party that is responsible for the activities giving rise to the doubts shall consult with a view to removing the doubts. If the doubts persist, the State Party having such doubts shall notify the other States Parties, and the Parties concerned shall co-operate on such further procedures for verification as may be agreed, including appropriate inspection of objects, structures, installations or other facilities that reasonably may be expected to be of a kind described in Article I. The Parties in the region of the activities, including any coastal State, and any other Party so requesting, shall be entitled to participate in such consultation and co-operation. After completion of the further procedures for verification, an appropriate report shall be circulated to other Parties by the Party that initiated such procedures.

3. If the State responsible for the activities giving rise to the reasonable doubts is not identifiable by observation of the object, structure, installation or other facility, the State Party having such doubts shall notify and make appropriate inquiries of States Parties in the region of the activities and of any other State Party. If it is ascertained through these inquiries that a particular State Party is responsible for the activities, that State Party shall consult and co-operate with other Parties as provided in paragraph 2 of this Article. If the identity of the State responsible for the activities cannot be ascertained through these inquiries, then further verification procedures, including inspection, may be undertaken by the inquiring State Party, which shall invite the participation of the Parties in the region of the activities, including any coastal State, and of any other Party desiring to co-operate.

4. If consultation and co-operation pursuant to paragraphs 2 and 3 of this Article have not removed the doubts concerning the activities and there remains a serious question concerning fulfilment of the obligations assumed under this Treaty, a State Party may, in accordance with the provisions of the Charter of the United Nations, refer the matter to the Security Council, which may take action in accordance with the Charter.

5. Verification pursuant to this Article may be undertaken by any State Party using its own means, or with the full or partial assistance of any other State Party, or through appropriate international procedures within the framework of the United Nations and in accordance with its Charter.

6. Verification activities pursuant to this Treaty shall not interfere with activities of other States Parties and shall be conducted with due regard for rights recognized under international law including the freedoms of the high seas and the rights of coastal States with respect to the exploration and exploitation of their continental shelves.

Article IV

Nothing in this Treaty shall be interpreted as supporting or prejudicing the position of any State Party with respect to existing international conventions, including the 1958 Convention on the Territorial Sea and the Contiguous Zone, or with respect to right or claims which such State Party may assert, or with respect to recognition or non-recognition of rights or claims asserted by any other State, related to waters off its coasts; including inter alia territorial seas and contiguous zones, or the sea-bed and the ocean floor, including continental shelves.

Article V

The Parties of this Treaty undertake to continue negotiations in good faith concerning further measures in the field of disarmament for the prevention of an arms race on the sea-bed, the ocean floor and the subsoil thereof.

Article VI

Any State Party may propose amendments to this Treaty. Amendments shall enter into force for each State Party accepting the amendments upon their acceptance by a majority of the States Parties to the Treaty and thereafter for each remaining State Party on the date of acceptance by it.

Article VII

Five years after the entry into force of this Treaty,

a conference of Parties to the Treaty shall be held in Geneva, Switzerland, in order to review the operation of this Treaty with a view to assuring that the purposes of the preamble and the provisions of the Treaty are being realized. Such review shall take into account any relevant technological developments. The review conference shall determine in accordance with the views of a majority of those Parties attending whether and when an additional review conference shall be convened.

Article VIII

Each State Party to this Treaty shall in exercising its national sovereignty have the right to withdraw from this Treaty if it decides that extraordinary events related to the subject matter of this Treaty have jeopardized the supreme interests of its country. It shall give notice of such withdrawal to all other States Parties to the Treaty and to the United Nations Security Council three months in advance. Such notice shall include a statement of the extraordinary events it considers to have jeopardized its supreme interests.

Article IX

The provisions of this Treaty shall in no way affect the obligations assumed by States Parties to the Treaty under international instruments establishing zones free from nuclear weapons.

Article X

1. This Treaty shall be open for signature to all States. Any State which does not sign the Treaty before its entry into force in accordance with paragraph 3 of this Article may accede to it at any time.

2. This Treaty shall be subject to ratification by signatory States. Instruments of ratification and of accession shall be deposited with the Governments of the Union of Soviet Socialist Republics, the United Kingdom of Great Britain and Northern Ireland and the United States of America, which are hereby designated the Depositary Governments.

3. This Treaty shall enter into force after the deposit of instruments of ratification by twenty-two Governments, including the Governments designated as Depositary Governments of this Treaty.

4. For States whose instruments of ratification or accession are deposited after the entry into force of this Treaty it shall enter into force on the date of the deposit of their instruments of ratification or accession.

5. The Depositary Governments shall promptly inform the Governments of all signatory and acceding States of the date of each signature, of the date of deposit of each instrument of ratification or of accession, of the date of the entry into force of this Treaty, and of the receipt of other notices.

6. This Treaty shall be registered by the Depositary Governments pursuant to Article 102 of the Charter of the United Nations.

Article XI

This Treaty, the Chinese, English, French, Russian and Spanish texts of which are equally authentic, Governments. Duly certified copies of this Treaty shall be transmitted by the Depositary Governments to the Governments of the States signatory and acceding thereto.

Agreements to Reduce Risk of Nuclear War Between the United States and the Union of Soviet Socialist Republics

Date of signature: September 30, 1971
Place of signature: Washington, DC
Signatory states: The United States, The Soviet Union

The United States of America and the Union of Soviet Socialist Republics, hereinafter referred to as the Parties:
Taking into account the devastating consequences that nuclear war would have for all mankind, and recognizing the need to exert every effort to avert the risk of outbreak of such a war, including measures to guard against accidental or unauthorized use of nuclear weapons,
Believing that agreement on measures for reducing the risk of outbreak of nuclear war serves the interests of strengthening international peace and security, and is in no way contrary to the interests of any other country,
Bearing in mind that continued efforts are also needed in the future to seek ways of reducing the risk of outbreak of nuclear war,
Having agreed as follows:

Article 1

Each Party undertakes to maintain and to improve, as it deems necessary, its existing organizational and technical arrangements to guard against the accidental or unauthorized use of nuclear weapons under its control.

Article 2

The Parties undertake to notify each other immediately in the event of an accidental, unauthorized or any other unexplained incident involving a possible detonation of a nuclear weapon which could create a risk of outbreak of nuclear war. In the event of such an incident, the Party whose nuclear weapon is involved will immediately make every effort to take necessary measures to render harmless or destroy such weapon without its causing damage.

Article 3

The Parties undertake to notify each other immediately in the event of detection by missile warning systems of unidentified objects, or in the event of signs of interference with these systems or with related communications facilities, if such occurrences could create a risk of outbreak of nuclear war between the two countries.

Article 4

Each Party undertakes to notify the other Party in advance of any planned missile launches if such launches will extend beyond its national territory in the direction of the other Party.

Article 5

Each Party, in other situations involving unex-plained nuclear incidents, undertakes to act in such a manner as to reduce the possibility of its actions being misinterpreted by the other Party. In any such situation, each Party may inform the other Party or request information when, in its view, this is warranted by the interests of averting the risk of outbreak of nuclear war.

Article 6

For transmission of urgent information, notifications and requests for information in situations requiring prompt clarification, the Parties shall make primary use of the Direct Communication Link between the Governments of the United States of America and the Union of Soviet Socialist Republics.

For transmission of other information, notifications and requests for information, the Parties, at their own discretion, may use any communications facilities, including diplomatic channels, depending on the degree of urgency.

Article 7

The Parties undertake to hold consultations, as mutually agreed, to consider questions relating to implementation of the provisions of this Agreement, as well as to discuss possible amendments thereto aimed ar further implementation of the purposes of this Agreement.

Article 8

This Agreement shall be of unlimited duration.

Article 9

This Agreement shall enter into force upon signature.

Agreement Between the United States of America and the Union of Soviet Socialist Republics on Measures to Improve the USA-USSR Direct Communications Link

Date of signature: September 30, 1971
Place of signature: Washington
Signatory states: The United States, The Union of Soviet Socialist Republics
Date of entry into force: September 30, 1971

The United States of America and the Union of Soviet Socialist Republics, herein after referred to as the Parties,

Noting the positive experience gained in the process of operating the existing Direct Communications Link between the United States of America and the Union of Soviet Socialist Republics, which was established for use in time of emergency pursuant to the Memorandum of Understanding Regarding the Establishment of a Direct Communications Link, signed on June 20, 1964,

Having examined, in a spirit of mutual understanding, matters relating to the improvement and modern-ization of the Direct Communications Link,

Having agreed as follows:

Article I

1. For the purpose of increasing the reliability of the Direct Communications Link, there shall be established and put into operation the following:

(a) Two additional circuits between the United States of America and the Union of Soviet Socialist Republics each using a satellite communications system, with each Party selecting a satellite communications system of its own choice,

(b) A system of terminals (more than one) in the territory of each Party for the Direct Communications Link, with the locations and number of terminals in the United State of America to be determined by the United States side, and the locations and number of terminals in the Union of Soviet Socialist Republics to be determined by the Soviet side.

2. Matters relating to the implementation of the aforementioned improvements of the Direct Communications Link are set forth in the Annex which is attached hereto and forms an integral part hereof.

Article II

Each Party confirms its intention to take all possible measures to assure the continuous and reliable operation, of the communications circuits and the system of terminals of the Direct Communications Link for which it is responsible in accordance with this Agreement and the Annex hereto, as well as to communicate to the head of its Government any messages received via the Direct Communications Link from the head of Government of the other Party.

Article III

The Memorandum of Understanding Between the United States of America and the Union of Soviet Socialist Republics Regarding the Establishment of a Direct Communications Link, signed on June 20, 1963, with the Annex thereto, shall remain in force, except to the extent that its provisions are modified by this Agreement and Annex hereto.

Article IV

The undertakings of the Parties hereunder shall be carried out in accordance with their respective Constitutional processes.

Article V

This Agreement, including the Annex hereto, shall enter into force upon signature.

Convention on the Prohibition of the Development, Production and Stockpiling of Bacteriological (Biological) and Toxin Weapons and on their Destruction

Also known as: Biological Weapons Convention
Date of signature: April 10, 1972
Place of signature: London, Moscow, and Washington, DC
Signatory states: Afghanistan, Argentina, Australia, Austria, Barbados, Belgium, Benin, Bolivia, Botswana, Brazil, Bulgaria, Burma, Burundi, Byelorussia, Canada, Central African Republic, Chile, Congo, Costa Rica, Cuba, Cyprus, Czechoslovakia, Denmark, Dominican Republic, Ecuador, Egypt, El Salvador, Ethiopia, Fiji, Finland, Gabon, Gambia, German Democratic Republic, Federal Republic of Germany, Ghana, Greece, Guatemala, Guyana, Haiti, Honduras,

Hungary, Iceland, India, Indonesia, Iran, Iraq, Ireland, Italy, Ivory Coast, Japan, Jordan, Kampuchea, Republic of Korea, Kuwait, Laos, Lebanon, Lesotho, Liberia, Luxembourg, Madagascar, Malawi, Malaysia, Malai, Malta, Mauritius, Mexico, Mongolia, Morocco, Nepal, Netherlands, New Zealand, Nicaragua, Niger, Nigeria, Norway, Pakistan, Panama, Peru, Philippines, Poland, Portugal, Qatar, Romania, Rwanda, San Marino, Saudi Arabia, Senegal, Sierra Leone, Singapore, Somalia, South Africa, Soviet Union, Spain, Sri Lanka, Sweden, Switzerland, Syria, Taiwan, Tanzania, Thailand, Togo, Tunisia, Turkey, Ukraine, United Arab Emirates, United Kingdom, United States, Venezuela,

Yemen Arab Republic, People's Democratic Republic of Yemen, Yugoslavia, Zaire
Ratifications: *Afghanistan, Argentina, Australia, Austria, Barbados, Belgium, Benin, Bhutan, Bolivia, Brazil, Bulgaria, Byelorussia, Canada, Cape Verde, Chile, Congo, Costa Rica, Cuba, Cyprus, Czechoslovakia, Denmark, Dominican Republic, Ecuador, Ethiopia, Fiji, Finland, German Democratic Republic, Ghana, Greece, Guatemala, Guinea-Bissau, Honduras, Hungary, Iceland, India, Iran, Ireland, Italy, Jamaica, Jordan, Kenya, Kuwait, Laos, Lebanon, Lesotho, Luxembourg, Malta, Mauritius, Mexico, Mongolia, Netherlands, New Zealand, Nicaragua, Niger, Nigeria, Norway, Pakistan, Panama, Papua New Guinea, Paraguay, Philippines, Poland, Portugal, Qatar, Romania, Rwanda, San Marino, Sao Tome, Saudi Arabia, Senegal, Seychelles, Sierra Leone, Singapore, Solomon Islands, South Africa, Soviet Union, Spain, Sweden, Switzerland, Taiwan, Thailand, Togo, Tonga, Tunisia, Turkey, Ukraine, United Kingdom, United States, Uruguay, Venezuela, Vietnam, People's Democratic Republic of Yemen, Yugoslavia, Zaire*
Date of entry into force: *March 26, 1975*

The General Assembly,
Recalling its resolution 2662 (XXV) of 7 December 1970,
Convinced of the importance and urgency of eliminating from the arsenals of States, through effective measures, such dangerous weapons of mass destruction as those using chemical or bacteriological (biological) agents,
Having considered the report of the Conference of the Committee on Disarmament dated 6 October 1971, and being appreciative of its work on the draft Convention on the Prohibition of the Development, Production and Stockpiling of Bacteriological (Biological) and Toxin Weapons and on Their Destruction, annexed to the report,
Recognizing the important significance of the Protocol for the Prohibition of the Use in War of Asphyxiating, Poisonous or Other Gases, and of Bacteriological Methods of Warfare, signed at Geneva on 17 June 1925, and conscious also of the contribution which the said Protocol has already made, and continues to make, to mitigating the horrors of war,
Noting that the Convention provides for the parties to reaffirm their adherence to the principles and objectives of that Protocol and to call upon all States to comply strictly with them,
Further noting that nothing in the Convention shall be interpreted as in any way limiting or detracting from the obligations assumed by any State under the Geneva Protocol,
Determined, for the sake of all mankind, to exclude completely the possibility of bacteriological (biological) agents and toxins being used as weapons,
Recognizing that an agreement on the prohibition of bacteriological (biological) and toxin weapons represents a first possible step towards the achievement of agreement on effective measures also for the prohibition of the development, production and stockpiling of chemical weapons,
Noting that the Convention contains an affirmation of the recognized objective of effective prohibition of chemical weapons and, to this end, an undertaking to continue negotiations in good faith with a view to reaching early agreement on effective measures for the prohibition of their development, production and stockpiling and for their destruction, and on appropriate measures concerning equipment and means of delivery specifically designed for the production or use of chemical agents for weapons purposes,
Convinced that the implementation of measures in the field of disarmament should release substantial additional resources which should promote economic and social development, particularly in the developing countries,
Convinced that the Convention will contribute to the realization of the purposes and principles of the Charter of the United Nations,

1. *Commends* the Convention on the Prohibition of the Development, Production and Stockpiling of Bacteriological (Biological) and Toxin Weapons and on Their Destruction, the text of which is annexed to the present resolution;

2. *Requests* the depositary Governments to open the Convention for signature and ratification at the earliest possible date;

3. *Expresses the hope* for the widest possible adherence to the Convention.

ANNEX

Convention on the Prohibition of the Development, Production and Stockpiling of Bacteriological (Biological) and Toxin Weapons and on Their Destruction

The States Parties to this Convention,

Determined to act with a view to achieving effective progress towards general and complete disarmament, including the prohibition and elimination of all types of weapons of mass destruction, and convinced that the prohibition of the development, production and stockpiling of chemical and bacteriological (biological) weapons and their elimination, through effective measures, will facilitate the achievement of general and complete disarmament under strict and effective international control,

Recognizing the important significance of the Protocol for the Prohibition of the Use in War of Asphyxiating, Poisonous or Other Gases, and of Bacteriological Methods of Warfare, signed at Geneva on 17 June 1925, and conscious also of the contribution which the said Protocol has already made, and continues to make, to mitigating the horrors of war,

Reaffirming their adherence to the principles and objectives of that protocol and calling upon all States to comply strictly with them,

Recalling that the General Assembly of the United Nations has repeatedly condemned all actions contrary to the principles and objectives of the Geneva Protocol of 17 June 1925,

Desiring to contribute to the strengthening of confidence between peoples and the general improvement of the international atmosphere,

Desiring also to contribute to the realization of the purposes and principles of the Charter of the United Nations,

Convinced of the importance and urgency of eliminating from the arsenals of States, through effective measures, such dangerous weapons of mass destruction as those using chemical or bacteriological (biological) agents,

Recognizing that an agreement on the prohibition of bacteriological (biological) and toxin weapons represents a first possible step towards the achievement of agreement on effective measures also for the prohibition of the development, production and stockpiling of chemical weapons, and determined to continue negotiations to that end,

Determined, for the sake of all mankind, to exclude completely the possibility of bacteriological (biological) agents and toxins being used as weapons,

Convinced that such use would be repugnant to the conscience of mankind and that no effort should be spared to minimize this risk,

Have agreed as follows:

Article I

Each State Party to this Convention undertakes never in any circumstances to develop, produce, stockpile or otherwise acquire or retain:

1. Microbiological or other biological agents, or toxins whatever their origin or method of production, of types and in quantities that have no justification for prophylactic, protective or other peaceful purposes;

2. Weapons, equipment or means of delivery designed to use such agents or toxins for hostile purposes or in armed conflict.

Article II

Each State Party to this Convention undertakes to destroy or to divert to peaceful purposes, as soon as possible but not later than nine months after the entry into force of the convention, all agents, toxins, weapons, equipment and means of delivery specified in Article I of the Convention, which are in its possession or under its jurisdiction or control. In implementing the provisions of this Article all necessary safety precautions shall be observed to protect populations and the environment.

Article III

Each State Party to this Convention undertakes not to transfer to any recipient whatsoever, directly or indirectly, and not in any way to assist, encourage, or induce any State, group of States or international organizations to manufacture or otherwise acquire any of the agents, toxins, weapons, equipment or means of delivery specified in Article I of the Convention.

Article IV

Each State Party to this Convention shall, in accordance with its constitutional processes, take any necessary measures to prohibit and prevent the development, production, stockpiling, acquisition or retention of the agents, toxins, weapons, equipment and means of delivery specified in Article I of the Convention, within the territory of such State, under its jurisdiction or under its control anywhere.

Article V

The States Parties to this Convention undertake to consult one another and to co-operate in solving any problems which may arise in relation to the objective of, or in the application of the provisions of, the Convention. Consultation and co-operation pursuant to this Article may also be undertaken through appropriate international procedures within the framework of the United Nations and in accordance with its Charter.

Article VI

(1) Any State Party to this Convention which finds that any other State Party is acting in breach of obligations deriving from the provisions of the Convention may lodge a complaint with the Security Council of the United Nations. Such a complaint should include all possible evidence confirming its validity, as well as a request for its consideration by the Security Council.

(2) Each State Party to this Convention undertakes to co-operate in carrying out any investigation which the Security Council may initiate, in accordance with the provisions of the Charter of the United Nations, on the basis of the complaint received by the Council. The Security Council shall inform the States Parties to the Convention of the results of the investigation.

Article VII

Each State Party to this Convention undertakes to provide or support assistance, in accordance with the United Nations Charter, to any Party to the Convention which so requests, if the Security Council decides that such Party has been exposed to danger as a result of violation of the Convention.

Article VIII

Nothing in this Convention shall be interpreted as in any way limiting or detracting from the obligations assumed by any State under the Protocol for the Prohibition of the Use in War of Asphyxiating, Poisonous or Other Gases, and of Bacteriological Methods of Warfare, signed at Geneva on 17 June 1925.

Article IX

Each State Party to this Convention affirms the recognized objective of effective prohibition of chemical weapons and, to this end, undertakes to continue negotiations in good faith with a view to reaching early agreement on effective measures for the prohibition of their development, production and stockpiling and for their destruction, and on appropriate measures concerning equipment and means of delivery specifically designed for the production or use of chemical agents for weapons purposes.

Article X

(1) The States Parties to this Convention undertake to facilitate, and have the right to participate in, the fullest possible exchange of equipment, materials and scientific and technological information for the use of bacteriological (biological) agents and toxins for peaceful purposes. Parties to the Convention in a position to do so shall also co-operate in contributing individually or together with other States or international organizations to the further development and application of scientific discoveries in the field of bacteriology (biology) for the prevention of disease, or for other peaceful purposes.

(2) This Convention shall be implemented in a manner designed to avoid hampering the economic or technological development of States Parties to the Convention or international co-operation in the field of peaceful bacteriological (biological) activities, including the international exchange of bacteriological (biological) agents and toxins and equipment for the processing, use or production of bacteriological (biological) agents and toxins for peaceful purposes in accordance with the provisions of the Convention.

Article XI

Any State Party may propose amendments to this Convention. Amendments shall enter into force for each State Party accepting the amendments upon their acceptance by a majority of the States Parties to the Convention and thereafter for each remaining State Party on the date of acceptance by it.

Article XII

Five years after the entry into force of this Convention, or earlier if it is requested by a majority of Parties to the Convention by submitting a proposal to this effect to the Depositary Governments, a conference of State Parties to the Convention shall be held at Geneva, Switzerland, to review the operation of the Convention, with a view to assuring that the purposes of the preamble and the provisions of the Convention, including the provisions concerning negotiations on chemical weapons, are being realized. Such review shall take into account any new scientific and technological developments relevant to the Convention.

Article XIII

(1) This Convention shall be of unlimited duration.

(2) Each State Party to this Convention shall in exercising its national sovereignty have the right to withdraw from the Convention if it decides that

extraordinary events, related to the subject matter of the Convention, have jeopardized the supreme interests of its country. It shall give notice of such withdrawal to all other States Parties to the Convention and to the United Nations Security Council three months in advance. Such notice shall include a statement of the extraordinary events it regards as having jeopardized its supreme interests.

Article XIV

(1) This Convention shall be open to all States for signature. Any State which does not sign the Convention before its entry into force in accordance with paragraph 3 of this Article may accede to it at any time.

(2) This Convention shall be subject to ratification by signatory States. Instruments of ratification and instruments of accession shall be deposited with the Governments of the Union of Soviet Socialist Republics, the United Kingdom of Great Britain and Northern Ireland and the United States of America, which are hereby designated the Depositary Governments.

(3) This Convention shall enter into force after the deposit of instruments of ratification by twenty-two Governments, including the Governments designated as Depositaries of the Convention.

(4) For States whose instruments of ratification or accession are deposited subsequent to the entry into force of this Convention, it shall enter into force on the date of the deposit of their instruments of ratification or accession.

(5) The Depositary Governments shall promptly inform all signatory and acceding States of the date of each signature, the date of deposit of each instrument of ratification or of accession and the date of the entry into force of this Convention, and of the receipt of other notices.

(6) This Convention shall be registered by the Depositary Governments pursuant to Article 102 of the Charter of the United Nations.

Article XV

This Convention, the Chinese, English, French, Russian and Spanish texts of which are equally authentic, shall be deposited in the archives of the Depositary Governments. Duly certified copies of the Convention shall be transmitted by the Depositary Governments to the Governments of the signatory and acceding States.

Agreement Between the Government of the United States of America and the Government of the Union of Soviet Socialist Republics on the Prevention of Incidents on and over the High Seas

Date of signature: May 25, 1972
Place of signature: Moscow
Signatory states: The United States, The Soviet Union

[The signatories],
Desiring to assure the safety of navigation of the ships of their respective armed forces on the high seas and flight of their military aircraft over the high seas, and
Guided by the principles and rules of international law,
Have decided to conclude this Agreement and have agreed as follows:

Article I

For the purposes of this Agreement, the following definitions shall apply:

1. "Ship" means:

(a) A warship belonging to the naval forces of the Parties bearing the external marks distinguishing warships of its nationality, under the command of an officer duly commissioned by the government and whose name appears in the Navy list, and manned by a crew who are under regular naval discipline;

(b) Naval auxiliaries of the Parties, which include all naval ships authorized to fly the naval auxiliary flag where such a flag has been established by either Party.

2. "Aircraft" means all military manned heavier-than-air and lighter-than-air craft, excluding space craft.

3. "Formation" means an ordered arrangement of two or more ships proceeding together and normalxly maneuvered together.

Article II

The Parties shall take measures to instruct the commanding officers of their respective ships to observe strictly the letter and spirit of the International Regulations for Preventing Collisions at Sea, hereinafter referred to as the Rules of the Road. The Parties recognize that their freedom to conduct operations on the high seas is based on the principles established under recognized international law and codified in the 1958 Geneva Convention on the High Seas.

Article III

1. In all cases ships operating in proximity to each other, except when required to maintain course and speed under the Rules of the Road, shall remain well clear to avoid risk of collision.

2. Ships meeting or operating in the vicinity of a formation of the other Party shall, while conforming to the Rules of the Road, avoid maneuvering in a manner which would hinder the evolutions of the formation.

3. Formations shall not conduct maneuvers through areas of heavy traffic where internationally recognized traffic separation schemes are in effect.

4. Ships engaged in surveillance of other ships shall stay at a distance which avoids the risk of collision and also shall avoid executing maneuvers embarrassing or endangering the ships under surveillance. Except when required to maintain course and speed under the Rules of the Road, a surveillant shall take positive early action so as, in the exercise of good seamanship, not to embarrass or endanger ships under surveillance.

5. When ships of both Parties maneuver in sight of one another, such signals (flag, sound, and light) as are prescribed by the Rules of the Road, the International Code of Signals, or other mutually agreed signals, shall be adhered to for signalling operations and intentions.

6. Ships of the Parties shall not simulate attacks by aiming guns, missile launchers, torpedo tubes, and other weapons in the direction of a passing ship of the other Party, not launch any object in the direction of passing ships of the other Party, and not use searchlights or other powerful illumination devices to illuminate the navigation bridges of passing ships of the other Party.

7. When conducting exercises with submerged submarines, exercising ships shall show the appropriate signals prescribed by the International Code of Signals to warn ships of the presence of submarines in the area.

8. Ships of one Party when approaching ships of the other Party conducting operations as set forth in Rule 4 (c) of the Rules of the Road, and particularly ships engaged in launching or landing aircraft as well as ships engaged in replenishment underway, shall take appropriate measures not to hinder maneuvers of such ships and shall remain well clear.

Article IV

Commanders of aircraft of the parties shall use the greatest caution and prudence in approaching aircraft and ships of the other Party operating on and over the high seas, in particular, ships engaged in launching or landing aircraft, and in the interest of mutual safety shall not permit: simulated attacks by the simulated use of weapons against aircraft and ships, or performance of various aerobatics over ships, or dropping various objects near them in such a manner as to be hazardous to ships or to constitute a hazard to navigation.

Article V

1. Ships of the Parties operating in sight of one another shall raise proper signals concerning their intent to begin launching or landing aircraft.

2. Aircraft of the Parties flying over the high seas in darkness or under instrument conditions shall, whenever feasible, display navigation lights.

Article VI

Both Parties shall:

1. Provide through the established system of radio broadcasts of information and warning to mariners, not less than 3 to 5 days in advance as a rule, notification of actions on the high seas which represent a danger to navigation or to aircraft in flight.

2. Make increased use of the informative signals contained in the International Code of Signals to signify the intentions of their respective ships when maneuvering in proximity to one another. At night, or in conditions of reduced visibility, or under conditions of lighting and such distances when signal flags are not distinct, flashing light should be used to inform ships of maneuvers which may hinder the movements of others or involve a risk of collision.

3. Utilize on a trial basis signals additional to those in the International Code of Signals, submitting such signals to the Intergovernmental Maritime Consultative Organization for its consideration and for the information of other States.

Article VII

The Parties shall exchange appropriate information concerning instances of collision, incidents which result in damage, or other incidents at sea between ships and aircraft of the Parties. The United States Navy shall provide such information through the Soviet Naval Attache in Washington and the Soviet Navy shall provide such information through the United States Naval Attache in Moscow.

Article VIII

This Agreement shall enter into force on the date of its signature and shall remain in force for a period of three years. It will thereafter be renewed without further action by the Parties for successive periods of three years each.

This Agreement may be terminated by either Party upon six months written notice to the other Party.

Article IX

The Parties shall meet within one year after the date of the signing of this Agreement to review the implementation of its terms. Similar consultations shall be held thereafter annually, or more frequently as the Parties may decide.

Article X

The Parties shall designate members to form a Committee which will consider specific measures in conformity with this Agreement. The Committee will, as a particular part of its work, consider the practical workability of concrete fixed distances to be observed in encounters between ships, aircraft, and ships and aircraft. The Committee will meet within six months of the date of signature of this Agreement and submit its recommendations for decision by the Parties during the consultations prescribed in Article IX.

Treaty Between the United States of America and the Union of the Soviet Socialist Republics on the Limitation of Anti-Ballistic Missile Systems

Also known as: Anti-Ballistic Missile Treaty, ABM *Treaty. The first of two treaties concluding the Strategic Arms Limitation Talks (SALT 1)*
Date of signature: May 26, 1972
Place of signature: Moscow
Signatory states: The United States, The Soviet Union
Date of entry into force: October 3, 1972

[The signatories], hereinafter referred to as the Parties,

Proceeding from the premise that nuclear war would have devastating consequences for all mankind,

Considering that effective measures to limit anti-ballistic missile systems would be a substantial factor in curbing the race in strategic offensive arms and would lead to a decrease in the risk of outbreak of war involving nuclear weapons,

Proceeding from the premise that the limitation of anti-ballistic missile systems, as well as certain agreed measures with respect to the limitation of strategic offensive arms, would contribute to the creation of more favorable conditions for further negotiations on limiting strategic arms,

Mindful of their obligations under Article VI of the Treaty on the Non-Proliferation of Nuclear Weapons,

Declaring their intention to achieve at the earliest possible date the cessation of the nuclear arms race and to take effective measures toward reductions in strategic arms, nuclear disarmament, and general complete disarmament,

Desiring to contribute to the relaxation of international tension and the strengthening of trust between States,

Have agreed as follows:

Article I

1. Each Party undertakes to limit anti-ballistic missile (ABM) systems and to adopt other measures in accordance with the provisions of this Treaty.

2. Each party undertakes not to deploy ABM systems for a defense of the territory of its country and not to provide a base for such a defense, and not to deploy ABM systems for defense of an individual region except as provided for in Article III of this Treaty.

Article II

1. For the purpose of this Treaty an ABM system is a system to counter strategic ballistic missiles or their elements in flight trajectory, currently consisting of:

(a) ABM interceptor missiles, which are interceptor missiles constructed and deployed for an ABM role, or of a type tested in an ABM mode;

(b) ABM launchers, which are launchers constructed and deployed for launching ABM interceptor missiles; and

(c) ABM radars, which are radars constructed and deployed for an ABM role, or of a type tested in an ABM mode.

2. The ABM system components listed in paragraph 1 of this Article include those which are:

(a) operational;

(b) under construction;

(c) undergoing testing;

(d) undergoing overhaul, repair or conversion; or

(e) mothballed.

Article III

Each Party undertakes not to deploy ABM systems or their components except that:

(a) within one ABM system deployment area having a radius of one hundred and fifty kilometers and centered on the Party's national capital, a Party may deploy: (1) no more than one hundred ABM launchers and no more than one hundred ABM interceptor missiles at launch sites, and (2) ABM radars within no more than six ABM radar complexes, the area of each complex being circular and having a diameter of no more than three kilometers; and

(b) within one ABM, system deployment area having a radius of one hundred and fifty kilometers and containing ICBM silo launchers, a Party may deploy: (1) no more than one hundred ABM launchers and no more than one hundred ABM interceptor missiles at launch sites, (2) two large phased-array ABM radars comparable in potential to corres-ponding ABM radars operational or under construction on the date of signature of the Treaty in an ABM system deployment area containing ICBM silo launchers, and (3) no more than eighteen ABM radars each having a potential less than the potential of the smaller of the above-mentioned two large phased array ABM radars.

Article IV

The limitations provided for in Article III shall not apply to ABM systems or their components used for development or testing, and located within current or additionally agreed test ranges. Each Party may have no more than a total of fifteen ABM launchers at test ranges.

Article V

1. Each Party undertakes not to develop, test, or deploy ABM systems or components which are seabased, air-based, space-based, or mobile land-based.

2. Each Party undertakes not to develop, test, or deploy ABM launchers for launching more than one ABM interceptor missile at a time from each launcher, nor to modify deployed launchers to provide them with such a capability, nor to develop, test, or deploy automatic or semi-automatic or other similar systems for rapid reload of ABM launchers.

Article VI

To enhance assurance of the effectiveness of the limitations on ABM systems and their components provided by this Treaty, each Party undertakes:

(a) not to give missiles, launchers, or radars, other than ABM interceptor missiles, ABM launchers, or ABM radars, capabilities to counter strategic ballistic missiles or their elements in flight trajectory, and not to test them in an ABM mode; and

(b) not to deploy in the future radars for early warning of strategic ballistic missile attack except at locations along the periphery of its national territory and oriented outward.

Article VII

Subject to the provisions of this Treaty, modernization and replacement of ABM systems or their components may be carried out.

Article VIII

ABM systems or their components in excess of the numbers or outside the areas specified in this Treaty, as well as ABM systems or their components prohibited by this Treaty, shall be destroyed or dismantled under agreed procedures within the shortest possible agreed period of time.

Article IX

To assure the viability and effectiveness of this Treaty, each Party undertakes not to transfer to other

States, and not to deploy outside its national territory, ABM systems or their components limited by this Treaty.

Article X

Each Party undertakes not to assume any international obligations which would conflict with this Treaty.

Article XI

The Parties undertake to continue active negotiations for limitations on strategic offensive arms.

Article XII

1. For the purpose of providing assurance of compliance with the provisions of this Treaty, each Party shall use national technical means of verification at its disposal in a manner consistent with generally recognized principles of international law.

2. Each Party undertakes not to interfere with the national technical means of verification of the other Party operating in accordance with paragraph 1 of this Article.

3. Each Party undertakes not to use deliberate concealment measures which impede verification by national technical means of compliance with the provisions of this Treaty. This obligation shall not require changes in current construction, assembly, conversion, or overhaul practices.

Article XIII

1. To promote the objectives and implementation of the provisions of this Treaty, the Parties shall establish promptly a Standing Consultative Commission, within the framework of which they will:

(a) consider questions concerning compliance with the obligations assumed and related situations which may be considered ambiguous;

(b) provide on a voluntary basis such information as either Party considers necessary to assure confidence in compliance with the obligations assumed;

(c) consider questions involving unintended interference with national technical means of verification;

(d) consider possible changes in the strategic situa-

tion which have a bearing on the provisions of this Treaty;

(e) agree upon procedures and dates for destruction or dismantling of ABM systems or their components in cases provided for by the provisions of this Treaty;

(f) consider, as appropriate, possible proposals for further increasing the viability of this Treaty, including proposals for amendments in accordance with the provisions of this Treaty;

(g) consider, as appropriate, proposals for further measures aimed at limiting strategic arms.

2. The Parties through consultation shall establish, and may amend as appropriate, Regulations for the Standing Consultative Commission governing procedures, composition and other relevant matters.

Article XIV

1. Each Party may propose amendments to this Treaty. Agreed amendments shall enter into force in accordance with the procedures governing the entry into force of this Treaty.

2. Five years after entry into force of this Treaty, and at five-year intervals thereafter, the Parties shall together conduct a review of this Treaty.

Article XV

1. This Treaty shall be of unlimited duration.

2. Each Party shall, in exercising its national sovereignty, has the right to withdraw from this Treaty if it decides that extraordinary events related to the subject matter of this Treaty have jeopardized its supreme interests. It shall give notice of its decision to the other Party six months prior to withdrawal from the Treaty. Such notice shall include a statement of the extraordinary events the notifying Party regards as having jeopardized its supreme interests.

Article XVI

1. This Treaty shall be subject to ratification in accordance with the constitutional procedures of each Party. The Treaty shall enter into force on the day of the exchange of instruments of ratification.

2. This Treaty shall be registered pursuant to Article 102 of the Charter of the United Nations.

Interim Agreement Between the United States of America and the Union of Soviet Socialist Republics on Certain Measures with Respect to the Limitation of Strategic Offensive Arms

Also known as: Interim Agreement. The second of two treaties concluding the Strategic Arms Limitation Talks (SALT I)
Date of signature: May 26, 1972
Place of signature: Moscow
Signatory states: The United States, The Soviet Union
Date of entry into force: October 3, 1972

[The signatories], hereinafter referred to as the Parties,
Convinced that the Treaty on the Limitation of Anti-Ballistic Missile Systems and this Interim Agreement on Certain Measures with Respect to the Limitation of Strategic Offensive Arms will contribute to the creation of more favorable conditions for active negotiations on limiting strategic arms as well as to the relaxation of international tension and the strengthening of trust between States,
Taking into account the relationship between strategic offensive and defensive arms,
Mindful of their obligations under Article VI of the Treaty on the Non-Proliferation of Nuclear Weapons,
Having agreed as follows:

Article I

The Parties undertake not to start construction of additional fixed land-based intercontinental ballistic missile (ICBM) launchers after July 1, 1972.

Article II

The Parties undertake not to convert land-based launchers for light ICBMs, or for ICBMs of older types deployed prior to 1964, into land-based launchers for heavy ICBMS of types deployed after that time.

Article III

The Parties undertake to limit submarine-launched ballistic missile (SLBM) launchers and modern ballistic missile submarines to the numbers operational and under construction on the date of signature of this Interim Agreement, and in addition to launchers and submarines constructed under procedures established by the Parties as replacements for an equal number of ICBM launchers of older types deployed prior to 1964 or for launchers on older submarines.

Article IV

Subject to the provisions of this Interim Agreement, modernization and replacement of strategic offensive ballistic missiles and launchers covered by this Interim Agreement may be undertaken.

Article V

1. For the purpose of providing assurance of compliance with the provisions of this Interim Agreement, each Party shall use national technical means of verification at its disposal in a manner consistent with generally recognized principles of international law.
2. Each Party undertakes not to interfere with the national technical means of verification of the other Party operating in accordance with paragraph 1 of this Article.
3. Each Party undertakes not to use deliberate concealment measures which impede verification by national technical means of compliance with the provisions of this Interim Agreement. This obligation shall not require changes in current construction, assembly, conversion, or overhaul practices.

Article VI

To promote the objectives and implementation of the provisions of this Interim Agreement, the Parties shall use the Standing Consultative Commission established under Article XIII of the Treaty on the Limitation of Anti-Ballistic Missile Systems in accordance with the provisions of that Article.

Article VII

The Parties undertake to continue active negotiations for limitations on strategic offensive arms. The obligations provided for in this Interim Agreement shall not prejudice the scope or terms of the limitation on strategic offensive arms which may be worked out in the course of further negotiations.

Article VIII

1. This Interim Agreement shall enter into force upon exchange of written notices of acceptance by each Party, which exchange shall take place simultaneously with the exchange of instruments of ratification of the Treaty on the Limitation of Anti-Ballistic

Missile Systems.

2. This Interim Agreement shall remain in force for a period of five years unless replaced earlier by an agreement on more complete measures limiting strategic offensive arms. It is the objective of the Parties to conduct active follow-on negotiations with the aim of concluding such an agreement as soon as possible.

3. Each Party shall, in exercising its national sovereignty, have the right to withdraw from this Interim Agreement if it decides that extraordinary events related to the subject matter of this Interim Agreement have jeopardized its supreme interests. It shall give notice of its decision to the other Party six months prior to withdrawal from this Interim Agreement. Such notice shall include a statement of the extraordinary events the notifying Party regards as having jeopardized its supreme interests.

Protocol

To the Interim Agreement Between the United States of America and the Union of Soviet Socialist Republics on Certain Measures with Respect to the Limitation of Strategic Offensive Arms

[The signatories], hereinafter referred to as the Parties,

Having agreed on certain limitations relating to submarine-launched ballistic missile launchers and modern ballistic missile submarines, and to replacement procedures, in the Interim Agreement,
Have agreed as follows:

The Parties understand that, under Article III of the Interim Agreement, for the period during which that Agreement remains in force:

The US may have no more than 710 ballistic missile launchers on submarines (SLBMs) and no more than 44 modern ballistic missile submarines. The Soviet Union may have no more than 950 ballistic missile launchers on submarines and no more than 62 modern ballistic missile submarines.

Additional ballistic missile launchers on submarines up to the above-mentioned levels, in the US—over 656 ballistic missile launchers on nuclear-powered submarines, and in the USSR—over 740 ballistic missile launchers on nuclear-powered submarines, operational and under construction, may become operational as replacements for equal numbers of ballistic missile launchers of older types deployed prior to 1964 or of ballistic missile launchers on older submarines.

The deployment of modern SLBMS on any submarine, regardless of type, will be counted against the total level of SLBMs permitted for the US and the USSR.

This Protocol shall be considered an integral part of the Interim Agreement.

Basic Principles of Negotiations on the Further Limitation of Strategic Offensive Arms

Date of signature: June 21, 1973
Place of signature: Washington, DC
Signatory states: The United States, The Soviet Union

The President of the United States of America, Richard Nixon, and the General Secretary of the Central Committee of the CPSU, L. I. Brezhnev,
Having thoroughly considered the question of the further limitation of strategic arms, and the progress already achieved in the current negotiations,
Reaffirming their conviction that the earliest adoption of further limitations of strategic arms would be a major contribution in reducing the danger of an outbreak of nuclear war and in strengthening international peace and security,

Having agreed as follows:
First. The two Sides will continue active negotiations in order to work out a permanent agreement on more complete measures on the limitation of strategic offensive arms as well as their subsequent reduction, proceeding from the Basic Principles of Relations between the United States of America and the Union of Soviet Socialist Republics signed in Moscow on May 29, 1972, and from the Interim Agreement between the United States of America and the Union of Soviet Socialist Republics of May 26, 1972 on Certain Measures with Respect to the Limitation of Strategic Offensive Arms.

Over the course of the next year the two Sides will make serious efforts to work out the provisions of the permanent agreement on more complete measures on the limitation of strategic offensive arms with the objective of signing it in 1974.

Second. New agreements on the limitation of strategic offensive armaments will be based on the principles of the American-Soviet documents adopted in Moscow in May 1972 and the agreements reached in Washington in June 1973; and in particular, both Sides will be guided by the recognition of each other's equal security interests and by the recognition that efforts to obtain unilateral advantage, directly or indirectly, would be inconsistent with the strengthening of peaceful relations between the United States of America and the Union of Soviet Socialist Republics.

Third. The limitations placed on strategic offensive weapons can apply both to their quantitative aspects as well as to their qualitative improvement.

Fourth. Limitations on strategic offensive arms must be subject to adequate verification by national technical means.

Fifth. The modernization and replacement of strategic offensive arms would be permitted under conditions which will be formulated in the agreements to be concluded.

Sixth. Pending the completion of a permanent agreement on more complete measures of strategic offensive arms limitation, both Sides are prepared to reach agreements on separate measures to supplement the existing Interim Agreement of May 26, 1972.

Seventh. Each Side will continue to take necessary organizational and technical measures for preventing accidental or unauthorized use of nuclear weapons under its control in accordance with the Agreement of September 30, 1971 between the United States of America and the Union of Soviet Socialist Republics.

Agreement Between the United States of America and the Union of Soviet Socialist Republics on the Prevention of Nuclear War

Date of signature: June 22, 1973
Place of signature: Washington, DC
Signatory states: The United States, The Soviet Union

The United States of America and the Union of Soviet Socialist Republics, hereinafter referred to as the Parties,
Guided by the objectives of strengthening world peace and international security,
Conscious that nuclear war would have devastating consequences for mankind,
Proceeding from the desire to bring about conditions in which the danger of an outbreak of nuclear war anywhere in the world would be reduced and ultimately eliminated,
Proceeding from their obligations under the Charter of the United Nations regarding the maintenance of peace, refraining from the threat or use of force, and the avoidance of war, and in conformity with the agreements to which either Party has subscribed,
Proceeding from the Basic Principles of Relations between the United States of America and the Union of Soviet Socialist Republics singed in Moscow on May 29, 1972,
Reaffirming that the development of relations between the United States of America and the Union of Soviet Socialist Republics is not directed against other countries and their interests,
Have agreed as follows:

Article I

The United States and the Soviet Union agree that an objective of their policies is to remove the danger of nuclear war and of the use of nuclear weapons.

Accordingly, the Parties agree that they will act in such a manner as to prevent the development of situations capable of causing a dangerous exacerbation of their relations, as to avoid military confrontations, and as to exclude the outbreak of nuclear war between them and between either of the Parties and other countries.

Article II

The Parties agree, in accordance with Article I and to realize the objectives stated in that Article, to proceed from the premise that each Party will refrain from the threat or use of force against the other Party, against the allies of the other Party and against other countries, in circumstances which may endanger international peace and security. The Parties in the formulation of their foreign policies and in their actions in the field of international relations.

Article III

The Parties undertake to develop their relations

with each other and with countries in a way consistent with the purposes of this Agreement.

Article IV

If at any time relations between the Parties or between either Party and other countries appear to involve the risk of a nuclear conflict, or if relations between countries not parties to this Agreement appear to involve the risk of nuclear war between the United States of America and the Union of Soviet Socialist Republics or between either Party and other countries, the United States and the Soviet Union, acting in accordance with the provisions of this Agreement, shall immediately enter into urgent consultations with each other and make every effort to avert this risk.

Article V

Each Party shall be free to inform the Security Council of the United Nations, the Secretary General of the United Nations and the Governments of allied or other countries of the progress and outcome of consultations initiated in accordance with Article IV of this Agreement.

Article VI

Nothing in this Agreement shall affect or impair:

(a) the inherent right of individual or collective self-defense as envisaged by Article 51 of the Charter of the United Nations,

(b) the provisions of the Charter of the United Nations, including those relating to the maintenance or restoration of international peace and security, and

(c) the obligations undertaken by either Party towards its allies or other countries in treaties, agreements, and other appropriate documents.

Article VII

This Agreement shall be of unlimited duration.

Article VIII

This Agreement shall enter into force upon signature.

Agreement Between the United States of America and the Union of Soviet Socialist Republics on the Prevention of Nuclear War

Date of signature: June 22, 1973
Place of signature: Washington
Signatory states: The United States of America,
The Union of Soviet Socialist Republics
Date of entry into force: June 22, 1973

The United States of America and the Union of Soviet Socialist Republics, hereinafter referred to as the Parties,

Guided by the objective of strengthening world peace and international security,

Conscious that nuclear war would have devastating consequences for mankind,

Proceeding from the desire to bring about conditions in which the danger of an outbreak of nuclear war anywhere in the world would be reduced and ultimately eliminated,

Proceeding from their obligations under the Charter of the United Nations regarding the maintenance of peace, refraining from the threat or use of force, and the avoidance of war, and in conformity with the agreements to which either Party has subscribed,

Proceeding from the Basic Principles of Relations between the United States of America and the Union of Soviet Socialist Republics signed in Moscow on May 29, 1972,

Reaffirming that the development of relations between the United States of America and the Union of Soviet Socialist Republics is not directed against other countries and their interests,

Have agreed as follows:

Article I

The United States and the Soviet Union agree that an objective of their policies is to remove the danger of nuclear war and of the use of nuclear weapons.

Accordingly, the Parties agree that they will act in such a manner as to prevent the development of situations capable of causing a dangerous exacerbation of their relations, as to avoid military confrontations, and as to exclude the outbreak of nuclear war between them and between either of the Parties and other countries.

Article II

The Parties agree, in accordance with Article I and to realize the objective stated in that Article, to proceed from the premise that each Party will refrain from the threat or use of force against the other Party, against the allies of the other Party and against other countries, in circumstances which may endanger international peace and security. The Parties agree that they will be guided by these considerations in the formulation of their foreign policies and in their actions in the field of international relations.

Article III

The Parties undertake to develop their relations with each other and with other countries in a way consistent with the purposes of this Agreement.

Article IV

If at any time relations between the Parties or between either Party and other countries appear to involve the risk of a nuclear conflict, or if relations between countries not parties to this Agreement appear to involve the risk of nuclear war between the Union States of America and the Union of Soviet Socialist Republics or between either Party and other countries, the United States and the Soviet Union, acting in accordance with the provisions of this Agreement, shall immediately enter into urgent consultations with each other and make every effort to avert this risk.

Article V

Each Party shall be free to inform the Security Council of the United Nations, the Secretary General of the United Nations and the Governments of allied or another countries of the progress and outcome of consultations initiated in accordance with Article IV of this Agreement.

Article VI

Nothing in this Agreement shall affect or impair.

(a) the inherent right of individual or collective self-defense as envisaged by Article 51 of the Charter of the United Nations

(b) the provisions of the Charter of the United Nations, including those relating to the maintenance or restoration of international peace and security, and

(c) the obligations undertaken by either Party towards its allies or other countries in treaties, agreements, and other appropriate documents.

Article VII

This Agreement shall be of unlimited duration.

Article VIII

This Agreement shall enter into force upon signature.

Treaty Between the United States of America and the Union of Soviet Socialist Republics on the Limitation of Underground Nuclear Weapon Tests

Also known as: Threshold Test Ban Treaty, (TTBT)
Date of signature: July 3, 1974
Place of signature: Moscow
Signatory states: The United States, The Soviet Union

[The signatories],
Declaring their intention to achieve at the earliest possible date the cessation of the nuclear arms race and to take effective measures toward reductions in strategic arms, nuclear disarmament, and general and complete disarmament under strict and effective international control,
Recalling the determination expressed by the Parties to the 1963 Treaty Banning Nuclear Weapon Tests in the Atmosphere, in Outer Space and Under Water in its Preamble to seek to achieve the discontinuance of all test explosions of nuclear weapons for all time, and to continue negotiations to this end.
Noting that the adoption of measures for the further limitation of underground nuclear weapon tests would contribute to the achievement of these objectives and would meet the interests of strengthening peace and the further relaxation of international tension.
Reaffirming their adherence to the objective and principles of the Treaty Banning Nuclear Weapon Tests in the Atmosphere, in Outer Space and Under Water and of the Treaty on the Non-Proliferation of Nuclear Weapons,

Have agreed as follows:

Article I

1. Each Party undertakes to prohibit, to prevent, and not to carry out any underground nuclear weapon test having a yield exceeding 150 kilotons at any place under its jurisdiction of control, beginning March 31, 1976.

2. Each Party shall limit the number of its underground nuclear weapon tests to a minimum.

3. The Parties shall continue their negotiations with a view toward achieving a solution to the problem of the cessation of all underground nuclear weapon tests.

Article II

1. For the purpose of providing assurance of compliance with the provisions of the Treaty, each Party shall use national technical means of verification at its disposal in a manner consistent with the generally recognized principles of international law.

2. Each Party undertakes not to interfere with the national technical means of verification of the other Party operating in accordance with paragraph 1 of this Article.

3. To promote the objectives and implementation of the provisions of this Treaty the Parties shall, as necessary, consult with each other, make inquiries and furnish information in response to such inquiries.

Article III

The provisions of this Treaty do not extend to underground nuclear explosions carried out by the Parties for peaceful purposes. Underground nuclear explosions for peaceful purposes shall be governed by an agreement which is to be negotiated and concluded by the Parties at the earliest possible time.

Article IV

This Treaty shall be subject to ratification in accordance with the constitutional procedures of each Party. This Treaty shall enter into force on the day of the exchange of instruments of ratification.

Article V

1. This Treaty shall remain in force for a period of five years. Unless replaced earlier by an agreement in implementation of the objectives specified in paragraph 3 of Article I of this Treaty, it shall be extended for successive five-year periods unless either

Party notifies the other of its termination no later than six months prior to the expiration of the Treaty. Before the expiration of this period the Parties may, as necessary, hold consultations to consider the situation relevant to the substance of this Treaty and to introduce possible amendments to the text of the Treaty.

2. Each Party shall, in exercising its national sovereignty, have the right to withdraw from this Treaty if it decides that extraordinary events related to the subject matter of this Treaty have jeopardized its supreme interests. It shall give notice of its decision to the other Party six months prior to withdrawal from this Treaty. Such notice shall include a statement of the extraordinary events the notifying Party regards as having jeopardized its supreme interests.

3. This Treaty shall be registered pursuant to Article 102 of the Charter of the United Nations.

Protocol to the Treaty between the United States of America and the Union of Soviet Socialist Republics on the Limitation of Underground Nuclear Weapon Tests

[The signatories], hereinafter referred to as the Parties,
Having agreed to limit underground nuclear weapon tests,
Have agreed as follows:

1. For the purpose of ensuring verification of compliance with the obligations of the Parties under the Treaty by national technical means, the Parties shall, on the basis of reciprocity, exchange the following data:

a. The geographic coordinates of the boundaries of each test site and of the boundaries of the geophysically distinct testing areas therein.

b. Information on the geology of the testing areas of the sites (the rock characteristics of geological formations and the basic physical properties of the rock, i.e., density, seismic velocity, water saturation, porosity and depth of water table).

c. The geographic coordinates of underground nuclear weapon tests, after they have been conducted.

d. Yield, date, time, depth and coordinates for two nuclear weapon tests for calibration purposes from each geophysically distinct testing area where underground nuclear weapon tests have been and are to be conducted. In this connection the yield of such explosions for calibration purposes should be as near as possible to the limit defined in Article I of the Treaty and not less than one-tenth of that limit. In the case of testing areas where data are not available on two tests for calibration purposes, the data pertaining to one such test shall be exchanged, if available, and the data pertaining to the second test shall be exchanged as soon as possible after a second test having a yield in the above-mentioned range. The provisions of the Protocol shall not require the Parties to conduct tests solely for calibration purposes.

2. The Parties agree that the exchange of data pursuant to subparagraphs a, b, and d of paragraph 1 shall be carried out simultaneously with the exchange of instruments of ratification of the Treaty, as provided in Article IV of the Treaty, having in mind that the Parties shall, on the basis of reciprocity, afford each other the opportunity to familiarize themselves with these data before the exchange of instruments of ratification.

3. Should a Party specify a new test site or testing area after the entry into force of the Treaty, the data called for by subparagraphs a and b of paragraph 1 shall be transmitted to the other Party in advance of use of that site or area. The data called for by subparagraph d of paragraph 1 shall also be transmitted in advance of use of that site or area if they are available; if they are not available, they shall be transmitted as soon as possible after they have been obtained by the transmitting Party.

4. The Parties agree that the test sites of each Party shall be located at places under its jurisdiction or control and that all nuclear weapon tests shall be conducted solely within the testing areas specified in accordance with paragraph 1.

5. For the purposes of the Treaty, all underground nuclear explosions at the specified test sites shall be considered nuclear weapon tests and shall be subject to all the provisions of the Treaty relating to nuclear weapon tests. The provisions of Article III of the Treaty apply to all underground nuclear explosions conducted outside of the specified test sites, and only to such explosions.

This Protocol shall be considered an integral party of the Treaty.

Protocol to the Treaty Between the United States of America and the Union of Soviet Socialist Republics on the Limitation of Anti-Ballistic Missile Systems

Date of signature: July 3, 1974
Place of signature: Moscow
Signatory states: The United States, The Soviet Union
Date of entry into force: May 25, 1976

[The signatories],
Proceeding from the basic principles of relations between the United States of America and the Union of Soviet Socialist Republics signed on May 29, 1972,
Desiring to further the objectives of the Treaty between the United States of America and the Union of Soviet Socialist Republics on the Limitation of Anti-Ballistic Missile Systems signed on May 26, 1972, hereinafter referred to as the Treaty,
Reaffirming their conviction that the adoption of further measures for the limitation of strategic arms would contribute to strengthening international peace and security,
Proceeding from the premise that further limitation of anti-ballistic missile systems will create more favorable conditions for the completion of work on a permanent agreement on more complete measures for the limitation of strategic offensive arms,
Have agreed as follows:

Article I

1. Each Party shall be limited at any one time to a single area out of the two provided in Article III of the Treaty for deployment of anti-ballistic missile (ABM) systems or their components and accordingly shall not exercise its right to deploy an ABM system or its components in the second of the two ABM system deployment areas permitted by Article III of the Treaty, except as an exchange of one permitted area for the other in accordance with Article II of this Protocol.

2. Accordingly, except as permitted by Article II of this Protocol: The United States of America shall not deploy an ABM system or its components in the area centered on its capital, as permitted by Article III (a) of the Treaty, and the Soviet Union shall not deploy an ABM system or its components in the deployment area of intercontinental ballistic missile (ICBM) silo launchers as permitted by Article III (b) of the Treaty.

Article II

1. Each Party shall have the right to dismantle or destroy its ABM system and the components thereof in the area where they are presently deployed and to deploy an ABM system or its components in the alternative area permitted by Article III of the Treaty, provided that prior to initiation of construction, notification is given in accord with the procedure agreed to by the Standing Consultative Commission during the year beginning October 3, 1977 and ending October 2, 1978, or during any year which commences at five year intervals thereafter, those being the years for periodic review of the Treaty, as provided in Article XIV of the Treaty. This right may be exercised only once:

2. Accordingly, in the event of such notice, the United States would have the right to dismantle or destroy the ABM system and its components in the deployment area of ICBM silo launchers and to deploy and ABM system or its components in an area centered on its capital, as permitted by Article III (a) of the Treaty, and the Soviet Union would have the right to dismantle or destroy the ABM system and its components in the area centered on its capital and to deploy an ABM system or its components in an area containing ICBM silo launchers, as permitted by Article III (b) of the Treaty.

3. Dismantling or destruction and deployment of ABM systems or their components and the notification thereof shall be carried out in accordance with Article VIII of the ABM Treaty and procedures agreed to in the Standing Consultative Commission.

Article III

The rights and obligations established by the Treaty remain in force and shall be complied with by the Parties except to the extent modified by this Protocol. In particular, the deployment of an ABM system or its components within the area selected shall remain limited by the levels and other requirements established by the Treaty.

Article IV

This Protocol shall be subject to ratification in accordance with the constitutional procedures of each Party. It shall enter into force on the day of the exchange of instruments of ratification and shall thereafter be considered an integral part of the Treaty.

Document on Confidence-Building Measures and Certain Aspects of Security and Disarmament Included in the Final Act of the Conference on Security and Cooperation in Europe

Also known as: Helsinki Final Act, Document on Confidence-Building Measures
Date of signature: August 1, 1975
Place of signature: Helsinki
Signatory states: Austria, Belgium, Bulgaria, Canada, Cyprus, Czechoslovakia, Denmark, Finland, France, German Democratic Republic, Federal Republic of Germany, Greece, Holy See, Hungary, Iceland, Ireland, Italy, Liechtenstein, Luxembourg, Malta, Monaco, Netherlands, Norway, Poland, Portugal, Rumania, San Marino, Soviet Union, Spain, Sweden, Switzerland, Turkey, United Kingdom, United States, Yugoslavia

The participating States,
Desirous of eliminating the causes of tension that may exist among them and thus of contributing to the strengthening of peace and security in the world;

Determined to strengthen confidence among them and thus to contribute to increasing stability and security in Europe;

Determined further to refrain in their mutual relations, as well as in their international relations in general, from the threat or use of force against the territorial integrity or political independence of any State, or in any other manner inconsistent with the purposes of the United Nations and with the Declaration on Principles Guiding Relations between Participating States as adopted in this Final Act;

Recognizing the need to contribute to reducing the dangers of armed conflict and of misunderstanding or miscalculation of military activities which could give rise to apprehension, particularly in a situation where the participating States lack clear and timely information about the nature of such activities;

Taking into account considerations relevant to efforts aimed at lessening tension and promoting disarmament;

Recognizing that the exchange of observers by invitation at military manoeuvres will help to promote contacts and mutual understanding;

Having studied the question of prior notification of major military movements in the context of confidence-building;

Recognizing that there are other ways in which individual States can contribute further to their common objectives;

Convinced of the political importance of prior notification of major military manoeuvres for the promotion of mutual understanding and the strengthening of confidence, stability and security;

Accepting the responsibility of each of them to promote these objectives and to implement this measure, in accordance with the accepted criteria and modalities, as essentials for the realization of these objectives;

Recognizing that this measure deriving from political decision rests upon a voluntary basis;

Have adopted the following:

I

Prior notification of major military manoeuvres

They will notify their major manoeuvres to all other participating States through usual diplomatic channels in accordance with the following provisions:

Notification will be given of major military manoeuvres exceeding a total of 25,000 troops, independently or combined with any possible air or naval components (in this context the word "troops" includes amphibious and airborne troops). In the case of independent manoeuvres of amphibious or airborne troops, or of combined manoeuvres involving them, these troops will be included in this total. Furthermore, in the case of combined manoeuvres which do not reach the above total but which involve land forces together with significant numbers of either amphibious or airborne troops, or both, notification can also be given.

Notification will be given of major military manoeuvres which take place on the territory, in Europe, of any participating State as well as, if applicable, in the adjoining sea area and air space.

In the case of a participating State whose territory extends beyond Europe, prior notification need be given only of maneuvres which take place in an area within 250 kilometres from its frontier facing or shared with any other European participating State, the participating State need not, however, give notification in cases in which that area is also contiguous to the participating State's frontier facing or shared

with a non-European non-participating State.

Notification will be given 21 days or more in advance of the start of the manoeuvre or in the case of a manoeuvre arranged at shorter notice at the earliest possible opportunity prior to its starting date.

Notification will contain information of the designation, if any, the general purpose of and the States involved in the manoeuvres, the type or types and numerical strength of the forces engaged, the area and estimated time-frame of its conduct. The participating States will also, if possible, provide additional relevant information, particularly that related to the components of the forces engaged and the period of involvement of these forces.

Prior notification of other military manoeuvres

The participating States recognize that they can contribute further to strengthening confidence and increasing security and stability, and to this end may also notify smaller-scale military manoeuvres to other participating States, with special regard for those near the area of such manoeuvres.

To the same end, the participating States also recognize that they may notify other military manoeuvres conducted by them.

Exchange of observers

The participating States will invite other participating States, voluntarily and on a bilateral basis, in a spirit of reciprocity and goodwill towards all participating States, to send observers to attend military manoeuvres.

The inviting State will determine in each case the number of observers, the procedures and conditions of their participation, and give other information which it may consider useful. It will provide appropriate facilities and hospitality.

The invitation will be given as far ahead as is conveniently possible through usual diplomatic channels.

Prior notification of major military movements

In accordance with the Final Recommendations of the Helsinki Consultations the participating States studied the question of prior notification of major military movements as a measure to strengthen confidence.

Accordingly, the participating States recognize that they may, at their own discretion and with a view to contributing to confidence-building, notify their major military movements.

In the same spirit, further consideration will be given by the States participating in the Conference on Security and Co-operation in Europe to the question of prior notification of major military movements, bearing in mind, in particular, the experience gained by the implementation of the measures which are set forth in this document.

Other confidence-building measures

The participating States recognize that there are other means by which their common objectives can be promoted.

In particular, they will, with due regard to reciprocity and with a view to better mutual understanding, promote exchanges by invitation among their military personnel, including visits by military delegations.

* * *

In order to make a fuller contribution to their common objective of confidence-building, the participating States, when conducting their military activities in the area covered by the provisions for the prior notification of major military manoeuvres, will duly take into account and respect this objective.

They also recognize that the experience gained by the implementation of the provisions set forth above, together with further efforts, could lead to developing and enlarging measures aimed at strengthening confidence.

II

Question relating to disarmament

The participating States recognize the interest of all of them in efforts aimed at lessening military confrontation and promoting disarmament which are designed to complement political détente in Europe

and to strengthen their security. They are convinced of the necessity to take effective measures in these fields which by their scope and by their nature constitute steps towards the ultimate achievement of general and complete disarmament under strict and effective international control, and which should result in strengthening peace and security throughout the world.

III

General considerations

Having considered the views expressed on various subjects related to the strengthening of security in Europe through joint efforts aimed at promoting detente and disarmament, the participating States, when engaged in such efforts, will, in this context, proceed, in particular, from the following essential considerations:

—The complementary nature of the political and military aspects of security;

—The interrelation between the security of each participating State and security in Europe as a whole and the relationship which exists, in the broader context of world security, between security in Europe and security in the Mediterranean area;

—Respect for the security interests of all States participating in the Conference on Security and Cooperation in Europe inherent in their sovereign equality;

—The importance that participants in negotiating fora see to it that information about relevant developments, progress and results is provided on an appropriate basis to other States participating in the Conference on Security and Co-operation in Europe and, in return, the justified interest of any of those States in having their views considered.

Agreement Between the Government of the Republic of Korea and the International Atomic Energy Agency for the Application of Safeguards in Connection with the Treaty on the Non-Proliferation of Nuclear Weapons

Date of signature: October 31, 1975
Place of signature: Seoul
Signatory states: The Republic of Korea,
the International Atomic Energy Agency
Date of entry into force: November 14, 1975

WHEREAS the Republic of Korea is a party to the Treaty on the Non-Proliferation of Nuclear Weapons

(hereinafter referred to as "the Treaty") opened for signature at London, Moscow and Washington on 1 July 1968 and which entered into force on 5 March 1970:

WHEREAS paragraph 1 of Article 3 of the Treaty reads as follows:

"Each non-nuclear-weapon States Party to the Treaty undertakes to accept safeguards, as set forth in an agreement to be negotiated and concluded with the International Atomic Energy Agency in accordance with the Statute of the International Atomic Energy Agency in accordance with the Statute of the International Atomic Energy Agency and the Agency's safeguards system, for the exclusive purpose of verification of the fulfillment of its obligations assumed under this Treaty with a view to preventing diversion of nuclear energy from peaceful uses to nuclear weapons or other nuclear explosive devices. Procedures for the safeguards required by this Article shall be followed with respect to source or special fissionable material whether it is being produced, processed or used in any principal nuclear facility or is outside any such facility. The safeguards required by this Article shall be applied on all source or special fissionable material in all peaceful nuclear activities within the territory of such States, under its jurisdiction, or carried out under its control anywhere."

WHEREAS the International Atomic Energy Agency (hereinafter referred to as "the Agency") is authorized, pursuant to Article 3 of its Statute, to conclude such agreements;

NOW THEREFOR the Government of the Republic of Korea and the Agency have agreed as follows:

Part I

Basic Undertaking

Article 1

The Government of the Republic of Korea undertakes, pursuant to paragraph 1 of Article 3 of the Treaty, to accept safeguards, in accordance with the terms of this Agreement, on all source of special fissionable materials in all peaceful nuclear activities within its territory, under its jurisdiction or carried out under its control anywhere, for the exclusive purpose of verifying that such materials is not diverted to nuclear or other nuclear explosive devices.

Application of Safeguards

Article 2

The Agency shall have the right and the obligation to ensure that safeguards will be applied in accordance with the terms of this Agreement, on all source or special fissionable material in all peaceful nuclear activities within the territory of the Republic of Korea under its jurisdiction or carried out under its control anywhere, for the exclusive purpose of verifying that such material is not diverted to nuclear

weapons or other nuclear explosive devices.

Co-operation between the Government of the Republic of Korea and the Agency

Article 3

The Government of the Republic of Korea and the Agency shall co-operate to facilitate the implementation of the safeguards provided for in this Agreement.

Implementation of Safeguards

Article 4

The safeguards provided for in this Agreement shall be implemented in a manner designed:

(a) To avoid hampering the economic and technological development of the Republic of Korea or international co-operation in the field of peaceful nuclear activities, including international exchange of nuclear material;

(b) To avoid undue interference in the Republic of Korea's peaceful nuclear activities, and in particular in the operation of facilities; and

(c) To be consistent with prudent management practices required for the economic and safe conduct of nuclear activities.

Article 5

(a) The Agency shall take every precaution to protect commercial and industrial secrets and other confidential information coming to its knowledge in the implementation of this Agreement.

(b) (i) The Agency shall not make public or communicate to any State, organization or person any information obtained by it in connection with the implementation of this Agreement, except that specific information relating to the implementation thereof may be given to the Board of Governors of the Agency (hereinafter referred to as "the Board") and to such staff members as require such knowledge by reason of their official duties in connection with safeguards, but only to the extent necessary for the Agency to fulfill its responsibilities in implementing this Agreement.

(ii) Summarized information on nuclear material subject to safeguards under this Agreement may be published upon decision of the Board if the

States directly concerned agree thereto.

Article 6

(a) The Agency Shall, in implementing safeguards pursuant to this Agreement, take full account of technological developments in the field of safeguards, and shall make every effort to ensure optimum cost-effectiveness and the application of the principle of safeguarding effectively the flow of nuclear material subject to safeguards under this Agreement by use of instruments and other techniques at certain strategic points to the extent that present or future technology permits.

(b) In order to ensure optimum cost-effectiveness, use shall be made, for example, of such means as:

(i) Containment as a means of defining material balance areas for accounting purposes:

(ii) Statistical techniques and random sampling in evaluating the flow of nuclear material; and

(iii) Concentration of verification procedures on those stages in the nuclear fuel cycle involving the production, processing, use or storage of nuclear material from which nuclear weapons or other nuclear explosive devices could readily be make, and minimization of verification procedures in respect of other nuclear material, on condition that this does not hamper the Agency in applying safeguards under this Agreement.

National System of Materials Control

Article 7

(a) The Government of the Republic of Korea shall establish and maintain a system of accounting for and control of all nuclear material subject to safeguards under this Agreement.

(b) The Agency shall apply safeguards in such a manner as to enable it to verify, in ascertaining that there has been no diversion of nuclear material from peaceful uses to nuclear weapons or other nuclear explosive devices, findings of the Republics of Korea's system. The Agency's verification shall include, inter alia, independent measurements and observations conducted by the Agency in accordance with the procedures specified in Party II of this Agreement. The Agency, in its verification, shall take due account of the technical effectiveness of the Republic of

Korea's system.

Provision of Information to the Agency

Article 8

(a) In order to ensure the effective implementation of safeguards under this Agreement, the Government of the Republic of Korea shall, in accordance with the provisions set out in Part II of this Agreement, provide the Agency with information concerning nuclear material subject to safeguards under this Agreement and the features of facilities relevant to safeguarding such material.

(b) (i) The Agency shall require only the minimum amount of information and data consistent with carrying out its responsibilities under this Agreement.

(ii) Information pertaining to facilities shall be the minimum necessary for safeguarding nuclear material subject to safeguards under this Agreement.

(c) If the Government of the Republic of Korea so requests, the Agency shall be prepared to examine on premises of the Republic of Korea designated information which the Government of the Republic of Korea regards as being of particular sensitivity. Such information need not be physically transmitted to the Agency provided that it remains readily available for further examination by the Agency on premises of the Republic of Korea.

Agency Inspectors

Article 9

(a) (i) The Agency shall secure the consent of the Government of the Republic of Korea to the designation of Agency inspectors to the Republic of Korea

(ii) If the Government of the Republic of Korea, either upon proposal of a designation or at any other time after a designation has been made, objects to the designation, the Agency shall propose to the Government of the Republic of Korea an alternative designation or designations.

(iii) If, as a result of the repeated refusal of the Government of the Republic of Korea to accept the designation of Agency inspectors, inspections to be conducted under this Agreement would be impeded, such refusal shall be considered by the Board, upon referral by the Director General of the Agency (hereinafter referred to as "the Director General"), with a view to its taking appropriate action.

(b) The Government of the Republic of Korea shall take the necessary steps to ensure that Agency inspectors can effectively discharge their functions under this Agreement.

(c) The visits and activities of Agency inspectors shall be so arranged as:

(i) To reduce to a minimum the possible inconvenience and disturbance to the Government of the Republic of Korea and to the peaceful nuclear activities inspected; and

(ii) To ensure protection of industrial secrets or any other confidential information coming to the inspectors's knowledge.

Privileges and Immunities

Article 10

The Government of the Republic of Korea shall apply to the Agency (including its property, funds and assets) and to its inspectors and other officials, performing function under this Agreement, the relevant provisions of the Agreement on the Privileges and Immunities of the International Atomic Energy Agency.

Termination of Safeguards

Article 11

Consumption or dilution of nuclear material

Safeguards shall terminate on nuclear material upon determination by the Agency that the material has been consumed, or has been diluted in such a way that it is no longer usable for any nuclear activity from the point of view of safeguards, or has become practically irrecoverable.

Article 12

Transfer of nuclear material out of the Republic of Korea

The Government of the Republic of Korea shall give the Agency advance notification of intended transfers of nuclear material subject to safeguards under this Agreement out of the Republic of Korea,

in accordance with the provisions set out in Part II of this Agreement. The Agency shall terminate safeguards on nuclear material under this Agreement when the recipient State has assumed responsibility therefor, as provided for Part II of this Agreement. The Agency shall maintain records indicating each transfer and, where applicable, the re-application of safeguards to the transferred nuclear material.

Article 13

Provisions relating to nuclear material to be used in non-nuclear activities

Where nuclear material subject to safeguards under this Agreement is to be used in non-nuclear activities, such as the production of alloys or ceramics, the Government of the Republic of Korea shall agree with the Agency, before the material is so used, on the circumstance under which the safeguards on such material may be terminated.

Non-application of Safeguards to Nuclear Material to be used in Non-peaceful activities

Article 14

If the Government of the Republic of Korea intends to exercise its discretion to use nuclear material which is required to be safeguarded under this Agreement in a nuclear activity which does not require the application of safeguards under this Agreement, the following procedures shall apply:

(a) The Government of the Republic of Korea shall inform the Agency of the activity, making it clear;

(i) That the use of the nuclear material in a non-prescribed activity will be in conflict with an undertaking the Government of the Republic of Korea may have given and in respect of which Agency safeguards apply that the material will be used only in a peaceful nuclear activity; and

(ii) That during the period of non-application of safeguards the nuclear material will not be used for the production of the nuclear weapons or other nuclear explosive devices;

(b) The Government of the Republic of Korea and the Agency shall make an arrangement so that, only while the nuclear materials is in such an activity, the safeguards provided for in period or circumstances during which safeguards will not be applied. In any event, the safeguards provided for in this Agreement shall apply again as soon as the nuclear material is reintroduced into a peaceful nuclear activity. The Agency shall be kept informed of the total quantity and composition of such unsafeguarded material in the Republic of Korea and of any export of such material; and

(c) Even arrangement shall be made in agreement with the Agency. Such agreement shall be given as promptly as possible and shall relate only to such matters as, inter alia, temporal and procedural provisions and reporting arrangements, but shall not involve any approval or classified knowledge of the military activity or relate to the use of the nuclear material therein.

Finance

Article 15

The Government of the Republic of Korea and the Agency will bear the expenses incurred by them implementing their respective responsibilities under this Agreement. However, if the Government of the Republic of Korea or persons under its jurisdiction incur extraordinary expenses as a result of a specific request by the Agency shall reimburse such expenses provided that it has agreed in advance to do so. In any case the Agency shall bear the cost of any additional measuring or sampling which inspectors may request.

Third Party Liability for Nuclear Damage

Article 16

The Government of the Republic of Korea shall ensure that any protection against third party liability in respect of nuclear damage, including any insurance or other financial security, which may be available under its laws or regulations shall apply to the Agency and its officials for the purpose of the implementation of this Agreement in the same way as that protection applies to nationals of the Republic of Korea.

International Responsibility

Article 17

Any claim by the Government of the Republic of Korea against the Agency or by the Agency against the Government of the Republic of Korea in respect of any damage resulting from the implementation of safeguards under this Agreement, other than damage arising out of a nuclear incident, shall be settled in accordance with international law.

Measures in Relation to Verification of Non-diversion

Article 18

If the Board, upon report of the Director General, decides that an action by the Government of the Republic of Korea is essential and urgent in order to ensure verification that nuclear material subject to safeguards under this Agreement is not diverted to nuclear weapons or other nuclear explosive devices, the Board may call upon the Government of the Republic of Korea to take the required action without delay, irrespective of whether procedures have been invoked pursuant to Article 22 of this Agreement for the settlement of a dispute.

Article 19

If the Board, upon examination of relevant information reported to it by the Director General, finds that the Agency is not able to verify that there has been no diversion of nuclear material required to be safeguarded under this Agreement, to nuclear weapons or other nuclear explosive device, it may make the reports provided for in paragraph C of Article XII of the Statute of the Agency (hereinafter referred to as "the Stature") and may also take where applicable, the other measures provided for in that paragraph. In taking such action the Board shall take account of the degree of assurance provided by the safeguards measures that have been applied and shall afford the Government of the Republic of Korea every reasonable opportunity to furnish the Board with any necessary reassurance.

Interpretation and Application of the Agreement and Settlement of Disputes

Article 20

The Government of the Republic of Korea and the Agency shall, at the request of either, consult about any question arising out of the interpretation or application of this Agreement.

Article 21

The Government of the Republic of Korea shall have the right to request that any question arising out of the interpretation or application of this Agreement be considered by the Board. The Board shall invite the Government of the Republic of Korea to participate in the discussion of any such question by the Board.

Article 22

Any dispute arising out of the interpretation or application of this Agreement, except a dispute with regard to a finding by the Board under Article 19 or an action taken by the Board pursuant to such finding, which is not settled by negotiation or another procedure agreed to by the Government of the Republic of Korea and the Agency shall, at the request of either, be submitted to an arbitral tribunal composed as follows: the Government of the Republic of Korea and the Agency shall each designate one arbitrator, and the town arbitrators so designated shall elect a third, who shall be the Chairman. If, within thirty days of the request for arbitration, either the Government of the Republic of Korea or the Agency has not designated an arbitrator, either the Government of the Republic of Korea or the Agency may request the President of the International Court of Justice to appoint an arbitrator. The same procedure shall apply if, within thirty days of the designation or appointment of the second arbitrator, the third arbitrator has not been elected. A majority of the members of the arbitral tribunal shall constitute a quorum, and all decision shall require the concurrence of two arbitrators. The arbitral procedure shall be fixed by the tribunal. The decision of the tribunal shall be binding on the Government of the Republic of Korea and the Agency.

Suspension of Application of Agency Safeguards under other Agreements

Article 23

The application of Agency safeguards in the Republic of Korea under other safeguards agreements with the Agency shall be suspended while this Agreement is in force.

Review of the Operation of the Agreement

Article 24

At any time after three years from the entry into force of this Agreement, the Government of the Republic of Korea and the Agency shall, at the request of either, review jointly the operation of this Agreement.

Amendment of the Agreement

Article 25

(a) The Government of the Republic of Korea and the Agency shall, at the request of either, consult each other on amendment to this Agreement.

(b) All amendments shall require the agreement of the Government of the Republic of Korea and the Agency.

(c) Amendments to this Agreement shall enter into force in the same conditions as entry into force of the Agreement itself.

(d) Amendments to Part II of this Agreement may, if convenient to the Government of the Republic of Korea, be archived by recourse to a simplified procedure.

(e) The Director General shall promptly inform all Member States of the Agency of any amendment to this Agreement.

Entry into Force and Duration

Article 26

(a) This Agreement shall enter into force on the date upon which the Agency receives from the Government of the Republic of Korea written notification that the Republic of Korea's statutory and constitutional requirements for entry into force have been met. The Director General shall promptly inform all Members States of the Agency of the entry into force of this Agreement.

(b) This Agreement shall remain in force as long as the Republic of Korea is party to the Treaty.

Part II

Introduction

Article 27

The purpose of this part of the Agreement is to specify the procedure to be applied in the implementation of the safeguards provisions of Part I.

Objective of Safeguards

Article 28

The objective of the safeguards procedures set

forth in this part of the Agreement is the timely detection of diversion of significant quantities of nuclear material from peaceful nuclear activities to the manufacture of nuclear weapons or of other nuclear explosive devices or for purposes unknown, and deterrence of such diversion by the risk of early detection.

Article 29

For the purpose of achieving the objective set forth in Article 28, material accountancy shall be used as a safeguard measure of fundamental importance, with containment and surveillance as important complementary measures.

Article 30

The technical conclusion of the Agency's verification activities shall be a statement, in respect of each material balance area, of the amount of material unaccounted for over a specific period, and giving the limits of accuracy of the amounts stated.

National System of Accounting for and Control of Nuclear Material

Article 31

Pursuant to Article 7 the Agency, in carrying out its verification activities, shall make full use of the Republic of Korea's system of accounting for and control of all nuclear material subject to safeguards under this Agreement and shall avoid unnecessary duplication of the Republic of Korea's accounting and control activities.

Article 32

The Republic of Korea's system of accounting for and control of all nuclear material subject to safeguards under this Agreement shall be based on a structure of material balance areas, and shall make provision, as appropriate and specified in the Subsidiary Arrangements, for the establishment of such measures as:

(a) A measurement system for the determination of the quantities of nuclear material received produced, shipped, lost or otherwise removed from inventory, and the quantities on inventory;

(b) The evaluation of precision and accuracy of measurements and the estimation of measurement uncertainty;

(c) Procedures for identifying, reviewing and evaluating differences in shipper receiver measurements;

(d) Procedures for taking a physical inventory;

(e) Procedures for the evaluation of accumulations of unmeasured inventory and unmeasured losses;

(f) A system of records and reports showing, for each material balance area, the inventory of nuclear material and the changes in that inventory including receipts into and transfers out of the material balance area;

(g) Provisions to ensure that the accounting procedures and arrangements are being operated correctly; and

(h) Procedures for the provision of reports to the Agency in accordance with Article 59 to 65 and 67 to 69.

Exemptions from Safeguards

Article 36

At the request of the Government of the Republic of Korea, the Agency shall exempt nuclear material from safeguards, as follows:

(a) Special fissionable material, when it is used in gram quantities or less as a sensing component in instruments;

(b) Nuclear material, when it is used in non-nuclear activities in accordance with Article 13, if such nuclear material is recoverable; and

(c) Plutonium with an isotopic concentration of plutonium-238 exceeding 80%.

Article 37

At the request of the Government of the Republic of Korea the Agency shall exempt from safeguards nuclear material that would otherwise be subject to safeguards provided that the total quantity of nuclear material which has been exempted in the Republic of Korea in accordance with this Article may not at any time exceed

(a) One kilogram in total of special fissionable material, which may consist of one or more of the following:

(i) Plutonium

(ii) Uranium with an enrichment of 0.2 (20%) and above, taken account of by multiplying its weight by its enrichment; and

(iii) Uranium with an enrichment below 0.2 (20%) and above that of natural uranium, taken account of by multiplying its weight by five times the square of its enrichment;

(b) Ten metric tons in total of natural uranium and depleted uranium with an enrichment above 0.005 (0.5%)

(c) Twenty metric tons of depleted uranium with an enrichment of 0.005 (0.5%) or below; and

(d) Twenty metric tons of thorium;

or such greater amounts as may be specified by the Board for uniform application.

Article 38

If exempted nuclear material is to be processed or stored together with nuclear material subject to safeguards under this Agreement, provision shall be made for the reapplication of safeguards thereto.

Subsidiary Arrangements

Article 39

The Government of the Republic of Korea and the Agency shall make Subsidiary Arrangement which shall specify in detail, to the extent necessary to permit the Agency to fulfill its responsibility under this Agreement in an effective and efficient manner, how the procedures laid down in this Agreement are to be applied. The Subsidiary Arrangements may be extended or changed by agreement between the Government of the Republic of Korea and the Agency without amendment of this Agreement.

Article 40

This Subsidiary Arrangements shall enter into force at the same time as, or soon as possible after, the entry into force of this Agreement. The Government of the Republic of Korea and the Agency shall make every effort to achieve their entry into force within ninety days of the entry into force of this Agreement; an extension of that period shall require agreement between the Government of the Republic of Korea and the Agency. The Government of the Republic of Korea shall provide the Agency promptly with the information required for completing the Subsidiary Arrangements. Upon the entry into force of this Agreement, the Agency shall have the right to apply the procedure laid down therein in respect of

the nuclear material listed in the inventory provided for in Article 41, even if the Subsidiary Arrangements have not yet entered into force.

Inventory

Article 41

On the basis of the initial referred to in Article 62, the Agency shall establish a unified inventory of all nuclear material in the Republic of Korea subject to safeguards under this Agreement, irrespective of its origin, and shall maintain this inventory on the basis of subsequent reports and of the results of its verification activities. Copies of the inventory shall be made available to the Government of the Republic of Korea at intervals to be agreed.

Design Information General Provisions

Article 42

Pursuant to Article 8, design information in respect of existing facilities shall be provided to the Agency during the discussion of the Subsidiary Arrangement. The time limits for the provision of design information in respect of the new facilities shall be specified in the Subsidiary Arrangements and such information shall be provided as early as possible before nuclear material is introduced into a new facility.

Article 43

The design information to be provided to the Agency shall include, in respect of each facility, when applicable:

(a) The identification of the facility stating its general character, purpose, nominal capacity and geographic location, and the name and address to be used of routine business purposes;

(b) A description of the general arrangement of the facility with reference, to the extent feasible, to the form, location and flow of nuclear material and to the general layout of important items of equipment which use, produce or process nuclear material;

(c) A description of features of the facility relating to material accountancy, containment and surveillance; and

(d) A description of the existing and proposed procedures at the facility for nuclear material accountancy and control, with special reference to material balance areas established by the operator, measurements of flow and procedures for physical inventory taking.

Article 44

Other information relevant to the application of safeguards shall also be provided to the Agency in respect of each facility, in particular on organizational responsibility for material accountancy and control. The Government of the Republic of Korea shall provide the Agency with supplementary information on the health and safety procedures which the Agency shall observe and with which the inspectors shall comply at the facility.

Article 45

The Agency shall be provided with design information in respect of a modification relevant for safeguards purposes, for examination, and shall be informed of any change in the information provided to it under Article 44, sufficiently in advance for the safeguards procedures to be adjusted when necessary.

Article 46

Purposes of examination of design information

The design information provided to the Agency shall be used for the following purposes:

(a) To identify the features of facilities and nuclear material relevant to the application of safeguards to nuclear material in sufficient detail to facilitate verification;

(b) To determine material balance areas to be used for Agency accounting purposes under this Agreement and to select those strategic points which are key measurement points and which will be used to determine flow and inventory of nuclear material; in determining such material balance areas the Agency shall, inter alia, use the following criteria:

(i) The size of the material balance area shall be related to the accuracy with which the material balance can be established;

(ii) In determining the material balance area advantage shall be taken of any opportunity to use containment and surveillance to help ensure the completeness of flow measurements and thereby to simplify the application of safeguards and to concentrate measurement efforts at key measurement points;

(iii) A number of material balance areas in use at a facility or at distinct sites may be combined in one material balance area to be used for Agency accounting purposes when the Agency determines that this is consistent with its verification requirements; and

(iv) A special material balance area may be established at the request of the Government of the Republic of Korea around a process step involving commercially sensitive information.

(c) To establish the nominal timing and procedure for taking of physical inventory of nuclear material for Agency accounting purposes;

(d) To establish the records and reports requirements and records evaluation procedures;

(e) To establish requirements and procedures for verification of the quantity and location of nuclear material; and

(f) To select appropriate combinations of containment and surveillance methods and techniques and the strategic points at which they are to be applied.

The results of the examination of the design information, as agreed upon between the Agency and the Government of the Republic of Korea, shall be included in the Subsidiary Arrangements.

Article 47

Re-examination of design information

Designs information shall be re-examined in the light of changes in operating conditions, of developments in safeguards technology or of experience in the application of verification procedures, with a view to modifying the action the Agency has taken pursuant to Article 46.

Article 48

Verification of design information

The Agency, in co-operation with the Government of the Republic of Korea, may send inspectors to facilities to verify the design information provided to the Agency pursuant to Article 42-45, for the purposes stated in Article 46.

Information in Respect of Nuclear Material outside Facilities

Article 49

The Agency shall be provided with the following information when nuclear material is to be customarily used outside facilities, as applicable:

(a) A general description of the use of the nuclear material, its geographic locations, and the user's name and address for routine business purposes; and

(b) A general description of the existing and proposed procedure for nuclear material accountancy and control including organization responsibility for material accountancy and control.

The Agency shall be informed, on a timely basis, of any change in the information provided to it under this Articles.

Article 50

The information provided to the Agency pursuant to Article 49 may be used, to the extent relevant, for the purposes set out in Article 46 (b)~(f).

Records System

General Provisions

Article 51

In establishing its systems of material control as referred to in Article 7, the Government of the Republic of Korea shall arrange that records are kept in respect of each material balance area. The records to be kept shall be described in the Subsidiary Arrangements.

Article 52

The Government of the Republic of Korea shall make arrangements to facilitate the examination of records by inspectors, particularly if the records are not kept in English, French, Russian or Spanish.

Article 53

Records shall be retained for at least five years.

Article 54

Records shall consist, as appropriate, of:

(a) Accounting records of all nuclear material subject to safeguards under this Agreement; and

(b) Operating records for facilities containing such nuclear material.

Article 55

The system of measurements on which the records used for the preparation of reports are based shall either conform to the latest international standards or be equivalent in quality to such standards.

Accounting Records

Article 56

The accounting records shall set forth the following in respect of each material balance area:

(a) All inventory changes, so as to permit a determination of the book inventory at any time;

(b) All measurement result that are used for determination of the physical inventory; and

(c) All adjustments and corrections that have been made in respect of inventory changes, book inventories and physical inventories.

Article 57

For all inventory changes and physical inventories the records shall show, in respect of each batch of nuclear material; material identification, batch data and source data. The records shall account for uranium, thorium and plutonium separately in each batch of nuclear material. For each inventory changes, the date of the inventory change and, when appropriate, the originating material balance area and receiving material balance area or the recipient, shall be indicated.

Article 58

Operating records

The operating records shall set forth, as appropriate, in respect of each material balance area:

(a) Those operating data which are used to establish in the quantities and composition of nuclear material;

(b) The data obtained from the calibration of tanks and instruments and from sampling and analysis, the procedures to control the quality of measurements and the derived estimates of random and systematic error;

(c) A description of the sequence of the actions taken in preparing for, and in taking, a physical inventory, in order to ensure that it is correct and complete; and

(d) A description of the actions taken in order to ascertain the cause and the magnitude of any accidental or unmeasured loss that might occur.

Reports System

General Provisions

Article 59

The Government of the Republic of Korea shall provide the Agency with reports as detailed in Articles 60-69 in respect of nuclear material subject to safeguards under this Agreement.

Article 60

Reports shall be made in English.

Article 61

Reports shall be based on the records kept in accordance with Article 51-58 and shall consist, as appropriate, of accounting reports and special reports.

Accounting Reports

Article 62

The Agency shall be provided with an initial report on all nuclear material subject to safeguards under this Agreement. The initial report shall be dispatched by the Government of the Republic of Korea to the Agency within thirty days of the last day of the calendar month in which this Agreement enters into force, and shall reflect the situation as of the last day of that month.

Article 63

The Government of the Republic of Korea shall provide the Agency with the following accounting reports for each material balance area:

(a) Inventory change reports showing all changes in the inventory of nuclear material. The reports shall be dispatched as soon as possible and in any event within thirty days after the end of the month in which the inventory changes occurred or were established unless otherwise agreed in the Subsidiary Arrangements; and

(b) Material balance reports showing the material balance based on a physical inventory of nuclear material actually present in the material balance area. The reports shall be dispatched as soon as possible and in any event within thirty days after the physical inventory has been taken unless otherwise agreed in the Subsidiary Arrangements.

The reports shall be based on data available as of the date of reporting and may be corrected at a later date, as required.

Article 64

Inventory change reports shall specify identification and batch data for each batch of nuclear material, the date of the inventory change and, as appropriate, the originating material balance area and the receiving material balance area or the recipient. These reports shall be accompanied by concise notes:

(a) Explaining the inventory changes, on the basis of the operating data contained in the operating records provided for under Article 58(a); and

(b) Describing, as specified in the Subsidiary Arrangements, the anticipated operational programme, particularly the taking of a physical inventory.

Article 65

The Government of the Republic of Korea shall report each inventory change, adjustment and correction, either periodically in a consolidated list or individually. Inventory changes shall be reported in terms of batches. As specified in the Subsidiary Arrangements, small changes in inventory of nuclear material, such as transfers of analytical samples, may be combined in one batch and reported as one inventory change.

Article 66

The Agency shall provide the Government of the Republic of Korea with semiannual statements of book inventory of nuclear material subject to safeguards under this Agreement, for each material balance area, as based on the inventory change reports for the period covered by each such statement.

Article 67

Material balance reports shall include the following entries, unless otherwise agreed by the Government of the Republic of Korea and the Agency:

(a) Beginning physical inventory;

(b) Inventory changes (first increases, then decreases);

(c) Ending book inventory;

(d) Shipper/receiver differences;

(e) Adjusted ending book inventory;

(f) Ending physical inventory; and

(g) Material unaccounted for.

A statement of the physical inventory, listing all batches separately and specifying material identification and batch data for each batch shall be attached to each material balance report.

Article 68

Special reports

The Government of the Republic of Korea shall make special reports without delay:

(a) If any unusual incident or circumstances lead the Government of the Republic of Korea to believe that there is or may have been loss of nuclear material that exceeds the limits specified for this purpose in the Subsidiary Arrangements; or

(b) If the containment has unexpectedly changed from that specified in the Subsidiary Arrangements to the extent that unauthorized removal of nuclear material has become possible.

Article 69

Amplification and clarification of reports

If the Agency so requests, the Government of the Republic of Korea shall provide it with amplification or clarifications of any report, in so far as relevant for the purpose of safeguards.

Inspections

Article 70

General provisions

The Agency shall have the right to make inspections as provided for in Articles 71-82.

Purposes of inspections

Article 71

The Agency may make ad hoc inspections in order to:

(a) Verify the information contained in the initial report on the nuclear material subject to safeguards under this Agreement;

(b) Identify and verify changes in the situation which have occurred since the data of the initial report; and

(c) Identify, and if possible verify the quantity and composition of, nuclear material in accordance with Article 93 and 96, before its transfer out of or upon its transfer into the Republic of Korea.

Article 72

The Agency may make routine inspections in order to:

(a) Verify that reports are consistent with records:

(b) Verify the location, identity, quantity and composition of all nuclear material subject to safeguards under this Agreement; and

(c) Verify information on the possible causes of material unaccounted for, shipper/receiver differences and uncertainties in the book inventory.

Article 73

Subject to the procedures laid down in Article 77, the Agency may make special inspections:

(a) In order to verify the information contained in special reports; or

(b) If the Agency considers that information made available by the Government of the Republic of Korea including explanations from the Government of the Republic of Korea and information obtained from routine inspection, is not adequate for the Agency to fulfill its responsibilities under this Agreement.

An inspection shall be deemed to be special when it is either additional to the routine inspection effort provided for in Article 78-82 or involves access to information or locations in addition to the access specified in Article 76 for ad hoc and routine inspections, or both.

Scope of inspections

Article 74

For the purposes specified in Articles 71-73, the Agency may:

(a) Examine the records kept pursuant to Article 51-58.

(b) Make independent measurements of all nuclear material subject to safeguards under this Agreement;

(c) Verify the functioning and calibration of instruments and other measuring and control equipment;

(d) Apply and make use of surveillance and containment measures; and

(e) Use other objective methods which have been demonstrated to be technically feasible.

Article 75

Within the scope of Article 74, the Agency shall be enabled:

(a) To observe that sample at key measurement points for material samples, to observe the treatment and analysis of the samples and to obtain duplicates of such samples;

(b) To observe that the measurements of nuclear material at key measurement point for material balance accountancy are representative and to observe the calibration of the instruments and equipment involved;

(c) To make arrangements with the Government of the Republic of Korea that, if necessary;

(i) Additional measurements are made and additional samples taken for the Agency's use;

(ii) The Agency's standard analytical samples are analyzed;

(iii) Appropriate absolute standards are used in calibrating instruments and other equipment; and

(iv) Other calibrations are carried out;

(d) To arrange to use its own equipment for independent measurement and surveillance, and if so agreed and specified in the Subsidiary Arrangements to arrange to install such equipment;

(e) To apply its seals and other identifying and tamper-indicating devices to containment, if so agreed and specified in the Subsidiary Arrangements; and

(f) To make arrangements with the Government of the Republic of Korea for the shipping of samples taken for the Agency's use.

Access for inspections

Article 76

(a) For the purposes specified in Article 71(a) and (b) and until such time as the strategic point have been specified in the Subsidiary Arrangements, the Agency inspectors shall have access to any location where the initial report or any inspections carried out in connection with it indicate that nuclear material is present;

(b) For the purpose specified in Article 71(c) the inspectors shall have access to any location of which the Agency has been notified in accordance with Article 92(d) (iii) or 95(d) (iii);

(c) For the purposes specified in Article 72 the inspectors shall have access only to the strategic points specified in the Subsidiary Arrangements and to the records maintained pursuant to Article 51-58; and

(d) In the event of the Government of the Republic of Korea concluding that any unusual circumstances require extended limitations on access by the Agency, the Government of the Republic of Korea and the Agency shall promptly make arrangements with a view to enabling the Agency to discharge its safeguards responsibilities in the light of these limitations. The Director General shall report each such arrangement to the Board.

Article 77

In circumstances which may lead to special inspections for the purposes specified in Article 73 the Government of the Republic of Korea and the Agency shall consult forthwith.

As a result of such consultations the Agency may:

(a) Make inspections in addition to the routine inspection effort provided for in Article 78-82; and

(b) Obtain access, in agreement with the Government of the Republic of Korea, to information or locations in addition to those specified in Article 76. Any disagreement concerning the need for additional access shall be resolved in accordance with Articles 21 and 22; in case action by the Government of the Republic of Korea is essential and urgent, Article 18 shall apply.

Frequency and intensity of routine inspections

Article 78

The Agency shall keep the number, intensity and duration of routine inspections, applying optimum timing, to the minimum consistent with the effective implementation of the safeguards procedures set forth in this Agreement, and shall make the optimum and most economical use of inspection resources available to it.

Article 79

The Agency may carry out one routine inspection per year in respect of facilities and material balance areas outside facilities with a content or annual throughput, whichever is greater, of nuclear material not exceeding five effective kilograms.

Article 80

The number, intensity, duration, timing and mode of routine inspections in respect of facilities with a content or annual throughout of nuclear material exceeding five effective kilograms shall be determined on the basis that in the maximum or limiting case the inspection regime shall be no more intensive than is necessary and sufficient to maintain continuity of knowledge of the flow and inventory of nuclear material, and the maximum routine inspection effort in respect of such facilities shall be determined as follows:

(a) For reactors and sealed storage installations the maximum total of routine inspection per year shall be determined by allowing one sixth of a man-year of inspection for each such facility;

(b) For facilities, other than reactors or sealed storage installations, involving plutonium or uranium enriched to more than 5%, the maximum total of routine inspection per year shall be determined by allowing for each such facility $30 \times \sqrt{E}$ man-days of inspection per year, where E is the inventory or annual throughput of nuclear material, whichever is greater, expressed in effective kilograms. The maximum established for any such facility shall not, however, be less than 1.5 man-year of inspection; and

(c) For facilities not covered by paragraphs (a) or (b), the maximum total of routine inspection per year shall be determined by allowing for each such facility one third of a man-year of inspection plus $0.4 \times E$ man-days of inspection per year, where E is the inventory or annual throughput of nuclear material, whichever is greater, expressed in effective kilograms.

The Government of the Republic of Korea and the Agency may agree to amend the figures for the maximum inspection effort specified in this Article, upon determination by the Board that such amendment is reasonable.

Article 81

Subject to Articles 78-80 the criteria to be used for determining the actual number, intensity, duration, timing and mode of routine inspections in respect of any facility shall include:

(a) The form of the nuclear material, in particular, whether the nuclear material is in bulk form or contained in a number of separate items; its chemical composition and, in the case of uranium, whether it is of low or high enrichment; and its accessibility;

(b) The effectiveness of the Republic of Korea's accounting and control system, including the extent to which the operators of facilities are functionally independent of the Republic of Korea's accounting and control system; the extent to which the measures specified in Article 32 have been implemented by the Government of the Republic of Korea; the promptness of reports provided to the Agency; their consistency with the Agency's independent verification; and the amount and accuracy of the material unaccounted for, as verified by the Agency;

(c) Characteristics of the Republic of Korea's nuclear fuel cycle, in particular, the number and types of facilities containing nuclear material subject to safeguards, the characteristics of such facilities relevant to safeguards, notably the degree of containment; the extent to which the design of such facilities facilitates verification of the flow and inventory of nuclear material; and the extent to which information from different material balance areas can be correlated;

(d) International interdependence, in particular, the extent to which nuclear material is received from or sent to other States for use or processing; any verification activities by the Agency in connection therewith; and the extent to which the Republic of Korea's nuclear activities are interrelated with those of other States; and

(e) Technical developments in the field of safeguards, including the use of statistical techniques and random sampling in evaluating the flow of nuclear material.

Article 82

The Government of the Republic of Korea and the Agency shall consult if the Government of the Republic of Korea considers that the inspection effort is being deployed with undue concentration on particular facilities.

Notice of inspections

Article 83

The Agency shall give advance notice to the Government of the Republic of Korea before arrival of inspectors at facilities or material balance areas outside facilities, as follows:

(a) For ad hoc inspections pursuant to Article 71(c), at least 24 hours; for those pursuant to Article 71(c) and (b) as well as the activities provided for in Article 48, at least one week;

(b) For special inspections pursuant to Article 73, as promptly as possible after the Government of the Republic of Korea and the Agency have consulted as provided for in Article 77, it being understood that notification of arrival normally will constitute part of the consultations; and

(c) For routine inspections pursuant to Article 72, at least 24 hours in respect of the facilities referred to in Article 80(b) and sealed storage installations containing plutonium or uranium enriched to more than 5%, and one week in all other cases.

Such notice of inspections shall include the name of the inspectors and shall indicate the facilities and the material balance areas outside facilities to be visited and the periods during which they will be visited. If the inspectors are to arrive from outside the Republic of Korea the Agency shall also give advance notice of the place and time of their arrival in the Republic of Korea.

Article 84

Notwithstanding the provisions of Article 83, the Agency may, as a supplementary measure, carry out without advance notification a portion of the routine inspections pursuant to Article 80 in accordance with the principle of random sampling. In performing any unannounced inspections, the Agency shall fully take into account any operational programme provided by the Government of the Republic of Korea pursuant to Article 64(b). Moreover, whenever practicable, and on the basis of the operational programme, it shall advise the Government of the Republic of Korea periodically of its general programme of announced and unannounced inspections, specifying the general periods when inspections are foreseen. In carrying out any unannounced inspections, the Agency shall make every effort to minimize any practical difficulties for the Government of the Republic of Korea and for facility operators, bearing in mind the relevant provisions of Article 44 and 89. Similarly the Government of the Republic of Korea shall make every effort to facilitate the task of the Inspectors.

Designation of Inspectors

Article 85

The following procedures shall apply to the designation of inspectors:

(a) The Director General shall inform the Government of the Republic of Korea in writing of the name; qualifications, nationality, grade and such other particulars as may be relevant, of each Agency official he proposes for designations as an inspector for the Republic of Korea;

(b) The Government of the Republic of Korea shall inform the Director General within thirty days of the receipt of such a proposal whether it accepts the proposal.

(c) The Director General may designate each official who has been accepted by the Government of the Republic of Korea as one of inspectors for the Republic of Korea, and shall inform the Government of the Republic of Korea of such designations; and

(d) The Director General, acting in response to a request by the Government of the Republic of Korea or on his own initiative, shall immediately inform the Government of the Republic of Korea of the withdrawal of the designation of any official as an inspector for the Republic of Korea.

However, in respect of inspectors needed for the activities provided for in Articles 48 and to carry out ad hoc inspections pursuant to Article 7(a) and (b) the designation procedures shall be completed if possible within thirty days after the entry into force of this Agreement. If such designation appears impossible within this time limit, inspectors for such purposes shall be designated on a temporary basis.

Article 86

The Government of the Republic of Korea shall grant or renew as quickly as possible appropriate visas, where required, for each inspector designated for the Republic of Korea.

Conduct and visits of inspectors

Article 87

Inspectors, in exercising their functions under Article 48 and 71-75, shall carry out their activities in a manner designed to avoid hampering or delaying the construction, commissioning or operation of facilities, or affecting their safety. In particular inspectors shall not operate any facility themselves or direct the staff of ability to carry out any operation. If inspectors consider that in pursuance of Article 74 and 75, particular operations in a facility should be carried out by the operator, they shall make a request therefor.

Article 88

When inspectors require services available in the Republic of Korea, including the use of equipment, in connection with the performance of inspections, the Government of the Republic of Korea shall facilitate the procurement of such services and the use of such equipment by inspectors.

Article 89

The Government of the Republic of Korea shall have the right to have inspectors accompanied during their inspections by representatives of the Government of the Republic of Korea, provided that inspect-

ors shall not thereby be delayed or otherwise impeded in the exercise of their functions.

Statements on the Agency's Verification Activities

Article 90

The Agency shall inform the Government of the Republic of Korea of:

(a) The results of inspections, at intervals to be specified in the Subsidiary Arrangements; and

(b) The conclusions it has drawn from its verification activities in the Republic of Korea, in particular by means of statements in respect of each material balance area, which shall be made as soon as possible after a physical inventory has been taken and verified by the Agency and a material balance has been struck.

International Transfers

Article 91

General provisions

Nuclear material subject or required to be subject to safeguards under this Agreement which is transferred internationally shall, for purposes of this Agreement, be regarded as being the responsibility of the Government of the Republic of Korea.

(a) In the case of import into the Republic of Korea, from the time that such responsibility ceases to lie with the exporting State, and no later than the time at which the material reaches its destination; and

(b) In the case of export out of the Republic of Korea, up to the time at which the recipient State assumes such responsibility, and no later than the time at which the nuclear material reaches its destination.

The point at which the transfer of responsibility will take place shall be determined in accordance with suitable arrangements to be made by the States concerned. Neither the Government of the Republic of Korea nor any other State shall be deemed to have such responsibility for nuclear material merely by reason of the fact that the nuclear material is in transit on or over its territory or that it is being transported on a ship under its flag or in its aircraft.

Transfers out of the Republic of Korea

Article 92

(a) The Government of the Republic of Korea shall notify the Agency of any intended transfer out of the Republic of Korea of nuclear material subject to safeguards under this Agreement if the shipment exceeds one effective kilogram, or if, within, a period of three months, several separate shipments are to be made to the same State, each of less than one effective kilogram but the total of which exceeds one effective kilogram.

(b) Such notification shall be given to the Agency after the conclusion of the contractual arrangements leading to the transfer and normally at least two weeks before the nuclear material is to be prepared for shipping.

(c) The Government of the Republic of Korea and the Agency may agree on different procedures for advance notification.

(d) The notification shall specify:

(i) The identification and, if possible, the expected quantity and composition of the nuclear material to be transferred, and the material balance area from which it will come;

(ii) The State for which the nuclear material is destined;

(iii) The dates on and locations at which the nuclear material is to be prepared for shipping;

(iv) The approximate dates of dispatch and arrival of the nuclear material; and

(v) At what point of the transfer the recipient States will assume responsibility for the nuclear material for the purposes of this Agreement, and the probable date on which that point will be reached.

Article 93

The notification referred to in Article 92 shall be such as to enable the Agency to make, if necessary, an ad hoc inspection to identify, and if possible verify the quantity and composition of, the nuclear material before it is transferred out of the Republic of Korea and, if the Agency wishes or the Government of the Republic of Korea so requests, to affix seals to the nuclear material when it has been prepared for shipping. However, the transfer of the nuclear material shall not be delayed in any way by any action taken or contemplated by the Agency pursuant to such a notification.

Article 94

If the nuclear material will not be subject to Agency safeguards in the recipient State, the Government of the Republic of Korea shall make arrangements for the Agency to receive, within three months of the time when the recipient State accepts responsibility for the nuclear material from the Republic of Korea, confirmation by the recipient State of the transfer.

Transfers into the Republics of Korea

Article 95

(a) The Government of the Republic of Korea shall notify the Agency of any expected transfer into the Republic of Korea of nuclear material required to be subject to safeguards under this Agreement if the shipment exceeds one effective kilogram, or if, within a period of three months, several separate shipments are to be received from the same State, each of less than one effective kilogram but the total of which exceeds one effective kilogram.

(b) The Agency shall be notified as much advance as possible of the expected arrival of the nuclear material, and in any case not later than the date on which the Government of the Republic of Korea assumes responsibility for the nuclear material.

(c) The Government of the Republic of Korea and the Agency may agree on different procedures for advance notification.

(d) The notification shall specify:

(i) The identification and, if possible, the expected quantity and composition of the nuclear material;

(ii) At what point of the transfer the Government of the Republic of Korea will assume responsibility for the nuclear material for the purpose of this Agreement, and the probable date on which that point will be reached; and

(iii) The expected date of arrival; the location where, and the date on which, the nuclear material is intended to be unpacked.

Article 96

The notification referred to in Article 95 shall be such as to enable the Agency to make, if necessary, an ad hoc inspection to identify, and if possible verify the quantity and composition of, the nuclear material at the time the consignment is unpacked. However, unpacking shall not be delayed by any action taken or contemplated by the Agency pursuant to such a notification.

Article 97

Special reports

The Government of the Republic of Korea shall make a special report as envisaged in Article 68 if any unusual incident or circumstances lead the Government of the Republic of Korea to believe that there is or may have been loss of nuclear material, including the occurrence of significant delay, during an international transfer.

Definitions

Article 98

For the purposes of this Agreement:

A. "Adjustment" means an entry into an accounting record or a report showing a shipper/receiver difference or material unaccounted for.

B. "Annual throughput" means, for the purposes of Article 79 and 80, the amount of nuclear material transferred annually out of a facility handled as a unit for accounting purposes at a key measurement point and for which the composition and quantity are defined by a single set of specifications or measurements. The nuclear material may be in bulk form or contained in a number of separate items.

D. "Batch data" means the total weight of each element of nuclear material and, in the case of plutonium and uranium, the isotopic composition when appropriate. The units of account shall be as follow:

(a) Grams of contained plutonium;

(b) Grams of total uranium and grams of contained uranium-235 plus uranium-233 for uranium enriched in these isotope; and

(c) Kilograms of contained thorium, natural uranium or depleted uranium.

For reporting purposes the weights of individual items in the batch shall be added together before rounding to the nearest unit.

E. "Book inventory" of a material balance area means the algebraic sum of the most recent physical inventory of that material balance area and of all inventory changes that have occurred since the physical inventory is taken.

F. "Correction" means an entry into an accounting record or a report to rectify an identified mistake or to reflect an improved measurement of a quantity previously entered into the record or report. Each correction must identify the entry to which it pertains.

G. "Effective kilogram" means a special unit used in safeguarding nuclear material. The quantity in effective kilograms is obtained by taking:

(a) For plutonium, the weight in kilograms;

(b) For uranium with an enrichment of 0.01 (1%) and above, its weight in kilograms multiplied by the square of its enrichment;

(c) For uranium with an enrichment below 0.01 (1%) and above 0.005 (0.5%), its weight in kilograms multiplied by 0.0001; and

(d) For depleted uranium with an enrichment of 0.005 (0.5%) or below, and for thorium, its weight in kilograms multiplied by 0.0005.

H. "Enrichment" means the ratio of the combined weight of the isotope uranium-233 and uranium-235 to that of the total uranium in question.

I. "Facility" means:

(a) A reactor, a critical facility, a conversion plant, a fabrication plant, a reprocessing plant, an isotope separation plant or a separate storage installation; or

(b) Any location where nuclear material in amounts greater than one effective kilogram is customarily used.

J. "Inventory change" means an increase or decrease, in terms of batches, of nuclear material in a material balance area; such a change shall involve one of the following:

(a) Increases:

(i) Import;

(ii) Domestic receipt: receipts from other material balance areas, receipts from a non-safeguarded(non-peaceful) activity or receipts at the starting point of safeguards;

(iii) Nuclear production: production of special fissionable material in a reactor; and

(iv) De-exemption; re-application of safeguards on nuclear material previously exempted therefrom on account of its use or quantity

(b) Decreases:

(i) Export;

(ii) Domestic shipment: shipments to other material balance areas of shipments for a non-safeguarded(non-peaceful) activity;

(iii) Nuclear loss: loss of nuclear material due to its transformation into other elements(s) or isotope(s) as a result of nuclear reactions;

(iv) Measured discard: nuclear material which has been measured, or estimated on the basis of measurements, and disposed of in such a way that is not suitable for further nuclear use;

(v) Retained waste: nuclear material generated from processing or from an operational accident, which is deemed to be unrecoverable for the time being but which is stored;

(vi) Exemption: exemption of nuclear material from safeguards on account of its use or quantity; and

(vii) Other loss: for example, accidental loss (that is, irretrievable and inadvertent loss of nuclear material as the result of an operational accident) or theft.

K. "Key Measurement point" means a location where nuclear material appears in such a form that it may be measured to determine material flow or inventory. Key measurement points thus include, but are not limited to, the inputs and outputs (including measured discards) and storage in material balance areas.

L. "Man-year of inspection" means, for the purposes of Article 80,300 man-days of inspection, a man-day being a day during which a single inspector has access to a facility at any time for a total of not more than eight hours.

M. "Material balance area" means an area in or outside or a facility such that:

(a) The quantity of nuclear material in each transfer into or out of each material balance area can be determined; and

(b) The physical inventory of nuclear material in each material balance area can be determined when necessary, in accordance with specified procedures, in order that the material balance for

Agency safeguards purposes can be established.

N. "Material unaccounted for" means the difference between book inventory and physical inventory.

O. "Nuclear material" means any source of any special fissionable material as defined in Article XX of the Statute. The term source material shall not be interpreted as applying to ore or ore residue. Any determination by the Board under Article XX of the Statute after the entry into force of the Agreement which ads to the material considered to be source material or special fissionable material shall have effect under this Agreement only upon acceptance by the Government of the Republic of Korea.

P. "Physical inventory" means the sum of all the measured or derived estimates of batch quantities of nuclear material on hand at a given time within a material balance area, obtained in accordance with specified procedures.

Q. "Shipper/receiver difference" means the difference between the quantity of nuclear material in a batch as stated by the shipping material balance area and as measured at the receiving material balance area.

E. "Source data" means those data, recorded during measurement or calibration or used to derive empirical relationships, which identify nuclear material and provide batch data. Source data may include, for example, weight of compounds, conversion factors to determine weight of element, specific gravity element concentration, isotopic ratios, relationship between volume and manometer readings and relationship between plutonium produced and power generated.

S. "Strategic point" means a location selected during examination of design information where, under normal conditions and when combined with the information from all strategic points taken together, the information necessary and sufficient for the implementation of safeguards measures is obtained and verified; a strategic point may include any location where key measurements related to material balance accountancy are made and where containment and surveillance measures are executed.

Treaty Between the United States of America and the Union of Soviet Socialist Republics on Underground Nuclear Explosions for Peaceful Purposes

Also known as: PNE Treaty

Date of signature: May 28, 1976

Place of signature: Moscow and Washington, DC
Signatory states: the United States, the Soviet Union

[The signatory states],

Proceeding from a desire to implement Article III of the Treaty between the United States of America and the Union of Soviet Socialist Republics on the Limitation of Underground Nuclear Weapon Tests, which calls for the earliest possible conclusion of an agreement on underground nuclear explosions for peaceful purposes,

Reaffirming their adherence to the objectives and principles of the Treaty Banning Nuclear Weapon Tests in the Atmosphere, in Outer Space and Under Water, the Treaty on Non-Proliferation of Nuclear Weapons, and the Treaty on the Limitation of Underground Nuclear Weapon Tests, and their determination to observe strictly the provisions of these international agreements,

Desiring to assure that underground nuclear explosions for peaceful purposes shall not be used for purposes related to nuclear weapons,

Desiring that utilization of nuclear energy be directed only toward peaceful purposes,

Desiring to develop appropriately cooperation in the field of underground nuclear explosions for peaceful purposes,

Have agreed as follows:

Article I

1. The Parties enter into this Treaty to satisfy the obligations in Article III of the Treaty on the Limitation of Underground Nuclear Weapon Tests, and assume additional obligations in accordance with the provisions of this Treaty.

2. This Treaty shall govern all underground nuclear explosions for peaceful purposes conducted by the Parties after March 31, 1976.

Article II

For the purposes of this Treaty:

(a) "explosion" means any individual or group underground nuclear explosion for peaceful purposes;

(b) "explosive" means any device, mechanism or system for producing an individual explosion;

(c) "group explosion" means two or more individual explosions for which the time interval between successive individual explosions does not exceed five seconds and for which the emplacement points of all explosives can be interconnected by straight line segments, each of which joins two emplacement points and each of which does not exceed 40 kilometers.

Article III

1. Each Party, subject to the obligations assumed under this Treaty and other international agreements, reserves the right to:

(a) carry out explosions at any place under its jurisdiction or control outside the geographical boundaries of test sites specified under the provisions of the Treaty on the Limitation of Underground Nuclear Weapon Tests; and

(b) carry out, participate or assist in carrying out explosions in the territory of another State at the request of such other State.

2. Each Party undertakes to prohibit, to prevent and not to carry out at any place under its jurisdiction, or control, and further undertakes not to carry out, participate or assist in carrying out anywhere:

(a) any individual explosion having a yield exceeding 150 kilotons;

(b) any group explosion:

(1) having any aggregate yield exceeding 150 kilotons except in ways that will permit identification of each individual explosion and determination of the yield of each individual explosion in the group in accordance with the provisions of Article IV of and the Protocol to this Treaty;

(2) having an aggregate yield exceeding one and one-half megatons;

(c) any explosion which does not carry out a peaceful application;

(d) any explosion except in compliance with the provisions of the Treaty Banning Nuclear Weapon Tests in the Atmosphere, in Outer Space and Under Water, the Treaty on the Non-Proliferation of Nuclear Weapons, and other international agreements entered into by that Party.

3. The question of carrying out any individual explosion having a yield exceeding the yield specified in paragraph 2(a) of this Article will be considered by the Parties at an appropriate time to be agreed.

Article IV

1. For the purpose of providing assurance of com-

pliance with the provisions of this Treaty, each Party shall:

(a) use national technical means of verification at its disposal in a manner consistent with generally recognized principles of international law; and

(b) provide to the other Party information and access to sites of explosions and furnish assistance in accordance with the provisions set forth in the Protocol to this Treaty.

2. Each Party undertakes not to interfere with the national technical means of verification of the other Party operating in accordance with paragraph 1(a) of this article, or with the implementation of the provisions of paragraph 1(b) of this article.

Article V

1. To promote the objectives and implementation of the provisions of this Treaty, the Parties shall establish promptly a Joint Consultative Commission within the framework of which they will:

(a) consult with each other, make inquiries and furnish information in response to such inquiries, to assure confidence in compliance with the obligations assumed;

(b) consider questions concerning compliance with the obligations assumed and related situations which may be considered ambiguous;

(c) consider questions involving unintended interference with the means for assuring compliance with the provisions of this Treaty;

(d) consider changes in technology or other new circumstances which have a bearing on the provisions of this Treaty; and

(e) consider possible amendments to provisions governing underground nuclear explosions for peaceful purposes.

2. The Parties through consultation shall establish, and may amend as appropriate, Regulations for the Joint Consultative Commission governing procedures, composition and other relevant matters.

Article VI

1. The Parties will develop cooperation on the basis of mutual benefit, equality, and reciprocity in various areas related to carrying out underground nuclear explosions for peaceful purposes.

2. The Joint Consultative Commission will facili-

tate this cooperation by considering specific areas and forms of cooperation which shall be determined by agreement between the Parties in accordance with their constitutional procedures.

3. The Parties will appropriately inform the International Atomic Energy Agency of results of their cooperation in the field of underground nuclear explosions for peaceful purposes.

Article VII

1. Each Party shall continue to promote the development of the international agreement or agreements and procedures provided for in Article V of the Treaty on the Non-Proliferation of Nuclear Weapons, and shall provide appropriate assistance to the International Atomic Energy Agency in this regard.

2. Each Party undertakes not to carry out, participate or assist in the carrying out of any explosion in the territory of another State unless that State agrees to the implementation in its territory of the international observation and procedures contemplated by Article V of the Treaty on the Non-Proliferation of Nuclear Weapons and the provisions of Article IV of and the Protocol to this Treaty, including the provision by that State of the assistance necessary for such implementation and of the privileges and immunities specified in the Protocol.

Article VIII

1. This Treaty shall remain in force for a period of five years, and it shall be extended for successive five-year periods unless either Party notifies the other of its termination no later than six months prior to its expiration. Before the expiration of this period the Parties may, as necessary, hold consultations to consider the situation relevant to the substance of this Treaty. However, under no circumstances shall either Party be entitled to terminate this Treaty while the Treaty on the Limitation of Underground Nuclear Weapon Tests remains in force.

2. Termination of the Treaty on the Limitation of Underground Nuclear Weapon Tests shall entitle either Party to withdraw from this Treaty at any time.

3. Each Party may propose amendments to this Treaty. Amendments shall enter into force on the day of the exchange of instruments of ratification of such amendments.

Article IX

1. This Treaty including the Protocol which forms an integral part hereof, shall be subject to ratification

in accordance with the constitutional procedures of each Party. This Treaty shall enter into force on the day of the exchange of instruments of ratification which exchange shall take place simultaneously with the exchange of instruments of ratification of the Treaty on the Limitation of Underground Nuclear Weapon Tests.

2. This Treaty shall be registered pursuant to Article 102 of the Charter of the United Nations.

Protocol to the Treaty Between the United States of America and the Union of Soviet Socialist Republics on Underground Nuclear Explosions for Peaceful Purposes

[The signatories],
Having agreed to the provisions in the Treaty on Underground Nuclear Explosions for Peaceful Purposes, hereinafter referred to as the Treaty,
Have agreed as follows:

Article I

1. No individual explosion shall take place at a distance in meters, from the ground surface which is less than 30 times the 3.4 root of its planned yield in kilotons.

2. Any group explosion with a planned aggregate yield exceeding 500 kilotons shall not include more than five individual explosions, each of which has a planned yield not exceeding 50 kilotons.

Article II

1. For each explosion, the Party carrying out the explosion shall provide the other Party:

(a) not later than 90 days before the beginning of emplacement of the explosives when the planned aggregate yield of the explosion does not exceed 100 kilotons, or not later than 180 days before the beginning of emplacement of the explosives when the planned aggregate yield of the explosion exceeds 100 kilotons, with the following information to the extent and degree of precision available when it is conveyed:

(1) the purpose of the planned explosion;

(2) the location of the explosion expressed in geographical coordinates with a precision of four or less kilometers, planned date and aggregate yield of the explosion;

(3) the type or types of rock in which the explosion will be carried out, including the degree of liquid saturation of the rock at the point of emplacement of each explosive; and

(4) a description of specific technological features of the project, of which the explosion is a part, that could influence the determination of its yield and confirmation of purpose; and

(b) not later than 60 days before the beginning of emplacement of the explosives the information specified in subparagraph 1(a) of this Article to the full extent and with the precision indicated in that subparagraph.

2. For each explosion with a planned aggregate yield exceeding 50 kilotons, the Party carrying out the explosion shall provide the other Party, not later than 60 days before the beginning of emplacement of the explosives, with the following information:

(a) the number of explosives, the planned yield of each explosive, the location of each explosive to be used in a group explosion relative to all other explosives in the group with a precision of 100 or less meters, the depth of emplacement of each explosive with a precision of one meter and the time intervals between individual explosions in any group explosion with a precision of one-tenth second; and

(b) a description of specific features of geological structure or other local conditions that could influence the determination of the yield.

3. For each explosion with a planned aggregate yield exceeding 75 kilotons, the Party carrying out the explosion shall provide the other Party, not later than 60 days before the beginning of emplacement of the explosives, with a description of the geological and geophysical characteristics of the site of each explosion which could influence determination of the yield, which shall include: the depth of the water table; a stratigraphic column above each emplacement point; the position of each emplacement point relative to nearby geological and other features which influenced the design of the project of which the explosion is a part; and the physical parameters of the rock, including density, seismic velocity, porosity, degree of liquid saturation, and rock strength, within the sphere centered on each emplacement point and having a radius, in meters, equal to 30 times the cube root of the planned yield in kilotons of the explosive emplaced at that point.

4. For each explosion with a planned aggregate yield exceeding 100 kilotons, the Party carrying out the explosion shall provide the other Party, not later

than 60 days before the beginning of emplacement of the explosives, with:

(a) information on locations and purposes of facilities and installations which are associated with the conduct of the explosion;

(b) information regarding the planned date of the beginning of emplacement of each explosive; and

(c) a topographic plan in local coordinates of the areas specified in paragraph 7 of Article IV, at a scale of 1:24,000 or 1:25,000 with a contour interval of 10 meters or less.

5. For application of an explosion to alleviate the consequences of an emergency situation involving an unforeseen combination of circumstances which calls for immediate action for which it would not be practicable to observe the timing requirements of paragraphs 1,2 and 3 of this Article, the following conditions shall be met:

(a) the Party carrying out an explosion for such purposes shall inform the other Party of that decision immediately after it has been made and describe such circumstances;

(b) the planned aggregate yield of an explosion for such purpose shall not exceed 100 kilotons; and

(c) the Party carrying out an explosion for such purpose shall provide to the other Party the information specified in paragraph 1 of this Article, and the information specified in paragraphs 2 and 3 of this Article if applicable, after the decision to conduct the explosion is taken, but not later than 30 days before the beginning of emplacement of the explosives.

6. For each explosion, the Party carrying out the explosion shall inform the other Party, not later than two days before the explosion, of the planned time of detonation of each explosive with a precision of one second.

7. Prior to the explosion, the Party carrying out the explosion shall provide the other Party with timely notification of changes in the information provided in accordance with this Article.

8. The explosion shall not be carried out earlier than 90 days after notification of any change in the information provided in accordance with this Article which requires more extensive verification procedures than those required on the basis of the original information, unless an earlier time for carrying out the explosion is agreed between the Parties.

9. Not later than 90 days after each explosion the Party carrying out the explosion shall provide the

other Party with the following information:

(a) the actual time of the explosion with a precision of one-tenth second and its aggregate yield;

(b) when the planned aggregate yield of a group explosion exceeds 50 kilotons, the actual time of the first individual explosion with a precision of one-tenth second, the time interval between individual explosions with a precision of one millisecond and the yield of each individual explosion; and

(c) confirmation of other information provided in accordance with paragraphs 1, 2, 3 and 4 of this Article and explanation of any changes or corrections based on the results of the explosion.

10. At any time, but not later than one year after the explosion, the other Party may request the Party carrying out the explosion to clarify any item of the information provided in accordance with this Article. Such clarification shall be provided as soon as practicable, but not later than 30 days after the request is made.

Article III

1. For the purposes of this Protocol:

(a) "designated personnel" means those nationals of the other Party identified to the Party carrying out an explosion as the persons who will exercise the rights and functions provided for in the Treaty and this Protocol; and

(b) "emplacement hole" means the entire interior of any drill-hole, shaft, adit or tunnel in which an explosive and associated cables and other equipment are to be installed.

2. For any explosion with a planned aggregate yield exceeding 100 kilotons but not exceeding 150 kilotons if the Parties, in consultation based on information provided in accordance with Article II and other information that may be introduced by either Party, deem it appropriate for the confirmation of the yield of the explosion, and for any explosion with a planned aggregate yield exceeding 150 kilotons, the Party carrying out the explosion shall allow designated personnel within the areas and at the locations described in Article V to exercise the following rights and functions:

(a) confirmation that the local circumstances, including facilities and installations associated with the project, are consistent with the stated peaceful purposes;

(b) confirmation of the validity of the geological and

geophysical information provided in accordance with Article II through the following procedures:

(1) examination by designated personnel of research and measurement data of the Party carrying out the explosion and of rock core or rock fragments removed from each emplacement hole, and of any logs and drill core from existing exploratory holes which shall be provided to designated personnel upon their arrival at the site of the explosion;

(2) examination by designated personnel of rock core or rock fragments as they become available in accordance with the procedures specified in subparagraph 2(b)(3) or this article; and

(3) observation by designated personnel of implementation by the Party carrying out the explosion of one of the following four procedures, unless this right is waived by the other Party:

(i) construction of that portion of each emplacement hole starting from a point nearest the entrance of the emplacement hole which is at a distance, in meters, from the nearest emplacement point equal to 30 times the cube root of the planned yield in kilotons of the explosive to be emplaced at that point and continuing to the completion of the emplacement hole; or

(ii) construction of that portion of each emplacement hole starting from a point nearest the entrance of the emplacement hole which is at a distance, in meters, from the nearest emplacement point equal to six times the cube root of the planned yield in kilotons of the explosive to be emplaced at that point and continuing to the completion of the emplacement hole as well as the removal of rock core or rock fragments from the wall of an existing exploratory hole, which is substantially parallel with and at no point more than 100 meters from the emplacement hole, at locations specified by designated personnel which lie within a distance, in meters, from the same horizon as each emplacement point of 30 times the cube root of the planned yield in kilotons of the explosive to be emplaced at that point; or

(iii) removal of rock core or rock fragments from the wall of each emplacement hole at locations specified by designated personnel which lie within a distance, in meters, from each emplacement point of 30 times the cube root of the planned yield in kilotons of the explosive to be emplaced at each such point; or

(iv) construction of one or more new exploratory holes so that for each emplacement hole there will be a new exploratory hole to the same depth as that of the emplacement of the explosive, substantially parallel with and at no point more than 100 meters from each emplacement hole, from which rock cores would be removed at locations specified by designated personnel which lie within a distance, in meters, from the same horizon as each emplacement point of 30 times the cube root of the planned yield in kilotons of the explosive to be emplaced at each such point;

(c) observation of the emplacement of each explosive, confirmation of the depth of its emplacement and observation of the stemming of each emplacement hole;

(d) unobstructed visual observation of the area of the entrance to each emplacement hole at any time from the time of emplacement of each explosive until all personnel have been withdrawn from the site for the detonation of the explosion; and

(e) observation of each explosion.

3. Designated personnel, using equipment provided in accordance with paragraph 1 of Article IV, shall have the right, for any explosion with a planned aggregate yield exceeding 150 kilotons, to determine the yield of each individual explosion in a group explosion in accordance with the provisions of Article VI.

4. Designated personnel, when using their equipment in accordance with paragraph 1 of Article IV, shall have the right, for any explosion with a planned aggregate yield exceeding 500 kilotons, to emplace, install and operate under the observation and with the assistance of personnel of the Party carrying out the explosion, if such assistance is requested by designated personnel, a local seismic network in accordance with the provisions of paragraph 7 of Article IV. Radio links may be used for the transmission of data and control signals between the seismic stations and the control center. Frequencies, maximum power output of radio transmitters, directivity of antennas and times of operation of the local seismic network radio transmitters before the explosion shall be agreed between the Parties in accordance with Article X and time of operation after the explosion shall conform to the time specified in paragraph 7 of Article IV.

5. Designated personnel shall have the right to:

(a) acquire photographs under the following conditions:

(1) the Party carrying out the explosion shall identify to the other Party those personnel of the Party carrying out the explosion who shall take photographs as requested by designating personnel;

(2) photographs shall be taken by personnel of the Party carrying out the explosion in the presence of designated personnel and at the time requested by designated personnel for taking such photographs. Designated personnel shall determine whether these photographs are in conformity with their requests and, if not, additional photographs shall be taken immediately;

(3) photographs shall be taken with cameras provided by the other Party having built-in, rapid developing capability and a copy of each photograph shall be provided at the completion of the development process to both Parties;

(4) cameras provided by designated personnel shall be kept in agreed secure storage when not in use; and

(5) the request for photographs can be made, at any time, of the following:

(i) exterior views of facilities and installations associated with the conduct of the explosion as described in subparagraph 4(a) of Article II;

(ii) geological samples used for confirmation of geological and geophysical information, as provided for in subparagraph 2(b) of this Article and the equipment utilized in the acquisition of such samples;

(iii) emplacement and installation of equipment and associated cables used by designated personnel for yield determination;

(iv) emplacement and installation of the local seismic network used by designated personnel;

(v) emplacement of the explosives and the stemming of the emplacement hole; and

(vi) containers, facilities and installations for storage and operation of equipment used by designated personnel;

(b) photographs of visual displays and records produced by the equipment used by designated personnel and photographs within the control centers taken by cameras which are component parts of such equipment; and

(c) receive at the request of designated personnel and with the agreement of the Party carrying out the explosion supplementary photographs taken by the Party carrying out the explosion.

Article IV

1. Designated personnel in exercising their rights and functions may choose to use the following equipment of either Party, of which choice the Party carrying out the explosion shall be informed not later than 150 days before the beginning of emplacement of the explosives:

(a) electrical equipment for yield determination and equipment for a local seismic network as described in paragraphs 3, 4 and 7 of this Article; and

(b) geologist's field tools and kits and equipment for recording of field notes.

2. Designated personnel shall have the right in exercising their rights and functions to utilize the following additional equipment which shall be provided by the Party carrying out the explosion, under procedures to be established in accordance with Article X to ensure that the equipment meets the specifications of the other Party: portable short-range communication equipment, field glasses, optical equipment for surveying and other items which may be specified by the other Party. A description of such equipment and operating instructions shall be provided to the other Party not later than 90 days before the beginning of emplacement of the explosives in connection with which such equipment is to be used.

3. A complete set of electrical equipment for yield determination shall consist of:

(a) sensing elements and associated cables for transmission of electrical power, control signals and data;

(b) equipment of the control center, electrical power supplies and cables for transmission of electrical power, control signals and data; and

(c) measuring and calibration instruments, maintenance equipment and spare parts necessary for ensuring the functioning of sensing elements, cables and equipment of the control center.

4. A complete set of equipment for the local seismic network shall consist of:

(a) seismic stations each of which contains a seismic instrument, electrical power for receiving and transmission of control signals and data or equipment for recording control signals and data;

(b) equipment of the control center and electrical power supplies; and

(c) measuring and calibration instruments, maintenance equipment and spare parts necessary for ensuring the functioning of the complete network.

5. In case designated personnel, in accordance with paragraph 1 of this Article, choose to use equipment of the Party carrying out the explosion for yield determination or for a local seismic network, a description of such equipment and installation and operating instructions shall be provided to the other Party not later than 90 days before the beginning of emplacement of the explosives in connection with which such equipment is to be used. Personnel of the Party carrying out the explosion shall emplace, install and operate the equipment in the presence of designated personnel. After the explosion, designated personnel shall receive duplicate copies of the recorded data. Equipment for yield determination shall be emplaced in accordance with Article VI. Equipment for a local seismic network shall be emplaced in accordance with paragraph 7 of this Article.

6. In case designated personnel, in accordance with paragraph 1 of this Article, choose to use their own equipment for yield determination and their own equipment for a local seismic network, the following procedures shall apply:

(a) the Party carrying out the explosion shall be provided by the other Party with the equipment and information specified in subparagraphs (a)(1) and (a)(2) of this paragraph not later than 150 days prior to the beginning of emplacement of the explosives in connection with which such equipment is to be used in order to permit the Party carrying out the explosion to familiarize itself with such equipment, if such equipment and information has not been previously provided, which equipment shall be returned to the other Party not later than 90 days before the beginning of emplacement of the explosives. The equipment and information to be provided are:

(1) one complete set of electrical equipment for yield determination as described in paragraph 3 of this Article, electrical and mechanical design information, specifications and installation and operating instructions concerning this equipment; and

(2) one complete set of equipment for the local seismic network described in paragraph 4 of this Article, including one seismic station, electrical and mechanical design information, specifications and installation and operating instructions concerning this equipment;

(b) not later than 35 days prior to the beginning of emplacement of the explosives in connection with which the following equipment is to be used, two complete sets of electrical equipment for yield determination as described in paragraph 3 of this Article and specific installation instructions for the emplacement of the sensing elements based on information provided in accordance with subparagraph 2(a) of Article VI and two complete sets of equipment for the local seismic network as described in paragraph 4 of this Article, which sets of equipment shall have the same components and technical characteristics as the corresponding equipment specified in subparagraph 6(a) of this Article, shall be delivered in sealed containers to the port of entry;

(c) the Party carrying out the explosion shall choose one of each of the two sets of equipment described above which shall be used by designated personnel in connection with the explosion;

(d) the set or sets of equipment not chosen for use in connection with the explosion shall be at the disposal of the Party carrying out the explosion for a period that may be as long as 30 days after the explosion at which time such equipment shall be returned to the other Party;

(e) the set or sets of equipment chosen for use shall be transported by the Party carrying out the explosion in the sealed containers in which this equipment arrived, after seals of the Party carrying out the explosion have been affixed to them, to the site of the explosion, so that this equipment is delivered to designated personnel for emplacement, installation and operation not later than 20 days before the beginning of emplacement of the explosives. This equipment shall remain in the custody of designated personnel in accordance with paragraph 7 of Article V or in agreed secure storage. Personnel of the Party carrying out the explosion shall have the right to observe the use of this equipment by designated personnel during the time the equipment is at the site of the explosion. Before the beginning of emplacement of the explosives, designated personnel shall demonstrate to personnel of the Party carrying out the explosion that this equipment is in working order;

(f) each set of equipment shall include two sets of components for recording data and associated calibration equipment. Both of these sets of components in the equipment chosen for use shall simultaneously record data. After the explosion, and after duplicate copies of all data have been obtained by designated personnel and the Party carrying out the explosion, one of each of the two sets of components for recording data and associated calibration equipment shall be selected, by an agreed process of chance, to be retained by designated personnel. Designated personnel shall pack and seal such components for recording data and associated calibration equipment which shall accompany them from the site of the explosion to the port of exit; and

(g) all remaining equipment may be retained by the Party carrying out the explosion for a period that may be as long as 30 days, after which time this equipment shall be returned to the other Party.

7. For any explosion with a planned aggregate yield exceeding 500 kilotons, a local seismic network, the number of stations of which shall be determined by designated personnel but shall not exceed the number of explosives in the group plus five, shall be emplaced, installed and operated at agreed sites of emplacement within an area circumscribed by circles of 15 kilometers in radius centered on points on the surface of the earth above the points of emplacement of the explosives during a period beginning not later than 20 days before the beginning of emplacement of the explosives and continuing after the explosion not later than three days unless otherwise agreed between the Parties.

8. The Party carrying out the explosion shall have the right to examine in the presence of designated personnel all equipment, instruments and tools of designated personnel specified in subparagraph 1 (b) of this Article.

9. The Joint Consultative Commission will consider proposals that either Party may put forward for the joint development of standardized equipment for verification purposes.

Article V

1. Except as limited by the provisions of paragraph 5 of this Article, designated personnel in the exercise of their rights and functions shall have access along agreed routes:

(a) for an explosion with a planned aggregate yield exceeding 100 kilotons in accordance with paragraph 2 of Article III:

(1) to the locations of facilities and installations associated with the conduct of the explosion provided in accordance with subparagraph 4(a) of Article II; and

(2) to the locations of activities described in paragraph 2 of Article III; and

(b) for any explosion with a planned aggregate yield exceeding 150 kilotons, in addition to the access described in subparagraph 1(a) of this Article:

(1) to other locations within the area circumscribed by circles of 10 kilometers in radius centered on points on the surface of the earth above the points of emplacement of the explosives in order to confirm that the local circumstances are consistent with the stated peaceful purposes;

(2) to the locations of the components of the electrical equipment for yield determination to be used for recording data when, by agreement between the Parties, such equipment is located outside the area described in subparagraph 1(b) (1) of this Article; and

(c) to the sites of emplacement of the equipment of the local seismic network provided for in paragraph 7 of Article IV.

2. The Party carrying out the explosion shall notify the other Party of the procedure it has chosen from among those specified in subparagraph 2(b)(3) or Article III not later than 30 days before beginning the implementation of such procedure. Designated personnel shall have the right to be present at the site of the explosion to exercise their rights and functions in the areas and at the locations described in paragraph 1 of this Article for a period of time beginning two days before the beginning of the implementation of the procedure and continuing for a period of three days after the completion of this procedure.

3. Except as specified in paragraph 4 of this Article; designated personnel shall have the right to be present in the areas and at the locations described in paragraph 1 of this Article:

(a) for an explosion with a planned aggregate yield exceeding 100 kilotons but not exceeding 150 kilotons, in accordance with paragraph 2 of Article III, at any time beginning five days before the beginning of emplacement of the explosives and continuing after the explosion and after safe access to evacuated areas has been established according to standards determined by the Party carrying out the explosion for a period of two days; and

(b) for any explosion with a planned aggregate yield exceeding 150 kilotons, at any time beginning 20 days before the beginning of emplacement of the explosives and continuing after the explosion and after safe access to evacuated areas has been established according to standards determined by the Party carrying out the explosion for a period of:

(1) five days in the case of an explosion with a planned aggregate yield exceeding 150 kilotons but not exceeding 500 kilotons; or

(2) eight days in the case of an explosion with a planned aggregate yield exceeding 500 kilotons.

4. Designated personnel shall not have the right to be present in those areas from which all personnel have been evacuated in connection with carrying out an explosion, but shall have the right to re-enter those areas at the same time as personnel of the Party carrying out the explosion.

5. Designated personnel shall not have or seek access by physical, visual or technical means to the interior of the canister containing an explosive, to documentary or other information descriptive of the design of an explosives. The Party carrying out the explosion shall not locate documentary or other information descriptive of the design of an explosive in such ways as to impede the designated personnel in the exercise of their rights and functions.

6. The number of designated personnel present at the site of an explosion shall not exceed:

(a) for the exercise of their rights and functions in connection with the confirmation of the geological and geophysical information in accordance with the provisions of subparagraph 2(b) and applicable provisions of paragraph 5 of Article III—the number of emplacement holes plus three;

(b) for the exercise of their rights and functions in connection with confirming that the local circumstances are consistent with the information provided and with the stated peaceful purposes in accordance with the provisions in subparagraphs 2(a), 2(c), 2(d) and 2(e) and applicable provisions of paragraph 5 of Article III—the number of explosives plus two;

(c) for the exercise of their rights and functions in connection with confirming that the local circumstances are consistent with the information provided and with the stated peaceful purposes in accordance with the provisions in subparagraphs 2(a), 2(c), 2(d) and 2(e) with applicable provisions of paragraph 5 of Article III and in connection with the use of electrical equipment for determination of the yield in accordance with paragraph 3 of Article III—the number of explosives plus seven; and

(d) for the exercise of their rights and functions in connection with confirming that the local circumstances are consistent with the information provided and with the stated peaceful purposes in accordance with the provisions in subparagraph 2(a), 2(c), 2(d) and 2(e) and applicable provisions of paragraph 5 of Article III and in connection with the use of electrical equipment for determination of the yield in accordance with paragraph 3 of Article III and with the use of the local seismic network in accordance with paragraph 4 of Article III—the number of explosives plus 10.

7. The Party carrying out the explosion shall have the right to assign its personnel to accompany designated personnel while the latter exercise their rights and functions.

8. The Party carrying out an explosion shall assure for designated personnel telecommunications with their authorities, transportation and other services appropriate to their presence and to the exercise of their rights and functions at the site of the explosion.

9. The expenses incurred for the transportation of designated personnel and their equipment to and from the site of the explosion, telecommunications provided for in paragraph 8 of this Article, their living and working quarters, subsistence and all other personal expenses shall be the responsibility of the Party other than the Party carrying out the explosion.

10. Designated personnel shall consult with the Party carrying out the explosion in order to coordinate the planned program and schedule of activities of designated personnel with the program of the Party carrying out the explosion for the conduct of the project so as to ensure that designated personnel are able to conduct their activities in an orderly and timely way that is compatible with the implementation of the project. Procedures for such consultations shall be established in accordance with Article X.

Article VI

For any explosion with a planned aggregate yield exceeding 150 kilotons, determination of the yield of each explosive used shall be carried out in accordance with the following provisions:

1. Determination of the yield of each individual explosion in the group shall be based on measurements of the velocity of propagation, as a function of time, of the hydrodynamic shock wave generated by the explosion, taken by means of electrical equipment described in paragraph 3 of Article IV.

2. The Party carrying out the explosion shall pro-

vide the other Party with the following information:

(a) not later than 60 days before the beginning of emplacement of the explosives, the length of each canister in which the explosives will be contained in the corresponding emplacement hole, the dimensions of the tube or other device used to emplace the canister and the cross-sectional dimensions of the emplacement hole to a distance, in meters, from the emplacement point of 10 times the cube root of its yield in kilotons;

(b) not later than 60 days before the beginning of emplacement of the explosives, a description of materials, including their densities, to be used to stem each emplacement hole; and

(c) not later than 30 days before the beginning of emplacement of the explosives, for each emplacement hole of a group explosion, the local coordinates of the point of emplacement of the explosive, the entrance of the emplacement hole, the point of the emplacement hole most distant from the entrance, the location of the emplacement hole at each 200 meters distance from the entrances and the configuration of any known voids larger than one cubic meter located within the distance, in meters, of 10 times the cube root of the planned yield in kilotons measured from the bottom of the canister containing the explosive. The error in these coordinates shall not exceed one percent of the distance between the emplacement hole and the nearest other emplacement hole or one percent of the distance between the point of measurement and the entrance of the emplacement hole, whichever is smaller, but in no case shall the error be required to be less than one meter.

3. The Party carrying out the explosion shall emplace for each explosive that portion of the electrical equipment for yield determination described in subparagraph 3(a) of Article IV, supplied in accordance with paragraph 1 of Article IV, in the same emplacement hole as the explosive in accordance with the installation instructions supplied under the provisions of paragraph 5 or 6 of Article IV. Such emplacement shall be carried out under the observation of designated personnel. Other equipment specified in subparagraph 3(b) of Article IV shall be emplaced and installed:

(a) by designated personnel under the observation and with the assistance of personnel of the Party carrying out the explosion, if such assistance is requested by designated personnel; or

(b) in accordance with paragraph 5 of Article IV.

4. That portion of the electrical equipment for yield determination described in subparagraph 3(a) of Article IV that is to be emplaced in each emplacement hole shall be located so that the end of the electrical equipment which is farthest from the entrance to the emplacement hole is at a distance, in meters, from the bottom of the canister containing the explosive equal to 3.5 times the cube root of the planned yield in kilotons of the explosive when the planned yield is less than 20 kilotons and three times the cube root of the planned yield in kilotons of the explosive when the planned yield is 20 kilotons or more. Canisters longer than 10 meters containing the explosive shall only be utilized if there is prior agreement between the Parties establishing provisions for their use. The Party carrying out the explosion shall provide the other Party with data on the distribution of density inside any other canister in the emplacement hole with a transverse cross-sectional area exceeding 10 square centimeters located within a distance, in meters, of 10 times the cube root of the planned yield in kilotons of the explosion from the bottom of the canister containing the explosive. The Party carrying out the explosion shall provide the other Party with access to confirm such data on density distribution within any such canister.

5. The Party carrying out an explosion shall fill each emplacement hole, including all pipes and tubes contained therein which have at any transverse section an aggregate cross-sectional area exceeding 10 square centimeters in the region containing the electrical equipment for yield determination and to a distance, in meters, of six times the cube root of the planned yield in kilotons of the explosive from the explosive emplacement point, with material having a density not less than seven-tenths of the average density of the surrounding rock, and from that point to a distance of not less than 60 meters from the explosive emplacement point with material having a density greater than one gram per cubic centimeter.

6. Designated personnel shall have the right to:

(a) confirm information provided in accordance with subparagraph 2(a) of this Article;

(b) confirm information provided in accordance with subparagraph 2(b) of this Article and be provided, upon request, with a sample of each batch of stemming material as that material is put into the emplacement hole; and

(c) confirm the information provided in accordance with subparagraph 2(c) of this Article by having access to the data acquired and by observing, upon their request, the making of measurements.

7. For those explosives which are emplaced in separate emplacement holes, the emplacement shall be such that the distance D, in meters, between any explosive and any portion of the electrical equipment for determination of the yield of any other explosive in the group shall be not less than 10 times the cube root of the planned yield in kilotons of the larger explosive of such a pair of explosives. Individual explosions shall be separated by time intervals, in milliseconds, not greater than one-sixth the amount by which the distance D, in meters, exceeds 10 times the cube root of the planned yield in kilotons of the larger explosive of such a pair of explosives.

8. For those explosives in a group which are emplaced in a common emplacement hole, the distance, in meters, between each explosive and any other explosive in that emplacement hole shall be not less than 10 times the cube root of the planned yield in kilotons of the larger explosive of such a pair of explosives, and the explosives shall be detonated in sequential order, beginning with the explosive farthest from the entrance to the emplacement hole, with the individual detonations separated by time intervals, in milliseconds, of not less than one times the cube root of the planned yield in kilotons of the largest explosive in this emplacement hole.

Article VII

1. Designated personnel with their personal baggage and their equipment as provided in Article IV shall be permitted to enter the territory of the Party carrying out the explosion at an entry port to be agreed upon by the Parties, to remain in the territory of the Party carrying out the explosion for the purpose of fulfilling their rights and functions provided for in the Treaty and this Protocol, and to depart from an exit port to be agreed upon by the Parties.

2. At all times while designated personnel are in the territory of the Party carrying out the explosion, their persons, property, personal baggage, archives and documents as well as their temporary official and living quarters shall be accorded the same privileges and immunities as provided in Articles 22, 23, 24, 29, 30, 31, 34 and 36 of the Vienna Convention on Diplomatic Relations of 1961 to the persons, property, personal baggage, archives and documents of diplomatic agents as well as to the premises of diplomatic missions and private residences of diplomatic agents.

3. Without prejudice to their privileges and immunities it shall be the duty of designated personnel to respect the laws and regulations of the State in whose territory the explosion is to be carried out insofar as they do not impede in any way whatsoever the proper exercising of their rights and functions provided for by the Treaty and this Protocol.

Article VIII

The Party carrying out an explosion shall have sole and exclusive control over and full responsibility for the conduct of the explosion.

Article IX

1. Nothing in the Treaty and this Protocol shall affect proprietary rights in information made available under the Treaty and this Protocol and in information which may be disclosed in preparation for and carrying out of explosions; however, claims to such proprietary rights shall not impede implementation of the provisions of the Treaty and this Protocol.

2. Public release of the information provided in accordance with Article II or publication of material using such information, as well as public release of the results of observation and measurements obtained by designated personnel, may take place only by agreement with the Party carrying out an explosion; however, the other Party shall have the right to issue statements after the explosion that do not divulge information in which the Party carrying out the explosion has rights which are referred to in paragraph 1 of this Article.

Article X

The Joint Consultative Commission shall establish procedures through which the Parties will, as appropriate, consult with each other for the purpose of ensuring efficient implementation of this Protocol.

United Nations Convention on the Prohibition of Military or Any Other Hostile Use of Environmental Modification Techniques

Also known as: ENMOD Convention   *Date of signature:* May 18, 1977

Place of signature: *Geneva*
Signatory states: *Australia, Belgium, Benin, Bolivia, Brazil, Bulgaria, Byelorussia, Canada, Cuba, Cyprus, Czechoslovakia, Denmark, Ethiopia, Finland, German Democratic Republic, Federal Republic of Germany, Ghana, Holy See, Hungary, Iceland, India, Iran, Iraq, Ireland, Italy, Laos, Lebanon, Liberia, Luxembourg, Mongolia, Morocco, Netherlands, Nicaragua, Norway, Poland, Portugal, Rumania, Sierra Leone, Soviet Union, Spain, Sri Lanka, Syria, Tunisia, Turkey, Uganda, Ukraine, United Kingdom, United States, Yemen Arab Republic, Zaire*
Ratifications: *Bangladesh, Bulgaria, Byelorussia, Canada, Cape Verde, Cuba, Cyprus, Czechoslovakia, Denmark, Finland, German Democratic Republic, Ghana, Hungary, India, Kuwait, Laos, Malawi, Mexico, Norway, Papua New Guinea, Poland, Sao Tome, Solomon Islands, Soviet Union, Spain, Sri Lanka, Tunisia, Ukraine, United Kingdom, United States, Vietnam, Yemen Arab Republic, People's Democratic Republic of Yemen*
Date of entry into force: *October 5, 1978*

The General Assembly,
Recalling its resolutions 3264 (XXIX) of 9 December 1974 and 3475 (XXX) of 11 December 1975,
Recalling its resolution 1722 (XVI) of 20 December 1961, in which it recognized that all States have a deep interest in disarmament and arms control negotiations,
Determined to avert the potential dangers of military or any other hostile use of environmental modification techniques,
Convinced that broad adherence to a convention on the prohibition of such action would contribute to the cause of strengthening peace and averting the threat of war,
Noting with satisfaction that the Conference of the Committee on Disarmament has completed and transmitted to the General Assembly, in the report of its work in 1976, the text of a draft Convention on the Prohibition of Military or Any Other Hostile Use of Environmental Modification Techniques,
Noting further that the Convention is intended to prohibit effectively military or any other hostile use of environmental modification techniques in order to eliminate the dangers to mankind from such use,
Bearing in mind that draft agreements on disarmament and arms control measures submitted to the

General Assembly by the Conference of the Committee on Disarmament should be the result of a process of effective negotiations, and that such instruments should duly take into account the views and interests of all States so that they can be adhered to by the widest possible number of countries,
Bearing in mind that Article VIII of the Convention makes provision for a conference to review the operation of the Convention five years after its entry into force, with a view to ensuring that its purposes and provisions are being realized,
Also bearing in mind all relevant documents and negotiating records of the Conference of the committee on Disarmament on the discussion of the draft Convention,
Convinced that the Convention should not affect the use of environmental modification techniques for peaceful purposes, which could contribute to the preservation and improvement of the environment for the benefit of present and future generations,
Convinced that the Convention will contribute to the realization of the purposes and principles of the Charter of the United Nations,
Anxious that during its 1977 session the Conference of the Committee on Disarmament should concentrate on urgent negotiations on disarmament and arms limitation measures,
1. *Refers* the Convention on the Prohibition of Military or Any Other Hostile Use of Environmental Modification Techniques, the text of which is annexed to the present resolution, to all States for their consideration, signature and ratification;
2. *Requests* the Secretary-General, as Depositary of the Convention, to open it for signature and ratification at the earliest possible date;
3. *Expresses its hope* for the widest possible adherence to the Convention;
4. *Calls upon* the Conference of the Committee on Disarmament, without prejudice to the priorities established in its programme of work, to keep under review the problem of effectively averting the dangers of military or any other hostile use of environmental modification techniques;
5. *Requests* the Secretary-General to transmit to the Conference of the Committee on Disarmament all documents relating to the discussion by the General Assembly at its thirty-first session of the question of the prohibition of military or any other hostile use of environmental modification techniques.

ANNEX

The States Parties to this Convention,

Guided by the interest of consolidating peace, and wishing to contribute to the cause of halting the arms race, and of bringing about general and complete disarmament under strict and effective international control, and of saving mankind from the danger of using new means of warfare,

Determined to continue negotiations with a view to achieving effective progress towards further measures in the field of disarmament,

Recognising that scientific and technical advances may open new possibilities with respect to modification of the environment,

Recalling the Declaration of the United Nations Conference on the Human Environment, adopted at Stockholm on 16 June 1972,

Realizing that the use of environmental modification techniques for peaceful purposes could improve the interrelationship of man and nature and contribute to the preservation and improvement of the environment for the benefit of present and future generations.

Recognizing, however, that military or any other hostile use of such techniques could have effects extremely harmful to human welfare,

Desiring to prohibit effectively military or any other hostile use of environmental modification techniques in order to eliminate the dangers to mankind from such use, and affirming their willingness to work towards the achievement of this objective,

Desiring also to contribute to the strengthening of trust among nations and to the further improvement of the international situation in accordance with the purposes and principles of the Charter of the United Nations,

Have agreed on the following:

Article I

1. Each State Party to this Convention undertakes not to engage in military or any other hostile use of environmental modification techniques having widespread, long-lasting or severe effects as the means of destruction, damage or injury to any other State Party.

2. Each State Party to this Convention undertakes not to assist, encourage or induce any State, group of States or international organization to engage in activities contrary to the provisions of paragraph 1 of this Article.

Article II

As used in Article I, the term "environmental modification techniques" refers to any technique for changing—through the deliberate manipulation of natural processes—the dynamics, composition or structure of the earth, including its biota, lithosphere, hydrosphere and atmosphere, or of outer space.

Article III

1. The provisions of this Convention shall not hinder the use of environmental modification techniques for peaceful purposes and shall be without prejudice to the generally recognized principles and applicable rules of international law concerning such use.

2. The States Parties to this Convention undertake to facilitate, and have the right to participate in, the fullest possible exchange of scientific and technological information on the use of environmental modification techniques for peaceful purposes. States Parties in a position to do so shall contribute, alone or together with other States or international organizations, to international economic and scientific co-operation in the preservation, improvement and peaceful utilization of the environment, with due consideration for the needs of the developing areas of the world.

Article IV

Each State Party to this Convention undertakes to take any measures it considers necessary in accordance with its constitutional processes to prohibit and prevent any activity in violation of the provisions of the Convention anywhere under its jurisdiction or control.

Article V

1. The States Parties to this Convention undertake to consult one another and to co-operate in solving any problems which may arise in relation to the objectives of, or in the application of the provisions of, the Convention. Consultation and co-operation pursuant to this Article may also be undertaken through appropriate international procedures within the framework of the United Nations and in accordance with its Charter. These international procedures may include the services of appropriate international organizations, as well as of a Consultative Committee of Experts as provided for in paragraph 2 of this Article.

2. For the purposes set forth in paragraph 1 of this Article, the Depositary shall, within one month of the receipt of a request from any State Party to this Convention, convene a Consultative Committee of Experts. Any State Party may appoint an expert to this Committee whose functions and rules of procedure are set out

in the annex, which constitutes an integral part of the Convention. The committee shall transmit to the Depositary a summary of its findings of fact, incorporating all views and information presented to the Committee during its proceedings. The Depositary shall distribute the summary to all States Parties.

3. Any State Party to this Convention which has reasons to believe that any other State Party is acting in breach of obligations deriving from the provisions of the Convention may lodge a complaint with the Security Council of the United Nations. Such a complaint should include all relevant information as well as all possible evidence supporting its validity.

4. Each State Party to this Convention undertakes to co-operate in carrying out any investigation which the Security Council may initiate, in accordance with the provisions of the Charter of the United Nations, on the basis of the complaint received by the Council shall inform the States Parties of the results of the investigation.

5. Each State Party to this Convention undertakes to provide or support assistance, in accordance with the provisions of the Charter of the United Nations, to any State Party which so requests, if the Security Council decides that such Party has been harmed or is likely to be harmed as a result of violation of the Convention.

Article VI

1. Any State Party may propose amendments to this Convention. The text of any proposed amendment shall be submitted to the Depositary, who shall promptly circulate it to all States Parties.

2. An amendment shall enter into force for all States Parties which have accepted it, upon the deposit with the Depositary of instruments of acceptance by a majority of States Parties. Thereafter it shall enter into force for any remaining State Party on the date of deposit of its instrument of acceptance.

Article VII

This Convention shall be of unlimited duration.

Article VIII

1. Five years after the entry into force of this Convention, a conference of the States Parties to the Convention shall be convened by the Depositary at Geneva. The conference shall review the operation of the Convention with a view to ensuring that its purposes and provisions are being realized, and shall in particular examine the effectiveness of the provisions of Article I, paragraph 1, in eliminating the dangers of military or any other hostile use of environmental modification techniques.

2. At intervals of not less than five years thereafter, a majority of the States Parties to this Convention may obtain, by submitting a proposal to this effect to the Depositary, the convening of a conference with the same objectives.

3. If no review conference has been convened pursuant to paragraph 2 of this Article within ten years following the conclusion of a previous review conference, the Depositary shall solicit the views of all States Parties to this Convention on the holding of such a conference. If one third or ten of the States Parties, whichever number is less, respond affirmatively, the Depositary shall take immediate steps to convene the conference.

Article IX

1. This Convention shall be open to all States for signature. Any State which does not sign the Convention before its entry into force in accordance with paragraph 3 of this Article may accede to it at any time.

2. This Convention shall be subject to ratification by signatory States. Instruments of ratification and of accession shall be deposited with the Secretary-General of the United Nations.

3. This Convention shall enter into force upon the deposit with the Depositary of instruments of ratification by twenty Governments in accordance with paragraph 2 of this Article.

4. For those States whose instruments of ratification or accession are deposited after the entry into force of this Convention, it shall enter into force on the date of the deposit of their instruments of ratification or accession.

5. The Depositary shall promptly inform all signatory and acceding States of the date of each signature, the date of deposit of each instrument of ratification or accession and the date of the entry into force of this Convention and of any amendments thereto, as well as of the receipt of other notices.

6. This Convention shall be registered by the Depositary in accordance with Article 102 of the Charter of the United Nations.

Article X

This Convention, of which the Arabic, Chinese, English, French, Russian and Spanish texts are equally authentic, shall be deposited with the Secretary-General of the United Nations who shall send certified copies thereof to the Governments of the signatory and acceding States.

Annex to the Convention

Consultative Committee of Experts

1. The Consultative Committee of Experts shall undertake to make appropriate findings of fact and provide expert views relevant to any problem raised pursuant to article V, paragraph 1, of this Convention by the State Party requesting the convening of the Committee.

2. The work of the Consultative Committee of Experts shall be organized in such a way as to permit it to perform the functions set forth in paragraph 1 of this annex. The Committee shall decide procedural questions relative to the organization of its work, where possible by consensus, but otherwise by a majority of those present and voting. There shall be no voting on matters of substance.

3. The Depositary or his representative shall serve as the Chairman of the Committee.

4. Each expert may be assisted at meetings by one or more advisers.

5. Each expert shall have the right, through the Chairman, to request from States, and from international organizations, such information and assistance as the expert considers desirable for the accomplishment of the Committee's work.

Guidelines for Nuclear Transfers Agreed by the Nuclear Suppliers Group

Date of signature: September 21, 1977
Place of signature: London
Signatory states: The guidelines were agreed by the members of the Nuclear Supplier Group, known as the London Club. The members are: Belgium, Canada, Czechoslovakia, France, German Democratic Republic, Federal Republic of Germany, Italy, Japan, Poland, Soviet Union, Sweden, Switzerland, United Kingdom, United States

COMMUNICATIONS RECEIVED FROM CERTAIN MEMBER STATES REGARDING GUIDELINES FOR THE EXPORT OF NUCLEAR MATERIAL, EQUIPMENT OR TECHNOLOGY

1. On 11 January 1978, the Director General received similar letters, all of that date, from the Resident Representatives to the Agency of Czechoslovakia, France, the German Democratic Republic, Japan, Poland, Switzerland, the Union of Soviet Socialist Republics and the United States of America, relating to the export of nuclear material, equipment or technology. In the light of the request at the end of each of those letters, the text is reproduced below as Letter I.

2. On the same day, the Resident Representatives to the Agency of Canada and Sweden also addressed analogous letters to the Director General. In the light of the request expressed at the end of each of those letters, their texts are reproduced below as Letter II

and Letter III respectively.

3. On the same day, the Director General received similar letters from the Resident Representatives to the Agency of Belgium, the Federal Republic of Germany, the Netherlands and the United Kingdom of Great Britain and Northern Ireland, Members of the European Communities, relating to the export of nuclear material, equipment or technology. In the light of the request expressed at the end of each of those letters, the text is reproduced below as Letter IV.

4. On 11 January 1978 the Resident Representative to the Agency of Italy, a Member of the European Communities, addressed a letter to the Director General relating to the same subject, the text of which is reproduced below as Letter V.

5. On 11 January 1978 the Director General received complementary letters, all of that date, from the Resident Representatives to the Agency of Belgium, Czechoslovakia, the German Democratic Republic, Japan, Poland, Switzerland and the Union of Soviet Socialist Republics, the texts of which are reproduced below as Letters VI, VII, VIII, IX, X, XI, and XII respectively.

6. The attachments to Letters I-V, which are in every case identical, setting forth the Guidelines for Nuclear Transfers with their Annexes, are reproduced in the Appendix.

Letter I

The Permanent Mission of . . . presents its compliments to the Director General of the International Atomic Energy Agency and has the honour to enclose copies of three documents which have been the subject of discussion between the Government of . . . and a number of other Governments.

The Government of . . . has decided that, when considering the export of nuclear material, equipment or technology, it will act in accordance with the principles contained in the attached documents.

In reaching this decision, the Government of . . . is fully aware of the need to contribute to the development of nuclear power in order to meet world energy requirements, while avoiding contributing in any way to the dangers of proliferation of nuclear weapons or other nuclear explosive devices, and of the need to remove safeguards and non-proliferation assurances from the field of commercial competition.

The Government of . . . hopes that other Governments may also decide to base their own nuclear export policies upon these documents.

The Government of . . . requests that the Director General of the International Atomic Energy Agency should circulate the texts of this note and its enclosures to all Member Governments for their information and as a demonstration of support by the Government of . . . for the Agency's non-proliferation objectives and safeguards activities.

The Permanent Mission of . . . avails itself of this opportunity to renew to the Director General of the International Atomic Energy Agency the assurances of its highest consideration.

Letter II

The Permanent Mission of Canada to the IAEA Presents its compliments to the Director General and has the honour to enclose copies of three documents that have been the subject of discussion between the Government of Canada and a number of other Governments.

The Government of Canada has decided that, when considering the export of nuclear material, equipment or technology, it will act in accordance with the principles contained in the attached documents as well as other principles considered pertinent by it.

In reaching this decision, the Government of Canada is fully aware of the need to contribute to the development of nuclear power in order to meet world energy requirements, while avoiding contributing in any way to the dangers of a proliferation of nuclear weapons or other nuclear explosive devices, and of the need to remove safeguards and non-proliferation assurances from the field of commercial competition.

The Government of Canada hopes that other Governments may also decide to base their own nuclear export policies upon these documents and such further principles as may be agreed upon.

The Government of Canada requests that the Director General of the International Atomic Energy Agency should circulate the text of this Note and its enclosures to all Member Governments for their information and as a demonstration of support by the Government of Canada for the Agency's non-proliferation objectives and safeguard activities.

The permanent Mission of Canada to the IAEA avails itself of this opportunity to renew to the Director General the assurances of its highest consideration.

Letter III

The Permanent Mission of Sweden present their compliments to the Director General of the International Atomic Energy Agency have the honour to enclose copies of three documents which have been the subject of discussion between the Government of Sweden and a number of other Governments.

The Government of Sweden have decided that, when considering the export of nuclear material, equipment or technology, they will act in accordance with the principles contained in the attached documents.

In reaching this decision, the Government of Sweden is fully aware of the need to avoid contributing in any way to the dangers of a proliferation of nuclear weapons or other nuclear explosive devices, and of the need to remove safeguards and non-proliferation assurances from the field of commercial competition.

The Government of Sweden hope that other Governments may also decide to base their own nuclear export policies upon these documents.

The Government of Sweden request that the Director General of the International Atomic Energy Agency should circulate the text of this Note and its enclosures to all Member Governments for their information and as a demonstration of support by the Government of Sweden for the Agency's non-proliferation objectives and safeguards activities.

The Permanent Mission of Sweden take this opportunity to renew to the Director General of the International Atomic Agency the assurances of their highest consideration.

Letter IV

The Permanent Mission of . . . to the International Organizations in Vienna presents its compliments to the Director General of the International Atomic Energy Agency and has the honour to enclose copies of three documents which have been the subject of discussion between the ... and a number of other Governments.

The Government of ... has decided that, when considering the export of nuclear material, equipment or technology, it will act in accordance with the principles contained in the attached documents.

In reaching this decision, the Government of ... is fully aware of the need to contribute to the development of nuclear power in order to meet world energy requirements, while avoiding contributing in any way to the dangers of a proliferation of nuclear weapons or other nuclear explosive devices, and of the need to remove safeguards and non-proliferation assurances from the field of commercial competition.

As a Member of the European Community, the Government of ... so far as trade within the Community is concerned, will implement these documents in the light of its commitments under the Treaties of Rome where necessary.

The Government of ... hopes that other Governments may also decide to base their own nuclear export policies upon these documents.

The Government of ... requests that the Director General of the International Atomic Energy Agency should circulate the texts of this Note and its enclosures to all Member Governments for their information and as a demonstration of support by the Governments of ... for the Agency's non-proliferation objectives and safeguards activities.

The Permanent Mission of ... to the International Organizations in Vienna avails itself of this opportunity to renew to the Director General of the International Atomic Energy Agency the assurances of its highest consideration.

Letter V

The Permanent Mission of Italy present their compliments and have the honour to enclose copies of three documents which have been the subject of discussion between the Government of Italy and a number of other Governments.

The Government of Italy have decided that, when considering the export of nuclear material, equipment or technology, they will act in accordance with the principles contained in the attached documents.

In reaching this decision, the Government of Italy are fully aware of the need to contribute to the development of nuclear power in order to meet world energy requirements, while avoiding contributing in any way to dangers of a proliferation of nuclear weapons or other nuclear explosive devices, and of

the need to remove safeguards and non-proliferation assurances from the field of commercial competition.

The Italian Government underline that the undertaking referred to cannot limit in any way the rights and obligations arising for Italy out of agreements to which she is a Party, and in particular those arising out of Article IV of the Non-Proliferation Treaty.

As a member of the European Community, the Government of Italy, so far as trade within the Community is concerned, will implement these documents in the light of their commitments under the Treaties of Rome where necessary.

The Government of Italy hope that other Governments may also decide to base their own nuclear export policies upon these documents.

The Government of Italy request that the Director General of the International Atomic Energy Agency should circulate the texts of this Note and its enclosures to all Member Governments for their information and as a demonstration of support by the Governments of Italy for the Agency's non-proliferation objectives and safeguards activities.

Letter VI

The Permanent Mission of Belgium presents its compliments to the Director General of the IAEA and, in addition to its Note P 10-92/24 of 11 January 1978, would like to draw the attention to the following:

The Government of Belgium at present are not in a position to implement fully the principles for technology transfer set out in the documents attached to the above-mentioned Note because of the lack of appropriate laws and regulations. However, the Government of Belgium intend to implement these principles fully when appropriate laws and regulations for this purpose are put into force as necessary.

The Government of Belgium request that the Director General of the IAEA should circulate the text of this Note to all Member Governments for their information.

The Permanent Mission of Belgium take this opportunity to renew to the Director General of the IAEA the assurance of its highest consideration.

Letter VII

The Permanent Mission of the Czechoslovak Socialist Republic to the International Organizations presents its compliments to the Director General of the International Atomic Energy Agency and has the honour to refer to its Note No. 1036/78 regarding standards of the nuclear export policies which have been adopted by the members of the Nuclear Suppliers

Group.

The Government of the Czechoslovak Socialist Republic greatly appreciates the role of the International Atomic Energy Agency in the sphere of control of the provisions of the Non-Proliferation Treaty. This activity has been an important instrument of preventing proliferation of nuclear weapons. Sharing the opinion that further strengthening of safeguards lies in the interest of universal peace, the Government of the Czechoslovak Socialist Republic has decided that it would deliver nuclear material, equipment and technology defined in a trigger list, to any non-nuclear-weapon State only in a case when the whole nuclear activity of a recipient country, and not only material, equipment and technology being transferred, are subject to the Agency's safeguards.

The Government of the Czechoslovak Socialist Republic expresses its opinion that this principle, if observed by all the States-nuclear suppliers, could have made a great contribution toward strengthening and universality of the Non-Proliferation Treaty.

The Permanent Mission of the Czechoslovak Socialist Republic to the International Organizations avails itself of this opportunity to renew to the Director General of the International Atomic Energy Agency the assurances of its highest consideration.

Letter VIII

The Permanent Mission of the German Democratic Republic to the International Organizations in Vienna presents its compliments to the Director General of the International Atomic Agency and has the honour, in connection with Note No. 2/78-III addressed to the Director General of the IAEA on 11 January 1978, to state the following: in the view of the Government of the German Democratic Republic, the guidelines for nuclear exports are such as to strengthen the regime of non-proliferation of nuclear weapons and the IAEA safeguards system. The German Democratic Republic will also in future advocate agreements to the effect that nuclear exports under the trigger list mentioned in the above Note should go only to those non-nuclear-weapon States that accept IAEA safeguards for all of their nuclear activities.

The Government of the German Democratic Republic is convinced that any reinforcement of the regime of non-proliferation of nuclear weapons will promote the peaceful uses of nuclear energy and international co-operation in this area.

The Permanent Mission requests that the present text be circulated as an official document of the International Atomic Energy Agency.

The Permanent Mission of the German Democratic Republic to the International Organizations in Vienna avails itself of this opportunity to renew to the Director General of the International Atomic Energy Agency the assurances of its highest consideration.

Letter IX

The Embassy of Japan presents its compliments to the International Atomic Energy Agency and, in reference to its Note No. J.M. 78/21 of January 11, 1978, has the honour to inform the International Atomic Energy Agency of the following.

The Government of Japan at present is not in a position to implement fully the Principles for Technology Transfers set out in the documents attached to the above-mentioned Note because of the lack of appropriate laws and regulations.

However, the Government of Japan intends to implement these principles fully when appropriate laws and regulations for this purpose are put into force as necessary.

The Government of Japan requests that the Director General of the International Atomic Energy Agency be good enough to circulate the texts of this Note to all Member Governments for their information.

The Embassy of Japan avails itself of this opportunity to renew to the International Atomic Energy Agency the assurances of its highest consideration.

Letter X

The Permanent Mission of the Polish People's Republic to the International Atomic Energy Agency presents its compliments to the Director General of the IAEA and has the honour to refer to its Note No. 10-96/77 regarding standards of the nuclear export policies which have been adopted by the members of the Nuclear Suppliers Group.

The Government of the Polish People's Republic greatly appreciates the role of the International Atomic Energy Agency in the sphere of control of the provisions of the Non-Proliferation Treaty. This activity has been an important instrument of preventing proliferation of nuclear weapons. Sharing the opinion that further strengthening of safeguards lies in the interest of universal peace, the Government of the Polish People's Republic has decided that it would deliver nuclear material, equipment and technology defined in a trigger list, to any non-nuclear-weapon State only in a case when the whole nuclear activity of a recipient country, and not only material, equipment and technology being transferred, are subject to the

Agency's safeguards.

The Government of the Polish People's Republic expresses its opinion that this principle, if observed by all the States-nuclear suppliers, could have made a great contribution toward strengthening and universality of the Non-Proliferation Treaty.

The Government of the Polish People's Republic requests that the Director General of the IAEA should circulate the text of this Note to all Member Governments.

The Permanent Mission of the Polish People's Republic to the International Atomic Energy Agency avails itself of this opportunity to renew to the Director General of the IAEA the assurances of the highest consideration.

Letter XI

The Permanent Mission of Switzerland presents its compliments to the Director General of the International Atomic Energy Agency and, with reference to its today's Note No. 003, has the honour to emphasize the following.

The Government of Switzerland at present is not in a position to implement fully the principles for Technology Transfers set out in the documents attached to the above-mentioned Notes because of the lack of appropriate laws and regulations. However, the Government of Switzerland intends to implement these principles fully when appropriate laws and regulations for this purpose are put into force as necessary.

The Government of Switzerland requests that the Director General of the International Atomic Energy Agency should circulate the text of this Note to all Member Governments for their information.

The Permanent Mission of Switzerland avails itself of this opportunity to renew to the Director General of the International Atomic Energy Agency the assurances of its highest consideration.

Letter XII

With reference to Note Verbale No. 1 from the Permanent Mission of the USSR, dated 11 January 1978, I have the honour to send you the following Declaration of the Government of the USSR:

The Government of the Union of Soviet Socialist Republics emphasizes its determination to continue its efforts to secure agreement between countries supplying nuclear materials, equipment and technology on the principle that IAEA safeguards must be applied to all nuclear activities of non-nuclear-weapon States when those States receive

any of the items mentioned in the initial list referred to in the above-mentioned Note Verbale. In this connection the Government of the USSR takes the view that the principle of full control is a necessary condition for ensuring effective safeguards which can prevent nuclear materials, equipment and technology from being used for manufacturing nuclear weapons or other explosive devices.

The Government requests that the text of the present letter be distributed as an official document of the IAEA.

APPENDIX

Guidelines for Nuclear Transfers

1. The following fundamental principles for safeguards and export controls should apply to nuclear transfers to any non-nuclear-weapon State for peaceful purposes. In this connection, suppliers have defined an export trigger list and agreed on common criteria for technology transfers.

Prohibition on Nuclear Explosives

2. Suppliers should authorise transfer of items identified in the trigger list only upon formal governmental assurances from recipients explicitly excluding uses which would result in any nuclear explosive device.

Physical Protection

3.

(a) All nuclear materials and facilities identified by the agreed trigger list should be placed under effective physical protection to prevent unauthorised use and handling. The levels of physical protection to be ensured in relation to the type of materials, equipment and facilities, have been agreed by suppliers, taking account of international recommendations.

(b) The implementation of measures of physical protection in the recipient country is the responsibility of the Government of that country. However, in order to implement the terms agreed upon amongst suppliers, the levels of physical protection on which these measures have to be based should be the subject of an agreement between supplier and recipient.

(c) In each case special arrangements should be made for a clear definition of responsibilities for the transport of trigger list items.

Safeguards

4. Suppliers should transfer trigger list items only when covered by IAEA safeguards, with duration and coverage provisions in conformance with the GOV/1621 guidelines. Exceptions should be made only after consultation with the parties to this understanding.

5. Suppliers will jointly reconsider their common safeguards requirements, whenever appropriate.

Safeguards Triggered by the Transfer of Certain Technology

6.

(a) The requirements of paragraphs 2, 3 and 4 above should also apply to facilities for reprocessing enrichment, or heavy-water production, utilizing technology directly transferred by the supplier or derived from transferred facilities, or major critical components thereof.

(b) The transfer of such facilities, or major critical components thereof, or related technology, should require an undertaking (1) that IAEA safeguards apply to any facilities of the same type (i.e., if the design, construction or operating processes are based on the same or similar physical or chemical processes, as defined in the trigger list) constructed during an agreed period in the recipient country and (2) that there should at all times be in effect a safeguards agreement permitting the IAEA to apply Agency safeguards with respect to such facilities identified by the recipient, or by the supplier in consultation with the recipient, as using transferred technology.

Special Controls on Sensitive Exports

7. Suppliers should exercise restraint in the transfer of sensitive facilities, technology and weapons usable materials. If enrichment or reprocessing facilities, equipment or technology are to be transferred, suppliers should encourage recipients to accept, as an alternative to national plants, supplier involvement and/or other appropriate multinational participation in resulting facilities. Suppliers should also promote international (including IAEA) activities concerned with multinational regional fuel cycle centres.

Special Controls on Export of Enrichment Facilities, Equipment and Technology

8. For a transfer of an enrichment facility, or technology therefor, the recipient nation should agree that neither the transferred facility, nor any facility based on such technology, will be designed or operated for the production of greater than 20% enriched uranium without the consent of the supplier nation, of which the IAEA should be advised.

Controls on Supplies or Derived Weapons-Usable Material

9. Suppliers recognize the importance, in order to advance the objectives of these guidelines and to provide opportunities further to reduce the risks of proliferation, of including in agreements on supply of nuclear materials or of facilities which produce weapons-usable material, provisions calling for mutual agreement between the supplier and the recipient on arrangements for reprocessing, storage, alteration, use, transfer or retransfer of any weapons usable material involved. Suppliers should endeavour to include such provisions whenever appropriate and practicable.

Controls on Retransfer

10.

(a) Suppliers should transfer trigger list items, including technology defined under paragraph 6, only upon the recipient's assurance that in the case of:

(1) retransfer of such items, or

(2) transfer of trigger list items derived from facilities originally transferred by the supplier, or with the help of equipment or technology originally transferred by the supplier, the recipient of the retransfer or transfer will have provided the same assurances as those required by the supplier for the original transfer.

(b) In addition the supplier's consent should be required for: (1) and retransfer of the facilities, major critical components, or technology described in paragraph 6; (2) any transfer of facilities or major critical components derived from those items; (3) any retransfer of heavy water or weapons-usable material.

Supporting Activities

Physical Security

11. Suppliers should promote international co-

operation on the exchange of physical security information, protection of nuclear materials in transit, and recovery of stolen nuclear materials and equipment.

Support for Effective IAEA Safeguards

12. Suppliers should make special efforts in support of effective implementation of IAEA safeguards. Suppliers should also support the Agency's efforts to assist Member States in the improvement of their national systems of accounting and control of nuclear material and to increase the technical effectiveness of safeguards.

Similarly, they should make every effort to support the IAEA in increasing further the adequacy of safeguards in the light of technical developments and the rapidly growing number of nuclear facilities, and to support appropriate initiatives aimed at improving the effectiveness of IAEA safeguards.

Sensitive Plant Design Features

13. Suppliers should encourage the designers and makers of sensitive equipment to construct it in such a way as to facilitate the application of safeguards.

Consultations

14.

(a) Suppliers should maintain contact and consult through regular channels on matters connected with the implementation of these guidelines.

(b) Suppliers should consult, as each deems appropri-

ate, with other Governments concerned on specific sensitive cases, to ensure that any transfer does not contribute to risks of conflict or instability.

(c) In the event that one or more suppliers believe that there has been a violation of supplier/recipient understandings resulting from these guidelines, particularly in the case of an explosion of a nuclear device, or illegal termination or violation of IAEA safeguards by a recipient, suppliers should consult promptly through diplomatic channels in order to determine and assess the reality and extent of the alleged violation.

Pending the early outcome of such consultations, suppliers will not act in a manner that could prejudice any measure that may be adopted by other suppliers concerning their current contacts with that recipient.

Upon the findings of such consultations, the suppliers, bearing in mind Article XII of the IAEA Statute, should agree on an appropriate response and possible action which could include the termination of nuclear transfers to that recipient.

15. In considering transfers, each supplier should exercise prudence having regard to all the circumstances of each case, including any risk that technology transfers not covered by paragraph 6, or subsequent retransfers, might result in unsafeguarded nuclear materials.

16. Unanimous consent is required for any changes in these guidelines, including any which might result from the reconsideration mentioned in paragraph 5.

Protocol I Additional to the Geneva Conventions of 1949 Relating to the Protection of Victims of International Armed Conflicts

Also known as: Protocol I
Date of signature: December 12, 1977
Place of signature: Berne
Signatory states: Bangladesh, Bahamas, Botswana, Cyprus, Ecuador, El Salvador, Finland, Gabon, Ghana, Jordan, Libya, Laos, Mauritania, Niger, Sweden, Tunisia, Vietnam, Yugoslavia
Date of entry into force: December 7, 1978

The High Contracting Parties,
Proclaiming their earnest wish to see peace prevail

among peoples,
Recalling that every State has the duty, in conformity with the Charter of the United Nations, to refrain in its international relations from the threat or use of force against the sovereignty, territorial integrity or political independence of any State, or in any other manner inconsistent with the purposes of the United Nations,
Believing it necessary nevertheless to reaffirm and develop the provisions protecting the victims of armed conflicts and to supplement measures intended to reinforce their application,
Expressing their conviction that nothing in this Pro-

tocol or in the Geneva Conventions of 12 August 1949 can be construed as legitimizing or authorizing any act of aggression or any other use of force inconsistent with the Charter of the United Nations,

Reaffirming further that the provisions of the Geneva Conventions of 12 August 1949 and of this Protocol must be fully applied in all circumstances to all persons who are protected by those instruments, without any adverse distinction based on the nature or origin of the armed conflict or on the causes espoused by or attributed to the Parties to the conflict,

Have agreed on the following:

PART I

GENERAL PROVISIONS

Article 1

General Principles and Scope of Application

1. The High Contracting Parties undertake to respect and to ensure respect for this Protocol in all circumstances.

2. In cases not covered by this Protocol or by other international agreements, civilians and combatants remain under the protection and authority of the principles of international law derived from established custom, from the principles of humanity and from dictates of public conscience.

3. This Protocol, which supplements the Geneva Conventions of 12 August 1949 for the protection of war victims, shall apply in the situations referred to in Article 2 common to those Conventions.

4. The situations referred to in the preceding paragraph include armed conflicts in which peoples are fighting against colonial domination and alien occupation and against racist régimes in the exercise of their right of self-determination, as enshrined in the Charter of the United Nations and the Declaration on Principles of International Law concerning Friendly Relations and Co-operation among States in accordance with the Charter of the United Nations.

Article 2

Definitions

For the purposes of this Protocol:

(a) "First Convention", "Second Convention", "Third Convention" and "Fourth Convention" mean, respectively, the Geneva Convention for the Amelioration of the Condition of the Wounded and Sick in Armed Forces in the Field of 12 August 1949;

the Geneva Convention for the Amelioration of the Condition of Wounded, Sick and Shipwrecked Members of Armed Forces at Sea of 12 August 1949; the Geneva Convention relative to the Treatment of Prisoners of War of 12 August 1949; the Geneva Convention relative to the Protection of Civilian Persons in Time of War of 12 August 1949; "the Conventions" means the four Geneva Conventions of 12 August 1949 for the protection of war victims;

(b) "Rules of international law applicable in armed conflict" means the rules applicable in armed conflict set forth in international agreements to which the Parties to the conflict are Parties and the generally recognized principles and rules of international law which are applicable to armed conflict;

(c) "Protecting Power" means a neutral or other State not a Party to the conflict which has been designated by a Party to the conflict and accepted by the adverse Party and has agreed to carry out the functions assigned to a Protecting Power under the Conventions and this Protocol;

(d) "Substitute" means an organization acting in place of a Protecting Power in accordance with Article 5.

Article 3

Beginning and End of Application

Without prejudice to the provisions which are applicable at all times:

(a) the Conventions and this Protocol shall apply from the beginning of any situation referred to in Article 1 of this Protocol;

(b) the application of the Conventions and of this Protocol shall cease, in the territory of Parties to the conflict, on the general close of military operations and, in the case of occupied territories, on the termination of the occupation, except, in either circumstance, for those persons whose final release, repatriation or re-establishment takes place thereafter. These persons shall continue to benefit from the relevant provisions of the Conventions and of this Protocol until their final release repatriation or re-establishment.

Article 4

Legal Status of the Parties to the Conflict

The application of the Conventions and of this Protocol, as well as the conclusion of the agreements provided for therein, shall not affect the legal status of the Parties to the conflict. Neither the occupation of a territory nor the application of the Conventions and this Protocol shall affect the legal status of the territory in question.

Article 5

Appointment of Protecting Powers and of their Substitute

[At the outset of any conflict, Protecting Powers shall be designated with responsibility for supervising and implementing this Convention.]

Article 6

Qualified Persons

1. The High Contracting Parties shall, also in peacetime, endeavour, with the assistance of the national Red Cross (Red Crescent, Red Lion and Sun) Societies, to train qualified personnel to facilitate the application of the Conventions and of this Protocol, and in particular the activities of the Protecting Powers.

2. The recruitment and training of such personnel are within domestic jurisdiction.

3. The International Committee of the Red Cross shall hold at the disposal of the High Contracting Parties the lists of persons so trained which the High Contracting Parties may have established and may have transmitted to it for that purpose.

4. The conditions governing the employment of such personnel outside the national territory shall, in each case, be the subject of special agreements between the Parties concerned.

PART II

WOUNDED, SICK AND SHIPWRECKED

Section I

General Protection

Article 8

Terminology

[This article gives definitions of the wounded, sick, shipwrecked, medical personnel, religious personnel etc.]

Article 9

Field of Application

1. This Part, the provisions of which are intended

to ameliorate the condition of the wounded, sick and shipwrecked, shall apply to all those affected by a situation referred to in Article 1, without any adverse distinction founded on race, colour, sex, language, religion or belief, political or other opinion, national or social origin, wealth, birth or other status, or on any other similar criteria.

Article 10

Protection and Care

1. All the wounded, sick and shipwrecked, to whichever Party they belong, shall be respected and protected.

2. In all circumstances they shall be treated humanely and shall receive, to the fullest extent practicable and with the least possible delay, the medical care and attention required by their condition. There shall be no distinction among them founded on any grounds other than medical ones.

Article 11

Protection of Persons

1. The physical or mental health and integrity of persons who are in the power of the adverse Party or who are interned, detained or otherwise deprived of liberty as a result of a situation referred to in Article 1 shall not be endangered by any unjustified act or omission. Accordingly, it is prohibited to subject the persons described in this Article to any medical procedure which is not indicated by the state of health of the person concerned and which is not consistent with generally accepted medical standards which would be applied under similar medical circumstances to persons who are nationals of the Party conducting the procedure and who are in no way deprived of liberty.

2. It is, in particular, prohibited to carry out on such persons, even with their consent:

(a) physical mutilations:

(b) medical or scientific experiments:

(c) removal of tissue or organs for transplantation, except where these acts are justified in conformity with the conditions provided for in paragraph 1.

3. Exceptions to the prohibition in paragraph 2 (c) may be made only in the case of donations of blood for transfusion or of skin for grafting, provided that they are given voluntarily and without any coercion or inducement, and then only for therapeutic purposes, under conditions consistent with generally accept-

ed medical standards and controls designed for the benefit of both the donor and the recipient.

Article 12

Protection of Medical Units

1. Medical units shall be respected and protected at all times and shall not be the object of attack.

2. Paragraph 1 shall apply to civilian medical units, provided that they:

(a) belong to one of the Parties to the conflict;

(b) are recognized and authorized by the competent authority of one of the Parties to the conflict; or

(c) are authorized in conformity with Article 9, paragraph 2, of this Protocol or Article 27 of the First Convention.

3. The Parties to the conflict are invited to notify each other of the location of their fixed medical units. The absence of such notification shall not exempt any of the Parties from the obligation to comply with the provisions of paragraph 1.

4. Under no circumstances shall medical units be used in an attempt to shield military objectives from attack. Whenever possible, the Parties to the conflict shall ensure the medical units are so sited that attacks against military objectives do not imperil their safety.

Article 13

Discontinuance of Protection of Civilian Medical Units

[The protection of civilian medical units shall be discontinued, after reasonable warning, if they commit acts harmful to the enemy.]

Article 14

Limitations on Requisition of Civilian Medical Units

1. The Occupying Power has the duty to ensure that the medical needs of the civilian population in occupied territory continue to be satisfied.

2. The Occupying Power shall not, therefore, requisition civilian medical units, their equipment, their *matériel* or the services of their personnel, so long as these resources are necessary for the provision of adequate medical services for the civilian population and for the continuing medical care of any wounded and sick already under treatment.

Article 15

Protection of Civilian Medical and Religious Personnel

[Civilian medical personnel and civilian religious personnel shall be clearly identified and fully protected at all times.]

Article 16

General Protection of Medical Duties

1. Under no circumstances shall any person be punished for carrying out medical activities compatible with medical ethics, regardless of the person benefiting therefrom.

2. Persons engaged in medical activities shall not be compelled to perform acts or to carry out work contrary to the rules of medical ethics or to other medical rules designed for the benefit of the wounded and sick or to the provisions of the Conventions or of this Protocol, or to refrain from performing acts or from carrying out work required by those rules and provisions.

3. No person engaged in medical activities shall be compelled to give to anyone belonging either to an adverse Party, or to his own Party except as required by the law of the latter Party, any information concerning the wounded and sick who are, or who have been, under his care, if such information would, in his opinion, prove harmful to the patients concerned or to their families. Regulations for the compulsory notification of communicable diseases shall, however, be respected.

Article 17

Role of the Civilian Population and of Aid Societies

1. The civilian population shall respect the wounded, sick and shipwrecked, even if they belong to the adverse Party, and shall commit no act of violence against them. The civilian population and aid societies, such as national Red Cross (Red Crescent, Red Lion and Sun) Societies, shall be permitted, even on their own initiative, to collect and care for the wounded, sick and shipwrecked, even in invaded or occupied areas. No one shall be harmed, prosecuted, convicted or punished for such humanitarian acts.

2. The Parties to the conflict may appeal to the civilian population and the aid societies referred to in paragraph 1 to collect and care for the wounded, sick and shipwrecked, and to search for the dead and report their location; they shall grant both protection and the necessary facilities to those who respond to this

appeal. If the adverse Party gains or regains control of the area, that Party also shall afford the same protection and facilities for so long as they are needed.

Article 18

Identification

[This article specifies regulations concerning the identification of medical and religious personnel, and of medical units and transport.]

Article 19

Neutral and other States not Parties to the Conflict

Neutral and other States not Parties to the conflict shall apply the relevant provisions of this Protocol to persons protected by this Part who may be received or interned within their territory, and to any dead of the Parties to that conflict whom they may find.

Article 20

Prohibition of Reprisals

Reprisals against the persons and objects protected by this Part are prohibited.

Section II

Medical Transportation

Article 21

Medical Vehicles

Medical vehicles shall be respected and protected in the same way as mobile medical units under the Conventions and this Protocol.

Article 22

Hospital Ships and Coastal Rescue Craft

Protection for hospital ships and coastal rescue craft.

Article 23

Other Medical Ships and Craft

[Other medical ships and craft shall be clearly identified and shall be protected.]

Article 24

Protection of Medical Aircraft

Medical aircraft shall be respected and protected, subject to the provisions of this Part.

Articles 25-27

[Medical aircraft shall be protected; provided that prior agreement for flights over enemy territory has been obtained from the enemy.]

Article 28

Restrictions on Operations of Medical Aircraft

[Medical aircraft shall not be used for military purposes, nor for collecting or transmitting medical data.]

Article 29

Notifications and Agreements Concerning Medical Aircraft

[Notifications and agreements regarding medical aircraft.]

Article 30

Landing and Inspection of Medical Aircraft

[Medical aircraft flying over enemy territory may be ordered to land, and may be subject to inspection.]

Article 31

Neutral or other States not Parties to the Conflict

[Medical aircraft flying over neutral territory may be required to land and shall be subject to inspection.]

Section III

Missing and Dead Persons

Article 32

General Principle

In the implementation of this Section, the activities of the High Contracting Parties, of the Parties to the conflict and of the international humanitarian organizations mentioned in the Conventions and in this Protocol shall be prompted mainly by the right of families to know the fate of their relatives.

Article 33

Missing Persons

1. As soon as circumstances permit, and at the latest from the end of active hostilities, each Party to the conflict shall search for the persons who have been reported missing by an adverse Party. Such

adverse Party shall transmit all relevant information concerning such persons in order to facilitate such searches.

2. In order to facilitate the gathering of information pursuant to the preceding paragraph, each Party to the conflict shall, with respect to persons who would not receive more favourable consideration under the Conventions and this Protocol:

(a) record the information specified in Article 138 of the Fourth Convention in respect of such persons who have been detained, imprisoned or otherwise held in captivity for more than two weeks as a result of hostilities or occupation, or who have died during any period of detention;

(b) to the fullest extent possible, facilitate and, if need be, carry out the search for and the recording of information concerning such persons if they have died in other circumstances as a result of hostilities or occupation.

3. Information concerning persons reported missing pursuant to paragraph 1 and requests for such information shall be transmitted either directly or through the Protecting Power or the Central Tracing Agency of the International Committee of the Red Cross or national Red Cross (Red Crescent, Red Lion and Sun) Societies. Where the information is not transmitted through the International Committee of the Red Cross and its Central Tracing Agency, each Party to the conflict shall ensure that such information is also supplied to the Central Tracing Agency.

4. The Parties to the conflict shall endeavour to agree on arrangements for teams to search for, identify and recover the dead from battlefield areas, including arrangements, if appropriate, for such teams to be accompanied by personnel of the adverse Party while carrying out these missions in areas controlled by the adverse Party. Personnel of such teams shall be respected and protected while exclusively carrying out these duties.

Article 34

Remains of Deceased

[The remains of the deceased shall be respected and gravesites maintained. Relatives shall be granted access to graves as soon as circumstances permit.]

PART III

METHODS AND MEANS OF WARFARE COMBATANT

AND PRISONER-OF-WAR STATUS

Section I

Methods and Means of Warfare

Article 35

Basic Rules

1. In any armed conflict, the right of the Parties to the conflict to choose methods or means of warfare is not unlimited.

2. It is prohibited to employ weapons, projectiles and material and methods of warfare of a nature to cause superfluous injury or unnecessary suffering.

3. It is prohibited to employ methods or means of warfare which are intended, or may be expected, to cause widespread, long-term and severe damage to the natural environment.

Article 36

New Weapons

In the study, development, acquisition or adoption of a new weapon, means or method of warfare, a High Contracting Party is under an obligation to determine whether its employment would, in some or all circumstances, be prohibited by this Protocol or by any other rule of international law applicable to the High Contracting Party.

Article 37

Prohibition of Perfidy

1. It is prohibited to kill, injure or capture an adversary by resort to perfidy. Acts inviting the confidence of an adversary to lead him to believe that he is entitled to, or is obliged to accord, protection under the rules of international law applicable in armed conflict, with intent to betray that confidence, shall constitute perfidy. The following acts are examples of perfidy:

(a) the feigning of an intent to negotiate under a flag of truce or of a surrender;

(b) the feigning of an incapacitation by wounds or sickness;

(c) the feigning of civilian, non-combatant status; and

(d) the feigning of protected status by the use of signs, emblems or uniforms of the United Nations or of neutral or other States not Parties to the conflict.

2. Ruses of war are not prohibited. Such ruses are acts which are intended to mislead an adversary or to induce him to act recklessly but which infringe no rule of international law applicable in armed conflict and which are not perfidious because they do not invite the confidence of an adversary with respect to protection under that law. The following are examples of such ruses; the use of camouflage, decoys, mock operations and misinformation.

Article 38

Recognised Emblems

[Improper use shall not be made of the red cross, red crescent, or other comparable emblems.]

Article 39

Emblems of Nationality

[Improper use shall not be made of the emblems of neutral states.]

Article 40

Quarter

It is prohibited to order that there shall be no survivors, to threaten an adversary therewith or to conduct hostilities on this basis.

Article 41

Safeguard of an Enemy Hors de Combat

[An enemy who is hors de combat shall not be attacked.]

Article 42

Occupants of Aircraft

[No-one parachuting from an aircraft in distress shall be attacked.]

Section II

Combatant and Prisoner-of-War Status

Article 43

Armed Forces

1. The armed forces of a Party to a conflict consist of all organized armed forces, groups and units which are under a command responsible to that Party for the conduct of its subordinates, even if that Party is represented by a government or an authority not recognized by an adverse Party. Such armed forces shall be subject to an internal disciplinary system which, *inter alia*, shall enforce compliance with the rules of international law applicable in armed conflict.

2. Members of the armed forces of a Party to a conflict (other than medical personnel and chaplains covered by Article 33 of the Third Convention) are combatants, that is to say, they have the right to participate directly in hostilities.

3. Whenever a Party to a conflict incorporates a paramilitary or armed law enforcement agency into its armed forces it shall so notify the other Parties to the conflict.

Article 44

Combatants and Prisoners of War

[Combatants as defined in Article 43 who fall into enemy hands shall be treated as prisoners of war.]

Article 45

Protection of Persons who Have Taken Part in Hostilities

[A person who has taken part in hostilities and falls into enemy hands shall be presumed to be a prisoner of war.]

Article 46

Spies

1. Notwithstanding any other provision of the Conventions or of this Protocol, any member of the armed forces of a Party to the conflict who falls into the power of an adverse Party while engaging in espionage shall not have the right to the status of prisoner of war and may be treated as a spy.

2. A member of the armed forces of a Party to the conflict who, on behalf of that Party and in territory controlled by an adverse Party, gathers or attempts to gather information shall not be considered as engaging in espionage if, while so acting, he is in the uniform of his armed forces.

3. A member of the armed forces of a Party to the conflict who is a resident of territory occupied by an adverse Party and who, on behalf of the Party on which he depends, gathers or attempts to gather information of military value within that territory shall not be considered as engaging in espionage unless he does so through an act of false pretences or deliberately in a clandestine manner. Moreover, such a resident shall not lose his right to the status of prisoner of war and may not be treated as a spy unless he

is captured while engaging in espionage.

4. A member of the armed forces of a Party to the conflict who is not a resident of territory occupied by an adverse Party and who has engaged in espionage in that territory shall not lose his right to the status of prisoner of war and may not be treated as a spy unless he is captured before he has rejoined the armed forces to which he belongs.

Article 47

Mercenaries

1. A mercenary shall not have the right to be a combatant or a prisoner of war.

2. A mercenary is any person who:

(a) is specially recruited locally or abroad in order to fight in an armed conflict;

(b) does, in fact, take a direct part in the hostilities;

(c) is motivated to take part in the hostilities essentially by the desire for private gain and, in fact, is promised, by or on behalf of a Party to the conflict, material compensation substantially in excess of that promised or paid to combatants of similar ranks and functions in the armed forces of that Party;

(d) is neither a national of a Party to the conflict nor a resident of territory controlled by a Party to the conflict;

(e) is not a member of the armed forces of a Party to the conflict; and

(f) has not been sent by a State which is not a Party to the conflict on official duty as a member of its armed forces.

PART III

CIVILIAN POPULATION

Section I

General Protection Against Effects of Hostilities

Chapter I

Basic Rule and Field of Application

Article 48

Basic Rule

In order to ensure respect for and protection of the civilian population and civilian objects, the Parties to the conflict shall at all times distinguish between the civilian population and combatants and between civilian objects and military objectives and accordingly shall direct their operations only against military objectives.

Article 49

Definition of Attacks and Scope of Application

[This article gives the definition of attacks and scope of application.]

Chapter II

Civilians and Civilian Population

Article 50

Definition of Civilians and Civilian Population

[This article gives the definition of civilians and civilian populations.]

Article 51

Protection of the Civilian Population

[The civilian population shall enjoy general protection. Indiscriminate attacks on civilians and reprisals against civilians are specifically forbidden.]

Chapter III

Civilian Objects

Article 52

General Protection of Civilian Objects

1. Civilian objects shall not be the object of attack or of reprisals. Civilian objects are all objects which are not military objectives as defined in paragraph 2.

2. Attacks shall be limited strictly to military objectives. In so far as objects are concerned, military objectives are limited to those objects which by their nature, location, purpose or use make an effective contribution to military action and whose total or partial destruction, capture or neutralization, in the circumstances ruling at the time, offers a definite military advantage.

3. In case of doubt whether an object which is normally dedicated to civilian purposes, such as a place of worship, a house or other dwelling or a school, is being used to make an effective contribution to military action, it shall be presumed not to be so used.

Article 53

Protection of Cultural Objects and of Places of Worship

[Historic monuments, works of art, and places of worship are specifically protected from hostile acts.]

Article 54

Protection of Objects Indispensable to the Survival of the Civilian Population

[Starvation of civilians is forbidden. Destruction of food-stuffs, crops, livestock, or drinking water installations is forbidden.]

Article 55

Protection of the Natural Environment

[Protection of the natural environment.]

Article 56

Protection of Works and Installations Containing Dangerous Forces

1. Works or installations containing dangerous forces, namely dams, dykes and nuclear electrical generating stations, shall not be made the object of attack, even where these objects are military objectives, if such attack may cause the release of dangerous forces and consequent severe losses among the civilian population. Other military objectives located at or in the vicinity of these works or installations shall not be made the object of attack if such attack may cause the release of dangerous forces from the works or installations and consequent severe losses among the civilian population.

Chapter III

Precautionary Measures

Article 57

Precautions in Attack

[Military attacks shall take precautions in order to minimize loss of civilian life, injury to civilians, and damage to civilian objects.]

Article 58

Precautions Against the Effects of Attacks

The Parties to the conflict shall, to the maximum extent feasible:

(a) without prejudice to Article 49 of the Fourth Convention, endeavour to remove the civilian population, individual civilians and civilian objects under their control from the vicinity of military objectives;
(b) avoid locating military objectives within or near densely populated areas;
(c) take the other necessary precautions to protect the civilian population, individual civilians and civilian objects under their control against the dangers resulting from military operations.

Chapter V

Localities and Zones Under Special Protection

Article 59

Non-defended Localities

1. It is prohibited for the Parties to the conflict to attack, by any means whatsoever, non-defended localities.

2. The appropriate authorities of a Party to the conflict may declare as a non-defended locality any inhabited place near or in a zone where armed forces are in contact which is open for occupation by an adverse Party. Such a locality shall fulfil the following conditions:

(a) all combatants, as well as mobile weapons and mobile military equipment must have been evacuated;

(b) no hostile use shall be made of fixed military installations or establishments;

(c) no acts of hostility shall be committed by the authorities or by the population; and

(d) no activities in support of military operations shall be undertaken.

Article 60

Demilitarized Zones

[Parties to the conflict shall not extend their military operations into areas that have already been designated demilitarized zones.]

Chapter VI

Civil Defence

Article 61

Definitions and Scope

[This article gives the definition and scope of civil defence.]

Article 62

General Protection

1. Civilian civil defence organizations and their personnel shall be respected and protected, subject to the provisions of this Protocol, particularly the provisions of this section. They shall be entitled to perform their civil defence tasks except in case of imperative military necessity.

2. The provisions of paragraph 1 shall also apply to civilians who, although not members of civilian civil defence organizations, respond to an appeal from the competent authorities and perform civil defence tasks under their control.

3. Buildings and *matériel* used for civil defence purposes and shelters provided for the civilian population are covered by Article 52. Objects used for civil defence purposes may not be destroyed or diverted from their proper use except by the Party to which they belong.

Article 63

Civil Defence in Occupied Territories

1. In occupied territories, civilian civil defence organizations shall receive from the authorities the facilities necessary for the performance of their tasks. In no circumstances shall their personnel be compelled to perform activities which would interfere with the proper performance of these tasks.

The Occupying power shall not change the structure or personnel of such organizations in any way which might jeopardize the efficient performance of their mission. These organizations shall not be required to give priority to the nationals or interests of that Power.

2. The Occupying Power shall not compel, coerce or induce civilian civil defence organizations to perform their tasks in any manner prejudicial to the interests of the civilian population.

3. The Occupying Power may disarm civil defence personnel for reasons of security.

Article 64

Civilian Civil Defence Organizations of Neutral or other States not Parties to the Conflict and International Co-ordinating Organizations

1. Articles 62, 63, 65, and 66 shall also apply to the personnel and *matériel* of civilian civil defence organizations of neutral or other States not Parties to the conflict which perform civil defence tasks mentioned in Article 61 in the territory of a Party to the conflict, with the consent and under the control of that Party. Notification of such assistance shall be given as soon as possible to any adverse Party concerned. In no circumstances shall this activity be deemed to be an interference in the conflict. This activity should, however, be performed with due regard to the security interests of the Parties to the conflict concerned.

Article 65

Cessation of Protection

[The protection afforded to civil defence organizations shall be withdrawn, after warning, if they commit acts harmful to the enemy.]

Article 66

Identification

1. Each Party to the conflict shall endeavour to ensure that its civil defence organizations, their personnel, buildings and *matériel*, are identifiable while they are exclusively devoted to the performance of civil defence tasks. Shelters provided for the civilian population should be similarly identifiable.

2. Each Party to the conflict shall also endeavour to adopt and implement methods and procedures which will make it possible to recognize civilian shelters as well as civil defence personnel, buildings and *matériel* on which the international distinctive sign of civil defence is displayed.

3. In occupied territories and in areas where fighting is taking place or is likely to take place, civilian civil defence personnel should be recognizable by the international distinctive sign of civil defence and by an identity card certifying their status.

Article 67

Members of the Armed Forces and Military Units Assigned to Civil Defence Organizations

1. Members of the armed forces and military units assigned to civil defence organizations shall be respected and protected, provided that:

(a) such personnel and such units are permanently assigned and exclusively devoted to the performance of any of the tasks mentioned in Article 61;

(b) if so assigned, such personnel do not perform any other military duties during the conflict;

(c) such personnel are clearly distinguishable from

the other members of the armed forces by prominently displaying the international distinctive sign of civil defence, which shall be as large as appropriate, and such personnel are provided with the identity card referred to in Chapter V of Annex I to this Protocol certifying their status;

Section II

Relief in Favour of the Civilian Population

Article 68

Field of Application

The provisions of this Section apply to the civilian populations as defined in this Protocol and are supplementary to Articles 23, 55, 59, 60, 61 and 62 and other relevant provisions of the Fourth Convention.

Article 69

Basic Needs in Occupied Territories

1. In addition to the duties specified in Article 55 of the Fourth Convention concerning food and medical supplies, the Occupying Power shall, to the fullest extent of the means available to it and without any adverse distinction, also ensure the provision of clothing, bedding, means of shelter, other supplies essential to the survival of the civilian population of the occupied territory and objects necessary for religious worship.

2. Relief actions for the benefit of the civilian population of occupied territories are governed by Articles 59, 60, 61, 62, 108, 109, 110 and 111 of the Fourth Convention, and by Article 71 of this Protocol, and shall be implemented without delay.

Article 70

Relief Actions

1. If the civilian population of any territory under the control of a Party to the conflict, other than occupied territory, is not adequately provided with the supplies mentioned in Article 69, relief actions which are humanitarian and impartial in character and conducted without any adverse distinction shall be undertaken, subject to the agreement of the Parties concerned in such relief actions. Offers of such relief shall not be regarded as interference in the armed conflict or as unfriendly acts. In the distribution of relief consignments, priority shall be given to those persons, such as children, expectant mothers, maternity cases and nursing mothers, who, under the Fourth Convention or under this Protocol, are to be accorded privileged treatment or special protection.

2. The Parties to the conflict and each High Contracting Party shall allow and facilitate rapid and unimpeded passage of all relief consignments, equipment and personnel provided in accordance with this Section, even if such assistance is destined for the civilian population of the adverse Party.

3. The Parties to the conflict and each High Contracting Party which allows the passage of relief consignments, equipment and personnel in accordance with paragraph 2:

(a) shall have the right to prescribe the technical arrangements, including search, under which such passage is permitted;

(b) may make such permission conditional on the distribution of this assistance being made under the local supervision of a Protecting Power;

(c) shall, in no way whatsoever, divert relief consignments from the purpose for which they are intended nor delay their forwarding, except in cases of urgent necessity in the interest of the civilian population concerned.

4. The Parties to the conflict shall protect relief consignments and facilitate their rapid distribution.

5. The Parties to the conflict and each High Contracting Party concerned shall encourage and facilitate effective international co-ordination of the relief actions referred to in paragraph 1.

Article 71

Personnel Participating in Relief Actions

1. Where necessary, relief personnel may form part of the assistance provided in any relief action, in particular for the transportation and distribution of relief consignments; the participation of such personnel shall be subject to the approval of the Party in whose territory they will carry out their duties.

2. Such personnel shall be respected and protected.

3. Each Party in receipt of relief consignments shall, to the fullest extent practicable, assist the relief personnel referred to in paragraph 1 in carrying out their relief mission. Only in case of imperative military necessity may the activities of the relief personnel be limited or their movements temporarily restricted.

Section III

Treatment of Persons in the Power of a Party to the Conflict

Chapter 1

Field of Application and Protection of Persons and Objects

Article 72

Field of Application

The provisions of this Section are additional to the rules concerning humanitarian protection of civilians and civilian objects in the power of a Party to the conflict contained in the Fourth Convention, particularly Parts I and III thereof, as well as to other applicable rules of international law relating to the protection of fundamental human rights during international armed conflict.

Article 73

Refugees and Stateless Persons

Persons who, before the beginning of hostilities, were considered as stateless persons or refugees under the relevant international instruments accepted by the Parties concerned or under the national legislation of the State of refuge or State of residence shall be protected persons within the meaning of Parts I and III of the Fourth Convention, in all circumstances and without any adverse distinction.

Article 74

Reunion of Dispersed Families

The High Contracting Parties and the Parties to the conflict shall facilitate in every possible way the reunion of families dispersed as a result of armed conflicts and shall encourage in particular the work of the humanitarian organizations engaged in this task in accordance with the provisions of the Conventions and of this Protocol and in conformity with their respective security regulations.

Article 75

Fundamental Guarantees

1. In so far as they are affected by a situation referred to in Article 1 of this Protocol, persons who are in the power of a Party to the conflict and who do not benefit from more favourable treatment under the Conventions or under this Protocol shall be treated humanely in all circumstances and shall enjoy, as a minimum, the protection provided by this Article without any adverse distinction based upon race, colour, sex, language, religion or belief, political or other opinion, national or social origin, wealth, birth or other status, or on any other similar criteria. Each Party shall respect the person, honour, convictions and religious practices of all such persons.

2. The following acts are and shall remain prohibited at any time and in any place whatsoever, whether committed by civilian or by military agents:

(a) violence to the life, health, or physical or mental well-being of persons, in particular:

(i) murder;

(ii) torture of all kinds, whether physical or mental;

(iii) corporal punishment; and

(iv) mutilation;

(b) outrages upon personal dignity, in particular humiliating and degrading treatment, enforced prostitution and any form of indecent assault;

(c) the taking of hostages;

(d) collective punishments; and

(e) threats to commit any of the foregoing acts.

3. Any person arrested, detained or interned for actions related to the armed conflict shall be informed promptly, in a language he understands, of the reasons why these measures have been taken. Except in cases of arrest or detention for penal offences, such persons shall be released with the minimum delay possible and in any event as soon as the circumstances justifying the arrest, detention of internment have ceased to exist.

4. No sentence may be passed and no penalty may be executed on a person found guilty of a penal offence related to the armed conflict except pursuant to a conviction pronounced by an impartial and regularly constituted court respecting the generally recognized principles of regular judicial procedure, which include the following:

(a) the procedure shall provide for an accused to be informed without delay of the particulars of the offence alleged against him and shall afford the accused before and during his trial all necessary rights and means of defence;

(b) no one shall be convicted of an offence except on the basis of individual penal responsibility;

(c) no one shall be accused or convicted of a criminal offence on account of any act or omission which did not constitute a criminal offence under the national or international law to which he was subject at the time it was committed; nor shall a heavier penalty be imposed than that which was applicable at the time when the criminal offence was committed; if, after the commission of the offence, provision is made by law for the imposition of a lighter penalty, the offender shall benefit thereby;

(d) anyone charged with an offence is presumed innocent until proved guilty according to law;

(e) anyone charged with an offence shall have the right to be tried in his presence;

(f) no one shall be compelled to testify against himself or to confess guilt;

(g) anyone charged with an offence shall have the right to examine, or have examined, the witnesses against him and to obtain the attendance and examination of witnesses on his behalf under the same conditions as witnesses against him;

(h) no one shall be prosecuted or punished by the same Party for an offence in respect of which a final judgement acquitting or convicting that person has been previously pronounced under the same law and judicial procedure;

(i) anyone prosecuted for an offence shall have the right to have the judgement pronounced publicly; and

(j) a convicted person shall be advised on conviction of his judicial and other remedies and of the time-limits within which they may be exercised.

Chapter II

Measures in Favour of Women and Children

Article 76

Protection of Women

1. Women shall be the object of special respect and shall be protected in particular against rape, forced prostitution and any other form of indecent assault.

2. Pregnant women and mothers having dependent infants who are arrested, detained or interned for reasons related to the armed conflict, shall have their cases considered with the utmost priority.

3. To the maximum extent feasible, the Parties to the conflict shall endeavour to avoid the pronouncement of the death penalty on pregnant women or mothers having dependent infants, for an offence related to the armed conflict. The death penalty for such offences shall not be executed on such women.

Article 77

Protection of Children

1. Children shall be the object of special respect and shall be protected against any form of indecent assault. The Parties to the conflict shall provide them with the care and aid they require, whether because of their age or for any other reason.

2. The Parties to the conflict shall take all feasible measures in order that children who have not attained the age of fifteen years do not take a direct part in hostilities and, in particular, they shall refrain from recruiting them into their armed forces. In recruiting among those persons who have attained the age of fifteen years but who have not attained the age of eighteen years the Parties to the conflict shall endeavour to give priority to those who are oldest.

3. If, in exceptional cases, despite the provisions of paragraph 2, children who have not attained the age of fifteen years take a direct part in hostilities and fall into the power of an adverse Party, they shall continue to benefit from the special protection accorded by this Article, whether or not they are prisoners of war.

4. If arrested, detained or interned for reasons related to the armed conflict, children shall be held in quarters separate from the quarters of adults, except where families are accommodated as family units as provided in Article 75, paragraph 5.

5. The death penalty for an offence related to the armed conflict shall not be executed on persons who had not attained the age of eighteen years at the time the offence was committed.

Article 78

Evacuation of Children

[Children shall only be evacuated to a foreign country for compelling reasons of their health or safety. Written consent of parents or guardians is required.]

Chapter III

Journalists

Article 79

Measures of Protection for Journalists

[Journalists working in areas of armed conflict shall be clearly identified and protected at all times.]

PART V

EXECUTION OF THE CONVENTIONS AND OF THIS PROTOCOL

Section I

General Provisions

Article 80

Measures for Execution

1. The High Contracting Parties and the Parties to the conflict shall without delay take all necessary measures for the execution of their obligations under the Conventions and this Protocol.

2. The High Contracting Parties and the Parties to the conflict shall give orders and instructions to ensure observance of the Conventions and this Protocol, and shall supervise their execution.

Article 81

Activities of the Red Cross and Other Humanitarian Organizations

[The Red Cross, Red Crescent, and comparable organizations shall be granted facilities to carry out their humanitarian and relief activities.]

Article 82

Legal Advisers in Armed Forces

The High Contracting Parties at all times, and the Parties to the conflict in time of armed conflict, shall ensure that legal advisers are available, when necessary, to advise military commanders at the appropriate level on the application of the Conventions and this Protocol and on the appropriate instruction to be given to the armed forces on this subject.

Article 83

Dissemination

1. The High Contracting Parties undertake, in time of peace as in time of armed conflict, to disseminate the Conventions and this Protocol as widely as possible in their respective countries and, in particular, to include the study thereof in their programmes of military instruction and to encourage the study thereof by the civilian population, so that those instruments may become known to the armed forces and to the civilian population.

2. Any military or civilian authorities who, in time of armed conflict, assume responsibilities in respect of the application of the Conventions and this Protocol shall be fully acquainted with the text thereof.

Article 84

Rules of Application

The High Contracting Parties shall communicate to one another, as soon as possible, through the deposi-

tory and, as appropriate, through the Protecting Powers, their official translations of this Protocol, as well as the laws and regulations which they may adopt to ensure its application.

Section II

Repression of Breaches of the Conventions and of this Protocol

Article 85

Repression of Breaches of this Protocol

[This article gives the definition of breaches and grave breaches of this Convention. Grave breaches shall be regarded as war crimes.]

Article 86

Failure to Act

1. The High contracting Parties and the Parties to the conflict shall repress grave breaches, and take measures necessary to suppress all other breaches, of the Conventions or of this Protocol which result from a failure to act when under a duty to do so.

2. The fact that a breach of the Conventions or of this Protocol was committed by a subordinate does not absolve his superiors from penal disciplinary responsibility, as the case may be, if they knew, or had information which should have enabled them to conclude in the circumstances at the time, that he was committing or was going to commit such a breach and if they did not take all feasible measures within their power to prevent or repress the breach.

Article 87

Duty of Commanders

[Military commanders will be responsible for ensuring that the Convention is not breached by persons under their control.]

Article 88

Mutual Assistance in Criminal Matters

1. The High Contracting Parties shall afford one another the greatest measure of assistance in connection with criminal proceedings brought in respect of grave breaches of the Conventions or of this Protocol.

2. Subject to the rights and obligations established in the Conventions and in Article 85, paragraph 1 of this Protocol, and when circumstances permit, the High Contracting Parties shall co-operate in the matter of extradition. They shall give due consideration

to the request of the State in whose territory the alleged offence has occurred.

3. The law of the High Contracting Party requested shall apply in all cases. The provisions of the preceding paragraphs shall not, however, affect the obligations arising from the provisions of any other treaty of a bilateral or multilateral nature which governs or will govern the whole or part of the subject of mutual assistance in criminal matters.

Article 89

Co-operation

In situations of serious violations of the Conventions or of this Protocol, the High Contracting Parties undertake to act jointly or individually, in cooperation with the United Nations and in conformity with the United Nations Charter.

Article 90

International Fact-Finding Commission

[This article specifies the establishment, terms of reference, and scope of an International Fact-Finding Commission. Such Commissions shall investigate grave breaches of this Convention.]

Article 91

Responsibility

A Party to the conflict which violates the provisions of the Conventions or of this Protocol shall, if the case demands, be liable to pay compensation. It shall be responsible for all acts committed by persons forming part of its armed forces.

PART VI

FINAL PROVISIONS

Article 92

Signature

This Protocol shall be open for signature by the Parties to the Conventions six months after the signing of the Final Act and will remain open for a period of twelve months.

Article 93

Ratification

This Protocol shall be ratified as soon as possible. The instruments of ratification shall be deposited with the Swiss Federal Council, depositary of the Conventions.

Article 94

Accession

This Protocol shall be open for accession by any Party to the Conventions which has not signed it. The instruments of accession shall be deposited with the depositary.

Treaty Between the United States of America and the Union of Soviet Socialist Republics on the Limitations of Strategic Offensive Arms

Also known as: The treaty concluding
the Strategic Arms Limitation Talks II (SALT II)
Date of signature: June 18, 1979
Place of signature: Vienna
Signatory states: The United States, The Soviet Union

[The signatories],
Conscious that nuclear war would have devastating consequences for all mankind,
Proceeding from the Basic Principles of Relations Between the United States of America and the Union of Soviet Socialist Republics of May 29, 1972,

Attaching particular significance to the limitation of strategic arms and determined to continue their efforts begun with the Treaty on the Limitation of Anti-Ballistic Missile Systems and the Interim Agreement on Certain Measures with Respect to the Limitation of Strategic Offensive Arms, of May 26, 1972,
Convinced that the additional measures limiting strategic offensive arms provided for in this Treaty will contribute to the improvement of relations between the Parties, help to reduce the risk of outbreak of nuclear war and strengthen international peace and security,
Mindful of their obligations under Article VI of the

Treaty on the Non-Proliferation of Nuclear Weapons,

Guided by the principle of equality and equal security,

Recognizing that the strengthening of strategic stability meets the interests of the Parties and the interests of international security,

Reaffirming their desire to take measures for the further limitation and for the further reduction of strategic arms, having in mind the goal of achieving general and complete disarmament,

Declaring their intention to undertake in the near future negotiations further to limit and further to reduce strategic offensive arms,

Have agreed as follows:

Article I

Each Party undertakes, in accordance with the provisions of this Treaty, to limit strategic offensive arms quantitatively and qualitatively, to exercise restraint in the development of new types of strategic offensive arms, and to adopt other measures provided for in this Treaty.

Article II

For the purposes of this Treaty:

1. Intercontinental ballistic missile (ICBM) launchers are land-based launchers of ballistic missiles capable of a range in excess of the shortest distance between the northeastern border of the continental part of the territory of the United States of America and the northwestern border of the continental part of the territory of the Union of Soviet Socialist Republics, that is, a range in excess of 5,500 kilometers.

First Agreed Statement

The term "intercontinental ballistic missile launchers," as defined in paragraph 1 of Article II of the Treaty, includes all launchers which have been developed and tested for launching ICBMs. If a launcher has been developed and tested for launching an ICBM, all launchers of that type shall be considered to have been developed and tested for launching ICBMs.

First Common Understanding

If a launcher contains or launches an ICBM, that launcher shall be considered to have been developed and tested for launching ICBMs.

Second Common Understanding

If a launcher has been developed and tested for launching an ICBM, all launchers of that type, except for ICBM test and training launchers, shall be included in the aggregate numbers of strategic offensive arms provided for in Article III of the Treaty, pursuant to the provisions of Article VI of the Treaty.

Third Common Understanding

The one hundred and seventy-seven former Atlas and Titan 1 ICBM launchers of the United States of America, which are no longer operational and are partially dismantled, shall not be considered as subject to the limitations provided for in the Treaty.

Second Agreed Statement

After the date on which the Protocol ceases to be in force, mobile ICBM launchers shall be subject to the relevant limitations provided for in the Treaty which are applicable to ICBM launchers, unless the Parties agree that mobile ICBM launchers shall not be deployed after that date.

2. Submarine-launched ballistic missile (SLBM) launchers are launchers of ballistic missiles installed on any nuclear-powered submarine or launchers of modern ballistic missiles installed on any submarine, regardless of its type.

Agreed Statement

Modern submarine-launched ballistic missiles are: for the United States of America, missiles installed in all nuclear-powered submarines; for the Union of Soviet Socialist Republics, missiles of the type installed in nuclear-powered submarines made operational since 1965; and for both Parties, submarine-launched ballistic missiles first flight-tested since 1965 and installed in any submarine, regardless of its type.

3. Heavy bombers are considered to be:

(a) currently, for the United States of America, bombers of the B-52 and B-1 types, and for the Union of Soviet Socialist Republics, bombers of the Tupolev-95 and Myasishchev types;

(b) in the future, types of bombers which can carry out the mission of a heavy bomber in a manner similar or superior to that of bombers listed in subparagraph (a) above;

(c) types of bombers equipped for cruise missiles capable of a range in excess of 600 kilometers; and

(d) types of bombers equipped for ASBMs.

First Agreed Statement

The term "bombers," as used in paragraph 3 of Article II and other provisions of the Treaty, means airplanes of types initially constructed to be equipped for bombs or missiles.

Second Agreed Statement

The Parties shall notify each other on a case-by-case basis in the Standing Consultative Commission of inclusion of types of bombers as heavy bombers pursuant to the provisions of paragraph 3 of Article II of the Treaty; in this connection the Parties shall hold consultations, as appropriate, consistent with the provisions of paragraph 2 of Article XVII of the Treaty.

Third Agreed Statement

The criteria the Parties shall use to make case-by-case determinations of which types of bombers in the future can carry out the mission of a heavy bomber in a manner similar or superior to that of current heavy bombers, as referred to in subparagraph 3(b) of Article II of the Treaty, shall be agreed upon in the Standing Consultative Commission.

Fourth Agreed Statement

Having agreed that every bomber of a type included in paragraph 3 of Article II of the Treaty is to be considered a heavy bomber, the Parties further agree that:

(a) airplanes which otherwise would be bombers of a heavy bomber type shall not be considered to be bombers of a heavy bomber type if they have functionally related observable differences which indicate that they cannot perform the mission of a heavy bomber;

(b) airplanes which otherwise would be bombers of a type equipped for cruise missiles capable of a range in excess of 600 kilometers shall not be considered to be bombers of a type equipped for cruise missiles capable of a range in excess of 600 kilometers if they have functionally related observable differences which dictate that they cannot perform the mission of a bomber equipped for cruise missiles capable of a range in excess of 600 kilometers, except that heavy bombers of current types, as designated in subparagraph 3(a) of Article II of the Treaty, which otherwise would be of a type equipped for cruise missiles capable of a range in excess of 600 kilometers shall not be considered to be heavy bombers of a type equipped for cruise missiles capable of a range in excess of 600 kilometers if they are distinguishable on the basis of externally observable differences from heavy bombers of a type equipped for cruise missiles capable of a range in excess of 600 kilometers; and

(c) airplanes which otherwise would be bombers of a type equipped for ASBMs shall not be considered to be bombers of a type equipped for ASBMs if they have functionally related observable differences which indicate that they cannot perform the mission of a bomber equipped for ASBMs, except that heavy bombers of current types, as designated in subparagraph 3(a) of Article II of the Treaty, which otherwise would be of a type equipped for ASBMs shall not be considered to be heavy bombers of a type equipped for ASBMs if they are distinguishable on the basis of externally observable differences from heavy bombers of a type equipped for ASBMs.

First Common Understanding

Functionally related observable differences are differences in the observable features of airplanes which indicate whether or not these airplanes can perform the mission of a heavy bomber, or whether or not they can perform the mission of a bomber equipped for cruise missiles capable of a range in excess of 600 kilometers or whether or not they can perform the mission of a bomber equipped for ASBMs. Functionally related observable differences shall be verifiable by national technical means. To this end, the Parties may take, as appropriate, cooperative measures contributing to the effectiveness of verification by national technical means.

Fifth Agreed Statement

Tupolev-142 airplanes in their current configuration, that is, in the configuration for anti-submarine warfare, are considered to be airplanes of a type different from types of heavy bombers referred to in subparagraph 3(a) of Article II of the Treaty. This Agreed Statement does not preclude improvement of Tupolev-142 airplanes as an antisubmarine system, and does not prejudice or set a precedent for designation in the future of types of airplanes as heavy bombers pursuant to subparagraph 3(b) of Article II of the Treaty of for application of the Fourth Agreed Statement to paragraph 3 of Article II of the Treaty to such airplanes.

Second Common Understanding

Not later than six months after entry into force of the Treaty the Union of Soviet Socialist Republics will give its thirty-one Myasishchev airplanes used as tankers in existence as of the date of signature of the treaty functionally related observable differences which indicate that they cannot perform the mission of a heavy bomber.

Third Common Understanding

The designations by the United States of America and by the Union of Soviet Socialist Republics for heavy bombers referred to in subparagraph 3(a) of Article II of the Treaty correspond in the following manner:

Heavy bombers of the types designated by the United States of America as the B-52 and the B-1 are known to the Union of Soviet Socialist Republics by the same designations;

Heavy bombers of the type designated by the Union of Soviet Socialist Republics as the Tupolev-95 are known to the United States of America as heavy bombers of the Bear type; and

Heavy bombers of the type designated by the Union of Soviet Socialist Republics as the Mya-sishchev are known to the United States of America as heavy bombers of the Bison type.

4. Air-to-surface ballistic missiles (ASBMS) are any such missiles capable of a range in excess of 600 kilometers and installed in an aircraft or on its external mountings.

5. Launchers of ICBMS and SLBMS equipped with multiple independently targetable reentry vehicles (MIRVS) are launchers of the types developed and tested for launching ICBMS or SLBMS equipped with MIRVS.

First Agreed Statement

If a launcher has been developed and tested for launching an ICBM or an SLBM equipped with MIRVS, all launchers of that type shall be considered to have been developed and tested for launching ICBMS or SLBMS equipped with MIRVS.

First Common Understanding

If a launcher contains or launches an ICBM or an SLBM equipped with MIRVS, that launcher shall be considered to have been developed and tested for launching ICBMS or SLBMS equipped with MIRVS.

Second Common Understanding

If a launcher has been developed and tested for launching an ICBM or an SLBM equipped with MIRVS, all launchers of that type, except for ICBM and SLBM test and training launchers, shall be included in the corresponding aggregate numbers provided for in Article V of the Treaty, pursuant to the provisions of Article VI of the Treaty.

Second Agreed Statement

ICBMS and SLBMS equipped with MIRVS are ICBM and SLBMS of the types which have been flight-tested with two or more independently targetable reentry vehicles, regardless of whether or not they have also been flight-tested with a single reentry vehicle or with multiple reentry vehicles which are not independently targetable. As of the date of signature of the Treaty, such as ICBMS and SLBMS are IV for the United States of America, Minuteman III ICBMS, Poseidon C-3 SLBMS, and Trident C-4 SLBMS; and for the Union of Soviet Socialist Republics, RS-16, RS-18, RS-20 ICBMS and RSM-50 SLBMS.

Each Party will notify the other Party in the Standing Consultative Commission on a case-by-case basis of the designation of the one new type of light ICBMS, if equipped with MIRVS, permitted pursuant to paragraph 9 of Article IV of the Treaty when first flight-tested; of designations of additional types of SLBMS equipped with MIRVS when first installed on a submarine; and of designations of types of ASBMS equipped with MIRVS when first flight-tested.

Third Common Understanding

The designations by the United States of America and by the Union of Soviet Socialist Republics for ICBMS and SLBMS equipped with MIRVS correspond in the following manner:

Missiles of the type designated by the United States of America as the Minuteman III and known to the Union of Soviet Socialist Republics by the same designation, a light ICBM that has been flight-tested with multiple independently targetable reentry vehicles;

Missiles of the type designated by the United States of America as the Poseidon C-3 and known to the Union of Soviet Socialist Republics by the same designation, and SLBM that was first flight-tested in 1968 and has been flight-tested with multiple independently targetable reentry vehicles;

Missiles of the type designated by the United

States of America as the Trident C-4 and known to the Union of Soviet Socialist Republics by the same designation, an SLBM that was first flight-tested in 1977 and that has been flight-tested with multiple independently targetable reentry vehicles;

Missiles of the type designated by the Union of Soviet Socialist Republics as the RS-16 and known to the United States of America as the SS-17, a light ICBM that has been flight-tested with a single reentry vehicle and with multiple independently targetable reentry vehicles;

Missiles of the type designated by the Union of Soviet Socialist Republics as the RS-18 and known to the United States of America as the SS-19, the heaviest in terms of launch-weight and throw-weight of light ICBMs, which has been flight-tested with a single reentry vehicle and with multiple independently targetable reentry vehicles;

Missiles of the type designated by the Union of Soviet Socialist Republics as the RS-20 and known to the United States of America as the SS-18, the heaviest in terms of launch-weight and throw-weight of heavy ICBMs, which has been flight-tested with a single reentry vehicle and with multiple independently targetable reentry vehicles;

Missiles of the type designated by the Union of Soviet Socialist Republics as the RSM-50 and known to the United States of America as the SS-N-18, an SLBM that has been flight-tested with a single reentry vehicle and with multiple independently targetable reentry vehicles.

Third Agreed Statement

Reentry vehicles are independently targetable:

(a) if, after separation from the booster, maneuvering and targeting of the reentry vehicles to separate aim points along trajectories which are unrelated to each other are accomplished by means of devices which are installed in a selfcontained dispensing mechanism or on the reentry vehicles, and which are based on the use of electronic or other computers in combination with devices using jet engines, including rocket engines, or aerodynamic systems;

(b) if maneuvering and targeting of the reentry vehicles to separate aim points along trajectories which are unrelated to each other are accomplished by means of other devices which may be developed in the future.

Fourth Common Understanding

For the purposes of this Treaty, all ICBM launchers in the Derazhnya and Pervomaysk areas in the Union of Soviet Socialist Republics are included in the aggregate numbers provided for in Article V of the Treaty.

Fifth Common Understanding

If ICBM or SLBM launchers are converted, constructed or undergo significant changes to their principal observable structural design features after entry into force of the Treaty, any such launchers which are launchers of missiles equipped with MIRVs shall be distinguishable from launchers of missiles not equipped with MIRVs, and any such launchers which are launchers of missiles not equipped with MIRVs shall be distinguishable from launchers of missiles equipped with MIRVs, on the basis of externally observable design features of the launchers. Submarines with launchers of SLBMs equipped with MIRVs shall be distinguishable from submarines with launchers of SLBMs not equipped with MIRVs on the basis of externally observable design features of the submarines.

This Common Understanding does not require changes to launcher conversion or construction programs, or to programs including significant changes to the principal observable structural design features of launchers, underway as of the date of signature of the Treaty.

6. ASBMs equipped with MIRVs are ASBMs of the types which have been flight-tested with MIRVs.

First Agreed Statement

ASBMs of the types which have been flight-tested with MIRVs are all ASBMs of the types which have been flight-tested with two or more independently targetable reentry vehicles, regardless of whether or not they have also been flight-tested with a single reentry vehicle or with multiple reentry vehicles which are not independently targetable.

Second Agreed Statement

Reentry vehicles are independently targetable:

(a) if, after separation from the booster, maneuvering and targeting of the reentry vehicles to separate aim points along trajectories which are unrelated to each other are accomplished by means of devices which are installed in a selfcontained dispensing mechanism or on the reentry vehicles, and which are based on the use of electronic or other computers in combination with devices using jet engines, including rocket engines, or aerodynamic systems;

(b) if maneuvering and targeting of the reentry vehicles to separate aim points along trajectories which are unrelated to each other are accomplished by means of other devices which may be developed in the future.

7. Heavy ICBMs are ICBMs which have a launch weight greater or a throw-weight greater than that of the heaviest, in terms of either launch-weight or throw-weight, respectively, of the light ICBMs deployed by either Party as of the date of signature of this Treaty.

First Agreed Statement

The launch-weight of an ICBM is the weight of the fully loaded missile itself at the time of launch.

Second Agreed Statement

The throw-weight of an ICBM is the sum of the weight of:

(a) its reentry vehicle or reentry vehicles;

(b) any self-contained dispensing mechanisms or other appropriate devices for targeting one reentry vehicle, or for releasing or for dispensing and targeting two or more reentry vehicles; and

(c) its penetration aids, including devices for their release.

Common Understanding

The term "other appropriate devices," as used in the definition of the throw-weight of an ICBM in the Second Agreed Statement to paragraph 7 of Article II of the Treaty, means any devices for dispensing and targeting two or more reentry vehicles; and any devices for releasing two or more reentry vehicles or for targeting one reentry vehicle, which cannot provide their reentry vehicles or reentry vehicle with additional velocity of more than 1,000 meters per second.

8. Cruise missiles are unmanned, self-propelled, guided, weapon-delivery vehicles which sustain flight through the use of aerodynamic lift over most of their flight path and which are flight-tested from or deployed on aircraft, that is, air-launched cruise missiles, or such vehicles which are referred to as cruise missiles in subparagraph 1(b) of Article IX.

First Agreed Statement

If a cruise missile is capable of a range in excess of 600 kilometers, all cruise missiles of that type shall be considered to be cruise missiles capable of a range in excess of 600 kilometers.

First Common Understanding

If a cruise missile has been flight-tested to a range in excess of 600 kilometers, it shall be considered to be a cruise missile capable of a range in excess of 600 kilometers.

Second Common Understanding

Cruise missiles not capable of a range in excess of 600 kilometers shall not be considered to be of a type capable of a range in excess of 600 kilometers if they are distinguishable on the basis of externally observable design features from cruise missiles of types capable of a range in excess of 600 kilometers.

Second Agreed Statement

The range of which a cruise missile is capable is the maximum distance which can be covered by the missile in its standard design mode flying until fuel exhaustion, determined by projecting its flight path onto the Earth's sphere from the point of launch to the point of impact.

Third Agreed Statement

If an unmanned, self-propelled, guided vehicle which sustains flight through the use of aerodynamic lift over most of its flight path has been flight-tested or deployed for weapon delivery, all vehicles of that type shall be considered to be weapon-delivery vehicles.

Third Common Understanding

Unmanned, self-propelled, guided vehicles which sustain flight through the use of aerodynamic lift over most of their flight path and are not weapon-delivery vehicles, that is, unarmed, pilotless, guided vehicles, shall not be considered to be cruise missiles if such vehicles are distinguishable from cruise missiles on the basis of externally observable design features.

Fourth Common Understanding

Neither Party shall convert unarmed, pilotless,

guided vehicles into cruise missiles capable of a range in excess of 600 kilometers, nor shall either Party convert cruise missiles capable of a range in excess of 600 kilometers into unarmed, pilotless, guided vehicles.

Fifth Common Understanding

Neither Party has plans during the term of the Treaty to flight-test from or deploy on aircraft unarmed, pilotless, guided vehicles which are capable of a range in excess of 600 kilometers. In the future, should a Party have such plans, that Party will provide notification thereof to the other Party well in advance of such flight-testing or deployment. This Common Understanding does not apply to target drones.

Article III

1. Upon entry into force of this Treaty, each Party undertakes to limit ICBM launchers, SLBM launchers, heavy bombers, and ASBMs to an aggregate number not to exceed 2,400.

2. Each Party undertakes to limit, from January 1, 1981, strategic offensive arms referred to in paragraph 1 of this Article to an aggregate number not to exceed 2,250, and to initiate reductions of those arms which as of that date would be in excess of this aggregate number.

3. Within the aggregate number provided for in paragraphs 1 and 2 of this Article and subject to the provisions of this Treaty, each Party has the right to determine the composition of these aggregates.

4. For each bomber of a type equipped for ASBMs, the aggregate numbers provided for in paragraphs 1 and 2 of this Article shall include the maximum number of such missiles for which a bomber of that type is equipped for one operational mission.

5. A heavy bomber equipped only for ASBMs shall not itself be included in the aggregate numbers provided for in paragraphs 1 and 2 of this Article.

6. Reductions of the numbers of strategic offensive arms required to comply with the provisions of paragraphs 1 and 2 of this Article shall be carried out as provided for in Article XI.

Article IV

1. Each Party undertakes not to start construction of additional fixed ICBM launchers.

2. Each Party undertakes not to relocate fixed ICBM launchers.

3. Each Party undertakes not to convert launchers of light ICBMs, or of ICBMs of older types deployed prior to 1964, into launchers of heavy ICBMs of types deployed after that time.

4. Each Party undertakes in the process of modernization and replacement of ICBM silo launchers not to increase the original internal volume of an ICBM silo launcher by more than thirty-two percent. Within this limit each Party has the right to determine whether such an increase will be made through an increase in the original diameter or in the original depth of an ICBM silo launcher, or in both of these dimensions.

Agreed Statement

The word "original" in paragraph 4 of Article IV of the Treaty refers to the internal dimensions of an ICBM silo launcher, including its internal volume, as of May 26, 1972, or as of the date on which such launcher becomes operational, whichever is later.

Common Understanding

The obligations provided for in paragraph 4 of Article IV of the Treaty and in the Agreed Statement thereto mean that the original diameter or the original depth of an ICBM silo launcher may not be increased by an amount greater than that which would result in an increase in the original internal volume of the ICBM silo launcher by thirty-two percent solely through an increase in one of these dimensions.

5. Each Party undertakes:

(a) not to supply ICBM launcher deployment areas with intercontinental ballistic missiles in excess of a number consistent with normal deployment, maintenance, training, and replacement requirements;

(b) not to provide storage facilities for or to store ICBMs in excess of normal deployment requirements at launch sites of ICBM launchers;

(c) not to develop, test, or deploy systems for rapid reload of ICBM launchers.

Agreed Statement

The term "normal deployment requirements," as used in paragraph 5 of Article IV of the Treaty, means the deployment of one missile at each ICBM launcher.

6. Subject to the provisions of this Treaty, each Party undertakes not to have under construction at any time strategic offensive arms referred to in para-

graph 1 of Article III in excess of numbers consistent with a normal construction schedule.

Common Understanding

A normal construction schedule, in paragraph 6 of Article IV of the Treaty, is understood to be one consistent with the past or present construction practices of each Party.

7. Each Party undertakes not to develop, test, or deploy ICBMs which have a launch-weight greater or a throw-weight greater than that of the heaviest, in terms of either launch-weight or throw-weight, respectively, of the heavy ICBMs, deployed by either Party as of the date of signature of this Treaty.

First Agreed Statement

The launch-weight of an ICBM is the weight of the fully loaded missile itself at the time of launch.

Second Agreed Statement

The throw-weight of an ICBM is the sum of the weight of:

(a) its reentry vehicle or reentry vehicles;

(b) any self-contained dispensing mechanisms or other appropriate devices for targeting one reentry vehicle, or for releasing or for dispensing and targeting two or more reentry vehicles; and

(c) its penetration aids, including devices for their release.

Common Understanding

The term "other appropriate devices," as used in the definition of the throw-weight of an ICBM in the Second Agreed Statement to paragraph 7 of Article IV of the Treaty, means any devices for dispensing and targeting two or more reentry vehicles; and any devices for releasing two or more reentry vehicles or for targeting one reentry vehicle, which cannot provide their reentry vehicles or reentry vehicle with additional velocity of more than 1,000 meters per second.

8. Each Party undertakes not to convert landbased launchers of ballistic missiles which are not ICBMs into launchers for launching ICBMs, and not to test them for this purpose.

Common Understanding

During the term of the Treaty, the Union of Soviet Socialist Republics will not produce, test, or deploy ICBMs of the type designated by the Union of Soviet Socialist Republics as the RS-14 and known to the United States of America as the SS-16, a light ICBM first flight-tested after 1970 and flight-tested only with a single reentry vehicle; this Common Understanding also means that the Union of Soviet Socialist Republics will not produce the third stage of that missile, the reentry vehicle of that missile, or the appropriate device for targeting the reentry vehicle of that missile.

9. Each Party undertakes not to flight-test or deploy new types of ICBMs, that is, types of ICBMs not flight-tested as of May 1, 1979, except that each Party may flight-test and deploy one new type of light ICBM.

First Agreed Statement

The term "new types of ICBMs," as used in paragraph 9 of Article IV of the Treaty, refers to any ICBM which is different from those ICBMs flight-tested as of May 1, 1979 in any one or more of the following respects:

(a) the number of stages, the length, the largest diameter, the launch-weight, or the throw weight, of the missile;

(b) the type of propellant (that is, liquid or solid) of any of its stages.

First Common Understanding

As used in the First Agreed Statement to paragraph 9 of Article IV of the Treaty, the term "different," referring to the length, the diameter, the launch-weight, and the throw-weight, of the missile, means a difference in excess of five percent.

Second Agreed Statement

Every ICBM of the one new type of light ICBM permitted to each Party pursuant to paragraph 9 of Article IV of the Treaty shall have the same number of stages and the same type of propellant (that is, liquid or solid) of each stage as the first ICBM of the one new type of light ICBM launched by that Party. In addition, after the twenty-fifth launch of an ICBM of that type, or after the last launch before deployment begins of ICBMs of that type, whichever occurs earlier, ICBMs of the one new type of light ICBM permitted to that Party shall not be different in any one or more of the following respects: the length, the largest diameter, the launch-weight, or the throw-weight, of the missile.

A Party which launches ICBMs of the one new type of light ICBM permitted pursuant to paragraph 9 of Article IV of the Treaty shall promptly notify the other Party of the date of the first launch and of the date of either the twenty-fifth or the last launch before deployment begins of ICBMs of that type, whichever occurs earlier.

Second Common Understanding

As used in the Second Agreed Statement to paragraph 9 of Article IV of the Treaty, the term "different," referring to the length, the diameter, the launch-weight, and the throw-weight, of the missile, means a difference in excess of five percent from the value established for each of the above parameters as of the twenty-fifth launch or as of the last launch before deployment begins, whichever occurs earlier. The values demonstrated in each of the above parameters during the last twelve of the twenty-five launches or during the last twelve launches before deployment begins, whichever twelve launches occur earlier, shall not vary by more than ten percent from any other of the corresponding values demonstrated during those twelve launches.

Third Common Understanding

The limitations with respect to launch-weight and throw-weight, provided for in the First Agreed Statement and the First Common Understanding to paragraph 9 of Article IV of the Treaty, do not preclude the flight-testing or the deployment of ICBMs with fewer reentry vehicles, or fewer penetration aids, or both, than the maximum number of penetration aids with which ICBMs of that type have been flight-tested as of May 1, 1979, even if this results in a decrease in launch-weight or in throw-weight in excess of five percent.

In addition to the aforementioned cases, those limitations do not preclude a decrease in launch-weight or in throw-weight in excess of five percent, in the case of the flight-testing or the deployment of ICBMs with a lesser quantity of propellant, including the propellant of a self-contained dispensing mechanism or other appropriate device, than the maximum quantity of propellant, including the propellant of a self-contained dispensing mechanism or other appropriate device, with which ICBMs of that type have been flight-tested as of May 1, 1979, provided that such an ICBM is at the same time flight-tested or deployed with fewer reentry vehicles, or fewer penetration aids, or both,

than the maximum number of reentry vehicles and the maximum number of penetration aids with which ICBMs of that type have been flight-tested as of May 1, 1979, and the decrease in launch-weight and throw-weight in such cases results only from the reduction in the number of reentry vehicles, or penetration aids, or both, and the reduction in the quantity of propellant.

Fourth Common Understanding

The limitations with respect to launch-weight and throw-weight, provided for in the Second Agreed Statement and the Second Common Understanding to paragraph 9 of Article IV of the Treaty, do not preclude the flight-testing or the deployment of ICBMs of the one new type of light ICBM permitted to each Party pursuant to paragraph 9 of Article IV of the Treaty with fewer reentry vehicles, or fewer penetration aids, or both, than the maximum number of reentry vehicles and the maximum number of penetration aids with which ICBMs of that type have been flight-tested, even if this results in a decrease in launch-weight or in throw-weight in excess of five percent.

In addition to the aforementioned cases, those limitations do not preclude a decrease in launch-weight or in throw-weight in excess of five percent, in the case of the flight-testing or the deployment of ICBMs of that type with a lesser quantity of propellant, including the propellant of a self-contained dispensing mechanism or other appropriate device, than the maximum quantity of propellant, including the propellant of a self-contained dispensing mechanism or other appropriate device, with which ICBMs of that type have been flight-tested, provided that such an ICBM is at the same time flight-tested or deployed with fewer reentry vehicles, or fewer penetration aids, or both, than the maximum number of reentry vehicles and the maximum number of penetration aids with which ICBMs of that type have been flight-tested, and the decrease in launch-weight and throw-weight in such cases results only from the reduction in the number of reentry vehicles, or penetration aids, or both, and the reduction in the quantity of propellant.

10. Each Party undertakes not to flight-test or deploy ICBMs of a type flight-tested as of May 1, 1979 with a number of reentry vehicles greater than the maximum number of reentry vehicles with which an ICBM of that type has been light-tested as of that date.

First Agreed Statement

The following types of ICBMs and SLBMs equipped with MIRVs have been flight-tested with the maximum number of reentry vehicles set forth below:

For the United States of America
ICBMs of the Minuteman III type-seven reentry vehicles;
SLBMs of the Poseidon C-3 type-fourteen, reentry vehicles;
SLBMs of the Trident C-4 type-seven reentry vehicles.
For the Union of Soviet Socialist Republics
ICBMs of the RS-16 type-four reentry vehicles;
ICBMs of the RS-18 type-six reentry vehicles;
ICBMs of the RS-20 type-ten reentry vehicles;
SLBMs of the RSM-50 type-seven reentry vehicles.

Common Understanding

Minuteman III ICBMs of the United States of America have been deployed with no more than three reentry vehicles. During the term of the Treaty the United States of America has no plans to and will not flight-test or deploy missiles of this type with more than three reentry vehicles.

Second Agreed Statement

During the flight-testing of any ICBM, SLBM, or ASBM after May 1, 1979, the number of procedures for releasing or for dispensing may not exceed the maximum number of reentry vehicles established for missiles of corresponding types as provided for in paragraphs 10, 11, 12 and 13 of Article IV of the Treaty. In this Agreed Statement "procedures for releasing or for dispensing" are understood to mean maneuvers of a missile associated with targeting and releasing or dispensing its reentry vehicles to aim points, whether or not a reentry vehicle is actually released or dispensed.

Procedures for releasing anti-missile defense penetration aids will not be considered to be procedures for releasing or for dispensing a reentry vehicle so long as the procedures for releasing anti-missile defense penetration aids differ from those for releasing or for dispensing reentry vehicles.

Third Agreed Statement

Each party undertakes:

(a) not to flight-test or deploy ICBMs equipped with multiple reentry vehicles, of a type flight-tested as of May 1, 1979, with reentry vehicles the weight of any of which is less than the weight of the lightest of those reentry vehicles with which an ICBM of that type has been flight-tested as of that date:

(b) not to flight-test or deploy ICBMs equipped with a single reentry vehicle and without an appropriate device for targeting a reentry vehicle, of a type flight-tested as of May 1, 1979, with a reentry vehicle the weight of which is less than the weight of the lightest reentry vehicle on an ICBM of a type equipped with MIRVs and flight-tested by that Party as of May 1, 1979; and

(c) not to flight-test or deploy ICBMs equipped with a single reentry vehicle and with an appropriate device for targeting a reentry vehicle, of a type flight-tested as of May 1, 1979, with a reentry vehicle the weight of which is less than fifty percent of the throw-weight of that ICBM.

11. Each Party undertakes not to flight-test or deploy ICBMs of the one new type permitted pursuant paragraphs 9 of this Article with a number of reentry vehicles greater than the maximum number of reentry vehicles with which an ICBM of either Party between flight-tested as of May 1, 1979, that is, ten.

First Agreed Statement

Each Party undertakes not to flight-test or deploy one new type of light ICBM permitted to each Party pursuant to paragraph 9 of Article IV of the Treaty with a number of reentry vehicles greater than the maximum number of reentry vehicles with which an ICBM of that type has been flight-tested as of the twenty-fifth launch or the last launch before deployment begins of ICBMs of that type, whichever occurs earlier.

Second Agreed Statement

During the flight-testing of any ICBM, SLBM, or ASBM after May 1, 1979 the number of procedures for releasing or for dispensing may not exceed the maximum number of reentry vehicles established for missiles of corresponding types as provided for in paragraphs 10, 11, 12, and 13 of Article IV of the Treaty. In this Agreed Statement "procedures for releasing and for dispensing" are understood to mean maneuvers of a missile associated with targeting and releasing or dispensing its reentry vehicles to aim points, whether or not a reentry vehicle is actually released or dispensed. Procedures for releasing anti-missile defense penetration aids will not be considered to be procedures for releasing or for dispensing a reentry vehicle so long as the procedures for releasing anti-missile defense penetration aids differ from those for releasing or for dispensing reentry vehicles.

12. Each Party undertakes not to flight-test or deploy SLBMs with a number of reentry vehicles with which an SLBM of either Party has been flight-tested as of May 1, 1979, that is fourteen.

First Agreed Statement

The following types of ICBMs and SLBMs equipped with MIRVs have been flight-tested with the maximum number of reentry vehicles set forth below:

For the United States of America
ICBMs of the Minuteman III type-seven reentry vehicles;
SLBMs of the Poseidon C-3 type-fourteen reentry vehicles;
SLBMs of the Trident C-4 type-seven reentry vehicles.
For the Union of Soviet Socialist Republics
ICBMs of the RS-16 type-four reentry vehicles;
ICBMs of the RS-18 type-six reentry vehicles;
ICBMs of the RS-20 type-ten reentry vehicles;
SLBMs of the RSM-50 type-seven reentry vehicles.

Second Agreed Statement

During the flight-testing of any ICBM, SLBM, or ASBM after May 1, 1979 the number of procedures for releasing or for dispensing may not exceed the maximum number of reentry vehicles established for missiles of corresponding types as provided for in paragraphs 10, 11, 12 and 13 of Article IV of the Treaty. In this Agreed Statement "procedures for releasing or dispensing" are understood to mean maneuvers of a missile associated with targeting and releasing or dispensing its reentry vehicles to aim points, whether or not a reentry vehicle is actually released or dispensed. Procedures for releasing anti-missile defense penetration aids will not be considered to be procedures for releasing or for dispensing a reentry vehicle so long as the procedures for releasing anti-missile defense penetration aids differ from those for releasing or for dispensing reentry vehicles.

13. Each Party undertakes not to flight-test or deploy ASBMs with a number of reentry vehicles greater than the maximum number of reentry vehicles with which an ICBM of either Party has been flight-tested as of May 1, 1979, that is, ten.

Agreed Statement

During the flight-testing of any ICBM, SLBM, or ASBM after May 1, 1979 the number of procedures for releasing or for dispensing may not exceed the maximum number of reentry vehicles established for missiles of corresponding types as provided for in paragraphs 10, 11, 12 and 13 of Article IV of the Treaty. In this Agreed Statement "procedures for releasing or for dispensing" are understood to mean maneuvers of a missile associated with targeting and releasing or dispensing its reentry vehicles to aim points, whether or not a reentry vehicle is actually released or dispensed. Procedures for releasing anti-missile defense penetration aids will not be considered to be procedures for releasing or for dispensing a reentry vehicle so long as the procedures for releasing anti-missile defense penetration aids differ from those for releasing or for dispensing reentry vehicles.

14. Each Party undertakes not to deploy at any one time on heavy bombers equipped for cruise missiles capable of a range in excess of 600 kilometers a number of such cruise missiles which exceeds the product of 28 and the number of such heavy bombers.

First Agreed Statement

For the purpose of the limitation provided for in paragraph 14 of Article IV of the Treaty, there shall be considered to be deployed on each heavy bomber of a type equipped for cruise missiles capable of a range in excess of 600 kilometers the maximum number of such missiles for which any bomber of that type is equipped for one operational mission.

Second Agreed Statement

During the term of the Treaty no bomber of the B-52 or B-1 types of the United States of America and no bomber of the Tupolev-95 or Myasishchev types of the Union of Soviet Socialist Republics will be equipped for more than twenty cruise missiles capable of a range in excess of 600 kilometers.

Article V

1. Within the aggregate numbers provided for in paragraphs 1 and 2 of Article III, each Party undertakes to limit launchers of ICBMs and SLBMs equipped with MIRVs, ASBMs equipped with MIRVs, and heavy bombers equipped for cruise missiles capable of a range in excess of 600 kilometers to an aggregate number not to exceed 1,320.

2. Within the aggregate number provided for in

paragraph 1 of this Article, each Party undertakes to limit launchers of ICBMs and SLBMs equipped with MIRVs and ASBMs equipped with MIRVs to an aggregate number not to exceed 1,200.

3. Within the aggregate number provided for in paragraph 2 of this Article, each Party undertakes to limit launchers of ICBMs equipped with MIRVs to an aggregate number not to exceed 820.

4. For each bomber of a type equipped for ASBMs equipped with MIRVs, the aggregate numbers provided for in paragraphs 1 and 2 of this Article shall include the maximum number of ASBMs for which a bomber of that type is equipped for one operational mission.

Agreed Statement

If a bomber is equipped for ASBMs equipped with MIRVs all bombers of that type shall be considered to be equipped for ASBMs equipped with MIRVs.

5. Within the aggregate numbers provided for in paragraphs 1, 2 and 3 of this Article and subject to the provisions of this Treaty, each Party has the right to determine the composition of these aggregates.

Article VI

1. The limitations provided for in this Treaty shall apply to those arms which are:

(a) operational;

(b) in the final stage of construction;

(c) in reserve, in storage, or mothballed;

(d) undergoing overhaul, repair, modernization, or conversion.

2. Those arms in the final stage of construction are:

(a) SLBM launchers on submarines which have begun sea trials;

(b) ASBMs after a bomber of a type equipped for such missiles has been brought out of the shop, plant, or other facility where final assembly or conversion for the purpose of equipping it for such missiles has been performed;

(c) other strategic offensive arms which are finally assembled in a shop, plant or other facility after they have been brought out of the shop, plant, or other facility where their final assembly has been perfomed.

3. ICBM and SLBM launchers of a type not subject to the limitation provided for in Article V, which under-go conversion into launchers of a type subject to that limitation, shall become subject to that limitation as follows:

(a) fixed ICBM launchers when work on their conversion reaches the stage which first definitely indicates that they are being so converted;

(b) SLBM launchers on a submarine when that submarine first goes to sea after their conversion has been performed.

Agreed Statement

The procedures referred to in paragraph 7 of Article VI of the Treaty shall include procedures determining the manner in which mobile ICBM launchers of a type not subject to the limitation provided for in Article V of the Treaty, which undergo conversion into launchers of a type subject to that limitation, shall become subject to that limitation, unless the Parties agree that mobile ICBM launchers shall not be deployed after the date on which the Protocol ceases to be in force.

4. ASBMs on a bomber which undergoes conversion from a bomber of a type equipped for ASBMs which are not subject to the limitation provided for in Article V into a bomber of a type equipped for ASBMs which are subject to that limitation shall become subject to that limitation when the bomber is brought out of the shop, plant, or other facility where such conversion has been performed.

5. A heavy bomber of a type not subject to the limitation provided for in paragraph 1 of Article V shall become subject to that limitation when it is brought out of the shop, plant, or other facility where it has been converted into a heavy bomber of a type equipped for cruise missiles capable of a range in excess of 600 kilometers. A bomber of a type not subject to the limitation provided for in paragraph 1 or 2 of Article III shall become subject to that limitation and to the limitation provided for in paragraph 1 of Article V when it is brought out of the shop, plant, or other facility where it has been converted into a bomber of a type equipped for cruise missiles capable of a range in excess of 600 kilometers.

6. The arms subject to the limitations provided for in this Treaty shall continue to be subject to these limitations until they are dismantled, are destroyed, or otherwise cease to be subject to these limitations under procedures to be agreed upon.

Agreed Statement

The procedures for removal of strategic offensive

arms from the aggregate numbers provided for in the Treaty, which are referred to in paragraph 6 of Article IV of the Treaty, and which are to be agreed upon in the Standing Consultative Commission, shall include:

(a) procedures for removal from the aggregate numbers, provided for in Article V of the Treaty, of ICBM and SLBM launchers which are being converted from launchers of a type subject to the limitation provided for in Article V of the Treaty, into launchers of a type not subject to that limitation;

(b) procedures for removal from the aggregate numbers, provided for in Articles III and V of the Treaty, of bombers which are being converted from bombers of a type subject to the limitations provided for in Article III of the Treaty or in Articles III and V of the Treaty into airplanes or bombers of a type not so subject.

Common Understanding

The procedures referred to in subparagraph (b) of the Agreed Statement to paragraph 6 of Article (of the Treaty for removal of bombers from the aggregate numbers provided for in Articles III and V of the Treaty shall be based upon the existence of functionally related observable differences which indicate whether or not they can perform the mission of a heavy bomber, or whether or not they can perform the mission of a bomber equipped for cruise missiles capable of a range in excess of 600 kilometers.

7. In accordance with the provisions of Article XVII, the Parties will agree in the Standing Consultative Commission upon procedures to implement the provisions of this Article.

Article VII

1. The limitations provided for in Article III shall not apply to ICBM and SLBM test and training launchers or to space vehicle launchers for exploration and use of outer space. ICBM and SLBM test and training launchers are ICBM and SLBM launchers used only for testing or training.

Common Understanding

The term "testing," as used in Article VII of the Treaty, includes research and development.

2. The Parties agree that:

(a) there shall be no significant increase in the number of ICBM of SLBM test and training launchers or

in the number of such launchers of heavy ICBMs;

(b) construction or conversion of ICBM launchers at test ranges shall be undertaken only for purposes of testing and training;

(c) there shall be no conversion of ICBM test and training launchers or of space vehicle launchers into ICBM launchers subject to the limitations provided for in Article III.

First Agreed Statement

The term "significant increase," as used in subparagraph 2(a) of Article VII of the Treaty, means an increase of fifteen percent or more. Any new ICBM test and training launchers which replace ICBM test and training launchers at test ranges will be located only at test ranges.

Second Agreed Statement

Current test ranges where ICBMs are tested are located: for the United States of America, near Santa Maria, California, and at Cape Canaveral, Florida; and for the Union of Soviet Socialist Republics, in the areas of Tyura-Tam and Plesetskaya. In the Standing Consultative Commission of the location of any other test range used by the Party to test ICBMs.

First Common Understanding

At test ranges where ICBMs are tested, other arms, including those not limited by the Treaty, may also be tested.

Second Common Understanding

Of the eighteen launchers of fractional orbital missiles at the test range where ICBMs are tested in the area of Tyura-Tam, twelve launchers shall be dismantled or destroyed and six launchers may be converted to launchers for testing missiles undergoing modernization.

Dismantling or destruction of the twelve launchers shall begin upon entry into force of the Treaty and shall be completed within eight months, under procedures for dismantling or destruction of these launchers to be agreed upon in the Standing Consultative Commission. These twelve launchers shall not be replaced.

Conversion of the six launchers may be carried out after entry into force of the Treaty, fractional orbital missiles shall be removed and shall be destroyed pursuant to the provisions of subparagraph I(c) of Article IX and of Article XI of the Treaty and shall not be replaced by other missiles, except in the case of conversion of these six launchers for testing missiles undergoing modernization. After removal of the fractional orbital missiles, and prior to such conversion, any activities associated with these launchers shall be limited to normal maintenance requirements for launchers in which missiles are not deployed. These six launchers shall be subject to the provisions of Article VII of the Treaty and, if converted, to the provisions of the Fifth Common Understanding to paragraph 5 of Article II of the Treaty.

Article VIII

1. Each Party undertakes not to flight-test cruise missiles capable of a range in excess of 600 kilometers or ASBMs from aircraft other than bombers or to convert such aircraft into aircraft equipped for such missiles.

Agreed Statement

For purposes of testing only, each Party has the right, through initial construction or, as an exception to the provisions of paragraph 1 of Article VIII of the Treaty, by conversion, to equip for cruise missiles capable of a range in excess of 600 kilometers of for ASBMs no more than sixteen airplanes, including airplanes which are prototypes of bombers equipped for such missiles. Each Party also has the right, as an exception to the provisions of paragraph 1 of Article VIII of the Treaty, to flight-test from such airplanes cruise missiles capable of a range in excess of 600 kilometers and, after the date on which the Protocol ceases to be in force, to flight-test ASBMs from such airplanes as well, unless the Parties agree that they will not flight-test ASBMs after that date. The limitations provided for in Article III of the Treaty shall not apply to such airplanes.

The aforementioned airplanes may include only:

(a) airplanes other than bombers which, as an exception to the provisions of paragraph 1 of Article VIII of the Treaty, have been converted into airplanes equipped for cruise missiles capable of a range in excess of 600 kilometers or for ASBMs;

(b) airplanes considered to be heavy bombers pursuant to subparagraph 3(c) or 3(d) or Article II of the Treaty; and

(c) airplanes other than heavy bombers which, prior to March 7, 1979, were used for testing cruise missiles capable of a range in excess of 600 kilometers.

The airplanes referred to in subparagraphs (a) and (b) of this Agreed Statement shall be distinguishable on the basis of functionally related observable differences from airplanes which otherwise would be of the same type but cannot perform the mission of a bomber equipped for cruise missiles capable of a range in excess of 600 kilometers or for ASBMs.

The airplanes referred to in subparagraph (c) of this Agreed Statement shall not be used for testing cruise missiles capable of a range in excess of 600 kilometers after the expiration of a six-month period from the date of entry into force of the Treaty, unless by the expiration of that period they are distinguishable on the basis of functionally related observable differences from airplanes which otherwise would be of the same type but cannot perform the mission of a bomber equipped for cruise missiles capable of a range in excess of 600 kilometers.

First Common Understanding

The term "testing," as used in the Agreed Statement to paragraph 1 of Article VIII of the Treaty, includes research and development.

Second Common Understanding

The Parties shall notify each other in the Standing Consultative Commission of the number of airplanes, according to type, used for testing pursuant to the Agreed Statement to paragraph 1 of Article VIII of the Treaty. Such notification shall be provided at the first regular session of the Standing Consultative Commission held after an airplane has been used for such testing.

Third Common Understanding

None of the sixteen airplanes referred to in the Agreed Statement to paragraph 1 of Article VIII of the Treaty may be replaced, except in the event of the involuntary destruction of any such airplane or in the case of the dismantling or destruction of any such airplane. The procedures for such replacement and for removal of any such airplane from that number, in case of its conversion, shall be agreed upon in the Standing Consultative Commission.

2. Each Party undertakes not to convert aircraft other than bombers into aircraft which can carry out the mission of a heavy bomber as referred to in subparagraph 3(b) of Article II.

Article IX

1. Each Party undertakes not to develop, test, or deploy:

(a) ballistic missiles capable of a range in excess of 600 kilometers for installation on waterborne vehicles other than submarines, or launchers of such missiles;

Common Understanding to subparagraph (a)

The obligations provided for in subparagraph 1(a) of Article IX of the Treaty do not affect current practices for transporting ballistic missiles.

(b) fixed ballistic or cruise missile launchers for emplacement on the ocean floor, on the seabed, or on the beds of internal waters and inland waters, or in the subsoil thereof, or mobile launchers of such missiles, which move only in contact with the ocean floor, the seabed, or the beds of internal waters and inland waters, or missiles for such launchers;

Agreed Statement to subparagraph (b)

The obligations provided for in subparagraph 1(b) of Article IX of the Treaty shall apply to all areas of the ocean floor and the seabed, including the seabed zone referred to in Articles I and II of the 1971 Treaty on the Prohibition of the Emplacement of Nuclear Weapons and Other Weapons of Mass Destruction on the Seabed and the Ocean Floor and in the Subsoil Thereof.

(c) systems for placing into Earth orbit nuclear weapons or any other kind of weapons of mass destruction, including fractional orbital missiles;

Common Understanding to subparagraph (c)

The provisions of subparagraph 1(c) of Article IX of the Treaty do not require the dismantling or destruction of any existing launchers of either Party.

(d) mobile launchers of heavy ICBMs;

(e) SLBMs which have a launch-weight greater or a throw-weight greater than that of the heaviest, in terms of either launch-weight or throw-weight, respectively, of the light ICBMs deployed by either Party as of the date of signature of this Treaty, or launchers of such SLBMs; or

(f) ASBMs which have a launch-weight greater or a throw-weight greater than that of the heaviest, in terms of either launch-weight or throw-weight, respectively, of the light ICBMs deployed by either Party as of the date of signature of this Treaty.

First Agreed Statement to subparagraphs (e) and (f)

The launch-weight of an SLBM or of an ASBM is the weight of the fully loaded missile itself at the time of launch.

Second Agreed Statement to subparagraphs (e) and (f)

The throw-weight of an SLBM or of an ASBM is the sum of the weight of:

(a) its reentry vehicle or reentry vehicles;

(b) any self-contained dispensing mechanisms or other appropriate devices for targeting one reentry vehicle, or for releasing or for dispensing and targeting two or more reentry vehicles; and

(c) its penetration aids, including devices for their release.

Common Understanding to subparagraphs (e) and (f)

The term "other appropriate devices," as used in the definition of the throw-weight of an SLBM or of an ASBM in the Second Agreed Statement to subparagraphs 1(e) and 1(f) of Article IX of the Treaty, means any devices for dispensing and targeting two or more reentry vehicles; and any devices for targeting one reentry vehicle, which cannot provide their reentry vehicles or reentry vehicle with additional velocity of more than 1,000 meters per second.

2. Each Party undertakes not to flight-test from aircraft cruise missiles capable of a range in excess of 600 kilometers which are equipped with multiple independently targetable warheads and not to deploy such cruise missiles on aircraft.

Agreed Statement

Warheads of a cruise missile are independently targetable if maneuvering or targeting of the warheads to separate aim points along ballistic trajectories or any other flight paths, which are unrelated to each other, is accomplished during a flight of a cruise missile.

Article X

Subject to the provisions of this Treaty, modernization and replacement of strategic offensive arms may be carried out.

Article XI

1. Strategic offensive arms which would be in excess of the aggregate numbers provided for in this

Treaty as well as strategic offensive arms prohibited by this Treaty shall be dismantled or destroyed under procedures to be agreed upon in the Standing Consultative Commission.

2. Dismantling or destruction of strategic offensive arms which would be in excess of the aggregate number provided for in paragraph 1 of Article III shall begin on the date of the entry into force of this Treaty and shall be completed within the following periods from that date: four months for ICBM launchers; six months for SLBM launchers; and three months for heavy bombers.

3. Dismantling or destruction of strategic offensive arms which would be in excess of the aggregate number provided for in paragraph 2 of Article III shall be initiated no later than January 1, 1981, shall be carried out throughout the ensuing twelve-month period, and shall be completed no later than December 31, 1981.

4. Dismantling or destruction of strategic offensive arms prohibited by this Treaty shall be completed within the shortest possible agreed period of time, but not later than six months after the entry into force of this Treaty.

Article XII

1. In order to ensure the viability and effectiveness of this Treaty, each Party undertakes not to circumvent the provisions of this Treaty, through any other state or states, or in any other manner.

Article XIII

1. Each Party undertakes not to assume any international obligations which would conflict with this Treaty.

Article XIV

The Parties undertake to begin, promptly after the entry into force of this Treaty, active negotiations with the objective of achieving, as soon as possible, agreement on further measures for the limitation and reduction of strategic arms. It is also the objective of the Parties to conclude well in advance of 1985 an agreement limiting strategic offensive arms to replace this Treaty upon its expiration.

Article XV

1. For the purpose of providing assurance of compliance with the provisions of this Treaty, each Party shall use national technical means of verification at its disposal in a manner consistent with generally recognized principles of international law.

2. Each party undertakes not to interfere with the national technical means of verification of the other Party operating in accordance with paragraph 1 of this Article.

3. Each Party undertakes not to use deliberate concealment measures which impede verification by national technical means of compliance with the provisions of this Treaty. This obligation shall not require changes in current construction, assembly, conversion, or overhaul practices.

First Agreed Statement

Deliberate concealment measures, as referred to in paragraph 3 of Article XV of the Treaty, are measures carried out deliberately to hinder or deliberately to impede verification by national technical means of compliance with the provisions of the Treaty.

Second Agreed Statement

The obligation not to use deliberated concealment measures, provided for in paragraph 3 of Article XV of the Treaty, does not preclude the testing of anti-missile defense penetration aids.

First Common Understanding

The provisions of paragraph 3 of Article XV of the Treaty and the First Agreed Statement thereto apply to all provisions of the Treaty, including provisions associated with testing. In this connection, the obligation not to use deliberate concealment measures includes the obligation not to use deliberate concealment measures associated with testing, including those measures aimed at concealing the association between ICBMs and launchers during testing.

Second Common Understanding

Each Party is free to use various methods of transmitting telemetric information during testing, including its encryption, except that, in accordance with the provisions of paragraph 3 of Article XV of the Treaty, neither Party shall engage in deliberate denial of telemetric information, such as through the use of telemetry encryption, whenever such denial impedes verification of compliance with the provisions of the Treaty.

Third Common Understanding

In addition to the obligations provided for in paragraph 3 of Article XV of the Treaty, no shelters which impede verification by national technical means of compliance with the provisions of the Treaty shall be used over ICBM silo launchers.

Article XVI

1. Each Party undertakes, before conducting each planned ICBM launch, to notify the other Party well in advance on a case-by-case basis that such a launch will occur, except for single ICBM launches from test ranges or from ICBM launcher deployment areas, which are not planned to extend beyond its national territory.

First Common Understanding

ICBM launches to which the obligations provided for in Article XVI of the Treaty apply, include, among others, those ICBM launches for which advance notification is required pursuant to the provisions of the Agreement on Measures to Reduce the Risk of Outbreak of Nuclear War Between the United States of America and the Union of Soviet Socialist Republics, signed September 30, 1971, and the Agreement Between the Government of the United States of America and the Government of the Union of Soviet Socialist Republics on the Prevention of Incidents On and Over the High Seas, signed May 25, 1972. Nothing in Article XVI of the Treaty is intended to inhibit advance notification, on a voluntary basis, of any ICBM launches not subject to its provisions, the advance notification of which would enhance confidence between the Parties.

Second Common Understanding

A multiple ICBM launch conducted by a Party, as distinct from single ICBM launches referred to in Article XVI of the Treaty, is a launch which would result in two or more of its ICBMs being in flight at the same time.

Third Common Understanding

The test ranges referred to in Article XVI of the Treaty are those covered by the Second Agreed Statement to paragraph 2 of Article VII of the Treaty.

2. The Parties shall agree in the Standing Consultative Commission upon procedures to implement the provisions of this Article.

Article XVII

1. To promote the objectives and implementation of the provisions of this Treaty, the Parties shall use the Standing Consultative Commission established by the Memorandum of Understanding Between the Government of the United States of America and the Government of the Union of Soviet Socialist Republics Regarding the Establishment of a Standing Consultative Commission of December 21, 1972.

2. Within the framework of the Standing Consultative Commission, with respect to this Treaty, the Parties will:

(a) consider questions concerning compliance with the obligations assumed and related situations which may be considered ambiguous;

(b) provide on a voluntary basis such informations as either Party considers necessary to assure confidence in compliance with the obligations assumed;

(c) consider questions involving unintended interference with national technical means of verification, and questions involving unintended impeding of verification by national technical means of compliance with the provisions of this Treaty;

(d) consider possible changes in the strategic situation which have a bearing on the provisions of this Treaty;

(e) agree upon procedures for replacement, conversion, and dismantling or destruction, of strategic offensive arms in cases provided for in the provisions of this Treaty and upon procedures for removal of such arms from the aggregate numbers when they otherwise cease to be subject to the limitations provided for in this Treaty, and at regular sessions of the Standing Consultative Commission, notify each other in accordance with the aforementioned procedures, at least twice annually, of actions completed and those in process;

(f) consider, as appropriate, possible proposals for further increasing the viability of this Treaty, including proposals for amendments in accordance with the provisions of this Treaty;

(g) consider, as appropriate, proposals for further measures limiting strategic offensive arms.

3. In the Standing Consultative Commission the Parties shall maintain by category the agreed data base on the numbers of strategic offensive arms established by the Memorandum of Understanding Between the United States of America and the Union

of Soviet Socialist Republics Regarding the Establishment of a Data Base on the Numbers of Strategic Offensive Arms of June 18, 1979.

Agreed Statement

In order to maintain the agreed data base on the number of strategic offensive arms subject to the limitations provided for in the Treaty in accordance with paragraph 3 of Article XVII of the Treaty, at each regular session of the Standing Consultative Commission the Parties will notify each other of and consider changes in those numbers in the following categories: launchers of ICBMs; fixed launchers of ICBMs; launchers of ICBMs equipped with MIRVs; launchers of SLBMs; launchers of SLBMs equipped with MIRVs; heavy bombers; heavy bombers equipped for cruise missiles capable of a range in excess of 600 kilometers; heavy bombers equipped only for ASBMs; ASBMs; and ASBMs equipped with MIRVs.

Article XVIII

Each Party may propose amendments to this Treaty. Agreed amendments shall enter into force in accordance with the procedures governing the entry into force of this Treaty.

Article XIV

1. This Treaty shall be subject to ratification in accordance with the constitutional procedures of each Party. This Treaty shall enter into force on the day of the exchange of instruments of ratification and shall remain in force through December 31, 1985, unless replaced earlier by an agreement further limiting strategic offensive arms.

2. This Treaty shall be registered pursuant to article 102 of the Charter of the United Nations.

3. Each Party shall, in exercising its national sovereignty, have the right to withdraw from this Treaty if it decides that extraordinary events related to the subject matter of this Treaty have jeopardized its supreme interests. It shall give notice of its decision to the other Party six months prior to withdrawal from the Treaty. Such notice shall include a statement of the extraordinary events the notifying Party regards as having jeopardized its supreme interests.

United Nations Agreement Governing the Activities of States on the Moon and Other Celestial Bodies

Opened for signature: *December 5, 1979*
Place of signature: *New York*
Ratifications: *Australia, Austria, Chile, Netherlands, Pakistan, Philippines, Uruguay*
Date of entry into force: *July 11, 1984*

The States Parties to this Agreement,
Noting the achievements of States in the exploration and use of the moon and other celestial bodies,
Recognizing that the moon, as a natural satellite of the earth, has an important role to play in the exploration of outer space,
Determined to promote on the basis of equality the further development of co-operation among States in the exploration and use of the moon and other celestial bodies,
Desiring to prevent the moon from becoming an area of international conflict,
Bearing in mind the benefits which may be derived from the exploitation of the natural resources of the moon and other celestial bodies,

Recalling the Treaty on Principles Governing the Activities of States in the Exploration and Use of Outer Space, including the Moon and Other Celestial Bodies, the Agreement on the Rescue of Astronauts, the Return of Astronauts and the Return of Objects Launched into Outer Space, the Convention on International Liability for Damage Caused by Space Objects, and the Convention on Registration of Objects Launched into Outer Space,
Taking into account the need to define and develop the provisions of these international instruments in relation to the moon and other celestial bodies, having regard to further progress in the exploration and use of outer space,
Have agreed on the following:

Article 1

1. The provisions of this Agreement relating to the moon shall also apply to other celestial bodies within the solar system, other than the earth, except in so far as specific legal norms enter into force with respect

to any of these celestial bodies.

2. For the purposes of this Agreement reference to the moon shall include orbits around or the trajectories to or around it.

3. This Agreement does not apply to extraterrestrial materials which reach the surface of the earth by natural means.

Article 2

All activities on the moon, including its exploration and use, shall be carried out in accordance with international law, in particular the Charter of the United Nations, and taking into account the Declaration on Principles of International Law concerning Friendly Relations and Co-operation among States in accordance with the Charter of the United Nations, adopted by the General Assembly on 24 October 1970, in the interests of maintaining international peace and security and promoting international co-operation and mutual understanding, and with due regard to the corresponding interests of all other States Parties.

Article 3

1. The moon shall be used by all States Parties exclusively for peaceful purposes.

2. Any threat or use of force or any other hostile act or threat of hostile act on the moon is prohibited. It is likewise prohibited to use the moon in order to commit any such act or to engage in any such threat in relation to the earth, the moon, spacecraft, the personnel of spacecraft or man-made space objects.

3. States Parties shall not place in orbit around or other trajectory to or around the moon objects carrying nuclear weapons or any other kinds of weapons of mass destruction or place or use such weapons on or in the moon.

4. The establishment of military bases, installations and fortifications, the testing of any type of weapons and the conduct of military manoeuvres on the moon shall be forbidden. The use of military personnel for scientific research or for any other peaceful purposes shall not be prohibited.

The use of any equipment of facility necessary for peaceful exploration and use of the moon shall also not be prohibited.

Article 4

1. The exploration and use of the moon shall be the province of all mankind and shall be carried out for the benefit and in the interests of all countries, irrespective of their degree of economic or scientific development. Due regard shall be paid to the interests of present and future generations as well as to the need to promote higher standards of living and conditions of economic and social progress and development in accordance with the Charter of the United Nations.

2. States Parties shall be guided by the principle of co-operation and mutual assistance in all their activities concerning the exploration and use of the moon. International co-operation in pursuance of this Agreement should be as wide as possible and may take place on a multilateral basis, on a bilateral basis or through international intergovernmental organizations.

Article 5

1. States Parties shall inform the Secretary-General of the United Nations as well as the public and the international scientific community, to the greatest extent feasible and practicable, of their activities concerned with the exploration and use of the moon. Information on the time, purposes, locations, orbital parameters and duration shall be given in respect of each mission to the moon as soon as possible after launching, while information on the results of each mission, including scientific results, shall be furnished upon completion of the mission. In the case of a mission lasting more than thirty days, information on conduct of the mission, including any scientific results, shall be given periodically at thirty days' intervals. For missions lasting more than six months, only significant additions to such information need to be reported thereafter.

2. If a State Party becomes aware that another State Party plans to operate simultaneously in the same area of or in the same orbit around or trajectory to or around the moon, it shall promptly inform the other State of the timing of and plans for its own operations.

3. In carrying out activities under this Agreement, States Parties shall promptly inform the Secretary-General, as well as the public and the international scientific community, of any phenomena they discover in outer space, including the moon, which could endanger human life or health, as well as of any indication of organic life.

Article 6

1. There shall be freedom of scientific investigation on the moon by all states Parties without discrimination of any kind, on the basis of equality and in accordance with international law.

2. In carrying out scientific investigations and in furtherance of the provisions of this Agreement, the States Parties shall have the right to collect on and remove from the moon samples of its mineral and other substances. Such samples shall remain at the disposal of those States Parties which caused them to be collected and may be used by them for scientific purposes. States Parties shall have regard to the desirability of making a portion of such samples available to other interested States Parties and the international scientific community for scientific investigation. States Parties may in the course of scientific investigations also use mineral and other substances of the moon in quantities appropriate for the support of their missions.

3. States Parties agree on the desirability of exchanging scientific and other personnel on expeditions to or installations on the moon to the greatest extent feasible and practicable.

Article 7

1. In exploring and using the moon, States Parties shall take measures to prevent the disruption of the existing balance of its environment whether by introducing adverse changes in that environment, by its harmful contamination through the introduction of extra-environmental matter or otherwise. States Parties shall also take measures to avoid harmfully affecting the environment of the earth through the introduction of extraterrestrial matter or otherwise.

2. States Parties shall inform the Secretary-General of the United Nations of the measures being adopted by them in accordance with paragraph 1 of this article and shall also, to the maximum extent feasible, notify him in advance of all placements by them of radio-active materials on the moon and of the purposes of such placements.

3. States Parties shall report to other States Parties and to the Secretary-General concerning areas of the moon having special scientific interest in order that, without prejudice to the rights of other States Parties, consideration may be given to the designation of such areas as international scientific preserves for which special protection arrangements are to be agreed upon in consultation with the competent bodies of the United Nations.

Article 8

1. States Parties may pursue their activities in the exploration and use of the moon anywhere on or below its surface, subject to the provisions of this Agreement.

2. For these purposes States Parties may, in particular:

(a) Land their space objects on the moon and launch them from the moon;

(b) Place their personnel, space vehicles, equipment, facilities, stations and installations anywhere on or below the surface of the moon.

Personnel, space vehicles, equipment, facilities, stations and installations may move or be moved freely over or below the surface of the moon.

3. Activities of States Parties in accordance with paragraphs 1 and 2 of this Article shall not interfere with the activities of other States Parties on the moon. Where such interference may occur, the States Parties concerned shall undertake consultations in accordance with article 15, paragraphs 2 and 3 of this Agreement.

Article 9

1. States Parties may establish manned and unmanned stations on the moon. A State Party establishing a station shall use only that area which is required for the needs of the station and shall immediately inform the Secretary-General of the United Nations of the location and purposes of that station. Subsequently, at annual intervals that State shall likewise inform the Secretary-General whether the station continues in use and whether its purposes have changed.

2. Stations shall be installed in such a manner that they do not impede the free access to all areas of the moon by personnel, vehicles and equipment of other States Parties conducting activities on the moon in accordance with the provisions of this Agreement or of Article I of the Treaty on Principles Governing the Activities of States in the Exploration and Use of Outer Space, including the Moon and other Celestial Bodies.

Article 10

1. States Parties shall adopt all practicable measures to safeguard the life and health of persons on the moon. For this purpose they shall regard any person on the moon as an astronaut within the meaning of Article V of the Treaty on Principles Governing the Activities of States in the Exploration and Use of Outer Space, including the Moon and Other Celestial Bodies and as part of the personnel of a spacecraft within the meaning of the Agreement on the Rescue of Astronauts, the Return of Astronauts and the

Return of Objects Launched into Outer Space.

2. States Parties shall offer shelter in their stations, installations, vehicles and other facilities to persons in distress on the moon.

Article 11

1. The moon and its natural resources are the common heritage of mankind, which finds its expression in the provisions of this Agreement and in particular in paragraph 5 of this article.

2. The moon is not subject to national appropriation by any claim of sovereignty, by means of use or occupation, or by any other means.

3. Neither the surface nor the subsurface of the moon, nor any part thereof or natural resources in place, shall become property of any State, international intergovernmental or non-governmental organization, national organization or non-governmental entity or of any natural person. The placement of personnel, space vehicles, equipment, facilities, stations and installations on or below the surface of the moon, including structures connected with its surface or subsurface, shall not create a right of ownership over the surface or the subsurface of the moon or any areas thereof. The foregoing provisions are without prejudice to the international régime referred to in paragraph 5 of this article.

4. States Parties have the right to exploration and use of the moon without discrimination of any kind, on a basis of equality and in accordance with international law and the terms of this Agreement.

5. States Parties to this Agreement hereby undertake to establish an international régime, including appropriate procedures, to govern the exploitation of the natural resources of the moon as such exploitation is about to become feasible. This provision shall be implemented in accordance with Article 18 of this Agreement.

6. In order to facilitate the establishment of the international régime referred to in paragraph 5 of this Article, States Parties shall inform the Secretary-General of the United Nations as well as the public and the international scientific community, to the greatest extent feasible and practicable, of any natural resources they may discover on the moon.

7. The main purposes of the international régime to be established shall include:

(a) The orderly and safe development of the natural resources of the moon;

(b) The rational management of those resources;

(c) The expansion of opportunities in the use of those resources;

(d) An equitable sharing by all States Parties in the benefits derived from those resources, whereby the interest and needs of the developing countries, as well as the efforts of those countries which have contributed either directly or indirectly to the exploration of the moon, shall be given special consideration.

8. All the activities with respect to the natural resources of the moon shall be carried out in a manner compatible with the purposes specified in paragraph 7 of this Article and the provisions of Article 6, paragraph 2, of this Agreement.

Article 12

1. States Parties shall retain jurisdiction and control over their personnel, vehicles, equipment, facilities, stations and installations on the moon. The ownership of space vehicles, equipment, facilities, stations and installations shall not be affected by their presence on the moon.

2. Vehicles, installations and equipment or their component parts found in places other than their intended location shall be dealt with in accordance with Article 5 of the Agreement on Rescue of Astronauts, the Return of Astronauts and the Return of Objects Launched into Outer Space.

3. In the event of an emergency involving a threat to human life, States Parties may use the equipment, vehicles, installations, facilities or supplies of other States Parties on the moon. Prompt notification of such use shall be made to the Secretary-General of the United Nations or the State Party concerned.

Article 13

A State Party which learns of the crash landing, forced landing or other unintended landing on the moon of a space object, or its component parts, that were not launched by it, shall promptly inform the launching State Party and the Secretary-General of the United Nations.

Article 14

1. States Parties to this Agreement shall bear international responsibility for national activities on the moon, whether such activities are carried on by governmental agencies or by non-governmental entities, and for assuring that national activities are carried out in conformity with the provisions set forth in this Agreement. States Parties shall ensure that non-

governmental entities under their jurisdiction shall engage in activities on the moon only under the authority and continuing supervision of the appropriate State Party.

2. States Parties recognize that detailed arrangements concerning liability for damage caused on the moon, in addition to the provisions of the Treaty on Principles Governing the Activities of States in the Exploration and Use of Outer Space, including the Moon and Other Celestial Bodies and the Convention on International Liability for Damage Caused by Space Objects, may become necessary as a result of more extensive activities on the moon. Any such arrangements shall be elaborated in accordance with the procedure provided for in Article 18 of this Agreement.

Article 15

1. Each State Party may assure itself that the activities of other States Parties in the exploration and use of the moon are compatible with the provisions of this Agreement. To this end, all space vehicles, equipment, facilities, stations and installations on the moon shall be open to other States Parties. Such States Parties shall give reasonable advance notice of a projected visit, in order that appropriate consultations may be held and that maximum precautions may be taken to assure safety and to avoid interference with normal operations in the facility to be visited. In pursuance of this article, any State Party may act on its own behalf or with the full or partial assistance of any other State Party or through appropriate international procedures within the framework of the United Nations and in accordance with the Charter.

2. A State Party which has reason to believe that another State Party is not fulfilling the obligations incumbent upon it pursuant to this Agreement or that another State Party is interfering with the rights which the former State has under this Agreement may request consultations with that State Party. A State Party receiving such a request shall enter into such consultations without delay. Any other State Party which requests to do so shall be entitled to take part in the consultations. Each State Party participating in such consultations shall seek a mutually acceptable resolution of any controversy and shall bear in mind the rights and interests of all States Parties.

The Secretary-General of the United Nations shall be informed of the results of the consultations and shall transmit the information received to all States Parties concerned.

3. If the consultations do not lead to a mutually acceptable settlement which has due regard for the rights and interests of all States Parties, the parties concerned shall take all measures to settle the dispute by other peaceful means of their choice appropriate to the circumstances and the nature of the dispute. If difficulties arise in connexion with the opening of consultations or if consultations do not lead to a mutually acceptable settlement, any State Party may seek the assistance of the Secretary-General, without seeking the consent of any other State Party concerned, in order to resolve the controversy. A State Party which does not maintain diplomatic relations with another State Party concerned shall participate in such consultations, at its choice, either itself or through another State Party or the Secretary-General as intermediary.

Article 16

With the exception of Articles 17 to 21, references in this Agreement to States shall be deemed to apply to any international intergovernmental organization which conducts space activities if the organization declares its acceptance of the rights and obligations provided for in this Agreement and if a majority of the States members of the organization are States Parties to this Agreement and to the Treaty on Principles Governing the Activities of States in the Exploration and Use of Outer Space, including the Moon and Other Celestial Bodies. States members of any such organization which are States Parties to this Agreement shall take all appropriate steps to ensure that the organization makes a declaration in accordance with the foregoing.

Article 17

Any State Party to this Agreement may propose amendments to the Agreement. Amendments shall enter into force for each State Party to the Agreement accepting the amendments upon their acceptance by a majority of the States Parties to the Agreement and thereafter for each remaining State Party to the Agreement on the date of acceptance by it.

Article 18

Ten years after the entry into force of this Agreement, the question of the review of the Agreement shall be included in the provisional agenda of the General Assembly of the United Nations in order to consider, in the light of past application of the Agreement, whether it requires revision. However, at any time after the Agreement has been in force for five years, the Secretary-General of the United Nations, as depository, shall, at the request of one third of the States Parties to the Agreement and with the concurrence of the majority of the States Parties, convene a conference of the States Parties to review this Agreement. A review conference shall also consider the question of the implementation of the provisions of Article 11, paragraph 5, on the basis of the principle referred to in paragraph 1 of that Article and taking into account in particular any relevant technological developments.

Article 19

1. This Agreement shall be open for signature by all States at United Nations Headquarters in New York.

2. This Agreement shall be subject to ratification by signatory States. Any State which does not sign this Agreement before its entry into force in accordance with paragraph 3 of this Article may accede to it at any time. Instruments of ratification or accession shall be deposited with the Secretary-General of the United Nations.

3. This Agreement shall enter into force on the thirtieth day following the date of deposit of the fifth instrument of ratification.

4. For each State depositing its instrument of ratification or accession after the entry into force of this Agreement, it shall enter into force on the thirtieth day following the date of deposit of any such instrument.

5. The Secretary-General shall promptly inform all signatory and acceding States of the date of each signature, the date of deposit of each instrument of ratification or accession to this Agreement, the date of its entry into force and other notices.

Article 20

Any State Party to this Agreement may give notice of its withdrawal from the Agreement one year after its entry into force by written notification to the Secretary-General of the United Nations.

Such withdrawal shall take effect one year from the date of receipt of this notification.

Article 21

The Original of this Agreement, of which the Arabic, Chinese, English, French, Russian and Spanish texts are equally authentic, shall be deposited with the Secretary-General of the United Nations, who shall send certified copies thereof to all signatory and acceding States.

Convention on the Physical Protection of Nuclear Material

Date of adoption: October 10, 1979 (Opened for signature: March 3, 1980)
Place of signature: Vienna and New York
Signatory states: Austria, Belgium, Brazil, Bulgaria, Canada, Czechoslovakia, Denmark, Dominican Republic, European Atomic Energy Community, Finland, France, German Democratic Republic, Federal Republic of Germany, Greece, Guatemala, Haiti, Hungary, Ireland, Italy, Republic of Korea, Luxembourg, Morocco, Netherlands, Paraguay, Philippines, Poland, Romania, South Africa, Soviet Union, Sweden, United Kingdom, United States, Yugoslavia

The States Parties to This Convention,
Recognizing the right of all States to develop and apply nuclear energy for peaceful purposes and their legitimate interests in the potential benefits to be derived from the peaceful application of nuclear energy,
Convinced of the need for facilitating international cooperation in the peaceful application of nuclear energy,
Desiring to avert the potential dangers posed by the unlawful taking and use of nuclear material,
Convinced that offenses relating to nuclear material are a matter of grave concern and that there is an urgent need to adopt appropriate and effective measures to ensure the prevention, detection and punishment of such offenses,
Aware of the need for international cooperation to establish, in conformity with the national law of each State Party and with this Convention, effective measures for the physical protection of nuclear material,
Convinced that this Convention should facilitate the safe transfer of nuclear material,
Stressing also the importance of the physical protection of nuclear material in domestic use, storage and transport,
Recognizing the importance of effective physical pro-

tection of nuclear material used for military purposes, and understanding that such material is and will continue to be accorded stringent physical protection,
Have agreed as follows:

Article 1

For the purposes of this Convention:

(a) "nuclear material" means plutonium except that with isotopic concentration exceeding 80% in plutonium-238; uranium-233; uranium enriched in the isotopes 235 or 233; uranium containing the mixture of isotopes as occurring in nature other than in the form of ore or ore-residue; any material containing one or more of the foregoing;

(b) "uranium enriched in the 235 or 233" means uranium containing the isotopes 235 or 233 or both in an amount such that the abundance ratio of the sum of these isotopes to the isotope 238 is greater than the ratio of the isotope 235 to the isotope 238 occurring in nature;

(c) "international nuclear transport" means the carriage of a consignment of nuclear material by any means of transportation intended to go beyond the territory of the State where the shipment originates beginning with the departure from a facility of the shipper in that State and ending with the arrival at a facility of the receiver within the State of ultimate destination.

Article 2

1. The Convention shall apply to nuclear material used for peaceful purposes while in international nuclear transport.

2. With the exception of Articles 3 and 4 and paragraph 3 of Article 5, this Convention shall also apply to nuclear material used for peaceful purposes while in domestic use, storage and transport.

3. Apart from the commitments expressly undertaken by States Parties in the articles covered by paragraph 2 with respect to nuclear material used for peaceful purposes while in domestic use, storage and transport, nothing in this Convention shall be interpreted as affecting the sovereign rights of a State regarding the domestic use, storage and transport of such nuclear material.

Article 3

Each State Party shall take appropriate steps within the framework of its national law and consistent with international law to ensure as far as practicable that,

during international nuclear transport, nuclear material within its territory, or on board a ship or aircraft under its jurisdiction insofar as such ship or aircraft is engaged in the transport to or from that State, is protected at the levels described in Annex I.

Article 4

1. Each State Party shall not export or authorize the export of nuclear material unless the State Party has received assurances that such material will be protected during the international nuclear transport at the levels described in Annex I.

2. Each State Party shall not import or authorize the import of nuclear material from a State not party to this Convention unless the State Party has received assurances that such material will during the international nuclear transport be protected at the levels described in Annex I.

3. A State Party shall not allow the transit of its territory by land or internal waterways or through its airports or seaports of nuclear material between States that are not parties to this Convention unless the State Party has received assurances as far as practicable that this nuclear material will be protected during international nuclear transport at the levels described in Annex I.

4. Each State Party shall apply within the framework of its national law the levels of physical protection described in Annex I to nuclear material being transported from a part of that State to another part of the same State through international waters or airspace.

5. The State Party responsible for receiving assurances that the nuclear material will be protected at the levels described in Annex I according to paragraphs 1 to 3 shall identify and inform in advance States which the nuclear material is expected to transit by land or internal waterways, or whose airports or seaports it is expected to enter.

6. The responsibility for obtaining assurances referred to in paragraph 1 may be transferred, by mutual agreement, to the State Party involved in the transport as the importing State.

7. Nothing in this Article shall be interpreted as in any way affecting the territorial sovereignty and jurisdiction of a State, including that over its airspace and territorial sea.

Article 5

1. States Parties shall identify and make known to each other directly or through the International Atomic Energy Agency their central authority and

point of contact having responsibility for physical protection of nuclear material and for coordinating recovery and response operations in the event of any unauthorized removal, use or alteration of nuclear material or in the event of credible threat thereof.

2. In the case of theft, robbery or any other unlawful taking of nuclear material or of credible threat thereof, States Parties shall, in accordance with their national law, provide cooperation and assistance to the maximum feasible extent in the recovery and protection of such material to any State that so requests. In particular:

(a) a State Party shall take appropriate steps to inform as soon as possible other States, which appear to it to be concerned, of any theft, robbery or other unlawful taking of nuclear material or credible threat thereof and to inform, where appropriate, international organizations;

(b) as appropriate, the States Parties concerned shall exchange information with each other or international organizations with a view to protecting threatened nuclear material, verifying the integrity of the shipping container, or recovering unlawfully taken nuclear material and shall:

(i) coordinate their efforts through diplomatic and other agreed channels;

(ii) render assistance, if requested;

(iii) ensure the return of nuclear material stolen or missing as a consequence of the above-mentioned events.

The means of implementation of this cooperation shall be determined by the States Parties concerned.

3. States Parties shall cooperate and consult as appropriate, with each other directly or through international organizations, with a view to obtaining guidance on the design, maintenance and improvement of systems of physical protection of nuclear material in international transport.

Article 6

1. States Parties shall take appropriate measures consistent with their national law to protect the confidentiality of any information, which they receive in confidence by virtue of the provisions of this Convention from another State Party or through participation in an activity carried out for the implementation of this Convention. If States Parties provide information to international organizations in confidence, steps shall be taken to ensure that the confi-

dentiality of such information is protected.

2. States Parties shall not be required by this Convention to provide any information which they are not permitted to communicate pursuant to national law or which would jeopardize the security of the State concerned or the physical protection of nuclear material.

Article 7

1. The intentional commission of:

(a) an act without lawful authority which constitutes the receipt, possession, use, transfer, alteration, disposal or dispersal of nuclear material and which causes or is likely to cause death or serious injury to any person or substantial damage to property;

(b) a theft or robbery of nuclear material;

(c) an embezzlement or fraudulent obtaining of nuclear material;

(d) an act constituting a demand for nuclear material by threat or use of force or by any other form of intimidation;

(e) a threat:

(i) to use nuclear material to cause death or serious injury to any person or substantial property damage, or

(ii) to commit an offense described in subparagraph (b) in order to compel a natural or legal person, international organization or State to do or to refrain from doing any act;

(f) an attempt to commit any offense described in paragraphs (a), (b) or (c); and

(g) an act which constitutes participation in any offense described in paragraphs (a) to (f) shall be made a punishable offense by each State Party under its national law.

2. Each State Party shall make the offenses described in this article punishable by appropriate penalties which take into account their grave nature.

Article 8

1. Each State Party shall take such measures as may be necessary to establish its jurisdiction over the offenses set forth in Article 7 in the following cases:

(a) when the offense is committed in the territory of that State or on board a ship or aircraft registered in the State;

(b) when the alleged offender is a national of that State.

2. Each State Party shall likewise take such measures as may be necessary to establish its jurisdiction over these offenses in cases where the alleged offender is present in its territory and it does not extradite him pursuant to Article II to any of the States mentioned in paragraph 1.

3. This Convention does not exclude any criminal jurisdiction exercised in accordance with national law.

4. In addition to the State Parties mentioned in paragraphs 1 and 2, each State Party may, consistent with international law, establish its jurisdiction over the offenses set forth in Article 7 when it is involved in international nuclear transport as the exporting or importing State.

Article 9

Upon being satisfied that the circumstances so warrant, the State Party in whose territory the alleged offender is present shall take appropriate measures, including detention, under its national law to ensure his presence for the purpose of prosecution or extradition. Measures taken according to this Article shall be notified without delay to the States required to establish jurisdiction pursuant to Article 8 and, where appropriate, all other States concerned.

Article 10

The State Party in whose territory the alleged offender is present shall, if it does not extradite him, submit, without exception whatsoever and without undue delay, the case to its competent authorities for the purpose of prosecution, through proceedings in accordance with the laws of that State.

Article 11

1. The offenses in Article 7 shall be deemed to be included as extraditable offenses in any extraditions treaty existing between States Parties. States Parties undertake to include those offenses as extraditable offenses in every future extradition treaty to be concluded between them.

2. If a State Party which makes extradition conditional on the existence of a treaty receives a request for extradition from another State Party with which it has no extradition treaty, it may at its option consider this Convention as the legal basis for extradition in respect of those offenses. Extradition shall be subject to the other conditions provided by the law of the requested State.

3. States Parties which do not make extradition conditional on the existence of a treaty shall recognize those offenses as extraditable offenses between themselves subject to the conditions provided by the law of the requested State.

4. Each of the offenses shall be treated, for the purpose of extradition between States Parties, as if it had been committed not only in the place in which it occurred but also in the territories of the States Parties required to establish their jurisdiction in accordance with paragraph 1 of Article 8.

Article 12

Any person regarding whom proceedings are being carried out in connection with any of the offenses set forth in Article 7 shall be guaranteed fair treatment at all stages of the proceedings.

Article 13

1. States Parties shall afford one another the greatest measure of assistance in connection with criminal proceedings brought in respect of the offenses set forth in Article 7, including the supply of evidence at their disposal necessary for the proceedings. The law of the State requested shall apply in all cases.

2. The provisions of paragraph 1 shall not affect obligations under any other treaty, bilateral or multilateral, which governs or will govern, in whole or in part, mutual assistance in criminal matters.

Article 14

1. Each State Party shall inform the depositary of its laws and regulations which give effect to this Convention. The depositary shall communicate such information periodically to all States Parties.

2. The State Party where an alleged offender is prosecuted shall, wherever practicable, first communicate the final outcome of the proceedings to the States directly concerned. The State Party shall also communicate the final outcome to the depositary who shall inform all States.

3. Where an offense involves nuclear material used for peaceful purposes in domestic use, storage or transport, and both the alleged offender and the nuclear material remain in the territory of the State Party in which the offense was committed, nothing in this Convention shall be interpreted as requiring that State Party to provide information concerning criminal proceedings arising out of such an offense.

Article 15

The Annexes constitute an integral part of this Convention.

Article 16

1. A conference of States Parties shall be convened by the depositary five years after the entry into force of this Convention to review the implementation of the Convention and its adequacy as concerns the preamble, the whole of the operative part and the annexes in the light of the then prevailing situation.

2. At intervals of not less than five years thereafter, the majority of States Parties may obtain, by submitting a proposal to this effect to the depositary, the convening of further conferences with the same objective.

Article 17

1. In the event of a dispute between two or more States Parties concerning the interpretation or application of this Convention, such States Parties shall consult with a view to the settlement of the dispute by negotiation, or by any other peaceful means of settling disputes acceptable to all parties to the dispute.

2. Any dispute of this character which cannot be settled in the manner prescribed in paragraph 1 shall, at the request of any party to such dispute, be submitted to arbitration or referred to the International Court of Justice for decision. Where a dispute is submitted to arbitration, if, within six months from the date of the request, the parties to the dispute are unable to agree on the organization of the arbitration, a party may request the President of the International Court of Justice or the Secretary-General of the United Nations to appoint one or more arbitrators. In case of conflicting requests by the parties to the dispute, the request to the Secretary-General of the United Nations shall have priority.

3. Each State Party may at the time of signature, ratification, acceptance or approval of this Convention or accession thereto declare that it does not consider itself bound by either or both of the dispute settlement procedures provided for in paragraph 2. The other States Parties shall not be bound by a dispute settlement procedure provided for in paragraph 2, with respect to a State Party which has made a reservation to that procedure.

4. Any State Party which has made a reservation in accordance with paragraph 3 may at any time withdraw that reservation by notification to the depositary.

Article 18

1. This Convention shall be open for signature by all States at the Headquarters of the International Atomic Energy Agency in Vienna and at the Headquarters of the United Nations in New York from 3 March 1980 until its entry into force.

2. This Convention is subject to ratification, acceptance or approval by the signatory States.

3. After its entry into force, this Convention will be open for accession by all States.

4.

(a) This Convention shall be open for signature or accession by international organizations and regional organizations of an integration or other nature, provided that any such organization is constituted by sovereign States and has competence in respect of the negotiation, conclusion and application of international agreements in matters covered by this Convention.

(b) In matters within their competence, such organizations shall, on their own behalf, exercise the rights and fulfill the responsibilities which this Convention attributes to States Parties.

(c) When becoming party to this Convention such an organization shall communicate to the depositary a declaration indicating which States are members thereof and which articles of this Convention do not apply to it.

(d) Such an organization shall not hold any vote additional to those of its Member States.

5. Instruments of ratification, acceptance, approval or accession shall be deposited with the depositary.

Article 19

1. This Convention shall enter into force on the thirtieth day following the date of deposit of the twenty-first instrument of ratification, acceptance or approval with the depositary.

2. For each State ratifying, accepting, approving or acceding to the Convention after the date of deposit of the twenty-first instrument of ratification, acceptance or approval, the Convention shall enter into force on the thirtieth day after the deposit by such State of its instrument of ratification, acceptance, approval or accession.

Article 20

1. Without prejudice to Article 16 a State Party may propose amendments to this Convention. The pro-

posed amendment shall be submitted to the depositary who shall circulate it immediately to all States Parties. If a majority of States Parties request the depositary to convene a conference to consider the proposed amendments, the depositary shall invite all States Parties to attend such a conference to begin not sooner than thirty days after the invitations are issued. Any amendment adopted at the conference by a two-thirds majority of all States Parties shall be promptly circulated by the depositary to all States Parties.

2. The amendment shall enter into force for each State Party that deposits its instrument of ratification, acceptance or approval of the amendment on the thirtieth day after the date on which two-thirds of the States Parties day after the date on which two-thirds of the States Parties have deposited their instruments of ratification, acceptance or approval with the depositary. Thereafter, the amendment shall enter into force for any other State Party on the day on which that State Party deposits its instrument of ratification, acceptance or approval of the amendment.

Article 21

1. Any State Party may denounce this Convention by written notification to the depositary.

2. Denunciation shall take effect one hundred and eighty days following the date on which notification is received by the depositary.

Article 22

The depositary shall promptly notify all States of :

(a) each signature of this Convention;

(b) each deposit of an instrument of ratification, acceptance, approval or accession;

(c) any reservation or withdrawal in accordance with Article 17;

(d) any communication made by an organization in accordance with paragraph 4(c) of Article 18;

(e) the entry into force of this Convention;

(f) the entry into force of any amendment to this Convention; and

(g) any denunciation made under Article 21.

Article 23

The original of this Convention, of which the Arabic, Chinese, English, French, Russian and Spanish texts are equally authentic, shall be deposited with the Director General of the International Atomic Energy Agency who shall send certified copies thereof to all States.

ANNEX I

LEVELS OF PHYSICAL PROTECTION TO BE APPLIED IN INTERNATIONAL TRANSPORT OF NUCLEAR MATERIAL AS CATEGORIZED IN ANNEX II

1. Levels of physical protection for nuclear material during storage incidental to international nuclear transport include:

(a) For Category III materials, storage within an area to which access in controlled;

(b) For Category II materials, storage within an area under constant surveillance by guards or electronic devices, surrounded by a physical barrier with a limited number of points of entry under appropriate control or any area with an equivalent level of physical protection;

(c) For Category I material, storage within a protected area as defined for Category II above, to which, in addition, access is restricted to persons whose trustworthiness has been determined, and which is under surveillance by guards who are in close communication with appropriate response forces. Specific measures taken in this context should have as their object the detection and prevention of any assault, unauthorized access or unauthorized removal of material.

2. Levels of physical protection for nuclear material during international transport include:

(a) For Category II and III materials, transportation shall take place under special precautions including prior arrangement between natural or legal persons subject to the jurisdiction and regulation of exporting and importing States, specifying time, place and procedures for transferring transport responsibility;

(b) For Category I materials, transportation shall take place under special precautions identified above for transportation of Category II and III materials, and in addition, under constant surveillance by escorts and under conditions which assure close communication with appropriate response forces;

(c) For natural uranium other than in the form of ore or ore-residue, transportation protection for quanti-

ANNEX II
TABLE: CATEGORIZATION OF NUCLEAR MATERIAL

Material	Form	Category I	Category II	Category III [3]
1. Plutonium [1]	Unirradiated [2]	2 kg. or more	Less than 2 kg. but more than 500 g.	500 g. or less but more than 15 g.
2. Uranium-235	Unirradiated [2]: —uranium enriched to 20% U^{235} or more	5 kg. or more	Less than 5 kg. but more than 1 kg.	1 kg. or less but more than 15 g.
	—uranium enriched to 10% U^{235} but less than 20%		10 kg or more	Less than 10 kg. but more than 1 kg.
	—uranium enriched above natural, but less than 10% U^{235}.			10 kg. or more.
3. Uranium-233	Unirradiated [2]	2 kg. or more	Less than 2 kg. but more than 500 g.	500 g or less but more than 15 g.
4. Irradiated fuel			Depleted or natural uranium, thorium or low-enriched fuel (less than 10% fissile content). [4][5]	

1 All plutonium except that with isotopic concentration exceeding 80% in plutonium-238.

2 Material not irradiated in a reactor or material irradiated in a reactor but with a radiation level equal to or less than 100 rads/hour at one metre unshielded.

3 Quantities not falling in Category III and natural uranium should be protected in accordance with prudent management practice.

4 Although this level of protection is recommended, it would be open to States, upon evaluation of the specific circumstances, to assign a different category of physical protection.

5 Other fuel which by virtue of its original fissile material content is classified as Category I and II before irradiation may be reduced one category level while the radiation level from the fuel exceeds 100 rads/hour at one metre unshielded.

ties exceeding 500 kilograms U shall include advance notification of shipment specifying mode of transport, expected time of arrival and confirmation of receipt of shipment.

Convention on Prohibitions or Restrictions on the Use of Certain Conventional Weapons Which may be Deemed to be Excessively Injurious or to Have Indiscriminate Effects

Also known as: UN *Weaponry Convention, Convention on Specific Conventional Weapons*
Date of adoption: October 10, 1980 (Opened for signature: April 10, 1981)
Place of signature: Geneva
Signatory states: Afghanistan, Australia,

Belgium, Bulgaria, Byelorussia, Canada, People's Republic of China, Cuba, Czechoslovakia, Denmark, Ecuador, Egypt, Finland, France, German Democratic Republic, Federal Republic of Germany, Greece, Guatemala, Hungary, Iceland, India,

Ireland, Italy, Japan, Laos, Liechtenstein, Luxembourg, Mexico, Mongolia, Morocco, Netherlands, New Zealand, Nicaragua, Nigeria, Norway, Pakistan, Philippines, Poland, Portugal, Romania, Sierra Leone, Soviet Union, Spain, Sudan, Sweden, Switzerland, Togo, Turkey, United Kingdom, United States, Vietnam, Yugoslavia
Date of entry into force: *December 2, 1983*

The High Contracting Parties,

Recalling that every State has the duty, in conformity with the Charter of the United Nations, to refrain in its international relations from the threat or use of force against the sovereignty, territorial integrity or political independence of any State, or in any other manner inconsistent with the purposes of the United Nations.

Further recalling the general principle of the protection of the civilian population against the effects of hostilities, basing themselves on the principle of international law that the right of the parties to an armed conflict to choose methods or means of warfare is not unlimited, and on the principle that prohibits the employment in armed conflicts of weapons, projectiles and material and methods of warfare of a nature to cause superfluous injury or unnecessary suffering,

Also recalling that it is prohibited to employ methods or means of warfare which are intended, or may be expected, to cause widespread, long-term and severe damage to the natural environment,

Confirming their determination that in cases not covered by this Convention and its annexed Protocols or by other international agreements, the civilian population and the combatants shall at all times remain under the protection and authority of the principles of international law derived from established custom, from the principles of humanity and from the dictates of public conscience,

Desiring to contribute to international détente, the ending of the arms race and the building of confidence among States, and hence to the realization of the aspiration of all peoples to live in peace,

Recognizing the importance of pursuing every effort which may contribute to progress towards general and complete disarmament under strict and effective international control,

Reaffirming the need to continue the codification and progressive development of the rules of international law applicable in armed conflict,

Wishing to prohibit or restrict further the use of cer-

tain conventional weapons and believing that the positive results achieved in this area may facilitate the main talks on disarmament with a view to putting an end to the production, stockpiling and proliferation of such weapons,

Emphasizing the desirability that all States become parties to this Convention and its annexed Protocols, especially the militarily significant States,

Bearing in mind that the General Assembly of the United Nations and the United Nations Disarmament Commission may decide to examine the question of a possible broadening of the scope of the prohibitions and restrictions contained in this Convention and its annexed Protocols,

Further bearing in mind that the Committee on Disarmament may decide to consider the question of adopting further measures to prohibit or restrict the use of certain conventional weapons,

Have agreed as follows:

Article 1

Scope of Application

This convention and its annexed Protocols shall apply in the situations referred to in Article 2 common to the Geneva Conventions of 12 August 1949 for the Protection of War Victims, including any situation described in paragraph 4 of Article 1 of Additional Protocol I to these conventions.

Article 2

Relations with other International Agreements

Nothing in this Convention or its annexed Protocols shall be interpreted as detracting from other obligations imposed upon the High contracting Parties by international humanitarian law applicable in armed conflict.

Article 3

Signature

This Convention shall be open for signature by all States at United Nations Headquarters in New York for a period of twelve months from 10 April 1981.

Article 4

Ratification, Acceptance, Approval or Accession

1. This Convention is subject to ratification, Acceptance or approval by the Signatories. Any State which has not signed this Convention may accede to

it.

2. The instruments of ratification, acceptance, approval or accession shall be deposited with the Depositary.

3. Expressions of consent to be bound by any of the Protocols annexed to this Convention shall be optional for each State, provided that at the time of the deposit of its instrument of ratification, acceptance or approval of this Convention or of accession thereto, that State shall notify the Depositary of its consent to be bound by any two or more of these Protocols.

4. At any time after the deposit of its instrument of ratification, acceptance or approval of this Convention or of accession thereto, a State may notify the Depositary of its consent to be bound by any annexed Protocol by which it is not already bound.

5. Any Protocol by which a High contracting Party is bound shall for that Party form an integral part of this Convention.

Article 5

Entry into Force

1. This Convention shall enter into force six months after the date of deposit of the twentieth instrument of ratification, acceptance, approval or accession.

2. For any State which deposits its instrument of ratification, acceptance, approval or accession after the date of the deposit of the twentieth instrument of ratification, acceptance, approval or accession, this Convention shall enter into force six months after the date on which that State has deposited its instrument of ratification, acceptance, approval or accession.

3. Each of the Protocols annexed to this Convention shall enter into force six months after the date by which twenty States have notified their consent to be bound by it in accordance with paragraph 3 or 4 of Article 4 of this Convention.

4. For any State which notifies its consent to be bound by a Protocol, annexed to this Convention after the date by which twenty States have notified their consent to be bound by it, the Protocol shall enter into force six months after the date on which that State has notified its consent so to be bound.

Article 6

Dissemination

The High contracting Parties undertake, in time of peace as in time of armed conflict, to disseminate this Convention and those of its annexed Protocols by which they are bound as widely as possible in their respective countries and, in particular, to include the study thereof in their programmes of military instruction, so that those instruments may become known to their armed forces.

Article 7

Treaty Relations upon Entry into Force of this Convention

1. When one of the parties to a conflict is not bound by an annexed Protocol, the parties bound by this Convention and that annexed Protocol shall remain bound by them in their mutual relations.

2. Any High Contracting Party shall be bound by this Convention and any Protocol annexed thereto which is in force for it, in any situation contemplated by Article 1, in relation to any State which is not a party to this Convention or bound by the relevant annexed Protocol, if the latter accepts and applies this convention or the relevant Protocol, and so notifies the Depositary.

3. The Depositary shall immediately inform the High Contracting Parties concerned of any notification received under paragraph 2 of this Article.

4. This convention, and the annexed Protocols by which a High Contracting Party is bound, shall apply with respect to an armed conflict against that High Contracting Party of the type referred to in Article 1, paragraph 4, of Additional Protocol I to the Geneva Conventions of 12 August 1949 for the Protection of War Victims:

(a) where the High Contracting Party is also a party to Additional Protocol I and an authority referred to in Article 96 paragraph 3, of that Protocol has undertaken to apply the Geneva Conventions and Additional Protocol I in accordance with Article 96, paragraph 3, of the said Protocol, and undertakes to apply this Convention and the relevant annexed Protocols in relation to that conflict; or

(b) where the High contracting Party is not a party to Additional Protocol I and an authority of the type referred to in subparagraph (a) above accepts and applies the obligations of the Geneva Conventions and of this Convention and the relevant annexed Protocols in relation to that conflict. Such an acceptance and applications shall have in relation to that conflict the following effects:

(i) the Geneva Conventions and this Convention and its relevant annexed Protocols are brought into force for the parties to the conflict with immediate effect;

(ii) the said authority assumes the same rights and

obligations as those which have been assumed by a High contracting Party to the Geneva Conventions, this Convention and its relevant annexed Protocols; and

(iii) the Geneva Conventions, this Convention and its relevant annexed Protocols are equally binding upon all parties to the conflict.

The High Contracting Party and the authority may also agree to accept and apply the obligations of Additional Protocol I to the Geneva Conventions on a reciprocal basis.

Article 8

Review and Amendments

1.

(a) At any time after the entry into force of this Convention any High Contracting Party may propose amendments to this Convention or any annexed Protocol by which it is bound. Any proposal for an amendment shall be communicated to the Depositary, who shall notify it to all the High Contracting Parties and shall seek their views on whether a conference should be convened to consider the proposal. If a majority, that shall not be less than eighteen of the High Contracting Parties so agree, he shall promptly convene a conference to which all High Contracting Parties shall be invited. States not parties to this Convention shall be invited to the conference as observers.

(b) Such a conference may agree upon amendments which shall be adopted and shall enter into force in the same manner as this Convention and the annexed Protocols, provided that amendments to this Convention may be adopted only by the High Contracting Parties and that amendments to a specific annexed Protocol may be adopted only by the High Contracting Parties which are bound by that Protocol.

2.

(a) At any time after the entry into force of this Convention any High Contracting Party may propose additional protocols relating to other categories of conventional weapons not covered by the existing annexed Protocols. Any such proposal for an additional protocol shall be communicated to the Depositary, who shall notify it to all the High Contracting Parties in accordance with subparagraph 1 (a) of this Article. If a majority, that shall not be less than eighteen of the High Contracting Parties

so agree, the Depositary shall promptly convene a conference to which all States shall be invited.

(b) Such a conference may agree, with the full participation of all States represented at the conference, upon additional protocols which shall be adopted in the same manner as this Convention, shall be annexed thereto and shall enter into force as provided in paragraphs 3 and 4 of Article 5 of this Convention.

3.

(a) If, after a period of ten years following the entry into force of this Convention, no conference has been convened in accordance with subparagraph 1 (a) or 2 (a) of this Article, any High Contracting Party may request the Depositary to convene a conference to which all High Contracting Parties shall be invited to review the scope and operation of this Convention and the Protocols annexed thereto and to consider any proposal for amendments of this Convention or of the existing Protocols. States not parties to this Convention shall be invited as observers to the conference. The conference may agree upon amendments which shall be adopted and enter into force in accordance with subparagraph 1 (b) above.

(b) At such conference consideration may also be given to any proposal for additional protocols relating to other categories of conventional weapons not covered by the existing annexed Protocols. All States represented at the conference may participate fully in such consideration. Any additional protocols shall be adopted in the same manner as this Convention, shall be annexed thereto and shall enter into force as provided in paragraphs 3 and 4 of Article 5 of this convention.

(c) Such a conference may consider whether provision should be made for the convening of a further conference at the request of any High Contracting Party if, after a similar period to that referred to in subparagraph 3 (a) of this Article, no conference has been convened in accordance with subparagraph 1 (a) or 2 (a) of this Article.

Article 9

Denunciation

1. Any High Contracting Party may denounce this convention or any of its annexed Protocols by so notifying the Depositary.

2. Any such denunciation shall only take effect one

year after receipt by the Depositary of the notification of denunciation. If, however, on the expiry of that year the denouncing High Contracting Party is engaged in one of the situations referred to in Article 1, the Party shall continue to be bound by the obligations of this Convention and of the relevant annexed Protocols until the end of the armed conflict or occupation and, in any case, until the termination of operations connected with the final release, repatriation or re-establishment of the person protected by the rules of international law applicable in armed conflict, and in the case of any annexed Protocol containing provisions concerning situations in which peace-keeping, observation or similar functions are performed by United Nations forces or missions in the area concerned, until the termination of those functions.

3. Any denunciation of this Convention shall be considered as also applying to all annexed Protocols by which the denouncing High contracting Party is bound.

4. Any denunciation shall have effect only in respect of the denouncing High Contracting Party.

5. Any denunciation shall not affect the obligations already incurred, by reason of an armed conflict, under this Convention and its annexed Protocols by such denouncing High Contracting Party in respect of any act committed before this denunciation becomes effective.

Article 10

Depositary

1. The Secretary-General of the United Nations shall be the Depositary of this Convention and of its annexed Protocols.

2. In addition to his usual functions, the Depositary shall inform all States of:

(a) signatures affixed to this Convention under Article 3;

(b) deposits of instruments of ratification, acceptance or approval of or accession to this Convention deposited under Article 4;

(c) notifications of consent to be bound by annexed Protocols under Article 4;

(d) the dates of entry into force of this Convention and of each of its annexed Protocols under Article 5; and

(e) notifications of denunciation received under Article 9, and their effective date.

Article 11

Authentic Texts

The original of this Convention with the annexed Protocols, of which the Arabic, Chinese, English, French, Russian and Spanish texts are equally authentic, shall be deposited with the Depositary, who shall transmit certified true copies thereof to all States.

APPENDIX B

Protocol on Non-detectable Fragments (PROTOCOL I)

It is prohibited to use any weapon the primary effect of which is to injure by fragments which in the human body escape detection by X-rays.

Charter of the Cooperation Council for the Arab States of the Gulf

Date of signature: May 25, 1981
Place of signature: Abu Dhabi City, UAE
Signatory states: Bahrain, Kuwait, Oman, Qatar, Saudi Arabia, United Arab Emirates
Date of entry into force: May 25, 1981

Being fully aware of their mutual bonds of special relations, common characteristics and similar systems founded on the Creed of Islam; and
Based on their faith in the common destiny and destination that link their peoples; and
In view of their desire to effect coordination, integration and interconnection between them in all fields; and
Based on their conviction that coordination, cooperation and integration between them serve the higher goals of the Arab Nation; and, In order to strengthen their cooperation and reinforce their common links; and
In an endeavor to complement efforts already begun in all vital scopes that concern their peoples and real-

ize their hopes in a better future on the path to unity of their States; and

In conformity with the Charter of the League of Arab States which calls for the realization of closer relations and stronger bonds; and

In order to channel their efforts to reinforce and serve Arab and Islamic causes

Have agreed as follows:

Article 1

Establishment of Council

A council shall be established hereby to be named The Cooperation Council for the Arab States, of the Gulf hereinafter referred to as Cooperation Council.

Article 2

Headquarters

The Cooperation Council shall have its headquarters in Riyadh, Saudi Arabia.

Article 3

Cooperation Council Meetings

The Council shall hold its meetings in the state where it has its headquarters, and may convene in any member state.

Article 4

Objectives

The basic objectives of the Cooperation Council are:

1. To effect coordination, integration and interconnection between member states in all fields in order to achieve unity between them.

2. Deepen and strengthen relations, links and scopes of cooperation now prevailing between their peoples in various fields.

3. Formulate similar regulations in various fields including the following:

a. Economic and financial affairs
b. Commerce, customs and communications
c. Education and culture
d. Social and health affairs
e. Information and tourism
f. Legislation and administrative affairs.

4. Stimulate scientific and technological progress in the fields of industry, minerology, agriculture, water and animal resources; the establishment of sci-

entific research centers; implementation of common projects, and encourage cooperation by the private sector for the good of their peoples.

Article 5

Council Membership

The Cooperation Council shall be formed of the six states that participated in the Foreign Ministers' meeting held at Riyadh on 4 February 1981.

Article 6

Organizations of the Cooperation Council

The Cooperation Council shall have the following main organizations:

1. Supreme Council to which shall be attached the Commission for Settlement of Disputes.

2. Ministerial Council.

3. Secretariat-General.

Each of these organizations may establish branch organs as necessary.

Article 7

Supreme Council

1. The Supreme Council is the highest authority of the Cooperation Council and shall be formed of heads of member states. Its presidency shall be rotatory based on the alphabetical order of the names of the member states.

2. The Supreme Council shall hold one regular session every year. Extraordinary sessions may be convened at the request of any member seconded by another member.

3. The Supreme Council shall hold its sessions in the territories of member states.

4. A Supreme Council's meeting shall be considered valid if attended by two thirds of the member states.

Article 8

Supreme Council's Functions

The Supreme Council shall endeavor to achieve the objectives of the Cooperation Council, particularly as concerns the following:

1. Review matters of interest to the member states.

2. Lay down the higher policy for the Cooperation Council and the basic lines it should follow.

3. Review the recommendations, reports, studies and common projects submitted by the Ministerial Council for approval.

4. Review reports and studies which the Secretary-General is charged to prepare.

5. Approve the bases for dealing with other states and international organizations.

6. Approve the rules of procedures of the Commission for Settlement of Disputes and nominate its members.

7. Appoint the Secretary-General.

8. Amend the Charter of the Cooperation Council.

9. Approve the Council's Internal Rules.

10. Approve the budget of the Secretariat-General.

Article 9

Voting in Supreme Council

1. Each member of the Supreme Council shall have one vote.

2. Resolutions of the Supreme Council in substantive matters shall be carried by unanimous approval of the member states participating in the voting, while resolutions on procedural matters shall be carried by majority vote.

Article 10

Commission for Settlement of Disputes

1. The Cooperation Council shall have a commission called "Commission for Settlement of Disputes" and shall be attached to the Supreme Council.

2. The Supreme Council shall form the Commission for every case separately based on the nature of the dispute.

3. If a dispute arises over interpretation or implementation of the Charter and such dispute is not resolved within the Ministerial Council or the Supreme Council, the Supreme Council may refer such dispute to the Commission for Settlement of Disputes.

4. The Commission shall submit its recommendations or opinion, as applicable, to the Supreme Council for appropriate action.

Article 11

Ministerial Council

1. The Ministerial Council shall be formed of the Foreign Ministers of the member states or other delegated Ministers. The Council's presidency shall rotate among members every three months by alphabetical order of the states.

2. The Ministerial Council shall convene every three months and may hold extraordinary sessions at the invitation of any member seconded by another member.

3. The Ministerial Council shall decide the venue of its next session.

4. A Council's meeting shall be deemed valid if attended by two thirds of the member states.

Article 12

Functions of the Ministerial Council

The Ministerial Council's functions shall include the following:

1. Propose policies, prepare recommendations, studies and projects aimed at developing cooperation and coordination between member states in the various fields and adopt required resolutions or recommendations concerning thereof.

2. Endeavor to encourage, develop and coordinate activities existing between member states in all fields. Resolutions adopted in such matters shall be referred to the Ministerial Council for further submission, with recommendations, to the Supreme Council for appropriate action.

3. Submit recommendations to the Ministers concerned to formulate policies whereby the Cooperation Council's resolutions may be put into action.

4. Encourage means of cooperation and coordination between the various private sector activities, develop existing cooperation between the member states' chambers of commerce and industry, and encourage the flow of working citizens of the member states among them.

5. Refer any of the various facets of cooperation to one or more technical or specialized committee for study and presentation of relevant proposals.

6. Review proposals related to amendments to this Charter and submit appropriate recommendations to the Supreme Council.

7. Approve the Ministerial Council's Rules of Procedures as well as the Rules of Procedures of the Secretariat-General.

8. Appoint the Assistant Secretaries-General, as nominated by the Secretary-General, for a renewable period of three years.

9. Approve periodic reports as well as internal rules and regulations related to administrative and financial affairs proposed by the Secretary-General, and submit recommendations to the Supreme Council for approval of the budget of the Secretariat-General.

10. Make arrangements for the Supreme Council's meetings and prepare its agenda.

11. Review matters referred to it by the Supreme Council.

Article 13

Voting at Ministerial Council

1. Every member of the Ministerial Council shall have one vote.

2. Resolutions of the Ministerial Council in substantive matters shall be carried by unanimous vote of the member states present and participating in the vote, and in procedural matters by majority vote.

Article 14

Secretariat-General

1. The Secretariat General shall be composed of a Secretary-General who shall be assisted by assistants and a number of staff as required.

2. The Supreme Council shall appoint the Secretary-General, who shall be a citizen of one of the Cooperation Council states, for a period of three years which may be renewed for one time only.

3. The Secretary-General shall nominate the assistant secretaries general.

4. The Secretary-General shall appoint the Secretariat-General's staff from among the citizens of member states, and may not make exceptions without the approval of the Ministerial Council.

5. The Secretary-General shall be directly responsible for the work of the Secretariat-General and the smooth flow of work in its various organizations. He shall represent the Cooperation Council with other parties within the powers vested in him.

Article 15

Functions of the Secretariat-General

The Secretariat-General shall undertake the following functions:

1. Prepare studies related to cooperation and coordination, and to integrated plans and programs for member states' common action.

2. Prepare periodic reports on the Cooperation Council's work.

3. Follow up the execution by the member states of the resolutions and recommendations of the Supreme Council and Ministerial Council.

4. Prepare reports and studies ordered by the Supreme Council or Ministerial Council.

5. Prepare the draft of administrative and financial regulations commensurate with the growth of the Cooperation Council and its expanding responsibilities.

6. Prepare the Cooperation Council's budgets and closing accounts.

7. Make preparations for meetings and prepare agendas and draft resolutions for the Ministerial Council.

8. Recommend to the Chairman of the Ministerial Council the convocation of an extraordinary session of the Council whenever necessary.

9. Any other tasks entrusted to it by the Supreme Council or Ministerial Council.

Article 16

The Secretary-General and the assistant secretaries general and all the Secretariat-General's staff shall carry out their duties in complete independence and for the common interest of the member states.

They shall refrain from any action or behavior that is incompatible with their duties and from divulging the secrets of their jobs either during or after their tenure of office.

Article 17

Privileges and Immunities

1. The Cooperation Council and its organizations shall enjoy on the territories of all member states such legal competence, privileges and immunities as required to realize their objectives and carry out their functions.

2. Representatives of the member states on the Council, and the Council's employees, shall enjoy such privileges and immunities as are specified in agreements to be concluded for this purpose between the member states. A special agreement shall organize the relation between the Council and the state in which it has its headquarters.

3. Until such time as the two agreements mentioned in item 2 above are prepared and put into effect, the representatives of the member states in the Cooperation Council and its staff shall enjoy the diplomatic privileges and immunities established for similar organizations.

Article 18

Budget of the Secretariat General

The Secretariat General shall have a budget to which the member states shall contribute equal amounts.

Article 19

Charter Implementation

1. This Charter shall go into effect as of the date it is signed by the heads of states of the six member

states named in this Charter's preamble.

2. The original copy of this Charter shall be deposited with Saudi Arabia's Ministry of Foreign Affairs which shall act as custodian and shall deliver a true copy thereof to every member state, pending the establishment of the Secretariat General at which time the latter shall become depository.

Article 20

Amendments to Charter

1. Any member state may request an amendment of this Charter.

2. Requests for Charter amendments shall be submitted to the Secretary-General who shall refer them to the member states at least four months prior to submission to the Ministerial Council.

3. An amendment shall become effective if unanimously approved by the Supreme Council.

Article 21

Closing Provisions

No reservations may be voiced in respect of the provisions of this Charter.

Article 22

The Secretariat-General shall arrange to deposit and register copies of this Charter with the League of Arab States and the United Nations, by resolution of the Ministerial Council.

The Cooperation Council for the Arab States of the Gulf, Rules of Procedures, Commission for Settlement of Disputes

Preamble

In accordance with the provisions of Article Six of the Charter of the Gulf Arab States Cooperation Council; and

In execution of the provision of Article Ten of the Cooperation Council Charter,

A Commission for Settlement of Disputes, hereinafter referred to as The Commission, shall be set up and its jurisdiction and rules for its proceedings shall be as follows:

Article 1

Terminology

Terms used in these Rules of Procedures shall have the same meanings established in the Charter of the Gulf Arab States Cooperation Council.

Article 2

Commission's Seat and Meetings

The Commission shall have its headquarters at Riyadh, Saudi Arabia, and shall hold its meetings on the territory of the state where its headquarters is located, but may hold its meetings elsewhere, when necessary.

Article 3

Jurisdiction

The Commission shall, once installed, have jurisdiction to consider the following matters referred to it by the Supreme Council:

a. Disputes between member states.

b. Differences of opinion as to the interpretation or execution of the Cooperation Council Charter.

Article 4

Commission's Membership

a. The Commission shall be formed of an appropriate number of citizen of member states not involved in the dispute as the Council selects in every case separately depending on the nature of the dispute, provided that the number shall not be less than three members.

b. The Commission may seek the advice of any such experts as it may deem necessary.

c. Unless the Supreme Council decides otherwise, the Commission's task shall end with the submission of its recommendations or opinion to the Supreme Council which, after the conclusion of the Commission's task, may summon it at any time to explain or elaborate on its recommendations or opinions.

Article 5

Meetings and Internal Procedures

a. The Commission's meeting shall be valid if attended by all members.

b. The Secretariat-General of the Cooperation Council shall prepare procedures required to conduct the Commission's affairs, and such procedures shall go into effect as of the date of approval by the Ministerial Council.

c. Each party to the dispute shall send representatives to the Commission who shall be entitled to follow proceedings and present their defense.

Article 6

Chairmanship

The Commission shall select a chairman from among its members.

Article 7

Voting

Every member of the Commission shall have one vote, and shall issue its recommendations or opinions on matters referred to it by majority of the members. In case of a tie, the party with chairman vote shall prevail.

Article 8

Commission's Secretariat

a. The Secretary-General shall appoint a recorder for the Commission, and a sufficient number of employees to carry out the secretarial work.

b. The Supreme Council may create an independent organization to carry out the Commission's secretarial work when the need arises.

Article 9

Recommendations and Opinions

a. The Commission shall issue its recommendations or opinions in accordance with the Cooperation Council's Charter, international laws and practices, and the principles of Islamic Shari'ah. The Commission shall submit its findings on the case on hand to the Supreme Council for appropriate action.

b. The Commission may, while considering any dispute referred to it and pending the issue of its final recommendations thereon, ask the Supreme Council to take interim action called for by necessity or circumstances.

c. The Commission's recommendations or opinions shall spell out the reasons on which they were based

and shall be signed by the chairman and recorder.

d. If an opinion is passed wholly or partially by unanimous vote of the members, the dissenting members shall be entitled to document their dissenting opinion.

Article 10

Immunities and Privileges

The Commission and its members shall enjoy such immunities and privileges in the territories of the member states as are required to realize its objectives and in accordance with Article Seventeen of the Cooperation Council Charter.

Article 11

Commission's Budget

The Commission's budget shall be considered part of the Secretariat-General's budget. Remunerations of the Commission's members shall be established by the Supreme Council.

Article 12

Amendments

a. Any member state may request for amendments of these Rules of Procedures.

b. Requests for amendments shall be submitted to the Secretary-General who shall relay them to the member states by at least four months before submission to the Ministerial Council.

c. An amendment shall be effective if approved unanimously by the Supreme Council.

Article 13

Effective Date

These Rules of Procedures shall go into effect as of the date of approval by the Supreme Council.

The Unified Economic Agreement Between the Countries of the Gulf Cooperation Council

Date of signature: November 11, 1982
Place of signature: Riyadh, Saudi Arabia
Signatory states: United Arab Emirates, Bahrain, Saudi Arabia, Oman, Qatar, Kuwait

With the help of God the Almighty;
The Governments of the Member States of the Arab Gulf Cooperation Council;
In accordance with the Charter thereof, which calls for closer relations and stronger links; and, desiring

to develop, extend and enhance their economic ties on solid foundations, in the best interest of their peoples and for the sake of working to coordinate and standardize their economic, financial and monetary policies, as well as their commercial and industrial legislation, and Customs regulations have agreed as follows:

Chapter 1

Trade Exchange

Article 1

a. The Member States shall permit the importation and exportation of agricultural, animal, industrial and natural resource products that are of national origin. Also, they shall permit exportation thereof to other Member States.

b. All agricultural, animal, industrial and natural resource products that are from Member States shall receive the same treatment as national products.

Article 2

1. All agricultural, animal, industrial and natural resource products that are of national origin shall be exempted from reciprocal charges.

2. Fees charged for specific services such as demurrage, storage, transportation, freight of unloading, shall not be considered as customs duties when they are levied on domestic products.

Article 3

1. For products of national origin to qualify as national manufactured products, the value added ensuing from their production in Member States shall not be less than 40% of their final value as at the termination of the production phase. In addition Member States citizens' share in the ownership of the producing plant shall not be less than 51%.

2. Every item enjoying exemption hereby shall be accompanied by a certificate of origin duly authenticated by the appropriate government agency concerned.

Article 4

1. Member States shall establish a uniform minimum Customs tariff applicable to the products of countries other than G.C.C. Member States.

2. One of the objectives of the uniform Customs tariff shall be the protection of national products from foreign competition.

3. The uniform Customs tariff shall be implemented gradually within five years from the date on which this agreement becomes effective. Arrangements for its gradual implementation shall be agreed upon within one year from the said date.

Article 5

Member States shall grant all facilities for the transit of any Member State's goods to other Member States, exempting them from all duties and taxes whatsoever, without prejudice to the provisions of Paragraph 2 of Article 2.

Article 6

Transit shall be denied to any goods that are barred from entry into the territory of a Member State by its local regulations. Lists of such goods shall be exchanged between the Customs authorities of the Member States.

Article 7

Member States shall coordinate their commercial policies and relations with other states and regional economic groupings and blocs with a view to creating balanced trade relations and equitable circumstances and terms of trade therewith.

To achieve this goal, the Member States shall make the following arrangements:

1. Coordination of import/export policies and regulations.

2. Coordination of policies for building up strategic food stocks.

3. Conclusion of collective economic agreements in cases where joint benefits to Member States would be realized.

4. Taking of action for the creation of collective negotiating power to strengthen their negotiating position vis-a-vis foreign parties in the field of importation of basic needs and exportation of major products.

Chapter 2

The Movement of Capital and Individuals and the Exercise of Economic Activities

Article 8

The Member States shall agree on executive principles to ensure that each Member State shall grant the citizens of all other Member States the same treatment as is granted to its own citizens without any discrimination of differentiation in the following fields:

1. Freedom of movement, work and residence.
2. Right of ownership, inheritance and bequest.
3. Freedom of exercising economic activity.
4. Free movement of capital.

Article 9

The Member States shall encourage their respective private sectors to establish joint ventures in order to link their citizens' economic interests in various spheres of activity.

Chapter 3

Coordination of Development

Article 10

The Member States shall endeavour to achieve the coordination and harmonization of their respective development plans with a view to achieving integration in economic affairs.

Article 11

1. The Member States shall endeavour to coordinate their policies with regard to all aspects of the oil industry including extraction, refining, marketing, processing, pricing, the exploitation of natural gas, and development of energy sources.
2. The Member States shall endeavour to formulate unified oil policies and adopt common positions vis-a-vis the outside world, and in international and specialized organizations.

Article 12

To achieve the objectives specified in this Agreement, the Member States shall

1. Coordinate industrial activities, formulate policies and mechanisms which will lead to industrial development and the diversification of their products on an integrated basis.
2. Standardize their industrial legislation and regulations and guide their local production units to meet their needs.
3. Allocate industries between Member States according to relative advantages and economic feasibility, and encourage the establishment of basic as well as ancillary industries.

Article 13

Within the framework of their coordinating activi-

ties, the Member States shall pay special attention to the establishment of joint ventures in the fields of industry, agriculture and services, and shall support them with public, private or mixed capital in order to achieve economic integration, productive interface, and common development on sound economic bases.

Chapter 4

Technical Cooperation

Article 14

The Member States shall collaborate in finding spheres for common technical cooperation aimed at building a genuine local base founded on encouragement and support of research and applied sciences and technology as well as adapting imported technology to meet the needs of the region and to achieve the objectives of progress and development.

Article 15

Member States shall establish procedures, make arrangement and lay down terms for the transfer of technology, selecting the most suitable or introducing such changes thereto as would serve their various needs. Member States shall also, whenever feasible, conclude uniform agreements with foreign governments and scientific or commercial organizations to achieve these objectives.

Article 16

Member States shall formulate policies and implement coordinated programs for technical, vocational and professional training and qualification at all levels and stages. They shall also develop educational curricula at all levels to link education and technology with the development needs of the Member States.

Article 17

Member States shall coordinate their manpower policies and shall formulate uniform and standardized criteria and classifications for the various categories of occupations and crafts in different sectors in order to avoid harmful competition among themselves and to optimize the utilization of available human resources.

Chapter 5

Transport and Communications

Article 18

Member States shall accord passenger and cargo transportation belonging to citizens of the other Member States, when transiting or entering its territory, the same treatment they accord to the means of passenger and cargo transportation belonging to their own citizens, including exemption from all duties and taxes, whatsoever. However, local means of transportation are excluded.

Article 19

1. Member States shall cooperate in the fields of land and sea transportation, and communications. They shall also coordinate and establish infrastructure projects such as seaports, airports, water and power stations and roads, with a view to realizing joint economic development and the linking of their economic activities with each other.

2. The contracting states shall coordinate aviation and air transport policies among them and promote all areas of joint action at various levels.

Article 20

Member States shall allow steamers, ships and boats and their cargoes, belonging to any Member State freely to use the various port facilities and grant them the same treatment and privileges granted to their own in docking or calling at the ports as concerns fees, pilotage and docking services, freight, loading and unloading, maintenance, repair, storage of goods and other similar services.

Chapter 6

Financial and Monetary Cooperation

Article 21

Member States shall seek to unify investment rules and regulations in order to achieve a joint investment policy aimed at directing their domestic and foreign investments towards serving their interest, and realizing their peoples' aspirations for development and progress.

Article 22

Member States shall seek to coordinate their financial, monetary and banking policies and enhance cooperation between monetary agencies and central banks, including the endeavour to establish a joint currency in order to further their desired economic development.

Article 23

Member States shall seek to coordinate their external policies in the sphere of international and regional development aid.

Chapter 7

Closing Provisions

Article 24

In the execution of the Agreement and determination of the procedures resulting therefrom, consideration shall be given to differences in the levels of development as between Member States and the local development priorities of each. Any Member State may be temporarily exempted from applying such provisions of this Agreement as may be necessitated by temporary local situations in that state or specific circumstances faced by it. Such exemption shall be for a specified period and shall be decided by the Supreme Council of the Cooperation Council of the Arab States of the Gulf.

Article 25

No Member State shall grant any non-member state any preferential privilege exceeding that granted herein.

Article 26

a. This Agreement shall enter into force four months after its approval by the Supreme Council.

b. This Agreement may be amended by consent of the Supreme Council.

Article 27

In case of conflict with local laws and regulations of Member States, execution of the provisions of this Agreement shall prevail.

Article 28

Provisions herein shall supercede any similar provisions contained in bilateral agreements. Drawn up at Riyadh on 15 Muharram 1402, corresponding to 11 November 1982.

Treaty for The Establishment of The Economic Community of Central African States

Date of Signature: October 19, 1983
Place of Signature: Libreville
Signatory States: Angola, Burundi, Cameroon, The Central African Republic, Chad, Congo, Gabon, Guinea, Rwanda, Sao Tome and Principe, Zaire

Preamble

[The signatories],
Conscious of the need to promote the economic and social development of their States in order to improve the living standards of their people,

Recalling:

— the aims expressed in the Charter of the Organization of African Unity, particularly Article 2, paragraph 1(b) and paragraph 2,

— the African Declaration on Co-operation, Development and Economic Independence adopted by the Tenth Assembly of Heads of State and Government of the Organization of African Unity (May 1973),

— the Declaration of Commitment of Monrovia (July 1979) on the guidelines to be observed and the measures to be taken to achieve national and collective self-sufficiency in the economic and social fields in order to initiate a new international economic order,

— the Plan of Action and Final Act of Lagos (April 1980), notably the measures aimed at the economic, social and culture development of Africa and defining *inter alia* those relating to the establishment of subregional structures and the strengthening of existing structures with a view to the gradual and progressive establishment of an African common market as a prelude to an African economic community,

— their solemn commitment in the Declaration of Libreville (December 1981) to do everything in their power to set up an Economic Community of Central African States,

Bearing in mind the principles of international law governing relationships, between States, notably the principles of sovereignty, equality and independence of all States, non-interference in their internal affairs and the principle of the rule of law in their mutual relations,

Convinced that efficient co-operation in large groups, backed up by a resolute and concerted policy, will foster the accelerated and harmonious economic development of their States,

Conscious that progress towards subregional economic co-operation can be achieved only by having regard to the situation and interests of every State,

Conscious of the different levels of development in the countries of the subregions, more particularly of the situation in countries which are land-locked or semi-land-locked, islands and/or belong to the category of the least advanced countries,

Convinced that present forms of economic co-operation in the subregion are decisive stages on the way to broader co-operation,

Recognizing that efforts at subregional co-operation should not conflict with or hamper similar efforts being made to foster wider co-operation in Africa,

Determined to lay the foundations for a greater subregional economic zone,

Undertaking to collaborate sincerely and effectively in pursuance of the aims defined by this Treaty *inter alia* by abstaining from any measures likely to jeopardize the achievement of such aims,

Resolved to make every effort and take the necessary steps to secure the enactment of such legislation as is necessary to implement the obligations arising from this Treaty or from the institutions of the Community,

Deciding to establish an Economic Community of Central African States,

HEREBY AGREE AS FOLLOWS:

Chapter I

Terminology

Article 1

Terminology

In this Treaty:

(a) "barter agreement" means any agreement whereby articles possibly subject to import controls which are imported into a Member State shall be paid for wholly or partly by a direct exchange of goods;

(b) "Committee" means any committee established by Article 26 of this Treaty;

(c) "Commission" means the Consultative Commission established by Article 23 of this Treaty;

(d) "Community" means the Economic Community of Central African States set up by Article 2 of this Treaty;

(e) "Conference" means the meeting of Heads of State and Government of the Community under Article 8 of this Treaty;

(f) "Council" means any meeting of ministers under Article 12 of this Treaty;

(g) "Court of Justice" means the Court of Justice of the Community established under Article 16 of this Treaty;

(h) "customs duties" means the protective duty and equivalent charges levied on goods by virtue of their importation;

(i) "fiscal charges on imports" means the non-protective duty and equivalent charges levied on goods by virtue of their importation;

(j) "export duties and charges" means export duty and equivalent charges levied on goods by virtue of their exportation;

(k) "customs duties and charges" means all the duties and charges as defined in the foregoing;

(l) "Member States" means any Member States of the Community;

(m) "third State" means any States other than a Member State;

(n) "Fund" means the Co-operation and Development Fund set up under Article 75 of this Treaty;

(o) "goods in transit" means goods being conveyed between two Member States or between a Member State and a third State and passing through one or more Member States;

(p) "person" means a natural or legal person;

(q) "intra-Community trade treatment" means the advantages given to the goods mentioned in Article 30 (1) of this Treaty;

(r) "national of the Community" means any natural person regarded as a national of a Member State in accordance with its laws; legal persons established under the existing legislation of a Member State shall be deemed to be natural persons provided that their business is established in such State and at least 30 per cent of their equity is held by nationals or public organizations of such State;

(s) "Secretary-General" means the Secretary-General of the Community as established by Article 19 hereof;

(t) "General Secretariat" means the General Secretariat of the Community as established by Article 19 of this Treaty;

(u) " Treaty" means the Treaty establishing the Community.

Chapter II

Establishment, Principles, Aims and Procedures

Article 2

Establishment of the Community

THE HIGH CONTRACTING PARTIES hereby establish between them an Economic Community of Central African States (ECCAS), hereinafter called "the Community."

Article 3

Principles

THE HIGH CONTRACTING PARTIES undertake to observe the principles of international law governing relations between States, notably the principles of sovereignty, equality and independence of all States, good neighbourliness, non-interference in their internal affairs, non-use of force to settle disputes and the respect of the rule of law in their mutual relations.

Article 4

Aims of the Community

1. It shall be the aim of the Community to promote and enhance a harmonious co-operation and a balanced and self-maintaining development in all fields of economic and social activity particularly in the fields of industry, transport and communications, energy, agriculture, natural resources, trade, customs, monetary and financial questions, human resources, tourism, education, further training, culture, science, technology and the movement of people in order to

achieve collective self-reliance, raise the standards of living of its peoples, increase and maintain economic stability, foster close peaceful relations between Member States and contribute to progress and development of the African continent.

2. For the purposes set out in paragraph 1 of this Article and in accordance with the relevant provisions of this Treaty, the aims of the Community are as follows:

(a) the elimination between Member States of customs duties and any other equivalent charges levied on the import and export of goods;

(b) the abolition between any Member States of quantitative restrictions and other hindrances to trade;

(c) the establishment and maintenance of a common external customs tariff;

(d) the establishment of a trade policy vis-à-vis third States;

(e) the gradual abolition between Member States of obstacles to the free movement of people, goods, services and capital and to the rights of establishment;

(f) the harmonization of national policies in order to promote Community activities, notably in the industry, transport and communications, energy, agriculture, natural resources, trade, currency and finance, human resources, tourism, education and culture, science and technology;

(g) the setting-up of a Co-operation and Development Fund;

(h) the rapid development of States which are fully or partly land-locked and fully or partly islands and/ or belong to the category of the least advanced countries;

(i) any other joint activities by Member States for achieving Community aims.

Article 5

General Undertaking

1. The Member States shall direct their endeavours with a view to creating favourable conditions for the development of the Community and the achievement of its aims and the harmonization of their policies for achievement of such aims through Community institutions. Member States shall refrain any unilateral action likely to impair such achievement.

2. Each Member State shall take all steps under its

constitutional procedures to secure the enactment and circulation of such legislation as is necessary to give effect to this Treaty.

Article 6

Procedures for Establishing the Community

1. The Economic Community of Central African States shall be established progressively over a twelve year-period subdivided into three four-year stages.

2. Each stage shall have allotted to it a schedule of actions to be undertaken and pursued concurrently, as follows:

(a) first stage: stability of the fiscal and customs regime existing at the date of entry into force of the Treaty, and the carrying out of studies to determine the timetable for the gradual removal of tariff and non-tariff obstacles to intra-Community trade; setting a timetable for increases or decreases in the customs tariffs of Member States in adaptation to a common external tariff;

(b) second stage: setting up a free trade zone (application of the timetable for the gradual elimination of tariff and non-tariff obstacles to intra-Community trade);

(c) third stage: establishment of the customs union (adoption of the common external tariff).

3. Change-overs between stages shall be subject to confirmation that the essential elements of the specific aims of this Treaty or the Conference have been achieved and undertakings observed.

At the proposal of the Council the Conference shall confirm that the aims allotted to a stage have been achieved and shall decide on the change-over to the next stage.

4. The total duration of the stages may be lengthened or shortened only by a consensual decision. However, decisions taken shall not be effective to shorten the transition period to ten years or prolong it for more than twenty years from the entry force of this Treaty.

Chapter III

Institutions of the Community

Article 7

Institutions

1. The institutions of the Community shall be:

(a) the Conference of the Heads of State and Government;

(b) the Council of Ministers;

(c) the Court of Justice;

(d) the General Secretariat;

(e) the Consultative Commission;

(f) any specialized technical committee or organ set up or provided for by this Treaty.

2. The institutions of the Community shall perform their duties and act within the limits of the powers conferred on them by this Treaty.

CONFERENCE OF HEADS OF STATE AND GOVERNMENT

Article 8

Establishment and Composition

1. There is established a Conference of Heads of State and Government of the Community.

2. The Conference of Heads of State and Government is the supreme organ of the Community.

3. It shall be composed of the Heads of State and Government of the Member States.

Article 9

Powers

1. The Conference shall be responsible for implementing the aims of the Community.

2. The Conference shall accordingly;

(a) define the general policy and basic attitudes of the Community and direct and harmonize the socio-economic policies of Member States;

(b) take any action under this Treaty for achieving the aims of the Community;

(c) oversee the operation of Community institutions;

(d) establish its rules of procedure and approve the rules of procedure of Council of Ministers;

(e) approve the organizational chart of the General Secretariat of the Community;

(f) appoint the Secretary-General, the Deputy Secretaries-General, the Financial Controller and the Accountant;

(g) appoint a board of Auditors at the proposal of the Council of Ministers;

(h) prepare the Community budget and determine the annual contribution of each Member State at the proposal of the Council of Ministers;

(i) if it wishes, delegate to the Council of Ministers the authority to take decisions and issue directives in matters coming under it;

(j) when it confirms by a two-thirds majority vote that a Member State is failing in one or more of its obligations under this Treaty, submit to the Court of Justice decision or a directive of the Conference or a decision of the Council of Ministers;

(k) if it wishes, request the Court of Justice to give an advisory opinion on any legal questions;

(l) determine the personnel regulations of the General Secretariat.

3. The Conference shall be assisted by the Council of Ministers in the performance of its duties.

4. The Conference shall exercise any other powers granted to it by this Treaty.

Article 10

Organization

1. The Conference shall meet once a year in ordinary session. The special session may be convened by its Chairman or at the request of a Member State provided that such a request is supported by two thirds of the Conference members.

2. The Office of Chairman shall be filled every year by one of the Heads of State in alphabetical order of listing of the Member States specified in this Treaty.

3. In the event of further States acceding to the Community, their Heads of State will fill the Office of Chairman of the Conference after that Member State signatory of this Treaty which is last in alphabetical order.

Article 11

Decisions and Directives

1. The Conference shall act by decisions and directives.

2. Its decisions shall be binding on the Member States and institutions of the Community except for the Court of Justice and shall be enforceable as of right in Member States thirty (30) days after the date of their publication in the official bulletin of the Community.

3. Directives shall be binding on the institutions concerned except for the Court of Justice.

They shall come into force upon notification and shall be published in the official bulletin of the Community.

4. Unless otherwise specified in this Treaty, decisions and directives of the Conference shall be taken by consensus.

COUNCIL OF MINISTERS

Article 12

Establishment and Composition

1. There is established a Council of Ministers of the Community.

2. The Council of Ministers shall be composed of the Ministers for economic development or any other Minister appointed for the purpose by each Member State.

Article 13

Powers

1. The Council shall be responsible for the operation and development of the Community.

2. Accordingly it shall:

(a) formulate recommendations for the Conference on any action aimed at achieving the aims of the Community in the context of the general policy and basic attitudes defined and ordered by the Conference;

(b) guide the activities of the other subordinate institutions of the Community;

(c) submit the draft budget of the Community to the Conference and propose to the Conference the annual contribution of each Member State;

(d) propose the appointment of the Board of Auditors to the Conference;

(e) prepare its rules of procedure and submit them for the approval of the Conference;

(f) exercise any powers granted to it by this Treaty or any power delegated to it by the Conference;

(g) if it wishes, request the Court of Justice for advisory opinion on any legal question.

Article 14

Organization

1. The Council shall meet twice a year in ordinary sessions, one of which shall precede the ordinary session of the Conference.

A special session may be called by the Chairman of the Council or at the request of a Member State provided that two thirds of its Members approve.

2. The Office of Chairman shall be filled by the Minister of the Member State whose Head of State is the Chairman of the Conference.

Article 15

Regulation

1. The Council shall act by regulation.

2. Regulations shall be binding on the Member States and institutions concerned except for the Court of Justice.

They shall be enforceable as of right in Member States thirty (30) days after the date of their publication in the official bulletin of the Community.

They shall become effective for the institutions concerned immediately upon notification.

3. Unless otherwise specified in this Treaty, regulations of the Council shall be adopted by consensus.

COURT OF JUSTICE

Article 16

Establishment and Powers

1. There is established a Court of Justice of the Community.

2. The Court of Justice shall be responsible for observance of the law in the interpretation and application of this Treaty and shall decide disputes submitted to it under this Treaty.

3. The Court of Justice shall accordingly;

(a) oversee the legality of the decisions, directives and regulations of Community institutions;

(b) decide on appeals lodged by Member States of the Conference on the grounds of lack of jurisdiction, exceeding jurisdiction and infringement of the substance of the provisions of this Treaty;

(c) make interlocutory decisions on:
— the interpretation of this Treaty;
— the effectiveness of the decisions, directives and regulations formulated by Community institutions;

(d) give advisory opinions on any legal matter at the request of the Conference or Council.

4. Powers to deal with other disputes may be grant-

ed to the Court by decisions taken by the Conference by virtue of this Treaty.

Article 17

Decisions of the Court

The decisions of the Court of Justice shall be binding on Member States and institutions of the Community.

Article 18

Organization

The composition, procedure and constitution of the Court and other matters concerning it shall be determined by the Conference.

GENERAL SECRETARIAT

Article 19

Establishment and Composition

1. There is established a General Secretariat of the Community.

2. The General Secretariat shall comprise a Secretary-General, Deputy Secretaries-General, a Financial Controller, an Accountant and the personnel required for operation of the Community.

Article 20

Powers

1. The Secretary-General shall be the chief executive official of the Community.

2. Accordingly his duties shall be:

(a) to prepare and carry out the decisions and directives of the Conference and the regulations of the Council;

(b) to promote development programmes and Community projects;

(c) to prepare the draft budget of the Community and have it implemented;

(d) to prepare the Community's programme of work;

(e) to submit a report on Community activities to all Conference and Council meetings;

(f) to prepare Conference and Council meetings and provide the secretariat for them;

(g) to carry out studies with a view to achieving the aims of the Community and to make proposals likely to enhance the operation and harmonious development of the Community, to which end he may request a Member State to supply him with all the necessary information;

(h) to recruit the personnel of the General Secretariat and make appointments for duties other than those specified in Article 9, paragraph 2 (f) of this Treaty.

Article 21

Appointments

1. The Secretary-General and the Deputy Secretaries-General shall be appointed by the Conference for a four-year term which can be renewed once.

2. Citizens of the State where the Community Headquarters are situated may not be appointed to the post of Secretary-General.

3. The Financial Controller and the Accountant shall be appointed by the Conference for a renewable term of three years.

4. In the appointment of General Secretariat personnel consideration shall be given not only to moral integrity and skill but also to equitable geographic distribution of posts among all the Member States.

Article 22

Relationships between the Personnel of the General Secretariat and the Member States

1. In the performance of their duties the Secretary-General, the Deputy Secretary-General, the Financial Controller, the Accountant and the personnel of the General Secretariat shall be responsible only to Community.

Accordingly, they may neither seek nor accept instructions from any Government or any national or international authority outside the Community.

They must refrain from any attitude incompatible with the nature of their duties as an international official.

2. Every Member State undertakes not to influence the personnel of the General Secretariat in the performance of their duties and to respect the international character of the duties of Secretary-General, Deputy Secretaries-General, Financial Controller, Accountant and any other official of the General Secretariat.

3. The Member States undertake to co-operate with the General Secretariat and to aid it in the performance of its duties hereunder.

CONSULTATIVE COMMISSION

Article 23

Establishment and Composition

1. There is established a Consultative Commission of the Community.

2. The Consultative Commission shall consist of experts appointed by the Member States.

Article 24

Powers

1. The Consultative Commission shall be responsible for studying or investigating, under the Council's responsibility, questions and projects submitted to it by other Community institutions.

2. Accordingly it shall:

(a) assist the Council in the performance of its duties;

(b) study the reports of the specialized technical committees and make recommendations to the Council;

(c) carry out any other duties given it hereunder.

Article 25

Organization

1. Subject to Council regulations the Commission shall meet as often as necessary for the satisfactory performance of the Committee.

2. It shall prepare its rules of procedure and submit them to the Council for approval.

SPECIALIZED TECHNICAL COMMITTEES

Article 26

1. The specialized technical committees shall be established under the Protocols hereto or may be established by the Conference at the Council's recommendation.

2. They shall act in connection with the duties given them.

3. Subject to Council regulations the specialized technical committees shall meet as often as necessary for the proper performance of their duties.

4. They shall prepare their rules of procedure and submit them to the Council for approval.

Chapter IV

Liberalization of Trade

Article 27

Customs Union

The Member States agree gradually to establish between them during a transition period, as specified in Article 5 of the pre-Treaty, a Customs Union involving:

(a) the elimination between Member States of customs duties, quotas, trade restrictions and bans and administrative obstacles to trade;

(b) the adoption by Member States of a common external customs tariff.

Article 28

Elimination of Customs Duties between Member States

1. In the first stage Member States shall refrain from the establishment of any new customs duties between them and from increasing those they apply in their mutual trade relations. They shall make regular submissions to the Secretary-General of any information concerning customs duties, for study.

2. At the end of the first stage Member States shall progressively reduce and eventually eliminate customs duties between them in accordance with a programme to be determined by the Conference on a Council proposal.

3. The Conference may at any time on the Council's recommendation decide that any customs duty may be reduced more rapidly or eliminated sooner. However, the Council shall study the question at least twelve months before the date on which such reduction or elimination is to apply to some or all of the goods and to some or all of the Member States and shall submit the result of this study to the Conference for a decision.

Article 29

Establishment of a Common External Customs Tariff

1. The Member States agree to the gradual establishment of a common external customs tariff applicable to goods imported into Member States from third countries.

2. At the end of the first stage and during the second stage Member States shall, in accordance with a programme to be proposed by the Council, eliminate differences between customs duties in their respective customs tariffs.

3. At the end of the second stage and during the third stage the Council shall propose to the Confer-

ence the adoption of a common and statistical nomenclature for all Member States.

Article 30

Treatment of Intra-Community Trade

1. At the end of the second stage no Member State shall levy customs duties on goods originating from one Member State and transferred to another Member State. Similar considerations shall apply to goods from third countries which are traded in freely in the Member States and transferred from one Member State to another.

2. The definition of this concept of products originating from Member States and the rules governing the application of this Article shall be given in the protocol annexed hereto as Annex I.

3. Goods originating from third-party countries in respect of which import formalities have been completed and customs duties paid in a Member State and which have not benefited from a partial or total rebate of such duties shall be considered as being traded in freely in such a Member State.

4. Member States shall not adopt legislation implying direct or indirect discrimination directed against identical or similar products of any other Member State.

Article 31

Deflection of Trade

1. For the purposes of this Article, trade is said to be deflected if:

(a) imports of any particular product by a Member State from another Member State increase significantly; and

(b) this increase in imports causes or would cause serious injury to production which is carried on in the territory of the importing Member State.

2. In case of deflection of trade to the detriment of a Member State resulting from the abusive reduction or elimination of duties and changes levied by another Member State as a result of unregistered trade or for any other reason, the Member State concerned shall submit a report to the Secretary-General who shall submit the matter to the Council.

The Council shall propose the necessary measures to the Conference.

Article 32

Internal Taxation

1. Member States shall not apply directly or indi-

rectly to goods originating from Member States and imported into every Member State internal taxation in excess of that applied to like domestic goods and otherwise impose such taxation for the effective protection of such goods.

2. Member States shall progressively eliminate all internal taxation made for the protection of like domestic goods in the same conditions as specified in Article 28 hereof. Where by virtue of obligations under an existing contract entered into by a Member State the latter is unable to comply with the provisions of this Article, the Member State shall duly notify the Council of Ministers of this fact and shall not, subject to Article 31, extend or renew such contract at its expiry.

Article 33

Non-tariff Restrictions on Intra-Community Trade

1. Except as is provided in this Article, each of the Member States undertakes that upon the definitive entry into force of this Treaty it shall gradually relax and eventually remove, at the latest by the end of the second stage and in accordance with paragraph 2 of this Article, prohibitions which apply to the transfer to that State of goods originating in the other Member States and that, except as may be provided or permitted by this Treaty, it will thereafter refrain from imposing any further restrictions or prohibitions on such goods.

2. Except as is provided in this Article, the Commission shall, after considering proposals submitted to it by the Secretary-General, recommend to the Council for its approval a programme for the gradual relaxation and eventual elimination, at the latest by the end of the second stage, of all the existing quota, restrictions or prohibitions which apply in a Member State to the import of goods originating in the other Member States, provided that the Council may subsequently decide that all the quotas, restrictions or prohibitions shall be relaxed more rapidly or removed earlier than is approved under the provisions of this paragraph.

3. The special provisions on restrictions, prohibitions, quotas, dumpings, grants and discriminatory practices shall be the subject of a protocol on non-tariff hindrances to trade annexed hereto as Annex II.

Article 34

Exceptions

1. Notwithstanding the provisions of Article 33, a Member State may, after having given notice to the

other Member states of its intention to do so, introduce or continue to impose restrictions or prohibitions affecting:

(a) the application of security laws and regulations;

(b) the control of arms, ammunition and other war equipment and military items;

(c) the protection of human, animal or plant health or life or the protection of public morality;

(d) the transfer of gold, silver, platinum and precious stones;

(e) the protection of national treasures of artistic or archaeological value or the protection of industrial and commercial property;

(f) the control of nuclear materials, radio-active products or any other equipment used in the development or exploitation of nuclear energy;

(g) the control of strategic products.

2. However, such prohibitions or restrictions shall in no case be a means of arbitrary discrimination nor a disguised restriction on trade between Member States.

3. If a Member State encounters balance-of-payments difficulties arising from the application of the provisions of this Chapter, that Member State may, provided that it has taken all reasonable steps to overcome the difficulties, impose for the purpose only of overcoming such difficulties for a specified period to be determined by the Council, quantitative or the like restrictions or prohibitions on goods originating from the other Member States.

4. For the purpose of protecting an infant or strategic industry a Member State may, provided that it has taken all reasonable steps to protect such industry, impose for the purpose only of protecting such industry for a specified period to be determined by the Council, impose quantitative or the like restrictions or prohibitions, on similar goods originating from the other Member States.

5. A Member State imposing quantitative or the like restrictions or prohibitions under paragraphs 3, 5 and 6 of this Article shall send a report to the Secretary-General who shall submit the matter to the Council in order to determine for how long such measures may continue.

6. The Council shall keep under review the operation of any quantitative or the like restrictions or prohibitions imposed under the provisions of Articles 1, 3 and 4 of this Article and take appropriate action.

Article 35

Most-favoured-nation Treatment

1. The Member States shall accord to one another in relation to intra-Community trade the most-favoured-nation treatment. In no case shall trade concessions granted to a third country under an agreement with a Member State be more favourable than those applicable under this Treaty.

2. The text of agreements coming under paragraph 1 of this Article shall be sent to the Secretary-General by the States parties to it.

3. Any agreement between a Member State and a third country under which tariff concessions are granted shall not be incompatible with obligations of that Member State hereunder.

4. No Member State may conclude with any third country an agreement whereby the latter would grant such Member State tariff concessions not granted to the other Member States.

Article 36

Re-export of Goods and Intra-Community Transit

Under this Article the Member States undertake:

(a) to facilitate the re-export of goods among them in accordance with the Protocol on the Re-Export of Goods annexed hereunto as Annex III while awaiting the stage of establishment of the customs union;

(b) to grant freedom of transit through their territories to goods proceeding to or from another Member State in accordance with the provision of the Protocol on Intra-Community Transit annexed hereto as Annex IV.

Article 37

Customs Administration

The Member States shall in accordance with the provisions of the Protocol on Customs Co-operation annexed hereto as Annex V take measures to harmonize and standardize their customs regulations and procedures to ensure the effective application of the provisions of this provisions of this Chapter and to facilitate the movement of goods and services across their frontiers.

Article 38

Deflection of Trade Arising from Barter Agreements

1. If a barter agreement in a specific category of articles between a Member State or a physical or

legal person thereof and a third country or a physical or legal person thereof leads to a substantial deflection of trade in such category to the detriment of articles imported from and manufactured in any other Member State in favour of articles imported under the barter agreement, the Member State importing such articles shall take effective steps to obviate such deflection.

2. To determine whether a deflection of trade has occurred in a specific category of articles within the meaning of this Article, consideration shall be given to all the relevant trade statistics and other data on the category of articles available for the six months prior to a complaint from a Member State affected concerning deflection of trade and to the average of two comparable six-month periods during the 24 months prior to the first importation of goods under the barter agreement.

3. The Secretary-General shall submit the matter to the Council which shall consider it and submit it to the Conference for a decision.

Article 39

Establishment of the Fund for Compensation for Loss of Revenue

1. There is established a Fund for Compensation for Loss of Revenue.

2. A Protocol concerning the resources and use of the Fund is attached hereto as Annex VI.

Chapter V

Freedom of Movement, Presidency and Right of Establishment

Article 40

1. Citizens of Member States shall be deemed to be citizens of the Community. Accordingly, Member States agree, in accordance with the Protocol on Freedom of Movement and Right of Establishment annexed hereto as Annex VII, gradually to facilitate procedures for the freedom of movement and right of establishment within the Community.

2. For the purposes of Protocol VII legal persons complying with existing legislation in a Member State shall be deemed to be natural persons.

Chapter VI

Co-operation in the Currency, Financial and Payments Field

Article 41

Currency, Finance and Payments

1. Member States agree to harmonize their currency, financial and payments policies in order to create confidence in their respective currencies, to ensure satisfactory operation of the Community and to further the achievement of its aims and to improve currency and financial co-operation between them and the other African countries.

2. For the purposes of paragraph 1 of this Article the General Secretariat acting in liaison with the particular subregional committees concerned with the Association of Central African Banks shall:

(a) prepare for the Council's attention recommendations on harmonization of the economic and financial policies of Member States;

(b) give continuous attention to the balance-of-payments problems of Member States and undertake any studies relating thereto;

(c) study the development of the economies of Member States;

(d) make recommendations to the Council about the short-term creation of bilateral clearing systems among Member States and the long-term establishment of a multilateral clearing system and monetary union.

3. Under the Protocol on the Clearing House annexed hereto as Annex VIII, Member States undertake to boost intra-Community trading in goods and services through the channel of a compensation chamber.

Article 42

Movement of Capital

Upon the entry into force hereof the Conference shall, at the proposal of the Council and subject to the approval of the Consultative Commission, take steps for the progressive co-ordination of national exchange policies with regard to movements of capital between Member States and third States.

Chapter VII

Co-operation in Agriculture and Food

Article 43

1. Member States agree to co-operate in agriculture, silviculture, livestock and fishing. The aims of the co-operation are as follows:

(a) raising the standard of life of rural populations, more particularly by raising incomes by increasing agricultural, forestry and fishery production and job creation;

(b) satisfying the food requirements of populations and enhancing food security, *inter alia* by the quantitative and qualitative improvement of food-stuffs and the definition of a food reserves and trade policy;

(c) improving rural living and working conditions;

(d) *in situ* upgrading of agricultural production by the processing of vegetable and animal products;

(e) development of the self-development ability of populations, notably by greater mastery of their technical and economic environment.

2. Accordingly, Member States shall:

(a) take concerted action to harmonize their agricultural policies;

(b) have regular exchanges of information on experiments and the results of the research work proceeding in their respective countries and on rural development programmes;

(c) prepare as required joint training and retraining programmes for cadres in existing or future institutions;

(d) take any necessary action for the gradual preparation of a joint policy, *inter alia* in the research and training production, processing and marketing of agricultural and forest products, livestock and fishery.

3. For the purposes of this Chapter Member States shall agree to co-operate in accordance with Protocol IX annexed hereto.

Article 44

To implement the co-operation activities under Article 43 hereof and to improve the effectiveness of services the General Secretariat shall make proposals to the Council for the application of this common agricultural policy.

Chapter VIII

Co-operation in Industry

Article 45

1. In order to integrate their economies Member States agree to harmonize their industrialization policies in the subregion.

2. Accordingly they undertake to:

(a) inform the General Secretariat of their development plans and corresponding action programmes with a view to the preparation of basic programmes for the harmonious development of the subregion;

(b) exchange information on any industrial project for the subregion;

(c) inform one another of their industrial experiences;

(d) exchange experts and information on industrial, commercial and technological research.

Article 46

1. To achieve a rational and harmonious industrial development the Member States agree to:

(a) harmonize measures for stimulating industrial development by gradually establishing a homogeneous industrial environment in the subregion, *inter alia* by the preparation of a common investment code;

(b) promote the establishment of large industrial units of a Community character and of an industrial development centre;

(c) distribute Community projects in a balanced and harmonious manner among all Member States;

(d) refuse permission to national industries which might compete with Community industries meeting the demands of Member States of the Community satisfactorily;

(e) create subregional training and further training centres at all levels of skill to satisfy their personnel requirements in industry, trade and technology.

2. For the purposes of this Chapter the Member States shall agree to co-operate under Protocol X annexed hereto.

Chapter IX

Co-operation in Infrastructure and Equipment, Transport and Communications

Article 47

Transport and Communications

1. To achieve a harmonious and integrated development of the subregional transport and communications network and gradually to prepare a common policy, the Member States agree to:

(a) promote the integration of transport and communications infrastructures;

(b) co-ordinate the various modes of transport in order to increase their effectiveness;

(c) progressively harmonize their transport and communications laws and regulations;

(d) encourage the use of local material and human resources, the standardization of networks and equipment, the research and publicizing of appropriate technologies for constructing appropriate infrastructures and equipment;

(e) expand and modernize transport and communications infrastructures by mobilizing the necessary technological and financial resources;

(f) promote subregional industry in the field of equipment for transport and communications;

(g) organize, structure and promote subregional sector of passenger and freight transport activities.

2. The Member States shall accordingly:

(a) prepare co-ordinated programmes for structuring the road transport sector;

(b) prepare plans for improving and re-organizing different railways systems of Member States with a view to their interconnection, and construct new railways;

(c) harmonize:

— their policies on international sea and river transport;

— their air transport policies;

— their work on basic and further training of specialist cadres in transport and communications;

(d) modernize and standardize their equipment in order that all Member States may be linked with one another and with the exterior by scheduled flights.

Article 48

Member States shall make every effort to establish Community sea, river and airline companies.

Article 49

Post and Telecommunications

Member States undertake to:

— reorganize, modernize and develop their telecom-

munications systems, in order to meet the requirements of international traffic and to provide reliable interconnection between Member States;

— devise as soon as possible a regional satellite communication system to complete the Pan-African Telecommunications Network in Central Africa;

— provide rapid and frequent postal services within the Community and develop close collaboration between postal administrations.

Article 50

For the purposes of this Chapter Member States shall agree to co-operate in accordance with Protocol XI annexed hereto.

Chapter X

Co-operation in Science and Technology

Article 51

1. The Member States agree:

(a) to develop an adequate scientific and technological base able to initiate the socio-economic changes needed to improve the quality of life of their populations, particularly rural populations;

(b) to arrange for an appropriate application of science and technology in the development of agriculture, transport and communications, industry, health and hygiene, energy, education and manpower and preservation of the environment;

(c) to reduce their dependence and promote their individual and collective technological self-reliance by seeking a favourable socio-economic balance between foreign contributions and contributions from local technology.

2. In the implementation of this co-operation the Member States shall:

(a) harmonize their national policies on scientific and technological research with a view to improving their integration at national levels of economic and social development;

(b) co-ordinate their applied research, research and development and scientific and technological services programmes;

(c) harmonize their national technological development plans by placing special emphasis on local technologies and their control of industrial property and the transfer of foreign technologies;

(d) co-ordinate their positions on all scientific and technological questions forming the subject of international negotiations;

(e) arrange for a permanent exchange of information and documentation and the establishment of Community data networks and data bank;

(f) develop joint programmes for training scientific and technological cadres including the basic and further training of skilled manpower.;

(g) promote exchanges of researchers and specialists among Member States in order to make full use of the technical skills available in the Community.

Article 52

1. The Member States shall take all the necessary measures to prepare and implement a joint scientific research and technological development programme.
2. The General Secretariat shall therefore undertake jointly with the competent national and subregional bodies the technical studies needed to define priority sectors and sectors of joint interest and shall submit its conclusions to the Council.

Article 53

For the purposes of this Chapter the Member States agree to co-operate in accordance with Protocol XII annexed hereto.

Chapter XI

Co-operation in Energy and Natural Resources

Article 54

1. The Member States agree to:

(a) rapidly increase the Community's energy resources availabilities;

(b) establish the appropriate trade machinery to ensure a regular supply of hydrocarbons;

(c) promote renewable energy sources in connection with the policy of diversification of energy sources.

2. To achieve the aims of paragraph 1 of this Article, the Member States shall:

(a) harmonize their national energy development plans;

(b) establish a joint energy policy more particularly for exploitation, production and distribution;

(c) establish an adequate system of concentration and

co-ordination for jointly solving the Community's energy development problems, notably those relating to energy transmission, shortage of skilled cadres and shortage of funds for implementing their energy projects;

(d) promote the basic and further training of cadres.

Article 55

The Member States shall agree to assess and upgrade the mineral and hydraulic resources *inter alia* by;

(a) endeavours to improve their knowledge of their natural resource potentialities;

(b) gradually reducing their dependence on transnational companies for upgrading such resources, notably by mastering exploitation technologies;

(c) improving methods of pricing and marketing raw materials.

Article 56

To promote this co-operation the Member States shall:

(a) harmonize their policies of prospecting for producing and processing mineral resources and prospecting, exploiting and distributing hydraulic resources;

(b) co-ordinate their development and utilization programmers for mineral and hydraulic resources in order to exploit similarities and complementarities within the Community and promote vertical and horizontal interindustrial relationships arising between Member States subsequently to the upgrading of such resources;

(c) co-ordinate their positions in all international negotiations on raw materials in order to safeguard their interests;

(d) develop a system of transfer of know-how and exchange of scientific, technical and economic data among Member States;

(e) prepare and implement joint basic and further training programmes for cadre in order to develop the human resources and appropriate local technological capacities needed for the exploration, exploitation and processing of mineral and hydraulic resources.

Article 57

To implement the co-operation activities under

Articles 54-56 hereof the Secretary-General shall submit proposals to the Council for preparing a joint policy for upgrading mineral and hydraulic resources.

Article 58

For the purposes of this Chapter the Member States shall agree to co-operate in accordance with the Protocols XIII and XIV annexed hereto.

Chapter XII

Co-operation in Human Resource and Social Affairs

Article 59

Human Resources

1. The Member States shall agree to co-operate in the development and use of their human resources, *inter alia* with regard to the programming, planning and preparation of policies, training and career orientation, providing the basic requirements of economic and social development and the use of human resources in general.

2. They shall accordingly:

(a) adopt and promote a joint policy on the programming, planning and preparation of policies;

(b) co-ordinate their policies and activities in education, training, career planning, guidance and expert advice;

(c) co-operate in the development of human resources in order to meet the basic requirements of their economic and social development;

(d) co-operate in order to use their human resources potential.

Article 60

Social Affairs

1. Member States agree to participate fully and make rational use of human resources in community development efforts.

2. They shall accordingly:

(a) promote exchanges of experience and information on literacy, vocational training and employment;

(b) develop collective research by appropriate policies aimed at improving the economic, social and cultural situation of urban and rural women and increasing their integration in development activities;

(c) gradually harmonize their labour laws, social securities systems and legal and administrative systems concerning individuals;

(d) initiate subregional co-operation in public health, medical research, promotion of the studies of traditional medicine, pharmacopoeias and exchange of experiences.

3. For the purposes of this Chapter the Member States agree to co-operate in accordance with Protocol XV annexed hereto.

Chapter XIII

Co-operation in Education, Training and Culture

Article 61

Education and Training

1. Member States agree to prepare a common educational policy including educational models more closely tailored to the economic and socio-cultural realities of the subregion in order to train men and women who are rooted in their environment and able to promote the changes necessary for social progress and development.

2. For the purposes of paragraph 1 of this Article, Member States shall:

(a) improve the efficiency of existing educational systems by promoting the training of trainers and using appropriate methods and equipment;

(b) establish new national and subregional training institutions and strengthen the existing ones;

(c) prepare joint training programmes better suited to development problems with a view to gradually achieving self-sufficiency in skilled personnel;

(d) promote the systematic exchange of experience and information on education policy and planning.

Article 62

Culture

1. The Member States agree to promote all forms of expression of their culture in order to make it more widely known.

2. For the purposes of paragraph 1 of this Article the Member States shall:

(a) make every endeavour to preserve their cultural heritage;

(b) inform one another of their cultural programmes

and their experiences, notably in art, literature, spectacles, sport and leisure activities;

(c) exchange cinema, TV and radio programme materials and works;

(d) seek ways and means aimed at developing infrastructures and facilities of joint interest.

Article 63

For the purposes of this Chapter the Member States shall agree to co-operate in accordance with the Protocol XV annexed hereto.

Chapter XIV
Co-operation in Tourism
Article 64

The Member States agree to:

(a) develop and promote subregional tourism;

(b) prepare a joint policy on subregional tourism;

(c) send the Secretary-General documents summarizing their plans and programmes for tourist development.

Article 65

For the purpose of application of the provisions of Article 64 the Secretary-General shall undertake jointly with the competent national and subregional organizations the technical studies necessary to devise a Community tourist development plan.

Article 66

For the purposes of this Chapter the Member States agree to co-operate in accordance with Protocol XVI annexed hereto.

Chapter XV
Trade Documents and Procedures
Article 67
Trade Documents and Procedures

The Member States agree to simplify and harmonize their trade documents and procedures in accordance with the provisions of the Protocol on the Simplification and Harmonization of Trade Documents and Procedures annexed hereto as Annex XVII so as to facilitate intra-Community trade in goods and services.

Chapter XVI
Co-operation in Other Fields
Article 68

Subject to the provisions hereof the Member States shall consult with one another through appropriate Community institutions for the purpose of harmonizing their respective policies in such fields as they may, from time to time, consider necessary or desirable for the efficient and harmonious functioning and development of the Community and for the application of the provisions hereof.

Article 69
Accounts, Taxation and Data Processing

1. The Member States agree to co-operate in standardizing and harmonizing their accounting procedures with the two aims of:

(a) standardizing methods of recording accounts data, assessing assets and liabilities and presenting results in order that they may be comparable and that accounts may be consolidated at both national and subregional levels;

(b) improving methods of management and control of the performances of businesses, administrative units and State organizations.

2. Member States shall harmonize existing laws and plans on accounting or make and promote every effort and every instrument likely to help achieve the aims of paragraph 1 of this Article.

3. Member States shall, within four years from the date of entry into force of this Treaty, harmonize their tax laws, notably with regard to determination of rates and to the levels of indirect taxes other than customs duties, in order to favour the establishment of businesses in the Community.

4. Member States shall make every effort to integrate and interconnect their data-processing networks.

Article 70
Planning of Development, Statistics and Demography

1. To achieve the aims of collective subregional development the Member States agree to:

(a) harmonize and integrate their development plans;

(b) promote and execute Community projects;

(c) prepare subregional sectoral programmes in areas

of joint interest.

2. Accordingly the Member States shall:

(a) inform one another and the Secretary-General of national economic data likely to foster trade, stimulate joint projects or facilitate the establishment of similar economic units in Member States;

(b) exchange their experiences in planning, statistics and demography and in the basic and further training of cadres in these areas.

3. The Secretary-General shall formulate proposals for:

(a) harmonizing and rationalizing current statistics;

(b) promoting, developing, improving and standardizing economic, demographic, social and cultural information, *inter alia* by preparing national and subregional statistical projects.

4. The Secretary-General shall prepare statistics on inter-State trade and shall centralize and disseminate statistical information about the Community.

Chapter XVII

Special Provision in Respect of Land-locked, Island, Part-island, Semi-land-locked and/or Least Developed Countries

Article 71

1. Member States, aware of the special economic and social situation of land-locked, island, part-island and semi-land-locked countries, agree to grant them special treatment in respect of the application of some provisions hereof and in accordance herewith.

2. Accordingly, Member States agree to aid the efforts of land-locked, island, part-island and semi-land-locked countries in their desire to reduce the geographical handicaps as far as possible so as to improve and promote the establishment of an integrated transport and communications infrastructure, *inter alia* by facilitating their access to the sea.

Article 72

1. Member States, aware of the economic and social situation of the least developed countries, agree to grant them special treatment in respect of the application of some provisions hereof and in accordance herewith.

2. Member States shall accordingly support all measures likely to facilitate the promotion of their economic and social development.

Article 73

The Council shall order appropriate measures to facilitate the application of Articles 71 and 72 hereof.

Article 74

For the purposes of the application of this Chapter Member States agree to adopt a protocol on the situation of land-locked, island, part-island, semi-land-locked and/or least developed countries annexed hereto as Annex XVIII.

Chapter XVIII

Means and Instruments of Co-operation

Article 75

Establishment of the Community Co-operation and Development Fund

There is established a Community Co-operation and Development Fund.

Article 76

Aims of the Fund

The aims of the Fund are *inter alia* as follows:

(a) to provide financial and technical assistance to promote the economic and social development of Member States in the light of the various economic and other conditions within the Community;

(b) to finance projects in Member States.

Article 77

Constitution of the Fund

1. The constitution of the Fund shall be determined by the Conference.

2. The Constitution shall determine *inter alia* the share capital and the authorized resources of the Fund, Members' countributions, the rules governing the payment of contributions and the currencies in which they are payable, the operation, organization and management of the Fund and any related and subsidiary questions.

Article 78

Members of the Fund

Membership of the Fund shall be open to Member States of the Community and to institutions permitted by the Conference to affiliate to it.

Chapter XIX

Financial Provisions

Article 79

Budget of the Community

1. There is established an annual budget of the Community.

2. The Secretary-General shall prepare a draft budget for each financial year and submit it to the Council for consideration, which shall submit it, together with its recommendations, to the Conference for approval.

3. All the expenditure of the Community except for Fund-related expenditure shall be approved for each financial year by the Conference and charged to the budget.

4. The resources for the budget shall come from the annual contributions of Member States and all the other sources determined by the Conference. The contributions of Member States shall be determined on the basis of the budget approved by the Conference.

Article 80

Contribution of the Member States

1. The Conference shall determine the contributions of Member States to the Community budget and the currencies in which the contributions shall be paid.

2. Where a Member State is in arrears for more than one year in the payment of its contribution for reasons other than public or natural calamity or exceptional circumstances that gravely affect its economy, such Member States may, by a resolution of the Community, be suspended from taking part in the activities of the Community and shall cease to enjoy the benefits provided for hereunder.

Article 81

Financial Regulations

The Conference shall at the Council's proposal approve the financial regulations for the application of the provisions of this Chapter including the terms and conditions of employment and the powers of the auditors.

Article 82

Board of Auditors

A board of three auditors of the Community shall be appointed and discharged from its duties by the Conference at the Council's recommendation.

Chapter XX

Settlement of Disputes

Article 83

Procedure for the Settlement of Disputes

Any dispute regarding the interpretation and application of the provisions hereof shall in the first place be amicably settled by direct agreement between the parties concerned. In the event of failure to settle such disputes, the matter may be referred to the Court of Justice by a party to such dispute.

Chapter XXI

General and Transitional Provisions

Article 84

Headquarters of the Community

The Headquarters of the Community shall be determined by the Conference.

Article 85

Official Languages

The official languages of the Community shall be English, French, Portuguese and Spanish.

Article 86

Relationships of Member States with Other Groups and Third States

1. Member States may join other regional or subregional groups or conclude individual agreements with other Member or non-Member States provided that the joining of such groups or the agreements concluded with third States are not incompatible with the provisions hereof.

2. Any Member State which is or becomes a Member of other economic co-operation organizations shall inform the Secretary-General and transmit the constitutional instruments of such organizations to him. The Secretary-General shall notify the Council.

3. Right and obligations under agreements concluded before the definitive entry into force hereof shall not be affected by the provisions hereof.

However, in the event of such agreements being incompatible with the provisions hereof, each Member State concerned shall make every appropriate effort to eliminate the incompatibilities. Member States shall, if necessary, assist one another to achieve this aim and shall, if necessary, adopt a common attitude.

4. In the application of agreements coming under paragraph 1 of this Article, Member States shall take into account that the advantages granted herein by each Member State are an integral part of the establishment of the Community and are therefore indissolubly linked with the establishment of common institutions, the granting of powers to them and the granting of the same advantages by all the other Member States.

5. The Community shall maintain with the Organization of African Unity, the Economic Commission for Africa and other inter-governmental organizations of the subregion relations likely to enhance application of the provisions hereof.

Article 87

Legal Capacity, Privileges and Immunities

1. The Community shall have legal capacity and be authorized to:

(a) contract;

(b) purchase and assign movable and immovable property essential for the achievement of its objectives;

(c) borrow;

(d) be a party to legal proceedings;

(e) accept donations, legacies and gifts of every kind.

2. The Community shall be represented for this purpose by its Secretary-General.

The authority to contract, purchase and dispose of movable and immovable property and to borrow shall be vested in the Secretary-General subject to the prior consent of the Conference.

3. The privileges and immunities granted to Community officials shall be the same as those enjoyed by diplomats in the country of the Community Headquarters and in Member States. Similarly, the privileges and immunities granted to the General Secretariat shall be the same as those enjoyed by diplomatic missions in the country of the Community Headquarters and in the Member States.

Article 88

Establishment of Institutions

The Conference shall at its first meeting:

(a) appoint the Secretary-General and Deputy Secretaries-General;

(b) determine where the Community headquarters shall be and, if necessary, take the necessary mea-

sures to set up a temporary secretariat;

(c) give the Council and other Community institutions the directives needed for rapid and effective application hereof.

Article 89

Co-operation between the Community and Third States

1. Any African State wishing to conclude co-operation agreements with the Community shall make application to the Conference which, having taken the Council's advice, shall take a unanimous decision.

2. Such agreements shall be subject to ratification by Member States in accordance with their respective national legislations.

Article 90

Amendment

1. Any Member State may submit proposals for the amendment of this Treaty.

2. Amendment proposals shall be submitted to the Secretary-General who shall transmit them to Member States at the latest by 30 days after receiving them.

3. The Conference shall examine the proposals at its next meeting.

4. Amendments shall be adopted by consensus and shall be subject to the ratification of all Member States in accordance with their respective national legislations. They shall enter into force 30 days after deposit of the instruments of ratification by the seventh Member State.

Article 91

Withdrawal and Dissolution

1. Any Member State wishing to withdraw from the Community shall give the Chairman in Office of the Conference one year's written notice of its intention to withdraw. At the end of such period such Member State shall, if the notice is not withdrawn, cease to be a Member State of the Community.

2. During the period of one year referred to in paragraph 1 of this Article, a Member State wishing to withdraw from the Community shall nevertheless observe the provisions hereof and shall remain liable for the discharge of its obligations hereunder.

3. The withdrawal of one or more Member States shall not entail the dissolution of the Community.

4. Only the Conference may decide to dissolve the

Community and decide on the terms and conditions for distributing assets or liabilities.

Article 92

Annexes to the Treaty

The Annexes hereto shall form an integral part hereof.

Article 93

Entry into Force, Ratification and Accession

1. This Treaty shall be ratified by the High Contracting Parties in accordance with their respective national legislations. The instruments of ratification shall be deposited with the Government of . . . .

2. This Treaty shall enter into force thirty days after the deposit of the instruments of ratification by the seventh signatory State.

3. The terms and conditions of the accession of a State and the adaptations hereof caused by such accession shall be the subject of an agreement between the Community and the petitioning State.

This agreement shall be subject to ratification by all Member States in accordance with their respective national legislations.

4. This Treaty shall enter into force in relation to an acceding State on such date its instruments of accession are deposited.

Article 94

Depositary

1. This Treaty, drafted in single original in the English, French, Portuguese and Spanish languages, all four texts being equally authentic, shall be deposited in the archives of the Government of the Headquarters State, which shall transmit a certified true copy to the Government of every signatory State.

2. The depositary Government shall notify Member States of the dates of deposits of the instruments of ratification and accession and shall register this Treaty with the United Nations and the Organization of African Unity.

Memorandum of Understanding Between the United States of America and the Union of Soviet Socialist Republics on the US-USSR Direct Communications Link

Date of signature: July 17, 1984
Place of signature: Washington, DC
Signatory states: The United States of America, The Union of Soviet Socialist Republics
Date of entry into force: July 17, 1984

The Department of State, referring to the Memorandum of Understanding between the United States of America and the Union of Soviet Socialist Republics regarding the Establishment of a Direct Communications Link, signed June 20, 1963; to the Agreement on Measures to Improve the Direct Communications Link, signed September 30, 1971; and to the exchange of views between the two parties in Moscow and Washington during which it was deemed desirable to arrange for facsimile communication in addition to the current teletype Direct Communications Link, proposes that for this purpose the parties shall:

1. Establish and maintain three transmission links employing INTELSAT and STATSIONAR satellites and cable technology with secure orderwire circuit for operational monitoring. In this regard:

(a) Each party shall provide communication circuits capable of simultaneously transmitting and receiving 4800 bits per second.

(b) Operation of facsimile communication shall begin with the operation over the INTELSAT satellite channel as soon as development, procurement and delivery of the necessary equipment by the sides are completed.

(c) Facsimile communication via STASIONAR shall be established after transition of the Direct Communications Link teletype circuit from MOLNIYA to STATSIONAR using mutually agreeable transition procedures and after successful tests of facsimile communication via INTELSAT and cable.

2. Employ agreed-upon information security devices to assure secure transmission of facsimile materials. In this regard:

(a) The information security devices shall consist of microprocessor that will combine the digital of facsimile output with buffered random data read from standard 51/4 inch floppy disks. The American side shall provide a specification describing the key data format and necessary keying material resident on a floppy disk for both parties until such time as the Soviet side develops this capability. Beyond that time, each party shall provide necessary keying material to the other.

(b) The American side shall provide to the Soviet side the floppy disk drives integral to the operation of the microprocessor.

(c) The necessary security devices as well as spare parts for the said equipment shall be provided by the American side to the Soviet side in return for payment of costs thereof by the Soviet side.

3. Establish and maintain at each operating end of the Direct Communications Link facsimile terminals of the same make and model. In this regard:

(a) Each party shall be responsible for the acquisition, installation, operation and maintenance of its own facsimile machines, the related information security devices, and local transmission circuits appropriate to the implementation of this understanding, except as otherwise specified.

(b) A Group III facsimile unit which meets CCITT Recommendations T. 4 and T. 30 and operates at 4800 bits per second shall be used for this purpose.

(c) The necessary facsimile equipment as well as spare parts for the said equipment shall be provided to the Soviet side by the American side in return for payment of costs thereof by the Soviet side.

4. Establish and maintain secure orderwire communications necessary for coordination of facsimile operation. In this regard:

(a) The orderwire terminals used with the information security devices described in Paragraph 2(a) shall incorporate standard U.S.S.R. Cyrillic and United States Latin keyboards and cathode ray tube displays to permit telegraphic exchange of information between operators. The specific layout of the Cyrillic keyboard shall be as specified by the Soviet side.

(b) To coordinate the work of the facsimile equipment operators, an orderwire shall be configured so as to permit, prior to the transmission and reception of facsimile messages, the exchange of all information pertinent to the coordination of such messages.

(c) Orderwire message concerning facsimile transmis-

sions shall be encoded using the same information security devices specified in Paragraph 29a).

(d) The orderwire shall use the same modem and communications link as used for facsimile transmission.

(e) A printer shall be included to provide a record copy of all information exchanged on the orderwire.

(f) The necessary orderwire equipment as well as spare parts for the said equipment shall be provided by the American side to the Soviet side, in return for payment of costs thereof by the Soviet side.

5. Ensure the exchange of information necessary for the operation and maintenance of the facsimile system.

6. Take all possible measures to assure the continuous, secure and reliable operation of the facsimile equipment, information security devices and communications links including orderwire, for which each party is responsible in accordance with this agreement.

The Department of State also proposes that the parties, in consideration of the continuing advance in information and communications technology, conduct reviews as necessary regarding questions concerning improvement of the Direct Communications Link and its technical maintenance.

It is also proposed to note that the Memorandum of Understanding between the United States of America and the Union of Soviet Socialist Republics regarding the Establishment of a Direct Communications Link, signed on June 20, 1963, with the Annex thereto; the Agreement between the United States of America and the Union of the Soviet Socialist Republics on Measures to Improve the Direct Communications Link, with the Annex thereto, signed on September 30, 1971; those Understandings, with Attached Annexes, reached between the United States and Union of Soviet Socialist Republics delegations of technical specialists and experts signed on September 11, 1972, December 10, 1973, March 22, 1976, and the exchange of notes at Moscow on March 20 and April 29, 1975, constituting an Agreement Amending the Agreement of September 30, 1971, remain in force, except to the extent that their provisions are modified by this agreement.

If the foregoing is acceptable to the Soviet side, it is proposed that this note, together with the reply of the Embassy of the Union of Soviet Socialist Republic, shall constitute an agreement, effective on the date of the Embassy's reply.

Agreement for Cooperation Between the Government of the United States of America and the Government of the People's Republic of China Concerning Peaceful Uses of Nuclear Energy

Date of signature: July 23, 1985
Place of signature: Washington, DC
Signatory states: The United States, China

[The signatories],
Desiring to establish extensive cooperation in the peaceful uses of nuclear energy on the basis of mutual respect for sovereignty, non-interference in each other's internal affairs, equality and mutual benefit,

Noting that such cooperation is one between two nuclear weapon states,

Affirming their support of the objectives of the statute of the International Atomic Energy Agency (IAEA),

Affirming their intention to carry out such cooperation on a stable, reliable and predictable basis,

Mindful that peaceful nuclear activities must be undertaken with a view to protecting the international environment from radioactive, chemical and thermal contamination,

Have agreed as follows:

Article 1

Definitions

For the purposes of this agreement:

(1) "parties" means the Government of the United States of America and the Government of the People's Republic of China;

(2) "authorized person" means any individual or any entity under the jurisdiction of either party and authorized by that party to receive, possess, use, or transfer material, facilities or components;

(3) "person" means any individual or any entity subject to the jurisdiction of either party but does not include the parties to this agreement;

(4) "Peaceful purposes" include the use of information, technology, material, facilities and components in such fields as research, power generation, medicine, agriculture and industry but do not include use in research specifically on or development of any nuclear explosive device, or any military purpose;

(5) "material' means source material; special nuclear material or by product material, radioisotopes other than by product material, moderator material, or any other such substance so designated by agreement of the parties;

(6) "source material" means (i) uranium, thorium, or any other material so designated by agreement of the parties, or (ii) ores containing one or more of the foregoing materials, in such concentration as the parties may agree from time to time;

(7) "special nuclear material" means (i) plutonium, uranium 233, or uranium enriched in the isotope 235, or (ii) any other material so designated by agreement of the parties;

(8) "by product material" means any radioactive material (except special nuclear material) yielded in or made radioactive by exposure to the radiation incident to the process of producing or utilizing special nuclear material;

(9) "moderator material" means heavy water, or graphite or beryllium of a purity suitable for use in a reactor to slow down high velocity neutrons and increase the likelihood of further fission, or any other such material so designated by agreement of the parties;

(10) "high enriched uranium" means uranium enriched to twenty percent or greater in the isotope 235;

(11) "low enriched uranium" means uranium enriched to less than twenty percent in the isotope 235 ;

(12) "facility" means any reactor, other than one designed or used primarily for the formation of plutonium or uranium 233, or any other item so designated by agreement of the parties;

(13) "reactor" is defined in Annex I, which may be modified by mutual consent of the parties.

(14) "sensitive nuclear facility" means any plant designed or used primarily for uranium enrichment, reprocessing of nuclear fuel, heavy water production or fabrication of nuclear fuel containing plutonium;

(15) "component" means a component part of a facility or other item, so designated by agreement of

the parties;

(16) "major critical component" means any part or group of parts essential to the operation of a sensitive nuclear facility;

(17) "sensitive nuclear technology" means any information (including information incorporated in a facility or an important component) which is not in the public domain and which is important to the design, construction, fabrication, operation or maintenance of any sensitive nuclear facility, or such other information so designated by agreement of the parties.

Article 2

Scope of Cooperation

1. The parties shall cooperate in the use of nuclear energy for peaceful purposes in accordance with the provisions of this agreement. Each party shall implement this agreement in accordance with its respective applicable treaties, national laws, regulations and license requirements concerning the use of nuclear energy for peaceful purposes. The parties recognize, with respect to the observance of this agreement, the principle of international law that provides that a party may not invoke the provisions of its internal law as justification for its failure to perform a treaty.

2. Transfers of information, technology, material, facilities and components under this agreement may be undertaken directly between the parties or through authorized persons. Such cooperation shall be subject to this agreement and to such additional terms and conditions as may be agreed by the parties.

3. Material, facilities and components will be regarded as having been transferred pursuant to this agreement only upon receipt of confirmation by the supplier party, from the appropriate Government authority of the recipient party that such material, facilities or components will be subject to this agreement and that the proposed recipient of such material, facilities or components, if other than the recipient party, is an authorized person.

4. Any transfer of sensitive nuclear technology, sensitive nuclear facilities, or major critical components will, subject to the principles of this agreement, require additional provisions as an amendment to this agreement.

Article 3

Transfer of Information and Technology

Information and technology concerning the use of nuclear energy for peaceful purposes may be transferred. Transfers of such information and technology shall be that which the parties are permitted to transfer and may be accomplished through various means, including reports, data banks, computer programs, conferences, visits and assignments of persons to facilities. Fields which may be covered include, but shall not be limited to, the following:

(1) research, development, experiment, design, construction, operation, maintenance and use and retirement of reactors and nuclear fuel fabrication technology;

(2) the use of material in physical and biological research, medicine, agriculture and industry;

(3) nuclear fuel cycle research, development and industrial application to meet civil nuclear needs, including multilateral approaches to guaranteeing nuclear fuel supply and appropriate techniques for management of nuclear wastes;

(4) health, safety, environment, and research and development related to the foregoing;

(5) assessing the role nuclear power may play in international energy plans;

(6) codes, regulations and standards for the nuclear energy industry; and

(7) such other fields as may be agreed by the parties.

Article 4

Transfer of Material, Facilities and Components

1. Material, facilities and components may be transferred pursuant to this agreement for applications consistent with this agreement. Any special nuclear material to be transferred under this agreement shall be low enriched uranium except as provided in paragraph 4 of this Article.

2. Low enriched uranium may be transferred for use as fuel in reactors and reactor experiments, for conversion or fabrication, or for such other purposes as may be agreed by the parties.

3. The quantity of special nuclear material transferred under this agreement shall be the quantity which the parties agree is necessary for any of the following purposes: the loading of reactors or use in reactor experiments, the efficient and continuous operation of such reactors or conduct of such reactor experiments, and the accomplishment of such other purposes as may be agreed by the parties.

4. Small quantities of special nuclear material may

be transferred for use as samples, standards, detectors, targets, radiation sources and for such other purposes as the parties may agree.

Article 5

Retransfers, Storage, Reprocessing, Enrichment, Alteration, and No Use for Military Purposes

1. Material, facilities, components or special nuclear material transferred pursuant to this agreement and any special nuclear material produced through the use of such material or facilities may be retransferred by the recipient party, except that any such material, facility, components or special nuclear material shall not be retransferred to unauthorized persons or, unless the parties agree, beyond its territory.

2. Neither party has any plans to enrich to twenty percent or greater, reprocess, or alter in form or content material transferred pursuant to this agreement or material used in or produced through the use of any material or facility so transferred. Neither party has any plans to change locations for storage of plutonium, uranium 233 (except as contained in irradiated fuel elements), or high enriched uranium transferred pursuant to this agreement or used in or produced through the use of any material or facility so transferred. In the event that a party would like at some future time to undertake such activities, the parties will promptly hold consultations to agree on a mutually acceptable arrangement. The parties undertake the obligation to consider such activities favorably, and agree to provide pertinent information on the plans during the consultations. In as much as any such activities will be solely for peaceful purposes and will be in accordance with the provisions of this agreement, the parties will consult immediately and will seek agreement within six months on long-term arrangements for such activities. In the spirit of cooperation the parties agree not to act within that period of time. If such an arrangement is not agreed upon within that period of time, the parties will promptly consult for the purpose of agreeing on measures which they consider to be consistent with the provisions of the agreement in order to undertake such activities on an interim basis. The parties agree to refrain from actions which either party believes would prejudice the long-term arrangements for undertaking such activities or adversely affect cooperation under this agreement. The parties agree that the consultations referred to above will be carried out promptly and mutual agreement reached in a manner to avoid hampering, delay or undue interference in their respective nuclear programs. Neither party will

seek to gain commercial advantage. Nothing in this article shall be used by either party to inhibit the legitimate development and exploitation of nuclear energy for peaceful purposes in accordance with this agreement.

3. Material, facilities or components transferred pursuant to this agreement and material used in or produced through the use of any material facility or components so transferred shall not be used for any nuclear explosive device, for research specifically on or development of any nuclear explosive device, or for any military purpose.

Article 6

Physical Security

1. Each party shall maintain adequate physical security with respect to any material, facility or components transferred pursuant to this agreement and with respect to any special nuclear material used in or produced through the use of any material or facility so transferred.

2. The parties agree to the levels for the application of physical security set forth in Annex II, which levels may be modified by mutual consent of the parties. The parties shall maintain adequate physical security measures in accordance with such levels. These measures, as minimum protection measures, shall be comparable to the recommendation set forth in IAEA document INFCIRC/225/Revision 1 entitled "The Physical Protection of Nuclear Material", or in any revision of that document agreed to by the parties.

3. The parties shall consult at the request of either party regarding the adequacy of physical security measures maintained pursuant to this article.

4. Each party shall identify those agencies or authorities responsible for ensuring that levels of physical security are adequately met and having responsibility for coordinating response and recovery operations in the event of unauthorized use or handling of material subject to this article. Each party shall also designate points of contact within its national authorities to cooperate on matters of out-of-country transportation and other physical security matters of mutual concern.

Article 7

Cessation of Cooperation

1. Each party shall endeavor to avoid taking any actions that affect cooperation under this agreement. If either party at any time following entry into force

of this agreement does not comply with the provisions of this agreement, the parties shall promptly hold consultations on the problem, it being understood that the other party shall have the rights to cease further cooperation under this agreement.

2. If either party decides to cease further cooperation under this agreement, the parties shall make appropriate arrangements as may be required.

Article 8

Consultations

1. The parties shall consult at the request of either party regarding the implementation of this agreement, the development of further cooperation in the field of peaceful uses of nuclear energy, and other matters of mutual concern.

2. The parties recognize that this cooperation in the peaceful uses of nuclear energy is between two nuclear-weapon states and that bilateral safeguards are not required. In order to exchange experience, strengthen technical cooperation between the parties, ensure that the provisions of this agreement are effectively carried out, and enhance a stable, reliable, and predictable nuclear cooperation relationship, in connection with transfers of material, facilities and components under this agreement the parties will use diplomatic channels to establish mutually acceptable arrangements for exchanges of information and visits to material, facilities and components subject to this agreement.

3. The parties shall exchange views and information on the establishment and operation of their respective national accounting and control systems for source and special nuclear material subject to this agreement.

Article 9

Environmental Protection

The parties shall consult, with regard to activities under this agreement, to identify the international environmental implications arising from such activities and shall cooperate in protecting the international environment from radioactive, chemical or thermal contamination arising from peaceful nuclear cooperation under this agreement and in related matters of health and safety.

Article 10

Entry Into Force and Duration

1. This agreement shall enter into force on the date of mutual notifications of the completion of legal procedures by the parties and shall remain in force for a period of thirty years. This term may be extended by agreement of the parties in accordance with their respective applicable procedures.

2. Notwithstanding the suspension, termination or expiration of this agreement or any cooperation hereunder for any reason, the provisions of Articles 5, 6, 7, and 8 shall continue in effect so long as any material, facility or components subject to these Articles remain in the territory of the party concerned or any material, facility or components subject to these articles remain subject to that party's right to exercise jurisdiction or to direct disposition elsewhere.

South Pacific Nuclear Free Zone Treaty

Also known as: The Treaty of Rarotonga
Date of signature: August 6, 1985
Place of signature: Rarotonga
Signatory states: Australia, Cook Islands, Fiji, Kiribati, Nauru, New Zealand, Niue, Papua New Guinea, Solomon Islands, Tonga, Tuvalu, Vanuatu, Western Samoa
Ratification: Australia, Cook Islands, Fiji, Kiribati, Nauru, New Zealand, Niue, Papua New Guinea, Solomon Islands, Tuvalu, Vanuatu, Western Samoa
Date of entry into force: December 11, 1986

Preamble

The Parties to this Treaty

United in their commitment to a world at peace;

Gravely concerned that the continuing nuclear arms race presents the risk of nuclear war which would have devastating consequences for all people;

Convinced that all countries have an obligation to make every effort to achieve the goal of eliminating nuclear weapons, the terror which they hold for humankind and the threat which they pose to life on earth;

Believing that regional arms control measures can contribute to global efforts to reverse the nuclear arms race and promote the national security of each country in the region and the common security of all;

Determined to ensure, so far as lies within their power, that the bounty and beauty of the land and sea in their region shall remain the heritage of their peoples and their descendants in perpetuity to be enjoyed by all in peace;

Reaffirming the importance of the Treaty on the Non-Proliferation of Nuclear Weapons (NPT) in preventing the proliferation of nuclear weapons and in contributing to world security;

Noting, in particular, that Article VII of the NPT recognises the right of any group of States to conclude regional treaties in order to assure the total absence of nuclear weapons in their respective territories;

Noting that the prohibitions of emplantation and emplacement of nuclear weapons on the seabed and the ocean floor and in the subsoil thereof contained in the Treaty on the Prohibition of the Emplacement of Nuclear Weapons and Other Weapons of Mass Destruction on the Seabed and the Ocean Floor and in the Subsoil Thereof apply in the South Pacific;

Noting also that the prohibition of testing of nuclear weapons in the atmosphere or under water, including territorial waters or high seas, contained in the Treaty Banning Nuclear Weapon Tests in the Atmosphere, in Outer Space and Under Water applies in the South Pacific;

Determined to keep the region free of environmental pollution by radioactive wastes and other radioactive matter.

Guided by the decision of the Fifteenth South Pacific Forum at Tuvalu that a nuclear free zone should be established in the region at the earliest possible opportunity in accordance with the principles set out in the communique of that meeting;

Have Agreed as follows:

Article 1

Usage of Terms

For the purposes of this Treaty and its Protocols:

(a) "South Pacific Nuclear Free Zone" means the areas described in Annex 1 as illustrated by the map attached to that Annex;

(b) "territory" means internal waters, territorial sea and archipelagic waters, the seabed and subsoil beneath, the land territory and the airspace above them;

(c) "nuclear explosive device" means any nuclear weapon or other explosive device capable of releasing nuclear energy, irrespective of the purpose for which it could be used. The term includes such a weapon or device in unassembled and partly assembled forms, but does not include the means of transport or delivery of such a weapon or device if separable from and not an indivisible part of it;

(d) "stationing" means emplantation, emplacement, transportation on land or inland waters, stockpiling, storage, installation and deployment.

Article 2

Application of the Treaty

1. Except where otherwise specified, this Treaty and its Protocols shall apply to territory within the South Pacific Nuclear Free Zone.

2. Nothing in this Treaty shall prejudice or in any way affect the rights, or the exercise of the rights, of any State under international law with regard to freedom of the seas.

Article 3

Renunciation or Nuclear Explosive Devices

Each Party undertakes:

(a) not to manufacture or otherwise acquire, possess or have control over any nuclear explosive device by any means anywhere inside or outside the South Pacific Nuclear Free Zone;

(b) not to seek or receive any assistance in the manufacture or acquisition of any nuclear explosive device;

(c) not to take any action to assist or encourage the manufacture or acquisition of any nuclear explosive device by any State.

Article 4

Peaceful Nuclear Activities

Each Party undertakes:

(a) not to provide source or special fissionable material, or equipment or material especially designed or prepared for the processing, use or production of special fissionable material for peaceful purposes to:

(i) any non-nuclear-weapon State unless subject to the safeguards required by Article III.1 of the NPT, or

(ii) any nuclear-weapon States unless subject to applicable safeguards agreements with the International Atomic Energy Agency (IAEA).

Any such provision shall be in accordance with strict non-proliferation measures to provide assurance of exclusively peaceful non-explosive use;

(b) to support the continued effectiveness of the international non-proliferation system based on the NPT and the IAEA safeguards system.

Article 5

Prevention of Stationing of Nuclear Explosive Devices

1. Each Party undertakes to prevent in its territory the stationing of any nuclear explosive device.

2. Each Party in the exercise of its sovereign rights remains free to decide for itself whether to allow visits by foreign ships and aircraft to its ports and airfields, transit of its airspace by foreign aircraft, and navigation by foreign ships in its territorial sea or archipelagic waters in a manner not covered by the rights of innocent passage, archipelagic sea lane passage or transit passage of straits.

Article 6

Prevention of Testing of Nuclear Explosive Devices

Each Party undertakes:

(a) to prevent in its territory the testing of any nuclear explosive device;

(b) not to take any action to assist or encourage the testing of any nuclear explosive device by any State.

Article 7

Prevention of Dumping

1. Each Party undertakes:

(a) not to dump radioactive wastes and other radioactive matter at sea anywhere within the South Pacific Nuclear Free Zone;

(b) to prevent the dumping of radioactive wastes and other radioactive matter by anyone in its territorial sea;

(c) not to take any action to assist or encourage the dumping by anyone of radioactive wastes and other radioactive matter at sea anywhere within the South Pacific Nuclear Free Zone;

(d) to support the conclusion as soon as possible of the proposed Convention relating to the protection of the natural resources and environment of the South Pacific region and its Protocol for the prevention of pollution of the South Pacific region by dumping, with the aim of precluding dumping at sea of radioactive wastes and other radioactive matter by anyone anywhere in the region.

2. Paragraphs 1(a) and 1(b) of this Article shall not apply to areas of the South Pacific Nuclear Free Zone in respect of which such a Convention and Protocol have entered into force.

Article 8

Control System

1. The Parties hereby establish a control system for the purpose of verifying compliance with their obligations under this Treaty.

2. The control system shall comprise:

(a) reports and exchange of information as provided for in Article 9;

(b) consultations as provided for in Article 10 and Annex 4 (1);

(c) the application to peaceful nuclear activities of safeguards by the IAEA as provided for in Annex 2;

(d) a complaints procedure as provided for in Annex (4).

Article 9

Reports and Exchanges of Information

1. Each Party shall report to the Director of the South Pacific Bureau for Economic Co-operation (the Director) as soon as possible any significant event within its jurisdiction affecting the implementation of this Treaty. The Director shall circulate such reports promptly to all Parties.

2. The Parties shall endeavour to keep each other informed on matters arising under or in relation to this Treaty. They may exchange information by communicating it to the Director, who shall circulate it to all Parties.

3. The Director shall report annually to the South Pacific Forum on the states of this Treaty and matters arising under or in relation to it, incorporating reports and communications made under paragraphs 1 and 2

of this Article and matters arising under Articles 8(2)(d) and 10 and Annex 2(4).

Article 10

Consultations and Review

Without prejudice to the conduct of consultations among Parties by other means, the Director, at the request of any Party, shall convene a meeting of the Consultative Committee established by Annex 3 for consultation and co-operation on any matter arising in relation to this Treaty or for reviewing its operation.

Article 11

Amendment

The Consultative Committee shall consider proposals for amendment of the provisions of this Treaty proposed by any Party and circulated by the Director to all Parties not less than three months prior to the convening of the Consultative Committee for this purpose. Any proposal agreed upon by consensus by the Consultative Committee shall be communicated to the Director who shall circulate it for acceptance to all Parties. An amendment shall enter into force thirty days after receipt by the depository of acceptances from all Parties.

Article 12

Signature and Ratification

1. This Treaty shall be open for signature by any Member of the South Pacific Forum.

2. This Treaty shall be subject to ratification. Instruments or ratification shall be deposited with the Director who is hereby designated depository of this Treaty and its Protocols.

3. If a Member of the South Pacific Forum whose territory is outside the South Pacific Nuclear Free Zone becomes a Party to this Treaty, Annex 1 shall be deemed to be amended so far as is required to enclose at least the territory of that Party within the boundaries of the South Pacific Nuclear Free Zone. The

delineation of any area added pursuant to this paragraph shall be approved by the South Pacific Forum.

Article 13

Withdrawal

1. This Treaty is of a permanent nature and shall remain in force indefinitely, provided that in the event of a violation by any Party of a provision of this Treaty essential to the achievement of the objectives of the Treaty or of the spirit of the Treaty, every other Party shall have the right to withdraw from the Treaty.

2. Withdrawal shall be effected by giving notice twelve months in advance to the Director who shall circulate such notice to all other Parties.

Article 14

Reservations

This Treaty shall not be subject to reservations.

Article 15

Entry into Force

1. This Treaty shall enter into force on the date of deposit of the eighth instrument of ratification.

2. For a signatory which ratifies this Treaty after the date of deposit of the eighth instrument of ratification, the Treaty shall enter into force on the date of deposit of its instrument of ratification.

Article 16

Depository Functions

The depository shall register this Treaty and its Protocols pursuant to Article 102 of the Charter of the United Nations and shall transmit certified copies of the Treaty and its protocols to all Members of the South Pacific Forum and all States eligible to become Party to the Protocols to the Treaty and shall notify them of signatures and ratifications of the Treaty and its Protocols.

Agreement Between the UK and the USSR Concerning the Prevention of Incidents at Sea Beyond the Territorial Sea

Date of signature: July 15, 1986
Place of signature: London
Signatory states: The United Kingdom, The Union

of Soviet Socialist Republics
Date of entry into force: July 15, 1986

[The signatories],

Desiring to ensure the safety of navigation of the ships of their respective armed forces, and of the fight of their military aircraft beyond the territorial sea;

Acknowledging that actions prohibited by this Agreement should also not be taken against non-military ships of the Parties;

Guided by the principles and rules of international law;

Have agreed as follows;

Article I

For the purposes of this Agreement the following definitions shall apply:

1. 'Ship' means:

(a) a warship belonging to the armed forces of the Parties bearing the external marks distinguishing warships of its nationality, under the command of an officer duly commissioned by the Government and whose name appears in the appropriate service list or its equivalent, and manned by a crew who are under regular armed forces discipline; and

(b) auxiliary ships belonging to the armed forces of the Parties, which include all ships authorized to fly the auxiliary ship flag where such a flag has been established by either Party;

2. 'aircraft' means all military manned heavier-than-air lighter-than-air craft, excluding space craft.

3. 'formation' means an ordered arrangement of two or more ships proceeding in company and normally manoeuvring together.

This Agreement shall apply to ships and aircraft operating beyond the territorial sea.

Article II

The Parties shall take measures to instruct the Commanding Officers of their respective ships to observe strictly the letter and spirit of the 1972 International Regulations for Preventing Collision at Sea, hereinafter referred to as 'the 1972 Collision Regulations'. The Parties recognize that their freedom to conduct operations beyond the territorial sea is based on the principles established under recognized international law and codified in the 1958 Geneva Convention on the High Seas.

Article III

1. In the cases ships of the Parties operating in proximity to each other, except when required to maintain course and speed under the 1972 Collision Regulations, shall remain well clear to avoid risk of collision.

2. Ships meeting or operating in the vicinity of a formation of the other Party shall, while conforming to the 1972 Collision Regulations, avoid manoeuvring in a manner which would hinder the evolution of the formation.

3. Formation shall not conduct manoeuvres through areas of heavy traffic where internationally recognized traffic separation schemes are in effect.

4. Ships engaged in surveillance of ships of the other Party shall stay at a distance which avoids the risk of collision and shall also avoid executing maneuvers to maintain course and speed under the 1972 Collision Regulations, a surveillant shall take positive early action so as, in the exercise of good seamanship, not to embarrass or endanger ships under surveillance.

5. When ships of both Parties manoeuvre in sight of one another, such signals (flag, sound and light) as are prescribed by the 1972 Collision Regulations, the International Code of Signals and the Table of Special Signals set forth in the Annex to this Agreement shall be adhered to for signalling operations and intentions. At night or in conditions of reduced visibility, or under conditions of lighting and at such distances when signal flags are not distinct, flashing light or Very High Frequency Radio Channel 16 (156.8 MHz) should be used.

6. Ships of the Parties shall not simulate attacks by aiming guns, missile launcher, torpedo tubes and other weapons in the direction of passing ships of the other Party; nor launch any object in the direction of passing ships of the other Party in such a manner as to be hazardous to those ships or to constitute a hazard to navigation; nor use searchlights or other powerful illumination devices for the purpose of illuminating the navigation bridge of passing ships of the other Party.

Such actions shall also not be taken by ships of each Party against non-military ships of the other Party.

7. When conducting exercises with submerged submarines, supporting ships shall show the appropriate signals prescribed by the International Code of Signals, or in the Table of Special Signals set forth in the Annex to this Agreement, to warn ships of the presence of submarines in the area.

8. Ships of one Party when approaching ships of the other Party conducting operations which in accordance with Rule 3(g) of the 1972 Collision Regulations are restricted in their ability to manoeuvre, and parti-

cularly ships engaged in replenishment underlay, shall take appropriate measures not to hinder manoeuvres of such ships and shall remain well clear.

Article IV

1. Commanders of aircraft of the Parties shall use greatest caution and prudence in approaching aircraft and ships of the other Party, in particular ships engaged in launching or landing aircraft, and, in the interest of mutual safety, shall not permit simulated attacks by the simulated use of weapons against aircraft and ships of the other Party, or the performance of aerobatics over ships of the other Party, or dropping objects near them in such a manner as to be hazardous to ships or to constitute a hazard to navigation.

Such actions shall also not be taken by aircraft of each Party against non-military ships of the other Party.

2. Aircraft of the Parties flying in darkness or under instrument conditions shall, whenever feasible, display navigation lights.

Article V

The Parties shall take measures to notify the non-military ships of each Party about the provisions of this Agreement directed at securing mutual safety.

Article VI

The Parties shall provide through the established system of radio broadcasts of information and warning to mariners, normally not less than three to five days in advance, notification of actions beyond the territorial sea which represent a danger to navigation or to aircraft in flight.

Article VII

The Parties shall exchange in a timely manner appropriate information concerning instances of collisions, incidents which result in damage, and other incidents at sea between ships and aircraft of the Parties. The Royal Navy shall provide such information through the Soviet Naval or other Military Attache in London and the Soviet Navy shall provide such information through the British Naval or other Military Attache in Moscow.

Article VIII

This Agreement shall enter into force on the date of its signature. It may be terminated by either Party giving six months' written notice of termination to the other Party.

Article IX

Representatives of the Parties shall meet within one year after the date of the signing of this Agreement to review the implementation of its terms, as well as possible ways of promoting a higher level of safety of navigation of their ships and flight of their aircraft beyond the territorial sea. Similar consultations shall be held thereafter annually, or more frequently as the Parties may decide.

In witness whereof the undersigned, duly authorized thereto by their respective Governments, have signed this Agreement.

Annex

Table of Special Signals[1] Yankee Victor One (YV1)

The following signals are to be preceded by the above group:

Signal Meaning of Signals

Signal	Meaning of Signals
IR1	I am engaged in oceanographic operations
IR2(...)	I am streaming/towing hydrographic survey
IR3	I am recovering hydrographic survey equipment.
IR4	I am conducting salvage operations.
JH1	I am attempting to retract a grounded vessel.
MH1	Request you not cross my course ahead of me.
NB1(...)	I have my unattached hydrographic survey equipment bearing in a direction from me as indicated . . . (Table 3 of ICS)
PJ1	I am unable to alter course to my starboard.
PJ2	I am unable to alter course to my port.
PJ3	Caution, I have a steering casualty.
PP8(...)	Dangerous operations in progress. Request you keep clear of the direction indicated from me . . . (Table 3 of ICS)
QF1	Caution, I have stopped the engines.
QS6(...)	I am proceeding to anchorage on course . . .
QV2	I am in a fixed multiple leg moor using two or more anchors or buoys fore and aft. Request you remain clear.
QV3	I am anchored in deep water with hydrographic survey equipment streamed.
RT2	I intend to pass you on your port side.
RT3	I intend to pass you on your starboard side.
RT4	I will overtake you on port side.
RT5	I will overtake you on your starboard side.
RT6(...)	I am manoeuvring (or the formation is manoeuvring). Request you keep clear of

the direction indicated from me . . . (Table 3 of ICS).

RT7(...) I shall approach your ship on starboard side to a distance of . . . 100's of meters (yards).

RT8(...) I shall approach your ship on port side to distance of . . . 100's of meters (yards)

RT9(...) I shall cross altern at a distance of . . . 100's of meters (yards).

RU2(...) I am beginning a port turn in approximately . . . minutes.

RU3(...) I am beginning a starboard turn in approximately . . . minutes.

RU4 The formation is preparing to alter course to port.

RU5 The formation is preparing to alter course to starboard.

RU6 I am engaged in manoeuvring exercise. It is dangerous to be inside the formation.

RU7 I am preparing to submerge.

RU8 A submarine will surface within two miles of me within 30 minutes. Request you remain clear.

SL2 Request your course speed and passing intention.

TX1 I am engaged in fisheries patrol.

UY1(...) I am preparing to launch/recover aircraft on course . . .

UY2(...) I am preparing to conduct missile exercises. Request you keep clear of the direction

indicated from me . . . (Table 3 of ICS)

UY3(...) I am preparing to conduct gunnery exercises. Request you keep clear of the direction indicated from me . . . (Table 3 of ICS).

UY4(...) I am preparing to conduct/am conducting operations employing explosive charges.

UY5(...) I am manoeuvring in preparation for torpedo launching exercises in a direction from me as indicated . . . (Table 3 o ICS).

UY6(...) I am preparing to conduct/am conducting underlay replenishment on course . . . Request you remain clear.

UK7 I am preparing to conduct extensive small boat and ship to shore amphibious training operations.

UY8 I am manoeuvring to launch/recover landing craft/boasts.

UK9 I am preparing to conduct/am conducting helicopter operations over my stern.

UY10 I am checking gunnery systems.*

UY11 I am checking rocket systems.*

UY12 I am preparing to conduct/I am conducting/ gunnery exercises/bombing/by aircraft of the towed target. Request you keep clear of the direction indicated from me . . . (Table 3 of ISC).

ZL1 I have received and understood your signal.

ZL2 Do you understand? Request acknowledgement.

Indo-Sri Lanka Agreement to Establish Peace and Normalcy in Sri Lanka

Date of signature: July 29,1987
Place of signature: Colombo, Sri Lanka
Signatory states: India, Sri Lanka

[The signatories],

Attaching utmost importance to nurturing, intensifying and strengthening the traditional friendship of Sri Lanka and India, and acknowledging the imperative need of resolving the ethnic problem of Sri Lanka, and the consequent violence, and for the safety, well-being and prosperity of people belonging to all communities in Sri Lanka;

Have this day entered into the following agreement to fulfill this objective.

1. In This Context,

1.1 Desiring to preserve the unity, sovereignty and

territorial intergrity of Sri Lanka:

1.2 Acknowledging that Sri Lanka is a multi-ethnic and a multi-lingual plural society consisting, *inter alia*, of Sinhalese, Tamils, Muslims (moors), and Burghers:

1.3 Recognising that each ethnic group has a distinct cultural and linguistic identity which has to be carefully nurtured:

1.4 Also recognising that the northern and the eastern provinces have been areas of historical habitation of Sri Lanka Tamil speaking peoples, who have at all times hitherto lived together in this territory with other ethnic groups:

1.5 Conscious of the necessity of strengthening the forces contributing to the unity, sovereignty and territorial integrity of Sri Lanka, and preserving its character as a multi-ethnic, multi-lingual and multi-religious plural society in which all citizens can live in equality, safety and harmony, and prosper and fulfill their aspirations:

2. *Resolve that:*

2.1 Since the government of Sri Lanka proposes to permit adjoining provinces to join to form one administrative unit and also by a referendum to separate as may be permitted to the northern and eastern provinces as outlined below:

2.2 During the period, which shall be considered an interim period, (i.e., from the date of the elections to the provincial council, as specified in para 2.8 to the date of the referendum as specified in para 2.3, the northern and eastern provinces as now constituted, will form one administrative unit, having one elected provincial council. Such a unit will have one Governor, one Chief Minister and one Board of Ministers.

2.3 There will be a referendum on or before 31st December, 1988 to enable the people of the eastern province to decide whether:

(a) The Eastern province should remain linked with the Northern province as one administrative unit, and continue to be governed together with the Northern province as specified in para 2.2 or

(b) The Eastern province should constitute a separate administrative unit having its own distinct provincial council with a separate Governor, Chief Minister and Board of Ministers.

The President may, at his discretion, decide to postpone such a referendum.

2.4 All persons who have been displaced due to ethnic violence, or other reasons, will have the right to vote in such a referendum. Necessary conditions to enable them to return to areas from where they were displaced will be created.

2.5 The referendum, when held, will be monitored by a committee headed by the Chief Justice, a member appointed by the President, nominated by the government of Sri Lanka, and a member appointed by the President, nominated by the representatives of the Tamil speaking people of the eastern province.

2.6 A simple majority will be sufficient to determine the result of the referendum.

2.7 Meetings and other forms of propaganda, permissible within the laws of the country, will be allowed before the referendum.

2.8 Elections to provincial councils will be held within the next three months, in any event before 31st December 1987. Indian observers will be invited for elections to the provincial council of the North and East.

2.9 The emergency will be lifted in the eastern and northern provinces by August 15, 1987. A cessation of hostilities will come into effect all over the island within 48 hours of the signing of this agreement. All arms presently held by militant groups will be surrendered in accordance with an agreed procedure to authorities to be designated by the government of Sri Lanka.

Consequent to the cessation of hostilities and the surrender of arms by militant groups, the army and other security personnel will be confined to barracks in camps as on 25 May 1987. The process of surrendering of arms and the confining of security personnel moving back to barracks shall be completed within 72 hours of the cessation of hostilities coming into effect.

2.10 The government of Sri Lanka will utilise for the purpose of law enforcement and maintenance of security in the northern and eastern provinces same organizations and mechanisms of government as are used in the rest of the country.

2.11 The President of Sri Lanka will grant a general amnesty to political and other prisoners now held in custody under the prevention of terrorism act and other emergency laws, and to combatants. As well as to those persons accused, charged and/or convicted under these laws. The Government of Sri Lanka will make special efforts to rehabilitate militant youth with a view to bringing them back into the mainstream of national life. India will cooperate in the process.

2.12 The Government of Sri Lanka will accept and abide by the above provisions and expect all others to do likewise.

2.13 If the framework for the resolutions is accepted, the Government of Sri Lanka will implement the relevant proposals forthwith.

2.14 The Government of India will underwrite and guarantee the resolutions, and co-operate in the implementation of these proposals.

2.15 These proposals are conditional to an acceptance of the proposals negotiated from 4.5.1986 to 19.12.1986. Residual matters not finalised during the above negotiations shall be resolved between India and Sri Lanka within a period of six weeks of signing this agreement. These proposals are also conditional to the Government of India co-operating directly with the government of Sri Lanka in their implementations.

2.16 These proposals are also conditional to the Government of India taking the following actions if any militant groups operating in Sri Lanka do not accept this framework of proposals for a settlement, namely:

(a) India will take all necessary steps to ensure that Indian territory is not used for activities prejudicial to the unity, integrity and security of Sri Lanka.

(b) The Indian navy/coast guard will co-operate with the Sri Lanka navy in preventing Tamil militant activites from affecting Sri Lanka.

(c) In the event that the government of Sri Lanka requests the government of India to afford military assistance to implement these proposals the Government of India will co-operate by giving to the Government of Sri Lanka such military assistance as and when requested.

(d) The government of India will expedite repatriation from Sri Lanka of Indian citizens to India who are resident here, concurrently with the repatriation of Sri Lanka refugees from Tamil Nadu.

(e) The Governments of Sri Lanka and India will co-operate in ensuring the physical security and safety of all communities inhabiting the Northern and Eastern provinces.

2.17 The Government of Sri Lanka shall ensure free, full and fair participation of voters from all communities in the Northern and Eastern provinces in electoral processes envisaged in this agreement. The Government of India will extend full co-operation to the Government of Sri Lanka in this regard.

2.18 The official language of Sri Lanka shall be Sinhala. Tamil and English will also be official languages.

3. This agreement and the Annexure thereto shall come into force upon signature.

Text of Agreements by the Presidents of Central America

Date of signature: August 7, 1987
Place of signature: Guatemala City
Signatory states: Costa Rica, El Salvador, Guatemala, Honduras, Nicaragua

Preamble

The Presidents of the Republics of Guatemala, El Salvador, Honduras, Nicaragua and Costa Rica, meeting in Guatemala City on August 6-7, 1987, encouraged by the farsighted and steadfast desire for peace of the Contadora and the Support Groups, strengthened by the firm support of all the governments and peoples of the world, and their priciple international organizations—particularly the European Economic Community and His Holiness John Paul II—based on the Declaration of Esquipulas I, and coming together in Guatemala to discuss the peace plan presented by the Government of Costa Rica, have decided:

To face fully the historic challenge of forging a peaceful future for Central America,

To undertake the commitment to fight for peace and eliminate war,

To make dialogue prevail over violence, and reason over rancor,

To dedicate these efforts for peace to the youth of Central America, whose legitimate aspirations for peace, social justice, freedom and reconciliation have been frustrated for many generations,

To make the Central American Parliament a symbol for the freedom, independence and reconciliation to which Central America aspires.

We ask for respect and assistance from the international community for our efforts,

We have Central American avenues for peace and development, but we need help to make them effective. We ask for an international treatment that will ensure development so that the peace we seek will be lasting,

We repeat firmly that peace and development are inseparable,

We thank President Vinicio Cerezo Arévalo and the noble people of Guatemala for hosting this meeting.

The generosity of the President and people of Guatemala were decisive elements in creating the climate in which the peace agreements were adopted.

Procedure for Establishing Firm and Lasting Peace in Central America

The governments of the Republics of Costa Rica, El Salvador, Guatemala, Honduras and Nicaragua, determined to achieve the objectives and to develop the principles established in the Charter of the United Nations, the Charter of the Organization of American States, the Document of Objectives, the Message of Caraballeda for Peace, Security and Democracy in Central America, the Declaration of Guatemala, the Communique of Punta del Este, the Message of Panama, the Declaration of Esquipulas, and the draft Contadora Act for Peace and Cooperation in Central America of June 6, 1986, have agreed on the following procedure to establish firm and lasting peace in Central America.

1. National Reconciliation

A. Dialogue

To undertake on an urgent basis, in those cases where deep divisions have occurred in society, actions for national reconciliation that will permit the participation of the people, with full guarantees in genuine democratic political processes, on the basis of justice, freedom and democracy, and to that end, to establish mechanisms that will make dialogue with opposing groups possible under the law.

For this purpose, the governments involved shall initiate a dialogue with all unarmed internal political opposition groups and with those that have availed themselves of amnesty.

B. Amnesty

In each Central American country, except those where the International Commission for Verification and Fol-

low-up determines that it is not necessary, decrees for amnesty shall be issued that will establish all of the provisions to ensure inviolability of life, freedom in all of its forms, material property and safety of the persons to whom those decrees are applicable. Simultaneously with the issuance of the amnesty decrees, the irregular forces of the country concerned shall release all prisoners under their control.

C. National Commission of Reconciliation

To verify compliance with the commitments that the five Central American Governments undertake by signing this document, regarding amnesty, cease-fire, democratization and free elections, a National Commission of Reconciliation shall be established that will have the duties of verifying the actual carrying out of the national reconciliation process, and the unrestricted respect for all the civil and political rights of Central American citizens that are guaranteed in this document.

The National Commission of Reconciliation shall be composed of a principal and alternate delegate representing the Executive Branch, a principal and alternate delegate suggested by the Episcopal Conference and selected by the Government from a panel of three bishops to be submitted within fifteen days after receipt of the formal invitation. This invitation shall be issued by the governments within five working days following the signature of this document. The same procedure using a panel of three shall be employed to select a principal and alternative representative of the legally-registered political opposition parties. The panel of three shall be submitted by the same deadline mentioned above. Each Central American Government shall also select as a member of that committee an outstanding citizen and an alternate for him who are not members either of the government or of the government's party. The decision or decree establishing the National Commission shall be reported immediately to the other Central American governments.

2. Exhortation for the Cessation of Hostilities

The governments strongly urge the countries in the area that are now undergoing attacks by irregular or insurgent groups to agree to ceasing hostilities. The governments of those countries undertake to carry out all actions required to achieve an effective cease-fire under the constitutional framework.

3. Democratization

The governments commit themselves to promote an authentic participatory and pluralistic democratic process involving promotion of social justice, respect for human rights, sovereignty, territorial integrity of the States, and the right of all nations to determine freely and without outside interference of any kind their economic, political and social models, and they shall take in a verifiable manner measures that are conducive to the establishment, and where necessary, the improvement of democratic, representative and pluralistic systems that guarantee the organization of political parties and effective participation of the people in decision-making and that ensure free access of different currents of opinion to honest periodic elections, based on the full observance of the rights of citizens.

In order to verify the good faith in the carrying out of this process of democratization, it shall be understood that:

(a) There shall be freedom of the press, radio and television. This complete freedom shall include opening and keeping in operation mass media communications for all ideological groups and operating those media without subjecting them to prior censorship.

(b) There shall be total pluralism of political parties. In this regard, political groups shall have full access to the mass media, shall enjoy fully the right of association and the right of public assembly in the unrestricted exercise of oral, written and televised publicity, as well as freedom of movement for the members of political parties in their efforts to proselytize.

(c) In addition, the Central American Government that has put in effect a state of exception, siege of emergency, shall lift it and shall put into effect the rule of law with full observance of all constitutional guarantees.

4. Free Elections

Having established the conditions inherent in any democracy, there shall be free, pluralistic and honest elections.

As a joint expression of the Central American countries to find reconciliation and lasting peace for their peoples, elections shall be held to select members of the Central American Parliament, whose establishment was proposed by the "Declaration of Esquipulas" of May 25, 1986.

For the above purposes, the Presidents expressed their resolve to proceed in organizing this Parliament, for which purpose the Preparatory Commission of the Central American Parliament shall conclude its deliberations and submit to the Central American Presidents the respective Draft Treaty within 150 days.

These elections shall be held simultaneously in all the countries of Central America in the first half of 1988 on a date that shall be agreed upon at the proper time by the Presidents of the Central American States. The elections shall be monitored by the appropriate electoral bodies, and the governments concerned commit themselves to extend invitations to the Organization of American States, the United Nations, and the Governments of third states, to send observers who shall verify that the electoral processes have been carried out in accordance with the strictest rules of equal access for all political parties to the social communication media, and to ample facilities to hold public meetings and to conduct any other kind of proselytizing propaganda.

So that the elections for members of the Central American Parliament are held within the period indicated in this section, the constituent treaty shall be submitted to the five countries for approval of ratification.

After the elections for the Central American Parliament are held, there shall take place in each country, with international observers and the same guarantees, within the deadlines set and the schedules that shall be proposed under the current political constitutions, equally free and democratic elections to select people's representatives in the municipalities, congresses and legislative assemblies, and the Presidency of the Republic.

5. Cessation of Assistance to Irregular Forces or to Insurrectional Movements

The Governments of the five Central American States shall request the Governments in the region and the governments outside the region that overtly, or covertly provide assistance, be it military, logistic, financial propagandist, in manpower, armament, munitions, and equipment to irregular forces or insurrectionist movements, to cease such assistance, as an indispensable element for achieving stable and durable peace in the region.

Not included in the foregoing is assistance for repatriation, or in its place, relocation and the assistance necessary for the return to normal life of those persons who were members of such groups or forces. In addition, irregular forces and insurgent groups operating in Central America shall be requested to refrain from receiving such assistance, for the sake of an authentic Latin American spirit. These requests shall be made pursuant to the provisions of the Document of Objectives regarding the elimination of the traffic in arms, whether within the region or from outside the region, intended for persons, organizations or groups that attempt to destabilize the governments of the Central American countries.

6. Non-use of Territory for Aggression Against Other States

The five countries signing this document reiterate their commitment to deny the use of their own territory to, and not to provide or permit logistic military support for persons, organizations or groups that seek to destabilize the governments of the Central American countries.

7. Negotiation on Matters of Security, Verification and Limitation of Armaments

The Governments of the five Central American States with the participation of the Contadora Group, in the exercise of its role as mediator, shall continue negotiations on points still pending of agreement regarding matters of security, verification and control in the Draft Act of Contadora for Peace and Cooperation in Central America.

These negotiations shall also cover measures for the disarmament of the irregular forces that are ready to avail themselves of the amnesty decrees.

8. Refugees and Displaced Persons

The Central American Governments commit themselves to provide urgent relief to the flows of refugees or displaced persons that the regional crisis has brought about, by furnishing protection and assistance particularly in areas of health, education, employment and security, and to facilitate their repatriation, resettlement or relocation, provided that it is voluntary and is requested individually.

They also commit themselves to seek assistance from the international community for Central American refugees and displaced persons, both directly under bilateral or multilateral agreements, and through the United Nations High Commissioner for Refugees

(UNHCR) and other agencies and organizations.

9. Cooperation, Democracy and Freedom for Peace and Development

In the climate of freedom that democracy ensure, the Central American countries shall take decisions to accelerate development in order to achieve societies that are more egalitarian and free from poverty.

Consolidation of democracy involves the establishment of an economy of wellbeing and an economic and social democracy. To achieve these objectives, the governments shall jointly make arrangements to obtain special economic assistance from the international community.

10. International Follow-up and Verification

A. International Commission for Verification and Follow-up

An International Commission for Verification and Follow-up shall be established composed of the Secretary Generals, or their representatives, of the Organization of American States and the United Nations, and the Ministers of Foreign Affairs of Central America, the Contadora Group and the Support Group. This Commission shall have the duty of verification and follow-up on compliance with the commitments set forth in this document.

B. Support for and Facilitation of the Mechanisms for Reconciliation and for Verification and Follow-up

In order to strengthen the actions of the International Commission for Verification and Follow-up, the Governments of the five Central American States shall issue declarations supporting its work. These declarations may be endorsed by any countries interested in promoting the cause of freedom, democracy and peace in Central America.

The five governments shall provide all the facilities needed for proper performance of the duties of verification and follow-up by the National Commission of Reconciliation of each country and the International Commission for Verification and Follow-up.

11. Schedule of Execution of Agreements

Within a period of fifteen days from the signature of this document, the Ministers of Foreign Affairs of Central America shall meet as an Executive Commission to establish regulations, promote and make viable the implementation of the commitments contained in this document, and to organize the working committees so that, beginning on that date, the processes that will lead to compliance with the commitments contracted shall be initiated within the stipulated deadlines, by means of consultations, negotiations and any other mechanisms deemed necessary.

Within ninety days following the signature of this document the commitments relating to amnesty, cease-fire, democratization, cessation of aid to irregular forces or to insurrectional movements, and the non-use of territory for aggression against other states, as defined in this document, shall enter into force simultaneously and publicly.

Within one hundred and twenty days following signature of this document, the International Commission for Verification and Follow-up shall review the progress made in complying with the agreements set forth in this document.

Within one hundred and fifty days, the five Central American presidents shall meet and shall receive a report from the International Commission for Verification and Follow-up and shall make the pertinent decisions.

Final Provisions

The points contained in this document comprise an harmonious and indivisible whole. The signing of the document involves the obligation, accepted in good faith, of complying simultaneously with the agreements entered into within the stipulated deadlines.

Agreement Between the United States of America and the Union of Soviet Socialist Republics on the Establishment of Nuclear Risk Reduction Centers

Date of signature: September 15, 1987
Place of signature: Washington
Signatory states: the United States of America, the Union of Soviet Socialist Republics
Date of entry into force: September 15, 1987

[The signatories], hereinafter referred to as the Parties,

Affirming their desire to reduce and ultimately eliminate the risk of outbreak of nuclear war, in particular, as a result of misinterpretation, miscalculation, or accident,

Believing that a nuclear war cannot be won and must never be fought,

Believing that agreement on measures for reducing the risk of outbreak of nuclear war serves the interests of strengthening international peace and security,

Reaffirming their obligations under the Agreement on Measures to Reduce the Risk of Outbreak of Nuclear War between the United States of America and the Union of Soviet Socialist Republics of September 30, 1971, and the Agreement between the Government of the United States of America and the Government of the Union of Soviet Socialist Republics on the Prevention of Incidents on and over the High Seas of May 25, 1972,

Have agreed as follows:

Article 1

Each Party shall establish, in its capital, a national Nuclear Risk Reduction Center that shall operate on behalf of and under the control of its respective Government.

Article 2

The Parties shall use the Nuclear Risk Reduction Centers to transmit notifications identified in Protocol I which constitutes an integral part of this Agreement.

In the future, the list of notifications transmitted through the Centers may be altered by agreement between the Parties, as relevant new agreements are reached.

Article 3

The Parties shall establish a special facsimile communications link between their national Nuclear Risk Reduction Centers in accordance with Protocol II which constitutes an integral part of this Agreement.

Article 4

The Parties shall staff their national Nuclear Risk Reduction Centers as they deem appropriate, so as to ensure their normal functioning.

Article 5

The Parties shall hold regular meetings between representatives of the Nuclear Risk Reduction Centers at least once each year to consider matters related to the functioning of such Centers.

Article 6

This Agreement shall not affect the obligations of either Party under other agreements.

Article 7

This Agreement shall enter into force on the date of its signature.

The duration of this Agreement shall not be limited.

This Agreement may be terminated by either Party upon 12 months written notice to the other Party.

PROTOCOL I

To the Agreement between the United States of America and the Union of Soviet Socialist Republics on the Establishment of Nuclear Risk Reduction Centers

Pursuant to provisions and in implementation of the Agreement between the United States of America and the Union of Soviet Socialist Republics on the Establishment of Nuclear Risk Reduction Centers, the Parties have agreed as follows:

Article 1

The Parties shall transmit the following types of notifications through the Nuclear Risk Reduction Centers:

(a) notifications of ballistic missile launches under Article 4 of the Agreement on Measures to Reduce the Risk of Outbreak of Nuclear War between the United States of America and the Union of Soviet Socialist Republics of September 30, 1971;

(b) notifications of ballistic missile launches under paragraph 1 of Article 6 of the Agreement between the Government of the United States of America and the Government of the Union of Soviet Socialist Republics on the Prevention of Incidents on and over the High Seas of May 25, 1972.

Article 2

The scope and format of the information to be transmitted through the Nuclear Risk Reduction Cen-

ters shall be agreed upon.

Article 3

Each Party also may, at its own discretion as a display of good will and with a view to building confidence, transmit through the Nuclear Risk Reduction Centers communications other than those provided for under Article 1 of this Protocol.

Article 4

Unless the Parties agree otherwise, all communications transmitted through and communications procedures of the Nuclear Risk Reduction Centers' communication link will be confidential.

Article 5

This Protocol shall enter into force on the date of its signature and shall remain in force as long as the Agreement between the United States of America and the Union of Soviet Socialist Republics on the Establishment of Nuclear Risk Reduction Centers of September 15, 1987, remains in force.

PROTOCOL II

To the Agreement between the United States of America and the Union of Soviet Socialist Republic on the Establishment of Nuclear Reduction Centers

Pursuant to the provisions and in implementation of the Agreement between the United States of America and the Union of Soviet Socialist Republics on the Establishment of Nuclear Risk Reduction Centers, the Parties have agreed as follows:

Article 1

To establish and maintain for the purpose of providing direct facsimile communications between their national Nuclear Risk Reduction Centers, established in accordance with Article 1 of this Agreement, hereinafter referred to as the national Centers, an INTELSAT satellite circuit and a STATSIONAR satellite circuit, each with a secure orderwire communications capability for operational monitoring. In this regard:

(a) There shall be terminals equipped for communication between the national Centers;

(b) Each Party shall provide communications circuits capable of simultaneously transmitting and receiving 4800 bits per second;

(c) Communication shall begin with test operation of the INTELSAT satellite circuit, as soon as purchase, delivery and installation of the necessary equipment by the Parties are completed. Thereafter, taking into account the results of test operations, the Parties shall agree on the transition to a fully operational status;

(d) To the extent practicable, test operation of the STATSIONAR satellite circuit shall begin simultaneously with test operation of the INTELSAT satellite circuit. Taking into account the results of test operations, the Parties shall agree on the transition to a fully operational status.

Article 2

To employ agreed-upon information security devices to assure secure transmission of facsimile messages. In the regard:

(a) The information security devices shall consist of microprocessors that will combine the digital message output with buffered random data read from standard 5 1/4 inch floppy disks;

(b) Each Party shall provide, through its Embassy, necessary keying material to the other.

Article 3

To establish and maintain at each operating end of the two circuits, facsimile terminals of the same make and model. In this regard:

(a) Each Party shall be responsible for the purchase, installation, operation and maintenance of its own terminals, the related information security devices, and local transmission circuits appropriate to the implementation of this Protocol;

(b) A Group III facsimile unit which meets CCITT Recommendations T.4 and T.30 and operates at 4800 bits per second shall be used;

(c) Direct facsimile messages from the USSR national Center to the U.S. national Center shall be transmitted and received in the Russian language, and from the U.S. national Center to the USSR national Center in the English language;

(d) Transmission and operating procedures shall be in conformity with procedures employed on the Direct Communications Link and adapted as necessary for the purpose of communications between the national Centers.

Article 4

To establish and maintain a secure orderwire communications capability necessary to coordinate facsimile operation. In this regard:

(a) The orderwire terminals used with the information security devices described in paragraph (a) of Article 2 shall incorporate standard USSR Cyrillic and United States Latin keyboards and cathode ray tube displays to permit the exchange of messages between operators. The specific layout of the Cyrillic keyboard shall be as specified by the Soviet side;

(b) To coordinate the work of operators, the orderwire shall be configured so as to permit, prior to the transmission and reception of messages, the exchange of all information pertinent to the coordination of such messages;

(c) Orderwire messages concerning transmissions shall be encoded using the same information security devices specified in paragraph (a) of Article 2;

(d) The orderwire shall use the same modem and communications link as used for facsimile message transmission;

(e) A printer shall be included to provide a record copy of all information exchange on the orderwire.

Article 5

To use the same type of equipment and the same maintenance procedures as currently in use for the Direct Communications Link for the establishment of direct facsimile communications between the national Centers. The equipment, security devices, and spare parts necessary for telecommunications links and the orderwire shall be provided by the United States side to the Soviet side in return for payment of costs thereof by the Soviet side.

Article 6

To ensure the exchange of information necessary for the operation and maintenance of the telecommunication system and equipment configuration.

Article 7

To take all possible measures to assure the continuous, secure and reliable operation of the equipment and communications link, including the orderwire, for which each Party is responsible in accordance with this Protocol.

Article 8

To determine, by mutual agreement between technical experts of the Parties, the distribution and calculation of expenses for putting into operation the communication link, its maintenance and further development.

Article 9

To convene meetings of technical experts of the Parties in order to consider initially questions pertaining to the practical implementation of the activities provided for in this Protocol and, thereafter, by mutual agreement and as necessary for the purpose of improving telecommunications and information technology in order to achieve the mutually agreed functions of the national centers.

Article 10

This Protocol shall enter into force on the date of its signature and shall remain in force as long as the Agreement between the United States of America and the Union of Soviet Socialist Republics on the Establishment of Nuclear Risk Reduction Centers of September 15, 1987, remains in force.

Treaty Between the United States of America and the Union of Soviet Socialist Republics on the Elimination of their Intermediate-Range and Shorter-Range Missiles

Also known as: INF Treaty
Date of signature: *December 8, 1987*
Place of signature: *Washington*
Signatory states: *The United States, The Union of Soviet Socialist Republics*
Date of entry into force: *June 1, 1988*

[The signatories], hereinafter referred to as the Parties,

Conscious that nuclear war would have devastating consequences for all mankind,

Guided by the objective of strengthening strategic stability,

Convinced that the measures set forth in this Treaty will help to reduce the risk of outbreak of war and strengthen international peace and security, and

Mindful of their obligations under Article VI of the Treaty on the Non-Proliferation of Nuclear Weapons,

Have agreed as follows:

Article 1

In accordance with the provisions of this Treaty which includes the Memorandum of Understanding and Protocols which form an integral part thereof, each Party shall eliminate its intermediate-range and shorter-range missiles, not have such systems thereafter, and carry out the other obligations set forth in this Treaty.

Article 2

For the purposes of this Treaty:

1. The term "ballistic missile" means a missile that has a ballistic trajectory over most of its flight path. The term "ground-launched ballistic missile (GLBM)" means a ground-launched ballistic missile that is a weapon-delivery vehicle.

2. The term "cruise missile" means an unmanned, self-propelled vehicle that sustains flight through the use of aerodynamic lift over most of its flight path. The term "ground-launched cruise missile (GLCM)" means a ground-launched cruise missile that is a weapon-delivery vehicle.

3. The term "GLBM launcher" means a fixed launcher or a mobile land-based transporter-erector-launcher mechanism for launching a GLBM.

4. The term "GLBM launcher" means a fixed launcher or a mobile land-based transporter-erector-launcher mechanism for launching a GLBM.

5. The term "intermediate-range missile" means a GLBM or a GLBM having a range capability in excess of 1,000 kilometers but not in excess of 5,500 kilometers.

6. The term "shorter-range missile" means a GLBM or a GLBM having a range capability equal to or in excess of 500 kilometers but not in excess of 1,000 kilometers.

7. The term "deployment area" means a designated area within which intermediate-range missiles and launchers of such missiles may operate and within which one or more missile operating bases are located.

8. The term "missile operating base" means:

(a) in the case of intermediate-range missiles, a complex of facilities, located within a deployment area, at which intermediate-range missiles and launchers of such missiles normally operate, in which support structures associated with such missiles and launchers are also located and in which support equipment associated with such missiles and launchers is normally located; and

(b) in the case of shorter-range missiles, a complex of facilities, located any place, at which shorter-range missiles and launchers of such missiles normally operate and in which support equipment associated with such missiles and launchers is normally located.

9. The term "missile support facility," as regards intermediate-range or shorter-range missiles and launchers of such missiles, means a missile production facility or a launcher production facility, a missile repair facility or a launcher repair facility, a training facility, a missile storage facility or a launcher storage facility, a test range, or an elimination facility as those terms are defined in the Memorandum of Understanding.

10. The term "transit" means movement, notified in accordance with paragraph 5(f) of Article IX of this Treaty, of an intermediate-range missile or a launcher of such a missile between missile support facilities, between such a facility and a deployment area or between deployment areas, or of a shorter-range missile or a launcher of such a missile from a missile support facility or a missile operating base to an elimination facility.

11. The term "deployed missile" means an intermediate-range missile located within a deployment area or a shorter-range missile located outside a missile operating base.

12. The term "non-deployed missile " means an intermediate-range missile located outside a deployment area or a shorter-range missile located outside a missile operating base.

13. The term "deployed launcher" means a launcher of an intermediate-range missile located within a deployment area or a·launcher of a shorter-range missile located at a missile operating base.

14. The term "non-deployed launcher" means a launcher of an intermediate-range missile located outside a deployment area or a launcher of a shorter-range missile located outside a missile operating base.

15. The term "basing country" means a country other than the United States of America or the Union of Soviet Socialist Republics on whose territory intermediate-range or shorter-range missiles of the Parties, launchers of such missiles or support structures associated with such missiles and launchers were located at any time after November 1, 1987. Missiles or launchers in transit are not considered to be "located".

Article 3

1. For the purposes of this Treaty, existing types of intermediate-range missiles are:

(a) for the United States of America, missiles of the types designated by the United States of America as the Pershing II and the BGM-109G, which are known to the Union of Soviet Socialist Republics by the same designations; and

(b) for the Union of Soviet Socialist Republics, missiles of the types designated by the Union of Soviet Socialist Republics as the RSD-10, the R-12 and the R-14, which are known to the United States of America as the SS-20, the SS-4 and the SS-5, respectively.

2. For the purposes of this Treaty, existing types of shorter-range missiles are:

(a) for the United States of America, missiles of the type designated by the United States of America as the Pershing IA, which is known to the Union of Soviet Socialist Republics by the same designation; and

(b) for the Union of Soviet Socialist Republics, missiles of the types designated by the Union of Soviet Socialist Republics as the OTR-22 and the OTR-23, which are known to the United States of America as the SS-12 and the SS-23, respectively.

Article 4

1. Each Party shall eliminate all its intermediate-range missiles and launchers of such missiles, and all support structures and support equipment of the categories listed in the Memorandum of Understanding associated with such missiles and launchers, so that no later than three years after entry into force of this Treaty and thereafter no such missiles, launchers, support structures or support equipment shall be possessed by either Party.

2. To implement paragraph 1 of this Article, upon entry into force of this Treaty, both Parties shall begin and continue throughout the duration of each

phase, the reduction of all types of their deployed and non-deployed intermediate-range missiles and deployed and non-deployed launchers of such missiles and support structures and support equipment associated with such missiles and launchers in accordance with the provisions of this Treaty. These reductions shall be implemented in two phases so that:

(a) by the end of the first phase, that is, no later than 29 months after entry into force of this Treaty:

(i) the number of deployed launchers of intermediate-range missiles for each Party shall not exceed the number of launchers that are capable of carrying or containing at one time missiles considered by the Parties to carry 171 warheads;

(ii) the number of deployed intermediate-range missiles for each Party shall not exceed the number of such missiles considered by the Parties to carry 180 warheads;

(iii) the aggregate number of deployed and non-deployed launchers of intermediate-range missiles for each Party shall not exceed the number of launchers that are capable of carrying or containing at one time missiles considered by the Parties to carry 200 warheads;

(iv) the aggregate number of deployed and non-deployed intermediate-range missiles for each Party shall not exceed the number of such missiles considered by the Parties to carry 200 warheads; and

(v) the ratio of the aggregate number of deployed and non-deployed intermediate-range GLBMs of existing types for each party to the aggregate number of deployed and non-deployed intermediate-range missiles of existing types possessed by the Party shall not exceed the ratio of such intermediate-range GLBMs to such intermediate-range missiles for that Party as of November 1, 1987, as set forth in the Memorandum of Understanding; and

(b) by the end of the second phase, that is, no later than three years after entry into force of this Treaty, all intermediate-range missiles of each Party, launchers of such missiles and all support structures and support equipment of the categories listed in the Memorandum of Understanding associated with such missiles and launchers, shall be eliminated.

Article 5

1. Each Party shall eliminate all its shorter-range missiles and all support equipment of the categories listed in the Memorandum of Understanding associated with such missiles and launchers, so that no later than 18 months after entry into force of this Treaty and thereafter no such missiles, launchers or support equipment shall be possessed by either Party.

2. No later than 90 days after entry into force of this Treaty, each Party shall complete the removal of all its deployed and non-deployed launchers of such missiles to elimination facilities and shall retain them at those locations until they are eliminated in accordance with the procedures set forth in the Protocol on Elimination. No later than 12 months after entry into force of this Treaty, each Party shall complete the removal of all its non-deployed shorter-range missiles to elimination facilities and shall retain them at those locations until they are eliminated in accordance with the procedures set forth in the Protocol on Elimination.

3. Shorter-range missiles and launchers of such missiles shall not be located at the same elimination facility. Such facilities shall be separated by no less than 1,000 kilometers.

Article 6

1. Upon entry into force of this Treaty and thereafter, neither Party shall:

(a) produce or flight-test any intermediate-range missiles or produce any stages of such missiles or any launchers of such missiles; or

(b) produce, flight-test or launch any shorter-range missiles or produce any stages of such missiles or any launchers of such missiles.

2. Notwithstanding paragraph 1 of this Article, each Party shall have the right to produce a type of GLBM not limited by this Treaty which uses a stage which is outwardly similar to, but not interchangeable with, a stage of an existing type of intermediate-range GLBM having more than one stage, providing that that Party does not produce any other stage which is outwardly similar to, but not interchangeable with, any other stage of an existing type of intermediate-range GLBM.

Article 7

For the purposes of this Treaty:

1. If a ballistic missile or a cruise missile has been flight-tested or deployed for weapon delivery, all missiles of that type shall be considered to be weapon-delivery vehicles.

2. If a GLBM or GLCM is an intermediate-range missile, all GLBMs or GLCMs of that type shall be considered to be intermediate-range missiles. If a GLBM or GLCM is a shorter-range missiles, all GLBMs or GLCMs of that type shall be considered to be shorter-range missiles.

3. If a GLBM is of a type developed and tested solely to intercept and counter objects not located on the surface of the earth, it shall not be considered to be a missile to which the limitations of this Treaty apply.

4. The range capability of a GLBM not listed in Article III of this Treaty shall be considered to be the maximum range to which it has been tested. The range capability of a GLBM not listed in Article III of this Treaty shall be considered to be the maximum distance which can be covered by the missile in its standard design mode flying until fuel exhaustion, determined by projecting its flight path onto the earth's sphere from the point of launch to the point of impact. GLBMs or GLCMs that have a range capability equal to or in excess of 500 kilometers but not in excess of 1,000 kilometers shall be considered to be shorter-range missiles. GLBMs or GLCMs that have a range capability in excess of 1,000 kilometers but not in excess of 5,500 kilometers shall be considered to be intermediate-range missiles.

5. The maximum number of warheads an existing type of intermediate-range missile or shorter-range missile carries shall be considered to be the number listed for missiles of that type in the Memorandum of Understanding.

6. Each GLBM or GLCM shall be considered to carry the maximum number of warheads listed for a GLBM or GLCM of that type in the Memorandum of Understanding.

7. If a launcher has been tested for launching a GLBM or a GLCM, all launchers of that type shall be considered to have been tested for launching GLBMs or GLCMs.

8. If a launcher has contained or launched a particular type of GLBM or GLCM, all launchers of that type shall be considered to be launchers of that type of GLBM or GLCM.

9. The number of missiles each launcher of an existing type of intermediate-range missile or shorter-range missile shall be considered to be capable of carrying or containing at one time the number listed for launchers of missiles of that type in the Memorandum of Understanding.

10. Except in the case of elimination in accordance with the procedures set forth in the Protocol on Elimination, the following shall apply:

(a) for GLBMs which are stored or moved in separate stages, the longest stage of an intermediate-range or shorter-range GLBM shall be counted as a complete missile;

(b) for GLBMs which are not stored or moved in separate stages, a canister of the type used in the launch of an intermediate-range GLBM, unless a Party proves to the satisfaction of the other Party that it does not contain such a missile, or an assembled intermediate-range or shorter-range GLBM, shall be counted as a complete missile; and

(c) for GLBMs, the airframe of an intermediate-range or shorter-range GLBM shall be counted as a complete missile.

11. A ballistic missile which is not a missile to be used in a ground-based mode shall not be considered to be a GLBM if it is test-launched at a test site from a fixed land-based launcher which is used solely for test purposes and which is distinguishable from GLBM launchers. A cruise missile which is not a missile to be used in a ground-based mode shall not be considered to be a GLBM if it is test-launched at a test site from a fixed land-based launcher which is used solely for test purposes and which is distinguishable from GLBM launchers.

12. Each Party shall have the right to produce and use for booster systems, which might otherwise be considered to be intermediate-range or shorter-range missiles, only existing types of booster stages for such booster systems. Launches of such booster systems shall not be considered to be flight-testing of intermediate-range or shorter-range missiles provided that:

(a) stages used in such booster systems are different from stages used in those missiles listed as existing types intermediate-range or shorter-range missiles in Article 3 of this Treaty;

(b) such booster systems are used only for research and development purposes to test objects other than the booster systems themselves;

(c) the aggregate number of launchers for such booster systems shall not exceed 35 for each Party at any one time; and

(d) the launchers for such booster systems are fixed, emplaced above ground and located only at research and development launch sites which are specified in the Memorandum of Understanding.

Research and development launch sites shall not be subject to inspection pursuant to Article 11 of this Treaty.

Article 8

1. All intermediate-range missiles and launchers of such missiles shall be located in deployment areas, at missile support facilities or shall be in transit. Intermediate-range missiles or launchers of such missiles shall not be located elsewhere.

2. Stages of intermediate-range missiles shall be located in deployment areas, at missiles support facilities or moving between deployment areas, between missiles support facilities or between missile support facilities and deployment areas.

3. Until their removal to elimination facilities as required by paragraph 2 of Article 5 of this Treaty, all shorter-range missiles and launchers of such missiles shall be located at missile operating bases, at missile support facilities or shall be in transit. Shorter-range missiles or launchers of such missiles shall not be located elsewhere.

4. Transit of a missile or launcher subject to the provisions of this Treaty shall be completed within 25 days.

5. All deployment areas, missile operating bases and missile support facilities are specified in the Memorandum of Understanding or in subsequent updates of data pursuant to paragraphs 3, 5 (a) or 5 (b) of Article 9 of this Treaty. Neither Party shall increase the number of, or change the location or boundaries of, deployment areas, missile operating bases or missile support facilities, except for elimination facilities, from those set forth in the Memorandum of Understanding. A missile support facility shall not be considered to be part of a deployment area even though it may be located within the geographic boundaries of a deployment area.

6. Beginning 30 days after entry into force of this Treaty, neither Party shall locate intermediate-range or shorter-range missiles, including stages of such missiles, or launchers of such missiles at missile production facilities, launcher production facilities or test ranges listed in the Memorandum of Understanding.

7. Neither Party shall locate any intermediate-range or shorter-range missiles at training facilities.

8. A non-deployed intermediate-range or shorter-range missile shall not be carried on or contained within a launcher of such a type of missile, except as required for maintenance conducted at repair facilities or for elimination by means of launching conducted at elimination facilities.

9. Training missiles and training launchers for intermediate-range or shorter-range missiles shall be subject to the same locational restrictions as are set forth for intermediate-range and shorter-range missiles and launchers of such missiles in paragraphs 1 and 3 of this Article.

Article 9

1. The Memorandum of Understanding contains categories of data relevant to obligations undertaken with regard to this Treaty and lists all intermediate-range and shorter-range missiles, launchers of such missiles, and support structures and support equipment associated with such missiles and launchers, possessed by the Parties as of November 1, 1987. Updates of that data and notifications required by this Article shall be provided according to the categories of data contained in the Memorandum of Understanding.

2. The Parties shall update that data and provide the notifications required by this Treaty through the Nuclear Risk Reduction Centers, established pursuant of the Agreement Between the United States of America and the Union of Soviet Socialist Republics on the Establishment of Nuclear Risk Reduction Centers of September 15, 1987.

3. No later than 30 days after entry into force of this Treaty, each Party shall provide the other Party with updated data, as of the date of entry into force of this Treaty, for all categories of data contained in the Memorandum of Understanding.

4. No later than 30 days after the end of each six-month interval following the entry into force of this Treaty, each Party shall provide data for all categories of data contained in the Memorandum of Understanding by informing the other Party of all changes, completed and in process, in that data, which have occurred during, the six-month interval since the preceding data exchange, and the net effect of those changes.

5. Upon entry into force of this Treaty and thereafter, each Party shall provide the following notifications to the other Party:

(a) notification, no less than 30 days in advance, of the scheduled date of the elimination of a specific deployment area, missile operating base or missile support facility;

(b) notification, no less than 30 days in advance, of changes in the number or location of elimination facilities, including the location and scheduled date of each change;

(c) notification, except with respect to launches of intermediate-range missiles for the purpose of their eliminating, no less than 30 days in advance, of the scheduled date of the initiation of the elimination of intermediate-range and shorter-range missiles, and stages of such missiles, and launchers of such missiles and support structures and support equipment associated with such missiles and launchers, including:

(i) the number and type of items of missile systems to be eliminated;

(ii) the elimination site;

(iii) for intermediate-range missiles, the location from which such missiles, launchers of such missiles and support equipment associated with such missiles and launchers are moved to the elimination facility; and

(iv) expect in the case of support structures, the point of entry to be used by and inspection team conducting an inspection pursuant to paragraph 7 of Article 11 of this Treaty and the estimated time of departure of an inspection team from the point of entry to the elimination facility;

(d) notification, no less than ten days in advance, of the scheduled date of the launch, or the scheduled date of the initiation of a series of launches, of intermediate-range missiles for the purpose of their elimination, including:

(i) the type of missiles to be eliminated;

(ii) the location of the launch, or, if elimination is by a series of launches, the location of such launches and the number of launches in the series;

(iii) the point of entry to be used by an inspection team conducting an inspection pursuant to paragraph 7 of Article 11 of this Treaty; and

(iv) the estimated time of departure of an inspection team from the point of entry to the elimination facility;

(e) notification, no later than 48 hours after they occur, of changes in the number of intermediate-range and shorter-range missiles, launchers of such missiles and support structures and support equipment associated with such missiles and launchers resulting from elimination as described in the Protocol on Elimination, including:

(i) the number and type of item of a missile system which were eliminated; and

(ii) the date and location of such elimination; and

(f) notification of transit of intermediate-range or shorter-range missiles or launchers of such mis-

siles, or the movement of training missiles or training launchers for such intermediate-range and shorter-range missiles, no later than 48 hours after it has been completed, including:

(i) the number of missiles or launchers;

(ii) the points, dates and times of departure and arrival;

(iii) the mode of transport; and

(iv) the location and time at that location at least once every four days during the period of transit.

6. Upon entry into force of this Treaty and thereafter, each Party shall notify the other Party, no less than ten days in advance, of the scheduled date and location of the launch of a research and development booster system as described in paragraph 12 of Article 7 of this Treaty.

Article 10

1. Each Party shall eliminate its intermediate-range and shorter-range missiles and launchers of such missiles and support structures and support equipment associated with such missiles and launchers in accordance with the procedures set forth in the Protocol on Elimination.

2. Verification by on-site inspection of the elimination of items of missile systems specified in the Protocol on Elimination shall be carried out in accordance with Article 11 of this Treaty, the Protocol on Elimination and the Protocol on Inspection.

3. When a Party removes its intermediate-range missiles, launchers of such missiles and support equipment associated with such missiles and launchers from deployment areas to elimination facilities for the purpose of their elimination, it shall do so in complete deployed organization units. For the United States of America, these units shall be Pershing II batteries and BGM-109G flights. For the Union of Soviet Socialist Republics, these units shall be SS-20 regiments composed of two or three battalions.

4. Elimination of intermediate-range and shorter-range missiles and launchers of such missiles and support equipment associated with such missiles and launchers shall be carried out at the facilities that are specified in the Memorandum of Understanding or notified in accordance with paragraph 5(b) of Article 9 of this Treaty, unless eliminated in accordance with Sections IV or V of the Protocol on Elimination. Support structures, associated with the missiles and launchers subject to this Treaty, that are subject to

elimination shall be eliminated *in situ*.

5. Each Party shall have the right, during the first six months after entry force of this Treaty, to eliminate by means of launching no more than 100 of its intermediate-range missiles.

6. Intermediate-range and shorter-range missiles which have been tested prior to entry into force of this Treaty, but never deployed, and which are not existing types of intermediate-range or shorter-range missiles listed in Article 3 of this Treaty, and launchers of such missiles, shall be eliminated within six months after entry into force of this Treaty in accordance with the procedures set forth in the Protocol on Elimination. Such missiles are:

(a) for the United States of America, missiles of the type designated by the United States of America as the Pershing IB, which is known to the Union of Soviet Socialist Republics by the same designation; and

(b) for the Union of Soviet Socialist Republics, missiles of the type designated by the Union of Soviet Socialist Republics as the RK-55, which is known to the United States of America as the SSC-X-4.

7. Intermediate-range and shorter-range missiles and launchers of such missiles and support structures and support equipment associated with such missiles and launchers shall be considered to be eliminated after completion of the procedures set forth in the Protocol on Elimination and upon the notification provided for in paragraph 5 (e) of Article 7 of this Treaty.

8. Each Party shall eliminate its deployment areas, missile operating bases and missile support facilities. A Party shall notify the other Party pursuant to paragraph 5 (a) of Article 9 of this Treaty once the conditions set forth below are fulfilled:

(a) all intermediate-range and shorter-range missiles, launchers of such missiles and support equipment associated with such missiles and launchers located there have been removed;

(b) all support structures associated with such missiles and launchers located there have been eliminated; and

(c) all activity related to production, flight-testing, training, repair, storage or deployment of such missiles and launchers has ceased there.

Such deployment areas, missile operating bases missile support facilities shall be considered to be eliminated either when they have been inspected pur-

suant to paragraph 4 of Article 11 of this Treaty or when 60 days have elapsed since the date of the scheduled elimination which was notified pursuant to paragraph 5(a) of Article 7 of this Treaty. A deployment area, missile operating base or missile support facility listed in the Memorandum of Understanding that met the above conditions prior to entry into force of this Treaty, and is not included in the initial data exchange pursuant to paragraph 3 of Article 9 of this Treaty, shall be considered to be eliminated.

9. If a Party intends to convert a missile operating base listed in the Memorandum of Understanding for use as a base associated with GLBM or GLCM systems not subject, to this Treaty, then that Party shall notify the other Party no less than 30 days in advance of the scheduled date of the initiation of the conversion, of the scheduled and the purpose for which the base will be converted.

Article 11

1. For the purpose of ensuring verification of compliance with the provisions of this Treaty, each Party shall have the right to conduct on-site inspections. The Parties shall implement on-site inspections in accordance with this Article, the Protocol on Inspection and the Protocol on Elimination.

2. Each Party shall have the right to conduct inspections provided for by this Article both within the territory of the other Party and within the territories of basing countries.

3. Beginning 30 days after entry into force of this Treaty, each Party shall have the right to conduct inspections at all missile operating bases and missile support facilities specified in the Memorandum of Understanding other than missile production facilities, and at all elimination facilities included in the initial data update required by paragraph 3 of Article 9 of this Treaty. These inspections shall be completed no later than 90 days after entry into force of this Treaty. The purpose of these inspections shall be to verify the number of missiles, launchers, support structures and support and other data, as of the date of entry into force of this Treaty, provided pursuant to paragraph 3 of Article 9 of this Treaty.

4. Each Party shall have the right to conduct inspections to verify the elimination, notified pursuant to paragraph 5(a) of Article 9 of this Treaty, of missile operating bases and missile support facilities other than missile production facilities, which are thus no longer subject to inspections pursuant to paragraph 5(a) of this Article. Such an inspection shall be carried out within 60 days after the sched-

uled date of the elimination of that facility. If a Party conducts an inspection at a particular facility pursuant to paragraph 3 of this Article after the scheduled date of the elimination of that facility, then no additional inspection of that facility pursuant to this paragraph shall be permitted.

5. Each Party shall have the right to conduct inspections pursuant to this paragraph for 13 years after entry into force of this Treaty. Each Party shall have the right to conduct 20 such inspections per calendar year during the first three years after entry into force of this Treaty, 15 such inspections per calendar year during the subsequent five years, and ten such inspections per calendar year during the last five years. Neither Party shall use more than half of its total number of these inspections per calendar year within the territory of any one basing country. Each Party shall have the right to conduct:

(a) inspections, beginning 90 days after entry into force of this Treaty, of missile operating bases and missile support facilities other than elimination facilities and missile production facilities, to ascertain, according to the categories of data specified in the Memorandum of Understanding, the numbers of missiles, launchers, support structures and support equipment located at each missile operating base or missile support facility at the time of the inspection; and

(b) inspections of former missile operating bases and former missile support facilities eliminated pursuant to paragraph 8 of Article 10 of this Treaty other than former missile production facilities.

6. Beginning 30 days after entry into force of this Treaty, each Party shall have the right, for 13 years after entry into force of this Treaty, to inspect by means of continuous monitoring:

(a) the portals of any facility of the other Party to which the final assembly of a GLBM using stages, any of which is outwardly similar to a stage of a solid-propellant GLBM listed in Article 3 of this Treaty, is accomplished; or

(b) if a Party has no such facility, the portals of an agreed former missile production facility at which existing types of intermediate-range or shorter-range GLBMs were produced.

The Party whose facility is to be inspected pursuant to this paragraph shall ensure that the other Party is able to establish a permanent continuous monitoring system at that facility within six months

after entry into force of this Treaty or within six months of initiation of the process of final assembly described in subparagraph (a). If, after the end of the second year after entry into force of this Treaty, neither Party conducts the process of final assembly described in subparagraph (a) for a period of 12 consecutive months, then neither Party shall have the right to inspect by means of continuous monitoring any missile production facility of the other Party unless the process of final assembly as described in subparagraph (a) is initiated again. Upon entry into force of this Treaty, the facilities to be inspected by continuous monitoring shall be; in accordance with subparagraph (b), for the United States of America, Hercules Plant Number 1, at Magna, Utah; in accordance with subparagraph (a), for the Union of Soviet Socialist Republics, the Votkinsk Machine Building Plant, Udmurt Autonomous Soviet Socialist Republic, Russian Soviet Federative Socialist Republic.

7. Each Party shall conduct inspections of the process of elimination, including elimination of intermediate-range missiles, by means of launching, of intermediate-range and shorter-range missiles and launchers of such missiles and support equipment associated with such missiles and launchers carried out at elimination facilities in accordance with Article 10 of this Treaty and the Protocol on Elimination. Inspectors conducting inspections provided for in this paragraph shall determine that the processing specified for the elimination of the missiles, launchers and support equipment have been completed.

8. Each Party shall have the right to conduct inspections to confirm the completion of the process of elimination of intermediate-range and shorter-range missiles and launchers of such missiles and support equipment associated with such missiles and launchers eliminated pursuant to Section 5 of the Protocol on Elimination, and of training missiles, training missile stages, training launch canisters and training launchers eliminated pursuant to Sections 2, 4 and 5 of the Protocol on Elimination.

Article 12

1. For the purpose of ensuring verification of compliance with the provisions of this Treaty, each Party shall use national technical means of verification at its disposal in a manner consistent with generally recognized principles of international law.

2. Neither Party shall:

(a) interfere with national technical means of verification of the other Party operating in accordance with paragraph 1 of this Article; or

(b) use concealment measures which impede verification of compliance with the provisions of this Treaty by national technical means of verification carried out in accordance with paragraph 1 of this Article. This obligation does not apply to cover or concealment practices, within a deployment area, associated with normal training, maintenance and operations, including the use of environmental shelters to protect missiles and launchers.

3. To enhance observation by national technical means of verification, each Party shall have the right until a treaty between the Parties reducing and limiting strategic offensive arms enters into force, but in any event for no more than three years after entry into force of this Treaty, to request the implementation of cooperative measures at deployment bases for road-mobile GLBMs with a range capability in excess of 5,500 kilometers, which are not former missile operating bases eliminated pursuant to paragraph 8 of Article 10 of this Treaty. The Party making such a request shall inform the other Party of the deployment base at which cooperative measures shall be implemented. The Party whose base is to be observed shall carry out the following cooperative measures:

(a) no later than six hours after such a request, the Party shall have opened the roofs of all fixed structures for launchers located at the base, removed completely all missiles on launchers from such fixed structures for launchers and displayed such missiles on launchers in the open without using concealment measures; and

(b) the Party shall leave the roofs open and the missiles on launchers in place until twelve hours have elapsed from the time of the receipt of a request for such an observation.

Each Party shall have the right to make six such requests per calendar year. Only one deployment base shall be subject to these cooperative measures at any one time.

Article 13

1. To promote the objectives and implementation of the provisions of this Treaty, the Parties hereby establish the Special Verification Commission. The Parties agree that, if either Party so requests, they shall meet within the framework of the Special Verification Commission to:

(a) resolve questions relating to compliance with the obligations assumed; and

(b) agree upon such measures as may be necessary to improve the viability and effectiveness of this Treaty

2. The Parties shall use the Nuclear Risk Reduction Centers, which provide for continuous communication between the Parties, to:

(a) exchange data and provide notifications as required by paragraphs 3, 4, 5 and 6 of Article 9 of this Treaty and the Protocol on Elimination;

(b) provide and receive the information required by paragraph 9 of Article 10 of this Treaty;

(c) provide and receive notifications of inspections as required by Article 11 of this Treaty and the Protocol on Inspection; and

(d) provide and receive requests for cooperative measures as provided for in paragraph 3 of Article 12 of this Treaty.

Article 14

The Parties shall comply with this Treaty and shall not assume any international obligations or undertakings which would conflict with its provisions.

Article 15

1. This Treaty shall be of unlimited duration.

2. Each Party shall, in exercising its national sovereignty, have the right to withdraw from this Treaty if it decides that extraordinary events related to the subject matter of this Treaty have jeopardized its supreme interests. It shall give notice of its decision to withdraw to the other Party six months prior to withdrawal from this Treaty. Such notice shall include a statement of the extraordinary events the notifying Party regards as having jeopardized its supreme interests.

Article 16

Each Party may propose amendments to this Treaty. Agreed amendments shall enter into force in accordance with the procedures set forth in Article 17 governing the entry into force of this Treaty.

Article 17

1. This Treaty including the Memorandum of Understanding and Protocols, which form an integral part thereof, shall be subject to ratification in accordance with the constitutional procedures of each Party. This Treaty shall enter into force on the date of the exchange of instruments of ratification.

2. This Treaty shall be registered pursuant to Article 102 of the Charter of the United Nations.

PROTOCOL

On Procedures Governing the Elimination of the Missile Systems Subject to the Treaty between the United States of America and the Union of Soviet Socialist Republics on the Elimination of Their Intermediate-Range and Shorter-Range Missiles

Pursuant to and in implementation of the Treaty Between the United States of America and the Union of Soviet Socialist Republics on the Elimination of Their Intermediate-Range and Shorter-Range Missiles of December 8, 1987, hereinafter referred to as the Treaty, the Parties hereby agree upon procedures governing the elimination of the missile systems subject to the Treaty.

I. Items of Missile Systems Subject to Elimination

The specific items for each type of missile system to be eliminated are:

1. For the United States of America:
Pershing II: missile, launcher and launch pad shelter;
BGM-109G: missile, launch canister and launcher;
PERSHING IA: missile and launcher: and
PERSHING IB: missile.

2. For the Union of Soviet Socialist Republics:
SS-20: missile, launcher canister, launcher, missile transporter vehicle and fixed structure for a launcher;
SS-4: missile, missile transporter vehicle, missile erector, launch stand and propellant tanks;
SS-5: missile;
SS-X-4: missile, launch canister and launcher;
SS-12: missile, launcher and missile transporter vehicle; and
SS-23: missile, launcher and missile transporter vehicle.

3. For both Parties, all training missiles, training missile stages, training launch canisters and training launchers shall be subject to elimination.

4. For both Parties, all stages of intermediate-range and shorter-range GLBMs shall be subject to elimination.

5. For both Parties, all front sections of deployed intermediate-range and shorter-range missiles shall be subject to elimination.

II. Procedures for Elimination at Elimination Facilities

1. In order to ensure the reliable determination of the type and number of missiles, missile stages, front sections, launch canisters, launchers, missile transporter vehicles, missile erectors and launch stands as well as training missiles, training missile stages, training launch canisters and training launchers, indicated in Section I of this Protocol, being eliminated at elimination facilities, and to preclude the possibility of restoration of such items for purposes inconsistent with the provisions of the Treaty, the Parties shall fulfill the requirements below.

2. The conduct of the elimination procedures for the items of missile systems listed in paragraph 1 of this Section, except for training missiles, training missile stages, training launch canisters and training launchers, shall be subject to on-site inspection in accordance with Article 11 of the treaty and the Protocol on Inspection. The Parties shall have the right to conduct on-site inspections to confirm the completion of the elimination procedures set forth in paragraph 11 of this Section for training missiles, training missile stages, training launch canisters and training launchers. The Party possessing such a training missile training missile stage, training launch canister or training launcher shall inform the other Party of the name and coordinates of the elimination facility at which the on-site inspection may be conducted as well as the date on which it may be conducted. Such information shall be provided no less than 30 days in advance of that date.

3. Prior to a missile's arrival at the elimination facility, its nuclear warhead device and guidance elements may be removed.

4. Each Party shall select the particular technological means necessary to implement the procedures required in paragraphs 10 and 11 of this Section and to allow for on-site inspection of the conduct of the elimination procedures required in paragraph 10 of this Section in accordance with Article 11 of the Treaty, this Protocol and the Protocol on Inspection.

5. The initiation of the elimination of the items of missile systems subject to this Section shall be considered to be the commencement of the procedures set forth in paragraph 10 or 11 of this Section.

6. Immediately prior to the initiation of the elimination procedures set forth in paragraph 10 of this Section, an inspector from the Party receiving the pertinent notification required by paragraph 5(c) of Article 9 of the Treaty shall confirm and record the type and number of items of missile systems, listed

in paragraph 1 of this Section, which are to be eliminated. If the inspecting Party deems it necessary, this shall include a visual inspection of the contents of launch canisters.

7. A missile stage being eliminated by burning in accordance with the procedures set forth in paragraph 10 of this Section shall not be instrumented for data collection. Prior to the initiation of the elimination procedures set forth in paragraph 10 of this Section, an inspector from the inspecting Party shall confirm that such missile stages are not instrumented for data collection. Those missile stages shall be subject to continuous observation by such an inspector from the time of that inspection until the burning is completed.

8. The completion of the elimination procedures set forth in this Section, except those for training missile, training missile stages, training launch canisters and training launchers, along with the type and number of item of missile systems for which those procedures have been completed, shall be confirmed in writing by the representative of the Party carrying out the elimination and by the inspection team leader of the other Party. The elimination of a training missile, training missile stage, training launch canister or training launcher shall be considered to have been completed upon completion of the procedures set forth in paragraph 11 of this Section and notification as required by paragraph 5(e) of Article 9 of the Treaty following the date specified pursuant to paragraph 2 of this Section.

9. The Parties agree that all United States and Soviet intermediate-range and shorter-range missiles and their associated reentry vehicles shall be eliminated within an agreed overall period of elimination. It is further agreed that all such missiles shall in fact, be eliminated fifteen days prior to the end of the overall period of elimination. During the last fifteen days, a Party shall withdraw to its national territory reentry vehicles which, by unilateral decision, have been released from existing programs of cooperation and eliminate them during the same timeframe in accordance with the procedures set forth in this Section.

10. The specific procedures for the elimination of the items of missile systems listed in paragraph 1 of this Section shall be as follows, unless the Parties agree upon different procedures to achieve the same result as the procedures identified in this paragraph:

For the Pershing II:
Missile:

(a) missile stages shall be eliminated by explosive demolition or burning;

(b) solid fuel, rocket nozzles and motor cases not destroyed in this process shall be burned, crushed, flattened or destroyed by explosion; and

(c) front section, minus nuclear warhead device and guidance elements, shall be crushed or flattened.

Launcher:

(a) erector-launcher mechanism shall be removed from launcher chassis;

(b) all components of erector-launcher mechanism shall be cut at locations that are not assembly joints into two pieces of approximately equal size;

(c) missile launch support equipment, including external instrumentation compartments, shall be removed from launcher chassis; and

(d) launcher chassis shall be cut at a location that is not an assembly joint into two pieces of approximately equal size.

For the BGM-109G:

(a) missile airframe shall be cut longitudinally into two pieces;

(b) wings and tail section shall be served from missile airframe at locations that are not assembly joints; and

(c) front section, minus nuclear warhead device and guidance elements, shall be crushed or flattened.

Launch Canister:

launch canister shall be crushed, flattened, cut into two pieces of approximately equal size or destroyed by explosion.

Launcher:

(a) erector-launcher mechanism shall be removed from launcher chassis;

(b) all components of erector-launcher mechanism shall be cut at locations that are not assembly joints into two pieces of approximately equal size;

(c) missile launch support equipment, including external instrumentation compartments, shall be removed from launcher chassis; and

(d) launcher chassis shall be cut at a location that is not an assembly joint into two pieces of approximately equal size.

For the Pershing IA:
Missile:

(a) missile stages shall be eliminated by explosive demolition or burning;

(b) solid fuel, rocket nozzles and motor cases not destroyed in this process shall be burned, crushed, flattened or destroyed by explosion; and

(c) front section, minus nuclear warhead device and guidance elements, shall be crushed or flattened.

Launcher:

(a) erector-launcher mechanism shall be removed from launcher chassis;

(b) all components of erector-launcher mechanism shall be cut at locations that are not assembly joints into two pieces of approximately equal size;

(c) missile launch support equipment, including external instrumentation compartments, shall be removed from launcher chassis; and

(d) launcher chassis shall be cut at a location that is not an assembly joint into two pieces of approximately equal size.

For the Pershing IB:
Missile:

(a) missile stage shall be eliminated by explosive demolition or burning;

(b) solid fuel, rocket nozzle and motor case not destroyed in this process shall be burned, crushed, flattened or destroyed by explosion; and

(c) front section, minus nuclear warhead device and guidance elements, shall be crushed or flattened.

For the SS-20:
Missile:

(a) missile shall be eliminated by explosive demolition of the missile in its launch canister or by burning missile stages;

(b) solid fuel, rocket nozzles and motor cases not destroyed in this process shall be burned, crushed, flattened or destroyed by explosion; and

(c) front section, including reentry vehicles, minus nuclear warhead devices, and instrumentation compartment, minus guidance elements, shall be crushed or flattened.

Launch Canister:

launch canister shall be destroyed by explosive demolition together with a missile, or shall be destroyed separately by explosion, cut into two pieces of approximately equal size, crushed or flattened.

Launcher:

(a) erector-launcher mechanism shall be removed from launcher chassis;

(b) all components of erector-launcher mechanism shall be cut at locations that are not assembly joints into two pieces of approximately equal size;

(c) missile launch support equipment, including external instrumentation compartments, shall be removed from launcher chassis;

(d) mountings of erector-launcher mechanism and launcher leveling supports shall be cut off launcher chassis;

(e) launcher leveling supports shall be cut at locations that are not assembly joints into two pieces of approximately equal size; and

(f) a portion of the launcher chassis, at least 0.78 meters in length, shall be cut off aft of the rear axle.

Missile Transporter Vehicle:

(a) all mechanisms associated with missile loading and mounting shall be removed from transporter vehicle chassis;

(b) all mountings of such mechanisms shall be cut off transporter vehicle chassis;

(c) all components of the mechanisms associated with missile loading and mounting shall be cut at locations that are not assembly joints into two pieces of approximately equal size;

(d) external instrumentation compartments shall be removed from transporter vehicle chassis;

(e) transporter vehicle leveling supports shall be cut off transporter vehicle chassis and cut at locations that are not assembly joints into two pieces of approximately equal size; and

(f) a portion of the transporter vehicle chassis, at least 0.78 meters in length, shall be cut off aft of the rear axle.

For the ss-4:
Missile:

(a) nozzles of propulsion system shall be cut off at locations that are not assembly joints;

(b) all propellant tanks shall be cut into two pieces of approximately equal size;

(c) instrumentation compartment, minus guidance elements, shall be cut into two pieces of approximately equal size; and

(d) front section, minus nuclear warhead device, shall be crushed or flattened.

Launch Stand:

launch stand components shall be cut at locations that are not assembly joints into two pieces of approximately equal size.

Missile Erector:

(a) jib, missile erector leveling supports and missile erector mechanism shall be cut off missile erector at locations that are not assembly joints; and

(b) jib and missile erector leveling supports shall be cut into two pieces of approximately equal size.

Missile Transporter Vehicle:

mounting components for a missile and for a missile erector mechanism as well as supports for erecting a missile onto a launcher shall be cut off transporter vehicle at locations that are not assembly joints.

For the ss-5:
Missile:

(a) nozzles of propulsion system shall be cut off at locations that are not assembly joints;

(b) all propellant tanks shall be cut into two pieces of approximately equal size; and

(c) instrumentation compartment, minus guidance elements, shall be cut into two pieces of approximately equal size;

For the ssc-x-4:
Missile:

(a) missile airframe shall be cut longitudinally into two pieces;

(b) wings and tail section shall be severed from missile airframe at locations that are not assembly joints; and

(c) front section, minus nuclear warhead device and guidance elements, shall be crushed or flattened.

Launch Canister:

launch canister shall be crushed, flattened, cut into two pieces of approximately equal size destroyed by explosion.

Launcher:

(a) erector-launcher mechanism shall be removed from launcher chassis;

(b) all components of erector-launcher mechanism shall be cut at locations that are not assembly joints into two pieces of approximately equal size;

(c) missile launch support equipment, including external instrumentation compartments, shall be removed from launcher chassis;

(d) mountings of erector-launcher mechanism and launcher leveling supports shall be cut off launcher chassis;

(e) launcher leveling supports shall be cut at locations that are not assembly joints into two pieces of approximately equal size; and

(f) the launcher chassis shall be severed at a location determined by measuring no more than 0.70 meters rearward from the rear axle.

For the ss-12:
Missile:

(a) missile shall be eliminated by explosive demolition or by burning missile stages;

(b) solid fuel, rocket nozzles and motor cases not destroyed in this process shall be burned, crushed, flattened or destroyed by explosion; and

(c) front section, minus nuclear warhead device, and instrumentation compartment, minus guidance elements, shall be crushed, flattened or destroyed by explosive demolition together with a missile.

Launcher:

(a) erector-launcher mechanism shall be removed from launcher chassis;

(b) all components of erector-launcher mechanism shall be cut at locations that are not assembly joints into two pieces of approximately equal size;

(c) missile launch support equipment, including external instrumentation compartments, shall be removed from launcher chassis;

(d) mountings of erector-launcher mechanism and launcher leveling supports shall be cut off launcher chassis;

(e) launcher leveling supports shall be cut at locations that are not assembly joints into two pieces of approximately equal size; and

(f) a portion of the launcher chassis, at least 1.10 meters in length, shall be cut off aft of the rear axle.

Missile Transporter Vehicle:

(a) all mechanisms associated with missile loading and mounting shall be removed from transporter vehicle chassis;

(b) all mountings of such mechanisms shall be cut off transporter vehicle chassis;

(c) all components of the mechanisms associated with missile loading and mounting shall be cut at location that are not assembly joints into two pieces of approximately equal size;

(d) external instrumentation compartments shall be removed from transporter vehicle chassis;

(e) transporter vehicle leveling supports shall be cut off transporter vehicle chassis and cut at locations that are not assembly joints into two pieces of approximately equal size; and

(f) a portion of the transporter vehicle chassis, at least 1.10 meters in length, shall be cut off aft of the rear axle.

For the ss-23
Missile:

(a) missile shall be eliminated by explosive demolition or by burning the missile stage;

(b) solid fuel, rocket nozzle and motor case not destroyed in this process shall be burned, crushed, flattened or destroyed by explosion; and

(c) front section, minus nuclear warhead device, and instrumentation compartment, minus guidance elements, shall be crushed, flattened, or destroyed by explosive demolition together with a missile.

Launcher:

(a) erector-launcher mechanism shall be removed from launcher body;

(b) all components of erector-launcher mechanism shall be cut at locations that are not assembly joints into two pieces of approximately equal size;

(c) missile launch support equipment shall be removed from launcher body;

(d) mountings of erector-launcher mechanism and launcher leveling supports shall be cut off launcher body;

(e) launcher leveling supports shall be cut at locations that are not assembly joints into two pieces of approximately equal size;

(f) each environmental cover of the launcher body shall be removed and cut into two pieces of approximately equal size; and

(g) a portion of the launcher body, at least 0.85 meters in length, shall be cut off aft of the rear axle.

Missile Transporter Vehicle

(a) all mechanisms associated with missile loading and mounting shall be removed from transporter vehicle body;

(b) all mounting of such mechanisms shall be cut off transporter vehicle body;

(c) all components of mechanisms associated with missile loading and mounting shall be cut at locations that are not assembly joints into two pieces of approximately equal size;

(d) control equipment of the mechanism associated with missile loading shall be removed from transporter vehicle body;

(e) transporter vehicle leveling supports shall be cut off transporter vehicle body and cut at locations that are not assembly joints into two pieces of approximately equal size; and

(f) a portion of the transporter vehicle body, at least 0.85 meters in length, shall be cut off aft of the rear axle.

11. The specific procedures for the elimination of the training missiles, training missile stages, training launch canisters and training launchers indicated in paragraph 1 of this Section shall be as follows:

Training Missile and Training Missile Stages:

training missile and training missile stage shall be

crushed, flattened, cut into two pieces of approximately equal size or destroyed by explosion.

Training Launch Canister:

training launch canister shall be crushed, flattened cut into two pieces of approximately equal size or destroyed by explosion.

Training Launcher:

training launcher chassis shall be cut at the same location designated in paragraph 10 of this Section for launcher of the same type of missile.

III. Elimination of Missiles by Means of Launching

1. Elimination of missiles by means of launching pursuant to paragraph 5 of Article 10 of the Treaty shall be subject to on-site inspection in accordance with paragraph 7 of Article 11 of the Treaty and the Protocol on Inspection. Immediately prior to each launch conducted for the purpose of elimination, an inspector from the inspecting Party shall confirm by visual observation the type of missile to be launched.

2. All missiles being eliminated by means of launching shall be launched from designated elimination facilities to existing impact areas for such missiles. No such missile shall be used as a target vehicle for a ballistic missile interceptor.

3. Missile being eliminated by means of launching shall be launched one at a time, and no less than six hours shall elapse between such launches.

4. Such launches shall involve ignition of all missile stages. Neither Party shall transmit or recover data from missiles being eliminated by means of launching except for unencrypted data used for range safety purposes.

5. The completion of the elimination procedures set forth in this Section, and the type and number of missiles for which those procedures have been completed, shall be confirmed in writing by the representative of the Party carrying out the elimination and by the inspection team leader of the other Party.

6. A missile shall be considered to be eliminated by means of launching after completion of the procedures set forth in this Section and upon notification required by paragraph 5(e) of Article 9 of the Treaty.

IV. Procedures for Elimination In Site

1. Support Structures

(a) Support structures listed in Section I of this Protocol shall be eliminated in site.

(b) The initation of the elimination of support structures shall be considered to be commencement of the elimination procedures required in paragraph 1(d) of this Section.

(c) The elimination of support structures shall be subject to verification by on-site inspection in accordance with paragraph 4 of Article 11 of the Treaty.

(d) The specific elimination procedures for support structures shall be as follows:

(i) the superstructure of the fixed structure or shelter shall be dismantled or demolished, and removed from its base of foundation;

(ii) the base or foundation of the fixed structure or shelter shall be destroyed by excavation or explosion;

(iii) the destroyed base or foundation of a fixed structure or shelter shall remain visible to national technical means of verification for six months or until completion of an on-site inspection conducted in accordance with Article 11 of the Treaty; and

(iv) upon completion of the above requirements, the elimination procedures shall be considered to have been completed.

2. Propellant Tanks for ss-4 Missiles

Fixed and transportable propellant tanks for ss-4 missiles shall be removed from launch sites.

3. Training Missiles, Training Missile Stages, Training Launch Canisters and Training Launchers

(a) Training missiles, training missile stages, training launch canisters and training launchers not eliminated at elimination facilities shall be eliminated *in situ*.

(b) Training missiles, training missile stage, training launch canisters and training launchers being eliminated *in situ* shall be eliminated in accordance with the specific procedures set forth in paragraph 11 of Section 2 of this Protocol.

(c) Each Party shall have the right to conduct an on-site inspection to confirm the completion of the elimination procedures for training missiles, training missile stages, training launch canisters and training launchers.

(d) The Party possessing such a training missile, training missile stage, training launch canister or training launcher shall inform the other Party of the place-name and coordinates of the location at which the on-site inspection provided for in paragraph 3(c) of this Section may be conducted as well as the date on which it may be conducted. Such information shall be provided no less than 30 days in advance of that date.

(e) Elimination of a training missile, training missile stage, training launch canister or training launcher shall be considered to have been completed upon the completion of the procedures required by this paragraph and upon notification as required by paragraph 5(e) of Article 9 of the Treaty following the date specified pursuant to paragraph 3(d) of this Section.

V. Other Types of Elimination

1. Loss or Accidental Destruction

(a) If an item listed in Section I of this Protocol is lost or destroyed as a result of an accident, the possessing Party shall notify the other Party within 48 hours, as required in paragraph 5(e) of Article 9 of the Treaty, that the item has been eliminated.

(b) Such notification shall include the type of the eliminated item, its approximate or assumed location and the circumstances related to the loss or accidental destruction.

(c) In such a case, the other Party shall have the right to conduct an inspection of the specific point at which the accident occurred to provide confidence that the item has been eliminated.

2. Static Display

(a) The Parties shall have the right to eliminate missiles, launch canisters and launchers, as well as training missiles, training launch canisters and training launchers, listed in Section I of this Protocol by placing them in static display. Each Party shall be limited to a total of 15 missiles, 15 launch canisters and 15 launchers on such static display.

(b) Prior to being placed on static display, a missile, launch canister or launcher shall be rendered unusable for purposes inconsistent with the Treaty. Missile propellant shall be removed and erector-launcher mechanisms shall be rendered inoperative.

(c) The party possessing a missile, launch canister or launcher, as well as a training missile, training launch canister or training launcher that is to be eliminated by placing it on static display shall pro-

vide the other Party with the place-name and coordinates of the location at which such a missile launch canister or launcher is to be on static display, as well as the location at which the on-site inspection provided for in paragraph 2(d) of this Section, may take place.

(d) Each Party shall have the right to conduct an on-site inspection of such a missile, launch canister or launcher within 60 days of receipt of the notification required in paragraph 2(c) of this Section.

(e) Elimination of a missile, launch canister of launcher, as well as training missile launcher, by placing it on static display shall be considered to have been completed upon completion of the procedures required by this paragraph and notification as required by paragraph 5(e) of Article 9 of the Treaty.

This Protocol is an integral part of the Treaty. It shall enter into force on the date of the entry into force of the Treaty and shall remain in force so long as the Treaty remains in force. As provided for in paragraph 1(b) of Article 13 of the Treaty, the Parties may agree upon such measures as may be necessary to improve the viability and effectiveness of this Protocol. Such measures shall not be deemed amendments to the Treaty.

PROTOCOL

Regarding inspections relating to the Treaty Between The United States of America and the Union of Soviet Socialist Republics on the Elimination of Their Intermediate-Range and Shorter-Range Missiles

Pursuant to and in implementation of the Treaty Between the United States of America and the Union of Soviet Socialist Republics on the Elimination of Their Intermediate-Range and Shorter-Range Missiles of December 8, 1987, hereinafter referred to as the Treaty, the Parties hereby agree upon procedures governing the conduct of inspections provided for in Article 11 of the Treaty.

I. Definitions

For the purposes of this Protocol, the Treaty, the Memorandum of Understanding and the Protocol on Elimination:

1. The term "inspected Party" means the Party to the Treaty whose sites are subject to inspection as provided for by Article 11 of the Treaty.

2. The term "inspection Party" means the Party to the Treaty carrying out an inspection.

3. The term "inspector" means an individual designated by one of the Parties to carry out inspections and included on that Party's list of inspectors in accordance with the provisions of Section III of this Protocol.

4. The term "inspection team" means the group of inspectors assigned by the inspecting Party to conduct a particular inspection,

5. The term "inspection site" means an area, location or facility at which an inspection is carried out.

6. The term "period of inspection" means the period of time from arrival of the inspection team at the inspection site until its departure from the inspection site, exclusive of time spent on any pre- and post-inspection procedures.

7. The term "point of entry" means: Washington, D.C., or San Francisco, California, the United States of America; Brussels (National Airport), The Kingdom of Belgium; Frankfurt (Rhein Main Airbase), The Federal Republic of Germany; Rome (Ciampino), The Republic of Italy; Schiphol, The Kingdom of the Netherlands; RAF Greenham Common, The United Kingdom of Great Britain and Northern Ireland; Moscow, or Irkutsk, the Union of Soviet Socialist Republics; Schkeuditz, the German Democratic Republic; and International Airport Ruzyne, the Czechoslovak Socialist Republic.

8. The term "in-country period" means the period from the arrival of the inspection team at the point of entry until its departure from the country through the point of entry.

9. The term "in-country escort" means individuals specified by the inspected Party to accompany and assist inspectors and aircrew members as necessary throughout the in-country period.

10. The term "aircrew member" means an individual who performs duties related to the operation of an airplane and who is included on a Party's list of aircrew members in accordance with the provisions of Section III of this Protocol.

II. General Obligations

1. For the purpose of ensuring verification of compliance with the provisions of the Treaty, each Party shall facilitate inspection by the other Party pursuant to this Protocol.

2. Each Party takes note of the assurances received from the other Party regarding understanding reached between the other Party and the basing countries to the effect that the basing countries have agreed to the conduct of inspections in accordance with the provisions of this Protocol, on their territories.

III. Pre-Inspection Requirements

1. Inspections to ensure verification of compliance by the Parties with the obligations assumed under the Treaty shall be carried out by inspectors designated in accordance with paragraphs 3 and 4 of this Section.

2. No later than one day after entry info force of the Treaty, each Party shall provide to the other Party: a list of its proposed aircrew members; a list of its proposed inspectors who will carry out inspections pursuant to paragraphs 3, 4, 5, 7 and 8 of Article 11 of the Treaty; and a list of its proposed inspectors who will carry out inspection activities pursuant to paragraph 6 of Article 11 of the Treaty. None of these lists shall contain at any time more than 200 individuals.

3. Each Party shall review the lists of inspectors and aircrew members proposed by the other Party. With respect to an individual included on the list of proposed inspectors who will carry out inspection activities pursuant to paragraph 6 of Article 11 of the Treaty, if such an individual is unacceptable to the Party reviewing the list, that Party shall, within 20 days, so inform the Party providing the list, and the individual shall be deemed not accepted and shall be deleted from the List. With respect to an individual on the list of proposed aircrew members or the list of proposed inspectors who will carry out inspections pursuant to paragraphs 3, 4, 5, 7 and 8 of Article 11 of the Treaty, each Party, within 20 days after the receipt of such lists, shall inform the other Party of its agreement to the designation of each inspector and aircrew member proposed. Inspectors shall be citizens of the inspecting Party.

4. Each Party shall have the right to amend its lists of inspectors and aircrew members. New inspectors and aircrew members shall be designated in the same manner as set forth in paragraph 3 of this Section with respect to the initial lists.

5. Within 30 days of receipt of the initial lists of inspectors and aircrew members, or of subsequent changes thereto, the Party receiving such information shall provide, or shall ensure the provision of, such visas and other documents to each individual to whom it has agreed as may be required to ensure that each inspector or aircrew member may enter and remain in the territory of the Party or basing country

in which an inspection site is located throughout the in-country period for the purpose of carrying out inspection activities in accordance with the provisions of this Protocol. Such visas and documents shall be valid for a period of at least 24 months.

6. To exercise their functions effectively, inspectors and aircrew members shall be accorded, throughout the in-country period, privileges and immunities in the country of the inspection site as set forth in the Annex to this Protocol.

7. Without prejudice to their privileges and immunities, inspectors and aircrew members shall be obliged to respect the laws and regulations of the State on whose territory an inspection is carried out and shall be obliged not to interfere in the internal affairs of that State. In the event the inspected Party determines that an inspector or aircrew member of the other Party has violated the conditions governing inspection activities set forth in this Protocol, or has ever committed a criminal offense on the territory of the inspected Party or a basing country, or expelled by the inspected Party or a basing country, the inspected Party making such a determination shall so notify the inspecting Party, which shall immediately strike the individual from the lists of inspectors or the list of aircrew members. If, at that time, the individual is on the territory of the inspected Party or a basing country, the inspection Party shall immediately remove that individual from the country.

8. Within 30 days after entry into force of the Treaty, each Party shall inform the other Party of the standing diplomatic clearance number for airplanes of the Party transporting inspectors and equipment necessary for inspection into and out of the territory of the Party or basing country in which an inspection site is located. Aircraft routings to and from the designated point of entry shall be along established international airways that are agreed upon by the Parties as the basis for such diplomatic clearance.

IV. Notifications

1. Notification of an intention to conduct an inspection shall be made through the Nuclear Risk Reduction Centers. The receipt of this notification shall be acknowledged through the Nuclear Risk Reduction Centers by the inspected Party within one hour of its receipt.

(a) For inspections conducted pursuant to paragraphs 3, 4 or 5 of Article 11 of the Treaty, such notifications shall be made no less than 16 hours in advance of the estimated time of arrival of the inspection team at the point of entry and shall

include:

(i) the point of entry;

(ii) the date and estimated time of arrival at the point of entry;

(iii) the date and time when the specification of the inspection site will be provided; and

(iv) the names of inspectors and aircrew members.

(b) For inspections conducted pursuant to paragraphs 7 or 8 of Article 11 of the Treaty, such notifications shall be made no less than 72 hours in advance of the estimated time of arrival of the inspection team at the point of entry and shall include:

(i) the point of entry;

(ii) the date and estimated time of arrival at the point of entry;

(iii) the site to be inspected and the type of inspection; and

(iv) the names of inspectors and aircrew members.

2. The date and time of the specification of the inspection site as notified pursuant to paragraph 1(a) of this Section shall fall within the following time intervals:

(a) for inspections conducted pursuant to paragraphs 4 or 5 of Article 11 of the Treaty, neither less than four hours nor more than 24 hours after the estimated date and time of arrival at the point of entry; and

(b) for inspections conducted pursuant to paragraph 3 of Article 11 of the Treaty, neither less than four hours nor more than 48 hours after the estimated date and time of arrival at the point of entry.

3. The inspecting Party shall provide the inspected Party with a flight plan, through the Nuclear Risk Reduction Centers, for its flight from the last airfield prior to entering the airspace of the country in which the inspection site is located to the point of entry, no less than six hours before the scheduled departure time from that airfield. Such a plan shall be filed in accordance with the procedures of the International Civil Aviation Organization applicable to civil aircraft. The inspecting Party shall include in the remarks section of each flight plan the standing diplomatic clearance number and the notation: "Inspection aircraft. Priority clearance processing required".

4. No less than three hours prior to the scheduled

departure of the inspection team from the last airfield prior to entering the airspace of the country in which the inspection is to take place, the inspected Party shall ensure that the flight plan filed in accordance with paragraph 3 of this Section is approved so that the inspection team may arrive at the point of entry by the estimated arrival time.

5. Either Party may change the point or points of entry to the territories of the countries within which its deployment areas, missile operation bases or missile support facilities are located, by giving notice of such change to the other Party. A change in a point of entry shall become effective five months after receipt of such notification by the other Party.

V. Activities Beginning Upon Arrival at the Point of Entry

1. The in-country escort and a diplomatic aircrew escort accredited to the Government of either the inspected Party or the basing country in which the inspection site is located shall meet the inspection team and aircrew members at the point of entry as soon as the airplane of the inspecting Party lands. The number of aircrew members for each airplane shall not exceed ten. The in-country escort shall expedite the entry of the inspection team and aircrew, their baggage, and equipment and supplies necessary for inspection, into the country in which the inspection site is located. A diplomatic aircrew escort shall have the right to accompany and assist aircrew members throughout the in-country period. In the case of an inspection taking place on the territory of a basing country the in-country escort may include representatives of that basing country.

2. An inspector shall be considered to have assumed his duties upon arrival at the point of entry on the territory of the inspected Party or a basing country, and shall be considered to have ceased performing those duties when he has left the territory of the inspected Party or basing country.

3. Each Party shall ensure that equipment and supplies are exempt from all customs duties.

4. Equipment and supplies which the inspecting Party brings into the country in which an inspection site is located shall be subject to examination at the point of entry each time they are brought into that country. This examination shall be completed prior to the departure of the inspection team from the point of entry to conduct an inspection. Such equipment and supplies shall be examined by the in-country escort in the presence of the inspection team members to ascertain to the satisfaction of each Party that

the equipment and supplies cannot perform functions unconnected with the inspection requirements of the Treaty. If it is established upon examination that the equipment or supplies are unconnected with these inspection requirements, then they shall not be cleared for use and shall be impounded at the point entry until the departure of the inspection team from the country where the inspection is conducted. Storage of the inspecting Party's equipment and supplies at each point of entry shall be within tamper-proof containers within a secure facility. Access to each secure facility shall be controlled by a "dual key" system requiring the presence of both Parties to gain access to the equipment and supplies.

5. Throughout the in-country period the inspected Party shall provide, or arrange for the provision of, meals, lodging, work space, transportation and, as necessary, medical care for the inspection team and aircrew of the inspection Party. All the costs in connection with the stay of inspectors carrying out inspection activities pursuant to paragraph 6 of Article 11 of the Treaty, on the territory of the inspected Party, including meals, services, lodging, work space, transportation and medical care shall be borne by the inspecting Party.

6. The inspected Party shall provide parking, security protection, servicing and fuel for the airplane of the inspecting Party at the point of entry. The inspecting Party shall bear the cost of such fuel and servicing.

7. For inspections conducted on the territory of the Parties, the inspection team shall enter at the point of entry on the territory of the inspected Party that is closest to the inspection site. In the case of inspections carried out in accordance with paragraphs 3, 4 or 5 of Article 11 of the Treaty, the inspection team leader shall, at or before the time notified pursuant to paragraph 1(a) (iii) of Section IV of this Protocol, inform the inspected Party at the point of entry through the in-country escort of the type of inspection and the inspection site, by place-name geographic coordinates.

VI. General Rules for Conducting Inspections

1. Inspectors shall discharge their functions in accordance with this Protocol.

2. Inspectors shall not disclose information received during inspections except with the expressed permission of the inspecting Party. They shall remain bound by this obligation after their assignment as inspectors has ended.

3. In discharging their functions, inspectors shall not interfere directly with on-going activities at the

inspection site and shall avoid unnecessarily hampering or delaying the operation of a facility or taking actions affecting its safe operation.

4. Inspections shall be conducted in accordance with the objectives set forth in Article 11 of the Treaty as applicable for the type of inspection specified by the inspecting Party under paragraph 1(b) of Section IV or paragraph 7 of Section V of this Protocol.

5. The in-country escort shall have the right to accompany and assist inspectors and aircrew members as considered necessary by the inspected Party throughout the in-country period. Except as otherwise provided in this Protocol, the movement and travel of inspections and aircrew members shall be at the discretion of the in-country escort.

6. Inspectors carrying out inspection activities pursuant to paragraph 6 of Article 11 of the Treaty shall be allowed to travel within 50 kilometers from the inspection site with the permission of the in-country escort, and as considered necessary by the inspected party, shall be accompanied by the in-country escort. Such travel shall be taken solely as a leisure activity.

7. Inspectors shall have the right throughout the period of inspection to be in communication with the embassy of the inspecting Party located within the territory of the country where the inspection is taking place using the telephone communications provided by the inspected Party.

8. At the inspection site, representatives of the inspected facility shall be included among the in-country escort.

9. This inspection team may bring onto the inspection site such documents as needed to conduct the inspection, as well as linear measurement devices; cameras; portable weighing devices; radiation detection devices; and other equipment, as agreed by the Parties. The characteristics and method of use of the equipment listed above, shall also be agreed upon within 30 days after entry into force of the Treaty. During inspections conducted pursuant to paragraphs 3, 4, 5(a), 7 or 8 Article 11 of the Treaty, the inspection team may use any of the equipment listed above, except for cameras, which shall be for use only by the inspected Party at the request of the inspecting Party. During inspections conducted pursuant to paragraph 5(b) of Article 11 of the Treaty, all measurements shall be made by the inspected Party at the request of the inspecting Party. At the request of inspectors, the in-country escort shall take photographs of the inspected facilities using the inspecting Party's camera systems which are capable of producing duplicate, instant development photographic prints. Each Party shall receive one copy of every photograph.

10. For inspections conducted pursuant to paragraphs 3, 4, 5, 7 or 8 of Article 11 of the Treaty, inspectors shall permit the in-country escort to observe the equipment used during the inspection by the inspection team.

11. Measurements recorded during inspections shall be certified by the signature of a member of the inspection team and a member of the in-country escort when they are taken. Such certified data shall be included in the inspection report.

12. Inspectors shall have the right to request clarifications in connection with ambiguities that arise during an inspection. Such request shall be made promptly through the in-country escort. The in-country escort shall provide the inspection team, during the inspection, with such clarifications as may be necessary to remove the ambiguity. In the event questions ralating to an object or building located within the inspection site are not resolved, the inspected Party shall photograph the object or building as requested by the inspecting Party for the purpose of clarifying its nature and function. If the ambiguity cannot be removed during the inspection, then the question, relevant clarifications and a copy of any photographs taken shall be included in the inspection report.

13. In carrying out their activities, inspectors shall observe safety regulations established at the inspection site, including those for the protection of controlled environments within a facility and for personal safety. Individual protective clothing and equipment shall be provided by the inspected Party, as necessary.

14. For inspections pursuant to paragraphs 3, 4, 5, 7 or 8 of Article 11 of the Treaty, pre-inspection procedures, including briefings and safety-related activities, shall begin upon arrival of the inspection team at the inspection site and shall be completed within one hour. The inspection team shall begin the inspection immediately upon completion of the pre-inspection procedures. The period of inspection shall not exceed 24 hours except for inspections pursuant to paragraphs 6, 7 or 8 of Article 11 of the Treaty. The period of inspection may be extended, by agreement with the in-country escort, by no more than eight hours. Post-inspection procedures, which include completing the inspection report in accordance with the provisions of Section XI of this Protocol, shall begin immediately upon completion of the inspection and shall be completed at the inspection site within four hours.

15. An inspection team conducting an inspection

pursuant to Article 11 of the Treaty shall include no more than ten inspectors, except for an inspection team conducting an inspection pursuant to paragraphs 7 or 8 of that Article, which shall include no more than 20 inspectors and an inspection team conducting inspection activities pursuant to paragraph 6 of that Article, which shall include no more than 30 inspectors. At least two inspectors on each team must speak the language of the inspected Party. An inspection team shall operate under the direction of the team leader and deputy team leader. Upon arrival at the inspection site, the inspection team may divide itself into subgroups consisting of no fewer than two inspectors each. There shall be no more than one inspection team at an inspection site at any one time.

16. Except in the case of inspections conducted pursuant to paragraph 3, 4, 7 or 8 of Article 11 of the Treaty, upon completion of the post-inspection procedures, the inspection team shall return promptly to the point of entry from which it commenced inspection activities and shall then leave, within 24 hours, the territory of the country in which the inspection site is located, using its own airplane. In the case of inspections conducted pursuant to paragraphs 3, 4, 7 or 8 of Article 11 of the Treaty, if the inspection team intends to conduct another inspection it shall either:

(a) notify the inspected Party of its intent upon return to the point of entry; or

(b) notify the inspected Party of the type of inspection and the inspection site upon completion of the post-inspection procedures. In this case it shall be the responsibility of the inspected Party to ensure that the inspection team reaches the next inspection site without unjustified delay. The inspected Party shall determine the means of transportation and route involved in such travel.

With respect to subparagraph (a), the procedures set forth in paragraph 7 of Section V of this Protocol and paragraphs 1 and 2 of Section VII of this Protocol shall apply.

VII. Inspections Conducted Pursuant to Paragraphs 3, 4 or 5 of Article 11 of the Treaty

1. Within one hour after the time for the specification of the inspection site notified pursuant to paragraph 1(a) of Section IV of this Protocol, the inspected Party shall implement pre-inspection movement restrictions at the inspection site, which shall remain in effect until the inspection team arrives at the inspection site. During the period that pre-inspection movement restrictions are in effect, missiles, stages of such missiles, launchers or support equipment subject to the Treaty shall not be removed from the inspection site.

2. The inspected Party shall transport the inspection team from the point of entry to the inspection site so that the inspection team arrives at the inspection site no later than nine hours after the time for the specification of the inspection site notified pursuant to paragraph 1(a) of Section IV of this Protocol.

3. In the event that an inspection is conducted in a basing country, the aircrew of the inspected Party may include representatives of the basing country.

4. Neither Party shall conduct more than one inspection pursuant to paragraph 5(a) of Article 11 of the Treaty at any one time, more than one inspection pursuant to paragraph 5(b) of Article 11 of the Treaty at any one time, or more than 10 inspections pursuant to paragraph 3 of Article 11 of the Treaty at any one time.

5. The boundaries of the inspection site at the facility to be inspected shall be the boundaries of that facility set forth in the Memorandum of Understanding.

6. Except in the case of an inspection conducted pursuant to paragraphs 4 or 5(b) of Article 11 of the Treaty, upon arrival of the inspection team at the inspection site, the in-country escort shall inform the inspection team leader of the number of missiles, stages of missiles, launchers, support structures and support equipment at the site that are subject to the Treaty and provide the inspection team leader with a diagram of the inspection site indicating the location of these missiles, stages of missiles, launchers, support structures and support equipment at the inspection site.

7. Subject to the procedures of paragraphs 8 through 14 of this Section, inspectors shall have the right to inspect the entire inspection site, including the interior of structures, containers or vehicles, or including covered objects, whose dimensions are equal to or greater than the dimensions specified in Section VI of the Memorandum of Understanding for the missiles, stages of such missiles, launchers or support equipment of the inspected Party.

8. A missile, a stage of such a missile or a launcher subject to the Treaty shall be subject to inspection only by external visual observation, including measuring, as necessary, the dimensions of such a missile, stage of such a missile or launcher. A container that the inspected Party declares to contain a missile or stage of a missile subject to the Treaty, and which is not sufficiently large to be capable of containing more than one missile or stage of such a missile of

the inspected Party subject to the Treaty, shall be subject to inspection only by external visual observation, including measuring, as necessary, the dimensions of such a container to confirm that it cannot contain more than one missile or stage of such a missile of the inspected Party subject to the Treaty. Except as provided for in paragraph 14 of this Section, a container that is sufficiently large to contain a missile or stage of such a missile of the inspected Party subject to the Treaty that the inspected Party declares not to contain a missile or stage of such a missile subject to the Treaty shall be subject to inspection only by means of weighing or visual observation of the interior of the container, as necessary, to confirm that it does not, in fact, contain a missile or stage of such a missile of the inspected Party subject to the Treaty. If such a container is a launch canister associated with a type of missile not subject to the Treaty, and declared by the inspected Party to contain such a missile, it shall be subject to external inspection only, including use of radiation detection devices, visual observation and linear measurement, as necessary, of the dimensions of such a canister.

9. A structure or container that is not sufficiently large to contain a missile, stage of such a missile or launcher of the inspected Party subject to the Treaty shall be subject to inspection only by external visual observation including measuring, as necessary, the dimensions of such a structure or container to confirm that it is not sufficiently large to be capable of containing a missile, stage of such a missile or launcher of the inspected Party subject to the Treaty.

10. Within a structure, a space which is sufficiently large to contain a missile, stage of such a missile or launcher of the inspected Party subject to the Treaty, but which is demonstrated to the satisfaction of the inspection team not be accessible by the smallest missile, stage of a missile or launcher of the inspected Party subject to the Treaty shall not be subject to further inspection. If the inspected Party demonstrates to the satisfaction of the inspection team by means of a visual inspection of the interior of an enclosed space from its entrance that the enclosed space does not contain any missile, stage of such a missile or launcher of the inspected Party subject to the Treaty, such an enclosed space shall not be subject to further inspection,

11. The inspection team shall be permitted to patrol the perimeter of the inspection site and station inspectors at the exits of the site for the duration of the inspection.

12. The inspection team shall be permitted to inspect any vehicle capable of carrying missiles, stage of such missiles, launchers or support equipment of the inspected Party subject to the Treaty at any time during the course of an inspection and no such vehicle shall leave the inspection site during the course of the inspection until inspected at site exits by the inspection team.

13. Prior to inspection of a building within the inspection site, the inspection team may station subgroups at the exits of the building that are large enough to permit passage of any missile, stage of such a missile, launcher or support equipment of the inspected Party subject to the Treaty. During the time that the building is being inspected, no vehicle or object capable of containing any missile, stage of such a missile launcher or support equipment of the inspected Party subject to the Treaty shall be permitted to leave the building until inspected.

14. During an inspection conducted pursuant to paragraph 5(b) of Article 11 of the Treaty, it shall be the responsibility of the inspected Party to demonstrate that a shrouded or environmentally protected object which is equal to or larger than the smallest missile, stage of a missile or launcher of the inspected Party subject to the Treaty is not, in fact, a missile, stage of such a missile or launcher of the inspected Party subject to the Treaty. This may be accomplished by partial removal of the shroud or environmental protection cover, measuring, or weighing the covered object or by other methods. If the inspected Party satisfies the inspection team by its demonstration that the object is not a missile, stage of such a missile or launcher of the inspected Party to the Treaty, then there shall be no further inspection of that object. If the container is a launch canister associated with a type of missile not subject to the Treaty, and declared by the inspected party to contain such a missile, then it shall be subject to external inspection only, including use of radiation detection devices, visual observation and linear measurement, as necessary, of the dimensions of such a canister.

VIII. Inspections Conducted Pursuant to Paragraphs 7 or 8 of Article 11 of the Treaty

1. Inspections of the process of elimination of items of missile systems specified in the Protocol on Elimination carried out pursuant to paragraph 7 of Article 11 of the Treaty shall be conducted in accordance with the procedures set forth in this paragraph and the Protocol on Elimination.

(a) Upon arrival at the elimination facility, inspectors shall be provided with a schedule of elimination activities.

(b) Inspectors shall check the data which are specified in the notification provided by the inspected Party regarding the number and type of items of missile systems to be eliminated against the number and type of such items which are at the elimination facility prior to the initiation of the elimination procedures.

(c) Subject to paragraphs 3 and 11 of Section VI of this Protocol, inspectors shall observe the execution of the specific procedures for the elimination of the items of missile systems as provided for in the Protocol on Elimination. If any deviations from the agreed elimination procedures are found, the inspectors shall have the right to call the attention of the in-country escort to the need for strict compliance with the above-mentioned procedures. The completion of such procedures shall be confirmed in accordance with the procedures specified in the Protocol on Elimination.

(d) During the elimination of missiles by means of launching, the inspectors shall have the right to ascertain by visual observation that a missile prepared for launch is a missile of the type subject to elimination. The inspectors shall also be allowed to observe such a missile from a safe location specified by the inspected Party until the completion of its launch. During the inspection of a series of launches for the elimination of missiles by means of launching, the inspected Party shall determine the means of transport and route for the transportion of inspectors between inspection sites.

2. Inspections of the elimination of items of missile systems specified in the Protocol on Elimination carried out pursuant to paragraph 8 of Article 11 of the Treaty shall be conducted in accordance with the procedures set forth in Sections II, IV or V of the Protocol on Elimination or as otherwise agreed by the Parties.

IX. Inspection Activities Conducted Pursuant to Paragraph 6 of Article 11 of the Treaty

1. The inspected Party shall maintain an agreed perimeter around the periphery of the inspection site and shall designate a portal with not more than one rail line and one road which shall be within 50 meters of each other. All vehicles which can contain an intermediate-range GLBM or longest stage of such a GLBM of the inspected Party shall exit only through this portal.

2. For the purposes of this Section, the provisions of paragraph 10 of Article 7 of the Treaty shall be applied to intermediate-range GLBMs of the inspected Party and the longest stage of such GLBMs.

3. There shall not be more than two other exits from the inspection site. Such exits shall be monitored by appropriate sensors. The perimeter of and exits from the inspection site may be monitored as provided for by paragraph 11 of Section VII of this Protocol.

4. The inspecting Party shall have the right to establish continuous monitoring systems at the portal specified in paragraph 1 of this Section and appropriate sensors at the exits specified in paragraph 3 of this Section and carry out necessary engineering surveys, construction, repair and replacement of monitoring systems.

5. The inspected Party shall, at the request of and at the expense of the inspecting Party, provide the following:

(a) all necessary utilities for the construction and operation of the monitoring systems, including electrical power, water, fuel, heating and sewage;

(b) basic construction materials including concrete and lumber;

(c) the site preparation necessary to accommodate the installation of continuously operating systems for monitoring the portal specified in paragraph 1 of this Section, appropriate sensors for other exits specified in paragraph 3 of this Section and the center for collecting data obtained during inspections, laying of concrete foundations, trenching between equipment locations and utility connections;

(d) transportation for necessary installation tools, materials and equipment from the point of entry to the inspection site; and

(e) a minimum of two telephone lines and, as necessary, high frequency radio equipment capable of allowing direct communication with the embassy of the inspecting Party in the country in which the site is located.

6. Outside the perimeter of the inspection site, the inspecting Party shall have the right to:

(a) build no more than three buildings with a total floor space of not more than 150 square meters for a data center and inspection team headquarters, and one additional building with floor space not to exceed 500 square meters for the storage of supplies and equipment;

(b) install systems to monitor the exits to include weight sensors, vehicle sensors, surveillance systems and vehicle dimensional measuring equipment;

(c) install at the portal specified in paragraph 1 of this Section equipment for measuring the length and diameter of missile stages contained inside of launch canisters or shipping containers;

(d) install at the portal specified in paragraph 1 of this Section non-damaging image producing equipment for imaging the contents of launch canisters or shipping containers declared to contain missiles or missile stages as provided for in paragraph 11 of this Section;

(e) install a primary and back-up power source; and

(f) use, as necessary, data authentication devices.

7. During the installation or operation of the monitoring systems, the inspecting Party shall not deny the inspected Party access to any existing structures or security systems. The inspecting Party shall not take any actions with respect to such structures without consent of the inspected Party. If the Parties agree that such structures are to be rebuilt or demolished, either partially or completely, the inspecting Party shall provide the necessary compensation.

8. The inspected Party shall not interfere with the installed equipment or restrict the access of the inspection team to such equipment.

9. The inspecting Party shall have the right to use its own two-way systems of radio communication between inspectors patrolling the perimeter and the data collection center. Such systems shall conform to power and frequency restrictions established on the territory of the inspected Party.

10. Aircraft shall not be permitted to land within the perimeter of the monitored site except for emergencies at the site and with prior notification to the inspection team.

11. Any shipment exiting through the portal specified in paragraph 1 of this Section which is large enough and heavy enough to contain an intermediate-range GLBM or longest stage of such a GLBM of the inspected Party shall be declared by the inspected Party to the inspection team before the shipment arrives at the portal. The declaration shall state whether such a shipment contains a missile or missile stage as large or larger than and as heavy or heavier than an intermediate-range GLBM or longest stage of such a GLBM of the inspected Party.

12. The inspection team shall have the right to weigh and measure the dimensions of any vehicle, including railcars, exiting the site to ascertain whether it is large enough and heavy enough to contain an intermediate-range GLBM or longest stage of such a GLBM of the inspected Party. These measurements shall be performed so as to minimize the delay of vehicles exiting the site. Vehicles that are either not large enough or not heavy enough to contain an intermediate-range GLBM or longest stage of such a GLBM of the inspected Party shall not be subject to further inspection.

13. Vehicles exiting through the portal specified in paragraph 1 of this Section that are large enough and heavy enough to contain an intermediate-range GLBM or longest stage of such a GLBM of the inspected Party but that are declared not to contain a missile or missile stage as large or larger than and as heavy or heavier than an intermediate-range GLBM or longest stage of such a GLBM of the inspected Party shall be subject to the following procedures.

(a) The inspecting Party shall have the right to inspect the interior of all such vehicles.

(b) If the inspection Party can determine by visual observation or dimensional measurement that, inside a particular vehicle, there are no containers or shrouded objects large enough to be or to contain an intermediate-range GLBM or longest stage of such a GLBM of the inspected Party, then that vehicle shall not be subject to further inspection.

(c) If inside a vehicle there are one or more containers or shrouded objects large enough to be or to contain an intermediate-range GLBM or longest stage of such a GLBM of the inspected Party, it shall be the responsibility of the inspected Party to demonstrate that such containers or shrouded objects are not and do not contain intermediate-range GLBMs or the longest stages of such GLBMs of the inspected Party.

14. Vehicles exiting through the portal specified in paragraph 1 of this Section that are declared to contain a missile or missile stage as large or larger than and as heavy or heavier than an intermediate-range GLBM or longest stage of such a GLBM of the inspected Party shall be subject to the following procedures.

(a) The inspecting Party shall preserve the integrity of the inspected missile or stage of a missile.

(b) Measuring equipment shall be placed only outside of the launch canister or shipping container; all measurements shall be made by the inspecting Party using the equipment provided for in paragraph 6 of this Section. Such measurements shall be observed and certified by the in-country escort.

(c) The inspecting Party shall have the right to weigh and measure the dimensions of any launch canister or of any shipping container declared to contain such a missile or missile stage and to image the contents of any launch canister or of any shipping container declared to contain such a missile or missile stage; it shall have the right to view such missiles or missile stages contained in launch canisters or shipping containers eight times per calendar year. The in-country escort shall be present during all phases of such viewing. During such interior viewing:

(i) the front end of the launch canister or the cover of the shipping container shall be opened;

(ii) the missile or missile stage shall not be removed from its launch canister or shipping container; and

(iii) the length and diameter of the stages of the missile shall be measured in accordance with the methods agreed by the Parties so as to ascertain that the missile or missile stage is not an intermediate-range GLBM of the inspected Party, or the longest stage of such a GLBM, and that the missile has no more than one stage which is outwardly similar to a stage of an existing type of intermediate-range GLBM.

(d) The inspecting Party shall also have the right to inspect any other containers or shrouded objects inside the vehicle containing such a missile or missile stage in accordance with the procedures in paragraph 13 of this Section.

X. Cancellation of Inspection

An inspection shall be cancelled if, due to circumstances brought about by force majeure, it cannot be carried out. In the case of a delay that prevents an inspection team performing an inspection pursuant to paragraphs 3, 4 or 5 of Article 11 of the Treaty, from arriving at the inspection site during the time specified in paragraph 2 of Section VII of this Protocol, the inspecting Party may either cancel or carry out the inspection. If an inspection is cancelled due to circumstances brought about by force majeure or delay, then the number of inspections to which the inspecting Party is entitled shall not be reduced.

XI. Inspection Report

1. For inspections conducted pursuant to paragraph 3, 4, 5, 7 or 8 of Article 11 of the Treaty, during post-inspection procedures, and no later than two hours after the inspection has been completed, the inspection team leader shall provide the in-country escort with a written inspection report in both the English and Russian languages. The report shall be factual. It shall include the type of inspection carried out, the inspection site, the number of missiles, stages of missiles, launchers and items of support equipment subject to the Treaty observed during the period of inspection and any measurements recorded pursuant to paragraph 10 of Section VI of this Protocol. Photographs taken during the inspection site diagram provided for by paragraph 6 of Section VII of this Protocol, shall be attached to this report.

2. For inspection activities conducted pursuant to paragraph 6 of Article 11 of the Treaty, within 3 days after the end of each month, the inspection team leader shall provide the in-country escort with a written inspection report both in the English and Russian languages. The report shall be factual. It shall include the number of vehicles declared to contain a missile or stage of a missile as large or larger than and as heavy or heavier than an intermediate-range GLBM or longest stage of such a GLBM of the inspected Party that left the inspection site through the portal specified in paragraph 1 of Section IX of this Protocol during that month. The report shall also include any measurements of launch canisters or shipping containers contained in these vehicles recorded pursuant to paragraph 11 of Section VI of this Protocol. In the event the inspecting Party, under the provisions of paragraph 14(c) of Section IX of this Protocol, has viewed the interior of a launch canister or shipping container declared to contain a missile or stage of a missile as large or larger than and as heavy or heavier than an intermediate-range GLBM or longest stage of such a GLBM of the inspected Party, the report shall also include the measurements of the length and diameter of missile stages obtained during the inspection and recorded pursuant to paragraph 11 of Section VI of this Protocol. Photographs taken during the inspection in accordance with agreed procedures shall be attached to this report.

3. The inspected Party shall have the right to include written comments in the report.

4. The Parties shall, when possible, resolve ambiguities regarding factual information contained in the inspection report. Relevant clarifications shall be recorded in the report. The report shall be signed by the inspection team leader and by one of the members of the in-country escort. Each Party shall retain one copy of the report.

This Protocol is an integral part of the Treaty. It shall enter into force on the date of entry into force of the Treaty and shall remain in force as long as the Treaty remains in force. As provided for in paragraph 1(b) of Article 13 of the Treaty, the Parties may agree upon such measures as may be necessary to improve the viability and effectiveness of this Protocol. Such measures shall not be deemed amendments to the Treaty.

Agreement among the United States of America and the Kingdom of Belgium, the Federal Republic of Germany, the Republic of Italy, the Kingdom of the Netherlands and the United Kingdom of Great Britain and Northern Ireland Regarding Inspections Relating to the Treaty Between the United States of America and the Union of Soviet Socialist Republics on the Elimination of their Intermediate-Range and Shorter-Range Missiles

Date of signature: December 11, 1987
Place of signature: Brussels
Signatory states: Belgium, The Federal Republic of Germany, Italy, Netherlands, Great Britain, Northern Ireland, The United States of America

[The signatories],
Noting the terms agreed between the United States of America and the Union of Soviet Socialist Republics for the elimination of their intermediate-range and shorter-range missiles,

Have agreed as follows;

Article I

General Obligations

1. Inspection activities related to Article 11 of the Treaty between the United States of America and the Union of Soviet Socialist Republics on the Elimination of Their Intermediate-Range and Shorter-Range Missiles, signed at Washington on December 8, 1987, may take place on the territory of the Kingdom of Belgium, the Federal Republic of Germany, the Republic of Italy, the Kingdom of the Netherlands and the United Kingdom of Great Britain and Northern Ireland and shall be carried out in accordance with the requirements, procedures and arrangements set forth in the Protocol Regarding Inspections Relating to the Treaty between the United States of America and the Union of Soviet Socialist Republics on the Elimination of Their Intermediate-Range and Shorter-Range Missiles and this Agreement.

2. The Kingdom of Belgium, the Federal Republic of Germany, the Republic of Italy, the Kingdom of the Netherlands and the United Kingdom of Great Britain and Northern Ireland, hereinafter the Basing Countries, hereby agree to facilitate the implementation by the United States of America of its obligations under the Treaty, including the inspection Protocol thereto, on their Territories in accordance with the requirements, procedures and arrangements set forth in this Agreement.

3. Except as herein agreed by the United States of America and the Basing Countries, nothing shall affect the sovereign authority of each state to enforce its laws and regulations with respect to persons entering, and activities taking place within, its jurisdiction.

4. The Basing Countries do not by this Agreement assume any obligations or grant any rights deriving from the Treaty or the Inspection Protocol other than those expressly undertaken or granted in this Agreement or otherwise with their specific consent.

5. The United States of America:

(a) Remains fully responsible towards the Soviet Union for the implementation of its obligations under the Treaty and the Inspection Protocol in respect of United States facilities located on the territories of the Basing Countries;

(b) Undertakes on request at any time to take such action, in exercise of its rights under the Treaty, including the Inspection Protocol, as may be required to protect and preserve the rights of the Basing Countries under this Agreement.

Article II

Definitions

For purposes of the present Agreement:

1. The term "Treaty" means the Treaty between the United States of America and the Union of Soviet Socialist Republics on the Elimination of Their Inter-mediate-Range and Shorter-Range Missiles;

2. The term "Inspection Protocol" means the Protocol Regarding Inspections Relating to the Treaty between the United States of America and the Union of Soviet Socialist Republics on the Elimination of Their Intermediate-Range and Shorter-Range Mis-siles;

3. The term "Inspected Party" means the United States of America;

4. The term "Inspecting Party" means Union of Soviet Socialist Republics;

5. The term "inspection team" means those inspect-ors designated by the Inspecting Party to conduct a particular inspection activity;

6. The term "inspector" means an individual pro-posed by the Union of Soviet Socialist Republics to carry out inspections pursuant to Article 11 of the Treaty, and included on its list of inspectors in accord-ance with Section III of the Inspection Protocol;

7. The term "diplomatic aircrew escort" means that individual accredited to the government of the Bas-ing Country in which the inspection site is located who is designated by the Inspecting Party to assist the aircrew of the Inspecting Party;

8. The term "inspection site" means the area, facili-ty, or location in a Basing Country at which an inspection provided for in Article 11 of the Treaty is carried out;

9. The term "period of inspection" means period from initiation of the inspection at the inspection site, until completion of the inspection at the inspection site, exclusive of time spent on any pre- and post-inspection procedures;

10. The term "point of entry" means: in respect of Belgium, Brussels (National); in respect of the Fede-ral Republic of Germany, Frankfurt (Rhein Main Air-base); in respect of Italy Rome (Ciampino); in respect of the Kingdom of the Netherlands, Schiphol; and in respect of the kingdom of the Great Britain and Northern Ireland, RAF Greenham Common;

11. The term "in-country period" means the period from the arrival of the inspection team at the point of entry until departure of the inspection team from the point of entry to depart the country;

12. The term "in-country escort" means official or officials specified by the Inspected Party, one or more of whom may be nominated by Basing Country within whose territory the inspection site is located, who shall accompany an inspection team throughout the in-country period and provide appropriate assist-ance to an inspection team, in accordance with the provisions of the Inspection Protocol, throughout the in-country period;

13. The term "aircrew member" means an indivi-dual, other than the member of an inspection team, diplomatic aircrew escort and in-country escort, on the aircraft of the Inspecting Party. The number of aircrew members per aircraft shall not exceed ten.

Article III

Notifications

1. Upon entry into force of this Agreement, the Inspected Party and each Basing Country shall estab-lish channels which shall be available to receive and acknowledge receipt of notifications on a 24 hour continous basis.

2. Immediately upon receipt of notice from the Inspecting Party of its intention to conduct an inspect-ion in a Basing Country, the Inspected Party shall notify the Basing Country concerned thereof and of the date and estimated time of arrival of the inspect-ion team at the point of entry, the date and estimated time arrival of the inspection team at the point of entry to the inspection site, the names of the aircrew and inspection team members, the flight plan (includ-ing the type of aircraft as specified therein) filed by the Inspecting Party in accordance with the Interna-tional Civil Aviation Organization, hereinafter ICAO, procedures applicable to civil aircraft, and any other information relevant to the inspection provided by the Inspecting Party.

3. No less than one hour prior to the estimated time of departure of the inspection team the point of entry for the inspection site, or in the case of successive inspections conducted pursuant to paragraphs 3, 4, 7 or 8 of Article 11 of the Treaty no less than one hour prior to the inspection team's departure from an inspection site for another inspection site, the Inspected Party shall inform the Basing Country of the inspection site, described by place name and geo-graphic coordinates, at which the inspection will be carried out.

Article IV

Pre-Inspection Arrangements

1. The Inspected Party shall provide the Basing Countries with the initial lists of inspectors and air-crew members, or any modification thereto, proposed by the Inspecting Party immediately upon receipt thereof. Within 15 days of receipt of the initial lists or proposed additions thereto, each Basing Country

shall notify the Inspected Party if it objects to the inclusion of any inspector or aircrew member on the basis that such individual had ever committed a criminal offense on the territory of the Inspected Party or the Basing Country, or been sentenced for committing a criminal offense or expelled by the Inspected Party or the Basing Country. The Inspected Party shall thereupon exercise its right under the Inspection Protocol to prevent the named individual from serving as an inspector or aircrew member.

2. Within 25 days of receipt of the initial lists of inspectors or aircrew member, or of any subsequent change thereto, each Basing Country shall provide such visas and related documentation as may be necessary to ensure that each inspector or aircrew member may enter its territory for the purpose of carrying out inspection activities in accordance with the provisions of the Treaty and the Inspection Protocol. Such visas and documentation shall be valid for a period of at least 24 months. The Inspected Party shall immediately notify the Inspecting Party's lists of inspectors or aircrew members, and the Basing Countries may thereupon cancel forthwith any visas and related documentation issued to such person pursuant to this paragraph.

3. Within 25 days after entry into force of this Agreement, each Basing Country shall inform the Inspected Party of the standing diplomatic clearance number for the aircraft of the Inspecting Party which will transport inspectors and equipment into its territory. At the same time each Basing Country shall inform the Inspected Party of the established international airways along which aircraft of the Inspecting Party shall enter the airspace of the Basing Country for the purpose of carrying out inspection activities under the Treaty.

4. Each Basing Country shall accord inspectors and aircrew members of the Inspecting Party entering its territory for the purpose of conducting inspection activities pursuant to the Treaty, including the Inspection Protocol, the privileges and immunities set forth in the Privileges and Immunities Annex to this Agreement. In the event the Inspecting Party refuses or fails to carry out its obligation under Section III, paragraph 7 of the Inspection Protocol to remove an inspector or aircrew member who has violated the conditions governing inspections, the inspector or aircrew member may be refused continued recognition as being entitled to such privileges and immunities.

5. Each Basing Country shall issue, at the point of entry, appropriate authorizations waiving customs duties and expediting customs processing requirements in respect of all equipment relating to inspect-

ion activities.

6. Each Basing Country shall provide, if requested, facilities at the point of entry for loading and the provision of food for inspectors and aircrew members.

7. The Basing Country in which the inspection is to take place shall have the right to examine jointly with Inspected Party each item of equipment brought in by the Inspecting Party to ascertain that the equipment cannot be used to perform functions unconnected with the inspection requirements of the Treaty. If it is established upon examination that a piece of equipment is unconnected with these inspection requirements, it shall not be cleared for use and shall be impounded at the point of entry until the departure of the inspection team from the country.

Article V

Conduct of Inspections

1. Within 90 minutes of receipt from the Inspected Party of notification that a flight plan for an aircraft of the Inspecting Party has been filed in accordance with ICAO procedures applicable to civil aircraft, the Basing Country in whose territory the inspection site is located shall provide the Inspected Party with its approval for the aircraft of the Inspecting Party to proceed to the point of entry via the filed routing, or an amended routing if necessary.

2. The Basing Country in whose territory the inspection site is located shall facilitate the entry of inspectors and aircrew into the country, and shall take the steps necessary to ensure that the baggage and equipment of the inspection team is identified and transported expeditiously through customs.

3. Upon notification by the Inspected Party, in accordance with Article III above, of the inspection site, the Basing Country in whose territory the inspection is to take place shall take the steps necessary to ensure that the inspection team is granted all clearances and assistance necessary to enable it to proceed expeditiously to the inspection site and to arrive at the inspection site within nine hours of the Inspecting Party's notification of the site to be inspected. The Inspected Party and the Basing Country in which the inspection site is located shall consult with respect to the mode of transport to be utilized, and the Basing Country shall have the right to designate the routing between the point of entry and the inspection site.

4. Each Basing Country shall assist the Inspected Party, as necessary, in providing two-way voice communication capability for an inspection team between an inspection site within its territory and the embassy

of the Inspecting Party.

5. The Inspected Party and the Basing Country within whose territory an inspection site is located shall consult with respect to aircraft servicing and provision of meals, lodging, and services for inspectors and aircrew member at the point of entry and inspected site. The cost of foregoing requested by the Inspected Party and provided by the Basing Country shall be borne by the Inspected Party.

6. In the event the Inspecting Party requests an extension, which shall not exceed eight hours beyond the original 24-hour period of inspection as provided for in Section VI, paragraph 14 of the Inspection Protocol, the Inspected Party shall immediately notify the Basing Country in whose territory the inspection site is located of the extension.

Article VI

Consultations

1. Within five days after entry into force of this Agreement, the Inspected Party and the Basing Countries shall meet to coordinate implementation of the inspection activities provided for in Article 11 of the Treaty, the Inspection Protocol and this Agreement.

2. A meeting between the Inspected Party and any Basing Country to discuss implementation of this Agreement shall be held within five days of a request for such a meeting by the Inspected Party or a Basing Country

3. Should any question arise which in the opinion of a Basing Country requires immediate attention, the Basing Country may contact the inspection notification authority of the Inspected Party. The Inspected Party will immediately acknowledge receipt of the inquiry or question and give urgent attention to the question or problem.

4. In the event that a Basing Country determines that an inspector or aircrew member has violated the conditions governing inspection within its territory, the Basing Country may notify the Inspected Party which shall inform the Inspecting Party of the disqualification of the inspector or aircrew member. The name of the individual will be removed from the list of inspectors or aircrew members.

5. A Basing Country may change the point of entry for its territory by giving six month's notice of such change to the Inspected Party.

6. Upon completion of an inspection, the Inspected Party shall advise the Basing Country within whose territory the inspection took place that the inspection has been completed, and upon request of the Basing Country provide a briefing for the Basing Country on the inspection.

7. The United States of America shall not, without the express agreement of the Basing Countries, propose or accept any amendment to Article 11 of the Treaty or to the Inspection Protocol that directly affects the rights, interests or obligations of the Basing Countries.

Article VII

Entry into Force and Duration

This Agreement shall be subject to approval in accordance with the constitutional procedures of each Party, which approval shall be notified by each Party to each of the other Parties. Following such notification by all Parties, the Agreement shall enter into force simultaneously with the entry into force of the Treaty and shall remain in force for a period of thirteen years.

Annex

Provisions on privileges and immunities of inspectors and aircrew members

In order to exercise their functions effectively, for the purpose of implementing the Treaty and not for their personal benefit, inspectors and aircrew members shall be accorded the privileges and immunities contained herein. Privileges and immunities shall be accorded for the entire in-country period in the country in which an inspection site is located, and thereafter with respect to acts previously performed in the exercise of official function as an inspector aircrew member.

1. Inspectors and aircrew members shall be accorded the inviolability enjoyed by diplomatic agents pursuants to Article 29 of the Vienna Convention on Diplomatic Relations of April 18, 1961.

2. The papers and correspondence of inspectors and aircrew members shall enjoy the inviolability accorded to the papers and correspondence of diplomatic agents pursuant to Article 30 of the Vienna Convention on Diplomatic Relations. In addition, the aircraft of the inspection team shall be inviolable.

3. Inspectors and aircrew members shall be accorded the immunities accorded diplomatic agents pursuant to paragraphs (1), (2) and (3) of Article 31 of the Vienna Convention on Diplomatic Relations. The immunity from jurisdiction of an inspector or an aircrew member may be waived by the Inspecting Party in those cases when it is of the opinion that immunity would impede the course of justice and that it can be

waived without prejudice to the implementation of the provisions of the Treaty. Waiver must always be expressed.

4. Inspectors and aircrew members of the Inspecting Party shall be permitted to bring into the territory of a Basing Country in which an inspection site is located, without payment of any customs duties or related charges, articles for their personal use, with the exception of articles the import or export of which is prohibited by law or controlled by quarantine regulations.

5. An inspectors or aircrew member shall not engaged in any professional or commercial activity for personal profit on the territory of the Basing Countries.

Bilateral Agreement Between the Republic of Afghanistan and the Islamic Republic of Pakistan on the Principles of Mutual Relations, in Particular on Non-Interference and Non-Intervention

Date of signature: April 14, 1988
Place of signature: Geneva
Signatory states: Afghanistan, Pakistan,
The United States, The Union of Soviet Socialist Republics
Date of entry into force: May 15, 1988

[The signatories], hereinafter referred to as the High Contracting Parties,

Desiring to normalize relations and promote good-neighbourliness and co-operation as well as to strengthen international peace and security in the region,

Considering that full observance of the principle of non-interference and non-intervention in the internal and external affairs of states is of the greatest importance for the maintenance of international peace and security and for the fulfillment of the purposes and principles of the charter of the United Nations,

Reaffirming the inalienable right of states freely to determine their own political, economic, cultural and social systems in accordance with the will of their peoples, without outside intervention, interference, subversion, coercion or threat in any form whatsoever,

Mindful of the provisions of the Charter of the United Nations as well as the resolutions adopted by the United Nations on the principle of non-interference and non-intervention, in particular the declaration on principles of international law concerning friendly relations and co-operation among States in accordance with the charter of the United Nations, of 24 October 1970, as well as the declaration on the inadmissibility of intervention and interference in the internal affairs of States, of 9 December 1981,

Have agreed as follows:

Article 1

Relations between the high Contracting Parties shall be conducted in strict compliance with the principle of non-interference and non-intervention by States in the affairs of other States.

Article 2

For the purpose of implementing the principle of non-interference and non-intervention each High Contracting Party undertakes to comply with the following obligations:

(1) To respect the sovereignty, political independence, territorial integrity, national unity, security and non-alignment of the other High Contracting Party, as well as the national identity and cultural heritage of its people;

(2) To respect the sovereign and inalienable right of the other High Contracting Party freely to determine its own political, economic, cultural and social systems, to develop its international relations and to exercise permanent sovereignty over its natural resources, in accordance with the will of its people, and without outside intervention, interference, subversion, coercion or threat in any form whatsoever;

(3) To refrain from the threat or use of force in any form whatsoever so as not to violate the boundaries of each other, to disrupt the political, social or economic order of the other high contracting party, to overthrow or change the political system of the other High Contracting Party or its government, or to cause tension between the High Contracting Parties;

(4) To ensure that its territory is not used in any manner which would violate the sovereignty, political independence, territorial integrity and national unity or disrupt the political, economic and social stability of the other High Contracting Party;

(5) To refrain from armed intervention, subversion, military occupation or any other form of intervention and interference, overt or covert, directed at the other High Contracting Party, or any act of military, political or economic interference in the internal affairs of the other High Contracting Party, including acts of reprisal involving the use of force;

(6) To refrain from any action or attempt in whatever form or under whatever pretext to destabilize or to undermine the stability of the other High Contracting Party or any of its institutions;

(7) To refrain from the promotion, encouragement or support, direct or indirect, of rebellious or secessionist activities against the other High Contracting Party, under any pretext whatsoever, or from any other action which seeks to disrupt the unity or to undermine or subvert the political order of the other High Contracting Party;

(8) To prevent within its territory the training, equipping, financing and recruitment of mercenaries from whatever origin for the purpose of hostile activities against the other High Contracting Party, or the sending of such mercenaries into the territory of the other high contracting party and accordingly to deny facilities, including financing for the training, equipping and transit of such mercenaries;

(9) To refrain from making any agreements or arrangements with other States designed to intervene or interfere in the internal and external affairs of the other High Contracting Party;

(10) To abstain from any defamatory campaign, vilification or hostile propaganda for the purpose of intervening or interfering in the internal affairs of the other high contracting party;

(11) To prevent any assistance to or use of or tolerance of terrorist groups, saboteurs or subversive agents against the other High Contracting Party;

(12) To prevent within its territory the presence, harbouring, in camps and bases or otherwise, organizing, training, financing, equipping and arming of individuals and political, ethnic and any other groups for the purpose of creating subversion, disorder or unrest in the territory of the other High Contracting Party and accordingly also to prevent the use of mass media and the transportation of arms, ammunition and equipment by such individuals and groups;

(13) Not to resort to or to allow any other action that could be considered as interference or intervention.

Article 3

The present Agreement shall enter into force on 15 May 1988.

Article 4

Any steps that may be required in order to enable the high contracting parties to comply with the provisions of Article 2 of this agreement shall be completed by the date on which this Agreement enters into force.

Article 5

This Agreement is drawn up in the English, Pashtu, and Urdu languages, all texts being equally authentic. In case of any divergence of interpretation, the English text shall prevail.

Declaration on International Guarantees

The Governments of the United States of America and of the Union of Soviet Socialist Republics,

Expressing support that the Republic of Afghanistan and the Islamic Republic of Pakistan have concluded a negotiated political settlement designed to normalize relations and promote good-neighbourliness between the two countries as well as to strengthen international peace and security in the region;

Wishing in turn to contribute to the achievement of the objectives that the Republic of Afghanistan and the Islamic Republic of Pakistan have set themselves, and with a view to ensuring respect for their sovereignty, independence, territorial integrity and non-alignment;

Undertake to invariably refrain from any form of interference and intervention in the internal affairs of the Republic of Afghanistan and the Islamic Republic of Pakistan and to respect the commitments contained in the bilateral agreement between the Republic of Afghanistan and the Islamic Republic of Pakistan on the principles of mutual relations, in particular on non-interference and non-intervention;

The present declaration shall enter into force on 15 May 1988.

Agreement on the Interrelationships for the Settlement of the Situation Relating to Afghanistan

1. The diplomatic process initiated by the Secretary General of the United Nations with the support of all Governments concerned and aimed at achieving, through negotiations, a political settlement of the situation relating to Afghanistan has been successfully brought to an end.

2. Having agreed to work towards a comprehensive settlement designed to resolve the various issues involved and to establish a framework for good-neighbourliness and co-operation, the government of the Republic of Afghanistan and the government of the Islamic Republic of Pakistan entered into negotiations through the intermediary of the personal representative of the Secretary General at Geneva from 16 to 24 June 1982. Following consultations held by the personal representative in Islamabad, Kabul and Teheran from 21 January to 7 February 1983, the negotiations continued at Geneva from 11 to 22 April and from 12 to 24 June 1983. The personal representative again visited the area for high level discussions from 3 to 15 April 1984. It was then agreed to change the format of the negotiations and, in pursuance thereof, proximity talks through the intermediary of the personal representative were held at Geneva from 24 to 30 August 1984. Another visit to the area by the personal representative from 25 to 31 May 1985 preceded further rounds of proximity talks held at Geneva from 20 to 25 June from 27 to 30 August and from 16 to 19 December 1985. The personal representative paid an additional visit to the area from 8 to 18 March 1986 for consultations. The final round of negotiations began as proximity talks at Geneva on 5 May 1986, was suspended on 23 May 1986, and was resumed from 31 July to 8 August 1986. The personal representative visited the area from 20 November to 3 December 1986 for further consultations and the talks at Geneva were resumed again from 25 February to 9 March 1987, and from 7 to 11 September 1987. The personal representative again visited the area from 18 January to 9 February 1988 and the talks resumed at Geneva from 2 March to 8 April 1988. The format of the negotiations was changed on 14 April 1988, when the instruments comprising the settlement were finalized, and, accordingly, direct talks were held at that stage. The government of the Islamic Republic of Iran was kept informed of the progress of the negotiations throughout the diplomatic process.

3. The government of the Republic of Afghanistan and the government of the Islamic Republic of Pakistan took part in the negotiations with the expressed conviction that they were acting in accordance with their rights and obligations under the charter of the United Nations and agreed that the political settlement should be based on the following principles of international law:

• The principle that states shall refrain in their international relations from the threat or use of force against the territorial integrity or political independence of any state, or in any other manner inconsistent with the purposes of the United Nations;

• The principle that states shall settle their international disputes by peaceful means in such a manner that international peace and security and justice are not endangered;

• The duty not to intervene in matters within the domestic jurisdiction of any state, in accordance with the Charter of the United Nations;

• The duty of States to co-operate with one another in accordance with the Charter of the United Nations;

• The principle of equal rights and self-determination of peoples;

• The principle of sovereign equality of States;

• The principle that States shall fulfill in good faith the obligations assumed by them in accordance with the Charter of the United Nations.

The two governments further affirmed the right of the Afghan refugees to return to their homeland in a voluntary and unimpeded manner.

4. The following instruments were concluded on this date as component parts of the political settlement:

A Bilateral Agreement between the Republic of Afghanistan and the Islamic Republic of Pakistan on the principles of mutual relations, in particular on non-interference and non-intervention;

A declaration on international guarantees by the United States of America and the Union of Soviet Socialist Republics;

A Bilateral Agreement between the Republic of Afghanistan and the Islamic Republic of Pakistan on the voluntary Return of refugees;

The present Agreement on the interrelationships for the settlement of the situation relating to Afghanistan.

5. The Bilateral Agreement on the principles of mutual relations, in particular on non-interference

and non-intervention; the declaration on international guarantees; the Bilateral Agreement on the voluntary return of refugees; and the present Agreement on the interrelationships for the settlement of the situation relating to Afghanistan will enter into force on 15 May 1988. In accordance with the timeframe agreed upon between the Republic of Afghanistan and the Union of Soviet Socialist Republics there will be a phased withdrawal of the foreign troops which will start on the date of entry into force mentioned above. One half of the troops will be withdrawn by 15 August 1988 and the withdrawal of all troops will be completed within nine months.

6. The interrelationships in paragraph 5 above have been agreed upon in order to achieve effectively the purpose of the political settlement, namely, that from 15 May 1988, there will be no interference and intervention in any form in the affairs of the parties; the international guarantees will be in operation; the voluntary return of the refugees to their homeland will start and be completed within the timeframe specified in the agreement on the voluntary return of the refugees; and the phased withdrawal of the foreign troops will start and be completed within the timeframe envisaged in paragraph 5. It is therefore, essential that all the obligations deriving from the instruments concluded as component parts of the settlement be strictly fulfilled and that all the steps required to ensure full compliance with all the provisions of the instruments be completed in good faith.

7. To consider alleged violations and to work out prompt and mutually satisfactory solutions to questions that may arise in the implementation of the instruments comprising the settlement representatives of the Republic of Afghanistan and the Islamic Republic of Pakistan shall meet whenever required.

A representative of the Secretary General of the United Nations shall lend his good offices to the parties and in that context he will assist in the organization of the meetings and participate in them. He may submit to the parties for their consideration and approval suggestions and recommendations for prompt, faithful and complete observance of the provisions of the instruments.

In order to enable him to fulfill his tasks, the representative shall be assisted by such personnel under his authority as required. On his own initiative, or at the request of any of the parties, the personnel shall investigate any possible violations of any of the provisions of the instruments and prepare a report thereon. For that purpose, the representative and his personnel shall receive all the necessary co-operation from the parties, including all freedom of movement within their respective territories required for effective investigation. Any report submitted by the representative to the two governments shall be considered in a meeting of the Parties no later than forty-eight hours after it has been submitted.

The modalities and logistical arrangements for the work of the representative and the personnel under his authority as agreed upon with the Parties are set out in the Memorandum of Understanding which is annexed to and is part of this Agreement.

8. The present instrument will be registered with the Secretary General of the United Nations. It has been examined by the representatives of Parties to the Bilateral Agreements and of the States Guarantors, who have signified their consent with its provision. The representatives of the Parties, being duly authorized thereto by their respective governments, have affixed their signatures hereunder. The Secretary General of the United Nations was present.

Agreement Between the United States of America and the Union of Soviet Socialist Republics on Notifications of Launches of Intercontinental Ballistic Missiles and Submarine-Launched Ballistic Missiles

Date of signature: May 31, 1988
Place of signature: Moscow
Signatory states: The United States of America,
The Union of Soviet Socialist Republics
Date of entry into force: May 31, 1988

[The signatories], hereinafter referred to as the Parties.

Affirming their desire to reduce and ultimately eliminate the risk of outbreak of nuclear war, in particular, as a result of misinterpretation, miscalculation, or accident,

Believing that a nuclear war cannot be won and must never be fought,

Believing that agreement on measures for reducing

the risk of outbreak of nuclear war serves the interests of strengthening international peace and security,

Reaffirming their obligations under the Agreement on Measures to Reduce the Risk of Outbreak of Nuclear War between the United States of America and the Union of Soviet Socialist Republics of September 30, 1971, the Agreement between the United States of America and the Government of the Union of Soviet Socialist Republics on the Prevention of Incidents on and over the High Seas of May 25, 1972, and the Agreement between the United States of America and the Union of Soviet Socialist Republics on the Establishment of Nuclear Risk Reduction Centers of September 15, 1987.

Have agreed as follows:

Article I

Each Party shall provide the other Party notification, through the Nuclear Risk Reduction Centers of the United States of America and the Union of Soviet Socialist Republics, no less than twenty-four hours in advance, of the planned date, launch area, and area of impact for any launch of a strategic ballistic missile: an intercontinental ballistic missile (hereinafter "ICBM") or a submarine-launched ballistic missile (hereinafter "SLBM")

Article II

A notification of a planned launch of an ICBM or an SLBM shall be valid for four days counting from the launch date indicated in such a notification. In case of postponement of the launch date within the indicated four days, or cancellation of the launch, no notification thereof shall be required.

Article III

1. For launches of ICBMS or SLBMS from land, the notification shall indicate the area from which the launch is planned to take place.

2. For launches of SLBMs from submarines, the notification shall indicate the general area from which the missile will be launched. Such notification shall indicate either the quadrant within the ocean (that is, the ninety-degree sector encompassing approximately one-fourth of the the area of the ocean) or the body of water (for example, sea or bay) from which the launch is planned to take place.

3. For all launches of ICBMS or SLBMS, the notification shall indicate the geographic coordinates of the planned impact area or areas of the reentry vehicles. Such an area shall be specified either by indicating the geographic coordinates of the boundary points of the area, or by indicating the geographic coordinates of the center of a circle with a radius specified in kilometers or nautical miles. The size of the impact area shall be determined by the notifying Party at its discretion.

Article IV

The Parties undertake to hold consultations, as mutually agreed, to consider questions relating to implementation of the provisions of this Agreement, as well as to discuss possible amendments thereto aimed at furthering the implementation of the objectives of this Agreement. Amendments shall enter into force in accordance with procedures to be agreed upon.

Article V

This Agreement shall not affect the obligations of either Party under other agreements.

Article VI

This Agreement shall enter into force on the date of its signature.

The duration of this Agreement shall not be limited.

This Agreement may be terminated by either Party upon 12 months written notice to the other Party.

Agreement Between the Government of the United States of America and the Government of the Union of Soviet Socialist Republics on the Prevention of Dangerous Military Activities

Date of signature: June 12, 1989
Place of signature: Moscow
Signatory states: The United States, The Union of

Soviet Republics
Date of entry into force: January 1, 1990

[The signatories], hereinafter referred to as the Parties.

Confirming their desire to improve relations and deepen mutual understanding. Convinced of the necessity to prevent dangerous military activities, and thereby to reduce the possibility of incidents arising between their armed forces.

Committed to resolving expeditiously and peacefully any incident between their armed forces which may arise as a result of dangerous military activities.

Desiring to ensure the safety of the personnel and equipment of their armed force when operating in proximity to one another during peacetime, and

Guided by generally recognized principles and rules of international law,

Have agreed as follow:

Article I

For the purpose of this Agreement:

1. "Armed forces" means, for the United States of America: the armed forces of the United States, including the United States Coast Guard; for the Union of Soviet Socialist Republics: the armed forces of the USSR, and the Border Troops of the USSR.

2. "Personnel" means any individual, military or civilian, who is serving in or employed by the armed force of the Parties.

3. "Equipment" means any ship, aircraft or ground hardware of the armed forces of the Parties.

4. "Ship" means any warship or auxiliary ship of the armed forces of the Parties.

5. "Aircraft" means any military aircraft of the armed forces of the Parties, excluding spacecraft.

6. "Ground hardware" means any material of the armed forces of the Parties designed for use on land.

7. "Laser" means any source of intense, coherent, highly directional electromagnetic radiation in the visible, infrared, or ultraviolet regions that is based on the stimulated radiation of elections, atoms or molecules.

8. "Special Caution Area" means a region, designated mutually by the Parties, in which personnel and equipment of their armed force are present and, due to circumstances in the region, in which special measures shall be undertaken in accordance with this Agreement.

9. "Interference with command and control networks" means actions that hamper, interrupt or limit the operation of the signals and information transmission means and systems providing for the control of personnel and equipment of the armed forces of a Party.

Article II

1. In accordance with the provisions of this Agreement, each Party shall take necessary measures directed toward preventing dangerous military activities, which are the following activities of personnel and equipment of its armed forces when operating in proximity to personnel and equipment of the armed forces of the other Party during peacetime:

(a) Entering by personnel and equipment of the armed forces of one Party into the national territory of the other Party owing to circumstances brought about by *force majeure*, or as a result of unintentional actions by such personnel;

(b) Using a laser in such a manner that its radiation could cause harm to personnel or damage to equipment of the armed forces of the other Party;

(c) Hampering the activities of the personnel and equipment of the armed forces of the other Party in a Special Caution Area in a manner which could cause harm to personnel or damage to equipment; and

(d) Interfering with command and control networks in a manner which could cause harm to personnel or damage to equipment of the armed forces of the other party.

2. The Parties shall take measures to ensure expeditious termination and resolution by peaceful means, without resort to the threat or use of force, of any incident which may arise as a result of dangerous military activities.

3. Additional provisions concerning prevention of dangerous military activities and resolution of any incident which may arise as a result of those activities are contained in Articles III, IV, V and VI of this Agreement and the Annexes thereto.

Article III

1. In the interest of mutual safety, personnel of the armed forces of the Parties shall exercise great caution and prudence while operating near the national territory of the other Party.

2. If, owing to circumstances brought about by *force majeure* or as a result of unintentional actions, as set forth in Article II, subparagraph 1(a) of this Agreement, personnel and equipment of the armed forces of one Party enter into the national territory of the other Party, such personnel shall adhere to the procedures set forth in Annexes 1 and 2 to this Agreement.

Article IV

1. When personnel of the armed forces of one Party, in proximity to personnel and equipment of the armed forces of the other Party, intend to use a laser and that use could cause harm to personnel or damage to equipment of the armed forces of that other Party, the personnel of the armed forces of the Party intending such use of a laser shall attempt to notify the relevant personnel of the armed forces of the other Party. In any case, personnel of the armed forces of the Party intending use of a laser shall follow appropriate safety measures.

2. If personnel of the armed forces of one Party believe that personnel of the armed forces of the other Party are using a laser in a manner which could cause harm to them or damage to their equipment, they shall immediately attempt to establish communications to seek termination of such use. If the personnel of the armed forces of the Party having received such notification are actually using a laser in proximity to the area indicated in the notification, they shall investigate the relevant circumstances. If their use of a laser could in fact cause harm to personnel or damage to equipment of the armed forces of other Party, they shall terminate such use.

3. Notifications with respect to the use of a laser shall be made in the manner provided for in Annex 1 to this Agreement.

Article V

1. Each Party may propose to the other Party that the Parties agree to designate a region as a Special Caution Area. The other Party may accept or decline the proposal. Either Party also has the right to request that a meeting of the Joint Military Commission be convened, in accordance with Article IX of this Agreement, to discuss such a proposal.

2. Personnel of the armed forces of the Parties present in a designated Special Caution Area shall establish and maintain communications, in accordance with Annex 1 to this Agreement, and undertake other measures as may be later agreed upon by the Parties, in order to prevent dangerous military activities and resolve any incident which may arise as a result of such activities.

3. Each Party has the right to terminate an arrangement with respect to a designated Special Caution Area. The Party intending to exercise this right shall provide timely notification of such intent to the other Party, including the date and time of termination of such an arrangement, through use of the communications channel set forth in paragraph 3 of Article VII

of this Agreement.

Article VI

1. When personnel of the armed forces of one Party, in proximity to personnel and equipment of the armed forces of the other Party, detect interference with their command and control networks which could cause harm to them or damage to their equipment, they may inform the relevant personnel of the armed forces of the other Party if they believe that the interference is being caused by such personnel and equipment of the armed forces of that Party.

2. If the personnel of the armed forces of the Party having received such information establish that this interference with the command and control networks is being caused by their activities, they shall take expeditious measure to terminate the interference.

Article VII

1. For the purpose of preventing dangerous military activities, and expeditiously resolving any incident which may arise as a result of such activities, the armed forces of the Parties shall establish and maintain communications as provided for in Annex 1 to Agreement.

2. The Parties shall exchange appropriate information on instances of dangerous military activities or incidents which may arise as a result of such activities, as well as on other issues related to this Agreement.

3. The Chairman of the Joint Chiefs of Staff of the United States shall convey information referred to in paragraph 2 of this Article through the Defense Attache of the Union of Soviet Socialist Republics in Washington, D.C. The Chief of the General Staff of the Armed Forces of the Union of Soviet Socialist Republics shall convey such information through the Defense Attache of the United States in Moscow.

Article XIII

1. This Agreement shall not affect the rights and obligations of the Parties under other international agreements and arrangements in force between the Parties, and the right of individual or collective self-defense and of navigation and overflight, in accordance with international law. Consistent with the foregoing, the Parties shall implement the provisions of this Agreement, taking into account the sovereign interests of both Parties.

2. Nothing in this Agreement shall be directed against any Third Party. Should an incident encompassed by this Agreement occur in the territory of an

ally of a Party, that Party shall have the right to consult with its ally as to appropriate measures to be taken.

Article IX

1. To promote the objectives and implementation of the provisions of this Agreement, the Parties hereby establish a Joint Military Commission. Within the framework of the Commission, the Parties shall consider:

(a) Compliance with the obligations assumed in this Agreement;

(b) Possible ways to ensure a higher level of safety for the personnel and equipment of their armed forces; and

(c) Other measures as may be necessary to improve the viability and effectiveness of this Agreement.

2. Meetings of the Joint Military Commission shall be convened annually or more frequently as may be agreed upon by the Parties.

Article X

1. This Agreement, including its Annexes, which form an integral part thereof, shall enter into force on January 1, 1990.

2. This Agreement may be terminated by either Party six months after written notice thereof is given to the other Party.

3. This Agreement shall be registered in accordance with Article 102 of the Charter of the United Nations.

Agreement Between the Government of the United States of America and the Government of the Union of Soviet Socialist Republics on Reciprocal Advance Notification of Major Strategic Exercises

Date of signature: September 23, 1989
Place of signature: Jackson Hole, Wyoming
Signatory states:The United States, The Union of Soviet Socialist Republics
Date of Entry into Force: January 1, 1990

[The signatories], hereinafter referred to as the Parties,

Affirming their desire to reduce and ultimately eliminate the risk of outbreak of nuclear war, in particular as a result of misinterpretation, miscalculation, or accident,

Believing that a nuclear war cannot be won and must never be fought,

Recognizing the necessity to promote the increase of mutual trust and the strengthening of strategic stability,

Acknowledging the importance of exchanging advance notification of major strategic exercises on the basis of reciprocity,

Reaffirming their obligations under the Agreement between the United States of America and the Union of Soviet Socialist Republics on the Establishment of Nuclear Risk Reduction Centers of September 15, 1987.

Have agreed as follows:

Article I

On the basis of reciprocity, each Party shall notify the other Party no less than 14 days in advance about the beginning of one major strategic forces exercise which includes the participation of heavy bomber aircraft to be held during each calendar year.

Article II

1. Each Party shall provide to the other Party the notifications required by Article I through the Nuclear Risk Reduction Centers established by the Agreement between the United States of America and the Union of Soviet Socialist Republics on the Establishment of Nuclear Risk Reduction Centers of September 15, 1987.

2. The notifications required by Article I shall be provided no less than 14 days prior to the date in Coordinated Universal Time (UTC) during which the relevant exercise will commence.

Article III

The Parties shall undertake to hold consultations, as mutually agreed, to consider questions relating to implementation of the provisions of this Agreement, as well as to discuss possible amendments thereto aimed at furthering the implementation of the objectives of this Agreement. Amendments shall enter into force in accordance with procedures to be agreed upon.

Article IV

This Agreement shall not affect the obligations of either Party under other agreements.

Article V

1. This Agreement shall be of unlimited duration.
2. This Agreement may be terminated by either Party upon 12 months written notice to the other Party.

Article VI

This Agreement shall enter into force on January 1, 1990, and notifications pursuant to this Agreement shall commence with the calendar year 1990.

Agreement Between the United States of America and the Union of Soviet Socialist Republics on Destruction and Non-Production of Chemical Weapons and on Measures to Facilitate the Multilateral Convention on Banning Chemical Weapons

Date of signature: June 1, 1990
Place of signature: Washington, DC
Signatory states: The United States, The Union of Soviet Socialist Republics

[The signatories], hereinafter referred to as "the Parties,"

Determined to make every effort to conclude and to bring into force at the earliest date a convention providing for a global ban on the development, production, stockpiling and use of chemical weapons and on their destruction, hereinafter referred to as "the multilateral convention,"

Aware of their special responsibility in the area of chemical weapons disarmament,

Desiring to halt the production of chemical weapons and to begin the destruction of the preponderance of their chemical weapons stockpiles, without waiting for the multilateral convention to enter into force,

Recalling the Memorandum of Understanding between the Government of the United States of America and the Government of the Union of Soviet Socialist Republics Regarding a Bilateral Verification Experiment and Data Exchange Related to Prohibition of Chemical Weapons, signed at Jackson Hole, Wyoming on September 23, 1989, hereinafter referred to as "the Memorandum,"

Recalling the bilateral commitment to co-operate

with respect to the destruction of chemical weapons, contained in the joint statement on chemical weapons issued at Jackson Hole, Wyoming on September 23, 1989, and

Mindful of the efforts of each Party aimed at the destruction of chemical weapons and desiring to cooperate in this area,

Have agreed as follows:

Article I

General Provisions and Areas of Cooperation

1. In accordance with provisions of this Agreement, the Parties undertake:

(a) to cooperate regarding methods and technologies for the safe and efficient destruction of chemical weapons;

(b) not to produce chemical weapons;

(c) to reduce their chemical weapons stockpiles to equal, low levels;

(d) to cooperate in developing, testing, and carrying out appropriate inspection procedures; and

(e) to adopt practical measures to encourage all chemical weapons-capable states to become parties to the multilateral convention.

2. Each Party, during its destruction of chemical weapons, shall assign the highest priority to ensuring the safety of people and to protecting the environment. Each Party shall destroy its chemical weapons

in accordance with stringent national standards for safety and emissions.

Article 2

Cooperation Regarding Methods and Technologies of Destruction

1. To implement their undertaking to cooperate regarding the destruction of chemical weapons, the Parties shall negotiate a specific program of cooperation. For this purpose, the Parties may create special groups of experts, as appropriate. The program may include matters related to: methods and specific technologies for the destruction of chemical weapons; measures to ensure safety and protection of people and the environment; construction and operation of destruction facilities; the appropriate equipment for destruction; past, current and planned destruction activities; monitoring of destruction of chemical weapons; or such other topics as the Parties may agree. Activities to implement this program may include: exchanges of visits to relevant facilities; exchanges of documents; meetings and discussions among experts; or such other activities as the Parties may agree.

2. Each Party shall, as appropriate, cooperate with other states that request information or assistance regarding the destruction of chemical weapons. The Parties may respond jointly to such requests.

Article 3

Cessation of the Production of Chemical Weapons

Upon entry into force of this Agreement and thereafter, each Party shall not produce chemical weapons.

Article 4

Destruction of Chemical Weapons

1. Each Party shall reduce and limit its chemical weapons so that, by no later than December 31, 2002, and thereafter, its aggregate quantity of chemical weapons does not exceed 5,000 agent tons. In this Agreement, "tons" means metric tons.

2. Each Party shall begin its destruction of chemical weapons by no later than December 31, 1992.

3. By no later than December 31, 1999, each Party shall have destroyed at least 50 per cent of its aggregate quantity of chemical weapons. The aggregate quantity of chemical weapons of a Party shall be the amount of chemical weapons declared in the data exchange carried out on December 29, 1989, or declared thereafter, pursuant to the Memorandum, as updated in accord-

ance with paragraph 6 (b) of this article.

4. In the event that a Party determines that it cannot achieve an annual rate of destruction of chemical weapons of at least 1,000 agent tons during 1995, or that it cannot destroy at least 1,000 agent tons during each year after 1995, that Party shall, at the earliest possible time, notify the other Party, in accordance with Paragraph 10 of this Article.

5. Each Party, in its destruction of chemical weapons, shall also destroy the munitions, devices and containers from which the chemicals have been removed. Each Party shall reduce and limit its other empty munitions and devices for chemical weapons purposes so that, by no later than December 31, 2002, and thereafter, the aggregate capacity of such munitions and devices does not exceed the volume of the remaining bulk agent of that Party.

6. Thirty days after the entry into force of this Agreement, each Party shall inform the other Party of the following:

(a) its current general plan for the destruction of chemical weapons pursuant to this Agreement and its detailed plan for the destruction of chemical weapons during the calendar year following the year in which this Agreement enters into force. The detailed plan shall encompass all of the chemical weapons to be destroyed during the calendar year, and shall include their locations, types and quantities, the methods of their destruction, and the locations of the destruction facilities that are to be used; and

(b) any changes, as of the entry into force of this Agreement, in the data contained in the data exchange carried out on December 29, 1989, or provided thereafter, pursuant to the Memorandum.

7. Beginning in the calendar year following the year in which this Agreement enters into force, each Party shall inform the other Party annually, by no later than November 30, of its detailed plan for the destruction of chemical weapons during the following calendar year.

8. Beginning in the calendar year following the year in which this Agreement enters into force, each Party shall inform the other Party annually, by no later than April 15, of the following:

(a) any further changes, as of December 31, of the previous year, to the data contained in the data exchange carried out on December 29 ,1989, or provided thereafter, pursuant to the Memorandum;

(b) the implementation during the previous calendar year of its detailed plan for the destruction of chemical weapons; and

(c) any update to the general and detailed plans provided pursuant to paragraphs 6 (a) or 7 of this Article.

9. Each Party shall limit its chemical weapons storage facilities so that, by no later than December 31, 2002, and thereafter, the number of such facilities does not exceed eight. Each Party plans to have all such facilities located on its national territory. This is without prejudice to its rights and obligations, including those under the Protocol for the Prohibition of the Use in War of Asphyxiating, Poisonous or Other Gases, and of Bacteriological Methods of Warfare, signed at Geneva on June 17, 1925.

10. If a Party experiences problems that will prevent it from destroying its chemical weapons at a rate sufficient to meet the levels specified in this Article, that Party shall immediately notify the other Party and provide a full explanation. The Parties shall promptly consult on measures necessary to resolve the problems. Under no circumstances shall the Party not experiencing problems in its destruction of chemical weapons be required to destroy its chemical weapons at a more rapid rate than the Party that has experienced such problems.

Article 5

Inspection Activities

1. Each Party shall provide access to each of its chemical weapons production facilities for systematic on-site inspection to confirm that production of chemical weapons is not occurring at those facilities.

2. Each Party shall identify and provide access to each of its chemical weapons destruction facilities and the chemical weapons holding areas within these destruction facilities for systematic on-site inspection of the destruction of chemical weapons. Such inspection shall be accomplished through the continuous presence of inspectors and continuous monitoring with on-site instruments.

3. When a Party has removed all of its chemical weapons from a particular chemical weapons storage facility, it shall promptly notify the other Party. The Party receiving the notification shall have the right to conduct, promptly after its receipt of the notification, an on-site inspection to confirm that no chemical weapons are present at that facility. Each Party shall also have the right to inspect, not more than once each calendar year, subsequent to the year of the notification and until such time as the multilateral convention enters into force, each chemical weapons storage facility for which it has received a notifica-

tion pursuant to this paragraph, to determine that chemical weapons are not being stored there.

4. When a Party has completed its destruction of chemical weapons pursuant to this Agreement, it shall promptly notify the other Party. In its notification, the Party shall specify the chemical weapons storage facilities where its remaining chemical weapons are located and provide a detailed inventory of the chemical weapons at each of these storage facilities. Each Party, promptly after it has received such a notification, shall have the right to inspect each of the chemical weapons storage facilities specified in the notification, to determine the quantities and types of chemical weapons at each facility.

5. Each Party shall also have the right to inspect, not more than once each calendar year, subsequent to the year in which destruction begins and until such time as the multilateral convention enters into force, each chemical weapons storage facility of the other Party that is not already subject to annual inspection pursuant to paragraph 3 of this Article, to determine the quantities and types of chemical weapons that are being stored there.

6. On the basis of the reports of its inspectors and other information available to it, each Party shall determine whether the provisions of this Agreement are being satisfactorily fulfilled and shall communicate its conclusions to the other Party.

7. Detailed provisions for the implementation of the inspection measures provided for in this Article shall be set forth in the document on inspection procedures. The Parties shall work to complete this document by December 31, 1990.

Article 6

Measures to Facilitate the Multilateral Convention

The Parties shall cooperate in making every effort to conclude the multilateral convention at the earliest date and to implement it effectively. Toward those ends, the Parties agree, in addition to their other obligations in this Agreement, to the following:

1. Each Party shall reduce and limit its chemical weapons so that, by no later than the end of the eighth year after entry into force of the multilateral convention, its aggregate quantity of chemical weapons does not exceed 500 agent tons.

2. Upon signature of this Agreement, the Parties shall enter into consultations with other participants in the multilateral negotiations and shall propose that a special conference of states parties to the multilateral convention be held at the end of the eighth year after its entry into force. This special conference

would, *inter alia*, determine, in accordance with agreed procedures, whether the participation in the multilateral convention is sufficient for proceeding to the total elimination of all remaining chemical weapons stocks over the subsequent two years.

3. The Parties shall intensify their cooperation with each other and with other states to ensure that all chemical weapon-capable states become parties to the multilateral convention.

4. The Parties declare their intention to be among the original parties to the multilateral convention.

5. To gain experience and thereby facilitate the elaboration and implementation of the multilateral convention, the Parties agree to conduct bilateral verification experiments involving trial challenge inspections at facilities not declared under the Memorandum or subsequently. The detailed modalities for such experiments, including the number and location of the facilities to be inspected, as well as the procedures to be used, shall be agreed between the Parties no later than six months after the signing of this Agreement.

Article 7

Consultations

The Parties, in order to resolve questions related to this Agreement that may arise, shall use normal diplomatic channels, specifically-designated representatives, or such other means as they may agree.

Article 8

Relationship to Other Documents

1. After the multilateral convention enters into force, the provisions of the multilateral convention shall take precedence over the provisions of this Agreement in cases of incompatible obligations therein. Otherwise, the provisions of this Agreement shall supplement the provisions of the multilateral convention in its operation between the Parties. After the multilateral convention is signed, the Parties to this Agreement shall consult with each other in order to resolve any questions concerning the relationship of this Agreement to the multilateral convention.

2. The chemical weapons, chemical weapons storage facilities, and chemical weapons production facilities subject to this Agreement are those that are subject to declaration under the Memorandum.

Article 9

Amendments

Each Party may propose amendments to this Agreement. Agreed amendments shall enter into force in accordance with the procedures governing the entry into force of this Agreement.

Article 10

Entry into Force; Duration; Withdrawal

1. This Agreement shall enter into force upon an exchange of instruments stating acceptance of the Agreement by each Party.

2. This Agreement shall be of unlimited duration, unless the Parties agree to terminate it after the entry into force of the multilateral convention.

3. Each Party shall, in exercising its national sovereignty, have the right to withdraw from this Agreement if it decides that extraordinary events related to the subject matter of this Agreement have jeopardized its supreme interests. It shall give notice of its decision to the other Party six months prior to withdrawal from the Agreement. Such notice shall include a statement of the extraordinary events the notifying Party regards as having jeopardized its supreme interests.

Agreed Statement in Connection with the Agreement between the United States of America and the Union of Soviet Socialist Republics on Destruction and Non-Production of Chemical Weapons and on Measures to Facilitate the Multilateral Convention on Banning Chemical Weapons

Paragraph 2 of Article 6 of the Agreement stipulates that, "Upon signature of this Agreement, the Parties shall enter into consultation with other participants in the multilateral negotiations and shall propose that a special conference of states parties to the multilateral convention be held at the end of eighth year after its entry to force this special conference would, *inter alia*, determine, in accordance with agreed procedures, whether the participation in the multilateral convention is sufficient for proceeding to the total elimination of all remaining chemical weapons stocks over the subsequent two years."

In this connection, the Parties agree that an affirmative decision would require the agreement of a majority of the states parties that attend the special conference, with such majority including those states parties attending the special conference that had taken the following three steps:

(a) presented officially and publicly, before December 31, 1991, before the Conference on Disarmament, a written declaration that they were at the time of that declaration in possession of chemical weapons;

(b) signed the multilateral convention within thirty days after it was opened for signature; and

(c) became a party to the multilateral convention by no later than one year after its entry into force.

Treaty Between the Federal Republic of Germany and the German Democratic Republic on the Establishment of German Unity

— Unification Treaty —

Date of signature: August 31, 1990
Place of signature: Berlin
Signatory states: Federal Republic of Germany, German Democratic Republic

[The signatories],
Resolved to achieve in free self-determination the unity of Germany in peace and freedom as an equal partner in the community of nations,

Mindful of the desire of the people in both parts of Germany to live together in peace and freedom in a democratic and social federal state governed by the rule of law,

In grateful respect to those who peacefully helped freedom prevail and who have unswervingly adhered to the task of establishing German unity and are achieving it,

Aware of the continuity of German history and bearing in mind the special responsibility arising from our past for a democratic development in Germany committed to respect for human rights and to peace,

Seeking through German unity to contribute to the unification of Europe and to the building of a peaceful European order in which borders no longer divide and which ensures that all European nations can live together in a spirit of mutual trust,

Aware that the inviolability of frontiers and of the territorial integrity and sovereignty of all states in Europe within their frontiers constitutes a fundamental condition for peace,

Have agreed to conclude a Treaty on the Establishment of German Unity, containing the following provisions:

Chapter I

Effect of Accession

Article 1

Länder

(1) Upon the accession of the German Democratic Republic to the Federal Republic of Germany in accordance with Article 23 of the Basic Law taking effect on 3 October 1990 the Länder of Brandenburg, Mecklenburg-Western Pomerania, Saxony, Saxony-Anhalt and Thuringia shall become Länder of the Federal Republic of Germany. The establishment of these Länder and their boundaries shall be governed by the provisions of the Constitutional Act of 22 July 1990 on the Establishment of Länder in the German Democratic Republic (Länder Establishment Act) (Law Gazette I, No. 51, p. 955) in accordance with Annex II.

(2) The 23 boroughs of Berlin shall form Land Berlin.

Article 2

Capital City, Day of German Unity

(1) The capital of Germany shall be Berlin. The seat of the parliament and government shall be decided after the establishment of German unity.

(2) 3 October shall be a public holiday known as the Day of German Unity.

Chapter II

Basic Law

Article 3

Entry into Force of the Basic Law

Upon the accession taking effect, the Basic Law of

the Federal Republic of Germany, as published in the Federal Law Gazette Part III, No. 100-1, and last amended by the Act of 21 December 1983 (Federal Law Gazette I, p. 1481), shall enter into force in the Länder of Brandenburg, Mecklenburg-Western Pomerania, Saxony, Saxony-Anhalt and Thuringia and in that part of Land Berlin where it has not been valid to date, subject to the amendments arising from Article 4, unless otherwise provided in this Treaty.

Article 4

Amendments to the Basic Law Resulting from Accession

The Basic Law of the Federal Republic of Germany shall be amended as follows:

1. The preamble shall read as follows:

"Conscious of their responsibility before God and men,

Animated by the resolve to serve world peace as an equal partner in a united Europe, the German people have adopted, by virtue of their constituent power, this Basic Law.

The Germans in the Länder of Baden-Württemberg, Bavaria, Berlin, Brandenburg, Bremen, Hamburg, Hesse, Lower Saxony, Mecklenburg-Western Pomerania, North-Rhine/Westphalia, Rhineland-Palatinate, Saarland, Saxony, Saxony-Anhalt, Schleswig-Holstein and Thuringia have achieved the unity and freedom of Germany in free self-determination. This Basic Law is thus valid for the entire German people."

2. Article 23 shall be repealed.

3. Article 51 (2) shall read as follows:

"(2) Each Land shall have at least three votes; Länder with more than two million inhabitants shall have four, Länder with more than six million inhabitants five, and Länder with more than seven million inhabitants six votes."

4. The existing text of Article 135a shall become paragraph 1. The following paragraph shall be inserted after paragraph 1:

"(2) Paragraph 1 above shall be applied *mutatis mutandis* to liabilities of the German Democratic Republic or its legal entities as well as to liabilities of the Federation or other corporate bodies and institutions under public law which are connected with the transfer of properties of the German Democratic

Republic to the Federation, Länder and communes (Gemeinden), and to liabilities arising from measures taken by the German Democratic Republic or its legal entities."

5. The following new Article 143 shall be inserted in the Basic Law:

Article 143

(1) Law in the territory specified in Article 3 of the Unification Treaty may deviate from provisions of this Basic Law for a period not extending beyond 31 December 1992 in so far as and as long as no complete adjustment to the order of the Basic Law can be achieved as a consequence of the different conditions. Deviations must not violate Article 19 (2) and must be compatible with the principles set out in Article 79 (3).

(2) Deviations from sections II, VIII, VIIIa, IX, X and XI are permissible for a period not extending beyond 31 December 1995.

(3) Notwithstanding paragraphs 1 and 2 above, Article 41 of the Unification Treaty and the rules for its implementation shall remain valid in so far as they provide for the irreversibility of interferences with property in the territory specified in Article 3 of the said Treaty."

6. Article 146 shall read as follows:

Article 146

This Basic Law, which is valid for the entire German people following the achievement of the unity and freedom of Germany, shall cease to be in force on the day on which a constitution adopted by a free decision of the German people comes into force."

Article 5

Future Amendments to the Constitution

The Governments of the two contracting Parties recommend to the legislative bodies of the united Germany that within two years they should deal with the questions regarding amendments or additions to the Basic Law as raised in connection with German unification, in particular

— with regard to the relationship between the Federation and the Länder in accordance with the Joint Resolution of the Minister-Presidents of 5 July 1990,

— with regard to the possibility of restructuring the

Berlin/Brandenburg area in derogation of the provisions of Article 29 of the Basic Law by way of an agreement between the Länder concerned,

— with considerations on introducing state objectives into the Basic Law, and

— with the question of applying Article 146 of the Basic Law and of holding a referendum in this context.

Article 6

Exception

For the time being, Article 131 of the Basic Law shall not be applied in the territory specified in Article 3 of this Treaty.

Article 7

Financial System

(1) The financial system of the Federal Republic of Germany shall be extended to the territory specified in Article 3 unless otherwise provided in this Treaty.

(2) Article 106 of the Basic Law shall apply to the apportionment of tax revenue among the Federation as well as the Länder and communes (associations of communes) in the territory specified in Article 3 of this Treaty with the proviso that

1. paragraph 3, fourth sentence, and paragraph 4 shall not apply up to 31 December 1994;

2. up to 31 December 1996 the share of income tax revenue received by the communes in accordance with Article 106 (5) of the Basic Law shall be passed on from the Länder to the communes not on the basis of the amount of income tax paid by their inhabitants, but according to the number of inhabitants in the communes;

3. up to 31 December 1994, in derogation of Article 106 (7) of the Basic Law, an annual share of at least 20 per cent of the Land share of total revenue from joint taxes and of the total revenue from Land taxes as well as 40 per cent of the Land share from the German Unity Fund according to paragraph 5, item 1, shall accrue to the communes (associations of communes).

(3) Article 107 of the Basic Law shall be valid in the territory specified in Article 3 of this Treaty with the proviso that up to 31 December 1994 the provision of paragraph 1, fourth sentence, shall not be applied between the Länder which have until now

constituted the Federal Republic of Germany and the Länder in the territory specified in Article 3 of this Treaty and that there shall be no all-German financial equalization between the Länder (Article 107 (2) of the Basic Law).

The Land share of turnover tax throughout Germany shall be divided up into an eastern component and a western component in such a way that the average share of turnover tax per inhabitant in the Länder of Brandenburg, Mecklenburg-Western Pomerania, Saxony, Saxony-Anhalt and Thuringia amounts

in 1991 to 55 per cent
in 1992 to 60 per cent
in 1993 to 65 per cent
in 1994 to 70 per cent

of the average share of turnover tax per inhabitant in the Länder of Baden-Württemberg, Bavaria, Bremen, Hesse, Hamburg, Lower Saxony, North-Rhine/Westphalia, Rhineland-Palatinate, Saarland and Schleswig-Holstein. The share of Land Berlin shall be calculated in advance on the basis of the number of inhabitants. The provisions contained in this paragraph shall be reviewed for 1993 in the light of the conditions obtaining at the time.

(4) The territory specified in Article 3 of this Treaty shall be incorporated into the provisions of Articles 91a, 91b and 104a (3) and (4) of the Basic Law, including the pertinent implementing provisions, in accordance with this Treaty with effect from 1 January 1991.

(5) Following the establishment of German unity the annual allocations from the German Unity Fund shall be distributed as follows:

1. 85 per cent as special assistance to the Länder of Brandenburg, Mecklenburg-Western Pomerania, Saxony, Saxony-Anhalt and Thuringia as well as to Land Berlin to cover their general financial requirements and divided up among these Länder in proportion to their number of inhabitants, excluding the inhabitants of Berlin (West), and

2. 15 per cent to meet public requirements at a central level in the territory of the aforementioned Länder.

(6) In the event of a fundamental change in conditions, the Federation and the Länder shall jointly examine the possibilities of granting further assistance in order to ensure adequate financial equalization for the Länder in the territory specified in Article 3 of this Treaty.

Chapter III

Harmonization of Law

Article 8

Extension of Federal Law

Upon the accession taking effect, federal law shall enter into force in the territory specified in Article 3 of this Treaty unless its area of application is restricted to certain Länder or parts of Länder of the Federal Republic of Germany and unless otherwise provided in this Treaty, notably Annex I.

Article 9

Continued Validity of Law of the German Democratic Republic

(1) Law of the German Democratic Republic valid at the time of signing of this Treaty which is Land law according to the distribution of competence under the Basic Law shall remain in force in so far as it is compatible with the Basic Law, notwithstanding Article 143, with the federal law put in force in the territory specified in Article 3 of this Treaty and with the directly applicable law of the European Communities, and unless otherwise provided in this Treaty. Law of the German Democratic Republic which is federal law according to the distribution of competence under the Basic Law and which refers to matters not regulated uniformly at the federal level shall continue to be valid as Land law under the conditions set out in the first sentence pending a settlement by the federal legislator.

(2) The law of the German Democratic Republic referred to in Annex II shall remain in force with the provisos set out there in so far as it is compatible with the Basic Law, taking this Treaty into consideration, and with the directly applicable law of the European Communities.

(3) Law of the German Democratic Republic enacted after the signing of this Treaty shall remain in force to the extent agreed between the Contracting Parties. Paragraph 2 above shall remain unaffected.

(4) Where law remaining in force according to paragraphs 2 and 3 above refers to matters within the exclusive legislative power of the Federation, it shall remain in force as federal law. Where it refers to matters within concurrent legislative powers or outlining legislation, it shall continue to apply as federal law if and to the extent that it relates to fields which are regulated by federal law in the remaining area of application of the Basic Law.

(5) The church tax legislation enacted by the German Democratic Republic in accordance with Annex II shall continue to apply as Land law in the Länder named in Article 1 (1) of this Treaty.

Article 10

Law of the European Communities

(1) Upon the accession taking effect, the Treaties on the European Communities together with their amendments and supplements as well as the international agreements, treaties and resolutions which have come into force in connection with those Treaties shall apply in the territory specified in Article 3 of this Treaty.

(2) Upon the accession taking effect, the legislative acts enacted on the basis of the Treaties on the European Communities shall apply in the territory specified in Article 3 of this Treaty unless the competent institutions of the European Communities enact exemptions. These exemptions are intended to take account of administrative requirements and help avoid economic difficulties.

(3) Legislative acts of the European Communities whose implementation or execution comes under the responsibility of the Länder shall be implemented or executed by the latter through provisions under Land law.

Chapter IV

International Treaties and Agreements

Article 11

Treaties of the Federal Republic of Germany

The Contracting Parties proceed on the understanding that international treaties and agreements to which the Federal Republic of Germany is a contracting party, including treaties establishing membership of international organizations or institutions, shall retain their validity and that the rights and obligations arising therefrom, with the exception of the treaties named in Annex I, shall also relate to the territory specified in Article 3 of this Treaty. Where adjustments become necessary in individual cases, the all-German Government shall consult with the respective contracting parties.

Article 12

Treaties of the German Democratic Republic

(1) The Contracting Parties are agreed that, in connection with the establishment of German unity, international treaties of the German Democratic Republic shall be discussed with the contracting parties concerned with a view to regulating or confirming their continued application, adjustment or expiry, taking into account protection of confidence, the interests of the states concerned, the treaty obligations of the Federal Republic of Germany as well as the principles of a free, democratic basic order governed by the rule of law, and respecting the competence of the European Communities.

(2) The united Germany shall determine its position with regard to the adoption of international treaties of the German Democratic Republic following consultations with the respective contracting parties and with the European Communities where the latter's competence is affected.

(3) Should the united Germany intend to accede to international organizations or other multilateral treaties of which the German Democratic Republic but not the Federal Republic of Germany is a member, agreement shall be reached with the respective contracting parties and with the European Communities where the latter's competence is affected.

Chapter V

Public Administration and the Administration of Justice

Article 13

Future Status of Institutions

(1) Administrative bodies and other institutions serving the purposes of public administration or the administration of justice in the territory specified in Article 3 of this Treaty shall pass under the authority of the government of the Land in which they are located. Institutions whose sphere of activities transcends the boundaries of a Land shall come under the joint responsibility of the Länder concerned. Where institutions consist of several branches each of which is in a position to carry out its activities independently, the branches shall come under the responsibility of the government of the respective Land in which they are located. The Land government shall be responsible for the transfer or winding-up. Section 22 of the Länder Establishment Act of 22 July 1990 shall remain unaffected.

(2) To the extent that before the accession took effect the institutions or branches mentioned in paragraph 1, first sentence, performed tasks that are incumbent upon the Federation according to the distribution of competence under the Basic Law, they shall be subject to the competent supreme federal authorities. The latter shall be responsible for the transfer or winding-up.

(3) Institutions under paragraphs 1 and 2 above shall also include such

1. cultural, educational, scientific and sports institutions,

2. radio and television establishments

as come under the responsibility of public administrative bodies.

Article 14

Joint Institutions of the Länder

(1) Institutions or branches of institutions which, before the accession took effect, performed tasks that are incumbent upon the Länder according to the distribution of competence under the Basic Law shall continue to operate as joint institutions of the Länder pending a final settlement by the Länder named in Article 1 (1) of this Treaty. This shall apply only to the extent that it is necessary for them to remain in place under this transitional arrangement so as to allow the Länder to carry out their responsibilities.

(2) The joint institutions of the Länder shall be under the authority of the Land plenipotentiaries pending the election of minister-presidents in the Länder. Subsequently they shall be under the authority of the minister-presidents. The latter may charge the responsible Land minister with their supervision.

Article 15

Transitional Arrangements for Land Administration

(1) The Land spokesmen in the Länder named in Article 1 (1) of this Treaty and the government plenipotentiaries in the districts shall continue to discharge their present responsibilities on behalf of the Federal Government and subject to its instructions, from the date when the accession takes effect until the election of minister-presidents. The Land spokesmen shall, as Land plenipotentiaries, be in charge of the administration of their respective Länder and have the right to give instructions to district administrative

authorities and, in the case of delegated responsibilities, also to communes and rural districts. Where Land commissioners were appointed in the Länder named in Article 1 (1) of this Treaty before the accession took effect, they shall be vested with the responsibilities and powers of the Land spokesman as set out in the first and second sentences.

(2) The other Länder and the Federation shall render administrative assistance in setting up Land administrative authorities.

(3) At the request of the minister-presidents of the Länder named in Article 1 (1) of this Treaty the other Länder and the Federation shall render administrative assistance in the execution of certain technical responsibilities for a period not extending beyond 30 June 1991. The minister-president shall grant any agencies and individuals from the Länder and the Federation a right to give instructions to the extent that they render administrative assistance in the execution of technical responsibilities.

(4) The Federation shall make available the necessary budget resources to the extent that it renders administrative assistance in the execution of technical responsibilities. The resources employed shall be deducted from the share of the respective Land in the German Unity Fund allocations or from its share of import turnover tax.

Article 16

Transitional Provision Pending the Constitution of a Single Land Government for Berlin

Until the constitution of a single Land government for Berlin its responsibilities shall be discharged by the Berlin Senat jointly with the Magistrat.

Article 17

Rehabilitation

The Contracting Parties reaffirm their intention to create without delay a legal foundation permitting the rehabilitation of all persons who have been victims of a politically motivated punitive measure or any court decision contrary to the rule of law or constitutional principles. The rehabilitation of these victims of the iniquitous SED regime shall be accompanied by appropriate arrangements for compensation.

Article 18

Continued Validity of Court Decisions

(1) Decisions handed down by the courts of the German Democratic Republic before the accession took effect shall retain their validity and may be executed in conformity with the law put into force according to Article 8 of this Treaty or remaining in force according to Article 9. This law shall be taken as the yardstick when checking the compatibility of decisions and their execution with the principles of the rule of law. Article 17 of this Treaty shall remain unaffected.

(2) Subject to Annex I, persons sentenced by criminal courts of the German Democratic Republic are granted by this Treaty a right of their own to seek the quashing of final divisions through the courts.

Article 19

Continued Validity of Decisions Taken by Public Administrative Bodies

Administrative acts of the German Democratic Republic performed before the accession took effect shall remain valid. They may be revoked if they are incompatible with the principles of the rule of law or with the provisions of this Treaty. In all other respects the rules on the validity of administrative acts shall remain unaffected.

Article 20

Legal Status of Persons in the Public Service

(1) The agreed transitional arrangements set out in Annex I shall apply to the legal status of persons in the public service at the time of accession.

(2) The exercise of public responsibilities (state authority as defined in Article 33 (4) of the Basic Law) shall be entrusted as soon as possible to professional civil servants. Public service law shall be introduced in accordance with the agreed arrangements set out in Annex I. Article 92 of the Basic Law shall remain unaffected.

(3) Military personnel law shall be introduced in accordance with the agreed arrangements set out in Annex I.

Chapter VI

Public Assets and Debts

Article 21

Administrative Assets

(1) The assets of the German Democratic Republic which are used directly for specific administrative

purposes (administrative assets) shall become federal assets unless their designated purpose as of 1 October 1989 was primarily to meet administrative responsibilities which, under the Basic Law, are to be exercised by Länder, communes (associations of communes) or other agencies of public administration. Where administrative assets were primarily used for the purposes of the former Ministry of State Security/National Security Office, they shall accrue to the Trust Agency unless they have already been given over to new social or public purposes since the above-mentioned date.

(2) Where administrative assets are not federal assets under paragraph 1 above, they shall accrue, upon the accession taking effect, to the agency of public administration which, under the Basic Law, is responsible for the relevant administrative purpose.

(3) Assets which have been made available free of charge by another corporate body under public law to the central government or to the Länder and communes (associations of communes) shall be returned free of charge to this corporate body or its legal successor; former Reich assets shall become federal assets.

(4) Where administrative assets become federal assets under paragraphs 1 to 3 above or by virtue of a federal law, they shall be used for public purposes in the territory specified in Article 3 of this Treaty. This shall also apply to the use of proceeds from the sale of assets.

Article 22

Financial Assets

(1) Public assets of legal entities in the territory specified in Article 3 of this Treaty, including landed property and assets in agriculture and forestry, which do not directly serve specific administrative purposes (financial assets), with the exception of social insurance assets, shall, unless they have been handed over to the Trust Agency or will be handed over by law according to Section 1 (1), second and third sentences, of the Trusteeship Act, to communes, towns and cities or rural districts, come under federal trusteeship upon the accession taking effect. Where financial assets were primarily used for the purposes of the former Ministry of State Security/National Security Office, they shall accrue to the Trust Agency unless they have already been given over to new social or public purposes since 1 October 1989. Financial assets shall be divided by federal law between the Federation and the Länder named in

Article 1 of this Treaty in such a way that the Federation and the Länder named in Article 1 each receive one half of the total value of the assets. The communes (associations of communes) shall receive an appropriate share of the Länder portion. Assets accruing to the Federation under this provision shall be used for public purposes in the territory specified in Article 3 of this Treaty. The Länder share should in principle be distributed to the respective Länder in such a way that the relationship between the total values of the assets apportioned to the respective Länder corresponds to the relationship between the population sizes of these Länder on the date the accession takes effect, excluding the inhabitants of Berlin (West). Article 21 (3) of this Treaty shall be applied *mutatis mutandis*.

(2) Pending legislative arrangements the financial assets shall be administered by the authorities currently responsible unless the Federal Minister of Finance orders the assumption of administrative responsibilities by authorities responsible for the administration of assets at the federal level.

(3) On demand the federal, regional or local authorities referred to in paragraphs 1 and 2 above shall provide each other with information about, and grant each other access to, land registers, files and other materials containing information on assets whose assignment in law and in fact is unresolved or the subject of dispute between the said authorities.

(4) Paragraph 1 above shall not apply to publicly owned property used for residential purposes and coming under the legal responsibility of publicly owned housing enterprises. This shall also apply to publicly owned property which is already the subject of concrete plans for residential use. Upon the accession taking effect, these assets shall become the property of the local authorities, which shall also assume their respective shares of the debts. Taking into consideration social concerns, the local authorities shall step by step place their housing stock on the basis obtaining in a market economy. Privatization shall be speeded up in this context, among other things to encourage individual home ownership. As regards the publicly owned housing stock of state institutions, in so far as it does not come under Article 21 of this Treaty, paragraph 1 above shall remain unaffected.

Article 23

Debt Arrangements

(1) Upon the accession taking effect, the total debts

of the central budget of the German Democratic Republic which have accumulated up to this date shall be taken over by a federal Special Fund without legal capacity, which shall meet the obligations arising from debt servicing. The Special Fund shall be empowered to raise loans:

1. to pay off debts of the Special Fund,
2. to cover due interest and loan procurement costs,
3. to purchase debt titles of the Special Fund for the purposes of market cultivation.

(2) The Federal Minister of Finance shall administer the Special Fund. The Special Fund may, in his name, conduct legal transactions, sue and be sued. The general legal domicile of the Special Fund shall be at the seat of the Federal Government. The Federation shall act as guarantor for the liabilities of the Special Fund.

(3) From the day the accession takes effect until 31 December 1993 the Federation and the Trust Agency shall each repay one half of the interest payments made by the Special Fund.

Repayment shall be made by the first of the month following the month in which the Special Fund has made the payments referred to in the first sentence.

(4) With effect from 1 January 1994 the Federation and the Länder named in Article 1 of this Treaty as well as the Trust Agency shall take over the total debts which have accumulated in the Special Fund up to 31 December 1993 in accordance with Article 27 (3) of the Treaty of 18 May 1990 between the Federal Republic of Germany and the German Democratic Republic Establishing a monetary, Economic and Social Union. The distribution of the debts shall be settled in detail by a separate law in accordance with Article 34 of the Act of 25 July 1990 concerning the Treaty of 18 May 1990 (Federal Law Gazette 1990 II, p. 518). The portions of the total amount for the Länder named in Article 1 of this Treaty to be taken over by each of the Länder named in Article 1 shall be calculated in relation to their number of inhabitants on the date the accession takes effect, excluding the inhabitants of Berlin (West).

(5) The Special Fund shall be abolished at the end of 1993.

(6) Upon the accession taking effect, the Federal Republic of Germany shall take over the sureties, guarantees and warranties assumed by the German Democratic Republic and debited to its state budget prior to unification. The Länder named in Article 1 (1) of this Treaty and Land Berlin for that part in which the Basic Law has not been in force to date shall assume jointly and severally a counter-surety to the amount of 50 per cent of the total debt transferred in the form of sureties, guarantees and warranties to the Federal Republic of Germany. The losses shall be divided among the Länder in proportion to their number of inhabitants on the date the accession takes effect, excluding the inhabitants of Berlin (West).

(7) The German Democratic Republic's share of the Statsbank Berlin may be transferred to the Länder named in Article 1 of this Treaty. The rights arising from the German Democratic Republic's share of the Staatsbank Berlin shall accrue to the Federation pending the transfer of the share according to the first sentence or a transfer according to the third sentence. The Contracting parties shall, notwithstanding an examination from the viewpoint of antitrust legislation, provide for the possibility of transferring the Staatsbank Berlin wholly or partially to a credit institution under public law in the Federal Republic of Germany or to other legal entities. In the event that not all assets and liabilities are covered by a transfer, the remaining part of the Staatsbank Berlin shall be wound up. The Federation shall assume the liabilities resulting from the German Democratic Republic acting as guarantor for the Staatsbank Berlin. This shall not apply to liabilities arising after the transfer of the share according to the first sentence or a transfer according to the third sentence. The fifth sentence shall apply *mutatis mutandis* to new liabilities created by the Staatsbank Berlin during winding-up. If claims are made on the Federation in its capacity as guarantor, the burden shall be incorporated upon the accession taking effect into the total debt of the central budget of the German Democratic Republic and be taken over by the Special Fund under paragraph 1 above, which has no legal capacity.

Article 24

Settlement of Claims and Liabilities Vis-à-vis Foreign Countries and the Federal Republic of Germany

(1) In so far as they arise from the monopoly on foreign trade and foreign currency or from the performance of other state tasks of the German Democratic Republic vis-à-vis foreign countries and the Federal Republic of Germany up to 1 July 1990, the settlement of the claims and liabilities remaining when the accession takes effect shall take place under instruct-

ions from, and under the supervision of, the Federal Minister of Finance. Debt rescheduling agreements contracted by the Government of the Federal Republic of Germany after the accession takes effect shall also incorporate the claims mentioned in the first sentence. The claims concerned shall be held in trust by the Federal Minister of Finance or transferred to the Federation to the extent that the claims are adjusted.

(2) The Special Fund as defined in Article 23 (1) of this Treaty shall, up to 30 November 1993, assume payment of the necessary administrative expenditure, the interest costs arising from the difference between interest payments and interest revenue and the other losses incurred by the institutions charged with the settlement of claims and liabilities during the settlement period in so far as the institutions are unable to balance them out of their own resources. After 30 November 1993 the Federation and the Trust Agency shall each assume one half of the expenditure and costs referred to in the first sentence and of the loss compensation. Further details shall be determined by federal law.

(3) Claims and liabilities arising from membership of the German Democratic Republic or its institutions in the council for Mutual Economic Assistance may be the subject of separate arrangements by the Federal Republic of Germany. These arrangements may also refer to claims and liabilities which will arise or have arisen after 30 June 1990.

Article 25

Assets Held in Trust

The Privatization and Reorganization of Publicly Owned Assets Act (Trusteeship Act) of 17 June 1990 (Law Gazette I, No. 33, p. 300) shall continue to apply after the accession takes effect with the following proviso:

(1) The Trust Agency shall continue to be charged, in accordance with the provisions of the Trusteeship Act, with restructuring and privatizing the former publicly owned enterprises to bring them into line with the requirements of a competitive economy. It shall become a direct institution of the Federation vested with legal capacity and subject to public law. Technical and legal supervision shall be the responsibility of the Federal Minister of Finance, who shall exercise technical supervision in agreement with the Federal Minister of Economics and the respective federal minister. Stakes held by the Trust Agency shall be indirect stakes of the Federation. Amend-

ments to the Charter shall require the agreement of the Federal Government.

(2) The number of members of the Administrative Board of the Trust Agency shall be raised from 16 to 20, and for the first Administrative Board to 23. Mark. The interest payments due shall be repaid to the Deutsche Kreditbank AG and the other banks by the Trust Agency.

Article 26

Special Fund of the Deutsche Reichsbahn

(1) Upon the accession taking effect, the property and all other property rights of the German Democratic Republic and the Reich property in Berlin (West) belonging to the special fund of the Deutsche Reichsbahn within the meaning of Article 26 (2) of the Treaty of 18 May 1990 shall become the property of the Federal Republic of Germany as the special fund of the Deutsche Reichsbahn. This further includes all property rights acquired since 8 May 1945 with resources from the special fund of the Deutsche Reichsbahn as well as those which were attached to its operation or that of its predecessor administrations, regardless of which legal entity they were acquired for, unless they were subsequently given over to another purpose with the consent of the Deutsche Reichsbahn. Property rights claimed by the Deutsche Reichsbahn up to 31 January 1991 pursuant to Section 1 (4) of the Decree of 11 July 1990 on the Registration of Claims with Regard to Property Rights (Law Gazette I, No. 44, p. 718) shall not be regarded as property given over to another purpose with the consent of the Deutsche Reichsbahn.

(2) Associated liabilities and claims shall be transferred simultaneously with the property rights to the special fund of the Deutsche Reichsbahn.

(3) The Chairman of the Board of the Deutsche Bundesbahn and the Chairman of the Board of the Deutsche Reichsbahn shall be responsible for coordinating the two special funds. In carrying out this responsibility they shall work towards the objective of technically and organizationally merging the two railways.

Article 27

Special Fund of the Deutsche Post

(1) The property and all other property rights belonging to the special fund of the Deutsche Post shall become the property of the Federal Republic of Germany. They shall be combined with the special

fund of Deutsche the Bundespost. Associated liabilities and claims shall be transferred simultaneously with the property rights to the special fund of the Deutsche Bundespost. Property serving sovereign and political purposes, together with associated liabilities and claims, shall not become part of the special fund of the Deutsche Bundespost.

The special fund of the Deutsche Post shall also include all property rights which, as of 8 May 1945, belonged to the special fund of the Deutsche Reichspost or, after 8 May 1945, were either acquired with resources from the former special fund of the Deutsche Reichspost or attached to the operation of the Deutsche Post, regardless of which legal entity they were acquired for, unless they were subsequently given over to another purpose with the consent of the Deutsche Post up to 31 January 1991 pursuant to Section 1 (4) of the Decree of 11 July 1990 on the Registration of Claims with Regard to Property Rights shall not be regarded as property given over to another purpose with the consent of the Deutsche Post.

(2) After consulting the enterprises of the Deutsche Bundespost, the Federal Minister of Posts and Telecommunications shall finally determine the division of the special fund of the Deutsche Post among the partial special funds of the three enterprises. After consulting the three enterprises of the Deutsche Bundespost, the Federal Minister of Posts and Telecommunications shall, within a transitional period of three years, determine which items of property serve sovereign and political purposes. He shall take them over without compensation.

Article 28

Economic Assistance

(1) Upon the accession taking effect, the territory specified in Article 3 of this Treaty shall be incorporated into the arrangements of the Federation existing in the territory of the Federal Republic for economic assistance, taking into consideration the competence of the European Communities. The specific requirements of structural adjustment shall be taken into account during a transitional period. This will make a major contribution to the speediest possible development of a balanced economic structure with particular regard for small and medium-sized businesses.

(2) The relevant ministries shall prepare concrete programmes to speed up economic growth and structural adjustment in the territory specified in Article 3 of this Treaty. The programmes shall cover the following fields:

measures of regional economic assistance accompanied by a special programme for the benefit of the territory specified in Article 3 of this Treaty; preferential arrangements shall be ensured for this territory;

measures to improve the general economic conditions in the communes, with particular emphasis being given to infrastructure geared to the needs of the economy;

measures to foster the rapid development of small and medium-sized businesses;

measures to promote the modernization and restructuring of the economy, relying on restructuring schemes drawn up by industry of its own accord (e.g., rehabilitation programmes, including ones for exports to COMECON countries);

debt relief for enterprises following the examination of each case individually.

Article 29

Foreign Trade Relations

(1) The established foreign trade relations of the German Democratic Republic, in particular the existing contractual obligations vis-à-vis the countries of the Council for Mutual Economic Assistance, shall enjoy protection of confidence. They shall be developed further and expanded, taking into consideration the interests of all parties concerned and having regard for the principles of a market economy as well as the competence of the European Communities. The all-German Government shall ensure that appropriate organizational arrangements are made for these foreign trade relations within the framework of departmental responsibility.

(2) The Federal Government, or the all-German Government, shall hold consultations with the competent institutions of the European Communities on which exemptions are required for a transitional period in the field of foreign trade, having regard to paragraph 1 above.

Chapter VII

Labour, Social Welfare, Family, Women, Public Health and Environmental Protection

Article 30

Labour and Social Welfare

(1) It shall be the task of the all-German legislator

1. to recodify in a uniform manner and as soon as possible the law on employment contracts and the provisions on working hours under public law, including the admissibility of work on Sundays and public holidays, and the specific industrial safety regulations for women;

2. to bring public law on industrial safety into line with present-day requirements in accordance with the law of the European Communities and the concurrent part of the industrial safety law of the German Democratic Republic.

(2) Employed persons in the territory specified in Article 3 of this Treaty shall be entitled, upon reaching the age of 57, to receive early retirement payments for a period of three years, but not beyond the earliest possible date on which they become entitled to receive a retirement pension under the statutory pension scheme. The early retirement payment shall amount to 65 per cent of the last average net earnings; for employed persons whose entitlement arises on or before 1 April 1991 early retirement payments shall be raised by an increment of five percentage points for the first 312 days. The early retirement payments shall be made by the Federal Institute for Employment along similar lines to unemployment pay, notably the provisions of Section 105c of the Employment Promotion Act. The Federal Institute for Employment may reject an application if it is established that there is a clear lack of manpower in the region to carry out the occupational duties so far discharged by the applicant. The early retirement payments shall be refunded by the Federation in so far as they reach beyond the period of entitlement to unemployment pay. The provisions on early retirement payments shall be applied to new claims up to 31 December 1991. The period of validity may be prolonged by one year.

In the period from this Treaty taking effect up to 31 December 1990, women shall be entitled, on reaching the age of 55, to receive early retirement payments for a period not exceeding five years.

(3) The social welfare supplement to pension, accident and unemployment payments introduced in the territory specified in Article 3 of this Treaty in conjunction with the Treaty of 18 May 1990 shall be limited to new cases up to 31 December 1991. The payments shall be made for a period not extending beyond 30 June 1995.

(4) The transfer of tasks incumbent upon the social insurance scheme to separate agencies shall take place in such a way as to ensure that payments are made and financed and sufficient staff is available to perform the said tasks. The distribution of assets and liabilities among the separate agencies shall be definitively settled by law.

(5) The details regarding the introduction of Part VI of the Social Code (pension insurance) and the provisions of Part III of the Reich Insurance Code (accident insurance) shall be settled in a federal Act.

For persons whose pension under the statutory pension scheme begins in the period from 1 January 1992 to 30 June 1995

1. a pension shall be payable which is in principle at least as high as the amount they would have received on 30 June 1990 in the territory specified in Article 3 of this Treaty according to the pension law valid until that time, without regard for payments from supplementary or special pension schemes.

2. a pension shall also be paid where, on 30 June 1990, a pension entitlement would have existed in the territory specified in Article 3 of this Treaty under the pension law valid until that time.

In all other respects, the introduction should have the goal of ensuring that as wages and salaries in the territory specified in Article 3 of this Treaty are brought into line with those in the other Länder, so are pensions.

(6) In developing further the ordinance on occupational diseases it shall be examined to what extent the arrangements which have applied until now in the territory specified in Article 3 of this Treaty can be taken into account.

Article 31

Family and Women

(1) It shall be the task of the all-German legislator to develop further the legislation on equal rights for men and women.

(2) In view of different legal and institutional starting positions with regard to the employment of mothers and fathers, it shall be the task of the all-German legislator to shape the legal situation in such a way as to allow a reconciliation of family and occupational life.

(3) In order to ensure that day care centres for children continue to operate in the territory specified in Article 3 of this Treaty, the Federation shall contribute to the costs of these centres for a transitional period up to 30 June 1991.

(4) It shall be the task of the all-German legislator to introduce regulations no later than 31 December 1992 which ensure better protection of unborn life and provide a better solution in conformity with the Constitution of conflict situations faced by pregnant women—notable through legally guaranteed entitlements for women, first and foremost to advice and public support—than is the case in either part of Germany at present. In order to achieve these objectives, a network of advice centres run by various agencies and offering blanket coverage shall be set up without delay with financial assistance from the Federation in the territory specified in Article 3 of this Treaty. The advice centres shall be provided with sufficient staff and funds to allow them to cope with the task of advising pregnant women and offering them necessary assistance, including beyond the time of confinement. In the event that no regulations are introduced within the period stated in the first sentence, the substantive law shall continue to apply in the territory specified in Article 3 of this Treaty.

Article 32

Voluntary Organizations

Voluntary welfare and youth welfare organizations play an indispensable part through their institutions and services in fashioning the socially oriented state described in the Basic Law. The establishment and expansion of voluntary welfare and youth welfare organizations shall be promoted in the territory specified in Article 3 of this Treaty in line with the distribution of competence under the Basic Law.

Article 33

Public Health

(1) It shall be the task of the legislators to create the conditions for effecting a rapid and lasting improvement in in-patient care in the territory specified in Article 3 of this Treaty and for bringing it into line with the situation in the remainder of the federal territory.

(2) In order to avoid deficits arising from expenditure on prescribed drugs by the health insurance scheme in the territory specified in Article 3 of this Treaty, the all-German legislator shall introduce temporary regulations providing for a reduction in producers' prices within the meaning of the Ordinance on the Price of Drugs corresponding to the gap between the income subject to insurance contributions in the territory specified in Article 3 of this

Treaty and that in the present federal territory.

Article 34

Protection of the Environment

(1) On the basis of the German environmental union established under Article 16 of the Treaty of 18 May 1990 in conjunction with the Skeleton Environment Act of the German Democratic Republic of 29 June 1990 (Law Gazette I, No. 42, p. 649), it shall be the task of the legislators to protect the natural basis of man's existence, with due regard for prevention, the polluter-pays principle, and cooperation, and to promote uniform ecological conditions of a high standard at least equivalent to that reached in the Federal Republic of Germany.

(2) With a view to attaining the objective defined in paragraph 1 above, ecological rehabilitation and development programmes shall be drawn up for the territory specified in Article 3 of this Treaty, in line with the distribution of competence under the Basic Law. Measures to ward off dangers to public health shall be accorded priority.

Chapter VIII

Culture, Education and Science, Sport

Article 35

Culture

(1) In the years of division, culture and the arts—despite different paths of development taken by the two states in Germany—formed one of the foundations for the continuing unity of the German nation. They have an indispensable contribution to make in their own right as the Germans cement their unity in a single state on the road to European unification. The position and prestige of a united Germany in the world depend not only on its political weight and its economic strength, but also on its role in the cultural domain. The overriding objective of external cultural policy shall be cultural exchange based on partnership and cooperation.

(2) The cultural substance in the territory specified in Article 3 of this Treaty shall not suffer any damage.

(3) Measures shall be taken to provide for the performance of cultural tasks, including their financing, with the protection and promotion of culture and the arts being the responsibility of the new Länder and local authorities in line with the distribution of com-

petence under the Basic Law.

(4) The cultural institutions which have been under central management to date shall come under the responsibility of the Länder or local authorities in whose territory they are located. In exceptional cases, the possibility of the Federation making a contribution to financing shall not be ruled out, particularly in Land Berlin.

(5) The parts of the former Prussian state collections which were separated as a result of post-war events (including State Museums, State Libraries, Secret State Archives, Ibero-American Institute, State Musicology Institute) shall be joined together again in Berlin. The Prussian Cultural Heritage Foundation shall assume responsibility for the time being. Future arrangements shall likewise involve an agency that is responsible for the former Prussian state collections in their entirety and is based in Berlin.

(6) The Cultural Fund shall be continued up to 31 December 1994 on a transitional basis in the territory specified in Article 3 of this Treaty to promote culture, the arts and artists. The possibility of the Federation making a contribution to financing in line with the distribution of competence under the Basic Law shall not be ruled out. Discussions on a successor institution shall be held in the framework of the talks on the accession of the Länder named in Article 1 (1) of this Treaty to the Cultural Foundation of the Länder.

(7) In order to offset the effects of the division of Germany the Federation may help to finance, on a transitional basis, individual cultural programmes and institutions in the territory specified in Article 3 of this Treaty to enhance the cultural infrastructure.

Article 36

Broadcasting

(1) The Rundfunk der DDR and the Deutscher Fernsehfunk shall be continued as an autonomous joint institution having legal capacity by the Länder named in Article 1 of this Treaty and by Land Berlin in respect of that part where the Basic Law has not been valid to date for a period not extending beyond 31 December 1991 in so far as they perform tasks coming under the responsibility of the Länder. The institution shall have the task of providing the population in the territory specified in Article 3 of this Treaty with a radio and television service in accordance with the general principles governing broadcasting

establishments coming under public law. The studio equipment which has belonged to Deutsche Post to date shall be made over to the institution together with the immovable property serving production and administrative purposes for radio and television. Article 21 of this Treaty shall be applied *mutatis mutandis*.

(2) The executive bodies of the institution shall be

1. the Broadcasting Commissioner,
2. the Advisory Council on Broadcasting.

(3) The Broadcasting Commissioner shall be elected by the Volkskammer on the proposal of the Prime Minister of the German Democratic Republic. Should the Volkskammer fail to elect a Broadcasting Commissioner, he shall be elected by the Land spokesmen of the Länder named in Article 1(1) of this Treaty and by the First Mayor of Berlin by a majority vote. The Broadcasting Commissioner shall be in charge of the institution and represent it in and out of court. He shall be responsible for fulfilling the mission of the institution within the limits of the available resources and shall, without delay, draw up a budget for 1991 in which revenue and expenditure are balanced.

(4) The Advisory Council on Broadcasting shall comprise 18 acknowledged public figures as representatives of socially relevant groups. The parliaments of the Länder named in Article 1(1) of this Treaty and the Berlin Municipal Assembly shall each elect three members. The Advisory Council on Broadcasting shall have a consultative voice on all questions of programming and a right to participation in major personnel, economic and budget decisions. The Advisory Council on Broadcasting may recall the Broadcasting Commissioner by a majority vote of two thirds of its members. It may elect a new Broadcasting Commissioner by a majority vote of two thirds of its members.

(5) The institution shall be financed mainly by revenue raised through licence fees paid by radio and television users resident in the territory specified in Article 3 of this Treaty. To that extent it shall be the recipient of radio and television licence fees. For the rest, it shall cover its expenditure by advertising revenue and other revenue.

(6) Within the period laid down in paragraph 1 above the institution shall be dissolved in accordance with the federal structure of broadcasting through a joint treaty between the Länder named in Article 1 of this Treaty or converted to agencies under public law

of one or more Länder. Should a treaty under the first sentence fail to materialize by 31 December 1991, the institution shall be deemed to have been dissolved on that date. The assets and liabilities existing on that date shall be shared out among the Länder named in Article 1 of this Treaty. The amount of the shares to be transferred shall be calculated in proportion to the licence fee revenues as of 30 June 1991 in the territory specified in Article 3 of this Treaty. This shall not affect the obligation of the Länder to continue to provide a broadcasting service in the territory specified in Article 3 of this Treaty.

(7) Upon the entry into force of the treaty under paragraph 6 above, but no later than 31 December 1991, paragraphs 1 to 6 above shall cease to have effect.

Article 37

Education

(1) School, vocational or higher education certificates or degrees obtained or officially recognized in the German Democratic Republic shall continue to be valid in the territory specified in Article 3 of this Treaty. Examinations passed and certificates obtained in the territory specified in Article 3 or in the other Länder of the Federal Republic of Germany, including Berlin (West), shall be considered equal and shall convey the same rights if they are of equal value. Their equivalence shall be established by the respective competent agency on application. Legal provisions of the Federation and the European Communities regarding the equivalence of examinations and certificates, and special provisions set out in this Treaty shall have priority. In all cases this shall not affect the right to use academic professional titles and degrees obtained or officially recognized or conferred.

(2) The usual recognition procedure operated by the Conference of Ministers of Education and Cultural Affairs shall apply to teaching diploma examinations. The said Conference shall make appropriate transitional arrangements.

(3) Examination certificates issued under the trained occupation scheme and the skilled workers' training scheme as well as final examinations and apprentices' final examinations in recognized trained occupations shall be considered equal.

(4) The regulations necessary for the reorganization of the school system in the territory specified in Article 3 of this Treaty shall be adopted by the Länder named in Article 1. The necessary regulations for the recognition of examinations under educational law shall be agreed by the Conference of Ministers of Education and Cultural Affairs. In both cases they shall be based on the Hamburg Agreement and the other relevant agreements reached by the said Conference.

(5) Undergraduates who move to another institution of higher education before completing their studies shall have their study and examination record up to that point recognized according to the principles laid down in Section 7 of the General Regulations on Degree Examination Procedures (ABD) or within the terms of the rules governing admission to state examinations.

(6) The entitlements to study at an institution of higher education confirmed on leaving certificates issued by engineering and technical schools of the German Democratic Republic shall be valid in accordance with the resolution of 10 May 1990 of the Conference of Ministers of Education and Cultural Affairs and its Annex B. Further principles and procedures for the recognition of technical school and higher education certificates for the purpose of school and college studies based on them shall be developed within the framework of the Conference of Ministers of Education and Cultural Affairs.

Article 38

Science and Research

(1) In the united Germany science and research shall continue to constitute important foundations of the state and society. The need to renew science and research in the territory specified in Article 3 of this Treaty while preserving efficient institutions shall be taken into account by an expert report on publicly maintained institutions prepared by the Science Council and to be completed by 31 December 1991, with individual results to be implemented step by step before that date.

The following provisions are intended to make possible the preparation of this report and ensure the incorporation of science and research in the territory specified in Article 3 of this Treaty into the joint research structure of the Federal Republic of Germany.

(2) Upon the accession taking effect, the Academy of Sciences of the German Democratic Republic shall be separated as a learned society from the research institutes and other institutions. The deci-

sion as to how the learned society of the Academy of Sciences of the German Democratic Republic is to be continued shall be taken under Land law. For the time being the research institutes and other institutions shall continue to exist up to 31 December 1991 as institutions of the Länder in the territory specified in Article 3 of this Treaty in so far as they have not been previously dissolved or transformed. Transitional arrangements shall be made for the financing of these institutes and institutions up to 31 December 1991; the requisite funds shall be provided in 1991 by the Federation and the Länder named in Article 1 of this Treaty.

(3) The employment contracts of the staff employed at the research institutes and other institutions of the Academy of Sciences of the German Democratic Republic shall continue to exist up to 31 December 1991 as limited employment contracts with the Länder to which these institutes and institutions are transferred. The right to cancel these employment contracts with or without notice under the conditions listed in Annex I to this Treaty shall remain unaffected.

(4) Paragraphs 1 to 3 above shall apply *mutatis mutandis* to the Academy of Architecture and the Academy of Agricultural Sciences of the German Democratic Republic and to the scientific institutions subordinate to the Ministry of Food, Agriculture and Forestry.

(5) The Federal Government shall begin negotiations with the Länder with a view to adapting or renewing the Federation-Länder agreements under Article 91b of the Basic Law in such a way that educational planning and the promotion of institutions and projects of scientific research of supra-regional importance are extended to the territory specified in Article 3 of this Treaty.

(6) The Federal Government shall seek to ensure that the proven methods and programmes of research promotion in the Federal Republic of Germany are applied as soon as possible to the entire federal territory and that the scientists and scientific institutions in the territory specified in Article 3 of this Treaty are given access to current research promotion schemes. Furthermore, certain schemes for promoting research and development which have expired in the territory of the Federal Republic of Germany shall be reopened for the territory specified in Article 3 of this Treaty; this shall not include fiscal measures.

(7) Upon the accession of the German Democratic Republic taking effect, the Research Council of the German Democratic Republic shall be dissolved.

Article 39

Sport

(1) The sporting structures which are in a process of transformation in the territory specified in Article 3 of this Treaty shall be placed on a self-governing basis. The public authorities shall give moral and material support to sport in line with the distribution of competence under the Basic Law.

(2) To the extent that it has proved successful, top-level sport and its development shall continue to receive support in the territory specified in Article 3 of this Treaty. Support shall be given within the framework of the rules and principles existing in the Federal Republic of Germany and in line with the public-sector budgets in the territory specified in Article 3 of this Treaty. Within this framework, the Physical Training and Sport Research Institute (FKS) in Leipzig, the doping control laboratory recognized by the International Olympic Committee (IOC) in Kreischa (near Dresden) and the Sports Equipment Research and Development Centre (FES) in Berlin (East) shall—each in an appropriate legal form and to the extent necessary—be continued as institutions in the united Germany or attached to existing institutions.

(3) The Federation shall support sport for the disabled for a transitional period until 31 December 1992.

Chapter IX

Transitional and Final Provisions

Article 40

Treaties and Agreements

(1) The obligations under the Treaty of 18 May 1990 between the Federal Republic of Germany and the German Democratic Republic on the Establishment of a Monetary, Economic and Social Union shall continue to be valid unless otherwise provided in this Treaty and unless they become irrelevant in the process of establishing German unity.

(2) Where rights and duties arising from other treaties and agreements between the Federal Republic of Germany or its Länder and the German Democratic Republic have not become irrelevant in the process of establishing German unity, they shall be assumed, adjusted or settled by the competent national entities.

Article 41

Settlement of Property Issues

(1) The Joint Declaration of 15 June 1990 on the Settlement of Open Property Issues (Annex III) issued by the Government of the Federal Republic of Germany and the Government of the German Democratic Republic shall form an integral part of this Treaty.

(2) In accordance with separate legislative arrangements there shall be no return of property rights to real estate or buildings if the real estate or building concerned is required for urgent investment purposes to be specified in detail, particularly if it is to be used for the establishment of an industrial enterprise and the implementation of this investment decision deserves support from a general economic viewpoint, above all if it creates or safeguards jobs. The investor shall submit a plan showing the major features of his project and shall undertake to carry out the plan on this basis. The legislation shall also contain arrangements for compensation to the former owner.

(3) The Federal Republic of Germany shall not otherwise enact any legislation contradicting the Joint Declaration referred to in paragraph 1 above.

Article 42

Delegation of Parliamentary Representatives

(1) Before the accession of the German Democratic Republic takes effect, the Volkskammer shall, on the basis of its composition, elect 144 Members of Parliament to be delegated to the 11th German Bundestag together with a sufficient number of reserve members. Relevant proposals shall be made by the parties and groups represented in the Volkskammer.

(2) The persons elected shall become members of the 11th German Bundestag by virtue of a statement of acceptance delivered to the President of the Volkskammer, but not until the accession takes effect. The President of the Volkskammer shall without delay communicate the result of the election, together with the statement of acceptance, to the President of the German Bundestag.

(3) The eligibility for election to, and loss of membership of, the 11th German Bundestag shall otherwise be subject to the provisions of the Federal Election Act as promulgated on 1 September 1975 (Ferderal Law Gazette 1, p. 2325) and last amended by the Act of 29 August 1990 (Federal Law Gazette 11, p. 813).

In the event of cessation of membership, the member concerned shall be replaced by the next person on the reserve list. He must belong to the same party as, at the time of his election, the member whose membership has ceased. The reserve member to take his seat in the German Bundestag shall, before the accession takes effect, be determined by the President of the Volkskammer, and thereafter by the President of the German Bundestag.

Article 43

Transitional Rule for the Bundesrat Pending the Formation of Länder Governments

From the formation of the Länder named in Article 1 (1) of this Treaty until the election of minister-presidents, the Land plenipotentiaries may take part in the meetings of the Bundesrat in a consultative capacity.

Article 44

Preservation of Rights

Rights arising from this Treaty in favour of the German Democratic Republic or the Länder named in Article 1 of this Treaty may be asserted by each of these Länder after the accession has taken effect.

Article 45

Entry into Force of the Treaty

(1) This Treaty, including the attached Protocol and Annexes I to III, shall enter into force on the day on which the Governments of the Federal Republic of Germany and the German Democratic Republic have informed each other that the internal requirements for such entry into force have been fulfilled.

(2) The Treaty shall remain valid as federal law after the accession has taken effect.

Treaty on Conventional Armed Forces in Europe

Date of signature: *November 19, 1990*
Place of signature: *Paris*

Signatory states: *Belgium, Bulgaria, Canada, the Czech and Slovak Federal Republic, Denmark,*

France, Federal Republic of Germany,
The Hellenic Republic, Hungary, Iceland, Italy,
Luxembourg, Netherlands, Norway, Poland,
Portugal, Romania, Spain, Turkey, Union of Soviet
Socialist Republics, United Kingdom and Northern
Ireland, The United States
Date of entry into force: November 9, 1992

[The signatories], hereinafter referred to as the States Parties,

Guided by the Mandate for Negotiation on Conventional Armed Forces in Europe of January 10, 1989, and having conducted this negotiation in Vienna beginning on March, 9, 1989,

Guided by the objectives and the purposes of the Conference on Security and Cooperation in Europe, within the framework of which the negotiation of this Treaty was conducted,

Recalling their obligation to refrain in their mutual relations, as well as in their international relations in general, from the threat or use against the territorial integrity or political independence of any State, or in any other manner inconsistent which the purposes and principles of the Charter of the United Nations,

Conscious of the need to prevent any military conflict in Europe,

Conscious of the common responsibility which they all have for seeking to achieve greater stability and security in Europe,

Striving to replace military confrontation with a new pattern of security relations among all the States Parties based on peaceful cooperation and thereby to contribute to overcoming the division of Europe,

Committed to the objectives of establishing a secure and stable balance of conventional armed forces in Europe at lower levels than heretofore, of eliminating disparities prejudicial to stability and security and of eliminating, as a matter of high priority, the capability for launching surprise attack and for initiating large-scale offensive action in Europe,

Recalling that they signed or acceded to the Treaty of Brussels of 1948, the Treaty of Washington of 1949 or the Treaty of Warsaw of 1995 and that they have the right to be or not to be a party to treaties of alliance,

Committed to the objective of ensuring that the numbers of conventional armaments and equipment limit-ed by the Treaty within the area of application of this Treaty do not exceed 40,000 battle tanks, 60,000 armoured combat vehicles, 40,000 pieces of artillery, 13,600 combat aircraft and 4,000 attack helicopters,

Affirming that this Treaty is not intended to affect adversely the security interests of any State,

Affirming their commitment to continue the conventional arms control process including negotiations, taking into account future requirements for European stability and security in the light of political developments in Europe,

Have agreed as follows:

Article 1

1. Each State Party shall carry out the obligations set forth in this Treaty in accordance with its provisions, including those obligations relating to the following five categories of conventional armed forces: battle tanks, armoured combat vehicles, artillery, combat aircraft and combat helicopters.

2. Each State Party also shall carry out the other measures set forth in this Treaty designed to ensure security and stability both during the period of reduction of conventional armed forces and after the completion of reductions.

3. This Treaty incorporates the Protocol on Existing Types of Conventional Armaments and Equipment, hereinafter referred to as the Protocol on Existing Types, with an Annex thereto: the Protocol on Procedures Governing the Reclassification of Specific Models or Versions of Combat-Capable Trainer Aircraft Into Unarmed Trainer Aircraft, hereinafter referred to as the Protocol on Aircraft Reclassification: the Protocol on Procedures Governing the Reduction of Conventional Armaments and Equipment Limited by the Treaty on Conventional Armed Forces in Europe, hereinafter referred to as the Protocol on Reduction: the Protocol on Procedures Governing the Categorisation of Combat Helicopters and Recategorisation of Multi-Purpose Attack Helicopters, hereinafter referred to as the Protocol on Helicopter Recategorisation: the Protocol on Notification and Exchange of Information, hereinafter referred to as the Protocol on Information Exchange, with an Annex on the Format for the Exchange of Information, hereinafter referred to as the Annex on Format, the Protocol on Inspection, the Protocol on the Joint Consultative Group, and the Protocol on the Provisional Application of Certain Provisions of the Treaty on Conventional Armed Forces in Europe, hereinafter referred to as the Protocol on Provisional

Application. Each of these documents constitutes an integral part of this Treaty.

Article 2

1. For the purposes of this Treaty:

(A) The term "group of States Parties" means the group of States Parties that signed the Treaty of Warsaw of 1955 consisting of the Republic of Bulgaria, the Czech and Slovak Federal Republic of Hungary, the Republic of Poland, Rumania and the Union of Soviet Socialist Republics, or the group of States Parties that signed or acceded to the Treaty of Brussels of 1948 or the Treaty of Washington of 1949 consisting of the Kingdom of Belgium, Canada, the Kingdom of Denmark, the French Republic, the Federal Republic of Germany, the Hellenic Republic, the Republic of Iceland, the Italian Republic, the Grand Duchy of Luxembourg, the Kingdom of the Netherlands, the Kingdom of Norway, the Portuguese Republic, the Kingdom of Spain, the Republic of Turkey, the United Kingdom of Great Britain and Northern Ireland and the United States of America.

(B) The term "area of application" means the entire land territory of the States Parties in Europe from the Atlantic Ocean to the Ural Mountains, which includes all the European island territories of the States Parties, including the Faroe Islands of the Kingdom of Denmark, Svalbard including Bear Island of the Kingdom of Norway, the islands of Azores and Madeira of the Portuguese Republic, the Canary Islands of the Kingdom of Spain and Franz Josef Land Novaya Zemlya of the Union of Soviet Socialist Republics. In the case of the Union of Soviet Socialist Republics, the area of application includes all territory lying west of the Ural River and the Caspian Sea. In the case of the Republic of Turkey, the area of application includes the territory of the Republic of Turkey north and west of a line extending from the point of intersection of the Turkish border with the 39th parallel to Muradiye, Patnos, Karayazi, Tekman, Kemaliye, Feke, Ceyhan, Dogankent, Cözne and thence to the sea.

(C) The term "battle tank" means a self-propelled armoured fighting vehicle, capable of heavy firepower, primarily of a high muzzle velocity direct fire main gun necessary to engage armoured and other targets, with high cross-country mobility, with a high level of self-protection, and which is not designed and equipped primarily to transport combat troops. Such armoured vehicles serve as the principal weapon system of ground-force tank and other armoured formations.

Battle tanks are tracked armoured fighting vehicles which weigh at least 16.5 metric tonnes unladen weight and which are armed with a 360-degree traverse gun of a 75 millimeters calibre. In addition, any wheeled armoured fighting vehicles entering into service which meet all the other criteria stated above shall also be deemed battle tanks.

(D) The term "armoured combat vehicle" means a self-propelled vehicle with armoured protection and cross-country capability. Armoured combat vehicles include armoured personnel carriers, armoured infantry fighting vehicles and heavy armament combat vehicles.

The term "armoured personnel carrier" means an armoured combat vehicle which is designed and equipped to transport a combat infantry squad and which, as a rule, is armed with an integral or organic weapon of less than 20 millimeters calibre.

The term "armoured infantry fighting vehicles" means an armoured combat vehicle which is designed and equipped primarily to transport a combat infantry squad, which normally provides the capability for the troops to deliver fire from inside the vehicle under armoured protection, and which is armed with an integral or organic cannon of at least 20 millimeters calibre and sometimes an antitank missile launcher. Armoured infantry fighting vehicles serve as the principal weapon system of armoured infantry or mechanised infantry or motorised infantry formations and units of ground forces.

The term "heavy armament combat vehicle" means an armoured combat vehicle with an integral or organic direct fire gun of at least 75 millimeters calibre, weighing at least 6.0 metric tonnes unladen weight, which does not fall within the definitions of an armoured personnel carrier, or an armoured infantry fighting vehicle or a battle tank.

(E) The term "unladen weight" means the weight of a vehicle excluding the weight of ammunition; fuel, oil and lubricants; removable reactive armour; spare parts, tools and accessories; removable snorkeling equipment; and crew and their personal kit.

(F) The term "artillery" means large calibre systems capable of engaging ground targets by delivering primarily indirect fire. Such artillery systems provide the essential indirect fire support to combined arms formations.

Large calibre artillery systems are guns, howitzers, artillery pieces combining the characteristics of guns and howitzers, mortars and multiple launch rocket systems with a calibre of 100 millimeters and above. In addition any future large calibre direct fire system which has a secondary effective indirect fire capability shall be counted against the artillery ceilings.

(G) The term "stationed conventional armed forces" means conventional armed forces of a State Party that are stationed within the area of application on the territory of another State Party.

(H) The term "designated permanent storage site" means a place with a clearly defined physical boundary containing conventional armaments and equipment limited by the Treaty, which are counted within overall ceilings but which are not subject to limitations on conventional armaments and equipment limited by the Treaty in active units.

(I) The term "armoured vehicle launched bridge" means a self-propelled armoured transporter-launcher vehicle capable of carrying and, through built-in mechanisms, of emplacing and retrieving a bridge structure. Such a vehicle with a bridge structure operates as an integrated system.

(J) The term "conventional armaments and equipment limited by the Treaty" means battle tanks, armoured combat vehicles, artillery combat aircraft and attack helicopters subject to the numerical limitations set forth in Articles 4, 5 and 6.

(K) The term "combat aircraft" means a fixed-wing or variable-geometry wing aircraft armed and equipped to engage targets by employing guided missiles, unguided rockets, bombs, guns, cannons, or other weapons of destruction, as well as any model or version of such an aircraft which performs other military functions such as reconnaissance or electronic warfare. The term "combat aircraft" does not include primary trainer aircraft.

(L) The term "combat helicopter" means a rotary wing aircraft armed equipped to engage targets or equipped to perform other military functions. The term "combat helicopter" comprises attack helicopters and combat support helicopters. The term "combat helicopter" does not include unarmed transport helicopters.

(M) The term "attack helicopter" means a combat helicopter equipped to employ antiarmour, air-to-ground, or air-to-air guided weapons and equipped with an integrated fire control and aiming system for these weapons. The term "attack helicopter" comprises specialized attack helicopters and multi-purpose attack helicopters.

(N) The term "specialized attack helicopter" means an attack helicopter that is designed primarily to employ guided weapons.

(O) The term "multi-purpose attack helicopter" means an attack helicopter designed to perform multiple military functions and equipped to employ guided weapons.

(P) The term "combat support helicopter" means a combat helicopter which does not fulfill the requirements to qualify as an attack helicopter and which may be equipped with a variety of self-defense and area suppression weapons, such as guns, cannons and unguided rockets, bombs or cluster bombs, or which may be equipped to perform other military functions.

(Q) The term "conventional armaments and equipment subject to the Treaty" means battle tanks, armoured combat vehicles, artillery, combat aircraft, primary trainer aircraft, unarmed trainer aircraft, combat helicopters, unarmed transport helicopters, armoured vehicle launched bridges, armoured personnel carrier look-alikes and armoured infantry fighting vehicle look-alikes subject to information exchange in accordance with the Protocol on Information Exchange.

(R) The term "in service," as it applies to conventional armed forces and conventional armaments and equipment, means battle tanks, armoured combat vehicles, artillery combat aircraft, primary trainer aircraft, unarmed trainer aircraft, combat helicopters unarmed transport helicopters, armoured vehicle, launched bridges, armoured personnel carrier look-alikes and armoured infantry fighting vehicle look-alikes that are within the area of application, except for those that are held by organizations designed and structured to perform in peacetime internal security functions or that meet any of the exceptions set forth in Article 3.

(S) The terms "armoured personnel carrier look-alike" and "armoured infantry fighting vehicle look-alike" means an armoured vehicle based on the same chassis as, and externally similar to, an armoured personnel carrier or armoured infantry fighting vehicle, respectively, which does not have a cannon or gun of 20 millimeters calibre or greater and which has been constructed or modified in such a way as not to permit the transportation of a combat infantry squad. Taking into account the provisions of the Geneva Convention "For the Amelioration of the Conditions of the Wounded and Sick in Armed Forces in the Field" of 12 August 1949 that confer a special status on ambulances, armoured personnel carrier ambulances shall not be deemed armoured combat vehicles or armoured personnel carrier look-alikes.

(T) The term "reduction site" means a clearly designated location where the reduction of conventional armaments and equipment limited by the Treaty in accordance with Article 8 takes place.

(U) The term "reduction liability" means the number in each category of conventional armaments and equipment limited by the Treaty that a State Party commits itself to reduce during the period of 40 months following the entry into force of this Treaty in order to ensure compliance with Article 7.

2. Existing types of conventional armaments and equipment subject to the Treaty are listed in the Protocol on Existing Types. The lists of existing types shall be periodically updated in accordance with Article XVI, paragraph 2, subparagraph (D) and Section IV of the Protocol on Existing Types. Such updates to the existing types lists shall not be deemed amendments to this Treaty.

3. The existing types of combat helicopters listed in the Protocol on Existing Types shall be categorized in accordance with Section I of the Protocol on Helicopter Recategorisation.

Article 3

1. For the purpose of this Treaty, the States Parties shall apply the following counting rules:

All battle tanks, armoured combat vehicles, artillery, combat aircraft and attack helicopters, as defined in Article 2, within the area of application shall be subject to the numerical limitations and other provision set forth in Article 4, 5 and 6, with the exception of those which in a manner consistent with a State Party's normal practices;

(A) are in the process of manufacture, including manufacturing-related testing;

(B) are used exclusively for the purposes of research and development;

(C) belong to historical collections;

(D) are awaiting disposal, having been decommissioned from service in accordance with the provisions of Article 9;

(E) are awaiting, or are being refurbished for, export or re-export and are temporarily retained within the area of application. Such battle tanks, armoured combat vehicles, artillery, combat aircraft and attack helicopters shall be located elsewhere than at sites declared under the terms of Section V of the Protocol on Information Exchange or at no more than 10 such declared sites which shall have been notified in the previous year's annual information exchange. In the latter case, they shall be separately distinguishable from conventional armaments and equipment limited by the Treaty;

(F) are, in the case of armoured personnel carriers, armoured infantry fighting vehicles, heavy armament combat vehicles or multi-purpose attack helicopters, held by organizations designed and structured to perform in peacetime internal security functions; or

(G) are in transit through the area of application from a location outside the area of application to a final destination outside the area of application, and are in the area of application for no longer than a total of seven days.

2. If in respect of any such battle tanks, armoured combat vehicles, artillery, combat aircraft or attack helicopters, the notification of which is required under Section IV of the Protocol on Information Exchange, a State Party notifies an unusually high number in more than two successive annual information exchanges, it shall explain the reasons in the Joint Consultative Group, if so requested.

Article 4

1. Within the area of application, as defined in Article 2, each State Party shall limit and, as necessary, reduce its battle tanks, armoured combat vehicles artillery, combat aircraft and attack helicopters so that, 40 months after entry into force of this Treaty and thereafter, for the group of States Parties to which it belongs, as defined in Article 2, the aggregate numbers do not exceed:

(A) 20,000 battle tanks, of which no more than 16,500 shall be in active units;

(B) 30,000 armoured combat vehicles, of which no more than 27,300 shall be in active units. Of the 30,000 armoured combat vehicles, no more than 18,000 shall be armoured infantry fighting vehicles and heavy armament combat vehicles; of armoured infantry fighting vehicles and heavy armament combat vehicles, no more than 1,500 shall be heavy armament combat vehicles;

(C) 20,000 pieces of artillery, of which no more than 17,000 shall be in active units;

(D) 6,800 combat aircraft; and

(E) 2,000 attack helicopters.

Battle tanks, armoured combat vehicles and artillery not in active units shall be placed in designated permanent storage sites, as defined in Article 2, and shall be located only in the area described in paragraph 2 of this Article. Such designated permanent storage sites may also be located in that part of the territory of the Union of Soviet Socialist Republics comprising the Odessa Military District and the southern part of Leningrad Military District. In the Odessa Military District, no more than 400 battle tanks and no more than 500 pieces of artillery may be thus stored. In the southern part of the Leningrad Military District, no more than 600 battle tanks, no more than 800 armoured combat vehicles, including no more than 300 armoured combat vehicles of any type with the remaining number consisting of armoured personnel carriers, and no more than 400 pieces of artillery may be thus stored. The southern part of the Leningrad Military District is understood to mean the territory within that military district south of the line East-West 60 degrees 15 minutes northern latitude.

2. Within the area consisting of the entire land territory in Europe, which includes all the European island territories, of the Kingdom of Belgium, the Czech and Slovak Federal Republic, the Kingdom of Denmark including the Faroe Island, the French Republic, the Federal Republic of Germany, the Republic of Hungary, the Italian Republic, the Grand Duchy of Luxembourg, the Kingdom of the Netherlands, the Republic of Poland, the Portuguese Republic including the islands of Azores and Madeira, the Kingdom of Spain including the Canary Islands, the United Kingdom of Great Britain and Northern Ireland and that part of the territory of the Union of Soviet Socialist Republics west of the Ural Military Districts, each State Party shall limit and as necessary, reduce its battle tanks, armoured combat vehi-

cles and artillery so that 40 months after entry into force of this Treaty and thereafter, for the group of States Parties to which it belongs the aggregate numbers do not exceed:

(A) 15,300 battle tanks, of which no more than 11,800 shall be in active units;

(B) 24,100 armoured combat vehicles, of which no more than 21,400 shall be in active units; and

(C) 14,000 pieces of artillery of which no more than 11,000 shall be in active units.

3. Within the area consisting of the entire land territory in Europe, which includes all the European island territories, of the Kingdom of Belgium, the Czech and Slovak Federal Republic, the Kingdom of Denmark including the Faroe Islands, the French Republic, the Federal Republic of Germany, the Republic of Hungary, the Italian Republic, the Grand Duchy of Luxembourg, the Kingdom of the Netherlands, the Republic of Poland, the United Kingdom of Great Britain and Northern Ireland and that part of the territory of the Union of Soviet Socialist Republic comprising the Baltic, Bevelorussian, Carpathian and Kiev Military Districts, each State Party shall limit and, as necessary, reduce its battle tanks, armored combat vehicles and artillery so that, 40 months after entry into force of this Treaty and thereafter, for the group of States Parties to which it belongs the aggregate numbers in active units do not exceed:

(A) 10,300 battle tanks;

(B) 19,260 armored combat vehicles; and

(C) 9,100 pieces of artillery; and

(D) in the Kiev Military District, the aggregate numbers in active units and designated permanent storage sites together shall not exceed:

(1) 2,250 battle tanks;

(2) 2,500 armoured combat vehicles; and

(3) 1,500 pieces of artillery.

4. Within the area consisting of the entire land territory in Europe, which includes all the European island territories, of the Kingdom of Belgium, the Czech and Slovak Federal Republic, the Federal Republic of Germany, the Republic of Hungary, the Grand Duchy of Luxembourg, the Kingdom of the Netherlands and the Republic of Poland, each State Party shall limit and, as necessary, reduce its battle tanks, armoured combat vehicles and artillery so that

40 months after entry into force of this Treaty and thereafter, for the group of States Parties to which it belongs the aggregate numbers in active units do not exceed:

(A) 7,500 battle tanks:

(B) 11,250 armoured combat vehicles; and

(C) 5,000 pieces of artillery.

5. States Parties belonging to the same group of States Parties may locate battle tanks, armoured combat vehicles and artillery in active units in each of the areas described in this Article and Article 5, paragraph 1, subparagraph (A) up to the numerical limitations applying in that area, consistent with the maximum levels for holdings notified pursuant to Article 7 and provided that no State Party stations conventional armed forces on the territory of another States Party without the agreement of that State Party.

6. If a group of States Parties' aggregate numbers of battle tanks, armoured combat vehicles and artillery in active units within the area described in paragraph 4 of this Article are less than the numerical limitations set forth in paragraph 4 of this Article, and provided that no State Party is thereby prevented from reaching its maximum levels for holdings notified in accordance with Article 7, paragraphs 2, 3 and 5, then amounts equal to the difference between the aggregate numbers in each of the categories of battle tanks, armoured combat vehicles and artillery and the specified numerical limitations for that area may be located by States Parties belonging to that group of States Parties in the area described in paragraph 3 of this Article, consistent with the numerical limitations specified in paragraph 3 of this Article.

Article 5

1. To ensure that the security of each State Party is not affected adversely at any stage:

(A) within the area consisting of the entire land territory in Europe, which includes all the European island territories, of the Republic of Bulgaria, the Hellenic Republic, the Republic of Iceland, the Kingdom of Norway, Romania, the part of the Republic of Turkey within the area of application and that part of the Union of Soviet Socialist Republics comprising the Leningrad, Odessa, Transcaucasus and North Caucasus Military Districts, each State Party shall limit and, as necessary, reduce its battle tanks, armoured combat vehicles and artillery so that, 40 months after entry

into force of this Treaty and thereafter, for the group of States Parties to which it belongs the aggregate numbers in active units do not exceed the difference between the overall numerical limitations set forth in Article 4, paragraph 1 and those in Article 4, paragraph 2, that is:

(1) 4,700 battle tanks;

(2) 5,900 armoured combat vehicles; and

(3) 6,000 pieces of artillery;

(B) notwithstanding the numerical limitations set forth in subparagraph (A) of this paragraph, a State Party or States Parties may on a temporary basis deploy into the territory belonging to the members of the same group of States Parties within the area described in subparagraph (A) of this paragraph additional aggregate numbers in active units for each group of States not to exceed:

(1) 459 battle tanks;

(2) 723 armoured combat vehicles; and

(3) 420 pieces of artillery; and

(C) provided that for each group of States Parties no more than one-third of each of these additional aggregate numbers shall be deployed to any States Party with territory within the area described in subparagraph (A) of this paragraph, that is:

(1) 153 battle tanks;

(2) 241 armoured combat vehicles; and

(3) 140 pieces of artillery.

2. Notification shall be provided to all other States Parties no later than at the start of the deployment by the State Party or States Parties conducting the development and by the recipient State Party or States Parties, specifying the total number in each category of battle tanks, armoured combat vehicles and artillery deployed. Notification also shall be provided to all other States Parties by the State Party or States Parties conducting the deployment and by the recipient State Party or States Parties within 30 days of the withdrawal of those battle tanks, armoured combat vehicles and artillery that were temporarily deployed.

Article 6

With the objective of ensuring that no single State Party possesses more than approximately one-third of the conventional armaments and equipment limited by the Treaty within the area of application, each

State Party shall limit and, as necessary, reduce its battle tanks, armoured combat vehicles, artillery, combat aircraft and attack helicopters so that, 40 months after entry into force of this Treaty and thereafter, the numbers within the area of application for that State Party do not exceed:

(A) 13,300 battle tanks;

(B) 20,000 armoured combat vehicles;

(C) 13,700 pieces of artillery;

(D) 5,150 combat aircraft; and

(E) 1,500 attack helicopters.

Article 7

1. In order that the limitations set forth in Articles 4, 5 and 6 are not exceeded, no State Party shall exceed, from 40 months after entry into force of this Treaty, the maximum levels which it has previously agreed upon within its group of States Parties, in accordance with paragraph 7 of this Article, for its holdings of conventional armaments and equipment limited by the Treaty and of which it has provided notification pursuant to the provisions of this Article.

2. Each State Party shall provide at the signature of this Treaty notification to all other States Parties of the maximum levels for its holdings of conventional armaments and equipment limited by the Treaty. The notification of the maximum levels for holdings of conventional armaments and equipment limited by the Treaty provided by each State Party at the signature of this Treaty shall remain valid until the date specified in a subsequent notification pursuant to paragraph 3 of this Article.

3. In accordance with the limitations set forth in Article 4, 5 and 6, each State Party shall have the right to change the maximum levels for its holdings of conventional armaments and equipment limited by the Treaty. Any change in the maximum levels for holdings of a State Party shall be notified by that State Party to all other States Parties at least 90 days in advance of the date, specified in the notification, on which such a change takes effect. In order not to exceed any of the limitations set forth in Articles 4 and 5, any increase in the maximum levels for holdings of a State Party that would otherwise cause those limitations to be exceeded shall be preceded or accompanied by a corresponding reduction in the previously notified maximum levels for holdings of conventional armaments and equipment limited by the Treaty of one or more States Parties belonging to the same group of States Parties. The notification of

a change in the maximum levels for holdings shall remain valid from the date specified in the notification until the date specified in a subsequent notification of change pursuant to this paragraph.

4. Each notification required pursuant to paragraph 2 or 3 of this Article for armoured combat vehicles shall also include maximum levels for the holding of armoured infantry fighting vehicles and heavy armament combat vehicles of the State Party providing the notification.

5. Ninety days before expiration of the 40-month period of reductions set forth in Article 8 and subsequently at the time of any notification of a change pursuant to paragraph 3 of this Article, each State Party shall provide notification of the maximum levels for its holdings of battle tanks, armoured combat vehicles and artillery with respect to each of the areas described in Article 4, paragraphs 2 to 4 and Article V, paragraph 1, subparagraph (A).

6. A decrease in the number of conventional armaments and equipment limited by the Treaty held by a State Party and subject to notification pursuant to the Protocol on Information Exchange shall by itself confer no right on any other States Party to increase the maximum levels for its holdings subject to notification pursuant to this Article.

7. It shall be the responsibility solely of each individual State Party to ensure that the maximum levels for its holdings notified pursuant to the provisions of this Article are not exceeded. States Parties belonging to the same group of States Parties shall consult in order to ensure that the maximum levels for holding notified pursuant to the provisions of this Article, taken together as appropriate, do not exceed the limitations set forth in Articles 4, 5 and 6.

Article 8

1. The numerical limitations set forth in Article 4, 5 and 6 shall be achieved only by means of reduction in accordance with the Protocol on Reduction, the Protocol on Helicopter Recategorisation, the Protocol on Aircraft Reclassification, the Footnote to Section 1, paragraph 2, subparagraph (A) of the Protocol on Existing Types and the Protocol on Inspection.

2. The categories of conventional armaments and equipment subject to reductions are battle tanks, armoured combat vehicles, artillery combat aircraft and attack helicopters. The specific types are listed in the Protocol on Existing Types.

(A) Battle tanks and armoured combat vehicles shall be reduced by destruction, conversion for non-military purposes, placement on static display, use as ground targets, or in the case of armoured personnel carriers, modification in accordance with the Footnote to Section 1, paragraph 2, subparagraph (A) of the Protocol on Existing Types.

(B) Artillery shall be reduced by destruction or placement on static display, or, in the case of self-propelled artillery, by use as ground targets.

(C) Combat aircraft shall be reduced by destruction, placement on static display, use for ground instructional purposes or in the case of specific models or versions of combat-capable trainer aircraft reclassification into unarmed trainer aircraft.

(D) Specialised attack helicopters shall be reduced by destruction, placement on static display, or use for ground instructional purposes.

(E) Multi-purpose attack helicopters shall be reduced by destruction, placement on static display, use for ground instructional purposes, or recategorisation.

3. Conventional armaments and equipment limited by the Treaty shall be deemed to be reduced upon execution of the procedures set forth in the Protocols listed in paragraph 1 of this Article and upon notification as required by these Protocols. Armaments and equipment so reduced shall no longer be counted against the numerical limitations set forth in Articles 4, 5 and 6.

4. Reductions shall be effected in three phases and completed no later than 40 months after entry into force of this Treaty, so that:

(A) by the end of the first reduction phase, that is no later than 16 months after entry into force of this Treaty, each State Party shall have ensured that at least 25 percent of its total reduction liability in each of the categories of conventional armaments and equipment limited by the Treaty has been reduced;

(B) by the end of the second reduction phase, that is, no later than 28 months after entry into force of this Treaty, each State Party shall have ensured that at least 60 percent of its total reduction liability in each of the categories of conventional armaments and equipment limited by the Treaty has been reduced;

(C) by the end of the third reduction phase, that is, no later than 40 months after entry into force of this Treaty, each State Party shall have reduced its total reduction liability in each of the categories of conventional armaments and equipment limited by the Treaty. States Parties carrying out conversion for

non-military purposes shall have ensured that the conversion of all battle tanks in accordance with Section VIII of the Protocol on Reduction shall have been completed by the end of the third reduction phases; and

(D) armoured combat vehicles deemed reduced by reason of having been partially destroyed in accordance with Section VIII, paragraph 6 of the Protocol on Reduction shall have been fully converted for non-military purposes, or destroyed in accordance with Section IV of the Protocol on Reduction, no later than 64 months after entry into force of this Treaty.

5. Conventional armaments and equipment limited by the Treaty to be reduced shall have been declared present within the area of application in the exchange of information at signature of this Treaty.

6. No later than 30 days after entry into force of this Treaty, each State Party shall provide notification to all other States Parties of its reduction liability.

7. Except as provided for in paragraph 8 of this Article, a State Party's reduction liability in each category shall be no less than the difference between its holdings notified in accordance with the Protocol on Information Exchange, at signature or effective upon entry into force of this Treaty, whichever is the greater, and the maximum levels for holdings it notified pursuant to Article 7.

8. Any subsequent revision of a State Party's holdings notified pursuant to the Protocol on Information Exchange or of its maximum levels for holdings notified pursuant to Article 7 shall be reflected by a notified adjustment to its reduction liability. Any notification of a decrease in a State Party's reduction liability shall be preceded or accompanied by either a notification of a corresponding increase in holdings not exceeding the maximum levels for holdings notified pursuant to Article 7 by one or more States belonging to the same group of States Parties, or a notification of a corresponding increase in the reduction liability of one or more such States Parties.

9. Upon entry into force of this Treaty, each State Party shall notify all other States Parties, in accordance with the Protocol on Information Exchange, of the locations of its reduction sites, including those where the final conversion of battle tanks and armoured combat vehicles for non-military purposes will be carried out.

10. Each State Party shall have the right to designate as many reduction sites as it wishes, to revise without restricting its designation of such sites and to carry out reduction and final conversion simultane-

ously at a maximum of 20 sites. States Parties shall have the right to share or co-locate reduction sites by mutual agreement.

11. Notwithstanding paragraph 10 of this Article, during the baseline validation period, that is the interval between entry into force of this Treaty and 120 days after entry into force of this Treaty, reduction shall be carried out simultaneously at no more than two reduction sites for each State Party.

12. Reduction of conventional armaments and equipment limited by the Treaty shall be carried out at reduction sites unless otherwise specified in the Protocols listed in paragraph 1 of this Article, within the area of application.

13. The reduction process, including the results of the conversion of conventional armaments and equipment limited by the Treaty for non-military purposes both during the reduction period and in the 24 months following the reduction period, shall be subject to inspection, without right of refusal, in accordance with the Protocol on Inspection.

Article 9

1. Other than removal from service in accordance with the provisions of Article 8, battle tanks, armoured combat vehicles, artillery, combat aircraft and attack helicopters within the area of application shall be removed from service only by decommisioning, provided that:

(A) such conventional armaments and equipment limited by the Treaty are decommissioned and awaiting disposal at no more than eight sites which shall be notified as declared sites in accordance with the Protocol on Information Exchange and shall be identified in such notifications as holding areas for decommissioned conventional armaments and equipment limited by the Treaty. If sites containing conventional armaments and equipment limited by the Treaty decommissioned from service also contain any other conventional armaments and equipment subject to the Treaty, the decommissioned conventional armaments and equipment limited by the Treaty shall be separately distinguishable; and

(B) the numbers of such decommissioned conventional armaments and equipment limited by the Treaty do not exceed, in the case of any individual State Party, one percent of its notified holdings of conventions armaments and equipment limited by the Treaty or a total of 250, whichever is greater, of which no more than 200 shall be battle tanks,

armoured combat vehicles and pieces of artillery, and no more than 50 shall be attack helicopters and combat aircraft.

2. Notification of decommissioning shall include the number and type of conventional armaments and equipment limited by the Treaty decommissioned and the location of decommissioning and shall be provided to all other States Parties in accordance with Section IX, paragraph 1, subparagraph (B) of the Protocol on Information Exchange.

Article 10

1. Designated permanent storage sites shall be notified in accordance with the Protocol on Information Exchange to all other States Parties by the State Party to which the conventional armaments and equipment limited by the Treaty contained at designated permanent storage sites belong. The notification shall include the designation and location, including geographic coordinates, of designated permanent storage sites and the numbers by type of each category of its conventional armaments and equipment limited by the Treaty at each such storage site.

2. Designated permanent storage sites shall contain only facilities appropriate for the storage and maintenance of armaments and equipment (e.g., warehouses, garages, workshops and associated stores as well as other support accommodation). Designated permanent storage sites shall not contain firing ranges or training areas associated with conventional armaments and equipment limited by the Treaty. Designated permanent storage sites shall contain only armaments and equipment belonging to the conventional armed forces of a State Party.

3. Each designated permanent storage site shall have a clearly defined physical boundary that shall consist of a continuous perimeter fence at least 1.5 meters in height. The perimeter fence shall have no more than three gates providing the sole means of entrance and exit for armaments and equipment.

4. Conventional armaments and equipment limited by the Treaty located within designated permanent storage sites shall be counted as conventional armaments and equipment limited by the Treaty not in active units, including when they are temporarily removed in accordance with paragraph 7, 8, 9 and 10 of this Article. Conventional armaments and equipment limited by the Treaty in storage other than in designated permanent storage sites shall be counted as conventional armaments and equipment limited by the Treaty in active units.

5. Active units or formations shall not be located

within designated permanent storage sites except as provided for in paragraph 6 of this Article.

6. Only personnel associated with the security or operation of designated permanent storage sites, or the maintenance of the armaments and equipment stored therein, shall be located within the designated permanent storage sites.

7. For the purpose of maintenance repair or modification of conventional armaments and equipment limited by the Treaty located within designated permanent storage sites, each State Party shall have the right, without prior notification to remove from and retain outside designated permanent storage sites simultaneously up to 10 percent rounded up to the nearest even whole number, of the notified holdings of each category of conventional armaments and equipment limited by the Treaty in each designated permanent storage site, or 10 items of the conventional armaments and equipment limited by the Treaty in each category in each designated permanent storage site, whichever is less.

8. Except as provided for in paragraph 7 of this Article, no State Party remove conventional armaments and equipment limited by the Treaty designated permanent storage sites unless notification has been provided to all other States Parties at least 42 days in advance of such removal. Notification shall be given by the State Party to which the conventional armaments and equipment limited by the Treaty belong. Such notification shall specify:

(A) the location of the designated permanent storage site from which conventional armaments and equipment limited by the Treaty are to be removed and the numbers by type of conventional armaments and equipment limited by the Treaty of each category to be removed.

(B) the dates of removal and return of conventional armaments and equipment limited by the Treaty; and

(C) the intended location and use of conventional armaments and equipment limited by the Treaty while outside the designated permanent storage site.

9. Except as provided for in paragraph 7 of this Article, the aggregate numbers of conventional armaments and equipment limited by the Treaty removed from and retained outside designated permanent storage sites by States belonging to the same group of States Parties shall at no time exceed the following levels:

(A) 550 battle tanks;

(B) 1,000 armoured combat vehicles; and

(C) 300 pieces of artillery.

10. Conventional armaments and equipment limited by the Treaty removed from designated permanent storage sites pursuant to paragraphs 8 and 9 of this Article shall be returned to designated permanent storage sites no later than 42 days after their removal, except for those items of conventional armaments and equipment limited by the Treaty removed for industrial rebuild. Such items shall be returned to designated permanent storage sites immediately on completion of the rebuild.

11. Each State Party shall have the right to replace conventional armaments and equipment limited by the Treaty located in designated permanent storage sites. Each State Party shall notify all other States Parties at the beginning of replacement of the number, location, type and disposition of conventional armaments and equipment limited by the Treaty being replaced.

Article 11

1. Each State Party shall limit its armoured vehicle launched bridges so that, 40 months after entry into force of this Treaty and thereafter, for the group of States Parties to which it belongs the aggregate number of armoured vehicle launched bridges, in active units within the area of application does not exceed 740.

2. All armoured vehicle launched bridges within the area of application in excess of the aggregate number specified in paragraph 1 of this Article for each group of States Parties shall be placed in designated permanent storage sites as defined in Article 10. When armoured vehicle launched bridges are placed in a designated permanent storage site, either on their own or together with conventional armaments and equipment limited by the Treaty, Article 10, paragraphs 1 to 6 shall apply to armoured vehicle launched bridges as well as to conventional armaments and equipment limited by the Treaty. Armoured vehicle bridges placed in designated permanent storage sites shall not be considered as being in active units.

3. Except as provided for in paragraph 6 of this Article, armoured vehicle launched bridges may be removed, subject to the provisions of paragraphs 4 and 5 of this Article, from designated permanent storage sites only after notification has been provided to all other States Parties at least 42 days prior to such removal. This notification shall specify:

(A) the location of the designated permanent storage from which armoured vehicle launched bridges are to be removed and the numbers of armoured vehicle launched bridges to be removed from each such site;

(B) the dates of removal of armoured vehicle launched bridges from and return to designated permanent storage sites; and

(C) the intended use of armoured vehicle launched bridges during the period of their removal from designated permanent storage sites.

4. Except as provided for in paragraph 6 of this Article, armoured vehicle launched bridges removed from designated permanent storage sites shall be returned to them no later than 42 days after the actual date of removal.

5. The aggregate number of armoured vehicle launched bridges from and retained outside of designated permanent storage sites by each group of States shall not exceed 50 at any one time.

6. States Parties shall have the right, for the purpose of maintenance or modification to remove and have outside of designated permanent storage sites simultaneously up to 10 percent rounded up to the nearest even whole number, of their notified holdings of armoured vehicle launched bridges in each designated permanent storage site, or 10 armoured vehicle launched bridges from each designated permanent storage site,

7. In the event of natural disasters involving flooding or damage to permanent bridge, States Parties shall have the right to withdraw armoured vehicle launched bridges from designated permanent storage sites. Notification to all other States Parties of such withdrawals shall be given at the time of withdrawal.

Article 12

1. Armoured infantry fighting vehicles held by organizations of a State Party designed and structured to perform in peacetime internal security functions, which are not structured and organised for ground combat against an external enemy, are not limited by this Treaty. The foregoing notwithstanding, in order to enhance the implementation of this Treaty and to provide assurance that the number of such armaments held by such organizations shall not be used to circumvent the provisions of this Treaty, any such armaments in excess of 1,000 armoured infantry fighting vehicles assigned by a State Party to organizations designed and structured to perform in peacetime internal security functions shall constitute

a portion of the permitted levels specified in Article 4, 5 and 6. No more than 600 such armoured infantry fighting vehicles of a State Party, assigned to such organizations may be located in that part of the area of application described in Article 5, paragraph 1, subparagraph (A). Each State Party shall further ensure that such organizations refrain from the acquisition of combat capabilities in excess of those necessary for meeting internal security requirements.

2. A State Party that intends to reassign battle tanks, armoured infantry fighting vehicles artillery combat aircraft, attack helicopters and armoured vehicle launched bridges in service with its conventional armed forces to any organisation of that State Party not a part of its conventional armed forces shall notify all other States Parties no later than the date such reassignment takes effect. Such notification shall specify the effective date of reassignment the date such equipment is physically transferred as well as the numbers, by type, of the conventional armaments equipment limited by the Treaty being reassigned.

Article 13

1. For the purpose of ensuring verification of compliance with the provisions of this Treaty each State Party shall provide notifications and exchange information pertaining to its conventional armaments and equipment in accordance with the Protocol on Information Exchange.

2. Such notifications and exchange of information shall be provided in accordance with Article 17.

3. Each State Party shall be responsible for its own information; receipt of such information and of notifications shall not imply validation or acceptance of the information provided.

Article 14

1. For the purpose of ensuring verification of compliance with the provisions of this Treaty, each State Party shall have the right to conduct, and the obligation to accept, within the area of application, inspections in accordance with the provisions of the Protocol on Inspection.

2. The purpose of such inspection shall be:

(A) to verify, on the basis of the information provided pursuant to the Protocol on Information Exchange, the compliance of States Parties with the numerical limitations set forth in Article 4, 5 and 6;

(B) to monitor the process of reduction of battle tanks, armoured combat vehicles, artillery, combat aircraft and attack helicopters carried out reduction sites in accordance with Article 8 and the Protocol on Reduction; and

(C) to monitor the certification of recategorised multi-purpose attack helicopters and reclassified combat-capable trainer aircraft carried out in accordance with the Protocol on Helicopter Recategorisation and the Protocol on Aircraft Reclassification, respectively.

3. No State Party shall exercise the rights set forth in paragraphs 1 and 2 of this Article in respect of States Parties which belong to the group of States Parties to which it belongs in order to elude the objectives of the verification regime.

4. In the case of an inspection conducted jointly by more than one State Party, one of them shall be responsible for the execution of the provisions of this Treaty.

5. The number of inspections pursuant to Sections VII and VIII of the Protocol on Inspection which each State Party shall have the right to conduct and the obligation to accept during each specified time period shall be determined in accordance with the provisions of Section II of that Protocol.

6. Upon completion of the 120-day residual level validation period, each State Party shall have the right to conduct, and each State Party with territory within the area of application shall have the obligation to accept, an agreed number of aerial inspections, within the area of application. Such agreed numbers and other applicable provisions shall be developed during negotiations referred to in Article 18.

Article 15

1. For the purpose of ensuring verification of compliance with the provisions of this Treaty, a State Party shall have the right to use, in addition to the procedures referred to in Article 14, national or multinational technical means of verification at its disposal in a manner consistent with generally recognized principles of international law.

2. A State Party shall not interfere with national or multinational technical means of verification of another State Party operating in accordance with paragraph 1 of this Article.

3. A State Party shall not use concealment measures that impede verification of compliance with the provisions of this Treaty by national or multinational technical means of verification of another State Party operating in accordance with paragraph 1 of this Article. This obligation does not apply to cover or concealment practices associated with normal personnel training, maintenance or operations involving conventional armaments and equipment limited by the Treaty.

Article 16

1. To promote the objectives and implementation of the provisions of this Treaty, the States Parties hereby establish a Joint Consultative Group.

2. Within the framework of the Joint Consultative Group, the States Parties shall:

(A) address questions relating to compliance with or possible circumvention of the provisions of this Treaty;

(B) seek to resolve ambiguities and differences of interpretation that may become apparent in the way this Treaty is implemented;

(C) consider and, if possible, agree on measures to enhance the viability and effectiveness of this Treaty;

(D) update the lists contained in the Protocol on Existing Types, as required by Article 2, paragraph 2;

(E) resolve technical questions in order to seek common practices among the States Parties in the way this Treaty is implemented;

(F) work out or revise, as necessary, rules of procedure, working methods, the scale of distribution of expenses of the Joint Consultative Group and of conferences convened under this Treaty and the distribution of costs of inspections between or among States Parties;

(G) consider and work out appropriate measures to ensure that information obtained through exchanges of information among the States Parties or as a result of inspections pursuant to this Treaty is used solely for the purposes of this Treaty, taking into account the particular requirements of each State Party in respect of safeguarding information which that State Party specifies as being sensitive;

(H) consider, upon the request of any State Party, any matter that a State Party wishes to propose for examination by any conference to be convened in accordance with Article 21; such consideration shall not prejudice the right of any State Party to resort to the procedures set forth in Article 21; and

(I) consider matters of dispute arising out of the

implementation of this Treaty.

3. Each State Party shall have the right to raise before the Joint Consultative Group, and have placed on its agenda, any issue relating to this Treaty.

4. The Joint Consultative Group shall take decisions or make recommendations by consensus. Consensus shall be understood to mean the absence of any objection by any representative of a State Party to the taking of a decision or the making of a recommendation.

5. The Joint Consultative Group may propose amendments to this Treaty for consideration and confirmation in accordance with Article 20. The Joint Consultative Group may also agree on improvements to the viability and effectiveness of this Treaty, consistent with its provisions. Unless such improvements relate only to minor matters of an administrative or technical nature they shall be subject to consideration and confirmation in accordance with Article 20 before they can take effect.

6. Nothing in this Article shall be deemed to prohibit or restrict any State Party from requesting information from or undertaking consultations with other States Parties on matters relating to this Treaty and its implementation in channels or fora other than the Joint Consultative Group.

7. The Joint Consultative Group shall follow the procedures set forth in the Protocol on the Joint Consultative Group.

Article 17

The States Parties shall transmit information and notifications required by this Treaty in written form. They shall use diplomatic channels or other official channels designated by them, including in particular a communications network to be established by a separate arrangement.

Article 18

1. The States Parties, after signature of this Treaty, shall continue the negotiations on conventional armed forces with the same Mandate and with the goal of building on this Treaty.

2. The objective for these negotiations shall be to conclude an agreement on additional measures aimed at further strengthening security and stability in Europe, and pursuant to the Mandate, including measures to limit the personnel strength of their conventional armed forces within the area of application.

3. The States Parties shall seek to conclude these negotiations no later than the follow-up meeting of the Conference on Security and Cooperation in Europe to be held in Helsinki in 1992.

Article 19

1. This Treaty shall be of unlimited duration. It may be supplemented by a further treaty.

2. Each State Party shall, in exercising its national sovereignty, have the right to withdraw from this Treaty if it decides that extraordinary events related to the subject matter of this Treaty have jeopardised its supreme interest, A State Party intending to withdraw shall give notice of its decision to do so to the Depositary and to all other States Parties. Such notice shall be given at least 150 days prior to the intended withdrawal from this Treaty. It shall include a statement of the extraordinary events the State Party regards as having jeopardised its supreme interests.

3. Each State Party shall, in particular, in exercising its national sovereignty, have the right to withdraw from this Treaty if another State Party increases its holdings in battle tanks, armoured combat vehicles, artillery, combat aircraft or attack helicopters, as defined in Article II, which are outside the scope of the limitations of this Treaty, in such proportions as to pose an obvious threat to the balance of forces within the area of application.

Article 20

1. Any State Party may propose amendments to this Treaty. The text of a proposed amendment shall be submitted to the Depositary, which shall circulate it to all the States Parties.

2. If an amendment is approved by all the States Parties, it shall enter into force in accordance with the procedures set forth in Article 22 governing the entry into force of this Treaty.

Article 21

1. Forty-six months after entry into force of this Treaty, and at five-year intervals thereafter, the Depositary shall convene a conference of the States Parties to conduct a review of the operation of this Treaty.

2. The Depositary shall convene an extraordinary conference of the States Parties, if requested to do so by any State Party which considers that exceptional circumstances relating to this Treaty have arisen, in particular, in the event that a State Party has announced its intention to leave its group of States Parties or to join the other group of States Parties as defined in Article II, Paragraph 1, subparagraph (A). In order to enable the other States Parties to prepare for this conference, the

request shall include the reason why that State Party deems an extraordinary conference to be necessary. The conference shall consider the circumstances set forth in the request and their effect on the operation of this Treaty. The conference shall open no later than 15 days after receipt of the request and unless it decides otherwise, shall last no longer than three weeks.

3. The Depositary shall convene a conference of the States Parties to consider an amendment proposed pursuant to Article 20, if requested to do so by three or more States Parties. Such a conference shall open no later than 31 days after receipt of the necessary requests.

4. In the event that a State Party gives notice of its decision to withdraw from this Treaty pursuant to Article 19, the Depositary shall convene a conference of the States Parties which shall open no later than 21 days after receipt of the notice of withdrawal in order to consider questions relating to the withdrawal from this Treaty.

Article 22

1. This Treaty shall be subject to ratification by each State Party in accordance with its constitutional procedures. Instruments of ratification shall be deposited with the Government of the Kingdom of the Netherlands, hereby designated the Depositary.

2. This Treaty shall enter into force 10 days after instruments of ratification have been deposited by all States Parties listed in the Preamble.

3. The Depositary shall promptly inform all States Parties of:

(A) the deposit of each instrument of ratification;

(B) the entry into force of this Treaty;

(C) any withdrawal in accordance with Article 19 and its effective date;

(D) the text of any amendment proposed in accordance with Article 20;

(E) the entry into force of any amendment to this Treaty;

(F) any request to convene a conference in accordance with Article 21;

(G) the convening of a conference pursuant to Article 21; and

(H) any other matter of which the Depositary is required by this Treaty to inform the States Parties.

4. This Treaty shall be registered by the Depositary pursuant to Article 102 of the Charter of the United Nations.

Article 23

The original of this Treaty, of which the English, French, German, Italian, Russian and Spanish texts are equally authentic, shall be deposited in the archives of the Depositary. Duly certified copies of this Treaty shall be transmitted by the Depositary to all the States Parties.

Agreement on a Comprehensive Political Settlement of the Cambodia Conflict

Date of signature: October 23, 1991
Place of signature: Paris
Signatory states: Australia, Brunei, Darussalam, Cambodia, Canada, The People's Republic of China, The French Republic, the Republic of India, The Republic of Indonesia, Japan, the Lao People's Democratic Republic, Malaysia, The Republic of the Philippines, The Republic of Singapore, The Kingdom of Thailand, The Union of Soviet Socialist Republics, The United Kingdom of Great Britain and Northern Ireland, The United States of America, The Socialist Republic of Vietnam, and the Socialist Federal Republic of Yugoslavia
Date of entry into force: October 23, 1991

The States participating in the Paris Conference on Cambodia, namely Australia, Brunei Darussalam, Cambodia, Canada, the People's Republic of China, the French Republic, the Republic of India, the Republic of Indonesia, Japan, the Lao People's Democratic Republic, Malaysia, the Republic of the Philippines, the Republic of Singapore, the Kingdom of Thailand, the Union of Soviet Socialist Republics, the United Kingdom of Great Britain and Northern Ireland, the United States of America, the Socialist Republic of Vietnam and the Socialist Federal Republic of Yugoslavia,

In the presence of the Secretary-General of the United Nations,

In order to maintain, preserve and defend the sovereignty, independence, territorial integrity and inviolability, neutrality and national unity of Cambodia,

Desiring to restore and maintain peace in Cambodia, to promote national reconciliation and to ensure the exercise of the right to self-determination of the Cambodian people through free and fair elections,

Convinced that only a comprehensive political settlement to the Cambodia conflict will be just and durable and will contribute to regional and international peace and security,

Welcoming the Framework document of 28 August 1990, which was accepted by the Cambodian Parties in its entirety as the basis for settling the Cambodia conflict, and which was subsequently unanimously endorsed by Security Council resolution 668 (1990) of 20 September 1990 and General Assembly resolution 45/3 of 15 October 1990,

Noting the formation in Jakarta on 10 September 1990 of the Supreme National Council of Cambodia as the unique legitimate body and source of authority in Cambodia in which, throughout the transitional period, national sovereignty and unity are enshrined, and which represents Cambodia externally,

Welcoming the unanimous election, in Beijing on 17 July 1991, of H.R.H. Prince NORDOM SIHANOUK as the President of the Supreme National Council,

Recognizing that an enhanced United Nations role requires the establishment of a United Nations Transitional Authority in Cambodia (UNTAC) with civilian and military components, which will act with full respect for the national sovereignty of Cambodia,

Noting the statements made at the conclusion of the meetings held in Jakarta on 9-10 September 1990, in Paris on 21-23 December 1990, in Pattaya on 24-26 June 1991, in Beijing on 16-17 July 1991, in Pattaya on 26-29 August 1991, and also the meetings held in Jakarta on 4-6 June 1991 and in New York on 19 September 1991,

Welcoming United Nations Security Council resolution 717 (1991) of 16 October 1991 on Cambodia,

Recognizing that Cambodia's tragic recent history requires special measures to assure protection of human rights, and the non-return to the policies and practices of the past,

Have agreed as follows:

PART I

Arrangements During the Transitional Period

Section I

Transitional Period

Article 1

For the purposes of this Agreement, the transitional period shall commence with the entry into force of this Agreement and terminate when the constituent assembly elected through free and fair elections, organized and certified by the United Nations, has approved the constitution and transformed itself into a legislative assembly, and thereafter a new government has been created.

Section II

United Nations Transitional Authority in Cambodia

Article 2

(1) The Signatories invite the United Nations Security Council to establish a United Nations Transitional Authority in Cambodia (hereinafter referred to as "UNTAC") with civilian and military components under the direct responsibility of the Secretary-General of the United Nations. For this purpose the Secretary-General will designate a Special Representative to act on his behalf.

(2) The Signatories further invite the United Nations Security Council to provide UNTAC with the mandate set forth in this Agreement and to keep its implementation under continuing review through periodic reports submitted by the Secretary-General.

Section III

Supreme National Council

Article 3

The Supreme National Council (hereinafter referred to as "the SNC") is the unique legitimate body and source of authority in which, throughout the transitional period, the sovereignty, independence and unity of Cambodia are enshrined.

Article 4

The members of the SNC shall be committed to the holding of free and fair elections organized and conducted by the United Nations as the basis for forming a new and legitimate Government.

Article 5

The SNC shall, throughout the transitional period, represent Cambodia externally and occupy the seat of Cambodia at the United Nations, in the United Nations specialized agencies, and in other international institutions and international conferences.

Article 6

The SNC hereby delegates to the United Nations all powers necessary to ensure the implementation of this Agreement, as described in annex 1.

In order to ensure a neutral political environment conducive to free and fair general elections, administrative agencies, bodies and offices which could directly influence the outcome of elections will be placed under direct United Nations supervision or control. In that context, special attention will be given to foreign affairs, national defence, finance, public security and information. To reflect the importance of these subjects, UNTAC needs to exercise such control as is necessary to ensure the strict neutrality of the bodies responsible for them. The United Nations, in consultation with the SNC, will identify which agencies, bodies and offices could continue to operate in order to ensure normal day-to-day life in the country.

Article 7

The relationship between the SNC, UNTAC and existing administrative structures is set forth in annex 1.

Section IV

Withdrawal of Foreign Forces and Its Verification

Article 8

Immediately upon entry into force of this Agreement, any foreign forces, advisers, and military personnel remaining in Cambodia, together with their weapons, ammunition, and equipment, shall be withdrawn from Cambodia and not be returned. Such withdrawal and non-return will be subject to UNTAC verification in accordance with annex 2.

Section V

Cease-fire and Cessation of Outside Military Assistance

Article 9

The cease-fire shall take effect at the time this Agreement enters into force. All forces shall immediately disengage and refrain from all hostilities and from any deployment, movement or action which would extend the territory they control or which might lead to renewed fighting.

The Signatories hereby invite the Security Council of the United Nations to request the Secretary-General to provide good offices to assist in this process until such time as the military component of UNTAC is in position to supervise, monitor and verify it.

Article 10

Upon entry into force of this Agreement, there shall be an immediate cessation of all outside military assistance to all Cambodian Parties.

Article 11

The objectives of military arrangements during the transitional period shall be to stabilize the security situation and build confidence among the parties to the conflict, so as to reinforce the purposes of this Agreement and to prevent the risks of a return to warfare.

Detailed provisions regarding UNTAC's supervision, monitoring, and verification of the cease-fire and related measures, including verification of the withdrawal of foreign forces and the regrouping, cantonment and ultimate disposition of all Cambodian forces and their weapons during the transitional period are set forth in annex 1, section C, and annex 2.

PART II

Elections

Article 12

The Cambodian people shall have the right to determine their own political future through the free and fair election of a constituent assembly, which will draft and approve a new Cambodian Constitution in accordance with Article 23 and transform itself into a legislative assembly, which will create the new Cambodian Government. This election will be held under United Nations auspices in a neutral political environment with full respect for the national sovereignty of Cambodia.

Article 13

UNTAC shall be responsible for the organization and

conduct of these elections based on the provisions of annex 1, section D, and annex 3.

Article 14

All Signatories commit themselves to respect the results of these elections once certified as free and fair by the United Nations.

PART III

Human Rights

Article 15

1. All persons in Cambodia and all Cambodian refugees and displaced persons shall enjoy the right and freedoms embodied in the Universal Declaration of Human Rights and other relevant international human rights instruments.

2. To this end,

(a) Cambodia undertakes:

— to ensure respect for and observance of human rights and fundamental freedoms in Cambodia;

— to support the right of all Cambodian citizens to undertake activities which would promote and protect human rights and fundamental freedoms;

— to take effective measures to ensure that the policies and practices of the past shall never be allowed to return;

— to adhere to relevant international human rights instruments;

(b) the other Signatories to this Agreement undertake to promote and encourage respect for and observance of human rights and fundamental freedoms in Cambodia as embodied in the relevant international instruments and the relevant resolutions of the United Nations General Assembly, in order, in particular, to prevent the recurrence of human right abuses.

Article 16

UNTAC shall be responsible during the transitional period for fostering an environment in which respect for human rights shall be ensured, based on the provisions of annex 1, section E.

Article 17

After the end of the transitional period, the United Nations Commission on Human Rights should con-

tinue to monitor closely the human rights situation in Cambodia, including, if necessary, the appointment of a Special Rapporteur who would report his findings annually to the Commission and to the General Assembly.

PART IV

International Guarantees

Article 18

Cambodia undertakes to maintain, preserve and defend, and the other Signatories undertake to recognize and respect, the sovereignty, independence, territorial integrity and inviolability, neutrality and national unity of Cambodia, as set forth in a separate Agreement.

PART V

Refugees and Displaced Persons

Article 19

Upon entry into force of this Agreement, every effort will be made to create in Cambodia political, economic and social conditions conducive to the voluntary return and harmonious integration of Cambodian refugees and displaced persons.

Article 20

(1) Cambodian refugees and displaced persons, located outside Cambodia, shall have the right to return to Cambodia and to live in safety, security and dignity, free from intimidation or coercion of any kind.

(2) The Signatories request the Secretary-General of the United Nations to facilitate the repatriation in safety and dignity of Cambodian refugees and displaced persons, as an integral part of the comprehensive political settlement and under the overall authority of the Special Representative of the Secretary-General, in accordance with the guidelines and principles on the repatriation of refugees and displaced persons as set forth in annex 4.

PART VI

Release of Prisoners of War and Civilian Internees

Article 21

The release of all prisoners of war and civilian

internees shall be accomplished at the earliest possible date under the direction of the International Committee of the Red Cross (ICRC) in co-ordination with the Special Representative of the Secretary-General, with the assistance, as necessary, of other appropriate international humanitarian organizations and the Signatories.

Article 22

The expression "civilian internees" refers to all persons who are not prisoners of war and who, having contributed in any way whatsoever to the armed or political struggle, have been arrested or detained by any of the parties by virtue of their contribution thereto.

PART VII

Principles for a New Constitution for Cambodia

Article 23

Basic principles, including those regarding human rights and fundamental freedoms as well as regarding Cambodia's status of neutrality, which the new Cambodian Constitution will incorporate, are set forth in annex 5.

PART VIII

Rehabilitation and Reconstruction

Article 24

The Signatories urge the international community to provide economic and financial support for the rehabilitation and reconstruction of Cambodia, as provided in a separate declaration.

PART IX

Final Provisions

Article 25

The Signatories shall, in good faith and in a spirit of co-operation, resolve through peaceful means any disputes with respect to the implementation of this Agreement.

Article 26

The Signatories request other States, international organizations and other bodies to co-operate and assist in the implementation of this Agreement and in

the fulfillment by UNTAC of its mandate.

Article 27

The Signatories shall provide their full co-operation to the United Nations to ensure the implementation of its mandate, including the provision of privileges and immunities, and by facilitating freedom of movement and communication within and through their respective territories. In carrying out its mandate UNTAC shall exercise due respect for the sovereignty of all States neighboring Cambodia.

Article 28

(1) The Signatories shall comply in good faith with all obligations undertaken in this Agreement and shall extend full co-operation to the United Nations, including the provision of the information which UNTAC requires in the fulfillment of its mandate.

(2) The signature on behalf of Cambodia by the members of the SNC shall commit all Cambodian parties and armed forces to the provisions of this Agreement.

Article 29

Without prejudice to the prerogatives of the Security Council of the United Nations, and upon the request of the Secretary-General, the two Co-Chairmen of the Paris Conference on Cambodia, in the event of a violation or threat of violation of this Agreement, will immediately undertake appropriate consultations, including members of the Paris Conference on Cambodia, with a view to taking appropriate steps to ensure respect for these commitments.

Article 30

This Agreement shall enter into force upon signature.

Article 31

This Agreement shall remain open for accession by all States. The instruments of accession shall be deposited with the Governments of the French Republic and the Republic of Indonesia. For each State acceding to the Agreement it shall enter into force on the date of deposit of its instruments of accession. Acceding States shall be bound by the same obligations as the Signatories.

Article 32

The originals of this Agreement, of which the Chinese, English, French, Khmer and Russian texts are equally authentic, shall be deposited with the Governments of the French Republic and the Republic of Indonesia, which shall transmit certified true copies to the Governments of the other States participating in the Paris Conference on Cambodia, as well as the Secretary-General of the United Nations.

Resolution Adopted by The UN General Assembly on General and Complete Disarmament

Forty-sixth session
Agenda item 60

Resolution adopted by the General Assembly [on the report of the first committee (A/46/673)]
46/36. General and complete disarmament

The General Assembly,

A

Second Review Conference of the Parties to the Convention on the Prohibition of Military or Any Other Hostile Use of Environmental Modification Techniques

The General Assembly,

Recalling its resolution 31/72 of 10 December 1976, in which it referred the Convention on the Prohibition of Military or Any other Hostile Use of Environmental Modification Techniques to all States for their consideration, signature and ratification and expressed the hope for the widest possible adherence to the Convention,

Noting that the second paragraph of article VIII of the Final Declaration of the First Review Conference of the Parties to the Convention, held in September 1984, provides that:

"The Conference, recognizing the importance of the review mechanism provided in Article VIII, decides that a second Review Conference may be held at Geneva at the request of a majority of States Parties not earlier than 1989. If no Review Conference is held before 1994 the Depositary is requested to solicit the views of all States Parties concerning the convening of such a Conference in accordance with Article VIII, paragraph 3, of the Convention,"

1. *Notes* that, as a result of consultations, a majority of States parties to the Convention on the Prohibition of Military or Any Other Hostile Use of Envi-

ronmental Modification Techniques have expressed their wish to convene the Second Review Conference of the Parties to the Convention in September 1992 and that, to that end, the Secretary-General of the United Nations, as Depositary of the Convention, will hold consultations with the parties to the Convention with regard to questions relating to the Conference and its preparation, including the establishment of a preparatory committee for the Conference;

2. *Requests* the Secretary-General to render the necessary assistance and to provide such services, including summary records, as may be required for the Second Review Conference and its preparation;

3. *Also notes* that arrangements for meeting the costs of the Second Review Conference and its preparation are to be made by the Conference.

65th Plenary Meeting
6 December 1991

B

Study on Charting Potential Uses of Resources Allocated to Military Activities for Civilian Endeavours to Protect the Environment

The General Assembly,

Recalling the report of the Secretary-General transmitting the study on charting potential uses of resources allocated to military activities for civilian endeavors to protect the environment,

Desirous of benefiting from progress in disarmament within the endeavours to protect the environment,

1. *Takes note* of the report of the Secretary-General;

2. *Requests* the Secretary-General to submit the report to the Preparatory Committee for the United Nations Conference on Environment and Development;

3. *Also requests* the Secretary-General to arrange for

the reproduction of the study as a United Nations publication and to give it the widest possible distribution;

4. *Commends* the study to the attention of all Member States.

65th Plenary Meeting
6 December 1991

C

Relationship between Disarmament and Development

The General Assembly,

Recalling the provisions of the Final Document of the Tenth Special Session of the General Assembly related to the relationship between disarmament and development,

Recalling also the adoption on 11 September 1987 of the Final Document of the International Conference on the Relationship between Disarmament and Development,

Stressing the growing importance of the relationship between disarmament and development in current international relations,

1. *Welcomes* the report of the Secretary-General and actions undertaken in accordance with the Final Document of the International Conference on the Relationship between Disarmament and Development;

2. *Requests* the Secretary-General to continue to take action, through appropriate organs and within available resources, for the implementation of the action programme adopted at the International Conference;

3. *Also requests* the Secretary-General to submit a report to the General Assembly at its forty-seventh session;

4. *Decides* to include in the provisional agenda of its forty-seventh session the item entitled "Relationship between disarmament and development."

65th Plenary Meeting
6 December 1991

D

Prohibition of the Production of Fissionable Material for Weapons Purposes

The General Assembly,

Recalling its resolution 45/58 L of 4 December 1990 and previous resolutions, in which it requested the Conference on Disarmament, at an appropriate stage of the implementation of the Programme of Action set forth in section III of the Final Document of the Tenth Special Session of the General Assembly, and of its work on the item entitled "Nuclear weapons in all aspects", to consider urgently the question of adequately verified cessation and prohibition of the production of fissionable material for nuclear weapons and other nuclear explosive devices and to keep the Assembly informed of the progress of that consideration,

Noting that the agenda of the Conference on Disarmament for 1991 included the item entitled "Nuclear weapons in all aspects" and that the programme of work of the Conference for all three parts of its 1991 session contained the item entitled "Cessation of the nuclear arms race and nuclear disarmament",

Recalling the proposals and statements made in the Conference on Disarmament on those item,

Welcoming the improved relationship between the Union of Soviet Socialist Republics and the United States of America and their consequent announcements of significant measures, which could signal the reversal of the nuclear arms race,

Considering that the cessation of production of fissionable material for weapons purposes and the progressive conversion and transfer of stocks to peaceful uses would also be a significant step towards halting and reversing the nuclear arms race,

Considering also that the prohibition of the production of fissionable material for nuclear weapons and other explosive devices would be an important measure in facilitating the prevention of the proliferation of nuclear weapons and explosive devices,

1. *Requests* the Conference on Disarmament, under the item entitled "Nuclear weapons in all aspects", to continue to pursue its consideration of the question of adequately verified cessation and prohibition of the production of fissionable material for nuclear weapons and other nuclear explosive devices and to keep the General Assembly informed of the progress of that consideration;

2. *Decides* to include in the provisional agenda of its forty-seventh session the item entitled "Prohibition of the production of fissionable material for weapons purposes."

65th Plenary Meeting
6 December 1991

E

Prohibition of the Development, Production, Stockpiling and Use of Radiological Weapons

The General Assembly,

Recalling its resolution 45/58 F of 4 December 1990,

1. *Takes note* of the part of the report of the Conference on Disarmament on its 1991 session that deals with the question of radiological weapons, in particular the report of the Ad Hoc Committee on Radiological Weapons;

2. *Recognizes* that in 1991 the Ad Hoc Committee made a further contribution to the clarification and better understanding of different approaches that continue to exist with regard to both of the important matters under Consideration;

3. *Takes note also* of the recommendation of the Conference on Disarmament that the Ad Hoc Committee on Radiological Weapons should be reestablished at the beginning of its 1992 session;

4. *Requests* the Conference on Disarmament to continue its substantive negotiation on the subject with a view to the prompt conclusion of its work, taking into account all proposals presented to the Conference to this end and drawing upon the annexes to the report of the Ad Hoc Committee as a basic of its future work, the result of which should be submitted to the General Assembly at its forty-seventh session;

5. *Requests* the Secretary-General to transmit to the Conference on Disarmament all relevant documents relating to the discussion of all aspects of the issue by the General Assembly at its forty-sixth session;

6. *Decides* to include in the provisional agenda of its forty-seventh session the item entitled "Prohibition of the development, production, stockpiling and use of radiological weapons."

65th Plenary Meeting
6 December 1991

F

Regional Disarmament, Including Confidence-building Measures

The General Assembly,

Recalling its resolutions 44/116 S, 44/116 U and 44/117 B of 15 December 1989 and 45/58 M and

45/58 P of 4 December 1990,

Considering that the adoption of regional disarmament measures is one of the most effective means by which States can contribute to international security, arms limitation and disarmament,

Recognizing that the regional and global approaches to disarmament complement each other and can be pursued simultaneously in the promotion of regional and international peace and security,

Noting that the recent events in the Middle East have underlined the importance of regional disarmament and that they justify in particular the search for a comprehensive and balanced control of armaments in the region, notably through a dialogue among the States of that region,

Convinced that disarmament can be carried out only in a climate of confidence based on mutual respect and aimed at ensuring better relations founded on justice, solidarity and cooperation,

Noting also that the volume of resources consumed for potentially destructive purposes is in stark contrast to social and economic development needs but that reduction in military expenditure following, *inter alia*, the conclusion of regional disarmament agreements could entail benefits in both the social and economic fields,

Considering that regional disarmament measures should be aimed at establishing a military balance at the lowest level while not diminishing the security of each State and eliminating as a matter of priority the capability for surprise attacks and large-scale offensive action,

Noting further that disarmament measure in one region should not lead to increased arms transfers to other regions,

Considering also that measure of transparency are one of the essential elements in the implementation of regional disarmament,

Persuaded that verification measures are important to ensure compliance with regional agreements on arms control and disarmament,

1. *Reaffirms* that the regional approach to disarmament is one of the essential elements in the global process of disarmament;

2. *Is convinced* of the importance and effectiveness of regional disarmament measures taken at the initiative of States of the region and with the participation

of all States concerned and taking into account the specific characteristics of each region, in that they can contribute to the security and stability of all States, in accordance with the principles of the Charter of the United Nations and in compliance with international law and existing treaties;

3. *Stresses* the importance of confidence-building measures in ensuring the success of this process;

4. *Notes with satisfaction* the important progress made in various regions of the world through the conclusion of peace, security and cooperation agreements and following from the implementation of measures intended to enhance confidence in the fields of political, economic and military cooperation;

5. *Affirms* that regional and subregional agreements on arms control and disarmament can contribute to the peaceful settlement of disputes and conflicts;

6. *Recognizes* the useful role played by the regional centres of the United Nations;

7. *Encourages* States of the same region to examine the possibility of creating, on their own initiative, regional mechanisms and/or institutions for the establishment of measures in the framework of an effort of regional disarmament or for the prevention and the peaceful settlement of disputes and conflicts with the assistance, if requested, of the United Nations;

8. *Stresses* that confidence-building measures, including objective information on military activities and capabilities, are essential to the promotion of arms control and disarmament at the regional level;

9. *Believes* that regional initiatives should enjoy the support of all States of the region concerned and the respect of those outside that region;

10. *Invites and encourages* all States to conclude, whenever possible, agreement on disarmament and confidence-building measures at the regional level.

65th plenary meeting
6 December 1991

G

Confidence- and Security-building Measures and Conventional Disarmament in Europe

The General Assembly,

Determined to achieve progress in disarmament,

Stressing that confidence-building and disarmament measures have a positive impact on international security and are facilitated by the reduction of tensions,

Noting the work accomplished in 1991 by the Disarmament Commission within the framework of the working Groups on its agenda item 4 and 6,

Expressing the hope that the improved international climate will facilitate the necessary efforts to build confidence, to lessen the risk of military confrontation and to enhance mutual security,

Recalling its resolutions 43/75 P of 7 December 1988, 44/116 I of 15 December 1989 and 45/58 I of 4 December 1990,

Reaffirming the great importance of increasing security and stability in Europe through the establishment of a stable, secure and verifiable balance of conventional armed forces at lower levels, as well as through increased openness and predictability of military activities,

Considering that the positive results of the negotiations on confidence and security-building measures, as well as of those on conventional armaments and forces, both within the framework of the Conference on Security and Cooperation in Europe, have considerably increased confidence and improved security and cooperation in Europe, thereby contributing to international peace and security,

Welcoming the prospects for the early implementation of the measures agreed upon and the continuation of negotiations in these fields among the States participating in the Conference on Security and Cooperation in Europe,

1. *Notes with satisfaction* the progress achieved so far in the process of disarmament and the strengthening of confidence and security in Europe;

2. *Welcomes* the determination of the States signatories of the Treaty on Conventional Armed Forces in Europe fully to implement its provisions and the determination of all the States participating in the Conference on Security and Cooperation in Europe fully to implement the provisions of the Vienna Document of the negotiations on confidence- and security-building measures, as well as the decision of these States to continue negotiations in these fields;

3. *Invites* all States to consider the possibility of taking appropriate measures with a view to reducing the risk of confrontation and strengthening security, taking due account of their specific regional conditions.

65th Plenary Meeting
6 December 1991

H

International Arms Transfers

The General Assembly,

Realizing the urgent need to resolve underlying conflicts, to diminish tensions and to accelerate efforts towards general and complete disarmament with a view to maintaining regional and international peace and security in a world free from the scourge of war and the burden of armaments.

Recognizing that the international transfer and production of conventional arms, including advanced weapons, delivery systems and military technology, have in recent decades acquired a dimension and qualitative characteristics that can give rise to serious and urgent concerns,

Greatly concerned by the illicit arms trade, a most disturbing and dangerous phenomenon, because of its destabilizing and destructive effects, particularly for the internal situation of affected States and the violation of human rights,

Recalling that in paragraph 85 of the Final Document of the Tenth Special Session of the General Assembly it urged major arms supplier and recipient countries to consult on the limitation of all types of international transfers of conventional arms,

Reaffirming the role of the United Nations in the field of disarmament and the commitment of Member States to take concrete steps in order to strengthen that role,

Realizing that arms obtained through the illicit arms trade are most likely to be used for violent purposes, and that even small arms when so obtained, directly or indirectly, by terrorist groups, drug traffickers or underground organizations can pose a danger to regional and international security, and certainly to the security and political stability of the countries affected,

Considering that the illicit arms trade, representing a distinctly unique phenomenon, by its clandestine nature defies transparency and could not be dealt with by an arms transfers register,

Recalling its resolution 43/75 I of 7 December 1988.

Welcoming the study submitted by the Secretary-General, pursuant to paragraph 5 of resolution 43/75 I and prepared with the assistance of governmental experts, on ways and means of promoting transparency in international transfers of conventional arms,[11] as well as the problem of the illicit arms trade,

1. *Expresses its appreciation* to the Secretary-General for the study on ways and means of promoting transparency in international transfers of conventional arms;

2. *Calls upon* all States to give high priority to eradicating the illicit trade in all kinds of weapons and military equipment, a most disturbing and dangerous phenomenon often associated with terrorism, drug trafficking, organized crime and mercenary and other destabilizing activities, and to take urgent action towards this end, as recommended in the study submitted by the Secretary-General;

3. *Urges* Member States to exercise effective control over their weapons and military equipment and their arms imports and exports to prevent them from getting into the hands of parties engaged in the illicit arms trade;

4. *Also urges* Member States to ensure that they have in place an adequate body of laws and administrative machinery for regulating and monitoring effectively their transfer of arms, to strengthen or adopt strict measures for their enforcement, and to cooperate at the international, regional and subregional levels to harmonize, where appropriate, relevant laws, regulations and administrative procedures as well as their enforcement measures, with the goal of eradicating the illicit arms trade as stated in the recommendations in the study;

5. *Invites* Member States to provide the Secretary-General with relevant information on their national legislation and/or regulations on arms exports, imports and procurement, and administrative procedures, as regards both authorization of arms transfers and prevention of the illicit arms trade;

6. *Calls upon* affected States to provide the Secretary-General, in accordance with national judicial procedures, information regarding arms and military equipment, seized by authorities, destined for the use of terrorists, drug traffickers and organized crime and for mercenary and other destabilizing activities, when this would assist the eradication of the illicit arms trade;

7. *Requests* the Secretary-General to make the necessary arrangements to make available for consultation by Member States the information referred to in paragraph 5 above, and to publish the information provided in connection with paragraph 6 above;

8. *Also requests* the Secretary-General to assist, upon request and within available resources, in holding meetings and seminars at the national, regional and international levels, as pertinent, with a view to:

(*a*) Promoting the concept of transparency as a confidence-building measure;

(*b*) Increasing the awareness of the destructive and destabilizing effects of the illicit traffic in arms and to exploring ways and means for its eradications;

(*c*) Promoting the development of internationally harmonized laws and administrative procedures relating to official arms procurement and arms transfer policies;

(*d*) Promoting regional and international efforts to eradicate the illicit traffic in arms and providing advisory assistance to Member States, when so requested, on measures for enforcement of relevant rules and administrative procedures as recommended in the study, with a view to, *inter alia*, facilitating cooperation between Member States in the training of their customs and other appropriate officials;

9. *Further requests* the Secretary-General to report to the General Assembly at its forty-seventh session on progress made in implementing the present resolution;

10. *Requests* the Disarmament Commission, at its organizational session in 1992, to consider including the issue of international arms transfers in the agenda of its substantive session in 1993;

11. *Decides* to include in the provisional agenda of its forty-seventh session the item entitled "International arms transfers."

65th plenary meeting
6 December 1991

I

Regional Disarmament

The General Assembly,

Recalling its resolution 45/58 P of 4 December 1990 on regional disarmament,

Believing that the efforts of the international community to move towards the ideal of general and complete disarmament are guided by the inherent human desire for genuine peace and security, the elimination of the danger of war and the release of economic, intellectual and other resources for peaceful pursuits,

Affirming the abiding commitment of all States to the purposes and principles enshrined in the Charter of the United Nations in the conduct of their international relations,

Noting that essential guidelines for progress towards general and complete disarmament were adopted at the tenth special session of the General Assembly,

Welcoming the prospects of genuine progress in the field of disarmament engendered in recent years as a result of negotiations between the two super-Powers,

Taking note of the recent proposals for disarmament and nuclear non-proliferation at the regional and subregional levels,

Recognizing the importance of confidence-building measures for regional and international peace and security,

Convinced that endeavours by countries to promote regional disarmament, taking into account the specific characteristics of each region and in accordance with the principle of undiminished security at the lowest level of armaments, would enhance the security of smaller States and would thus contribute to international peace and security by reducing the risk of regional conflicts,

1. *Stresses* that sustained efforts are needed, within the framework of the Conference on Disarmament and under the umbrella of the United Nations, to make progress on the entire range of disarmament issues;

2. *Affirms* that global and regional approaches to disarmament complement each other and should therefore be pursued simultaneously to promote regional and international peace and security;

3. *Calls upon* States to conclude agreements, wherever possible, for nuclear non-proliferation, disarmament and confidence-building measures at regional and subregional levels;

4. *Welcomes* the initiatives towards disarmament, nuclear non-proliferation and security undertaken by some countries at the regional and subregional levels;

5. *Supports and encourages* efforts aimed at promoting confidence-building measures at regional and subregional levels in order to ease regional tensions

and to further disarmament and nuclear non-proliferation measures at regional and subregional levels;

6. *Decides* to include in the provisional agenda of its forty-seventh session the item entitled "Regional disarmament."

65th plenary meeting
6 December 1991

J

Bilateral Nuclear-arms Negotiations

The General Assembly,

Recalling its previous relevant resolutions,

Mindful that it is the responsibility and obligation of all States to contribute to the process of the relaxation of tension and to the strengthening of international security,

Stressing the importance of the strengthening of international security through disarmament and the halting of the qualitative and quantitative escalation of the arms race,

Stressing also that general and complete disarmament under effective international control is by its very nature unattainable unless all States have the responsibility and join in adopting and implementing measures towards that objective,

Emphasizing that nuclear disarmament and the prevention of nuclear war remains one of the principal tasks of our times,

Concerned that the world is still threatened by the significant nuclear arsenals and that the primary responsibility for nuclear disarmament, with the objective of the total elimination of nuclear weapons, rests with the nuclear-weapon States, in particular those which possess the largest nuclear arsenals,

Noting with satisfaction the positive development in the current international scene, in particular the cooperation between the Union of Soviet Socialist Republics and the United States of America, which contributes to the process of general and complete disarmament and the strengthening of international security,

Recalling that, at their meeting in Washington in 1990, the leaders of the two major nuclear Powers, the Union of Soviet Socialist Republics and the United States of America, agreed to pursue, among other efforts, new talks on the relationship between strategic offensive and defensive arms,

Welcoming the decision of the Union of Soviet Socialist Republic to suspend all nuclear tests throughout the next twelve months as a contribution towards the achievement of a comprehensive test-ban treaty,

Convinced that the international community should encourage the Government of the Union of Soviet Socialist Republics and the Government of the United States of America in their endeavours in the process leading to the complete elimination of nuclear weapons,

Affirming that bilateral and multilateral negotiations on disarmament should facilitate and complement each other,

1. *Expresses its satisfaction* at the continued implementation of the Treaty between the United States of America and the Union of Soviet Socialist Republics on the Elimination of Their Intermediate-Range and Shorter-Range Missiles, in particular at the completion by both parties of the destruction of all their declared missiles subject to elimination under the Treaty;

2. *Welcomes* the signing of the Treaty on the Reduction and Limitation of Strategic Offensive Arms by the President of the Union of Soviet Socialist Republics and the President of the United States of America in Moscow on 31 July 1991;

3. *Also welcomes* the unilateral decision announced by the President of the United States of America on 27 September 1991 significantly to reduce the size and nature of United States nuclear deployments worldwide and to enhance stability, as well as the similar steps announced by the President of the Union of Soviet Socialist Republics on 5 October 1991, in response to that decision;

4. *Recalls* the stated intention of the two Governments concerned to intensify, following the signature of the Treaty on the Reduction and Limitation of Strategic Offensive Arms, further negotiations on other issues, in particular on preventing an arms race in space and achieving a comprehensive nuclear-test ban;

5. *Encourages and supports* the Union of Soviet Socialist Republics and the United States of America in their efforts to reduce their nuclear armaments and to give future negotiations the highest priority;

6. *Invites* the Union of Soviet Socialist Republics

and the United States of America to keep other Members of the United Nations duly informed of progress in their negotiations.

65th plenary meeting
6 December 1991

K

Prohibition of the Dumping of Radioactive Wastes

The General Assembly,

Bearing in mind resolutions CM/Res. 1153 (XLVIII) of 1988 and CM/Res. 1225 (L) of 1989 concerning the dumping of nuclear and industrial wastes in Africa, adopted by the Council of Ministers of the Organization of African Unity,

Welcoming resolution GC (XXXIII)/RES/509 on the dumping of nuclear wastes, adopted on 29 September 1989 by the General Conference of the International Atomic Energy Agency at its thirty-third regular session,

Welcoming also resolution GC (XXXIV)/RES/530 establishing a Code of Practice on the International Transboundary Movement of Radioactive Waste, adopted on 21 September 1990 by the General Conference of the International Atomic Energy Agency at its thirty-fourth regular session,

Considering its resolution 2602 C (XXIV) of 16 December 1969, in which it requested the Conference of the Committee in Disarmament, *inter alia*, to consider effective methods of control against the use of radiological methods of warfare,

Recalling resolution CM/Res.1356 (LIV) of 1991, adopted by the Council of Ministers of the Organization of African Unity, on the Bamako Convention on the Ban on the Import of Hazardous Wastes into Africa and on the Control of Their Transboundary Movements within Africa,

Aware of the potential hazards underlying any use of radioactive wastes that would constitute radiological warfare and its implications for regional and international security and in particular for the security of developing countries,

Desirous of promoting the implementation of paragraph 76 of the Final Document of the Tenth Special Session of the General Assembly,

Aware also of the consideration of the question of dumping of radioactive wastes in the Conference on Disarmament during its 1991 session,

Recalling its resolution 45/58 k of 4 December 1990, in which it requested the Conference on Disarmament to include in its report to the General Assembly at its forty-sixth session the development in the ongoing negotiations on this subject,

1. *Takes note* of the part of the report of the Conference on Disarmament relating to a future convention on the prohibition of radiological weapons;

2. *Expresses grave concern* regarding any use of nuclear wastes that would constitute radiological warfare and have grave implications for the national security of all States;

3. *Calls upon* all states to take appropriate measures with a view to preventing any dumping of nuclear or radioactive waste that would infringe upon the sovereignty of States;

4. Requests the Conference on Disarmament to take into account, in the ongoing negotiations for a convention on the prohibition of radiological weapons, radioactive waste as part of the scope of such a convention;

5. *Also requests* the Conference on Disarmament to intensify efforts towards an early conclusion of such a convention and to include in its report to the General Assembly at its forty-seventh session the progress recorded in the ongoing negotiations on this subject;

6. *Takes note* of resolution CM/Res.1356(LIV) of 1991, adopted by the Council of Ministers of the Organization of African Unity, on the Bamako Convention on the Ban of the Import of Hazardous Wastes into Africa and on the Control of Their Transboundary Movements within Africa;

7. *Expresses the hope* that the effective implementation of the International Atomic Energy Agency Code of Practice on the International Transboundary Movement of Radioactive Waste will enhance the protection of all States from the dumping of radioactive wastes on their territories;

8. *Requests* the International Atomic Energy Agency to continue keeping the subject under active review, including the desirability of concluding a legally binding instrument in this field;

9. *Decides* to include in the provisional agenda of its forty-seventh session the item entitled "Prohibition of the dumping of radioactive wastes."

65th plenary meeting
6 December 1991

L

Transparency in Armaments

The General Assembly,

Realizing that excessive and destabilizing arms build-ups pose a threat to national, regional and international peace and security, particularly by aggravating tensions and conflict situations, giving rise to serious and urgent concerns,

Noting with satisfaction that the current international environment and recent agreements and measures in the field of arms limitation and disarmament make it a propitious time to work towards easing tensions and a just resolution of conflict situations, as well as more openness and transparency in military matters,

Recalling the consensus among Member States on implementing confidence-building measures, including transparency and exchange of relevant information on armaments, likely to reduce the occurrence of dangerous misperceptions about the intentions of States and to promote trust among States,

Considering that increased openness and transparency in the field of armaments could enhance confidence, ease tensions, strengthen regional and international peace and security and contribute to restraint in military production and the transfer of arms,

Realizing the urgent need to resolve underlying conflicts, to diminish tensions and to accelerate efforts towards general and complete disarmament under strict and effective international control with a view to maintaining regional and international peace and security in a world free from the scourge of war and the burden of armaments,

Recalling also that in paragraph 85 of the Final Document of the Tenth Special Session of the General Assembly it urged major arms supplier and recipient countries to consult on the limitation of all types of international transfer of conventional arms,

Disturbed by the destabilizing and destructive effects of the illicit arms trade, particularly for the internal situation of affected States and the violation of human rights,

Bearing in mind that, in accordance with the Charter of the United Nations, Member States have undertaken to promote the establishment and maintenance of international peace and security with the least diversion for armaments of the world's human and economic resources, and that the reduction of world military expenditures could have a significant positive impact for the social and economic development of all peoples,

Reaffirming the important role of the United Nations in the field of disarmament and the commitment of Member States to take concrete steps in order to strengthen that role,

Recalling its resolution 43/75 I of 7 December 1988.

Welcoming the study submitted by the Secretary-General, pursuant to paragraph 5 of resolution 43/75 I and prepared with the assistance of governmental experts, on ways and means of promoting transparency in international transfers of conventional arms, as well as the problem of the illicit arms trade, taking into account views of Member States and other relevant informations,

Recognizing the major contribution of an enhanced level of transparency in armaments to confidence-building and security among States, and also recognizing the urgent need to establish, under the auspices of the United Nations, as a first step in this direction, a universal and non-discriminatory register to include data on international arms transfer, as well as other interrelated information provided to the Secretary-General,

Stressing the importance of greater transparency in the interest of promoting readiness to exercise restraint in accumulation of armaments,

Considering that the standardized reporting of international arms transfers together with the provision of other interrelated information to a United Nations register will constitute further important steps forward in the promotion of transparency in military matters and, as such, will enhance the role and effectiveness of the United Nations in promoting arms limitation and disarmament, as well as in maintaining international peace and security;

Recognizing also the importance of the prevention of the proliferation of nuclear weapons and other weapons of mass destruction,

1. *Recognizes* that an increased level of openness and transparency in the field of armaments would enhance confidence, promote stability, help States to exercise restraint, ease tensions and strengthen regional and international peace and security;

2. *Declares its determination* to prevent the exces-

sive and destabilizing accumulation of arms, including conventional arms, in order to promote stability and strengthen regional or international peace and security, taking into account the legitimate security needs of States and the principle of undiminished security at the lowest possible level of armaments;

3. *Reaffirms* the inherent right to individual or collective self-defense recognized in Article 51 of the Charter of the United Nations, which implies that States also have the right to acquire arms with which to defend themselves;

4. *Reiterates its conviction*, as expressed in its resolution 43/75 I, that arms transfers in all their aspects deserve serious consideration by the international community, *inter alia*, because of:

(a) Their potential effects in further destabilizing areas where tension and regional conflict threaten international peace and security and national security;

(b) Their potentially negative effects on the progress of the peaceful social and economic development of all peoples;

(c) The danger of increasing illicit and covert arms trafficking;

5. *Calls upon* all Member States to exercise due restraint in exports and imports of conventional arms, particularly in situations of tension or conflict, and to ensure that they have in place an adequate body of laws and administrative procedures regarding the transfer of arms and to adopt strict measures for their enforcement;

6. *Expresses its appreciation* to the Secretary-General for his study on ways and means of promoting transparency in international transfers of conventional arms, which also addressed the problem of the illicit arms trade;

7. *Requests* the Secretary-General to establish and maintain at United Nations Headquarters in New York a universal and non-discriminatory Register of Conventional Arms, to include data on international arms transfers as well as information provided by Member States on military holdings, procurement through national production and relevant policies, as set out in paragraph 10 below and in accordance with procedures and input requirements initially comprising those set out in the annex to the present resolution and subsequently incorporating any adjustments to the annex decided upon by the General Assembly at its forty-seventh session in the light of the recom-

mendations of the panel referred to in paragraph 8 below;

8. *Also requests* the Secretary-General, with the assistance of a panel of governmental technical experts to be nominated by him on the basis of equitable geographical representation, to elaborate the technical procedures and to make any adjustments to the annex to the present resolution necessary for the effective operation of the Register, and to prepare a report on the modalities for early expansion of the scope of the Register by the addition of further categories of equipment and inclusion of data on military holdings and procurement through national production, and to report to the General Assembly at its forty-seventh session;

9. *Calls upon* all Member States to provide annually for the Register data on imports and exports of arms in accordance with the procedures established by paragraphs 7 and 8 above;

10. *Invites* Member States, pending the expansion of the Register, also to provide to the Secretary-General, with their annual report on imports and exports of arms, available background information regarding their military holdings, procurement through national production and relevant policies, and requests the Secretary-General to record this material and to make it available for consultation by Member States at their request;

11. *Decides*, with a view to future expansion, to keep the scope of and the participation in the Register under review, and, to this end:

(a) *Invites* member States to provide the Secretary-General with their views, not later than 30 April 1994, on:

(i) The operation of the Register during its first two years;

(ii) The addition of further categories of equipment and the elaboration of the Register to include military holdings and procurement through national production;

(b) *Requests* the Secretary-General, with the assistance of a group of governmental experts convened in 1994 on the basis of equitable geographical representation, to prepare a report on the continuing operation of the Register and its further development, taking into account the work of the Conference on Disarmament as set forth in paragraphs 12 to 15 below and the views expressed by Member States, for submission to the General Assembly with a view to a decision at its forty-ninth session;

12. *Requests* the Conference on Disarmament to address, as soon as possible, the question of the inter-related aspects of the excessive and destabilizing accumulation of arms, including military holdings and procurement through national production, and to elaborate universal and non-discriminatory practical means to increase openness and transparency in this field;

13. *Also requests* the Conference on Disarmament to address the problems of, and the elaboration of practical means to increase, openness and transparency related to the transfer of high technology with military applications and to weapons of mass destruction, in accordance with existing legal instruments;

14. *Invites* the Secretary-General to provide to the Conference on Disarmament all relevant information, including, *inter alia*, views submitted to him by Member States and information provided under the United Nations system for the standardized reporting of military expenditures, as well as on the work of the Disarmament Commission under its agenda item entitled "Objective information on military matters";

15. *Further requests* the Conference on Disarmament to include in its annual report to the General Assembly a report on its work on this issue;

16. *Invites* all Member States, in the meantime, to take measures on a national, regional and global basis, including within the appropriate forums, to promote openness and transparency in armaments;

17. *Calls upon* all Member States to cooperate at a regional and subregional level, taking fully into account the specific conditions prevailing in the region or subregion, with a view to enhancing and coordinating international efforts aimed at increased openness and transparency in armaments;

18. *Also invites* all Member States to inform the Secretary-General of their national arms import and export policies, legislation and administrative procedures, both as regards authorization of arms transfers and prevention of illicit transfers;

19. *Requests* the Secretary-General to report to the General Assembly at its forty-seventh session on progress made in implementing the present resolution, including relevant information provided by Member States;

20. *Notes* that effective implementation of the present resolution will require an up-to-date database

system in the Department for Disarmament Affairs of the Secretariat;

21. *Decides* to include in the provisional agenda of its forty-seventh session an item entitled "Transparency in armaments."

66th plenary meeting
9 December 1991

ANNEX

Register of Conventional Arms

1. The Register of Conventional Arms ("the Register") shall be established, with effect from 1 January 1992, and maintained at the Headquarters of the United Nations in New York.

2. Concerning international arms transfers:

(a) Member States are requested to provide data for the Register, addressed to the Secretary-General, on the number of items in the following categories of equipment imported into or exported from their territory:

I

Battle tanks

A tracked or wheeled self-propelled armoured fighting vehicle with high cross-country mobility and a high level of self-protection, weighing at least 16.5 metric tonnes unladen weight, with a high muzzle velocity direct fire main gun of at least 75 millimeters calibre.

II

Armoured combat vehicles

A tracked or wheeled self-propelled vehicle, with armoured protection and cross-country capability, either: (a) designed and equipped to transport a squad of four or more infantrymen, or (b) armed with an integral or organic weapon of at least 20 millimeters calibre or an anti-tank missile launcher.

III

Large calibre artillery systems

A gun, howitzer, artillery piece combining the characteristics of a gun and a howitzer, mortar of multiple-launch rocket system, capable of engaging surface targets by delivering primarily indirect fire, with a calibre of 100 millimeters and above.

IV

Combat aircraft

A fixed-wing or variable-geometry wing aircraft armed and equipped to engage targets by employing guided missiles, unguided rockets, bombs, guns, cannons, or other weapons of destruction.

V

Attack helicopters

A rotary-wing aircraft equipped to employ anti-armour, air-to-ground, or air-to-air guided weapons and equipped with an integrated fire control and aiming system for these weapons.

VI

Warships

A vessel or submarine with a standard displacement of 850 metric tonnes or above, armed or equipped for military use.

VII

Missiles or missile systems

A guided rocket, ballistic or cruise missile capable of delivering a payload to a range of at least 25 kilometres, or a vehicle, apparatus or device designed or modified for launching such munitions.

(b) Data on imports provided under the present paragraph shall also specify the supplying State; data on exports shall also specify the recipient State and the State of origin if not the exporting State;

(c) Each Member State is requested to provide data on an annual basis by 30 April each year in respect of imports into and exports from their territory in the previous calendar year;

(d) The first such registration shall take place by 30 April 1993 in respect of the calendar year 1992;

(e) The data so provided shall be recorded in respect of each Member State;

(f) Arms "exports and imports" represent in the present resolution, including its annex, all forms of arms transfers under of grant, credit, barter or cash.

3. Concerning other interrelated information:

(a) Member States are invited also to provide to the Secretary-General available background information regarding their military holdings, procurement through national production, and relevant policies;

(b) The information so provided shall be recorded in respect of each Member State.

4. The Register shall be open for consultation by representatives of Member States at any time.

5. In addition, the Secretary-General shall provide annually a consolidated report to the General Assembly of the data registered, together with an index of the other interrelated information.

Agreement Establishing the Commonwealth of Independent States

Date of signature: December 8, 1991
Place of signature: Minsk
Signatory states: Belarus, The Russian Federation, Ukraine

We, the Republic of Belarus, the Russian Federation (RSFSR) and Ukraine, as founder States of the Union of Soviet Socialist Republics and signatories of the Union Treaty of 1992, hereinafter referred to as the High Contracting Parties, hereby declare that the Union of Soviet Socialist Republics as a subject of international law and a geopolitical reality no longer exists.

On the basis of the historical communality of our peoples and the ties that have developed between them, and bearing in mind the bilateral agreement concluded between High Contracting Parties,

Desirous of setting up lawfully constituted democratic States,

Intending to develop our relations on the basis of mutual recognition of and respect for State sovereignty, the inalienable right to self-determination, the principles of equality and non-intervention in internal affairs, of abstention from the use of force and from economic or other means of applying pressure and of settling controversial issues through agreement, and other universally recognized principles and norms of international law,

Considering that the further development and strengthening of relations of friendship, good-neigh-bourliness and mutually advantageous cooperation between our States are in accord with the vital national interests of their peoples and serve the cause of peace and security,

Confirming our adherence to the purposes and principles of the Charter of the United Nations, the Helsinki Final Act and the other documents of the Conference on Security and Cooperation in Europe,

Undertaking to abide by the universally recognized international norms relating to human and peoples' rights,

We have agreed as follows:

Article 1

The High Contracting Parties hereby establish the Commonwealth of Independent States.

Article 2

The High Contracting Parties guarantee to their citizens, regardless of their nationality or other differences, equal rights and freedoms. Each of the High Contracting Parties guarantees to the citizens of the other Parties, and also to stateless persons resident in their territory, regardless of national affiliation or other differences, civil, political, social, economic and cultural rights and freedoms in accordance with the universally recognized international norms relating to human rights.

Article 3

The High Contracting Parties, desirous of facilitating the expression, preservation and development of the distinctive ethnic, cultural, linguistic and religious characteristics of the national minorities resident in their territories and of the unique ethno-cultural regions that have come into being, will extend protection to them.

Article 4

The High Contracting Parties will develop equitable and mutually advantageous cooperation between their peoples and States in the spheres of politics, economics, culture, education, health care, environmental protection, science and trade and in the humanitarian and other spheres, will promote the broad exchange of information and will discharge their mutual obligations conscientiously and in full.

The Parties deem it necessary to conclude an agreement on cooperation in the above-mentioned spheres.

Article 5

The High Contracting Parties acknowledge and respect each other's territorial integrity and the inviolability of existing borders within the Commonwealth.

They guarantee openness of borders, freedom of movement of citizens and freedom of transmission of information within the Commonwealth.

Article 6

The States members of the Commonwealth will cooperate in safeguarding international peace and security and implementing effective measures for the reduction of armaments and military expenditures. They are striving to eliminate all nuclear weapons and achieve universal and complete disarmament under strict international control.

The Parties will respect each other's efforts to achieve the status of a nuclear-free zone and a neutral State.

The States members of the Commonwealth will maintain, and retain under joint command, a common military and strategic space, including joint control over nuclear weapons, the procedure for implementing which will be regulated by a special agreement.

They also jointly guarantee the necessary conditions for the deployment and functioning and the material and social security of the strategic armed forces. The Parties undertake to pursue an agreed policy on issues of the social welfare and provision of pensions for military personnel and their families.

Article 7

The High Contracting Parties recognize that the sphere of their joint activity, conducted on an equitable basis through common coordinating institutions of the Commonwealth, embraces:

— coordination of foreign policy;
— cooperation in the formation and development of a common economic space and Europe-wide and Eurasian markets and in the field of cus-

toms policy;
— cooperation in developing the transport and communications systems;
— cooperation in the protection of the environment and participation in establishing a comprehensive international system of environmental security;
— issues of migration policy;
— combating organized crime.

Article 8

The Parties recognize the planet-wide nature of the Chernobyl disaster, and undertake to unite and coordinate their efforts to minimize and overcome its consequences.

They have agreed to conclude for these purposes a special agreement which takes into account the seriousness of the disaster's consequences.

Article 9

Disputes regarding the interpretation and application of the provisions of this Agreement shall be resolved by means of negotiations between the appropriate organs, and if necessary at the state and governmental level.

Article 10

Each of the High Contracting Parties reserves the right to suspend the application of this Agreement or individual articles thereof by giving the Parties to the Agreement one year's notice of such suspension.

The provisions of this Agreement may be supplemented or modified by mutual agreement among the High Contracting Parties.

Article 11

From the moment of signature of the present Agreement, application of the laws of third States, including the former Union of Soviet Socialist Republics, shall not be permitted in the territories of the signatory States.

Article 12

The High Contracting Parties undertake to discharge the international obligations incumbent on them under treaties and agreements entered into by the former Union of Soviet Socialist Republics.

Article 13

This Agreement shall not affect the obligations of the High Contracting Parties towards third States.

This Agreement is open for accession by all States members of the former Union of Soviet Socialist Republics, and also by other States sharing the purposes and principles of this Agreement.

Article 14

The official location of the coordinating organs of the Commonwealth shall be the city of Minsk.

The activities of organs of the former Union of Soviet Socialist Republics in the territories of the States members of the Commonwealth are hereby terminated.

Agreement on Reconciliation, Nonaggression and Exchanges and Cooperation Between the South and the North

Date of signature: December 13, 1991
Place of signature: Seoul
Signatory states: The Republic of Korea, Democratic People's Republic of Korea
Date of entry into force: February 19, 1992

The South and the North,

In keeping with the yearning of the entire Korean people for the peaceful unification of the divided land;

Reaffirming the three principles of unification set forth in the July 4 (1972) South-North Joint Communique;

Determined to remove the state of political and military confrontation and achieve national reconciliation;

Also determined to avoid armed aggression and hostilities, reduce tension and ensure peace;

Expressing the desire to realize multi-faceted exchanges and cooperation to advance common national interests and prosperity;

Recognizing that their relations, not being a relationship between states, constitute a special interim relationship stemming from the process towards unification;

Pledging to exert joint efforts to achieve peaceful unification;

Hereby have agreed as follows;

Chapter I
South-North Reconciliation

Article 1

The South and the North shall recognize and respect each other's system.

Article 2

The two sides shall not interfere in each other's internal affairs.

Article 3

The two sides shall not slander or vilify each other.

Article 4

The two sides shall not attempt any action of sabotage or overthrow against each other.

Article 5

The two sides shall endeavor together to transform the present state of armistice into a solid state of peace between the South and the North and shall abide by the present Military Armistice Agreement (of July 27, 1953) until such a state of peace has been realized.

Article 6

The two sides shall cease to compete or confront each other and shall cooperate and endeavor together to promote national prestige and interests in the international arena.

Article 7

To ensure close consultations and liaison between the two sides, South-North Liaison Offices shall be established at Panmunjom within three (3) months after the coming into force of this Agreement.

Article 8

A South-North Political Committee shall be established within the framework of the South-North High-Level Talks within one (1) month of the coming into force of this Agreement with a view to discussing concrete measures to ensure the implementation and observance of the accords on South-North reconciliation.

Chapter II
South-North Non-Aggression

Article 9

The two sides shall not use force against each other and shall not undertake armed aggression against each other.

Article 10

Differences of views and disputes arising between the two sides shall be resolved peacefully through dialogue and negotiation.

Article 11

The South-North demarcation line and areas for non-aggression shall be identical with the Military Demarcation Line specified in the Military Armistice Agreement of July 27, 1953 and the areas that have been under the jurisdiction of each side until the present time.

Article 12

To implement and guarantee non-aggression, the two sides shall set up a South-North Joint Military Commission within three (3) months of the coming into force of this Agreement. In the said Commission, the two sides shall discuss and carry out steps to build military confidence and realize arms reduction, including the mutual notification and control of major movements of military units and major military exercises, the peaceful utilization of the Demilitarized Zone, exchanges of military personnel and information, phased reductions in armaments including the elimination of weapons of mass destruction and attack capabilities, and verifications thereof.

Article 13

A telephone hotline shall be installed between the military authorities of the two sides to prevent accidental armed clashes and their escalation.

Article 14

A South-North Military Committee shall be established within the framework of the South-North High-Level Talks within one (1) month of the coming into force of this agreement in order to discuss concrete measures to ensure the implementation and observance of the accords on non-aggression and to remove military confrontation.

Chapter III

South-North Exchanges and Cooperation

Article 15

To promote an integrated and balanced development of the national economy and the welfare of the entire people, the two sides shall engage in economic exchanges and cooperation, including the joint development of resources, the trade of goods as domestic commerce and joint ventures.

Article 16

The two sides shall carry out exchanges and cooperation in various fields such as science and technology, education, literature and the arts, health, sports, environment, and publishing and journalism including newspapers, radio, and television broadcasts, and publications.

Article 17

The two sides shall promote free intra-Korean travel and contacts for the residents of their respective areas.

Article 18

The two sides shall permit free correspondence, meeting and visits between dispersed family members and other relatives and shall promote the voluntary reunion of divided families and shall take measures to resolve other humanitarian issues.

Article 19

The two sides shall reconnect railroads and roads that have been cut off and shall open South-North sea and air transport routes.

Article 20

The two sides shall establish and link facilities needed for South-North postal and telecommunications services and shall guarantee the confidentiality of intra-Korean mail and telecommunications.

Article 21

The two sides shall cooperate in the economic, cultural and various other fields in the international arena and carry out joint undertakings abroad.

Article 22

To implement accords on exchanges and cooperation in the economic, cultural and various other fields, the two sides shall establish joint commissions for specific sectors, including a Joint South-North Economic Exchange and Cooperation Commission, within three (3) months of the coming into force of this Agreement.

Article 23

A South-North Exchanges and Cooperation Committee shall be established within the framework of the South-North High-Level Talks within one (1) month of the coming into force of this Agreement with a view to discussing concrete measures to ensure the implementation and observance of the accords on South-North exchanges and cooperation.

Chapter IV

Amendments and Effectuation

Article 24

This agreement may be amended or supplemented by concurrence between the two sides.

Article 25

This Agreement shall enter into force as of the day the two sides exchange appropriate instruments following the completion of their respective procedures for bringing it into effect.

Agreement on Joint Measures with Respect to Nuclear Weapons

Date of signature: December 21, 1991
Place of signature: Alma Ata

Signatory states: Belarus, Kazakhstan, The Russian Federation, Ukraine

[The signatories], hereinafter referred to as "the participating States",

Confirming their commitment to the non-proliferation of nuclear weapons,

Aspiring to the elimination of all nuclear weapons,

Desirous of promoting the strengthening of international stability,

Have agreed as follows:

Article 1

The nuclear weapons with which the Joint Strategic Armed Forces are equipped safeguard the collective security of all participants in the Commonwealth of Independent States.

Article 2

The participating States in the present Agreement confirm the obligation relating to the non-first-use of nuclear weapons.

Article 3

The participating States in the present Agreement shall jointly develop a policy on nuclear issues.

Article 4

Pending the complete elimination of nuclear weapons from the territories of the Republic of Belarus and Ukraine, the decision regarding the need to use such weapons shall be taken with the consent of the Heads of the participating States of the Agreement by the President of the RSFSR on the basis of procedures drawn up jointly by the participating States.

Article 5

1. The Republic of Belarus and Ukraine undertake to accede to the 1968 Treaty on the Non-proliferation of Nuclear Weapons as non-nuclear States and to conclude with IAEA the corresponding safeguards agreement.

2. The participating States in the present Agreement undertake not to transfer to any party whatsoever nuclear weapons or other nuclear explosive devices in technology, or control, either direct or indirect, over such weapons and explosive devices, and not in any way to assist, encourage or incite any States not possessing nuclear weapons to produce or acquire by any other means nuclear weapons or other nuclear explosive devices or control over such weapons or explosive devices.

3. The provisions of paragraph 2 of this Article shall not prevent the transfer of nuclear weapons from the territory of the Republic of Belarus, the Republic of Kazakhzstan and Ukraine to the territory of the RSFSR for the purpose of their destruction.

Article 6

The participating States of the present Agreement shall in conformity with the international Treaty promote the elimination of nuclear weapons. By 1 July 1992 the Republic of Belarus, the Republic of Kazakhstan and Ukraine shall ensure the withdrawal of tactical nuclear weapons to central bases adjacent to the manufacturing plants for dismantling under joint control.

Article 7

The Governments of the Republic of Belarus, the Republic of Kazakhstan, the Russian Federation (RSFSR) and Ukraine undertake to submit the Treaty on the Reduction and Elimination of Strategic Offensive Arms to the Supreme Soviets of their States for ratification.

Article 8

This Agreement is subject to ratification. It shall enter into force 30 days after deposit of all the instruments of ratification with the Government of the RSFSR.

Joint Declaration of the Denuclearization of the Korean Peninsula

Date of signature: January 20, 1992
Place of signature: Seoul, Pyongyang
Signatory states: the Republic of Korea, Democratic People's Republic of Korea
Date of entry into force: February 19, 1992

The South and the North,

Desiring to eliminate the danger of nuclear war through denuclearization of the Korean peninsula, and thus to create an environment and conditions favorable for peace and peaceful unification of our country and contribute to peace and security in Asia and the world.

Declare as follows;

1. The South and the North shall not test, manufacture, produce, receive, possess, store, deploy or use nuclear weapons.

2. The South and the North shall use nuclear energy solely for peaceful purposes.

3. The South and the North shall not possess nuclear reprocessing and uranium enrichment facilities.

4. The South and the North, in order to verify the denuclearization of the Korean peninsula, shall conduct inspection of the objects selected by the other side and agreed upon between the two sides, in accordance with procedures and methods to be determined by the South-North Joint Nuclear Control Commission.

5. The South and the North, in oder to implement this joint declaration, shall establish and operate a South-North Joint Nuclear Control Commission within one (1) month of the effectuation of this joint declaration.

6. This Joint Declaration shall enter into force as of the day the two sides exchange appropriate instruments following the completion of their respective procedures for bringing it into effect.

Agreement Between the Government of the Democractic People's Republic of Korea and the International Atomic Energy Agency for the Application of Safeguards in Connection with the Treaty on the Non-Proliferation of Nuclear Weapons

Data of signature: January 30, 1992
Place of signature: Vienna
Signatory states: Democratic People's Republic of Korea, International Atomic Energy Agency

WHEREAS the Government of the Democratic People's Republic of Korea (hereinafter referred to as "the Democratic People's Republic of Korea") is a party to the Treaty on the Non-Proliferation of Nuclear Weapons (hereinafter referred to as "the Treaty") opened for signature at London, Moscow and Washington on 1 July 1968 and which entered into force on 5 March 1970;

WHEREAS paragraph 1 of Article III of the Treaty reads as follows:

"Each non-nuclear-weapon State Party to the Treaty undertakes to accept safeguards, as set forth in an agreement to be negotiated and concluded with the International Atomic Energy Agency in accordance with the Statute of the International Atomic Energy Agency and the Agency's safeguards system, for the exclusive purpose of verification of the fulfillment of its obligations assumed under this Treaty with a view to preventing diversion of nuclear energy from peaceful uses to nuclear weapons or other nuclear explosive devices. Procedures for the safeguards required by this Article shall be followed with respect to source or special fissionable material whether it is being produced, processed or used in any principal nuclear facility or is outside any such facility. The safeguards required by this Article shall be applied on all source or special fissionable material in all peaceful nuclear activities within the territory of such State, under its jurisdiction, or carried out under its control anywhere".

WHEREAS the International Atomic Energy Agency (hereinafter referred to as "the Agency") is authorized, pursuant to Article III of its Statute, to conclude such agreements;

NOW THEREFORE the Democratic People's Republic of Korea and the Agency have agreed as follow:

PART I

BASIC UNDERTAKING

Article 1

The Democratic People's Republic of Korea undertakes, pursuant to paragraph 1 of Article III of the Treaty, to accept safeguards in accordance with the terms of this Agreement, on all source or special fissionable material in all peaceful nuclear activities within its territory, under its jurisdiction or carried out under its control anywhere, for the exclusive purpose of verifying that such material is not diverted to nuclear weapon or other nuclear explosive devices.

Application of Safeguards

Article 2

The Agency shall have the right and the obligation to ensure that safeguards will be applied, in accordance with the terms of this Agreement, on all source or special fissionable material in all peaceful nuclear activities within the territory of the Democratic People's Republic of Korea, under its jurisdiction or carried out under its control anywhere, for the exclusive purpose of verifying that such material is not diverted to nuclear weapons or other nuclear explosive devices.

Co-operation between the Democratic People's Republic of Korea and the Agency

Article 3

The Democratic People's Republic of Korea and the Agency shall co-operate to facilitate the implementation of the safeguards provided for in this Agreement.

Implementation of Safeguards

Article 4

The safeguards provided for in this Agreement shall be implemented in a manner designed:

(a) to avoid hampering the economic and technological development of the Democratic People's Republic of Korea or international co-operation in the field of peaceful nuclear activities, including international exchange of nuclear material;

(b) to avoid undue interference in the Democratic People's Republic of Korea's peaceful nuclear activities, and in particular in the operation of facilities; and

(c) to be consistent with prudent management practices required for the economic and conduct of nuclear activities.

Article 5

(a) The Agency shall take every precaution to protect commercial and industrial secrets and other confidential information coming to its knowledge in the implementation of this Agreement.

(b) (i) The Agency shall not make public or communicate to any State, organization or person any information obtained by it in connection with the implementation of this Agreement, except that specific information relating to the implementation thereof may be given to the Board of Governors of the Agency (hereinafter referred to as "the Board") and to such Agency staff members as require such knowledge by reason of their official duties in connection with safeguards, but only to the extent necessary for the Agency to fulfill its responsibilities in implementing this Agreement.

(ii) Summarized information on nuclear material subject to safeguards under this Agreement may be published upon decision of the Board if the States directly concerned agree thereto.

Article 6

(a) The Agency shall, in implementing safeguards pursuant to this Agreement, take full account of technological developments in the field of safeguards, and shall make every effort to ensure optimum cost-effectiveness and the application of the principle of safeguarding effectively the flow of nuclear material subject to safeguards under this Agreement by use of instruments and other techniques at certain strategic points to the extent that present or future technology permits.

(b) In order to ensure optimum cost-effectiveness, use shall be made, for example, of such means as:

(i) containment as a means of defining material balance areas for accounting purposes;

(ii) statistical techniques and random sampling in evaluating the flow of nuclear material; and

(iii) concentration of verification procedures on those stages in the nuclear fuel cycle involving the production, processing, use or storage of nuclear material from which nuclear weapon or other nuclear explosive devices could readily be made, and minimization of verification procedures in respect of other nuclear material, on condition that this does not hamper the Agency in applying safeguards under this Agreement.

National System of Materials Control

Article 7

(a) The Democratic People's Republic of Korea shall establish and maintain a system of accounting for and control of all nuclear material subject to safeguards under this Agreement.

(b) The Agency shall apply safeguards in such a manner as to enable it to verify, in ascertaining that there has been no diversion of nuclear material from peaceful uses to nuclear weapons or other nuclear explosive devices, finding of the Democratic People's Republic of Korea's system. The Agency's verification shall include, *inter alia*, independent measurements and observations conducted by the Agency in accordance with the procedures specified in Part II of this Agreement. The Agency, in its verification, shall take due account of the technical effectiveness of the Democratic People's Republic of Korea's system.

Provision of Information to the Agency

Article 8

(a) In order to ensure the effective implementation of safeguards under this Agreement, the Democratic People's Republic of Korea shall, in accordance with the provisions set out in Part II of this Agreement, provide the Agency with information concerning nuclear material subject to safeguards under this Agreement and the features of facilities relevant to safeguarding such material.

(b) (i) The Agency shall require only the minimum amount of information and data consistent with carrying out its responsibilitie under this Agreement.

(ii) Information pertaining to facilities shall be the minimum necessary for safeguarding nuclear material subject to sagefuards under this Agreement.

(c) If the Democratic People's Republic of Korea so requests, the Agency shall be prepared to examine on premises of the Democratic People's Republic of Korea design information which the Democratic People's Republic of Korea regards as being of particular sensitivity. Such information need not be physically transmitted to the Agency provided that it remains readily available for further examination by the Agency on premises of the Democratic People's Republic of Korea.

Agency Inspectors

Article 9

(a) (i) The Agency shall secure the consent of the Democratic People's Republic of Korea to the designation of Agency inspectors to the Democratic People's Republic of Korea.

(ii) If the Democratic People's Republic of Korea, either upon proposal of a designation or at any other time after a designation has been made, objects to the designation, the Agency shall secure the consent of the Democratic People's Republic of Korea to an alternative designation or designations.

(iii) If, as a result of the repeated refusal of the Democratic People's Republic of Korea to accept the designation of Agency inspectors, inspections to be conducted under this Agreement would be impeded, such refusal shall be considered by the Board, upon referral by "the Director General of the Agency (hereinafter referred to as "the Director General"), with a view to its taking appropriate action.

(b) The Democratic People's Republic of Korea shall take necessary steps to ensure that Agency inspectors can effectively discharge their functions under this Agreement. The Agency shall, as far as compatible with the other terms of this Agreement, respect legal procedures and regulations of the Democratic People's Republic relevant to such steps.

(c) The visits and activities of Agency inspectors shall be so arranged as:

(i) to reduce to a minimum the possible inconvenience and disturbance to the Democratic People's Republic of Korea and to the peaceful nuclear activities inspected; and

(ii) to ensure protection of industrial secrets or any other confidential information coming to the inspectors' knowledge.

Privileges and Immunities

Article 10

The Democratic People's Republic of Korea shall accord to the Agency (including its property, funds and assets) and to its inspectors and other officials, performing functions under this Agreement, the same privileges and immunities as those set forth in the relevant provisions of the Agreement on the Privileges and Immunities of the International Atomic Energy Agency.

Termination of Safeguards

Article 11

Consumption or Dilution of Nuclear Material

Safeguards shall terminate on nuclear material upon determination by the Agency that the material has been consumed, or has been diluted in such a way that it is no longer usable for any nuclear activity relevant from the point of view of safeguards, or has become practically irrecoverable.

Article 12

Transfer of Nuclear Material out of the Democratic People's Republic of Korea

The Democratic People's Republic of Korea shall give the Agency advance notification of intended transfers of nuclear material subject to safeguards under this Agreement out of the Democratic People's Republic of Korea, in accordance with the provisions set out in Part II of this Agreement. The Agency shall terminate safeguards on nuclear material under this Agreement when the recipient State has assumed responsibility therefor, as provided for in Part II of this Agreement. The Agency shall maintain records indicating each transfer and, where applicable, the re-application of safeguards to the transferred nuclear material.

Article 13

Provisions Relating to Nuclear Material to be Used in Non-Nuclear Activities

Where nuclear material subject to safeguards under this Agreement is to be used in non-nuclear activities, such as the production of alloys or ceramics, the Democratic People's Republic of Korea shall agree with the Agency, before the material is so used, on the circumstances under which the safeguards on such material may be terminated.

Non-Application of Safeguards to Nuclear Material to be Used in Non-Peaceful Activities

Article 14

If the Democratic People's Republic of Korea intends to exercise its discretion to use nuclear material which is required to be safeguarded under this Agreement in a nuclear activity which does not require the application of safeguards under this Agreement, the following procedures shall apply:

(a) the Democratic People's Republic of Korea shall inform the Agency of the activity, making it clear:

(i) that the use of the nuclear material in a non-proscribed military activity will not be in conflict with an undertaking the Democratic People's Republic of Korea may have given and in respect of which Agency safeguards apply, that the material will be

used only in a peaceful nuclear activity; and

(ii) that during the period of non-application of safeguards the nuclear material will not be used for the production of nuclear weapons or other nuclear explosive devices;

(b) the Democratic People's Republic of Korea and the Agency shall make an arrangement so that, only while the nuclear material is in such an activity, the safeguards provided for in this Agreement will not be applied. The arrangement shall identify, to the extent possible, the period or circumstances during which safeguards will not be applied. In any event, the safeguards provided for in this Agreement shall apply again as soon as the material is reintroduced into a peaceful nuclear activity. The Agency shall be kept informed of the total quantity and composition of such unsafeguarded material in the Democratic People's Republic of Korea and of any export of such material; and

(c) each arrangement shall be made in agreement with the Agency. Such agreement shall be given as promptly as possible and shall relate only to such matters as, inter alia, temporal and procedural provisions and reporting arrangements, but not involved any approval or classified knowledge of the military activity or relate to the use of the nuclear material therein.

Finance

Article 15

The Democratic People's Republic of Korea and the Agency will bear the expenses incurred by them in implementing their respective responsibilities under this Agreement. However, if the Democratic People's Republic of Korea or persons under its jurisdiction incur extraordinary expenses as a result of a specific request by the Agency, the Agency shall reimburse such expenses provided that it has agreed in advance to do so. In any case the Agency shall bear the cost of any additional measuring or sampling which inspectors may request.

Third Party Liability for Nuclear Damage

Article 16

The Democratic People's Republic of Korea shall ensure that any protection against third party liability in respect of nuclear damage, including any insurance or other financial security, which may be available under its laws or regulations shall apply to the

Agency and its officials for the purpose of the implementation of this Agreement, in the same way as that protection applies to nationals of the Democratic People's Republic of Korea.

International Responsibility

Article 17

Any claim by the Democratic People's Republic of Korea against the Agency or by the Agency against the Democratic People's Republic of Korea in respect of any damage resulting from the implementations of safeguards under this Agreement, other than damage arising out of a nuclear incident, shall be settled in accordance with international law.

Measures in Relation to Verification of Non-Division

Article 18

If the Board, upon report of the Director General, decides that an action by the Democratic People's Republic of Korea is essential and urgent in order to ensure verification that nuclear material subject to safeguards under this Agreement is not diverted to nuclear weapons or other nuclear explosive devices, the Board may call upon the Democratic People's Republic of Korea to take the required action without delay, irrespective of whether procedures have been invoked pursuant to Article 22 of this Agreement for the settlement of a dispute.

Article 19

If the Board, upon examination of relevant information reported to it by the Director General, finds that the Agency is not able to verify that there has been no diversion of nuclear material required to be safeguarded under this Agreement to nuclear weapons or other nuclear explosive devices, it may make the reports provided for in paragraph C of Article XII of the Statute of the Agency (hereinafter referred to as "the Statute") and may also take, where applicable, the other measures provided for in that paragraph. In taking such action the Board shall take account of the degree of assurance provided by the safeguards measures that have been applied and shall afford the Democratic People's Republic of Korea every reasonable opportunity to furnish the Board with any necessary reassurance.

Interpretation and Application of the Agreement and Settlement of Disputes

Article 20

The Democratic People's Republic of Korea and the Agency shall, at the request of either, consult about any question arising out of the interpretation or application of this Agreement.

Article 21

The Democratic People's Republic of Korea shall have the right to request that any question arising out of the interpretation or application of this Agreement be considered by the Board. The Board shall invite the Democratic People's Republic of Korea to participate in the discussion of any such question by the Board.

Article 22

Any dispute arising out of the interpretation or application of this Agreement, except a dispute with regard to a finding by the Board under Article 19 or an action taken by the Board pursuant to such a finding, which is not settled by negotiation or another procedure agreed to by the Democratic People's Republic of Korea and the Agency shall, at the request of either, be submitted to an arbitral tribunal composed as follows: the Democratic People's Republic of Korea and the Agency shall each designate one arbitrator, and the two arbitrators so designated shall elect a third, who shall be the Chairman. If, within thirty days of the request for arbitration, either the Democratic People's Republic of Korea or the Agency has not designated an arbitrator, either the Democratic People's Republic of Korea or the Agency may request the President of the International Court of Justice to appoint an arbitrator. The same procedure shall apply if, within thirty days of the designation or appointment of the second arbitrator, the third arbitrator has not been elected. A majority of the members of the arbitral tribunal shall constitute a quorum, and all decisions shall require the concurrence of two arbitrators. The arbitral procedure shall be fixed by the tribunal. The decisions of the tribunal shall be binding on the Democratic People's Republic of Korea and the Agency.

Suspension of Application of Agency Safeguards Under Other Agreements

Article 23

The application of Agency safeguards in the Democratic People's Republic of Korea under other safeguards agreements with the Agency shall be suspended while this Agreement is in force. If the Democratic People's Republic of Korea has received assistance from the Agency for a project, the Democratic People's Republic of Korea's undertaking in the Project Agreement not to use items which are subject thereto in such a way as to further any military purpose shall continue to apply.

Amendment of the Agreement

Article 24

(a) The Democratic People's Republic of Korea and the Agency shall, at the request of either, consult each other on amendment to this Agreement.

(b) All amendments shall require the agreement of the Democratic People's Republic of Korea and the Agency.

(c) Amendments to this Agreement shall enter into force in the same conditions as entry into force of the Agreement itself.

(d) The Director General shall promptly inform all Member States of the Agency of any amendment of this Agreement.

Entry into Force and Duration

Article 25

This Agreement shall enter into force on the date upon which the Agency receives from the Democratic People's Republic of Korea written notification that the Democratic People's Republic of Korea's statutory and constitutional requirements for entry into force have been met. The Director General shall promptly inform all Member States of the Agency of the entry into force of this Agreement.

Article 26

This Agreement shall remain in force as long as the Democratic People's Republic of Korea is party to the Treaty.

PART II

Introduction

Article 27

The purpose of this part of the Agreement is to specify the procedures to be applied in the implementation of the safeguards provisions of Part I.

Objective of Safeguards

Article 28

The objective of the safeguards procedures set forth in this part of the Agreement is the timely detection of diversion of significant quantities of nuclear material from peaceful nuclear activities to the manufacture of nuclear weapons or of other nuclear explosive devices or for purposes unknown, and deterrence of such diversion by the risk of early detection.

Article 29

For the purpose of achieving the objective set forth in Article 28, material accountancy shall be used as a safeguard measure of fundamental importance, with containment and surveillance as important complementary measures.

Article 30

The technical conclusion of the Agency's verification activities shall be a statement, in respect of each material balance area, of the amount of material unaccounted for over a specific period, and giving the limits of accuracy of the amounts stated.

National System of Accounting for and Control of Nuclear Material

Article 31

Pursuant to Article 7 the Agency, in carrying out its verification activities, shall make full use of the Democratic People's Republic of Korea's system of accounting for and control of all nuclear material subject to safeguards under this Agreement and shall avoid unnecessary duplication of the Democratic People's Republic of Korea's accounting and control activities.

Article 32

The Democratic People's Republic of Korea's system of accounting for and control of all nuclear material subject to safeguards under this Agreement shall be based on a structure of material balance areas, and shall make provision, as appropriate and specified in the Subsidiary Arrangements, for the establishment of such measures as:

(a) a measurement system for the determination of the quantities of nuclear material received, produced, shipped, lost or otherwise removed from inventory, and the quantities on inventory;

(b) the evaluation of precision and accuracy of measurements and the estimation of measurement uncertainty;

(c) procedures for identifying, reviewing and evaluating differences in shipper/receiver measurements;

(d) procedures for taking a physical inventory;

(e) procedures for the evaluation of accumulations of unmeasured inventory and unmeasured losses;

(f) a system of records and reports showing, for each material balance area, the inventory of nuclear material and the changes in that inventory including receipts into and transfers out of the material balance area;

(g) provisions to ensure that the accounting procedures and arrangements are being operated correctly; and

(h) procedures for the provision of reports to the Agency in accordance with Article 59-69.

Starting Point of Safeguards

Article 33

Safeguards under this Agreement shall not apply to material in mining or ore processing activities.

Article 34

(a) When any material containing uranium or thorium which has not reached the stage of the nuclear fuel cycle described in paragraph (c) is directly or indirectly exported to a non-nuclear-weapon States, the Democratic People's Republic of Korea shall inform the Agency of its quantity, composition and destination, unless the material is exported for specifically non-nuclear purposes;

(b) When any material containing uranium or thorium which has not reached the stage of the nuclear fuel cycle described in paragraph (c) is imported, the Democratic People's Republic of Korea shall inform the Agency of its quantity and composition, unless the material is imported for specifically non-nuclear purpose; and

(c) When any nuclear material of a composition and purity suitable for fuel fabrication or for isotopic enrichment leaves the plant or the process stage in which it has been produced, or when such nuclear material, or any other nuclear material produced at a later stage in the nuclear fuel cycle, is imported into the Democratic People's Republic of Korea, the

nuclear material shall become subject to the other safeguards procedures specified in this Agreement.

Termination of Safeguards

Article 35

(a) Safeguards shall terminate on nuclear material subject to safeguards under this Agreement, under the conditions set forth in Article 11, where the conditions of that Article are not met. But the Democratic People's Republic of Korea considers that the recovery of safeguarded nuclear material from residues is not for the time being practicable or desirable, the Democratic People's Republic of Korea and the Agency shall consult on the appropriate safeguards measures to be applied.

(b) Safeguards shall terminate on nuclear material subject to safeguards under this Agreement, under the conditions set forth in Article 13, provided that the Democratic People's Republic of Korea and the Agency agree that such nuclear material is practicably irrecoverable.

Exemptions from Safeguards

Article 36

At the request of the Democratic People's Republic of Korea, the Agency shall exempt nuclear material from safeguards, as follows:

(a) special fissionable material, when it is used in gram quantities or less as a sensing component in instruments;

(b) nuclear material, when it is used in non-nuclear activities in accordance with Article 13, if such nuclear material is recoverable; and

(c) plutonium with an isotopic concentration of plutonium-238 exceeding 80%.

Article 37

At the request of the Democratic People's Republic of Korea the Agency shall exempt from safeguards nuclear material that would otherwise be subject to safeguards, provided that the total quantity of nuclear material which has been exempted in the Democratic People's Republic of Korea in accordance with this Article may not at any time exceed:

(a) one kilogram in total of special fissionable material, which may consist of one or more of the following:

(i) plutonium;

(ii) uranium with an enrichment of 0.2 (20%) and above, taken account of by multiplying its weight by its enrichment; and

(iii) uranium with an enrichment below 0.2 (20%) and above that of natural uranium, taken account of by multiplying its weight by five times the square of its enrichment;

(b) ten metric tons in total of natural uranium and depleted uranium with an enrichment above 0.005 (0.5%);

(c) twenty metric tons of depleted uranium with an enrichment of 0.005 (0.5%) or below; and

(d) twenty metric tons of thorium;

or such greater amounts as may be specified by the Board for uniform application.

Article 38

If exempted nuclear material is to be processed or stored together with nuclear material subject to safeguards under this Agreement, provision shall be made for the re-application of safeguards thereto.

Subsidiary Arrangements

Article 39

The Democratic People's Republic of Korea and the Agency shall make Subsidiary Arrangements which shall specify in detail, to the extent necessary to permit the Agency to fulfill its responsibilities under this Agreement in an effective and efficient manner, how the procedures laid down in this Agreement are to be applied. The Subsidiary Arrangements may be extended or changed by agreement between the Democratic People's Republic of Korea and the Agency without amendment of this Agreement.

Article 40

The Subsidiary Arrangements shall enter into force at the same time as, or as soon as possible after, the entry into force of this Agreement. The Democratic People's Republic of Korea and the Agency shall make every effort to achieve their entry into force within ninety days of the entry into force of this Agreement; an extension of that period shall require agreement between the Democratic People's Republic of Korea and the Agency. The Democratic People's Republic of Korea shall provide the Agency promptly with the information required for completing the Subsidiary Arrangements. Upon the entry into force of this Agreement, the Agency shall have the right to apply the procedures laid down therein in respect of the nuclear material listed in the inventory provided for in Article 41, even if the Subsidiary Arrangements have not yet entered into force.

Inventory

Article 41

On the basis of the initial report referred to in Article 62, the Agency shall establish a unified inventory of all nuclear material in the Democratic People's Republic of Korea subject to safeguards under this Agreement, irrespective of its origin, and shall maintain this inventory on the basis of subsequent reports and of the results of its verification activities. Copies of the inventory shall be made available to the Democratic People's Republic of Korea at intervals to be agreed.

Design Information

General Provisions

Article 42

Pursuant to Article 8, design information in respect of existing facilities shall be provided to the Agency during the discussion of the Subsidiary Arrangements. The time limits for the provision of design information in respect of the new facilities shall be specified in the Subsidiary Arrangements and such information shall be provided as early as possible before nuclear material is introduced into a new facility.

Article 43

The design information to be provided to the Agency shall include, in respect of each facility, when applicable:

(a) the identification of the facility, stating its general character, purpose, nominal capacity and geographic location, and the name and address to be used for routine business purposes;

(b) a description of the general arrangement of the facility with reference, to the extent feasible, to the form, location and flow of nuclear material and to the general layout of important items of equipment which use, produce or process nuclear material;

(c) a description of features of the facility relating to material accountancy, containment and surveillance; and

(d) a description of the existing and proposed procedures at the facility for nuclear material accountancy and control, with special reference to material balance areas established by the operator, measurements of flow and procedures for physical inventory taking.

Article 44

Other information relevant to the application of safeguards shall also be provided to the Agency in respect of each facility, in particular on organizational responsibility for material accountancy and control. The Democratic People's Republic of Korea shall provide the Agency with supplementary information on the health and safety procedures which the Agency shall observe and with which the inspectors shall comply at the facility.

Article 45

The Agency shall be provided with design information in respect of a modification relevant for safeguards purposes, for examination, and shall be informed of any change in the information provided to it under Article 44, sufficiently in advance for the safeguards procedures to be adjusted when necessary.

Article 46

Purpose of Examination of Design Information

The design information provided to the Agency shall be used for the following purposes:

(a) to identify the features of facilities and nuclear material relevant to the application of safeguards to nuclear material in sufficient detail to facilitate verification;

(b) to determine material balance areas to be used for Agency accounting purposes and to select those strategic points which are key measurement points and which will be used to determine flow and inventory of nuclear material; in determining such material balance areas the Agency shall *inter alia*, use the following criteria:

(i) the size of the material balance area shall be related to the accuracy with which the material balance can be established;

(ii) in determining the material balance area advantage shall be taken of any opportunity to use containment and surveillance to help ensure the completeness of flow measurements and thereby to simplify the application of safeguards and to concentrate measurement efforts at key measurement points;

(iii) a number of material balance areas in use at a facility or at distinct sites may be combined in one material balance area to be used for Agency accounting purposes when the Agency determines that this is consistent with its verification requirements; and

(iv) a special material balance area may be established at the request of the Democratic People's Republic of Korea around a process step involving commercially sensitive information;

(c) to establish the nominal timing and procedures for taking of physical inventory of nuclear material for Agency accounting purposes;

(d) to establish the records and reports requirements and records evaluation procedures;

(e) to establish requirements and procedures for verification of the quantity and location of nuclear material; and

(f) to select appropriate combinations of containment and surveillance methods and techniques and the strategic points at which they are to be applied.

The results of the examination of the design information shall be included in the Subsidiary Arrangements.

Article 47

Re-examination of Design Information

Design information shall be re-examined in the light of changes in operating conditions, of developments in safeguards technology or of experience in the application of verification procedures, with a view to modifying the action the Agency has taken pursuant to Article 46.

Article 48

Verification of Design Information

The Agency, in co-operation with the Democratic People's Republic of Korea, may send inspectors to facilities to verify the design information provided to the Agency pursuant to Articles 42-45, for the purposes stated in Article 46.

Information in Respect of Nuclear Material Outside Facilities

Article 49

The Agency shall be provided with the following information when nuclear material is to be customarily used outside facilities, as applicable:

(a) a general description of the use of the nuclear material, its geographic location, and the user's name and address for routine business purposes; and

(b) a general description of the existing and proposed procedures for nuclear material accountancy and control, including organizational responsibility for material accountancy and control.

The Agency shall be informed, on a timely basis, of any change in the information provided to it under this Article.

Article 50

The information provided to the Agency pursuant to Article 49 may be used, to the extent relevant, for the purposes set out in Article 46(b)-(f).

Records System

General Provisions

Article 51

In establishing its system of materials control as referred to in Article 7, the Democratic People's Republic of Korea shall arrange that records are kept in respect of each material balance area. The records to be kept shall be described in the Subsidiary Arrangements.

Article 52

The Democratic People's Republic of Korea shall make arrangements to facilitate the examination of records by inspectors, particularly if the records are not kept in English, French, Russian or Spanish.

Article 53

Records shall be retained for at least five years.

Article 54

Records shall consist, as appropriate, of:

(a) accounting records of all nuclear material subject to safeguards under this Agreement; and

(b) operating records for facilities containing such nuclear material.

Article 55

The system of measurements on which the records used for the preparation of reports are based shall either conform to the latest international standards or be equivalent in quality to such standards.

Accounting Records

Article 56

The accounting records shall set forth the following in respect of each material balance area:

(a) all inventory changes, so as to permit a determination of the book inventory at any time;

(b) all measurement results that are used for determination of the physical inventory; and

(c) all adjustments and corrections that have been made in respect of inventory changes, book inventories and physical inventories.

Article 57

For all inventory changes and physical inventories the records shall show, in respect of each batch of nuclear material: material identification, batch data and source data. The records shall account for uranium, thorium and plutonium separately in each batch of nuclear material. For each inventory change, the date of the inventory change and, when appropriate, the originating material balance area and the receiving material balance area or the recipient, shall be indicated.

Article 58

Operating Records

The operating records shall set forth, as appropriate, in respect of each material balance area:

(a) those operating data which are used to establish changes in the quantities and composition of nuclear material;

(b) the data obtained from the calibration of tanks and instruments and from sampling and analyses, the procedures to control the quality of measurements and the derived estimates of random and systematic error;

(c) a description of the sequence of the actions taken in preparing for, and in taking, a physical inventory, in order to ensure that it is correct and complete; and

(d) a description of the actions taken in order to ascertain the cause and magnitude of any accidental or unmeasured loss that might occur.

Reports System

General Provisions

Article 59

The Democratic People's Republic of Korea shall provide the Agency with reports as detailed in Articles 60-69 in respect of nuclear material subject to safeguards under this Agreement.

Article 60

Reports shall be made in English, French, Russian or Spanish, except as otherwise specified in the Subsidiary Arrangements.

Article 61

Reports shall be based on the records kept in accordance with Articles 51-58 and shall consist, as appropriate, of accounting reports and special reports.

Accounting Reports

Article 62

The Agency shall be provided with an initial report on all nuclear material subject to safeguards under this Agreement. The initial report shall be dispatched by the Democratic People's Republic of Korea to the Agency within thirty days of the last day of the calendar month in which this Agreement enters into force, and shall reflect the situation as of the last day of that month.

Article 63

The Democratic People's Republic of Korea shall provide the Agency with the following accounting reports for each material balance area:

(a) inventory change reports showing all change in the inventory of nuclear material. The reports shall be dispatched as soon as possible and in any event within thirty days after the end of the month in which the inventory changes occurred or were established; and

(b) material balance reports showing the material balance based on a physical inventory of nuclear material actually present in the material balance area. The reports shall be dispatched as soon as possible and in any event within thirty days after

the physical inventory has been taken.

The reports shall be based on data available as of the date of reporting and may be corrected at a later date, as required.

Article 64

Inventory change reports shall specify identification and batch data for each batch of nuclear material, the data of the inventory change and, as appropriate, the originating material balance area and the receiving material balance area or the recipient. These reports shall be accompanied by concise notes:

(a) explaining the inventory changes, on the basis of the operating data contained in the operating records provided for under Article 58(a); and

(b) describing, as specified in the Subsidiary Arrangements, the anticipated operational programme, particularly the taking of a physical inventory.

Article 65

The Democratic People's Republic of Korea shall report each inventory change, adjustment and correction, either periodically in a consolidated list or individually. Inventory changes shall be reported in terms of batches. As specified in the Subsidiary Arrangements, small changes in inventory of nuclear material, such as transfers of analytical samples, may be combined in one batch and reported as one inventory change.

Article 66

The Agency shall provide the Democratic People's Republic of Korea with semi-annual statements of book inventory of nuclear material subject to safeguards under this Agreement, for each material balance area, as based on the inventory change reports for the period covered by each statement.

Article 67

Material balance reports shall include the following entries, unless otherwise agreed by the Democratic People's Republic of Korea and the Agency:

(a) beginning physical inventory;

(b) inventory changes (first increases, then decreases);

(c) ending book inventory;

(d) shipper/receiver differences;

(e) adjusted ending book inventory;

(f) ending physical inventory; and

(g) material unaccounted for.

A statement of the physical inventory, listing all batches separately and specifying material identification and batch data for each batch, shall be attached to each material balance report.

Article 68

Special Reports

The Democratic People's Republic of Korea shall make special reports without delay:

(a) if any unusual incident or circumstances lead the Democratic People's Republic of Korea to believe that there is or may have been loss of nuclear material that exceeds the limits specified for this purpose in the Subsidiary Arrangements; or

(b) if the containment has unexpectedly changed from that specified in the Subsidiary Arrangements to the extent that unauthorized removal of nuclear material has become possible.

Article 69

Amplification and Clarification of Reports

If the Agency so requests, the Democratic People's Republic of Korea shall provide it with amplification or clarifications of any report, in so far as relevant for the purpose of safeguards.

Inspections

Article 70

General Provisions

The Agency shall have the right to make inspections as provided for in Article 71-82.

Purposes of Inspections

Article 71

The Agency may make ad hoc inspections in order to:

(a) verify the information contained in the initial report on the nuclear material subject to safeguards under this Agreement;

(b) identify and verify changes in the situation which have occurred since the date of the initial report; and

(c) identify, and if possible verify the quantity and composition of, nuclear material in accordance with Article 93 and 96, before its transfer out of or upon its transfer into the Democratic People's Republic of Korea.

Article 72

The Agency may make routine inspections in order to:

(a) verify that reports are consistent with records;

(b) verify the location, identity, quantity and composition of all nuclear material subject to safeguards under this Agreement; and

(c) verify information on the possible causes of material unaccounted for, shipper/receiver differences and uncertainties in the book inventory.

Article 73

Subject to the Procedure Laid Down in Article 77, the Agency may Make Special Inspections:

(a) in order to verify the information contained in special reports; or

(b) if the Agency considers that information made available by the Democratic People's Republic of Korea, including explanations from the Democratic People's Republic of Korea and information obtained from routine inspections, is not adequate for the Agency to fulfill its responsibilities under this Agreement.

An inspection shall be deemed to be special when it is either additional to the routine inspection effort provided for in Articles 78-82 or involves access to information or locations in addition to the access specified in Article 76 for ad hoc and routine inspections, or both.

Scope of Inspections

Article 74

For the purposes specified in Article 71-73, the Agency may:

(a) examine the records kept pursuant to Articles 51-58;

(b) make independent measurements of all nuclear material subject to safeguards under this Agreement;

(c) verify the functioning and calibration of instruments and other measuring and control equipment;

(d) apply and make use of surveillance and containment measures; and

(e) use other objective methods which have been demonstrated to be technically feasible.

Article 75

Within the scope of Article 74, the Agency shall be enabled:

(a) to observe that samples at key measurement points for material balance accountancy are taken in accordance with procedures which produce representative samples, to observe the treatment and analysis of the samples and to obtain duplicates of such samples;

(b) to observe that the measurements of nuclear material at key measurement points for material balance accountancy are representative, and to observe the calibration of the instruments and equipment involved;

(c) to make arrangements with the Democratic People's Republic of Korea that, if necessary:

(i) additional measurements are made and additional samples taken for the Agency's use;

(ii) the Agency's standard analytical samples are analysed;

(iii) appropriate absolute standards are used in calibrating instruments and other equipment; and

(iv) other calibrations are carried out;

(d) to arrange to use its own equipment for independent measurement and surveillance, and if so agreed and specified in the Subsidiary Arrangements, to arrange to install such equipment;

(e) to apply its seals and other identifying and tamper-indicating devices to containments, if so agreed and specified in the Subsidiary Arrangements; and

(f) to make arrangements with the Democratic People's Republic of Korea for the shipping of samples taken for the Agency's use.

Access for Inspections

Article 76

(a) For the purposes specified in Article 71(a) and (b) and until such time as the strategic points have been specified in the Subsidiary Arrangements, the Agency inspectors shall have access to any location where the initial report or any inspections carried out in connection with it indicate that nuclear material is present;

(b) For the purposes specified in Article 71(c) the inspectors shall have access to any location of which the Agency has been notified in accordance with Articles 92(d)(iii) or 95(d)(iii);

(c) For the purposes specified in Article 72 the inspectors shall have access only to the strategic points specified in the Subsidiary Arrangements and to the records maintained pursuant to Articles 51-58; and

(d) In the event of the Democratic People's Republic of Korea concluding that any unusual circumstances require extended limitations on access by the Agency, the Democratic People's Republic of Korea and the Agency shall promptly make arrangements with a view to enabling the Agency to discharge its safeguards responsibilities in the light of these limitations. The Director General shall report each such arrangement to the Board.

Article 77

In circumstances which may lead to special inspections for the purposes specified in Article 73 the Democratic People's Republic of Korea and the Agency shall consult forthwith. As a result of such consultations the Agency may:

(a) make inspections in addition to the routine inspection effort provided for in Articles 78-82; and

(b) obtain access, in agreement with the Democratic People's Republic of Korea, to information or locations in addition to those specified in Article 76. Any disagreement concerning the need for additional access shall be resolved in accordance with Articles 21 and 22; in case action by the Democratic People's Republic of Korea is essential and urgent, Article 18 shall apply.

Frequency and Intensity of Routine Inspections

Article 78

The Agency shall keep the number, intensity and duration of routine inspections, applying optimum timing, to the minimum consistent with the effective implementation of the safeguards procedures set forth in this Agreement, and shall make the optimum and most economical use of inspection resources available to it.

Article 79

The Agency may carry out one routine inspection per year in respect of facilities and material balance areas outside facilities with a content or annual throughput, whichever is greater, of nuclear material not exceeding five effective kilograms.

Article 80

The number, intensity, duration, timing and mode of routine inspections in respect of facilities with a content or annual throughput of nuclear material exceeding five effective kilograms shall be determined on the basis that in the maximum or limiting case the inspection regime shall be no more intensive than is necessary and sufficient to maintain continuity of knowledge of the flow and inventory of nuclear material, and the maximum routine inspection effort in respect of such facilities shall be determined as follows;

(a) for reactors and sealed storage installations the maximum total of routine inspection per year shall be determined by allowing one sixth of a man-year of inspection for each such facility;

(b) for facilities, other than reactors or sealed storage installations, involving plutonium uranium enriched to more than 5%, the maxium total of routine inspection per year shall be determined by allowing for each such facility $30 \times \sqrt{E}$ man-days of inspection per year, where E is the inventory or annual throughput of nuclear material, whichever is greater, expressed in effective kilograms. The maximum established for any such facility shall not, however, be less than 1.5 man-years of inspection; and

(c) for facilities not covered by paragraphs (a) or (b), the maximum total of routine inspection per year shall be determined by allowing for each such facility one third of a man-year of inspection plus $0.4 \times E$ man-days of inspection per year, where E is the inventory or annual throughput of nuclear material, whichever is greater, expressed in effective kilograms.

The Democratic People's Republic of Korea and the Agency may agree to amend the figures for the maximum inspection effort specified in this Article, upon determination by the Board that such amendment is reasonable.

Article 81

Subject to Article 78-80 the criteria to be used for determining the actual number, intensity, duration, timing and mode of routine inspections in respect of any facility shall include:

(a) *the form of the nuclear material*, in particular, whether the nuclear material is in bulk form or contained in a number of separate items; its chemical composition and, in the case of uranium, whether it is of low or high enrichment; and its accessibility;

(b) *the effectiveness of the Democratic People's Republic of Korea's accounting and control system*, including the extent to which the operators of facilities are functionally independent of the Democratic People's Republic of Korea's accounting and control system; the extent to which the measures specified in Article 32 have been implemented by the Democratic People's Republic of Korea; the promptness of reports provided to the Agency; their consistency with the Agency's independent verification; and the amount and accuracy of the material unaccounted for, as verified by the Agency;

(c) *characteristics of the Democratic People's Republic of Korea's nuclear fuel cycle*, in particular, the number and types of facilities containing nuclear material subject to safeguards, the characteristics of such facilities relevant to safeguards, notably the degree of containment; the extent to which the design of such facilities facilitates verification of the flow and inventory of nuclear material; and the extent to which information from different material balance areas can be correlated;

(d) *international interdependence*, in particular, the extent to which nuclear material is received from or sent to other States for use or processing; any verification activities by the Agency in connection therewith; and the extent to which the Democratic People's Republic of Korea's nuclear activities are interrelated with those of other States; and

(e) *technical developments in the field of safeguards*, including the use of statistical techniques and random sampling in evaluating the flow of nuclear material.

Article 82

The Democratic People's Republic of Korea and the Agency shall consult if the Democratic People's Republic of Korea considers that the inspection effort is being deployed with undue concentration on particular facilities.

Notice of Inspections

Article 83

The Agency shall give advance notice to the Democratic People's Republic of Korea before arrival of inspectors at facilities or material balance areas outside facilities, as follows:

(a) for ad hoc inspections pursuant to Article 71(c), at least 24 hours; for those pursuant to Article 71(a) and (b) as well as the activities provided for in Article 48, at least one week;

(b) for special inspections pursuant to Article 73, as promptly as possible after the Democratic People's Republic of Korea and the Agency have consulted as provided for in Article 77, it being understood that notification of arrival normally will constitute part of the consultations; and

(c) for routine inspections pursuant to Article 72, at least 24 hours in respect of the facilities referred to in Article 80(b) and sealed storage installations containing plutonium or uranium enriched to more than 5%, and one week in all other cases.

Such notice of inspection shall include the name of the inspectors and shall indicate the facilities and the material balance areas outside facilities to be visited and the periods during which they will be visited. If the inspectors are to arrive from outside the Democratic People's Republic of Korea the Agency shall also give advance notice of the place and time of their arrival in the Democratic People's Republic of Korea.

Article 84

Notwithstanding the provisions of Article 83, the Agency may, as a supplementary measure, carry out without advance notification a portion of the routine inspections pursuant to Article 80 in accordance with the principle of random sampling. In performing any unannounced inspections, the Agency shall fully take into account any operational programme provided by the Democratic People's Republic of Korea pursuant to Article 64(b). Moreover, whenever practicable, and on the basis of the operational programme, it shall advise the Democratic People's Republic of Korea periodically of its general programme of announced and unannounced inspections, specifying the general periods when inspections are foreseen. In carrying out any unannounced inspections, the Agency shall make every effort to minimize any practical difficulties for the Democratic People's Republic of Korea and for facility operators, bearing in mind the relevant provisions of Articles 44 and 89. Similarly the Democratic People's Republic of Korea shall make every effort to facilitate the task of the inspectors.

Designation of Inspectors

Article 85

The following procedures shall apply to the designation of inspectors:

(a) the Director General shall inform the Democratic People's Republic of Korea in writing of the name, qualifications, nationality, grade and such other particulars as may be relevant, of each Agency official he proposes for designation as an inspector for the Democratic People's Republic of Korea;

(b) the Democratic People's Republic of Korea shall inform the Director General within thirty days of the receipt of such a proposal whether it accepts the proposal;

(c) the Director General may designate each official who has been accepted by the Democratic People's Republic of Korea as one of the inspectors for the Democratic People's Republic of Korea, and shall inform the Democratic People's Republic of Korea of such designations; and

(d) the Director General, acting in response to a request by the Democratic People's Republic of Korea or on his own initiative, shall immediately inform the Democratic People's Republic of Korea of the withdrawal of the designation of any official as an inspector for the Democratic People's Republic of Korea.

However, in respect of inspectors needed for the activities provided for in Article 48 and to carry out ad hoc inspections pursuant to Article 71(a) and (b) the designation procedures shall be completed if possible within thirty days after the entry into force of this Agreement. If such designation appears impossible within this time limit, inspectors for such purposes shall be designated on a temporary basis.

Article 86

The Democratic People's Republic of Korea shall grant or renew as quickly as possible appropriate visas, where required, for each inspector designated for the Democratic People's Republic of Korea.

Conduct and Visits of Inspectors

Article 87

Inspectors, in exercising their functions under Articles 48 and 71-75, shall carry out their activities in a manner designed to avoid hampering or delaying the construction, commissioning or operation of facilities, or affecting their safety. In particular inspectors shall not operate any facility themselves or direct the staff of a facility to carry out any operation. If inspectors consider that in pursuance of Articles 74 and 75, particular operations in a facility should be carried out by the operator, they shall make a request therefor.

Article 88

When inspectors require services available in the Democratic People's Republic of Korea, including the use of equipment, in connection with the performance of inspections, the Democratic People's Republic of Korea shall facilitate the procurement of such services and the use of such equipment by inspectors.

Statements on the Agency's Verification Activities

Article 90

The Agency shall inform the Democratic People's Republic of Korea of:

(a) the results of inspections, at intervals to be specified in the Subsidiary Arrangements; and

(b) the conclusions it has drawn from its verification activities in the Democratic People's Republic of Korea, in particular by means of statements in respect of each material balance area, which shall be made as soon as possible after a physical inventory has been taken and verified by the Agency and a material balance has been struck.

International Transfers

Article 91

General Provisions

Nuclear material subject or required to be subject to safeguards under this Agreement which is transferred internationally shall, for purpose of this Agreement, be regarded as being the responsibility of the Democratic People's Republic of Korea.:

(a) in the case of import into the Democratic People's Republic of Korea, from the time that such responsibility ceases to lie with the exporting States, and no later than the time at which the material reaches its destination; and

(b) in the case of export out of the Democratic People's Republic of Korea, up to the time at which the recipient State assumes such responsibility, and no later than the time at which the nuclear material reaches its destination.

The point at which the transfer of responsibility will take place shall be determined in accordance with suitable arrangements to be made by the States concerned. Neither the Democratic People's Republic of Korea nor any other State shall be deemed to have such responsibility for nuclear material merely by reason of the fact that the nuclear material is in transit on or over its territory, or that it is being transported on a ship under its flag or in its aircraft.

Transfers out of the Democratic People's Republic of Korea

Article 92

(a) The Democratic People's Republic of Korea shall notify the Agency of any intended transfer out of the Democratic People's Republic of Korea of nuclear material subject to safeguards under this Agreement if the shipment exceeds one effective kilogram, or if, within a period of three months, several separate shipments are to be made to the same State, each of less than one effective kilogram but the total of which exceeds one effective kilogram.

(b) Such notification shall be given to the Agency after the conclusion of the contractual arrangements leading to the transfer and normally at least two weeks before the nuclear material is to be prepared for shipping.

(c) The Democratic People's Republic of Korea and the Agency may agree on different procedures for advance notification.

(d) The notification shall specify:

(i) the identification and, if possible, the expected quantity and composition of the nuclear material to be transferred, and the material balance area from which it will come;

(ii) the State for which the nuclear material is destined;

(iii) the dates on and locations at which the nuclear

material is to be prepared for shipping;

(iv) the approximate dates of dispatch and arrival of the nuclear material; and

(v) at what point of the transfer the recipient State will assume responsibility for the nuclear material for the purpose of this Agreement, and the probable date on which that point will be reached.

Article 93

The notification referred to in Article 92 shall be such as to enable the Agency to make, if necessary, an ad hoc inspection to identify, and if possible verify the quantity and composition of, the nuclear material before it is transferred out of the Democratic People's Republic of Korea and, if the Agency so wishes or the Democratic People's Republic of Korea so requests, to affix seals to the nuclear material when it has been prepared for shipping. However, the transfer of the nuclear material shall not be delayed in any way by any action taken or contemplated by the Agency pursuant to such a notification.

Article 94

If the nuclear meterial will not be subject to Agency safeguards in the recipient State, the Democratic People's Republic of Korea shall make arrangement for the Agency to receive, within three months of the time when the recipient States accepts responsibility for the nuclear material from the Democratic People's Republic of Korea, confirmation by the recipient State of the transfer.

Transfers into the Democratic People's Republic of Korea

Article 95

(a) The Democratic People's Republic of Korea shall notify the Agency of any expected transfer into the Democratic People's Republic of Korea of nuclear material required to be subject to safeguards under this Agreement if the shipment exceeds one effective kilogram, or if, within a period of three months, several separate shipments are to be received from the same State, each of less than one effective kilogram but the total of which exceeds one effective kilogram.

(b) The Agency shall be notified as much in advance as possible of the expected arrival of the nuclear material, and in any case not later than the date on which the Democratic People's Republic of Korea

assumes responsibility for the nuclear material.

(c) The Democratic People's Republic of Korea and the Agency may agree on different procedures for advance notification.

(d) The notification shall specify:

(i) the identification and, if possible, the expected quantity and composition of the nuclear material;

(ii) at what point of the transfer the Democratic People's Republic of Korea will assume responsibility for the nuclear material for the purpose of this Agreement, and the probable date on which that point will be reached; and

(iii) the expected date of arrival, the location where, and the date on which, the nuclear material is intended to be unpacked.

Article 96

The notification referred to in Article 95 shall be such as to enable the Agency to make, if necessary, an ad hoc inspection to identify, and if possible verify the quantity and composition of, the nuclear material at the time the consignment is unpacked. However, unpacking shall not be delayed by any action taken or contemplated by the Agency pursuant to such a notification.

Article 97

Special Reports

The Democratic People's Republic of Korea shall make a special report as envisaged in Article 68 if any unusual incident or circumstances lead the Democratic People's Republic of Korea to believe that there is or may have been loss of nuclear material, including the occurrence of significant delay, during an international transfer.

Definitions

Article 98

For the purposes of this Agreement:

A. *adjustment* means an entry into an accounting record or a report showing a shipper/receiver difference or material unaccounted for.

B. *annual throughput means,* for the purposes of Article 79 and 80, the amount of nuclear material transferred annually out of a facility working at nominal capacity.

C. *batch* means a portion of nuclear material handled as a unit for accounting purposes at a key measurement point and for which the composition and quantity are defined by a single set of specifications or measurements. The nuclear material may be in bulk form or contained in a number of separate items.

D. *batch data* means the total weight of each element of nuclear material and, in the case of plutonium and uranium, the isotopic composition when appropriate. The units of account shall be as follows:

(a) grams of contained plutonium;

(b) grams of total uranium and grams of contained uranium-235 plus uranium-233 for uranium enriched in these isotopes; and

(c) kilograms of contained thorium, natural uranium or depleted uranium.

For reporting purposes the weights of individual items in the batch shall be added together before rounding to the nearest unit.

E. *book inventory* of a material balance area means the algebraic sum of the most recent physical inventory of that material balance area and of all inventory change that have occurred since that physical inventory was taken.

F. *correction* means an entry into an accounting record or a report to rectify an identified mistake or to reflect an improved measurement of a quantity previously entered into the record or report. Each correction must identify the entry to which it pertains.

G. *effective kilogram* means a special unit used in safeguarding nuclear material. The quantity in effective kilograms is obtained by taking:

(a) for plutonium, its weight in kilograms;

(b) for uranium with an enrichment of 0.01 (1%) and above, its weight in kilograms multiplied by the square of its enrichment;

(c) for uranium with an enrichment below 0.01 (1%) and above 0.005 (0.5%), its weight in kilograms multiplied by 0.0001; and

(d) for depleted uranium with enrichment of 0.005 (0.5%) or below, and for thorium, its weight in kilograms multiplied by 0.00005.

H. *enrichment* means the ratio of the combined weight of the isotopes uranium-233 and uranium-235 to that of the total uranium in question.

I. *facility* means:

(a) a reactor, a critical facility, a conversion plant, a fabrication plant, a reprocessing plant, an isotope separation plant or a separate storage installation; or

(b) any location where nuclear material in amounts greater than one effective kilogram is customarily used.

J. *inventory change* means an increase or decrease, in terms of batches, of nuclear material in a material balance area; such a change shall involve one of the following:

(a) increases:

(i) import;

(ii) domestic receipt: receipts from other material balance areas, receipts from a non-safeguarded (non-peaceful) activity or receipts at the starting point of safeguards;

(iii) nuclear production: production of special fissionable material in a reactor; and

(iv) de-exemption: re-application of safeguards on nuclear material previously exempted therefrom on account of its use or quantity.

(b) decreases:

(i) export;

(ii) domestic shipment: shipments to other material balance areas or shipments for a non-safeguarded (non-peaceful) activity;

(iii) nuclear loss: loss of nuclear material due to its transformation into other element(s) or isotope(s) as a result of nuclear reactions;

(iv) measured discard: nuclear material which has been measured, or estimated on the basis of measurements, and disposed of in such a way that it is not suitable for further nuclear use;

(v) retained waste: nuclear material generated from processing or from an operational accident, which is deemed to be unrecoverable for the time being but which is stored;

(vi) exemption: exemption of nuclear material from safeguards on account of its use or quantity; and

(viii) other loss: for example, accidental loss (that is, irretrievable and inadvertent loss of nuclear material as the result of an operational accident) or theft.

K. *key measurement point* means a location where nuclear material appears in such a form that it may be measured to determine material flow or inventory. Key measurement points thus include, but are not limited to, the inputs and outputs (including measured discards) and storages in material balance areas.

L. *man-year of inspection* means, for the purposes of Article 80, 300 man-days of inspection, a man-day being a day during which a single inspector has access to a facility at any time for a total of not more than eight hours.

M. *material balance area* means an area in or outside of a facility such that:

(a) the quantity of nuclear material in each transfer into out of each material balance area can be determined; and

(b) the physical inventory of nuclear material in each material balance area can be determined when necessary, in accordance with specified procedures,

in order that the material balance for Agency safeguards purposes can be established.

N. *material unaccounted for* means the difference between book inventory and physical inventory.

O. *nuclear material* means any source or any special fissionable material as defined in Article XX of the Statute. The term source material shall not be interpreted as applying to ore or ore residue. Any determination by the Board under Article XX of the Statute after the entry into force of this Agreement which adds to the materials considered to be source material or special fissionable material shall have effect under this Agreement only upon acceptance by the Democratic People's Republic of Korea.

P. *physical inventory* means the sum of all the measured or derived estimates of batch quantities of nuclear material on hand at a given time within a material balance area, obtained in accordance with specified procedures.

Q. *shipper/receiver difference* means the difference between the quantity of nuclear material in a batch as stated by the shipping material balance area and as measured at the receiving material balance area.

R. *source data* means those data, recorded during measurement or calibration or used to derive empirical relationships, which identify nuclear material and provide batch data. Source data may include, for example, weight of compounds, conversion factors to determine weight of element, specific gravity, element concentration, isotopic ratios, relationship between volume and manometer readings and relationship between plutonium produced and power generated.

S. *strategic point* means a location selected during examination of design information where, under normal conditions and when combined with the information from all strategic points taken together, the information necessary and sufficient for the implementation of safeguards measures is obtained and verified; a strategic point may include any location where key measurements related to material balance accountancy are made and where containment and surveillance measures are executed.

Treaty on European Union

Also known as: Maastricht Treaty
Date of signature: February 7, 1992
Place of signature: Maastricht
Signatory states: Belgium, Denmark, Germany, The Hellenic Republic, Spain, The French Republic, Ireland, The Italian Republic, Luxembourg, Netherlands, The Portuguese Republic, Great Britain and Northern Ireland
Date of entry into force: January 1, 1993

RESOLVED to mark a new stage in the process of

European integration undertaken with the establishment of the European Communities,

RECALLING the historic importance of the ending of the division of the European continent and the need to create firm bases for the construction of the future Europe,

CONFIRMING their attachment to the principle of liberty, democracy and respect for human rights and fundamental freedoms and of the rule of law,

DESIRING to deepen the solidarity between their

peoples while respecting their history, their culture and their traditions,

DESIRING to enhance further the democratic and efficient functioning of the institutions so as to enable them better to carry out, within a single institutional framework, the tasks entrusted to them,

RESOLVED to achieve the strengthening and the convergence of their economies and to establish an economic and monetary union including, in accordance with the provisions of this Treaty, a single and stable currency,

DETERMINED to promote economic and social progress for their peoples, within the context of the accomplishment of the internal market and of reinforced cohesion and environmental protection, and to implement policies ensuring that advances in economic integration are accompanied by parallel progress in other fields,

RESOLVED to establish a citizenship common to nationals of their countries,

RESOLVED to implement a common foreign and security policy including the eventual framing of a common defense policy, which might in time lead to a common defense, thereby reinforcing the European identity and its independence in order to promote peace, security and progress in Europe and in the world,

REAFFIRMING their objectives to facilitate the free movement of persons, while ensuring the safety and security of their peoples, by including provisions on justice and home affairs in this Treaty,

RESOLVED to continue the process of creating an ever closer union among the peoples of Europe, in which decisions are taken as closely as possible to the citizen in accordance with the principle of subsidiarity,

IN VIEW of further steps to be taken in order to advance European integration,

HAVE DECIDED to establish a European Union and to this end have designated as their plenipotentiaries:

WHO, having exchanged their full powers, found in good and due form, have agreed as follows:

TITLE 1

COMMON PROVISIONS

Article A

By this treaty, the High Contracting Parties establish among themselves a European Union, hereafter called "the Union".

This Treaty marks a new stage in the process of creating an ever closer union among the peoples of Europe, in which decisions are taken as closely as possible to the citizen.

The Union shall be founded on the European Communities, supplemented by the policies and forms of cooperation established by this Treaty. Its task shall be to organize, in a manner demonstrating consistency and solidarity, relations between the Member States and between their peoples.

Article B

The Union shall set itself the following objectives:

– to promote economic and social progress which is balanced and sustainable, in particular through the creation of an area without internal frontiers, through the strengthening of economic and social cohesion and through the establishment of economic and monetary union, ultimately including a single currency in accordance with the provisions of this Treaty;

– to assert its identity on the international scene, in particular through the implementation of a common foreign and security policy including the eventual framing of a common defence policy, which might in time lead to a common defence;

– to strengthen the protection of the rights and interests of the nationals of its Member States through the introduction of a citizenship of the Union;

– to develop close cooperation on justice and home affairs;

– to maintain in full the "acquis communautaire" and build on it with a view to considering, through the procedure referred to in Article N(2), to what extent the policies and forms of cooperation introduced by this Treaty may need to be revised with the aim of ensuring the effectiveness of the mechanisms and the institutions of the Community.

The objectives of the Union shall be achieved as provided in this Treaty and in accordance with the condition and the timetable set out therein while respecting the principle of subsidiarity as defined in Article 3b of the Treaty establishing the European Community.

Article C

The Union shall be served by a single institutional

framework which shall ensure the consistency and the continuity of the activities carried out in order to attain its objectives while respecting and building upon the "acquis communautaire".

The Union shall in particular ensure the consistency of its external activities as a whole in the context of its external relations, security, economic and development policies. The Council and the Commission shall be responsible for ensuring such consistency. They shall ensure the implementation of these policies, each in accordance with its respective powers.

Article D

The European Council shall provide the Union with the necessary impetus for its development and shall define the general political guidelines thereof.

The European Council shall bring together the Heads of State or of Government of the Member States and the President of the Commission. They shall be assisted by the Ministers for Foreign Affairs of the Member States and by a Member of the Commission. The European Council shall meet at least twice a year, under the chairmanship of the Head of State or of Government of the Member State which holds the Presidency of the Council.

The European Council shall submit to the European Parliament a report after each of its meetings and a yearly written report on the progress achieved by the Union.

Article E

The European Parliament, the Council, the Commission and the Court of Justice shall exercise their powers under the conditions and for the purposes provided for, on the one hand, by the provisions of the Treaties establishing the European Communities and of the subsequent Treaties and Acts modifying and supplementing them and, on the other hand, by the other provisions of this Treaty.

Article F

1. The Union shall respect the national identities of its Member States, whose systems of government are founded on the principles of democracy.

2. The Union shall respect fundamental rights, as guaranteed by the European Convention for the Protection of Human Rights and Fundamental Freedoms signed in Rome on 4 November 1950 and as they result from the constitutional traditions common to the Member States, as general principles of Community law.

3. The Union shall provide itself with the means necessary to attain its objectives and carry through its policies.

TITLE II

PROVISIONS AMENDING THE TREATY ESTABLISHING THE EUROPEAN ECONOMIC COMMUNITY WITH A VIEW TO ESTABLISHING THE EUROPEAN COMMUNITY

Article G

The Treaty establishing the European Economic Community shall be amended in accordance with the provisions of this Article, in order to establish a European Community.

A. Throughout the Treaty:

1) The term "European Economic Community" shall be replaced by the term "European Community".

B. In Part One "Principles":

2) Article 2 shall be replaced by the following:

Article 2

The Community shall have as its task, by establishing a common market and an economic and monetary union and by implementing the common policies or activities referred to in Articles 3 and 3a, to promote throughout the Community a harmonious and balanced development of economic activities, sustainable and non-inflationary growth respecting the environment, a high degree of convergence of economic performance, a high level of employment and of social protection, the raising of the standard of living and quality of life, and economic and social cohesion and solidarity among Member States.'

3) Article 3 shall be replaced by the following:

Article 3

For the purposes set out in Article 2, the activities of the Community shall include, as provided in this Treaty and in accordance with the timetable set out therein:

(a) the elimination, as between Member States, of customs duties and quantitative restrictions on the import and export of goods, and of all other measures having equivalent effect;

(b) a common commercial policy;

(c) an internal market characterized by the abolition, as between Member States of obstacles to the free movement of goods, persons, services and capital;

(d) measures concerning the entry and movement of persons in the internal market as provided for in Article l00c;

(e) a common policy in the sphere of agriculture and fisheries;

(f) a common policy in the sphere of transport;

(g) a system ensuring that competition in the internal market is not distorted;

(h) the approximation of the laws of Member States to the extent required for the functioning of the common market;

(i) a policy in the social sphere comprising a European Social Fund;

(j) the strengthening of economic and social cohesion;

(k) a policy in the sphere of the environment;

(l) the strengthening of the competitiveness of Community industry;

(m) the promotion of research and technological development;

(n) encouragement for the establishment and development of trans-European networks;

(o) a contribution to the attainment of a high level of health protection;

(p) a contribution to education and training of quality and to the flowering of the cultures of the Member States;

(q) a policy in the sphere of development cooperation;

(r) the association of the overseas countries and territories in order to increase trade and promote jointly economic and social development;

(s) a contribution to the strengthening of consumer protection;

(t) measures in the spheres of energy, civil protection and tourism."

4) The following Article shall be inserted:

Article 3a

1. For the purposes set out in Article 2, the activities of the Member States and the Community shall include, as provided in this Treaty and in accordance with the timetable set out therein, the adoption of an economic policy which is based on the close coordination of Member States' economic policies, on the internal market and on the definition of common objectives, and conducted in accordance with the principle of an open market economy with free competition.

2. Concurrently with the foregoing, and as provided in this Treaty and in accordance with the timetable and the procedures set out therein, these activities shall include the irrevocable fixing of exchange rates leading to the introduction of a single currency, the ECU, and the definition and conduct of a single monetary policy and exchange rate policy the primary objective of both of which shall be to maintain price stability and, without prejudice to this objective, to support the general economic policies in the Community, in accordance with the principle of an open market economy with free competition.

3. These activities of the Member States and the Community shall entail compliance with the following guiding principles: stable prices, sound public finances and monetary conditions and a sustainable balance of payments."

5) The following Article shall be inserted:

Article 3b

The Community shall act within the limit of the powers conferred upon it by this Treaty and of the objectives assigned to it therein.

In areas which do not fall within its exclusive competence, the Community shall take action, in accordance with the principle of subsidiarity, only if and in so far as the objectives of the proposed action cannot be sufficiently achieved by the Member States and can therefore, by reason of the scale or effects of the proposed action, be better achieved by the Community.

Any action by the Community shall not go beyond what is necessary to achieve the objectives of this Treaty."

6) Article 4 shall be replaced by the following:

Article 4

1. The tasks entrusted to the Community shall be carried out by the following institutions:

– EUROPEAN Parliament,

– a COUNCIL,

– a COMMISSION,

– a COURT OF JUSTICE,

– a COURT OF AUDITORS.

Each institution shall act within the limits of the powers conferred upon it by this Treaty.
2. The Council and the Commission shall be assisted by an Economic and Social Committee and a Committee of the Regions acting in an advisory capacity."

7) The following Articles shall be inserted:

Article 4a

A European System of Central Banks (hereinafter referred to as "ESCB") and a European Central Bank (hereinafter referred to as "ECB") shall be established in accordance with the procedures laid down in this Treaty; they shall act within the limits of the powers conferred upon them by this Treaty and by the Statute of the ESCB and of the ECB (hereinafter referred to as "Statute of the ESCB") annexed thereto.

Article 4b

A European Investment Bank is hereby established, which shall act within the limit of the powers conferred upon it by this Treaty and the Statute annexed thereto."

8) Article 6 shall be deleted and Article 7 shall become Article 6. Its second paragraph shall be replaced by the following:

"The Council, acting in accordance with the procedure referred to in Article 189c, may adopt rules designed to prohibit such discrimination."

9) Articles 8, 8a, 8b and 8c shall become respectively Article 7, 7a, 7b and 7c.

C. The following Part shall be inserted:

PART TWO
CITIZENSHIP OF THE UNION

Article 8

1. Citizenship of the Union is hereby established.
Every person holding the nationality of a Member State shall be a citizen of the Union.
2. Citizens of the Union shall enjoy the rights conferred by this Treaty and shall be subject to the duties imposed thereby.

Article 8a

1. Every citizen of the Union shall have the right to move and reside freely within the territory of the Member States, subject to the limitations and conditions laid down in this Treaty and by the measures adopted to give it effect.
2. The Council may adopt provisions with a view to facilitating the exercise of the rights referred to in paragraph 1; save as otherwise provided in this Treaty, the Council shall act unanimously on a proposal from the Commission after obtaining the assent of the European Parliament.

Article 8b

1. Every citizen of the Union residing in a Member State of which he is not a national shall have the right to vote and to stand as a candidate at municipal elections in the Member State in which he resides, under the same conditions as nationals of that State. This right shall be exercised subject to detailed arrangements to be adopted before 31 December 1994 by the Council, acting unanimously, on a proposal from the Commission and after consulting the European Parliament; these arrangements may provide for derogations where warranted by problems specific to a Member State.
2. Without prejudice to Article 138(3) and to the provisions adopted for its implementation, every citizen of the Union residing in a Member State of which he is not a national shall have the right to vote and to stand as a candidate in elections to the European Parliament in the Member State in which he resides, under the same conditions as nationals of that State. This right shall be exercised subject to detailed arrangements to be adopted before 31 December 1993 by the Council, acting unanimously on a proposal from the Commission and after consulting the European Parliament; these arrangements may provide for derogations where warranted by problems specific to a Member State.

Article 8c

Every citizen of the Union shall, in the territory of a third country in which the Member State of which he is a national is not represented, be entitled to protection by the diplomatic or consular authorities of any Member State, on the same conditions as the nationals of that State. Before 31 December 1993, Member States shall establish the necessary rules among themselves and start the international negotiations required to secure this protection.

Article 8d

Every citizen of the Union shall have the right to petition the European Parliament in accordance with Article 138d.

Every citizen of the Union may apply to the Ombudsman established in accordance with Article 138e.

Article 8e

The Commission shall report to the European Parliament, to the Council and to the Economic and Social Committee before 31 December 1993 and then every three years on the application of the provisions of this Part. This report shall take account of the development of the Union.

On this basis, and without prejudice to the other provisions of this Treaty, the Council, acting unanimously on a proposal from the Commission and after consulting the European Parliament, may adopt provisions to strengthen or to add to the rights laid down in this Part, which it shall recommend to the Member States for adoption in accordance with their respective constitutional requirements."

D. Parts Two and Three shall be grouped under the following Title:

PART THREE
COMMUNITY POLICIES

and in this Part:

10) The first sentence of Article 49 shall be replaced by the following:

"As soon as this Treaty enters into force, the Council shall, acting in accordance with the procedure referred to in Article 189b and after consulting the Economic and Social Committee, issue directives or make regulations setting out the measures required to bring about, by progressive stages, freedom of movement for workers, as defined in Article 48, in particular."

11) Article 54(2) shall be replaced by the following:

"2. In order to implement this general programme or, in the absence of such programme, in order to achieve a stage in attaining freedom of establishment as regards a particular activity, the Council, acting in accordance with the Procedure referred to in Article 189b and after consulting the Economic and Social Committee, shall act by means of directives."

12) Article 56(2) shall be replaced by the following:

"2. Before the end of the transitional period, the Council shall, acting unanimously on a proposal from the Commission and after consulting the European Parliament, issue directives for the coordination of the above mentioned provisions laid down by law, regulation or administrative action. After the end of the second stage, however, the Council shall, acting in accordance with the procedure referred to in Article 189b, issue directives for the coordination of such provisions as, in each Member State, are a matter for regulation or administrative action."

13) Article 57 shall be replaced by the following:

Article 57

1. In order to make it easier for persons to take up and pursue activities as self-employed persons, the Council shall, acting in accordance with the procedure referred to in Article 189b, issue directives for the mutual recognition of diplomas, certificates and other evidence of formal qualifications.

2. For the same purpose, the Council shall, before the end of the transitional period, issue directives for the coordination of the provisions laid down by law, regulation or administrative action in Member States concerning the taking up and pursuit of activities as self-employed persons. The Council, acting unanimously on a proposal from the Commission and after consulting the European Parliament, shall decide on directives the implementation of which involves in at least one Member State amendment of the existing principles laid down by law governing the professions with respect to training and conditions of access for natural persons. In other cases the Council

shall act in accordance with the procedure referred to in Article 189b.

3. In the case of the medical and allied and pharmaceutical professions, the progressive abolition of restrictions shall be dependent upon coordination of the conditions for their exercise in the various Member States."

14) The title of Chapter 4 shall be replaced by the following:

CHAPTER 4

CAPITAL AND PAYMENTS

15) The following Articles shall be inserted:

"Article 73a

As from 1 January 1994, Articles 67 to 73 shall be replaced by Articles 73b, c, d, e, f and g.

Article 73b

1. Within the framework of the provisions set out in this Chapter, all restrictions on the movement of capital between Member States and between Member States and third countries shall be prohibited.

2. Within the framework of the provisions set out in this Chapter, all restrictions on payments between Member States and between Member States and third countries shall be prohibited.

Article 73c

1. The Provisions of Article 73b shall be without prejudice to the application to third countries, of any restrictions which exist on 31 December 1993 under national or Community law adopted in respect of the movement of capital to or from third countries involving direct investment—including investment in real estate—establishment, the provision of financial services or the admission of securities to capital markets.

2. Whilst endeavouring to achieve the objective of free movement of capital between Member States and third countries to the greatest extent possible and without prejudice to the other Chapters of this Treaty, the Council may, acting by a qualified majority on a proposal from the Commission, adopt measures on the movement of capital to or from third countries involving direct investment—including investment in real estate—, establishment, the provision of financial services or the admission of securities to capital markets. Unanimity shall be required

for measures under this paragraph which constitute a step back in Community law as regards the liberalization of the movement of capital to or from third countries.

Article 73d

1. The provisions of Article 73b shall be without prejudice to the right of Member States:

(a) to apply the relevant provision of their tax law which distinguish between tax-payers who are not in the same situation with regard to their place of residence or with regard to the place where their capital is invested;

(b) to take all requisite measures to prevent infringement of national law and regulations, in particular in the field taxation and the prudential supervision of financial institutions, or to lay down procedures for the declaration of capital movements for purposes of administrative or statistical information, or to take measures which are justified on grounds of public policy or public security.

2. The provisions of this Chapter shall be without prejudice to the applicability of restrictions on the right of establishment which are compatible with this Treaty.

3. The measures and procedures referred to in paragraphs 1 and 2 shall not constitute a means of arbitrary discrimination or a disguised restriction on the free movement of capital and payments as defined in Article 73b.

Article 73e

By way of derogation from Article 73b, Member States which, on 31 December 1993, enjoy a derogation on the basis of existing Community law, shall be entitled to maintain, until 31 December 1995 at the latest, restrictions on movement of capital authorized by such derogations as exist on that date.

Article 73f

Where, in exceptional circumstances, movement of capital to or from third countries cause, or threaten to cause, serious difficulties for the operation of economic and monetary union, the Council, acting by a qualified majority on a proposal from the Commission and after consulting the ECB, may take safeguard measures with regard to third countries for a period not exceeding six months if such measures are strictly necessary.

Article 73g

1. If, in the cases envisaged in Article 228a, action by the Community is deemed necessary, the Council may, in accordance with the procedure provided for in Article 228a, take the necessary urgent measures on the movement of capital and on payments as regards the third countries concerned.

2. Without prejudice to Article 224 and as long as the Council has not taken measures pursuant to paragraph 1, a Member State may, for serious political reasons and on grounds of urgency, take unilateral measures against a third country with regard to capital movements and payments. The Commission and the other Member States shall be informed of such measures by the date of their entry into force at the latest.

The Council may, acting by a qualified majority on a proposal from the Commission, decide that the Member State concerned shall amend or abolish such measures. The President of the Council shall inform the European Parliament of any such decision taken by the Council.

Article 73h

Until 1 January 1994, the following provisions shall be applicable:

1) Each Member State undertakes to authorize, in the currency of the Member State in which the creditor or the beneficiary resides, any payment connected with the movement of goods, services or capital, and any transfers of capital and earnings, to the extent that the movement of goods, services, capital and persons between Member States has been liberalized pursuant to this Treaty.

The Member States declare their readiness to undertake the liberalization of payments beyond the extent provided in the preceding subparagraph, in so far as their economic situation in general and the state of their balance of payment in particular so permit.

2) In so far as movement of goods, services and capital are limited only by restrictions on payments connected therewith, these restrictions shall be progressively abolished by applying, *mutatis mutandis*, the provisions of this Chapter and the Chapters relating to the abolition of qualitative restrictions and to the liberalization of services.

3) Member States undertake not to introduce between themselves any new restrictions on transfers connected with the invisible transactions listed in Annex III to this Treaty.

The progressive abolition of existing restrictions shall be effected in accordance with the provisions of Articles 63 to 65, in so far as such abolition is not governed by the provisions contained in paragraphs 1 and 2 or by the other provisions of this Chapter.

4) If need be, Member States shall consult each other on the measures to be taken to enable the payment and transfers mentioned in this Article to be effected; such measures shall not prejudice the attainment of the objectives set out in this Treaty."

16) Article 75 shall be replaced by the following:

Article 75

1. For the purpose of implementing Article 74, and taking into account the distinctive features of transport, the Council shall, acting in accordance with the procedure referred to in Article 189c and after consulting the Economic and Social Committee, lay down:

(a) common rules applicable to international transport to or from the territory of a Member State or passing across the territory of one or more Member States;

(b) the conditions under which non-resident carriers may operate transport services within a Member State;

(c) measures to improve transport safety;

(d) any other appropriate provisions.

2. The Provisions referred to in (a) and (b) of paragraph 1 shall be laid down during the transitional period.

3. By way of derogation from the procedure provided for in paragraph 1, where the application of provisions concerning the principles of the regulatory system for transport would be liable to have a serious effect on the standard of living and on employment in certain areas and on the operation of transport facilities, they shall be laid down by the Council acting unanimously on a proposal from the Commission, after consulting the European Parliament and the Economic and Social Committee. In so doing, the Council shall take into account the need for adaptation to the economic development which will result from establishing the common market."

17) The title of Title I in Part Three shall be replaced by the following:

TITLE V

COMMON RULES ON COMPETITION AND APPROXIMATION OF LAWS

18) In Article 92(3):

- the following point shall be inserted:

"(d) aid to promote culture and heritage conservation where such aid does not affect trading conditions and competition in the Community to an extent that is contrary to the common interest."

- the present point (d) shall become (e).

19) Article 94 shall be replaced by the following:

Article 94

"The Council, acting by a qualified majority on a proposal from the Commission and after consulting the European Parliament, may make any appropriate regulations for the application of Articles 92 and 93 and may in particular determine the conditions in which Article 93(3) shall apply and the categories of aid exempted from this procedure."

20) Article 99 shall be replaced by the following:

Article 99

"The Council shall, acting unanimously on a proposal from the Commission and after consulting the European Parliament and the Economic and Social Committee, adopt provisions for the harmonization of legislation concerning turnover taxes, excise duties and other forms of indirect taxation to the extent that such harmonization is necessary to ensure the establishment and the functioning of the internal market within the time limit laid down in Article 7a."

21) Article 100 shall be replaced by the following:

Article 100

"The Council shall, acting unanimously on a proposal from the Commission and after consulting the European Parliament and the Economic and Social Committee, issue directives for the approximation of such laws, regulations or administrative provisions of the Member States as directly affects the establishment or functioning of the common market."

22) Article l00a(1) shall be replaced by the following:

"1. By way of derogation from Article 100 and save where otherwise provided in this Treaty, the following provisions shall apply for the achievement of the objectives set out in Article 7a. The Council shall, acting in accordance with the procedure referred to in Article 189b and after consulting the Economic and Social Committee, adopt the measures for the approximation of the provisions laid down by law, regulation or administrative action in Member States which have as their object the establishment and functioning of the internal market."

23) The following Article shall be inserted:

Article l00c

1. The Council, acting unanimously on a proposal from the Commission and after consulting the European Parliament, shall determine the third countries whose nationals must be in possession of a visa when crossing the external borders of the Member States.

2. However, in the event of an emergency situation in a third country posing a threat of a sudden inflow of nationals from that country into the Community, the Council, acting by a qualified majority on a recommendation from the Commission, may introduce, for a period not exceeding six months, a visa requirement for nationals from the country in question. The visa requirement established under this paragraph may be extended in accordance with the procedure referred to in paragraph 1.

3. From 1 January 1996, the Council shall adopt the decisions referred to in paragraph 1 by a qualified majority. The Council shall, before that date, acting by a qualified majority on a proposal from the Commission and after consulting the European Parliament, adopt measures relating to a uniform format for visas.

4. In the areas referred to in this Article, the Commission shall examine any request made by a Member State that it submit a proposal to the Council.

5. This Article shall be without prejudice to the exercise of the responsibilities incumbent upon the Member States with regard to the maintenance of law and order and the safeguarding of internal security.

6. This Article shall apply to other areas if so decided pursuant to Article K.9 of the provisions of the Treaty on European Union which relate to cooperation in the fields of justice and home affairs, subject to the voting conditions determined at the same time.

7. The provisions of the conventions in force between the Member States governing areas covered by this Article shall remain in force until their content has been replaced by directives or measures adopted pursuant to this Article."

24) The following Article shall be inserted:

Article l00d

"The Coordinating Committee consisting of senior officials set up by Article K.4 of the Treaty on European Union shall contribute, without prejudice to the provisions of Article 151, to the preparation of the proceedings of the Council in the fields referred to in Article l00c."

25) Title II, Chapters 1, 2 and 3 in Part Three shall be replaced by the following:

TITLE VI

ECONOMIC AND MONETARY POLICY

CHAPTER 1

ECONOMIC POLICY

Article 102a

Member States shall conduct their economic policies with a view to contributing to the achievement of the objectives of the Community, as defined in Article 2, and in the context of the broad guidelines referred to in Article 103(2). The Member States and the Community shall act in accordance with the principle of an open market economy with free competition, favouring an efficient allocation of resources, and in compliance with the principle set out in Article 3a.

Article 103

1. Member States shall regard their economic policies as a matter of common concern and shall coordinate them within the Council, in accordance with the provisions of Article 102a.

2. The Council shall, acting by a qualified majority on a recommendation from the Commission, formulate a draft for the broad guidelines of the economic policies of the Member States and of the Community, and shall report its findings to the European Council.

The European Council shall, acting on the basis of the report from the Council, discuss a conclusion on the broad guidelines of the economic policies of the Member States and of the Community.

On the basis of this conclusion, the Council shall, acting by a qualified majority, adopt a recommendation setting out these broad guidelines. The Council shall inform the European Parliament of its recommendation.

3. In order to ensure closer coordination of economic policies and sustained convergence of the economic performances of the Member States, the Council shall, on the basis of reports submitted by the Commission, monitor economic development in each of the Member States and in the Community as well as the consistency of economic policies with the broad guidelines referred to in paragraph 2, and regularly carry out an overall assessment.

For the purpose of this multilateral surveillance, Member States shall forward information to the Commission about important measures taken by them in the field of their economic policy and other information as they deem necessary.

4. Where it is established, under the procedure referred in paragraph 3, that the economic policies of a Member State are not consistent with the broad guidelines referred to in paragraph 2 or that they risk jeopardizing the proper functioning of economic and monetary union, the Council may, acting by a qualified majority on a recommendation from the Commission, make the necessary recommendations to the Member State concerned. The Council may, acting by a qualified majority on a proposal from the Commission, decide to make its recommendations public.

The President of the Council and the Commission shall report to the European Parliament on the result of multilateral surveillance. The President of the Council may be invited to appear before the competent Committee of the European Parliament if the Council has made its recommendations public.

5. The Council, acting in accordance with the procedure referred to in Article 189c, may adopt detailed rules for the multilateral surveillance procedure referred to in paragraphs 3 and 4 of this Article.

Article 103a

1. Without prejudice to any other procedures provided for in this Treaty, the Council may, acting unanimously on a proposal from the Commission, decide upon the measures appropriate to the economic situation, in particular if severe difficulties arise in the supply of certain products.

2. Where a Member State is in difficulties or is seriously threatened with severe difficulties caused by exceptional occurrences beyond its control, the

Council may, acting unanimously on a proposal from the Commission, grant, under certain conditions, Community financial assistance to the Member State concerned. Where the severe difficulties are caused by natural disasters, the Council shall act by qualified majority. The President of the Council shall inform the European Parliament of the decision taken.

Article 104

1. Overdraft facilities or any other type of credit facility with the ECB or with the central banks of the Member States (hereinafter referred to as "national central banks") in favour of Community institutions or bodies, central governments, regional, local or other public authorities, other bodies governed by public law, or public undertakings of Member States shall be prohibited, as shall the purchase directly from them by the ECB or national central banks of debt instruments.

2. The provisions of Paragraph 1 shall not apply to publicly-owned credit institutions which, in the context of the supply of reserves by central banks, shall be given the same treatment by national central banks and the ECB as private credit institutions.

Article 104a

1. Any measure, not based on prudential considerations, establishing privileged access by Community institutions or bodies, central governments, regional, local or other public authorities, other bodies governed by public law, or public undertakings of Member States to financial institutions shall be prohibited.

2. The Council, acting in accordance with the procedure referred to in Article 189c, shall, before 1 January 1994, specify definitions for the application of the prohibition referred to in paragraph 1.

Article 104b

1. The Community shall not be liable for or assume the commitments of central governments, regional, local or other public authorities, other bodies governed by public law, or public undertakings of any Member State, without prejudice to mutual financial guarantees for the joint execution of a specific project. A Member State shall not be liable for or assume the commitment of central governments, regional, local or other public authorities, other bodies governed by public law or public undertakings of another Member State, without prejudice to mutual financial guarantees for the joint execution of a specific project.

2. If necessary, the Council, acting in accordance with the procedure referred to in Article 189c, may specify definitions for the application of the prohibitions referred to in Article 104 and in this Article.

Article 104c

1. Member States shall avoid excessive governmental deficits.

2. The Commission shall monitor the development of the budgetary situation and of the stock of government debt in the Member States with a view to identifying gross errors. In particular it shall examine compliance with budgetary discipline on the basis of the following two criteria:

(a) whether the ratio of the planned or actual government deficit to gross domestic product exceeds a reference value, unless

– either the ratio has declined substantially and continuously and reached a level that comes close to the reference value;

– or, alternatively, the excess over the reference value is only exceptional and temporary and the ratio remains close to the reference value;

(b) whether the ratio of government debt to gross domestic product exceeds a reference value, unless the ratio is sufficiently diminishing and approaching the reference value at a satisfactory pace.

The reference values are specified in the Protocol on the excessive deficit procedure annexed to this Treaty.

3. If a Member State does not fulfil the requirements under one or both of these criteria, the Commission shall prepare a report. The report of the Commission shall also take into account whether the government deficit exceeds government investment expenditure and take into account all other relevant factors, including the medium term economic and budgetary position of the Member State.

The Commission may also prepare a report if, notwithstanding the fulfillment of the requirement under the criteria, it is of the opinion that there is a risk of an excessive deficit in a Member State.

4. The Committee provided for in Article 109c shall formulate an opinion on the report of the Commission.

5. If the Commission considers that an excessive deficit in a Member State exists or may occur, the Commission shall address an opinion to the Council.

6. The Council shall, acting by a qualified majority

on a recommendation from the Commission, and having considered any observations which the Member State concerned may wish to make, decide after an overall assessment whether an excessive deficit exists.

7. Where the existence of an excessive deficit is decided according to paragraph 6, the Council shall make recommendations to the Member State concerned with a view to bringing that situation to an end within a given period. Subject to the provisions of paragraph 8, these recommendations shall not be made public.

8. Where it establishes that there has been no effective action in response to its recommendations within the period laid down, the Council may make its recommendations public.

9. If a Member State persists in failing to put into practice the recommendations of the Council, the Council may decide to give notice to the Member State to take, within a specified time limit, measures for the deficit reduction which is judged necessary by the Council in order to remedy the situation.

In such a case, the Council may request the Member State concerned to submit reports in accordance with a specific timetable in order to examine the adjustment efforts of that Member State.

10. The right to bring actions provided for in Articles 169 and 170 may not be exercised within the framework of paragraphs 1 to 9 of this Article.

11. As long as a Member State fails to comply with a decision taken in accordance with paragraph 9, the Council may decide to apply or, as the case may be, intensify one or more of the following measures:

– to require the Member State concerned shall publish additional information, to be specified by the Council, before issuing bonds and securities;

– to invite the European Investment Bank to reconsider its lending policy towards the Member State concerned;

– to require the Member State concerned to make a non-interest-bearing deposit of an appropriate size with the Community until the excessive deficit has, in the view of the Council, been corrected;

– to impose fines of an appropriate size.

The President of the Council shall inform the European Parliament of the decisions taken.

12. The Council shall abrogate some or all of its decisions referred to in paragraphs 6 to 9 and 11 to the extent that the excessive deficit in the Member State concerned has, in the view of the Council, been corrected. If the Council has previously made public recommendations, it shall, as soon as the decision under paragraph 8 has been abrogated, make a public statement that an excessive deficit in the Member State concerned no longer exists.

13. When taking the decisions referred to in paragraphs 7 to 9, 11 and 12, the Council shall act on a recommendation from the Commission by a majority of two thirds of the votes of its members weighted in accordance with Article 148(2), excluding the votes of the representative of the Member State concerned.

14. Further provisions relating to the implementation of the procedure described in this Article are set out in the Protocol on the excessive deficit procedure annexed to this Treaty.

The Council shall, acting unanimously on a proposal from the Commission and after consulting the European Parliament and the ECB, adopt the appropriate provisions which shall then replace the said Protocol.

Subject to the other provisions of this paragraph the Council shall, before 1 January 1994, acting by a qualified majority on a proposal from the Commission and after consulting the European Parliament, lay down detailed rules and definitions for the application of the provisions of the said Protocol.

CHAPTER 2

MONETARY POLICY

Article 105

1. The primary objective of the ESCB shall be to maintain price stability. Without prejudice to the objective of price stabilty, the ESCB shall support the general economic policies in the Community with a view to contributing to the achievement of the objectives of the Community as laid down in Article 2. The ESCB shall act in accordance with the principle of an open market economy with free competition, favouring an efficient allocation of resources, and in compliance with the principles set out in Article 3a.

2. The basic tasks to be carried out through the ESCB shall be:

– to define and implement the monetary policy of the Community;

– to conduct foreign exchange operations consistent with the provisions of Article 109;

– to hold and manage the official foreign reserves of the Member States;

– to promote the smooth operation of payment systems.

3. The third indent of paragraph 2 shall be without prejudice to the holding and management by the government of Member States of foreign exchange working balances.

4. The ECB shall be consulted:

– on any proposed Community act in its fields of competence;

– by national authorities regarding any draft legislative provision in its fields of competence, but within the limits and under the conditions set out by the Council in accordance with the procedure laid down in Article 106(6).

The ECB may submit opinions to the appropriate Community institutions or bodies or to national authorities on matters within its fields of competence.

5. The ESCB shall contribute to the smooth conduct of policies pursued by the competent authorities relating to the prudential supervision of credit institutions and the stability of the financial system.

6. The Council may, acting unanimously on a proposal from the Commission and after consulting the ECB and after receiving the assent of the European Parliament, confer upon the ECB specific tasks concerning policies relating to the prudential supervision of credit institutions and other financial institutions with the exception of insurance undertakings.

Article 105a

1. The ECB shall have the exclusive right to authorize the issue of bank note within the Community. The ECB and the national central banks may issue such notes. The bank notes issued by the ECB and the national central banks shall be the only such notes to have the status of legal tender within the Community.

2. Member States may issue coins subject to approval by the ECB of the volume of the issue. The Council may, acting in accordance with the procedure referred to in Article 189c and after consulting the EDB, adopt measures to harmonize the denominations and technical specifications of all coins intended for circulation to the extent necessary to permit their smooth circulation within the Community.

Article 106

1. The ESCB shall be composed of the ECB and of the national central banks.

2. The ECB shall have legal personality.

3. The ESCB shall be governed by the decision-making bodies of the ECB which shall be the Governing Council and the Executive Board.

4. The Statute of the ESCB is laid down in a Protocol annexed to this Treaty.

5. Articles 5.1, 5.2, 5.3, 17, 18, 19.1, 22, 23, 24, 26, 32.2, 32.3. 32.4, 32.6, 33.l(a) and 36 of the Statute of the ESCB may be amended by the Council, acting either by a qualified majority on a recommendation from the ECB and after consulting the Commission or unanimously on a proposal from the Commission and after consulting the ECB. In either case, the assent of the European Parliament shall be required.

6. The Council, acting by a qualified majority either on a proposal from the Commission and after consulting the European Parliament and the ECB or on a recommendation from the ECB and after consulting the European Parliament and the Commission, shall adopt the provisions referred to in Articles 4, 5.4, 19.2, 20, 28-1, 29.2, 30.4 and 34.3 of the Statute of the ESCB.

Article 107

When exercising the powers and carrying out the tasks and duties conferred upon them by this Treaty and the Statute of the ESCB, neither the ECB, nor a national central bank, nor any member of their decision-making bodies shall seek or take instructions from Community institutions or bodies, from any government of a Member State or from any other body. The Community institutions and bodies and the governments of the Member States undertake to respect this principle and not to seek to influence the members of the decision-making bodies of the ECB or of the national central banks in the performance of their tasks.

Article 108

Each Member State shall ensure, at the latest at the date of the establishment of the ESCB, that its national legislation including the statutes of its national central bank is compatible with this Treaty and the Statute of the ESCB.

Article 108a

1. In order to carry out the tasks entrusted to the ESCB, the ECB shall, in accordance with the provisions of this Treaty and under the conditions laid down in the Statute of the ESCB:

– make regulations to the extent necessary to implement the tasks defined in Article 3.1, first indent,

Articles 19.1, 22 or 25.2 of the Statute of the ESCB and in cases which shall be laid down in the acts of the Council referred to in Article 106(6);

– take decisions necessary for carrying out the tasks entrusted to the ESCB under this Treaty and the Statute of the ESCB;

– make recommendations and deliver opinions.

2. A regulation shall have general application. It shall be binding in its entirety and directly applicable in all Member States.

Recommendations and opinions shall have no binding force.

A decision shall be binding in its entirety upon those to whom it is addressed.

Articles 190 to 192 shall apply to regulations and decisions adopted by the ECB.

The ECB may decide to publish its decisions, recommendations and opinions.

3. Within the limits and under the conditions adopted by the Council under the procedure laid down in Article 106(6), the ECB shall be entitled to impose fines or periodic penalty payments on undertakings for failure to comply with obligations under its regulations and decisions.

Article 109

1. By way of derogation from Article 228, the Council may, acting unanimously on a recommendation from the ECB or from the Commission, and after consulting the ECB in an endeavour to reach a consensus consistent with the objective of price stability, after consulting the European Parliament, in accordance with the procedure in paragraph 3 for determining the arrangements, conclude formal agreements on an exchange rate system for the ECU in relation to non-Community currencies. The Council may, acting by a qualified majority on a recommendation from the ECB or from the Commission, and after consulting the ECB in an endeavour to reach a consensus consistent with the objective of price stability, adopt, adjust or abandon the central rates of the ECU within the exchange rate system. The President of the Council shall inform the European Parliament of the adoption, adjustment or abandonment of the ECU central rates.

2. In the absence of an exchange rate system in relation to one or more non-Community currencies as referred to in paragraph 1, the Council, acting by a qualified majority either on a recommendation from the Commission and after consulting the ECB or on a recommendation from the ECB, may formulate gene-

ral orientations for exchange-rate policy in relation to these currencies. These general orientations shall be without prejudice to the primary objective of the ESCB to maintain price stability.

3. By way of derogation from Article 228, where agreements concerning monetary or foreign exchange regime matters need to be negotiated by the Community with one or more States or international organizations, the Council, acting by a qualified majority on a recommendation from the Commission and after consulting the ECB, shall decide the arrangements for the negotiation and for the conclusion of such agreements. These arrangements shall ensure that the Community expresses a single position. The Commission shall be fully associated with the negotiations.

Agreements concluded in accordance with this paragraph shall be binding on the institutions of the Community, on the ECB and on Member States.

4. Subject to paragraph 1, the Council shall, on a proposal from the Commission and after consulting the ECB, acting by a qualified majority decide on the position of the Community at international level as regards issues of particular relevance to economic and monetary union and, acting unanimously, decide its representation in compliance with the allocation of powers laid down in Articles 103 and 105.

5. Without prejudice to Community competence and Community agreements as regards Economic and Monetary Union, Member States may negotiate in international bodies and conclude international agreements.

CHAPTER 3

INSTITUTIONAL PROVISION

Article 109a

1. The Governing Council of the ECB shall comprise the members of the Executive Board of the ECB and the Governors of the national central banks.

2 (a) The Executive Board shall comprise the President, the Vice-President and four other members.

(b) The President, the Vice-President and the other members of the Executive Board shall be appointed from among the persons of recognized standing and professional experience in monetary or banking matters by common accord of the Governments of the Member States at the level of Heads of State or of Government, on a recommendation from the Council, after it has consulted the European Parliament and the Governing Council of the ECB.

Their term of office shall be eight years and shall not be renewable.

Only nationals of Member States may be members of the Executive Board.

Article 109b

1. The President of the Council and a member of the Commission may participate, without having the right to vote, in meetings of the Governing Council of the ECB.

The President of the Council may submit a motion for deliberation to the Governing Council of the ECB.

2. The President of the ECB shall be invited to participate in Council meetings when the Council is discussing matters relating to the objectives and tasks of the ESCB.

3. The ECB shall address an annual report on the activities of the ESCB and on the monetary policy of both the previous and current year to the European Parliament, the Council and the Commission, and also to the European Council. The President of the ECB shall present this report to the Council and to the European Parliament, which may hold a general debate on that basis.

The President of the ECB and the other members of the Executive Board may, at the request of the European Parliament or on their own initiative, be heard by the competent Committees of the European Parliament.

Article 109c

1. In order to promote coordination of the policies of Member States to the full extent needed for the functioning of the internal market, a Monetary Committee with advisory status is hereby set up.

It shall have the following tasks:

– to keep under review the monetary and financial situation of the Member States and of the Community and the general payments system of the Member States and to report regularly thereon to the Council and to the Commission;

– to deliver opinions at the request of the Council or of the Commission, or on its own initiative for submission to those institutions;

– without prejudice to Article 151, to contribute to the preparation of the work of the Council referred to in Articles 73f, 73g, 103(2), (3), (4) and (5), 103a, 104a, 104b, 104c, 109e(2), 109f(6), 109h, 109i, 109j(2) and 109k(1);

– to examine, at least once a year, the situation regarding the movement of capital and the freedom of payments, as they result from the application of this Treaty and of measures adopted by the Council; the examination shall cover all measures relating to capital movements and payments; the Committee shall report to the Commission and to the Council on the outcome of this examination.

The Member States and the Commission shall each appoint two members of the Monetary Committee.

2. At the start of the third stage, and Economic and Financial Committee shall be set up. The Monetary Committee provided for in paragraph 1 shall be dissolved.

The Economic and Financial Committee shall have the following tasks:

– to deliver opinions at the request of the Council or of the Commission, or on its own initiative for submission to those institutions;

– to keep under review the economic and financial situation of the Member States and of the Community and to report regularly thereon to the Council and to the Commission, in particular on financial relations with third countries and international institutions;

– without prejudice to Article 151, to contribute to the preparation of the work of the Council referred to in Articles 73f, 73g, 103(2), (3),(4) and (5), 103a, 104a, 104b, 104c, 105(6), 105a(2), 106(5) and (6), 109, 109h, 109i(2) and (3), 109k(2), 109l(4) and (5), and to carry out other advisory and preparatory tasks assigned to it by the Council;

– to examine, at least once a year, the situation regarding the movement of capital and the freedom of payments, as they result from the application of this Treaty and of measures adopted by the Council; the examination shall cover all measures relating to capital movements and payments; the committee shall report to the Commission and to the Council on the outcome of this examination.

The Member States, the Commission and the ECB shall each appoint no more than two members of the Committee.

3. The Council shall, acting by qualified majority on a proposal from the Commission and after consulting the ECB and the Committee referred to in the Article, lay down detailed provisions concerning the composition of the Economic and Financial Committee. The President of the Council shall inform the European Parliament of such a decision.

4. In addition to the tasks set out in paragraph 2, if

and as long as there are Member States with a derogation as referred to in Articles 109k and 109l, the Committee shall keep under review the monetary and financial situation and the general payments system of those Member States and report regularly thereon to the Council and to the Commission.

Article 109d

For matters within the scope of Articles 103(4), 104c with the exception of paragraph 14, 109, 109j, 109k and 109l(4) and (5), the Council or a Member State may request the Commission to make a recommendation or a proposal, as appropriate. The Commission shall examine this request and submit its conclusions to the Council without delay.

CHAPTER 4

TRANSITIONAL PROVISIONS

Article 109e

1. The second stage for achieving economic and monetary union shall begin on 1 January 1994.

2. Before that date

(a) each Member State shall:

- adopt, where necessary, appropriate measures to comply with the prohibitions laid down in Article 73b, without prejudice to Article 73e, and in Articles 104 and 104a(1);

- adopt, if necessary, with a view to permitting the assessment provided for in subparagraph (b), multiannual programmes intended to ensure the lasting convergence necessary for the achievement of economic and monetary union, in particular with regard to price stability and sound public finances;

(b) the Council shall, on the basis of a report from the Commission, assess the progress made with regard to economic and monetary convergence, in particular with regard to price stability and sound public finances, and the progress made with the implementation of Community law concerning the internal market.

3. The provisions of Articles 104, 104a(1), 104b(1), and 104c with the exception of paragraphs 1,9,11 and 14 shall apply from the beginning of the second stage.

The provision of Articles 103a(2), 104c(1), (9) and (11), 105, 105a, 107, 109, 109a, 109b and 109c(2) and (4) shall apply from the beginning of the third stage.

4. In the second stage, Member States shall endeavour to avoid excessive government deficits.

5. During the second stage, each Member State shall, as appropriate, start the process leading to the independence of its central bank, and in accordance with Article 108.

Article 109f

1. At the start of the second stage, a European Monetary Institute (hereinafter referred to as "EMI") shall be established and take up its duties; it shall have legal personality and be directed and managed by a Council, consisting of a President and the Governors of the national central banks, one of whom shall be Vice-President.

The President shall be appointed by common accord of the Governments of the Member States at the level of Heads of State or of Government, on a recommendation from, as the case may be, the Committee of Governors of the central banks of the Member States (hereinafter referred to as "Committee of Governors") or the Council of the EMI, and after consulting the European Parliament and the Council. The President shall be selected from among persons of recognized standing and professional experience in monetary or banking matters. Only nationals of Member States may be President of the EMI. The Council of the EMI shall appoint the Vice-President.

The Statute of the EMI is laid down in a Protocol annexed to this Treaty.

The Committee of Governors shall be dissolved at the start of the second stage.

2. The EMI shall:

- strengthen cooperation between the national central banks;

- strengthen the coordination of monetary policies of the Member States, with the aim of ensuring price stability;

- monitor the functioning of the European Monetary System;

- hold consultations concerning issues falling within the competence of the national central banks and affecting the stability of financial institutions and markets;

- take over the tasks of the European Monetary Cooperation Fund, which shall be dissolved; the modalities of dissolution are laid down in the Statute of the EMI;

- facilitate the use of the ECU and oversee its development, including the smooth functioning of the ECU clearing system.

3. For the preparation of the third stage, the EMI shall:

– prepare the instruments and procedures necessary for carrying out a single monetary policy in the third stage;

– promote the harmonization, where necessary, of the rules and practices governing the collection, compilation and distribution of statistics in the areas in the areas within its field of competence;

– prepare the rules for operations to be undertaken by the national central banks within the framework of the ESCB;

– promote the efficiency of cross-border payments;

– supervise the technical preparation of ECU bank notes.

At the latest by 31 December 1996, the EMI shall specify the regulatory, organizational and logistical framework necessary for the ESCB to perform its tasks in the third stage. This framework shall be submitted for decision to the ECB at the date of its establishment.

4. The EMI, acting by a majority of two thirds of the members of its Council, may:

– formulate opinions or recommendations on the overall orientation of monetary policy and exchange rate policy as well as on related measures introduced in each Member State;

– submit opinions or recommendations to Governments and to the Council on policies which might affect the internal or external monetary situation in the Community and, in particular, the functioning of the European Monetary System;

– make recommendations to the monetary authorities of the Member States concerning the conduct of monetary policy.

5. The EMI, acting unanimously, may decide to publish its opinions and its recommendations.

6. The EMI shall be consulted by the Council regarding any proposed Community act within its field of competence.

Within the limits and under the conditions set out by the Council, acting by a qualified majority on a proposal from the Commission and after consulting the European Parliament and the EMI, the EMI shall be consulted by the authorities of the Member States on

any draft legislative provision within its field of competence.

7. The Council may, acting unanimously on a proposal from the Commission and after consulting the European Parliament and the EMI, confer upon the EMI other tasks for the preparation of the third stage.

8. Where this Treaty provides for a consultative role for the ECB, reference to the ECB shall be read as referring to the EMI before the establishment of the ECB. Where this Treaty provides for a consultative role for the EMI, references to the EMI shall be read, before 1 January 1994, as referring to the Committee of Governors.

9. During the second stage, the term "ECB" used in Articles 173, 175, 176, 177, 180 and 215 shall be read as referring to the EMI.

Article 109g

The currency composition of the ECU basket shall not be changed.

From the start of the third stage, the value of the ECU shall be irrevocably fixed in accordance with Article 109l(4).

Article 109h

1. Where a Member State is in difficulties or is seriously threatened with difficulties as regards its balance of payments either as a result of an overall disequilibrium in its balance of payments, or as a result of the type of currency at its disposal, and where such difficulties are liable in particular to jeopardize the functioning of the common market or the progressive implementation of the common commercial policy, the Commission shall immediately investigate the position of the State in question and the action which, making use of all means at its disposal, that State has taken or may take in accordance with the provisions of this Treaty. The Commission shall state what measures it recommends the State concerned to take.

If the action taken by a Member States and the measures suggested by the Commission do not prove sufficient to overcome the difficulties which have arisen or which threaten, the Commission shall, after consulting the Committee referred to in Article 109c, recommend to the Council the granting of mutual assistance and appropriate methods therefor.

The Commission shall keep the Council regularly informed of the situation of how it is developing.

2. The Council, acting by a qualified majority, shall grant such mutual assistance; it shall adopt directives or decisions laying down the conditions

and details of such assistance, which may take such forms as:

(a) a concerted approach to or within any other international organizations to which Member States may have recourse;

(b) measures needed to avoid deflection of trade where the State which is in difficulties maintains or reintroduces quantitative restrictions against third countries;

(c) the granting of limited credits by other Member States, subject to their agreement.

3. If the mutual assistance recommended by the Commission is not granted by the Council or if the mutual assistance granted and the measures taken are insufficient, the Commission shall authorize the State which is in difficulties to take protective measures, the conditions and details of which the Commission shall determine.

Such authorization may be revoked and such conditions and details may be changed by the Council acting by a qualified majority.

4. Subject to Article 109k(6), this Article shall cease to apply from the beginning of the third stage.

Article 109i

1. Where a sudden crisis in the balance of payments occurs and a decision within the meaning of Article 109h(2) is not immediately taken, the Member State concerned may, as a precaution, take the necessary protective measures. Such measures must cause the least possible disturbance in the functioning of the common market and must not be wider in scope than is strictly necessary to remedy the sudden difficulties which have arisen.

2. The Commission and the other Member State shall be informed of such protective measures not later than when they enter into force. The Commission may recommend to the Council the granting of mutual assistance under Article 109h.

3. After the Commission has delivered an opinion and the Committee referred to in Article 109c has been consulted, the Council may, acting by a qualified majority, decide that the State concerned shall amend, suspend or abolish the protective measures referred to above.

4. Subject to Article 109k(6), this Article shall cease to apply from the beginning of the third stage.

Article 109j

1. The Commission and the EMI shall report to the Council on the progress made in the fulfilment by the Member States of their obligations regarding the achievement of economic and monetary union. These reports shall include an examination of the compatibility between each Member State's national legislation, including the statutes of its national central bank, and Articles 107 and 108 of this Treaty and the Statute of the ESCB. The report shall also examine the achievement of a high degree of sustainable convergence by reference to the fulfilment by each Member State of the following criteria:

– the achievement of a high degree of price stability; this will be apparent from rate of inflation which is close to that of, at most, the three best performing Member States in terms of price stability;

– the sustainability of the government financial position; this will be apparent from having achieved a government budgetary position without a deficit that is excessive as determined in accordance with Article 104c(6);

– the observance of the normal fluctuation margins provided for by the Exchange Rate Mechanism of the European Monetary System, for at least two years, without devaluing against the currency of any other Member State;

– the durability of convergence achieved by the Member State and of its participation in the Exchange Rate Mechanism of the European Monetary System being reflected in the long-term interest rate levels.

The four criteria mentioned in this paragraph and the relevant periods over which they are to be respected are developed further in a Protocol annexed to this Treaty. The reports of the Commission and the EMI shall also take account of the development of the ECU, the results of the integration of markets, the situation and development of the balances of payments on current account and an examination of the development of unit labour costs and other price indices.

2. On the basis of these reports, the Council, acting by a qualified majority on a recommendation from the Commission, shall assess:

– for each Member State, whether it fulfils the necessary conditions for the adoption of a single currency;

– where a majority of the Member States fulfil the necessary conditions for the adoption of a single currency,

and recommend its findings to the Council, meeting in the composition of the Heads of State or of Government. The European Parliament shall be consulted and forward its opinion to the Council, meeting in the composition of the Heads of State or of Government.

3. Taking due account of the reports referred to in paragraph 1 and the opinion of the European Parliament referred to in paragraph 2, the Council, meeting in the composition of Heads of State or of Government, shall acting by a qualified majority, not later than 31 December 1996:

– decide, on the basis of the recommendations of the Council referred to in paragraph 2, whether a majority of the Member States fulfil the necessary conditions for the adoption of a single currency;

– decide whether it is appropriate for the Community to enter the third stage,

and if so

– set the date for the beginning of the third stage.

4. If by the end of 1997 the date for the beginning of the third stage has not been set, the third stage shall start on 1 January 1999. Before 1 July 1998, the Council, meeting in the composition of heads of State or of Government, after a repetition of the procedure provided for in paragraphs 1 and 2, with the exception of the second indent of paragraph 2, taking into account the reports referred to in paragraph 1 and the opinion of the European parliament, shall, acting by a qualified majority and on the basis of the recommendations of the Council referred to in paragraph 2, confirm which member States fulfil the necessary conditions for the adoption of a single currency.

Article 109k

1. If the decision has been taken to set the date in accordance with Article 109j(3), the Council shall, on the basis of its recommendation as referred to in Article 109j(2), acting by a qualified majority on a recommendation from the Commission, decide whether any, and if so which, Member States shall have a derogation as defined in paragraph 3 of this Article. Such Member States shall in this Treaty be referred to as "Member States with a derogation".

If the Council has confirmed which Member States fulfil the necessary conditions for the adoption of a single currency, in accordance with Article 109j(4), those Member States which do not fulfil the conditions shall have a derogation as defined in paragraph 3 of this Article. Such Member States shall in this Treaty be referred to as "Member States with a derogation".

2. At least once every two years, or at the request of a Member State with a derogation, the Commission and the ECB shall report to the Council in accordance with the procedure laid down in Article 109j(1). After consulting the European Parliament and after discussion in the Council, meeting in the composition of the Heads of State or of Government, the Council shall, acting by a qualified majority on a proposal from the Commission, decide which Member States with a derogation fulfil the necessary conditions on the basis of the criteria set out in Article 109j(1), and abrogate the derogations of the Member States concerned.

3. A derogation referred to in paragraph 1 shall entail that the following Articles do not apply to the Member State concerned: Articles 104c(9) and (11), 105(1),(2), (3) and (5), 105a, 108a, 109, 109a(2)(b). The exclusion of such a Member State and its national central bank from rights and obligations within the ESCB is laid down in Chapter IX of the Statute of the ESCB.

4. In Articles 105(1), (2) ,and (3), 105a, 108a, 109 and 109a(2)(b), "Member States" shall be read as "Member States without a derogation".

5. The voting rights of Member States with a derogation shall be suspended for the Council decisions referred to in the Articles of this Treaty mentioned in paragraph 3. In that case, by way of derogation from Articles 148 and 189a(1), a qualified majority shall be defined as two thirds of the votes of the representatives of the Member States without derogation weighted in accordance with Article 148(2), and unanimity of those Member States shall be required for an act requiring unanimity.

6. Articles 109h and 109i shall continue to apply to a Member State with a derogation.

Article 109l

1. Immediately after the decision on the date for the beginning of the third stage has been taken in accordance with Article 109j(3), or, as the case may be, immediately after 1 July 1998:

– the Council shall adopt the provisions referred to in Article 106(6);

– the governments of the Member States without a

derogation shall appoint, in accordance with the procedure set out in Article 50 of the Statute of the ESCB, the President, the Vice-President and the other members of the Executive Board of the ECB. If there are Member States with a derogation, the number of members of the Executive Board may be smaller than provided for in Article 11.1 of the Statute of the ESCB, but in no circumstances shall it be less than four.

As soon as the Executive Board is appointed, the ESCB and the ECB shall be established and shall prepare for their full operation as described in this Treaty and the Statute of the ESCB. The full exercise of their powers shall start from the first day of the third stage.

2. As soon as the ECB is established, it shall, if necessary, take over tasks of the EMI. The EMI shall go into liquidation upon the establishment of the ECB; the modalities of liquidation are laid down in the Statute of the EMI.

3. If and as long as there are Member States with a derogation, and without prejudice to Article 106(3) of this Treaty, the General Council of the ECB referred to in Article 45 of the Statute of the ESCB shall be constituted as a third decision-making body of the ECB.

4. At the starting date of the third stage, the Council shall, acting with the unanimity of the Member States without derogation, on a proposal from the Commission and after consulting the ECB, adopt the conversion rates at which their currencies shall be irrevocably fixed and at which irrevocably fixed rate the ECU shall be substituted for these currencies, and the ECU will become a currency in its own right. This measure shall by itself not modify the external value of the ECU. The Council shall, acting according to the same procedure, also take the other measures necessary for the rapid introduction of the ECU as the single currency of those Member States.

5. If it is decided, according to the procedure set out in Article 109k(2), to abrogate a derogation, the Council shall, acting with the unanimity of the Member States without a derogation and the Member State concerned, on a proposal from the Commission and after consulting the ECB, adopt the rate at which the ECU shall be substituted for the currency of the Member State concerned, and take the other measures necessary for the introduction of the ECU as the single currency in the Member State concerned.

Article 109m

1. Until the beginning of the third stage, each Member State shall treat its exchange rate policy as a matter of common interest. In doing so, Member States shall take account of the experience acquired in cooperation within the framework of the European Monetary System (EMS) and in developing the ECU, and shall respect existing powers in this field.

2. From the beginning of the third stage and for as long as a member State has a derogation, paragraph 1 shall apply by analogy to the exchange rate policy of that Member State."

26) In Title II of Part Three, the title of Chapter 4 shall be replaced by the following:

TITLE VII

COMMON COMMERCIAL POLICY

27) Article 111 shall be repealed.

28) Article 113 shall be replaced by the following:

Article 113

1. The common commercial policy shall be based on uniform principles, particularly in regard to changes in tariff rates, the conclusion of tariff and trade agreements, the achievement of uniformity in measures of liberalization, export policy and measures to protect trade such as those to be taken in the event of dumping or subsidies.

2. The Commission shall submit proposals to the Council for implementing the common commercial policy.

3. Where agreements with one or more States or international organizations need to be negotiated, the Commission shall make recommendations to the Council, which shall authorize the Commission to open the necessary negotiations.

The Commission shall conduct these negotiations in consultation with a special committee appointed by the Council to assist the Commission in this task and within the framework of such directives as the Council may issue to it.

The relevant provision of Article 228 shall apply.

4. In exercising the powers conferred upon it by this Article, the Council shall act by a qualified majority."

29) Article 114 shall be repealed.

30) Article 115 shall be replaced by the following:

Article 115

In order to ensure that the execution of measures of commercial policy taken in accordance with this Treaty by any Member State is not obstructed by deflection of trade, or where differences between such measures lead to economic difficulties in one or more Member States, the Commission shall recommend the methods for the requisite cooperation between Member States. Failing this, the Commission may authorise Member States to take the necessary protective measures, the conditions and details of which it shall determine.

In case of urgency, Member States shall request authorization to take the necessary measures themselves from the Commission, which shall take a decision as soon as possible; the Member States concerned shall then notify the measures to the other Member States. The Commission may decide at any time that the Member States concerned shall amend or abolish the measures in question.

In the selection of such measures, priority shall be given to those which cause the least disturbance to the functioning of the common market."

31) Article 116 shall be repealed.

[This section includes provisions on social policy, education, vocational training and youth; culture; public health; consumer protection; Trans-European networks; industry; economic and social cohesion; research and technological development; environment; and development cooperation.]

TITLE VIII: Social Policy, Education, Vocational Training and Youth [. . .]

TITLE IX: Culture [. . .]

TITLE X: Public Health [. . .]

TITLE XI: Consumer Protection [. . .]

TITLE XII: Trans-European networks [. . .]

TITLE XIII: Industry [. . .]

TITLE XIV: Economic and social cohesion [. . .]

TITLE XV: Research and technological development [. . .]

TITLE XVI: Environment [. . .]

TITLE XVII: Development cooperation [. . .]

E. In Part Five "Institutions of the Community

39) Article 137 shall be replaced by the following:

Article 137

"The European Parliament, which shall consist of representatives of the peoples of the States brought together in the Community, shall exercise the powers conferred upon it by this Treaty."

40) Paragraph 3 of Article 138 shall be replaced by the following:

"3. The European Parliament shall draw up proposals for elections by direct universal suffrage in accordance with a uniform procedure in all Member States.

The Council shall, acting unanimously after obtaining the assent of the European Parliament, which shall act by a majority of its component members, lay down the appropriate provision, which it shall recommend to Member States for adoption in accordance with their respective constitutional requirements."

41) The following Article shall be inserted:

Article 138a

Political parties at European level are important as a factor for integration within the Union. They contribute to forming a European awareness and to expressing the political will of the citizens of the Union.

Article 138b

In so far as provided in this Treaty, the European Parliament shall participate in the process leading up to the adoption of Community acts by exercising its powers under the procedures laid down in Articles 189b and 189c and by giving its assent or delivering advisory opinions.

The European Parliament may, acting by a majority of its members, request the Commission to submit any appropriate proposal on matters on which it considers that a Community act is required for the purpose of implementing this Treaty.

Article 138c

In the course of its duties, the European Parliament may, at the request of a quarter of its members, set up a temporary Committee of Inquiry to investigate, without prejudice to the powers conferred by this Treaty on other institutions or bodies, alleged contraventions or maladministration in the implementation of Community law, except where the alleged facts are being examined before a court and while the case is still subject to legal proceedings.

The temporary Committee of Inquiry shall cease to exist on the submission of its report.

The detailed provisions governing the exercise of the right of inquiry shall be determined by common accord of the European Parliament, the Council and the Commission.

Article 138d

Any citizen of the Union, and any natural or legal person residing or having his registered office in a Member State, shall have the right to address, individually or in association with other citizens or persons, a petition to the European Parliament on a matter which comes within the Community's fields of activity and which affects him, her or it directly.

Article 138e

1. The European Parliament shall appoint an Ombudsman empowered to receive complaints from any citizen of the Union or any natural or legal person residing or having his registered office in a Member State concerning instances of maladministration in the activities of the Community institutions or bodies, with the exception of the Court of Justice and the Court of First Instance acting in their judicial role.

In accordance with his duties, the Ombudsman shall conduct inquiries for which he finds grounds, either on his own initiative or on the basis of complaints submitted to him direct or through a member of the European Parliament, except where the alleged facts are or have been the subject of legal proceedings. Where the Ombudsman establishes an instance of maladministration, he shall refer the matter to the institution concerned, which shall have a period of three months in which to inform him of its views. The Ombudsman shall then forward a report to the European Parliament and the institution concerned. The person lodging the complaint shall be informed of the outcome of such inquiries.

The Ombudsman shall submit an annual report to the European Parliament on the outcome of his inquiries.

2. The Ombudsman shall be appointed after each election of the European Parliament for the duration of its term of office. The Ombudsman shall be eligible for reappointment.

The Ombudsman may be dismissed by the Court of Justice at the request of the European Parliament if he no longer fulfils the conditions required for the performance of his duties or if he is guilty of serious misconduct.

3. The Ombudsman shall be completely independent in the performance of his duties. In the performance of those duties he shall neither seek nor take instructions from any body. The Ombudsman may not, during his term of office, engage in any other occupation, whether gainful or not.

4. The European Parliament shall, after seeking an opinion from the Commission and with the approval of the Council acting by a qualified majority, lay down the regulations and general conditions governing the performance of the Ombudsman's duties."

42) The second subparagraph of Article 144 shall be supplemented by the following sentence:

"In this case, the term of office of the members of the Commission appointed to replace them shall expire on the date on which the term of office of the members of the Commission obliged to resign as a body would have expired."

43) The following Article shall be inserted:

Article 146

The Council shall consist of a representative of each Member State at ministerial level, authorized to commit the government of that Member State.

The office of President shall be held in turn by each Member State in the Council for a term of six months, in the following order of Member States:

– for a first cycle of six years: Belgium, Denmark, Germany, Greece, Spain, France, Ireland, Italy, Luxembourg, Netherlands, Portugal, United Kingdom;

– for the following cycle of six years: Denmark, Belgium, Greece, Germany, France, Spain, Italy, Ireland, Netherlands, Luxembourg, United Kingdom, Portugal.

44) The following Article shall be inserted:

Article 147

The Council shall meet when convened by its President on his own initiative or at the request of one of its members or of the Commission."

45) Article 149 shall be repealed.

46) The following Article shall be inserted:

Article 151

1. A committee consisting of the Permanent Representatives of the Member States shall be responsible for preparing the work of the Council and for carrying out the tasks assigned to it by the Council.

2. The Council shall be assisted by a General Secretariat, under the direction of a Secretary-General. The Secretary-General shall be appointed by the Council acting unanimously.

The Council shall decide on the organization of the General Secretariat.

3. The Council shall adopt its rules of procedure."

47) The following Article shall be inserted:

Article 154

The Council shall, acting by a qualified majority, determine the salaries, allowances and pensions of the President and members of the Commission, and of the President, Judges, Advocates-General and Registrar of the Court of Justice. It shall also, again by a qualified majority, determine any payment to be made instead of remuneration."

48) The following Articles shall be inserted:

Article 156

The Commission shall publish annually, not later than one month before the opening of the session of the European Parliament, a general report on the activities of the Community.

Article 157

1. The Commission shall consist of seventeen members, who shall be chosen on the grounds of their general competence and whose independence is beyond doubt.

The number of members of the Commission may be altered by the Council, acting unanimously.

Only nationals of Member States may be members of the Commission.

The Commission must include at least one national of each of the Member States, but may not include more than two members having the nationality of the same State.

2. The members of the Commission shall, in the general interest of the Community, be completely independent in the performance of their duties.

In the performance of these duties, they shall neither seek nor take instructions from any government or from any other body. They shall refrain from any action incompatible with their duties. Each Member State undertakes to respect this principle and not to seek to influence the members of the Commission in the performance of their tasks.

The members of the Commission may not, during their term of office, engage in any other occupation, whether gainful or not. When entering upon their duties they shall give a solemn undertaking that, both during and after their term of office, they will respect the obligations arising therefrom and in particular their duty to behave with integrity and discretion as regards the acceptance, after they have ceased to hold office, of certain appointments or benefits. In the events of any breach of these obligations, the Court of Justice may, on application by the Council or the Commission, rule that the member concerned be, according to the circumstances, either compulsorily retired in accordance with Article 160 or deprived of his rights to a pension or other benefits in its stead.

Article 158

1. The members of the Commission shall be appointed, in accordance with the procedure referred to in paragraph 2, for a period of five years, subject, if need be, to Article 144.

Their term of office shall be renewable.

2. The governments of the Member States shall nominate by common accord, after consulting the European Parliament, the person they intend to appoint as President of the Commission.

The governments of the Member States shall, in consultation with the nominee for President, nominate the other persons whom they intend to appoint as members of the Commission.

The President and the other members of the Commission thus nominated shall be subject as a body to a vote of approval by the European Parliament. After approval by the European Parliament, the President and the other members of the Commission shall be appointed by common accord of the governments of the Member States.

3. Paragraphs 1 and 2 shall be applied for the first time to the President and the other members of the Commission whose term of office begins on 7 Janu-

ary 1995.

The President and the other members of the Commission whose term of office begins on 7 January 1993 shall be appointed by common accord of the governments of the Member States. Their term of office shall expire on 6 January 1995.

Article 159

Apart from normal replacement, or death, the duties of a member of the Commission shall end when he resigns or is compulsorily retired.

The vacancy thus caused shall be filled for the remainder of the member's term of office by a new member appointed by common accord of the governments of the Member States. The Council may, acting unanimously, decide that such a vacancy need not be filled.

In the event of resignation, compulsory retirement or death, the President shall be replaced for the remainder of his term of office. The procedure laid down in Article 158(2) shall be applicable for the replacement of the President.

Save in the case of compulsory retirement under Article 160, members of the Commission shall remain in office until they have been replaced.

Article 160

If any member of the Commission no longer fulfills the conditions required for the performance of his duties or if he has been guilty of serious misconduct, the Court of Justice may, on application by the Council or the Commission, compulsorily retire him.

Article 161

The Commission may appoint a Vice-President or two Vice-Presidents from among its members.

Article 162

1. The Council and the Commission shall consult each other and shall settle by common accord their methods of cooperation.

2. The Commission shall adopt its rules of procedure so as to ensure that both it and its departments operate in accordance with the provisions of this Treaty. It shall ensure that these rules are published.

Article 163

The Commission shall act by a majority of the number of members provided for in Article 157. A meeting of the Commission shall be valid only if the number of members laid down in its rules of procedure is present.

49) Article 165 shall be replaced by the following:

Article 165

The Court of Justice shall consist of thirteen judges.

The Court of Justice shall sit in plenary session. It may, however, form chambers, each consisting of three of five judges, either to undertake certain preparatory inquiries or to adjudicate on particular categories of cases in accordance with rules laid down for these purposes.

The Court of Justice shall sit in plenary session when a Member State or a Community institution that is a party to the proceedings so requests.

Should the Court of Justice so request, the Council may, acting unanimously, increase the number of judges and make necessary adjustments to the second and third paragraphs of this Article and to the second of Article 167.

50) Article 168a shall be replaced by the following:

Article 168a

1. The Court of First Instance shall be attached to the Court of Justice with jurisdiction to hear and determine at first instance, subject to a right of appeal to the Court of Justice on points of law only and in accordance with the conditions laid down by Statute, certain classes of action or proceeding defined in accordance with the conditions laid down in paragraph 2. The Court of First Instance shall not be competent to hear and determine questions referred for a preliminary ruling under Article 177.

2. At the request of the Court of Justice and after consulting the European Parliament and the Commission, the Council, acting unanimously, shall determine the classes of action or proceeding referred to in paragraph 1 and the composition of the Court of First Instance and shall adopt the necessary adjustments and additional provisions to the Statute of the the Court of Justice. Unless the Council decides otherwise, the provisions of this Treaty relating to the Court of Justice, in particular the provisions of the Protocol on the Statute of the Court of Justice, shall apply to the Court of First Instance.

3. The members of the Court of First Instance shall be chosen from persons whose independence is beyond doubt and who possess the ability required for

appointment to judicial office; they shall be appointed by common accord of the governments of the Member States for a term of six years. The membership shall be partially renewed every three years. Retiring members shall be eligible for re-appointment.

4. The Court of First Instance shall establish its rules of procedure in agreement with the Court of Justice. Those rules shall require the unanimous approval of the Council.

51) Article 171 shall be replaced by the following:

Article 171

1. If the Court of Justice finds that a Member State has failed to fulfil an obligation under this Treaty, the State shall be required to take the necessary measures to comply with the judgment of the Court of Justice.

2. If the Commission considers that the Member State concerned has not taken such measures it shall, after giving that State the opportunity to submit its observations, issue a reasoned opinion specifying the points on which the Member State concerned has not complied with the judgment of the Court of Justice.

If the Member State concerned fails to take the necessary measures to comply with the Court's judgment within the time-limit laid down by the Commission, the latter may bring the case before the Court of Justice. In so doing it shall specify the amount of lump sum or penalty payment to be paid by the Member State concerned which it considers appropriate in the circumstances.

If the Court of Justice finds that the Member State concerned has not complied with its judgment it may impose a lump sum or penalty payment on it.

This procedure shall be without prejudice to Article 170.

52) Article 172 shall be replaced by the following:

Article 172

Regulations adopted jointly by the European Parliament and the Council, and by the Council, pursuant to the provisions of this Treaty, may give the Court of Justice unlimited jurisdiction with regard to the penalties provided for in such regulations."

53) Article 173 shall be replaced by the following:

Article 173

The Court of Justice shall review the legality of acts adopted jointly by the European Parliament and the Council, of acts of the Council, of the Commission and of the ECB, other than recommendations and opinions, and of acts of the European Parliament intended to produce legal effects vis-à-vis third parties.

It shall for this purpose have jurisdiction in actions brought by a Member State, the Council or the Commission on grounds of lack of competence, infringement of an essential procedural requirement, infringement of this Treaty or of any rule of law relating to its application, or misuse of powers.

The Court shall have jurisdiction under the same conditions, in actions brought by the European Parliament and by the ECB for the purpose of protecting their prerogatives.

Any natural or legal person may, under the same conditions, institute proceedings against a decision addressed to that person or against a decision which, although in the form of a regulation or a decision addressed to another person, is of direct and individual concern to the former.

The proceedings provided for in this Article shall be instituted within two months of the publication of the measure, or of its notification to the plaintiff, or, in the absence thereof, of the day on which it came to the knowledge of the latter, as the case may be.

54) Article 175 shall be replaced by the following:

Article 175

Should the European Parliament, the Council or the Commission, in infringement of this Treaty, fail to act, the Member States and the other institutions of the Community may bring an action before the Court of Justice to have the infringement established.

The action shall be admissible only if the institution concerned has first been called upon to act. If, within two months of being so called upon, the institution concerned has not defined its position, the action may be brought within a further period of two months.

Any natural or legal person may, under the conditions laid down in the preceding paragraphs, complain to the Court of Justice that an institution of the Community has failed to address to that person any act other than a recommendation or an opinion.

The Court of Justice shall have jurisdiction, under the same conditions, in actions or proceedings brought by the ECB in the areas falling within the latter's field of competence and in actions or proceedings brought against the latter.

55) Article 176 shall be replaced by the following:

Article 176

The institution or institutions whose act has been declared void or whose failure to act has been declared contrary to this Treaty shall be required to take the necessary measures to comply with the judgment of the Court of Justice.

This obligation shall not affect any obligation which may result from the application of the second paragraph of Article 215.

This Article shall also apply to the ECB.

56) Article 177 shall be replaced by the following:

Article 177

The Court of Justice shall have jurisdiction to give preliminary rulings concerning:

(a) the interpretation of this Treaty;

(b) the validity and interpretation of acts of the institutions of the Community and of the ECB;

(c) the interpretation of the statutes of bodies established by an act of the Council, where those statutes so provide.

Where such a question is raised before any court or tribunal of a Member State, that court or tribunal may, if it considers that a decision on the question is necessary to enable it to give judgment, request the Court of Justice to give a ruling thereon.

Where any such question is raised in a case pending before a court or tribunal of a Member State against whose decisions there is no judicial remedy under national law, that court or tribunal shall bring the matter before the Court of Justice."

57) Article 180 shall be replaced by the following:

Article 180

The Court of Justice shall, within the limits hereinafter laid down, have jurisdiction in disputes concerning:

(a) the fulfillment by Member States of obligations under the Statute of the European Investment Bank. In this connection, the Board of Directors of the Bank shall enjoy the powers conferred upon the Commission by Article 169;

(b) measures adopted by the Board of Governors of the European Investment Bank. In this connection, any Member State, the Commission or the Board of Directors of the Bank may institute proceedings under the conditions laid down in Article 173;

(c) measures adopted by the Board of Directors of the European Investment Bank. Proceedings against such measures may be instituted only by Member States or by the Commission, under the conditions laid down in Article 173, and solely on the grounds of non-compliance with the procedure provided for in Article 21(2), (5), (6) and (7) of the Statute of the Bank;

(d) the fulfillment by the national central banks of obligations under this Treaty and the Statute of the ESCB. In this connection the powers of the Council of the ECB in respect of national central banks shall be the same as those conferred upon the Commission in respect of Member States by Article 169. If the Court of Justice finds that a national central bank has failed to fulfill an obligation under this Treaty, that bank shall be required to take the necessary measures to comply with the judgment of the Court of Justice.

58) Article 184 shall be replaced by the following:

Article 184

Notwithstanding the expiry of the period laid down in the fifth paragraph of Article 173, any party may, in proceedings in which a regulation adopted jointly by the European Parliament and the Council, or a regulation of the Council, of the Commission, or of the ECB is at issue, plead the grounds specified in the second paragraph of Article 173 in order to invoke before the Court of Justice the inapplicability of that regulation."

[This section includes provisions on the court of auditors; the committee of the regions; and the European Investment Bank. Also, it provides for the amendments on the treaties of the ECSC and EAEC.]

SECTION 5 THE COURT OF AUDITORS [. . .]

CHAPTER 4 THE COMMITTEE OF THE REGIONS [. . .]

CHAPTER 5 EUROPEAN INVESTMENT BANK [. . .]

TITLE III: PROVISIONS AMENDING THE

TREATY ESTABLISHING THE EUROPEAN COAL AND STEEL COMMUNITY [...]

TITLE IV: PROVISIONS AMENDING THE TREATY ESTABLISHING THE EUROPEAN ATOMIC ENERGY COMMUNITY [...]

TITLE V

PROVISIONS ON A COMMON FOREIGN AND SECURITY POLICY

Article J

A common foreign and security policy is hereby established which shall be governed by the following provisions.

Article J.1

1. The union and its Member States shall define and implement a common foreign and security policy, governed by the provisions of the Title and covering all areas of foreign and security policy.

2. The objectives of the common foreign and security policy shall be:

– to safeguard the common values, fundamental interests and independence of the Union;

– to strengthen the security of the Union and its Member States in all ways;

– to preserve peace and strengthen international security, in accordance with the principles of the United Nations Charter as well as the principles of the Helsinki Final Act and the objectives of the Paris Charter;

– to promote international cooperation;

– to develop and consolidate democracy and the rule of law, and respect for human rights and fundamental freedoms.

3. The Union shall pursue these objectives;

– by establishing systematic cooperation between Member States in the conduct of policy, in accordance with Article J.2;

– by gradually implementing, in accordance with Article J.3, joint action in the areas in which the Member States have important interests in common.

4. The Member States shall support the Union's external and security policy actively and unreservedly in a spirit of loyalty and mutual solidarity. They shall refrain from any action which is contrary to the interests of the Union or likely to impair its effectiveness as a cohesive force in international relations. The Council shall ensure that these principles are complied with.

Article J.2

1. Member States shall inform and consult one another within the Council on any matter of foreign and security policy of general interest in order to ensure that their combined influence is exerted as effectively as possible by means of concerted and convergent action.

2. Whenever it deems it necessary, the Council shall define a common position. Member States shall ensure that their national policies conform on the common positions.

3. Member States shall coordinate their action in international organizations and at international conferences. They shall uphold the common positions in such fora.

In international organizations and at international conferences where not all the Member States participate, those which do take part shall uphold the common positions.

Article J.3

The procedure for adopting joint action in matters covered by foreign and security policy shall be the following:

1. The Council shall decide, on the basis of general guidelines from the European Council, that a matter should be the subject of joint action.

Whenever the Council decides on the principle of joint action, it shall lay down the specific scope, the Union's general and specific objectives in carrying out such action, if necessary its duration, and the means, procedures and conditions for its implementation.

2. The Council shall, when adopting the joint action and at any stage during its development, define those matters on which decisions are to be taken by a qualified majority.

Where the Council is required to act by a qualified majority pursuant to the preceding subparagraph, the votes of its members shall be weighted in accordance with Article 148(2) of the Treaty establishing the European Community, and for their adoption, acts of the Council shall require at least fifty-four votes in favour, cast by at least eight members.

3. If there is a change in circumstances having a

substantial effect on a question subject to joint action, the Council shall review the principles and objectives of that action and take the necessary decisions. As long as the Council has not acted, the joint action shall stand.

4. Joint actions shall commit the Member States in the positions they adopt and in the conduct of their activity.

5. Whenever there is any plan to adopt a national position or take national action pursuant to a joint action, information shall be provided in time to allow, if necessary, for prior consultations within the Council. The obligation to provide prior information shall not apply to measures which are merely a national transposition of Council decisions.

6. In cases of imperative need arising from changes in the situation and failing a Council decision, Member States may take the necessary measures as a matter of urgency having regard to the general objectives of the joint action. The Member State concerned shall inform the Council immediately of any such measures.

7. Should there be any major difficulties in implementing a joint action, a Member State shall refer them to the Council which shall discuss them and seek appropriate solutions. Such solutions shall not run counter to the objectives of the joint action or impair its effectiveness.

Article J.4

1. The common foreign and security policy shall include all questions related to the security of the Union, including the eventual framing of a common defence policy, which might in time lead to a common defence.

2. The Union requests the Western European Union (WEU), which is an integral part of the development of the Union, to elaborate and implement decisions and actions of the Union which have defence implications. The Council shall, in agreement with the institutions of the WEU, adopt the necessary practical arrangements.

3. Issues having defence implications dealt with under this Article shall not be subject to the procedures set out in Article J.3.

4. The policy of the Union in accordance with this Article shall not prejudice the specific character of the security and defence policy of certain Member States and shall respect the obligations of certain Member States under the North Atlantic Treaty and be compatible with the common security and defence policy established within that framework.

5. The provisions of this Article shall not prevent the development of closer cooperation between two or more Member States on a bilateral level, in the framework of the WEU and the Atlantic Alliance, provided such cooperation does not run counter to or impede that provided for in this Title.

6. With a view to furthering the objective of this Treaty, and having in view the date of 1998 in the context of Article XII of the Brussels Treaty, the provisions of this Article may be revised as provided for in Article N(2) on the basis of a report to be presented in 1996 by the Council to the European Council, which shall include an evaluation of the progress made and the experience gained until then.

Article J.5

1. The Presidency shall represent the Union in matters coming within the common foreign and security policy.

2. The Presidency shall be responsible for the implementation of common measures; in that capacity it shall in principle express the position of the Union in international organizations and international conferences.

3. In the tasks referred to in paragraphs 1 and 2, the Presidency shall be assisted if needs be by the previous and next Member States to hold the Presidency. The Commission shall be fully associated in these tasks.

4. Without prejudice to Article J.2(3) and Article J.3(4), Member States represented in international organizations or international conferences where not all the Member States participate shall keep the latter informed of any matter of common interest.

Member States which are also members of the United Nations Security Council will concert and keep the other Member States fully informed. Member States which are permanent members of the Security Council will, in the execution of their functions, ensure the defence of the positions and the interests of the Union, without prejudice to their responsibilities under the provisions of the United Nations Charter.

Article J.6

The diplomatic and consular missions of the Member States and the Commission Delegations in third countries and international conferences, and their representations to international organizations, shall cooperate in ensuring that the common positions and common measures adopted by the Council are complied with and implemented.

They shall step up cooperation by exchanging

information, carrying out joint assessments and contributing to the implementation of the provisions referred to in Article 8c of the Treaty establishing the European Community.

Article J.7

The Presidency shall consult the European Parliament on the main aspects and the basic choices of the common foreign and security policy and shall ensure that the views of the European Parliament are duly taken into consideration. The European Parliament shall be kept regularly informed by the Presidency and the Commission of the development of the Union's foreign and security policy.

The European Parliament may ask questions of the Council or make recommendations to it. It shall hold an annual debate on progress in implementing the common foreign and security policy.

Article J.8

1. The European Council shall define the principles of and general guidelines for the common foreign and security policy.

2. The Council shall take the decisions necessary for defining and implementing the common foreign and security policy on the basis of the general guidelines adopted by the European Council. It shall ensure the unity, consistency and effectiveness of action by the Union.

The Council shall act unanimously, except for procedural questions and in the case referred to in Article J.3(2).

3. Any Member State or the Commission may refer to the Council any question relating to the common foreign and security policy and may submit proposals to the Council.

4. In cases requiring a rapid decision, the Presidency, of its own motion, or at the request of the Commission or a Member State, shall convene an extraordinary Council meeting within forty-eight hours or, in an emergency, within a shorter period.

5. Without prejudice to Article 151 of the Treaty establishing the European Community, a Political Committee consisting of Political Directors shall monitor the international situation in the areas covered by common foreign and security policy and contribute to the definition of policies by delivering opinions to the Council at the request of the Council or on its own initiative. It shall also monitor the implementation of agreed policies, without prejudice to the responsibility of the Presidency and the Commission.

Article J.9

The Commission shall be fully associated with the work carried out in the common foreign and security policy field.

Article J.10

On the occasion of any review of the security provisions under Article J.4, the Conference which is convened to that effect shall also examine whether any other amendments need to be made to provisions relating to the common foreign and security policy.

Article J.11

1. The provisions referred to in Articles 137, 138, to 142, 146, 147, 150 to 153, 157 to 163 and 217 of the Treaty establishing the European Community shall apply to the provisions relating to the areas referred to in this Title.

2. Administrative expenditure which the provisions relating to the areas referred to in this Title entail for the institutions shall be charged to the budget of the European Communities.

The Council may also:

– either decide unanimously that operating expenditure to which the implementation of those provisions gives rise is to be charged to the budget of the European Communities; in that event, the budgetary procedure laid down in the Treaty establishing the European Community shall be applicable;

– or determine that such expenditure shall be charged to the Member States, where appropriate in accordance with a scale to be decided.

TITLE VI

PROVISIONS ON COOPERATION IN THE FIELDS OF JUSTICE AND HOME AFFAIRS

Article K

Cooperation in the fields of justice and home affairs shall be governed by the following provisions.

Article K.1

For the purposes of achieving the objectives of the Union, in particular the free movement of persons, and without prejudice to the powers of the European Community, Member States shall regard the following areas as matters of common interest:

1. asylum policy;

2. rules governing the crossing by persons of the external borders of the Member States and the exercise of controls thereon;

3. immigration policy and policy regarding nationals of third countries;

(a) conditions of entry and movement by nationals of third countries on the territory of Member States;

(b) conditions of residence by nationals of third countries on the territory of Member States, including family reunion and access to employment;

(c) combatting unauthorized immigration, residence and work by nationals of third countries on the territory of Member States;

4. combatting drug addiction in so far as this is not covered by 7 to 9;

5. combating fraud on an international scale in so far as this is not covered by 7 to 9;

6. judicial cooperation in civil matters;

7. judicial cooperation in criminal matters;

8. customs cooperation;

9. police cooperation for the purposes of preventing and combating terrorism, unlawful drug trafficking and other serious forms of international crime, including if necessary certain aspects of customs cooperation, in connection with the organization of a Union-wide system for exchanging information within a European Police Office (Europol).

Article K.2

1. The matters referred to in Article K.1 shall be dealt with in compliance with the European Convention for the Protection of Human Rights and Fundamental Freedoms of 4 November 1950 and the Convention relating to the Status of Refugees of 28 July 1951 and having regard to the protection afforded by Member States to persons persecuted on political grounds.

2. This Title shall not affect the exercise of the responsibilities incumbent upon Member States with regard to the maintenance of law and order and the safeguarding of internal security.

Article K.3

1. In the areas referred to in Article K.1, Member States shall inform and consult one another within the Council with a view to co-ordinating their action. To that end, they shall establish collaboration between the relevant departments of their administrations.

2. The Council may:

– on the initiative of any Member State or of the Commission, in the areas referred to in Article K.1(1) to (6);

– on the initiative of any Member State, in the areas referred to Article K1(7) to (9):

(a) adopt joint positions and promote, using the appropriate form and procedures, any cooperation contributing to the pursuit of the objectives of the Union;

(b) adopt joint action in so far as the objectives of the Union can be attained better by joint action than by the Member States acting individually on account of the scale or effects of the action envisaged; it may decide that measures implementing joint action are to be adopted by a qualified majority;

(c) without prejudice to Article 220 of the Treaty establishing the European Community, draw up conventions which it shall recommend to the Member States for adoption in accordance with their respective constitutional requirements.

Unless otherwise provided by such conventions, measures implementing them shall be adopted within the Council by a majority of two-thirds of the High Contracting Parties.

Such conventions may stipulate that the Court of Justice shall have jurisdiction to interpret their provisions and to rule on any disputes regarding their application, in accordance with such arrangements as they may lay down.

Article K.4

1. A Coordinating Committee shall be set up consisting of senior officials. In addition to its coordinating role, it shall be the task of the Committee to:

– give opinions for the attention of the Council, either at the Councils request or on its own initiative.

– contribute, without prejudice to Article 151 of the Treaty establishing the European Community, to the preparation of the Council's discussions in the areas referred to in Article K.1 and, in accordance with the conditions laid down in Article 100d of the Treaty establishing the European Community, in the areas referred to in Article 100c of that Treaty.

2. The Commission shall be fully associated with the work in the areas referred to in this Title.

3. The Council shall act unanimously, except on matters of procedure and in cases where Article K.3 expressly provides for other voting rules.

Where the Council is required to act by a qualified majority, the votes of its members shall be weighted as laid down in Article 148(2) of the Treaty establishing the European Community, and for their adoption, acts of the Council shall require at least fifty-four votes in favour, cast by at least eight members.

Article K.5

Within international organizations and at international conferences in which they take part, Member States shall defend the common positions adopted under the provisions of this Title.

Article K.6

The Presidency and the Commission shall regularly inform the European Parliament of discussions in the areas covered by this Title.

The Presidency shall consult the European Parliament on the principal aspects of activities in the areas referred to in this Title and shall ensure that the views of the European Parliament are duly taken into consideration.

The European Parliament may ask questions of the Council or make recommendations to it. Each year, it shall hold a debate on the progress made in implementation of the areas referred to in this Title.

Article K.7

The provisions of this Title shall not prevent the establishment or development of closer cooperation between two or more Member States in so far as such cooperation does not conflict with, or impede, that provided for in this Title.

Article K.8

1. The provisions referred to in Article 137, 138 to 142, 146, 147, 150 to 153, 157 to 163 and 217 of the Treaty establishing the European Community shall apply to the provisions relating to the areas referred

to in this Title.

2. Administrative expenditure which the provisions relating to the areas referred to in this Title entail for the institutions shall be charged to the budget of European Communities.

The Council may also:

– either decide unanimously that operating expenditure to which the implementation of those provisions gives rise is to be charged to the budget of the European Communities; in that event, the budgetary procedure laid down in the Treaty establishing the European Community shall be applicable;

– or determine that such expenditure shall be charged to the Member States, where appropriate in accordance with a scale to be decided.

Article K.9

The Council, acting unanimously on the initiative of the Commission or a Member State, may decide to apply Article 100c of the Treaty establishing the European Community to action in areas referred to in Article K.1(1) to (6), and at the same time determine the relevant voting conditions relating to it. It shall recommend the Member States to adopt that decision in accordance with their respective constitutional requirements.

TITLE VII

FINAL PROVISIONS

Article L

The provisions of the Treaty establishing the European Community, the Treaty establishing the European Coal and Steel Community and the Treaty establishing the European Atomic Energy Community concerning the powers of the Court of Justice of the European Communities and the exercise of those powers shall apply only to the following provisions of this Treaty:

(a) provisions amending the Treaty establishing the European Economic Community, the Treaty establishing the European Coal and Steel Community and the Treaty establishing the European Atomic Energy Community;

(b) the third subparagraph of Article K.3(2)(c);

(c) Articles L to S.

Article M

Subject to the provisions amending the Treaty establishing the European Economic Community with a view to establishing the European Community, the Treaty establishing the European Coal and Steel Community and the Treaty establishing the European Atomic Energy Community, and to these final provisions, nothing in this Treaty shall effect the Treaties establishing the European Communities or the subsequent Treaties and Acts modifying or supplementing them.

Article N

1. The government of any Member State or the Commission may submit to the Council proposals for the amendment of the Treaties on which the Union is founded.

If the Council, after consulting the European Parliament and, where appropriate, the Commission, delivers an opinion in favour of calling a conference of representatives of the governments of the Member States, the conference shall be convened by the President of the Council for the purpose of determining by common accord the amendments to be made to those Treaties. The European Central Bank shall also be consulted in the case of institutional changes in the monetary area.

The amendments shall enter into force after being ratified by all the Member States in accordance with their respective constitutional requirements.

2. A conference of representatives of the governments of the Member States shall be convened in 1996 to examine those provisions of this Treaty for which revision is provided, in accordance with the objectives set out in Articles A and B.

Article O

Any European State may apply to become a Member of the Union. It shall address its application to the Council, which shall act unanimously after consulting the Commission and after receiving the assent of the European Parliament, which shall act by an absolute majority of its component members.

The conditions of admission and the adjustments to the Treaties on which the Union is founded which such admission entails shall be the subject of an agreement between the Member States and the applicant State. This agreement shall be submitted for ratification by all the contracting States in accordance with their respective constitutional requirements.

Article P

1. Articles 2 to 7 and 10 to 19 of the Treaty establishing a single Council and a single Commission of the European Communities, signed in Brussels on 8 April 1965, are hereby repealed.

2. Article 2, Article 3(2) and Title III of the Single European Act signed in Luxembourg on 17 February 1986 and in the Hague on February 1986 are hereby repealed.

Article Q

This Treaty is concluded for an unlimited period.

Article R

1. This Treaty shall be ratified by the High Contracting Parties in accordance with their respective constitutional requirements. The instruments of ratification shall be deposited with the government of the Italian Republic.

2. This Treaty shall enter into force on 1 January 1993, provided that all the instruments of ratification have been deposited, or, failing that, on the first day of the month following the deposit of the instrument of ratification by the last signatory State to take this step.

Article S

This Treaty, drawn up in a single original in the Danish, Dutch, English, French, German, Greek, Irish, Italian, Portuguese and Spanish languages, the texts in each of these languages being equally authentic, shall be deposited in the archives of the government of the Italian Republic, which will transmit a certified copy to each of the governments of the other signatory States.

IN WITNESS WHEREOF, the undersigned Plenipotentiaries have signed this Treaty.

Agreement to Establish a South-North Joint Nuclear Control Commission

Date of signature: March 19, 1992
Place of signature: Seoul, Pyongyang
Signatory states: the Republic of Korea,

Democratic People's Republic of Korea
Date of entry into force: March 19, 1992

The South and the North, in order to implement the Joint Declaration of the Denuclearization of the Korean Peninsula, have agreed to organize and operate a South-North Joint Nuclear Control Commission (to be referred to as the Joint Nuclear Control Commission) as follows:

Article 1

The Joint Nuclear Control Commission shall be composed as follows:

1. The Joint Nuclear Control Commission shall be composed of seven members, including a chairman and a vice chairman, from each side. Only one or two of them shall be military officers on active duty. The chairmanship shall be filled by officials with the rank of vice minister.

2. Both parties shall notify the other side in advance if and when a member or members of the Joint Nuclear Control Commission are to be replaced.

3. Each side shall have a staff of six. When necessary, the size of the staffs may be readjusted by concurrence by both parties.

Article 2

The Joint Nuclear Control Commission shall discuss and carry out the following matters:

1. The adoption and disposition of protocols based on discussions of ways to implement the Joint Declaration of the Denuclearization of the Korean Peninsula and actions on other related matters.

2. Exchanges of information needed to verify the denuclearization of the Korean Peninsula (the range of such information to include nuclear facilities and nuclear materials, and suspected nuclear weapons and bases).

3. The composition and operation of inspection teams to verify the denuclearization of the Korean Peninsula.

4. The selection of objects of inspections to verify the denuclearization of the Korean Peninsula (such objects to include nuclear facilities and nuclear materials, and suspected nuclear weapons and bases), and the formulation of procedures and methods for such inspections.

5. Matters pertaining to equipment that may be used for nuclear inspections.

6. Remedial measures based on the results of nuclear inspections.

7. Settlement of disputes arising from the implementation of the Joint Declaration of the Denu-

clearization of the Korean Peninsula and inspections related thereto.

Article 3

The Joint Nuclear Control Commission shall be operated as follows:

1. The Joint Nuclear Control Commission shall in principle meet once every two months, providing, however, that it may meet at anytime by concurrence between both parties.

2. The Joint Nuclear Control Commission shall in principle meet alternately at the Peace House in the southern sector of Panmunjom and Tong-ilgak (the Unification Pavilion) in the northern sector. However, it may meet at any other place agreed to by both parties.

3. Meeting of the Joint Nuclear Control Commission shall be jointly presided over by the chairmen from both sides and shall in principle be held behind closed doors.

4. Guarantees of personal safety and provision of the necessary services for the personnel traveling from the other area to attend meetings of the Joint Nuclear Commission, and such administrative matters as the recording of proceeding of meetings shall comply with past practices.

5. Other matters necessary to operate the Joint Nuclear Control Commission shall be decided by consultation between both sides of the Commission.

Article 4

Accords reached at the Joint Nuclear Control Commission shall enter into force as of the day Prime Ministers of both sides sign the agreed documents. Depending on the situation, an important document agreed to by both sides shall enter into force as of the day when the appropriate instruments are exchanged after the procedures needed to bring it into force have been completed following its signature by the Prime Ministers of both sides.

Article 5

This Agreement may be revised or supplemented by concurrence between both parties.

Article 6

This Agreement shall enter into force as of the day its text is exchanged after it has been signed by the Prime Ministers of both sides.

Treaty on Open Skies

Date of signature: March 24, 1992
Place of signature: Helsinki
Signatory states: Belarus, Belgium, Bulgaria,
Canada, Czech Republic, Denmark, France,
Georgia, Germany, Greece, Hungary, Iceland,
Italy, Kyrgyzstan, Luxembourg, Netherlands,
Norway, Poland, Portugal, Romania, Russia,
Slovak Republic, Spain, Turkey, United Kingdom,
Ukraine, United States (as of September 6, 1996)
Ratification: Belgium, Bulgaria, Canada, Czech
Republic, Denmark, France, Germany, Greece,
Hungary, Iceland, Italy, Luxembourg, Netherlands,
Norway, Poland, Portugal, Romania, Slovak
Republic, Spain, Turkey, United Kingdom, United
States (Ratification by Russia, Belarus and
Ukraine is required for the Treaty to enter into
force, as of September 6, 1996)

The States concluding this Treaty, hereinafter referred to collectively as the States Parties or individually as a State Party,

Recalling the commitments they have made in the Conference on Security and Co-operation in Europe to promoting greater openness and transparency in their military activities and to enhancing security by means of confidence- and security-building measures,

Welcoming the historic events in Europe which have transformed the security situation from Vancouver to Vladivostok,

Wishing to contribute to the further development and strengthening of peace, stability and co-operative security in that area by the creation of an Open Skies regime for aerial observation,

Recognizing the potential contribution which an aerial observation regime of this type could make to security and stability in other regions as well,

Noting the possibility of employing such a regime to improve openness and transparency, to facilitate the monitoring of compliance with existing or future arms control agreements and to strengthen the capacity for conflict prevention and crisis management in the framework of the Conference on Security and Co-operation in Europe and in other relevant international institutions,

Envisaging the possible extension of the Open Skies regime into additional fields, such as the protection of the environment,

Seeking to establish agreed procedures to provide for aerial observation of all the territories of States Parties, with the intent of observing a single State Party or groups of States Parties, on the basis of equity and effectiveness while maintaining flight safety,

Noting that the operation of such an Open Skies regime will be without prejudice to States not participating in it,

Have agreed as follows:

Article I

General Provisions

1. This Treaty establishes the regime, to be known as the Open Skies regime, for the conduct of observation flights by States Parties over the territories of other States Parties, and sets forth the rights and obligations of the States Parties relating thereto.

2. Each of the Annexes and their related Appendices constitutes an integral part of this Treaty.

Article II

Definitions

For the purposes of this Treaty:

1. The term "observed Party" means the State Party or group of States Parties over whose territory an observation flight is conducted or is intended to be conducted, from the time it has received notification thereof from an observing Party until completion of the procedures relating to that flight, or personnel acting on behalf of that State Party or group of States Parties.

2. The term "observing Party" means the State Party or group of States Parties that intends to conduct or conducts an observation flight over the territory of another State Party or group of States Parties, from the time that it has provided notification of its intention to conduct an observation flight until completion of the procedures relating to that flight, or personnel acting on behalf of that State Party or group of States Parties.

3. The term "group of States Parties" means two or more States Parties that have agreed to form a group for the purposes of this Treaty.

4. The term "observation aircraft" means an unarmed, fixed wing aircraft designated to make observation flights, registered by the relevant authorities of a State Party and equipped with agreed sensors. The term "unarmed" means that the observation aircraft used for the purposes of this Treaty is not equipped

to carry and employ weapons.

5. The term "observation flight" means the flight of the observation aircraft conducted by an observing Party over the territory of an observed Party, as provided in the flight plan, from the point of entry or Open Skies airfield to the point of exit or Open Skies airfield.

6. The term "transit flight" means a flight of an observation aircraft or transport aircraft conducted by or on behalf of an observing Party over the territory of a third State Party enroute to or from the territory of the observed Party.

7. The term "transport aircraft" means an aircraft other than an observation aircraft that, on behalf of the observing Party, conducts flights to or from the territory of the observed Party exclusively for the purposes of this Treaty.

8. The term "territory" means the land, including islands, and internal and territorial waters, over which a State Party exercises sovereignty.

9. The term "passive quota" means the number of observation flights that each State Party is obliged to accept as an observed Party.

10. The term "active quota" means the number of observation flights that each State Party has the right to conduct as an observing Party.

11. The term "maximum flight distance" means the maximum distance over the territory of the observed Party from the point at which the observation flight may commence to the point at which that flight may terminate, as specified in Annex A to this Treaty.

12. The term "sensor" means equipment of a category specified in Article IV, paragraph 1 that is installed on an observation aircraft for use during the conduct of observation flights.

13. The term "ground resolution" means the minimum distance on the ground between two closely located objects distinguishable as separate objects.

14. The term "infra-red line-scanning device" means a sensor capable of receiving and visualizing thermal electro-magnetic radiation emitted in the invisible infra-red part of the optical spectrum by objects due to their temperature and in the absence of artificial illumination.

15. The term "observation period" means a specified period of time during an observation flight when a particular sensor installed on the observation aircraft is operating.

16. The term "flight crew" means individuals from any State Party who may include, if the State Party so decides, interpreters and who perform duties associated with the operation or servicing of an observation aircraft or transport aircraft.

17. The term "pilot-in-command" means the pilot on board the observation aircraft who is responsible for the operation of the observation aircraft, the execution of the flight plan, and the safety of the observation aircraft.

18. The term "flight monitor" means an individual who, on behalf of the observed Party, is on board an observation aircraft provided by the observing Party during the observation flight and who performs duties in accordance with Annex G to this Treaty.

19. The term "flight representative" means an individual who, on behalf of the observing Party, is on board an observation aircraft provided by the observed Party during an observation flight and who performs duties in accordance with Annex G to this Treaty.

20. The term "representative" means an individual who has been designated by the observing Party and who performs activities on behalf of the observing Party in accordance with Annex G during an observation flight on an observation aircraft designated by a State Party other than the observing Party or the observed Party.

21. The term "sensor operator" means an individual from any State Party who performs duties associated with the functioning, operation and maintenance of the sensors of an observation aircraft.

22. The term "inspector" means an individual from any State Party who conducts an inspection of sensors or observation aircraft of another State Party.

23. The term "escort" means an individual from any State Party who accompanies the inspectors of another State Party.

24. The term "mission plan" means a document, which is in a format established by the Open Skies Consultative Commission, presented by the observing Party that contains the route, profile, order of execution and support required to conduct the observation flight, which is to be agreed upon with the observed Party and which will form the basis for the elaboration of the flight plan.

25. The term "flight plan" means a document elaborated on the basis of the agreed mission plan in the format and with the content specified by the International Civil Aviation Organization, hereinafter referred to as the ICAO, which is presented to the air traffic control authorities and on the basis of which the observation flight will be conducted.

26. The term "mission report" means a document describing an observation flight completed after its termination by the observing Party and signed by both the observing and observed Parties, which is in a format established by the Open Skies Consultative

Commission.

27. The term "Open Skies airfield" means an airfield designated by the observed Party as a point where an observation flight may commence or terminate.

28. The term "point of entry" means a point designated by the observed Party for the arrival of personnel of the observing Party on the territory of the observed Party.

29. The term "point of exit" means a point designated by the observed Party for departure of personnel of the observing Party from the territory of the observed Party.

30. The term "refuelling airfield" means an airfield designated by the observed Party used for fuelling and servicing of observation aircraft and transport aircraft.

31. The term "alternate airfield" means an airfield specified in the flight plan to which an observation aircraft or transport aircraft may proceed when it becomes inadvisable to land at the airfield of intended landing.

32. The term "hazardous airspace" means the prohibited areas, restricted areas and danger areas, defined on the basis of Annex 2 to the Convention on International Civil Aviation, that are established in accordance with Annex 15 to the Convention on International Civil Aviation in the interests of flight safety, public safety and environmental protection and about which information is provided in accordance with ICAO provisions.

33. The term "prohibited area" means an airspace of defined dimensions, above the territory of a State Party, within which the flight of aircraft is prohibited.

34. The term "restricted area" means an airspace of defined dimensions, above the territory of a State Party, within which the flight of aircraft is restricted in accordance with specified conditions.

35. The term "danger area" means an airspace of defined dimensions within which activities dangerous to the flight of aircraft may exist at specified times.

Section I

General Provisions

Article III

Quotas

1. Each State Party shall have the right to conduct observation flights in accordance with the provisions of this Treaty.

2. Each State Party shall be obliged to accept observation flights over its territory in accordance with the provisions of this Treaty.

3. Each State Party shall have the right to conduct a number of observation flights over the territory of any other State Party equal to the number of observation flights which that other State Party has the right to conduct over it.

4. The total number of observation flights that each State Party is obliged to accept over its territory is the total passive quota for that State Party. The allocation of the total passive quota to the States Parties is set forth in Annex A, Section I to this Treaty.

5. The number of observation flights that a State Party shall have the right to conduct each year over the territory of each of the other States Parties is the individual active quota of that State Party with respect to that other State Party. The sum of the individual active quotas is the total active quota of that State Party. The total active quota of a State Party shall not exceed its total passive quota.

6. The first distribution of active quotas is set forth in Annex A, Section II to this Treaty.

7. After entry into force of this Treaty, the distribution of active quotas shall be subject to an annual review for the following calendar year within the framework of the Open Skies Consultative Commission. In the event that it is not possible during the annual review to arrive within three weeks at agreement on the distribution of active quotas with respect to a particular State Party, the previous year's distribution of active quotas with respect to that State Party shall remain unchanged.

8. Except as provided for by the provisions of Article VIII, each observation flight conducted by a State Party shall be counted against the individual and total active quotas of that State Party.

9. Notwithstanding the provisions of paragraphs 3 and 5 of this Section, a State Party to which an active quota has been distributed may, by agreement with the State Party to be overflown, transfer a part or all of its total active quota to other States Parties and shall promptly notify all other States Parties and the Open Skies Consultative Commission thereof. Paragraph 10 of this Section shall apply.

10. No State Party shall conduct more observation flights over the territory of another State Party than a number equal to 50 percent, rounded up to the nearest whole number, of its own total active quota, or of the total passive quota of that other State Party, whichever is less.

11. The maximum flight distances of observation flights over the territories of the States Parties are set forth in Annex A, Section III to this Treaty.

Section II

Provisions for a Group of States Parties

1.

A. Without prejudice to their rights and obligations under this Treaty, two or more States Parties which hold quotas may form a group of States Parties at signature of this Treaty and thereafter. For a group of States Parties formed after signature of this Treaty, the provisions of this Section shall apply no earlier than six months after giving notice to all other States Parties, and subject to the provisions of paragraph 6 of this Section.

B. A group of States Parties shall co-operate with regard to active and passive quotas in accordance with the provisions of either paragraph 2 or 3 of this Section.

2.

A. The members of a group of States Parties shall have the right to redistribute amongst themselves their active quotas for the current year, while retaining their individual passive quotas. Notification of the redistribution shall be made immediately to all third States Parties concerned.

B. An observation flight shall count as many observation flights against the individual and total active quotas of the observing Party as observed Parties belonging to the group are overflown. It shall count one observation flight against the total passive quota of each observed Party.

C. Each State Party in respect of which one or more members of a group of States Parties hold active quotas shall have the right to conduct over the territory of any member of the group 50 percent more observation flights, rounded up to the nearest whole number, than its individual active quota in respect of that member of the group or to conduct two such overflights if it holds no active quota in respect of that member of the group.

D. In the event that it exercises this right the State Party concerned shall reduce its active quotas in respect of other members of the group in such a way that the total sum of observation flights it conducts over their territories shall not exceed the sum of the individual active quotas that the State Party holds in respect of all the members of the group in the current year.

E. The maximum flight distances of observation flights over the territories of each member of the group shall apply. In case of an observation flight conducted over several members, after completion of the maximum flight distance for one member all sensors shall be switched off until the observation aircraft reaches the point over the territory of the next member of the group of States Parties where the observation flight is planned to begin. For such follow-on observation flight the maximum flight distance related to the Open Skies airfield nearest to this point shall apply.

3.

A. A group of States Parties shall, at its request, be entitled to a common total passive quota which shall be allocated to it and common individual and total active quotas shall be distributed in respect of it.

B. In this case, the total passive quota is the total number of observation flights that the group of States Parties is obliged to accept each year. The total active quota is the sum of the number of observation flights that the group of States Parties has the right to conduct each year. Its total active quota shall not exceed the total passive quota.

C. An observation flight resulting from the total active quota of the group of States Parties shall be carried out on behalf of the group.

D. Observation flights that a group of States Parties is obliged to accept may be conducted over the territory of one or more of its members.

E. The maximum flight distances of each group of States Parties shall be specified pursuant to Annex A, Section III and Open Skies airfields shall be designated pursuant to Annex E to this Treaty.

4. In accordance with the general principles set out in Article X, paragraph 3, any third State Party that considers its rights under the provisions of Section I, paragraph 3 of this Article to be unduly restricted by the operation of a group of States Parties may raise this problem before the Open Skies Consultative Commission.

5. The group of States Parties shall ensure that procedures are established allowing for the conduct of observation flights over the territories of its members during one single mission, including refuelling if necessary. In the case of a group of States Parties established pursuant to paragraph 3 of this Section, such observation flights shall not exceed the maximum flight distance applicable to the Open Skies air-

fields at which the observation flights commence.

6. No earlier than six months after notification of the decision has been provided to all other States Parties:

A. a group of States Parties established pursuant to the provisions of paragraph 2 of this Section may be transformed into a group of States Parties pursuant to the provisions of paragraph 3 of this Section;

B. a group of States Parties established pursuant to the provisions of paragraph 3 of this Section may be transformed into a group of States Parties pursuant to the provisions of paragraph 2 of this Section;

C. a State Party may withdraw from a group of States Parties; or

D. a group of States Parties may admit further States Parties which hold quotas.

7. Following entry into force of this Treaty, changes in the allocation or distribution of quotas resulting from the establishment of or an admission to or a withdrawal from a group of States Parties according to paragraph 3 of this Section shall become effective on 1 January following the first annual review within the Open Skies Consultative Commission occurring after the six-month notification period. When necessary, new Open Skies airfields shall be designated and maximum flight distances established accordingly.

Article IV

Sensors

1. Except as otherwise provided for in paragraph 3 of this Article, observation aircraft shall be equipped with sensors only from amongst the following categories:

A. optical panoramic and framing cameras;

B. video cameras with real-time display;

C. infra-red line-scanning devices; and

D. sideways-looking synthetic aperture radar.

2. A State Party may use, for the purposes of conducting observation flights, any of the sensors specified in paragraph 1 above, provided that such sensors are commercially available to all States Parties, subject to the following performance limits:

A. in the case of optical panoramic and framing cameras, a ground resolution of no better than 30 centimetres at the minimum height above ground level determined in accordance with the provisions of Annex D, Appendix 1, obtained from no more than one panoramic camera, one vertically-mounted framing camera and two obliquely-mounted framing cameras, one on each side of the aircraft, providing coverage, which need not be continuous, of the ground up to 50 kilometres of each side of the flight path of the aircraft;

B. in the case of video cameras, a ground resolution of no better than 30 centimetres determined in accordance with the provisions of Annex D, Appendix 1;

C. in the case of infra-red line-scanning devices, a ground resolution of no better than 50 centimetres at the minimum height above ground level determined in accordance with the provisions of Annex D, Appendix 1, obtained from a single device; and

D. in the case of sideways-looking synthetic aperture radar, a ground resolution of no better than three metres calculated by the impulse response method, which, using the object separation method, corresponds to the ability to distinguish on a radar image two corner reflectors, the distance between the centres of which is no less than five metres, over a swath width of no more than 25 kilometres, obtained from a single radar unit capable of looking from either side of the aircraft, but not both simultaneously.

3. The introduction of additional categories and improvements to the capabilities of existing categories of sensors provided for in this Article shall be addressed by the Open Skies Consultative Commission pursuant to Article X of this Treaty.

4. All sensors shall be provided with aperture covers or other devices which inhibit the operation of sensors so as to prevent collection of data during transit flights or flights to points of entry or from points of exit over the territory of the observed Party. Such covers or such other devices shall be removable or operable only from outside the observation aircraft.

5. Equipment that is capable of annotating data collected by sensors in accordance with Annex B, Section II shall be allowed on observation aircraft. The State Party providing the observation aircraft for an observation flight shall annotate the data collected by sensors with the information provided for in Annex B, Section II to this Treaty.

6. Equipment that is capable of displaying data collected by sensors in real-time shall be allowed on

observation aircraft for the purposes of monitoring the functioning and operation of the sensors during the conduct of an observation flight.

7. Except as required for the operation of the agreed sensors, or as required for the operation of the observation aircraft, or as provided for in paragraphs 5 and 6 of this Article, the collection, processing, retransmission or recording of electronic signals from electro-magnetic waves are prohibited on board the observation aircraft and equipment for such operations shall not be on that observation aircraft.

8. In the event that the observation aircraft is provided by, the observing Party, the observing Party shall have the right to use an observation aircraft equipped with sensors in each sensor category that do not exceed the capability specified in paragraph 2 of this Article.

9. In the event that the observation aircraft used for an observation flight is provided by the observed Party, the observed Party shall be obliged to provide an observation aircraft equipped with sensors from each sensor category specified in paragraph 1 of this Article, at the maximum capability and in the numbers specified in paragraph 2 of this Article, subject to the provisions of Article XVIII, Section II, unless otherwise agreed by the observing and observed Parties. The package and configuration of such sensors shall be installed in such a way so as to provide coverage of the ground provided for in paragraph 2 of this Article. In the event that the observation aircraft is provided by the observed Party, the latter shall provide a sideways-looking synthetic aperture radar with a ground resolution of no worse than six metres, determined by the object separation method.

10. When designating an aircraft as an observation aircraft pursuant to Article V of this Treaty, each State Party shall inform all other States Parties of the technical information on each sensor installed on such aircraft as provided for in Annex B to this Treaty.

11. Each State Party shall have the right to take part in the certification of sensors installed on observation aircraft in accordance with the provisions of Annex D. No observation aircraft of a given type shall be used for observation flights until such type of observation aircraft and its sensors has been certified in accordance with the provisions of Annex D to this Treaty.

12. A State Party designating an aircraft as an observation aircraft shall, upon 90-day prior notice to all other States Parties and subject to the provisions of Annex D to this Treaty, have the right to remove, replace or add sensors, or amend the technical information it has provided in accordance with the provi-

sions of paragraph 10 of this Article and Annex B to this Treaty. Replacement and additional sensors shall be subject to certification in accordance with the provisions of Annex D to this Treaty prior to their use during an observation flight.

13. In the event that a State Party or group of States Parties, based on experience with using a particular observation aircraft, considers that any sensor or its associated equipment installed on an aircraft does not correspond to those certified in accordance with the provisions of Annex D, the interested States Parties shall notify all other States Parties of their concern. The State Party that designated the aircraft shall:

A. take the steps necessary to ensure that the sensor and its associated equipment installed on the observation aircraft correspond to those certified in accordance with the provisions of Annex D, including, as necessary, repair, adjustment or replacement of the particular sensor or its associated equipment; and

B. at the request of an interested State Party, by means of a demonstration flight set up in connection with the next time that the aforementioned observation aircraft is used, in accordance with the provisions of Annex F, demonstrate that the sensor and its associated equipment installed on the observation aircraft correspond to those certified in accordance with the provisions of Annex O. Other States Parties that express concern regarding a sensor and its associated equipment installed on an observation aircraft shall have the right to send personnel to participate in such a demonstration flight.

14. In the event that, after the steps referred to in paragraph 13 of this Article have been taken, the States Parties remain concerned as to whether a sensor or its associated equipment installed on an observation aircraft correspond to those certified in accordance with the provisions of Annex D, the issue may be referred to the Open Skies Consultative Commission.

Article V

Aircraft Designation

1. Each State Party shall have the right to designate as observation aircraft one or more types or models of aircraft registered by the relevant authorities of a State Party.

2. Each State Party shall have the right to designate types or models of aircraft as observation aircraft or add new types or models of aircraft to those designa-

ted earlier by it, provided that it notifies all other States Parties 30 days in advance thereof. The notification of the designation of aircraft of a type or model shall contain the information specified in Annex C to this Treaty.

3. Each State Party shall have the right to delete types or models of aircraft designated earlier by it, provided that it notifies all other States Parties 90 days in advance thereof.

4. Only one exemplar of a particular type and model of aircraft with an identical set of associated sensors shall be required to be offered for certification in accordance with the provisions of Annex D to this Treaty.

5. Each observation aircraft shall be capable of carrying the flight crew and the personnel specified in Article VI, Section III.

Section I

Choice of Observation Aircraft and General Provisions for the Conduct of Observation Flights

Article VI

Choice of Observation Aircraft, General Provisions for the Conduct of Observation Flights, and Requirements for Mission Planning

1. Observation flights shall be conducted using observation aircraft that have been designated by a State Party pursuant to Article V. Unless the observed Party exercises its right to provide an observation aircraft that it has itself designated, the observing Party shall have the right to provide the observation aircraft. In the event that the observing Party provides the observation aircraft, it shall have the right to provide an aircraft that it has itself designated or an aircraft designated by another State Party. In the event that the observed Party provides the observation aircraft, the observing Party shall have the right to be provided with an aircraft capable of achieving a minimum unrefuelled range, including the necessary fuel reserves, equivalent to one-half of the flight distance, as notified in accordance with paragraph 5, subparagraph(G) of this Section.

2. Each State Party shall have the right, pursuant to paragraph 1 of this Section, to use an observation aircraft designated by another State Party for observation flights. Arrangements for the use of such aircraft shall be worked out by the States Parties involved to allow for active participation in the Open Skies regime.

3. States Parties having the right to conduct observation flights may co-ordinate their plans for conducting observation flights in accordance with Annex H to this Treaty. No State Party shall be obliged to accept more than one observation flight at any one time during the 96-hour period specified in paragraph 9 of this Section, unless that State Party has requested a demonstration flight pursuant to Annex F to this Treaty. In that case, the observed Party shall be obliged to accept an overlap for the observation flights of up to 24 hours. After having been notified of the results of the co-ordination of plans to conduct observation flights, each State Party over whose territory observation flights are to be conducted shall inform other States Parties, in accordance with the provisions of Annex H, whether it will exercise, with regard to each specific observation flight, its right to provide its own observation aircraft.

4. No later than 90 days after signature of this Treaty, each State Party shall provide notification to all other States Parties:

A. of the standing diplomatic clearance number for Open Skies observation flights, flights of transport aircraft and transit flights; and

B. of which language or languages of the Open Skies Consultative Commission specified in Annex L, Section I, paragraph 7 to this Treaty shall be used by personnel for all activities associated with the conduct of observation flights over its territory, and for completing the mission plan and mission report, unless the language to be used is the one recommended in Annex 10 to the Convention on International Civil Aviation, Volume II, paragraph 5.2.1.1.2.

5. The observing Party shall notify the observed Party of its intention to conduct an observation flight, no less than 72 hours prior to the estimated time of arrival of the observing Party at the point of entry of the observed Party. States Parties providing such notifications shall make every effort to avoid using the minimum pre-notification period over weekends. Such notification shall include:

A. the desired point of entry and, if applicable, Open Skies airfield where the observation flight shall commence;

B. the date and estimated time of arrival of the observing Party at the point of entry and the date and estimated time of departure for the flight from the point of entry to the Open Skies airfield, if applicable, indicating specific accommodation needs;

C. the location, specified in Annex E, Appendix 1, where the conduct of the pre-flight inspection is desired and the date and start time of such pre-flight inspection in accordance with the provisions of Annex F;

D. the mode of transport and, if applicable, type and model of the transport aircraft used to travel to the point of entry in the event that the observation aircraft used for the observation flight is provided by the observed Party;

E. the diplomatic clearance number for the observation flight or for the flight of the transport aircraft used to bring the personnel in and out of the territory of the observed Party to conduct an observation flight;

F. the identification of the observation aircraft, as specified in Annex C;

G. the approximate observation flight distance; and

H. the names of the personnel, their gender, date and place of birth, passport number and issuing State Party, and their function.

6. The observed Party that is notified in accordance with paragraph 5 of this Section shall acknowledge receipt of the notification within 24 hours. In the event that the observed Party exercises its right to provide the observation aircraft, the acknowledgement shall include the information about the observation aircraft specified in paragraph 5, subparagraph (F) of this Section. The observing Party shall be permitted to arrive at the point of entry at the estimated time of arrival as notified in accordance with paragraph 5 of this Section. The estimated time of departure for the flight from the point of entry to the Open Skies airfield where the observation flight shall commence and the location, the date and the start time of the pre-flight inspection shall be subject to confirmation by the observed Party.

7. Personnel of the observing Party may include personnel designated pursuant to Article XIII by other States Parties.

8. The observing Party, when notifying the observed Party in accordance with paragraph 5 of this Section, shall simultaneously notify all other States Parties of its intention to conduct the observation flight.

9. The period from the estimated time of arrival at the point of entry until completion of the observation flight shall not exceed 96 hours, unless otherwise agreed. In the event that the observed Party requests a demonstration flight pursuant to Annex F to the Treaty, it shall extend the 96-hour period pursuant to Annex F, Section III, paragraph 4, if additional time is required by the observing Party for the unrestricted execution of the mission plan.

10. Upon arrival of the observation aircraft at the point of entry, the observed Party shall inspect the covers for sensor apertures or other devices that inhibit the operation of sensors to confirm that they are in their proper position pursuant to Annex E, unless otherwise agreed by all States Parties involved.

11. In the event that the observation aircraft is provided by the observing Party, upon the arrival of the observation aircraft at the point of entry or at the Open Skies airfield where the observation flight commences, the observed Party shall have the right to carry out the pre-flight inspection pursuant to Annex F, Section I. In the event that, in accordance with paragraph 1 of this Section, an observation aircraft is provided by the observed Party, the observing Party shall have the right to carry out the pre-flight inspection of sensors pursuant to Annex F, Section II. Unless otherwise agreed, such inspections shall terminate no less than four hours prior to the scheduled commencement of the observation flight set forth in the flight plan.

12. The observing Party shall ensure that its flight crew includes at least one individual who has the necessary linguistic ability to communicate freely with the personnel of the observed Party and its air traffic control authorities in the language or languages notified by the observed Party in accordance with paragraph 4 of this Section.

13. The observed Party shall provide the flight crew, upon its arrival at the point of entry or at the Open Skies airfield where the observation flight commences, with the most recent weather forecast and air navigation information and information on flight safety, including Notices to Airmen. Updates of such information shall be provided as requested. Instrument procedures, and information about alternate airfields along the flight route, shall be provided upon approval of the mission plan in accordance with the requirements of Section II of this Article.

14. While conducting observation flights pursuant to this Treaty, all observation aircraft shall be operated in accordance with the provisions of this Treaty and in accordance with the approved flight plan. Without prejudice to the provisions of Section II, paragraph 2 of this Article, observation flights shall also be conducted in compliance with:

A. published ICAO standards and recommended practices; and

B. published national air traffic control rules, procedures and guidelines on flight safety of the State Party whose territory is being overflown.

15. Observation flights shall take priority over any regular air traffic. The observed Party shall ensure that its air traffic control authorities facilitate the conduct of observation flights in accordance with this Treaty.

16. On board the aircraft the pilot-in-command shall be the sole authority for the safe conduct of the flight and shall be responsible for the execution of the flight plan.

17. The observed Party shall provide:

A. a calibration target suitable for confirming the capability of sensors in accordance with the procedures set forth in Annex D, Section III to this Treaty, to be overflown during the demonstration flight or the observation flight upon the request of either Party, for each sensor that is to be used during the observation flight. The calibration target shall be located in the vicinity of the airfield at which the pre-flight inspection is conducted pursuant to Annex F to this Treaty;

B. customary commercial aircraft fuelling and servicing for the observation aircraft or transport aircraft at the point of entry, at the Open Skies airfield, at any refuelling airfield, and at the point of exit specified in the flight plan, according to the specifications that are published about the designated airfield;

C. meals and the use of accommodation for the personnel of the observing Party; and

D. upon the request of the observing Party, further services, as may be agreed upon between the observing and observed Parties, to facilitate the conduct of the observation flight.

18. All costs involved in the conduct of the observation flight, including the costs of the recording media and the processing of the data collected by sensors, shall be reimbursed in accordance with Annex L, Section I, paragraph 9 to this Treaty.

19. Prior to the departure of the observation aircraft from the point of exit, the observed Party shall confirm that the covers for sensor apertures or other devices that inhibit the operation of sensors are in their proper position pursuant to Annex E to this Treaty.

20. Unless otherwise agreed, the observing Party shall depart from the point of exit no later than 24 hours following completion of the observation flight, unless weather conditions or the airworthiness of the observation aircraft or transport aircraft do not permit, in which case the flight shall commence as soon as practicable.

21. The observing Party shall compile a mission report of the observation flight using the appropriate format developed by the Open Skies Consultative Commission. The mission report shall contain pertinent data on the date and time of the observation flight, its route and profile, weather conditions, time and eriod for each sensor, the approximate amount of data collected by sensors, and the result of inspection of covers for sensor apertures or other devices that inhibit the operation of sensors in accordance with Article VII and Annex E. The mission report shall be signed by the observing and observed Parties at the point of exit and shall be provided by the observing Party to all other States Parties within seven days after departure of the observing Party from the point of exit.

Section II

Requirements for Mission Planning

1. Unless otherwise agreed, the observing Party shall, after arrival at the Open Skies airfield, submit to the observed Party a mission plan for the proposed observation flight that meets the requirements of paragraphs 2 and 4 of this Section.

2. The mission plan may provide for an observation flight that allows for the observation of any point on the entire territory of the observed Party, including areas designated by the observed Party as hazardous airspace in the source specified in Annex I. The flight path of an observation aircraft shall not be closer than, but shall be allowed up to, ten kilometres from the border with an adjacent State that is not a State Party.

3. The mission plan may provide that the Open Skies airfield where the observation flight terminates, as well as the point of exit, may be different from the Open Skies airfield where the observation flight commences or the point of entry. The mission plan shall specify, if applicable, the commencement time of the observation flight, the desired time and place of planned refuelling stops or rest periods, and the time of continuation of the observation flight after a refuelling stop or rest period within the 96-hour period specified in Section I, paragraph 9 of this Article.

4. The mission plan shall include all information necessary to file the flight plan and shall provide that:

A. the observation flight does not exceed the relevant maximum flight distance as set forth in Annex A, Section I;

B. the route and profile of the observation flight satisfies observation flight safety conditions in conformity with ICAO standards and recommended practices, taking into account existing differences in national flight rules, without prejudice to the provisions of paragraph 2 of this Section;

C. the mission plan takes into account information on hazardous airspace, as provided in accordance with Annex I;

D. the height above ground level of the observation aircraft does not permit the observing Party to exceed the limitation on ground resolution for each sensor, as set forth in Article IV, paragraph 2;

E. the estimated time of commencement of the observation flight shall be no less than 24 hours after the submission of the mission plan, unless otherwise agreed;

F. the observation aircraft flies a direct route between the co-ordinates or navigation fixes designated in the mission plan in the declared sequence; and

G. the flight path does not intersect at the same point more than once, unless otherwise agreed, and the observation aircraft does not circle around a single point, unless otherwise agreed. The provisions of this subparagraph do not apply for the purposes of taking off, flying over calibration targets, or landing by the observation aircraft.

5. In the event that the mission plan filed by the observing Party provides for flights through hazardous airspace, the observed Party shall:

A. specify the hazard to the observation aircraft;

B. facilitate the conduct of the observation flight by co-ordination or suppression of the activity specified pursuant to subparagraph (A) of this paragraph; or

C. propose an alternative flight altitude, route, or time.

6. No later than four hours after submission of the mission plan, the observed Party shall accept the mission plan or propose changes to it in accordance with Article VIII, Section I, paragraph 4 and paragraph 5 of this Section. Such changes shall not preclude observation of any point on the entire territory of the observed Party, including areas designated by the observed Party as hazardous airspace in the source

specified in Annex I to this Treaty. Upon agreement, the mission plan shall be signed by the observing and observed Parties. In the event that the Parties do not reach agreement on the mission plan within eight hours of the submission of the original mission plan, the observing Party shall have the right to decline to conduct the observation flight in accordance with the provisions of Article VIII of this Treaty.

7. If the planned route of the observation flight approaches the border of other States Parties or other States, the observed Party may notify that State or those States of the estimated route, date and time of the observation flight.

8. On the basis of the agreed mission plan the State Party providing the observation aircraft shall, in coordination with the other State Party, file the flight plan immediately, which shall have the content specified in Annex 2 to the Convention on International Civil Aviation and shall be in the format specified by ICAO Document No. 4444-RAC/501/12, "Rules of the Air and Air Traffic Services", as revised or amended.

Section III

Special Provisions

1. In the event that the observation aircraft is provided by the observing Party, the observed Party shall have the right to have on board the observation aircraft two flight monitors and one interpreter, in addition to one flight monitor for each sensor control station on board the observation aircraft, unless otherwise agreed. Flight monitors and interpreters shall have the rights and obligations specified in Annex G to this Treaty.

2. Notwithstanding paragraph 1 of this Section, in the event that an observing Party uses an observation aircraft which has a maximum take-off gross weight of no more than 35,000 kilograms for an observation flight distance of no more than 1,500 kilometres as notified in accordance with Section I, paragraph 5, subparagraph (G) of this Article, it shall be obliged to accept only two flight monitors and one interpreter on board the observation aircraft, unless otherwise agreed.

3. In the event that the observation aircraft is provided by the observed Party, the observed Party shall permit the personnel of the observing Party to travel to the point of entry of the observed Party in the most expeditious manner. The personnel of the observing Party may elect to travel to the point of entry using ground, sea, or air transportation, including transportation by an aircraft owned by any State Party. Procedures regarding such travel are set forth in

Annex E to this Treaty.

4. In the event that the observation aircraft is provided by the observed Party, the observing Party shall have the right to have on board the observation aircraft two flight representatives and one interpreter, in addition to one flight representative for each sensor control station on the aircraft, unless otherwise agreed. Flight representatives and interpreters shall have the rights and obligations set forth in Annex G to this Treaty.

5. In the event that the observing State Party provides an observation aircraft designated by a State Party other than the observing or observed Party, the observing Party shall have the right to have on board the observation aircraft two representatives and one interpreter, in addition to one representative for each sensor control station on the aircraft, unless otherwise agreed. In this case, the provisions on flight monitors set forth in paragraph 1 of this Section shall also apply. Representatives and interpreters shall have the rights and obligations set forth in Annex G to this Treaty.

Article VII

Transit Flights

1. Transit flights conducted by an observing Party to and from the territory of an observed Party for the purposes of this Treaty shall originate on the territory of the observing Party or of another State Party.

2. Each State Party shall accept transit flights. Such transit flights shall be conducted along internationally recognized Air Traffic Services routes, unless otherwise agreed by the States Parties involved, and in accordance with the instructions of the national air traffic control authorities of each State Party whose airspace is transited. The observing Party shall notify each State Party whose airspace is to be transited at the same time that it notifies the observed Party in accordance with Article VI.

3. The operation of sensors on an observation aircraft during transit flights is prohibited. In the event that, during the transit flight, the observation aircraft lands on the territory of a State Party, that State Party shall, upon landing and prior to departure, inspect the covers of sensor apertures or other devices that inhibit the operation of sensors to confirm that they are in their proper position.

Section I

Prohibition of Observation Flights and Changes to Mission Plans

Article VIII

Prohibitions, Deviations from Plans and Emergency Situations

1. The observed Party shall have the right to prohibit an observation flight that is not in compliance with the provisions of this Treaty.

2. The observed Party shall have the right to prohibit an observation flight prior to its commencement in the event that the observing Party fails to arrive at the point of entry within 24 hours after the estimated time of arrival specified in the notification provided in accordance with Article VI, Section I, paragraph 5, unless otherwise agreed between the States Parties involved.

3. In the event that an observed State Party prohibits an observation flight pursuant to this Article or Annex F, it shall immediately state the facts for the prohibition in the mission plan. Within seven days the observed Party shall provide to all States Parties, through diplomatic channels, a written explanation for this prohibition in the mission report provided pursuant to Article VI, Section I, paragraph 21. An observation flight that has been prohibited shall not be counted against the quota of either State Party.

4. The observed Party shall have the right to propose changes to the mission plan as a result of any of the following circumstances:

A. the weather conditions affect flight safety;

B. the status of the Open Skies airfield to be used, alternate airfields, or refuelling airfields prevents their use; or

C. the mission plan is inconsistent with Article VI, Section II, paragraphs 2 and 4.

5. In the event that the observing Party disagrees with the proposed changes to the mission plan, it shall have the right to submit alternatives to the proposed changes. In the event that agreement on a mission plan is not reached within eight hours of the submission of the original mission plan, and if the observing Party considers the changes to the mission plan to be prejudicial to its rights under this Treaty with respect to the conduct of the observation flight, the observing Party shall have the right to decline to conduct the observation flight, which shall not be recorded against the quota of either State Party.

6. In the event that an observing Party declines to conduct an observation flight pursuant to this Article or Annex F, it shall immediately provide an explanation of its decision in the mission plan prior to the departure of the observing Party. Within seven days

after departure of the observing Party, the observing Party shall provide to all other States Parties, through diplomatic channels, a written explanation for this decision in the mission report provided pursuant to Article VI, Section I, paragraph 21.

Section II

Deviations from the Flight Plan

1. Deviations from the flight plan shall be permitted during the observation flight if necessitated by:

A. weather conditions affecting flight safety;

B. technical difficulties relating to the observation aircraft;

C. a medical emergency of any person on board; or

D. air traffic control instructions related to circumstances brought about by force *majeure*.

2. In addition, if weather conditions prevent effective use of optical sensors and infra-red line-scanning devices, deviations shall be permitted, provided that:

A. flight safety requirements are met;

B. in cases where national rules so require, permission is granted by air traffic control authorities; and

C. the performance of the sensors does not exceed the capabilities specified in Article IV, paragraph 2, unless otherwise agreed.

3. The observed Party shall have the right to prohibit the use of a particular sensor during a deviation that brings the observation aircraft below the minimum height above ground level for operating that particular sensor, in accordance with the limitation on ground resolution specified in Article IV, paragraph 2. In the event that a deviation requires the observation aircraft to alter its flight path by more than 50 kilometres from the flight path specified in the flight plan, the observed Party shall have the right to prohibit the use of all the sensors installed on the observation aircraft beyond that 50-kilometre limit.

4. The observing Party shall have the right to curtail an observation flight during its execution in the event of sensor malfunction. The pilot-in-command shall have the right to curtail an observation flight in the event of technical difficulties affecting the safety of the observation aircraft.

5. In the event that a deviation from the flight plan permitted by paragraph 1 of this Section results in curtailment of the observation flight, or a curtailment occurs in accordance with paragraph 4 of this Section, an observation flight shall be counted against the quotas of both States Parties, unless the curtailment is due to:

A. sensor malfunction on an observation aircraft provided by the observed Party;

B. technical difficulties relating to the observation aircraft provided by the observed Party;

C. a medical emergency of a member of the flight crew of the observed Party or of flight monitors; or

D. air traffic control instructions related to circumstances brought about by force majeure.

In such cases the observing Party shall have the right to decide whether to count it against the quotas of both States Parties.

6. The data collected by the sensors shall be retained by the observing Party only if the observation flight is counted against the quotas of both States Parties.

7. In the event that a deviation is made from the flight plan, the pilot-in-command shall take action in accordance with the published national flight regulations of the observed Party. Once the factors leading to the deviation have ceased to exist, the observation aircraft may, with the permission of the air traffic control authorities, continue the observation flight in accordance with the flight plan. The additional flight distance of the observation aircraft due to the deviation shall not count against the maximum flight distance.

8. Personnel of both States Parties on board the observation aircraft shall be immediately informed of all deviations from the light plan.

9. Additional expenses resulting from provisions of this Article shall be reimbursed in accordance with Annex L, Section I, paragraph 9 to this Treaty.

Section III

Emergency Situations

1. In the event that an emergency situation arises, the pilot-in-command shall be guided by "Procedures for Air Navigation Services - Rules of the Air and Air Traffic Services", ICAO Document No. 4444-RAC/ 501/12, as revised or amended, the national flight regulations of the observed Party, and the flight operation manual of the observation aircraft.

2. Each observation aircraft declaring an emergency shall be accorded the full range of distress and

navigational facilities of the observed Party in order to ensure the most expeditious recovery of the aircraft to the nearest suitable airfield.

3. In the event of an aviation accident involving the observation aircraft on the territory of the observed Party, search and rescue operations shall be conducted by the observed Party in accordance with its own regulations and procedures for such operations.

4. Investigation of an aviation accident or incident involving an observation aircraft shall be conducted by the observed Party, with the participation of the observing Party, in accordance with the ICAO recommendations set forth in Annex 13 to the Convention on International Civil Aviation ("Investigation of Aviation Accidents") as revised or amended and in accordance with the national regulations of the observed Party.

5. In the event that the observation aircraft is not registered with the observed Party, at the conclusion of the investigation all wreckage and debris of the observation aircraft and sensors, if found and recovered, shall be returned to the observing Party or to the Party to which the aircraft belongs, if so requested.

Section I

General Provisions

Article IX

Sensor Output from Observation Flights

1. For the purposes of recording data collected by sensors during observation flights, the following recording media shall be used:

A. in the case of optical panoramic and framing cameras, black and white photographic film;

B. in the case of video cameras, magnetic tape;

C. in the case of infra-red line-scanning devices, black and white photographic film or magnetic tape; and

D. in the case of sideways-looking synthetic aperture radar, magnetic tape.

The agreed format in which such data is to be recorded and exchanged on other recording media shall be decided within the Open Skies Consultative Commission during the period of provisional application of this Treaty.

2. Data collected by sensors during observation flights shall remain on board the observation aircraft until completion of the observation flight. The transmission of data collected by sensors from the observation aircraft during the observation flight is prohibited.

3. Each roll of photographic film and cassette or reel of magnetic tape used to collect data by a sensor during an observation flight shall be placed in a container and sealed in the presence of the States Parties as soon as is practicable after it has been removed from the sensor.

4. Data collected by sensors during observation flights shall be made available to States Parties in accordance with the provisions of this Article and shall be used exclusively for the attainment of the purposes of this Treaty.

5. In the event that, on the basis of data provided pursuant to Annex B, Section I to this Treaty, a data recording medium to be used by a State Party during an observation flight is incompatible with the equipment of another State Party for handling that data recording medium, the States Parties involved shall establish procedures to ensure that all data collected during observation flights can be handled, in terms of processing, duplication and storage, by them.

Section II

Output from Sensors that Use Photographic Film

1. In the event that output from duplicate optical cameras is to be exchanged, the cameras, film and film processing shall be of an identical type.

2. Provided that the data collected by a single optical camera is subject to exchange, the States Parties shall consider, within the Open Skies Consultative Commission during the period of provisional application of this Treaty, the issue of whether the responsibility for the development of the original film negative shall be borne by the observing Party or by the State Party providing the observation aircraft. The State Party developing the original film negative shall be responsible for the quality of processing the original negative film and producing the duplicate positive or negative. In the event that States Parties agree that the film used during the observation flight conducted on an observation aircraft provided by the observed Party shall be processed by the observing Party, the observed Party shall bear no responsibility for the quality of the processing of the original negative film.

3. All the film used during the observation flight shall be developed:

A. in the event that the original film negative is developed at a film processing facility arranged for by the observed Party, no làter than three days, unless otherwise agreed, after the arrival of the observation aircraft at the point of exit; or

B. in the event that the original film negative is developed at a film processing facility arranged for by the observing Party, no later than ten days after the departure of the observation aircraft from the territory of the observed Party.

4. The State Party that is developing the original film negative shall be obliged to accept at the film processing facility up to two officials from the other State Party to monitor the unsealing of the film cassette or container and each step in the storage, processing, duplication and handling of the original film negative, in accordance with the provisions of Annex K, Section II to this Treaty. The State Party monitoring the film processing and duplication shall have the right to designate such officials from among its nationals present on the territory on which the film processing facility arranged for by the other State Party is located, provided that such individuals are on the list of designated personnel in accordance with Article XIII, Section I of this Treaty. The State Party developing the film shall assist the officials of the other State Party in their functions provided for in this paragraph to the maximum extent possible.

5. Upon completion of an observation flight, the State Party that is to develop the original film negative shall attach a 21-step sensitometric test strip of the same film type used during the observation flight or shall expose a 21-step optical wedge onto the leader or trailer of each roll of original film negative used during the observation flight. After the original film negative has been processed and duplicate film negative or positive has been produced, the States Parties shall assess the image quality of the 21-step sensitometric test strips or images of the 21-step optical wedge against the characteristics provided for that type of original film negative or duplicate film negative or positive in accordance with the provisions of Annex K, Section I to this Treaty.

6. In the event that only one original film negative is developed:

A. the observing Party shall have the right to retain or receive the original film negative; and

B. the observed Party shall have the right to select and receive a complete first generation duplicate or part thereof, either positive or negative, of the original film negative. Unless otherwise agreed, such duplicate shall be:

1. of the same format and film size as the original film negative;

2. produced immediately after development of the original film negative; and

3. provided to the officials of the observed Party immediately after the duplicate has been produced.

7. In the event that two original film negatives are developed:

A. if the observation aircraft is provided by the observing Party, the observed Party shall have the right, at the completion of the observation flight, to select either of the two original film negatives, and the original film negative not selected shall be retained by the observing Party; or

B. if the observation aircraft is provided by the observed Party, the observing Party shall have the right to select either of the original film negatives, and the original film negative not selected shall be retained by the observed Party.

Section III

Output from Sensors that Use other Recording Media

1. The State Party that provides the observation aircraft shall record at least one original set of data collected by sensors using other recording media.

2. In the event that only one original set is made:

A. if the observation aircraft is provided by the observing Party, the observing Party shall have the right to retain the original set and the observed Party shall have the right to receive a first generation duplicate copy; or

B. if the observation aircraft is provided by the observed Party, the observing Party shall have the right to receive the original set and the observed Party shall have the right to receive a first generation duplicate copy.

3. In the event that two original sets are made:

A. if the observation aircraft is provided by the observing Party, the observed Party shall have the right, at the completion of the observation flight, to select either of the two sets of recording media, and the set not selected shall be retained by the observing Party; or

B. if the observation aircraft is provided by the observed Party, the observing Party shall have the right to elect either of the two sets of recording media, and the set not selected shall be retained by the observed Party.

4. In the event that the observation aircraft is provided by the observing Party, the observed Party shall have the right to receive the data collected by a sideways-looking synthetic aperture radar in the form of either initial phase information or a radar image, at its choice.

5. In the event that the observation aircraft is provided by the observed Party, the observing Party shall have the right to receive the data collected by a sideways-looking synthetic aperture radar in the form of either initial phase information or a radar image, at its choice.

Section IV

Access to Sensor Output

Each State Party shall have the right to request and receive from the observing Party copies of data collected by sensors during an observation flight. Such copies shall be in the form of first generation duplicates produced from the original data collected by sensors during an observation flight. The State Party requesting copies shall also notify the observed Party. A request for duplicates of data shall include the following information:

A. the observing Party;

B. the observed Party;

C. the date of the observation flight;

D. the sensor by which the data was collected;

E. the portion or portions of the observation period during which the data was collected; and

F. the type and format of duplicate recording medium, either negative or positive film, or magnetic tape.

Article X

Open Skies Consultative Commission

1. In order to promote the objectives and facilitate the implementation of the provisions of this Treaty, the States Parties hereby establish an Open Skies Consultative Commission.

2. The Open Skies Consultative Commission shall take decisions or make recommendations by consensus. Consensus shall be understood to mean the absence of any objection by any State Party to the tak-

ing of a decision or the making of a recommendation.

3. Each State Party shall have the right to raise before the Open Skies Consultative Commission, and have placed on its agenda, any issue relating to this Treaty, including any issue related to the case when the observed Party provides an observation aircraft.

4. Within the framework of the Open Skies Consultative Commission the States Parties to this Treaty shall:

A. consider questions relating to compliance with the provisions of this Treaty;

B. seek to resolve ambiguities and differences of interpretation that may become apparent in the way this Treaty is implemented;

C. consider and take decisions on applications for accession to this Treaty; and

D. agree as to those technical and administrative measures, pursuant to the provisions of this Treaty, deemed necessary following the accession to this Treaty by other States.

5. The Open Skies Consultative Commission may propose amendments to this Treaty for consideration and approval in accordance with Article XVI. The Open Skies Consultative Commission may also agree on improvements to the viability and effectiveness of this Treaty, consistent with its provisions. Improvements relating only to modification of the annual distribution of active quotas pursuant to Article III and Annex A, to updates and additions to the categories or capabilities of sensors pursuant to Article IV, to revision of the share of costs pursuant to Annex L, Section I, paragraph 9, to arrangements for the sharing and availability of data pursuant to Article IX, Sections III and IV and to the handling of mission reports pursuant to Article VI, Section I, paragraph 21, as well as to minor matters of an administrative or technical nature, shall be agreed upon within the Open Skies Consultative Commission and shall not be deemed to be amendments to this Treaty.

6. The Open Skies Consultative Commission shall request the use of the facilities and administrative support of the Conflict Prevention Centre of the Conference on Security and Co-operation in Europe, or other existing facilities in Vienna, unless it decides otherwise.

7. Provisions for the operation of the Open Skies Consultative Commission are set forth in Annex L to this Treaty.

Article XI

Notifications and Reports

The States Parties shall transmit notifications and reports required by this Treaty in written form. The States Parties shall transmit such notifications and reports through diplomatic channels or, at their choice, through other official channels, such as the communications network of the Conference on Security and Co-operation in Europe.

Article XII

Liability

A State Party shall, in accordance with international law and practice, be liable to pay compensation for damage to other States Parties, or to their natural or juridical persons or their property, caused by it in the course of the implementation of this Treaty.

Section I

Designation of Personnel

Article XIII

Designation of Personnel and Privileges and Immunities

1. Each State Party shall, at the same time that it deposits its instrument of ratification to either of the Depositaries, provide to all other States Parties, for their review, a list of designated personnel who will carry out all duties relating to the conduct of observation flights for that State Party, including monitoring the processing of the sensor output. No such list of designated personnel shall include more than 400 individuals at any time. It shall contain the name, gender, date of birth, place of birth, passport number, and function for each individual included. Each State Party shall have the right to amend its list of designated personnel until 30 days after entry into force of this Treaty and once every six months thereafter.

2. In the event that any individual included on the original or any amended list is unacceptable to a State Party reviewing the list, that State Party shall, no later than 30 days after receipt of each list, notify the State Party providing that list that such individual shall not be accepted with respect to the objecting State Party. Individuals not declared unacceptable within that 30-day period shall be deemed accepted. In the event that a State Party subsequently determines that an individual is unacceptable, that State Party shall so notify the State Party that designated such individual. Individuals who are declared unac-ceptable shall be removed from the list previously submitted to the objecting State Party.

3. The observed Party shall provide visas and any other documents as required to ensure that each accepted individual may enter and remain on the territory of that State Party for the purpose of carrying out duties relating to the conduct of observation flights, including monitoring the processing of the sensor output. Such visas and any other necessary documents shall be provided either:

A. no later than 30 days after the individual is deemed to be accepted, in which case the visa shall be valid for a period of no less than 24 months; or

B. no later than one hour after the arrival of the individual at the point of entry, in which case the visa shall be valid for the duration of that individual's duties; or

C. at any other time, by mutual agreement of the States Parties involved.

Section II

Privileges and Immunities

1. In order to exercise their functions effectively, for the purpose of implementing this Treaty and not for their personal benefit, personnel designated in accordance with the provisions of Section I, paragraph 1 of this Article shall be accorded the privileges and immunities enjoyed by diplomatic agents pursuant to Article 29; Article 30, paragraph 2; Article 31, paragraphs 1, 2 and 3; and Articles 34 and 35 of the Vienna Convention on Diplomatic Relations of 18 April 1961, hereinafter referred to as the Vienna Convention. In addition, designated personnel shall be accorded the privileges enjoyed by diplomatic agents pursuant to Article 36, paragraph 1, subparagraph (b) of the Vienna Convention, except in relation to articles, the import or export of which is prohibited by law or controlled by quarantine regulations.

2. Such privileges and immunities shall be accorded to designated personnel for the entire period between arrival on and departure from the territory of the observed Party, and thereafter with respect to acts previously performed in the exercise of their official functions. Such personnel shall also, when transiting the territory of other States Parties, be accorded the privileges and immunities enjoyed by diplomatic agents pursuant to Article 40, paragraph 1 of the Vienna Convention.

3. The immunity from jurisdiction may be waived by the observing Party in those cases when it would impede the course of justice and can be waived without prejudice to this Treaty. The immunity of personnel who are not nationals of the observing Party may be waived only by the States Parties of which such personnel are nationals. Waiver must always be expressed.

4. Without prejudice to their privileges and immunities or the rights of the observing Party set forth in this Treaty, it is the duty of designated personnel to respect the laws and regulations of the observed Party.

5. The transportation means of the personnel shall be accorded the same immunities from search, requisition, attachment or execution as those of a diplomatic mission pursuant to Article 22, paragraph 3 of the Vienna Convention, except as otherwise provided for in this Treaty.

Article XIV

Benelux

1. Solely for the purposes of Articles II to IX and Article XI, and of Annexes A to I and Annex K to this Treaty, the Kingdom of Belgium, the Grand Duchy of Luxembourg, and the Kingdom of the Netherlands shall be deemed a single State Party, hereinafter referred to as the Benelux.

2. Without prejudice to the provisions of Article XV, the above-mentioned States Parties may terminate this arrangement by notifying all other States Parties thereof. This arrangement shall be deemed to be terminated on the next 31 December following the 60-day period after such notification.

Article XV

Duration and Withdrawal

1. This Treaty shall be of unlimited duration.

2. A State Party shall have the right to withdraw from this Treaty. A State Party intending to withdraw shall provide notice of its decision to withdraw to either Depositary at least six months in advance of the date of its intended withdrawal and to all other States Parties. The Depositaries shall promptly inform all other States Parties of such notice.

3. In the event that a State Party provides notice of its decision to withdraw from this Treaty in accordance with paragraph 2 of this Article, the Depositaries shall convene a conference of the States Parties no less than 30 days and no more than 60 days after they have received such notice, in order to consider the effect of the withdrawal on this Treaty.

Article XVI

Amendments and Periodic Review

1. Each State Party shall have the right to propose amendments to this Treaty. The text of each proposed amendment shall be submitted to either Depositary, which shall circulate it to all States Parties for consideration. If so requested by no less than three States Parties within a period of 90 days after circulation of the proposed amendment, the Depositaries shall convene a conference of the States Parties to consider the proposed amendment. Such a conference shall open no earlier than 30 days and no later than 60 days after receipt of the third of such requests.

2. An amendment to this Treaty shall be subject to the approval of all States Parties, either by providing notification, in writing, of their approval to a Depositary within a period of 90 days after circulation of the proposed amendment, or by expressing their approval at a conference convened in accordance with paragraph 1 of this Article. An amendment so approved shall be subject to ratification in accordance with the provisions of Article XVII, paragraph 1, and shall enter into force 60 days after the deposit of instruments of ratification by the States Parties.

3. Unless requested to do so earlier by no less than three States Parties, the Depositaries shall convene a conference of the States Parties to review the implementation of this Treaty three years after entry into force of this Treaty and at five-year intervals thereafter.

Article XVII

Depositaries, Entry Into Force and Accession

1. This Treaty shall be subject to ratification by each State Party in accordance with its constitutional procedures. Instruments of ratification and instruments of accession shall be deposited with the Government of Canada or the Government of the Republic of Hungary or both, hereby designated the Depositaries. This Treaty shall be registered by the Depositaries pursuant to Article 102 of the Charter of the United Nations.

2. This Treaty shall enter into force 60 days after the deposit of 20 instruments of ratification, including those of the Depositaries, and of States Parties whose individual allocation of passive quotas as set forth in Annex A is eight or more.

3. This Treaty shall be open for signature by Armenia, Azerbaijan, Georgia, Kazakhstan, Kirgistan, Moldova, Tajikistan, Turkmenistan and Uzbekistan and shall be subject to ratification by them. Any of

these States which do not sign this Treaty before it enters into force in accordance with the provisions of paragraph 2 of this Article may accede to it at any time by depositing an instrument of accession with one of the Depositaries.

4. For six months after entry into force of this Treaty, any other State participating in the Conference on Security and Co-operation in Europe may apply for accession by submitting a written request to one of the Depositaries. The Depositary receiving such a request shall circulate it promptly to all States Parties. The States applying for accession to this Treaty may also, if they so wish, request an allocation of a passive quota and the level of this quota. The matter shall be considered at the next regular meeting of the Open Skies Consultative Commission and decided in due course.

5. Following six months after entry into force of this Treaty, the Open Skies Consultative Commission may consider the accession to this Treaty of any State which, in the judgement of the Commission, is able and willing to contribute to the objectives of this Treaty.

6. For any State which has not deposited an instrument of ratification by the time of entry into force, but which subsequently ratifies or accedes to this Treaty, this Treaty shall enter into force 60 days after the date of deposit of its instrument of ratification or accession.

7. The Depositaries shall promptly inform all States Parties of:

A. the date of deposit of each instrument of ratification and the date of entry into force of this Treaty;

B. the date of an application for accession, the name of the requesting State and the result of the procedure;

C. the date of deposit of each instrument of accession and the date of entry into force of this Treaty for each State that subsequently accedes to it;

D. the convening of a conference pursuant to Articles XV and XVI;

E. any withdrawal in accordance with Article XV and its effective date;

F. the date of entry into force of any amendments to this Treaty; and

G. any other matters of which the Depositaries are required by this Treaty to inform the States Parties.

Article XVIII

Provisional Application and Phasing of Implementation of the Treaty

In order to facilitate the implementation of this Treaty, certain of its provisions shall be provisionally applied and others shall be implemented in phases.

Section I

Provisional Application

1. Without detriment to Article XVII, the signatory States shall provisionally apply the following provisions of this Treaty:

A. Article VI, Section I, paragraph 4;

B. Article X, paragraphs 1, 2, 3, 6 and 7;

C. Article XI;

D. Article XIII, Section I, paragraphs 1 and 2;

E. Article XIV; and

F. Annex L, Section I.

2. This provisional application shall be effective for a period of 12 months from the date when this Treaty is opened for signature. In the event that this Treaty does not enter into force before the period of provisional application expires, that period may be extended if all the signatory States so decide. The period of provisional application shall in any event terminate when this Treaty enters into force. However, the States Parties may then decide to extend the period of provisional application in respect of signatory States that have not ratified this Treaty.

Section II

Phasing of Implementation

1. After entry into force, this Treaty shall be implemented in phases in accordance with the provisions set forth in this Section. The provisions of paragraphs 2 to 6 of this Section shall apply during the period from entry into force of this Treaty until 31 December of the third year following the year during which entry into force takes place.

2. Notwithstanding the provisions of Article IV, paragraph 1, no State Party shall during the period specified in paragraph 1 above use an infra-red line-scanning device if one is installed on an observation aircraft, unless otherwise agreed between the observing and observed Parties. Such sensors shall not be subject to certification in accordance with Annex D.

If it is difficult to remove such sensor from the observation aircraft, then it shall have covers or other devices that inhibit its operation in accordance with the provisions of Article IV, paragraph 4 during the conduct of observation flights.

3. Notwithstanding the provisions of Article IV, paragraph 9, no State Party shall, during the period specified in paragraph 1 of this Section, be obliged to provide an observation aircraft equipped with sensors from each sensor category, at the maximum capability and in the numbers specified in Article IV, paragraph 2, provided that the observation aircraft is equipped with:

A. a single optical panoramic camera; or

B. not less than a pair of optical framing cameras.

4. Notwithstanding the provisions of Annex B, Section II, paragraph 2, subparagraph (A) to this Treaty, data recording media shall be annotated with data in accordance with existing practice of States Parties during the period specified in paragraph 1 of this Section.

5. Notwithstanding the provisions of Article VI, Section I, paragraph 1, no State Party during the period specified in paragraph 1 of this Section shall have the right to be provided with an aircraft capable of achieving any specified unrefuelled range.

6. During the period specified in paragraph 1 of this Section, the distribution of active quotas shall be established in accordance with the provisions of Annex A, Section II, paragraph 2 to this Treaty.

7. Further phasing in respect of the introduction of additional categories of sensors or improvements to the capabilities of existing categories of sensors shall be addressed by the Open Skies Consultative Commission in accordance with the provisions of Article IV, paragraph 3 concerning such introduction or improvement.

Article XIX

Authentic Texts

The originals of this Treaty, of which the English, French, German, Italian, Russian and Spanish texts are equally authentic, shall be deposited in the archives of the Depositaries. Duly certified copies of this Treaty shall be transmitted by the Depositaries to all the States Parties.

Agreement to Establish a South-North Joint Military Commission

Date of signature: May 7, 1992
Place of signature: Seoul
Signatory states: The Republic of Korea, Democratic People's Republic of Korea
Date of entry into force: May 7, 1992

The South and the North,

In order to achieve and guarantee nonaggression and to discuss and carry out steps to build military confidence and realize arms reduction in accordance with the provisions of Article 12 of the Agreement on Reconciliation, Nonaggression, and Exchanges and Cooperation Between the South and the North, have agreed to establish and operate the South-North Joint Military Commission (hereinafter referred to as the Joint Military Commission) as follows:

Article 1

The Joint Military Commission shall be organized as follows:
1. The Joint Military Commission shall be composed of seven members, including a chairman and a vice chairman, from each side.

2. The chairman shall be of vice-ministerial or higher rank and the ranks of the vice chairman and members shall be determined by each side at its own discretion.

3. Both parties shall notify the other side in advance if and when a member or members of the Joint Military Commission are to be replaced.

4. Each side shall have a staff of 15. When necessary, the size of the staffs may be readjusted by concurrence of both parties.

5. Each side of the Joint Military Commission shall have working-level consultative group(s), if necessary, to ensure the smooth operation of the Joint Military Commission.

Article 2

The Joint Military Commission shall discuss and act on the following matters:
1. Concrete and practical measures to implement, abide by and guarantee the nonaggression provisions of the basic agreement.

2. Preparation and implementation of an agreement designed to achieve, abide by and guarantee nonaggression.

3. Implementation of agreed measures to dissolve military confrontation.

4. Supervision and verification of the implementation of measures mentioned above.

Article 3

The Joint Military Commission shall be operated as follows:

1. The Joint Military Commission shall in principle meet once every three months, providing, however, that it may meet at anytime by concurrence between both parties.

2. The Joint Military Commission shall meet in P'anmunjom, Seoul, P'yongyang or at any other place agreed to by both parties.

3. Meetings of the Joint Military Commission shall be jointly presided over by the chairmen from both sides.

4. The meetings of the Joint Military Commission shall in principle be held behind closed doors, providing, however, that open meetings may be held by concurrence between both parties.

5. Guarantees of personal safety and provision of the necessary services for the personnel traveling from the other area to attend meetings of the Joint Military Commission, and such administrative matters as the recording of proceeding of meetings shall

comply with past practices.

6. Other matters necessary to operate the Joint Military Commission shall be decided by consultation between both sides of the Commission.

Article 4

Accords reached at the Joint Military Commission shall enter into force as of the day when the cochairmen of both sides sign the agreed documents. Depending on the situation, an important document agreed to by both sides shall enter into force as of the day when the appropriate instruments are exchanged after the procedures needed to bring it into force have been completed following its signature by the cochairmen of both sides. If and when an agreement reached by a working-level consultative group has been put into effect through an exchange of the text signed by the cochairmen of both sides, the said agreement shall be reported to a meeting of the Joint Military Commission.

Article 5

This agreement may be revised or supplemented by concurrence between both parties.

Article 6

This agreement shall enter into force as of the day its text is exchanged after it has been signed by both sides.

Treaty of the Southern African Development Community

Date of signature: July 17, 1992
Place of signature: Windhoek
Signatory states: Angola, Botswana, Lesotho, Malawi, Mauritius, Mozambique, Namibia, South Africa Swaziland, Tanzania, Zambia, Zimbabwe

Preamble

[The signatories],
HAVING REGARD to the objectives set forth in "SOUTHERN AFRICA: TOWARD ECONOMIC LIBERATION—A Declaration by the Governments of independent States of Southern Africa, made at Lusaka, on the 1st April, 1980";

IN PURSUANCE of the principles of "TOWARDS

A SOUTHERN AFRICAN DEVELOPMENT COMMUNITY—A Declaration made by the Heads of State or Government of Southern Africa at Windhoek, in August, 1992," which affirms our commitment to establish a Development Community in the Region;

DETERMINED to ensure, through common action, the progress and well-being of the peoples of Southern Africa;

CONSCIOUS of our duty to promote the interdependence and integration of our national economies for the harmonious, balanced and equitable development of the Region;

CONVINCED of the need to mobilise our own and

international resources to promote the implementation of national, interstate and regional policies, programmes and projects within the framework for economic integration;

DEDICATED to secure, by concerted action, international understanding, support and cooperation;

MINDFUL of the need to involve the peoples of the Region centrally in the process of development and integration, particularly through the guarantee of democratic rights, observance of human rights and the rule of law;

RECOGNISING that, in an increasingly interdependent world, mutual understanding, good neighbourliness, and meaningful cooperation among the countries of the Region are indispensable to the realisation of these ideals;

TAKING INTO ACCOUNT the Lagos Plan of Action and the Final Act of Lagos of April 1980, and the Treaty establishing the African Economic Community signed at Abuja, on the 3rd of June, 1991;

BEARING IN MIND the principles of international law governing relations between States;

HAVE DECIDED TO ESTABLISH AN INTERNATIONAL ORGANISATION TO BE KNOWN AS THE SOUTHERN AFRICAN DEVELOPMENT COMMUNITY (SADC), AND HEREBY AGREE AS FOLLOWS:

Chapter I

Article 1

Definitions

In this Treaty, unless the context otherwise requires:

1. "Treaty" means this Treaty establishing SADC;
2. "Protocol" means an instrument of implementation of this Treaty, having the same legal force as this Treaty;
3. "Community" means the organisation for economic integration established by Article 2 of this Treaty;
4. "Region" means the geographical area of the Member States of SADC;
5. "Member State" means a member of SADC;
6. "Summit" means the Summit of the Heads of State or Government of SADC established by Article 9

of this Treaty;
7. "High Contracting Parties" means States, herein represented by Heads of State or Government or their duly authorised representatives for purposes of the establishment of the Community;
8. "Council" means the Council of Ministers of SADC established by Article 9 of this Treaty;
9. "Secretariat" means the Secretariat of SADC established by Article 9 of this Treaty;
10. "Executive Secretary" means the chief executive officer of SADC appointed under Article 10 (7) of this Treaty;
11. "Commission" means a commission of SADC established by Article 9 of this Treaty;
12. "Tribunal" means the tribunal of the Community established by Article 9 of this Treaty;
13. "Sectoral Committee" means a committee referred to in Article 38 of this Treaty;
14. "Sector Coordinating Unit" means a unit referred to in Article 38 of this Treaty;
15. "Standing Committee" means the Standing Committee of Officials established by Article 9 of this Treaty;
16. "Fund" means resources available at any given time for application to programmes, projects and activities of SADC as provided by Article 26 of this Treaty.

Chapter II

Establishment and Legal Status

Article 2

Establishment

1. By this Treaty, the High Contracting Parties establish the Southern African Development Community (hereinafter referred to as SADC).
2. The Headquarters of SADC shall be at Gaborone, Republic of Botswana.

Article 3

Legal Status

1. SADC shall be an international organisation, and shall have legal personality with capacity and power to enter into contract, acquire, own or dispose of movable or immovable property and to sue and be sued.
2. In the territory of each Member State, SADC shall, pursuant to paragraph 1 of this Article, have such legal capacity as is necessary for the proper exercise of its functions.

Chapter III

Principles, Objectives and General Undertakings

Article 4

Principles

SADC and its Member States shall act in accordance with the following principles:

(a) sovereign equality of all Member States;

(b) solidarity, peace and security;

(c) human rights, democracy, and the rule of law;

(d) equity, balance and mutual benefit;

(e) peaceful settlement of disputes.

Article 5

Objectives

1. The objectives of SADC shall be to:

(a) achieve development and economic growth, alleviate poverty, enhance the standard and quality of life of the peoples of Southern Africa and support the socially disadvantaged through regional integration;

(b) evolve common political values, systems and institutions;

(c) promote and defend peace and security;

(d) promote self-sustaining development on the basis of collective self-reliance, and the interdependence of Member States;

(e) achieve complementarity between national and regional strategies and programmes;

(f) promote and maximise productive employment and utilisation of resources of the Region;

(g) achieve sustainable utilisation of natural resources and effective protection of the environment;

(h) strengthen and consolidate the long standing historical, social and cultural affinities and links among the peoples of the Region.

2. In order to achieve the objectives set out in paragraph 1 of this Article, SADC shall:

(a) harmonise political and socio-economic policies and plans of Member States;

(b) encourage the peoples of the Region and their institutions to take initiatives to develop economic, social and cultural ties across the Region, and to participate fully in the implementation of the programmes and projects of SADC;

(c) create appropriate institutions and mechanisms for the mobilisation of requisite resources for the implementation of programmes and operations of SADC and its Institutions;

(d) develop policies aimed at the progressive elimination of obstacles to the free movement of capital and labour, goods and services, and of the peoples of the Region generally, among Member States;

(e) promote the development of human resources;

(f) promote the development, transfer and mastery of technology;

(g) improve economic management and performance through regional cooperation;

(h) promote the coordination and harmonisation of the international relations of Member States;

(i) secure international understanding, cooperation and support, and mobilise the inflow of public and private resources into the Region;

(j) develop such other activities as Member States may decide in furtherance of the objectives of this Treaty.

Article 6

General Undertakings

1. Member States undertake to adopt adequate measures to promote the achievement of the objectives of SADC, and shall refrain from taking any measure likely to jeopardise the sustenance of its principles, the achievement of its objectives and the implementation of the provisions of this Treaty.

2. SADC and Member States shall not discriminate against any person on grounds of gender, religion, political views, race, ethnic origin, culture or disability.

3. SADC shall not discriminate against any Member State.

4. Member States shall take all steps necessary to ensure the uniform application of this Treaty.

5. Member States shall take all necessary steps to accord this Treaty the force of national law.

6. Member States shall cooperate with and assist institutions of SADC in the performance of their duties.

Chapter IV

Membership

Article 7

Membership

States listed in the Preamble hereto shall, upon signature and ratification of this Treaty, be members of SADC.

Article 8

Admission of New Members

1. Any state not listed in the Preamble to this Treaty may become a member of SADC upon being admitted by the existing members and acceding to this Treaty.

2. The admission of any such state to membership of SADC shall be effected by a unanimous decision of the Summit.

3. The Summit shall determine the procedures for the admission of new members and for accession to this Treaty by such members.

4. Membership of SADC shall not be subject to any reservations.

Chapter V

Institutions

Article 9

Establishment of Institutions

1. The following Institutions are hereby established:

(a) The Summit of Heads of State or Government;

(b) The Council of Ministers;

(c) Commissions;

(d) The Standing Committee of Officials;

(e) The Secretariat; and

(f) The Tribunal.

2. Other institutions may be established as necessary.

Article 10

The Summit

1. The Summit shall consist of the Heads of State of Government of all Member States, and shall be the supreme policy-making institution of SADC.

2. The Summit shall be responsible for the overall policy direction and control of the functions of SADC.

3. The Summit shall adopt legal instruments for the implementation of the provisions of this Treaty; provided that the Summit may delegate this authority to the Council or any other institution of SADC as the Summit may deem appropriate.

4. The Summit shall elect a Chairman and a Vice-Chairman of SADC from among its members for an agreed period, on the basis of rotation.

5. The Summit shall meet at least once a year.

6. The Summit shall decide on the creation of Commissions, other institutions, committees and organs as need arises.

7. The Summit shall appoint the Executive Secretary and the Deputy Executive Secretary, on the recommendation of Council.

8. Unless otherwise provided in this Treaty, the decisions of the Summit shall be by consensus and shall be binding.

Article 11

The Council

1. The Council shall consist of one Minister from each Member State, preferably a Minister responsible for economic planning or finance.

2. It shall be the responsibility of the Council to:

(a) oversee the functioning and development of SADC;

(b) oversee the implementation of the policies of SADC and the proper execution of its programmes;

(c) advise the Summit on matters of overall policy and efficient and harmonious functioning and development of SADC;

(d) approve policies, strategies and work programmes of SADC;

(e) direct, coordinate and supervise the operations of the institutions of SADC subordinate to it;

(f) define sectoral areas of cooperation and allocate to Member States responsibility for coordinating sectoral activities, or re-allocate such responsibilities;

(g) create its own committees as necessary;

(h) recommend to the Summit persons for appointment to the posts of Executive Secretary and Deputy Executive Secretary;

(i) determine the Terms and Conditions of Service of

the staff of the institutions of SADC;

(j) convene conferences and other meetings as appropriate, for purposes of promoting the objectives and programmes of SADC; and

(k) perform such other duties as may be assigned to it by the Summit or this Treaty.

3. The Chairman and Vice-Chairman of the Council shall be appointed by the Member States holding the Chairmanship and the Vice-Chairmanship of SADC respectively.

4. The Council shall meet at least once a year.

5. The Council shall report and be responsible to the Summit.

6. Decisions of the Council shall be by consensus.

Article 12

Commissions

1. Commissions shall be constituted to guide and coordinate cooperation and integration policies and programmes in designated sectoral areas.

2. The composition, powers, functions, procedures and other matters related to each Commission shall be prescribed by an appropriate protocol approved by the Summit.

3. The Commissions shall work closely with the Secretariat.

4. Commissions shall be responsible and report to the Council.

Article 13

The Standing Committee of Officials

1. The Standing Committee shall consist of one permanent secretary or an official of equivalent rank from each Member State, preferably from a ministry responsible for economic planning or finance.

2. The Standing Committee shall be a technical advisory committee to the Council.

3. The Standing Committee shall be responsible and report to the Council.

4. The Chairman and Vice-Chairman of the Standing Committee shall be appointed from the Member States holding the Chairmanship and the Vice-Chairmanship, respectively, of the Council.

5. The Standing Committee shall meet at least once a year.

6. Decisions of the Standing Committee shall be by consensus.

Article 14

The Secretariat

1. The Secretariat shall be the principal executive Institution of SADC, and shall be responsible for:

(a) strategic planning and management of the programmes of SADC;

(b) implementation of decisions of the Summit and of the Council;

(c) organisation and management of SADC meetings;

(d) financial and general administration;

(e) representation and promotion of SADC; and

(f) coordination and harmonisation of the policies and strategies of Member States.

2. The Secretariat shall be headed by the Executive Secretary.

3. The Secretariat shall have such other staff as may be determined by the Council from time to time.

Article 15

The Executive Secretary

1. The Executive Secretary shall be responsible to the Council for the following:

(a) consultation and coordination with the Governments and other institutions of Member States;

(b) pursuant to the direction of Council or Summit, or on his/her own initiative, undertaking measures aimed at promoting the objectives of SADC and enhancing its performance;

(c) promotion of cooperation with other organisations for the furtherance of the objectives of SADC;

(d) organising and servicing meetings of the Summit, the Council, the Standing Committee and any other meetings convened on the direction of the Summit or the Council;

(e) custodianship of the property of SADC;

(f) appointment of the staff of the Secretariat, in accordance with procedures, and under Terms and Conditions of Service determined by the Council;

(g) administration and finances of the Secretariat;

(h) preparation of Annual Reports on the activities of SADC and its institutions;

(i) preparation of the Budget and Audited Accounts of SADC for submission to the Council;

(j) diplomatic and other representations of SADC;

(k) public relations and promotion of SADC;

(l) such other functions as may, from time to time, be determined by the Summit and Council.

2. The Executive Secretary shall liaise closely with Commissions, and other institutions, guide, support and monitor the performance of SADC in the various sectors to ensure conformity and harmony with agreed policies, strategies, programmes and projects.

3. The Executive Secretary shall be appointed for four years, and be eligible for appointment for another period not exceeding four years.

Article 16

The Tribunal

1. The Tribunal shall be constituted to ensure adherence to and the proper interpretation of the provisions of this Treaty and subsidiary instruments and to adjudicate upon such disputes as may be referred to it.

2. The composition, powers, functions, procedures and other related matters governing the Tribunal shall be prescribed in a Protocol adopted by the Summit.

3. Members of the Tribunal shall be appointed for a specified period.

4. The Tribunal shall give advisory opinions on such matters as the Summit or the Council may refer to it.

5. The decisions of the Tribunal shall be final and binding.

Article 17

Specific Undertakings

1. Member States shall respect the international character and responsibilities of SADC, the Executive Secretary and other staff of SADC, and shall not seek to influence them in the discharge of their functions.

2. In the performance of their duties, the members of the Tribunal, the Executive Secretary and the other staff of SADC shall be committed to the international character of SADC, and shall not seek or receive instructions from any Member States, or from any authority external to SADC. They shall refrain from any action incompatible with their positions as international staff responsible only to SADC.

Chapter VI

Meetings

Article 18

Quorum

The quorum for all meetings of the Institutions of SADC shall be two-thirds of its Members.

Article 19

Decisions

Except as otherwise provided in this Treaty, decisions of the Institutions of SADC shall be taken by consensus.

Article 20

Procedure

Except as otherwise provided in this Treaty, the Institutions of SADC shall determine their own rules of procedure.

Chapter VII

Cooperation

Article 21

Areas of Cooperation

1. Member States shall cooperate in all areas necessary to foster regional development and integration on the basis of balance, equity and mutual benefit.

2. Member States shall, through appropriate institutions of SADC, coordinate, rationalise and harmonize their overall macro-economic and sectoral policies and strategies, programmes and projects in the areas of cooperation.

3. In accordance with the provisions of this Treaty, Member States agree to cooperate in the areas of:

(a) food security, land and agriculture;

(b) infrastructure and services;

(c) industry, trade, investment and finance;

(d) human resources development, science and technology;

(e) natural resources and environment;

(f) social welfare, information and culture; and

(g) politics, diplomacy, international relations, peace and security.

4. Additional areas of cooperation may be decided upon by the Council.

Article 22

Protocols

1. Member States shall conclude such Protocols as may be necessary in each area of cooperation, which shall spell out the objectives and scope of, and institutional mechanisms for, cooperation and integration.

2. Each Protocol shall be approved by the Summit on the recommendation of the Council, and shall thereafter become an integral part of this Treaty.

3. Each Protocol shall be subject to signature and ratification by the parties thereto.

Article 23

Non-Governmental Organisations

1. In pursuance of the objectives of this Treaty, SADC shall seek to involve fully, the peoples of the Region and non-governmental organisations in the process of regional integration.

2. SADC shall cooperate with, and support the initiatives of the peoples of the Region and non-governmental organisations, contributing to the objectives of this Treaty in the areas of cooperation in order to foster closer relations among the communities, associations and peoples of the Region.

Chapter VIII

Relations with other States, Regional and International Organisations

Article 24

1. Subject to the provisions of Article 6 (1), Member States and SADC shall maintain good working relations and other forms of cooperation, and may enter into agreements with other states, regional and international organisations, whose objectives are compatible with the objectives of SADC and the provisions of this Treaty.

2. Conferences and other meetings may be held between Member States and other Governments and organisations associated with the development efforts of SADC to review policies and strategies, and evaluate the performance of SADC in the implementation of its programmes and projects, identify and agree on future plans of cooperation.

Chapter IX

Resources, Fund and Assets

Article 25

Resources

1. SADC shall be responsible for the mobilisation of its own and other resources required for the implementation of its programmes and projects.

2. SADC shall create such institutions as may be necessary for the effective mobilisation and efficient application of resources for regional development.

3. Resources acquired by SADC by way of contributions, loans, grants or gifts, shall be the property of SADC.

4. The resources of SADC may be made available to Member States in pursuance of the objectives of this Treaty, on terms and conditions mutually agreed between SADC and the Member States involved.

5. Resources of SADC shall be utilised in the most efficient and equitable manner.

Article 26

Fund

The Fund of SADC shall consist of contributions of Member States, income from SADC enterprises and receipts from regional and non-regional sources.

Article 27

Assets

1. Property, both movable and immovable, acquired by or on behalf of SADC shall constitute the assets of SADC, irrespective of their location.

2. Property acquired by Member States, under the auspices of SADC, shall belong to the Member States concerned, subject to provisions of paragraph 3 of this Article, and Articles 25 and 34 of this Treaty.

3. Assets acquired by Member States under the auspices of SADC shall be accessible to all Member States on an equitable basis.

Chapter X

Financial Provisions

Article 28

The Budget

1. The budget of SADC shall be funded by contributions made by Member States, and such other sources as may be determined by the Council.

2. Member States shall contribute to the budget of SADC in proportions agreed upon by the Council.

3. The Executive Secretary shall cause to be prepared, estimates of revenue and expenditure for the Secretariat and Commissions, and submit them to the

Council, not less than three months before the beginning of the financial year.

4. The Council shall approve the estimates of revenue and expenditure before the beginning of the financial year.

5. The financial year of SADC shall be determined by the Council.

Article 29

External Audit

1. The Council shall appoint external auditors and shall fix their fees and remuneration at the beginning of each financial year.

2. The Executive Secretary shall cause to be prepared and audited annual statements of accounts for the Secretariat and Commissions, and submit them to the Council for approval.

Article 30

Financial Regulations

The Executive Secretary shall prepare and submit to the Council for approval financial regulations, standing orders and rules for the management of the affairs of SADC.

Chapter XI

Immunities and Privileges

Article 31

1. SADC, its Institutions and staff shall, in the territory of each Member State, have such immunities and privileges as are necessary for the proper performance of their functions under this Treaty, and which shall be similar to those accorded to comparable international organisations.

2. The immunities and privileges conferred by this Article shall be prescribed in a Protocol.

Chapter XII

Settlement of Disputes

Article 32

Any dispute arising from the interpretation or application of this Treaty, which cannot be settled amicably, shall be referred to the Tribunal.

Chapter XIII

Sanctions, Withdrawal and Dissolution

Article 33

Sanctions

1. Sanctions may be imposed against any Member State that:

(a) persistently fails, without good reason, to fulfill obligations assumed under this Treaty;

(b) implements policies which undermine the principles and objectives of SADC; or

(c) is in arrears for more than one year in the payment of contributions to SADC, for reasons other than those caused by natural calamity or exceptional circumstances that gravely affect its economy, and has not secured the dispensation of the Summit.

2. The sanctions shall be determined by the Summit on a case-by-case basis.

Article 34

Withdrawal

1. A Member State wishing to withdraw from SADC shall serve notice of its intention in writing, a year in advance, to the Chairman of SADC, who shall inform other Member States accordingly.

2. At the expiration of the period of notice, the Member State shall, unless the notice is withdrawn, cease to be a member of SADC.

3. During the one year period of notice referred to in paragraph 1 of this Article, the Member State wishing to withdraw from SADC shall comply with the provisions of this Treaty, and shall continue to be bound by its obligations.

4. A Member State which has withdrawn shall not be entitled to claim any property or rights until the dissolution of SADC.

5. Assets of SADC situated in the territory of a Member State which has withdrawn, shall continue to be the property of SADC and be available for its use.

6. The obligations assumed by Member States under this Treaty shall, to the extent necessary to fulfill such obligations, survive the termination of membership by any State.

Article 35

Dissolution

1. The Summit may decide by a resolution supported by three-quarters of all members to dissolve SADC or any of its Institutions, and determine the terms and conditions of dealing with its liabilities and disposal of its assets.

2. A proposal for the dissolution of SADC may be made to the Council by any Member State, for preliminary consideration, provided, however, that such a proposal shall not be submitted for the decision of the Summit until all Member States have been duly notified of it and a period of twelve months has elapsed after the submission to the Council.

Chapter XIV

Amendment of the Treaty

Article 36

1. An amendment of this Treaty shall be adopted by a decision of three-quarters of all the Members of the Summit.

2. A proposal for the amendment of this Treaty may be made to the Executive Secretary by any Member State for preliminary consideration by the Council, provided, however, that the proposed amendment shall not be submitted to the Council for preliminary consideration until all Member States have been duly notified of it, and a period of three months has elapsed after such notification.

Chapter XV

Language

Article 37

The working languages of SADC shall be English and Portuguese, and such other languages as the Council may determine.

Chapter XVI

Saving Provisions

Article 38

A Sectoral Committee, Sector Coordinating Unit or any other institution, obligation or arrangement of the Southern African Development Coordination Conference which exists immediately before the coming into force of this Treaty, shall to the extent that it is not inconsistent with the provisions of this Treaty, continue to subsist, operate or bind Member States or SADC as if it were established or undertaken under this Treaty, until the Council or Summit determines otherwise.

Chapter XVII

Signature, Ratification, Entry into Force, Accession and Depositary

Article 39

Signature

This Treaty shall be signed by the High Contracting Parties.

Article 40

Ratification

This Treaty shall be ratified by the signatory States in accordance with their constitutional procedures.

Article 41

Entry into Force

This Treaty shall enter into force thirty (30) days after the deposit of the instruments of ratification by two thirds of the States listed in the Preamble.

Article 42

Accession

This Treaty shall remain open for accession by any state subject to Article 8 of this Treaty.

Article 43

Depositary

1. The original texts of this Treaty and Protocols and all instruments of ratification and accession shall be deposited with the Executive Secretary of SADC, who shall transmit certified copies to all Member States.

2. The Executive Secretary shall register this Treaty with the Secretariats of the United Nations Organisation and the Organisation of African Unity.

Chapter XIX

Termination of the Memorandum of Understanding

Article 44

This Treaty replaces the Memorandum of Understanding on the Institutions of the Southern African Development Coordination Conference dated 20th July, 1981.

Protocol on the Compliance with and Implementation of Chapter II, Nonaggression, of the Agreement on Reconciliation, Nonaggression and Exchanges and Cooperation Between the South and the North

Date of signature: September 17, 1992
Place of signature: Pyongyang
Signatory states: The Republic of Korea,
Democratic People's Republic of Korea
Date of entry into force: September 17, 1992

The South and the North,

As a result of concrete negotiations to resolve military confrontation as well as to comply with and implement Chapter II, Nonaggression, of the Agreement on Reconciliation, Nonaggression and Exchanges and Cooperation Between the South and the North.

Have agreed as follows:

Chapter I

Nonuse of Military Power

Article 1

The South and the North shall prohibit the use of military power, including shooting, bombarding, bombing and other forms of attack and destruction, against the people, property, vehicles and civil and military ships and airplanes on the other side of its jurisdiction including the Demilitarized Zone. Neither side shall resort to armed provocation that inflicts damage to the other side.

Article 2

The South and the North shall not infiltrate into or attack by military force the administrative region of the other side or even temporarily occupy part or whole of the area of the other side. Under no circumstances, shall the South and the North infiltrate a regular or irregular force into the administrative region of the other side with any means or method whatsoever.

Article 3

The South and the North shall not engage in hostile acts against citizens from the other side, who are visiting in accordance with an agreement between the two sides, or their belongings or transportation vehicles nor block their way.

In addition, the issues of the nonreinforcement of military power along the Demilitarized Zone, suspension of scouting activities against the other side, and nonblocking of territorial waters and air space of the other side—all proposed by the North—and the issue of guaranteeing the security of Seoul and Pyongyang—proposed by Seoul—shall continue to be discussed in the South-North Military Commission.

Chapter II

Peaceful Settlement of Disputes and Prevention of Accidental Armed Clashes

Article 4

The South and the North, upon detection of any sign of deliberate armed aggression from the other side, shall immediately notify the other side and demand clarification and shall adopt necessary measures so as to prevent it from escalating into an armed clash.

The South and the North, upon the discovery of any unintentional armed clash or aggression due to misunderstanding, misperception, mistake or unavoidable accident, shall immediately notify the other side in accordance with the signals agreed to by both sides, and shall adopt precautionary measures to prevent such incidents.

Article 5

When an armed group, an individual, a vehicle, a civil or military ship or airplane has violated the administrative region of the other side due to natural calamity, navigational error or other unavoidable cause, the trespassing side shall immediately notify the other side of the incident along with the fact that it has no aggression intent and shall abide by instructions of the other side. The other side shall immediately confirm the incident, guarantee the safety of the persons and equipment concerned and take measures to repatriate them.

Repatriation shall be completed within a month in principle but may be further delayed.

Article 6

In the event of an outbreak of a dispute such as accidental aggression or armed clash between the South and the North, the military authorities of both sides shall immediately have the hostile acts of the armed group of its own side stopped, and shall immediately notify the military authorities of the other side through the military hotline or other available means of communications

Article 7

The South and the North shall discuss and resolve all military disputes and confrontation through a mechanism agreed to by the military authorities of both sides.

Article 8

The South and the North, whenever either side has violated this Protocol on the compliance with and implementation of the non-aggression chapter of the Basic Agreement, shall conduct a joint investigation to determine the cause of and responsibility for the violation and shall adopt measures to prevent the recurrence of such an incident.

Chapter III

Demarcation Line and Areas of Nonaggression

Article 9

The South-North demarcation line and areas for nonaggression shall be identical with the Military Demarcation Line specified in the Military Armistice Agreement and the areas that have been under the jurisdiction of each sides until the present time.

Article 10

The South-North sea nonaggression demarcation line shall continue to be discussed. Until the sea nonaggression demarcation line has been finalized, the sea nonaggression zones shall be identical with those that have been under the jurisdiction of each side until the present time.

Article 11

The air nonaggression demarcation line and zone shall be the skies over the land and sea demarcation lines.

Chapter IV

Establishment and Operation of Military Hotlines

Article 12

The South and the North, in order to prevent the outbreak or an escalation of any armed clash, shall establish and operate direct military hotlines between the Minister of National Defense in the South and the Minister of the People's Armed Forces in the North.

Article 13

The direct military hotlines shall use means of communication agreed to by both sides to send the texts of messages over telex, facsimile or telephone. If necessary, the military authorities of both sides may directly converse with each other over the telephone.

Article 14

Technical and practical matters concerning the establishment and operation of the hotlines shall be discussed and resolve by a working-level communications group, composed of five members from each side, as soon as possible following the coming into force of the Protocol.

Article 15

The South and the North shall open the military hotlines within 50 days of the effectuation of the Protocol.

Chapter V

Mechanisms for Consultation and Implementation

Article 16

The South-North Joint Military Commission shall carry out its duties and functions as provided in Article 12 of the Basic Agreement and Article 2 of the Agreement to Establish a South-North Joint Military Commission.

Article 17

The South-North Joint Military Commission shall discuss and adopt concrete measures on issues both side recognize need to be resolved to effectively comply with and implement the nonaggression chapter of the Basic Agreement and remove the military confrontation between the South and the North.

Chapter VI

Amendments and Effectuation

Article 18

This Protocol may be amended or supplemented by agreement between the two sides.

Article 19

This Protocol shall enter into force on the day it is signed and exchanged by the two sides.

Central European Free Trade Agreement

Date of signature: December 21, 1992
Place of signature: Kraków
Signatory states: the Czech Republic, Hungary, Poland, the Slovak Republic
Date of entry into force: March 1, 1993

Preamble

[The signatories], hereinafter called the Parties,

Reaffirming their commitment to pluralistic democracy based on the rule of law, human rights and fundamental freedoms,

Having regard to the Visegrad Declaration of 15 February 1991 and the Cracow Declaration of 6 October 1991 adopted as the results of the meetings of the highest representatives of the Parties,

Recalling their intention to participate actively in the process of economic integration in Europe and expressing their preparedness to co-operate in seeking ways and means to strengthen this process,

Reaffirming their firm commitment to the principles of a market economy, which constitutes the basis for their relations,

Recalling their firm commitment to the Final Act of the Conference on Security and Co-operation in Europe, the Paris Charter, and in particular the principles contained in the final document of the Bonn Conference on Economic Co-operation in Europe,

Resolved to this end to eliminate progressively the obstacles to substantially all their mutual trade, in accordance with the provisions of the General Agreement on Tariffs and Trade,

Firmly convinced that this Agreement will foster the intensification of mutually beneficial trade relations among them and contribute to the process of integration in Europe,

Considering that no provision of this Agreement may be interpreted as exempting the Parties from their obligations under other international agreements, especially the General Agreement on Tariffs and Trade,

Have decided as follows:

Article 1

Objectives

1. The Parties shall gradually establish a free trade area in accordance with the provisions of the present Agreement and in conformity with Article XXIV of the General Agreement on Tariffs and Trade in a transitional period ending on 1 January 2001, at the latest.

2. The objectives of the present Agreement are:

(a) to promote through the expansion of trade the harmonious development of the economic relations between the Parties and thus to foster in the Parties the advance of economic activity, the improvement of living and employment conditions, and increased productivity and financial stability,

(b) to provide fair conditions of competition for trade between the Parties,

(c) to contribute in this way, by the removal barriers to trade, to the harmonious development and expansion of world trade.

Chapter I

Industrial Products

Article 2

Scope

The provisions of this Chapter shall apply to industrial products originating in the Parties. The term "industrial products" means for the purpose of this Agreement the products falling within Chapters 25 to 97 of the Harmonized Commodity Description and Coding System, with the exception of the products listed in Annex I.

[Annex 1 not reproduced]

Article 3

Customs Duties on Imports

1. No new customs duty on imports shall be introduced in trade between the Parties.

2. Customs duties on imports shall be abolished in accordance with the provisions in Protocols 1, 2 and 3.

Provisions for the abolition of customs duties on imports between:

—the Czech Republic and the Slovak Republic on the one side and the Republic of Hungary on the other side are laid down in Protocol 1;

—the Czech Republic and the Slovak Republic on the one side and the Republic of Poland on the other side are laid down in Protocol 2;

—the Republic of Hungary and the Republic of Poland are laid down in Protocol 3.

Article 4

Basic Duties

1. For each product the basic duty to which the successive reductions set out in this Agreement are to be applied shall be the Most Favored Nation rate of duty applicable on 29 February 1992.

2. If, after entry into force of the Agreement, any tariff reduction is applied on an erga omens basis, in particular reductions resulting from the tariff agreement concluded as a result of the Uruguay Round of Multilateral Trade negotiations, such reduced duties shall replace the basic duties referred to in paragraph 1 as from that date when such reductions are applied.

3. The reduced duties calculated in accordance with Article 2 shall be applied rounded to the first decimal place.

4. The Parties shall communicate to each other their respective customs duties.

Article 5

Charges Equivalent to Duties

1. No new charge having an effect equivalent to a customs duty on imports shall be introduced in trade between the Parties.

2. All charges having an effect equivalent to customs duties on imports shall be abolished on the date of the entry into force of this Agreement, except as

provided for in Annex II.
[Annex II not reproduced]

Article 6

Fiscal Duties

The provisions of Article 3 shall also apply to customs duties of a fiscal nature.

Article 7

Customs Duties on Exports and Charges Having Equivalent Effect

1. No customs duty on exports or charge having equivalent effect shall be introduced in trade between the Parties.

2. The Parties shall progressively abolish among them at the latest by 1 January 1997 any customs duties on exports and charges having equivalent effect.

Article 8

Quantitative Restrictions on Imports and Measures Having Equivalent Effect

1. No new quantitative restrictions on imports or measures having equivalent effect shall be introduced in trade between the Parties.

2. All quantitative restrictions and measures having equivalent effect on imports of products originating in the Parties shall be abolished on the date of entry into force of the Agreement, except as provided for in Annexes III/a, III/b and III/c
[Annexes III/a, b, c not reproduced]

Article 9

Quantitative Restrictions on Exports and Measures Having Equivalent Effect

1. No new quantitative restrictions on exports or measures having equivalent effect shall be introduced in trade between the Parties.

2. All quantitative restrictions on exports from the Parties and measures having equivalent effect shall be abolished on the date of the entry into force of the Agreement, except as provided for in Annexes IV/a, IV/b and IV/c.
[Annexes IV/a, b, c not reproduced]

Article 10

Information Procedure on Draft Technical Regulations

1. The Parties shall notify each other at the earliest

practicable stage and in accordance with the provisions laid down in Annex V of draft technical regulations and draft amendments thereto, which they intend to issue.

2. The Joint Committee shall decide on the date for implementing the provisions in paragraph 1.

Chapter II

Agricultural Products

Article 11

Scope

1. The provisions of this Chapter shall apply to agricultural products originating in the Parties to this Agreement.

2. The term "agricultural products" means for the purpose of this Agreement the products falling within Chapters 1 to 24 of the Harmonized Commodity Description and Coding System and the products listed in Annex I.

Article 12

Exchange of Concessions

1. The Parties to this Agreement grant each other the concessions, specified in Protocols 4, 5 and 6 in accordance with provisions of this chapter and laid down in those Protocols.

Concessions exchanged between:

– the Czech Republic and the Slovak Republic on the one side and the Republic of Hungary on the other side are specified in Protocol 4;

– the Czech Republic and the Slovak Pepublic on the one side and the Republic of Poland on the other side are specified in Protocol 5;

– the Republic of Hungary and the Republic of Poland are specified in Protocol 6.

2. Taking account of:

– the role of agriculture in their economies,

– the development of trade in agricultural products between the Parties,

– the particular sensitivity of the agricultural products,

– the rules of their agricultural policies,

– the consequences of the multilateral trade negotiations under the General Agreement on Tariffs and Trade,

the Parties shall examine the possibilities of granting each other further concessions.

Article 13

Concessions and Agricultural Policies

1. Without prejudice to the concessions granted under Article 12, the provisions of this Chapter shall not restrict in any way the pursuance of the respective agricultural policies of the Parties or the taking of any measures under such policies, including the implementation of the results of the Uruguay Round agreements.

2. The Parties shall notify to the Joint Committee changes in their respective agricultural policies pursued or measures applied which may affect the conditions of agricultural trade among them as provided for in this Agreement. On the request of a Party prompt consultations shall be held to examine the situation.

Article 14

Specific Safeguards

Notwithstanding other provisions of this Agreement and in particular Article 27, if, given the particular sensitivity of the agricultural markets, imports of products originating in a Party, which are the subject to concessions granted under this Agreement, cause serious disturbance to the markets of the other Party of Parties, the Parties concerned shall enter into consultations immediately to find an appropriate solution. Pending such solution, the Parties concerned may take measures they deem necessary.

Article 15

Sanitary and Phitosanitary Measures

The Parties shall apply their regulations in veterinary, plant health and health matters in a non-discriminatory fashion and shall not introduce any new measures that have the effect of unduly obstructing trade.

Chapter III

General Provisions

Article 16

Rules of Origin and Co-operation in Customs Administration

1. Protocol 7 lays down the rules of origin and related methods of administrative co-operation.

2. The Parties shall take appropriate measures,

including regular reviews by the Joint Committee and arrangements for administrative co-operation, to ensure that the provisions of Protocol 7 and Articles 3 to 9, 12, 17 and 28 of the Agreement are effectively and harmoniously applied, and to reduce, as far as possible the formalities imposed on trade, and to achieve mutually satisfactory solutions to any difficulties arising from the operation of those provisions.

Article 17

Internal Taxation

1. The Parties shall refrain from any measure or practice of an internal fiscal nature establishing, whether directly or indirectly, discrimination between the products originating in the Parties.

2. Products exported to the territory of one of the Parties may not benefit from repayment of internal taxation in excess of the amount of direct or indirect taxation imposed on them.

Article 18

General Exceptions

This Agreement shall not preclude prohibitions or restrictions on imports, exports or goods in transit justified on grounds of public morality, public policy or public security; the protection of health and life of humans, animals or plants; the protection of national treasures possessing artistic, historic or archaeological value; protection of intellectual property or rules relating to gold or silver or the conservation of exhaustible natural resources if such measures are made effective in conjunction with restrictions on domestic production or consumption. Such prohibitions or restrictions shall not, however, constitute a means of arbitrary discrimination or a disguised restriction on trade between the Parties.

Article 19

Security Exceptions

Nothing in this Agreement shall prevent a Party from taking any measure which it considers necessary;

(a) to prevent the disclosure of information contrary to its essential security interests;

(b) for the protection of its essential security interests or for the implementation of international obligations or national policies;

(i) relating to the traffic in arms, ammunition and

implements of war, provided that such measures do not impair the conditions of competition in respect of products not intended for specifically military purposes, and to such traffic in other goods, materials and services as is carried on directly or indirectly for the purpose of supplying a military establishment; or

(ii) relating to the non-proliferation of biological and chemical weapons, nuclear weapons or other nuclear explosive devices; or

(iii) taken in time of war or other serious international tension.

Article 20

State Monopolies

1. The Parties shall adjust progressively any State monopoly of a commercial character so as to ensure that by the end of the fifth year after the entry into force of the Agreement, no discrimination regarding the conditions under which goods are procured and marketed exists between nationals of the Parties. The Joint Committee will be informed about the measures adopted to implement this objective.

2. The provisions of this Article shall apply to any body through which the competent authorities of the Parties, in law or in fact, either directly or indirectly supervise, determine or appreciably influence imports or exports between the Parties. These provisions shall likewise apply to monopolies delegated by the State to others.

Article 21

Payments

1. Payments in freely convertible currencies relating to trade in goods between the Parties and the transfer of such payments to the territory of the State, Party to this Agreement, where the creditor resides shall be free from any restrictions.

2. The Parties shall refrain from any exchange or administrative restrictions on the grant, repayment or acceptance of short and medium term credits to trade in goods in which a resident participates.

3. Notwithstanding paragraph 2, until Article VIII of the Articles of Agreement of the IMF becomes applicable for the Parties, the Parties reserve the right to apply exchange restrictions on the grant or acceptance of short and medium term credits related to trade in goods to the extent permitted according to their status under the IMF, provided that these restrict-

ions are applied in a non-discriminatory manner as regards the origin of the products and that they are not applied only to specific products or kind of products. The restrictions shall be of limited duration and shall be eliminated when conditions no longer justify their maintenance. The parties shall inform the Joint Committee promptly of the introduction of such measures and of any changes therein.

Article 22

Rules of Competition Concerning Undertakings

1. The following are incompatible with the proper functioning of this Agreement in so far as they may affect trade between the Parties:

(a) all agreements between undertakings, decisions by associations of undertakings and concerted practices between undertakings which have as their object or effect the prevention, restriction or distortion of competition;

(b) abuse by one or more undertakings of a dominant position in the territories of the Parties as a whole or in a substantial part thereof.

2. The provisions of paragraph 1 shall apply to the activities of all undertakings including public undertakings and undertakings to which the Parties grant special or exclusive rights.

Undertakings entrusted with the operation of services of general economic interest or having the character of a revenue-producing monopoly, shall be subject to provisions of paragraph 1 insofar as the application of these provisions does not obstruct the performance, in law or fact, of the particular public tasks assigned to them.

3. With regard to products referred to in Chapter II the provisions stipulated in paragraph 1 (a) shall not apply to such agreements, decisions and practices which form an integral part of a national market organization.

4. If a Party considers that a given practice is incompatible with paragraphs 1, 2 and 3 of this Article and if such practice causes or threatens to cause serious prejudice to the interest of that Party or material injury to its domestic industry, it may take appropriate measures under the conditions and in accordance with the procedure laid down in Article 31.

Article 23

State Aid

1. Any aid granted by a State being a Party to this Agreement or through State resources in any form whatsoever which distorts or threatens to distort competition by favoring certain undertakings or the production of certain goods shall, in so far as it may affect trade between this Party and other Parties to this Agreement, be incompatible with the proper functioning of this Agreement.

2. The provisions of paragraph 1 shall not apply to products referred to in Chapter II.

3. The Joint Committee shall, within three years from the entry into force of this Agreement, adopt the criteria on the basis of which the practices contrary to paragraph 1 shall be assessed, as well as the rules for their implementation.

4. The Parties shall ensure transparency in the area of state aid, inter alia by reporting annually to the Joint Committee on the total amount and the distribution af the aid given and by providing to the other Parties, upon request, information on aid schemes and on particular individual cases of state aid.

5. If a Party considers that a particular practice, including that in agriculture:

– is incompatible with the terms of paragraph 1, and is not adequately dealt with under the implementing rules referred to in paragraph 3, or
– in the absence of such rules, and if such practice causes or threatens to cause serious prejudice to the interest of that Party or material injury to its domestic industry,

it may take appropriate measures under the conditions of and in accordance with the provisions laid down in Article 31.

Such appropriate measures may only be taken in conformity with the procedures and under the conditions laid down by the GATT and any other relevant instrument negotiated under its auspices which are applicable between the Parties concerned.

Article 24

Government Procurement

1. The Parties consider the liberalization of their respective government procurement markets as an objective of this Agreement.

2. The Parties shall progressively develop their respective regulations for government procurement with a view to grant suppliers of the other Parties by the end of the transitional period referred to in Article 1 of this Agreement, at the latest, access to contract award procedures on their respective government procurement markets according to the provi-

sions of the GATT Agreement on Government Procurement of 12 April 1979, as amended by a Protocol of Amendments of 2 February 1987.

3. The Joint Committee shall examine developments related to the achievement of the objectives of this Article and may recommend practical modalities of implementing the provisions of paragraph 2 of this Article so as to ensure free access, transparency and full balance of rights and obligations.

4. During the examination referred to in paragraph 3 of this Article, the Joint Committee may consider, especially in the light of developments in this area in international relations, the possibility of extending the coverage and/or the degree of the market opening provided for in paragraph 2.

5. The Parties shall endeavor to accede to the relevant Agreements negotiated under the auspices of the GATT.

Article 25

Protection of Intellectual Property

1. The Parties shall grant and ensure protection of intellectual property rights on a non-discriminatory basis, including measures for the grant and enforcement of such rights. The protection shall be gradually improved and, before the end of the fifth year after the entry into force of this Agreement, of a level corresponding to the substantive standards of the multilateral agreements which are specified in Annex VI. **[Annex VI reproduced at 34 I.L.M. 19 (1995)]**

2. For the purpose of this Agreement "intellectual property protection" includes in particular protection of copyright, comprising computer programs and databases, and neighboring rights, trade marks, geographical indications, industrial designs, patents, topographies of integrated circuits, as well as undisclosed information on know-how.

3. Protection of topographies of integrated circuits ensured by any Party shall be granted on reciprocal basis.

4. The Parties shall co-operate in matters of intellectual property. They shall hold, upon request of any Party, expert consultations on these matters, in particular on activities relating to the existing or to future international conventions on harmonization, administration and enforcement of intellectual property and on activities in international organizations, such as the General Agreement on Tariffs and Trade, WIPO, as well as relations of Parties with third countries on matters concerning intellectual property.

Article 26

Dumping

If a Party finds that dumping within the meaning of Article 6 of the GATT is taking place in trade relations governed by this Agreement, it may take appropriate measures against that practice in accordance with Article 6 of the General Agreement on Tariffs and Trade and agreements related to that Article, under the conditions and in accordance with the procedure laid down in Article 31.

Article 27

General Safeguards

Where any product is being imported in such increased quantities and under such conditions as to cause or threaten to cause:

(a) serious injury to domestic producers of like or directly competitive products in the territory of the importing Party, or

(b) serious disturbances in any related sector of the economy or difficulties which could bring about serious deterioration in the economic situation of a region,

the Party concerned may take appropriate measures under the conditions and in accordance with the procedure laid down in Article 31.

Article 28

Structural Adjustment

1. Exceptional measures of limited duration which derogate from the provisions of Article 3 may be taken by any of the Parties in the form of increased customs duties.

2. These measures may only concern infant industries, or certain sectors undergoing restructuring or facing serious difficulties, particularly where these difficulties produce important social problems.

3. Customs duties on imports applicable in the Party concerned to products originating in the other Party introduced by these measures may not exceed 25% ad valorem and shall maintain an element of preference for products originating in the Parties. The total value of imports of the products which are subject to these measures may not exceed 15% of total imports of industrial products from the other Parties as defined in Chapter 1, during the last year for which statistics are available.

4. These measures shall be applied for a period not exceeding five years unless a longer duration is authorized by the Joint Committee. They shall cease to apply at the latest at the expiration of the transitional period.

5. No such measures can be introduced in respect of a product if more than three years elapsed since the elimination of all duties and quantitative restrictions or charges or measures having an equivalent effect concerning that product.

6. The Party concerned shall inform the Joint Committee of any exceptional measures it intends to take and, at the request of the other Parties, consultations shall be held in the Joint Committee on such measures and the sectors to which they apply before they are applied. When taking such measures the Party concerned shall provide the Joint Committee with a schedule for the elimination of the customs duties introduced under this Article. This schedule shall provide for a phasing out of these duties starting at the latest two years after their introduction, at equal annual rates. The Joint Committee may decide on a different schedule.

Article 29

Re-export and Serious Shortage

Where compliance with the provisions of Article 7 and 9 leads to:

(a) re-export towards a third country against which the exporting Party maintains for the product concerned quantitative export restrictions, export duties or measures or charges having equivalent effect; or

(b) a serious shortage, or threat thereof, of a product essential to the exporting Party;

and where the situations referred to above give rise or are likely to give rise to major difficulties for the exporting Party, that Party may take appropriate measures under the conditions and in accordance with the procedures laid down in Article 31.

Article 30

Fulfillment of Obligations

1. The Parties shall take any general or specific measures required to fulfill their obligations under the Agreement. They shall see to it that the objectives set out in the Agreement are attained.

2. If a Party considers that the other Party has failed to fulfill an obligation under this Agreement, the Party concerned may take appropriate measures under the conditions and in accordance with the procedure laid down in Article 31.

Article 31

Procedure for the Application of Safeguard Measures

1. Before initiating the procedure for the application of safeguard measures set out in the following paragraphs of the present Article, the Parties shall endeavor to solve any differences between them through direct consultations.

2. In the event of a Party subjecting imports of products liable to give rise to the situation referred to in Article 27 to an administrative procedure having as its purpose the rapid provision of information on the trend of trade flows, it shall inform the other Party.

3. Without prejudice to paragraph 7 of the present Article, a Party which considers resorting to safeguard measures shall promptly notify the other Party and the Joint Committee thereof and supply all relevant information. Consultations between the Parties shall take place without delay in the Joint Committee with a view to finding a solution.

4. (a) As regards Articles 26, 27 and 29, the Joint Committee shall examine the case or the situation and may take any decision needed to put an end to the difficulties notified by the Party concerned. In the absence of such decision within thirty days of the matter being referred to the Joint Committee, the Party concerned may adopt the measures necessary in order to remedy the situation.

(b) As regards Article 30, the Party concerned may take appropriate measures after the consultations have been concluded or a period of three months has elapsed from the date of notification.

(c) As regards Article 22 and 23, the Parties concerned shall give the Joint Committee all the assistance required in order to examine the case and, where appropriate, eliminate the practice objected to. If the Party in question fails to put an end to the practice objected to within the period fixed by the Joint Committee or if the Joint Committee fails to reach an agreement within thirty working days of the matter being referred to it, the Party concerned may adopt the appropriate measures to deal with the difficulties resulting from the practice in question.

5. The safeguard measures taken shall be notified immediately to the other Party and to the Joint Committee. They shall be restricted with regard to their extent and to their duration to what is strictly necessary in order to rectify the situation giving rise to their application and shall not be in excess of the injury caused by the practice or the difficulty in question. Priority shall be given to such measures as will least disturb the functioning of the Agreement. The measures taken by a Party against an action or an omission of another Party may only affect the trade with that Party.

6. The safeguard measures taken shall be the object of periodic consultations within the Joint Committee with a view to their relaxation as soon as possible or abolition when conditions no longer justify their maintenance.

7. Where exceptional circumstances requiring immediate action make prior examination impossible, the Party concerned may, in the cases of Articles 26, 27 and 29, apply forthwith the provisional measures strictly necessary to remedy the situation. The measures shall be notified without delay and consultations between the Parties shall take place as soon as possible within the Joint Committee.

Article 32

Balance of Payments Difficulties

1. The Parties shall endeavor to avoid the imposition of restrictive measures including measures relating to imports for balance of payments purposes.

2. Where one of the Parties is in serious balance of payments difficulties, or under imminent threat thereof, the Party concerned may, in accordance with the conditions established under the General Agreement on Tariffs and Trade, adopt restrictive measures, including measures related to imports, which shall be of limited duration and may not go beyond what is necessary to remedy the balance of payments situation. The measures shall be progressively relaxed as balance of payments conditions improve and they shall be eliminated when conditions no longer justify their maintenance. The Party shall inform the other Party forthwith of their introduction and, whenever practicable, of a time schedule for their removal.

Article 33

Evolutionary Clause

1. Where a Party considers that it would be useful in the interests of the economies of the Parties to develop and deepen the relations established by the Agreement by extending them to fields not covered thereby, it shall submit a reasoned request to the other Party. The Parties may instruct the Joint Committee to examine such a request and, where appropriate, to make recommendations, particularly with a view to opening negotiations.

2. Agreements resulting from the procedure referred to in paragraph 1 will be subject to ratification or approval by the Parties in accordance with their own procedures.

Article 34

The Joint Committee

1. The Parties agree to set up the Joint Committee composed of representatives of the Parties.

2. The implementation of this Agreement shall be supervised and administered by the Joint Committee.

3. For the purpose of the proper implementation of the Agreement, the Parties shall exchange information and, at the request of any Party, shall hold consultations within the Joint Committee. The Committee shall keep under review the possibility of further removal of the obstacles to trade between the Parties.

4. The Joint Committee may take decisions in the cases provided for in this Agreement. On other matters the Committee may make recommendations.

Article 35

Procedures of the Joint Committee

1. For the proper implementation of this Agreement the Joint Committee shall meet whenever necessary but at least once a year. Each Party may request that a meeting be held.

2. The Joint Committee shall act by common agreement.

3. If a representative in the Joint Committee of a Party to this Agreement has accepted a decision subject to the fulfillment of constitutional requirements, the decision shall enter into force, if no later date is contained therein, on the day the lifting of the reservation is notified.

4. For the purpose of this Agreement the Joint Committee shall adopt its rules of procedure which shall, inter alia, contain provisions for convening meetings and for the designation of the Chairman and his term of office.

5. The Joint Committee may decide to set up such subcommittees and working parties as it considers necessary to assist it in accomplishing its tasks.

Article 36

Trade Relations Governed by This and Other Agreements

1. This Agreement shall apply to trade relations among the Czech Republic, the Republic of Poland, the Republic of Hungary and the Slovak Republic but not to the trade relations between the Czech Republic and the Slovak Republic.

2. This Agreement shall not prevent the maintenance or establishment of customs unions, free trade areas or arrangements for frontier trade to the extent that these do not negatively affect the trade regime and in particular the provisions concerning rules of origin provided for by this Agreement.

Article 37

Annexes and Protocols

The Annexes and the Protocols to this Agreement are an integral part of it. The Joint Committee may decide to amend the Annexes and Protocols in accordance with the provisions of paragraph 3 of the Article 35.

Article 38

Territorial Application

This Agreement shall apply to the territories of the States Parties to the Agreement.

Article 39

Amendments

Amendments to this Agreement other than those referred to in paragraph 4 of Article 34 which are approved by the Joint Committee shall be submitted to the Parties to this Agreement for acceptance and shall enter into force if accepted by all the Parties. The instruments of acceptance shall be deposited with the Depositary.

Article 40

Entry into Force

1. This Agreement shall enter into force on 1 March 1993 provided that all Parties have deposited their instruments of ratification with the Depositary.

2. If this Agreement has not entered into force in accordance with the provision of paragraph 1, representatives of the Parties having deposited their instruments of ratification shall meet before 30 April 1993 and may decide when the Agreement shall enter into force in relation to those Parties.

3. In relation to a Party depositing its instruments of ratification after the meeting referred to in paragraph 2, this Agreement shall enter into force on the first day of the second month following the deposit of its instrument but not before the date decided upon in accordance with paragraph 2.

4. Any Party may already at the time of signature declare that, during an initial phase it shall apply the Agreement provisionally if the Agreement cannot enter into force in relation to that Party by 1 March 1993.

Article 41

Validity and Withdrawal

Each Party to this Agreement may withdraw therefrom, including from the provisional application by means of a written notification to the Depositary. The withdrawal shall take effect six months after the date on which the notification was received by the Depositary.

The Agreement remains in force for the other Parties.

Article 42

Depositary

The Government of Poland, acting as Depositary, shall notify all States that have signed this Agreement of the deposit of any instrument of ratification, the entry into force of this Agreement, any other act or notification relating to this Agreement or of its validity.

Treaty Between the United States of America and the Russian Federation on the Further Reduction and Limitation of Strategic Offensive Arms

Date of signature: January 3, 1993
Place of signature: Moscow

Signatory states: The United States of America; The Russian Federation

[The signatories], hereinafter referred to as the Parties,

Reaffirming their obligations under the Treaty Between the United States of America and the Union of Soviet Socialist Republics on the Reduction and Limitation of Strategic Offensive Arms of July 31, 1991, hereinafter referred to as the START Treaty.

Stressing their firm commitment to the Treaty on the Non-Proliferation of Nuclear Weapons of July 1, 1968, and their desire to contribute to its strengthening.

Taking into account the commitment by the Republic of Belarus, the Republic of Kazakhstan, and Ukraine to accede to the Treaty on the Non-Proliferation of Nuclear Weapons of July 1, 1968, as non-nuclear weapon States Parties.

Mindful of their undertaking with respect to strategic offensive arms under Article VI of the Treaty on the Non-Proliferation of Nuclear Weapons of July 1, 1968, and under the Treaty Between the United States of America and the Union of Soviet Socialist Republics on the Limitation of Anti-Ballistic Missile Systems of May 26, 1972, as well as the provisions of the Joint Understanding signed by the Presidents of the United States of America and the Russian Federation on June 17, 1992, and of the Joint Statement on a Global Protection System signed by the Presidents of the United States of America and the Russian Federation on June 17, 1992.

Desiring to enhance strategic stability and predictability, and in doing so, to reduce further strategic offensive arms, in addition to the reductions and limitations provided for in the START Treaty.

Considering that further progress toward that end will help lay a solid foundation for a world order built on democratic values that would preclude the risk of outbreak of war.

Recognizing their special responsibility as permanent members of the United Nations Security Council for maintaining international peace and security.

Taking note of United Nations General Assembly Resolution 47/52K of December 9, 1992.

Conscious of the new realities that have transformed the political and strategic relations between the Parties, and the relations of partnership that have been established between them,

Have agreed as follow:

Article I

1. Each Party shall reduce and limit its intercontinental ballistic missiles (ICBMS) and ICBM launchers, submarine-launched ballistic missiles (SLBMS) and SLBM launchers, heavy bombers, ICBM warheads, SLBM warheads, and heavy bomber armaments, so that seven years after entry into force to the START Treaty and thereafter, the aggregate number for each Party, as counted in accordance with Articles III and IV of this Treaty, does not exceed, for warheads attributed to deployed ICBMs, deployed SLBMs, and deployed heavy bombers, a number between 3800 and 4250 or such lower number as each Party shall decide for itself, but in no case shall such number exceed 4250.

2. Within the limitations provided for in paragraph 1 of this Article, the aggregate number for each Party shall not exceed:

(a) 2160, for warheads attributed to deployed SLBMs;

(b) 1200, for warheads attributed to deployed ICBMs of types to which more than one warhead is attributed; and

(c) 650, for warheads attributed to deployed heavy ICBMS.

3. Upon fulfillment of the obligations provided for in paragraph 1 of this Article, each Party shall further reduce and limit its ICBMS and ICBM launchers, heavy bombers, ICBMs warheads, SLBMs warheads and heavy bomber armaments so that no later than January, 2003, and thereafter, the aggregate number for each Party, as counted in accordance with Article III and IV of this Treaty, does not exceed, for warheads attributed to deployed ICBMs, deployed SLBMs, and deployed heavy bombers, a number between 3000 and 3500 or such lower number as each Party shall decide for itself, but in no case shall such number exceed 3500.

4. Within the limitations provided for in paragraph 3 of this Article, the aggregate numbers for each Party shall not exceed:

(a) a number between 1700 and 1750, for warheads attributed to deployed SLBMs or such lower number as each Party shall decide for itself, but in no case shall such number exceed 1750;

(b) zero, for warheads attributed to deployed ICBMS of types of which more than one warhead is attributed; and

(c) zero, for warheads attributed to deployed heavy ICBMS.

5. The process of reductions provided for in paragraph 1 and 2 of this Article shall begin upon entry into force of this Treaty, shall be sustained throughout the reductions period provided for in paragraph 1 of this Article, and shall be completed no later than

seven years after entry into force of the START Treaty, Upon completion of these reductions, the Parties shall begin further reductions provided for in paragraphs 3 and 4 of this Article, which shall also be sustained throughout the reductions period defined in accordance with paragraphs 3 and 6 of this Article.

6. Provided that the Parties conclude, within one year after entry into force of this Treaty, an agreement on a program of assistance to promote the fulfillment of the provisions of this Article, the obligations provided for in paragraph 3 and 4 of this Article and in Article II of this Treaty shall be fulfilled by each Party no later than December 31, 2000.

Article II

1. No later than January 1, 2003, each Party undertake to have eliminated or to have converted to launchers of ICBMs to which one warhead is attributed all its deployed and non-deployed launchers of ICBMs to which more than one warhead is attributed under Article III of this Treaty (including test launchers and training launchers), with the exception of those launchers of ICBMs other than heavy ICBMs at space launch facilities allowed under the START Treaty, and not to have thereafter launchers of ICBMs to which more than one warhead is attributed. ICBM Launchers that have been converted to launch an ICBM of different type shall not be capable of launching an ICBM of the former type. Each Party shall carry out such elimination or conversion using the procedures provided for in the START Treaty, except as otherwise provided for in paragraph 3 of this Article.

2. The obligations provide for in paragraph 1 of this Article shall not apply to silo launchers of ICBMs on which the number of warheads has been reduced to one pursuant to paragraph 2 of Article III of this Treaty.

3. Elimination of silo launchers of heavy ICBMs, including test launchers and training launcher, shall be implemented by means of either:

(a) elimination in accordance with the procedures provided for in Section II of the Protocol on Procedures Governing the Conversion or Elimination of the Items Subject to the START Treaty; or

(b) conversion to silo launchers of ICBMs other than heavy ICBMs in accordance with the procedures provided for in the Protocol on Procedures Governing Elimination of Heavy ICBMs and Procedures Governing Conversion of Silo Launchers of Heavy ICBMs Relating to the Treaty Between the United States of America and the Russian Federation on Further Reduction and Limitation of Strategic Offensive Arms, hereinafter referred to as the Elimination and Conversion Protocol. No more than 90 silo launchers of heavy ICBMs may be so converted.

4. Each Party undertakes not to emplace an ICBM, the launch canister of which has a diameter greater than 2.5 meters, in any silo launcher of heavy ICBMs converted in accordance with subparagraph 3(b) of this Article.

5. Elimination of launchers of heavy ICBMs at space launch facilities shall only be carried out in accordance with subparagraph 3(a) of this Article.

6. No later than January 1, 2003, each Party undertakes to have eliminated all of its deployed and non-deployed heavy ICBMs and their launch canisters in accordance with the procedure provided for in the Elimination and Conversion Protocol or by using such missiles for delivering objects into the upper atmosphere or space, and not to have such missiles or launch canisters thereafter.

7. Each Party shall have the right to conduct inspections in connection with the elimination of have ICBMs and their launch canisters, as well as inspections in connection with the conversion of silo launchers of heavy ICBMs. Except as otherwise provided for in the Elimination and Conversion Protocol, such inspections shall be conducted subject to the applicable provisions of the START Treaty.

8. Each Party undertakes not to transfer heavy ICBMs to any recipient whatsoever, including any other Party to the START Treaty.

9. Beginning on January 1, 2003, and thereafter, each Party undertakes not to produce, acquire, flight-test (except for flight tests from space launch facilities conducted in accordance with the provisions of the START Treaty), or deploy ICBMs to which more than one warhead is attributed under Article III of this Treaty.

Article III

1. For the purpose of attributing warheads to deployed ICBMs and deployed SLBMs under this Treaty, the Party shall use the provisions provided for in Article III of the START Treaty, except as otherwise provided for in paragraph 2 of this Article.

2. Each Party shall have the right to reduce the number of warheads attributed to deployed ICBMs or deployed SLBMs only of existing types, except for heavy ICBMs. Reduction in the number of warheads attributed to deployed ICBMs and deployed SLBMs of existing types that are not heavy ICBMs shall be car-

ried out in accordance with the provisions of paragraph 5 of Article III of the START Treaty, except that:

(a) the aggregate number by which warheads are reduced may exceed the 1250 limit provided for in paragraph 5 of Article III of the START Treaty;

(b) the number by which warheads are reduced on ICBMS and SLBMS, other than the Minuteman III ICBM for the United States of America and the SS-N-18 SLBM for the Russian Federation, may at any one time exceed the limit of 500 warheads for each Party provided for in subparagraph 5(c)(i) of Article III of the START Treaty;

(c) each Party shall have the right to reduce by more than four warheads, but not by more than five warheads, the number of warheads attributed to each ICBM out of no more than 105 ICBMs of one existing type of ICBM. An ICBM to which the number of warheads attributed has been reduced in accordance with this paragraph shall only be deployed in an ICBM launcher in which an ICBM of that type was deployed as of the date of signature of the START Treaty; and

(d) the reentry vehicle platform for an ICBM or SLBM to which a reduced number of warheads is attributed is not required to be destroyed and replaced with a new reentry vehicle platform.

3. Notwithstanding the number of warheads attributed to a type of ICBM or SLBM in accordance with the START Treaty, each Party undertakes not to:

(a) produce, flight-test, or deploy an ICBM or SLBM with a number of reentry vehicles greater than the number of warheads attributed to it under this Treaty; and

(b) increase the number of warheads attributed to an ICBM or SLBM that has had the number of warheads attributed to it reduced in accordance with the provision of this Article.

Article IV

1. For the purpose of this Treaty, the number of warheads attributed to each deployed heavy bomber shall be equal to the number of nuclear weapons for which any heavy bomber of the same type or variant of a type is actually equipped with the exception of heavy bomber reoriented to a conventional role as provided for in paragraph 7 of this Article. Each nuclear weapon for which a heavy bomber is actually equipped shall count as one warhead toward the limitations provided for in Article I of this Treaty. For the purpose of such counting, nuclear weapons include long-range nuclear air-launched cruise missiles (ALCMS), nuclear air-to-surface missiles with a range of less than 600 kilometers, and nuclear bombs.

2. For the purposes of this Treaty, the number of nuclear weapon for which a heavy bomber is actually equipped shall be the number specified for heavy bombers of that type and variant of a type in the Memorandum of Understanding on Warhead Attribution and Heavy Bomber Data Relating to the Treaty Between the United States of America and the Russian Federation on Further Reduction and Limitation of Strategic Offensive Arms, hereinafter referred to as the Memorandum on Attribution.

3. Each Party undertakes not to equip any heavy bomber with a great number of nuclear heavy bomber of each type and variant of a type specified in the Memorandum on Attribution. The purpose of the exhibition shall be to demonstrate to the other Party the number of nuclear weapons for which a heavy bomber of a given type or variant of a type is actually equipped.

4. If either Party intends to change the number of nuclear weapons specified in the Memorandum on Attribution, for which a heavy bomber of a type or variant of a type is actually equipped, it shall provide a 90-day advance notification of such intention to the other Party. Ninety days after providing such a notification, or at a later date agreed by the Parties, the Party changing the number of nuclear weapons for which a heavy bomber is actually equipped shall exhibit one heavy bomber of each such type or variant of a type. The purpose of the exhibition shall be to demonstrate to the other Party the revised number of nuclear weapons for which heavy bombers of the specified type or variant of a type are actually equipped. The number of nuclear weapons attributed to the specified type and variant of a type of heavy bomber shall change on the ninetieth day after the notification of such intent. On the day, the Party changing the number of nuclear weapons for which a heavy bombers is actually equipped shall provide to the other Party a notification of each change in data according to categories of data contained in the Memorandum on Attribution.

5. The exhibitions and inspections conducted pursuant to paragraphs 4 and 5 of this Article shall be carried out in accordance with the procedures provided for in the Protocol on Exhibitions and Inspections of Heavy Relating to the Treaty Between the United States of America and the Russian Federation on Further Reduction and Limitation of Strategic Offensive Arms, hereinafter referred to as the Protocol on

Exhibitions and Inspections.

6. Each Party shall have the right to reorient to a conventional role heavy bomber equipment for nuclear armaments other than long-range nuclear ALCMs. For the purpose of this Treaty, heavy bombers reoriented to a conventional role are those heavy bombers specified by a Party from among its heavy bombers equipped for nuclear armaments other than long-range nuclear ALCMs that have never been accountable under the START Treaty as heavy bombers equipped for long-range nuclear ALCMs. The reorienting Party shall provided to the other Party a notification of its intent to reorient a heavy bomber to a conventional role no less than 90 days in advance of such reorientation. No conversion procedures shall be required for such a heavy bomber to be specified as a heavy bomber reoriented to a conventional role.

7. Heavy bombers reoriented to a conventional role shall be subject to the following requirements:

(a) the number of such bombers shall not exceed 100 at any one time;

(b) such heavy bombers shall be based separately from heavy bombers with nuclear roles;

(c) such heavy bombers shall be used only for non-nuclear missions. Such heavy bombers shall not be used in exercises for nuclear missions, and their aircrew shall not train or exercises for such missions; and

(d) heavy bombers reoriented to a conventional role shall have differences from other heavy bombers of that type or variant of a type that are observable by national technical means of verification and visible during inspection.

8. Each Party shall have the right to return to a nuclear role heavy bombers that have been reoriented in accordance with paragraph 7 of this Article to a conventional role. The Party carrying out such action shall provide to the other Party through diplomatic channels notification of its intent to return a heavy bomber to a nuclear role no less than 90 days in advance of taking such action. Such a heavy bomber returned to a nuclear role shall not subsequently be reoriented to a conventional role. Heavy bombers reoriented to a conventional role that are subsequently returned to a nuclear role shall have differences observable by national technical means of verification and visible during inspection from other heavy bombers of that type and variant of a type that have not been reoriented to a conventional role, as well of

from heavy bombers of that type and variant of a type that are still reoriented to a conventional role.

9. Each Party shall storage areas for heavy bomber nuclear armaments no less than 100 kilometers from any air base where heavy bombers reoriented to a conventional role are based.

10. Except as otherwise provided for in this Treaty, heavy bombers reoriented to a conventional role shall remain subject to the provisions of the START Treaty, including the inspection provisions.

11. If not all heavy bombers of a given type or variant of a type are reoriented to a conventional role, one heavy bomber of each type or variant to a type of heavy bomber reoriented to a conventional role shall be exhibited in the open for the purpose of demonstrating to the other Party the differences referred to in subparagraph 8(d) of this Article. Such differences shall be subject to inspection by the other Party.

12. If not all heavy bomber of a given type or variant of a type reoriented to a conventional role are returned to a nuclear role, one heavy bomber of each type and variant of a type of heavy bomber returned to a nuclear role shall be exhibited in the open for the purpose of heavy bomber returned to a nuclear role shall be exhibited in the open for purpose of demonstrating to the other Party the differences referred to in paragraph 9 of this Article. Such differences shall be subject to inspection by the other Party.

13. The exhibitions and inspections provided for in paragraphs 12 and 13 of this Article shall be carried out in accordance with the procedures provided for in the Protocol on Exhibitions and Inspections.

Article V

1. Except as provided for in this Treaty, the provisions of the START Treaty, including the verification provisions, shall be used for implementation of this Treaty.

2. To promote the objective and implementation of the provisions of this Treaty, the Parties hereby establish the Bilateral Implementation Commission. The Parties agree that, if either Party so requests, they shall meet within the framework of the Bilateral Implementation Commission to:

(a) resolve question relating to compliance with the obligations assumed; and

(b) agree upon such additional measures as may be necessary to improve the viability and effectiveness of this Treaty.

Article VI

1. This treaty including its Memorandum on Attribution Elimination and Conversion Protocol, and Protocol on Exhibitions and Inspections, all of which are integral parts thereof, shall be subject to ratification in accordance with the constitutional procedures of each Party. This Treaty shall enter into force on the date of the exchange of instruments of ratification, but not prior to the entry into force of the START Treaty.

2. The provisions of paragraph 8 of Article II of this Treaty shall be applied provisionally by the Parties from the date of its signature.

3. This Treaty shall remain in force so long as the START Treaty remains in force.

4. Each Party shall, in exercising its national sovereignty, have the right to withdraw from this Treaty if it decides that extraordinary events related to the subject matter of this Treaty have jeopardized its supreme interests. It shall give notice of its decision to the other Party six months prior to withdrawal from this Treaty. Such notice shall include a statement of the extraordinary events the notifying Party regards as having jeopardized its supreme interests.

Article VII

Each Party may propose amendments to this Treaty. Agreed amendments shall enter into force in accordance with the procedures governing entry into force of this Treaty.

Article VIII

This Treaty shall be registered pursuant to Article 102 of the Charter of the United Nations.

Convention on the Prohibition of the Development, Production, Stockpiling and Use of Chemical Weapons and on Their Destruction

Date of signature: January 12, 1993
Place of signature: Paris
Signatory states: Afghanistan, Albania, Algeria, Argentina, Armenia, Australia, Austria, Azerbaijan, Bahamas, Bahrain, Bangladesh, Belarus, Belgium, Benin, Bhutan, Bolivia, Bosnia and Herzegovina, Botswana, Brazil, Brunei Darussalam, Bulgaria, Burkina Faso, Burundi, Cambodia, Cameroon, Canada, Cape Verde, Central African Republic, Chad, Chile, China, Colombia, Comoros, Congo, Cook Islands, Costa Rica, Cote d'Ivoire, Croatia, Cuba, Cyprus, Czech Republic, Democratic Republic of the Congo, Denmark, Djibouti, Dominica, Dominican Republic, Ecuador, El Salvador, Equatorial Guinea, Estonia, Ethiopia, Fiji, Finland, France, Gabon, Gambia, Georgia, Germany, Ghana, Greece, Grenada, Guatemala, Guinea, Guinea-Bissau, Guyana, Haiti, Holy See, Honduras, Hungary, Iceland, India, Indonesia, Iran (Islamic Republic of), Ireland, Israel, Italy, Jamaica, Japan, Jordan, Kazakhstan, Kenya, Kuwait, Kyrgyzstan, Lao People's Democratic Republic, Latvia, Lesotho, Liberia, Liechtenstein, Lithuania, Luxembourg, Madagascar, Malawi, Malaysia, Maldives, Mali, Malta, Marshall Islands, Mauritania, Mauritius, Mexico, Micronesia (Federated States of), Monaco, Mongolia, Morocco, Myanmar, Namibia, Nauru, Nepal, Netherlands, New Zealand, Nicaragua, Niger, Nigeria, Norway, Oman, Pakistan, Panama, Papua New Guinea, Paraguay, Peru, Philippines, Poland, Portugal, Qatar, Republic of Korea, Republic of Moldova, Romania, Russian Federation, Rwanda, Saint Kitts and Nevis, Saint Lucia, Saint Vincent and the Grenadines, Samoa, San Marino, Saudi Arabia, Senegal, Seychelles, Sierra Leone, Singapore, Slovak Republic, Slovenia, South Africa, Spain, Sri Lanka, Suriname, Swaziland, Sweden, Switzerland, Tajikistan, Thailand, The former Yugoslav Republic of Macedonia, Togo, Trinidad and Tobago, Tunisia, Turkey, Turkmenistan, Uganda, Ukraine, United Arab Emirates, United Kingdom of Great Britain and Northern Ireland, United Republic of Tanzania, United States of America, Uruguay, Uzbekistan, Venezuela, Viet Nam, Yemen, Zambia, Zimbabwe
Ratification: Albania, Algeria, Argentina, Armenia, Australia, Austria, Azerbaijan, Bahamas, Bahrain, Bangladesh, Belarus, Belgium, Benin, Bolivia, Bosnia and Herzegovina, Brazil, Brunei Darussalam, Bulgaria, Burkina Faso, Burundi, Cameroon, Canada, Chile, China, Cook Islands, Costa Rica, Côte d'Ivoire, Croatia, Cuba, Cyprus, Czech Republic, Denmark, Ecuador, El Salvador, Equatorial, Guinea, Ethiopia, Fiji, Finland, France, Gambia, Georgia, Germany, Ghana,

Greece, Guinea, Guyana, Hungary, Iceland, India, Indonesia, Iran (Islamic Republic of), Ireland, Italy, Japan, Kenya, Kuwait, Lao People's Democratic Republic, Latvia, Lesotho, Lithuania, Luxembourg, Malawi, Maldives, Mali, Malta, Marshall Islands, Mauritania, Mauritius, Mexico, Micronesia (Federated States of), Monaco, Mongolia, Morocco, Namibia, Nepal, Netherlands, New Zealand, Nicaragua, Niger, Nigeria, Norway, Oman, Pakistan, Panama, Papua New Guinea, Paraguay, Peru, Philippines, Poland, Portugal, Qatar, Republic of Korea, Republic of Moldova, Romania, Russian Federation, Saint Lucia, Saudi Arabia, Senegal, Seychelles, Singapore, Slovak Republic, Slovenia, South Africa, Spain, Sri Lanka, Suriname, Swaziland, Sweden, Switzerland, Tajikistan, Togo, Tunisia, Turkey, Turkmenistan, Ukraine, United Kingdom of Great Britain and Northern Ireland, United Republic of Tanzania, United States of America, Uruguay, Uzbekistan, Venezuela, Viet Nam, Zimbabwe
Date of entry into force: *April 29, 1997*

Preamble

The States Parties to this Convention,

Determined to act with a view to achieving effective progress towards general and complete disarmament under strict and effective international control, including the prohibition and elimination of all types of weapons of mass destruction,

Desiring to contribute to the realization of the purposes and principles of the Charter of the United Nations,

Recalling that the General Assembly of the United Nations has repeatedly condemned all actions contrary to the principles and objectives of the Protocol for the Prohibition of the Use in War of Asphyxiating, Poisonous or Other Gases, and of Bacteriological Methods of Warfare, signed at Geneva on 17 June 1925 (the Geneva Protocol of 1925),

Recognizing that this Convention reaffirms principles and objectives of and obligations assumed under the Geneva Protocol of 1925, and the Convention on the Prohibition of the Development, Production and Stockpiling of Bacteriological (Biological) and Toxin Weapons and on their Destruction signed at London, Moscow and Washington on 10 April 1972,

Bearing in mind the objective contained in Article IX of the Convention on the Prohibition of the Develop-

ment, Production and Stockpiling of Bacteriological (Biological) and Toxin Weapons and on their Destruction,

Determined for the sake of all mankind, to exclude completely the possibility of the use of chemical weapons, through the implementation of the provisions of this Convention, thereby complementing the obligations assumed under the Geneva Protocol of 1925,

Recognizing the prohibition, embodied in the pertinent agreements and relevant principles of international law, of the use of herbicides as a method of warfare,

Considering that achievements in the field of chemistry should be used exclusively for the benefit of mankind,

Desiring to promote free trade in chemicals as well as international cooperation and exchange of scientific and technical information in the field of chemical activities for purposes not prohibited under this Convention in order to enhance the economic and technological development of all States Parties.

Convinced that the complete and effective prohibition of the development, production, acquisition, stockpiling, retention, transfer and use of chemical weapons, and their destruction, represent a necessary step towards the achievement of these common objectives.

Have agreed as follows:

Article 1

General Obligations

1. Each State Party to this Convention undertakes never under any circumstances:

(a) To develop, produce, otherwise acquire, stockpile or retain chemical weapons, or transfer, directly or indirectly, chemical weapons to anyone;

(b) To use chemical weapons;

(c) To engage in any military preparations to use chemical weapons;

(d) To assist, encourage or induce, in any way, anyone to engage in any activity prohibited to a State Party under this Convention.

2. Each State Party undertakes to destroy chemical weapons it owns or possesses, or that are located in any place under its jurisdiction or control, in accord-

ance with the provisions of this Convention.

3. Each State Party undertakes to destroy all chemical weapons it abandoned on the territory of another State Party, in accordance with the provisions of this Convention.

4. Each State Party undertakes to destroy any chemical weapons production facilities it owns or possesses, or that are located in any place under its jurisdiction or control, in accordance with the provisions of this Convention.

5. Each State Party undertakes not to use riot control agents as a method of warfare.

Article 2

Definitions and Criteria

For the purposes of this Convention:

1. "Chemical Weapons" means the following, together or separately:

(a) Toxic chemicals and their precursors, except where intended for purposes not prohibited under this Convention, as long as the types and quantities are consistent with such purposes;

(b) Munitions and devices, specifically designed to cause death or other harm through the toxic properties of those toxic chemicals specified in subparagraph (a), which would be released as a result of the employment of such munitions and devices;

(c) Any equipment specifically designed for use directly in connection with the employment of munitions and devices specified in subparagraph (b).

2. "Toxic Chemical" means:

Any chemical which through its chemical action on life processes can cause death, temporary incapacitation or permanent harm to humans or animals. This includes all such chemicals, regardless of their origin or of their method of production, and regardless of whether they are produced in facilities, in munitions or elsewhere.

(For the purpose of implementing this Convention, toxic chemicals which have been identified for the application of verification measures are listed in Schedules contained in the Annex on Chemicals.)

3. "Precursor" means:

Any chemical reactant which takes part at any stage in the production by whatever method of a toxic chemical. This includes any key component of a binary or multicomponent chemical system.

(For the purpose of implementing this Convention, precursors which have been identified for the application of verification measures are listed in Schedules contained in the Annex on Chemicals.)

4. "Key Component of Binary or Multicomponent Chemical Systems" (hereinafter referred to as "key component") means:

The precursor which plays the most important role in determining the toxic properties of the final product and reacts rapidly with other chemicals in the binary or multicomponent system.

5. "Old Chemical Weapons" means:

(a) Chemical weapons which were produced before 1925; or

(b) Chemical weapons produced in the period between 1925 and 1946 that have deteriorated to such extent that they can no longer be used as chemical weapons.

6. "Abandoned Chemical Weapons" means:

Chemical weapons, including old chemical weapons, abandoned by a State after 1 January 1925 on the territory of another State without the consent of the latter.

7. "Riot Control Agent" means:

Any chemical not listed in a Schedule, which can produce rapidly in humans sensory irritation or disabling physical effects which disappear within a short time following termination of exposure.

8. "Chemical Weapons Production Facility":

(a) Means any equipment, as well as any building housing such equipment, that was designed, constructed or used at any time since 1 January 1946:

(i) As part of the stage in the production of chemicals ("final technological stage") where the material flows would contain, when the equipment is in operation:

(1) Any chemical listed in Schedule 1 in the Annex on Chemicals; or

(2) Any other chemical that has no use, above 1 tonne per year on the territory of a State Party or in any other place under the jurisdiction of a state Party, for purposes not prohibited under this Convention, but can be used for chemical weapons pur-

poses; or

(ii) For filling chemical weapons, including, inter alia, the filling of chemicals listed in Schedule 1 into munitions, devices or bulk storage containers; the filling of chemicals into containers that form part of assembled binary munitions and devices or into chemical submunitions that form part of assembled unitary munitions and devices, and the loading of the containers and chemical submunitions into the respective munitions and devices;

(b) Does not mean:

(i) Any facility having a production capacity for synthesis of chemicals specified in subparagraph (a) (i) that is less than 1 tonne;

(ii) Any facility in which a chemical specified in subparagraph (a) (i) is or was produced as an unavoidable by-product of activities for purposes not prohibited under this Convention, provided that the chemical does not exceed 3 per cent of the total product and that the facility is subject to declaration and inspection under the Annex on Implementation and Verification (hereinafter referred to as "Verification Annex"); or

(iii) The single small-scale facility for production of chemicals listed in Schedule 1 for purposes not prohibited under this Convention as referred to in Part VI of the verification Annex.

9. "Purposes Not Prohibited Under this Convention" means:

(a) Industrial, agricultural, research, medical, pharmaceutical or other peaceful purposes;

(b) Protective purposes, namely those purposes directly related to protection against toxic chemicals and to protection against chemical weapons;

(c) Military purposes not connected with the use of chemical weapons and not dependent on the use of the toxic properties of chemicals as a method of warfare;

(d) Law enforcement including domestic riot control purposes.

10. "Production Capacity" means:

The annual quantitative potential for manufacturing a specific chemical based on the technological process actually used or, if the process is not yet operational, planned to be used at the relevant facility. It shall be deemed to be equal to the nameplate capacity or, if the nameplate capacity is not available, to the design capacity. The maximum quantity for the production facility, as demonstrated by one or more test-runs. The design capacity is the corresponding theoretically calculated product output.

11. "Organization" means the Organization for the Prohibitions of Chemical Weapons established pursuant to Article 8 of this Convention.

12. For the purpose of Article 6:

(a) "Production" of a chemical means its formation through chemical reaction;

(b) "Processing" of a chemical means a physical process, such as formulation, extraction and purification, in which a chemical is not converted into another chemical;

(c) "Consumption" of a chemical means its conversion into another chemical via chemical reaction.

Article 3

Declarations

1. Each State Party shall submit to the Organization, not later than 30 days after this Convention enters into force for it, the following declarations, in which it shall:

(a) With respect to chemical weapons:

(i) Declare whether it owns or possesses any chemical weapons, or whether there are any chemical weapons located in any place under its jurisdiction or control;

(ii) Specify the precise location, aggregate quantity and detailed inventory of chemical weapons it owns or possesses, or that are located in any place under its jurisdiction or control, in accordance with Part IV(A), paragraph 1 to 3, of the Verification Annex, except for those chemical weapons referred to in sub-subparagraph (iii);

(iii) Report any chemical weapons on its territory that are owned and possessed by another State and located in any place under the jurisdiction or control of another State, in accordance with Part IV(A), paragraph 4, of the Verification Annex;

(iv) Declare whether it has transferred or received, directly or indirectly, any chemical weapons since 1 January 1946 and specify the transfer or receipt of such weapons, in accordance with Part IV(A), paragraph 5, of the Verification Annex;

(v) Provide its general plan for destruction of chemical weapons that it owns or possesses, or that are located in any place under its jurisdiction or control, in accordance with Part IV (A), paragraph 6, of the Verification Annex;

(b) With respect to old chemical weapons and abandoned chemical weapons:

(i) Declare whether it has on its territory old chemical weapons and provide all available information in accordance with Part IV (B), paragraph 3, of the Verification Annex;

(ii) Declare whether there are abandoned chemical weapons on its territory and provide all available information in accordance with Part IV (B), paragraph 8, of the Verification Annex;

(iii) Declare whether it has abandoned chemical weapons on the territory of other States and provide all available information in accordance with Part IV (B), paragraph 10, of the Verification Annex;

(c) With respect to chemical weapons production facilities:

(i) Declare whether it has or has had any chemical weapons production facility under its ownership or possession, or that is or has been located in any place under its jurisdiction or control at any time since 1 January 1946;

(ii) Specify any chemical weapons production facility it has or has had under its ownership or possession or that is or has been located in any place under its jurisdiction or control at any time since 1 January 1946, in accordance with Part V, paragraph 1 of the Verification Annex, except for those facilities referred to in sub-subparagraph (iii);

(iii) Report any chemical weapons production facility on its territory that another State has or has had under its ownership and possession and that is or has been located in any place under jurisdiction or control of another State at any time since 1 January 1946, in accordance with Part V, paragraph 2, of the Verification Annex;

(iv) Declare where it has transferred or received, directly or indirectly, any equipment for the production of chemical weapons since 1 January 1946 and specify the transfer or receipt of such equipment, in accordance with Part V, paragraphs 3 to 5, of the Verification Annex;

(v) Provide its general plan for destruction of any chemical weapons production facility it owns or possesses, or that is located in any place under its

jurisdiction or control, in accordance with Part V, paragraph 6, of the Verification Annex;

(vi) Specify actions to be taken for closure of any chemical weapons production facility it owns or possesses, or that is located in any place under its jurisdiction or control, in accordance with Part V, paragraph 1 (i), of the Verification Annex;

(vii) Provide its general plan for any temporary conversion of any chemical weapons production facility it owns or possesses, or that is located in any place under its jurisdiction or control, into a chemical weapons destruction facility, in accordance with Part V, paragraph 7, of the Verification Annex;

(d) With respect to other facilities:

Specify the precise location, nature and general scope of activities of any facility or establishment under its ownership or possession, or located in any place under its jurisdiction or control, and that has been designed, constructed or used since 1 January 1946 primarily for development of chemical weapons. Such declaration shall include, inter alia, laboratories and test and evaluation sites;

(e) With respect to riot control agents: Specify the chemical name, structural formula and Chemical Abstracts Service (CAS) registry number, if assigned, of each chemical it holds for riot control purposes. This declaration shall be updated not later than 30 days after any change becomes effective.

2. The provisions of this Article and the relevant provisions of Part IV of the Verification Annex shall not, at the discretion of a State Party, apply to chemical weapons buried on its territory before 1 January 1977 and which remain buried, or which had been dumped at sea before 1 January 1985.

Article 4

Chemical Weapons

1. The provisions of this Article and the detailed procedures for its implementation shall apply to all chemical weapons owned or possessed by a State Party, or that are located in any place under its jurisdiction or control, except old chemical weapons and abandoned chemical weapons to which Part IV(B) of the Verification Annex applies.

2. Detailed procedures for the implementation of this Article are set forth in the Verification Annex.

3. All locations at which chemical weapons speci-

fied in paragraph 1 are stored or destroyed shall be subject to systematic verification through on-site inspection and monitoring with on-site instruments, in accordance with Part IV(A) of the Verification Annex.

4. Each State Party shall, immediately after the declaration under Article III, paragraph 1 (a), has been submitted, provide access to chemical weapons specified in paragraph 1 for the purpose of systematic verification of the declaration through on-site inspection. Thereafter, each State Party shall not remove any of these chemical weapons, except to a chemical weapons destruction facility. It shall provide access to such chemical weapons, for the purpose of systematic on-site verification.

5. Each State Party shall provide access to any chemical weapons destruction facilities and their storage areas, that it owns or possesses, or that are located in any place under its jurisdiction or control, for the purpose of systematic verification through on-site inspection and monitoring with on-site instruments.

6. Each State Party shall destroy all chemical weapons specified in paragraph 1 pursuant to the Verification Annex and in accordance with the agreed rate and sequence of destruction (hereinafter referred to as "order of destruction"). Such destruction shall begin not later than two years after this Convention enters into force for it and shall finish not later than 10 years after entry into force of this Convention. A State Party is not precluded from destroying such chemical weapons at a faster rate.

7. Each State Party shall:

(a) Submit detailed plans for the destruction of chemical weapons specified in paragraph 1 not later than 60 days before each annual destruction period begins, in accordance with Part IV(A), paragraph 29, of the Verification Annex; the detailed plans shall encompass all stocks to be destroyed during the next annual destruction period;

(b) Submit declarations annually regarding the implementation of its plans for destruction of chemical weapons specified in paragraph 1, not later than 60 days after the end of each annual destruction period; and

(c) Certify, not later than 30 days after the destruction process has been completed, that all chemical weapons specified in paragraph 1 have been destroyed.

8. If a State ratifies or accedes to this Convention after the 10-year period for destruction set forth in paragraph 6, it shall destroy chemical weapons specified in paragraph 1 as soon as possible. The order of destruction and procedures for stringent verification for such a State Party shall be determined by the Executive Council.

9. Any Chemical weapon discovered by a State Party after the initial declaration of chemical weapons shall be reported, secured and destroyed in accordance with Part IV(A) of the Verification Annex.

10. Each State Party, during transportation, sampling, storage and destruction of chemical weapons, shall assign the highest priority to ensuring the safety of people and to protecting the environment. Each State Party shall transport, sample, store and destroy chemical weapons in accordance with its national standard for safety and emissions.

11. Any State Party which has on its territory chemical weapons that are owned or possessed by another State, or that are located in any place under the jurisdiction or control of another State, shall make the fullest efforts to ensure that these chemical weapons are removed from its territory not later than one year after this Convention enters into force for it. If they are not removed within one year, the State Party may request the Organization and other States Parties to provide assistance in the destruction of these chemical weapons.

12. Each State Party undertakes to cooperate with other States Parties that request information or assistance on a bilateral basis or through the Technical Secretariat regarding methods and technologies for the safe and efficient destruction of chemical weapons.

13. In carrying our verification activities pursuant to this Article and Part IV(A) of the Verification Annex, the Organization shall consider measures to avoid unnecessary duplication of bilateral or multilateral agreements on verification of chemical weapons storage and their destruction among States Parties.

To this end, the Executive Council shall decide to limit verification to measures complementary to those undertaken pursuant to such a bilateral or multilateral agreement, if it considers that:

(a) Verification provisions of such an agreement are consistent with the verification provisions of this Article and Part IV(A) of the Verification Annex;

(b) Implementation of such an agreement provides

for sufficient assurance of compliance with the relevant provisions of this Convention;

(c) Parties to the bilateral or multilateral agreement keep the Organization fully informed about their verification activities.

14. If the Executive Council takes a decision pursuant to paragraph 13, the Organization shall have the right to monitor the implementation of the bilateral or multilateral agreement.

15. Nothing in paragraphs 13 and 14 shall affect the obligation of a State Party to provide declarations pursuant to Article 3, this Article and Part IV (A) of the verification Annex.

16. Each State Party shall meet the costs of destruction of chemical weapons it is obliged to destroy. It shall also meet the costs of verification of storage and destruction of these chemical weapons unless the Executive Council decides otherwise. If the Executive Council decides to limit verification measures of the Organization pursuant to paragraph 13, the costs of complementary verification and monitoring by the Organization shall be paid in accordance with the United Nations scale of assessment, as specified in Article VIII, paragraph 7.

17. The provisions of this Article and the relevant provisions of Part IV of the Verification Annex shall not, at the discretion of a State Party, apply to chemical weapons buried on its territory before 1 January 1977 and which remain buried, or which had been dumped at sea before 1 January 1985.

Article 5

Chemical Weapons Production Facilities

1. The provisions of this Article and the detailed procedures for its implementation shall apply to any and all chemical weapons production facilities owned or possessed by a State Party, or that are located in any place under its jurisdiction or control.

2. Detailed procedures for the implementation of this Article are set forth in the Verification Annex.

3. All chemical weapons production facilities specified in paragraph 1 shall be subject to systematic verification through on-site inspection and monitoring with on-site instruments in accordance with Part V of the Verification Annex.

4. Each State Party shall cease immediately all activity at chemical weapons production facilities specified in paragraph 1, except activity required for closure.

5. No State Party shall construct any new chemical weapons production facilities or modify any existing facilities for the purpose of chemical weapons production or for any other activity prohibited under this Convention.

6. Each State Party shall, immediately after the declaration under Article 3, paragraph 1 (C), has been submitted, provide access to chemical weapons production facilities specified in paragraph 1, for the purpose of systematic verification of the declaration through on-site inspection.

7. Each State Party shall:

(a) Close, not later than 90 days after this Convention enters into force for it, all chemical weapon production facilities specified in paragraph 1, in accordance with Part V of the Verification Annex, and give notice thereof; and

(b) Provide access to chemical weapons production facilities specified in paragraph 1, subsequent to closure, for the purpose of systematic verification through on-site inspection and monitoring with on-site instruments in order to ensure that the facility remains closed and is subsequently destroyed.

8. Each State Party shall destroy all chemical weapons production facilities specified in paragraph 1 and related facilities and equipment, pursuant to the Verification Annex and in accordance with an agreed rate and sequence of destruction (hereinafter referred to as "order of destruction"). Such destruction shall begin not later than one year after this Convention enters into force for it, and shall finish not later than 10 years after entry into force of this Convention. A State Party is not precluded from destroying such facilities at a faster rate.

9. Each State Party shall:

(a) Submit detailed plans for destruction of chemical weapons production facilities specified in paragraph 1, not later than 180 days before the destruction of each facility begins;

(b) Submit declarations annually regarding the implementation of its plans for the destruction of all chemical weapons production facilities specified in paragraph 1, not later than 90 days after the end of each annual destruction period; and

(c) Certify, not later than 30 days after the destruction process has been completed, that all chemical weapons production facilities specified in paragraph 1 have been destroyed.

10. If a State ratifies or accedes to this Convention after the 10-year period for destruction set forth in paragraph 8, it shall destroy chemical weapons pro-

duction facilities specified in paragraph 1 as soon as possible. The order of destruction and procedures for stringent verification for such a State Party shall be determined by the Executive Council.

11. Each State Party, during the destruction of chemical weapons production facilities, shall assign the highest priority to ensuring the safety of people and to protecting the environment. Each State Party shall destroy chemical weapons production facilities in accordance with its national standards for safety and emissions.

12. Chemical weapons production facilities specified in paragraph 1 may be temporarily converted for destruction of chemical weapons in accordance with Part V, paragraphs 18 to 25, of the Verification Annex. Such a converted facility must be destroyed as soon as it is no longer in use for destruction of chemical weapons but, in any case, not later than 10 years after entry into force of this Convention.

13. A State Party may request, in exceptional cases of compelling need, permission to use a chemical weapons production facility specified in paragraph 1 for purpose not prohibited under this Convention. Upon the recommendation of the Executive Council, the Conference of the States Parties shall decide whether or not to approve the request and shall establish the conditions upon which approval is contingent in accordance with Part V, Section D, of the Verification Annex.

14. The chemical weapons production facility shall be converted in such a manner that the converted facility is not more capable for being reconverted into a chemical weapons production facility than any other facility used for industrial, agricultural, research, medical, pharmaceutical or other peaceful purposes not involving chemicals listed in Schedule 1.

15. All converted facilities shall be subject to systematic verification through on-site inspection and monitoring with on-site instruments in accordance with Part V, Section D, of the Verification Annex.

16. In carrying out verification activities pursuant to this Article and Part V of the Verification Annex, the Organization shall consider measures to avoid unnecessary duplication of bilateral or multilateral agreements on verification of chemical weapons production facilities and their destruction among States Parties.

To this end, the Executive Council shall decide to limit the verification to measures complementary to those undertaken pursuant to such a bilateral or multilateral agreement, if it considers that:

(a) Verification provisions of such an agreement are consistent with the verification provisions of this

Article and Part V of the Verification Annex;

(b) Implementation of the agreement provides for sufficient assurance of compliance with the relevant provisions of this convention; and

(c) Parties to the bilateral or multilateral agreement keep the Organization fully informed about their verification activities.

17. If the Executive Council takes a decision pursuant to paragraph 16, the Organization shall have the right to monitor the implementation of the bilateral or multilateral agreement.

18. Nothing in paragraphs 16 and 17 shall affect the obligation of a State Party to make declarations pursuant to Article 3, this Article and Part V of the Verification Annex.

19. Each State Party shall meet the costs of destruction of chemical weapons production facilities it is obliged to destroy. It shall also meet the costs of verification under this Article unless the Executive Council decides otherwise. If the Executive Council decides to limit verification measures of the Organization pursuant to paragraph 16, the costs of complementary verification and monitoring by the Organization shall be paid in accordance with the United Nations scale of assessment, as specified in Article 8, paragraph 7.

Article 6

Activities not Prohibited under This Convention

1. Each State Party has the right, subject to the provisions of this Convention, to develop, produce, otherwise acquire, retain, transfer and use toxic chemicals and their precursors for purposes not prohibited under this Convention.

2. Each State Party shall adopt the necessary measures to ensure that toxic chemicals and their precursors are only developed, produced, otherwise acquired, retained, transferred, or used within its territory or in any other place under its jurisdiction or control for purposes not prohibited under this Convention. To this end, and in order to verify that activities are in accordance with obligations under this Convention, each State Party shall subject toxic chemicals and their precursors listed in Schedules 1, 2 and 3 of the Annex on Chemicals, facilities related to such chemicals, and other facilities as specified in the Verification Annex, that are located on its territory or in any other place under its jurisdiction or control, to verification measures as provided in the Veri-

fication Annex.

3. Each State Party shall subject chemicals listed in Schedule 1 (hereinafter referred to as "Schedule 1 chemicals") to the prohibitions on production, acquisition, retention, transfer and use as specified in Part VI of the Verification Annex. It shall subject Schedule 1 chemicals and facilities specified in Part VI of the Verification Annex to systematic verification through on-site inspection and monitoring with on-site instruments in accordance with that Part of the Verification Annex.

4. Each States Party shall subject chemicals listed in Schedule 2 (hereinafter referred to as "Schedule 2 chemicals") and facilities specified in Part VII of the Verification Annex to data monitoring and on-site verification in accordance with that Part of the Verification Annex.

5. Each State Party shall subject chemicals listed in Schedule 3 (hereinafter referred to as "Schedule 3 chemicals") and facilities specified in Part VIII of the Verification Annex to data monitoring and on-site verification in accordance with that Part of the Verification Annex.

6. Each State Party shall subject facilities specified in Part IX of the Verification Annex to data monitoring and eventual on-site verification in accordance with that Part of the Verification Annex unless decided otherwise by the Conference of the States Parties pursuant to Part IX, paragraph 22, of the Verification Annex.

7. Not later than 30 days after this Convention enters into force for it, each State Party shall make an initial declaration on relevant chemicals and facilities in accordance with the Verification Annex.

8. Each State Party shall make annual declarations regarding the relevant chemicals and facilities in accordance with the Verification Annex.

9. For the purpose of on-site verification, each State Party shall grant to the inspectors access to facilities as required in the Verification.

10. In conducting verification activities, the Technical Secretariat shall avoid undue intrusion into the State Party's chemical activities for purposes not prohibited under this Convention and, in particular, abide by the provisions set forth in the Annex on the Protection of Confidential Information (hereinafter referred to as "Confidentiality Annex").

11. The provisions of this Article shall be implemented in a manner which avoids hampering the economic or technological development of States Parties, and international cooperation in the field of chemical activities for purposes not prohibited under this Convention including the international exchange of scientific and technical information and chemicals and equipment for the production, processing or use of chemicals for purposes not prohibited under this Convention.

Article 7

National Implementation Measures

General Undertaking

1. Each State Party shall, in accordance with its constitutional processes, adopt the necessary measures to implement its obligations under this Convention. In particular, it shall:

(a) Prohibit natural and legal persons anywhere on its territory or in any other place under its jurisdiction as recognized by international law from undertaking any activity prohibited to a State Party under this Convention, including enacting penal legislation with respect to such activity;

(b) Not permit in any place under its control any activity prohibited to a State Party under this Convention; and

(c) Extend its penal legislation enacted under subparagraph (a) to any activity prohibited to a State Party under this Convention undertaken anywhere by natural persons, possessing its nationality, in conformity with international law.

2. Each State Party shall cooperate with other States Parties and afford the appropriate form of legal assistance to facilitate the implementation of the obligations under paragraph 1.

3. Each State Party, during the implementation of its obligations under this Convention, shall assign the highest priority to ensuring the safety of people and to protecting the environment, and shall cooperate as appropriate with other States Parties in this regard.

Relation between the State Party and the Organization

4. In order to fulfill its obligations under this Convention, each State Party shall designate or establish a National Authority to serve as the national focal point for effective liaison with the Organization and other States Parties. Each State Party shall notify the Organization of its National Authority at the time that this Convention enters into force for it.

5. Each State Party shall inform the Organization of the legislative and administrative measures taken to implement this Convention.

6. Each State Party shall treat as confidential and afford special handling to information and data it receives in confidence from the Organization in connection with the implementation of this Convention. It shall treat such information and data exclusively in connection with its rights and obligations under this Convention and accordance with the provisions set forth in the Confidentiality Annex.

7. Each State Party undertakes to cooperate with the Organization in the exercise of all its functions and in particular to provide assistance to the Technical Secretariat.

Article 8

The Organization

A. General Provisions

1. The States Parties to this Convention hereby establish the Organization for the Prohibition of Chemical Weapons to achieve the object and purpose of this Convention, to ensure the implementation of its provisions, including those for international verification of compliance with it, and to provide a forum for consultation and cooperation among States Parties.

2. All States Parties to this Convention shall be members of the Organization. A State Party shall not be deprived of its membership in the Organization.

3. The seat of the Headquarters of the Organization shall be The Hague, Kingdom of the Netherlands.

4. There are hereby established as the organs of the Organization: the Conference of the States Parties, the Executive Council, and the Technical Secretariat.

5. The Organization shall conduct its verification activities provided for under this Convention in the least intrusive manner possible consistent with the timely and efficient accomplishment of their objectives. It shall request only the information and data necessary to fulfill its responsibilities under this Convention. It shall take every precaution to protect the confidentiality of information on civil and military activities and facilities coming to its knowledge in the implementation of this Convention and, in particular shall abide by the provisions set forth in the Confidentiality Annex.

6. In undertaking its verification activities the Organization shall consider measures to make use of advance in science and technology.

7. The costs of the Organization's activities shall be paid by States Parties in accordance with the United Nations scale of assessment adjusted to take into account differences in membership between the United Nations and this Organization, and subject to the provisions of Articles IV and V. Financial contributions of States Parties to the Preparatory Commission shall be deducted in an appropriate way from their contributions to the regular budget. The budget of the Organization shall comprise two separate chapters, one relating to administrative and other costs, and one relating to verification costs.

8. A member of the Organization which is in arrears in the payment of its financial contribution to the Organization shall have no vote in the Organization if the amount of its arrears equals or exceeds the amount of the contribution due from it for the preceding two full years. The Conference of the States Parties may, nevertheless, permit such a member to vote if it is satisfied that the failure to pay is due to conditions beyond the control of the member.

B. The Conference of the States Parties

Composition, procedures and decision-making

9. The Conference of the States Parties (hereinafter referred to as "the Conference") shall be composed of all members of this Organization. Each member shall have one representative in the Conference, who may be accompanied by alternates and advisers.

10. The first session of the Conference shall be convened by the depository not later than 30 days after the entry into force of this Convention.

11. The Conference shall meet in regular sessions which shall be held annually unless it decides otherwise.

12. Special sessions of the Conference shall be convened:

(a) When decided by the Conference;

(b) When requested by the Executive Council;

(c) When requested by any member and supported by one third of the members; or

(d) In accordance with paragraph 22 to undertake reviews of the operation of this Convention.

Except in the case of subparagraph (d), the special session shall be convened not later than 30 days after receipt of the request by the Director-General of the Technical Secretariat, unless specified otherwise in the request.

13. The Conference shall also be convened in the form of an Amendment Conference in accordance with Article XV, paragraph 2.

14. Session of the Conference shall take place at the seat of the Organization unless the Conference decides otherwise.

15. The Conference shall adopt its rules of procedure. At the beginning of each regular session, it shall elect its Chairman and such other officers as may be required. They shall hold office until a new Chairman and other officers are elected at the next regular session.

16. A majority of the members of the Organization shall constitute a quorum for the Conference.

17. Each member of the Organization shall have one vote in the Conference.

18. The conference shall take decisions on questions of procedure by a simple majority of the members present and voting. Decisions on matters of substance should be taken as far as possible by consensus. If consensus is not attainable when an issue comes up for decision, the Chairman shall defer any vote for 24 hours and during this period of deferment shall make every effort to facilitate achievement of consensus, and shall report to the Conference before the end of this period. If consensus is not possible at the end of 24 hours, the Conference shall take the decision by a two-thirds majority of members present and voting unless specified otherwise in this Convention. When the issue arises as to whether the question is one of substance or not, that question shall be treated as a matter of substance unless otherwise decided by the Conference by the majority required for decisions on matters of substance.

Powers and functions

19. The Conference shall be the principal organ of the Organization. It shall consider any questions, matters or issues within the scope of this Convention, including those relating to the powers and functions of the Executive Council and the Technical Secretariat. It may make recommendations and take decisions on any questions, matters or issues related to this Convention raised by a State Party or brought to its attention by the Executive Council.

20. The Conference shall oversee the implementation of this Convention, and act in order to promote its object and purpose. The Conference shall review compliance with this Convention. It shall also oversee the activities of the Executive Council and the Technical Secretariat and may issue guidelines in accordance with this Convention to either of them in the exercise of their functions.

21. The Conference shall:

(a) Consider and adopt at its regular sessions the report, programs and budget of the Organization, submitted by the Executive Council, as well as consider other reports;

(b) Decide on the scale of financial contributions to be paid by States Parties in accordance with paragraph 7;

(c) Elect the members of the Executive Council;

(d) Appoint the Director-General of the Technical Secretariat (hereinafter referred to as "the Director-General");

(e) Approve the rules of procedure of the Executive Council submitted by the latter;

(f) Establish such subsidiary organs as it finds necessary for the exercise of its functions in accordance with this Convention;

(g) Foster international cooperation for peaceful purposes in the field of chemical activities;

(h) Review scientific and technological developments that could affect the operation of this Convention and, in this context, direct the Director-General to establish a Scientific Advisory Board to enable him, in the performance of his functions, to render specialized advice in areas of science and technology relevant to this Convention, to the Conference, the Executive Council or States Parties. The Scientific Advisory Board shall be composed of independent experts appointed in accordance with terms of reference adopted by the Conference;

(i) Consider and approve at its first session any draft agreement, provisions and guidelines developed by the Preparatory Commission;

(j) Establish at its first session the voluntary fund for assistance in accordance with Article 5;

(k) Take the necessary measures to ensure compliance with this Convention and to redress and remedy any situation which contravenes the provisions of this Convention, in accordance with Article 7.

22. The Conference shall not later than one year after the expiry of the fifth and the tenth year after the entry into force of this Convention, and at such other times within that time period as may be decided upon, convene in special sessions to undertake reviews of the operation of this Convention. Such reviews shall take into account any relevant scientific and technological developments. At intervals of five years thereafter, unless otherwise decided upon, further sessions of the Conference shall be convened with the same objective.

C. The Executive Council

Composition, procedure and decision-making

23. The Executive Council shall consist of 41 members. Each State Party shall have the right, in accordance with the principle of rotation, to serve on the Executive Council. The members of the Executive Council shall be elected by the Conference for a term of two years. In order to ensure the effective functioning of this Convention, due regard being specially paid to equitable geographical distribution, to the importance of chemical industry, as well as to political and security interest, the Executive Council shall be composed as follows:

(a) Nine States Parties from Africa to be designated by States Parties located in this region. As a basis for this designation it is understood that, out of these nine States Parties, three members shall, as a rule, be the States Parties with the most significant national chemical industry in the region as determined by internationally reported and published data; in addition, the regional group shall agree also to take into account other regional factors in designating these three members.

(b) Nine States Parties from Asia to be designated by States Parties located in this region. As a basis for this designation it is understood that, out of these nine States Parties, four members shall, as a rule, be the States Parties with the most significant national chemical industry in the region as determined by internationally reported and published data; in addition, the regional group shall agree also to take into account other regional factors in designating these four members;

(c) Five States Parties from Eastern Europe to be designated by States Parties located in this region. As a basis for this designation it is understood that, out of these five States Parties, one member shall, as a rule, be the State Party with the most significant national chemical industry in the region as determined by internationally reported and published data; in addition, the regional group shall agree also to take into account other regional factors in designating this one member;

(d) Seven States Parties from Latin America and the Caribbean to be designated by States Parties located in this region. As a basis for this designation it is understood that, out of these seven States Parties, three members shall, as a rule, be the States Parties with the most significant national chemical industry in the region as determined by internationally reported and published data; in addition, the regional group shall agree also to take into account other regional factors in designating these three members;

(e) The States Parties from among Western European and other States to be designated by States Parties located in this region. As a basis for this designation it is understood that, out of these 10 States Parties, 5 members shall, as a rule, be the States Parties with the most significant national chemical industry in the region as determined by internationally reported and published data; in addition, the regional group shall agree also to take into account other regional factors in designating these five members;

(f) One further State Party to be designated consecutively by States Parties located in the regions of Asia and Latin America and the Caribbean. As a basis for this designation it is understood that this States Party shall be a rotating member from these regions.

24. For the first election of the Executive Council 20 members shall be elected for a term of one year, due regard being paid to the established numerical proportions as described in paragraph 23.

25. After the full implementation of Article 4 and 5 the conference may, upon the request of a majority of the numbers of the Executive Council, review the composition of the Executive Council taking into account developments related to the principles specified in paragraph 23 that are governing its composition.

26. The Executive Council shall elaborate its rules of procedure and submit them to the Conference for approval.

27. The Executive council shall elect its chairman from among its members.

28. The Executive Council shall meet for regular sessions. Between regular sessions it shall meet as often as may be required for the fulfillment of its powers and functions.

29. Each member of the Executive Council shall have one vote. Unless otherwise specified in this Convention, the Executive Council shall take decisions on matters of substance by a two-thirds majority of all its members. The Executive Council shall take decisions on questions of procedure by a simple majority of all its members. When the issue arises as to whether the question is one of substance or not, that question shall be treated as a matter of substance unless otherwise decided by the Executive Council

by the majority required for decisions on matters of substance.

Powers and functions

30. The Executive Council shall be the executive organ of the Organization. It shall be responsible to the Conference, The Executive Council shall carry out the powers and functions entrusted to it under this Convention as well as those functions delegated to it by the Conference. In so doing, it shall act in conformity with the recommendations, decisions and guidelines of the Conference and assure their proper and continuous implementation.

31. The Executive Council shall promote the effective implementation of, and compliance with, this Convention. It shall supervise the activities of the Technical Secretariat, cooperate with the National Authority of each State Party and facilitate consultations and cooperation among States Parties at their request.

32. The Executive Council shall;

(a) Consider and submit to the Conference the draft programs and budget of the Organization;

(b) Consider and submit to the Conference the draft report of the Organization on the implementation of this Convention, the report on the performance of its own activities and such special reports as it deems necessary or which the Conference may request;

(c) Make arrangement for the sessions of the Conference including the preparation of the draft agenda.

33. The Executive Council may request the convening of a special session of the Conference.

34. The Executive Council shall:

(a) Conclude agreements or arrangements with States and international organizations on behalf of the Organization, subject to prior approval by the Conference;

(b) Conclude agreements with States Parties on behalf of the organization in connection with Article 10 and supervise the voluntary fund referred to in Article 10;

(c) Approve agreements or arrangements relating to the implementation of verification activities, negotiated by the Technical Secretariat with States Parties.

35. The Executive Council shall consider any issue or matter within its competence affecting this Convention and its implementation, including concerns regarding compliance, and cases of non-compliance, and, as appropriate, inform States Parties and bring the issue or matter to the attention of Conference.

36. In its consideration of doubts or concerns regarding cases of non-compliance, including, inter alia, abuse of the rights provided for under this Convention, the Executive Council shall consult with the States Parties involved and, as appropriate, request the State Party to take measures to redress the situation within a specified time. To the extent that the Executive Council considers further action to be necessary, it shall take, inter alia, one or more of the following measures:

(a) Inform all States Parties of the issue or matter;

(b) Bring the issue or matter to the attention of the Conference;

(c) Make recommendations to the Conference regarding measures to redress the situation and to ensure compliance.

The Executive Council shall, in cases of particular gravity and urgency, bring the issue or matter, including relevant information and conclusions, directly to the attention of the United Nations General Assembly and the United Nations Security Council. It shall at the same time inform all States Parties of this step.

D. The Technical Secretariat

37. The Technical Secretariat shall assist the Conference and the Executive Council in the performance of their functions. The Technical Secretariat shall carry out the verification measures provided for in this Convention. It shall carry out the other functions entrusted to it under this Convention as well as those functions delegated to it by the Conference and the Executive Council.

38. The Technical Secretariat shall;

(a) Prepare and submit to the Executive Council the draft programme and budget of the Organization;

(b) Prepare and submit to the Executive Council the draft report of the Organization on the implementation of this Convention and such other reports as the Conference or the Executive Council may request;

(c) Provide administrative and technical support to the Conference, the Executive Council and subsidiary organ;

(d) Address and receive communications on behalf of

the Organization of and from States Parties on matters pertaining to the implementation of this Convention;

(e) Provide technical assistance and technical evaluation to States Parties in the implementation of the provisions of this Convention, including evaluation of scheduled and unscheduled chemicals.

39. The Technical Secretariat shall:

(a) Negotiate agreements or arrangements relating to the implementation of verification activities with States Parties, subject to approval by the Executive Council;

(b) Not later than 180 days after entry into force of this Convention, coordinate the establishment and maintenance of permanent stockpiles of emergency and humanitarian assistance by States Parties in accordance with Article 10, paragraph 7 (b) and (c). The Technical Secretariat may inspect the items maintained for serviceability. Lists of items to be stockpiled shall be considered and approved by the Conference pursuant to paragraph 21 (i) above;

(c) Administer the voluntary fund referred to in Article 10, compile declarations made by the States Parties and register, when requested, bilateral agreements concluded between States Parties or between a State Party and the Organization for the purpose of Article 10.

40. The Technical Secretariat shall inform the Executive Council of any problem that has arisen with regard to the discharge of its functions, including doubts, ambiguities or uncertainties about compliance with this Convention that have come to its notice in the performance of its verification activities and that it has been unable to resolve or clarify through its consultations with the State Party concerned.

41. The Technical Secretariat shall comprise a Director-General, who shall be its head and chief administrative officer, inspectors and such scientific, technical and other personnel as may be required.

42. The Inspectorate shall be a unit of the Technical Secretariat and shall act under the supervision of the Director-General.

43. The Inspector-General shall be appointed by the Conference upon the recommendation of the Executive Council for a term of four years, renewable for one further term, but not thereafter.

44. The Director-General shall be responsible to the Conference and the Executive Council for the appointment of the staff and the organization and functioning of the Technical Secretariat. The para-

mount consideration in the employment of the staff and in the determination of the conditions of service shall be the necessity of securing the highest standards of efficiency, competence and integrity. Only citizens of States Parties shall serve as the Director-General, as inspectors or as other members of the professional and clerical staff. Due regard shall be paid to the importance of recruiting the staff on as wide a geographical basis as possible. Recruitment shall be funded by the principle that the staff shall be kept to a minimum necessary for the proper discharge of the responsibilities of the Technical Secretariat.

45. The Director-General shall be responsible for the organization and functioning of the Scientific Advisory Board referred to in paragraph 21(h). The Director-General shall, in consultation with States Parties, appoint members of the Scientific Advisory Board, who shall serve in their individual capacity. The members of the Board shall be appointed on the basis of their expertise in the particular scientific fields relevant to the implementation of this Convention. The Director-General may also, as appropriate in consultation with members of the Board, establish temporary working groups of scientific experts to provide recommendations on specific issues. In regard to the above, States Parties may submit lists of experts to the Director-General.

46. In the performance of their duties, the Director-General, the inspectors and the other members of the staff shall not seek or receive instructions from any Government or from any other source external to the Organization. They shall refrain from any action that might reflect on their positions as international officers responsible only to the Conference and the Executive Council.

47. Each State Party shall respect the exclusively international character of the responsibilities of the Director-General, the inspectors and the other members of the staff and not seek to influence them in the discharge of their responsibilities.

E. Privileges and Immunities

48. The Organization shall enjoy on the territory and in any other place under the jurisdiction or control of a State Party such legal capacity and such privileges and immunities as are necessary for the exercise of its functions.

49. Delegates of States Parties, together with their alternates and advisers, representatives appointed to the Executive Council together with their alternates and advisers, the Director-General and the staff of the Organization shall enjoy such privileges and immuni-

ties as are necessary in the independent exercise of their functions in connection with the Organization.

50. The legal capacity, privileges, and immunities referred to in this Article shall be defined in agreements between the Organization and the States Parties as well as in an agreement between the Organization and the State in which the headquarters of the Organization and the State in which the headquarters of the Organization is seated. These agreements shall be considered and approved by the Conference pursuant to paragraph 21(i).

51. Notwithstanding paragraphs 48 and 49, the privileges and immunities enjoyed by the Director-General and the staff of the Technical Secretariat during the conduct of verification activities shall be those set forth in Part II, Section B, of the Verification Annex.

Article 9

Consultations, Cooperation and Fact-Finding

1. States Parties shall consult and cooperate, directly among themselves, or through the Organization or other appropriate international procedures, including procedures within the framework of the United Nations and in accordance with its Charter, on any matter which may be raised relating to the object and purpose, or the implementation of the provisions, of this Convention.

2. Without prejudice to the right of any State Party to request a challenge inspection, States Parties should, whenever possible, first make every effort to clarify and resolve, through exchange of information and consultations among themselves, any matter which may cause doubt about compliance with this Convention, or which gives rise to concerns about a related matter which may be considered ambiguous. A State Party which receives a request from another State Party for clarification of any matter which the requesting State Party believes causes such a doubt or concern shall provide the requesting State Party as soon as possible, but in any case not later than 10 days after the request, with information sufficient to answer the doubt or concern raised along with an explanation of how the information provided resolves the matter. Nothing in this Convention shall affect the right of any two or more States Parties to arrange by mutual consent for inspections or any other procedures among themselves to clarify and resolve any matter which may cause doubt about compliance or gives rise to a concern about a related matter which may be considered ambiguous. Such arrangements shall not affect the rights and obliga-

tions of any State Party under other provisions of this Convention.

Procedure for requesting clarification

3. A State Party shall have the right to request the Executive Council to assist in clarifying any situation which may be considered ambiguous or which gives rise to a concern about the possible non-compliance of another State Party with this Convention. The Executive Council shall provide appropriate information in its possession relevant to such a concern.

4. A State Party shall have the right to request the Executive Council to obtain clarification from another State Party on any situation which may be considered ambiguous or which gives rise to a concern about its possible non-compliance with this Convention. In such a case, the following shall apply:

(a) The Executive Council shall forward the request for clarification to the State Party concerned through the Director-General not later than 24 hours after its receipt;

(b) The requested State Party shall provide the clarification to the Executive Council as soon as possible, but in any case not later than 10 days after the receipt of the request;

(c) The Executive Council shall take note of the clarification and forward it to the requesting State Party not later than 24 hours after its receipt;

(d) If the requesting State Party deems the clarification to be inadequate, it shall have that right to request the Executive Council to obtain from the requested State Party further clarification;

(e) For the purpose of obtaining further clarification requested under subparagraph (d), the Executive Council may call on the Director-General to establish a group of experts from the technical Secretariat, or if appropriate staff are not available in the Technical Secretariat, from elsewhere, to examine all available information and data relevant to the situation causing the concern. The group of experts shall submit a factual report to the Executive Council on its findings;

(f) If the requesting State Party considers the clarification obtained under subparagraphs (d) and (e) to be unsatisfactory, it shall have the right to request a special session of the Executive Council in which States Parties involved that are not members of the Executive Council shall be entitled to take part. In such a special session, the Executive Council shall consider the matter and may recommend any measure it deems appropriate to resolve the situation.

5. A State Party shall also have the right to request the Executive Council to clarify any situation which has been considered ambiguous or has given rise to a concern about its possible non-compliance with this Convention . The Executive shall respond by providing such assistance as appropriate.

6. The Executive Council shall inform the States Parties about any request for clarification provided in this Article.

7. If the doubt or concern of a State Party about a possible non-compliance has not been resolved within 60 days after the submission of the request for clarification to the Executive Council, or it believes its doubts warrant urgent consideration, notwithstanding its right to request a challenge inspection, it may request a special session of the Conference in accordance with Article 8, paragraph 12 (c). At such a special session, the Conference shall consider the matter and may recommend any measure it deems appropriate to resolve the situation.

Procedures for challenge inspections

8. Each State Party has the right to request an on-site challenge inspection of any facility or location in the territory or in any other place under the jurisdiction or control of any other State Party for the sole purpose of clarifying and resolving any questions concerning possible non-compliance with the provisions of this Convention, and to have this inspection conducted anywhere without delay by an inspection team designated by the Director-General and in accordance with the Verification Annex.

9. Each State Party is under the obligation to keep the inspection request within the scope of this Convention and to provide in the inspection request all appropriate information on the basis of which a concern has arisen regarding possible non-compliance with this Convention as specified in the Verification Annex. Each State Party shall refrain from unfounded inspection requests, care being taken to avoid abuse. The challenge inspection shall be carried out for the sole purpose of determining facts relating to the possible non-compliance.

10. For the purpose of verifying compliance with the provisions of this Convention, each State Party shall permit the Technical Secretariat to conduct the on-site challenge inspection pursuant to paragraph 8.

11. Pursuant to a request for a challenge inspection of a facility or location, and in accordance with the procedures provided for in the Verification Annex,

the inspected State Party shall have:

(a) The right and the obligation to make every reasonable effort to demonstrate its compliance with this Convention and, to this end, to enable the inspection team to fulfill its mandate;

(b) The obligation to provide access within the requested site for the sole purpose of establishing facts relevant to the concern regarding possible non-compliance; and

(c) The right to take measures to protect sensitive installations, and to prevent disclosure of confidential information and data, not related to this Convention.

12. With regard to an observer, the following shall apply:

(a) The requesting State Party may, subject to the agreement of the inspected State Party, send a representative who may be a national either of the requesting State Party or of a third State Party, to observe the conduct of the challenge inspection.

(b) The inspected state shall then grant access to the observer in accordance with the verification Annex.

(c) The inspected State Party shall, as a rule, accept the proposed observer, but if the inspected State Party exercise a refusal, that fact shall be recorded in the final report.

13. The requesting State Party shall present an inspection request for an on-site challenge inspection to the Executive Council and at the same time to the Director-General for immediate processing.

14. The Director-General shall immediately ascertain that the inspection request meets the requests specified in Part X, paragraph 4, of the Verification Annex, and, if necessary, assist the requesting State Party in filing the inspection request accordingly. When the inspection request fulfills the requirements, preparations for the challenge inspection shall begin.

15. The Director-General shall transmit the inspection request to the inspected State Party not less than 12 hours before the planned arrival of the inspection team at the point of entry.

16. After having received the inspection request, the Executive Council shall take cognizance of the Director-General's actions on the request and shall keep the case under its consideration throughout the inspection procedure. However, its deliberations shall not delay the inspection process.

17. The Executive Council may, not later than 12

hours after having received the inspection request, decide by three-quarter majority of all its members against carrying out the challenge inspection, if it considers the inspection request to be frivolous, abusive or clearly beyond the scope of this Convention as described in paragraph 8. Neither the requesting nor the inspected State Party shall participate in such a decision. If the Executive Council decides against the challenge inspection, preparations shall be stopped, no further action on the inspection request shall be taken, and the States Parties concerned shall be informed accordingly.

18. The Director-General shall issue an inspection mandate for the conduct of the challenge inspection. The inspection mandate shall be the inspection request referred to in paragraphs 8 and 9 put into operational terms, and shall conform with the inspection request.

19. The challenge inspection shall be conducted in accordance with Part X or, in the case of alleged use, in accordance with Part XI of the Verification Annex. The inspection team shall be guided by the principle of conducting the challenge inspection in the least intrusive manner possible, consistent with the effective and timely accomplishment of its mission.

20. The inspected State Party shall assist the inspection team throughout the challenge inspection and facilitate its task. If the inspected State Party proposes, pursuant to Part X, Section C, of the Verification Annex, arrangements to demonstrate compliance with this Convention, alternative, to full and comprehensive access, it shall make every reasonable effort, through consultations with the inspection team, to reach agreement on the modalities for establishing the facts with the aim of demonstrating its compliance.

21. The final report shall contain the factual findings as well as an assessment by the inspection team of the degree and nature of access and cooperation granted for the satisfactory implementation of the challenge inspection. The Director-General shall promptly transmit the final report of the inspection team to the requesting State Party, to the inspected State Party, to the Executive Council and to all other States Parties. The Director-General shall further transmit promptly to the Executive Council the assessments of the requesting and of the inspected States Parties, as well as the views of other States Parties which may be conveyed to the Director-General for that purpose, and then provide them to all States Parties.

22. The Executive Council shall, in accordance with its powers and functions, review the final report of the inspection team as soon as it is presented, and address any concerns as to:

(a) Whether any non-compliance has occurred;

(b) Whether the request had been within the scope of this Convention; and

(c) Whether the right to request a challenge inspection had been abused.

23. If the Executive Council reaches the conclusion, in keeping with its powers and functions, that further action may be necessary with regard to paragraph 22, it shall take the appropriate measures to redress the situation and to ensure compliance with this Convention including specific recommendations to the Conference. In the case of abuse, the Executive Council shall examine whether the requesting State Party should bear any of the financial implications of the challenge inspection.

24. The requesting State Party and the inspected State Party shall have the right to participate in the review process. The Executive Council shall inform the States Parties and the next session of the Conference of the outcome of the process.

25. If the Executive Council has made specific recommendations to the Conference, the Conference shall consider action in accordance with Article XII.

Article 10

Assistance and Protection Against Chemical Weapons

1. For the purpose of this Article, "Assistance" means the coordination and delivery to States Parties of protection against chemical weapons, including, inter alia, the following: detection equipment and alarm systems; protective equipment; decontamination equipment and decontaminants; medical antidotes and treatments; and advice on any of these protective measures.

2. Nothing in this Convention shall be interpreted as impeding the right of any State Party to conduct research into, develop, produce, acquire, transfer or use means of protection against chemical weapons, for purposes not prohibited under this Convention.

3. Each State Party undertakes to facilitate, and shall have the right to participate in, the fullest possible exchange of equipment, material and scientific and technological information concerning means of protection against chemical weapons.

4. For the purposes of increasing the transparency of national programmer related to protective purposes, each State Party shall provide annually to the Technical Secretariat information on its programme,

in accordance with procedures to be considered and approved by the Conference pursuant to Article 8, paragraph 21 (i).

5. The Technical Secretariat shall establish, not later than 180 days after entry into force of this Convention and maintain, for the use of any requesting State Party, a data bank containing freely available information concerning various means of protection against chemical weapons as well as such information as may be provided by States Parties.

The Technical Secretariat shall also, within the resources available to it, and at the request of a State Party, provide expert advice and assist the State Party in identifying how its programmes for the development and improvement of a protective capacity against chemical weapons could be implemented.

6. Nothing in this Convention shall be interpreted as impeding the right of States Parties to request and provide assistance bilaterally and to conclude individual agreements with other States Parties concerning the emergency procurement of assistance.

7. Each State Party undertakes to provide assistance through the Organization and to this end to elect to take one or more of the following measures:

(a) To contribute to the voluntary fund for assistance to be established by the Conference at its first session;

(b) To conclude, if possible not later than 180 days after this Convention enters into force for it, agreements with the Organization concerning the procurement, upon demand, of assistance;

(c) To declare, not later than 180 days this Convention enters into force for it, the kind of assistance it might provide in response to an appeal by the Organization. If however, a State Party subsequently is unable to provide the assistance envisaged in its declaration, it is still under the obligation to provide assistance in accordance with this paragraph.

8. Each State Party has the right to request and, subject to the procedures set forth in paragraphs 9, 10 and 11, to receive assistance and protection against the use or threat of use of chemical weapons if it considers that:

(a) Chemical weapons have been used against it;

(b) Riot control agents have been used against it as a method of warfare; or

(c) It is threatened by actions or activities of any State that are prohibited for States Parties by Article 1.

9. The request, substantiated by relevant information, shall be submitted to the Director-General, who shall transmit it immediately to the Executive Council and to all States Parties. The Director-General shall immediately forward the request to States Parties which have volunteered, in accordance with paragraph 7(b) and (c), to dispatch emergency assistance in case of use of chemical weapons or use of riot control agents as a method of warfare, or humanitarian assistance in case of serious threat of use of chemical weapons or serious threat of use of riot control agents as a method of warfare to the States Party concerned not later than 12 hours after receipt of the request. The Director-General shall initiate, not later than 24 hours after receipt of the request, an investigation in order to provide foundation for further action. He shall complete the investigation within 72 hours and forward a report to the Executive Council. If additional time is required for completion of the investigation, an interim report shall be submitted within the same time-frame. The additional time required for investigation shall not exceed 72 hours. It may, however, be further extended by similar periods. Reports at the end of each additional period shall be submitted to the Executive Council. The investigation shall, as appropriate and in conformity with the request and the information accompanying the request, establish relevant facts related to the request as well as types and scope of supplementary assistance and protection needed.

10. The Executive Council shall meet not later than 24 hours after receiving an investigation report to consider the situation and shall take a decision by simple majority within the following 24 hours on whether to instruct the Technical Secretariat to provide supplementary assistance. The Technical Secretariat shall immediately transmit to all States Parties and relevant international organizations the investigation report and decision taken by the Executive Council. When so decided by the Executive Council, the Director-General shall provide assistance immediately. For this purpose, the Director-General may cooperate with the requesting State Party, other States Parties and relevant international organizations. The States Parties shall make the fullest possible efforts to provide assistance.

11. If the information available from the ongoing investigation or other reliable sources would give sufficient proof that there are victims of use of chemical weapons and immediate action is indispensable, the Director-General shall notify all States Parties and shall take emergency measures of assistance, using the resources. The Director-General shall keep the Executive Council informed of actions underta-

ken pursuant to this paragraph.

Article 11

Economic and Technological Development

1. The provisions of this Convention shall be implemented in a manner which avoids hampering the economic or technological development of States Parties, and international cooperation in the field of chemical activities for purposes not prohibited under this Convention including the international exchange of scientific and technical information and chemicals and equipment for the production, processing or use of chemicals for purposes not prohibited under this Convention.

2. Subject to the provision of this Convention and without prejudice to the principles and applicable rules of international law, the States Parties shall:

(a) Have the right, individually or collectively, to conduct research with, to develop, produce, acquire, retain, transfer, and use chemicals;

(b) Undertake to facilitate, and have the right to participate in, the fullest possible exchange of chemicals, equipment and scientific and technical information relating to the development and application of chemistry for purposes not prohibited under this Convention;

(c) Not maintain among themselves any restrictions, including those in any international agreements, incompatible with the obligations undertaken under this Convention, which would restrict or impede trade and the development and promotion of scientific and technological knowledge in the field of chemistry for industrial, agricultural, research, medical, pharmaceutical or other peaceful purposes;

(d) Not use this Convention as ground for applying any measures other than those provided for, or permitted, under this Convention nor use any other international agreement for pursuing an objective inconsistent with this Convention;

(e) Undertake to review their existing national regulations in the field of trade in chemicals in order to render them consistent with the object and purpose of this Convention.

Article 12

Measures to Redress a Situation and to Ensure Compliance, Including Sanctions

1. The Conference shall take the necessary measures, as set forth in paragraphs 2, 3 and 4, to ensure compliance with this Convention and to redress and remedy any situation which contravenes the provisions of this Convention. In considering action pursuant to this paragraph, the Conference shall take into account all information and recommendations on the issues submitted by the Executive Council.

2. In cases where a State Party has been requested by the Executive Council to take measures to redress a situation raising problems with regard to its compliance, and where the State Party fails to fulfill the request within the specified time, the Conference may, *inter alia*, upon the recommendation of the executive Council, restrict or suspend the State Party's rights and privileges under this Convention until it undertakes the necessary action to conform with its obligations under this Convention.

3. In cases where serious damage to the object and purpose of this Convention may result from activities prohibited under this Convention in particular by Article I, the Conference may recommend collective measures to States Parties in conformity with international law.

4. The Conference shall, in cases of particular gravity, bring the issue, including relevant information and conclusions, to the attention of the United Nations General Assembly and the United Nations Security Council.

Article 13

Relation to other International Agreements

Nothing in this Convention shall be interpreted as in any way limiting or detracting from the obligations assumed by any State under the Protocol for the Prohibition of the Use in War of Asphyxiating, Poisonous or other Gases, and of Bacteriological Methods of Warfare, signed at Geneva on 17 June 1925, and under the Convention on the Prohibition of the Development, Production and Stockpiling of Bacteriological (Biological) and Toxic Weapons and on Their Destruction, signed at London, Moscow and Washington on 10 April 1972.

Article 14

Settlement of Disputes

1. Disputes that may arise concerning the application or the interpretation of this Convention shall be settled in accordance with the relevant provisions of this Convention and in conformity with the provisions of the Charter of the United Nations.

2. When a dispute arises between two or more

States Parties, or between one or more States Parties and the Organization, relating to the interpretation or application of this Convention, the parties concerned shall consult together with a view to the expeditious settlement of the dispute by negotiation or by other peaceful means of the parties' choice, including recourse to appropriate organs of this Convention and, by mutual consent, referral to the International Court of Justice in conformity with the Statute of the Court. The States Parties involved shall keep the Executive Council informed of actions being taken.

3. The Executive Council may contribute to the settlement of a dispute by whatever means it deems appropriate, including offering its good offices, calling upon the States Parties to a dispute to start the settlement process of their choice and recommending a time-limit for any agreed procedure.

4. The Conference shall consider questions related to disputes raised by States Parties or brought to its attention by the Executive Council. The Conference shall, as it finds necessary, establish or entrust organs with tasks related to the settlement of these disputes in conformity with Article VIII, paragraph 21 (f).

5. The Conference and the Executive Council are separately empowered subject to authorization from the General Assembly of the United Nations, to request the International Court of Justice to give an advisory opinion on any legal question arising within the scope of the activities of the Organization. An agreement between the Organization and the United Nations shall be concluded for this purpose in accordance with Article VIII, paragraph 34 (a).

6. This Article is without prejudice to Article IX or to the provisions on measures to redress a situation and to ensure compliance, including sanctions.

Article 15

Amendments

1. Any State Party may propose amendments to this Convention. Any State Party may also propose changes, as specified in paragraph 4, to the Annexes of this Convention. Proposals for amendments shall be subject to the procedures in paragraphs 2 and 3. Proposals for changes, as specified in paragraph 4, shall be subject to the procedures in paragraph 5.

2. The text of a proposed amendment shall be submitted to the Director-General for circulation to all States Parties and to the Depositary. The proposed amendment shall be considered only by an Amendment Conference. Such an Amendment Conference shall be convened if one third or more of the States Parties notify the Director-General not later than 30

days after its circulation that they support further consideration of the proposal. The Amendment Conference shall be held immediately following a regular session of the Conference unless the requesting States Parties ask for an earliest meeting. In no case shall an Amendment Conference be held less than 60 days after the circulation of the proposed amendment.

3. Amendment shall enter into force for all States Parties 30 days after deposit of the instruments of ratification or acceptance by all the States Parties referred to under subparagraph (b) below;

(a) When adopted by the Amendment Conference by a positive vote of a majority of all States Parties with no State Party casting a negative vote; and

(b) Ratified or accepted by all those States Parties casting a positive vote at the Amendment Conference.

4. In order to ensure the viability and the effectiveness of this Convention, provisions in the Annexes shall be subject to changes in accordance with paragraph 5, if proposed changes are related only to matters of an administrative or technical nature. All changes to the Annex on Chemical shall be made in accordance with paragraph 5. Sections A and C of the Confidentiality Annex, Part X of the Verification Annex, and those definitions in Part I of the Verification Annex which relate exclusively to challenge inspections, shall not be subject to change in accordance with paragraph 5.

5. Proposed changes referred to in paragraph 4 shall be made in accordance with the following procedure:

(a) The next of the proposed changes shall be transmitted together with the necessary information to the Director-General. Additional information for the evaluation of the proposal may be provided by any State Party and the Director-General. The Director-General shall promptly communicate any such proposals and information to all States Parties, the Executive Council and the Depositary;

(b) Not later than 60 days after its receipt, the Director-General shall evaluate proposal to determine all its possible consequences for the provisions of this Convention and its implementation and shall communicate any such information to all States Parties and the Executive Council;

(c) The Executive Council shall examine the proposal in the light of all information available to it, including whether the proposal fulfills the requirements of paragraph 4. Not later than 90 days after its receipt, the Executive Council shall notify its recommendation, with appropriate explanations, to all States Parties for consideration. States Parties acknowledge receipt within 10 days;

(d) If the Executive Council recommends to all States Parties that the proposal be adopted, it shall be considered approved if no State Party objects to it within 90 days after receipt of the recommendation. If the Executive Council recommends that the proposal be rejected, it shall be considered rejected if no State Party objects to the rejection within 90 days after receipt of the recommendation;

(e) If a recommendation of the Executive Council does not meet with the acceptance required under subparagraph (d), a decision on the proposal, including whether it fulfills the requirements of paragraph 4, shall be taken as a matter of substance by the Conference at its next session;

(f) The Director-General shall notify all States Parties and the Depositary of any decision under this paragraph;

(g) Changes approved under this procedure shall enter into force for all States Parties 180 days after the date of notification by the Director-General of their approval unless another time period is recommended by the Executive Council or decided by the Conference.

Article 16

Duration and Withdrawal

1. This Convention shall be of unlimited duration.

2. Each State Party shall, in exercising its national sovereignty have the right to withdraw from this Convention if it decides that extraordinary events, related to the subject-matter of this Convention, have jeopardized the supreme interests of its country. It shall give notice of such withdrawal 90 days in advance to all other States Parties, the Executive Council, the Depositary and the United Nations Security Council. Such notice shall include a statement of the extraordinary events it regards as having jeopardized its supreme interests.

3. The withdrawal of a State Party from the Convention shall not in any way affect the duty of States to continue fulfilling the obligations assumed under any relevant rules of international law, particularly the Geneva Protocol of 1925.

Article 17

Status of the Annexes

The Annexes form an integral part of this Convention. Any reference to this Convention includes the Annexes.

Article 18

Signature

This Convention shall be open for signature for all States before its entry into force.

Article 19

Ratification

This Convention shall be subject to ratification by States Signatories according to their respective constitutional processes.

Article 20

Accession

Any State which does not sign this Convention before its entry into force may accede to it at any time thereafter.

Article 21

Entry into Force

1. This Convention shall enter into force 180 days after the date of the deposit of the 65th instrument of ratification, but in no case earlier than two years after its opening for signature.

2. For States whose instruments of ratification or accession are deposited subsequent to the entry into force of this Convention, it shall enter into force on the 30th day following the date of deposit of their instrument of ratification or accession.

Article 22

Preservations

The Article of this Convention shall not be subject to reservations. The Annexes of this Convention shall not be subject to reservations incompatible with its object and purpose.

Article 23

Depositary

The Secretary-General of the United Nations is hereby designated as the Depositary of this Convention and shall, *inter alia*:

(a) Promptly inform all signatory and acceding States

of the date of each signature, the date of deposit of each instrument of ratification or accession and the date of the entry into force of this Convention, and of the receipt of other notices;

(b) Transmit duly certified copies of this Convention to the Governments of all signatory and acceding States; and

(c) Register this Convention pursuant to Article 102

of the Charter of the United Nations.

Article 24

Authentic Texts

This Convention, of which the Arabic, Chinese, English, French, Russian and Spanish texts are equally authentic, shall be deposited with the Secretary-General of the United Nations.

Preliminary Agreement Concerning the Establishment of a Confederation Between the Federation of Bosnia and Herzegovina and the Republic of Croatia

Date of signature: March 14, 1994
Place of signature: Vienna
Signatory states: Bosnia and Herzegovina, Croatia

The Federation of Bosnia and Herzegovina (hereinafter "The Federation")
and
The Republic of Croatia (hereinafter "Croatia"),
Have agreed that:

Article 1

It is anticipated that a Confederation will be established between The Federation of Bosnia and Croatia (hereinafter "the Parties").

Article 2

The establishment of the Confederation shall not change the international identity or legal personality of Croatia or of the Federation.

Article 3

(1) The Parties shall constitute a Confederative Council in order to coordinate their policies and activities within the Confederation. Each Party shall have an equal number of members on the Council. Decisions of the Council shall require the approval of a majority of the members from each Party.

(2) The President of the Confederative Council shall be elected by the Council for a term of one year, rotating among the Council members of each Party.

Article 4

The Parties shall enact internal regulations and conclude agreements for the purpose of undertaking progressive steps in their economic collaboration as described in this Article, with the aim of establishing a common market and monetary union when conditions are appropriate.

(1) The Parties shall immediately propose cooperation and the development of common policies in the following areas:

(a) transport;

(b) energy;

(c) the environment;

(d) economic policy, including laws and regulations governing the development of free markets, finance, and customs;

(e) the reconstruction of the economy;

(f) health care;

(g) culture, science, and education;

(h) product standardization and consumer protection;

(i) migration, immigration, and asylum; and

(j) law enforcement, particularly with regard to terrorism, smuggling, drug abuse, and organized crime.

(2) The Parties shall consult with a view to establishing, in progressive steps over the next [ ] years:

(a) a free trade area providing for the free movement of goods of domestic origin;

(b) a customs union;

(c) a common market, in which goods, services, capital, and labor shall move freely; and

(d) a monetary union.

Article 5

Croatia and the Federation shall agree as soon as possible on defense arrangements, including the coordination of defense policies and the establishment of joint command staffs in the event of war or imminent peril to either Party.

Article 6

The Parties shall conclude the following agreement as soon as possible:

(i) Croatia shall grant the Federation unrestricted access to the Adriatic through Croatia, as specified in Annex I to this Agreement; and

(ii) The Federation shall grant Croatia unrestricted transit through Neum, as specified in Annex II to this Agreement. These could be concluded between the Republic of Croatia and the Republic of Bosnia and Herzegovina.

Article 7

This Agreement shall enter into force upon signature and remain in force until otherwise agreed by the Parties.

Agreement Establishing the World Trade Organization (WTO)

Date of signature: April 15, 1994
Place of signature: Marrakesh
Signatory states: Antigua and Barbuda, Argentina, Australia, Austria, Bahrain, Bangladesh, Barbados, Belgium, Belize, Benin, Bolivia, Botswana, Brazil, Brunei Darussalam, Burkina Faso, Burundi, Cameroon, Canada, Central African Republic, Chad, Chile, Colombia, Costa Rica, Côte d'Ivoire, Cuba, Cyprus, Czech Republic, Denmark, Djibouti, Dominica, Dominican Republic, Ecuador, Egypt, El Salvador, European Community, Fiji, Finland, France, Gabon, Germany, Ghana, Greece, Grenada, Guatemala, Guinea Bissau, Guinea, Rep. of, Guyana, Haiti, Honduras, Hong Kong, Hungary, Iceland, India, Indonesia, Ireland, Israel, Italy, Jamaica, Japan, Kenya, Korea, Kuwait, Lesotho, Liechtenstein, Luxembourg, Macau, Madagascar, Malawi, Malaysia, Maldives, Mali, Malta, Mauritania, Mauritius, Mexico, Morocco, Mozambique, Myanmar, Namibia, Netherlands, New Zealand, Nicaragua, Nigeria, Pakistan, Papua New Guinea, Paraguay, Peru, Philippines, Poland, Portugal, Qatar, Romania, Rwanda, Saint Lucia, Saint Kitts and Nevis, Saint Vincent & the Grenadines, Senegal, Sierra Leone, Singapore, Slovak Republic, Slovenia, Solomon Islands, South Africa, Spain, Sri Lanka, Suriname, Swaziland, Sweden, Switzerland, Tanzania, Thailand, Togo, Trinidad and Tobago, Tunisia, Turkey, Uganda, United Arab Emirates, United Kingdom, United States, Uruguay, Venezuela, Zambia, Zimbabwe (as of October 22, 1996)
Accessions: Albania, Algeria, Armenia, Belarus, Bulgaria, Cambodia, People's Republic of China, Chinese Taipei, Croatia, Estonia, Georgia, Jordan, Kazakhstan, Kirgyz Republic, Latvia, Lithuania, Former Yugoslav Republic of Macedonia, Moldova, Mongolia, Nepal, Panama, Russian Federation, Saudi Arabia, Seychelles, Sudan, Sultanate of Oman, Tonga, Ukraine, Uzbekistan, Vanuatu, Vietnam
Date of entry into force: January 1, 1995

The *Parties* to this Agreement,
Recognizing that their relations in the field of trade and economic endeavour should be conducted with a view to raising standards of living, ensuring full employment and a large and steadily growing volume of real income and effective demand, and expanding the production of and trade in goods and services, while allowing for the optimal use of the world's resources in accordance with the objective of sustainable development. Seeking both to protect and preserve the environment and to enhance the means for doing so in a manner consistent with their respective needs concerns at different levels of economic development,
Recognizing further that there is need for positive efforts designed to ensure that developing countries, and especially the least developed among them, secure a share in the growth in international trade commensurate with the needs of their economic

development,

Being desirous of contributing to these objectives by entering into reciprocal and mutually advantageous arrangements directed to the substantial reduction of tariffs and other barriers to trade and to the elimination of discriminatory treatment in international trade relations,

Resolved, therefore, to develop an integrated, more viable and durable multilateral trading system encompassing the General Agreement on Tariffs and Trade, the results of past trade liberalization efforts, and all of the results of the Uruguay Round of Multilateral Trade Negotiations,

Determined to preserve the basic principles and to further the objectives underlying this multilateral trading system,

Agree as follows:

Article 1

Establishment of the Organization

The World Trade Organization (hereinafter referred to as "the WTO") is hereby established.

Article 2

Scope of the WTO

1. The WTO shall provide the common institutional framework for the conduct of trade relations among its Members in matters related to the agreements and associated legal instruments included in the Annexes to this Agreement.

2. The agreements and associated legal instruments included in Annexes 1, 2 and 3 (hereinafter referred to as "Multilateral Trade Agreements") are integral parts of this Agreement, binding on all Members.

3. The agreements and associated legal instruments included in Annex 4 (hereinafter referred to as "Plurilateral Trade Agreements") are also part of this Agreement for those Members that have accepted them, and are binding on those Members. The Plurilateral Trade Agreement do not create either obligations or right for Members that have not accepted them.

4. The General Agreement on Tariffs and Trade 1994 as specified in Annex 1A (hereinafter referred to as "GATT 1994") is legally distinct from the General Agreement on Tariffs and Trade, dated 30 October 1947, annexed to the Final Act Adopted at the Conclusion of the Second Session of the Preparatory Committee of the United Nations Conference on Trade and Employment, as subsequently rectified, amended or modified (hereinafter referred to as "GATT 1947").

Article 3

Functions of the WTO

1. The WTO shall facilitate the implementation, administration and operation, and further the objectives, of this Agreement and of the Multilateral Trade Agreement, and shall also provide the framework for the implementation, administration and operation of the Plurilateral Trade Agreements.

2. The WTO shall provide the forum for negotiations among its Members concerning their multilateral trade relations in matters dealt with under the agreements in the Annexes to this Agreement. The WTO may also provide a forum for further negotiations among its Members concerning their multilateral trade relations, and a framework for the implementation of the results of such negotiations, as may be decided by the Ministerial Conference.

3. The WTO shall administer the Understanding on Rules and Procedures Governing the Settlement of Disputes (hereinafter referred to as the "Dispute Settlement Understanding" or "DSU") in Annex 2 to this Agreement.

4. The WTO shall administer the Trade Policy Review Mechanism (hereinafter referred to as the "TPRM") provided for in Annex 3 to this Agreement.

5. With a view to achieving greater coherence in global economic policy-making, the WTO shall cooperate, as appropriate, with the International Monetary Fund and with the International Bank for Reconstruction and Development and its affiliated agencies.

Article 4

Structure of the WTO

1. There shall be a Ministerial Conference composed of representatives of all the Members, which shall meet at least once every two years. The Ministerial Conference shall carry out the functions of the WTO and take actions necessary to this effect. The Ministerial Conference shall have the authority to take decisions on all matters under any of the Multilateral Trade Agreements, if so requested by a Member, in accordance with the specific requirements for decision-making in this Agreement and in the relevant Multilateral Trade Agreement.

2. There shall be a General Council composed of representatives of all the Members, which shall meet as appropriate. In the intervals between meetings of the Ministerial Conference, its functions shall be conducted by the General Council. The General Council shall also carry out the functions assigned to it by this Agreement. The General Council shall

establish its rules of procedure and approve the rules of procedure for the Committees provided for in paragraph 7.

3. The General Council shall convene as appropriate to discharge the responsibilities of the Dispute Settlement Body provided for in the Dispute Settlement Understanding. The Dispute Settlement Body may have its own chairman and shall establish such rules of procedures as it deems necessary for the fulfillment of those responsibilities.

4. The General Council shall convene as appropriate to discharge the responsibilities of the Trade Policy Review Body provided for in the TPRM. The Trade Policy Review Body may have its own chairman and shall establish such rules of procedure as it deems necessary for the fulfillment of those responsibilities.

5. There shall be a Council for Trade in Goods, a Council for Trade in Services and a Council for Trade-Related Aspects of Intellectual Property Rights (hereinafter referred to as the "Council for TRIPS"), which shall operate under the general guidance of the General Council. The Council for Trade in Goods shall oversee the functioning of the Multilateral Trade Agreements in Annex 1A. The Council for Trade in Services shall oversee the functioning of the General Agreement on Trade in Services (hereinafter referred to as "GATS"). The Council for TRIPS shall oversee the functioning of the Agreement on Trade-Related Aspects of Intellectual Property Right (hereinafter referred to as the "Agreement on TRIPS"). These Councils shall carry out the functions assigned to them by their respective agreements and by the General Council. They shall establish their respective rules of procedure subject to the approval of the General Council. Membership in these Councils shall be open to representatives of all Members. These Councils shall meet as necessary to carry out their functions.

6. The Council for Trade in Goods, the Council for Trade in Services and the Council for TRIPS shall establish subsidiary bodies as required. These subsidiary bodies shall establish their respective rules of procedures subject to the approval of their respective Councils.

7. The Ministerial Conference shall establish a Committee on Trade and Development, a Committee on Balance-of-Payments Restrictions and a Committee on Budget, Finance and Administration, which shall carry out the functions assigned to them by this Agreement and by the Multilateral Trade Agreements, and any additional functions assigned to them by the General Council, and may establish such additional Committees with such functions as it may deem appropriate. As part of its functions, the Committee on Trade and Development shall periodically review the special provisions in the Multilateral Trade Agreements in favor of the least-developed country Members and report to the General Council for appropriate action. Membership in these Committees shall be open to representatives of all Members.

8. The bodies provided for under the Plurilateral Trade Agreements shall carry out the functions assigned to them under those Agreements and shall operate within the institutional framework of the WTO. These bodies shall keep the General Council informed of their activities on a regular basis.

Article 5

Relations with Other Organizations

1. The General Council shall make appropriate arrangement for effective cooperation with other intergovernmental organizations that have responsibilities related to those of the WTO.

2. The General Council may make appropriate arrangements for consultation and cooperation with non-governmental organizations concerned with matters related to those of the WTO.

Article 6

The Secretariat

1. There shall be a Secretariat of the WTO (hereinafter referred to as "the Secretariat") headed by a Director-General.

2. The Ministerial Conference shall appoint the Director-General and adopt regulations setting out the powers, duties, conditions of service and term of office of the Director-General.

3. The Director-General shall appoint the numbers of the staff of the Secretariat and determine their duties and conditions of service in accordance with regulations adopted by the Ministerial Conference.

4. The responsibilities of the Director-General and of the staff of the Secretariat shall be exclusively international in character. In the discharge of their duties, the Director-General and the staff of the Secretariat shall not seek or accept instructions from any government or any to other authority external to the WTO. They shall refrain from any action which might adversely reflect on their position as international officials. The Members of the WTO shall respect the international character of the responsibilities of the Director-General and of the staff Secretariat and shall not seek to influence them in the discharge of their duties.

Article 7

Budget and Contributions

1. The Director-General shall present to the Committee on Budget, Finance and Administration the annual budget estimate and financial statement of the WTO. The Committee on Budget, Finance and Administration shall review the annual budget estimate and the financial statement presented by the Director-General and make recommendations thereon to the General Council. The annual budget estimate shall be subject to approval by the General Council.

2. The Committee on Budget, Finance and Administration shall propose to the General Council financial regulations which shall include provisions setting out:

(a) the scale of contributions apportioning the expenses of the WTO among its Members; and

(b) the measures to be taken in respect of Members in arrears.

The financial regulations shall be based, as far as practicable, on the regulations and practices of GATT 1947.

3. The General Council shall adopt the financial regulations and the annual budget estimate by a two-thirds majority comprising more than half of the Members of the WTO.

4. Each Member shall promptly contribute to the WTO its share in the expenses of the WTO in accordance with the financial regulations adopted by the General Council.

Article 8

Statutes of the WTO

1. The WTO shall have legal personality, and shall be accorded by each of its Members such legal capacity as may be necessary for the exercise of its functions.

2. The WTO shall be accorded by each of its Members such privileges and immunities as are necessary for the exercise of its functions.

3. The officials of the WTO and the representative of the Members shall similarly be accorded by each of its Members such privileges and immunities as are necessary for the independent exercise of their functions in connection with the WTO.

4. The privileges and immunities to be accorded by a Member to the WTO, its officials, and the representatives of its Members shall be similar to the privileges and immunities stipulated in the Convention on the Privileges and Immunities of the Specialized Agencies, approved by the General Assembly of the United Nations on 21 November 1947.

5. The WTO may conclude a headquarters agreement.

Article 9

Decision-Making

1. The WTO shall continue the practice of decision-making by consensus following under GATT 1947.[1] Except as otherwise provided, where a decision cannot be arrived at by consensus, the matter at issue shall be decided by voting. At meetings of the Ministerial Conference and the General Council, each Member of the WTO shall have one vote. Where the European Communities exercise their right to vote, they shall have a number of votes equal to the number of their member States[2] which are Members of the WTO. Decisions of the Ministerial Conference and the General Council shall be taken by a majority of the votes cast, unless otherwise provided in this Agreement or in the relevant Multilateral Trade Agreement.[3]

2. The Ministerial Conference and the General Council shall have exclusive authority to adopt interpretations of this Agreement and of the Multilateral Trade Agreements. In the case of an interpretation of a Multilateral Trade Agreement in Annex 1, they shall exercise their authority on the basis of a recommendation by the Council overseeing the functioning of that Agreement. The decision to adopt an interpretation shall be taken by a three-fourth majority of the Members. This paragraph shall not be used in a manner that would undermine the amendment provisions in Article X.

3. In exceptional circumstances, the Ministerial Conference may decide to waive an obligation imposed on a Member by this Agreement or any of the Multilateral Trade Agreements, provided that any such decision shall be taken by three-fourths[4] of the Members unless otherwise provided for in this paragraph.

(a) A request for a waiver concerning this Agreement shall be submitted to the Ministerial Conference for consideration pursuant to the practice of decision-making by consensus. The Ministerial Conference shall establish a time-period, which shall not exceed 90 days, to consider the request. If consensus is not reached during the time-period, any decision to grant a waiver shall be taken by three fourths[4] of the Members.

(b) A request for a waiver concerning the Multilateral Trade Agreements in Annexes 1A or 1B or 1C and their annexes shall be submitted initially to the Council for Trade in Goods, the Council for Trade in Services or the Council for TRIPS, respectively, for consideration during a time-period which shall not exceed 90 days. At the end of the time-period, the relevant Council shall submit a report to the Ministerial Conference.

4. A decision by the Ministerial Conference granting a waiver shall state the exceptional circumstances justifying the decision, the terms and conditions governing the application of the waiver, and the date on which the waiver shall terminate. Any waiver granted for a period of more than one year shall be reviewed by the Ministerial Conference not later than one year after it is granted, and thereafter annually until the waiver terminates. In each review, the Ministerial Conference shall examine whether the exceptional circumstances justifying the waiver still exist and whether the terms and conditions attached to the waiver have been met. The Ministerial Conference, on the basis of the annual review, may extend, modify or terminate the waiver.

5. Decisions under a Plurilateral Trade Agreement, including any decisions on interpretations and waivers, shall be governed by the provisions of that Agreement.

Article 10

Amendments

1. Any Member of the WTO may initiate a proposal to amend the provisions of this Agreement or the Multilateral Trade Agreements in Annex 1 by submitting such proposal to the Ministerial Conference. The Councils listed in paragraph 5 of Article IV may also submit to the Ministerial Conference proposals to amend the provisions of the corresponding Multilateral Trade Agreements in Annex 1 the functioning to which they oversee. Unless the Ministerial Conference decide on a longer period, for a period of 90 days after the proposal has been tabled formally at the Ministerial Conference any decision by the Ministerial Conference to submit the proposed amendment to the Members for acceptance shall be taken by consensus. Unless the provisions of paragraph 2, 5 or 6 apply, that decision shall specify whether the provisions of paragraphs 3 or 4 shall apply. If consensus is reached, the Ministerial Conference shall forthwith submit the proposed amendment to the Members for acceptance. If consensus is not reached at a meeting of the Ministerial Conference within the established

period, the Ministerial Conference shall decide by a two-thirds majority of the Members whether to submit the proposed amendment to the Members for acceptance. Except as provided in paragraphs 2, 5 and 6, the provisions of paragraph 3 shall apply to the proposed amendment, unless the Ministerial Conference decides by a three-fourths majority of the Members that the provisions of paragraph 4 shall apply.

2. Amendments to the provisions of this Article and to the provisions of the following Articles shall take effect only upon acceptance by all Members:

Article IX of this Agreement;
Article I and II of GATT 1994;
Article II.1 of GATS;
Article 4 of the Agreement on TRIPS.

3. Amendments to provisions of this Agreement, or of the Multilateral Trade Agreement in Annexes 1A and 1C, other than those listed in paragraphs 2 and 6, of a nature that would alter the rights and obligations of the Members, shall take effect for the Members that have accepted them upon acceptance by two-thirds of the Members and thereafter for each other Members upon acceptance by it. The Ministerial Conference may decide by a three-fourths majority of the Members that any amendment made effective under this paragraph is of such a nature that any Member which has not accepted it within a period specified by the Ministerial Conference in each case shall be free to withdraw from the WTO or to remain a Member with the consent of the Ministerial Conference.

4. Amendments to provisions of this Agreement or the Multilateral Trade Agreements in Annexes 1A and 1C, other than those listed in paragraphs 2 and 6, a nature that would not alter the rights and obligations of the Members, shall take effect for all Members upon acceptance by two-thirds of the Members.

5. Except as provided in paragraph 2 above, amendments to Parts I, II and III of GATS and the respective annexes shall take effect for the Members that have accepted them upon acceptance by two thirds of the Members and thereafter for each Member upon acceptance by it. The Ministerial Conference may decide by a three-fourths majority of the Members that any amendment made effective under the preceding provision is of such a nature that any Member which has not accepted it within a period specified by the Ministerial Conference in each case shall be free to withdraw from the WTO or to remain a Member with the consent of the Ministerial Conference. Amendments to Parts IV, V and VI of GATS and the respective annexes shall take effect for all Members upon acceptance by two thirds of the Members.

6. Notwithstanding the other provisions of this Article, amendments to the Agreement on TRIPS meeting the requirements of paragraph 2 of Article 71 thereof may be adopted by the Ministerial Conference without further formal acceptance process.

7. Any Member accepting an amendment to this Agreement or to a Multilateral Trade Agreement in Annex 1 shall deposit an instrument of acceptance with the Director-General of the WTO within the period of acceptance specified by the Ministerial Conference.

8. Any Member of the WTO may initiate a proposal to amend the provisions of the Multilateral Trade Agreements in Annexes 2 and 3 by submitting such proposal to the Ministerial Conference. The decision to approve amendments to the Multilateral Trade Agreement in Annex 2 shall be made by consensus and these amendments shall take effect for all Members upon approval by the Ministerial Conference. Decisions to approve amendments to the Multilateral Trade Agreement in Annex 3 shall take effect for all Members upon approval by the Ministerial Conference.

9. The Ministerial Conference, upon the request of the Members parties to a trade agreement, may decide exclusively by consensus to add that agreement to Annex 4. The Ministerial Conference, upon the request of the Members parties to a Plurilateral Trade Agreement, may decide to delete that Agreement from Annex 4.

10. Amendments to a Plurilateral Trade Agreement shall be governed by the provisions of that Agreement.

Article 11

Original Membership

1. The contracting parties to GATT 1947 as of the date of entry into force of this Agreement, and the European Communities, which accept this Agreement and the Multilateral Trade Agreements and for which Schedules of Concessions and Commitments are annexed to GATT 1994 and for which Schedules of Specific Commitments are annexed to GATS shall become original Members of the WTO.

2. The least-developed countries recognized as such by the United Nations will only be required to undertake commitments and concessions to the extent consistent with their individual development, financial and trade needs or their administrative and institutional capabilities.

Article 12

Accession

1. Any State or separate customs territory possess-

ing full autonomy in the conduct of its external commercial relations and for other matters provided for in this Agreement and the Multilateral Trade Agreements may accede to this Agreement, on terms to be agreed between it and the WTO. Such accession shall apply to this Agreement and the Multilateral Trade Agreement annexed thereto.

2. Decisions on accession shall be taken by the Ministerial Conference. The Ministerial Conference shall approve the agreement on the terms of accession by a two-thirds majority of the Members of the WTO.

3. Accession to a Plurilateral Trade Agreement shall be governed by the provisions of that Agreement.

Article 13

Non-Application of Multilateral Trade Agreements between Particular Members

1. This Agreement and the Multilateral Trade Agreement in Annexes 1 and 2 shall not apply as between any Member and any other Member if either of the Members, at the time either becomes a Member, does not consent to such application.

2. Paragraph 1 may be invoked between original Members of the WTO which were contracting parties to GATT 1947 only where Article XXXV of that Agreement had been invoked earlier and was effective as between those contracting parties at the time of entry into force for them of this Agreement.

3. Paragraph 1 shall apply between a Member and another Member which has acceded under Article XII only if the Member not consenting to the application has so notified the Ministerial Conference before the approval of the agreement on the terms of accession by the Ministerial Conference.

4. The Ministerial Conference may review the operation of this Article in particular cases at the request of any Member and make appropriate recommendations.

5. Non-application of a Plurilateral Trade Agreement between parties to that Agreement shall be governed by the provisions of that Agreement.

Article 14

Acceptance, Entry into Force and Deposit

1. This Agreement shall be open for acceptance, by signature or otherwise, by contracting parties to GATT 1947, and the European Communities, which are eligible to become original Members of the WTO in accordance with Article XI of this Agreement. Such acceptance shall apply to this Agreement and the

Multilateral Trade Agreements annexed hereto. This Agreement and the Multilateral Trade Agreements annexed hereto shall enter into force on the date determined by Ministers in accordance with paragraph 3 of the Final Act Embodying the Results of the Uruguay Round of Multilateral Trade Negotiations and shall remain open for acceptance for a period of two years following that date unless the Ministers decide otherwise. An acceptance following the entry into force of this Agreement shall enter into force on the 30th day following the date of such acceptance.

2. A Member which accepts this Agreement after its entry into force shall implement those concessions and obligations in the Multilateral Trade Agreements that are to be implemented over a period of time starting with the entry into force of this Agreement as it had accepted this Agreement on the date of its entry into force.

3. Until the entry into force of this Agreement, the text of this Agreement and the Multilateral Trade Agreements shall be deposited with the Director-General to the CONTRACTING PARTIES to GATT 1947. The Director-General shall promptly furnish a certified true copy of this Agreement and the Multilateral Trade Agreements, and a notification of each acceptance thereof, to each government and the European Communities having accepted this Agreement. This Agreement and the Multilateral Trade Agreements, and any amendments thereto, shall, upon the entry into force of this Agreement, be deposited with the Director-General of the WTO.

4. The acceptance and entry into force of a Plurilateral Trade Agreement shall be governed by the provisions of that Agreement. Such Agreements shall be deposited with the Director-General to the CONTRACTING PARTIES to GATT 1947. Upon the entry into force of this Agreement, such Agreement shall be deposited with the Director-General of the WTO.

Article 15

Withdrawal

1. Any Member may withdraw from this Agreement. Such withdrawal shall apply both to this Agreement and the Multilateral Trade Agreements and shall take effect upon the expiration of six months from the date on which written notice of withdrawal is received by the Director-General of the WTO.

2. Withdrawal from a Plurilateral Trade Agreement

shall be governed by the provisions of that Agreement.

Article 16

Miscellaneous Provisions

1. Except as otherwise provided under this Agreement or the Multilateral Trade Agreements, the WTO shall be guided by the decisions, procedures and customary practices followed by the CONTRACTING PARTIES to GATT 1947 and the bodies established in the framework of GATT 1947.

2. To the extent practicable, the Secretariat of GATT 1947 shall become the Secretariat of the WTO, and the Director-General to the CONTRACTING PARTIES to GATT 1947, until such time as the Ministerial Conference has appointed a Director-General in accordance with paragraph 2 of Article VI of this Agreement, shall serve as Director-General of the WTO.

3. In the event of a conflict between a provision of this Agreement and a provision of any of the Multilateral Trade Agreements, the provision of this Agreement shall prevail to the extent of the conflict.

4. Each Member shall ensure the conformity of its laws, regulations and administrative procedures with its obligations as provided in the annexed Agreements.

5. No reservations may be made in respect of any provision of this Agreement. Reservations in respect of any of the provisions of the Multilateral Trade Agreements may only be made to the extent provided for in those Agreements. Reservations in respect of a provision of a Plurilateral Trade Agreement shall be governed by the provisions of that Agreement.

6. This Agreement shall be registered in accordance with the provisions of Article 102 of the Charter of the United Nations.

Notes

1. The body concerned shall be deemed to have decided by consensus on a matter submitted of its consideration, if no Member, present at the meeting when the decision is taken, formally objects to the proposed decision.

2. The number of votes of the European Communities and their member States shall in no case exceed the number of the member States of the European Communities.

3. Decisions by the General Council when convened as the Dispute Settlement Body shall be taken only in accordance with the provisions of paragraph 4 of Article 2 of the Dispute Settlement Understanding.

4. A decision to grant a waiver in respect of any obligation a transition period or a period for staged implementation that the requesting Member has not performed by the end of the relevant period shall be taken only by consensus.

Agreement on the Gaza Strip and the Jericho Area

Date of signature: May 4, 1994
Place of signature: Cairo
Signatory states: Israel, The P.L.O.

Preamble

[The signatories],
WITHIN the framework of the Middle East peace process initiated at Madrid in October 1991;

REAFFIRMING their determination to live in peaceful coexistence, mutual dignity and security, while recognizing their mutual legitimate and political rights;

REAFFIRMING their desire to achieve a just, lasting and comprehensive peace settlement through the agreed political process;

REAFFIRMING their adherence to the mutual recognition and commitments expressed in the letters dated September 9, 1993, signed by and exchanged between the Prime Minister of Israel and the Chairman of the PLO;

REAFFIRMING their understanding that the interim self-government arrangements, including the arrangements to apply in the Gaza Strip and the Jericho Area contained in this Agreement, are an integral part of the whole peace process and that the negotiations on the permanent status will lead to the implementation of Security Council Resolutions 242 and 338;

DESIROUS of putting into effect the Declaration of Principles on Interim Self-Government Arrangements signed at Washington, D.C. on September 13, 1993, and the Agreed Minutes thereto (hereinafter "the Declaration of Principles"), and in particular the Protocol on withdrawal of Israeli forces from the Gaza Strip and the Jericho Area;

HEREBY AGREE to the following arrangements regarding the Gaza Strip and the Jericho Area:

Article 1

Definitions

For the purpose of this Agreement:

(a) the Gaza Strip and the Jericho Area are delineated on Nos. 1 and 2 attached to this Agreement;

(b) "the Settlements" means the Gush Katif and Erez settlement areas, as well as the other settlements in the Gaza Strip, as shown on attached map No. 1;

(c) "the Military Installation Area" means the Israeli military installation area along the Egyptian border in the Gaza Strip, as shown on map No. 1; and

(d) the term "Israelis" shall also include Israeli statutory agencies and corporations registered in Israel.

Article 2

Scheduled Withdrawal of Israeli Military Forces

1. Israel shall implement an accelerated and scheduled withdrawal of Israeli military forces from the Gaza Strip and from the Jericho Area to begin immediately with the signing of this Agreement. Israel shall complete such withdrawal within three weeks from this date.

2. Subject to the arrangements included in the Protocol Concerning Withdrawal of Israeli Military Forces and Security Arrangements attached as Annex I, the Israeli withdrawal shall include evacuating all military bases and other fixed installations to be handed over to the Palestinian Police, to be established pursuant to Article IX below (hereinafter "the Palestinian Police").

3. In order to carry out Israel's responsibility for external security and for internal security and public order of Settlements and Israelis, Israel shall, concurrently with the withdrawal, redeploy its remaining military forces to the Settlements and the Military Installation Area, in accordance with the provisions of this Agreement. Subject to the provisions of this Agreement, this redeployment shall constitute full implementation of Article XIII of the Declaration of Principles with regard to the Gaza Strip and the Jericho Area only.

4. For the purposes of this Agreement, "Israeli military forces" may include Israel police and other Israeli security forces.

5. Israelis, including Israeli military forces, may continue to use roads freely within the Gaza Strip and the Jericho Area. Palestinians may use public roads crossing the Settlements freely, as provided for in Annex I.

6. The Palestinian Police shall be deployed and shall assume responsibility for public order and internal security of Palestinians in accordance with this Agreement and Annex I.

Article 3

Transfer of Authority

1. Israel shall transfer authority as specified in this Agreement from the Israeli military government and its Civil Administration to the Palestinian Authority, hereby established, in accordance with Article V of this Agreement, except for the authority that Israel shall continue to exercise as specified in this Agreement.

2. As regards the transfer and assumption of authority in civil spheres, powers and responsibilities shall be transferred and assumed as set out in the Protocol Concerning Civil Affairs attached as Annex II.

3. Arrangements for a smooth and peaceful transfer of the agreed powers and responsibilities are set out in Annex II.

4. Upon the completion of the Israeli withdrawal and the transfer of powers and responsibilities as detailed in paragraphs 1 and 2 above and in Annex II, the Civil Administration in the Gaza Strip and the Jericho Area will be dissolved and the Israeli military government will be withdrawn. The withdrawal of the military government shall not prevent it from continuing to exercise the powers and responsibilities specified in this Agreement.

5. A Joint Civil Affairs Coordination and Cooperation Committee (hereinafter "the CAC") and two Joint Regional Civil Affairs Subcommittees for the Gaza Strip and the Jericho Area respectively shall be established in order to provide for coordination and cooperation in civil affairs between the Palestinian Authority and Israel, as detailed in Annex II.

6. The offices of the Palestinian Authority shall be located in the Gaza Strip and the Jericho Area pending the inauguration of the Council to be elected pursuant to the Declaration of Principles.

Article 4

Structure and Composition of the Palestinian Authority

1. The Palestinian Authority will consist of one body of 24 members which shall carry out and be responsible for all the legislative and executive powers and responsibilities transferred to it under this Agreement, in accordance with this Article, and shall be responsible for the exercise of judicial functions in accordance with Article VI, subparagraph 1. b. of this Agreement.

2. The Palestinian Authority shall administer the departments transferred to it and may establish, within its jurisdiction, other departments and subordinate administrative units as necessary for the fulfillment of its responsibilities. It shall determine its own internal procedures.

3. The PLO shall inform the Government of Israel of the names of the members of the Palestinian Authority and any change of members. Changes in the membership of the Palestinian Authority will take effect upon an exchange of letters between the PLO and the Government of Israel.

4. Each member of the Palestinian Authority shall enter into office upon undertaking to act in accordance with this Agreement.

Article 5

Jurisdiction

1. The authority of the Palestinian Authority encompasses all matters that fall within its territorial, functional and personal jurisdiction, as follows:

(a) The territorial jurisdiction covers the Gaza Strip and the Jericho Area territory, as defined in Article I, except for Settlements and the Military Installation Area.

Territorial jurisdiction shall include land, subsoil and territorial waters, in accordance with the provisions of this Agreement.

(b) The functional jurisdiction encompasses all powers and responsibilities as specified in this Agreement. This jurisdiction does not include foreign relations, internal security and public order of Settlements and the Military Installation Area and Israelis, and external security.

(c) The personal jurisdiction extends to all persons within the territorial jurisdiction referred to above, except for Israelis, unless otherwise provided in this Agreement.

2. The Palestinian Authority has, within its authority, legislative, executive and judicial powers and responsibilities, as provided for in this Agreement.

3. (a) Israel has authority over the Settlements, the Military Installation Area, Israelis, external security, internal security and public order of Settlements, the Military Installation Area and Israelis, and those agreed powers and responsibilities specified in this Agreement.

(b) Israel shall exercise its authority through its military government, which, for that end, shall continue to have the necessary legislative, judicial and executive powers and responsibilities, in accordance with international law. This provision shall not derogate from Israel's applicable legislation over Israelis in personam.

4. The exercise of authority with regard to the electromagnetic sphere and airspace shall be in accordance with the provisions of this Agreement.

5. The provisions of this Article are subject to the specific legal arrangements detailed in the Protocol Concerning Legal Matters attached as Annex III. Israel and the Palestinian Authority may negotiate further legal arrangements.

6. Israel and the Palestinian Authority shall cooperate on matters of legal assistance in criminal and civil matters through the legal subcommittee of the CAC.

Article 6

Powers and Responsibilities of the Palestinian Authority

1. Subject to the provisions of this Agreement, the Palestinian Authority, within its jurisdiction:

(a) has legislative powers as set out in Article VII of this Agreement, as well as executive powers;

(b) will administer justice through an independent judiciary;

(c) will have, inter alia, power to formulate policies, supervise their implementation, employ staff, establish departments, authorities and institutions, sue and be sued and conclude contracts; and

(d) will have, inter alia, the power to keep and administer registers and records of the population, and issue certificates, licenses and documents.

2. (a) In accordance with the Declaration of Principles, the Palestinian Authority will not have powers and responsibilities in the sphere of foreign relations, which sphere includes the establishment abroad of embassies, consulates or other types of foreign missions and posts or permitting their establishment in the Gaza Strip or the Jericho Area, the appointment of or admission of diplomatic and consular staff, and the exercise of diplomatic functions.

(b) Notwithstanding the provisions of this paragraph, the PLO may conduct negotiations and sign agreements with states or international organizations for the benefit of the Palestinian Authority in the fol-

lowing cases only:

(1) economic agreements, as specifically provided in Annex IV of this Agreement;

(2) agreements with donor countries for the purpose of implementing arrangements for the provision of assistance to the Palestinian Authority;

(3) agreements for the purpose of implementing the regional development plans detailed in Annex IV of the Declaration of Principles or in agreements entered into in the framework of the multilateral negotiations; and

(4) cultural, scientific and educational agreements.

(c) Dealings between the Palestinian Authority and representatives of foreign states and international organizations, as well as the establishment in the Gaza Strip and the Jericho Area of representative offices other than those described in subparagraph 2.a. above, for the purpose of implementing the agreements referred to in subparagraph 2.b. above, shall not be considered foreign relations.

Article 7

Legislative Powers of the Palestinian Authority

1. The Palestinian Authority will have the power, within its jurisdiction, to promulgate legislation, including basic laws, laws, regulations and other legislative acts.

2. Legislation promulgated by the Palestinian Authority shall be consistent with the provisions of this Agreement.

3. Legislation promulgated by the Palestinian Authority shall be communicated to a legislation subcommittee to be established by the CAC (hereinafter "the Legislation Subcommittee"). During a period of 30 days from the communication of the legislation, Israel may request that the Legislation Subcommittee decide whether such legislation exceeds the jurisdiction of the Palestinian Authority or is otherwise inconsistent with the provisions of this Agreement.

4. Upon receipt of the Israeli request, the Legislation Subcommittee shall decide, as an initial matter, on the entry into force of the legislation pending its decision on the merits of the matter.

5. If the Legislation Subcommittee is unable to reach a decision with regard to the entry into force of the legislation within 15 days, this issue will be referred to a board of review. This board of review shall be comprised of two judges, retired judges or senior jurists (hereinafter "Judges"), one from each

side, to be appointed from a compiled list of three Judges proposed by each.

In order to expedite the proceedings before this board of review, the two most senior Judges, one from each side, shall develop written informal rules of procedure.

6. Legislation referred to the board of review shall enter into force only if the board of review decides that it does not deal with a security issue which falls under Israel's responsibility, that it does not seriously threaten other significant Israeli interests protected by this Agreement and that the entry into force of the legislation could not cause irreparable damage or harm.

7. The Legislation Subcommittee shall attempt to reach a decision on the merits of the matter within 30 days from the date of the Israeli request. If this Subcommittee is unable to reach such a decision within this period of 30 days, the matter shall be referred to the Joint Israeli-Palestinian Liaison Committee referred to in Article XV below (hereinafter "the Liaison Committee"). This Liaison Committee will deal with the matter immediately and will attempt to settle it within 30 days.

8. Where the legislation has not entered into force pursuant to paragraphs 5 or 7 above, this situation shall be maintained pending the decision of the Liaison Committee on the merits of the matter, unless it has decided otherwise.

9. Laws and military orders in effect in the Gaza Strip or the Jericho Area prior to the signing of this Agreement shall remain in force, unless amended or abrogated in accordance with this Agreement.

Article 8

Arrangements for Security and Public Order

1. In order to guarantee public order and internal security for the Palestinians of the Gaza Strip and the Jericho Area, the Palestinian Authority shall establish a strong police force, as set out in Article IX below. Israel shall continue to carry the responsibility for defense against external threats, including the responsibility for protecting the Egyptian border and the Jordanian line, and for defense against external threats from the sea and from the air, as well as the responsibility for overall security of Israelis and Settlements, for the purpose of safeguarding their internal security and public order, and will have all the powers to take the steps necessary to meet this responsibility.

2. Agreed security arrangements and coordination mechanisms are specified in Annex I.

3. A joint Coordination and Cooperation Commit-

tee for mutual security purposes (hereinafter "the JSC"), as well as three joint District Coordination and Cooperation Offices for the Gaza district, the Khan Yunis district and the Jericho district respectively (hereinafter "the DCOs") are hereby established as provided for in Annex I.

4. The security arrangements provided for in this Agreement and in Annex I may be reviewed at the request of either Party and may be amended by mutual agreement of the Parties. Specific review arrangements are included in Annex I.

Article 9

The Palestinian Directorate of Police Force

1. The Palestinian Authority shall establish a strong police force, the Palestinian Directorate of Police Force (hereinafter "the Palestinian Police"). The duties, functions, structure, deployment and composition of the Palestinian Police, together with provisions regarding its equipment and operation, are set out in Annex I, Article III. Rules of conduct governing the activities of the Palestinian Police are set out in Annex I, Article VIII.

2. Except for the Palestinian Police referred to in this Article and the Israeli military forces, no other armed forces shall be established or operate in the Gaza Strip or the Jericho Area.

3. Except for the arms, ammunition and equipment of the Palestinian Police described in Annex I, Article III, and those of the Israeli military forces, no organization or individual in the Gaza Strip and the Jericho Area shall manufacture, sell, acquire, possess, import or otherwise introduce into the Gaza Strip or the Jericho Area any firearms, ammunition, weapons, explosives, gunpowder or any related equipment, unless otherwise provided for in Annex I.

Article 10

Passages

Arrangements for coordination between Israel and the Palestinian Authority regarding the Gaza-Egypt and Jericho-Jordan passages, as well as any other agreed international crossings, are set out in Annex I, Article X.

Article 11

Safe Passage between the Gaza Strip and the Jericho Area

Arrangements for safe passage of persons and transportation between the Gaza Strip and the Jericho

Area are set out in Annex I, Article IX.

Article 12

Relations between Israel and the Palestinian Authority

1. Israel and the Palestinian Authority shall seek to foster mutual understanding and tolerance and shall accordingly abstain from incitement, including hostile propaganda, against each other and, without derogating from the principle of freedom of expression, shall take legal measures to prevent such incitement by any organizations, groups or individuals within their jurisdiction.

2. Without derogating from the other provisions of this Agreement, Israel and the Palestinian Authority shall cooperate in combatting criminal activity which may affect both sides, including offenses related to trafficking in illegal drugs and psychotropic substances, smuggling, and offenses against property, including offenses related to vehicles.

Article 13

Economic Relations

The economic relations between the two sides are set out in the Protocol on Economic Relations signed in Paris on April 29, 1994 and the Appendices thereto, certified copies of which are attached as Annex IV, and will be governed by the relevant provisions of this Agreement and its Annexes.

Article 14

Human Rights and the Rule of Law

Israel and the Palestinian Authority shall exercise their powers and responsibilities pursuant to this Agreement with due regard to internationally-accepted norms and principles of human rights and the rule of law.

Article 15

The Joint Israeli-Palestinian Liaison Committee

1. The Liaison Committee established pursuant to Article X of the Declaration of Principles shall ensure the smooth implementation of this Agreement. It shall deal with issues requiring coordination, other issues of common interest and disputes.

2. The Liaison Committee shall be composed of an equal number of members from each Party. It may add other technicians and experts as necessary.

3. The Liaison Committee shall adopt its rules of procedure, including the frequency and place or places of its meetings.

4. The Liaison Committee shall reach its decisions by Agreement.

Article 16

Liaison and Cooperation with Jordan and Egypt

1. Pursuant to Article XII of the Declaration of Principles, the two Parties shall invite the Governments of Jordan and Egypt to participate in establishing further liaison and cooperation arrangements between the Government of Israel and the Palestinian representatives on the one hand, and the Governments of Jordan and Egypt on the other hand, to promote cooperation between them. These arrangements shall include the constitution of a Continuing Committee.

2. The Continuing Committee shall decide by agreement on the modalities of admission of persons displaced from the West Bank and the Gaza Strip in 1967, together with necessary measures to prevent disruption and disorder.

3. The Continuing Committee shall deal with other matters of common concern.

Article 17

Settlement of Differences and Disputes

Any difference relating to the application of this Agreement shall be referred to the appropriate coordination and cooperation mechanism established under this Agreement. The provisions of Article XV of the Declaration of Principles shall apply to any such difference which is not settled through the appropriate coordination and cooperation mechanism, namely:

1. Disputes arising out of the application or interpretation of this Agreement or any subsequent agreements pertaining to the interim period shall be settled by negotiations through the Liaison Committee.

2. Disputes which cannot be settled by negotiations may be settled by a mechanism of conciliation to be agreed between the Parties.

3. The Parties may agree to submit to arbitration disputes relating to the interim period, which cannot be settled through conciliation. To this end, upon the agreement of both Parties, the Parties will establish an Arbitration Committee.

Article 18

Prevention of Hostile Acts

Both sides shall take all measures necessary in

order to prevent acts of terrorism, crime and hostilities directed against each other, against individuals falling under the other's authority and against their property, and shall take legal measures against offenders. In addition, the Palestinian side shall take all measures necessary to prevent such hostile acts directed against the Settlements, the infrastructure serving them and the Military Installation Area, and the Israeli side shall take all measures necessary to prevent such hostile acts emanating from the Settlements and directed against Palestinians.

Article 19

Missing Persons

The Palestinian Authority shall cooperate with Israel by providing all necessary assistance in the conduct of searches by Israel within the Gaza Strip and the Jericho Area for missing Israelis, as well as by providing information about missing Israelis. Israel shall cooperate with the Palestinian Authority in searching for, and providing necessary information about, missing Palestinians.

Article 20

Confidence Building Measures

With a view to creating a positive and supportive public atmosphere to accompany the implementation of this Agreement, and to establish a solid basis of mutual trust and good faith, both Parties agree to carry out confidence building measures as detailed herewith:

1. Upon the signing of this Agreement, Israel will release, or turn over, to the Palestinian Authority within a period of 5 weeks, about 5,000 Palestinian detainees and prisoners, residents of the West Bank and the Gaza Strip. Those released will be free to return to their homes anywhere in the West Bank or the Gaza Strip. Prisoners turned over to the Palestinian Authority shall be obliged to remain in the Gaza Strip or the Jericho Area for the remainder of their sentence.

2. After the signing of this Agreement, the two Parties shall continue to negotiate the release of additional Palestinian prisoners and detainees, building on agreed principles.

3. The implementation of the above measures will be subject to the fulfillment of the procedures determined by Israeli law for the release and transfer of detainees and prisoners.

4. With the assumption of Palestinian authority, the Palestinian side commits itself to solving the problem of those Palestinians who were in contact with the Israeli authorities. Until an agreed solution is found, the Palestinian side undertakes not to prosecute these Palestinians or to harm them in any way.

5. Palestinians from abroad whose entry into the Gaza Strip and the Jericho Area is approved pursuant to this Agreement, and to whom the provisions of this Article are applicable, will not be prosecuted for offenses committed prior to September 13, 1993.

Article 21

Temporary International Presence

1. The Parties agree to a temporary international or foreign presence in the Gaza Strip and the Jericho Area (hereinafter "the TIP"), in accordance with the provisions of this Article.

2. The TIP shall consist of 400 qualified personnel, including observers, instructors and other experts, from 5 or 6 of the donor countries.

3. The two Parties shall request the donor countries to establish a special fund to provide finance for the TIP.

4. The TIP will function for a period of 6 months. The TIP may extend this period, or change the scope of its operation, with the agreement of the two Parties.

5. The TIP shall be stationed and operate within the following cities and villages: Gaza, Khan Yunis, Rafah, Deir El Ballah, Jabaliya, Absan, Beit Hanun and Jericho.

6. Israel and the Palestinian Authority shall agree on a special Protocol to implement this Article, with the goal of concluding negotiations with the donor countries contributing personnel within two months.

Article 22

Rights, Liabilities and Obligations

1. (a) The transfer of all powers and responsibilities to the Palestinian Authority, as detailed in Annex II, includes all related rights, liabilities and obligations arising with regard to acts or omissions which occurred prior to the transfer. Israel will cease to bear any financial responsibility regarding such acts or omissions and the Palestinian Authority will bear all financial responsibility for these and for its own functioning.

(b) Any financial claim made in this regard against Israel will be referred to the Palestinian Authority.

(c) Israel shall provide the Palestinian Authority with the information it has regarding pending and anticipated claims brought before any court or tribunal against Israel in this regard.

(d) Where legal proceedings are brought in respect of such a claim, Israel will notify the Palestinian Authority and enable it to participate in defending the claim and raise any arguments on its behalf.

(e) In the event that an award is made against Israel by any court or tribunal in respect of such a claim, the Palestinian Authority shall reimburse Israel the full amount of the award.

(f) Without prejudice to the above, where a court or tribunal hearing such a claim finds that liability rests solely with an employee or agent who acted beyond the scope of the powers assigned to him or her, unlawfully or with willful malfeasance, the Palestinian Authority shall not bear financial responsibility.

2. The transfer of authority in itself shall not affect rights, liabilities and obligations of any person or legal entity, in existence at the date of signing of this Agreement.

Article 23

Final Clauses

1. This Agreement shall enter into force on the date of its signing.
2. The arrangements established by this Agreement shall remain in force until and to the extent superseded by the Interim Agreement referred to in the Declaration of Principles or any other agreement between the Parties.

3. The five-year interim period referred to in the Declaration of Principles commences on the date of the signing of this Agreement.

4. The Parties agree that, as long as this Agreement is in force, the security fence erected by Israel around the Gaza Strip shall remain in place and that the line demarcated by the fence, shall be authoritative only for the purpose of this Agreement.

5. Nothing in this Agreement shall prejudice or pre-empt the outcome of the negotiations on the interim agreement or on the permanent status to be conducted pursuant to the Declaration of Principles. Neither Party shall be deemed, by virtue of having entered into this Agreement, to have renounced or waived any of its existing rights, claims or positions.

6. The two Parties view the West Bank and the Gaza Strip as a single territorial unit, the integrity of which will be preserved during the interim period.

7. The Gaza Strip and the Jericho Area shall continue to be an integral part of the West Bank and the Gaza Strip, and their status shall not be changed for the period of this Agreement. Nothing in this Agreement shall be considered to change this status.

8. The Preamble to this Agreement, and all Annexes, Appendices and maps attached hereto, shall constitute an integral part hereof.

Convention on Nuclear Safety

Date of signature: September 20, 1994
Place of signature: Vienna
Signatory states: Algeria, Argentina, Armenia, Australia, Austria, Belgium, Brazil, Bulgaria, Canada, Chile, China, Cuba, Czech Republic, Denmark, Egypt, Finland, France, Germany, Greece, Hungary, India, Indonesia, Ireland, Israel, Italy, Japan, Republic of Korea, Luxembourg, Mexico, Netherlands, Nicaragua, Nigeria, Norway (ratification on September 29, 1994), Pakistan, Peru, Philippines, Poland, Portugal, Romania, Russian Federation, Slovak Republic, Slovenia, South Africa, Spain, Sudan, Sweden, Syria, Tunisia, Turkey, Ukraine, United Kingdom, United States [as of November 15, 1994]
Ratification: Bangladesh, Bulgaria, Canada, China, Croatia, the Czech Republic, Finland,
France, Hungary, Ireland, Japan, the Republic of Korea, Lebanon, Lithuania, Mali, Mexico, Poland, Romania, the Russian Federation, the Slovak Republic, Spain, Sweden, Turkey, the United Kingdom (as of July 29, 1996)
Date of entry into force: October 24, 1996

Preamble

The Contracting Parties

(i) Aware of the importance to the international community of ensuring that the use of nuclear energy is safe, well regulated and environmentally sound;

(ii) Reaffirming the necessity of continuing to promote a high level of nuclear safety worldwide;

(iii) Reaffirming that responsibility for nuclear safety rests with the State having jurisdiction over a nuclear installation;

(iv) Desiring to promote an effective nuclear safety culture;

(v) Aware that accidents at nuclear installations have the potential for transboundary impacts;

(vi) Keeping in mind the Convention on the Physical Protection of Nuclear Material (1979), the Convention on Early Notification of a Nuclear Accident (1986), and the Convention on Assistance in the Case of a Nuclear Accident or Radiological Emergency (1986);

(vii) Affirming the importance of international co-operation for the enhancement of nuclear safety through existing bilateral and multilateral mechanisms and the establishment of this incentive Convention;

(viii) Recognizing that this Convention entails a commitment to the application of fundamental safety principles for nuclear installations rather than of detailed safety standards and that there are internationally formulated safety guidelines which are updated from time to time and so can provide guidance on contemporary means of achieving a high level of safety;

(ix) Affirming the need to begin promptly the development of an international convention on the safety of radioactive waste management as soon as the ongoing process to develop waste management safety fundamentals has resulted in broad international agreement;

(x) Recognizing the usefulness of further technical work in connection with the safety of other parts of the nuclear fuel cycle, and that this work may, in time, facilitate the development of current or future international instruments;

HAVE AGREED as follows:

Chapter I

Objectives, Definitions and Scope of Application

Article 1

Objectives

The objectives of this Convention are:

(i) to achieve and maintain a high level of nuclear safety worldwide through the enhancement of national measures and international co-operation including, where appropriate, safety-related technical co-operation;

(ii) to establish and maintain effective defenses in nuclear installations against potential radiological hazards in order to protect individuals, society and the environment from harmful effects of ionizing radiation from such installations;

(iii) to prevent accidents with radiological consequences and to mitigate such consequences should they occur.

Article 2

Definitions

For the purpose of this Convention:

(i) "nuclear installation" means for each Contracting Party any land-based civil nuclear power plant under its jurisdiction including such storage, handling and treatment facilities for radioactive materials as are on the same site and are directly related to the operation of the nuclear power plant. Such a plant ceases to be a nuclear installation when all nuclear fuel elements have been removed permanently from the reactor core and have been stored safely in accordance with approved procedures, and a decommissioning programme has been agreed to by the regulatory body.

(ii) "regulatory body" means for each Contracting Party any body or bodies given the legal authority by that Contracting Party to grant licenses and to regulate the siting, design, construction, commissioning, operation or decommissioning of nuclear installations.

(iii) "licence" means any authorization granted by the regulatory body to the applicant to have the responsibility for the siting, design, construction, commissioning, operation or decommissioning of a nuclear installation.

Article 3

Scope of Application

This Convention shall apply to the safety of nuclear installations.

Chapter II

Obligations

(a) General Provisions

Article 4

Implementing Measures

Each Contracting Party shall take, within the framework of its national law, the legislative, regulatory and administrative measures and other steps necessary for implementing its obligations under this Convention.

Article 5

Reporting

Each Contracting Party shall submit for review, prior to each meeting referred to in Article 20, a report on the measures it has taken to implement each of the obligations of this Convention.

Article 6

Existing Nuclear Installations

Each Contracting Party shall take the appropriate steps to ensure that the safety of nuclear installations existing at the time the Convention enters into force for that Contracting Party is reviewed as soon as possible. When necessary in the context of this Convention, the Contracting Party shall ensure that all reasonably practicable improvements are made as a matter of urgency to upgrade the safety of the nuclear installation. If such upgrading cannot be achieved, plans should be implemented to shut down the nuclear installation as soon as practically possible. The timing of the shut-down may take into account the whole energy context and possible alternatives as well as the social, environmental and economic impact.

(b) Legislation and Regulation

Article 7

Legislative and Regulatory Framework

1. Each Contracting Party shall establish and maintain a legislative and regulatory framework to govern the safety of nuclear installations.

2. The legislative and regulatory framework shall provide for:

(i) the establishment of applicable national safety requirements and regulations;

(ii) a system of licensing with regard to nuclear installations and the prohibition of the operation of a nuclear installation without a licence:

(iii) a system of regulatory inspection and assessment of nuclear installations to ascertain compliance with applicable regulations and the terms of licences;

(iv) the enforcement of applicable regulations and of the terms of licences, including suspension, modification or revocation.

Article 8

Regulatory Body

1. Each Contracting Party shall establish or designate a regulatory body entrusted with the implementation of the legislative and regulatory framework referred to in Article 7, and provided with adequate authority, competence and financial and human resources to fulfill its assigned responsibilities.

2. Each Contracting Party shall take the appropriate steps to ensure an effective separation between the functions of the regulatory body and those of any other body or organization concerned with the promotion or utilization of nuclear energy.

Article 9

Responsibility of the Licence Holder

Each Contracting Party shall ensure that prime responsibility for the safety of a nuclear installation rests with the holder of the relevant licence and shall take the appropriate steps to ensure that each of such licence holder meets its responsibility.

(c) General Safety Considerations

Article 10

Priority to Safety

Each Contracting Party shall take the appropriate steps to ensure that all organizations engaged in activities directly related to nuclear installations shall establish policies that give due priority to nuclear safety.

Article 11

Financial and Human Resources

1. Each Contracting Party shall take the appropriate steps to ensure that adequate financial resources are available to support the safety of each nuclear installation throughout its life.

2. Each Contracting Party shall take the appropri-

ate steps to ensure that sufficient numbers of qualified staff with appropriate education, training and retraining are available for all safety-related activities in or for each nuclear installation, throughout its life.

Article 12

Human Factors

Each Contracting Party shall take the appropriate steps to ensure that the capabilities and limitations of human performance are taken into account throughout the life of a nuclear installation.

Article 13

Quality Assurance

Each Contracting Party shall take the appropriate steps to ensure that quality assurance programmes are established and implemented with a view to providing confidence that specified requirements for all activities important to nuclear safety are satisfied throughout the life of a nuclear installation.

Article 14

Assessment and Verification of Safety

Each Contracting Party shall take the appropriate steps to ensure that:

(i) comprehensive and systematic safety assessments are carried out before the construction and commissioning of a nuclear installation and throughout its life. Such assessments shall be well documented, subsequently updated in the light of operating experience and significant new safety information, and reviewed under the authority of the regulatory body;

(ii) verification by analysis, surveillance, testing and inspection is carried out to ensure that the physical state and the operation of a nuclear installation continue to be in accordance with its design, applicable national safety requirements, and operational limits and conditions.

Article 15

Radiation Protection

Each Contracting Party shall take the appropriate steps to ensure that in all operational states the radiation exposure to the workers and the public caused by a nuclear installation shall be kept as low as reasonably achievable and that no individual shall be exposed to radiation doses which exceed prescribed

national dose limits.

Article 16

Emergency Preparedness

1. Each Contracting Party shall take the appropriate steps to ensure that there are on-site and off-site emergency plans that are routinely tested for nuclear installations and cover the activities to be carried out in the event of an emergency.

For any new nuclear installation, such plans shall be prepared and tested before it commences operation above a low power level agreed by the regulatory body.

2. Each Contracting Party shall take the appropriate steps to ensure that, insofar as they are likely to be affected by a radiological emergency, its own population and the competent authorities of the States in the vicinity of the nuclear installation are provided with appropriate information for emergency planning and response.

3. Contracting Parties which do not have a nuclear installation on their territory, insofar as they are likely to be affected in the event of a radiological emergency at a nuclear installation in the vicinity, shall take the appropriate steps for the preparation and testing of emergency plans for their territory that cover the activities to be carried out in the event of such an emergency.

(d) Safety of Installations

Article 17

Siting

Each Contracting Party shall take the appropriate steps to ensure that appropriate procedures are established and implemented:

(i) for evaluating all relevant site-related factors likely to affect the safety of a nuclear installation for its projected lifetime;

(ii) for evaluating the likely safety impact of a proposed nuclear installation on individuals, society and the environment;

(iii) for re-evaluating as necessary all relevant factors referred to in sub-paragraphs (i) and (ii) so as to ensure the continued safety acceptability of the nuclear installation;

(iv) for consulting Contracting Parties in the vicinity of a proposed nuclear installation, insofar as they are likely to be affected by that installation and, upon request providing the necessary information to such Contracting Parties, in order to enable them to evaluate and make their own assessment of the likely safety impact on their own territory of the nuclear installation.

Article 18

Design and Construction

Each Contracting Party shall take the appropriate steps to ensure that:

(i) the design and construction of a nuclear installation provides for several reliable levels and methods of protection (defense in depth) against the release of radioactive materials, with a view to preventing the occurrence of accidents and to mitigating their radiological consequences should they occur;

(ii) the technologies incorporated in the design and construction of a nuclear installation are proven by experience or qualified by testing or analysis;

(iii) the design of a nuclear installation allows for reliable, stable and easily manageable operation, with specific consideration of human factors and the man-machine interface.

Article 19

Operation

Each Contracting Party shall take the appropriate steps to ensure that:

(i) the initial authorization to operate a nuclear installation is based upon an appropriate safety analysis and a commissioning programme demonstrating that the installation, as constructed, is consistent with design and safety requirements;

(ii) operational limits and conditions derived from the safety analysis, tests and operational experience are defined and revised as necessary for identifying safe boundaries for operation;

(iii) operation, maintenance, inspection and testing of a nuclear installation are conducted in accordance with approved procedures;

(iv) procedures are established for responding to anticipated operational occurrences and to accidents;

(v) necessary engineering and technical support in all safety-related fields is available throughout the lifetime of a nuclear installation;

(vi) incidents significant to safety are reported in a timely manner by the holder of the relevant licence to the regulatory body;

(vii) programmes to collect and analyse operating experience are established, the results obtained and the conclusions drawn are acted upon and that existing mechanisms are used to share important experience with international bodies and with other operating organizations and regulatory bodies;

(viii) the generation of radioactive waste resulting from the operation of a nuclear installation is kept to the minimum practicable for the process concerned, both in activity and in volume, and any necessary treatment and storage of spent fuel and waste directly related to the operation and on the same site as that of the nuclear installation take into consideration conditioning and disposal.

Chapter III

Meetings of the Contracting Parties

Article 20

Review Meetings

1. The Contracting Parties shall hold meetings (hereinafter referred to as "review meetings") for the purpose of reviewing the reports submitted pursuant to Article 5 in accordance with the procedures adopted under Article 22.

2. Subject to the provisions of Article 24 subgroups comprised of representatives of Contracting Parties may be established and may function during the review meetings as deemed necessary for the purpose of reviewing specific subjects contained in the reports.

3. Each Contracting Party shall have a reasonable opportunity to discuss the reports submitted by other Contracting Parties and to seek clarification of such reports.

Article 21

Timetable

1. A preparatory meeting of the Contracting Parties shall be held not later than six months after the date of entry into force of this Convention.

2. At this preparatory meeting, the Contracting Parties shall determine the date for the first review meeting. This review meeting shall be held as soon as possible, but not later than thirty months after the date of entry into force of this Convention.

3. At each review meeting, the Contracting Parties

shall determine the date for the next such meeting. The interval between review meetings shall not exceed three years.

Article 22

Procedural Arrangements

1. At the preparatory meeting held pursuant to Article 21 the Contracting Parties shall prepare and adopt by consensus Rules of Procedure and Financial Rules. The Contracting Parties shall establish in particular and in accordance with the Rules of Procedure:

(i) guidelines regarding the form and structure of the reports to be submitted pursuant to Article 5;

(ii) a date for the submission of such reports;

(iii) the process for reviewing such reports.

2. At review meetings the Contracting Parties may, if necessary, review the arrangements established pursuant to sub-paragraphs (i)-(iii) above, and adopt revisions by consensus unless otherwise provided for in the Rules of Procedure. They may also amend the Rules of Procedure and the Financial Rules, by consensus.

Article 23

Extraordinary Meetings

An extraordinary meeting of the Contracting Parties shall be held:

(i) if so agreed by a majority of the Contracting Parties present and voting at a meeting, abstentions being considered as voting; or

(ii) at the written request of a Contracting Party, within six months of this request having been communicated to the Contracting Parties and notification having been received by the secretariat referred to in Article 28, that the request has been supported by a majority of the Contracting Parties.

Article 24

Attendance

1. Each Contracting Party shall attend meetings of the Contracting Parties and be represented at such meetings by one delegate, and by such alternates, experts and advisers as it deems necessary.

2. The Contracting Parties may invite, by consensus, any intergovernmental organization which is competent in respect of matters governed by this Convention to attend, as an observer, any meeting, or specific sessions thereof. Observers shall be required to accept in writing, and in advance, the provisions of Article 27.

Article 25

Summary Reports

The Contracting Parties shall adopt, by consensus, and make available to the public a document addressing issues discussed and conclusions reached during a meeting.

Article 26

Languages

1. The languages of meetings of the Contracting Parties shall be Arabic, Chinese, English, French, Russian and Spanish unless otherwise provided in the Rules of Procedure.

2. Reports submitted pursuant to Article 5 shall be prepared in the national language of the submitting Contracting Party or in a single designated language to be agreed in the Rules of Procedure. Should the report be submitted in a national language other than the designated language, a translation of the report into the designated language shall be provided by the Contracting Party.

3. Notwithstanding the provisions of paragraph 2, if compensated, the secretariat will assume the translation into the designated language of reports submitted in any other language of the meeting.

Article 27

Confidentiality

1. The provisions of this Convention shall not affect the rights and obligations of the Contracting Parties under their law to protect information from disclosure. For the purposes of this Article, "information" includes, inter alia, (i) personal data; (ii) information protected by intellectual property rights or by industrial or commercial confidentiality; and (iii) information relating to national security or to the physical protection of nuclear materials or nuclear installations.

2. When, in the context of this Convention, a Contracting Party provides information identified by it as protected as described in paragraph 1, such information shall be used only for the purposes for which it has been provided and its confidentiality shall be respected.

3. The content of the debates during the reviewing

of the reports by the Contracting Parties at each meeting shall be confidential.

Article 28

Secretariat

1. The International Atomic Energy Agency, (hereinafter referred to as the "Agency") shall provide the secretariat for the meetings of the Contracting Parties.

2. The secretariat shall:

(i) convene, prepare and service the meetings of the Contracting Parties;

(ii) transmit to the Contracting Parties information received or prepared in accordance with the provisions of this Convention.

The costs incurred by the Agency in carrying out the functions referred to in sub-paragraphs (i) and (ii) above shall be borne by the Agency as part of its regular budget.

3. The Contracting Parties may, by consensus, request the Agency to provide other services in support of meetings of the Contracting Parties. The Agency may provide such services if they can be undertaken within its programme and regular budget. Should this not be possible, the Agency may provide such services if voluntary funding is provided from another source.

Chapter IV

Final Clauses and Other Provisions

Article 29

Resolution of Disagreements

In the event of a disagreement between two or more Contracting Parties concerning the interpretation or application of this Convention, the Contracting Parties shall consult within the framework of a meeting of the Contracting Parties with a view to resolving the disagreement.

Article 30

Signature, Ratification, Acceptance, Approval, Accession

1. This Convention shall be open for signature by all States at the Headquarters of the Agency in Vienna from 20 September 1994 until its entry into force.

2. This Convention is subject to ratification, acceptance or approval by the signatory States.

3. After its entry into force, this Convention shall be open for accession by all States.

4. (i) This Convention shall be open for signature or accession by regional organizations of an integration or other nature, provided that any such organization is constituted by sovereign States and has competence in respect of the negotiation, conclusion and application of international agreements in matters covered by this Convention.

(ii) In matters within their competence, such organizations shall, on their own behalf, exercise the rights and fulfill the responsibilities which this Convention attributes to States Parties

(iii) When becoming party to this Convention, such an organization shall communicate to the Depository referred to in Article 34, a declaration indicating which States are members thereof, which articles of this Convention apply to it, and the extent of its competence in the field covered by those articles.

(iv) Such an organization shall not hold any vote additional to those of its Member States.

5. Instruments of ratification, acceptance, approval or accession shall be deposited with the Depository.

Article 31

Entry into Force

1. This Convention shall enter into force on the ninetieth day after the date of deposit with the Depository of the twenty-second instrument of ratification, acceptance or approval, including the instruments of seventeen States, each having at least one nuclear installation which has achieved criticality in a reactor core.

2. For each State or regional organization of an integration of other nature which ratifies, accepts, approves or accedes to this Convention after the date of deposit of the last instrument required to satisfy the conditions set forth in paragraph 1, this Convention shall enter into force on the ninetieth day after the date of deposit with the Depository of the appropriate instrument by such a State or organization.

Article 32

Amendments to the Convention

1. Any Contracting party may propose an amendment to this Convention. Proposed amendments shall

be considered at a review meeting or an extraordinary meeting.

2. The text of any proposed amendment and the reasons for it shall be provided to the Depository who shall communicate the proposal to the Contracting Parties promptly and at least ninety days before the meeting for which it is submitted for consideration. Any comments received on such a proposal shall be circulated by the Depository to the Contracting Parties.

3. The Contracting Parties shall decide after consideration of the proposed amendment whether to adopt it by consensus, or, in the absence of consensus, to submit it to a Diplomatic Conference. A decision to submit a proposed amendment to a Diplomatic Conference shall require a two-thirds majority vote of the Contracting parties present and voting at the meeting, provided that at least one half of the Contracting Parties are present at the time of voting. Abstentions shall be considered as voting.

4. The Diplomatic Conference to consider and adopt amendments to this Convention shall be convened by the Depository and held no later than one year after the appropriate decision taken in accordance with paragraph 3 of this Article. The Diplomatic Conference shall make every effort to ensure amendments are adopted by consensus. Should this not be possible, amendments shall be adopted with a two-thirds majority of all Contracting Parties.

5. Amendments to this Convention adopted pursuant to paragraphs 3 and 4 above shall be subject to ratification, acceptance, approval, or confirmation by the Contracting Parties and shall enter into force for those Contracting Parties which have ratified, accepted, approved or confirmed them on the ninetieth day after the receipt by the Depository of the relevant instruments by at least three fourths of the Contracting Parties. For a Contracting Party which subsequently ratifies, accepts, approves or confirms the said amendments, the amendments will enter into force on the ninetieth day after that Contracting Party has deposited its relevant instrument.

Article 33

Denunciation

1. Any Contracting Party may denounce this Convention by written notification to the Depository.

2. Denunciation shall take effect one year following the date of the receipt of the notification by the Depository, or on such later date as may be specified in the notification.

Article 34

Depository

1. The Director General of the Agency shall be the Depository of this Convention.

2. The Depository shall inform the Contracting Parties of:

(i) the signature of this Convention and of the deposit of instruments of ratification, acceptance, approval or accession, in accordance with Article 30;

(ii) the date on which the Convention enters into force, in accordance with Article 31;

(iii) the notifications of denunciation of the Convention and the date thereof, made in accordance with Article 33;

(iv) the proposed amendments to this Convention submitted by Contracting Parties, the amendments adopted by the relevant Diplomatic Conference or by the meeting of the Contracting Parties, and the date of entry into force of the said amendments, in accordance with Article 32.

Article 35

Authentic Texts

The original of this Convention of which the Arabic, Chinese, English, French, Russian and Spanish texts are equally authentic, shall be deposited with the Depository, who shall send certified copies thereof to the Contracting Parties.

Agreed Framework Between the United States of America and the Democratic People's Republic of Korea

Date of signature: October 21, 1994
Place of signature: Geneva
Signatory states: the United States,
the Democratic People's Republic of Korea

Delegations of the Governments of the United States of America (US) and the Democratic People's Republic of Korea (DPRK) held talks in Geneva from September 23 to October 21, 1994, to negotiate an overall resolution of the nuclear issue on the Korean Peninsula.

Both sides reaffirmed the importance of attaining the objectives contained in the August 12, 1994 Agreed Statement between the US and the DPRK and upholding the principles of the June 11, 1993 Joint Statement of the US and the DPRK to achieve peace and security on a nuclear-free Korean peninsula. The US and the DPRK decided to take the following actions for the resolution of the nuclear issue:

I. Both sides will cooperate to replace the DPRK's graphite-moderated reactors and related facilities with light-water reactor (LWR) power plants.

1) In accordance with the October 20, 1994 letter of assurance from the US President, the US will undertake to make arrangements for the provision to the DPRK of a LWR project with a total generating capacity of approximately 2,000 MW(e) by a target date of 2003.

— The US will organize under its leadership an international consortium or finance and supply the LWR project to be provided to the DPRK. The US, representing the international consortium, will serve as the principal point of contact with the DPRK for the LWR project.

— The US, representing the consortium, will make best efforts to secure the conclusion of a supply contract with the DPRK within six months of the date of this Document for the provision of the LWR project. Contract talks will begin as soon as possible after the date of this Document.

— As necessary, the US and the DPRK will conclude a bilateral agreement for cooperation in the field of peaceful uses of nuclear energy.

2) In accordance with the October 20, 1994 letter of assurance from the US President, the US, representing the consortium, will make arrangements to offset the energy foregone due to the freeze of the DPRK's graphite-moderated reactors and related facilities, pending completion of the first LWR unit.

— Alternative energy will be provided in the form of heavy oil heating and electricity production.

— Deliveries of heavy oil will begin within three months of the date of this Document and will reach a rate of 500,000 tons annually, in accordance with an agreed schedule of deliveries.

3) Upon receipt of US assurances for the provision of LWR's and for arrangements for interim energy alternatives, the DPRK will freeze its graphite-moderated reactors and related facilities and will eventually dismantle these reactors and related facilities.

— The freeze on the DPRK's graphite-moderated reactors and related facilities will be fully implemented within one month of the date of this Document. During this one-month period, and throughout the freeze, the International Atomic Energy Agency (IAEA) will be allowed to monitor this freeze, and the DPRK will provide full cooperation to the IAEA for this purpose.

— Dismantlement of the DPRK's graphite-moderated reactors and related facilities will be completed when the LWR project is completed.

— The US and the DPRK will cooperate in finding a method to store safely the spent fuel from the 5 MW (e) experimental reactor during the construction of the LWR project, and to dispose of the fuel in a safe manner that does not involve reprocessing in the DPRK.

4) As soon as possible after the date of this document US and DPRK experts will hold two sets of experts talks.

— At one set of talks, experts will discuss issues related to alternative energy and the replacement of the graphite-moderated reactor program with the LWR project.

— At the other set of talks, experts will discuss specific arrangements for spent fuel storage and ultimate disposition.

II. The two sides will move toward full normalization of political and economic relations.

1) Within three months of the date of this Document, both sides will reduce barriers to trade and investment, including restrictions on telecommunications services and financial transactions.

2) Each side will open a liaison office in the other's capital following resolution of consular and other technical issues through expert level discussions.

3) As progress is made on issues of concern to each side, the US and the DPRK will upgrade bilateral relations to the Ambassadorial level.

III. Both sides will work together for peace and security on a nuclear-free Korean peninsula.

1) The US will provide formal assurances to the DPRK, against the threat of weapons by the US.

2) The DPRK will consistently take steps to implement the North-South Joint Declaration on the Denu-clearization of the Korean Peninsula.

3) The DPRK will engage in North-South dialogue, as this Agreed Framework will help create an atmos-phere that promotes such dialogue.

IV. Both sides will work together to strengthen the international nuclear non-proliferation regime.

1) The DPRK will remain a party to the Treaty on the Non-Proliferation of Nuclear Weapons (NPT) and will allow implementation of its safeguards agree-ment under the Treaty.

2) Upon conclusion of the supply contract for the provision of the LWR project, ad hoc and routine inspections will resume under the DPRK's safe-guards agreement with the IAEA with respect to the facilities not subject to the freeze. Pending conclu-sion of the supply contract, inspections required by the IAEA for the continuity of safeguards will con-tinue at the facilities not subject to the freeze.

3) When a significant portion of the LWR project is completed, but before delivery of key nuclear com-ponents, the DPRK will come into full compliance with its safeguards agreement with the IAEA (INF-CIRC/403), including taking all steps that may be deemed necessary by the IAEA, following consulta-tions with the Agency with regard to verifying the accuracy and completeness of the DPRK's initial report on all nuclear material in the DPRK.

Treaty of Peace Between the State of Israel and the Hashimite Kingdom of Jordan

Date of signature: October 26, 1994
Place of signature: The Araba/Araba Crossing Point
Signatory states: Israel, Jordan

Preamble

[The signatories],
Bearing in mind the Washington Declaration, signed by them on 25th July, 1994. and which they are both committed to honour;
Aiming at the achievement of a just, lasting and com-prehensive peace in the Middle East based on Securi-ty Council resolutions 242 and 338 in all their aspects;
Bearing in mind the importance of maintaining and strengthening peace based on freedom, equality jus-tice and respect for fundamental human rights, there-by overcoming psychological barriers and promoting human dignity;
Reaffirming their faith in the purposes and principles of the Charter of the United Nations and recognizing their right and obligation to live in peace with each other as well as with all states, within secure and re-cognized boundaries;
Desiring to develop friendly relations and co-opera-tion between them in accordance with the principles of international law governing international relations in time of peace;
Desiring as well to ensure lasting security for both their States and in particular to avoid threats and the use of force between them;
Bearing in mind that in their Washington Declaration of 25th July, 1994, they declared the termination of the state of belligerency between them;
Deciding to establish peace between them in accord-ance with this Treaty of Peace;
Have agreed as follows:

Article 1

Establishment of Peace

Peace is hereby established between the State of lsrael and the Hashimite Kingdom of Jordan (the "Parties") effective from the exchange of the instru-ments of ratification of this Treaty.

Article 2

General Principles

The Parties will apply between them the provisions of the Charter of the United Nations and the princi-ples of international law governing relations among states in time of peace. In particular;

1. They recognise and will respect each other's

sovereignty, territorial integrity and political independence;

2. They recognise and will respect each other's right to live in peace within secure and recognized boundaries;

3. They will develop good neighborly relations of co-operation between them to ensure lasting security, will refrain from the threat or use of force against each other and will settle all disputes between them by peaceful means;

4. They respect and recognise the sovereignty, territorial integrity and political independence of every state in the region;

5. They respect and recognize the pivotal role of human development and dignity in regional and bilateral relationships;

6. They further believe that within their control, involuntary movements of persons in such a way as to adversely prejudice the security of either Party should not be permitted.

Article 3

International Boundary

1. The international boundary between Israel and Jordan is delimited with reference to the boundary definition under the Mandate as is shown in Annex I (a), on the mapping materials attached thereto and coordinates specified therein.

2. The boundary as set out in Annex I (a) is the permanent, secure and recognized international boundary between Israel and Jordan without prejudice to the status of any territories that came under Israeli military government control in 1967.

3. The Parties recognize the international boundary as well as each other's territory, territorial waters and airspace, as inviolable, and will respect and comply with them.

4. The demarcation of the boundary will take place as set forth in Appendix (1) to Annex I and will be concluded not later than 9 months after the signing of the Treaty.

5. It is agreed that where the boundary follows a river, in the event of natural changes in the course of the flow of the river as described in Annex I (a), the boundary shall follow the new course of the flow, in the event of any other changes the boundary shall not be affected unless otherwise agreed.

6. Immediately upon the exchange of the instruments of ratification of this Treaty, each Party will deploy on its side of the international boundary as defined in Annex I (a).

7. The Parties shall, upon the signature of the

Treaty, enter into negotiations to conclude, within 9 months, an agreement on the delimitation of their maritime boundary in the Gulf of Aqaba.

8. Taking into account the special circumstances of the Naharayim Baqura area, which is under Jordanian sovereignty, with Israeli private ownership rights. the Parties agree to apply the provisions set out in Annex I (b).

9. With respect to the Zofar Al-Ghamr area, the provisions set out in Annex i (c) will apply.

Article 4

Security

1. a. Both Parties, acknowledging that mutual understanding and cooperation in security-related matters will form a significant part of their relations and will further enhance the security of the region, take upon themselves to base their security relations on mutual trust, advancement of joint interests and co-operation, and to aim towards a regional framework of partnership in peace.

b. Towards that goal, the Parties recognize the achievements of the European Community and European Union in the development of the Conference on Security and Co-operation in Europe (CSCE) and commit themselves to the creation, in the Middle East, of a Conference on Security and Co-operation in the Middle East (CSCME).

This commitment entails the adoption of regional models of security successfully implemented in the post-World War era (along the lines of the Helsinki Process) culminating in a regional zone of security and stability.

2. The obligations referred to in this Article are without prejudice to the inherent right of self-defence in accordance with the United Nations Charter.

3. The parties undertake, in accordance with the provisions of this Article, the following:

a. to refrain from the threat or use of force or weapons. conventional, non-conventional or of any other kind, against each other, or of other actions or activities that adversely affect the security of the other party:

b. to refrain from organizing, instigating, inciting, assisting or participating in acts or threats of belligerency, hostility, subversion or violence against the other Party:

c. to take necessary and effective measures to ensure that acts or threats of belligerency, hostility, subversion or violence against the other Party do not originate from, and are not committed within, through or over their territory (hereinafter the term "territory" includes the airspace and territorial waters).

4. Consistent with the era of peace and with the efforts to build regional security and to avoid and prevent aggression and violence, the Parties further agree to refrain from the following:

a. joining or in any way assisting, promoting or co-operating with any coalition, organization or alliance with a military or security character with a third party, the objectives or activities of which include launching aggression or other acts of military hostility against the other party, in contravention of the provisions of the present Treaty;

b. allowing the entry, stationing and operating on their territory, or through it, of military forces, personnel or material of a third party, in circumstances which may adversely prejudice the security of the other Party.

5. Both parties will take necessary and effective measures, and will co-operate in combating terrorism of all kinds. The Parties undertake:

a. to take necessary and effective measures to prevent acts of terrorism, subversion or violence from being carried out from their territory or through it and to take necessary and effective measures to combat such activities and all their perpetrators;

b. without prejudice to the basic rights of freedom of expression and association, to take necessary and effective measures to prevent the entry, presence and operation in their territory of any group or organization, and their infrastructure, which threatens the security of the other Party by the use of, or incitement to the use of, violent means;

c. to co-operate in preventing and combating cross-boundary infiltrations.

6. Any question as to the implementation of this Article will be dealt with through a mechanism of consultations which will include a liaison system, verification, supervision, and where necessary, other mechanisms, and higher level consultations. The details of the mechanism of consultations will be contained in an agreement to be concluded by the Parties within 3 months of the exchange of the instruments of ratification of this Treaty.

7. The Parties undertake to work as a matter of priority, and as soon as possible, in the context of the Multilateral Working Group on Arms Control and Regional Security, and jointly, towards the following:

a. the creation in the Middle East of a region free from hostile alliances and coalitions:

b. the creation of a Middle East free from weapons of mass destruction, both conventional and non-conventional, in the context of a comprehensive, lasting and stable peace, characterized by the renunciation of the use of force, and by reconciliation and goodwill.

Article 5

Diplomatic and Other Bilateral Relations

1. The Parties agree to establish full diplomatic and consular relations and to exchange resident ambassadors within one month of the exchange of the instruments of ratification of this Treaty.

2. The Parties agree that the normal relationship between them will further include economic and cultural relations.

Article 6

Water

With the view to achieving a comprehensive and lasting settlement of all the water problems between them:

1. The Parties agree mutually to recognize the rightful allocations of both of them in Jordan River and Yarmouk River waters and Araba Arava ground water in accordance with the agreed acceptable principles, quantities and quality as set out in Annex II, which shall be fully respected and complied with.

2. The Parties, recognizing the necessity to find a practical, just and agreed solution to their water problems and with the view that the subject of water can form the basis for the advancement of co-operation between them, jointly undertake to ensure that the management and development of their water resources do not, in any way, harm the water resources of the other Party.

3. The Parties recognize that their water resources are not sufficient to meet their needs. More water should be supplied for their use through various methods, including projects of regional and international co-operation.

4. In light of paragraph 3 of this Article, with the understanding that co-operation in water-related subjects would be to the benefit of both Parties, and will help alleviate their water shortages, and that water issues along their entire boundary must be dealt with in their totality, including the possibility of transboundary water transfers, the Parties agree to search

for ways to alleviate water shortages and to co-operate in the following fields:

a. development of existing and new water resources, increasing the water availability, including cooperation on a regional basis as appropriate, and minimizing wastage of water resources through the chain of their uses;

b. prevention of contamination of water resources;

c. mutual assistance in the alleviation of water shortages;

d. transfer of information and joint research and development in water related subjects, and review of the potentials for enhancement of water resources development and use.

5. The implementation of both Parties' undertakings under this Article is detailed in Annex II.

Article 7

Economic Relations

1. Viewing economic development and prosperity as pillars of peace, security and harmonious relations between states, peoples and individual human beings, the Parties, taking note of understandings reached between them, affirm their mutual desire to promote economic co-operation between them, as well as within the framework of wider regional economic co-operation.

2. In order to accomplish this goal, the Parties agree to the following:

a. to remove all discriminatory barriers to normal economic relations, to terminate economic boycotts directed at the other party, and to co-operate in terminating boycotts against either Party by third parties;

b. recognizing that the principle of free and unimpeded flow of goods and services should guide their relations, the Parties will enter into negotiations with a view to concluding agreements on economic co-operation, including trade and the establishment of a free trade area or areas, investment, banking, industrial co-operation and labour, for the purpose of promoting beneficial economic relations, based on principles to be agreed upon, as well as on human development considerations on a regional basis. These negotiations will be concluded no later than 6 months from the exchange of the instruments of ratification of this Treaty;

c. to co-operate bilaterally, as well as in multilateral

forums, towards the promotion of their respective economies and of their neighborly economic relations with other regional parties.

Article 8

Refugees and Displaced Persons

1. Recognizing the massive human problems caused to both Parties by the conflict in the Middle East, as well as the contribution made by them towards the alleviation of human suffering, the Parties will seek to further alleviate those problems arising on a bilateral level.

2. Recognizing that the above human problems caused by the conflict in the middle East cannot be fully resolved on the bilateral level, the Parties will seek to resolve them in appropriate forums, in accordance with international law, including the following;

a. in the case of displaced persons, in a quadripartite committee together with Egypt and the Palestinians;

b. in the case of refugees:

i. in the framework of the Multilateral Working Group on Refugees;

ii. in negotiations, in a framework to be agreed, bilateral or otherwise, in conjunction with and at the same time as the permanent status negotiations pertaining to the Territories referred to in Article 3 of this Treaty;

c. through the implementation of agreed United Nations programmes and other agreed international economic programmes concerning refugees and displaced persons, including assistance to their settlement.

Article 9

Places of Historical and Religious Significance and Interfaith Relations

1. Each Party will provide freedom of access to places of religious and historical significance.

2. In this regard, in accordance with the Washington Declaration, Israel respects the present special role of the Hashimite Kingdom of Jordan in Muslim Holy shrines in Jerusalem. When negotiations on the permanent status will take place, Israel will give high priority to the Jordanian historic role in these shrines.

3. The Parties will act together to promote interfaith relations among the three monotheistic religions, with the aim of working towards religious understanding, moral commitment, freedom of reli-

gious worship, and tolerance and peace.

Article 10

Cultural and Scientific Exchanges

The Parties, wishing to remove biases developed through periods of conflict, recognize the desirability of cultural and scientific exchanges in all fields, and agree to establish normal cultural relations between them. Thus, they shall, as soon as possible and not later than 9 months from the exchange of the instruments of ratification of this Treaty, conclude the negotiations on cultural and scientific agreements.

Article 11

Mutual Understanding and Good Neighborly Relations

1. The Parties will seek to foster mutual understanding and tolerance based on shared historic values, and accordingly undertake:

a. to abstain from hostile or discriminatory propaganda against each other, and to take all possible legal and administrative measures to prevent the dissemination of such propaganda by any organization or individual present in the territory of either Party;

b. as soon as possible, and not later than 3 months from the exchange of the instruments of ratification of this Treaty, to repeal all adverse or discriminatory references and expressions of hostility in their respective legislation;

c. to refrain in all government publications from any such references or expressions;

d. to ensure mutual enjoyment by each other's citizens of due process of law within their respective legal systems and before their courts.

2. Paragraph 1 (a) of this Article is without prejudice to the right to freedom of expression as contained in the International Covenant on Civil and Political Rights.

3. A joint committee shall be formed to examine incidents where one Party claims there has been a violation of this Article.

Article 12

Combating Crime and Drugs

The parties will co-operate in combating crime, with an emphasis on smuggling, and will take all necessary measures to combat and prevent such activities as the production of, as well as the trafficking in illicit drugs, and will bring to trial perpetrators of such acts. In this regard, they take note of the understandings reached between them in the above spheres, in accordance with Annex III and undertake to conclude all relevant agreements not later than 9 months from the date of the exchange of the instruments of ratification of this Treaty.

Article 13

Transportation and Roads

Taking note of the progress already made in the area of transportation, the Parties recognize the mutuality of interest in good neighbourly relations in the area of transportation and agree to the following means to promote relations between them in this sphere:

1. Each party will permit the free movement of nationals and vehicles of the other into and within its territory according to the general rules applicable to nationals and vehicles of other states. Neither party will impose discriminatory taxes or restrictions on the free movement of persons and vehicles from its territory to the territory of the other.

2. The parties will open and maintain roads and border-crossings between their countries and will consider further road and rail links between them.

3. The parties will continue their negotiations concerning mutual transportation agreements in the above and other areas, such as joint projects, traffic safety, transport standards and norms, licensing of vehicles, land passages, shipment of goods and cargo, and meteorology, to be concluded not later than 6 months from the exchange of the instruments of ratification of this Treaty.

4. The Parties agree to continue their negotiations for a highway to be constructed and maintained between Egypt, Israel and Jordan near Eilat.

Article 14

Freedom of Navigation and Access to Ports

1. Without prejudice to the provisions of paragraph 3, each Party recognizes the right of the vessels of the other Party to innocent passage through its territorial waters in accordance with the rules of international law.

2. Each Party will grant normal access to its ports for vessels and cargoes of the other, as well as vessels and cargoes destined for or coming from the other Party. Such access will be granted on the same conditions as generally applicable to vessels and car-

goes of other nations.

3. The parties consider the Strait of Titan and the Gulf of Aqaba to be international waterways open to all nations for unimpeded and nonsuspendable freedom of navigation and overflight. The parties will respect each other's right to navigation and overflight for access to either Party through the Strait of Titan and the Gulf of Aqaba.

Article 15

Civil Aviation

1. The Parties recognize as applicable to each other the rights, privileges and obligations provided for by the multilateral aviation agreements to which they are both party, particularly by the 1944 Convention on International Civil Aviation (the Chicago Convention) and the 1944 International Air Services Transit Agreement.

2. Any declaration of national emergency by a Party under Article 89 of the Chicago Convention will not be applied to the other Party on a discriminatory basis.

3. The parties take note of the negotiations on the international air corridor to be opened between them in accordance with the Washington Declaration. In addition, the Parties shall, upon ratification of this Treaty, enter into negotiations for the purpose of concluding a Civil Aviation Agreement. All the above negotiations are to be concluded not later than 6 months from the exchange of the instruments of ratification of this Treaty.

Article 16

Posts and Telecommunications

The Parties take note of the opening between them, in accordance with the Washington Declaration, of direct telephone and facsimile lines. Postal links, the negotiations on which having been concluded, will be activated upon the signature of this Treaty. The Parties further agree that normal wireless and cable communications and television relay services by cable, radio and satellite, will be established between them, in accordance with all relevant international conventions and regulations. The negotiations on these subjects will be concluded not later than 9 months from the exchange of the instruments of ratification of this Treaty.

Article 17

Tourism

The Parties affirm their mutual desire to promote co-operation between them in the field of tourism. In order to accomplish this goal, the Parties—taking note of the understandings reached between them concerning tourism—agree to negotiate, as soon as possible, and to conclude not later than 3 months from the exchange of the instruments of ratification of this Treaty, an agreement to facilitate and encourage mutual tourism and tourism from third countries.

Article 18

Environment

The Parties will co-operate in matters relating to the environment, a sphere to which they attach great importance, including conservation of nature and prevention of pollution, as set forth in Annex IV. They will negotiate an agreement on the above, to be concluded not later than 6 months from the exchange of the instruments of ratification of this Treaty.

Article 19

Energy

1. The Parties will co-operate in the development of energy resources, including the development of energy related projects such as the utilization of solar energy.

2. The Parties, having concluded their negotiations on the interconnecting of their electric grids in the Eilat-Aqaba area, will implement the interconnecting upon the signature of this Treaty. The Parties view this step as a part of a wider binational and regional concept. They agree to continue their negotiations as soon as possible to widen the scope of their interconnected grids.

3. The Parties will conclude the relevant agreements in the field of energy within 6 months from the date of exchange of the instruments of ratification of this Treaty.

Article 20

Rift Valley Development

The Parties attach great importance to the integrated development of the Jordan Rift Valley area, including joint projects in the economic, environmental, energy related and tourism fields. Taking note of the Terms of Reference developed in the framework of the Trilateral Israel-Jordan-us Economic Committee towards the Jordan Rift Valley Development Master Plan, they will vigorously continue their efforts towards the completion of planning and towards implementation.

Article 21

Health

The Parties will co-operate in the area of health and shall negotiate with a view to the conclusion of an agreement within 9 months of the exchange of the instruments of ratification of this Treaty.

Article 22

Agriculture

The Parties will co-operate in the areas of agriculture, including veterinary services, plant protection, biotechnology and marketing, and shall negotiate with a view to the conclusion of an agreement within 6 months from the date of the exchange of instruments of ratification of this Treaty.

Article 23

Aqua and Eclat

The Parties agree to enter into negotiations, as soon as possible, and not later than one month from the exchange of the instruments of ratification of this Treaty, on arrangements that would enable the joint development of the towns of Aqaba and Eilat with regard to such matters, inter alia, as joint tourism development, joint customs posts, free trade zone, co-operation in aviation, prevention of pollution, maritime matters, police, customs and health co-operation. The Parties will conclude all relevant agreements within 9 months from the exchange of instruments of ratification of the Treaty.

Article 24

Claims

The Parties agree to establish a claims commission for the mutual settlement of all financial claims.

Article 25

Rights and Obligations

1. This Treaty does not affect and shall not be interpreted as affecting, in any way, the rights and obligations of the Parties under the Charter of the United Nations.
2. The parties undertake to fulfill in good faith their obligations under this Treaty, without regard to action or inaction of any other party and independently of any instrument inconsistent with this Treaty. For the purposes of this paragraph, each Party represents to the other that in its opinion and interpretation there is no inconsistency between their existing treaty obligations and this Treaty.
3. They further undertake to take all the necessary measures for the application in their relations of the provisions of the multilateral conventions to which they are parties, including the submission of appropriate notification to the Secretary General of the United Nations and other depositories of such conventions.
4. Both Parties will also take all the necessary steps to abolish all pejorative references to the other Party, in multilateral conventions to which they are parties, to the extent that such references exist.
5. The parties undertake not to enter into any obligation in conflict with this Treaty.
6. Subject to Article 103 of the United Nations Charter, in the event of a conflict between the obligations of the Parties under the present Treaty and any of their other obligations, the obligations under this Treaty will be binding and implemented.

Article 26

Legislation

Within 3 months of the exchange of the instruments of ratification of this Treaty, the Parties undertake to enact any legislation necessary in order to implement the Treaty, and to terminate any international commitments and to repeal any legislation that is inconsistent with the Treaty.

Article 27

Ratification and Annexes

1. This Treaty shall be ratified by both Parties in conformity with their respective national procedures. It shall enter into force on the exchange of the instruments of ratification.
2. The Annexes, Appendices, and other attachments to this Treaty shall be considered integral parts thereof.

Article 28

Interim Measures

The Parties will apply in certain spheres, to be agreed upon, interim measures pending the conclusion of the relevant agreements in accordance with this Treaty as stipulated in Annex V.

Article 29

Settlement of Disputes

1. Disputes arising out of the application or interpretation of this Treaty shall be resolved by negotiations.

2. Any such disputes which cannot be settled by negotiations shall be resolved by conciliation or submitted to arbitration.

Article 30

Registration

This Treaty shall be transmitted to the Secretary General of the United Nations for registration in accordance with the provisions of Article 102 of the Charter of the United Nations.

Vienna Document 1994

Adopted on November 28, 1994 by the Conference on Security and Cooperation in Europe (CSCE) Forum for Security Cooperation (FSC)

(1) Representatives of the participating States of the Conference on Security and Co-operation in Europe (CSCE), Albania, Armenia, Austria, Azerbaijan, Belarus, Belgium, Bosnia-Herzegovina, Bulgaria, Canada, Croatia, Cyprus, the Czech Republic, Denmark, Estonia, Finland, France, Georgia, Germany, Greece, the Holy See, Hungary, Iceland, Ireland, Italy, Kazakhstan, Kyrgyzstan, Latvia, Liechtenstein, Lithuania, Luxembourg, Malta, Moldova, Monaco, the Netherlands, Norway, Poland, Portugal, Romania, the Russian Federation, San Marino, Slovakia, Slovenia, Spain, Sweden, Switzerland, Tajikistan, Turkey, Turkmenistan, Ukraine, the United Kingdom, the United States of America, Uzbekistan and Yugoslavia[1], met in Vienna in accordance with the provisions relating to the Conference on Confidence- and Security-Building Measures and Disarmament in Europe contained in the Concluding Documents of the Madrid, Vienna and Helsinki Follow-up Meetings of the CSCE. The delegation of the former Yugoslav Republic of Macedonia attended the meetings as an observer as from 1993.

(2) The Negotiations were conducted from 1989 to 1994.

(3) The participating States recalled that the aim of the Conference on Confidence- and Security-Building Measures and Disarmament in Europe is, as a substantial and integral part of the multilateral process initiated by the Conference on Security and Co-operation in Europe, to undertake, in stages, new, effective and concrete actions designed to make progress in strengthening confidence and security and in achieving disarmament, so as to give effect and expression to the duty of States to refrain from the threat or use of force in their mutual relations as well as in their international relations in general.

(4) The participating States recognized that the mutually complementary confidence- and security-building measures which are adopted in the present document and which are in accordance with the mandates of the Madrid[2], Vienna and Helsinki Follow-up Meetings of the CSCE serve by their scope and nature and by their implementation to strengthen confidence and security among the participating States.

(5) The participating States recalled the declaration on Refraining from the Threat or Use of Force contained in paragraphs (9) to (27) of the Document of the Stockholm Conference and stressed its continuing validity as seen in the light of the Charter of Paris for a New Europe.

(6) On 17 November 1990, the participating States adopted the Vienna Document 1990, which built upon and added to the confidence- and security-building measures contained in the Document of the Stockholm Conference 1986. On 4 March 1992, the participating States adopted the Vienna Document 1992, which built upon and added to the confidence- and security-building measures contained in the Vienna Document 1990.

(7) In fulfilment of the Charter of Paris for a New Europe of November 1990 and the Programme for Immediate Action, set out in the Helsinki Document 1992, they continued the CSBM negotiations under the same mandate, and have adopted the present document which integrates a set of new confidence- and security-building measures with measures previously adopted.

(8) The participating States have adopted the following:

I. ANNUAL EXCHANGE OF MILITARY INFORMATION

INFORMATION ON MILITARY FORCES

(9) The participating States will exchange annually information on their military forces concerning the military organization, manpower and major weapon and equipment systems, as specified below, in the zone of application for confidence- and security-building measures (CSBMS). Participating States which have no military forces to be reported will so inform all other participating States.

(10) The information will be provided in an agreed format to all other participating States not later than 15 December of each year. It will be valid as of 1 January of the following year and will include:

(10.1) 1. Information on the command organization of those military forces referred to under points 2 and 3 specifying the designation and subordination of all formations[3] and units[4] at each level of command down to and including brigade/regiment or equivalent level. The information will be designed in such a way as to distinguish units from formations.

(10.1.1) Each participating State providing information on military forces will include a statement indicating the total number of units contained therein and the resultant annual evaluation quota as provided for in paragraph (107).

(10.2) 2. For each formation and combat unit[5] of land forces down to and including brigade/regiment or equivalent level the information will indicate:

(10.2.1) - the designation and subordination;

(10.2.2) - whether it is active or non-active[6];

(10.2.3) - the normal peacetime location of its headquarters indicated by exact geographic terms and/or co-ordinates;

(10.2.4) - the peacetime authorized personnel strength;

(10.2.5) - the major organic weapon and equipment systems, specifying the numbers of each type of:

(10.2.5.1) - battle tanks;

(10.2.5.2) - helicopters;

(10.2.5.3) - armoured combat vehicles (armoured personnel carriers, armoured infantry fighting vehicles, heavy armament combat vehicles);

(10.2.5.4) - armoured personnel carrier look-alikes and armoured infantry fighting vehicle look-alikes;

(10.2.5.5) - anti-tank guided missile launchers permanently/integrally mounted on armoured vehicles;

(10.2.5.6) - self-propelled and towed artillery pieces, mortars and multiple rocket launchers (100 mm calibre and above);

(10.2.5.7) - armoured vehicle launched bridges.

(10.3.1) For planned increases in personnel strength above that reported under paragraph (10.2.4) for more than 21 days by more than 1,500 troops for each active combat unit and by more than 5,000 troops for each active formation, excluding personnel increases in the formation's subordinate formations and/or combat units subject to separate reporting under paragraph (10.2); as well as

(10.3.2) for each non-active formation and non-active combat unit which is planned to be temporarily activated for routine military activities or for any other purpose with more than 2,000 troops for more than 21 days

(10.3.3) the following additional information will be provided in the annual exchange of military information:

(10.3.3.1) designation and subordination of the formation or combat unit;

(10.3.3.2) - purpose of the increase or activation;

(10.3.3.3) - for active formations and combat units the planned number of troops exceeding the personnel strength indicated under paragraph (10.2.4) or for non-active formations and combat units the number of troops involved during the period of activation;

(10.3.3.4) - start and end dates of the envisaged increase in personnel strength or activation;

(10.3.3.5) - planned location/area of activation;

(10.3.3.6) - the numbers of each type of the major weapon and equipment systems as listed in paragraphs (10.2.5.1) to (10.2.5.7) which are planned to be used during the period of the personnel increase or activation.

(10.3.4) In cases where the information required under paragraphs (10.3.1) to (10.3.3.6) cannot be provided in the annual exchange of military information, or in cases of changes in the information already provided, the required information will be communicated at least 42 days prior to such a personnel increase or temporary activation taking effect or, in cases when the personnel increase or temporary activation is carried out without advance notice to the troops involved, at the latest at the time the increase or the activation has taken effect.

(10.4) For each amphibious formation and amphibious combat unit[7] permanently located in the zone of application down to and including brigade/regiment or equivalent level, the information will include the items as set out above.

(10.5) 3. For each air formation and air combat unit[8] of the air forces, air defence aviation and of naval aviation permanently based on land down to and including wing/air regiment or equivalent level the information will include:

(10.5.1) - the designation and subordination;

(10.5.2) - the normal peacetime location of the headquarters indicated by exact geographic terms and/or co-ordinates;

(10.5.3) - the normal peacetime location of the unit indicated by the air base or military airfield on which the unit is based, specifying:

(10.5.3.1) - the designation or, if applicable, name of the air base or military airfield and

(10.5.3.2) - its location indicated by exact geographic terms and/or co-ordinates;

(10.5.4) - the peacetime authorized personnel strength[9];

(10.5.5) - the numbers of each type of:

(10.5.5.1) - combat aircraft;

(10.5.5.2) - helicopters

organic to the formation or unit.

DATA RELATING TO MAJOR WEAPON AND EQUIPMENT SYSTEMS

(11) The participating States will exchange data relating to their major weapon and equipment systems as specified in the provisions on Information on Military Forces within the zone of application for CSBMS.

(11.1) Data on existing weapon and equipment systems, if not already provided, will be provided once to all other participating States not later than 15 December 1995.

(11.2) Data on new types or versions of major weapon and equipment systems will be provided by each State when its deployment plans for the systems concerned are provided for the first time in accordance with paragraphs (13) and (14) below or, at the latest, when it deploys the systems concerned for the first time in the zone of application for CSBMS. If a participating State has already provided data on the same new type or version, other participating States may, if appropriate, certify the validity of those data as far as their system is concerned.

(12) The following data will be provided for each type or version of major weapon and equipment systems:

(12.1) BATTLE TANKS

(12.1.1) Type

(12.1.2) National Nomenclature/Name

(12.1.3) Main Gun Calibre

(12.1.4) Unladen Weight

(12.1.5) Data on new types or versions will, in addition, include:

(12.1.5.1) Night Vision Capability—yes/no

(12.1.5.2) Additional Armour—yes/no

(12.1.5.3) Track Width-cm

(12.1.5.4) Floating Capabilities—yes/no

(12.1.5.5) Snorkelling Equipment—yes/no

(12.2) ARMOURED COMBAT VEHICLES

(12.2.1) Armoured Personnel Carriers

(12.2.1.1) Type

(12.2.1.2) National Nomenclature/Name

(12.2.1.3) Type and Calibre of Armaments, if any

(12.2.1.4) Data on new types or versions will, in addition, include:

(12.2.1.4.1) Night Vision Capability—yes/no

(12.2.1.4.2) Seating Capacity

(12.2.1.4.3) Floating Capability—yes/no

(12.2.1.4.4) Snorkelling Equipment—yes/no

(12.2.2) Armoured Infantry Fighting Vehicles

(12.2.2.1) Type

(12.2.2.2) National Nomenclature/Name

(12.2.2.3) Type and Calibre of Armaments

(12.2.2.4) Data on new types or versions will, in addition, include:

(12.2.2.4.1) Night Vision Capability—yes/no

(12.2.2.4.2) Additional Armour—yes/no

(12.2.2.4.3) Floating Capability—yes/no

(12.2.2.4.4) Snorkelling Equipment—yes/no

(12.2.3) Heavy Armament Combat Vehicles

(12.2.3.1) Type

(12.2.3.2) National Nomenclature/Name

(12.2.3.3) Main Gun Calibre

(12.2.3.4) Unladen Weight

(12.2.3.5) Data on new types or versions will, in addition, include:

(12.2.3.5.1) Night Vision Capability—yes/no

(12.2.3.5.2) Additional Armour—yes/no

(12.2.3.5.3) Floating Capability—yes/no

(12.2.3.5.4) Snorkelling Equipment—yes/no

(12.3) ARMOURED PERSONNEL CARRIER LOOK-ALIKES AND ARMOURED INFANTRY FIGHTING VEHICLE LOOK-ALIKES

(12.3.1) Armoured Personnel Carrier Look-Alikes

(12.3.1.1) Type

(12.3.1.2) National Nomenclature/Name

(12.3.1.3) Type and Calibre of Armaments, if any

(12.3.2) Armoured Infantry Fighting Vehicle Look-Alikes

(12.3.2.1) Type

(12.3.2.2) National Nomenclature/Name

(12.3.2.3) Type and Calibre of Armaments, if any

(12.4) ANTI-TANK GUIDED MISSILE LAUNCHERS PERMANENTLY/INTEGRALLY MOUNTED ON ARMOURED VEHICLES

(12.4.1) Type

(12.4.2) National Nomenclature/Name

(12.5) SELF-PROPELLED AND TOWED ARTILLERY PIECES, MORTARS AND MULTIPLE ROCKET LAUNCHERS (100 mm CALIBRE AND ABOVE)

(12.5.1) Artillery pieces

(12.5.1.1) Type

(12.5.1.2) National Nomenclature/Name

(12.5.1.3) Calibre

(12.5.2) Mortars

(12.5.2.1) Type

(12.5.2.2) National Nomenclature/Name

(12.5.2.3) Calibre

(12.5.3) Multiple Launch Rocket Systems

(12.5.3.1) Type

(12.5.3.2) National Nomenclature/Name

(12.5.3.3) Calibre

(12.5.3.4) Data on new types or versions will, in addition, include:

(12.5.3.4.1) Number of Tubes

(12.6) ARMOURED VEHICLE LAUNCHED BRIDGES

(12.6.1) Type

(12.6.2) National Nomenclature/Name

(12.6.3) Data on new types or versions will, in addition, include:

(12.6.3.1) Span of the Bridge _____m

(12.6.3.2) Carrying Capacity/Load Classification _____metric tons

(12.7) COMBAT AIRCRAFT

(12.7.1) Type

(12.7.2) National Nomenclature/Name

(12.7.3) Data on new types or versions will, in addition, include:

(12.7.3.1) Type of Integrally Mounted Armaments, if any

(12.8) HELICOPTERS

(12.8.1) Type

(12.8.2) National Nomenclature/Name

(12.8.3) Data on new types or versions will, in addition, include:

(12.8.3.1) Primary Role (e.g., specialized attack, multi-purpose attack, combat support, transport)

(12.8.3.2) Type of Integrally Mounted Armaments, if any

(12.9) Each participating State will, at the time the data are presented, ensure that other participating States are provided with photographs presenting the right or left side, top and front views for each of the types of major weapon and equipment systems concerned.

(12.10) Photographs of armoured personnel carrier look-alikes and armoured infantry fighting vehicle look-alikes will include a view of such vehicles so as to show clearly their internal configuration illustrating the specific characteristic which distinguishes each particular vehicle as a look-alike.

(12.11) The photographs of each type will be accompanied by a note giving the type designation and national nomenclature for all models and versions of the type which the photographs represent. The photographs of a type will contain an annotation of the data for that type.

INFORMATION ON PLANS FOR THE DEPLOYMENT OF MAJOR WEAPON AND EQUIPMENT SYSTEMS

(13) The participating States will exchange annually information on their plans for the deployment of major weapon and equipment systems as specified in the provisions on Information on Military Forces within the zone of application for CSBMs.

(14) The information will be provided in an agreed format to all other participating States not later than 15 December of each year. It will cover plans for the following year and will include:

(14.1) the type and name of the weapon/equipment systems to be deployed;

(14.2) the total number of each weapon/equipment system;

(14.3) whenever possible, the number of each weapon/equipment system planned to be allocated to each formation or unit;

(14.4) the extent to which the deployment will add to or replace existing weapon/equipment systems.

DEFENCE PLANNING[10]

EXCHANGE OF INFORMATION

(15) General provisions

The participating States will exchange annually information as specified below in paragraphs (15.1) to (15.4), to provide transparency about each CSCE participating State's intentions in the medium to long term as regards size, structure, training and equipment of its armed forces, as well as defence policy, doctrines and budgets related thereto, based on their national practice and providing the background for a dialogue among the participating States. The information will be provided to all other participating States not later than two months after the military budget, referred to in paragraph (15.4.1), has been approved by the competent national authorities.

(15.1) Defence policy and doctrine

In a written statement participating States will address:

(15.1.1) their defence policy, including military strategy/doctrine as well as changes occurring thereto;

(15.1.2) their national procedures for defence planning, including the stages of defence planning, the institutions involved in the decision-making process as well as changes occurring thereto;

(15.1.3) their current personnel policy and the most substantial changes in it.

If the information under this point has remained the same, participating States may refer to the previously exchanged information.

(15.2) Force planning

In a written statement participating States will address in the form of a general description:

(15.2.1) the size, structure, personnel, major weapon and equipment systems and deployment of their armed forces and the envisaged changes thereto. In view of the reorganization of the defence structure in a number of participating States, similar information will be provided on other forces, including paramilitary forces, on a voluntary basis and as appropriate. The scope and the status of the information on such forces will be reviewed after their status has been further defined, in the process of reorganization;

(15.2.2) the training programmes for their armed forces and planned changes thereto in the forthcoming years;

(15.2.3) the procurement of major equipment and major military construction programmes on the basis of the categories as set out in the United Nations Instrument mentioned in paragraph (15.3), either ongoing or starting in the forthcoming years, if planned, and the implications of such projects, accompanied by explanations, where appropriate;

(15.2.4) the realization of the intentions previously reported under this paragraph.

In order to facilitate the understanding of the information provided, the participating States are encouraged to use illustrative charts and maps, wherever applicable.

(15.3) Information on previous expenditures

Participating States will report their defence expenditures of the preceding fiscal year on the basis of the categories as set out in the United Nations "Instrument for Standardized International Reporting of Military Expenditures" adopted on 12 December 1980.

They will provide, in addition, any appropriate clarification, if necessary, as to possible discrepancies between expenditures and previously reported budgets.

(15.4) Information on budgets

The written statement will be supplemented with the following information, where available:

(15.4.1) On the forthcoming fiscal year

(15.4.1.1) budget figures on the basis of the categories as set out in the United Nations Instrument mentioned in paragraph (15.3);

(15.4.1.2) status of budget figures.

The participating States will furthermore provide the following information in as far as available:

(15.4.2) On the two fiscal years following the forthcoming fiscal year

(15.4.2.1) the best estimates itemizing defence expenditures on the basis of the categories as set out in the United Nations Instrument mentioned in paragraph (15.3);

(15.4.2.2) status of these estimates.

(15.4.3) On the last two years of the forthcoming five fiscal years

(15.4.3.1) the best estimates specifying the total and figures for the following three main categories:

- operating costs,

- procurement and construction,

- research and development;

(15.4.3.2) status of these estimates.

(15.4.4) Explanatory data

(15.4.4.1) an indication of the year which has been used as the basis for any extrapolation;

(15.4.4.2) clarifications of the data as specified in paragraphs (15.3) and (15.4), especially with regard to inflation.

CLARIFICATION, REVIEW AND DIALOGUE

(15.5) Request for clarification

To increase transparency, each participating State may ask any other participating State for clarification of the information provided. Questions should be submitted within a period of two months following the receipt of a participating State's information. Participating States will make every effort to answer such questions fully and promptly. It should be understood that these exchanges are informational only. The questions and replies may be transmitted to all other participating States.

(15.6) Annual discussion meetings

Without prejudice to the possibility of having ad hoc discussions on the information and clarification provided, the participating States will hold each year a meeting for a focused and structured dialogue to discuss the issues relating to defence planning. The Annual Implementation Assessment Meeting as foreseen in Chapter X of the Vienna Document 1994 could be used for the purpose. Such discussions may extend to the methodology of defence planning and the implications originating from the information provided.

(15.7) Study visits

To increase knowledge of national defence planning procedures and promote dialogue, each participating State may arrange study visits for representatives of other CSCE participating States to meet with officials at the institutions involved in defence planning and appropriate bodies such as government agencies (planning, finance, economy), ministry of defence, general staff and relevant parliamentary committees.

Such exchanges could be organized within the framework of military contacts and co-operation.

POSSIBLE ADDITIONAL INFORMATION

(15.8) Participating States are encouraged to provide any other factual and documentary information relating to their defence planning. This may include:

(15.8.1) the list and, if possible, the texts of major publicly available documents, in any of the CSCE working languages, reflecting their defence policy, military strategies and doctrines;

(15.8.2) any other publicly available documentary reference material on their plans relating to paragraphs (15.1) and (15.2), e.g., military documents and/or "white papers".

(15.9) This documentary information may be provided to the CPC Secretariat, which will distribute lists of received information and make it available upon request.

II. RISK REDUCTION

MECHANISM FOR CONSULTATION AND

CO-OPERATION AS REGARDS UNUSUAL MILITARY ACTIVITIES

(16) Participating States will, in accordance with the following provisions, consult and co-operate with each other about any unusual and unscheduled activities of their military forces outside their normal peacetime locations which are militarily significant, within the zone of application for CSBMs and about which a participating State expresses its security concern.

(16.1) The participating State which has concerns about such an activity may transmit a request for an explanation to another participating State where the activity is taking place.

(16.1.1) The request will state the cause, or causes, of the concern and, to the extent possible, the type and location, or area, of the activity.

(16.1.2) The reply will be transmitted within not more than 48 hours.

(16.1.3) The reply will give answers to questions raised, as well as any other relevant information which might help to clarify the activity giving rise to concern.

(16.1.4) The request and the reply will be transmitted to all other participating States without delay.

(16.2) The requesting State, after considering the reply provided, may then request a meeting to discuss the matter.

(16.2.1) The requesting State may ask for a meeting with the responding State.

(16.2.1.1) Such a meeting will be convened within not more than 48 hours.

(16.2.1.2) The request for such a meeting will be transmitted to all participating States without delay.

(16.2.1.3) The responding State is entitled to ask other interested participating States, in particular those which might be involved in the activity, to participate in the meeting.

(16.2.1.4) Such a meeting will be held at a venue to be mutually agreed upon by the requesting and the responding States. If there is no agreement, the meeting will be held at the Conflict Prevention Centre.

(16.2.1.5) The requesting and responding States will, jointly or separately, transmit a report of the meeting to all other participating States without delay.

(16.2.2) The requesting State may ask for a meeting of all participating States.

(16.2.2.1) Such a meeting will be convened within not more than 48 hours.

(16.2.2.2) The Permanent Committee will serve as the forum for such a meeting.

(16.2.2.3) Participating States involved in the matter to be discussed undertake to be represented at such a meeting.

(16.2.2.4) In the light of its assessment of the situation, the Permanent Committee will use all its competences to contribute to a solution.

CO-OPERATION AS REGARDS HAZARDOUS INCIDENTS OF A MILITARY NATURE

(17) Participating States will co-operate by reporting and clarifying hazardous incidents of a military nature within the zone of application for CSBMs in order to prevent possible misunderstandings and mitigate the effects on another participating State.

(17.1) Each participating State will designate a point to contact in case of such hazardous incidents and will so inform all other participating States. A list of such points will be kept available at the Conflict Prevention Centre.

(17.2) In the event of such a hazardous incident the participating State whose military forces are involved in the incident should provide the information available to other participating States in an expeditious manner. Any participating State affected by such an incident may also request clarification as appropriate. Such requests will receive a prompt response.

(17.3) Matters relating to information about such hazardous incidents may be discussed by participating States at the Special Committee of the FSC, or at the annual implementation assessment meeting.

(17.4) These provisions will not affect the rights and obligations of participating States under any international agreement concerning hazardous incidents, nor will they preclude additional methods of reporting and clarifying hazardous incidents.

VOLUNTARY HOSTING OF VISITS TO DISPEL CONCERNS ABOUT MILITARY ACTIVITIES

(18) In order to help to dispel concerns about military activities in the zone of application for CSBMs, participating States are encouraged to invite other participating States to take part in visits to areas on the territory of the host State in which there may be cause for such concerns. Such invitations will be without prejudice to any action taken under paragraphs (16) to (16.2).

(18.1) States invited to participate in such visits will include those which are understood to have concerns. At the time invitations are issued, the host State will communicate to all other participating States its intention to conduct the visit, indicating the reasons for the visit, the area to be visited, the States invited and the general arrangements to be adopted.

(18.2) Arrangements for such visits, including the number of the representatives from other participating States to be invited, will be at the discretion of the host State, which will bear the in-country costs. However, the host State should take appropriate account of the need to ensure the effectiveness of the visit, the maximum amount of openness and transparency and the safety and security of the invited representatives. It should also take account, as far as practicable, of the wishes of visiting representatives as regards the itinerary of the visit. The host State and the States which provide visiting personnel may circulate joint or individual comments on the visit to all other participating States.

III. CONTACTS

VISITS TO AIR BASES

(19) Each participating State with air combat units reported under paragraph (10) will arrange visits for representatives of all other participating States to one of its normal peacetime air bases[11] on which such units are located in order to provide the visitors with the opportunity to view activity at the air base, including preparations to carry out the functions of the air base, and to gain an impression of the approximate number of air sorties and type of missions being flown.

(20) No participating State will be obliged to arrange more than one such visit in any five-year period. Prior indications given by participating States of forthcoming schedules for such visits for the subsequent year(s) may be discussed at the annual implementation assessment meetings.

(21) As a rule, up to two visitors from each participating State will be invited.

(22) When the air base to be visited is located on the territory of another participating State, the invitations will be issued by the participating State on whose territory the air base is located (host State). In such cases, the responsibilities as host delegated by this State to the participating State arranging the visit will be specified in the invitation.

(23) The State arranging the visit will determine the programme for the visit in co-ordination with the host State, if appropriate. The visitors will follow the instructions issued by the State arranging the visit in accordance with the provisions set out in this document.

(24) The modalities regarding visits to air bases will conform to the provisions in Annex II.

(25) The invited State may decide whether to send military and/or civilian visitors, including personnel accredited to the host State. Military visitors will normally wear their uniforms and insignia during the visit.

(26) The visit to the air base will last for a minimum of 24 hours.

(27) In the course of the visit, the visitors will be given a briefing on the purpose and functions of the air base and on its current activities, including appropriate information on the air force structure and operations so as to explain the specific role and subordination of the air base. The State arranging the visit will provide the visitors with the opportunity to view routine activities at the air base during the visit.

(28) The visitors will have the opportunity to communicate with commanders and troops, including those of support/logistic units located at the air base. They will be provided with the opportunity to view all types of aircraft located at the air base.

(29) At the close of the visit, the State arranging the visit will provide an opportunity for the visitors to meet together and also with State officials and senior air base personnel to discuss the course of the visit.

(30) PROGRAMME OF MILITARY CONTACTS AND CO-OPERATION MILITARY CONTACTS

(30.1) To improve further their mutual relations in the interest of strengthening the process of confidence- and security-building, the participating States will, on a voluntary basis and as appropriate, promote and facilitate:

(30.1.1) exchanges and visits between members of the armed forces at all levels, especially those between junior officers and commanders;

(30.1.2) contacts between relevant military institutions, especially between military units;

(30.1.3) exchanges of visits of naval vessels and air force units;

(30.1.4) reservation of places in military academies and schools and on military training courses for members of the armed forces from the participating States;

(30.1.5) - use of the language facilities of military training institutions for the foreign-language instruction of members of the armed forces from the participating States and the organization of language courses in military training institutions for military foreign-language instructors from the participating States;

(30.1.6) - exchanges and contacts between academics and experts in military studies and related areas;

(30.1.7) - participation and contribution by members of the armed forces of the participating States, as well as civil experts in security matters and defence policy, to academic conferences, seminars and symposia;

(30.1.8) - issuing of joint academic publications on security and defence issues;

(30.1.9) - sporting and cultural events between members of their armed forces.

MILITARY CO-OPERATION

Joint military exercises and training

(30.2) The participating States will conduct, on a voluntary basis and as appropriate, joint military training and exercises to work on tasks of mutual interest.

Visits to military facilities, to military formations and observation of certain military activities

(30.3) In addition to the provisions of the Vienna Document 1994 regarding visits to air bases, each participating State will arrange for representatives of all other participating States to visit one of its military facilities or military formations, or to observe military activities below thresholds specified in Chapter V. These events will provide the visitors or observers with the opportunity to view activity of that military facility, observe the training of that military formation or observe the conduct of that military activity.

(30.4) Each participating State will make every effort to arrange one such visit or observation in any five-year period.

(30.5) In order to ensure maximum efficiency and cost-effectiveness, the participating States may conduct such visits or observations in conjunction with, *inter alia*, other visits and contacts organized in accordance with provisions of the Vienna Document 1994.

(30.6) The modalities regarding visits to air bases specified in paragraphs (19)-(29) of the Vienna Document 1994 will, *mutatis mutandis*, be applied to the visits to military facilities and to military formations.

Observation visits

(30.7) Participating States conducting military activities subject to prior notification according to Chapter IV of the Vienna Document 1994, but at levels lower than those specified in Chapter V of the Vienna Document 1994, are encouraged to invite observers from other participating States, especially neighbouring States, to observe such military activities.

(30.8) Arrangements for such visits will be at the discretion of the host State.

Provision of experts

(30.9) The participating States express their willingness to provide to any other participating State available experts to be consulted on matters of defence and security.

(30.10) For that purpose participating States will designate a point of contact and will inform all other participating States accordingly. A list of such points will be kept available at the Conflict Prevention Centre.

(30.11) At the discretion of participating States, communications between them on this subject may be transmitted through the CSCE communications network.

(30.12) The modalities regarding provision of experts will be agreed directly between the participating States concerned.

Seminars on co-operation in the military field

(30.13) Subject to the approval of the appropriate CSCE bodies, the Conflict Prevention Centre will organize seminars on co-operation between the armed forces of the participating States.

(30.14) The agenda of the seminars will concentrate primarily on CSCE-oriented tasks, including the participation of the armed forces in peacekeeping operations, in disaster and emergency relief, in refugee crises and in providing humanitarian assistance.

Exchange of information on agreements on military contacts and co-operation

(30.15) The participating States will exchange information on agreements on programmes of military contacts and co-operation concluded with other participating States within the scope of these provisions.

* * *

(30.16) The participating States have decided that the Programme of Military Contacts and Co-operation will be open to all CSCE participating States in respect of all their armed forces and territory. The implementation of this Programme will be assessed at annual implementation assessment meetings as foreseen in Chapter X.

DEMONSTRATION OF NEW TYPES OF MAJOR WEAPON AND EQUIPMENT SYSTEMS

(31) The first participating State which deploys with its military forces in the zone of application a new type of major weapon and equipment system as specified in the provisions on Information on Military Forces will arrange at the earliest opportunity, but not later than one year after deployment has started, a demonstration for representatives of all other participating States[12], which may coincide with other events stipulated in this document.

(32) When the demonstration is carried out on the territory of another participating State, the invitation will be issued by the participating State on whose territory the demonstration is carried out (host State). In such cases, the responsibilities as host delegated by this State to the participating State arranging the demonstration will be specified in the invitation.

(33) The State arranging the demonstration will determine the programme for the demonstration in co-ordination with the host State, if appropriate. The visitors will follow the instructions issued by the State arranging the demonstration in accordance with the provisions set out in this document.

(34) The modalities regarding demonstration of new types of major weapon and equipment systems will conform to the provisions in Annex II.

(35) The invited State may decide whether to send military and/or civilian visitors, including personnel accredited to the host State. Military visitors will normally wear their uniforms and insignia during the visit.

IV. PRIOR NOTIFICATION OF CERTAIN MILITARY ACTIVITIES

(36) The participating States will give notification in writing in accordance with the provisions of Chapter IX to all other participating States 42 days or more in advance of the start of notifiable[13] military activities in the zone of application for CSBMs.

(37) Notification will be given by the participating State on whose territory the activity in question is planned to take place (host State) even if the forces of that State are not engaged in the activity or their strength is below the notifiable level. This will not

relieve other participating States of their obligation to give notification, if their involvement in the planned military activity reaches the notifiable level.

(38) Each of the following military activities in the field conducted as a single activity in the zone of application for CSBMs at or above the levels defined below will be notified:

(38.1) The engagement of formations of land forces[14] of the participating States in the same exercise activity conducted under a single operational command independently or in combination with any possible air or naval components.

(38.1.1) This military activity will be subject to notification whenever it involves at any time during the activity:

- at least 9,000 troops, including support troops, or

- at least 250 battle tanks, or

- at least 500 ACVs, as defined in paragraph (12.2), or

- at least 250 self-propelled and towed artillery pieces, mortars and multiple rocket-launchers (100 mm calibre and above)

if organized into a divisional structure or at least two brigades/regiments, not necessarily subordinate to the same division.

(38.1.2) The participation of air forces of the participating States will be included in the notification if it is foreseen that in the course of the activity 200 or more sorties by aircraft, excluding helicopters, will be flown.

(38.2) The engagement of military forces in an amphibious landing[15], heliborne landing or parachute assault in the zone of application for CSBMs.

(38.2.1) These military activities will be subject to notification whenever any of them involves at least 3,000 troops.

(38.3) The engagement of formations of land forces of the participating States in a transfer from outside the zone of application for CSBMs to arrival points in the zone, or from inside the zone of application for CSBMs to points of concentration in the zone, to participate in a notifiable exercise activity or to be concentrated.

(38.3.1) The arrival or concentration of these forces will be subject to notification whenever it involves, at any time during the activity:

- at least 9,000 troops, including support troops, or

- at least 250 battle tanks, or

- at least 500 ACVs, as defined in paragraph (12.2), or

- at least 250 self-propelled and towed artillery pieces, mortars and multiple rocket launchers (100 mm calibre and above)

if organized into a divisional structure or at least two brigades/regiments, not necessarily subordinate to the same division.

(38.3.2) Forces which have been transferred into the zone will be subject to all provisions of agreed CSBMs when they depart their arrival points to participate in a notifiable exercise or to be concentrated within the zone of application for CSBMs.

(39) Notifiable military activities carried out without advance notice to the troops involved are exceptions to the requirement for prior notification to be made 42 days in advance.

(39.1) Notification of such activities, above the agreed thresholds, will be given at the time the troops involved commence such activities.

(40) Notification will be given in writing of each notifiable military activity in the following agreed form:

(41) **A) General information**

(41.1) The designation of the military activity;

(41.2) The general purpose of the military activity;

(41.3) The names of the States involved in the military activity;

(41.4) The level of command organizing and commanding the military activity;

(41.5) The start and end dates of the military activity.

(42) B) Information on different types of notifiable military activities

(42.1) The engagement of formations of land forces of the participating State in the same exercise activity conducted under a single operational command independently or in combination with any possible air or naval components:

(42.1.1) The total number of troops taking part in the military activity (i.e., ground troops, amphibious troops, airmobile or heliborne and airborne troops) and the number of troops participating for each State involved, if applicable;

(42.1.2) The designation, subordination, number and type of formations and units participating for each State down to and including brigade/regiment or equivalent level;

(42.1.3) The total number of battle tanks for each State;

(42.1.4) The total number of armoured combat vehicles for each State and the total number of anti-tank guided missile launchers mounted on armoured vehicles;

(42.1.5) The total number of artillery pieces and multiple rocket launchers (100 mm calibre or above);

(42.1.6) The total number of helicopters, by category;

(42.1.7) Envisaged number of sorties by aircraft, excluding helicopters;

(42.1.8) Purpose of air missions;

(42.1.9) Categories of aircraft involved;

(42.1.10) The level of command organizing and commanding the air force participation;

(42.1.11) Naval ship-to-shore gunfire;

(42.1.12) Indication of other naval ship-to-shore support;

(42.1.13) The level of command organizing and commanding the naval force participation.

(42.2) The engagement of military forces in an amphibious landing, heliborne landing or parachute assault in the zone of application for CSBMs:

(42.2.1) The total number of amphibious troops involved in notifiable amphibious landings, and/or the total number of troops involved in notifiable parachute assaults or heliborne landings;

(42.2.2) In the case of a notifiable landing, the point or points of embarkation, if in the zone of application for CSBMs.

(42.3) The engagement of formations of land forces of the participating States in a transfer from outside the zone of application for CSBMs to arrival points in the zone, or from inside the zone of application for CSBMs to points of concentration in the zone, to participate in a notifiable exercise activity or to be concentrated:

(42.3.1) The total number of troops transferred;

(42.3.2) Number and type of formations participating in the transfer;

(42.3.3) The total number of battle tanks participating in a notifiable arrival or concentration;

(42.3.4) The total number of armoured combat vehicles participating in a notifiable arrival or concentration;

(42.3.5) The total number of artillery pieces and multiple rocket launchers (100 mm calibre and above) participating in a notifiable arrival or concentration;

(42.3.6) Geographical co-ordinates for the points of arrival and for the points of concentration.

(43) C) The envisaged area in the zone of application for CSBMs and timeframe of the activity

(43.1) The area of the military activity delimited by geographic features together with geographic co-ordinates, as appropriate;

(43.2) Start and end dates of each phase of activity in the zone of application for CSBMs of participating formations (e.g., transfer, deployment, concentration of forces, active exercise, recovery);

(43.3) Tactical purpose of each phase and corresponding geographical area delimited by geographic co-ordinates; and

(43.4) Brief description of each phase.

(44) D) Other information

(44.1) Changes, if any, in relation to information provided in the annual calendar regarding the activity;

(44.2) Relationship of the activity to other notifiable activities.

V. OBSERVATION OF CERTAIN MILITARY ACTIVITIES

(45) The participating States will invite observers from all other participating States to the following notifiable military activities:

(45.1) The engagement of formations of land forces[16] of the participating States in the same exercise activity conducted under a single operational command independently or in combination with any possible air or naval components.

(45.2) - The engagement of military forces in an amphibious landing, heliborne landing or parachute assault in the zone of application for CSBMs.

(45.3) - In the case of the engagement of formations of land forces of the participating States in a transfer from outside the zone of application for CSBMs to arrival points in the zone, or from inside the zone of application for CSBMs to points of concentration in the zone, to participate in a notifiable activity or to be concentrated, the concentration of these forces. Forces which have been transferred into the zone will be subject to all provisions of agreed confidence- and security-building measures when they depart their arrival points to participate in a notifiable exercise activity or to be concentrated within the zone of application for CSBMs.

(45.4) The above-mentioned activities will be subject to observation whenever the number of troops engaged equals or exceeds 13,000 or where the number of battle tanks engaged equals or exceeds 300, or where the number of armoured combat vehicles engaged as defined in paragraph (12.2) equals or exceeds 500, or where the number of self-propelled and towed artillery pieces, mortars and multiple

rocket launchers (100 mm calibre and above) engaged equals or exceeds 250. In the case of an amphibious landing, heliborne landing or parachute assault, the activity will be subject to observation whenever the number of troops engaged equals or exceeds 3,500.

(46) The host State will be the participating State on whose territory the notified activity will take place.

(47) The host State may delegate responsibilities as host to another participating State or States engaged in the military activity on the territory of the host State, which will be the delegated State. In such cases, the host State will specify the allocation of responsibilities in its invitation to observe the activity.

(48) Each participating State may send up to two observers to the military activity to be observed. The invited State may decide whether to send military and/or civilian observers, including personnel accredited to the host State. Military observers will normally wear their uniforms and insignia while performing their tasks.

(49) The modalities regarding observation of certain military activities will conform to the provisions in Annex II.

(50) The host or delegated State will determine a duration of observation which permits the observers to observe a notifiable military activity from the time that agreed thresholds for observation are met or exceeded until, for the last time during the activity, the thresholds for observation are no longer met.

(51) The observers may make requests with regard to the observation programme. The host or delegated State will, if possible, accede to them.

(52) The observers will be granted, during their mission, the privileges and immunities accorded to diplomatic agents in the Vienna Convention on Diplomatic Relations.

(53) The participating States will ensure that official personnel and troops taking part in an observed military activity, as well as other armed personnel located in the area of the military activity, are adequately informed regarding the presence, status and functions of observers.

(54) The host or delegated State will not be required to permit observation of restricted locations, installations or defence sites.

(55) In order to allow the observers to confirm that the notified activity is non-threatening in character and that it is carried out in conformity with the appropriate provisions of the notification, the host or delegated State will:

(55.1) - at the commencement of the observation programme give a briefing on the purpose, the basic situation, the phases of the activity and possible changes as compared with the notification, and provide the observers with an observation programme containing a daily schedule;

(55.2) - provide the observers with a map to a scale of one to not more than 250,000 depicting the area of the notified military activity and the initial tactical situation in this area. To depict the entire area of the notified military activity, smaller-scale maps may be additionally provided;

(55.3) - provide the observers with appropriate observation equipment; in addition, the observers will be permitted to use their own binoculars, maps, photo and video cameras, dictaphones and hand-held passive night-vision devices. The above-mentioned equipment will be subject to examination and approval by the host or delegated State. It is understood that the host or delegated State may limit the use of certain equipment in restricted locations, installations or defence sites;

(55.4) - be encouraged, whenever feasible and with due consideration for the security of the observers, to provide an aerial survey, preferably by helicopter, of the area of the military activity. If carried out, such a survey should provide the observers with the opportunity to observe from the air the disposition of forces engaged in the activity in order to help them gain a general impression of its scope and scale. At least one observer from each participating State represented at the observation should be given the opportunity to participate in the survey. Helicopters and/or aircraft may be provided by the host State or by another participating State at the request of and in agreement with the host State;

(55.5) - give the observers briefings, once daily at a minimum, with the help of maps on the various phases of the military activity and their development, and on the geographic location of the observers; in the case of a land force activity conducted in combination with air or naval components, briefings will be given by representatives of all forces involved;

(55.6) - provide opportunities to observe directly forces of the State(s) engaged in the military activity so that the observers get an impression of the flow of the entire activity; to this end, the observers will be given the opportunity to observe combat and support units of all participating formations of a divisional or equivalent level and, whenever possible, to visit units below divisional or equivalent level and communicate with commanders and troops. Commanders and other senior personnel of the participating formations as well as of the visited units will inform the observers of the mission and disposition of their respective units;

(55.7) - guide the observers in the area of the military activity; the observers will follow the instructions issued by the host or delegated State in accordance with the provisions set out in this document;

(55.8) - provide the observers with opportunities for timely communication with their embassies or other official missions and consular posts; the host or delegated State is not obligated to cover the communication expenses of the observers;

(55.9) - at the close of each observation, provide an opportunity for the observers to meet together and also with host State officials to discuss the course of the observed activity. Where States other than the host State have been engaged in the activity, military representatives of those States will also be invited to take part in this discussion.

(56) The participating States need not invite observers to notifiable military activities which are carried out without advance notice to the troops involved unless these notifiable activities have a duration of more than 72 hours. The continuation of these activities beyond this time will be subject to observation while the agreed thresholds for observation are met or exceeded. The observation programme will follow as closely as practically possible all the provisions for observation set out in this document.

(57) The participating States are encouraged to permit media representatives from all participating States to attend observed military activities in accordance with accreditation procedures set down by the host State. In such instances, media representatives

from all participating States will be treated without discrimination and given equal access to those facets of the activity open to media representatives.

(57.1) The presence of media representatives will not interfere with the observers carrying out their functions nor with the flow of the military activity.

(58) The host or delegated State will provide the observers with transportation from a suitable location announced in the invitation to the area of the notified activity so that the observers are in position before the start of the observation programme. It will also provide the observers with appropriate means of transportation in the area of the military activity, and return the observers to another suitable location announced in the invitation at the conclusion of the observation programme.

VI. ANNUAL CALENDARS

(59) Each participating State will exchange, with all other participating States, an annual calendar of its military activities subject to prior notification[17], within the zone of application for CSBMs, forecast for the subsequent calendar year. A participating State which is to host military activities subject to prior notification conducted by any other participating State(s) will include these activities in its annual calendar. It will be transmitted every year in writing, in accordance with the provisions of Chapter IX, not later than 15 November for the following year.

(60) If a participating State does not forecast any military activity subject to prior notification, it will so inform all other participating States in the same manner as prescribed for the exchange of annual calendars.

(61) Each participating State will list the above-mentioned activities chronologically and will provide information on each activity in accordance with the following model:

(61.1) number of military activities to be reported;

(61.2) - activity number;

(61.2.1) - type of military activity and its designation;

(61.2.2) - general characteristics and purpose of the military activity;

(61.2.3) - States involved in the military activity;

(61.2.4) - area of the military activity, indicated by geographic features, where appropriate, and defined by geographic co-ordinates;

(61.2.5) - planned duration of the military activity, indicated by envisaged start and end dates;

(61.2.6) - envisaged total number of troops[17] engaged in the military activity;

(61.2.7) - envisaged total number of troops for each State involved, if applicable. For activities involving more than one State, the host State will provide such information;

(61.2.8) - types of armed forces involved in the military activity;

(61.2.9) - envisaged level of the military activity and designation of the direct operational command under which this military activity will take place;

(61.2.10) - number and type of divisions whose participation in the military activity is envisaged;

(61.2.11) - any additional information concerning, *inter alia*, components of armed forces which the participating State planning the military activity considers relevant.

(62) Should changes regarding the military activities in the annual calendar prove necessary, they will be communicated to all other participating States no later than in the appropriate notification.

(63) Should a participating State cancel a military activity included in its annual calendar or reduce it to a level below notification thresholds, that State will inform the other participating States immediately.

(64) Information on military activities subject to prior notification not included in an annual calendar will be communicated to all participating States as soon as possible, in accordance with the model provided in the annual calendar.

VII. CONSTRAINING PROVISIONS

(65) The following provisions will apply to military activities subject to prior notification:[17]

(65.1) No participating State will carry out within two calendar years more than one military activity subject to prior notification involving more than 40,000 troops or 900 battle tanks.

(65.2) No participating State will carry out within a calendar year more than six military activities subject to prior notification each one involving more than 13,000 troops or 300 battle tanks, but not more than 40,000 troops or 900 battle tanks.

(65.2.1) Of these six military activities, no participating State will carry out within a calendar year more than three military activities subject to prior notification, each one involving more than 25,000 troops or 400 battle tanks.

(65.3) No participating State will carry out simultaneously more than three military activities subject to prior notification each one involving more than 13,000 troops or 300 battle tanks.

(66) Each participating State will communicate, in writing, in accordance with the provisions of Chapter IX, to all other participating States, by 15 November each year, information concerning military activities subject to prior notification involving more than 40,000 troops or 900 battle tanks, which it plans to carry out or host in the second subsequent calendar year. Such a communication will include preliminary information on the activity, as to its general purpose, timeframe and duration, area, size and States involved.

(67) If a participating State does not forecast any such military activity, it will so inform all other participating States in the same manner as prescribed for the exchange of annual calendars.

(68) No participating State will carry out a military activity subject to prior notification involving more than 40,000 troops or 900 battle tanks, unless it has been the object of a communication as defined above and unless it has been included in the annual calendar, not later than 15 November each year.

(69) If military activities subject to prior notification are carried out in addition to those contained in the annual calendar, they should be as few as possible.

VIII. COMPLIANCE AND VERIFICATION

(70) According to the Madrid mandate, the confidence- and security-building measures to be agreed upon "will be provided with adequate forms of verification which correspond to their content".

(71) The participating States recognize that national technical means can play a role in monitoring compliance with agreed confidence- and security-building measures.

INSPECTION

(72) In accordance with the provisions contained in this document each participating State has the right to conduct inspections on the territory of any other participating State within the zone of application for CSBMs. The inspecting State may invite other participating States to participate in an inspection.

(73) Any participating State will be allowed to address a request for inspection to another participating State within the zone of application for CSBMs.

(74) No participating State will be obliged to accept on its territory within the zone of application for CSBMs more than three inspections per calendar year.

(74.1) When a participating State has accepted three inspections in a calendar year, it will so inform all other participating States.

(75) No participating State will be obliged to accept more than one inspection per calendar year from the same participating State.

(76) An inspection will not be counted if, due to force majeure, it cannot be carried out.

(77) The participating State which has received such a request will reply in the affirmative to the request within the agreed period of time, subject to the provisions contained in paragraphs (74) and (75).

(78) The participating State which requests an inspection will be permitted to designate for inspection on the territory of another State within the zone of application for CSBMs, a specific area. Such an area will be referred to as the "specified area". The specified area will comprise terrain where notifiable military activities are conducted or where another participating State believes a notifiable military activity is taking place. The specified area will be defined and limited by the scope and scale of notifiable military activities but will not exceed that required for an army level military activity.

(79) In the specified area the inspection team accompanied by the representatives of the receiving State will be permitted access, entry and unobstructed survey, except for areas or sensitive points to which access is normally denied or restricted, military and other defence installations, as well as naval vessels, military vehicles and aircraft. The number and extent of the restricted areas should be as limited as possible. Areas where notifiable military activities can take place will not be declared restricted areas, except for certain permanent or temporary military installations which, in territorial terms, should be as small as possible, and consequently those areas will not be used to prevent inspection of notifiable military activities. Restricted areas will not be employed in a way inconsistent with the agreed provisions on inspection.

(80) Within the specified area, the forces of participating States other than the receiving State will also be subject to the inspection.

(81) Inspection will be permitted on the ground, from the air, or both.

(82) The representatives of the receiving State will accompany the inspection team, including when it is in land vehicles and an aircraft from the time of their first employment until the time they are no longer in use for the purposes of inspection.

(83) In its request, the inspecting State will notify the receiving State of:

(83.1) - the location of the specified area defined by geographical co-ordinates;

(83.2) - the preferred point(s) of entry for the inspection team;

(83.3) - mode of transport to and from the point(s) of entry and, if applicable, to and from the specified area;

(83.4) - where in the specified area the inspection will begin;

(83.5) - whether the inspection will be conducted from the ground, from the air, or both simultaneously;

(83.6) - whether aerial inspection will be conducted using an airplane, a helicopter, or both;

(83.7) - whether the inspection team will use land vehicles provided by the receiving State or, if mutually agreed, its own vehicles;

(83.8) - other participating States participating in the inspection, if applicable;

(83.9) - information for the issuance of diplomatic visas to inspectors entering the receiving State;

(83.10) - the preferred CSCE working language(s) to be used during the inspection.

(84) The reply to the request will be given in the shortest possible period of time, but within not more than twenty-four hours. Within thirty-six hours after the issuance of the request, the inspection team will be permitted to enter the territory of the receiving State.

(85) Any request for inspection as well as the reply thereto will be communicated to all participating States without delay.

(86) The receiving State should designate the point(s) of entry as close as possible to the specified area. The receiving State will ensure that the inspection team will be able to reach the specified area without delay from the point(s) of entry. The receiving State will, in its reply, indicate which of the six official working languages will be used during the inspection.

(87) All participating States will facilitate the passage of the inspection teams through their territory.

(88) Within 48 hours after the arrival of the inspection team at the specified area, the inspection will be terminated.

(89) There will be no more than four inspectors in an inspection team. The inspecting State may invite other participating States to participate in an inspection. The inspection team will be headed by a national of the inspecting State, which will have at least as many inspectors in the team as any invited State. The inspection team will be under the responsibility of the inspecting State, against whose quota the inspection is counted. While conducting the inspection, the inspection team may divide into two subteams.

(90) The inspectors and, if applicable, auxiliary personnel will be granted during their mission the privileges and immunities in accordance with the

Vienna Convention on Diplomatic Relations.

(91) The participating States will ensure that troops, other armed personnel and officials in the specified area are adequately informed regarding the presence, status and functions of inspectors and, if applicable, auxiliary personnel. The receiving State will ensure that no action is taken by its representatives which could endanger inspectors and, if applicable, auxiliary personnel. In carrying out their duties, inspectors and, if applicable, auxiliary personnel will take into account safety concerns expressed by representatives of the receiving State.

(92) The receiving State will provide the inspection team with appropriate board and lodging in a location suitable for carrying out the inspection, and, when necessary, medical care; however this does not exclude the use by the inspection team of its own tents and rations.

(93) The inspection team will have use of its own maps and charts, photo and video cameras, binoculars, hand-held passive night vision devices and dictaphones. Upon arrival in the specified area the inspection team will show the equipment to the representatives of the receiving State. In addition, the receiving State may provide the inspection team with a map depicting the area specified for the inspection.

(94) The inspection team will have access to appropriate telecommunications equipment of the receiving State for the purpose of communicating with the embassy or other official missions and consular posts of the inspecting State accredited to the receiving State.

(95) The receiving State will provide the inspection team with access to appropriate telecommunications equipment for the purpose of continuous communication between the subteams.

(96) Inspectors will be entitled to request and to receive briefings at agreed times by military representatives of the receiving State. At the inspectors' request, such briefings will be given by commanders of formations or units in the specified area. Suggestions of the receiving State as to the briefings will be taken into consideration.

(97) The inspecting State will specify whether aerial inspection will be conducted using an airplane, a helicopter or both. Aircraft for inspection will be chosen by mutual agreement between the inspecting and receiving States. Aircraft will be chosen which provide the inspection team with a continuous view of the ground during the inspection.

(98) After the flight plan, specifying, *inter alia*, the inspection team's choice of flight path, speed and altitude in the specified area, has been filed with the competent air traffic control authority the inspection aircraft will be permitted to enter the specified area without delay. Within the specified area, the inspection team will, at its request, be permitted to deviate from the approved flight plan to make specific observations provided such deviation is consistent with paragraph (79) as well as flight safety and air traffic requirements. Directions to the crew will be given through a representative of the receiving State on board the aircraft involved in the inspection.

(99) One member of the inspection team will be permitted, if such a request is made, at any time to observe data on navigational equipment of the aircraft and to have access to maps and charts used by the flight crew for the purpose of determining the exact location of the aircraft during the inspection flight.

(100) Aerial and ground inspectors may return to the specified area as often as desired within the 48-hour inspection period.

(101) The receiving State will provide for inspection purposes land vehicles with cross-country capability. Whenever mutually agreed, taking into account the specific geography relating to the area to be inspected, the inspecting State will be permitted to use its own vehicles.

(102) If land vehicles or aircraft are provided by the inspecting State, there will be one accompanying driver for each land vehicle, or accompanying aircraft crew.

(103) The inspecting State will prepare a report of its inspection using a format to be agreed by the participating States and will provide a copy of that report to all participating States without delay.

(104) The inspection expenses will be incurred by the receiving State except when the inspecting State uses its own aircraft and/or land vehicles. The inspecting State will be responsible for travel expenses to and from the point(s) of entry.

EVALUATION

(105) Information provided under the provisions on Information on Military Forces and on Information on Plans for the Deployment of Major Weapon and Equipment Systems will be subject to evaluation.

(106) Subject to the provisions below each participating State will provide the opportunity to visit active formations and units in their normal peacetime locations as specified in points 2 and 3 of the provisions on Information on Military Forces to allow the other participating States to evaluate the information provided.

(106.1) Non-active formations and combat units temporarily activated will be made available for evaluation during the period of temporary activation and in the area/location of activation indicated under paragraph (10.3.3). In such cases the provisions for the evaluation of active formations and units will be applicable, *mutatis mutandis*. Evaluation visits conducted under this provision will count against the quotas established under paragraph (107).

(107) Each participating State will be obliged to accept a quota of one evaluation visit per calendar year for every sixty units, or portion thereof, reported under paragraph (10). However, no participating State will be obliged to accept more than fifteen visits per calendar year. No participating State will be obliged to accept more than one fifth of its quota of visits from the same participating State; a participating State with a quota of less than five visits will not be obliged to accept more than one visit from the same participating State during a calendar year. No formation or unit may be visited more than twice during a calendar year and more than once by the same participating State during a calendar year.

(107.1) A participating State will inform all other participating States when, if applicable, its quota is filled.

(108) No participating State will be obliged to accept more than one visit at any given time on its territory.

(109) If a participating State has formations or units stationed on the territory of other participating States (host States) in the zone of application for CSBMs, the maximum number of evaluation visits permitted to its forces in each of the States concerned will be proportional to the number of its units in each State. The application of this provision will not alter the number of visits this participating State (stationing State) will have to accept under paragraph (107).

(110) Requests for such visits will be submitted giving five days notice.

(111) The request will specify:

(111.1) - the formation or unit to be visited;

(111.2) - the proposed date of the visit;

(111.3) - the preferred point(s) of entry as well as the date and estimated time of arrival for the evaluation team;

(111.4) - the mode of transport to and from the point(s) of entry and, if applicable, to and from the formation or unit to be visited;

(111.5) - the names and ranks of the members of the team and, if applicable, information for the issue of diplomatic visas;

(111.6) - the preferred CSCE working language(s) to be used during the visit.

(112) If a formation or unit of a participating State is stationed on the territory of another participating State, the request will be addressed to the host State and sent simultaneously to the stationing State.

(113) The reply to the request will be given within 48 hours after the receipt of the request.

(114) In the case of formations or units of a participating State stationed on the territory of another participating State, the reply will be given by the host State in consultation with the stationing State. After consultation between the host State and the stationing State, the host State will specify in its reply any of its responsibilities which it agrees to delegate to the stationing State.

(115) The reply will indicate whether the formation or unit will be available for evaluation at the proposed date at its normal peacetime location.

(116) Formations or units may be in their normal peacetime location but be unavailable for evaluation. Each participating State will be entitled in such cases

not to accept a visit; the reasons for the non-acceptance and the number of days that the formation or unit will be unavailable for evaluation will be stated in the reply. Each participating State will be entitled to invoke this provision up to a total of five times for an aggregate of no more than 30 days per calendar year.

(117) If the formation or unit is absent from its normal peacetime location, the reply will indicate the reasons for and the duration of its absence. The requested State may offer the possibility of a visit to the formation or unit outside its normal peacetime location. If the requested State does not offer this possibility, the requesting State will be able to visit the normal peacetime location of the formation or unit. The requesting State may however refrain in either case from the visit.

(118) Visits will not be counted against the quotas of receiving States, if they are not carried out. Likewise, if visits are not carried out, due to force majeure, they will not be counted.

(119) The reply will designate the point(s) of entry and indicate, if applicable, the time and place of assembly of the team. The point(s) of entry and, if applicable, the place of assembly will be designated as close as possible to the formation or unit to be visited. The receiving State will ensure that the team will be able to reach the formation or unit without delay. The receiving State will, in its reply, indicate which of the six official working languages will be used during the evaluation visit.

(120) The request and the reply will be communicated to all participating States without delay.

(121) Participating States will facilitate the passage of teams through their territory.

(122) The team will have no more than two members. It may be accompanied by an interpreter as auxiliary personnel.

(123) The members of the team and, if applicable, auxiliary personnel will be granted during their mission the privileges and immunities in accordance with the Vienna Convention on Diplomatic Relations.

(124) The visit will take place in the course of a single working day and last up to 12 hours.

(125) The visit will begin with a briefing by the officer commanding the formation or unit, or his deputy, in the headquarters of the formation or unit, concerning the personnel as well as the major weapon and equipment systems reported under paragraph (10).

(125.1) In the case of a visit to a formation, the receiving State may provide the possibility to see personnel and major weapon and equipment systems reported under paragraph (10) for that formation, but not for any of its formations or units, in their normal locations.

(125.2) In the case of a visit to a unit, the receiving State will provide the possibility to see the personnel and the major weapon and equipment systems of the unit reported under paragraph (10) in their normal locations.

(126) Access will not have to be granted to sensitive points, facilities and equipment.

(127) The team will be accompanied at all times by representatives of the receiving State.

(128) The receiving State will provide the team with appropriate transportation during the visit to the formation or unit.

(129) The evaluation team will have use of its own maps and charts, photo and video cameras, personal binoculars and dictaphones. Upon arrival at the location of the formation or unit being visited the evaluation team will show the equipment to the representatives of the receiving State.

(130) The visit will not interfere with activities of the formation or unit.

(131) The participating States will ensure that troops, other armed personnel and officials in the formation or unit are adequately informed regarding the presence, status and functions of members of teams and, if applicable, auxiliary personnel. Participating States will also ensure that no action is taken by their representatives which could endanger the members of teams and, if applicable, auxiliary personnel. In carrying out their duties, members of teams and, if applicable, auxiliary personnel will take into account safety concerns expressed by representatives of the receiving State.

(132) Travel expenses to and from the point(s) of entry, including expenses for refuelling, maintenance

and parking of aircraft and/or land vehicles of the visiting State, will be borne by the visiting State according to existing practices established under the CSBM inspection provisions.

(132.1) Expenses for evaluation visits incurred beyond the point(s) of entry will be borne by the receiving State, except when the visiting State uses its own aircraft and/or land vehicles in accordance with paragraph (111.4).

(132.2) The receiving State will provide appropriate board and, when necessary, lodging in a location suitable for carrying out the evaluation as well as any urgent medical care which may be required.

(132.3) In the case of visits to formations or units of a participating State stationed on the territory of another participating State, the stationing State will bear the costs for the discharge of those responsibilities which have been delegated to it by the host State under the terms of paragraph (114).

(133) The visiting State will prepare a report of its visit using a format to be agreed by the participating States which will be communicated to all participating States expeditiously.

(134) The communications concerning compliance and verification will be transmitted preferably through the CSBM communications network.

(135) Each participating State will be entitled to request and obtain clarification from any other participating State concerning the application of agreed confidence- and security-building measures. The requested participating State will provide promptly relevant clarification to the requesting participating State unless otherwise specified in this document. Communications in this context will, if appropriate, be transmitted to all other participating States.

* * *

(136) The participating States are encouraged to undertake, including on the basis of separate agreements, in a bilateral, multilateral or regional context, measures to increase transparency and confidence. Illustrative examples could be as follows:

(136.1) to provide their neighbouring participating States with information on certain military activities carried out below the thresholds for notification and close to borders between them;

(136.2) - to invite representatives from other, especially neighbouring participating States to observe exercises other than those subject to the provisions of this document.

(137) The participating States are encouraged to provide information on such measures to the CPC, which will distribute lists of received information and make it available upon request.

IX. COMMUNICATIONS

(138) *The CSCE Communications Network*

The participating States have established a network of direct communications between their capitals for the transmission of messages relating, *inter alia*, to agreed measures contained in this document. The network will complement the existing use of diplomatic channels. Participating States undertake to use the network flexibly, efficiently and in a cost-effective way in communications between States concerning agreed CSBMs and other CSCE-related matters.

(139) *Financial Arrangements*

The cost-sharing arrangements are set out in documents CSCE/WV/Dec.2 and CSCE/WV/Dec.4.

(140) *Points of Contact*

Each participating State will designate a point of contact capable of transmitting and receiving messages from other participating States on a 24-hour-a-day basis and will notify in advance any change in this designation.

(141) *Six CSCE Languages*

Communications may be in any one of the six working languages of the CSCE. Without prejudicing the future continued use of all six working languages of the CSCE, according to established rules and practice as set out in the Final Recommendations of the Helsinki Consultations, the participating States will:

(141.1) - in order to facilitate an efficient use of the communications network, give due consideration to practical needs of rapid transmission of their messages and of immediate understandability. A translation into another CSCE working language will be added where needed to meet that principle;

(141.2) - indicate at least two CSCE working languages in which they would prefer to receive the message or its translation.

(142) *Use of the Network*

Participating States will, whenever possible, use the Standard Operating Procedures (S.O.P.) and enforce user discipline to maximize the efficiency and cost-effectiveness of the network.

(142.1) Messages will always have headers as defined in the S.O.P.

(142.2) Messages will, whenever possible, be transmitted in formats with headings in all six CSCE working languages. Such formats, agreed among the participating States with a view to making transmitted messages immediately understandable by reducing the language element to a minimum, are annexed to document CSCE/WV/Dec.4. The formats may be subject to agreed modifications as required.

(142.3) Messages will be considered official communications of the sending State. If the content of a message is not related to an agreed measure, the receiving State has the right to reject it by so informing the other participating States.

(142.4) Any narrative text, to the extent it is required in such formats, and messages that do not lend themselves to formatting will be transmitted in the CSCE working languages chosen by the transmitting State, in accordance with the provisions of paragraph (141).

(142.5) Each participating State has the right to ask for clarification of messages in case of doubt.

(143) *Additional use of the Network*

Participating States may agree among themselves to use the network for other purposes.

(144) *The Communications Group*

A Communications Group will be established, composed of representatives of the participating States and chaired, on behalf of the Chairman-in-Office, by a representative of the Secretary General of the CSCE.

(144.1) The group will address questions relating to rules of procedure, working methods, formats and any other measures to enhance the viability and effectiveness of the communications network, including issues relating to use of modern information technologies for data exchange.

(144.2) The group will meet two times per year for at least one day. Additional meetings may be convened as necessary.

(144.3) The Chairman of the Group will report to the appropriate CSCE committee about the proceedings of the Communications Group and, if appropriate, present drafts for decisions to be taken as prepared by the Group.

X. ANNUAL IMPLEMENTATION ASSESSMENT MEETING

(145) The participating States will hold each year a meeting to discuss the present and future implementation of agreed CSBMs. Discussion may extend to:

(145.1) - clarification of questions arising from such implementation;

(145.2) - operation of agreed measures, including the use of additional equipment during inspections and evaluation visits;

(145.3) - implications of all information originating from the implementation of any agreed measures for the process of confidence- and security-building in the framework of the CSCE.

(146) Before the conclusion of each year's meeting the participating States will normally agree upon the agenda and dates for the subsequent year's meeting. Lack of agreement will not constitute sufficient reason to extend a meeting, unless otherwise agreed. Agenda and dates may, if necessary, be agreed between meetings.

(147) The Special Committee of the Forum for Security Co-operation will hold such meetings. It will consider, as required, suggestions made during the AIAM aiming at the improvement of the implementation of CSBMs.

Within one month after the AIAM, the Conflict Prevention Centre will circulate a survey of such suggestions.

(147.1) One month prior to the meeting, the Conflict Prevention Centre will circulate a survey of exchanged annual information and ask participating States to confirm or to correct applicable data.

(147.2) Any participating State may request assistance in implementing the provisions of this document from any other participating State.

(147.3) Participating States which, for whatever reason, have not exchanged annual information according to this document will during the meeting explain the reasons why and provide an expected date for their full compliance with this commitment.

* * *

(148) The participating States will implement this set of mutually complementary confidence-and security-building measures in order to promote security co-operation and to reduce the risk of military conflict.

(149) In order to strengthen compliance with agreed confidence- and security-building measures and in addition to other relevant provisions of this document, the participating States will, as necessary, consider in appropriate CSCE bodies how to ensure full implementation of those measures.

(150) The measures adopted in this document are politically binding and will come into force on 1 January 1995, unless specified otherwise.

(151) The Secretary General of the CSCE is requested to transmit the present document to the Secretary-General of the United Nations and to the Governments of the non-participating Mediterranean States, observer State, Japan and the Republic of Korea.

(152) The text of this document will be published in each participating State, which will disseminate it and make it known as widely as possible.

(153) The representatives of the participating States express their profound gratitude to the Government and people of Austria for the excellent arrangements they have made for the negotiations within the framework of the FSC and the warm hospitality they have extended to the delegations which participated in the negotiations.

Notes

1. On 13 December 1992 the CSCE Committee of Senior Officials agreed to maintain in force its decision of 8 July 1992 to suspend the participation of Yugoslavia in the CSCE and review it as appropriate.
2. The zone of application for CSBMs under the terms of the Madrid mandate is set out in Annex 1.
3. In this context, formations are armies, corps and divisions and their equivalents.
4. In this context, units are brigades, regiments and their equivalents.
5. In this context, combat units are infantry, armoured, mechanized, motorized rifle, artillery, combat engineer and army aviation units. Those combat units which are airmobile or airborne will also be included.
6. In this context, non-active formations or combat units are those manned from zero to fifteen percent of their authorized combat strength. This term includes low strength formations and units.
7. Combat units as defined above.
8. In this context, air combat units are units, the majority of whose organic aircraft are combat aircraft.
9. As an exception, this information need not be provided on air defence aviation units.
10. The application of the measures relating to defence planning is not restricted by the zone of application for CSBMs as set out in Annex I.
11. In this context, the term normal peacetime air base is understood to mean the normal peacetime location of the air combat unit indicated by the air base or military airfield on which the unit is based.
16. In this context, the term land forces includes amphibious, airmobile or heliborne forces and airborne forces.
17. As defined in the provisions on Prior Notification of Certain Military Activities.

Agreement on the Establishment of the Korean Peninsula Energy Development Organization

Date of signature: March 9, 1995
Place of signature: New York
Signatory states: the Republic of Korea, the United States, Japan

[The signatories],

Affirming the objective of an overall resolution of the North Korean nuclear issue, as referred to in the Agreed Framework Between the United States of

America and the Democratic People's Republic of Korea, signed in Geneva on October 21, 1994 (hereinafter referred to as "the Agreed Framework");

Recognizing the critical importance of the nonproliferation and other steps that must be taken by North Korea, as described in the Agreed Framework, as a condition of implementation of the Agreed Framework;

Bearing in mind the paramount importance of maintaining peace and security on the Korean Peninsula;

Wishing to cooperate in taking the steps necessary to implement the Agreed Framework, consistent with the Charter of the United Nations, the Treaty on the Non-Proliferation of Nuclear Weapons, and the Statute of the International Atomic Energy Agency; and

Convinced of the need to establish an organization, as contemplated in the Agreed Framework, to coordinate cooperation among interested parties and to facilitate the financing and execution of projects needed to implement the Agreed Framework;

Have agreed as follows:

Article 1

The Korean Peninsula Energy Development Organization (hereinafter referred to as "KEDO" or "the Organization") is established upon the terms and conditions hereinafter set forth.

Article 2

(a) The purpose of the Organization shall be to:

(1) provide for the financing and supply of a light-water reactor (hereinafter referred to as "LWR") project in North Korea (hereinafter referred to as "the DPRK"), consisting of two reactors of the Korean standard nuclear plant model with a capacity of approximately 1,000 MW (e) each, pursuant to a supply agreement to be concluded between the Organization and the DPRK.

(2) provided for the supply of interim energy alternatives in lieu of the energy from the DPRK's graphite-moderated reactors pending construction of the first light-water reactor unit; and

(3) provide for the implementation of any other measures deemed necessary to accomplish the foregoing or otherwise to carry out the objectives of the Agreed Framework.

(b) The Organization shall fulfill its purposes with a

view toward ensuring the full implementation by the DPRK of its undertaking as described in the Agreed Framework.

Article 3

In carrying out these purposes, the Organization may do any of the following:

(a) Evaluate and administer projects designed to further the purposes of the Organization;

(b) Receive funds from members of the Organization or other states entities for financing projects designed to further the purposes of the Organization, manage and disburse such funds, and retain for Organization purposes any interest that accumulates on such funds;

(c) Receive in-kind contributions from members of the Organization or other states or entities for projects designed to further the purposes of the Organization;

(d) Receive funds or other compensation from the DPRK in payment for the LWR project and other goods and services provided by the Organization;

(e) Cooperate and enter into agreements, contracts, or other arrangements with appropriate financial institutions, as may be agreed upon, for the handling of funds received by the Organization or designated for projects of the Organization;

(f) Acquire any property, facilities, equipment, or goods necessary for achieving the purposes of the Organization;

(g) Conclude or enter into agreements, contracts, or other arrangements, including loan agreements, with states, international organizations or other appropriate entities, as may be necessary for achieving the purposes and exercising the functions of the Organization;

(h) Coordinate with and assist states, local authorities and other public entities, national and international institutions, and private parties in carrying out activities that further the purpose of the Organization, including activities promoting nuclear safety;

(i) Dispose of any receipts, funds, accounts, or other assets of the Organization and distribute the proceeds in accordance with the financial obligations of the Organization, with any remaining assets or proceeds therefrom to be distributed in an equitable manner according to the contributions of each member of the Organization; and

(j) Exercise such other powers as shall be necessary in furtherance of its purposes and functions, consistent with this Agreement.

Article 4

(a) Activities undertaken by the Organization shall be carried out consistent with the Charter of the United Nations, the Treaty on the Non-Proliferation of Nuclear Weapons, and the Statute of the International Atomic Energy Agency.

(b) Activities undertaken by the Organization shall be subject to the DPRK's compliance with the terms of all agreements between the DPRK and KEDO and to the DPRK acting in a manner consistent with the Agreed Framework. In the event that these conditions are not satisfied, the Organization may take appropriate steps.

(c) The Organization shall obtain formal assurances from the DPRK that nuclear materials, equipment, or technology transferred to the DPRK in connection with projects undertaken by the Organization shall be used exclusively for such projects, only for peaceful purposes, and in a manner that ensures the safe use of nuclear energy.

Article 5

(a) The original members of the Organization shall be the United States of America, Japan, and the Republic of Korea (hereinafter referred to as the "original Members").

(b) Additional states that support the purposes of the Organization and offer assistance, such as providing funds, goods, or services to the Organization, may, with the approval of the Executive Board, also become members of the Organization (hereinafter jointly with the original Members referred to as "Members") in accordance with the procedures in Article XIV (b).

Article 6

(a) The authority to carry out the functions of the Organization shall be vested in the Executive Board.

(b) The Executive Board shall consist of one representative of each of the original Members.

(c) The Executive Board shall select a Chair from among the representatives serving on the Executive Board for a term of two years.

(d) The Executive Board shall meet whenever necessary at the request of the Chair of the Executive Board, the Executive Director, or any representative serving on the Executive Board, in accordance with rules of procedure it shall adopt.

(e) Decisions of the Executive Board shall be made by a consensus of the representatives of all the original Members.

(f) The Executive Board may approve such rules and regulations as may be necessary or appropriate to achieve the purposes of the Organization.

(g) The Executive Board may take any necessary action on any matter relating to the functions of the Organization.

Article 7

(a) The General Conference shall consist of representatives of all the Members.

(b) The General Conference shall be held annually to consider the annual report, as referred to in Article XII.

(c) Extraordinary meeting of the General Conference shall be held at the direction of the Executive Board to discuss matters submitted by the Executive Board.

(d) The General Conference may submit a report containing recommendations to the Executive Board for its consideration.

Article 8

(a) The staff of the Organization shall be headed by an Executive Director. The Executive Director shall be appointed by the Executive Board as soon as possible after this Agreement enters into force.

(b) The Executive Director shall be the chief administrative officer of the Organization and shall be under the authority and subject to the control of the Executive Board. The Executive Director shall exercise all the powers delegated to him or her by the Executive Board and shall be responsible for conducting the ordinary business of the Organization, including the organization and direction of a headquarters and a staff, the preparation of annual budgets, the procurement of financing, and the approval, execution and administration of contracts to achieve the purposes of the Organization. The Executive Director may delegate such powers to other officers or staff members as he or she deems appropriate. The Executive Director shall perform his or her duties in accordance with all rules and regulations approved by the Executive Board.

(c) The Executive Director shall be assisted by two Deputy Executive Directors. The two Deputy Executive Directors shall be appointed by the Executive Board.

(d) The Executive Director and the Deputy Executive Directors shall be appointed for terms of two years and may be reappointed. They shall be nationals of the original Members. The terms of employment, including salaries, of these officers shall be determined by the Executive Board. The Executive Director and the Deputy Executive Directors may be removed prior to the expiration of their terms by a decision of the Executive Board.

(e) The Executive Director shall have the authority to approve projects, execute contracts, and enter into other financial obligations on behalf of the Organization within the guidelines adopted by the Executive Board and the limits of the approved budget, provided that the Executive Director shall obtain the prior approval of the Executive Board for projects, contracts, or financial obligations that exceed a specified value, which shall be determined by the Executive Board based on the need for effective and efficient operation of the Organization.

(f) The Executive Director shall establish staff positions and terms of employment, including salaries, subject to the approval of the Executive Board. The Executive Director shall appoint qualified personnel to such staff positions and dismiss personnel as necessary, in accordance with rules and regulations to be approved by the Executive Board. The Executive Director shall seek to appoint a staff in which the nationals of the original Members are fairly represented, paying due regard to the importance of securing the highest standards of integrity, efficiency, and technical competence.

(g) The Executive Director shall report to the Executive Board and the General Conference on the activities and finances of the Organization. The Executive Director shall promptly bring to the notice of the Executive Board any matter that may require Executive Board action.

(h) The Executive Director, with the advice of the Deputy Executive Directors, shall prepare rules and regulations consistent with this Agreement and the purposes of the Organization. The rules and regulations shall be submitted to the Executive Board for its approval to implementation.

(i) In the performance of their duties, the Executive Director and the staff shall not seek or receive instructions from any government or from any other authority external to the Organization. They shall refrain from any action that might reflect on their position as international officials responsible only to the Organization. Each Member undertakes to respect the exclusively international character of the responsibilities of the Executive Director and the staff and not to seek to influence them in the discharge of their responsibilities.

Article 9

(a) The Executive Board shall establish Advisory Committees to provide advice to the Executive Director and the Executive Board, as appropriate, on specific projects being carried out by the Organization or proposed to be carried out by the Organization. Advisory Committees shall be established for the light-water reactor project, the project for the provision of interim energy alternatives, and such other projects as the Executive Board may determine.

(b) Each Advisory Committee shall include representatives of the original Members and other Members that support the project for which the Advisory Committee was established.

(c) The Advisory Committees shall meet at such times as they may determine.

(d) The Executive Director shall keep the Advisory Committees fully informed of matters pertinent to their respective projects, and the Executive Board and Executive Director shall give due consideration to the recommendations of the Advisory Committees.

Article 10

(a) The budget for each fiscal year shall be prepared by the Executive Director and shall be approved by the Executive Board. The Organization's fiscal year shall be from January 1 to December 31.

(b) Each Member may make voluntary contributions to the Organization by providing or making available such funds as it deems appropriate. Such contributions may be made directly to the Organization or by paying the Organization's contractors. Contributions shall be made by cash deposit, escrow, letter of credit, promissory note, or by such other legal means and in such currency as may be agreed between the Organization and the contributor.

(c) The Organization may seek contributions from such other public or private sources as it deems appropriate.

(d) The Organization shall establish an account or accounts to receive funds from Members or other sources, including independent accounts for those funds to be reserved for specific projects and the administration of the Organization. Interest or dividends accruing on such accounts shall be reinvested for activities of the Organization. Excess funds shall be distributed as set forth in Article III(i).

Article 11

(a) Members may make available to the Organization or its contractors goods, services, equipment, and facilities that may be of assistance in achieving the purposes of the Organization.

(b) The Organization may accept from such other public or private sources as it deems appropriate any goods, services, equipment, and facilities that may be of assistance in achieving the purposes of the Organization.

(c) The Executive Director shall be responsible for valuing in-kind contributions to the Organization, whether direct or indirect. Members shall cooperate with the Executive Director in the valuation process, including by providing regular reports of in-kind contributions and access to records necessary to verify the value of such contributions.

(d) In the event of a dispute concerning the value of an in-kind contribution, the Executive Board shall review the matter and render a decision.

Article 12

The Executive Director shall submit to the Executive Board for its approval an annual report on the activities of the Organization, which shall include a description of the status of the LWR project and other projects, a comparison of planned activities to completed activities, and an audited statement of the Organization's accounts. Upon the approval of the Executive Board, the Executive Director shall distribute the annual report to the Members. The Executive Director shall submit to the Executive Board such other reports as may be required by the Executive Board.

Article 13

(a) To carry out its purposes and functions, the organization shall possess legal capacity and, in particular, the capacity to: (1) contract; (2) lease or rent real property; (3) acquire and dispose of personal property; and (4) institute legal proceedings. Members may accord the Organization such legal capacity in accordance with their respective laws and regulations where necessary for the Organization to carry out its purposes and functions.

(b) No Member shall be liable, by reason of its status or participation as a Member for acts, omissions, or obligations of the Organization.

(c) Information provided to the Organization by a Member shall be used exclusively for the purposes of the Organization and shall not be publicly disclosed without the express consent of that Member.

(d) Implementation of this Agreement in the Members territories shall be in accordance with the laws and regulations, including budgetary appropriations, of such Members.

Article 14

(a) This Agreement shall enter into force upon signature by the original Members.

(b) States approved by the Executive Board for membership in accordance with Article V(b) may become Members by submitting an instrument of acceptance of this Agreement to the Executive Director, which shall become effective on the date of receipt by the Executive Director.

(c) This Agreement may be amended by written agreement of the original Members.

(d) This Agreement may be terminated or suspended by written agreement of the original Members.

Article 15

A Member may withdraw from this Agreement at any time by giving written notice of withdrawal to the Executive Director. The withdrawal shall become effective ninety days after receipt of the notice of withdrawal by the Executive Director.

Pelindaba Text of the African Nuclear-Weapon-Free Zone Treaty

Also known as: The Treaty of Pelindaba
Date of signature: June 21, 1995
Place of signature: Addis Abba
Signatory states: Algeria, Angola, Benin, Botswana, Burkina Faso, Burundi, Cameroon, Cape Verde, Central African Republic, Chad, Comoros, Congo, Cote d'Ivoire, Dem. Rep. of Congo, Djibouti, Egypt, Equatorial Guinea, Eritrea, Ethiopia, Gabon, Gambia, Ghana, Guinea-Bissau, Kenya, Lesotho, Liberia, Libya, Madagascar, Malawi, Mali, Mauritania, Mauritius, Morocco, Mozambique, Namibia, Niger, Nigeria, Rwanda, Sao Tome & Principe, Senegal, Seychelles, Sierra Leone, Somalia, South Africa, Sudan, Swaziland, Tanzania, Togo, Tunisia, Uganda, Zambia, Zimbabwe (as of November 19, 1998)
Also known as: Algeria, Burkina Faso, Gambia, Mauritania, Mauritius, South Africa, Tanzania, Zimbabwe (as of November 19, 1998)

The Parties to this Treaty:

Guided by the Declaration on the Denuclearisation of Africa, adopted by the Assembly of Heads of State and Government of the Organization of African Unity (hereinafter referred to as OAU) at its first ordinary session, held at Cairo from 17 to 21 July 1964 (AHG/Res. 11(1)), in which they solemnly declared their readiness to undertake, through an international agreement to be concluded under United Nations auspices, not to manufacture or acquire control of nuclear weapons,

Guided also, by the resolutions of the fifty-fourth and fifty-sixth ordinary sessions of the Council of Ministers of OAU, held at Abuja from 27 May to 1 June 1991 and at Dakar from 22 to 28 June 1992 respectively, (CM/Res. 1342 LIV) and CM/Res. 1395 (LVI)), which affirmed that the evolution of the international situation was conducive to the implementation of the Cairo Declaration, as well as the relevant provisions of the 1986 OAU Declaration on Security, Disarmament and Development,

Recalling United Nations General Assembly resolution 3472 B (XXX) of 11 December 1975, in which it considered nuclear-weapon-free zones one of the most effective means for preventing the proliferation, both horizontal and vertical, of nuclear weapons,

Convinced of the need to take all steps in achieving the ultimate goal of a world entirely free of nuclear weapons, as well as of the obligations of all States to contribute to this end,

Convinced also that the African nuclear-weapon-free zone will constitute an important step towards strengthening the non-proliferation regime, promoting cooperation in the peaceful uses of nuclear energy, promoting general and complete disarmament and enhancing regional and international peace and security.

Aware that regional disarmament measures contribute to global disarmament efforts,

Believing that the African nuclear-weapon-free zone will protect African States against possible nuclear attacks on their territories,

Noting with satisfaction existing NWFZs and recognizing that the establishment of other NWFZs, especially in the Middle East, would enhance the security of States Parties to the African NWFZ,

Reaffirming the importance of the Treaty on the Non-Proliferation of Nuclear Weapons (hereinafter referred to as the NPT) and the need for the implementation of all its provisions,

Desirous of taking advantage of article IV of the NPT, which recognizes the inalienable right of all States Parties to develop research on, production and use of nuclear energy for peaceful purposes without discrimination and to facilitate the fullest possible exchange of equipment, materials and scientific and technological information for such purposes,

Determined to promote regional cooperation for the development and practical application of nuclear energy for peaceful purposes in the interest of sustainable social and economic development of the Africa continent,

Determined to keep Africa free of environmental pollution by radioactive wastes and other radioactive matter,

Welcoming the cooperation of all States and governmental and non-governmental organizations for the attainment of these objectives,

Have decided by this treaty to establish the African NWFZ and hereby agree as follows:

Article 1

Definition/Usage of Terms

For the purpose of this Treaty and its Protocols:

(a) "African nuclear-weapon-free zone" means the territory of the continent of Africa, islands States members of OAU and all islands considered by the Organization of African Unity in its resolutions to be part of Africa;

(b) "Territory" means the land territory, internal waters, territorial seas and archipelagic waters and the airspace above them as well as the sea bed and subsoil beneath;

(c) "Nuclear explosive device" means any nuclear weapon or other explosive device capable of releasing nuclear energy, irrespective of the purpose for which it could be used. The term includes such a weapon or device in unassembled and partly assembled forms, but does not include the means of transport or delivery of such a weapon or device if separable from and not an indivisible part of it;

(d) "Stationing" means implantation, emplacement, transport on land or inland waters, stockpiling, storage, installation and deployment;

(e) "Nuclear installation" means a nuclear-power reactor, a nuclear research reactor, a critical facility, a conversion plant, a fabrication plant, a reprocessing plant, an isotope separation plant, a separate storage installation and any other installation or location in or at which fresh or irradiated nuclear material or significant quantities of radioactive materials are present.

(f) "Nuclear material" means any source material or special fissionable material as defined in Article XX of the Statute of the International Atomic Energy Agency (IAEA) and as amended from time to time by the IAEA.

Article 2

Application of the Treaty

1. Except where otherwise specified, this Treaty and its Protocols shall apply to the territory within the African nuclear-weapon-free zone, as illustrated in the map in annex I.

2. Nothing in this Treaty shall prejudice or in any way affect the rights, or the exercise of the rights, of any state under international law with regards to freedom of the seas.

Article 3

Renunciation of Nuclear Explosive Devices

Each Party undertakes:

(a) Not to conduct research on, develop, manufacture, stockpile or otherwise acquire, possess or have control over any nuclear explosive device by any means anywhere;

(b) Not to seek or receive any assistance in the research on, development, manufacture, stockpiling or acquisition, or possession of any nuclear explosive device;

(c) Not to take any action to assist or encourage the research on, development, manufacture, stockpiling or acquisition, or possession of any nuclear explosive device.

Article 4

Prevention of Stationing of Nuclear Explosive Devices

1. Each Party undertakes to prohibit, in its territory, the stationing of any nuclear explosive device.

2. Without prejudice to the purposes and objectives of the treaty, each party in the exercise of its sovereign rights remains free to decide for itself whether to allow visits by foreign ships and aircraft to its ports and airfields, transit of its airspace by foreign aircraft, and navigation by foreign ships in its territorial sea or archipelagic waters in a manner not covered by the rights of innocent passage, archipelagic sea lane passage or transit passage of straits.

Article 5

Prohibition of testing of nuclear explosive devices

Each Party undertakes:

(a) Not to test any nuclear explosive device;

(b) To prohibit in its territory the testing of any nuclear explosive device;

(c) Not to assist or encourage the testing of any nuclear explosive device by any State anywhere.

Article 6

Declaration, Dismantling, Destruction or Conversion of Nuclear Explosive Devices and the Facilities for Their Manufacture

Each Party undertakes:

(a) To declare any capability for the manufacture of

nuclear explosive devices;

(b) To dismantle and destroy any nuclear explosive device that it has manufactured prior to the coming into force of this Treaty;

(c) To destroy facilities for the manufacture of nuclear explosive devices or, where possible, to convert them to peaceful uses;

(d) To permit the International Atomic Energy Agency (hereinafter referred to as IAEA) and the Commission established in Article 12 to verify the processes of dismantling and destruction of the nuclear explosive devices, as well as the destruction or conversion of the facilities for their production.

Article 7

Prohibition of Dumping of Radioactive Wastes

Each Party undertakes:

(a) To effectively implement or to use as guidelines the measures contained in the Bamako Convention on the Ban of the Import into Africa and Control of Transboundary Movement and Management of Hazardous wastes within Africa in so far as it is relevant to radioactive waste;

(b) Not to take any action to assist or encourage the dumping of radioactive wastes and other radioactive matter anywhere within the African nuclear-weapon-free zone.

Article 8

Peaceful Nuclear Activities

1. Nothing in this Treaty shall be interpreted as to prevent the use of nuclear science and technology for peaceful purposes.

2. As part of their efforts to strengthen their security, stability and development, the Parties undertake to promote individually and collectively the use of nuclear science and technology for economic and social development. To this end they undertake to establish and strengthen mechanisms for cooperation at the bilateral, subregional and regional levels.

3. Parties are encouraged to make use of the programme of assistance available in IAEA and, in this connection, to strengthen cooperation under the African Regional Cooperation Agreement for Research, Training and Development Related to Nuclear Science and Technology (hereinafter referred to as AFRA).

Article 9

Verification of Peaceful Uses

(a) To conduct all activities for the peaceful use of nuclear energy under strict non-proliferation measures to provide assurance of exclusively peaceful uses;

(b) To conclude a comprehensive safeguards agreement with IAEA for the purpose of verifying compliance with the undertakings in subparagraph (a) of this article;

(c) Not to provide source or special fissionable material, or equipment or material especially designed or prepared for the processing, use or production of special fissionable material for peaceful purposes to any non-nuclear-weapon State unless subject to a comprehensive safeguards agreement concluded with IAEA.

Article 10

Physical Protection of Nuclear Materials and Facilities

Each Party undertakes to maintain the highest standards of security and effective physical protection of nuclear materials, facilities and equipment to prevent theft or unauthorized use and handling. To that end each Party, *inter alia*, undertakes to apply measures of physical protection equivalent to those provided for in the Convention on Physical Protection of Nuclear Material and in recommendations and guidelines developed by IAEA for that purpose.

Article 11

Prohibition of Armed Attack on Nuclear Installations

Each Party undertakes not to take, or assist, or encourage any action aimed at an armed attack by conventional or other means against nuclear installations in the African nuclear-weapon-free zone.

Article 12

Mechanism for Compliance

1. For the purpose of ensuring compliance with their undertakings under this Treaty, the Parties agree to establish the African Commission on Nuclear Energy (hereafter referred to as the Commission) as set out in annex III.

2. The Commission shall be responsible *inter alia* for:

(a) Collating the reports and the exchange of information as provided for in Article 13;

(b) Arranging consultations as convening conferences of Parties on the concurrence of simple majority of State Parties on any matter arising from the implementation of the Treaty;

(c) Reviewing the application to peaceful nuclear activities of safeguards by IAEA as elaborated in Annex II;

(d) Bringing into effect the complaints procedure elaborated in Annex IV;

(e) Encouraging regional and sub-regional programmes for cooperation in the peaceful uses of nuclear science and technology;

(f) Promoting international cooperation with extra-zonal States for the peaceful uses of nuclear science and technology.

3. The Commission shall meet in ordinary session once a year, and may meet in extraordinary session as may be required by the complaints and settlement of disputes procedure in Annex IV.

Article 13

Report and Exchanges of Information

1. Each Party shall submit an annual report to the Commission on its nuclear activities as well as other matters relating to the Treaty, in accordance with the format for reporting to be developed by the Commission.

2. Each Party shall promptly report to the Commission any significant event affecting the implementation of the Treaty.

3. The Commission shall request the IAEA to provide it with an annual report on the activities of AFRA.

Article 14

Conference of Parties

1. A Conference of all Parties to the Treaty shall be convened by the Depositary as soon as possible after the entry into force of the Treaty to, *inter alia*, elect members of the Commission and determine its headquarters. Further conferences of States Parties shall be held as necessary. Further conferences of States Parties shall be held as necessary and at least every two years, and convened in accordance with Paragraph 2 (b) of Article 12.

Article 15

Interpretation of the Treaty

Any dispute arising out of the interpretation of the Treaty shall be settled by negotiation, by recourse to the Commission or another procedure agreed to by the Parties, which may include recourse to an arbitral panel or to the International Court of Justice.

Article 16

Reservations

This Treaty shall not be subject to reservations.

Article 17

Duration

This Treaty shall be of unlimited duration and shall remain in force indefinitely.

Article 18

Signature, Ratification and Entry into Force

1. This Treaty shall be open for signature by any States in the African nuclear-weapon-free zone. It shall be subject to ratification.

2. It shall enter into force on the date of deposit of the twenty-eight instrument of ratification.

3. For a signatory that ratifies Treaty after the date of the deposit of the twenty-eight instrument of ratification, it shall enter into force for that signatory on the date of deposit of its instrument of ratification.

Article 19

Amendments

1. Any amendments to the Treaty proposed by a Party shall be submitted to the Commission, which shall circulate it to all Parties.

2. Decision on the adoption of such an amendment shall be taken by a two-thirds majority of the Parties either through written communication to the Commission or through a conference of Parties convened upon the concurrence of a simple majority.

3. An amendment so adopted shall enter into force for all parties after receipt by the Depositary of the instrument of ratification by the majority of Parties.

Article 20

Withdrawal

1. Each Party shall, in exercising its national sovereignty, have the right to withdraw from this Treaty

if it decides that extraordinary events, related to the subject-matter of this Treaty, have jeopardized its supreme interests.

2. Withdrawal shall be affected by a Party giving notice, which included a statement of the extraordinary events it regards as having jeopardized its supreme interest, twelve months in advance to the Depositary. The Depositary shall circulate such notice to all other parties.

Article 21

Depositary Functions

1. This Treaty, of which the Arabic, English, French and Portuguese texts are equally authentic, shall be deposited with the Secretary-General of OAU, who is hereby designated as Depositary of the Treaty.

2. The Depositary shall:

(a) Receive instruments of ratification;

(b) Register this Treaty and its Protocols pursuant to Article 102 of the Charter of the United Nations;

(c) Transmit certified copies of the Treaty and its Protocols to all States in the African nuclear-weapon-free zone and to all States eligible to become party to the Protocols to the Treaty, and shall notify them of signatures and ratification of the Treaty and its Protocols.

Article 22

Status of the Annexes

The annexes from an integral part of this Treaty. Any reference to this Treaty includes the annexes.

General Framework Agreement for Peace in Bosnia and Herzegovina

Also known as: Dayton Peace Accords
Date of signature: December 14, 1995
Place of signature: Paris
Signatory states: Bosnia and Herzegovina, Croatia, Yugoslavia

[The signatories], hereinafter called the Parties, (the "Parties"),

Recognizing the need for a comprehensive settlement to bring an end to the conflict in the region,

Desiring to contribute toward that end to promote an enduring peace and stability,

Affirming their commitment to the Agreed Basic Principles issued on September 8, 1995, the Further Agreed Basic Principles issued on September 26, 1995, and the cease-fire agreements of September 14 and October 5, 1995,

Noting the agreement of August 29, 1995, which authorized the delegation of the Federal Republic of Yugoslavia to sign, on behalf of the Republika Srpska, the parts of the peace plan concerning it, with the obligation to implement the agreement that is reached strictly and consequently,

Have agreed as follows:

Article 1

The Parties shall conduct their relations in accordance with the principles set forth in the United Nation Charter, as well as the Helsinki Final Act and other documents of the Organization for Security and Cooperation in Europe. In particular, the Parties shall fully respect the sovereign equality of one another, shall settle disputes by peaceful means, and shall refrain from any action, by threat or use of force or otherwise, against the territorial integrity or political independence of Bosnia and Herzegovina or any other State.

Article 2

The Parties welcome and endorse the arrangements that have been made concerning the military aspects of the peace settlement and aspects of regional stabilization, as set forth in the Agreement at Annex 1-A and Annex 1-B. The Parties shall fully respect and promote fulfillment of the commitments made in Annex 1-A, and shall comply fully with their commitment as set forth in Annex 1-B.

Article 3

The Parties welcome and endorse the arrangement that have been made concerning the boundary demarcation between the two Entities, the Federation of

Bosnia and Herzegovina and Republika Srpska, as set forth in the Agreement at Annex 2. The Parties shall fully respect and promote fulfillment of the commitments made therein.

Article 4

The Parties welcome and endorse elections program for Bosnia and Herzegovina as set forth in Annex 3. The Parties shall fully respect and promote fulfillment of that program.

Article 5

The Parties welcome and endorse the arrangement that have been made concerning the Constitution of Bosnia and Herzegovina, as set forth in Annex 4. The Parties shall fully respect and promote fulfillment of the commitments made therein.

Article 6

The Parties welcome and endorse the arrangement that have been made concerning the establishment of an arbitration tribunal, a Commission on Human Right, a Commission on Refugees and Displaced Persons, a Commission to Preserve National Monuments, and Bosnia and Herzegovina Public Corporations, as set forth in the Agreement at Annexes 5-9. The Parties shall fully respect and promote fulfillment of the commitments made therein.

Article 7

Recognizing that the observance of human rights and the protection of refugees and displaced persons are of vital importance in achieving a lasting peace, the Parties agree to and shall comply fully with the provision concerning human right set forth in Chapter One of the Agreement at Annex 6, as set forth in Chapter One of the Agreement at Annex 7.

Article 8

The Parties welcome and endorse the arrangement that have been made concerning the implementation of this peace settlement, including in particular those pertaining to the civilian (non-military) implementation, as set forth in the Agreement at Annex 10, and the international police task force, as set forth in the Agreement at Annex 11. The Parties shall fully respect and promote fulfillment of the commitments made therein.

Article 9

The Parties shall cooperate fully with all entities involved in implementation of this peace settlement, as described in the Annexes to this Agreement, or which are otherwise authorized by the United Nations Security Council, pursuant to the obligation of all Parties to cooperate in the investigation and prosecution, of war crimes and other violations of international humanitarian law.

Article 10

The Federal Republic of Yugoslavia and Republic of Bosnia and Herzegovina recognize each other as sovereign independent State within their international borders. Further aspects of their mutual recognition will be subject to subsequent discussions.

Article 11

This Agreement shall enter into force upon signature.

Treaty on the Southeast Asia Nuclear-Weapon-Free Zone

Date of signature: December 15, 1995
Place of signature: Bangkok
Signatory state: Brunei Darussalam, Cambodia, Indonesia, Laos, Malaysia, Myanmar, Philippines, Singapore, Thailand, Vietnam

The States Parties to this Treaty:

DESIRING to contribute to the realization of the purposes and principles of the Charter of the United Nations;

DETERMINED to take concrete action which will contribute to the progress towards general and complete disarmament of nuclear weapons, and to promotion of international peace and security;

REAFFIRMING the desire of the Southeast Asian States to maintain peace and stability in the region in the spirit of peaceful coexistence and mutual understanding and cooperation as enunciated in various communiques, declarations and other legal instruments;

RECALLING the Declaration on the Zone of Peace, Freedom and Neutrality (ZOPFAN) signed in Kuala Lumpur on 27 November 1971 and the Programme of Action on ZOPFAN adopted at the 26th ASEAN Ministerial Meeting in Singapore in July 1993;

CONVINCED that the establishment of a Southeast Asia Nuclear Weapon-Free Zone, as an essential component of the ZOPFAN will contribute towards strengthening the security of States within the Zone and towards enhancing international peace and security as a whole;

REAFFIRMING the importance of the Treaty on the Non-Proliferation of Nuclear Weapons (NPT) in preventing the proliferation of nuclear weapons and in contributing towards international peace and security;

RECALLING Article VII of the NPT which recognizes the right of any group of States to conclude regional treaties in order to assure the total absence of nuclear weapons in their respective territories;

RECALLING the Final Document of the Tenth Special Session of the United Nations General Assembly which encourages the establishment of nuclear weapon-free zones;

RECALLING the Principles and Objectives for Nuclear Non-Proliferation and Disarmament, adopted at the 1995 Review and Extension Conference of the Parties to the NPT, that the cooperation of all the nuclear-weapon States and their respect and support for the relevant protocols is important for the maximum effectiveness of this nuclear weapon-free zone treaty and its relevant protocols,

DETERMINED to protect the region from environmental pollution and the hazards posed by radioactive wastes and other radioactive material;

HAVE AGREED as follows:

Article 1

Use of Terms

For the purposes of this Treaty and its Protocol:

(a) "Southeast Asia Nuclear Weapon-Free Zone", hereinafter referred to as the "Zone", means the area comprising the territories of all States in Southeast Asia, namely, Brunei Darussalam, Cambodia, Indonesia, Laos, Malaysia, Myanmar, Philippines, Singapore, Thailand and Vietnam, and their respective continental shelves and Exclusive Economic Zones (EEZ);

(b) "territory" means the land territory, internal waters, territorial sea, archipelagic waters, the seabed and the sub-soil thereof and the airspace above them;

(c) "nuclear weapon" means any explosive device capable of releasing nuclear energy in an uncontrolled manner but does not include the means of transport or delivery of such device if separable from and not an indivisible part thereof;

(d) "station" means to deploy, emplace, implant, install, stockpile or store;

(e) "radioactive material" means material that contains radionuclides above clearance or exemption levels recommended by the International Atomic Energy Agency (IAEA);

(f) "radioactive wastes" means material that contains or is contaminated with radionuclides at concentrations or activities greater than clearance levels recommended by the IAEA and for which no use is foreseen; and

(g) "dumping" means

(i) any deliberate disposal at sea, including seabed and subsoil insertion, of radioactive wastes or other matter from vessels, aircraft, platforms or other man-made structures at sea, and

(ii) any deliberate disposal at sea, including seabed and subsoil insertion, of vessels, aircraft, platforms or other man-made structures at sea, containing radioactive material,

but does not include the disposal of wastes or other matter incidental to, or derived from the normal operations of vessels, aircraft, platforms or other man-made structures at sea and their equipment, other than wastes or other matter transported by or to vessels, aircraft, platforms or other man-made structures at sea, operating for the purpose of disposal of such matter or derived from the treatment of such wastes or other matter on such vessels, aircraft, platforms or structures.

Article 2

Application of the Treaty

1. This Treaty and its Protocol shall apply to the territories, continental shelves, and EEZ of the States Parties within the Zone in which this Treaty is on force.

2. Nothing in this Treaty shall prejudice the rights or the exercise of these rights by any State under the

provisions of the United Nations Convention on the Law of the Sea of 1982, in particular with regard to freedom of the high seas, rights of innocent passage, archipelagic sea lanes passage or transit passage of ships and aircraft, and consistent with the Charter of the United Nations.

Article 3

Basic Undertakings

1. Each State Party undertakes not to, anywhere inside or outside the Zone:

   (a) develop, manufacture or otherwise acquire, possess or have control over nuclear weapons;

   (b) station or transport nuclear weapons by any means; or

   (c) test or use nuclear weapons.

2. Each State Party also undertakes not to allow, in its territory, any other State to:

   (a) develop, manufacture or otherwise acquire, possess or have control over nuclear weapons;

   (b) station nuclear weapons; or

   (c) test or use nuclear weapons.

3. Each State Party also undertakes not to:

   (a) dump at sea or discharge into the atmosphere anywhere within the Zone any radioactive material or wastes;

   (b) dispose radioactive material or wastes on land in the territory of or under the jurisdiction of other States except as stipulated in Paragraph 2(e) of Article 4; or

   (c) allow, within its territory, any other State to dump at sea or discharge into the atmosphere any redioactive material or wastes.

4. Each State Party undertakes not to:

   (a) seek or receive any assistance in the commission of any act in violation of the provisions of Paragraph 1, 2 and 3 of this Article; or

   (b) take any action to assist or encourage the commission of any act in violation of the provisions of Paragraphs 1, 2 and 3 of this Article.

Article 4

Use of Nuclear Energy for Peaceful Purpose

1. Nothing in this Treaty shall prejudice the right of the States Parties to use nuclear energy, in particular for their economic development and social progress.

2. Each State Party therefore undertakes:

   (a) to use exclusively for peaceful purpose nuclear material and facilities which are within its territory and areas under its jurisdiction and control;

   (b) prior to embarking on its peaceful nuclear energy programme, to subject its programme to rigorous nuclear safety assessment conforming to guidelines and standards recommended by the IAEA for the protection of health and minimization of danger to life and property in accordance with Paragraph 6 of Article III of the Statute of the IAEA;

   (c) upon request, to make available to another State Party the assessment except information relating to person data, information protected by intellectual property rights or by industrial or commercial confidentiality and information relating to national security;

   (d) to support the continued effectiveness of the international non-proliferation system based on the Treaty on the Non-Proliferation of Nuclear Weapon (NPT) and the IAEA safeguards system; and

   (e) to dispose radioactive wastes and other radioactive material in accordance with IAEA standards and procedures on land within its territory or on land within the territory of another State which has consented to such disposal.

3. Each State Party further undertakes not to provide source or special fissionable material, or equipment or material especially designed or prepared for the processing, use or production of special fissionable material to:

   (a) any non-nuclear-weapon State except under conditions subject to the safeguards required by Paragraph 1 of Article III of the NPT; or

   (b) any nuclear-weapon State except in conformity with applicable safeguards agreements with the IAEA.

Article 5

IAEA Safeguards

Each State Party which has not done so shall conclude an agreement with the IAEA for the application of full scope safeguards to its peaceful nuclear activities not later than eighteen months after the entry into force for that State Party of this Treaty.

Article 6

Early Notification of a Nuclear Accident

Each State Party which has not acceded to the Convention on Early Notification of a Nuclear Accident shall endeavour to do so.

Article 7

Foreign Ships and Aircraft

Each State Party, on being notified, may decide for itself whether to allow visits by foreign ships and aircraft to its ports and airfields, transit of its airspace by foreign aircraft, and navigation by foreign ships through its territorial sea or archipelagic waters and overflight of foreign aircraft above those waters in a manner not governed by the rights of innocent passage, archipelagic sea lanes passage or transit passage.

Article 8

Establishment of the Commission for the Southeast Asia Nuclear Weapon-Free Zone

1. There is hereby established a Commission for the Southeast Asia Nuclear Weapon-Free Zone, hereinafter referred to as the "Commission".

2. All States Parties are ipso facto members of the Commission. Each State Party shall be represented by its Foreign Minister or his representative accompanied by alternates and advisers.

3. The function of the Commission shall be to oversee the implementation of this Treaty and ensure compliance with its provisions.

4. The Commission shall meet as and when necessary in accordance with the provisions of this Treaty including upon the request of any State Party. As far as possible, the Commission shall meet in conjunction with the ASEAN Ministerial Meeting.

5. At the beginning of each meeting, the Commission shall elect its Chairman and such other officers as may be required. They shall hold office until a new Chairman and other officers are elected at the next meeting.

6. Unless otherwise provided for in this Treaty, two-thirds of the members of the Commission shall be present to constitute a quorum.

7. Each member of the Commission shall have one vote.

8. Except as provided for in this Treaty, decisions of the Commission shall be taken by consensus or, failing consensus, by a two-thirds majority of the members present and voting.

9. The Commission shall, by consensus, agree upon and adopt rules of procedure for itself as well as financial rules governing its funding and that of its subsidiary organs.

Article 9

The Executive Committee

1. There is hereby established, as a subsidiary organ of the Commission, the Executive Committee.

2. The Executive Committee shall be composed of all States Parties to this Treaty. Each State Party shall be represented by one senior official as its representative, who may be accompanied by alternates and advisers.

3. The functions of the Executive Committee shall be to:

    (a) ensure the proper operation of verification measures in accordance with the provisions on the Control System as stipulated in Article 10;

    (b) consider and decide on requests for clarification and for a fact-finding mission;

    (c) set up a fact-finding mission in accordance with the Annex of this Treaty;

    (d) consider and decide on the findings of a fact-finding mission and report to the Commission;

    (e) request the Commission to convene a meeting when appropriate and necessary;

    (f) conclude such agreements with the IAEA or other international organizations as referred to in Article 18 on behalf of the Commission after being duly authorized to do so by the Commission; and

    (g) carry out such other tasks as may, from time to time, be assigned by the Commission.

4. The Executive Committee shall meet as and when necessary for the efficient exercise of its functions. As far as possible, the Executive Committee shall meet in conjunction with the ASEAN Senior officials Meeting.

5. The Chairman of the Executive Committee shall be the representative of the Chairman of the Com-

mission. Any submission or communication made by a State Party to the Chairman of the Executive Committee shall be disseminated to the other members of the Executive Committee.

6. Two-thirds of the members of the Executive Committee shall be present to constitute a quorum.

7. Each member of the Executive Committee shall have one vote.

8. Decisions of the Executive Committee shall be taken by consensus or, failing consensus, by a two-thirds majority of the members present and voting.

Article 10

Control System

1. There is hereby established a control system for the purpose of verifying compliance with the obligations of the States Parties under this Treaty.

2. The Control System shall comprise:

   (a) the IAEA safeguards system as provided for in Article 5;

   (b) report and exchange of information as provided for in Article 11;

   (c) request for clarification as provided for in Article 12; and

   (d) request and procedures for a fact-finding mission as provided for in Article 13.

Article 11

Report and Exchange of Information

1. Each State Party shall submit reports to the Executive Committee on any significant event within its territory and areas under its jurisdiction and control affecting the implementation of this Treaty.

2. The States Parties may exchange information on matters arising under or in relation to this Treaty.

Article 12

Request for Clarification

1. Each State Party has the right to request another State Party for clarification concerning any situations which may be considered ambiguous or which may give rise to doubts about the compliance of that State Party with this Treaty. It shall inform the Executive Committee of such a request. The requested State Party shall duly respond by

providing without delay the necessary information and inform the Executive Committee of its reply to the requesting State Party.

2. Each State Party shall have the right to request the Executive Committee to seek clarification from another State Party concerning any situation which may be considered ambiguous or which may give rise to doubts about compliance of that state Party with this Treaty. Upon receipt of such a request, the Executive Committee shall consult the State Party from which clarification is sought for the purpose of obtaining the clarification requested.

Article 13

Request for a Fact-Finding Mission

A State party shall have the right to request the Executive Committee to send a fact-finding mission to another State Party in order to clarify and resolve a situation which may be considered ambiguous or which may give rise to doubts about compliance with the provisions of this Treaty, in accordance with the procedure contained in the Annex to this Treaty.

Article 14

Remedial Measures

1. In case the Executive Committee decides in accordance with the Annex that there is a breach of this Treaty by a State Party, that State Party shall, within a reasonable time, take all steps necessary to bring itself in full compliance with this Treaty and shall promptly inform the Executive Committee of the action taken or proposed to be taken by it.

2. Where a State Party fails or refuses to comply with the provisions of paragraph 1 of this Article, the Executive Committee shall request the Commission to convene a meeting in accordance with the provisions of paragraph 3(e) of Article 9.

3. At the meeting convened pursuant to Paragraph 2 of this Article, the commission shall consider the emergent situation and shall decide on any measure it deems appropriate to cope with the situation, including the submission of the matter to the IAEA and, where the situation might endanger international peace and security, the Security Council and the General Assembly of the United Nations.

4. In the event of breach of the Protocol attached to this Treaty by State Party to the Protocol, the

Executive Committee shall convene a special meeting of the Commission to decide on, appropriate measures to be taken.

Article 15

Signature, Ratification, Accession, Deposit and Registration

1. This Treaty shall be open for signature by all States in Southeast Asia, namely, Brunei Darussalam, Cambodia, Indonesia, Laos, Malaysia, Myanmar, Philippines, Singapore, Thailand and Vietnam.

2. This Treaty shall be subject to ratification in accordance with the constitutional procedure of the signatory States. The instruments of ratification shall be deposited with the Government of the Kingdom of Thailand which is hereby designated as the Depositary State.

3. This Treaty shall be open for accession. The instruments of accession shall be deposited with the Depositary State.

4. The Depositary State shall inform the other States Parties to this Treaty on the deposit of instruments of ratification or accession.

5. The Depositary State shall register this Treaty and its Protocol pursuant to Article 102 of the Charter of the United Nations.

Article 16

Entry into Force

1. This Treaty shall enter into force on the date of the deposit of the seventh instrument of ratification and/or accession.

2. For States which ratify or accede to this Treaty after the date of this seventh instrument of ratification or accession, this Treaty shall enter into force on the date of deposit of its instrument of ratification or accession.

Article 17

Reservations

This Treaty shall not be subject to reservations.

Article 18

Relations with Other International Organizations

The Commission may conclude such agreements with the IAEA or other international organization as it considers likely to facilitate the efficient operation of the Control System established by this Treaty.

Article 19

Amendments

1. Any States Party may propose amendments to this Treaty and its Protocol and shall submit its proposals to the Executive Committee, which shall transmit them to all the other States Parties. The Executive Committee shall immediately request the Commission to convene a meeting to examine the proposed amendments. The quorum required for such a meeting shall be all the members of the Commission. Any amendment shall be adopted by a consensus decision of the Commission.

2. Amendments adopted shall enter into force 30 days after the receipt by the Depositary State of the seventh instrument of acceptance from the States Parties.

Article 20

Review

Ten years after this Treaty enters into force, a meeting of the Commission shall be convened for the purpose of reviewing the operation of this Treaty. A meeting of the Commission for the same purpose may also be convened at anytime thereafter if there is consensus among all its members.

Article 21

Settlement of Disputes

Any dispute arising from the interpretation of the provisions of this Treaty shall be settled by peaceful means as may be agreed upon by the States Parties to the dispute. If within one month, the parties to the dispute are unable to achieve a peaceful settlement of the dispute by negotiation, mediation, enquiry or conciliation, any of the parties concerned shall, with the prior consent of the other parties concerned, refer the dispute to arbitration or to the International Court of Justice.

Article 22

Duration and Withdrawal

1. This Treaty shall remain in force indefinitely.

2. In the event of a breach by any State Party of this Treaty essential to the achievement of the objectives of this Treaty, every other State Party shall

have the right to withdraw from this Treaty.

3. Withdrawal under Paragraph 2 of Article 22, shall be effected by giving notice twelve months in advance to the members of the Commission.

Annex

Procedure for a Fact-Finding Mission

1. The State Party requesting a fact-finding mission as provided in Article 13, hereinafter referred to as the "requesting State", shall submit the request to the Executive Committee specifying the following:

(a) the doubts or concerns and the reasons for such doubts or concerns;

(b) the location in which the situation which gives rise to doubts has allegedly occurred;

(c) the relevant provisions of this Treaty about which doubts of compliance have arisen; and

(d) any other relevant information.

2. Upon receipt of a request for a fact-finding mission, the Executive Committee shall:

(a) immediately inform the State Party to which the fact-finding mission is requested to be sent, hereinafter referred to as the "receiving State", about the receipt of the request; and

(b) not later than 3 weeks after receiving the request, decide if the request complies with the provisions of paragraph 1 and whether or not it is frivolous, abusive or clearly beyond the scope of this Treaty. Neither the requesting nor receiving State Party shall participate in such decisions.

3. In case the Executive Committee decides that the request does not comply with the provisions of Paragraph 1, or that it is frivolous, abusive or clearly beyond the scope of this Treaty, it shall take no further action on the request and inform the requesting State and the receiving State accordingly.

4. In the event that the Executive Committee decides that the request complies with the provisions of paragraph 1, and that it is not frivolous, abusive or clearly beyond the scope of this Treaty, it shall immediately forward the request for a fact-finding mission to the receiving State, indicating, inter alia, the proposed date for sending the mission. The proposed date shall not be later than 3 weeks from the time the receiving State receives the request for a fact-finding mission. The Executive

Committee shall also immediately set up a fact-finding mission consisting of 3 inspectors from the IAEA who are neither nationals of the requesting nor receiving State.

5. The receiving State shall comply with the request for a fact-finding mission referred to in Paragraph 4. It shall cooperate with the Executive Committee in order to facilitate the effective functioning of the fact-finding mission, inter alia, by promptly providing unimpeded access of the fact-finding mission to the location in question. The receiving State shall accord to the members of the fact-finding mission such privileges and immunities as are necessary for them to exercise their functions effectively, including inviolability of all papers and documents and immunity from arrest, detention and legal process for acts done and words spoken for the purpose of the mission.

6. The receiving State shall have the right to take measures to protect sensitive installations and to prevent disclosures of confidential information and data not related to this Treaty.

7. The fact-finding mission, in the discharge of its functions, shall;

(a) respect the laws and regulations of the receiving State;

(b) refrain from activities inconsistent with the objectives and purposes of this Treaty;

(c) submit preliminary or interim reports to the Executive Committee; and

(d) complete its task without undue delay and shall submit its final report to the Executive Committee within a reasonable time upon completion of its work.

8. The Executive Committee shall:

(a) consider the reports submitted by the fact-finding mission and reach a decision on whether or not there is a breach of this Treaty;

(b) immediately communicate its decision to the requesting State and the receiving State; and

(c) present a full report on its decision to the Commission.

9. In the event that the receiving State refuses to comply with the request for a fact-finding mission in accordance with Paragraph 4, the requesting State through the Executive Committee shall have the right to request for a meeting of the Commis-

sion. The Executive Committee shall immediately request the Commission to convene a meeting in accordance with Paragraph 3(e) of Article 9.

Protocol to the Treaty on Southeast Asia Nuclear Weapon-Free Zone

The States Parties to this Protocol,

DESIRING to contribute to efforts towards achieving general and complete disarmament of nuclear weapons, and thereby ensuring international peace and security, including in Southeast Asia;

NOTING the Treaty on the Southeast Asia Nuclear Weapon-Free Zone, signed at Bangkok on the fifteenth day of december, one thousand nine hundred and ninety-five;

HAVE AGREED as follows:

Article 1

Each State Party undertakes to respect the Treaty on the Southeast Asia Nuclear Weapon-Free Zone, hereinafter referred to as the "Treaty", and not to contribute to any act which constitutes a violation of the Treaty or its Protocol by States Parties to them.

Article 2

Each State Party undertakes not to use or threaten to use nuclear weapons against any States Party to the Treaty. It further undertakes not to use or threaten to use nuclear weapons within the Southeast Asia Nuclear Weapon-Free Zone.

Article 3

This Protocol shall be open for signature by the People's Republic of China, the French Republic, the Russian Federation, the United Kingdom of Great Britain and Northern Ireland and the United States of America.

Article 4

Each State Party undertakes, by written notification to the Depositary State, to indicate its acceptance or otherwise of any alteration to its obligation under this Protocol that may be brought by the entry into force of an amendment to the Treaty pursuant to Article 19 thereof.

Article 5

This Protocol is of a permanent nature and shall remain in force indefinitely, provided that each State Party shall, in exercising its national sovereignty, have the right to withdraw from this Protocol if it decides that extraordinary events, related to the subject-matter of this Protocol, have jeopardized its supreme national interest. It shall give notice of such withdrawal to the Depositary State twelve months in advance. Such notice shall include a statement of the extraordinary events it regards as having jeopardized its supreme national interest.

Article 6

This Protocol shall be subject to ratification.

Article 7

This Protocol shall enter into force for each State Party on the date of its deposit of its instrument of ratification with the Depositary State. The Depositary State shall inform the other States Parties to the Treaty and to this Protocol on the deposit of instruments of ratification.

Protocol on Prohibitions or Restrictions on the Use of Mines, Booby-Traps and Other Devices as Amended on 3 May 1996 (Protocol II as Amended on 3 May 1996) Annexed to the Convention on Prohibitions or Restrictions on the Use of Certain Conventional Weapons Which May be Deemed to be Excessively Injurious or to Have Indiscriminate Effects

Date of signature: May 3, 1996
Place of signature: Geneva
Signatory states: Argentina, Australia, Austria, Bulgaria, Cambodia, Canada, Cape Verde, China, Costa Rica, Czech Republic, Denmark, Finland, France, Germany, Greece, Hungary, Ireland, Italy, Japan, Liechtenstein, Lithuania, Monaco, New Zealand, Norway, Peru, Philippines, south Africa,

Spain, Sweden, Switzerland, United Kingdom, Uruguay
Date of entry into force: *December 3, 1998*

Article 1: Amended Protocol

The Protocol on Prohibitions or Restrictions on the Use of Mines, Booby-traps and Other Devices (Protocol II), annexed to the Convention on Prohibitions or Restrictions on the Use of Certain Conventional Weapons Which May Be Deemed to Be Excessively Injurious or to Have Indiscriminate Effects ("the Convention") is hereby amended. The text of the Protocol as amended shall read as follows:

"Protocol on Prohibitions or Restrictions on the Use of Mines, Booby-Traps and Other Devices as Amended on 3 May 1996
(Protocol II as amended on 3 May 1996)

Article 1

Scope of Application

1. This Protocol relates to the use on land of the mines, booby-traps and other devices, defined herein, including mines laid to interdict beaches, waterway crossings or river crossings, but does not apply to the use of anti-ship mines at sea or in inland waterways.

2. This Protocol shall apply, in addition to situations referred to in Article 1 of this Convention, to situations referred to in Article 3 common to the Geneva Conventions of 12 August 1949. This Protocol shall not apply to situations of internal disturbances and tensions, such as riots, isolated and sporadic acts of violence and other acts of a similar nature, as not being armed conflicts.

3. In case of armed conflicts not of an international character occurring in the territory of one of the High Contracting Parties, each party to the conflict shall be bound to apply the prohibitions and restrictions of this Protocol.

4. Nothing in this Protocol shall be invoked for the purpose of affecting the sovereignty of a State or the responsibility of the Government, by all legitimate means, to maintain or re-establish law and order in the State or to defend the national unity and territorial integrity of the State.

5. Nothing in this Protocol shall be invoked as a justification for intervening, directly or indirectly, for any reason whatever, in the armed conflict or in the internal or external affairs of the High Contracting Party in the territory of which that conflict occurs.

6. The application of the provisions of this Protocol to parties to a conflict, which are not High Contracting Parties that have accepted this Protocol, shall not change their legal status or the legal status of a disputed territory, either explicitly or implicitly.

Article 2

Definitions

For the purpose of this Protocol:

1. "Mine" means a munition placed under, on or near the ground or other surface area and designed to be exploded by the presence, proximity or contact of a person or vehicle.

2. "Remotely-delivered mine" means a mine not directly emplaced but delivered by artillery, missile, rocket, mortar, or similar means, or dropped from an aircraft. Mines delivered from a land-based system from less than 500 metres are not considered to be "remotely delivered", provided that they are used in accordance with Article 5 and other relevant Articles of this Protocol.

3. "Anti-personnel mine" means a mine primarily designed to be exploded by the presence, proximity or contact of a person and that will incapacitate, injure or kill one or more persons.

4. "Booby-trap" means any device or material which is designed, constructed, or adapted to kill or injure, and which functions unexpectedly when a person disturbs or approaches an apparently harmless object or performs an apparently safe act.

5. "Other devices" means manually-emplaced munitions and devices including improvised explosive devices designed to kill, injure or damage and which are actuated manually, by remote control or automatically after a lapse of time.

6. "Military objective" means, so far as objects are concerned, any object which by its nature, location, purpose or use makes an effective contribution to military action and whose total or partial destruction, capture or neutralization, in the circumstances ruling at the time, offers a definite military advantage.

7. "Civilian objects" are all objects which are not military objectives as defined in paragraph 6 of this Article.

8. "Minefield" is a defined area in which mines have been emplaced and "mined area" is an area which is dangerous due to the presence of mines. "Phoney minefield" means an area free of mines that simulates a minefield. The term "minefield" includes phoney minefields.

9. "Recording" means a physical, administrative

and technical operation designed to obtain, for the purpose of registration in official records, all available information facilitating the location of minefields, mined areas, mines, booby-traps and other devices.

10. "Self-destruction mechanism" means an incorporated or externally attached automatically-functioning mechanism which secures the destruction of the munition into which it is incorporated or to which it is attached.

11. "Self-neutralization mechanism" means an incorporated automatically-functioning mechanism which renders inoperable the munition into which it is incorporated.

12. "Self-deactivating" means automatically rendering a munition inoperable by means of the irreversible exhaustion of a component, for example, a battery, that is essential to the operation of the munition.

13. "Remote control" means control by commands from a distance.

14. "Anti-handling device" means a device intended to protect a mine and which is part of, linked to, attached to or placed under the mine and which activates when an attempt is made to tamper with the mine.

15. "Transfer" involves, in addition to the physical movement of mines into or from national territory, the transfer of title to and control over the mines, but does not involve the transfer of territory containing emplaced mines.

Article 3

General Restrictions on the Use of Mines, Booby-traps and Other Devices

1. This Article applies to:

(a) mines;
(b) booby-traps; and
(c) other devices.

2. Each High Contracting Party or party to a conflict is, in accordance with the provisions of this Protocol, responsible for all mines, booby-traps, and other devices employed by it and undertakes to clear, remove, destroy or maintain them as specified in Article 10 of this Protocol.

3. It is prohibited in all circumstances to use any mine, booby-trap or other device which is designed or of a nature to cause superfluous injury or unnecessary suffering.

4. Weapons to which this Article applies shall strictly comply with the standards and limitations specified in the Technical Annex with respect to each particular category.

5. It is prohibited to use mines, booby-traps or other devices which employ a mechanism or device specifically designed to detonate the munition by the presence of commonly available mine detectors as a result of their magnetic or other non-contact influence during normal use in detection operations.

6. It is prohibited to use a self-deactivating mine equipped with an anti-handling device that is designed in such a manner that the anti-handling device is capable of functioning after the mine has ceased to be capable of functioning.

7. It is prohibited in all circumstances to direct weapons to which this Article applies, either in offence, defence or by way of reprisals, against the civilian population as such or against individual civilians or civilian objects.

8. The indiscriminate use of weapons to which this Article applies is prohibited. Indiscriminate use is any placement of such weapons:

(a) which is not on, or directed against, a military objective. In case of doubt as to whether an object which is normally dedicated to civilian purposes, such as a place of worship, a house or other dwelling or a school, is being used to make an effective contribution to military action, it shall be presumed not to be so used;

(b) which employs a method or means of delivery which cannot be directed at a specific military objective; or

(c) which may be expected to cause incidental loss of civilian life, injury to civilians, damage to civilian objects, or a combination thereof, which would be excessive in relation to the concrete and direct military advantage anticipated.

9. Several clearly separated and distinct military objectives located in a city, town, village or other area containing a similar concentration of civilians or civilian objects are not to be treated as a single military objective.

10. All feasible precautions shall be taken to protect civilians from the effects of weapons to which this Article applies. Feasible precautions are those precautions which are practicable or practically possible taking into account all circumstances ruling at the time, including humanitarian and military considerations. These circumstances include, but are not limited to:

(a) the short- and long-term effect of mines upon the local civilian population for the duration of the minefield;

(b) possible measures to protect civilians (for example, fencing, signs, warning and monitoring);

(c) the availability and feasibility of using alternatives; and

(d) the short- and long-term military requirements for a minefield.

11. Effective advance warning shall be given of any emplacement of mines, booby-traps and other devices which may affect the civilian population, unless circumstances do not permit.

Article 4

Restrictions on the Use of Anti-personnel Mines

It is prohibited to use anti-personnel mines which are not detectable, as specified in paragraph 2 of the Technical Annex.

Article 5

Restrictions on the Use of Anti-personnel Mines Other than Remotely-delivered Mines

1. This Article applies to anti-personnel mines other than remotely-delivered mines.

2. It is prohibited to use weapons to which this Article applies which are not in compliance with the provisions on self-destruction and self-deactivation in the Technical Annex, unless:

(a) such weapons are placed within a perimeter-marked area which is monitored by military personnel and protected by fencing or other means, to ensure the effective exclusion of civilians from the area. The marking must be of a distinct and durable character and must at least be visible to a person who is about to enter the perimeter-marked area; and

(b) such weapons are cleared before the area is abandoned, unless the area is turned over to the forces of another State which accept responsibility for the maintenance of the protections required by this Article and the subsequent clearance of those weapons.

3. A party to a conflict is relieved from further compliance with the provisions of sub-paragraphs 2 (a) and 2 (b) of this Article only if such compliance is not feasible due to forcible loss of control of the area as a result of enemy military action, including situations where direct enemy military action makes it impossible to comply. If that party regains control of the area, it shall resume compliance with the provisions of sub-paragraphs 2 (a) and 2 (b) of this Article.

4. If the forces of a party to a conflict gain control of an area in which weapons to which this Article applies have been laid, such forces shall, to the maximum extent feasible, maintain and, if necessary, establish the protections required by this Article until such weapons have been cleared.

5. All feasible measures shall be taken to prevent the unauthorized removal, defacement, destruction or concealment of any device, system or material used to establish the perimeter of a perimeter-marked area.

6. Weapons to which this Article applies which propel fragments in a horizontal arc of less than 90 degrees and which are placed on or above the ground may be used without the measures provided for in sub-paragraph 2 (a) of this Article for a maximum period of 72 hours, if:

(a) they are located in immediate proximity to the military unit that emplaced them; and

(b) the area is monitored by military personnel to ensure the effective exclusion of civilians.

Article 6

Restrictions on the Use of Remotely-delivered Mines

1. It is prohibited to use remotely-delivered mines unless they are recorded in accordance with sub-paragraph 1 (b) of the Technical Annex.

2. It is prohibited to use remotely-delivered anti-personnel mines which are not in compliance with the provisions on self-destruction and self-deactivation in the Technical Annex.

3. It is prohibited to use remotely-delivered mines other than anti-personnel mines, unless, to the extent feasible, they are equipped with an effective self-destruction or self-neutralization mechanism and have a back-up self-deactivation feature, which is designed so that the mine will no longer function as a mine when the mine no longer serves the military purpose for which it was placed in position.

4. Effective advance warning shall be given of any delivery or dropping of remotely-delivered mines which may affect the civilian population, unless circumstances do not permit.

Article 7

Prohibitions on the Use of Booby-traps and Other Devices

1. Without prejudice to the rules of international law applicable in armed conflict relating to treachery and perfidy, it is prohibited in all circumstances to use booby-traps and other devices which are in any way attached to or associated with:

(a) internationally recognized protective emblems, signs or signals;

(b) sick, wounded or dead persons;

(c) burial or cremation sites or graves;

(d) medical facilities, medical equipment, medical supplies or medical transportation;

(e) children's toys or other portable objects or products specially designed for the feeding, health, hygiene, clothing or education of children;

(f) food or drink;

(g) kitchen utensils or appliances except in military establishments, military locations or military supply depots;

(h) objects clearly of a religious nature;

(i) historic monuments, works of art or places of worship which constitute the cultural or spiritual heritage of peoples; or

(j) animals or their carcasses.

2. It is prohibited to use booby-traps or other devices in the form of apparently harmless portable objects which are specifically designed and constructed to contain explosive material.

3. Without prejudice to the provisions of Article 3, it is prohibited to use weapons to which this Article applies in any city, town, village or other area containing a similar concentration of civilians in which combat between ground forces is not taking place or does not appear to be imminent, unless either:

(a) they are placed on or in the close vicinity of a military objective; or

(b) measures are taken to protect civilians from their effects, for example, the posting of warning sentries, the issuing of warnings or the provision of fences.

Article 8

Transfers

1. In order to promote the purposes of this Protocol, each High Contracting Party:

(a) undertakes not to transfer any mine the use of which is prohibited by this Protocol;

(b) undertakes not to transfer any mine to any recipient other than a State or a State agency authorized to receive such transfers;

(c) undertakes to exercise restraint in the transfer of any mine the use of which is restricted by this Protocol. In particular, each High Contracting Party undertakes not to transfer any anti-personnel mines to States which are not bound by this Protocol, unless the recipient State agrees to apply this Protocol; and

(d) undertakes to ensure that any transfer in accordance with this Article takes place in full compliance, by both the transferring and the recipient State, with the relevant provisions of this Protocol and the applicable norms of international humanitarian law.

2. In the event that a High Contracting Party declares that it will defer compliance with specific provisions on the use of certain mines, as provided for in the Technical Annex, sub-paragraph 1 (a) of this Article shall however apply to such mines.

3. All High Contracting Parties, pending the entry into force of this Protocol, will refrain from any actions which would be inconsistent with sub-paragraph 1 (a) of this Article.

Article 9

Recording and Use of Information on Minefields, Mined Areas, Mines, Booby-traps and Other Devices

1. All information concerning minefields, mined areas, mines, booby-traps and other devices shall be recorded in accordance with the provisions of the Technical Annex.

2. All such records shall be retained by the parties to a conflict, who shall, without delay after the cessation of active hostilities, take all necessary and appropriate measures, including the use of such information, to protect civilians from the effects of

minefields, mined areas, mines, booby-traps and other devices in areas under their control.

At the same time, they shall also make available to the other party or parties to the conflict and to the Secretary-General of the United Nations all such information in their possession concerning minefields, mined areas, mines, booby-traps and other devices laid by them in areas no longer under their control; provided, however, subject to reciprocity, where the forces of a party to a conflict are in the territory of an adverse party, either party may withhold such information from the Secretary-General and the other party, to the extent that security interests require such withholding, until neither party is in the territory of the other. In the latter case, the information withheld shall be disclosed as soon as those security interests permit. Wherever possible, the parties to the conflict shall seek, by mutual agreement, to provide for the release of such information at the earliest possible time in a manner consistent with the security interests of each party.

3. This Article is without prejudice to the provisions of Articles 10 and 12 of this Protocol.

Article 10

Removal of Minefields, Mined Areas, Mines, Booby-traps and Other Devices and International Cooperation

1. Without delay after the cessation of active hostilities, all minefields, mined areas, mines, booby-traps and other devices shall be cleared, removed, destroyed or maintained in accordance with Article 3 and paragraph 2 of Article 5 of this Protocol.

2. High Contracting Parties and parties to a conflict bear such responsibility with respect to minefields, mined areas, mines, booby-traps and other devices in areas under their control.

3. With respect to minefields, mined areas, mines, booby-traps and other devices laid by a party in areas over which it no longer exercises control, such party shall provide to the party in control of the area pursuant to paragraph 2 of this Article, to the extent permitted by such party, technical and material assistance necessary to fulfill such responsibility.

4. At all times necessary, the parties shall endeavour to reach agreement, both among themselves and, where appropriate, with other States and with international organizations, on the provision of technical and material assistance, including, in appropriate circumstances, the undertaking of joint operations necessary to fulfill such responsibilities.

Article 11

Technological Cooperation and Assistance

1. Each High Contracting Party undertakes to facilitate and shall have the right to participate in the fullest possible exchange of equipment, material and scientific and technological information concerning the implementation of this Protocol and means of mine clearance. In particular, High Contracting Parties shall not impose undue restrictions on the provision of mine clearance equipment and related technological information for humanitarian purposes.

2. Each High Contracting Party undertakes to provide information to the database on mine clearance established within the United Nations System, especially information concerning various means and technologies of mine clearance, and lists of experts, expert agencies or national points of contact on mine clearance.

3. Each high Contracting Party in a position to do so shall provide assistance for mine clearance through the United Nations System, other international bodies or on a bilateral basis, or contribute to the United Nations Voluntary Trust Fund for Assistance in Mine Clearance.

4. Requests by High Contracting Parties for assistance, substantiated by relevant information, may be submitted to the United Nations, to other appropriate bodies or to other States. These requests may be submitted to the Secretary-General of the United Nations, who shall transmit them to all High Contracting Parties and to relevant international organizations.

5. In the case of requests to the United Nations, the Secretary-General of the United Nations, within the resources available to the Secretary-General of the United Nations, may take appropriate steps to assess the situation and, in cooperation with the requesting High Contracting Party, determine the appropriate provision of assistance in mine clearance or implementation of the Protocol. The Secretary-General may also report to High Contracting Parties on any such assessment as well as on the type and scope of assistance required.

6. Without prejudice to their constitutional and other legal provisions, the High Contracting Parties undertake to cooperate and transfer technology to facilitate the implementation of the relevant prohibitions and restrictions set out in this Protocol.

7. Each High Contracting Party has the right to seek and receive technical assistance, where appropriate, from another High Contracting Party on specific relevant technology, other than weapons technology, as necessary and feasible, with a view to

reducing any period of deferral for which provision is made in the Technical Annex.

Article 12

Protection from the Effects of Minefields, Mined Areas, Mines, Booby-traps and Other Devices

1. Application

(a) With the exception of the forces and missions referred to in sub-paragraph 2(a) (i) of this Article, this Article applies only to missions which are performing functions in an area with the consent of the High Contracting Party on whose territory the functions are performed.

(b) The application of the provisions of this Article to parties to a conflict which are not High Contracting Parties shall not change their legal status or the legal status of a disputed territory, either explicitly or implicitly.

(c) The provisions of this Article are without prejudice to existing international humanitarian law, or other international instruments as applicable, or decisions by the Security Council of the United Nations, which provide for a higher level of protection to personnel functioning in accordance with this Article.

2. Peace-keeping and certain other forces and missions

(a) This paragraph applies to:

(i) any United Nations force or mission performing peace-keeping, observation or similar functions in any area in accordance with the Charter of the United Nations; and

(ii) any mission established pursuant to Chapter VIII of the Charter of the United Nations and performing its functions in the area of a conflict.

(b) Each High Contracting Party or party to a conflict, if so requested by the head of a force or mission to which this paragraph applies, shall:

(i) so far as it is able, take such measures as are necessary to protect the force or mission from the effects of mines, booby-traps and other devices in any area under its control;

(ii) if necessary in order effectively to protect such personnel, remove or render harmless, so far as it is able, all mines, booby-traps and other devices in

that area; and

(iii) inform the head of the force or mission of the location of all known minefields, mined areas, mines, booby-traps and other devices in the area in which the force or mission is performing its functions and, so far as is feasible, make available to the head of the force or mission all information in its possession concerning such minefields, mined areas, mines, booby-traps and other devices.

3. Humanitarian and fact-finding missions of the United Nations System

(a) This paragraph applies to any humanitarian or fact-finding mission of the United Nations System.

(b) Each High Contracting Party or party to a conflict, if so requested by the head of a mission to which this paragraph applies, shall:

(i) provide the personnel of the mission with the protections set out in sub-paragraph 2(b) (i) of this Article; and

(ii) if access to or through any place under its control is necessary for the performance of the mission's functions and in order to provide the personnel of the mission with safe passage to or through that place:

(aa) unless on-going hostilities prevent, inform the head of the mission of a safe route to that place if such information is available; or

(bb) if information identifying a safe route is not provided in accordance with sub-paragraph (aa), so far as is necessary and feasible, clear a lane through minefields.

4. Missions of the International Committee of the Red Cross

(a) This paragraph applies to any mission of the International Committee of the Red Cross performing functions with the consent of the host State or States as provided for by the Geneva Conventions of 12 August 1949 and, where applicable, their Additional Protocols.

(b) Each High Contracting Party or party to a conflict, if so requested by the head of a mission to which this paragraph applies, shall:

(i) provide the personnel of the mission with the protections set out in sub-paragraph 2(b) (i) of this Article; and

(ii) take the measures set out in sub-paragraph 3(b) (ii) of this Article.

5. *Other humanitarian missions and missions of enquiry*

(a) Insofar as paragraphs 2, 3 and 4 of this Article do not apply to them, this paragraph applies to the following missions when they are performing functions in the area of a conflict or to assist the victims of a conflict:

(i) any humanitarian mission of a national Red Cross or Red Crescent Society or of their International Federation;

(ii) any mission of an impartial humanitarian organization, including any impartial humanitarian demising mission; and

(iii) any mission of enquiry established pursuant to the provisions of the Geneva Conventions of 12 August 1949 and, where applicable, their Additional Protocols.

(b) Each High Contracting Party or party to a conflict, if so requested by the head of a mission to which this paragraph applies, shall, so far as is feasible:

(i) provide the personnel of the mission with the protections set out in sub-paragraph 2(b) (i) of this Article; and

(ii) take the measures set out in sub-paragraph 3(b) (ii) of this Article.

6. *Confidentiality*

All information provided in confidence pursuant to this Article shall be treated by the recipient in strict confidence and shall not be released outside the force or mission concerned without the express authorization of the provider of the information.

7. *Respect for laws and regulations*

Without prejudice to such privileges and immunities as they may enjoy or to the requirements of their duties, personnel participating in the forces and missions referred to in this Article shall:

(a) respect the laws and regulations of the host State; and

(b) refrain from any action or activity incompatible with the impartial and international nature of their duties.

Article 13

Consultations of High Contracting Parties

1. The High Contracting Parties undertake to consult and cooperate with each other on all issues related to the operation of this Protocol. For this purpose, a conference of High Contracting Parties shall be held annually.

2. Participation in the annual conferences shall be determined by their agreed Rules of Procedure.

3. The work of the conference shall include:

(a) review of the operation and status of this Protocol;

(b) consideration of matters arising from reports by High Contracting Parties according to paragraph 4 of this Article;

(c) preparation for review conferences; and

(d) consideration of the development of technologies to protect civilians against indiscriminate effects of mines.

4. The High Contracting Parties shall provide annual reports to the Depositary, who shall circulate them to all High Contracting Parties in advance of the conference, on any of the following matters:

(a) dissemination of information on this Protocol to their armed forces and to the civilian population;

(b) mine clearance and rehabilitation programmes;

(c) steps taken to meet technical requirements of this Protocol and any other relevant information pertaining thereto;

(d) legislation related to this Protocol;

(e) measures taken on international technical information exchange, on international cooperation on mine clearance, and on technical cooperation and assistance; and

(f) other relevant matters.

5. The cost of the Conference of High Contracting Parties shall be borne by the High Contracting Parties and States not parties participating in the work of the Conference, in accordance with the United Nations scale of assessment adjusted appropriately.

Article 14

Compliance

1. Each High Contracting Party shall take all appropriate steps, including legislative and other measures, to prevent and suppress violations of this

Protocol by persons or on territory under its jurisdiction or control.

2. The measures envisaged in paragraph 1 of this Article include appropriate measures to ensure the imposition of penal sanctions against persons who, in relation to an armed conflict and contrary to the provisions of this Protocol, willfully kill or cause serious injury to civilians and to bring such persons to justice.

3. Each High Contracting Party shall also require that its armed forces issue relevant military instructions and operating procedures and that armed forces personnel receive training commensurate with their duties and responsibilities to comply with the provisions of this Protocol.

4. The High Contracting Parties undertake to consult each other and to cooperate with each other bilaterally, through the Secretary-General of the United Nations or through other appropriate international procedures, to resolve any problems that may arise with regard to the interpretation and application of the provisions of this Protocol.

Agreement on Normalization of Relations Between the Federal Republic of Yugoslavia and the Republic of Croatia

Date of signature: August 23, 1996
Place of signature: Belgrade
Signatory states: Croatia, Yugoslavia

[The signatories], hereinafter "the Contracting Parties",

Aware of their responsibility for the establishment and maintenance of peace and security in the region,

Desiring to contribute to that end through the normalization of mutual relations,

Aimed at promoting relations between their peoples and citizens,

have agreed as follows:

Article 1

The Contracting Parties shall respect each other as independent, sovereign and equal States within international borders.

Article 2

Each Contracting Party shall respect, in accordance with international law, the sovereignty, territorial integrity and independence of the other Contracting Party. The Contracting Parties confirm that they shall carry out the regulation of their borders and the delimitation through mutual agreement only, that they shall solve disputes by peaceful means and refrain from threat or use of force in accordance with the Charter of the United Nations. The Contracting Parties shall seek to foster mutual confidence, good will and tolerance and shall cooperate in promoting peace, stability and development in the region.

Article 3

Within 15 days after the signing of this Agreement, the Contracting Parties shall establish full diplomatic and consular relations. The Contracting Parties shall promptly upgrade their existing representative offices to embassies and shall exchange ambassadors.

Article 4

The Contracting Parties are agreed to solve the disputed issue of Prevlaka through mutual negotiations. Thereby a contribution shall be made to the full security of the part of the territory of the Federal Republic of Yugoslavia in the Boka Kotorska Bay and the part of the territory of the Republic of Croatia in the area of the Dubrovnik region. The two Parties shall solve this important disputed issue through mutual negotiations in the spirit of the Charter of the United Nations and good-neighbourliness.

Until mutual agreement on Prevlaka is reached, the Contracting Parties are agreed to respect the existing security regime established through United Nations monitoring.

Article 5

Proceeding from the historical fact that Serbia and Montenegro existed as independent States before the creation of Yugoslavia, and bearing in mind the fact that Yugoslavia has continued the international legal personality of these States, the Republic of Croatia notes the existence of the State continuity of the Federal Republic of Yugoslavia.

Proceeding from the historical fact of the existence of the various forms of stratal organization of Croatia in the past, the Federal Republic of Yugoslavia notes the existence of the continuity of the Croatian statehood.

The Contracting Parties are agreed to solve the issue of the succession of the Socialist Federal Republic of Yugoslavia on the basis of the rules of international law on succession of States and through agreement.

Article 6

The Contracting Parties undertake to speed up forthwith the process of solving the questions of missing persons, and both Contracting Parties shall immediately exchange all available information about these persons.

Article 7

The Contracting Parties shall ensure conditions for a free and safe return of refugees and displaced persons to their places of residence or other places which they freely choose. The Contracting Parties shall ensure to these persons return into possession of their property or a just compensation.

The Contracting Parties shall ensure full security to the refugees and displaced persons who return. The Contracting Parties shall assist these persons to ensure necessary conditions for normal and safe life.

The Contracting Parties shall declare general amnesty for all acts committed in connection with the armed conflicts, except for the gravest violations of humanitarian law having the nature of war crimes.

The Contracting Parties shall encourage consistent and comprehensive implementation of the Erdut Agreement on Eastern Slavonia, Baranja and Western Sirmium.

Each Contracting Party shall guarantee the same legal protection to the property of physical persons and legal entities having the citizenship of the other Party, that is, being seated in the territory of the other Party, as the one enjoyed by its own citizens, that is, its legal entities.

Within six months from the date of the entry into force of this Agreement, the Contracting Parties shall conclude an agreement on compensation for all

destroyed, damaged or lost property. Such agreement shall define the procedures for the realization of the rights to fair compensation which shall not include court proceedings.

For the purpose of implementing the obligations under this article, a joint commission, consisting of three representatives of each Contracting Party, shall be established within 30 days from the signing of this Agreement.

Article 8

The Contracting Parties shall guarantee the Croats in the Federal Republic of Yugoslavia and the Serbs and Montenegrins in the Republic of Croatia all

Article 9

The Contracting Parties shall conclude, within six months, a separate agreement on social insurance which shall regulate disability, health and pension insurance, including the payment of pensions. The Contracting Parties shall conclude, if necessary, other agreement as well concerning the settlement of work—and status—related issues.

Article 10

The Contracting Parties shall continue to cooperate in normalizing road, railway, air and river traffic on the basis of the principle of reciprocity and good-neighbourliness.

Article 11

International regulations in force concerning the stay and movement of foreigners shall be applied without discrimination to the entry, movement and stay of the citizens and vehicles of one Contracting Party in the territory of the other Contracting Party.

Article 12

The Contracting Parties shall continue to promote post, telephone and other telecommunications.

Article 13

The Contracting Parties shall proceed, without delay, to concluding mutual agreements in the fields of economy, science, education, protection of the environment, as well as in other fields of the common interest of the Contracting Parties.

The Contracting Parties shall immediately conclude an agreement on cultural cooperation which shall include the preservation and restoration of cultural heritage.

Article 14

This Agreement has been done in two original copies, in the Serbian and Croatian languages, both texts being equally authentic.

This Agreement shall be provisionally applied from the day of signature and shall enter into force after the two Contracting Parties notify each other through diplomatic channels that it has been confirmed by their competent authorities.

Comprehensive Nuclear Test Ban Treaty

Date of signature: September 24, 1996
Place of signature: New York
Signatory states: Albania, Algeria, Andorra, Angola, Antigua and Barbuda, Argentina, Armenia, Australia, Austria, Azerbaijan, Bahrain, Bangladesh, Belarus, Belgium, Benin, Bolivia, Bosnia and Herzegovina, Brazil, Brunei Darussalam, Bulgaria, Burkina Faso, Burundi, Cambodia, Canada, Cape Verde, Chad, Chile, China, Colombia, Comoros, Congo, Republic of (Brazzaville), Congo, Democratic Republic of (Kinshasa), Cook Islands, Costa Rica, Cote d'Ivoire, Croatia, Cyprus, Czech Republic, Denmark, Djibouti, Dominican Republic, Ecuador, Egypt, El Salvador, Equatorial Guinea, Estonia, Ethiopia, Fiji, Finland, France, Gabon, Georgia, Germany, Ghana, Greece, Grenada, Guinea, Guinea-Bissau, Haiti, Holy See, Honduras, Hungary, Iceland, India, Indonesia, Iran (Islamic Rep. of), Ireland, Israel, Italy, Jamaica, Japan, Jordan, Kazakhstan, Kenya, Kuwait, Kyrgyzstan, Lao People's Democratic Republic, Latvia, Lesotho, Liberia, Liechtenstein, Lithuania, Luxembourg, Madagascar, Malawi, Malaysia, Maldives, Mali, Malta, Marshall Islands, Mauritania, Mexico, Micronesia (Federated States of), Moldova, Monaco, Mongolia, Morocco, Mozambique, Myanmar, Namibia, Nepal, Netherlands, New Zealand, Nicaragua, Niger, North Korea, Norway, Pakistan, Panama, Papua New Guinea, Paraguay, Peru, Philippines, Poland, Portugal, Qatar, Republic of Korea, Romania, Russian Federation, Saint Lucia, Samoa, San Marino, Sao Tome and Principe, Senegal, Seychelles, Slovakia, Slovenia, Solomon Islands, South Africa, Spain, Sri Lanka, Suriname, Swaziland, Sweden, Switzerland, Tajikistan, Thailand, The Former Yugoslav Republic of Macedonia, Togo, Tunisia, Turkey, Turkmenistan, Uganda, Ukraine, United Arab Emirates, United Kingdom, United States, Uruguay, Uzbekistan, Vanuatu, Venezuela, Vietnam, Yemen, Zambia (as of October 29, 1998)
Ratification: Australia, Austira, Brazil, Czech Republic, El Salvador, Fiji, France, Germany, Grenada, Japan, Jordan, Micronesia, Mongolia, Peru, Qatar, Slovakia, Spain, Turkmenistan, United Kingdom, Uzbekistan (as of October 29, 1998)

Preamble

The States Parties to this Treaty (hereinafter referred to as "the States Parties")

Welcoming the international agreements and other positive measures of recent years in the field of nuclear disarmament, including reductions in arsenals of nuclear weapons, as well as in the field of the prevention of nuclear proliferation in all its aspects,

Underlining the importance of the full and prompt implementation of such agreements and measures,

Convinced that the present international situation provides an opportunity to take further effective measures towards nuclear disarmament and against the proliferation of nuclear weapons in all its aspects, and *declaring* their intention to take such measures,

Stressing therefore the need for continued systematic and progressive efforts to reduce nuclear weapons globally, with the ultimate goal of eliminating those weapons, and of general and complete disarmament under strict and effective international control,

Recognizing that the cessation of all nuclear weapon test explosions and all other nuclear explosions, by constraining the development and qualitative improvement of nuclear weapons and ending the development of advanced new types of nuclear weapons, constitutes an effective measure of nuclear disarmament and non-proliferation in all its aspects,

Further recognizing that an end to all such nuclear explosions will thus constitute a meaningful step in the realization of a systematic process to achieve nuclear disarmament,

Convinced that the most effective way to achieve an end to nuclear testing is through the conclusion of a universal and internationally and effectively verifiable comprehensive nuclear test-ban treaty, which has long been one of the highest priority objectives of the international community in the field of disarmament and non-proliferation,

Noting the aspirations expressed by the Parties to the 1963 Treaty Banning Nuclear Weapon Tests in the Atmosphere, in Outer Space and Under Water to seek to achieve the discontinuance of all test explosions of nuclear weapons for all time,

Noting also the views expressed that this Treaty could contribute to the protection of the environment,

Affirming the purpose of attracting the adherence of all States to this Treaty and its objective to contribute effectively to the prevention of the proliferation of nuclear weapons in all its aspects, to the process of nuclear disarmament and therefore to the enhancement of international peace and security,

Have agreed as follows:

Article 1

Basic Obligations

1. Each State Party undertakes not to carry out any nuclear weapon test explosion or any other nuclear explosion, and to prohibit and prevent any such nuclear explosion at any place under its jurisdiction or control.

2. Each State Party undertakes, furthermore, to refrain from causing, encouraging, or in any way participating in the carrying out of any nuclear weapon test explosion or any other nuclear explosion.

Article 2

The Organization

A. General Provisions

1. The States Parties hereby establish the Comprehensive Nuclear Test-Ban Treaty Organization (hereinafter referred to as "the Organization") to achieve the object and purpose of this Treaty, to ensure the implementation of its provisions, including those for international verification of compliance with it, and to provide a forum for consultation and cooperation among States Parties.

2. All States Parties shall be members of the Organization. A State Party shall not be deprived of its membership in the Organization.

3. The seat of the Organization shall be Vienna, Republic of Austria.

4. There are hereby established as organs of the Organization: the Conference of the States Parties, the Executive Council and the Technical Secretariat, which shall include the International Data Centre.

5. Each State Party shall cooperate with the Organization in the exercise of its functions in accordance with this Treaty. States Parties shall consult, directly among themselves, or through the Organization or other appropriate international procedures, including procedures within the framework of the United Nations and in accordance with its Charter, on any matter which may be raised relating to the object and purpose, or the implementation of the provisions, of this Treaty.

6. The Organization shall conduct its verification activities provided for under this Treaty in the least intrusive manner possible consistent with the timely and efficient accomplishment of their objectives. It shall request only the information and data necessary to fulfill its responsibilities under this Treaty. It shall take every precaution to protect the confidentiality of information on civil and military activities and facilities coming to its knowledge in the implementation of this Treaty and, in particular, shall abide by the confidentiality provisions set forth in this Treaty.

7. Each State Party shall treat as confidential and afford special handling to information and data that it receives in confidence from the Organization in connection with the implementation of this Treaty. It shall treat such information and date exclusively in connection with its rights and obligations under this Treaty.

8. The Organization, as an independent body, shall seek to utilize existing expertise and facilities, as appropriate, and to maximize cost efficiencies, through cooperative arrangements with other international organizations such as the International Atomic Energy Agency. Such arrangements, excluding those of a minor and normal commercial and contractual nature, shall be set out in agreements to be submitted to the Conference of the States Parties for approval.

9. The costs of the activities of the Organization shall be met annually by the States Parties in accordance with the United Nations scale of assessments adjusted to take into account differences in membership between the United Nations and the Organization.

10. Financial contributions of States Parties to the Preparatory Commission shall be deducted in an appropriate way from their contributions to the regu-

lar budget.

11. A member of the Organization which is in arrears in the payment of its assessed contribution to the Organization shall have no vote in the Organization if the amount of its arrears equals or exceeds the amount of the contribution due from it for the preceding two full years. The Conference of the States Parties may, nevertheless, permit such a member to vote if it is satisfied that the failure to pay is due to conditions beyond the control of the member.

B. *The Conference of the States Parties*

Composition, Procedures and Decision-making

12. The Conference of the States Parties (hereinafter referred to as "the Conference") shall be composed of all States Parties. Each State party shall have one representative in the Conference, who may be accompanied by alternates and advisers.

13. The initial session of the Conference shall be convened by the Depositary no later than 30 days after the entry into force of this Treaty.

14. The Conference shall meet in regular sessions, which shall be held annually, unless it decides otherwise.

15. A special session of the Conference shall be convened:

(a) When decided by the Conference;

(b) When requested by the Executive Council; or

(c) When requested by any State Party and supported by a majority of the States Parties.

The special session shall be convened no later than 30 days after the decision of the Conference, the request of the Executive Council, or the attainment of the necessary support, unless specified otherwise in the decision or request.

16. The Conference may also be convened in the form of an Amendment Conference, in accordance with Article VII.

17. The Conference may also be convened in the form of a Review Conference, in accordance with Article VIII.

18. Sessions shall take place at the seat of the Organization unless the Conference decides otherwise.

19. The Conference shall adopt its rules of procedure. At the beginning of each session, it shall elect its President and such other officers as may be required. They shall hold office until a new President and other officers are elected at the next session.

20. A majority of the States Parties shall constitute a quorum.

21. Each State Party shall have one vote.

22. The Conference shall take decisions on matters of procedure by a majority of members present and voting. Decisions on matters of substance shall be taken as far as possible by consensus. If consensus is not attainable when an issue comes up for decision, the President of the Conference shall defer any vote for 24 hours and during this period of deferment shall make every effort to facilitate achievement of consensus, and shall report to the Conference before the end of this period. If consensus is not possible at the end of 24 hours, the Conference shall take a decision by a two-thirds majority of members present and voting unless specified otherwise in this Treaty. When the issue arises as to whether the question is one of substance or not, that question shall be treated as a matter of substance unless otherwise decided by the majority required for decisions on matters of substance.

23. When exercising its function under paragraph 26 (k), the Conference shall take a decision to add any State to the list of States contained in Annex 1 to this Treaty in accordance with the procedure for decisions on matters of substance set out in paragraph 22. Notwithstanding paragraph 22, the Conference shall take decisions on any other change to Annex 1 to this Treaty by consensus.

Powers and Functions

24. The Conference shall be the principal organ of the Organization. It shall consider any questions, matters or issues within the scope of this Treaty, including those relating to the powers and functions of the Executive Council and the Technical Secretariat, in accordance with this Treaty. It may make recommendations and take decisions on any questions, matters or issues within the scope of this Treaty raised by a State Party or brought to its attention by the Executive Council.

25. The Conference shall oversee the implementation of, and review compliance with, this Treaty and act in order to promote its object and purpose. It shall also oversee the activities of the Executive Council and the Technical Secretariat and may issue guidelines to either of them for the exercise of their functions.

26. The conference shall:

(a) Consider and adopt the report of the Organization on the implementation of this Treaty and the annual programme and budget of the Organization, submitted by the Executive Council, as well as consider other reports;

(b) Decide on the scale of financial contributions to

be paid by States Parties in accordance with paragraph 9;

(c) Elect the members of the Executive Council;

(d) Appoint the Director-General of the Technical Secretariat (hereinafter referred to as "the Director-General");

(e) Consider and approve the rules of procedure of the Executive Council submitted by the latter;

(f) Consider and review scientific and technological developments that could affect the operation of this Treaty. In this context, the Conference may direct the Director-General to establish a Scientific Advisory Board to enable him or her, in the performance of his or her functions, to render specialized advice in areas of science and technology relevant to this Treaty to the Conference, to the Executive Council, or to States Parties. In that case, the Scientific Advisory Board shall be composed of independent experts serving in their individual capacity and appointed, in accordance with terms of reference adopted by the Conference, on the basis of their expertise and experience in the particular scientific fields relevant to the implementation of this Treaty;

(g) Take the necessary measures to ensure compliance with this Treaty and to redress and remedy any situation that contravenes the provisions of this Treaty, in accordance with Article V;

(h) Consider and approve at its initial session any draft agreements, arrangements, provisions, procedures, operational manuals, guidelines and any other documents developed and recommended by the Preparatory Commission;

(i) Consider and approve agreements or arrangements negotiated by the Technical Secretariat with States Parties, other States and international organizations to be concluded by the Executive Council on behalf of the Organization in accordance with paragraph 38 (h);

(j) Establish such subsidiary organs as it finds necessary for the exercise of its functions in accordance with this Treaty; and

(k) Update Annex 1 to this Treaty, as appropriate, in accordance with paragraph 23.

C. The Executive Council

Composition, Procedures and Decision-making

27. The Executive Council shall consist of 51 members. Each State Party shall have the right, in accordance with the provisions of this Article, to serve on the Executive Council.

28. Taking into account the need for equitable geographical distribution, the Executive Council shall comprise:

(a) Ten States Parties from Africa;

(b) Seven States Parties from Eastern Europe;

(c) Nine States Parties from Latin America and the Caribbean;

(d) Seven States Parties from the Middle East and South Asia;

(e) Ten States Parties from North America and Western Europe; and

(f) Eight States Parties from South-East Asia, the Pacific and the Far East.

All states in each of the above geographical regions are listed in Annex I to this Treaty. Annex 1 to this Treaty shall be updated, as appropriate, by the Conference in accordance with paragraphs 23 and 26 (k). It shall not be subject to amendments or changes under the procedures contained in Article VII.

29. The members of the Executive Council shall be elected by the Conference. In this connection, each geographical region shall designate States parties from that region for election as members of the Executive Council as follows:

(a) At least one-third of the seats allocated to each geographical region shall be filled, taking into account political and security interests, by States Parties in that region designated on the basis of the nuclear capabilities relevant to the Treaty as determined by international data as well as all or any of the following indicative criteria in the order of priority determined by each region:

(i) Number of monitoring facilities of the International Monitoring System;

(ii) Expertise and experience in monitoring technology; and

(iii) Contribution to the annual budget of the Organization;

(b) One of the seats allocated to each geographical region shall be filled on a rotational basis by the State Party that is first in the English alphabetical order among the States Parties in that region that have not served as members of the Executive

Council for the longest period of time since becoming States Parties or since their last term, whichever is shorter. A State Party designated on this basis may decide to forgo its seat. In that case, such a State Party shall submit a letter of renunciation to the Director-General, and the seat shall be filled by the State Party following next-in-order according to this sub-paragraph; and

(c) The remaining seats allocated to each geographical region shall be filled by States Parties designated from among all the States Parties in that region by rotation or elections.

30. Each member of the Executive Council shall have one representative on the Executive Council, who may be accompanied by alternates and advisers.

31. Each member of the Executive Council shall hold office from the end of the session of the Conference at which that member is elected until the end of the second regular annual session of the Conference thereafter, except that for the first election of the Executive Council, 26 members shall be elected to hold office until the end of the third regular annual session of the Conference, due regard being paid to the established numerical proportions as described in paragraph 28.

32. The Executive Council shall elaborate its rules of procedure and submit them to the Conference for approval.

33. The Executive Council shall elect its Chairman from among its members.

34. The Executive Council shall meet for regular sessions. Between regular sessions it shall meet as may be required for the fulfillment of its powers and functions.

35. Each member of the Executive Council shall have one vote.

36. The Executive Council shall take decisions on matters of procedure by a majority of all its members. The Executive Council shall take decisions on matters of substance by a two-thirds majority of all its members unless specified otherwise in this Treaty. When the issue arises as to whether the question is one of substance or not, that question shall be treated as a matter of substance unless otherwise decided by the majority required for decisions on matters of substance.

Powers and Functions

37. The Executive Council shall be the executive organ of the Organization. It shall be responsible to the Conference. It shall carry out the powers and functions entrusted to it in accordance with this Treaty. In so doing, it shall act in conformity with the recommendations, decisions and guidelines of the Conference and ensure their continuous and proper implementation.

38. The Executive Council shall:

(a) Promote effective implementation of, and compliance with, this Treaty;

(b) Supervise the activities of the Technical Secretariat;

(c) Make recommendations as necessary to the Conference for consideration of further proposals for promoting the object and purpose of this Treaty;

(d) Cooperate with the National Authority of each State Party;

(e) Consider and submit to the Conference the draft annual programme and budget of the Organization, the draft report of the Organization on the implementation of this Treaty, the report on the performance of its own activities and such other reports as it deems necessary or that the Conference may request;

(f) Make arrangements for the sessions of the Conference, including the preparation of the draft agenda;

(g) Examine proposals for changes, on matters of an administrative or technical nature, to the Protocol or the Annexes thereto, pursuant to Article VII, and make recommendations to the States Parties regarding their adoption;

(h) Conclude, subject to prior approval of the Conference, agreements or arrangements with States Parties, other States and international organizations on behalf of the Organization and supervise their implementation, with the exception of agreements or arrangements referred to in sub-paragraph (i);

(i) Approve and supervise the operation of agreements or arrangements relating to the implementation of verification activities with States Parties and other States; and

(j) Approve any new operational manuals and any changes to the existing operational manuals that may be proposed by the Technical Secretariat.

39. The Executive Council may request a special session of the Conference.

40. The Executive Council shall:

(a) Facilitate cooperation among States Parties, and between States Parties and the Technical Secretariat, relating to the implementation of this Treaty through information exchanges;

(b) Facilitate consultation and clarification among States Parties in accordance with Article IV; and

(c) Receive, consider and take action on requests for, and reports on, on-site inspections in accordance with Article IV.

41. The Executive Council shall consider any concern raised by a State Party about possible non-compliance with this Treaty and abuse of the rights established by this Treaty. In so doing, the Executive Council shall consult with the States Parties involved and, as appropriate, request a State Party to take measures to redress the situation within a specified time. To the extent that the Executive Council considers further action to be necessary, it shall take, *inter alia*, one or more of the following measures:

(a) Notify all States Parties of the issue or matter;

(b) Bring the issue or matter to the attention of the Conference;

(c) Make recommendations to the Conference or take action, as appropriate, regarding measures to redress the situation and to ensure compliance in accordance with Article V.

D. The Technical Secretariat

42. The Technical Secretariat shall assist States Parties in the implementation of this Treaty. The Technical Secretariat shall assist the Conference and the Executive Council in the performance of their functions. The Technical Secretariat shall carry out the verification and other functions entrusted to it by this Treaty, as well as those functions delegated to it by the Conference or the Executive Council in accordance with this Treaty. The Technical Secretariat shall include, as an integral part, the International Data Centre.

43. The functions of the Technical Secretariat with regard to verification of compliance with this Treaty shall, in accordance with Article IV and the Protocol, include *inter alia*:

(a) Being responsible for supervising and coordinating the operation of the International Monitoring System;

(b) Operating the International Data Centre;

(c) Routinely receiving, processing, analyzing and reporting on International Monitoring System data;

(d) Providing technical assistance in, and support for, the installation and operation of monitoring stations;

(e) Assisting the Executive Council in facilitating consultation and clarification among States Parties;

(f) Receiving requests for on-site inspections and processing them, facilitating Executive Council consideration of such requests, carrying out the preparations for, and providing technical support during, the conduct of on-site inspections, and reporting to the Executive Council;

(g) Negotiating agreements or arrangements with States Parties, other States and international organizations and concluding, subject to prior approval by the Executive Council, any such agreements or arrangements relating to verification activities with States Parties or other States; and

(h) Assisting the States Parties through their National Authorities on other issues of verification under this Treaty.

44. The Technical Secretariat shall develop and maintain, subject to approval by the Executive Council, operational manuals to guide the operation of the various components of the verification regime, in accordance with Article IV and the Protocol. These manuals shall not constitute integral parts of this Treaty or the Protocol and may be changed by the Technical Secretariat subject to approval by the Executive Council. The Technical Secretariat shall promptly inform the States Parties of any changes in the operational manuals.

45. The functions of the Technical Secretariat with respect to administrative matters shall include:

(a) Preparing and submitting to the Executive Council the draft programme and budget of the Organization;

(b) Preparing and submitting to the Executive Council the draft report of the Organization on the implementation of this Treaty and such other reports as the Conference of the Executive Council may request;

(c) Providing administrative and technical support to the Conference, the Executive Council and other subsidiary organs;

(d) Addressing and receiving Communications on behalf of the Organization relating to the implementation of this Treaty; and

(e) Carrying out the administrative responsibilities related to any agreements between the Organization and other international organizations.

46. All requests and notifications by States Parties to the Organization shall be transmitted through their

National Authorities to the Director-General. Requests and notifications shall be in one of the official languages of this Treaty. In response the Director-General shall use the language of the transmitted request or notification.

47. With respect to the responsibilities of the Technical Secretariat for preparing and submitting to the Executive Council the draft programme and budget of the Organization, the Technical Secretariat shall determine and maintain a clear accounting of all costs for each facility established as part of the International Monitoring System. Similar treatment in the draft programme and budget shall be accorded to all other activities of the Organization.

48. The Technical Secretariat shall promptly inform the Executive Council of any problems that have arisen with regard to the discharge of its functions that have come to its notice in the performance of its activities and that it has been unable to resolve through consultations with the State Party concerned.

49. The Technical Secretariat shall comprise a Director-General, who shall be its head and chief administrative officer, and such scientific, technical and other personnel as may be required. The Director-General shall be appointed by the Conference upon the recommendation of the Executive Council for a term of four years, renewable for the further term, but not thereafter. The first Director-General shall be appointed by the Conference at its initial session upon the recommendation of the Preparatory Commission.

50. The Director-General shall be responsible to the Conference and the Executive Council for the appointment of the staff and for the organization and functioning of the Technical Secretariat. The paramount consideration in the employment of the staff and in the determination of the conditions of service shall be the necessity of securing the highest standards of professional expertise, experience, efficiency, competence and integrity. Only citizens of States Parties shall serve as the Director-General, as inspectors or as members of the professional and clerical staff. Due regard shall be paid to the importance of recruiting the staff on as wide a geographical basis as possible. Recruitment shall be guided by the principle that the staff shall be kept to the minimum necessary for the proper discharge of the responsibilities of the Technical Secretariat.

51. The Director-General may, as appropriate, after consultation with the Executive Council, establish temporary working groups of scientific experts to provide recommendations on specific issues.

52. In the performance of their duties, the Director-General, the inspectors, the inspection assistants and the members of the staff shall not seek or receive instructions from any Government or from any other source external to the Organization. They shall refrain from any action that might reflect adversely on their positions as international officers responsible only to the Organization. The Director-General shall assume responsibility for the activities of an inspection team.

53. Each State Party shall respect the exclusively international character of the responsibilities of the Director-General, the inspectors, the inspection assistants and the members of the staff and shall not seek to influence them in the discharge of their responsibilities.

E. Privileges and Immunities

54. The Organization shall enjoy on the territory and in any other place under the jurisdiction or control of a State Party such legal capacity and such privileges and immunities as are necessary for the exercise of its functions.

55. Delegates of States Parties, together with their alternates and advisers, representatives of members elected to the Executive Council, together with their alternates and advisers, the Director-General, the inspectors, the inspection assistants and the members of the staff of the Organization shall enjoy such privileges and immunities as are necessary in the independent exercise of their functions in connection with the Organization.

56. The legal capacity, privileges and immunities referred to in this Article shall be defined in agreement between the Organization and the States Parties as well as in an agreement between the Organization and the States in which the Organization in seated. Such agreements shall be considered and approved in accordance with paragraph 26 (h) and (i).

57. Notwithstanding paragraph 54 and 55, the privileges and immunities enjoyed by the Director-General, the inspectors, the inspection assistants and the members of the staff of the Technical Secretariat during the conduct of verification activities shall be those set forth in the Protocol.

Article 3

National Implementation Measures

1. Each State Party shall, in accordance with its constitutional processes, take any necessary measure to implement its obligations under this Treaty. In particular, it shall take any necessary measures:

(a) To prohibit natural and legal persons anywhere on its territory or in any other place under its jurisdiction as recognized by international law from undertaking any activity prohibited to a State Party under this Treaty;

(b) To prohibit natural and legal persons from undertaking any such activity anywhere under its control; and

(c) To prohibit, in conformity with international law, natural persons possessing its nationality from undertaking any such activity anywhere.

2. Each State Party shall cooperate with other States and afford the appropriate form of legal assistance to facilitate the implementation of the obligations under paragraph 1.

3. Each State Party shall inform the Organization of the measures taken pursuant to this Article.

4. In order to fulfill its obligations under the Treaty, each State Party shall designate or set up a National Authority and shall so inform the Organization upon entry into force of the Treaty for it. The National Authority shall serve as the national focal for liaison with the Organization and with other States Parties.

Article 4

Verification

A. General Provisions

1. In order to verify compliance with this Treaty, a verification regime shall be established consisting of the following elements;

(a) An International Monitoring System;

(b) Consultation and clarification;

(c) On-site inspections; and

(d) Confidence-building measures.

At entry into force of this Treaty, the verification regime shall be capable of meeting the verification requirements of this Treaty.

2. Verification activities shall be based on objective information, shall be limited to the subject matter of this Treaty, and shall be carried out on the basis of full respect for the sovereignty of States Parties and in the least intrusive manner possible consistent with the effective and timely accomplishment of their objectives. Each State Party shall refrain from any abuse of the right of verification.

3. Each State Party undertakes in accordance with this Treaty to cooperate through its National Authori-ty established pursuant to Article III, paragraph 4, with the Organization and with other States Parties to facilitate the verification of compliance with this Treaty by, *inter alia*;

(a) Establishing the necessary facilities to participate in these verification measures and establishing the necessary communication;

(b) Providing data obtained from national stations that are part of the International Monitoring System;

(c) Participating, as appropriate, in a consultation and clarification process;

(d) Permitting the conduct of on-site inspections; and

(e) Participating, as appropriate, in confidence-building measures.

4. All States Parties, irrespective of their technical and financial capabilities, shall enjoy the equal right of verification and assume the equal obligation to accept verification.

5. For the purpose of this Treaty, no State Party shall be precluded from using information obtained by national technical means of verification in a manner consistent with generally recognized principles of international law, including that of respect for the sovereignty of States.

6. Without prejudice to the right of State Parties to protect sensitive installations, activities or locations not related to this Treaty, States Parties shall not interfere with elements of the verification regime of this Treaty or with national technical means of verification operating in accordance with paragraph 5.

7. Each State Party shall have the right to take measures to protect sensitive installations and to prevent disclosure of confidential information and data not related to this Treaty.

8. Moreover, all necessary measures shall be taken to protect the confidentiality of any information related to civil and military activities and facilities obtained during verification activities.

9. Subject to paragraph 8, information obtained by the Organization through the verification regime established by this Treaty shall be made available to all States Parties in accordance with the relevant provisions of this Treaty and the Protocol.

10. The provisions of this Treaty shall not be interpreted as restricting the international exchange of data for scientific purposes.

11. Each State Party undertake to cooperate with the Organization and with other States Parties in the improvement of the verification regime, and in the examination of the verification potential of additional

monitoring technologies such as electromagnetic pulse monitoring or satellite monitoring, with a view to developing, when appropriate, specific measures to enhance the efficient and cost-effective verification of this Treaty. Such measures shall, when agreed, be incorporated in existing provisions in this Treaty, the Protocol or as additional sections of the Protocol, in accordance with Article VII, or, if appropriate, be reflected in the operational manuals in accordance with Article II, paragraph 44.

12. The States Parties undertake to promote cooperation among themselves to facilitate and participate in the fullest possible exchange relating to technologies used in the verification of this Treaty in order to enable all States Parties to strengthen their national implementation of verification measures and to benefit from the application of such technologies for peaceful purpose.

13. The provisions of this Treaty shall be implemented in a manner which avoids hampering the economic and technological development of the States Parties for further development of the application of atomic energy for peaceful purposes.

Verification Responsibilities of the Technical Secretariat

14. In discharging its responsibilities in the area of verification specified in this Treaty and the Protocol, in cooperation with the States Parties the Technical Secretariat shall, for the purpose of this Treaty:

(a) Make arrangements to receive and distribute data and reporting products relevant to the verification of this Treaty in accordance with its provisions, and to maintain a global communications infrastructure appropriate to this task;

(b) Routinely through its International Data Centre, which shall in principle be the focal point within the Technical Secretariat for data storage and data processing:

(i) Receive and initiate requests for data from the International Monitoring System;

(ii) Receive data, as appropriate, resulting from the process of consultation and clarification, from on-site inspections, and from confidence-building measures; and

(iii) Receive other relevant data from States Parties and international organizations in accordance with this Treaty and the Protocol;

(c) Supervise, coordinate and ensure the operation of the International Monitoring System and its component elements, and of the International Data Centre, in accordance with the relevant operational manuals;

(d) Routinely process, analyse and report on International Monitoring System data according to agreed procedures so as to permit the effective international verification of this Treaty and to contribute to the early resolution of compliance concerns;

(e) Make available all data, both raw and processed, and any reporting products, to all States Parties, each State Party taking responsibility for the use of International Monitoring System data in accordance with Article 2, paragraph 7, and with paragraphs 8 and 13 of this Article;

(f) Provide to all States Parties equal, open, convenient and timely access to all stored data;

(g) Store all data, both raw and processed, and reporting products;

(h) Coordinate and facilitate requests for additional data from the International Monitoring System;

(i) Coordinate requests for additional data from one State Party to another State Party;

(j) Provide technical assistance in, and support for, the installation and operation of monitoring facilities and respective communication means, where such assistance and support are required by the State concerned;

(k) Make available to any State Party, upon its request, techniques utilized by the Technical Secretariat and its International Data Centre in compiling, storing, processing, analyzing and reporting on data from the verification regime; and

(l) Monitor, assess and report on the overall performance of the International Monitoring System and of the International Data Centre.

15. The agreed procedure to be used by the Technical Secretariat in discharging the verification responsibilities referred to in paragraph 14 and detailed in the Protocol shall be elaborated in the relevant operational manuals.

B. The International Monitoring System

16. The International Monitoring System shall comprise facilities for seismological monitoring, radionuclide monitoring including certified laboratories, hydroacoustic monitoring, infrasound monitor-

ing, and respective means of communication, and shall be supported by the International Data Centre of the Technical Secretariat.

17. The International Monitoring System shall be placed under the authority of the Technical Secretariat. All monitoring facilities of the International Monitoring System shall be owned and operated by the States hosting or otherwise taking responsibility for them in accordance with the Protocol.

18. Each State Party shall have the right to participate in the international exchange of data and to have access to all data made available to the International Data Centre. Each State Party shall cooperate with the International Data Centre through its National Authority.

Funding the International Monitoring System

19. For facilities incorporated into the International Monitoring System and specified in Table 1-A, 2-A, 3 and 4 of Annex 1 to the Protocol, and for their functioning, to the extent that such facilities are agreed by the relevant State and the Organization to provide data to the International Data Centre in accordance with the technical requirements of the Protocol and relevant operational manuals, the Organization, as specified in agreements or arrangements pursuant to Part I, paragraph 4 of the Protocol, shall meet the costs of:

(a) Establishing any new facilities and upgrading existing facilities, unless the State responsible for such facilities meets these costs itself;

(b) Operating and maintaining International Monitoring System facilities, including facility physical security if appropriate, and application of agreed data authentication procedures;

(c) Transmitting International Monitoring System data (raw or processed) to the International Data Centre by the most direct and cost-effective means available, including, if necessary, via appropriate communications nodes, from monitoring stations, laboratories, analytical facilities or from national data centres; or such (including samples where appropriate) to laboratory and analytical facilities from monitoring stations; and

(d) Analyzing samples on behalf of the Organization.

20. For auxiliary network seismic stations specified in Table 1-B of Annex 1 to the Protocol the Organization, as specified in agreement or arrangements pursuant to Part I, paragraph 4 of the Protocol, shall meet the costs only of:

(a) Transmitting data to the International Data Centre;

(b) Authenticating data from such stations;

(c) Upgrading stations to the required technical standard, unless the State responsible for such facilities meets these costs itself;

(d) If necessary, establishing new stations for the purposes of this Treaty where no appropriate facilities currently exist, unless the State responsible for such facilities meets these costs itself; and

(e) Any other costs related to the provision of data required by the Organization as specified in the relevant operational manuals.

21. The Organization shall also meet the cost of provision to each State Party of its requested selection from the standard range of International Data Centre reporting products and services, as specified in Part I, Section F of the Protocol. The cost of preparation and transmission of any additional data or products shall be met by requesting State Party.

22. The agreements or, if appropriate, arrangements concluded with States Parties or States hosting or otherwise taking responsibility for facilities of the International Monitoring System shall contain provisions for meeting these costs. Such provisions may include modalities whereby a State Party meets any of the costs referred to in paragraphs 19 (a) and 20 (c) and (d) for facilities with it hosts or for which it is responsible, and is compensated by an appropriate reduction in its assessed financial contribution to the Organization. Such a reduction shall not exceed 50 per cent of the annual assessed financial contribution of a State Party, but may be spread over successive years. A State Party may share such a reduction with another State Party by agreement or arrangement between themselves and with the concurrence of the Executive Council. The agreements or arrangements referred to in this paragraph shall be approved in accordance with Article II, paragraphs 26 (h) and 38 (i).

Changes to the International Monitoring System

23. Any measure referred to in paragraph 11 affecting the International Monitoring System by means of addition or deletion of a monitoring technology shall, when agreed, be incorporated into this Treaty and the Protocol pursuant to Article VII, paragraphs 1 to 6.

24. The following changes to the International Monitoring System, subject to the agreement of those

States directly affected, shall be regarded as matters of an administrative or technical nature pursuant to Article VII, paragraphs 7 and 8:

(a) Change to the number of facilities specified in the Protocol for a given monitoring technology; and

(b) Changes to other details for particular facilities as reflected in the Tables of Annex 1 to the Protocol (including, inter alia, State responsible for the facility; location; name of facility; type of facility; and attribution of a facility between the primary and auxiliary seismic networks).

If the Executive Council recommends, pursuant to Article VII, paragraph 8 (d), that such changes be adopted, it shall as a rule also recommend pursuant to Article VII, paragraph 8(g), that such changes enter into force upon notification by the Director-General of their approval.

25. The Director-General, in submitting to the Executive Council and States Parties information and evaluation in accordance with Article VII, paragraph 8 (b), shall include in the case of any proposal made pursuant to paragraph 24:

(a) A technical evaluation of the proposal;

(b) A statement on the administrative and financial impact of the proposal; and

(c) A report on consultations with States directly affected by the proposal, including indication of their agreement.

Temporary Arrangements

26. In cases of significant or irretrievable breakdown of a monitoring facility specified in the Table of Annex 1 to the Protocol, or in order to cover other temporary reductions of monitoring coverage, the Director-General shall, in consultation and agreement with those States directly affected, and with the approval of the Executive Council, initiate temporary arrangements of no more than one year's duration, renewable if necessary by agreement of the Executive Council and of the States directly affected for another year. Such arrangements shall not cause the number of operational facilities of the International Monitoring System to exceed the number specified for the relevant network; shall meet as far as possible the technical and operational requirements specified in the operational manual for the relevant network; and shall be conducted within the budget of the Organization. The Director-General shall furthermore take steps to rectify the situation and make pro-

posals for its permanent resolution. The Director-General shall notify all States Parties of any decision taken pursuant to this paragraph.

Cooperating National Facilities

27. States Parties may also separately establish cooperative arrangements with the Organization, in order to make available to the International Data Centre supplementary data from national monitoring stations that are not formally part of the International Monitoring System.

28. Such cooperative arrangements may be established as follows;

(a) Upon request by a State Party, and at the expense of that State, the Technical Secretariat shall take the steps required to certify that a given monitoring facility meets the technical and operational requirements specified in the relevant operational manuals for an International Monitoring Subject to the agreement of the Executive Council, the Technical Secretariat shall then formally designate such a facility as a cooperating national facility. The Technical Secretariat shall take the steps required to revalidate its certification as appropriate;

(b) The Technical Secretariat shall maintain a current list of cooperating national facilities and shall distribute it to all States Parties; and

(c) The International Data Centre shall call upon data from cooperation national facilities, if so requested by a State Party, for the purposes of facilitating consultation and clarification and the consideration of on-site inspection requests, data transmission costs being borne by that State Party.

The conditions under which supplementary data from such facilities are made available, and under which the International Data Centre may request further or expedited reporting, or clarifications, shall be elaborated in the operational manual for the respective monitoring network.

C. Consultation and Clarification

29. Without prejudice to the right of any State Party to request an on-site inspection, States Parties should, whenever possible, first make every effort to clarify and resolve, among themselves or with or through the Organization, any matter which may cause concern about possible non-compliance with the basic obligations of this Treaty.

30. A State Party that receives a request pursuant to paragraph 29 directly from another State Party

shall provide the clarification to the requesting State Party as soon as possible, but in any case no later than 48 hours after the request. The requesting and requested States Parties may keep the Executive Council and the Director-General informed of the request and the respone.

31. A State Party shall have the right to request the Director-General to assist in clarifying any matter which may cause concern about possible non-compliance with the basic obligations of this Treaty. The Director-General shall provide appropriate information in the possession of the Technical Secretariat relevant to such a concern. The Director-General shall inform the Executive Council of the request and of the information provided in response, if so requested by the requesting States Party.

32. A State Party shall have the right to request the Executive Council to obtain clarification from another State Party on any matter which may cause concern about possible non-compliance with the basic obligations of this Treaty. In such a case, the following shall apply;

(a) The Executive Council shall forward the request for clarification to the requested State Party through the Director-General no later than 24 hours after its receipt;

(b) The requested State Party shall provide the clarification to the Executive Council as soon as possible, but in any case no later than 48 hours after receipt of the request;

(c) The Executive Council shall take note of the clarification and forward it to the requesting States Party no later than 24 hours after its receipt;

(d) If the requesting State Party deems the clarification to be inadequate, it shall have the right to request the Executive Council to obtain further clarification from the requested State Party.

The Executive Council shall inform without delay all other States Parties about any request for clarification pursuant to this paragraph as well as any response provided by the requested State Party.

33. If the requesting State Party considers the clarification obtained under paragraph 32 (d) to be unsatisfactory, it shall have the right to request a meeting of the Executive Council in which States Parties involved that are not members of the Executive Council shall be entitled to take part. At such a meeting, the Executive Council shall consider the matter and may recommend any measure in accordance with Article V.

D. On-Site Inspections

Request for an On-Site Inspection

34. Each State Party has the right to request an on-site inspection in accordance with the provisions of this Article and Part II of the Protocol in the territory or in any other place under the jurisdiction or control of any State Party, or in any area beyond the jurisdiction or control of any State.

35. The sole purpose of an on-site inspection shall be to clarify whether a nuclear weapon test explosion or any other nuclear explosion has been carried out in violation of Article I and, to the extent possible, to gather any facts which might assist in identifying any possible violator.

36. The requesting State Party shall be under the obligation to keep the on-site inspection request within the scope of this Treaty and to provide in the request information in accordance with paragraph 37. The requesting State Party shall refrain from unfounded or abusive inspection requests.

37. The on-site inspection request shall be based on information collected by the International Monitoring System, on any relevant technical information obtained by national technical means of verification in a manner consistent with generally recognized principles of international law, or on a combination thereof. The request shall contain information pursuant to Part II, paragraph 41 of the Protocol.

38. The requesting State Party shall present the on-site inspection request to the Executive Council and at the same time to the Director-General for the latter to begin immediate processing.

Follow-up After Submission of an On-Site Inspection Request

39. The Executive Council shall begin its consideration immediately upon receipt of the on-site inspection request.

40. The Director-General, after receiving the on-site inspection request, shall acknowledge receipt of the request to the requesting State Party within two hours and communicate the request to the State Party sought to be inspected within six hours. The Director-General shall ascertain that the request meets the requirements specified in Part II, paragraph 41 of the Protocol, and if necessary, shall assist the requesting State Party in filing the request accordingly, and shall communicate the request to the Executive Council and to all other States Parties within 24 hours.

41. When the on-site inspection request fulfills the requirements, the Technical Secretariat shall begin

preparations for the on-site inspection without delay.

42. The Director-General, upon receipt of an on-site inspection request referring to an inspection area under the jurisdiction or control of a State Party, shall immediately seek clarification from the State Party sought to be inspected in order to clarify and resolve the concern raised in the request.

43. A State Party that receives a request for clarification pursuant to paragraph 42 shall provide the Director-General with explanations and with other relevant information available as soon as possible, but no later than 72 hours after receipt of the request for clarification.

44. The Director-General, before the Executive Council takes a decision on the on-site inspection request, shall transmit immediately to the Executive Council any additional information available from the International Monitoring System or provided any State Party on the event specified in the request, including any clarification provided pursuant to paragraphs 42 and 43, as well as any other information from within the Technical Secretariat that the Director-General deems relevant or that is requested by the Executive Council.

45. Unless the requesting State Party considers the concern raised in the on-site inspection request to be resolved and withdraws the request, the Executive Council shall take a decision on the request in accordance with paragraph 46.

Executive Council Decisions

46. The Executive Council shall take a decision on the on-site inspection request no later than 96 hours after receipt of the request from the requesting State Party. The decision to approve the on-site inspection shall be made by at least 30 affirmative votes of members of the Executive Council. If the Executive Council does not approve the inspection, preparations shall be stopped and no further action on the request shall be taken.

47. No later than 25 days after the approval of the on-site inspection in accordance with paragraph 46, the inspection team shall transmit to the Executive Council, through the Director-General, a progress inspection report. The continuation of the inspection shall be considered approved unless the Executive Council, no later than 72 hours after receipt of the progress inspection report, decides by a majority of all its members not to continue the inspection, the inspection shall be terminated, and the inspection team shall leave the inspection area and the territory of the inspected State Party as soon as possible in accordance with Part II, paragraphs 109 and 110 of

the Protocol.

48. In the course of the on-site inspection, the inspection team may submit to the Executive Council, through the Director-General, a proposal to conduct drilling. The Executive Council shall take a decision on such a proposal no later than 72 hours after receipt of the proposal. The decision to approve drilling shall be made by a majority of all members of the Executive Council.

49. The inspection team may request the Executive Council, through the Director-General, to extend the inspection duration by a maximum of 70 days beyond the 60-day time-frame specified in Part II, paragraph 4 of the Protocol, if the inspection team considers such an extension essential to enable it to fulfill its mandate. The inspection team shall indicate in its request which of the activities and techniques listed in Part II, paragraph 69 of the Protocol it intends to carry out during the extension period. The Executive Council shall take a decision on the extension request no later than 72 hours after receipt of the request. The decision to approve an extension of the inspection duration shall be made by a majority of all members of the Executive Council.

50. Any time following the approval of the continuation of the on-site inspection in accordance with paragraph 47, the inspection team may submit to the Executive Council, through the Director-General, a recommendation to terminate the inspection. Such a recommendation shall be considered approved unless the Executive Council, no later than 72 hours after receipt of the recommendation, decides by a two-thirds majority of all its members not to approve the termination of the inspection. In case of termination of the inspection, the inspection team shall leave the inspection area and the territory of the inspected State Party as soon as possible in accordance with Part II, paragraphs 109 and 110 of the Protocol

51. The requesting State Party and the State Party sought to be inspected may participate in the deliberations of the Executive Council on the on-site inspection request without voting. The requesting State Party and the inspected State Party may also participate without voting in any subsequent deliberations of the Executive Council related to the inspection.

52. The Director-General shall notify all States Parties within 24 hours about any decision by and reports, proposals, requests and recommendations to the Executive Council pursuant to paragraphs 46 to 50.

Follow-up After Executive Council Approval of an On-Site Inspection

53. An on-site inspection approved by the Execu-

tive Council shall be conducted without delay by an inspection team designated by the Director-General and in accordance with the provisions of this Treaty and the Protocol. The inspection team shall arrive at the point of entry no later than six days following the receipt by the Executive Council of the on-site inspection request from the requesting State Party.

54. This Director-General shall issue an inspection mandate for the conduct of the on-site inspection. The inspection mandate shall contain the information specified in Part II, paragraph 42 of the Protocol.

55. The Director-General shall notify the inspected State Party of the inspection no less than 24 hours before the planned arrival of the inspection team at the point of entry, in accordance with Part II, paragraph 43 of the Protocol.

The Conduct of an On-Site Inspection

56. Each State Party shall permit the Organization to conduct an on-site inspection on its territory or at place under its jurisdiction or control in accordance with the provisions of this Treaty and the Protocol. However, no State Party shall have to accept simultaneous on-site inspections on its territory or at places under its jurisdiction or control.

57. In accordance with the provisions of this Treaty and the Protocol, the inspected States Party shall have:

(a) The right and the obligation to make every reasonable effort to demonstrate its compliance with this Treaty and, to this end, to enable the inspection team to fulfill its mandate;

(b) The right to take measures it deems necessary to protect national security interests and to prevent disclosure of confidential information not related to the purpose of the inspection;

(c) The obligation to provide access within the inspection area for the sole purpose of determining facts relevant to the purposes of the inspection, taking into account sub-paragraph (b) and any constitutional obligations it may have with regard to proprietary rights or searches and seizures;

(d) The obligation not to invoke this paragraph or Part II, paragraph 88 of the Protocol to conceal any violation of its obligations under Article I; and

(e) The obligation not to impede the ability of the inspection team to move within the inspection area and to carry out inspection activities in accordance with this Treaty and the Protocol.

Access, in the context of an on-site inspection, means both the physical access of the inspection team and the inspection equipment to, and the conduct of inspection activities within, the inspection area.

58. The on-site inspection shall be conducted in the least intrusive manner possible, consistent with the efficient and timely accomplishment of the inspection mandate, and in accordance with the procedures set forth in the Protocol. Wherever possible, the inspection team shall begin with the least intrusive procedures and then proceed to more intrusive procedures only as it deems necessary to collect sufficient information to clarify the concern about possible non-compliance with this Treaty. The inspectors shall seek only the information and data necessary for the purpose of the inspection and shall seek to minimize interference with normal operations of the inspected State Party.

59. The inspected State Party shall assist the inspection team throughout the on-site inspection and facilitate its task.

60. If the inspected State Party, acting in accordance with Part II, paragraphs 86 to 96 of the Protocol, restricts access within the inspection area, it shall make every reasonable effort in consultations with the inspection team to demonstrate through alternative means its compliance with this Treaty.

Observer

61. With regard to an observer, the following shall apply:

(a) The requesting State Party, subject to the agreement of the inspected State Party, may send a representative, who shall be a national either of the requesting State Party or of a third State Party, to observe the conduct of the on-site inspection;

(b) The inspected State Party shall notify its acceptance or non-acceptance of the proposed observer to the Director-General within 12 hours after approval of the on-site inspection by the Executive Council;

(c) In case of acceptance, the inspected State Party shall grant access to the observer in accordance with the Protocol;

(d) The inspected State Party shall, as a rule, accept the proposed observer, but if the inspected State Party exercises a refusal, that fact shall be recorded in the inspection report.

There shall be no more than three observers from an aggregate of requesting States Parties.

Reports of an On-Site Inspection

62. Inspection reports shall contain;

(a) A description of the activities conducted by the inspection team;

(b) The factual finding of the inspection team relevant to the purpose of the inspection;

(c) An account of the cooperation granted during the on-site inspection;

(d) A factual description of the extent of the access granted, including the alternative means provided to the team, during the on-site inspection; and

(e) Any other details relevant to the purpose of the inspection.

Differing observations made by inspection may be attached to the report.

63. The Director-General shall make draft inspection reports available to the inspected State Party. The inspected State Party shall have the right to provide the Director-General within 48 hours with its comments and explanations, and to identify any information and data which, in its view, are not related to the purpose of the inspection and should not be circulated outside the Technical Secretariat. The Director-General shall consider the proposals for changes to the draft inspection report made by the inspected Party and shall wherever possible incorporate them. The Director General shall also annex the comments and explanations provided by the inspected State Party to the inspection report.

64. The Director-General shall promptly transmit the inspection report to the requesting State Party, the inspected, the Executive Council and to all other State Parties. The Director-General shall further transmit promptly to the Executive Council and to all other States Parties any results of sample analysis in designated laboratories in accordance with Part II, paragraph 104 of the Protocol, relevant data from the International Monitoring System, the assessments of the requesting and inspected States Parties, as well as any other information that the Director-General deems relevant. In the case of the progress inspection report referred to in paragraph 47, the Director-General shall transmit the report to the Executive Council within the time-frame specified in that paragraph.

65. The Executive Council, in accordance with its powers and functions, shall review the inspection report and any material provided pursuant to paragraph 64, and shall address any concerns as to:

(a) Whether any non-compliance with this Treaty has occurred; and

(b) Whether the right to request an on-site inspection has been abused.

66. If the Executive Council reaches the conclusion, in keeping with its powers and functions, that further action may be necessary with regard to paragraph 65, it shall take the appropriate measures in accordance with Article V.

Frivolous or Abusive On-Site Inspection Requests

67. If the Executive Council does not approve the on-site inspection on the basis that the on-site inspection request is frivolous or abusive, or if the inspection is terminated for the same reasons, the Executive Council shall consider and decide on whether to implement appropriate measures to redress the situation, including the following;

(a) Requiring the requesting State Party to pay for the cost of any preparations made by the Technical Secretariat;

(b) Suspending the right of the requesting State Party to request an on-site inspection for a period of time, as determined by the Executive Council; and

(c) suspending the right of the requesting State Party to serve on the Executive Council for a period of time.

E. Confidence-Building Measures

68. In order to:

(a) Contribute to the timely resolution of any compliance concerns arising from possible misinterpretation of verification data relating to chemical explosions; and

(b) Assist in the calibration of the stations that are part of the component networks of the International Monitoring System,

Each State Party undertakes to cooperate with the Organization and with other States Parties in implementing relevant measures as set out in Part III of the Protocol.

Article 5

Measures to Redress a Situation and to Ensure Compliance, Including Sanctions

1. The Conference, taking into account, *inter alia,*

the recommendation of the Executive Council, shall take the necessary measures, as set forth in paragraph 2 and 3, to ensure compliance with this Treaty and to redress and remedy any situation which contravenes the provisions of this Treaty.

2. In cases where a State Party has been requested by the Conference or the Executive Council to redress a situation raising problems with regard to its compliance and fails to fulfill the request within the specified time, the Conference may, *inter alia*, decide to restrict or suspend the State Party from the exercise of its rights and privileges under this Treaty until the Conference decides otherwise.

3. In case where damage to the object and purpose of this Treaty may result from non-compliance with the basic obligations of this Treaty, the Conference may recommend to States Parties collective measures which are in conformity with international law.

4. The Conference, or alternatively, if the case is urgent, the Executive Council, may bring the issue, including relevant information and conclusions, to the attention of the United Nations.

Article 6

Settlement of Disputes

1. Disputes that may arise concerning the application or the interpretation of this Treaty shall be settled in accordance with the relevant provisions of this Treaty and in conformity with the provisions of the Charter of the United Nations.

2. When a dispute arises between two or more States Parties, or between one or more States Parties and the Organization, relating to the application or interpretation of this Treaty, the parties concerned shall consult together with a view to the expeditious settlement of the dispute by negotiation or by other peaceful means of the parties' choice, including recourse to appropriate organs of this Treaty and, by mutual consent, referred to the International Court of Justice in conformity with the State of the Court. The parties involved shall keep the Executive Council informed of actions being taken.

3. The Executive Council may contribute to the settlement of a dispute that may arise concerning the application or interpretation of this Treaty by whatever means it deems appropriate, including offering its good offices calling upon the States Parties to a dispute to seek a settlement through a process of their own choice, bringing the matter to the attention of the Conference and recommending time-limit for any agreed procedure.

4. The Conference shall consider questions related to disputes raised by States Parties or brought to its attention by the Council. The Conference shall, as it finds necessary, establish or entrust organs with tasks related to the settlement of these disputes in conformity with Article 2, paragraph 26 (j).

5. The Conference and the Executive Council are separately empowered subject to authorization from General Assembly of the United Nations, to request the International Court of Justice to give an advisory opinion on any legal question arising within the scope of the United Nations shall be concluded for this purpose in accordance with Article II, paragraph 38 (h).

6. This Article is without prejudice to Article IV and V.

Article 7

Amendments

1. At any time after the entry into force of this Treaty, any State Party may propose amendments to this Treaty, the Protocol, or the Annexes to the Protocol. Any State Party may also propose changes, in accordance with paragraph 7, to the Protocol or the Annexes thereto. Proposals for amendments shall be subject to the procedures in paragraphs 2 to 6. Proposals for change, in accordance with paragraph 7, shall be subject to the procedures in paragraph 8.

2. The proposed amendment shall be considered and adopted only by an Amendment Conference.

3. Any proposal for an amendment shall be communicated to the Director-General, who shall circulate it to all States Parties and the Depository and seek the views of the States Parties on whether an Amendment Conference should be convened to consider the proposal. If a majority of the States Parties notify the Director-General no later than 30 days after its Circulation that they support further consideration of the proposal, the Director-General shall convene an Amendment Conference to which all States Parties shall be invited.

4. The Amendment Conference shall be held immediately following a regular session of the Conference unless all States Parties that support the convening of an Amendment Conference request that it be held earlier. In no case shall an Amendment Conference be held less than 60 days after the circulation of the proposed amendment.

5. Amendments shall be adopted by the Amendment Conference by a positive vote of a majority of the States Parties with no States Party casting a negative vote.

6. Amendment shall enter into force for all States Parties 30 days after deposit of the instruments of ratification or acceptance by all those States Parties cast-

ing a positive vote at the Amendment Conference.

7. In order to ensure the viability and effectiveness of this Treaty, Parts I and III of the Protocol and Annexes 1 and 2 to the Protocol shall be subject to change in accordance with paragraph 8, if the proposed changes are related only to matters of an administrative or technical nature. All other provisions of the Protocol and the Annexes thereto shall not be subject to change in accordance with Paragraph 8.

8. Proposed changes referred to in paragraph 7 shall be made in accordance with the following procedures:

(a) The text of the proposed changes shall be transmitted together with the necessary information to the Director-General. Additional information for the evaluation of the proposal may be provided by any State Party and the Director-General. The Director-General shall promptly communicate any such proposals and information to all States Parties, the Executive Council and the Depositary;

(b) No later than 60 days after its receipt, the Director-General shall evaluate the proposal to determine all its possible consequences for the provisions of this Treaty and its implementation and shall communicate any such information to all States Parties and the Executive Council;

(c) The Executive Council shall examine the proposal in the light of all information available to it, including whether the proposal fulfills the requirements of paragraph 7. No later than 90 days after its receipt, the Executive Council shall notify its recommendation, with appropriate explanation, to all States Parties for consideration. States Parties shall acknowledge receipt within 10 days;

(d) If the Executive Council recommends to all States Parties that the proposal be adopted, it shall be considered approved if no State Party objects to it within 90 days after receipt of the recommendation. If the Executive Council recommends that the proposal be rejected, it shall be considered rejected if no State Party objects to the rejection within 90 days after receipt of the recommendation;

(e) If a recommendation of the Executive Council does not meet with the acceptance required under sub-paragraph (d), a decision on the proposal, including whether it fulfills the requirements of paragraph 7, shall be taken as a matter of substance by the Conference at its next session;

(f) The Director-General shall notify all State Parties and the Depositary of any decision under this paragraph;

(g) Changes approved under this procedure shall enter into force for all States Parties 180 days after the date of notification by the Director-General of their approval unless another time period is recommended by the Executive Council or decided by the Conference.

Article 8

Review of the Treaty

1. Unless otherwise decided by a majority of the States Parties, ten years after the entry into force of this Treaty a Conference of the States Parties shall be held to review the operation and effectiveness of this Treaty, with a view to assuring itself that the objectives and purposes in the Preamble and the provisions of the Treaty are being realized. Such review shall take into account any new scientific and technological developments relevant to this Treaty. On the basis of a request by any State Party, the Review Conference shall consider the possibility of permitting the conduct of underground nuclear explosions for peaceful purposes. If the review Conference decides by consensus that such nuclear explosions may be permitted. It shall commence work without delay, with a view to recommending to States Parties an appropriate amendment to this Treaty that shall preclude any military benefits to the Director-General by any State Party and shall be dealt with in accordance with the provisions of Article VII (*).

2. At intervals of ten years thereafter, further Review Conferences may be convened with the same objective, if the Conference so decides as a matter of procedure in the preceding year. Such Conferences may be convened after an interval of less than ten years if so decided by the Conference as a matter of substance.

3. Normally, any Review Conference shall be held immediately following the regular annual session of the Conference provided for in Article II.

Article 9

Duration and Withdrawal

1. This Treaty shall be of unlimited duration.

2. Each State Party shall, in exercising its national sovereignty, have the right to withdraw from this Treaty if it decides that extraordinary event related to the subject matter of this Treaty have jeopardized its

supreme interests.

3. Withdrawal shall be effected by giving notice six months in advance to all other States Parties, the Executive Council, the Depositary and the United Nations Security Council. Notice of withdrawal shall include a statement of the extraordinary event or events which a State Party regards as jeopardizing its supreme interests.

Article 10

Status of the Protocol and the Annexes

The Annexes to this Treaty, the Protocol, and the Annexes to the Protocol form an integral of the Treaty. Any reference to this Treaty includes the Annexes to this Treaty, the Protocol and the Annexes to the Protocol.

Article 11

Signature

This Treaty shall be open to all States for signature before its entry into force.

Article 12

Ratification

This Treaty shall be subject to ratification by States Signatories according to their respective constitutional processes.

Article 13

Accession

Any State which does not sign this Treaty before its entry into force may accede to it at any time thereafter.

Article 14

Entry into Force

1. This Treaty shall enter into force 180 days after the date of deposit of the instruments of ratification by all States listed in Annex 2 to this Treaty, but in no case earlier than two years after its opening for signature.

2. If this Treaty has not entered into force three years after the date of the anniversary of its opening for signature, the Depositary shall convene a Conference of the States that have already deposited their instruments of ratification upon the request of a majority of those States. That Conference shall examine the extent to which the requirement set out in paragraph 1 has been met and shall consider and decide by consensus what measure consistent with

international law may be undertaken to accelerate the ratification process in order to facilitate the early entry into force of this Treaty.

3. Unless otherwise decided by the Conference referred to in paragraph 2 or other such conferences, this process shall be repeated at subsequent anniversaries of the opening for signature of this Treaty, until its entry into force.

4. All States Signatories shall be invited to attend the Conference referred to in paragraph 2 and subsequent conferences as referred to in paragraph 3, as observers.

5. For States whose instruments of ratification or accession are deposited subsequent to the entry into force of this Treaty, it shall enter into force on the 30th day following the date of deposit of their instruments of ratification or accession.

Article 15

Reservations

The Articles of and the Annexes to this Treaty shall not be subject to reservations. The provisions of the Protocol to this Treaty and the Annexes to the Protocol shall not be subject to reservations incompatible with the object and purpose of this Treaty.

Article 16

Depositary

1. The Secretary-General of the United Nations shall be the Depositary of this Treaty and shall receive signatures, instruments of ratification and instruments of accession.

2. The Depositary shall promptly inform all States Signatories and acceding States of the date of each signature, the date of deposit of each instrument of ratification or accession, the date of the entry into force of this Treaty and of any amendments and changes thereto, and the receipt of other notices.

3. The Depositary shall send duly certified copies of this Treaty to the Governments of the States Signatories and acceding States.

4. This Treaty shall be registered by the Depositary pursuant to Article 102 of the Charter of the United Nations.

Article 17

Authentic Texts

This Treaty, of which the Arabic, Chinese, English, French, Russian and Spanish texts are equally authentic, shall be deposited with the Secretary-General of the United Nations.

The 1987 Montreal Protocol on Substances that Deplete the Ozone Layer

as adjusted and amended by the second Meeting of the Parties (London, 27-29 June 1990) and by the fourth Meeting of the Parties (Copenhagen, 23-25 November 1992) and further adjusted by the seventh Meeting of the Parties (Vienna, 5-7 December 1995) and further adjusted and amended by the ninth Meeting of the Parties (Montreal, 15-17 September 1997)

Date of signature (Montreal Amendment):
September 17, 1997
Place of signature (Montreal Amendment):
Montreal
Signatory states (Montreal Protocol): *Argentina, Australia, Austria, Belarus, Belgium, Burkina Faso, Canada, Chile, Congo, Denmark, European Community, Finland, France, Germany, Ghana, Greece, Indonesia, Ireland, Israel, Italy, Japan, Kenya, Luxembourg, Maldives, Malta, Mexico, Morocco, Netherlands, New Zealand, Norway, Panama, Philippines, Portugal, Russian Federation, Senegal, Spain, Sweden, Switzerland, Thiland, Togo, Uganda, Ukraine, United Kingdom, USA, Venezuela*
Ratification (Montreal Amendment): *Australia, Canada, Chile, Germany, Jordan, Korea, Republic of, Luxembourg, Norway (as of February 8, 1999)*
Date of entry into force: *Vienna Convention (September 22, 1988); Montreal Protocol (January 1, 1989); London Amendment (August 10, 1992); Copenhagen Amendment (June 14, 1994); Montreal Amendment (not yet in force, as of February 8, 1999)*

Preamble

The Parties to this Protocol,

Being Parties to the Vienna Convention for the Protection of the Ozone Layer,

Mindful of their obligation under that Convention to take appropriate measures to protect human health and the environment against adverse effects resulting or likely to result from human activities which modify or are likely to modify the ozone layer,

Recognizing that world-wide emissions of certain substances can significantly deplete and otherwise modify the ozone layer in a manner that is likely to result in adverse effects on human health and the environment,

Conscious of the potential climatic effects of emissions of these substances,

Aware that measures taken to protect the ozone layer from depletion should be based on relevant scientific knowledge, taking into account technical and economic considerations,

Determined to protect the ozone layer by taking precautionary measures to control equitably total global emissions of substances that deplete it, with the ultimate objective of their elimination on the basis of developments in scientific knowledge, taking into account technical and economic considerations and bearing in mind the developmental needs of developing countries,

Acknowledging that special provision is required to meet the needs of developing countries, including the provision of additional financial resources and access to relevant technologies, bearing in mind that the magnitude of funds necessary is predictable, and the funds can be expected to make a substantial difference in the world's ability to address the scientifically established problem of ozone depletion and its harmful effects,

Noting the precautionary measures for controlling emissions of certain chlorofluorocarbons that have already been taken at national and regional levels,

Considering the importance of promoting international co-operation in the research, development and transfer of alternative technologies relating to the control and reduction of emissions of substances that deplete the ozone layer, bearing in mind in particular the needs of developing countries,

HAVE AGREED AS FOLLOWS:

Article 1

Definitions

For the purposes of this Protocol:

1. "Convention" means the Vienna Convention for the Protection of the Ozone Layer, adopted on 22 March 1985.

2. "Parties" means, unless the text otherwise indicates, Parties to this Protocol.

3. "Secretariat" means the Secretariat of the Convention.

4. "Controlled substance" means a substance in Annex A, Annex B, Annex C or Annex E to this Protocol, whether existing alone or in a mixture. It includes the isomers of any such substance, except as specified in the relevant Annex, but excludes any controlled substance or mixture which is in a manufactured product other than a container used for the transportation or storage of that substance.

5. "Production" means the amount of controlled substances produced, minus the amount destroyed by technologies to be approved by the Parties and minus the amount entirely used as feedstock in the manufacture of other chemicals. The amount recycled and reused is not to be considered as "production".

6. "Consumption" means production plus imports minus exports of controlled substances.

7. "Calculated levels" of production, imports, exports and consumption means levels determined in accordance with Article 3.

8. "Industrial rationalization" means the transfer of all or a portion of the calculated level of production of one Party to another, for the purpose of achieving economic efficiencies or responding to anticipated shortfalls in supply as a result of plant closures.

Article 2

Control Measures

1. *Incorporated in Article 2A.*

2. *Replaced by Article 2B.*

3. *Replaced by Article 2A.*

4. *Replaced by Article 2A.*

5. Any Party may, for one or more control periods, transfer to another Party any portion of its calculated level of production set out in Articles 2A to 2E, and Article 2H, provided that the total combined calculated levels of production of the Parties concerned for any group of controlled substances do not exceed the production limits set out in those Articles for that group. Such transfer of production shall be notified to the Secretariat by each of the Parties concerned,

stating the terms of such transfer and the period for which it is to apply.

5 *bis* Any Party not operating under paragraph 1 of Article 5 may, for one or more control periods, transfer to another such Party any portion of its calculated level of consumption set out in Article 2F, provided that the calculated level of consumption of controlled substances in Group I of Annex A of the Party transferring the portion of its calculated level of consumption did not exceed 0.25 kilograms per capita in 1989 and that the total combined calculated levels of consumption of the Parties concerned do not exceed the consumption limits set out in Article 2F. Such transfer of consumption shall be notified to the Secretariat by each of the Parties concerned, stating the terms of such transfer and the period for which it is to apply.

6. Any Party not operating under Article 5, that has facilities for the production of Annex A or Annex B controlled substances under construction, or contracted for, prior to 16 September 1987, and provided for in national legislation prior to 1 January 1987, may add the production from such facilities to its 1986 production of such substances for the purposes of determining its calculated level of production for 1986, provided that such facilities are completed by 31 December 1990 and that such production does not raise that Party's annual calculated level of consumption of the controlled substances above 0.5 kilograms per capita.

7. Any transfer of production pursuant to paragraph 5 or any addition of production pursuant to paragraph 6 shall be notified to the Secretariat, no later than the time of the transfer or addition.

8. (a) Any Parties which are Member States of a regional economic integration organization as defined in Article 1 (6) of the Convention may agree that they shall jointly fulfil their obligations respecting consumption under this Article and Articles 2A to 2H provided that their total combined calculated level of consumption does not exceed the levels required by this Article and Articles 2A to 2H.

(b) The Parties to any such agreement shall inform the Secretariat of the terms of the agreement before the date of the reduction in consumption with which the agreement is concerned.

(c) Such agreement will become operative only if all Member States of the regional economic integration organization and the organization concerned are Parties to the Protocol and have notified the Secretariat of their manner of implementation.

9. (a) Based on the assessments made pursuant to Article 6, the Parties may decide whether:

(i) Adjustments to the ozone depleting potentials specified in Annex A, Annex B, Annex C and/or Annex E should be made and, if so, what the adjustments should be; and

(ii) Further adjustments and reductions of production or consumption of the controlled substances should be undertaken and, if so, what the scope, amount and timing of any such adjustments and reductions should be;

(b) Proposals for such adjustments shall be communicated to the Parties by the Secretariat at least six months before the meeting of the Parties at which they are proposed for adoption;

(c) In taking such decisions, the Parties shall make every effort to reach agreement by consensus. If all efforts at consensus have been exhausted, and no agreement reached, such decisions shall, as a last resort, be adopted by a two-thirds majority vote of the Parties present and voting representing a majority of the Parties operating under Paragraph 1 of Article 5 present and voting and a majority of the Parties not so operating present and voting;

(d) The decisions, which shall be binding on all Parties, shall forthwith be communicated to the Parties by the Depositary. Unless otherwise provided in the decisions, they shall enter into force on the expiry of six months from the date of the circulation of the communication by the Depositary.

10. Based on the assessments made pursuant to Article 6 of this Protocol and in accordance with the procedure set out in Article 9 of the Convention, the Parties may decide:

(a) whether any substances, and if so which, should be added to or removed from any annex to this Protocol, and

(b) the mechanism, scope and timing of the control measures that should apply to those substances;

11. Notwithstanding the provisions contained in this Article and Articles 2A to 2H Parties may take more stringent measures than those required by this Article and Articles 2A to 2H.

Introduction to the adjustments

The Second, Fourth, Seventh and Ninth Meetings of the Parties to the Montreal Protocol on Substances that Deplete the Ozone Layer decided, on the basis of assessments made pursuant to Article 6 of the Protocol, to adopt adjustments and reductions of production and consumption of the controlled substances in Annexes A, B, C and E to the Protocol as follows (the text here shows the cumulative effect of all the adjustments):

Article 2A

CFCs

1. Each Party shall ensure that for the twelve-month period commencing on the first day of the seventh month following the date of entry into force of this Protocol, and in each twelve-month period thereafter, its calculated level of consumption of the controlled substances in Group I of Annex A does not exceed its calculated level of consumption in 1986. By the end of the same period, each Party producing one or more of these substances shall ensure that its calculated level of production of the substances does not exceed its calculated level of production in 1986, except that such level may have increased by no more than ten per cent based on the 1986 level. Such increase shall be permitted only so as to satisfy the basic domestic needs of the Parties operating under Article 5 and for the purposes of industrial rationalization between Parties.

2. Each Party shall ensure that for the period from 1 July 1991 to 31 December 1992 its calculated levels of consumption and production of the controlled substances in Group I of Annex A do not exceed 150 per cent of its calculated levels of production and consumption of those substances in 1986; with effect from 1 January 1993, the twelve-month control period for these controlled substances shall run from 1 January to 31 December each year.

3. Each Party shall ensure that for the twelve-month period commencing on 1 January 1994, and in each twelve-month period thereafter, its calculated level of consumption of the controlled substances in Group I of Annex A does not exceed, annually, twenty-five per cent of its calculated level of consumption in 1986. Each Party producing one or more of these substances shall, for the same periods, ensure that its calculated level of production of the substances does not exceed, annually, twenty-five per cent of its calculated level of production in 1986. However, in order to satisfy the basic domestic needs of the Par-

ties operating under paragraph 1 of Article 5, its calculated level of production may exceed that limit by up to ten per cent of its calculated level of production in 1986.

4. Each Party shall ensure that for the twelve-month period commencing on 1 January 1996, and in each twelve-month period thereafter, its calculated level of consumption of the controlled substances in Group I of Annex A does not exceed zero. Each Party producing one or more of these substances shall, for the same periods, ensure that its calculated level of production of the substances does not exceed zero. However, in order to satisfy the basic domestic needs of the Parties operating under paragraph 1 of Article 5, its calculated level of production may exceed that limit by up to fifteen per cent of its calculated level of production in 1986. This paragraph will apply save to the extent that the Parties decide to permit the level of production or consumption that is necessary to satisfy uses agreed by them to be essential.

Article 2B

Halons

1. Each Party shall ensure that for the twelve-month period commencing on 1 January 1992, and in each twelve-month period thereafter, its calculated level of consumption of the controlled substances in Group II of Annex A does not exceed, annually, its calculated level of consumption in 1986. Each Party producing one or more of these substances shall, for the same periods, ensure that its calculated level of production of the substances does not exceed, annually, its calculated level of production in 1986. However, in order to satisfy the basic domestic needs of the Parties operating under paragraph 1 of Article 5, its calculated level of production may exceed that limit by up to ten per cent of its calculated level of production in 1986.

2. Each Party shall ensure that for the twelve-month period commencing on 1 January 1994, and in each twelve-month period thereafter, its calculated level of consumption of the controlled substances in Group II of Annex A does not exceed zero. Each Party producing one or more of these substances shall, for the same periods, ensure that its calculated level of production of the substances does not exceed zero. However, in order to satisfy the basic domestic needs of the Parties operating under paragraph 1 of Article 5, its calculated level of production may exceed that limit by up to fifteen per cent of its calculated level of production in 1986. This paragraph will apply save to the extent that the Parties decide to permit the level of

production or consumption that is necessary to satisfy uses agreed by them to be essential.

Article 2C

Other fully halogenated CFCs

1. Each Party shall ensure that for the twelve-month period commencing on 1 January 1993, its calculated level of consumption of the controlled substances in Group I of Annex B does not exceed, annually, eighty per cent of its calculated level of consumption in 1989. Each Party producing one or more of these substances shall, for the same period, ensure that its calculated level of production of the substances does not exceed, annually, eighty per cent of its calculated level of production in 1989. However, in order to satisfy the basic domestic needs of the Parties operating under paragraph 1 of Article 5, its calculated level of production may exceed that limit by up to ten per cent of its calculated level of production in 1989.

2. Each Party shall ensure that for the twelve-month period commencing on 1 January 1994, and in each twelve-month period thereafter, its calculated level of consumption of the controlled substances in Group I of Annex B does not exceed, annually, twenty-five per cent of its calculated level of consumption in 1989. Each Party producing one or more of these substances shall, for the same periods, ensure that its calculated level of production of the substances does not exceed, annually, twenty-five per cent of its calculated level of production in 1989. However, in order to satisfy the basic domestic needs of the Parties operating under paragraph 1 of Article 5, its calculated level of production may exceed that limit by up to ten per cent of its calculated level of production in 1989.

3. Each Party shall ensure that for the twelve-month period commencing on 1 January 1996, and in each twelve-month period thereafter, its calculated level of consumption of the controlled substances in Group I of Annex B does not exceed zero. Each Party producing one or more of these substances shall, for the same periods, ensure that its calculated level of production of the substances does not exceed zero. However, in order to satisfy the basic domestic needs of the Parties operating under paragraph 1 of Article 5, its calculated level of production may exceed that limit by up to fifteen per cent of its calculated level of production in 1989. This paragraph will apply save to the extent that the Parties decide to permit the level of production or consumption that is necessary to satisfy uses agreed by them to be essential.

Article 2D

Carbon tetrachloride

1. Each Party shall ensure that for the twelve-month period commencing on 1 January 1995, its calculated level of consumption of the controlled substance in Group II of Annex B does not exceed, annually, fifteen per cent of its calculated level of consumption in 1989. Each Party producing the substance shall, for the same period, ensure that its calculated level of production of the substance does not exceed, annually, fifteen per cent of its calculated level of production in 1989. However, in order to satisfy the basic domestic needs of the Parties operating under paragraph 1 of Article 5, its calculated level of production may exceed that limit by up to ten per cent of its calculated level of production in 1989.

2. Each Party shall ensure that for the twelve-month period commencing on 1 January 1996, and in each twelve-month period thereafter, its calculated level of consumption of the controlled substance in Group II of Annex B does not exceed zero. Each Party producing the substance shall, for the same periods, ensure that its calculated level of production of the substance does not exceed zero. However, in order to satisfy the basic domestic needs of the Parties operating under paragraph 1 of Article 5, its calculated level of production may exceed that limit by up to fifteen per cent of its calculated level of production in 1989. This paragraph will apply save to the extent that the Parties decide to permit the level of production or consumption that is necessary to satisfy uses agreed by them to be essential.

Article 2E

1.1.1-Trichloroethane (Methyl chloroform)

1. Each Party shall ensure that for the twelve-month period commencing on 1 January 1993, its calculated level of consumption of the controlled substance in Group III of Annex B does not exceed, annually, its calculated level of consumption in 1989. Each Party producing the substance shall, for the same period, ensure that its calculated level of production of the substance does not exceed, annually, its calculated level of production in 1989. However, in order to satisfy the basic domestic needs of the Parties operating under paragraph 1 of Article 5, its calculated level of production may exceed that limit by up to ten per cent of its calculated level of production in 1989.

2. Each Party shall ensure that for the twelve-month period commencing on 1 January 1994, and in each twelve-month period thereafter, its calculated level of consumption of the controlled substance in Group III of Annex B does not exceed, annually, fifty per cent of its calculated level of consumption in 1989. Each Party producing the substance shall, for the same periods, ensure that its calculated level of production of the substance does not exceed, annually, fifty per cent of its calculated level of production in 1989. However, in order to satisfy the basic domestic needs of the Parties operating under paragraph 1 of Article 5, its calculated level of production may exceed that limit by up to ten per cent of its calculated level of production in 1989.

3. Each Party shall ensure that for the twelve-month period commencing on 1 January 1996, and in each twelve-month period thereafter, its calculated level of consumption of the controlled substance in Group III of Annex B does not exceed zero. Each Party producing the substance shall, for the same periods, ensure that its calculated level of production of the substance does not exceed zero. However, in order to satisfy the basic domestic needs of the Parties operating under paragraph 1 of Article 5, its calculated level of production may exceed that limit by up to fifteen per cent of its calculated level of production for 1989. This paragraph will apply save to the extent that the Parties decide to permit the level of production or consumption that is necessary to satisfy uses agreed by them to be essential.

Article 2F

Hydrochlorofluorocarbons

1. Each Party shall ensure that for the twelve-month period commencing on 1 January 1996, and in each twelve-month period thereafter, its calculated level of consumption of the controlled substances in Group I of Annex C does not exceed, annually, the sum of:

(a) Two point eight per cent of its calculated level of consumption in 1989 of the controlled substances in Group I of Annex A; and

(b) Its calculated level of consumption in 1989 of the controlled substances in Group I of Annex C.

2. Each Party shall ensure that for the twelve month period commencing on 1 January 2004, and in each twelve-month period thereafter, its calculated level of consumption of the controlled substances in Group I of Annex C does not exceed, annually, sixty-five per cent of the sum referred to in paragraph 1 of this Article.

3. Each Party shall ensure that for the twelve-month period commencing on 1 January 2010, and in each twelve-month period thereafter, its calculated level of consumption of the controlled substances in Group I of Annex C does not exceed, annually, thirty-five per cent of the sum referred to in paragraph 1 of this Article.

4. Each Party shall ensure that for the twelve-month period commencing on 1 January 2015, and in each twelve-month period thereafter, its calculated level of consumption of the controlled substances in Group I of Annex C does not exceed, annually, ten per cent of the sum referred to in paragraph 1 of this Article.

5. Each Party shall ensure that for the twelve-month period commencing on 1 January 2020, and in each twelve-month period thereafter, its calculated level of consumption of the controlled substances in Group I of Annex C does not exceed, annually, zero point five per cent of the sum referred to in paragraph 1 of this Article. Such consumption shall, however, be restricted to the servicing of refrigeration and air conditioning equipment existing at that date.

6. Each Party shall ensure that for the twelve-month period commencing on 1 January 2030, and in each twelve-month period thereafter, its calculated level of consumption of the controlled substances in Group I of Annex C does not exceed zero.

7. As of 1 January 1996, each Party shall endeavour to ensure that:

(a) The use of controlled substances in Group I of Annex C is limited to those applications where other more environmentally suitable alternative substances or technologies are not available;

(b) The use of controlled substances in Group I of Annex C is not outside the areas of application currently met by controlled substances in Annexes A, B and C, except in rare cases for the protection of human life or human health; and

(c) Controlled substances in Group I of Annex C are selected for use in a manner that minimizes ozone depletion, in addition to meeting other environmental, safety and economic considerations.

Article 2G

Hydrobromofluorocarbons

Each Party shall ensure that for the twelve-month period commencing on 1 January 1996, and in each twelve-month period thereafter, its calculated level of consumption of the controlled substances in Group II

of Annex C does not exceed zero. Each Party producing the substances shall, for the same periods, ensure that its calculated level of production of the substances does not exceed zero. This paragraph will apply save to the extent that the Parties decide to permit the level of production or consumption that is necessary to satisfy uses agreed by them to be essential.

Article 2H

Methyl bromide

1. Each Party shall ensure that for the twelve-month period commencing on 1 January 1995, and in each twelve-month period thereafter, its calculated level of consumption of the controlled substance in Annex E does not exceed, annually, its calculated level of consumption in 1991. Each Party producing the substance shall, for the same period, ensure that its calculated level of production of the substance does not exceed, annually, its calculated level of production in 1991. However, in order to satisfy the basic domestic needs of the Parties operating under paragraph 1 of Article 5, its calculated level of production may exceed that limit by up to ten per cent of its calculated level of production in 1991.

2. Each Party shall ensure that for the twelve-month period commencing on 1 January 1999, and in the twelve-month period thereafter, its calculated level of consumption of the controlled substance in Annex E does not exceed, annually, seventy-five per cent of its calculated level of consumption in 1991. Each Party producing the substance shall, for the same periods, ensure that its calculated level of production of the substance does not exceed, annually, seventy-five per cent of its calculated level of production in 1991. However, in order to satisfy the basic domestic needs of the Parties operating under paragraph 1 of Article 5, its calculated level of production may exceed that limit by up to ten per cent of its calculated level of production in 1991.

3. Each Party shall ensure that for the twelve-month period commencing on 1 January 2001, and in the twelve-month period thereafter, its calculated level of consumption of the controlled substance in Annex E does not exceed, annually, fifty per cent of its calculated level of consumption in 1991. Each Party producing the substance shall, for the same periods, ensure that its calculated level of production of the substance does not exceed, annually, fifty per cent of its calculated level of production in 1991. However, in order to satisfy the basic domestic needs of the Parties operating under paragraph 1 of Article 5, its calculated level of production may exceed that

limit by up to ten per cent of its calculated level of production in 1991.

4. Each Party shall ensure that for the twelve-month period commencing on 1 January 2003, and in the twelve-month period thereafter, its calculated level of consumption of the controlled substance in Annex E does not exceed, annually, thirty per cent of its calculated level of consumption in 1991. Each Party producing the substance shall, for the same periods, ensure that its calculated level of production of the substance does not exceed, annually, thirty per cent of its calculated level of production in 1991. However, in order to satisfy the basic domestic needs of the Parties operating under paragraph 1 of Article 5, its calculated level of production may exceed that limit by up to ten per cent of its calculated level of production in 1991.

5. Each Party shall ensure that for the twelve-month period commencing on 1 January 2005, and in each twelve-month period thereafter, its calculated level of consumption of the controlled substance in Annex E does not exceed zero. Each Party producing the substance shall, for the same periods, ensure that its calculated level of production of the substance does not exceed zero. However, in order to satisfy the basic domestic needs of the Parties operating under paragraph 1 of Article 5, its calculated level of production may exceed that limit by up to fifteen per cent of its calculated level of production in 1991. This paragraph will apply save to the extent that the Parties decide to permit the level of production or consumption that is necessary to satisfy uses agreed by them to be critical uses.

6. The calculated levels of consumption and production under this Article shall not include the amounts used by the Party for quarantine and pre-shipment applications.

Article 3

Calculation of control levels

For the purposes of Articles 2, 2A to 2H and 5, each Party shall, for each group of substances in Annex A, Annex B, Annex C or Annex E determine its calculated levels of:

(a) Production by:

    (i) multiplying its annual production of each controlled substance by the ozone depleting potential specified in respect of it in Annex A, Annex B, Annex C or Annex E;

    (ii) adding together, for each such Group, the

resulting figures;

(b) Imports and exports, respectively, by following, *mutatis mutandis*, the procedure set out in subparagraph (a); and

(c) Consumption by adding together its calculated levels of production and imports and subtracting its calculated level of exports as determined in accordance with subparagraphs (a) and (b). However, beginning on 1 January 1993, any export of controlled substances to non-Parties shall not be subtracted in calculating the consumption level of the exporting Party.

Article 4

Control of trade with non-Parties

1. As of 1 January 1990, each party shall ban the import of the controlled substances in Annex A from any State not party to this Protocol.

1 *bis*. Within one year of the date of the entry into force of this paragraph, each Party shall ban the import of the controlled substances in Annex B from any State not party to this Protocol.

1 *ter*. Within one year of the date of entry into force of this paragraph, each Party shall ban the import of any controlled substances in Group II of Annex C from any State not party to this Protocol.

1 *qua. Within one year of the date of entry into force of this paragraph, each Party shall ban the import of the controlled substance in Annex E from any State not party to this Protocol.*

2. As of 1 January 1993, each Party shall ban the export of any controlled substances in Annex A to any State not party to this Protocol.

2 *bis*. Commencing one year after the date of entry into force of this paragraph, each Party shall ban the export of any controlled substances in Annex B to any State not party to this Protocol.

2 *ter*. Commencing one year after the date of entry into force of this paragraph, each Party shall ban the export of any controlled substances in Group II of Annex C to any State not party to this Protocol.

2 *qua. Commencing one year of the date of entry into force of this paragraph, each Party shall ban the export of the controlled substance in Annex E to any State not party to this Protocol.*

3. By 1 January 1992, the Parties shall, following the procedures in Article 10 of the Convention, ela-

borate in an annex a list of products containing controlled substances in Annex A. Parties that have not objected to the annex in accordance with those procedures shall ban, within one year of the annex having become effective, the import of those products from any State not party to this Protocol.

3 *bis*. Within three years of the date of the entry into force of this paragraph, the Parties shall, following the procedures in Article 10 of the Convention, elaborate in an annex a list of products containing controlled substances in Annex B. Parties that have not objected to the annex in accordance with those procedures shall ban, within one year of the annex having become effective, the import of those products from any State not party to this Protocol.

3 *ter*. Within three years of the date of entry into force of this paragraph, the Parties shall, following the procedures in Article 10 of the Convention, elaborate in an annex a list of products containing controlled substances in Group II of Annex C. Parties that have not objected to the annex in accordance with those procedures shall ban, within one year of the annex having become effective, the import of those products from any State not party to this Protocol.

4. By 1 January 1994, the Parties shall determine the feasibility of banning or restricting, from States not party to this Protocol, the import of products produced with, but not containing, controlled substances in Annex A. If determined feasible, the Parties shall, following the procedures in Article 10 of the Convention, elaborate in an annex a list of such products. Parties that have not objected to the annex in accordance with those procedures shall ban, within one year of the annex having become effective, the import of those products from any State not party to this Protocol.

4 *bis*. Within five years of the date of the entry into force of this paragraph, the Parties shall determine the feasibility of banning or restricting, from States not party to this Protocol, the import of products produced with, but not containing, controlled substances in Annex B. If determined feasible, the Parties shall, following the procedures in Article 10 of the Convention, elaborate in an annex a list of such products. Parties that have not objected to the annex in accordance with those procedures shall ban or restrict, within one year of the annex having become effective, the import of those products from any State not party to this Protocol.

4 *ter*. Within five years of the date of entry into force of this paragraph, the Parties shall determine the feasibility of banning or restricting, from States not party to this Protocol, the import of products produced with, but not containing, controlled substances in Group II of Annex C. If determined feasible, the Parties shall, following the procedures in Article 10 of the Convention, elaborate in an annex a list of such products. Parties that have not objected to the annex in accordance with those procedures shall ban or restrict, within one year of the annex having become effective, the import of those products from any State not party to this Protocol.

5. Each Party undertakes to the fullest practicable extent to discourage the export to any State not party to this Protocol of technology for producing and for utilizing controlled substances in Annexes A and B, Group II of Annex C *and Annex E*.

6. Each Party shall refrain from providing new subsidies, aid, credits, guarantees or insurance programmes for the export to States not party to this Protocol of products, equipment, plants or technology that would facilitate the production of controlled substances in Annexes A and B, Group II of Annex *C and Annex E*

7. Paragraphs 5 and 6 shall not apply to products, equipment, plants or technology that improve the containment, recovery, recycling or destruction of controlled substances, promote the development of alternative substances, or otherwise contribute to the reduction of emissions of controlled substances in Annexes A and B, Group II of Annex *C and Annex E*.

8. Notwithstanding the provisions of this Article, imports and exports referred to in paragraphs 1 to 4 *ter* of this Article may be permitted from, or to, any State not party to this Protocol, if that State is determined, by a meeting of the Parties, to be in full compliance with Article 2, Articles 2A to 2E, Articles 2G *and 2H* and this Article, and have submitted data to that effect as specified in Article 7.

9. For the purposes of this Article, the term "State not party to this Protocol" shall include, with respect to a particular controlled substance, a State or regional economic integration organization that has not agreed to be bound by the control measures in effect for that substance.

10. By 1 January 1996, the Parties shall consider whether to amend this Protocol in order to extend the measures in this Article to trade in controlled substances in Group I of Annex C and in Annex E with States not party to the Protocol.

Article 4A

Control of trade with Parties

1. *Where, after the phase-out date applicable to it for a controlled substance, a Party is unable, despite having taken all practicable steps to comply with its obligation under the Protocol, to cease production of that substance for domestic consumption, other than for uses agreed by the Parties to be essential, it shall ban the export of used, recycled and reclaimed quantities of that substance, other than for the purpose of destruction.*

2. *Paragraph 1 of this Article shall apply without prejudice to the operation of Article 11 of the Convention and the non-compliance procedure developed under Article 8 of the Protocol.*

Article 4B

Licensing

1. Each Party shall, by 1 January 2000 or within three months of the date of entry into force of this Article for it, whichever is the later, establish and implement a system for licensing the import and export of new, used, recycled and reclaimed controlled substances in Annexes A, B, C and E.

2. Notwithstanding paragraph 1 of this Article, any Party operating under paragraph 1 of Article 5 which decides it is not in a position to establish and implement a system for licensing the import and export of controlled substances in Annexes C and E, may delay taking those actions until 1 January 2005 and 1 January 2002, respectively.

3. Each Party shall, within three months of the date of introducing its licensing system, report to the Secretariat on the establishment and operation of that system.

4. The Secretariat shall periodically prepare and circulate to all Parties a list of the Parties that have reported to it on their licensing systems and shall forward this information to the Implementation Committee for consideration and appropriate recommendations to the Parties.

Article 5

Special situation of developing countries

1. Any Party that is a developing country and whose annual calculated level of consumption of the controlled substances in Annex A is less than 0.3 kilograms per capita on the date of the entry into force of the Protocol for it, or any time thereafter until 1 January 1999, shall, in order to meet its basic domestic needs, be entitled to delay for ten years its compliance with the control measures set out in Articles 2A to 2E, provided that any further amendments to the adjustments or Amendment adopted at the Second Meeting of the Parties in London, 29 June 1990, shall apply to the Parties operating under this paragraph after the review provided for in paragraph 8 of this Article has taken place and shall be based on the conclusions of that review.

1 *bis*. The Parties shall, taking into account the review referred to in paragraph 8 of this Article, the assessments made pursuant to Article 6 and any other relevant information, decide by 1 January 1996, through the procedure set forth in paragraph 9 of Article 2:

(a) With respect to paragraphs 1 to 6 of Article 2F, what base year, initial levels, control schedules and phase-out date for consumption of the controlled substances in Group I of Annex C will apply to Parties operating under paragraph 1 of this Article;

(b) With respect to Article 2G, what phase-out date for production and consumption of the controlled substances in Group II of Annex C will apply to Parties operating under paragraph 1 of this Article; and

(c) With respect to Article 2H, what base year, initial levels and control schedules for consumption and production of the controlled substance in Annex E will apply to Parties operating under paragraph 1 of this Article.

2. However, any Party operating under paragraph 1 of this Article shall exceed neither an annual calculated level of consumption of the controlled substances in Annex A of 0.3 kilograms per capita nor an annual calculated level of consumption of controlled substances of Annex B of 0.2 kilograms per capita.

3. When implementing the control measures set out in Articles 2A to 2E, any Party operating under paragraph 1 of this Article shall be entitled to use:

(a) For controlled substances under Annex A, either the average of its annual calculated level of consumption for the period 1995 to 1997 inclusive or a calculated level of consumption of 0.3 kilograms per capita, whichever is the lower, as the basis for determining its compliance with the control measures relating to consumption.

(b) For controlled substances under Annex B, the

average of its annual calculated level of consumption for the period 1998 to 2000 inclusive or a calculated level of consumption of 0.2 kilograms per capita, whichever is the lower, as the basis for determining its compliance with the control measures relating to consumption.

(c) For controlled substances under Annex A, either the average of its annual calculated level of production for the period 1995 to 1997 inclusive or a calculated level of production of 0.3 kilograms per capita, whichever is the lower, as the basis for determining its compliance with the control measures relating to production.

(d) For controlled substances under Annex B, either the average of its annual calculated level of production for the period 1998 to 2000 inclusive or a calculated level of production of 0.2 kilograms per capita, whichever is the lower, as the basis for determining its compliance with the control measures relating to production.

4. If a Party operating under paragraph 1 of this Article, at any time before the control measures obligations in Articles 2A to 2H become applicable to it, finds itself unable to obtain an adequate supply of controlled substances, it may notify this to the Secretariat. The Secretariat shall forthwith transmit a copy of such notification to the Parties, which shall consider the matter at their next Meeting, and decide upon appropriate action to be taken.

5. Developing the capacity to fulfil the obligations of the Parties operating under paragraph 1 of this Article to comply with the control measures set out in Articles 2A to 2E, and any control measures in Articles 2F to 2H that are decided pursuant to paragraph 1 bis of this Article, and their implementation by those same Parties will depend upon the effective implementation of the financial co-operation as provided by Article 10 and the transfer of technology as provided by Article 10A.

6. Any Party operating under paragraph 1 of this Article may, at any time, notify the Secretariat in writing that, having taken all practicable steps it is unable to implement any or all of the obligations laid down in Articles 2A to 2E, or any or all obligations in Articles 2F to 2H that are decided pursuant to paragraph 1 bis of this Article, due to the inadequate implementation of Articles 10 and 10A. The Secretariat shall forthwith transmit a copy of the notification to the Parties, which shall consider the matter at their next Meeting, giving due recognition to paragraph 5 of this Article and shall decide upon appro-

priate action to be taken.

7. During the period between notification and the Meeting of the Parties at which the appropriate action referred to in paragraph 6 above is to be decided, or for a further period if the Meeting of the Parties so decides, the non-compliance procedures referred to in Article 8 shall not be invoked against the notifying Party.

8. A Meeting of the Parties shall review, not later than 1995, the situation of the Parties operating under paragraph 1 of this Article, including the effective implementation of financial co-operation and transfer of technology to them, and adopt such revisions that may be deemed necessary regarding the schedule of control measures applicable to those Parties.

8 *bis.* Based on the conclusions of the review referred to in paragraph 8 above:

(a) With respect to the controlled substances in Annex A, a Party operating under paragraph 1 of this Article shall, in order to meet its basic domestic needs, be entitled to delay for ten years its compliance with the control measures adopted by the Second Meeting of the Parties in London, 29 June 1990, and reference by the Protocol to Articles 2A and 2B shall be read accordingly;

(b) With respect to the controlled substances in Annex B, a Party operating under paragraph 1 of this Article shall, in order to meet its basic domestic needs, be entitled to delay for ten years its compliance with the control measures adopted by the Second Meeting of the Parties in London, 29 June 1990, and reference by the Protocol to Articles 2C to 2E shall be read accordingly.

8 *ter.* Pursuant to paragraph 1 bis above:

(a) Each Party operating under paragraph 1 of this Article shall ensure that for the twelve-month period commencing on 1 January 2016, and in each twelve-month period thereafter, its calculated level of consumption of the controlled substances in Group I of Annex C does not exceed, annually, its calculated level of consumption in 2015;

(b) Each Party operating under paragraph 1 of this Article shall ensure that for the twelve-month period commencing on 1 January 2040, and in each twelve-month period thereafter, its calculated level of consumption of the controlled substances in Group I of Annex C does not exceed zero;

(c) Each Party operating under paragraph 1 of this Article shall comply with Article 2G;

(d) With regard to the controlled substance contained

in Annex E:

(i) As of 1 January 2002 each Party operating under paragraph 1 of this Article shall comply with the control measures set out in paragraph 1 of Article 2H and, as the basis for its compliance with these control measures, it shall use the average of its annual calculated level of consumption and production, respectively, for the period of 1995 to 1998 inclusive;

(ii) Each Party operating under paragraph 1 of this Article shall ensure that for the twelve-month period commencing on 1 January 2005, and in each twelve-month period thereafter, its calculated levels of consumption and production of the controlled substance in Annex E do not exceed, annually, eighty per cent of the average of its annual calculated levels of consumption and production, respectively, for the period of 1995 to 1998 inclusive;

(iii) Each Party operating under paragraph 1 of this Article shall ensure that for the twelve-month period commencing on 1 January 2015 and in each twelve-month period thereafter, its calculated levels of consumption and production of the controlled substance in Annex E do not exceed zero. This paragraph will apply save to the extent that the Parties decide to permit the level of production or consumption that is necessary to satisfy uses agreed by them to be critical uses;

(iv) The calculated levels of consumption and production under this subparagraph shall not include the amounts used by the Party for quarantine and pre-shipment applications.

9. Decisions of the Parties referred to in paragraph 4, 6 and 7 of this Article shall be taken according to the same procedure applied to decision-making under Article 10.

Article 6

Assessment and review of control measures

1. Beginning in 1990, and at least every four years thereafter, the Parties shall assess the control measures provided for in Article 2 and Articles 2A to 2H on the basis of available scientific, environmental, technical and economic information. At least one year before each assessment, the Parties shall convene appropriate panels of experts qualified in the fields mentioned and determine the composition and terms of reference of any such panels. Within one year of being convened, the panels will report their conclusions, through the Secretariat, to the Parties.

Article 7

Reporting of data

1. Each Party shall provide to the Secretariat, within three months of becoming a Party, statistical data on its production, imports and exports of each of the controlled substances in Annex A for the year 1986, or the best possible estimates of such data where actual data are not available.

2. Each Party shall provide to the Secretariat statistical data on its production, imports and exports of each of the controlled substances

• in Annexes B and C, for the year 1989;
• in Annex E, for the year 1991,

or the best possible estimates of such data where actual data are not available, not later than three months after the date when the provisions set out in the Protocol with regard to the substances in Annexes B, C and E respectively enter into force for that Party.

3. Each Party shall provide to the Secretariat statistical data on its annual production (as defined in paragraph 5 of Article 1) of each of the controlled substances listed in Annexes A, B, C and E and, separately, for each substance,

• Amounts used for feedstocks,
• Amounts destroyed by technologies approved by the Parties, and
• Imports from and exports to Parties and non-Parties respectively,

4. For the year during which provisions concerning the substances in Annexes A, B, C and E respectively entered into force for that Party and for each year thereafter. Data shall be forwarded not later than nine months after the end of the year to which the data relate.

3 *bis*. Each Party shall provide to the Secretariat separate statistical data of its annual imports and exports of each of the controlled substances listed in Group II of Annex A and Group I of Annex C that have been recycled.

4. For Parties operating under the provisions of paragraph 8 (a) of Article 2, the requirements in paragraphs 1, 2, 3 and 3 bis of this Article in respect of statistical data on imports and exports shall be sa-

tisfied if the regional economic integration organization concerned provides data on imports and exports between the organization and States that are not members of that organization.

Article 8

Non-compliance

The Parties, at their first meeting, shall consider and approve procedures and institutional mechanisms for determining non-compliance with the provisions of this Protocol and for treatment of Parties found to be in non-compliance.

Article 9

Research, development, public awareness and exchange of information

1. The Parties shall co-operate, consistent with their national laws, regulations and practices and taking into account in particular the needs of developing countries, in promoting, directly or through competent international bodies, research, development and exchange of information on:

(a) best technologies for improving the containment, recovery, recycling, or destruction of controlled substances or otherwise reducing their emissions;

(b) possible alternatives to controlled substances, to products containing such substances, and to products manufactured with them; and

(c) costs and benefits of relevant control strategies.

2. The Parties, individually, jointly or through competent international bodies, shall co-operate in promoting public awareness of the environmental effects of the emissions of controlled substances and other substances that deplete the ozone layer.

3. Within two years of the entry into force of this Protocol and every two years thereafter, each Party shall submit to the Secretariat a summary of the activities it has conducted pursuant to this Article.

Article 10

Financial mechanism

1. The Parties shall establish a mechanism for the purposes of providing financial and technical co-operation, including the transfer of technologies, to Parties operating under paragraph 1 of Article 5 of this Protocol to enable their compliance with the control mea-

sures set out in Articles 2A to 2E, and any control measures in Articles 2F to 2H that are decided pursuant to paragraph 1 bis of Article 5 of the Protocol. The mechanism, contributions to which shall be additional to other financial transfers to Parties operating under that paragraph, shall meet all agreed incremental costs of such Parties in order to enable their compliance with the control measures of the Protocol. An indicative list of the categories of incremental costs shall be decided by the meeting of the Parties.

2. The mechanism established under paragraph 1 shall include a Multilateral Fund. It may also include other means of multilateral, regional and bilateral co-operation.

3. The Multilateral Fund shall:

(a) Meet, on a grant or concessional basis as appropriate, and according to criteria to be decided upon by the Parties, the agreed incremental costs;

(b) Finance clearing-house functions to:

(i) Assist Parties operating under paragraph 1 of Article 5, through country specific studies and other technical co-operation, to identify their needs for co-operation;

(ii) Facilitate technical co-operation to meet these identified needs;

(iii) Distribute, as provided for in Article 9, information and relevant materials, and hold workshops, training sessions, and other related activities, for the benefit of Parties that are developing countries; and

(iv) Facilitate and monitor other multilateral, regional and bilateral co-operation available to Parties that are developing countries;

(c) Finance the secretarial services of the Multilateral Fund and related support costs.

4. The Multilateral Fund shall operate under the authority of the Parties who shall decide on its overall policies.

5. The Parties shall establish an Executive Committee to develop and monitor the implementation of specific operational policies, guidelines and administrative arrangements, including the disbursement of resources, for the purpose of achieving the objectives of the Multilateral Fund. The Executive Committee shall discharge its tasks and responsibilities, specified in its terms of reference as agreed by the Parties, with the co-operation and assistance of the International Bank for Reconstruction and Development (World Bank), the United Nations Environment Programme,

the United Nations Development Programme or other appropriate agencies depending on their respective areas of expertise. The members of the Executive Committee, which shall be selected on the basis of a balanced representation of the Parties operating under paragraph 1 of Article 5 and of the Parties not so operating, shall be endorsed by the Parties.

6. The Multilateral Fund shall be financed by contributions from Parties not operating under paragraph 1 of Article 5 in convertible currency or, in certain circumstances, in kind and/or in national currency, on the basis of the United Nations scale of assessments. Contributions by other Parties shall be encouraged. Bilateral and, in particular cases agreed by a decision of the Parties, regional co-operation may, up to a percentage and consistent with any criteria to be specified by decision of the Parties, be considered as a contribution to the Multilateral Fund, provided that such co-operation, as a minimum:

(a) Strictly relates to compliance with the provisions of this Protocol;

(b) Provides additional resources; and

(c) Meets agreed incremental costs.

7. The Parties shall decide upon the programme budget of the Multilateral Fund for each fiscal period and upon the percentage of contributions of the individual Parties thereto.

8. Resources under the Multilateral Fund shall be disbursed with the concurrence of the beneficiary Party.

9. Decisions by the Parties under this Article shall be taken by consensus whenever possible. If all efforts at consensus have been exhausted and no agreement reached, decisions shall be adopted by a two-thirds majority vote of the Parties present and voting, representing a majority of the Parties operating under paragraph 1 of Article 5 present and voting and a majority of the Parties not so operating present and voting.

10. The financial mechanism set out in this Article is without prejudice to any future arrangements that may be developed with respect to other environmental issues.

Article 10A

Transfer of technology

Each Party shall take every practicable step, consistent with the programmes supported by the financial mechanism, to ensure:

(a) that the best available, environmentally safe substitutes and related technologies are expeditiously transferred to Parties operating under paragraph 1 of Article 5; and

(b) that the transfers referred to in subparagraph (a) occur under fair and most favourable conditions.

Article 11

Meetings of the parties

1. The Parties shall hold meetings at regular intervals. The Secretariat shall convene the first meeting of the Parties not later than one year after the date of the entry into force of this Protocol and in conjunction with a meeting of the Conference of the Parties to the Convention, if a meeting of the latter is scheduled within that period.

2. Subsequent ordinary meetings of the parties shall be held, unless the Parties otherwise decide, in conjunction with meetings of the Conference of the Parties to the Convention. Extraordinary meetings of the Parties shall be held at such other times as may be deemed necessary by a meeting of the Parties, or at the written request of any Party, provided that within six months of such a request being communicated to them by the Secretariat, it is supported by at least one third of the Parties.

3. The Parties, at their first meeting, shall:

(a) adopt by consensus rules of procedure for their meetings;

(b) adopt by consensus the financial rules referred to in paragraph 2 of Article 13;

(c) establish the panels and determine the terms of reference referred to in Article 6;

(d) consider and approve the procedures and institutional mechanisms specified in Article 8; and

(e) begin preparation of workplans pursuant to paragraph 3 of Article 10.

[The Article 10 in question is that of the original Protocol adopted in 1987.]

4. The functions of the meetings of the Parties shall be to:

(a) review the implementation of this Protocol;

(b) decide on any adjustments or reductions referred to in paragraph 9 of Article 2;

(c) decide on any addition to, insertion in or removal from any annex of substances and on related control measures in accordance with paragraph 10 of Article 2;

(d) establish, where necessary, guidelines or procedures for reporting of information as provided for in Article 7 and paragraph 3 of Article 9;

(e) review requests for technical assistance submitted pursuant to paragraph 2 of Article 10;

(f) review reports prepared by the secretariat pursuant to subparagraph (c) of Article 12;

(g) assess, in accordance with Article 6, the control measures;

(h) consider and adopt, as required, proposals for amendment of this Protocol or any annex and for any new annex;

(i) consider and adopt the budget for implementing this Protocol; and

(j) consider and undertake any additional action that may be required for the achievement of the purposes of this Protocol.

5. The United Nations, its specialized agencies and the International Atomic Energy Agency, as well as any State not party to this Protocol, may be represented at meetings of the Parties as observers. Any body or agency, whether national or international, governmental or non-governmental, qualified in fields relating to the protection of the ozone layer which has informed the secretariat of its wish to be represented at a meeting of the Parties as an observer may be admitted unless at least one third of the Parties present object. The admission and participation of observers shall be subject to the rules of procedure adopted by the Parties.

Article 12

Secretariat

For the purposes of this Protocol, the Secretariat shall:

(a) arrange for and service meetings of the Parties as provided for in Article 11;

(b) receive and make available, upon request by a Party, data provided pursuant to Article 7;

(c) prepare and distribute regularly to the Parties reports based on information received pursuant to Articles 7 and 9;

(d) notify the Parties of any request for technical assistance received pursuant to Article 10 so as to facilitate the provision of such assistance;

(e) encourage non-Parties to attend the meetings of the Parties as observers and to act in accordance with the provisions of this Protocol;

(f) provide, as appropriate, the information and requests referred to in subparagraphs (c) and (d) to such non-party observers; and

(g) perform such other functions for the achievement of the purposes of this Protocol as may be assigned to it by the Parties.

Article 13

Financial provisions

1. The funds required for the operation of this Protocol, including those for the functioning of the Secretariat related to this Protocol, shall be charged exclusively against contributions from the Parties.

2. The Parties, at their first meeting, shall adopt by consensus financial rules for the operation of this Protocol.

Article 14

Relationship of this Protocol to the Convention

Except as otherwise provided in this Protocol, the provisions of the Convention relating to its protocols shall apply to this Protocol.

Article 15

Signature

This Protocol shall be open for signature by States and by regional economic integration organizations in Montreal on 16 September 1987, in Ottawa from 17 September 1987 to 16 January 1988, and at United Nations Headquarters in New York from 17 January 1988 to 15 September 1988.

Article 16

Entry into force

1. This Protocol shall enter into force on 1 January 1989, provided that at least eleven instruments of ratification, acceptance, approval of the Protocol or accession thereto have been deposited by States or regional economic integration organizations representing at least two-thirds of 1986 estimated global consumption of the controlled substances, and the provisions of paragraph 1 of Article 17 of the Convention have been fulfilled. In the event that these

conditions have not been fulfilled by that date, the Protocol shall enter into force on the ninetieth day following the date on which the conditions have been fulfilled.

2. For the purposes of paragraph 1, any such instrument deposited by a regional economic integration organization shall not be counted as additional to those deposited by member States of such organization.

3. After the entry into force of this Protocol, any State or regional economic integration organization shall become a Party to it on the ninetieth day following the date of deposit of its instrument of ratification, acceptance, approval or accession.

Article 17

Parties joining after entry into force

Subject to Article 5, any State or regional economic integration organization which becomes a Party to this Protocol after the date of its entry into force, shall fulfil forthwith the sum of the obligations under Article 2, as well as under Articles 2A to 2H and Article 4, that apply at that date to the States and regional economic integration organizations that became Parties on the date the Protocol entered into force.

Article 18

Reservations

No reservations may be made to this Protocol.

Article 19

Withdrawal

Any Party may withdraw from this Protocol by giving written notification to the Depositary at any time after four years of assuming the obligations specified in paragraph 1 of Article 2A. Any such withdrawal shall take effect upon expiry of one year after the date of its receipt by the Depositary, or on such later date as may be specified in the notification of the withdrawal.

Article 20

Authentic texts

The original of this Protocol, of which the Arabic, Chinese, English, French, Russian and Spanish texts are equally authentic, shall be deposited with the Secretary-General of the United Nations.

Convention on the Prohibition of the Use, Stockpiling, Production and Transfer of Anti-personnel Mines and on Their Destruction

Also known as: Oslo Treaty; Mine Ban Treaty
Date of signature: September 18, 1997
Place of signature: Oslo
Signatory states: Albania, Algeria, Andorra, Angola, Antigua and Barbuda, Argentina, Australia, Austria, Bahamas, Bangladesh, Barbados, Belgium, Belize, Benin, Bolivia, Bosnia and Herzegovina, Botswana, Brazil, Brunei Darussalam, Bulgaria, Burkina Faso, Burundi, Cambodia, Cameroon, Canada, Cape Verde, Chad, Chile, Colombia, Cook Islands, Costa Rica, Cote d'Ivoire, Croatia, Cyprus, Czech Republic, Denmark, Djibouti, Dominica, Dominican Republic, Ecuador, El Salvador, Equatorial Guinea, Ethiopia, Fiji, France, Gabon, Gambia, Germany, Ghana, Greece, Grenada, Guatemala, Guinea, Guinea-Bussau, Guyana, Haiti, Holy See, Honduras, Hungary, Iceland, Indonesia, Ireland, Italy, Jamaica, Japan, Jordan, Kenya, Lesotho, Liechtenstein, Luxembourg, Macedonia, FYR, Madagascar, Maldives, Malaysia, Malawi, Mali,

Malta, Marshall Islands, Mauritania, Mauritius, Mexico, Monaco, Mozambique, Namibia, Netherlands, New Zealand, Nicaragua, Niger, Niue, Norway, Panama, Paraguay, Peru, Philippines, Poland, Portugal, Qatar, Republic of Moldova, Rumania, Rwanda, Saint Kitts and Nevis, Saint Lucia, Saint Vincent and the Grenadines, Samoa, San Marino, Sao Tome and Principe, Senegal, Seychelles, Sierra Leone, Slovakia, Slovenia, Solomon Islands, South Africa, Spain, Sudan, Suriname, Swaziland, Sweden, Switzerland, Thailand, Togo, Trinidad and Tobago, Tunisia, Turkmenistan, Uganda, United Kingdom, United Republic of Tanzania, Uruguay, Vanuatu, Venezuela, Yemen, Zambia, Zimbabwe
Ratification: Andorra, Austria, Bahamas, Belgium, Belize, Benin, Bolivia, Bosnia and Herzegovina, Bulgaria, Burkina Faso, Canada, Croatia, Denmark, Djibouti, Fiji, France, Germany, Grenada, Guinea, Holy See, Honduras, Hungary, Ireland, Jamaica, Japan, Jordan, Malawi, Mali,

Maurituis, Mexico, Monaco, Mozambique, Namibia, Nicarqgua, Niue, Norway, Panama, Paraguay, Peru, Qatar, Samoa, San Marino, Senegal, Slovenia, South Africa, Sweden, Switzerland, Thailand, Trinidan and Tobago, Turkmenistan, United Kingdom, Yemen (as of December 1, 1998)
Date of entry into force: March 1, 1999

Preamble

The States Parties,

Determined to put an end to the suffering and casualties caused by antipersonnel mines, that kill or maim hundreds of people every week, mostly innocent and defenceless civilians and especially children, obstruct economic development and reconstruction, inhibit the repatriation of refugees and internally displaced persons, and have other severe consequences for years after emplacement,

Believing it necessary to do their utmost to contribute in an efficier.t and coordinated manner to face the challenge of removing anti-personnel mines placed throughout the world, and to assure their destruction,

Wishing to do their utmost in providing assistance for the care and rehabilitation, including the social and economic reintegration of mine victims,

Recognizing that a total ban of anti-personnel mines would also be an important confidence-building measure,

Welcoming the adoption of the Protocol on Prohibitions or Restrictions on the Use of Mines, Booby-Traps and Other Devices, as amended on 3 May 1996, annexed to the Convention on Prohibitions or Restrictions on the Use of Certain Conventional Weapons Which May Be Deemed to Be Excessively Injurious or to Have Indiscriminate Effects, and calling for the early ratification of this Protocol by all States which have not yet done so,

Welcoming also United Nations General Assembly Resolution 51/45 S of 10 December 1996 urging all States to pursue vigorously an effective, legally-binding international agreement to ban the use, stockpiling, production and transfer of antipersonnel landmines,

Welcoming furthermore the measures taken over the past years, both unilaterally and multilaterally, aiming at prohibiting, restricting or suspending the use, stockpiling, production and transfer of anti-personnel mines,

Stressing the role of public conscience in furthering the principles of humanity as evidenced by the call for a total ban of anti-personnel mines and recognizing the efforts to that end undertaken by the International Red Cross and Red Crescent Movement, the International Campaign to Ban Landmines and numerous other nongovernmental organizations around the world,

Recalling the Ottawa Declaration of 5 October 1996 and the Brussels Declaration of 27 June 1997 urging the international community to negotiate an international and legally binding agreement prohibiting the use, stockpiling, production and transfer of anti-personnel mines,

Emphasizing the desirability of attracting the adherence of all States to this Convention, and determined to work strenuously towards the promotion of its universalization in all relevant fora including, *inter alia*, the United Nations, the Conference on Disarmament, regional organizations, and groupings, and review conferences of the Convention on Prohibitions or Restrictions on the Use of Certain Conventional Weapons Which May Be Deemed to Be Excessively Injurious or to Have Indiscriminate Effects,

Basing themselves on the principle of international humanitarian law that the right of the parties to an armed conflict to choose methods or means of warfare is not unlimited, on the principle that prohibits the employment in armed conflicts of weapons, projectiles and materials and methods of warfare of a nature to cause superfluous injury or unnecessary suffering and on the principle that a distinction must be made between civilians and combatants,

Have agreed as follows:

Article 1

General Obligations

1. Each State Party undertakes never under any circumstances

a) To use anti-personnel mines;

b) To develop, produce, otherwise acquire, stockpile,

retain or transfer to anyone, directly or indirectly, anti-personnel mines;

c) To assist, encourage or induce, in any way, anyone to engage in any activity prohibited to a State Party under this Convention.

2. Each State Party undertakes to destroy or ensure the destruction of all antipersonnel mines in accordance with the provisions of this Convention.

Article 2

Definitions

1. "Anti-personnel mine" means a mine designed to be exploded by the presence, proximity or contact of a person and that will incapacitate, injure or kill one or more persons. Mines designed to be detonated by the presence, proximity or contact of a vehicle as opposed to a person, that are equipped with anti-handling devices, are not considered anti-personnel mines as a result of being so equipped.

2. "Mine" means a munition designed to be placed under, on or near the ground or other surface area and to be exploded by the presence, proximity or contact of a person or a vehicle.

3. "Anti-handling device" means a device intended to protect a mine and which is part of, linked to, attached to or placed under the mine and which activates when an attempt is made to tamper with or otherwise intentionally disturb the mine.

4. "Transfer" involves, in addition to the physical movement of anti-personnel mines into or from national territory, the transfer of title to and control over the mines, but does not involve the transfer of territory containing emplaced anti-personnel mines.

5. "Mined area" means an area which is dangerous due to the presence or suspected presence of mines.

Article 3

Exceptions

1. Notwithstanding the general obligations under Article 1, the retention or transfer of a number of anti-personnel mines for the development of and training in mine detection, mine clearance, or mine destruction techniques is permitted. The amount of such mines shall not exceed the minimum number absolutely necessary for the above-mentioned purposes.

2. The transfer of anti-personnel mines for the purpose of destruction is permitted.

Article 4

Destruction of stockpiled anti-personnel mines

Except as provided for in Article 3, each State Party undertakes to destroy or ensure the destruction of all stockpiled anti-personnel mines it owns or possesses, or that are under its jurisdiction or control, as soon as possible but not later than four years after the entry into force of this Convention for that State Party.

Article 5

Destruction of anti-personnel mines in mined areas

1. Each State Party undertakes to destroy or ensure the destruction of all antipersonnel mines in mined areas under its jurisdiction or control, as soon as possible but not later than ten years after the entry into force of this Convention for that State Party.

2. Each State Party shall make every effort to identify all areas under its jurisdiction or control in which anti-personnel mines are known or suspected to be emplaced and shall ensure as soon as possible that all anti-personnel mines in mined areas under its jurisdiction or control are perimeter-marked, monitored and protected by fencing or other means, to ensure the effective exclusion of civilians, until all antipersonnel mines contained therein have been destroyed. The marking shall at least be to the standards set out in the Protocol on Prohibitions or Restrictions on the Use of Mines, Booby-Traps and Other Devices, as amended on 3 May 1996, annexed to the Convention on Prohibitions or Restrictions on the Use of Certain Conventional Weapons Which May Be Deemed to Be Excessively Injurious or to Have Indiscriminate Effects.

3. If a State Party believes that it will be unable to destroy or ensure the destruction of all anti-personnel mines referred to in paragraph 1 within that time period, it may submit a request to a Meeting of the States Parties or a Review Conference for an extension of the deadline for completing the destruction of such anti-personnel mines, for a period of up to ten years.

4. Each request shall contain:

a) The duration of the proposed extension;

b) A detailed explanation of the reasons for the proposed extension, including:

(i) The preparation and status of work conducted under national demining programs;

(ii) The financial and technical means available to the State Party for the destruction of all the anti-personnel mines; and

(iii) Circumstances which impede the ability of the State Party to destroy all the anti-personnel mines in mined areas;

c) The humanitarian, social, economic, and environmental implications of the extension; and

d) Any other information relevant to the request for the proposed extension.

5. The Meeting of the States Parties or the Review Conference shall, taking into consideration the factors contained in paragraph 4, assess the request and decide by a majority of votes of States Parties present and voting whether to grant the request for an extension period.

6. Such an extension may be renewed upon the submission of a new request in accordance with paragraphs 3, 4 and 5 of this Article. In requesting a further extension period a State Party shall submit relevant additional information on what has been undertaken in the previous extension period pursuant to this Article.

Article 6

International cooperation and assistance

1. In fulfilling its obligations under this Convention each State Party has the right to seek and receive assistance, where feasible, from other States Parties to the extent possible.

2. Each State Party undertakes to facilitate and shall have the right to participate in the fullest possible exchange of equipment, material and scientific and technological information concerning the implementation of this Convention. The States Parties shall not impose undue restrictions on the provision of mine clearance equipment and related technological information for humanitarian purposes.

3. Each State Party in a position to do so shall provide assistance for the care and rehabilitation, and social and economic reintegration, of mine victims and for mine awareness programs. Such assistance may be provided, inter alia, through the United Nations system, international, regional or national organizations or institutions, the International Committee of the Red Cross, national Red Cross and Red Crescent societies and their International Federation, non-governmental organizations, or on a bilateral basis.

4. Each State Party in a position to do so shall provide assistance for mine clearance and related activities. Such assistance may be provided, *inter alia*, through the United Nations system, international or regional organizations or institutions, nongovernmental organizations or institutions, or on a bilateral basis, or by contributing to the United Nations Voluntary Trust Fund for Assistance in Mine Clearance, or other regional funds that deal with demining.

5. Each State Party in a position to do so shall provide assistance for the destruction of stockpiled anti-personnel mines.

6. Each State Party undertakes to provide information to the database on mine clearance established within the United Nations system, especially information concerning various means and technologies of mine clearance, and lists of experts, expert agencies or national points of contact on mine clearance.

7. States Parties may request the United Nations, regional organizations, other States Parties or other competent intergovernmental or non-governmental fore to assist its authorities in the elaboration of a national demining program to determine, inter alia:

a) The extent and scope of the anti-personnel mine problem;

b) The financial, technological and human resources that are required for the implementation of the program;

c) The estimated number of years necessary to destroy all anti-personnel mines in mined areas under the jurisdiction or control of the concerned State Party;

d) Mine awareness activities to reduce the incidence of mine-related injuries or deaths;

e) Assistance to mine victims;

f) The relationship between the Government of the concerned State Party and the relevant governmental, inter-governmental or non-governmental entities that will work in the implementation of the program.

8. Each State Party giving and receiving assistance under the provisions of this Article shall cooperate with a view to ensuring the full and prompt implementation of agreed assistance programs.

Article 7

Transparency measures

1. Each State Party shall report to the Secretary-General of the United Nations as soon as practicable, and in any event not later than 180 days after the entry into force of this Convention for that State Party on:

a) The national implementation measures referred to in Article 9;

b) The total of all stockpiled anti-personnel mines owned or possessed by it, or under its jurisdiction or control, to include a breakdown of the type, quantity and, if possible, lot numbers of each type of anti-personnel mine stockpiled;

c) To the extent possible, the location of all mined areas that contain, or are suspected to contain, anti-personnel mines under its jurisdiction or control, to include as much detail as possible regarding the type and quantity of each type of antipersonnel mine in each mined area and when they were emplaced;

d) The types, quantities and, if possible, lot numbers of all anti-personnel mines retained or transferred for the development of and training in mine detection, mine clearance or mine destruction techniques, or transferred for the purpose of destruction, as well as the institutions authorized by a State Party to retain or transfer antipersonnel mines, in accordance with Article 3;

e) The status of programs for the conversion or decommissioning of antipersonnel mine production facilities;

f) The status of programs for the destruction of anti-personnel mines in accordance with Articles 4 and 5, including details of the methods which will be used in destruction, the location of all destruction sites and the applicable safety and environmental standards to be observed;

g) The types and quantities of all anti-personnel mines destroyed after the entry into force of this Convention for that State Party, to include a breakdown of the quantity of each type of anti-personnel mine destroyed, in accordance with Articles 4 and 5, respectively, along with, if possible, the lot numbers of each type of antipersonnel mine in the case of destruction in accordance with Article 4;

h) The technical characteristics of each type of anti-personnel mine produced, to the extent known, and those currently owned or possessed by a State Party, giving, where reasonably possible, such categories of information as may facilitate identification and clearance of anti-personnel mines; at a minimum, this information shall include the dimensions, fusing, explosive content, metallic content, colour photographs and other information which may facilitate mine clearance; and

i) The measures taken to provide an immediate and effective warning to the population in relation to all areas identified under paragraph 2 of Article 5.

2. The information provided in accordance with this Article shall be updated by the States Parties annually, covering the last calendar year, and reported to the Secretary-General of the United Nations not later than 30 April of each year.

3. The Secretary-General of the United Nations shall transmit all such reports received to the States Parties.

Article 8

Facilitation and clarification of compliance

1. The States Parties agree to consult and cooperate with each other regarding the implementation of the provisions of this Convention, and to work together in a spirit of cooperation to facilitate compliance by States Parties with their obligations under this Convention.

2. If one or more States Parties wish to clarify and seek to resolve questions relating to compliance with the provisions of this Convention by another State Party, it may submit, through the Secretary-General of the United Nations, a Request for Clarification of

that matter to that State Party. Such a request shall be accompanied by all appropriate information. Each State Party shall refrain from unfounded Requests for Clarification, care being taken to avoid abuse. A State Party that receives a Request for Clarification shall provide, through the Secretary-General of the United Nations, within 28 days to the requesting State Party all information which would assist in clarifying this matter.

3. If the requesting State Party does not receive a response through the Secretary-General of the United Nations within that time period, or deems the response to the Request for Clarification to be unsatisfactory, it may submit the matter through the Secretary-General of the United Nations to the next Meeting of the States Parties. The Secretary-General of the United Nations shall transmit the submission, accompanied by all appropriate information pertaining to the Request for Clarification, to all States Parties. All such information shall be presented to the requested State Party which shall have the right to respond.

4. Pending the convening of any meeting of the States Parties, any of the States Parties concerned may request the Secretary-General of the United Nations to exercise his or her good offices to facilitate the clarification requested.

5. The requesting State Party may propose through the Secretary-General of the United Nations the convening of a Special Meeting of the States Parties to consider the matter. The Secretary-General of the United Nations shall thereupon communicate his proposal and all information submitted by the Stares Parties concerned, to all States Parties with a request that they indicate whether they favour a Special Meeting of the States Parties, for the purpose of considering the matter. In the event that within 14 days from the date of such communication, at least one-third of the States Parties favors such a Special Meeting, the Secretary-General of the United Nations shall convene this Special Meeting of the States Parties within a further 14 days. A quorum for this Meeting shall consist of a majority of States Parties.

6. The Meeting of the States Parties or the Special Meeting of the States Parties, as the case may be, shall first determine whether to consider the matter further, taking into account all information submitted by the States Parties concerned. The Meeting of the States Parties or the Special Meeting of the States

Parties shall make every effort to reach a decision by consensus. If despite all efforts to that end no agreement has been reached, it shall take this decision by a majority of States Parties present and voting.

7. All States Parties shall cooperate fully with the Meeting of the States Parties or the Special Meeting of the States Parties in the fulfilment of its review of the matter, including any fact-finding missions that are authorized in accordance with paragraph 8.

8. If further clarification is required, the Meeting of the States Parties or the Special Meeting of the States Parties shall authorize a fact-finding mission and decide on its mandate by a majority of States Parties present and voting. At any time the requested State Party may invite a fact-finding mission to its territory. Such a mission shall take place without a decision by a Meeting of the States Parties or a Special Meeting of the States Parties to authorize such a mission. The mission, consisting of up to 9 experts, designated and approved in accordance with paragraphs 9 and 10, may collect additional information on the spot or in other places directly related to the alleged compliance issue under the jurisdiction or control of the requested State Party.

9. The Secretary-General of the United Nations shall prepare and update a list of the names, nationalities and other relevant data of qualified experts provided by States Parties and communicate it to all States Parties. Any expert included on this list shall be regarded as designated for all fact-finding missions unless a State Party declares its non-acceptance in writing. In the event of non-acceptance, the expert shall not participate in fact-finding missions on the territory or any other place under the jurisdiction or control of the objecting State Party, if the non-acceptance was declared prior to the appointment of the expert to such missions.

10. Upon receiving a request from the Meeting of the States Parties or a Special Meeting of the States Parties, the Secretary-General of the United Nations shall, after consultations with the requested State Party, appoint the members of the mission, including its leader. Nationals of States Parties requesting the fact-finding mission or directly affected by it shall not be appointed to the mission. The members of the factfinding mission shall enjoy privileges and immunities under Article VI of the Convention on the Privileges and Immunities of the United Nations, adopted on 13 February 1946.

11. Upon at least 72 hours notice, the members of the fact-finding mission shall arrive in the territory of the requested State Party at the earliest opportunity. The requested State Party shall take the necessary administrative measures to receive, transport and accommodate the mission, and shall be responsible for ensuring the security of the mission to the maximum extent possible while they are on territory under its control.

12. Without prejudice to the sovereignty of the requested State Party, the factfinding mission may bring into the territory of the requested State Party the necessary equipment which shall be used exclusively for gathering information on the alleged compliance issue. Prior to its arrival, the mission will advise the requested State Party of the equipment that it intends to utilize in the course of its fact-finding mission.

13. The requested State Party shall make all efforts to ensure that the fact-finding mission is given the opportunity to speak with all relevant persons who may be able to provide information related to the alleged compliance issue.

14. The requested State Party shall grant access for the fact-finding mission to all areas and installations under its control where facts relevant to the compliance issue could be expected to be collected. This shall be subject to any arrangements that the requested State Party considers necessary for:

a) The protection of sensitive equipment, information and areas;

b) The protection of any constitutional obligations the requested State Party may have with regard to proprietary rights, searches and seizures, or other constitutional rights; or

c) The physical protection and safety of the members of the fact-finding mission. In the event that the requested State Party makes such arrangements, it shall make every reasonable effort to demonstrate through alternative means its compliance with this Convention.

15. The fact-finding mission may remain in the territory of the State Party concerned for no more than 14 days, and at any particular site no more than 7 days, unless otherwise agreed.

16. All information provided in confidence and not related to the subject matter of the fact-finding mission shall be treated on a confidential basis.

17. The fact-finding mission shall report, through the Secretary-General of the United Nations, to the Meeting of the States Parties or the Special Meeting of the States Parties the results of its findings.

18. The Meeting of the States Parties or the Special Meeting of the States Parties shall consider all relevant information, including the report submitted by the fact-finding mission, and may request the requested State Party to take measures to address the compliance issue within a specified period of time. The requested State Party shall report on all measures taken in response to this request.

19. The Meeting of the States Parties or the Special Meeting of the States Parties may suggest to the States Parties concerned ways and means to further clarify or resolve the matter under consideration, including the initiation of appropriate procedures in conformity with international law. In circumstances where the issue at hand is determined to be due to circumstances beyond the control of the requested State Party, the Meeting of the States Parties or the Special Meeting of the States Parties may recommend appropriate measures, including the use of cooperative measures referred to in Article 6.

20. The Meeting of the States Parties or the Special Meeting of the States Parties shall make every effort to reach its decisions referred to in paragraphs 18 and 19 by consensus, otherwise by a two-thirds majority of States Parties present and voting.

Article 9

National implementation measures

Each State Party shall take all appropriate legal, administrative and other measures, including the imposition of penal sanctions, to prevent and suppress any activity prohibited to a State Party under this Convention undertaken by persons or on territory under its jurisdiction or control.

Article 10

Settlement of disputes

1. The States Parties shall consult and cooperate with each other to settle any dispute that may arise with regard to the application or the interpretation of

this Convention. Each State Party may bring any such dispute before the Meeting of the States Parties.

2. The Meeting of the States Parties may contribute to the settlement of the dispute by whatever means it deems appropriate, including offering its good offices, calling upon the States parties to a dispute to start the settlement procedure of their choice and recommending a time-limit for any agreed procedure 3. This Article is without prejudice to the provisions of this Convention on facilitation and clarification of compliance.

Article 11

Meetings of the States Parties

1. The States Parties shall meet regularly in order to consider any matter with regard to the application or implementation of this Convention, including:

a) The operation and status of this Convention;

b) Matters arising from the reports submitted under the provisions of this Convention;

c) International cooperation and assistance in accordance with Article 6;

d) The development of technologies to clear anti-personnel mines;

e) Submissions of States Parties under Article 8; and

f) Decisions relating to submissions of States Parties as provided for in Article 5.

2. The First Meeting of the States Parties shall be convened by the Secretary-General of the United Nations within one year after the entry into force of this Convention. The subsequent meetings shall be convened by the Secretary-General of the United Nations annually until the first Review Conference.

3. Under the conditions set out in Article 8, the Secretary-General of the United Nations shall convene a Special Meeting of the States Parties 4. States not parties to this Convention, as well as the United Nations, other relevant international organizations or institutions, regional organizations, the International Committee of the Red Cross and relevant non-governmental organizations may be invited to attend these meetings as observers in accordance with the agreed Rules of Procedure.

Article 12

Review Conferences

1. A Review Conference shall be convened by the Secretary-General of the United Nations five years after the entry into force of this Convention. Further Review Conferences shall be convened by the Secretary-General of the United Nations if so requested by one or more States Parties, provided that the interval between Review Conferences shall in no case be less than five years. All States Parties to this Convention shall be invited to each Review Conference.

2. The purpose of the Review Conference shall be:

a) To review the operation and status of this Convention;

b) To consider the need for and the interval between further Meetings of the States Parties referred to in paragraph 2 of Article 11;

c) To take decisions on submissions of States Parties as provided for in Article 5; and

d) To adopt, if necessary, in its final report conclusions related to the implementation of this Convention.

3. States not parties to this Convention, as well as the United Nations, other relevant international organizations or institutions, regional organizations, the International Committee of the Red Cross and relevant non-governmental organizations may be invited to attend each Review Conference as observers in accordance with the agreed Rules of Procedure.

Article 13

Amendments

1. At any time after the entry into force of this Convention any State Party may propose amendments to this Convention. Any proposal for an amendment shall be communicated to the Depositary, who shall circulate it to all States Parties and shall seek their views on whether an Amendment Conference should be convened to consider the proposal. If a majority of the States Parties notify the Depositary no later than 30 days after its circulation that they support further consideration of the proposal, the Depositary shall convene an Amendment Conference to which all States Parties shall be invited.

2. States not parties to this Convention, as well as the United Nations, other relevant international organizations or institutions, regional organizations, the International Committee of the Red Cross and relevant non-governmental organizations may be invited to attend each Amendment Conference as observers in accordance with the agreed Rules of Procedure.

3. The Amendment Conference shall be held immediately following a Meeting of the States Parties or a Review Conference unless a majority of the States Parties request that it be held earlier.

4. Any amendment to this Convention shall be adopted by a majority of two-thirds of the States Parties present and voting at the Amendment Conference. The Depositary shall communicate any amendment so adopted to the States Parties. 5. An amendment to this Convention shall enter into force for all States Parties to this Convention which have accepted it, upon the deposit with the Depositary of instruments of acceptance by a majority of States Parties. Thereafter it shall enter into force for any remaining State Party on the date of deposit of its instrument of acceptance.

Article 14

Costs

1. The costs of the Meetings of the States Parties, the Special Meetings of the States Parties, the Review Conferences and the Amendment Conferences shall be borne by the States Parties and States not parties to this Convention participating therein, in accordance with the United Nations scale of assessment adjusted appropriately.

2. The costs incurred by the Secretary-General of the United Nations under Articles 7 and 8 and the costs of any fact-finding mission shall be borne by the States Parties in accordance with the United Nations scale of assessment adjusted appropriately.

Article 15

Signature

This Convention, done at Oslo, Norway, on 18 September 1997, shall be open for signature at Ottawa, Canada, by all States from 3 December 1997 until 4 December 1997, and at the United Nations Headquarters in New York from 5 December 1997 until its entry into force.

Article 16

Ratification, acceptance, approval or accession

1. This Convention is subject to ratification, acceptance or approval of the Signatories.

2. It shall be open for accession by any State which has not signed the Convention.

3. The instruments of ratification, acceptance, approval or accession shall be deposited with the Depositary.

Article 17

Entry into force

1. This Convention shall enter into force on the first day of the sixth month after the month in which the 40th instrument of ratification, acceptance, approval or accession has been deposited.

2. For any State which deposits its instrument of ratification, acceptance, approval or accession after the date of the deposit of the 40th instrument of ratification, acceptance, approval or accession, this Convention shall enter into force on the first day of the sixth month after the date on which that State has deposited its instrument of ratification, acceptance, approval or accession.

Article 18

Provisional application

Any State may at the time of its ratification, acceptance, approval or accession, declare that it will apply provisionally paragraph 1 of Article 1 of this Convention pending its entry into force.

Article 19

Reservations

The Articles of this Convention shall not be subject to reservations.

Article 20

Duration and withdrawal

1. This Convention shall be of unlimited duration.

2. Each State Party shall, in exercising its national sovereignty, have the right to withdraw from this Convention. It shall give notice of such withdrawal to all other States Parties, to the Depositary and to

the United Nations Security Council. Such instrument of withdrawal shall include a full explanation of the reasons motivating this withdrawal.

3. Such withdrawal shall only take effect six months after the receipt of the instrument of withdrawal by the Depositary. If, however, on the expiry of that six month period, the withdrawing State Party is engaged in an armed conflict, the withdrawal shall not take effect before the end of the armed conflict.

4. The withdrawal of a State Party from this Convention shall not in any way affect the duty of States to continue fulfilling the obligations assumed under any relevant rules of international law.

Article 21

Depositary

The Secretary-General of the United Nations is hereby designated as the Depositary of this Convention.

Article 22

Authentic texts

The original of this Convention, of which the Arabic, Chinese, English, French, Russian and Spanish texts are equally authentic, shall be deposited with the Secretary-General of the United Nations.

[RETURN TO CONTENTS]